MORNINGSTAR®

ETFs 150™

Annual Sourcebook
2008 Edition

Introduction by
Jeffrey Ptak, Editor

Published by John Wiley & Sons, Inc., Hoboken, New Jersey
Published simultaneously in Canada

For general information on our other products and services or for technical support, please contact our Customer Care Department within the United States at (800) 762-2974, outside the United States at (317) 572-3993 or fax (317) 572-4002.

For general information about Morningstar's other products and services, please contact Morningstar's product sales line at 866-608-9570 or visit www.morningstar.com.

Wiley also publishes its books in a variety of electronic formats. Some content that appears in print may not be available in electronic books. For more information about Wiley products, visit our web site at www.wiley.com.

Library of Congress Cataloging-in-Publication Data:

ISBN-978-0-470-12128-3

Printed in the United States of America

10 9 8 7 6 5 4 3 2 1

Table of Contents

2 Introduction
4 How to Use This Book
16 ETFs Basics
18 Constructing Winning Portfolios Using ETFs
22 Beating the Market with ETFs
26 ETFs on Our Buy List

Report Pages

29 U.S. Stock Funds: Diversified
87 U.S. Stock Funds: Sector
137 Foreign Stock Funds: Diversified
147 Foreign Stock Funds: Country/Region
167 Fixed Income
179 Specialty/Other Funds

Tables and Charts

190 Performance Summary—U.S.-Listed ETFs
214 Performance Summary—Indexes
217 Best and Worst Performing ETFs
218 Cheapest and Dearest Stock ETFs
219 Highest and Lowest Quality Stock ETFs
220 Least and Most Risky Stock ETFs
221 Largest and Most Heavily-Traded ETFs
222 Most and Least Popular ETFs
223 Highest Yielding ETFs
224 ETFs with Lowest Annual Expenses
225 Valuation Measures
226 Growth Measures
227 Profitability Measures
228 Least and Most Volatile

Glossary

229 Glossary

Change is good.

Well, let's hope so anyway. For 2007 was another year of momentous change in the ETF world, which saw an onslaught of new fund launches.

Foreign-bond, municipal-income, and commodity funds were among the new crop of ETFs that made their debuts last year. In addition, ETF providers flooded the market with specialty offerings that filleted the market into ever-finer slices or gave investors the opportunity to place sophisticated wagers on the market's direction. All told, a record 290 ETFs began trading in 2007.

It's wonderful to have a wealth of new options from which to choose. And with 671 ETFs now available to U.S. investors, there's a fund to fill just about any nook or cranny in your portfolio. But the trick is wading through an increasingly cluttered field to find the ETF that suits your needs. That, in a nutshell, is where this book comes in.

As in editions past, we've written *Morningstar ETFs 150* with novice and advanced ETF investors in mind. For instance, those of you who are relatively new to ETFs should find that the book's introductory section provides a high-level primer on ETFs, including what they are, how to use them, and factors to consider when choosing a fund. By the same token, even wizened old pros should find that the 150 report pages—which are the book's focal point—and the accompanying data tables deliver the right mix of insight and actionable data.

That said, we're hardly standing pat with this, our third edition of the book. We've made numerous enhancements in order to keep up with the changing ETF market and help you wring the most value out of the information we've compiled.

Chief among those improvements, we've retooled our analyst reports to more directly address whether a stock ETF is attractively valued. Investors have increasingly used ETFs as substitutes for positions in single stocks. Within that context, an ETF's fundamental attractiveness—that is, the quality, risk, and valuation of its underlying holdings—is important to investors' odds of success.

As it turns out, we're well equipped to gauge attributes like stock quality, risk, and valuation, as our 100-plus equity analysts cover more than 2,000 stocks. For instance, we can estimate the intrinsic worth of a stock ETF—such as SPDRs, which tracks the S&P 500 Index—based on the fair value estimates that our analysts place on the fund's underlying holdings. By comparing our estimate of an ETF's intrinsic worth with its market price, we can determine whether it's cheap, dear, or reasonably priced and, thus, help you to identify funds that sport the most compelling valuations. Our enhanced ETF reports set that information forth.

We've also made significant changes to the list of funds that comprise the ETF 150, which we think is the best yet. The 150 featured ETFs represent a sizable chunk of total industry trading volume and assets. What's more, we've nearly doubled the number of industry-, country-, and region-specific funds and bumped up the number of bond and commodity ETFs. This, should better serve investors who have made these types of ETFs a central part of their trading strategies.

Of course, these enhancements aren't likely to be worth much if you can't quickly find what you're looking for in the book. With that in mind, we've grouped the 150 ETF reports by major category (U.S. Stock—Diversified, U.S. Stock—Sector, Foreign Stock—Diversified, Foreign Stock—Country/Region, Fixed Income, Specialty/Other) and reorganized the data tables at the back of the book. This, we believe, should make it much easier for you to quickly home in on specific types of ETFs, or other information, you're seeking.

Change might not always bring clarity, especially where a profusion of new ETFs is concerned. But we sincerely hope that the changes we've made in this newest installment of *Morningstar ETFs 150* greatly enhance your research.

Jeffrey Ptak, Editor *Morningstar ETFs 150*

How to Use This Book

This book's goal is to help you make more-informed investment decisions using ETFs.

by Jeffrey Ptak, CPA, CFA
Editor, Morningstar ETF's 150

In the pages that follow, we'll walk you through the basics of ETFs, explore our distinctive approach to evaluating ETFs, provide examples of how ETFs can be used in practice, and offer our take on some of the newest and most-compelling ETFs to cross our radar.

But lest we get ahead of ourselves, let's pause to mull a simple question: What is an ETF? If you find yourself straining to come up with an answer, do not hang your head in shame. Your secret is safe with us! In all seriousness, before you plunge headlong into the details, you'll want to spend a few minutes reading through the "ETF Basics" tutorial, which will get you acquainted with the whats, hows, and whys of ETFs.

This Book's Layout

Before we delve into some of the more important tools and concepts featured in the book, let's take a moment to review its layout. We've organized the book with simplicity and ease of use in mind. To that end, we've divvied it up into four primary sections.

Introduction

In addition to this piece, you'll find in the introduction the following other educational and idea-centric articles that provide insight into ETFs and our approach.

ETF Basics: A quick introduction to ETFs and the advantages and disadvantages of using them.

Report Page Guide: An annotated guide to the Morningstar analyst report page.

Constructing a Winning Portfolio with ETFs: A primer on factors to consider when using ETFs to build an efficient, low-cost portfolio.

Beating the Market with ETFs: The low-down on the Morningstar approach to identifying, and profiting from, fundamentally attractive ETFs.

ETFs on Our Buy List: A short-list of the most-attractive ETFs on our radar.

Those of you who are relatively new to ETFs should make these introductory pieces your first stop, as they'll help orient you to concepts that are central to ETF investing.

Reports

This is the book's focal point: 150 analyst reports on funds spanning virtually every asset class and investment style. If you have a question regarding a particular ETF or want to bone up on a certain type of fund, make this your destination.

Though the annotated "Report Page Guide" provides a detailed illustration of the stock and bond analyst report page layout, here's a quick primer on the report page's major sections:

- Morningstar's Take: Our analysts' objective, plain-English take on a fund's merits. In cases in which Morningstar's stock analysts cover a significant number of an equity ETF's underlying holdings, the take includes a discussion of the stocks' quality, the risk of those holdings, and the portfolio's diversification. In other cases, the take is devoted to analyzing salient attributes like a fund's cost, portfolio construction, risk, and past performance.
- Valuation: In cases in which our equity analysts cover a large proportion of a stock ETF's holdings, this section will provide color on an ETF's valuation and how attractive we consider the ETF.
- Methodology: A concise description of which index the ETF tracks, how that index is constructed, and what portfolio biases or other traits it might confer.
- History: A year-by-year chronicle of a fund's performance. Also includes portfolio and expense data.
- Performance: A compilation of quarterly, annualized, and tax-adjusted return data, including relative return statistics.
- Rating and Risk: A breakdown of a fund's Morningstar rating, as well as other statistical risk and return measures.
- Portfolio Analysis: A listing of the ETF's top holdings; also includes a breakdown of the portfolio by sector and other key metrics, such as valuation, growth, or profitability.

To make it easier to browse these reports, we've broken the "Reports" section into subsections by major ETF category. Those subsections are:

- U.S. Stock-Diversified: This is home to ETFs whose stock holdings span multiple styles or market-cap strata. Examples include SPDRs (which tracks the S&P 500 Index, a commonly cited proxy for the U.S. equity market), Diamonds (which tracks another popular broad-market benchmark, the Dow Jones Industrial Average), and iShares Russell 2000 (which follows the small-cap Russell 2000 Index).

- U.S. Stock-Sector: Here you'll find reports on ETFs whose stock holdings cluster in a particular sector or industry or coalesce around a certain theme. Prominent examples include Energy Select Sector SPDRs, an ETF that devotes all of its assets to the stocks of energy-producing firms, and Powershares Water Resources, which invests in the stocks of companies that focus on the provision or treatment of water.

- Foreign Stock-Diversified: There are a number of ETFs that invest in the stocks of companies based overseas, be they in developed nations or emerging markets. In fact, iShares MSCI EAFE, an ETF that mimics the uber-popular MSCI EAFE Index (which tracks stocks in developed countries in Europe and Asia), is the second-largest ETF measured by assets under management. Diversified emerging-markets, foreign growth, foreign value, foreign small-cap, and a variety of other diversified foreign-stock ETFs call this section home.

- Foreign Stock-Country/Region: Interested in investing in the best that the country of Brazil has to offer? Or perhaps you prefer to fan out across Latin America. Australia caught your fancy? You can whet your appetite with a wide range of ETFs targeting specific regions or locales. This section contains reports on more than a dozen such offerings.

- Fixed Income: One of the fastest-growing segments of the ETF market, bond ETFs have sprouted left and right in recent years. Bond ETFs can take a variety of forms, ranging from funds that target the broad taxable investment-grade market, such as Vanguard Total Bond Market, to more-specialized offerings like iShares Lehman TIPS, which invests in Treasury Inflation-Protected Securities. There are now even ETFs that invest in municipal bonds. You'll find our reports on 10 bond ETFs in this section.

- Specialty/Other: ETFs aren't confined to investing solely in stocks or bonds. To the contrary, we've seen a profusion of funds targeting commodities, currencies, and precious metals. For instance, iPath Dow Jones-AIG Commodity Index is tied to the returns of a diversified basket of commodities. We've compiled reports on seven such offerings in this section.

We've sorted the reports in each of these subsections alphabetically by fund name in order to make paging through the book a snap.

Tables and Charts

It's one thing to research a single ETF, or compare and contrast a small group of ETFs—tasks that are straightforward and easy to pull off by browsing the 150 analyst reports that comprise the book's midsection. But what if you want to survey the broader ETF landscape and compare funds across a number of different metrics? Say, for instance, you want to know which ETF, regardless of type, put up the best returns in 2007. Or which is paying the fattest dividend yield. Or maybe even which ETF owned the highest-quality, or lowest-risk, stocks.

This book's tables and charts section—which immediately follows the reports section—is just the ticket. We've compiled a wealth of performance, portfolio, risk, and other data for you to crunch to your heart's content. To make it easier to pore through the data, we've subdivided this section into a few subsections, as follows:

- Performance Summary: Here you'll find risk, return, portfolio, and expense data for each of the nearly 700 ETFs listed in the U.S. as of December 2007. It's worth noting that where applicable, we've cross-referenced the data tables to the relevant report page of any ETF that we cover in the book. Thus, if you spy an ETF in the tables that looks intriguing, you can quickly jump to the relevant report, if available.

- Morningstar Research: These tables, which are a new addition to this year's edition, screen and rank ETFs based on our proprietary valuation, stock quality, and stock risk criteria. Using them, you can more-readily ascertain which ETFs our analysts rate highly or poorly.

- Size & Popularity Stats: Face it—we're interested in the consensus view, even if we don't always subscribe to it ourselves. So, knowing which ETFs investors are flocking to, or fleeing, can offer useful clues that become part of your decision-making process. For instance, heavy outflows from a particular fund or group of funds might be a contrarian buy signal. More prosaically, it can also be helpful to understand which ETFs investors are finding most useful, an insight that can be gleaned from our ranking of the largest funds.

- Yield and Cost Data: For you income-minded types, our table of highest-yielding ETFs is likely to prove quite valuable. And for those of you who don't want to spend one one-hundredth of a percentage point more than you have to, our table of ETFs with the lowest annual expenses should come in handy.

- Portfolio & Volatility Data: Here we compare ETFs across various valuation (price/earnings, etc.), growth (sales growth, etc.), and profitability measures (return on equity, etc.). In addition, we've ranked ETFs based on their trailing one-, three-, and five-year volatility stats to give you a sense of the wildest, and most sedate, funds the ETF world has to offer.

Glossary

Don't know a basis point from a bump on a log? Fear not. This book's glossary, which covers more than 150 commonly used terms and concepts, should bring you up to speed in no time.

Know Your Objective

As we explain further in our "ETF Basics" piece, ETFs can be used to accomplish a wide variety of goals. This book is primarily focused on two of them: constructing a more efficient portfolio and beating the market.

Portfolio-Builder

You're a portfolio-builder if your primary goal is to construct a portfolio that appropriately balances risk and reward. Typically, the need for diversification plays an important role in that process. Therefore, you pay a good deal of attention not just to the way a given ETF portfolio is constructed (including the types of securities it owns), but also to the relationship between various funds. You're interested in specialty ETFs, such as sector- or region-specific funds, only insofar as they fill gaps in your portfolio, thereby advancing your goal of achieving broad diversification.

You're also focused on minimizing expenses and taxes, as those factors can weigh on your long-term returns. Finally, while you'd like to beat the market (who wouldn't!), your paramount concern is ensuring that you meet your investing goals without taking on scads of risk. Some of you might even be skeptical of active managers' ability to beat the market over the long haul, reinforcing your conviction in the wisdom of constructing a well-diversified portfolio using low-cost ETFs that simply track an index.

Market-Beater

You're a market-beater if your goal is to beat the market on a risk-adjusted basis. Unlike the portfolio-builder, to whom portfolio diversification is paramount, you're primarily interested in identifying and seizing opportunities for excess returns, wherever they happen to reside. Therefore, you're not all that concerned if your portfolio skews toward certain parts of the market. Further, you're only too happy to invest in narrowly focused ETFs, like sector funds, when they present inviting opportunities, such as during a particular industry's sell-off, when buying opportunities are created.

An ETF portfolio's construction and composition are relevant as they relate to the quality, risk, and valuation of the fund's underlying holdings. All of these attributes play a role in determining the fund's expected future return and the degree of uncertainty associated with realizing that return.

Though you consider expenses important, you view them as a hurdle that a prospective investment must overcome, not a factor that governs your decisions.

The reality is that not every investor will fit either of these profiles to a T—at least some of you might be a mix of both. For instance, you might use a handful of low-cost ETFs to achieve broad-market diversification (as a portfolio-builder would) and surround those core funds with sector or specialty ETFs that you use to make opportunistic investments in certain parts of the market (like a market-beater).

The point is this: To get the biggest bang for your buck, you'll want to at least consider your objective, as it will play a part in determining which sections of the book are most relevant to you.

Putting the Pieces Together

So, you know how the book is laid out. You've also reflected on the goals you're seeking to achieve by using ETFs. Now what?

Below we've mapped the two types of ETF investors to this book's main sections. Within each column of the tables below, you'll find a listing of the various feature pieces, report-page sections, or tables that address a particular attribute. For instance, portfolio-builders can find commentary or data on a fund's returns in the "History", "Performance", "Rating and Risk", and "Morningstar's Take" sections of the report page. And so forth.

A Great Offer at an Unbeatable Price

When you purchase this book, you get a free 30-day research pass to Morningstar.com, where you'll find a wealth of additional ETF analysis. Importantly, you can use the research pass to bring yourself up to date on changes in the valuation of ETFs that might have taken place since this book was published. After all, the markets never sleep.

If you're not already a Morningstar.com Premium Member, it's an offer worth taking advantage of. M

Portfolio-Builder		Introduction	Reports	Tables & Charts
	Portfolio Construction	ETF Basics Constructing a Winning Portfolio with ETFs	• Methodology • Portfolio Analysis • Morningstar's Take	• Highest/Lowest Quality • Least/Most Risky • Valuation Measures • Growth Measures • Profitability Measures
	Returns	See all articles listed above.	• History • Performance • Rating and Risk • Morningstar's Take	• Performance Summary • Best/Worst Performing • Highest Yielding
	Risk	See all articles listed above.	• History • Rating and Risk • Morningstar's Take	• Least/Most Risky • Least/Most Volatile
	Cost	See all articles listed above.	• History • Morningstar's Take	• Lowest Expenses
	Tax Efficiency	See all articles listed above.	• Performance	• Performance Summary

Market-Beater		Introduction	Reports	Tables & Charts
	Company Quality	ETF Basics Beating the Market with ETFs ETFs on Our Buy List	• Valuation • Methodology • Portfolio Analysis • Morningstar's Take	• Highest/Lowest Quality • Growth Measures • Profitability Measures
	Business Risk	See all articles listed above.	• History • Performance • Rating and Risk • Morningstar's Take	• Least/Most Risky • Least/Most Volatile
	Valuation	See all articles listed above.	• Morningstar Fair Value • Valuation • Morningstar's Take • Portfolio Analysis	• Performance Summary • Cheapest/Dearest • Valuation Measures
	Portfolio Diversification	See all articles listed above.	• Methodology • Morningstar's Take • Portfolio Analysis	• Least/Most Volatile
	Cost	See all articles listed above.	• History • Morningstar's Take	• Performance Summary • Lowest Expenses

The Morningstar Stock-ETF Page

In this six-page walk-through, we briefly describe how each section of the page is relevant to your ETF research and offer some tips on using these features to better analyze ETFs. More-detailed discussions of the elements presented in this section appear in the Glossary.

Data through December 31, 2007

Vanguard TSM ETF VTI

Market Price	Mstar Category
$145.15	Large Blend

Morningstar Rating	Return	Risk	Yield	NAV	Avg Daily Vol. (k)	52 wk High/Low
★★★★	Above Avg	Average	1.8%	$145.27	389	$155.49 - $136.50

A Investment Value Graph

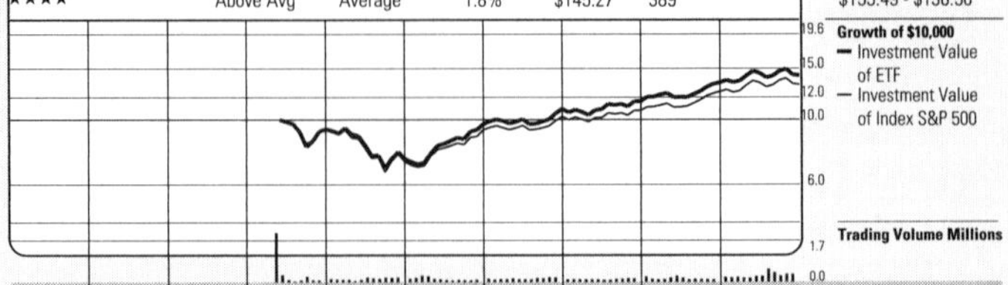

B Morningstar Fair Value

Morningstar Fair Value

Price/Fair Value Ratio	Coverage Rate %
0.90	92

C Valuation

Valuation

This ETF owns the entire U.S. stock market, but solid firms with real earnings and cash flow still carry more weight. That diversification gives the fund a stable risk profile. So, we'd only need an 8% discount to our fair value estimates to buy. Recently the fund was trading at a 10% discount, putting it in "bargain" territory.

D Methodology

Methodology

This ETF tracks the MSCI U.S. Broad Market Index, which includes almost every domestic stock. It ranks stocks by their free-float market capitalizations (or the value of all the shares that regularly trade) and covers 99.5% of the U.S. equity market. There are some differences between it and other total-market indexes. For example, unlike the Wilshire 5000 index, this benchmark includes the stocks of firms that are headquartered abroad but do most of their business in the U.S., such as Montpelier Re Holdings. In general it has and should correlate closely with other core stock indexes.

1998	1999	2000	2001	2002	2003	2004	2005	2006	2007	History
—	—	—	105.80	82.47	106.81	118.21	123.25	140.08	145.27	NAV $
—	—	—	105.39	82.52	106.46	118.05	123.33	140.21	145.15	Market Price $
—	—	—	4.84*	-20.93	31.44	12.55	6.10	15.66	5.56	NAV Return%
—	—	—	5.33*	-20.58	30.93	12.77	6.31	15.69	5.37	Market Price Return%
—	—	—	0.32	-0.09	-0.01	0.01	0.04	0.02	0.01	Avg Premium/Discount%
—	—	—	—	1.17	2.76	1.67	1.19	-0.13	0.07	NAV Rtrn% +/-S&P 500
—	—	—	—	—	—	0.16	-0.27	-0.06	-0.03	NAV Rtrn% +/-MSCI Tot Mkt
—	—	—	—	47	38	38	35	37	55	NAV Return% Rank in Cat
—	—	—	—	1.19	1.69	1.79	1.77	1.88	1.86	Income Return %
—	—	—	—	-22.12	29.75	10.76	4.33	13.78	3.70	Capital Return %
—	—	—	0.99	1.25	1.38	1.90	2.08	2.30	2.60	Income $
—	—	—	0.00	0.00	0.00	0.00	0.00	0.00	0.00	Capital Gains $
—	—	—	0.15	0.15	0.15	0.13	0.07	0.07	—	Expense Ratio %
—	—	—	1.26	1.38	1.54	1.79	1.74	1.78	—	Income Ratio %
—	—	—	7	4	11	4	12	4	—	Turnover Rate %
—	—	—	—	1,290	2,517	4,259	5,612	6,885	10,255	Net Assets $mil

E Performance

Performance 12-31-07

Historic Quarterly NAV Returns

	1st Qtr	2nd Qtr	3rd Qtr	4th Qtr	Total
2003	-3.13	16.46	3.62	12.43	31.44
2004	2.59	1.29	-1.83	10.33	12.55
2005	-2.38	2.20	4.05	2.19	6.10
2006	5.38	-1.94	4.52	7.09	15.66
2007	1.36	6.08	1.54	-3.32	5.56

Trailing	NAV Return%	Market Return%	NAV Rtrn% +/-S&P 500	%Rank Cat.(NAV)
3 Mo	-3.32	-3.49	0.01	50
6 Mo	-1.83	-1.90	-0.46	51
1 Yr	5.56	5.37	0.07	55
3 Yr Avg	9.01	9.03	0.39	48
5 Yr Avg	13.89	13.86	1.06	23
10 Yr Avg	—	—	—	—

F Tax Analysis

Tax Analysis	Tax-Adj Return%	Tax-Cost Ratio
3 Yr (estimated)	8.72	0.27
5 Yr (estimated)	13.57	0.28
10 Yr (estimated)	—	—

Rating and Risk

Time Period	Morningstar Rtn vs Cat	Morningstar Risk vs Cat	Morningstar Risk-Adj Rating
3 Yr	Avg	Avg	★★★
5 Yr	+Avg	Avg	★★★★
10 Yr	—	—	—

Other Measures	Standard Index S&P 500	Best Fit Index M* U.S. Mkt TR
Alpha	0.2	-0.3
Beta	1.05	1.01
R-Squared	98	100
Standard Deviation	8.28	
Mean	9.01	
Sharpe Ratio	0.57	

Portfolio Analysis 09-30-07

Share change since 06-07 Total Stocks:3623	Sector	PE	Tot Ret%	% Assets
⊕ ExxonMobil Corporation	Energy	13.6	24.34	3.08
⊕ General Electric Company	Ind Mtrls	16.6	2.69	2.51
⊕ AT&T, Inc.	Telecom	21.6	20.58	1.54
⊕ Microsoft Corporation	Software	23.4	20.83	1.50
⊕ Citigroup, Inc.	Financial	7.9	-44.93	1.36
⊕ Bank of America Corporat	Financial	9.4	-19.25	1.32
⊕ Procter & Gamble Company	Goods	23.1	16.63	1.31
⊕ Chevron Corporation	Energy	11.4	30.59	1.19
⊕ Cisco Systems, Inc.	Hardware	21.5	-0.95	1.19
⊕ Johnson & Johnson	Health	18.8	3.61	1.12
⊕ International Business M	Hardware	16.2	13.20	1.03
⊕ Pfizer Inc.	Health	22.5	-8.15	1.01
⊕ J.P. Morgan Chase & Co.	Financial	9.5	-7.24	0.92
⊕ Intel Corporation	Hardware	25.4	34.22	0.89
⊕ American International G	Financial	10.2	-17.96	0.88
⊕ Altria Group Inc.	Goods	13.2	22.10	0.86
⊕ ConocoPhillips	Energy	13.8	25.42	0.80
⊕ Apple, Inc.	Hardware	50.5	133.47	0.78
⊕ Google, Inc.	Business	54.0	50.17	0.78
⊕ Hewlett-Packard Company	Hardware	18.8	23.40	0.77

Current Investment Style

Value Blnd Growth — Large Mid Small

Market Cap	%
Giant	42.0
Large	30.5
Mid	19.3
Small	6.1
Micro	2.1
Avg $mil: 31,195	

Value Measures		Rel Category
Price/Earnings	15.97	1.01
Price/Book	2.58	1.01
Price/Sales	1.46	1.18
Price/Cash Flow	10.49	1.13
Dividend Yield %	1.63	0.86

Growth Measures	%	Rel Category
Long-Term Erngs	11.00	0.93
Book Value	10.20	1.10
Sales	-1.77	NMF
Cash Flow	3.02	0.35
Historical Erngs	11.78	0.70

Profitability	%	Rel Category
Return on Equity	20.72	0.93
Return on Assets	7.76	0.93
Net Margin	14.00	1.14

Sector Weightings	% of Stocks	Rel S&P 500	3 Year High	3 Year Low
Info	20.72	0.99		
Software	3.85	0.93	4	4
Hardware	10.06	0.99	10	9
Media	3.19	1.10	4	3
Telecom	3.62	1.00	4	3
Service	43.85	1.08		
Health	11.73	0.98	13	12
Consumer	7.55	1.11	10	8
Business	5.26	1.19	6	5
Financial	19.31	1.11	22	19
Mfg	35.44	0.92		
Goods	8.05	0.88	9	7
Ind Mtrls	12.83	0.99	13	11
Energy	10.95	0.87	11	8
Utilities	3.61	0.98	4	3

Composition

Cash	0.5
Stocks	99.4
Bonds	0.1
Other	0.0
Foreign (% of Stock)	0.2

G Morningstar's Take

Morningstar's Take by Dan Culloton 12-31-07

You'll find nearly the entire market here, warts and all. Formidable companies predominate, though, making it easy to own at a slight margin of safety.

Vanguard Total Stock Market ETF tracks the MSCI U.S. Broad Market Index, which includes nearly all publicly traded domestic stocks. Its 2,000 holdings include everything from market bellwethers such as General Electric and Bank of America, to speculative micro-caps like Human Genome Sciences and Standard Pacific.

Stocks with durable competitive advantages have the most influence, though. GE, which has a diverse portfolio of well-managed market-leading businesses, and Bank of America, which offers a hard-to-match branch system and services to retail customers, handily outweigh the profitless likes of Human Genome Sciences. In fact, the fund invests more than three quarters of assets in stocks that boast some kind of defensible advantage, or economic moat, which is higher than most equity ETFs. On balance, though, the portfolio's quality is middling, not an unexpected state of affairs considering that the fund purports to represent the entire U.S. stock market.

The portfolio's mediocre quality gives the ETF a middling risk profile, as well. Generally speaking, the more dominant the firm, the more certain its future results. In that sense, the presence of wide-moat companies like Procter & Gamble, whose unmatched and varied array of name brand consumer products help it weather economic cycles, offsets holdings like oil refiner Valero Energy, whose returns are at the mercy of the volatile spread between oil and refined products prices as well as a disappearing edge in processing high sulfur crude. All told, this fund's typical holding courts average risk in our analysts' view.

Taken together with its wide diversification across holdings and industries, the portfolio's middling-quality, moderate-risk profile has tamped down volatility. We'd be buyers at a modest 8% discount to our fair value estimate.

H Operations

Address:	PO Box 2600 United States 800-662-7447	Management Fee:	0.04%		
		Expense Projections:	3Yr:$23	5Yr:$40	10Yr:$90
		Income Distrib:	Quarterly		
Web Address:	www.vanguard.com	Exchange:	AMEX		
Inception:	05-24-01 *				
Advisor:	The Vanguard Group, Inc.				

79

MORNINGSTAR® ETFs 150

A Investment Value Graph

The Investment Value graph line shows an ETF's performance trend, derived from the ETF's historical growth of $10,000. It provides a visual depiction of how an ETF has amassed its returns, including the performance swings its shareholders have endured along the way. The growth of $10,000 begins at the date of the ETF's inception, or if the ETF has been in existence for more than 10 years, at the first year listed on the graph. Also, featured in the graph is the performance of an index (S&P 500 or MSCI EAFE, for example), which allows investors to compare the performance of the ETF with the benchmark index.

B Morningstar Fair Value

This section is home to the Morningstar Price/Fair Value and Coverage Rate % datapoints. The price/fair value ratio is a measure of a stock ETF's valuation based on Morningstar's analysis of its underlying holdings. The lower the price/fair value ratio, the cheaper our analysts consider the fund's holdings. The price/fair value ratio is only meaningful if our analysts cover a significant portion of the portfolio. With that in mind, the coverage rate indicates the percentage of fund assets represented by holdings that our analysts cover.

C Valuation

This section sets forth Morningstar analyst commentary on a stock ETF's valuation traits, including its recent valuation and whether it constitutes a bargain or not. Our analysts also provide historical context, such as how a fund's valuation compares to the recent past. If our analysts don't cover a significant portion of the portfolio, we'll indicate that here.

D Methodology

While the Morningstar Category gives investors an idea of the kind of investments an ETF makes; it does not fully capture the nuances of the ETFs methodology for capturing the returns of the market segment it claims to represent. In this section, Morningstar's analysts might explain how an ETF's benchmark selects securities for inclusion, how often it rebalances, when it decides to kick issues out, how it controls turnover, and how risky it may be. On the equity side, the strategy description often focuses on what size and type of company ETF's index focuses on. For style-based ETFs this includes a discussion of how the index defines growth and value stocks. With bond ETFs, the strategy section might explain how the ETF goes about matching the duration, credit quality, and maturity of its benchmark index.

E Performance

The quarterly returns show the performance investors have seen over each calendar quarter in the past five years. This section is a good spot to quickly test your risk tolerance. Find the largest quarterly loss; if it makes you uneasy, you should probably look for less-volatile ETFs. The trailing returns section illustrates performance over short and long periods. We compare returns against appropriate benchmarks and peers: 1 is the best percentile; 100 is the worst.

F Tax Analysis

This section lists an ETF's tax-adjusted returns and the percentage-point reduction in annualized returns that results from taxes, called the tax-cost ratio. For context, each figure is then given a percentile rank in the ETF's category (1 is the best percentile; 100 is the worst). Examine the two returns figures together because high tax-adjusted returns do not necessarily mean the ETF is tax-efficient. Also, an ETF could be very tax efficient, but if returns are poor to begin with, an investor will still pocket a low sum.

G Morningstar's Take

Our analysts interpret the data on the page and interview the ETF's manager to explain the methodologies guiding investment decisions. They then succinctly detail how and why an ETF has succeeded or failed, and what role—if any—it should play in your portfolio.

H Operations

Here we list where to write or call to obtain investment information from the ETF. We also list the ETF's management fee, income distribution frequency, inception date, and exchange on which it trades.

The Morningstar Stock-ETF Page (continued)

I Morningstar Category

J History

K Portfolio Analysis

L Rating and Risk

Data through December 31, 2007

Vanguard TSM ETF VTI

Market Price $145.15

Mstar Category Large Blend

Morningstar Fair Value

Price/Fair Value Ratio	Coverage Rate %
0.90	92

Morningstar Rating	Return	Risk	Yield	NAV	Avg Daily Vol. (k)	52 wk High/Low
★★★★	Above Avg	Average	1.8%	$145.27	389	$155.49 - $136.50

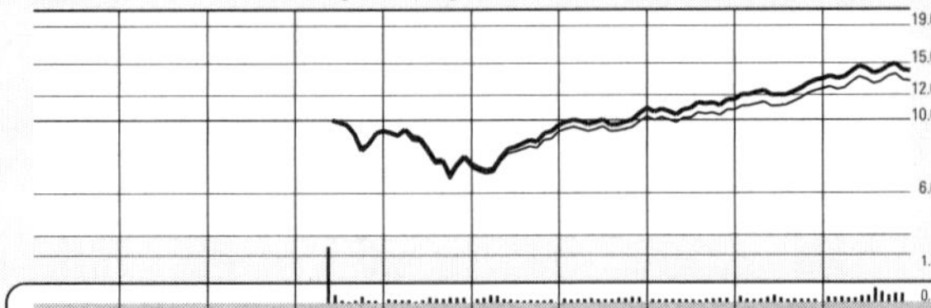

Valuation

This ETF owns the entire U.S. stock market, but solid firms with real earnings and cash flow still carry more weight. That diversification gives the fund a stable risk profile. So, we'd only need an 8% discount to our fair value estimates to buy. Recently the fund was trading at a 10% discount, putting it in "bargain" territory.

Methodology

This ETF tracks the MSCI U.S. Broad Market Index, which includes almost every domestic stock. It ranks stocks by their free-float market capitalizations (or the value of all the shares that regularly trade) and covers 99.5% of the U.S. equity market. There are some differences between it and other total-market indexes. For example, unlike the Wilshire 5000 index, this benchmark includes the stocks of firms that are headquartered abroad but do most of their business in the U.S., such as Montpelier Re Holdings. In general it has and should correlate closely with other core stock indexes.

1998	1999	2000	2001	2002	2003	2004	2005	2006	2007	History
—	—	—	105.80	82.47	106.81	118.21	123.25	140.08	145.27	NAV $
—	—	—	105.39	82.52	106.46	118.05	123.33	140.21	145.15	Market Price $
—	—	—	4.84*	-20.93	31.44	12.55	6.10	15.66	5.56	NAV Return%
—	—	—	5.33*	-20.58	30.93	12.77	6.31	15.69	5.37	Market Price Return%
—	—	—	0.32	-0.09	-0.01	0.01	0.04	0.02	0.01	Avg Premium/Discount%
—	—	—	—	1.17	2.76	1.67	1.19	-0.13	0.07	NAV Rtrn% +/-S&P 500
—	—	—	—	—	—	0.16	-0.27	-0.06	-0.03	NAV Rtrn% +/-MSCI Tot Mkt
—	—	—	—	47	38	38	35	37	55	NAV Return% Rank in Cat
—	—	—	—	1.19	1.69	1.79	1.77	1.88	1.86	Income Return %
—	—	—	—	-22.12	29.75	10.76	4.33	13.78	3.70	Capital Return %
—	—	—	0.99	1.25	1.38	1.90	2.08	2.30	2.60	Income $
—	—	—	0.00	0.00	0.00	0.00	0.00	0.00	0.00	Capital Gains $
—	—	—	0.15	0.15	0.15	0.13	0.07	0.07	—	Expense Ratio %
—	—	—	1.26	1.38	1.54	1.79	1.74	1.78	—	Income Ratio %
—	—	—	7	4	11	4	12	4	—	Turnover Rate %
—	—	—	—	1,290	2,517	4,259	5,612	6,885	10,255	Net Assets $mil

Performance 12-31-07

Historic Quarterly NAV Returns

	1st Qtr	2nd Qtr	3rd Qtr	4th Qtr	Total
2003	-3.13	16.46	3.62	12.43	31.44
2004	2.59	1.29	-1.83	10.33	12.55
2005	-2.38	2.20	4.05	2.19	6.10
2006	5.38	-1.94	4.52	7.09	15.66
2007	1.36	6.08	1.54	-3.32	5.56

Trailing	NAV Return%	Market Return%	NAV Rtrn% +/-S&P 500	%Rank Cat.(NAV)
3 Mo	-3.32	-3.49	0.01	50
6 Mo	-1.83	-1.90	-0.46	51
1 Yr	5.56	5.37	0.07	55
3 Yr Avg	9.01	9.03	0.39	48
5 Yr Avg	13.89	13.86	1.06	23
10 Yr Avg	—	—	—	—

Tax Analysis	Tax-Adj Return%	Tax-Cost Ratio
3 Yr (estimated)	8.72	0.27
5 Yr (estimated)	13.57	0.28
10 Yr (estimated)	—	—

Rating and Risk

Time Period	Morningstar Rtn vs Cat	Morningstar Risk vs Cat	Morningstar Risk-Adj Rating
3 Yr	Avg	Avg	★★★
5 Yr	+Avg	Avg	★★★★
10 Yr	—	—	—

Other Measures	Standard Index S&P 500	Best Fit Index M* U.S. Mkt TR
Alpha	0.2	-0.3
Beta	1.05	1.01
R-Squared	98	100
Standard Deviation	8.28	
Mean	9.01	
Sharpe Ratio	0.57	

Portfolio Analysis 09-30-07

Share change since 06-07 Total Stocks:3623	Sector	PE	Tot Ret%	% Assets
⊕ ExxonMobil Corporation	Energy	13.6	24.34	3.08
⊕ General Electric Company	Ind Mtrls	16.6	2.69	2.51
⊕ AT&T, Inc.	Telecom	21.6	20.58	1.54
⊕ Microsoft Corporation	Software	23.4	20.83	1.50
⊕ Citigroup, Inc.	Financial	7.9	-44.93	1.36
⊕ Bank of America Corporat	Financial	9.4	-19.25	1.32
⊕ Procter & Gamble Company	Goods	23.1	16.63	1.31
⊕ Chevron Corporation	Energy	11.4	30.59	1.19
⊕ Cisco Systems, Inc.	Hardware	21.5	-0.95	1.19
⊕ Johnson & Johnson	Health	18.8	3.61	1.12
⊕ International Business M	Hardware	16.2	13.20	1.03
⊕ Pfizer Inc.	Health	22.5	-8.15	1.01
⊕ J.P. Morgan Chase & Co.	Financial	9.5	-7.24	0.92
⊕ Intel Corporation	Hardware	25.4	34.22	0.89
⊕ American International G	Financial	10.2	-17.96	0.88
⊕ Altria Group Inc.	Goods	13.2	22.10	0.86
⊕ ConocoPhillips	Energy	13.8	25.42	0.80
⊕ Apple, Inc.	Hardware	50.5	133.47	0.78
⊕ Google, Inc.	Business	54.0	50.17	0.78
⊕ Hewlett-Packard Company	Hardware	18.8	23.40	0.77

Current Investment Style

Value Blnd Growth — Large Mid Small

Market Cap	%
Giant	42.0
Large	30.5
Mid	19.3
Small	6.1
Micro	2.1

Avg $mil: 31,195

Value Measures		Rel Category
Price/Earnings	15.97	1.01
Price/Book	2.58	1.01
Price/Sales	1.46	1.18
Price/Cash Flow	10.49	1.13
Dividend Yield %	1.63	0.86

Growth Measures	%	Rel Category
Long-Term Erngs	11.00	0.93
Book Value	10.20	1.10
Sales	-1.77	NMF
Cash Flow	3.02	0.35
Historical Erngs	11.78	0.70

Profitability	%	Rel Category
Return on Equity	20.72	0.93
Return on Assets	7.76	0.93
Net Margin	14.00	1.14

Sector Weightings	% of Stocks	Rel S&P 500	3 Year High	3 Year Low
Info	20.72	0.99		
Software	3.85	0.93	4	4
Hardware	10.06	0.99	10	9
Media	3.19	1.10	4	3
Telecom	3.62	1.00	4	3
Service	43.85	1.08		
Health	11.73	0.98	13	12
Consumer	7.55	1.11	10	8
Business	5.26	1.19	6	5
Financial	19.31	1.11	22	19
Mfg	35.44	0.92		
Goods	8.05	0.88	9	7
Ind Mtrls	12.83	0.99	13	11
Energy	10.95	0.87	11	8
Utilities	3.61	0.98	4	3

Composition

Cash	0.5
Stocks	99.4
Bonds	0.1
Other	0.0
Foreign (% of Stock)	0.2

Morningstar's Take by Dan Culloton 12-31-07

You'll find nearly the entire market here, warts and all. Formidable companies predominate, though, making it easy to own at a slight margin of safety.

Vanguard Total Stock Market ETF tracks the MSCI U.S. Broad Market Index, which includes nearly all publicly traded domestic stocks. Its 2,000 holdings include everything from market bellwethers such as General Electric and Bank of America, to speculative micro-caps like Human Genome Sciences and Standard Pacific.

Stocks with durable competitive advantages have the most influence, though. GE, which has a diverse portfolio of well-managed market-leading businesses, and Bank of America, which offers a hard-to-match branch system and services to retail customers, handily outweigh the profitless likes of Human Genome Sciences. In fact, the fund invests more than three quarters of assets in stocks that boast some kind of defensible advantage, or economic moat, which is higher than most equity ETFs. On balance, though, the portfolio's quality is middling, not an unexpected state of affairs considering that the fund purports to represent the entire U.S. stock market.

The portfolio's mediocre quality gives the ETF a middling risk profile, as well. Generally speaking, the more dominant the firm, the more certain its future results. In that sense, the presence of wide-moat companies like Procter & Gamble, whose unmatched and varied array of name brand consumer products help it weather economic cycles, offsets holdings like oil refiner Valero Energy, whose returns are at the mercy of the volatile spread between oil and refined products prices as well as a disappearing edge in processing high sulfur crude. All told, this fund's typical holding courts average risk in our analysts' view.

Taken together with its wide diversification across holdings and industries, the portfolio's middling-quality, moderate-risk profile has tamped down volatility. We'd be buyers at a modest 8% discount to our fair value estimate.

Address: PO Box 2600, United States, 800-662-7447
Web Address: www.vanguard.com
Inception: 05-24-01 *
Advisor: The Vanguard Group, Inc.

Management Fee: 0.04%
Expense Projections: 3Yr:$23 5Yr:$40 10Yr:$90
Income Distrib: Quarterly
Exchange: AMEX

79

MORNINGSTAR® ETFs 150

I Morningstar Category

This is the first stage of digging into the ETF's portfolio. We sort ETFs into peer groups based on the types of securities the ETFs hold. Each category is assigned by fundamental analyzing of an ETF's portfolio over a three-year period. It is important to analyze the types of securities an ETF holds. Portfolio analysis, and an ETF's category, can tell you a lot about an ETF's performance and future volatility. For example, investors can expect bumpier rides with ETFs in the small-cap growth category—those that focus on small, rapidly growing companies—than with large-cap value ETFs, which focus on well-established companies that are trading cheaply. In addition to portfolio analysis, the Morningstar categories also can help you diversify and evaluate the role an ETF might play in your portfolio. For example, you might head to the more-volatile categories (the small-cap groups or emerging markets) if you decided to spice up your large-cap-laden portfolio. Or you might want to tone down a growth-oriented portfolio with a value ETF or two.

J History

Use this table to spot trends over the past 10 years. Pay particular attention to the following statistics.

Avg. Premium/Discount %

As explained in the "ETF Basics" feature, because an ETF trades on an exchange, its market price can diverge from net asset value (NAV). Thus, it's worthwhile to eyeball this datapoint, which indicates how closely the fund's price has hewed to NAV over time.

NAV Rtrn % +/–

The first of these two datapoints indicates the degree to which the fund's returns surpassed, or skirted, the broad market. The second datapoint compares the fund's return to its target index (or a comparable substitute). Ideally, an ETF will perfectly track its target index. However, the typical ETF lags by the amount of its expense ratio. This datapoint helps you to pinpoint deviations from the target index, or "tracking error".

Expense Ratio

This percentage shows how much it costs to own the ETF.

Turnover Rate

Virtually all ETFs are index funds and, thus, should have low turnover compared to actively managed funds. Low turnover is generally a plus given that it keeps transaction costs low and enhances a fund's tax-efficiency.

K Portfolio Analysis

Analyzing an ETF's portfolio will give you an understanding of the ETF's performance and potential volatility. First, note the ETF's total holdings: The ETF with fewer stocks will get more kick from its best performers, but if just a few holdings falter, the ETF will lag. All things being equal, an ETF with 50 or fewer stocks will be more volatile than an ETF holding twice as many issues. Next, check the percentage of assets devoted to each security. An ETF following a concentrated index will have large chunks of the ETF's assets (more than 5% per stock) invested in its top holdings. Now identify each stock's sector to gain insight into where an ETF's top holdings are concentrated and where its vulnerabilities lie. Then check the stocks' P/E ratios; high P/Es are another indication of possible future volatility. Each stock's year-to-date returns tell you which securities in which sectors are driving the performance of the ETF.

L Rating and Risk

This section breaks down the ETF's risk, returns, and overall star rating over the three-, five-, and 10-year time periods. The return versus category section shows how the ETF's returns compare with those of ETFs and conventional open-end mutual funds in its peer group. We rate the top 10% ETFs "high", the next 22.5% "above average", and the middle 35% "average". We call the next 22.5% ETFs "below average", and the bottom 10% "low". Similarly, the Risk versus Category section ranks a fund's historical volatility versus that of its peer group, with those funds that have exhibited a lot of downside volatility faring worse than those that have not. The rationale here is highly volatile funds are risky, but those offerings that tend to lose a lot of money are most worrisome to investors. The historical star ratings offer some clues regarding the consistency of a fund's historical risk-adjusted performance. Those with 5-star three-, five-, and 10-year results have often put up consistently strong risk-adjusted results while those with poor marks have often languished year after year. Funds with markedly different short- and long-term results may have extreme strategies that produce feast-or-famine returns or they may have experienced a manager change that has materially affected performance.

The Morningstar Stock-ETF Page (continued)

M Style Box

N Sector Weightings

O Growth and Value Measures

P Composition Information

Data through December 31, 2007

Vanguard TSM ETF VTI

Market Price	Mstar Category
$145.15	Large Blend

Morningstar Fair Value

Price/Fair Value Ratio	Coverage Rate %
0.90	92

Valuation

This ETF owns the entire U.S. stock market, but solid firms with real earnings and cash flow still carry more weight. That diversification gives the fund a stable risk profile. So, we'd only need an 8% discount to our fair value estimates to buy. Recently the fund was trading at a 10% discount, putting it in "bargain" territory.

Methodology

This ETF tracks the MSCI U.S. Broad Market Index, which includes almost every domestic stock. It ranks stocks by their free-float market capitalizations (or the value of all the shares that regularly trade) and covers 99.5% of the U.S. equity market. There are some differences between it and other total-market indexes. For example, unlike the Wilshire 5000 index, this benchmark includes the stocks of firms that are headquartered abroad but do most of their business in the U.S., such as Montpelier Re Holdings. In general it has and should correlate closely with other core stock indexes.

Morningstar Rating	Return	Risk	Yield	NAV	Avg Daily Vol. (k)	52 wk High/Low
★★★★	Above Avg	Average	1.8%	$145.27	389	$155.49 - $136.50

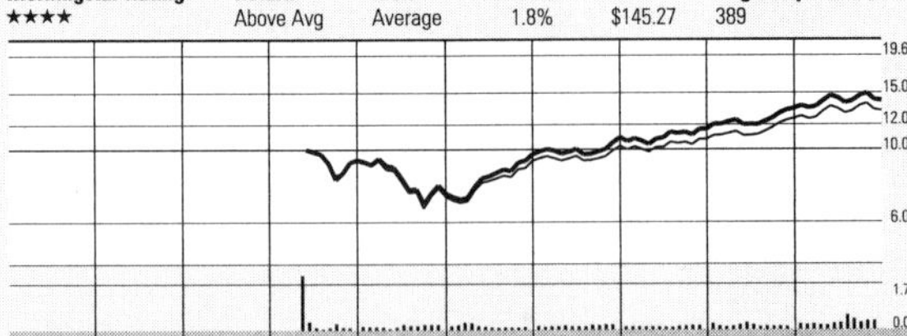

Growth of $10,000
— Investment Value of ETF
— Investment Value of Index S&P 500

Trading Volume Millions

1998	1999	2000	2001	2002	2003	2004	2005	2006	2007	History
—	—	—	105.80	82.47	106.81	118.21	123.25	140.08	145.27	NAV $
—	—	—	105.39	82.52	106.46	118.05	123.33	140.21	145.15	Market Price $
—	—	—	4.84*	-20.93	31.44	12.55	6.10	15.66	5.56	NAV Return%
—	—	—	5.33*	-20.58	30.93	12.77	6.31	15.69	5.37	Market Price Return%
—	—	—	0.32	-0.09	-0.01	0.01	0.04	0.02	0.01	Avg Premium/Discount%
—	—	—	—	1.17	2.76	1.67	1.19	-0.13	0.07	NAV Rtrn% +/-S&P 500
—	—	—	—	—	—	0.16	-0.27	-0.06	-0.03	NAV Rtrn% +/-MSCI Tot Mkt
—	—	—	—	47	38	38	35	37	55	NAV Return% Rank in Cat
—	—	—	—	1.19	1.69	1.79	1.77	1.88	1.86	Income Return %
—	—	—	—	-22.12	29.75	10.76	4.33	13.78	3.70	Capital Return %
—	—	—	0.99	1.25	1.38	1.90	2.08	2.30	2.60	Income $
—	—	—	0.00	0.00	0.00	0.00	0.00	0.00	0.00	Capital Gains $
—	—	—	0.15	0.15	0.15	0.13	0.07	0.07	—	Expense Ratio %
—	—	—	1.26	1.38	1.54	1.79	1.74	1.78	—	Income Ratio %
—	—	—	7	4	11	4	12	4	—	Turnover Rate %
—	—	—	—	1,290	2,517	4,259	5,612	6,885	10,255	Net Assets $mil

Performance 12-31-07

Historic Quarterly NAV Returns

	1st Qtr	2nd Qtr	3rd Qtr	4th Qtr	Total
2003	-3.13	16.46	3.62	12.43	31.44
2004	2.59	1.29	-1.83	10.33	12.55
2005	-2.38	2.20	4.05	2.19	6.10
2006	5.38	-1.94	4.52	7.09	15.66
2007	1.36	6.08	1.54	-3.32	5.56

Trailing	NAV Return%	Market Return%	NAV Rtrn% +/-S&P 500	%Rank Cat.(NAV)
3 Mo	-3.32	-3.49	0.01	50
6 Mo	-1.83	-1.90	-0.46	51
1 Yr	5.56	5.37	0.07	55
3 Yr Avg	9.01	9.03	0.39	48
5 Yr Avg	13.89	13.86	1.06	23
10 Yr Avg	—	—	—	—

Tax Analysis	Tax-Adj Return%	Tax-Cost Ratio
3 Yr (estimated)	8.72	0.27
5 Yr (estimated)	13.57	0.28
10 Yr (estimated)	—	—

Rating and Risk

Time Period	Morningstar Rtn vs Cat	Morningstar Risk vs Cat	Morningstar Risk-Adj Rating
3 Yr	Avg	Avg	★★★
5 Yr	+Avg	Avg	★★★★
10 Yr	—	—	—

Other Measures	Standard Index S&P 500	Best Fit Index M* U.S. Mkt TR
Alpha	0.2	-0.3
Beta	1.05	1.01
R-Squared	98	100
Standard Deviation	8.28	
Mean	9.01	
Sharpe Ratio	0.57	

Portfolio Analysis 09-30-07

Share change since 06-07 Total Stocks:3623	Sector	PE	Tot Ret%	% Assets
⊕ ExxonMobil Corporation	Energy	13.6	24.34	3.08
⊕ General Electric Company	Ind Mtrls	16.6	2.69	2.51
⊕ AT&T, Inc.	Telecom	21.6	20.58	1.54
⊕ Microsoft Corporation	Software	23.4	20.83	1.50
⊕ Citigroup, Inc.	Financial	7.9	-44.93	1.36
⊕ Bank of America Corporat	Financial	9.4	-19.25	1.32
⊕ Procter & Gamble Company	Goods	23.1	16.63	1.31
⊕ Chevron Corporation	Energy	11.4	30.59	1.19
⊕ Cisco Systems, Inc.	Hardware	21.5	-0.95	1.19
⊕ Johnson & Johnson	Health	18.8	3.61	1.12
⊕ International Business M	Hardware	16.2	13.20	1.03
⊕ Pfizer Inc.	Health	22.5	-8.15	1.01
⊕ J.P. Morgan Chase & Co.	Financial	9.5	-7.24	0.92
⊕ Intel Corporation	Hardware	25.4	34.22	0.89
⊕ American International G	Financial	10.2	-17.96	0.88
⊕ Altria Group Inc.	Goods	13.2	22.10	0.86
⊕ ConocoPhillips	Energy	13.8	25.42	0.80
⊕ Apple, Inc.	Hardware	50.5	133.47	0.78
⊕ Google, Inc.	Business	54.0	50.17	0.78
	Hardware	18.8	23.40	0.77

Current Investment Style

Value Blnd Growth / Large Mid Small

Market Cap	%
Giant	42.0
Large	30.5
Mid	19.3
Small	6.1
Micro	2.1
Avg $mil: 31,195	

Value Measures		Rel Category
Price/Earnings	15.97	1.01
Price/Book	2.58	1.01
Price/Sales	1.46	1.18
Price/Cash Flow	10.49	1.13
Dividend Yield %	1.63	0.86

Growth Measures	%	Rel Category
Long-Term Erngs	11.00	0.93
Book Value	10.20	1.10
Sales	-1.77	NMF
Cash Flow	3.02	0.35
Historical Erngs	11.78	0.70

Profitability	%	Rel Category
Return on Equity	20.72	0.93
Return on Assets	7.76	0.93
Net Margin	14.00	1.14

Sector Weightings	% of Stocks	Rel S&P 500	3 Year High	Low
Info	20.72	0.99		
Software	3.85	0.93	4	4
Hardware	10.06	0.99	10	9
Media	3.19	1.10	4	3
Telecom	3.62	1.00	4	3
Service	43.85	1.08		
Health	11.73	0.98	13	12
Consumer	7.55	1.11	10	8
Business	5.26	1.19	6	5
Financial	19.31	1.11	22	19
Mfg	35.44	0.92		
Goods	8.05	0.88	9	7
Ind Mtrls	12.83	0.99	13	11
Energy	10.95	0.87	11	8
Utilities	3.61	0.98	4	3

Composition

Cash	0.5
Stocks	99.4
Bonds	0.1
Other	0.0
Foreign (% of Stock)	0.2

Morningstar's Take by Dan Culloton 12-31-07

You'll find nearly the entire market here, warts and all. Formidable companies predominate, though, making it easy to own at a slight margin of safety.

Vanguard Total Stock Market ETF tracks the MSCI U.S. Broad Market Index, which includes nearly all publicly traded domestic stocks. Its 2,000 holdings include everything from market bellwethers such as General Electric and Bank of America, to speculative micro-caps like Human Genome Sciences and Standard Pacific.

Stocks with durable competitive advantages have the most influence, though. GE, which has a diverse portfolio of well-managed market-leading businesses, and Bank of America, which offers a hard-to-match branch system and services to retail customers, handily outweigh the profitless likes of Human Genome Sciences. In fact, the fund invests more than three quarters of assets in stocks that boast some kind of defensible advantage, or economic moat, which is higher than most equity ETFs. On balance, though, the portfolio's quality is middling, not an unexpected state of affairs considering that the fund purports to represent the entire U.S. stock market.

The portfolio's mediocre quality gives the ETF a middling risk profile, as well. Generally speaking, the more dominant the firm, the more certain its future results. In that sense, the presence of wide-moat companies like Procter & Gamble, whose unmatched and varied array of name brand consumer products help it weather economic cycles, offsets holdings like oil refiner Valero Energy, whose returns are at the mercy of the volatile spread between oil and refined products prices as well as a disappearing edge in processing high sulfur crude. All told, this fund's typical holding courts average risk in our analysts' view.

Taken together with its wide diversification across holdings and industries, the portfolio's middling-quality, moderate-risk profile has tamped down volatility. We'd be buyers at a modest 8% discount to our fair value estimate.

Address:	PO Box 2600, United States, 800-662-7447	Management Fee:	0.04%		
Web Address:	www.vanguard.com	Expense Projections:	3Yr:$23	5Yr:$40	10Yr:$90
Inception:	05-24-01 *	Income Distrib:	Quarterly		
Advisor:	The Vanguard Group, Inc.	Exchange:	AMEX		

79

MORNINGSTAR® ETFs 150

Alpha, Beta, and R-squared are three Modern Portfolio Theory statistics that measure how much you can expect an ETF to follow a market index and whether the ETF has added or subtracted value versus that benchmark. We compare all domestic- and international-equity ETFs with the S&P 500 and a Best Fit Index (the index with which the ETF has the highest correlation).

Alpha
Alpha measures excess returns per unit of risk. The higher the alpha the better. A positive alpha indicates the ETF performed better in the past than its beta would predict. A negative alpha indicates the ETF performed worse. Below these statistics, standard deviation measures risk as volatility by showing the range within which an ETF's monthly returns have landed. The larger the number, the wider the range and more volatile the ETF has been. To set an ETF's standard deviation in context, compare it with others in the ETF's category. The mean represents the annualized total return for an ETF over the trailing three years.

Beta
Beta measures an ETF's volatility relative to its benchmark. A beta of more than 1.0 means the ETF is more volatile than the index and should outperform it when the index is rising and underperform it when the index is falling. A beta of less than 1.0 works the opposite way. The iShares Dow Jones Real Estate Index's beta of 0.94 versus the Dow Jones Real Estate Index means it's just as volatile as that bogy. The ETF's beta of 1.47 versus the S&P 500 means it's more volatile than the broad market.

R-squared
For beta and alpha to be reliable measures of risk and reward, an ETF must have a high correlation with its index, as measured by R-squared. R-squared indicates how marketlike an ETF is. A high R-squared (between 85 and 100) indicates the ETF's performance patterns have been in line with the index's. An ETF with a low R-squared (70 or less) doesn't act much like the index. Index ETFs should have R-squared of 100 when compared against their own or similar indexes, but the measure can vary when they are compared against a different bogy. The iShares Dow Jones Real Estate Index, for example, has an R-squared of 99 versus the Dow Jones Real Estate Index, but an R-squared of 47 versus the S&P 500. That means the ETF is more like the REIT index.

Sharpe Ratio
The Sharpe ratio is a risk-adjusted performance measure. The higher the Sharpe ratio (1.0 is pretty good), the better the ETF's risk-adjusted performance has been.

M Style Box
For stock ETFs, Morningstar assigns style-box classifications based on portfolios' scores for Growth Measures, Value Measures, and average weighted market cap. For example, ETFs that invest predominantly in large-cap, fast-growing firms with high valuations typically land in large growth. By contrast, ETFs that specialize in smaller, slower-growing firms with modest valuations are assigned to the small-value style box.

N Sector Weightings
Learn which sectors of the economy the ETF invests in to gauge how diversified the ETF is. An ETF that has more than 25% of assets concentrated in one sector is likely to carry more risk than a more-diversified offering. Knowing the ETF's weightings can help you maintain a well-diversified portfolio. Weightings are displayed relative to the S&P 500 for domestic-stock ETFs and to the category for international-stock ETFs. (We show relative subsector breakdowns for ETFs in certain specialty categories.) The last two columns of the section give an ETF's historical range of the percentage of assets held in each sector.

O Growth and Value Measures
This section lists an ETF portfolio's current averages for various portfolio statistics, including price/earnings, price/cash flow, and historical earnings growth. To provide perspective, we compare these measures with the ETF's category average.

P Composition Information
This section shows the percentage of assets devoted to cash, stocks, bonds, and other, along with what percentage of stock assets are invested in foreign securities. All ETFs should be nearly fully invested, though they typically will carry a trace of cash for settlement purposes.

The Morningstar Bond-ETF Page

In this two-page walk-through, we spotlight sections that are unique to the bond-ETF page and offer some advice on using the page to select a bond ETF. More-detailed discussions of the elements presented in this section appear in the Glossary.

Data through December 31, 2007

iShares Lehman Aggregate AGG

Market Price	Mstar Category
$101.17	Intermediate-Term Bond

Morningstar Rating	Return	Risk	Yield	NAV	Avg Daily Vol. (k)	52 wk High/Low
★★★★	Above Avg	Above Avg	4.9%	$100.88	598	$102.17 - $97.20

Morningstar Fair Value

Price/Fair Value Ratio	Coverage Rate %
NA	NA

Valuation

This ETF primarily holds fixed-income securities, not stocks. That explains why the fund's price/fair value ratio does not appear above.

Methodology

The fund strives to approximate the performance of the Lehman Brothers Aggregate Bond Index, which is a commonly used proxy for the broad, investment-grade U.S. bond market. It uses representative sampling to do this because owning every fixed-income security in the domestic market would be unwieldy and costly because some of the issues are illiquid.

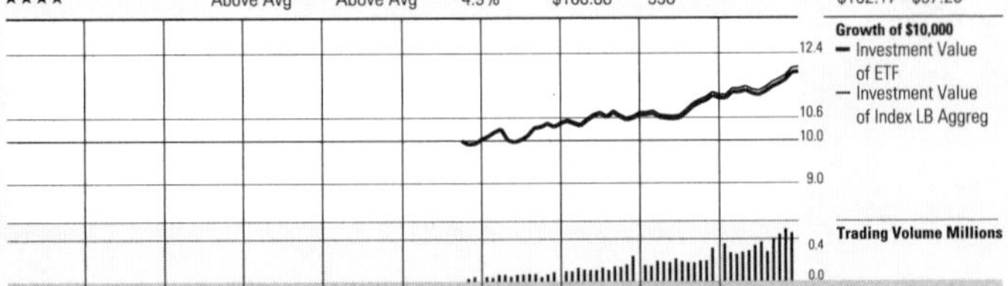

1998	1999	2000	2001	2002	2003	2004	2005	2006	2007	History
—	—	—	—	—	101.61	102.05	100.13	99.45	100.88	NAV $
—	—	—	—	—	102.15	102.40	100.59	99.70	101.17	Market Price $
—	—	—	—	—	4.31*	3.99	2.16	4.13	6.57	NAV Return%
—	—	—	—	—	4.38*	3.79	2.28	3.91	6.61	Market Price Return%
—	—	—	—	—	0.50	0.25	0.12	0.16	0.24	Avg Premium/Discount%
—	—	—	—	—	—	-0.35	-0.27	-0.20	-0.40	NAV Rtrn% +/-LB Aggreg
—	—	—	—	—	—	-0.35	-0.27	-0.20	-0.40	NAV Rtrn% +/-LB Aggreg
—	—	—	—	—	—	1	1	1	1	NAV Return% Rank in Cat
—	—	—	—	—	—	3.54	4.08	4.77	5.06	Income Return %
—	—	—	—	—	—	0.45	-1.92	-0.64	1.51	Capital Return %
—	—	—	—	—	0.92	3.54	4.09	4.68	4.91	Income $
—	—	—	—	—	0.00	0.00	0.00	0.00	0.00	Capital Gains $
—	—	—	—	—	—	0.20	0.20	0.20	0.20	Expense Ratio %
—	—	—	—	—	—	2.47	2.90	3.89	4.76	Income Ratio %
—	—	—	—	—	—	165	457	456	483	Turnover Rate %
—	—	—	—	—	213	990	2,894	4,913	7,738	Net Assets $mil

A Expense Ratio %

Performance 12-31-07

Historic Quarterly NAV Returns

	1st Qtr	2nd Qtr	3rd Qtr	4th Qtr	Total
2003	—	—	—	0.28	—*
2004	2.59	-2.66	3.22	0.88	3.99
2005	-0.60	3.01	-0.74	0.51	2.16
2006	-0.69	-0.16	3.73	1.24	4.13
2007	1.38	-0.63	2.71	2.99	6.57

Trailing	NAV Return%	Market Return%	NAV Rtrn% +/-LB Aggreg	%Rank Cat.(NAV)
3 Mo	2.99	2.82	-0.01	25
6 Mo	5.79	5.93	-0.14	38
1 Yr	6.57	6.61	-0.40	1
3 Yr Avg	4.27	4.25	-0.29	1
5 Yr Avg	—	—	—	—
10 Yr Avg	—	—	—	—

Tax Analysis	Tax-Adj Return%	Tax-Cost Ratio
3 Yr (estimated)	2.62	1.58
5 Yr (estimated)	—	—
10 Yr (estimated)	—	—

Rating and Risk

Time Period	Morningstar Rtn vs Cat	Morningstar Risk vs Cat	Morningstar Risk-Adj Rating
3 Yr	+Avg	+Avg	★★★★
5 Yr	—	—	—
10 Yr	—	—	—

Other Measures	Standard Index S&P 500	Best Fit Index LB Aggreg
Alpha	-0.3	-0.3
Beta	1.00	1.00
R-Squared	100	100
Standard Deviation	2.81	
Mean	4.27	
Sharpe Ratio	-0.03	

Portfolio Analysis 12-31-07

Total Fixed-Income:168	Date of Maturity	Amount $000	Value $000	% Net Assets
FNMA 5.5%	01-01-38	449,462	448,619	4.29
US Treasury Note 6%	08-15-09	385,801	403,359	3.86
FHLMC 4.75%	03-05-09	368,160	373,239	3.57
FHLMC 5%	01-01-38	323,674	315,734	3.02
FNMA 6%	01-01-38	297,596	302,153	2.89
US Treasury Bond 7.625%	02-15-25	216,294	296,522	2.84
FHLMC 5.5%	01-01-38	292,227	291,496	2.79
FNMA 6.5%	01-01-38	260,780	268,033	2.56
US Treasury Note 3.5%	02-15-10	238,537	240,674	2.30
US Treasury Note 4.5%	02-15-09	233,935	237,381	2.27
FHLMC 6%	01-01-38	201,721	204,652	1.96
US Treasury Bond 8.125%	08-15-19	122,720	165,429	1.58
FHLMC 4.5%	01-15-13	157,235	160,894	1.54
US Treasury Note 4.75%	05-15-14	148,798	158,195	1.51
FHLMC 5.5%	01-01-23	136,526	138,126	1.32
FNMA 7.25%	01-15-10	124,254	133,074	1.27
FNMA 5%	01-01-23	128,856	128,916	1.23
FNMA 4.5%	01-01-23	123,487	121,500	1.16
FHLMC 4.5%	01-01-23	123,487	121,422	1.16
FHLMC 5%	02-01-23	117,351	117,351	1.12

Morningstar's Take by Annie Sorich 12-31-07

IShares Lehman Aggregate Bond doesn't stand up to the competition.

Although this ETF was the first to offer diversified fixed-income exposure, it's no longer the only choice. In April, Vanguard introduced an ETF share class of its Vanguard Total Bond Market Index mutual fund called Vanguard Total Bond Market ETF, and State Street followed by launching SPDR Lehman Aggregate Bond in May. Each fund tracks the Lehman Aggregate Bond Index.

Unlike stock index funds, bond index funds are not typically mirror images of their benchmark indexes, many of which would be prohibitively expensive to duplicate bond for bond. The Lehman Aggregate Index contains more than 6,000 securities, making it virtually impossible to mimic. Although bond index funds do replicate the major characteristics of the index, there is room for managers to add value with issue selection and sector allocation.

Overall, the Vanguard fund looks better from a replication standpoint. It owned 2,300 issues through September 2007, while this fund's portfolio contained fewer than 170 securities on the same date, perhaps making it easier for the Vanguard fund to replicate the index's returns. When we compare this ETF's returns with those of the mutual fund version of the Vanguard ETF, which carries the same 0.20% expense ratio, the difference is obvious. This fund trailed the Lehman Aggregate by 0.31% since its September 2003 inception through the end of September 2007. In contrast, the mutual fund version of the Vanguard ETF trailed the index by only 0.12%.

On the expense front, the Vanguard ETF is also a clear winner. This fund's 0.20% expense ratio is not unreasonable, but the Vanguard ETF charges only 0.11% of assets, leaving more return for investors than even its mutual fund counterpart.

Given the strengths of the Vanguard ETF on replication and expenses, few reasons remain to invest in this ETF.

B Current Investment Style/ Duration Management

Current Investment Style

Duration: Short Int Long; Quality: High Med Low

Avg Eff Duration[1]	4.6 Yrs
Avg Eff Maturity	7.1 Yrs
Avg Credit Quality	AA
Avg Wtd Coupon	5.59%
Avg Wtd Price	104.16% of par

[1] figure provided by fund

Coupon Range	% of Bonds	Rel Cat
0% PIK	0.0	0.0
0% to 6%	77.2	1.1
6% to 8%	19.7	0.9
8% to 10%	3.1	0.7
More than 10%	0.0	0.0

1.00=Category Average

Sector Breakdown	% of assets
US Treasuries	18
TIPS	0
US Agency	9
Mortgage Pass-Throughs	27
Mortgage CMO	0
Mortgage ARM	0
US Corporate	18
Asset-Backed	0
Convertible	0
Municipal	0
Corporate Inflation-Protected	0
Foreign Corporate	1
Foreign Govt	1

Composition

Cash	26.8	Bonds	73.2
Stocks	0.0	Other	0.0

C Credit Analysis

Credit Analysis		% bonds 12-31-07	
US Govt	0	BB	0
AAA	74	B	0
AA	8	Below B	0
A	10	NR/NA	1
BBB	8		

Special Securities	
Restricted/Illiquid Secs	Trace
Exotic Mortgage-Backed	0
Emerging-Markets Secs	Trace
Options/Futures/Warrants	No

Address:	45 Fremont Street United States 800-474-2737
Web Address:	www.ishares.com
Inception:	09-22-03*
Advisor:	Barclays Global Fund Advisers

Management Fee:	0.20%		
Expense Projections:	3Yr:$77	5Yr:$135	10Yr:$306
Income Distrib:	Annually		
Exchange:	AMEX		

MORNINGSTAR® ETFs 150 172

(A) Expense Ratio %

It's critical to look for bond ETFs with low expenses. Expenses can eat into total returns and income payments.

(B) Current Investment Style / Duration

The bond style box is based on an ETF's credit quality and its duration. Check the ETF's average credit quality and average effective duration in the column next to the style box. Credit quality is an important aspect of any bond ETF, as it measures the creditworthiness of the ETF's holdings. An ETF with an average credit quality of AAA, for example, is less likely to get stung by defaults than an ETF with an average credit quality of BBB. Duration is equally important, as it measures an ETF's overall interest-rate risk. The longer an ETF's duration, the more sensitive the ETF is to shifts in interest rates. When rates fall, ETFs with longer durations benefit; when interest rates climb, shorter-duration ETFs are beneficial. First-time bond-ETF buyers, especially those looking to cushion their stock-heavy portfolios, probably should stick with ETFs in the intermediate-term range (3.5 to six years). Intermediate-term bond funds have offered yields and returns similar to long-term bond funds but with less volatility.

(C) Credit Analysis

Average credit quality provides a snapshot of a portfolio's overall credit quality, while the Credit Analysis section shows the percentage of fixed-income securities that fall within each credit-quality rating, as assigned by Standard & Poor's or Moody's. The lower a bond's rating, the greater its default risk and the higher its yield. Bonds rated BBB and above are considered investment-grade issues; those rated BB and below are high-yield, commonly called junk bonds. Pay particularly close attention to an ETF's weightings in below B and nonrated bonds. Often these issues are riskier bonds that are in danger of defaulting or that have already defaulted. They are also typically less liquid than higher-quality bonds. That's why it's a good idea to diversify with a good mix of high- and low-quality bonds. (Lean more toward the high-quality side.)

ETFs Basics

Here's a quick primer on ETFs and some suggestions for analyzing them and working them into your investment mix.

by Dan Culloton, Fund Analyst

Disclosure: Barclays Global Investors (BGI), which is owned by Barclays, currently licenses Morningstar's 16 style-based indexes for use in BGI's iShares exchange-traded funds. iShares are not sponsored, issued, or sold by Morningstar. Morningstar does not make any representation regarding the advisability of investing in iShares that are based on Morningstar indexes.

The Basics

ETFs are essentially mutual funds that can be bought and sold throughout the day like stocks on an exchange. Unlike conventional mutual funds (whose share prices are set once per day at 4 p.m. EST), ETFs' share prices are determined throughout the day by supply and demand. Anything you can do with a stock you can do with an ETF: You can sell them short (meaning sell borrowed shares with the intention of buying them back at a lower price and pocketing the difference), write options on many of them, and set market, limit, and stop-loss orders on them. And just like stocks, you can buy them through an online or full-service broker.

How They Work

The price of an ETF share fluctuates along with the values of the underlying securities in its portfolio. Occasionally there will be differences between the ETF share price and the value of the underlying securities. But the difference tends to be small because institutional investors can continuously create and redeem ETF shares in-kind, meaning that they can exchange ETF shares for the actual stocks or bonds in the ETF's portfolio.

The in-kind creation/redemption process creates an arbitrage opportunity for large institutional investors and market makers, known as authorized participants, who deal directly with the ETF. This helps keep ETF premiums and discounts narrow. When ETF shares trade at a discount to the NAVs of their underlying holdings, the APs buy the ETF shares and sell the underlying securities. If the ETF shares trade at a premium the APs buy the underlying securities and sell the ETF shares.

Advantages

Many institutional and individual investors have been drawn to ETFs because of the ability to pick their own entry and exit prices, as well as the chance to use fund portfolios in various trading and hedging strategies. Another advantage is transparency. Because all ETFs currently are index funds, it's easy to know what you own. ETFs also come in more exotic flavors. While conventional mutual funds still greatly outnumber ETFs, funds that drill down into specific sectors, industries, regions, countries, and asset classes make up a greater percentage of the ETF universe. They offer relatively inexpensive access to investments, such as currencies, precious metals, or emergent industries, that heretofore have been the sole province of larger institutional and wealthy investors.

Low expenses and tax efficiency are among the most attractive features of ETFs. They are able to offer much lower expense ratios than conventional mutual funds, because they're index funds that typically don't hire professional (and often expensive) researchers and stock-pickers in an effort to beat the market. Furthermore, because investors purchase ETFs via a broker on the open market instead of from the fund companies, the ETFs don't have all the record-keeping and shareholder-servicing costs that conventional mutual funds incur.

When it comes to taxes, the ETF structure has a lot of advantages, too. Index funds in general tend to be more tax efficient than actively managed funds because they don't trade as often. The in-kind creation/redemption mechanism also gives ETFs additional tools to sidestep capital gains. Because no one redeems their fund shares for cash, ETFs don't have to sell securities to pay off departing shareholders. Furthermore, ETFs can use in-kind redemptions to flush low-cost basis shares out of the portfolio, thereby reducing the chance of realizing capital gains when the ETFs have to sell securities to keep up with changes in their benchmarks.

Finally, ETFs can also be a good alternative to positions in single shares of stock. For instance, rather than invest in a single name like Citigroup, perhaps you prefer to spread your bets across numerous financial firms by purchasing an ETF like KBW Bank. In so doing, you diffuse risk across multiple stocks, potentially improving your risk/reward profile. And you do so with all of the collateral benefits that ETFs confer, including a high degree of transparency (which makes it easy to value what an ETF is holding) and low costs.

Disadvantages

There are hidden costs to ETFs, though. They can be more costly to use than conventional mutual funds after you factor in brokerage commissions. You can find discount brokerages, but even their transaction costs can

ETF Creation/Redemption Process

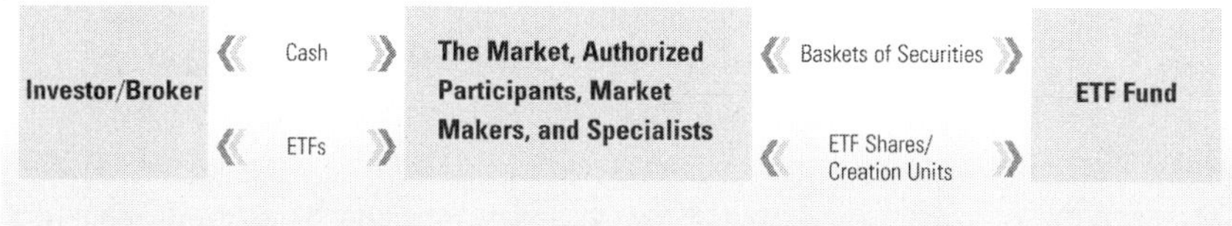

pile up quickly and negate ETFs' expense advantage if you trade frequently or make regular monthly investments. And don't forget the bid/ask spread, or the difference between the price at which you can buy an ETF and the price at which you can sell it (the market maker pockets this difference). For all of these reasons, ETFs are better suited to lump-sum investments than recurring purchases.

Because ETFs trade on the secondary market and price throughout the trading day, it's possible that an ETF's market price will diverge meaningfully from the net asset value of the securities in its portfolio. This risk is most acute for thinly traded ETFs or those funds that invest in relatively illiquid securities.

In addition, all ETFs are passively managed. While this has obvious benefits, including lower annual expenses and greater transparency, some investors prefer a full-blown active approach where a manager assembles a portfolio one security at a time. True, on balance, active managers haven't exactly covered themselves in glory, with most failing to even keep up with the prevailing market indexes. But if you're more comfortable with active management in some contexts, you'll have to broaden your gaze beyond ETFs.

Finally, most ETFs are relatively young, with many having launched in just the past few years. That poses a practical challenge: how to fully evaluate an ETF that lacks a lengthy track record. Though we think that challenge can be overcome, it's worth considering, especially if you're comfortable investing only in a fund that's been around the block a time or two, as evidenced by a long-term record.

How to Use ETFs

The ability to frequently trade, short, and buy ETFs on margin is alluring, but these are speculative tactics that require accurate short-term market calls, which few, if any, can get right consistently over the long term. Similarly, market-timing and sector-rotation strategies don't get any easier just because you use ETFs to implement them.

You're likely to be far better served by approaches that harness ETFs' advantages as part of a prudent long-term investing strategy. These strategies can take a variety of forms. For instance, you can cover the major asset classes—bonds, U.S. stocks, foreign stocks, and commodities—using as few as four ETFs. Thus, for those of you seeking a low-cost, no-frills portfolio, perhaps you invest in just a handful of broad-market ETFs, rebalance once a year, and call it a day.

For those of you who prefer a more active approach to ETF investing, there are other options. For instance, core and explore approaches, which involve using diversified funds or ETFs as your portfolio cornerstones and deploying more specialized ETFs around its edges to enhance returns, seem reasonable. But they require strict discipline and attention to detail lest you sabotage yourself with increased complexity and costs.

In addition, as mentioned previously, ETFs can be valid alternatives to positions in single stocks. Therefore, if you were seeking to beat the market, you could construct a portfolio consisting of ETFs whose underlying holdings were fundamentally attractive, such as a technology ETF trading at a significant discount to its intrinsic worth.

Beyond portfolio construction, ETFs also have become popular tax-management tools. Some investors and financial planners use them to maintain exposure to areas of the market while they realize tax losses. You can sell your losing funds and use up to $3,000 of net investment losses to offset income in the current year and capital gains indefinitely. (There's no limit to the amount of losses you can use to offset capital gains.) The problem is you can't buy that fund back within 31 days without running afoul of IRS rules. That's where ETFs can come in; you can use them to maintain exposure to the style or market segment while you wait. For example, at the end of 2005 many large-growth funds—even decent ones—were in the red over the past five years. You could have sold, booked a loss to offset gains elsewhere in your portfolio, and then bought an ETF, such as Vanguard Growth ETF. M

Constructing Winning Portfolios Using ETFs

Factors to consider when constructing an ETF portfolio.

by Jeffrey Ptak, CPA, CFA
Editor, Morningstar ETF's 150

Disclosure: Barclays Global Investors (BGI), which is owned by Barclays, currently licenses Morningstar's 16 style-based indexes for use in BGI's iShares exchange-traded funds. iShares are not sponsored, issued, or sold by Morningstar. Morningstar does not make any representation regarding the advisability of investing in iShares that are based on Morningstar indexes.

This book is devoted to helping investors use ETFs in two principal ways—to build an efficient portfolio or to beat the market. (For further detail on these two objectives, see the "How to Use This Book" feature piece.)

If you're more interested in constructing a well-diversified portfolio that appropriately balances risk and reward, a fund's potential role and utility in a portfolio takes center stage. So, in this section, let's turn our attention to the attributes that play the biggest role in determining an ETF's merit as a portfolio building block.

Cost

Given that ETFs are passively managed—meaning that they merely attempt to mimic a target index, not beat the benchmark—cost is king. Why? When you're comparing, say, one broad-market U.S. stock ETF with another, you'll find there's typically not all that much to distinguish them. IShares Russell 1000 Index and SPDRs Trust might track slightly different indexes (the Russell 1000 and S&P 500 indexes, respectively), but they both hold the largest U.S.-based firms. Given that similarity, cost is a key differentiator.

Cost is important in another regard: The success of indexing is predicated, in part, on the idea that the typical fund's return will approximate the market return before fees. That is, the average manager is, well, about average after all's said and done. (Active managers' general failure to keep pace with prevailing indexes provides ammunition for this argument, which is sometimes referred to as the "efficient market hypothesis.") By definition, index funds will do no better than the market. However, because index funds are typically much cheaper than their actively managed rivals, they pull ahead once fees are taken into account.

Of course, costs don't begin and end with an ETF's expense ratio. There are also transaction costs, such as brokerage commissions and bid/ask spreads, to consider. If you're investing a lump sum, transaction costs shouldn't be too onerous. (Because brokerage commissions should be similar from one fund to the next, they typically aren't a deciding factor when choosing between various ETFs.) What's more, if you're investing in a widely traded ETF like SPDRs or Diamonds, bid/ask spreads are likely to be infinitesimal.

However, if you're making regular investments via payroll deductions or purchasing a thinly traded ETF, it pays to crunch the numbers in order to ensure that transaction costs aren't blunting the expense advantage that the ETF's low expense ratio confers. You could be better off choosing a comparable traditional mutual fund.

Portfolio Construction

Think of portfolio construction in two dimensions—breadth and depth, where breadth represents the variety of securities that the portfolio encompasses and depth is the weight of those securities in the portfolio.

A portfolio's breadth can vary wildly. For instance, some ETFs span the entire stock or bond markets. Others zero in on narrower slices, such as particular market caps, styles, or industries. And still others corral certain types of securities that match designated attributes, like valuation, growth, price momentum, and other factors.

Similarly, ETFs can weight securities in a number of different ways. The largest stock ETFs typically weight securities based on market capitalization. But equal-weighting schemes are also common. And we've recently seen a wave of ETFs tied to "alternate" or "fundamental" indexes that weight stocks based on dividends, earnings, cash flow, or book value.

What's the upshot? There are innumerable ways to construct a portfolio using ETFs, ranging from totally hands-off approaches to those that only an ardent tinkerer could love. Ultimately, the "right" ETF is the fund that's best suited to your portfolio and needs. For instance, if you already own a U.S.-focused value fund, investing in Vanguard Total Stock Market—which tracks virtually the entire U.S. stock market—isn't the best option given the overlap it would create. Rather, a growth-oriented ETF would probably fit the bill.

Generally speaking, if your primary goal is to construct a diversified portfolio, you don't need sector-, region-, or even country-specific ETFs. True, funds like these can serve a purpose. For instance, if the ETFs that anchor your portfolio leave you underexposed to a certain slice of the market, then perhaps a narrowly focused ETF like a sector fund helps to plug that gap. But most widely diversified ETFs should afford ample exposure to virtually every part of the stock and bond markets, making thinly sliced ETFs redundant. (On the other hand, if you're seeking to outgun the market using ETFs, then narrowly sliced ETFs most definitely have a place, as we explain further in our "Beating the Market with ETFs" piece.)

With respect to weighting schemes, we think you should tune out a lot of the noise and focus on your long-term goals. Yes, it's possible that some ETFs have come up with a better mousetrap for weighting or screening stocks. But many of these approaches remain unproven while still others, such as equal-weighting, have drawbacks of their own, such as potentially higher transaction costs and tax inefficiency.

Returns

Returns are important, though not for the reason you might suspect.

Let's suppose iShares S&P 500's absolute returns were to surpass the returns of every other ETF for five years running. Should that make us any more enthused about its future prospects? Not necessarily. For one thing, as mentioned previously, the fund has to make sense in your portfolio, which is a function of your objectives and risk tolerance. A hot streak does not a suitable fund make. In addition, a strong record doesn't tell you why the fund performed as it did. For instance, did large caps, which predominate in the S&P 500, catch fire? If so, how sustainable is that trend? Recall that investors in S&P 500 Index funds were sitting pretty in the late 1990s, only to watch small-cap stocks roar back in the ensuing years.

So what can we learn from a fund's performance? First, we can glean some insights into the fund's tendencies. For instance, does it lag in rallies and hold its ground during downturns? Is it especially sensitive to changes in interest rates? Examining a fund's track record should yield answers to at least some of these questions.

• Absolute Returns

Take iShares MSCI Brazil, which, if you're judging from performance stats alone, probably looks like the greatest thing since sliced bread. The fund notched a 62% annualized return from 2003–2007, besting every other ETF in existence. Sterling as that performance seems, had you mistimed your purchase by just a few years, you would have seen more than half of your investment go up in smoke, as the fund lost roughly 70% of its value from its August 2000 inception through October 2002.

What could explain the fund's Jekyll and Hyde nature? It's very sensitive to two factors—the performance of its top holdings, which soak up most of its assets, and the trajectory of the Brazilian real, the currency in which most of its investments are denominated. In the five years ended October 2007, top holdings like miner Comphania Vale do Rio Doce went on a tear amid strong worldwide demand for iron ore. What's more, the Brazilian real rose smartly against the greenback, roughly doubling in value over that span. By contrast, some of those same holdings slumped in 2001 and 2002 while the real depreciated heavily against the dollar.

The moral of the story is that the fund's returns, while eye-popping, are sustainable only insofar as its top holdings continue to knock the cover off the ball and the Brazilian currency maintains its upward march against the dollar. Those are big "ifs" that should color your assessment of the fund's return potential.

• Relative Returns

Because we'd like our portfolio to beat the majority of competing alternatives, relative returns also figure into our assessment. Again, we have to be careful not to incorrectly extrapolate past results into the future. But one of the things we might want to consider is how well indexing has fared in that particular market segment. For instance, indexing has been less-resoundingly successful in small-cap land, as active managers have tended to trump the Russell 2000 Index on average. While we can build a case even for small-cap indexing, the fact remains that a purely passive approach may not necessarily be the only option. Thus, a fund's relative returns are worth checking to see how well it has stacked up. If poorly, then perhaps it's worth considering a low-cost active manager for that slot of your portfolio.

Relative returns, just like absolute returns, also must be put into the proper context. For instance, generally speaking, large-cap ETFs that skewed toward smaller and cheaper stocks fared better than their more broadly diversified peers during the bear market and through much of the subsequent rebound.

Consider Powershares Dynamic Market, which ruled the roost in its large-blend category in 2004 and 2005, in part because its quantitative screening models favored smaller, inexpensively priced stocks. But that trend reversed sharply in 2006 as larger stocks began to retake center stage. That malaise extended into 2007, explaining the fund's lackluster relative returns of late. That doesn't indict the fund, per se, as relative returns shouldn't govern your decision making to begin with. But it offers greater insights into the portfolio's biases and, in turn, how it's likely to perform in varying market conditions—useful information to be sure.

Second, an ETF's performance can help you judge how well it'll work with your other holdings. For instance, if a fund's returns seem to loosely parallel those of your other ETF holdings, perhaps it's an indication that the fund isn't the optimal diversifier.

Powershares Dynamic Market is one example, as the fund isn't the clear-cut choice to anchor the large-cap slot of a portfolio given its previously mentioned small-cap tilt. But other examples abound. For instance, high-yield corporate bond funds like iShares iBoxx High-Yield Corporate Bond aren't ideal diversifiers given their strong correlations to stocks. Any number of sector funds deliver returns that you're more or less already realizing via the holdings of broad-market ETFs that you own (as sector funds often significantly overlap with widely diversified offerings).

Risk

We can define risk in a number of ways. Volatility. Loss of principal. Lagging the market or peers. And so forth. Which is the best measure? It depends on the way you define risk. If you're scared stiff at the prospect of your investments losing their value, then a measure like drawdown, which quantifies the maximum loss an investment has suffered over a specified period, might be most useful.

Because risk is inseparable from return, it's important to be able to reconcile whatever measure you choose with your investment objective. For example, loss of principal seems like an especially apt measure for more-conservative fund holdings, like bond ETFs. But it's not a great fit where most stock ETFs are concerned given the inevitable ups and downs such funds experience. Instead, if you're willing to court the risk of losing the money you plunk down on a stock ETF, you're probably better off focusing on the degree to which the fund's value could change, making volatility the most salient measure.

And, of course, it's also vital to consider an ETF's risk profile in relation to your portfolio as a whole. For instance, while an investment in a bond ETF exposes you to the risk of losing out on outsized returns, it offers the benefits of added stability. Conversely, if a hyperaggressive ETF has caught your eye, and you're willing to ride out the inevitable bumps, you still have to consider the impact it'll have on your portfolio's overall risk/reward profile.

One other ETF-specific risk that's at least worth noting is tracking error, or the risk that a fund will fail to keep pace with its benchmark before fees. This risk tends to be most acute for ETFs that target difficult-to-track indexes, such as sprawling fixed-income benchmarks or indexes traversing less-liquid parts of the stock market like municipal bonds or foreign small caps. That said, most of the large indexers boast experience in spades and have the record to prove their acumen. Therefore, while it's worth kicking the tires, particularly where less-established ETF providers are concerned, tracking error is rarely a deal-breaker.

The same also applies to divergences from net asset value. As you may recall from our discussion in "ETF Basics," ETFs boast a built-in arbitrage mechanism that ordinarily keeps a fund's market price in line with the underlying value of its assets. However, it's not unheard of for thinly traded ETFs to experience significant deviations from net asset value. Our advice? Eyeball a prospective fund's average premium or discount to NAV over time. If the fund has traded within a narrow corridor, chances are that you won't see the fund spike above, or dip well below, net asset value in the future. Big deviations from NAV shouldn't necessarily eliminate a fund from consideration. But they up the ante, forcing you to more carefully time your purchases and sales, which can be more trouble than it's worth, especially when comparable alternatives that hew closely to NAV are available.

Tax Efficiency

ETFs are typically more tax-efficient that traditional mutual funds for a few reasons. First, because shares change hands in the secondary market, ETF managers aren't forced to sell securities in order to generate cash with which to pay investors who are selling out of the fund. Consequently, ETFs realize taxable gains far less frequently than a traditional mutual fund would. Second, due to the vagaries of the arbitrage process, ETF managers are able to essentially "flush out" low-cost-basis shares of stock. Because those shares would rack up the biggest taxes if sold in a cash transaction, this flushing-out process further reduces the incidence and magnitude of any taxable gains.

Probably the best way to gauge an ETF's tax efficiency is by examining the fund's capital gains distributions history. (To that end, check out the "Capital Gains $" row in the "History" section of each ETF analyst report in this book, as it sets forth the dollar amount per share of taxable gains that a fund distributed each year.) If the fund has been reasonably tax-efficient, chances are that it hasn't paid any capital gains at all.

True, past isn't always prologue and, thus, it's possible that a formerly tax-efficient fund can cease to be so. One way to evaluate the potential for future taxable gains is by considering portfolio turnover. Generally speaking, the higher a fund's turnover, the greater the likelihood that it will realize capital gains in the course of selling one security for another.

Also bear in mind that not even an ETF can provide a haven when it comes to certain types of securities. For instance, bond ETFs must distribute any income that their underlying holdings throw off. Those distributions, which represent the bulk of the return that a bond ETF is likely to generate, are taxed at ordinary income rates. M

Beating the Market with ETFs

Our formula for beating the indexes.

by Jeffrey Ptak, CPA, CFA
Editor, Morningstar ETF's 150

Disclosure: Barclays Global Investors (BGI), which is owned by Barclays, currently licenses Morningstar's 16 style-based indexes for use in BGI's iShares exchange-traded funds. iShares are not sponsored, issued, or sold by Morningstar. Morningstar does not make any representation regarding the advisability of investing in iShares that are based on Morningstar indexes.

For some of you, a market return simply won't do. Instead, you invest in ETFs with the goal of beating the pants off the market. There's nothing wrong with that—we think there's plenty of money to be made from opportunistic investments in stock ETFs.

But it requires patience and discipline, qualities that imbue Morningstar's approach to choosing market-beating ETFs. Here's a primer on how we pick ETFs that we think will best the market, along with some tips for you to consider as you conduct your own research.

A Fundamental(s) Question

What many investors forget is that an investment in a stock ETF isn't a wager on the value the market places on a piece of paper. It's an ownership stake in dozens, if not hundreds, of underlying businesses. Thus, we think the key to successful, market-beating ETF investing is an unerring focus on long-term business fundamentals.

But what does that mean? If an ETF investment gives you a stake in numerous businesses, the value of your investment should turn on the intrinsic worth of those firms. For instance, if the market is fairly valuing those businesses, then you're getting your money's worth. On the other hand, if the market is significantly undervaluing those firms, then you're getting an opportunity to buy in at a cut-rate price, and vice-versa for overvalued businesses.

Where the Rubber Meets the Road

You're probably wondering how this helps you beat the market. If we assume that the market, for all of its short-term gyrations, is efficient over the long haul, then we would expect the prices of assets to eventually converge to their intrinsic values. Thus, if the market is bidding down various businesses, perhaps because sentiment has turned sharply negative, but the intrinsic worth of those firms hasn't changed one iota, we'd expect the market to eventually see the error of its ways and push up the prices of those businesses to a level that approximates fair value.

When you invest in firms that the market has mispriced in this fashion, you should reap a tidy return when price converges to fair value, beating the market in the process. This calculus holds for an ETF just as it does for a single-stock investment, the only difference being that you own stakes in multiple businesses rather than a single one.

Valuing ETFs (with a Little Help from Your Friends)
The question that naturally arises is: How on earth am I supposed to estimate the value of iShares S&P 500 Index when it spans hundreds of businesses? And even if I could get my arms around the holdings of a less sprawling fund, like a sector ETF, how do I estimate the value of those businesses?

In a nutshell, that's where we come in: We have more than 100 equity analysts covering 2,000-plus stocks spanning numerous industries and geographic locales. As such, we follow many of the stocks that the most-prominent ETFs own. To wit, our analysts were recently covering more than 450 of the S&P 500 Index's 500 constituents, representing 99.5% of the index's assets. That's not an anomaly: Our analysts cover substantially all the portfolio holdings of nearly 300 stock ETFs. What's more, our analysts estimate the fair value of each stock they cover based on the rigorous analysis they conduct into company fundamentals. That is, they estimate a business' net worth and calculate the value of each shareholder's stake in that business.

To estimate a firm's fair value, our analysts conduct extensive fundamental research, examining the business' competitive profile, the durability of any advantages it might boast, and the economics of the markets in which it operates. This routinely entails combing through regulatory filings, meeting with company management, and conducting other industry research. Those efforts culminate in a discounted cash-flow model that our analysts build for each company that they cover. The model sets forth our analysts' forecasts of the cash flows that they expect the business to throw off, with those forecasts extending well into the future. (The model explicitly forecasts results from up to 20 years, which is far more extensive than the norm.) To arrive at our fair value estimate, we discount those cash flows back to the present at a certain discount rate and then divide that amount by the number of shares outstanding.

We can harness this comprehensive research to place a fair value estimate on a stock ETF. For instance, if an ETF holds 20 stocks and our analysts have placed fair value estimates on every last one of them, then the ETF's fair value is more or less the weighted average of the stocks' fair values.

Separating the Wheat from the Chaff

Once we've placed a fair value estimate on an ETF, the question becomes: Is it cheap, dear, or reasonably priced? We can begin to evaluate this by comparing the ETF's market price with our fair value estimate. If the fund is trading meaningfully below our fair value estimate, then it has the makings of a bargain. By contrast, if it's trading at a premium to our fair value estimate, we'd probably take a pass.

End of story? Not quite. Our analysts base their forecasts on assumptions that they make about various fundamental attributes of the firms they're analyzing. For instance, how quickly revenue will grow, how profitable the firm's business will be, how capital-intensive its operations will prove, and how long any good times might last. Because all of these assumptions are uncertain to varying degrees, we want to afford ourselves a margin of error when we invest. In that way, if our fair value estimates proves too rosy, we're not necessarily left in the lurch.

With that in mind, we probably wouldn't pound the table for an ETF trading at a 1 or 2 percentage point discount to our fair value estimate. Instead, we'd seek a larger discount to fair value, with that extra cushion protecting us should our fair value estimate end up being wrong.

Important Themes

In the report pages that follow, you're likely to hear us harp on a few recurring themes—company quality (i.e.,"economic moat"), business risk, portfolio diversification, and cost. All of these factors impact the fair value estimate that we place on an ETF and the margin of safety we demand when investing in it. Thus, they warrant further explanation, which we've provided below.

- **Company Quality:** Company quality has a straightforward relationship to an ETF's fair value—the higher-quality a fund's holdings, the greater the fund's intrinsic worth.

High-quality firms boast intractable competitive advantages that offer economic benefits to shareholders for years and years. We refer to these sorts of advantages as "economic moats." The wider a firm's moat, the more defensible its advantages and, thus, the higher its quality.

What makes a moat? Maybe it's scale in an industry where cost leadership is paramount (Anheuser Busch, CheckFree). Or barriers to entry like intellectual property protection (Abbott Laboratories, 3M) and massive capital outlays (ExxonMobil, Bank of America). In today's information age, network effects, which bind customers to a particular system or marketplace by sheer virtue of the critical mass those networks have attained, increasingly form the basis for moats (Microsoft, eBay, Chicago Mercantile Exchange). And in still other cases, good old fashion branding does the trick (Coca-Cola, Procter & Gamble, Harley Davidson). The common thread in these cases is that the moat keeps rivals at bay.

That's a key advantage given that outsized growth and profits, which often flow to an erstwhile market-leader, typically attract competition. And as rivals elbow their way in to get a piece of the action, it diminishes long-term profit potential for every player in the industry. By contrast, wide-moat firms' defenses fortify them against competitors' assaults, allowing them to continue churning out economic profits for shareholders.

Because those profits translate to excess cash flow, which is what we tally when estimating a company's intrinsic worth, it's fair to say that wide-moat firms are more valuable than their narrow- and no-moat counterparts. Consequently, an ETF that's chock-full of wide-moat stocks is worth more (i.e., sports a higher fair-value estimate) then a comparable fund that holds lower-quality names.

Thus, think of stock quality as the trait that most directly influences an ETF's intrinsic worth.

- **Business Risk:** As we mentioned earlier, the forecasts that underpin our analysts' fair value estimates are typically subject to varying levels of uncertainty. That is, our analysts could pin the wrong fair value estimates on the stocks that they cover. But what makes one forecast more- or less-uncertain than another? That variable is what we refer to as "business risk."

Our analysts assign every stock that they cover to one of four business-risk buckets—below-average, average, above-average, or speculative. The more uncertain our analysts' cash-flow forecasts, the higher the risk rating we're likely to assign to the company concerned, and vice versa.

Business risk is a function of two factors—company quality and "event risk." With respect to company quality, the results of wide-moat firms tend to be more predictable, on balance, because such businesses are often buoyed by recurring demand, stable cost structures, or strong pricing power, among other salutary traits. Wide-moat oil-and-gas pipeline operators like Buckeye Partners, L.P., for example, are very difficult to dislodge given regulatory constraints, the high cost of building new pipelines, and the absence of cost-effective alternative modes of transport. Consequently, Buckeye's business throws off cash flows like clockwork, making the firm's results easier to forecast; hence that firm's below-average business-risk rating.

Event risk encompasses a grab bag of concerns, including the extent of a firm's indebtedness, exposure to costly litigation, a history of shareholder-unfriendly governance practices, and the like. Though tobacco-maker Altria, for instance, boasts a wide moat, our analysts consider it an above-average risk principally because it could suffer a multibillion litigation judgment in the future.

The riskier our analysts consider a firm, the greater the margin of safety—that is, the discount to fair value—they'll demand before recommending an investment in the stock. For instance, we'd typically invest in a below-average risk stock only when it's trading at a 15% discount to our fair value estimate, whereas we'd demand a 36% discount for an above-average-risk stock. The same basic principle holds for an ETF as well. If the portfolio is crammed with risky energy-related stocks, we're likely to require a meaningfully larger margin of safety than we would for, say, a consumer-staples ETF.

Thus, whereas company quality influences our estimate of an ETF's intrinsic worth, business risk denotes the level of uncertainty associated with that estimate.

- **Portfolio Diversification:** It sounds obvious, but diversification across stocks and industries is a surefire way to tamp volatility. That principle is especially evident in very turbulent areas. For instance, given the boom/bust nature of the biotech business, investments in single biotech stocks are usually fraught with risk. But a funny thing happens when you throw a bunch of biotech names into a portfolio: Volatility falls dramatically.

What explains it? The odds of success associated with these various firms, many of them upstarts, aren't strongly correlated. For instance, the chance of one therapy being approved is, for all intents and purposes, independent of another drug's odds for approval. Thus, the range of possible outcomes narrows from all or nothing to something better resembling a bell-shaped curve. That phenomenon can be seen in widely diversified ETFs as well. For instance, the average broad-market fund, such as iShares Russell 1000 or Powershares Dynamic Market, is about half as volatile as the typical "below-average" risk stock.

So what's the rub? While we certainly want to pay attention to the margins of safety we're placing around an ETF's individual holdings, we also have to evaluate the level of portfolio diversification in deciding upon an appropriate margin of safety for the fund.

Consider this hypothetical: an ETF that equally weights 20 stocks, every one of which our analysts consider "average" risks. In that scenario, we'd be demanding a roughly 23% discount to fair value before recommending the typical holding. So, we should buy the ETF only at a 23% discount to our estimate of its fair value, right? Not necessarily. Remember that we place a margin of safety around a stock to account for the uncertainty associated with our forecasts. That is, the margin of safety accounts for the range of possible outcomes—our fair value estimate being on the money, slightly off the mark, wildly errant—and the probabilities associated with each outcome. But assuming that the portfolio's holdings aren't perfectly correlated, diversification should narrow the range of outcomes. For instance, the imprecision of one overly optimistic fair value estimate should be offset by an overly pessimistic one, and so forth.

Therefore, when placing a margin of safety around our estimate of an ETF's fair value, we consider the business risk of the underlying holdings in conjunction with the level of portfolio diversification. The more diversified the portfolio across stocks and industries, the more we're likely to narrow the margin of safety that we'd demand. In that sense, you should think of a portfolio's weighted average margin of safety as the maximum discount to fair value that we would demand when investing in an ETF and the fund's diversification as the property that can narrow that margin of safety.

The upshot is that we're typically demanding an 8% discount to our fair value estimate before recommending a broadly diversified ETF, and a 15%-plus discount for more narrowly focused funds.

- **Cost:** While an ETF's annual expenses might seem to pale in comparison to the potential rewards the fund offers, they're important nonetheless. Every basis point in expenses represents an additional hurdle that your investment must clear. All things being equal, if given the choice of two identical, or at least highly similar, ETFs, it's a no-brainer: Pick the fund that has the lower annual expenses.

Think of it this way: Expenses eat into the excess return you'd otherwise derive from an investment in an ETF that's trading at a hefty discount to our fair value estimate. For instance, if a diversified ETF's price was 8% below its intrinsic worth, it would certainly warrant a close look. But if the fund costs 1% per year, you're not going to capture the return implied by the fund's valuation. To capture that return, you'd need to first overcome the 1% expense hurdle. To overcome that hurdle, we essentially have to widen the margin of safety by demanding a slightly larger discount to fair value. Because each percentage point of expenses translates to roughly 2% in incremental margin of safety, you'd demand a 10% discount to fair value before recommending the diversified ETF in our example.

Walk the Talk

It's one thing to read up on these concepts. It's quite another to put them into practice.

With that in mind, the introductory section of this book includes a companion piece to this one, entitled "ETFs on Our Buy List," in which we sift through the ETF universe for the best bargains.

Therefore, if you're intrigued by what you'd read thus far, "ETFs on Our Buy List" is well worth checking out.

ETFs on Our Buy List

A collection of funds in the bargain bin.

by Jeffrey Ptak, CPA, CFA
Editor, Morningstar ETF's 150

Disclosure: Barclays Global Investors (BGI), which is owned by Barclays, currently licenses Morningstar's 16 style-based indexes for use in BGI's iShares exchange-traded funds. iShares are not sponsored, issued, or sold by Morningstar. Morningstar does not make any representation regarding the advisability of investing in iShares that are based on Morningstar indexes.

One of the many benefits that comes from covering more than 2,000 stocks is the ability to tap our research to value ETFs. Where others might use notoriously imprecise methods like top-down macro forecasting to gauge an ETF's fundamental attractiveness, we're able to go bottom-up, stock by stock.

To understand how, consider the largest ETF in the world, SPDRs Trust, which tracks the S&P 500 Index. We can roll up the fair value estimates that we've placed on more than 450 of the S&P's 500 constituent stocks (representing nearly 100% of the index's assets) in order to derive a fair value estimate for the SPDR. Once we've estimated an ETF's fair value, we can compare it with the fund's price, just as we do in our stock research. The lower an ETF's market price relative to our fair value estimate, the more attractive we'd consider it, and vice versa. (The SPDR was trading at a 12% discount to our fair value estimate as of Dec. 31, 2007, in case you were wondering.)

Which ETFs are in the bargain bin these days? Here's a short list that we've drawn from the nearly 300 stock ETFs for which we have comprehensive coverage of the underlying equities (defined as coverage on stocks accounting for at least 70% of the fund's assets).

Homebuilder ETFs

No group has taken a worse beating recently than the homebuilders. In 2007, the market had wiped out roughly one half of the average homebuilder's market value. Slumping real estate prices and a reeling mortgage market have left many investors wondering whether some of the most prominent homebuilders are on the road to financial ruin.

We're hardly sanguine about homebuilders' near-term prospects, which are dark indeed given a glut of vacant homes, pricing pressures, and the aforementioned mortgage meltdown. Yet, we don't subscribe to the doomsday scenario that the market seems to be pricing into the builders' shares, nearly all of which were recently trading below book value.

What are we seeing that the market isn't? A future that extends beyond the next year or two, for one thing, as investors' preoccupation with near-term challenges, as opposed to long-term fundamentals, seems to know no bounds. Take home builder M.D.C. Holdings, for instance, which boasts strong liquidity thanks to its asset- and debt-light business model, a fact underscored by the firm's ability to continue churning out free cash flow in the face of the current carnage. Despite that, investors have sold first and asked questions later, erasing roughly one third of the stock's value in 2007. (M.D.C. was recently trading at a 42% discount to our analysts' estimate of the firm's intrinsic worth.)

Not surprisingly, we see a pair of homebuilder ETFs that have "bargain" written all over them.

- **iShares Dow Jones U.S. Home Construction** (0.65 price/fair value) and
- **SPDR S&P Homebuilders** (0.69 price/fair value)

There's not much to differentiate these two funds, which share the bulk of their 20-plus holdings in common. The SPDR offering pulls in a passel of home supply-related concerns, like Home Depot, Lowe's, and Sherwin Williams. But it's pretty much a toss-up between these two ETFs.

Given the volatility of these stocks, none of which are for the faint of heart, we'd invest only at a hefty margin of safety, with a 20% discount to our fair value estimate sufficing. Even by that standard, these funds look like compelling values.

Financial-Services ETFs

You have plenty to choose from in this sector, which has been waylaid by cascading fears over higher interest rates, a slumping real estate market, and shoddy lending. The typical financial-services stock that we cover was trading at a 14% discount to its fair value estimate as of Dec. 31, 2007.

That's reflected in the valuation of the broad financials-market funds that we cover, which are typically trading at 20% to 30% discounts to our fair value estimate. Rydex S&P Equal-Weight Financials (21% discount) and iShares Dow Jones U.S. Financial Sector (24% discount) are two such examples.

But to find some of the biggest bargains, set your sights on the financials subsector ETFs, a number of which have gotten battered amid the sell-off. Here are our favorites at the moment:

- **KBW Bank** (0.68 price/fair value)
This fund teems with values—all but a handful of the portfolio's 25 stocks were trading at a discount to our fair value estimates as of Dec. 31. And many of those discounts were steep, with many of the fund's global bank (Citigroup, Bank of America, and J.P. Morgan Chase) and super-regional (Wachovia and Fifth Third, among others) holdings trading at 25% or larger discounts to fair value. The fund's narrow focus means we'd ordinarily demand a 15% discount to fair value before recommending it. By that standard, it screams "buy."

- **Regional Bank HOLDRs** (0.71 price/fair value) and **iShares Dow Jones U.S. Regional Banks** (0.70 price/fair value)
Don't let the names fool you—with top holdings including giants like J.P. Morgan Chase, Wachovia, and US Bancorp, these funds are hardly a dumping ground for toaster-peddling community savings banks or rinky-dink S&Ls. In some cases, such as Regions Financial, these firms have been punished by investors concerned about contracting net interest margins or mounting loan losses, subprime mortgage exposure in particular. We think the selling looks overdone, and many look cheap, explaining these regional bank funds' compelling valuations.

- **iShares Dow Jones U.S. Financial Services** (0.71 price/fair value)
This is the most diversified of the four financials ETFs profiled, spanning virtually every financials subsector. It isn't hard to figure out why: Its top three holdings—Citigroup, Bank of America, and J.P. Morgan Chase—recently soaked up nearly 30% of assets, and all three of those stocks are trading well below fair value, in our estimation.

Consumer-Related ETFs

Is the U.S. consumer rolling over? That question has bedeviled consumer stocks in recent months, as investors weighing the prospects of an economic slowdown or resurgent inflation have seemed to sell first and ask questions later. Housing-related concerns (think Home Depot and Lowe's) and firms believed to be heavily leveraged to a vibrant, unburdened consumer (apparel makers, restaurants, etc.) have been hit especially hard.

If not always deep, the selling has been fairly widespread, leaving roughly two in every three consumer stocks that we cover trading at least 10% below our fair value estimate. That, in turn, has put a number of consumer-related ETFs on sale, with the following being the cheapest of the bunch.

- **SPDR S&P Retail** (0.76 price/fair value)
Given that this portfolio is more or less equally weighted across 60 or so stocks, a few bargains do not a cheap ETF make. But with consumer stocks pulling back en masse lately, this fund finds itself flush with values. Well over half of the 49 portfolio holdings that we cover were trading at a 10% or greater discount to fair value, with apparel retailers (Coldwater Creek, Chico's, Foot Locker), department stores (J.C. Penney, Macy's), discount chains (Sears, Wal-Mart), and grocers (Whole Foods, SuperValu) looking particularly cheap.

- **Powershares Dynamic Retail** (0.78 price/fair value)
Because we cover a lesser percentage of this fund's underlying stocks—78% to be precise—than we do the other ETFs on our buy list, it's worth noting that our fair value estimate should be taken with the proverbial grain of salt. That said, there's nothing on the surface to suggest that our 0.78 price/fair value ratio is not representative of the whole. This ETF's bargain price owes mainly to a clutch of cheap discount retailers (Sears), auto suppliers (Advance Auto Parts, AutoNation), clothing stores (Collective Brands, Ann Taylor), and home supply giants (Home Depot, Lowe's).

- **Retail HOLDRs** (0.79 price/fair value)
It pays to scan the holdings list of this ETF. True, it looks cheap, even when we account for the 89% discount to fair value that we'd demand. However, the portfolio is crammed into just a handful of names, with the top five holdings recently soaking up around 55% of assets. Thus, our call turns to an unusually large extent on the precision of our fair value estimates on the five stocks in question—Wal-Mart, Home Depot, Target, Lowe's, and Walgreen. For that reason, we'd probably opt for the two better-diversified offerings mentioned above over this one.

Diversified ETFs

And then there are the handful of diversified ETFs where nicked financial-, consumer-, and homebuilder-related names converge. What's the common thread? Usually, it's a record of strong historical earnings growth, which is abundant in the financial-services and retail realms, though the market has apparently soured on many of these firms' growth prospects for now.

- **Claymore/Great Companies Large-Cap Growth** (0.87 price/fair value)
  This fund tracks an index that seeks firms with strong earnings growth, sane price multiples, and the traits of "great companies," the telltale of which include a global orientation. While those criteria are on the murky side (Research in Motion passes the index's valuation screen despite the fact that, by our estimate, it's trading at nearly twice its intrinsic value), the upshot is that financials, and retailers figure prominently, with many of those names trading comfortably in 5-star territory. Given the portfolio's respectably high quality (nearly half of the names boast wide economic moats), moderate risk profile (our analysts consider only a handful to be above-average risks), and wide diversification across sectors, we wouldn't demand an especially large margin of safety before investing here, with a 9% discount to fair value sufficing.

- **Powershares High Growth Rate Dividend Achievers** (0.79)
  This fund tracks an index that targets firms that have raised their annual dividend at least 10 years consecutively. Not surprisingly, stock quality is high—wide-moat stocks account for nearly 70% of assets—with mega-cap global banks (Bank of America, Citigroup), insurers (American International Group), drugmakers (Johnson & Johnson, Pfizer), and industrial conglomerates (United Technologies) filling out the portfolio's upper ranks. In short, these businesses have been able to exploit their manifold competitive advantages to churn out gobs of free cash year after year, returning a slug of that cash to shareholders each year in the form of dividends. In addition to the usual suspects in the banking, retail, and home improvement realms, this offering also prominently features a clutch of cheap health-care (Medtronic, Johnson & Johnson) and capital-markets-related names (Legg Mason, Lehman Brothers). IM

U.S. Stock Funds: Diversified

This section offers a full-page report on each diversified U.S. Stock ETF.

DIAMONDS Trust DIA

Market Price	Mstar Category
$132.55	Large Value

Morningstar Fair Value

Price/Fair Value Ratio	Coverage Rate %
0.88	100

Valuation

This ETF was recently trading at a 12% discount to our fair value estimate. Given the portfolio's diversification and high-quality tilt, we wouldn't require a large margin of safety in order to recommend it: An 8% discount to fair value should suffice. By that standard, the fund looks like a bargain at recent levels.

Methodology

This ETF tracks the Dow Jones Industrial Average, a price-weighted index composed of 30 U.S.-based non-utilities stocks. The index is maintained by the editors of The Wall Street Journal, who consider subjective factors, such as the strength of each firm's reputation and the degree to which the business is representative of the U.S. economy, in deciding which stocks to include. Befitting its name, the Dow has historically leaned toward industrials, although the financial services, consumer goods, and technology sectors now account for a sizable portion of the index as well.

Morningstar Rating	Return	Risk	Yield	NAV	Avg Daily Vol. (k)	52 wk High/Low
★★★	Average	Below Avg	2.1%	$132.50	13,891	$141.57 - $120.30

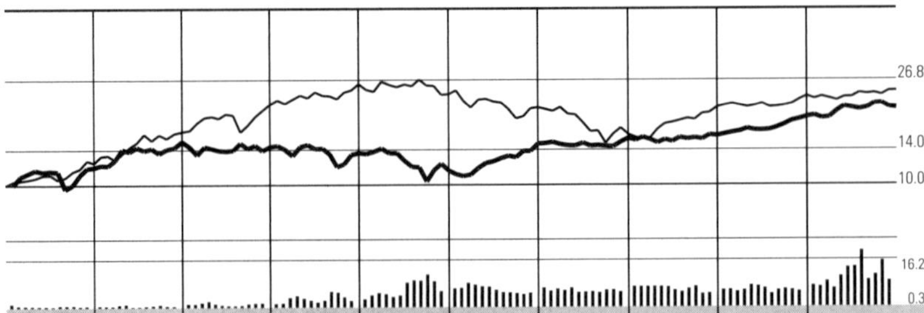

Growth of $10,000
— Investment Value of ETF
— Investment Value of Index S&P 500

Trading Volume Millions

1998	1999	2000	2001	2002	2003	2004	2005	2006	2007	History
91.81	114.99	107.82	100.29	83.52	104.67	107.71	107.08	124.45	132.50	NAV $
91.53	115.19	106.78	99.80	83.51	104.57	107.51	106.95	124.41	132.55	Market Price $
7.62*	26.95	-4.84	-5.52	-15.10	28.00	5.12	2.40	18.81	8.71	NAV Return%
7.42*	27.56	-5.92	-5.07	-14.69	27.90	5.02	2.47	18.91	8.79	Market Price Return%
-0.16	-0.12	-0.05	-0.12	-0.19	0.03	0.03	0.02	0.07	0.07	Avg Premium/Discount%
—	5.91	4.26	6.37	7.00	-0.68	-5.76	-2.51	3.02	3.22	NAV Rtrn% +/-S&P 500
—	-0.26	0.01	-0.08	-0.09	-0.28	-0.19	0.68	-0.24	-0.17	NAV Rtrn% +/-DJ Industr
—	1	20	39	20	75	100	100	64	16	NAV Return% Rank in Cat
—	1.57	1.37	1.46	1.75	2.33	2.12	2.94	2.39	2.23	Income Return %
—	25.38	-6.21	-6.98	-16.85	25.67	3.00	-0.54	16.42	6.48	Capital Return %
1.35	1.43	1.57	1.56	1.74	1.93	2.20	3.13	2.53	2.75	Income $
0.00	0.00	0.00	0.00	0.00	0.00	0.00	0.00	0.00	0.00	Capital Gains $
—	0.18	0.17	0.17	0.18	0.18	0.18	0.18	0.17	—	Expense Ratio %
—	1.37	1.34	1.51	1.85	2.12	1.89	2.27	2.21	—	Income Ratio %
—	35	24	13	1	9	14	8	—	—	Turnover Rate %
—	—	—	—	4,728	6,778	8,022	7,634	6,733	8,574	Net Assets $mil

Performance 12-31-07

Historic Quarterly NAV Returns

	1st Qtr	2nd Qtr	3rd Qtr	4th Qtr	Total
2003	-3.69	13.05	3.72	13.35	28.00
2004	-0.47	1.20	-2.94	7.53	5.12
2005	-1.27	-1.67	3.39	2.02	2.40
2006	4.19	0.90	5.29	7.34	18.81
2007	-0.36	9.06	4.14	-3.94	8.71

Trailing	NAV Return%	Market Return%	NAV Rtrn% +/-S&P 500	%Rank Cat.(NAV)
3 Mo	-3.94	-3.97	-0.61	23
6 Mo	0.04	-0.09	1.41	1
1 Yr	8.71	8.79	3.22	16
3 Yr Avg	9.77	9.85	1.15	12
5 Yr Avg	12.22	12.23	-0.61	100
10 Yr Avg	—	—	—	—

Tax Analysis	Tax-Adj Return%	Tax-Cost Ratio
3 Yr (estimated)	8.85	0.84
5 Yr (estimated)	11.32	0.80
10 Yr (estimated)	—	—

Rating and Risk

Time Period	Morningstar Rtn vs Cat	Morningstar Risk vs Cat	Morningstar Risk-Adj Rating
3 Yr	+Avg	Avg	★★★★
5 Yr	Avg	-Avg	★★★
10 Yr	—	—	—

Other Measures	Standard Index S&P 500	Best Fit Index DJ IndusAvg
Alpha	1.2	2.5
Beta	0.98	0.99
R-Squared	88	100
Standard Deviation	8.12	
Mean	9.77	
Sharpe Ratio	0.67	

Portfolio Analysis 12-31-07

Share change since 11-07 Total Stocks:30	Sector	PE	Tot Ret%	% Assets
⊕ International Business M	Hardware	16.2	13.20	6.61
⊕ ExxonMobil Corporation	Energy	13.6	24.34	5.73
⊕ Boeing Company	Ind Mtrls	16.9	-0.11	5.35
⊕ 3M Company	Ind Mtrls	14.1	10.53	5.15
⊕ United Technologies	Ind Mtrls	18.8	24.46	4.68
⊕ Altria Group Inc.	Goods	13.2	22.10	4.62
⊕ Procter & Gamble Company	Goods	23.1	16.63	4.49
⊕ Caterpillar Inc.	Ind Mtrls	14.0	20.48	4.44
⊕ Johnson & Johnson	Health	18.8	3.61	4.08
⊕ Honeywell International,	Ind Mtrls	20.8	38.65	3.76
⊕ Coca-Cola Company	Goods	26.3	30.44	3.75
⊕ McDonald's Corporation	Consumer	39.5	36.38	3.60
⊕ American International G	Financial	10.2	-17.96	3.56
⊕ Merck & Co., Inc.	Health	23.6	37.36	3.55
⊕ American Express Company	Financial	14.9	-13.18	3.18
⊕ Hewlett-Packard Company	Hardware	18.8	23.40	3.09
⊕ Wal-Mart Stores, Inc.	Consumer	15.4	4.91	2.91
⊕ E.I. du Pont de Nemours	Ind Mtrls	12.4	-6.63	2.70
⊕ Verizon Communications I	Telecom	21.7	22.19	2.67
⊕ J.P. Morgan Chase & Co.	Financial	9.5	-7.24	2.67

Current Investment Style

Value Blnd Growth — Large Mid Small

Market Cap	%
Giant	83.7
Large	16.3
Mid	0.0
Small	0.0
Micro	0.0

Avg $mil: 113,594

Value Measures		Rel Category
Price/Earnings	14.32	1.06
Price/Book	3.38	1.72
Price/Sales	1.16	0.97
Price/Cash Flow	9.51	1.14
Dividend Yield %	2.08	0.77

Growth Measures	%	Rel Category
Long-Term Erngs	—	—
Book Value	4.68	0.54
Sales	5.76	0.90
Cash Flow	11.70	2.22
Historical Erngs	18.52	1.23

Profitability	%	Rel Category
Return on Equity	29.95	1.52
Return on Assets	9.15	1.43
Net Margin	11.97	0.86

Sector Weightings	% of Stocks	Rel S&P 500	3 Year High	3 Year Low
Info	20.73	0.99		
Software	2.18	0.53	2	2
Hardware	11.35	1.11	12	9
Media	1.98	0.68	2	2
Telecom	5.22	1.44	5	4
Service	28.45	0.70		
Health	9.04	0.75	9	8
Consumer	8.17	1.21	9	8
Business	0.00	0.00	0	0
Financial	11.24	0.64	16	11
Mfg	50.81	1.32		
Goods	14.42	1.57	16	13
Ind Mtrls	30.65	2.36	35	29
Energy	5.74	0.45	6	4
Utilities	0.00	0.00	0	0

Composition

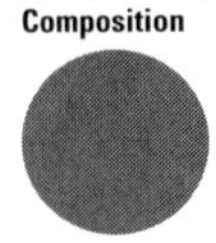

Cash	0.3
Stocks	99.8
Bonds	0.0
Other	0.0
Foreign (% of Stock)	0.0

Morningstar's Take by Emiko Kurotsu 12-31-07

We'd buy this high-quality, moderate-risk portfolio at a modest discount to our fair value estimate.

DIAMONDS Trust tracks the Dow Jones Industrial Average, an index of 30 U.S.-listed stocks selected by the editors of The Wall Street Journal. Although its approach is somewhat subjective, the selection committee aims to include stocks that are representative of the broad U.S. stock market. As a result, the index has long teemed with household names like McDonald's and IBM.

Not surprisingly, the quality of this fund's portfolio is high. Morningstar's stock analysts have awarded wide economic moats to 21 of the fund's 30 holdings--or nearly 72% of assets. A wide-moat rating denotes our analysts' belief that a firm's competitive advantages are durable, making it more difficult for competitors to chip away at the profits the business generates. Such firms are typically hard to find--as of December 2007, our analysts had doled out wide-moat ratings to about 10% of the 2,000-plus firms that they covered. Yet, blue-chip names abound here, ranging from branding titans (Procter & Gamble and Disney), to intellectual property leaders (3M and Johnson & Johnson) and vaunted scale competitors (Wal-Mart and ExxonMobil).

The fund's relatively temperate risk profile is also worth noting. In our analysts' view, 27 of its 30 holdings court below-average or average business risk, meaning that they're confident in the accuracy of the cash-flow forecasts that underpin their fair value estimates. That stems largely from the quality of these firms, whose industry-leading positions fortify them against most event-specific "shocks" while, in at least some cases, conferring a steady, more-predictable base of recurring sales.

Coupled with the fund's diversification across names and sectors, the holdings' risk profile has tamped volatility. We would not demand an especially large margin of safety before investing in the shares: An 8% discount to our fair value estimate is sufficient.

Address:	PDR Services, 86 Trinity Place United States 800-843-2639
Web Address:	www.amex.com
Inception:	01-13-98*
Advisor:	PDR Services

Management Fee:	0.07%		
Expense Projections:	3Yr: —	5Yr: —	10Yr: —
Income Distrib:	Monthly		
Exchange:	AMEX		

iShares DJ Sel Dividend DVY

Market Price	Mstar Category
$64.49	Large Value

Morningstar Fair Value

Price/Fair Value Ratio	Coverage Rate %
0.82	86

Valuation

This fund is a good deal. It was recently trading at a nearly 14% discount to our fair value estimate, well in excess of the 9% margin of safety we'd normally demand. The fund has gotten cheap due in large part to widespread weakness in the financial sector, as financial services stocks abound here.

Methodology

This fund tracks the Dow Jones Select Dividend Index, which consists of roughly 100 stocks from the broader Dow Jones U.S. Total Market Index with the highest dividend yields. The index omits firms that have cut the dividend in the past five years or that pay more than 60% of earnings in the form of dividends. The index ranks the stocks by annual yield and reconstitutes once a year. It excludes REITs outright. Like other dividend-focused funds, this portfolio stashes an inordinate amount--nearly 40% of assets--in financials, while eschewing low-payout tech stocks altogether.

Morningstar Rating	Return	Risk	Yield	NAV	Avg Daily Vol. (k)	52 wk High/Low
★★	Below Avg	Below Avg	3.7%	$64.72	836	$75.55 - $61.13

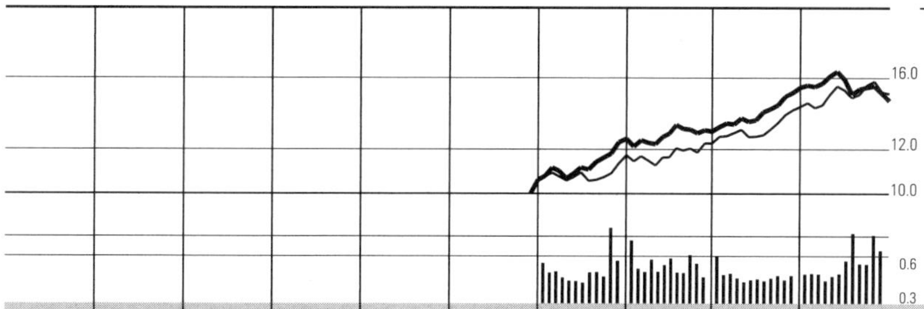

Growth of $10,000
— Investment Value of ETF
— Investment Value of Index S&P 500

Trading Volume Millions

1998	1999	2000	2001	2002	2003	2004	2005	2006	2007	History
—	—	—	—	—	53.80	61.34	61.30	70.76	64.72	NAV $
—	—	—	—	—	53.84	61.40	61.26	70.73	64.49	Market Price $
—	—	—	—	—	9.70*	17.90	2.98	19.41	-5.37	NAV Return%
—	—	—	—	—	9.60*	17.93	2.81	19.44	-5.67	Market Price Return%
—	—	—	—	—	0.10	0.11	0.03	0.02	-0.05	Avg Premium/Discount%
—	—	—	—	—	—	7.02	-1.93	3.62	-10.86	NAV Rtrn% +/-S&P 500
—	—	—	—	—	—	-0.24	-0.79	-0.15	-0.21	NAV Rtrn% +/-DJ Sel Div
—	—	—	—	—	—	100	75	57	89	NAV Return% Rank in Cat
—	—	—	—	—	—	3.59	3.05	3.68	3.39	Income Return %
—	—	—	—	—	—	14.31	-0.07	15.73	-8.76	Capital Return %
—	—	—	—	—	0.29	1.91	1.85	2.22	2.37	Income $
—	—	—	—	—	0.00	0.00	0.00	0.00	0.00	Capital Gains $
—	—	—	—	—	—	0.40	0.40	0.40	0.40	Expense Ratio %
—	—	—	—	—	—	3.43	3.39	3.35	3.28	Income Ratio %
—	—	—	—	—	—	2	20	14	6	Turnover Rate %
—	—	—	—	—	460	5,009	7,252	7,770	6,913	Net Assets $mil

Performance 12-31-07

Historic Quarterly NAV Returns

	1st Qtr	2nd Qtr	3rd Qtr	4th Qtr	Total
2003	—	—	—	—	—*
2004	3.58	1.47	4.01	7.85	17.90
2005	-1.59	3.78	1.62	-0.78	2.98
2006	2.90	1.66	6.25	7.44	19.41
2007	1.69	1.54	-3.09	-5.43	-5.37

Trailing	NAV Return%	Market Return%	NAV Rtrn% +/-S&P 500	%Rank Cat.(NAV)
3 Mo	-5.43	-6.05	-2.10	50
6 Mo	-8.36	-8.65	-6.99	77
1 Yr	-5.37	-5.67	-10.86	89
3 Yr Avg	5.18	5.02	-3.44	100
5 Yr Avg	—	—	—	—
10 Yr Avg	—	—	—	—

Tax Analysis	Tax-Adj Return%	Tax-Cost Ratio
3 Yr (estimated)	3.99	1.13
5 Yr (estimated)	—	—
10 Yr (estimated)	—	—

Rating and Risk

Time Period	Morningstar Rtn vs Cat	Morningstar Risk vs Cat	Morningstar Risk-Adj Rating
3 Yr	-Avg	-Avg	★★
5 Yr	—	—	—
10 Yr	—	—	—

Other Measures	Standard Index S&P 500	Best Fit Index M* U.S. Value TR
Alpha	-2.4	-3.0
Beta	0.79	0.78
R-Squared	66	78
Standard Deviation	7.62	
Mean	5.18	
Sharpe Ratio	0.14	

Morningstar's Take by Emiko Kurotsu 12-31-07

High yields aren't a harbinger for quality.

This fund tracks the Dow Jones Select Dividend Index, which sifts the Dow Jones U.S. Total Market Index for about 100 stocks that pay the highest dividends. To blunt the risk that financially unsound firms will predominate, the index omits those that have made a dividend cut in the past five years or dole out more than 60% of earnings in dividends.

That doesn't necessarily translate to high quality, a trait we associate with firms that boast intractable competitive advantages, or wide "economic moats." Of the 91 stocks our analysts cover, just 17 garner a wide moat. For every wide-moat stock such as Eli Lilly or Bank of America, there are several other lesser-quality names. For instance, narrow-moat bank Regions Financial lacks the breadth and depth of products that would allow it to play in the league of larger banks. Similarly, natural-gas distributor Nicor's fate is tied to the regulator that sets its rates to customers.

Although many of these firms boast some advantages, they're either fleeting in nature or don't translate to attractive shareholder returns. That might seem at odds with a history of paying hefty dividends. But because dividends represent a use of excess cash that a business throws off, and the supply of cash depends on a firm's ability to generate strong returns, then a firm's returns on invested capital are a far better gauge of company quality than dividend payouts. On that basis, many of the stocks here fall short.

Business risk is partly a function of quality, with stronger firms typically courting less risk because they're less likely to be thwarted by rivals. Not surprisingly, many of the firms here carry at least average business risk, reflecting the moderate level of uncertainty associated with the cash flows they're likely to churn out in the future.

Because the fund is reasonably well diversified, though, it hasn't been too volatile. We wouldn't demand a large margin of safety to invest here.

Address:	45 Fremont Street United States 800-474-2737
Web Address:	www.ishares.com
Inception:	11-03-03*
Advisor:	Barclays Global Fund Advisers

Management Fee:	0.40%		
Expense Projections:	3Yr:$128	5Yr:$224	10Yr:$505
Income Distrib:	Quarterly		
Exchange:	NYSE		

Portfolio Analysis 12-31-07

Share change since 11-07 Total Stocks:112	Sector	PE	Tot Ret%	% Assets
⊖ Altria Group Inc.	Goods	13.2	22.10	3.45
⊖ FirstEnergy Corporation	Utilities	17.3	23.71	3.07
⊖ FPL Group	Utilities	20.0	27.91	2.94
⊖ Merck & Co., Inc.	Health	23.6	37.36	2.87
⊖ DTE Energy Holding Compa	Utilities	8.9	-5.16	2.82
⊖ PNC Financial Services G	Financial	12.8	-8.29	2.77
⊖ Bank of America Corporat	Financial	9.4	-19.25	2.65
⊖ AT&T, Inc.	Telecom	21.6	20.58	2.62
⊖ Pinnacle West Capital	Utilities	14.0	-12.23	2.26
⊖ Chevron Corporation	Energy	11.4	30.59	2.10
⊖ PPL Corporation	Utilities	20.0	49.31	2.09
⊖ Bristol-Myers Squibb Com	Health	24.8	4.75	1.97
⊖ Lincoln National Corp.	Financial	10.9	-12.63	1.94
⊖ Unitrin, Inc.	Financial	12.4	-0.37	1.89
⊖ Regions Financial Corpor	Financial	10.1	-33.64	1.81
⊖ Eastman Chemical Company	Ind Mtrls	17.4	5.19	1.77
⊖ PPG Industries, Inc.	Ind Mtrls	14.1	12.49	1.72
⊖ Comerica Incorporated	Financial	9.1	-22.42	1.70
⊖ Energy East Corporation	Utilities	16.3	15.05	1.65
⊖ Lyondell Chemical Compan	Energy	—	—	1.58

Current Investment Style

Value Blnd Growth — Large Mid Small

Market Cap	%
Giant	17.3
Large	20.9
Mid	47.6
Small	13.4
Micro	0.8
Avg $mil: 10,257	

Value Measures		Rel Category
Price/Earnings	12.52	0.93
Price/Book	1.36	0.69
Price/Sales	1.10	0.92
Price/Cash Flow	6.12	0.73
Dividend Yield %	4.32	1.60

Growth Measures	%	Rel Category
Long-Term Erngs	—	—
Book Value	6.67	0.77
Sales	1.00	0.16
Cash Flow	2.31	0.44
Historical Erngs	6.78	0.45

Profitability	%	Rel Category
Return on Equity	14.88	0.75
Return on Assets	3.67	0.57
Net Margin	14.22	1.02

Sector Weightings	% of Stocks	Rel S&P 500	3 Year High	3 Year Low
Info	4.08	0.20		
Software	0.00	0.00	0	0
Hardware	0.00	0.00	0	0
Media	1.39	0.48	1	0
Telecom	2.69	0.74	4	2
Service	55.04	1.35		
Health	4.35	0.36	7	4
Consumer	2.33	0.34	3	1
Business	1.99	0.45	3	1
Financial	46.37	2.66	46	37
Mfg	40.88	1.06		
Goods	10.57	1.15	12	10
Ind Mtrls	9.07	0.70	11	7
Energy	2.18	0.17	9	2
Utilities	19.06	5.18	24	19

Composition

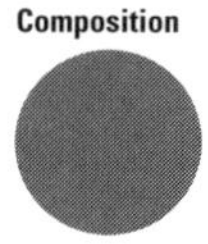

Cash	0.8
Stocks	99.2
Bonds	0.0
Other	0.0
Foreign (% of Stock)	0.0

iShares Dow Jones US Idx IYY

Market Price	Mstar Category
$71.54	Large Blend

Morningstar Rating	Return	Risk	Yield	NAV	Avg Daily Vol. (k)	52 wk High/Low
★★★★	Above Avg	Average	1.6%	$71.60	55	$76.33 - $67.03

Morningstar Fair Value

Price/Fair Value Ratio	Coverage Rate %
0.90	97

Valuation

This ETF looks cheap right now. It was recently trading at a 10% discount to our fair value estimate, which is more than the 8% minimum we'd demand to invest here. We're enthusiastic buyers of this broad-market fund while this attractive price lasts.

Methodology

This ETF tracks the Dow Jones U.S. Total Stock Market Index, a broad benchmark that represents about 95% of the total U.S. stock market. The fund is top-heavy due to its market-cap-weighted methodology, with less than 5% of the fund invested in small caps and micro-caps. Still, the index represents a comprehensive slice of the U.S. stock market and offers sector diversification in line with the broad domestic market (e.g., heavier stakes in financials, industrials, energy, and health care).

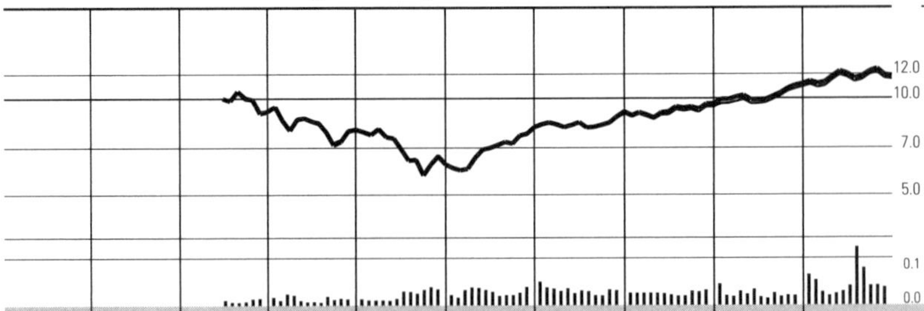

Growth of $10,000
— Investment Value of ETF
— Investment Value of Index S&P 500

Trading Volume Millions

1998	1999	2000	2001	2002	2003	2004	2005	2006	2007	History
—	—	61.42	53.39	41.00	52.71	57.94	60.53	68.72	71.60	NAV $
—	—	61.53	53.57	41.02	52.71	58.00	60.51	68.69	71.54	Market Price $
—	—	2.28*	-12.13	-22.17	30.42	11.78	6.14	15.31	5.81	NAV Return%
—	—	2.27*	-11.99	-22.40	30.36	11.90	6.00	15.30	5.78	Market Price Return%
—	—	0.13	0.02	0.10	0.12	0.04	0.01	-0.02	-0.04	Avg Premium/Discount%
—	—	—	-0.24	-0.07	1.74	0.90	1.23	-0.48	0.32	NAV Rtrn% +/-S&P 500
—	—	—	-0.18	-0.09	-0.33	-0.23	-0.18	-0.26	-0.20	NAV Rtrn% +/-DJ Tot Mkt
—	—	—	84	80	50	44	31	57	49	NAV Return% Rank in Cat
—	—	—	0.94	1.13	1.64	1.76	1.63	1.67	1.65	Income Return %
—	—	—	-13.07	-23.30	28.78	10.02	4.51	13.64	4.16	Capital Return %
—	—	0.24	0.57	0.60	0.67	0.92	0.94	1.01	1.12	Income $
—	—	0.01	0.00	0.00	0.00	0.00	0.00	0.00	0.00	Capital Gains $
—	—	—	0.20	0.20	0.20	0.20	0.20	0.20	0.20	Expense Ratio %
—	—	—	0.98	1.15	1.57	1.49	1.81	1.63	1.62	Income Ratio %
—	—	—	5	5	14	5	6	5	4	Turnover Rate %
—	—	37	104	143	335	435	472	539	684	Net Assets $mil

Performance 12-31-07

Historic Quarterly NAV Returns

	1st Qtr	2nd Qtr	3rd Qtr	4th Qtr	Total
2003	-3.09	16.12	3.16	12.35	30.42
2004	2.15	1.46	-1.93	9.98	11.78
2005	-2.12	2.10	3.92	2.20	6.14
2006	4.95	-1.83	4.71	6.89	15.31
2007	1.33	6.16	1.70	-3.28	5.81

Trailing	NAV Return%	Market Return%	NAV Rtrn% +/-S&P 500	%Rank Cat.(NAV)
3 Mo	-3.28	-3.31	0.05	47
6 Mo	-1.64	-1.65	-0.27	50
1 Yr	5.81	5.78	0.32	49
3 Yr Avg	9.00	8.94	0.38	52
5 Yr Avg	13.55	13.53	0.72	31
10 Yr Avg	—	—	—	—

Tax Analysis	Tax-Adj Return%	Tax-Cost Ratio
3 Yr (estimated)	8.41	0.54
5 Yr (estimated)	12.94	0.54
10 Yr (estimated)	—	—

Rating and Risk

Time Period	Morningstar Rtn vs Cat	Morningstar Risk vs Cat	Morningstar Risk-Adj Rating
3 Yr	Avg	Avg	★★★
5 Yr	+Avg	Avg	★★★★
10 Yr	—	—	—

Other Measures	Standard Index S&P 500	Best Fit Index M* U.S. Mkt TR
Alpha	0.2	-0.2
Beta	1.04	0.99
R-Squared	99	100
Standard Deviation	8.11	
Mean	9.00	
Sharpe Ratio	0.58	

Portfolio Analysis 12-31-07

Share change since 11-07 Total Stocks:1530	Sector	PE	Tot Ret%	% Assets
⊕ ExxonMobil Corporation	Energy	13.6	24.34	3.36
⊕ General Electric Company	Ind Mtrls	16.6	2.69	2.46
⊕ Microsoft Corporation	Software	23.4	20.83	1.95
⊕ AT&T, Inc.	Telecom	21.6	20.58	1.66
⊕ Procter & Gamble Company	Goods	23.1	16.63	1.50
⊕ Chevron Corporation	Energy	11.4	30.59	1.31
⊕ Johnson & Johnson	Health	18.8	3.61	1.26
⊕ Bank of America Corporat	Financial	9.4	-19.25	1.22
⊕ Apple, Inc.	Hardware	50.5	133.47	1.14
⊕ Cisco Systems, Inc.	Hardware	21.5	-0.95	1.08
⊕ Google, Inc.	Business	54.0	50.17	1.07
⊕ Altria Group Inc.	Goods	13.2	22.10	1.04
⊕ Pfizer Inc.	Health	22.5	-8.15	1.02
⊕ Intel Corporation	Hardware	25.4	34.22	1.02
⊕ J.P. Morgan Chase & Co.	Financial	9.5	-7.24	0.97
⊕ International Business M	Hardware	16.2	13.20	0.97
⊕ Citigroup, Inc.	Financial	7.9	-44.93	0.96
⊕ ConocoPhillips	Energy	13.8	25.42	0.86
⊕ Hewlett-Packard Company	Hardware	18.8	23.40	0.86
⊕ Coca-Cola Company	Goods	26.3	30.44	0.86

Current Investment Style

Value Blnd Growth; Large Mid Small

Market Cap	%
Giant	43.4
Large	32.1
Mid	20.1
Small	4.2
Micro	0.2
Avg $mil: 36,730	

Value Measures		Rel Category
Price/Earnings	14.44	0.92
Price/Book	2.37	0.93
Price/Sales	1.34	1.08
Price/Cash Flow	9.45	1.02
Dividend Yield %	1.71	0.90

Growth Measures	%	Rel Category
Long-Term Erngs	8.45	0.72
Book Value	7.76	0.84
Sales	7.08	0.87
Cash Flow	7.47	0.85
Historical Erngs	16.83	1.01

Profitability	%	Rel Category
Return on Equity	21.41	0.96
Return on Assets	8.27	0.99
Net Margin	13.79	1.12

Sector Weightings	% of Stocks	Rel S&P 500	3 Year High	3 Year Low
Info	20.90	1.00		
Software	4.35	1.05	4	4
Hardware	10.05	0.98	10	9
Media	3.02	1.04	4	3
Telecom	3.48	0.96	4	3
Service	41.67	1.03		
Health	12.20	1.01	14	12
Consumer	7.12	1.05	9	7
Business	5.34	1.21	5	4
Financial	17.01	0.98	22	17
Mfg	37.44	0.97		
Goods	8.72	0.95	9	7
Ind Mtrls	12.97	1.00	13	11
Energy	11.85	0.94	12	8
Utilities	3.90	1.06	4	3

Composition

Cash	0.6
Stocks	99.4
Bonds	0.0
Other	0.0
Foreign (% of Stock)	0.2

Morningstar's Take by Emiko Kurotsu 12-31-07

This total-market fund is of middling quality.

This ETF tracks the Dow Jones U.S. Total Stock Market Index, which broadly represents 95% of the U.S. stock market. Although the fund is stuffed with more than 1,500 names, the index's market-cap-weighted strategy makes it extremely top-heavy, with the first 300 names making up more than three fourths of the portfolio.

This large-cap tilt doesn't impact the proportion of high-quality stocks in the fund, though. In fact, just 139 out of 1,566 stocks--or about 10% of the fund--is invested in stocks with wide economic moats, or firms that our analysts believe possess enduring competitive advantages. That's not altogether surprising, though, given that only 10% of the 2,000-plus equities that our analysts cover boast wide-moat status. By the numbers, then, this fund's allocation to wide-moat stocks isn't shabby.

That said, the overall quality of the portfolio is middling, with the bulk of the fund devoted to narrow- and no-moat firms. This makes sense, as the fund's total-market coverage means the portfolio tends to regress to the mean. This phenomenon reflects the basic nature of competition--profitable firms attract rivals and only those with defensible advantages (i.e., wide moats) can withstand predatory competitors. Thus, this fund abounds with narrow-moat firms such as Google, whose dominance in Internet search and non-search advertising is tenuous amid a lack of switching costs.

Most of the stocks here court average business risk, meaning that there's not excessive uncertainty associated with the forecasts that underpin our fair value estimates. What's more, the portfolio's volatility is tamped by the sheer range of firms in the fund, which span the gamut of economic sectors and market caps.

Given this fund's temperate risk profile and wide diversification, we demand only a modest margin of safety here. An 8% or greater discount to our fair value estimate suffices.

Address:	45 Fremont Street United States 800-474-2737
Web Address:	www.ishares.com
Inception:	06-12-00*
Advisor:	Barclays Global Fund Advisers

Management Fee:	0.20%		
Expense Projections:	3Yr:$64	5Yr:$113	10Yr:$255
Income Distrib:	Quarterly		
Exchange:	NYSE		

iShares KLD Sel Soc Idx KLD

Market Price	Mstar Category
$60.82	Large Blend

Morningstar Rating	Return	Risk	Yield	NAV	Avg Daily Vol. (k)	52 wk High/Low
—	—	—	1.3%	$60.62	10	$65.31 - $57.05

Morningstar Fair Value

Price/Fair Value Ratio	Coverage Rate %
0.88	99

Valuation

This fund looks like a bargain right now. It was recently trading at an 11% or more discount to our fair value estimate, better than the 9% discount we'd demand. Given the fund's plethora of high-quality, moderate-risk stocks, we'd happily scoop up shares here at this attractive price.

Methodology

This ETF tracks the KLD Select Social Index, a large-cap socially screened benchmark that draws its holdings from the Russell 1000 and S&P 500 indexes. The index scores and ranks its eligible universe on the basis of social and environmental issues including diversity, employee relations, corporate governance, and human rights, and it excludes tobacco companies outright. The highest-scoring 200-300 companies are included in the index and weighted based on their scores. The portfolio skews heavily to technology, health-care, and consumer-goods firms while underweighting utilities and media stocks.

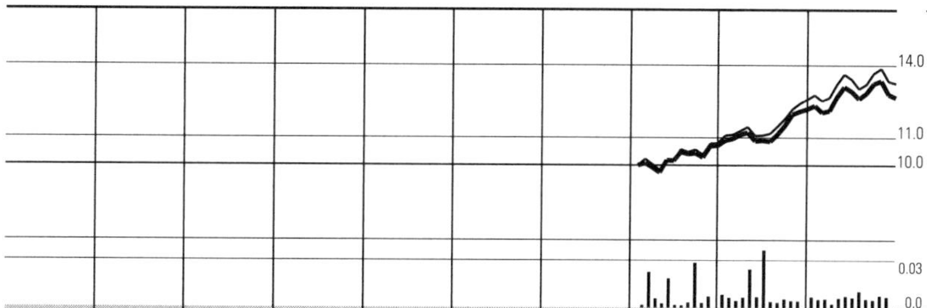

Growth of $10,000
— Investment Value of ETF
— Investment Value of Index S&P 500

Trading Volume Millions

History

1998	1999	2000	2001	2002	2003	2004	2005	2006	2007	History
—	—	—	—	—	—	—	53.14	59.02	60.62	NAV $
—	—	—	—	—	—	—	53.17	59.05	60.82	Market Price $
—	—	—	—	—	—	—	8.50*	12.85	4.03	NAV Return%
—	—	—	—	—	—	—	8.62*	12.84	4.31	Market Price Return%
—	—	—	—	—	—	—	-0.09	0.04	0.12	Avg Premium/Discount%
—	—	—	—	—	—	—	—	-2.94	-1.46	NAV Rtrn% +/-S&P 500
—	—	—	—	—	—	—	—	1.33	1.35	NAV Rtrn% +/-KLD Social
—	—	—	—	—	—	—	—	90	69	NAV Return% Rank in Cat
—	—	—	—	—	—	—	—	1.68	1.33	Income Return %
—	—	—	—	—	—	—	—	11.17	2.70	Capital Return %
—	—	—	—	—	—	—	0.61	0.89	0.78	Income $
—	—	—	—	—	—	—	0.00	0.00	0.00	Capital Gains $
—	—	—	—	—	—	—	0.50	0.50	0.50	Expense Ratio %
—	—	—	—	—	—	—	1.16	1.32	1.34	Income Ratio %
—	—	—	—	—	—	—	3	46	46	Turnover Rate %
—	—	—	—	—	—	—	117	68	124	Net Assets $mil

Performance 12-31-07

Historic Quarterly NAV Returns

	1st Qtr	2nd Qtr	3rd Qtr	4th Qtr	Total
2003	—	—	—	—	—
2004	—	—	—	—	—
2005	—	2.38	2.49	2.58	—*
2006	3.63	-1.85	5.06	5.60	12.85
2007	-0.54	6.79	2.56	-4.50	4.03

Trailing	NAV Return%	Market Return%	NAV Rtrn% +/-S&P 500	%Rank Cat.(NAV)
3 Mo	-4.51	-4.16	-1.18	70
6 Mo	-2.06	-2.20	-0.69	58
1 Yr	4.03	4.31	-1.46	69
3 Yr Avg	—	—	—	—
5 Yr Avg	—	—	—	—
10 Yr Avg	—	—	—	—

Tax Analysis	Tax-Adj Return%	Tax-Cost Ratio
3 Yr (estimated)	—	—
5 Yr (estimated)	—	—
10 Yr (estimated)	—	—

Rating and Risk

Time Period	Morningstar Rtn vs Cat	Morningstar Risk vs Cat	Morningstar Risk-Adj Rating
3 Yr	—	—	—
5 Yr	—	—	—
10 Yr	—	—	—

Other Measures	Standard Index S&P 500	Best Fit Index
Alpha	—	—
Beta	—	—
R-Squared	—	—
Standard Deviation	—	
Mean	—	
Sharpe Ratio	—	

Portfolio Analysis 12-31-07

Share change since 11-07 Total Stocks:227

Holding	Sector	PE	Tot Ret%	% Assets
⊕ Johnson & Johnson	Health	18.8	3.61	4.30
⊖ Wells Fargo Company	Financial	11.4	-12.13	2.94
⊕ Microsoft Corporation	Software	23.4	20.83	2.90
⊕ General Mills, Inc.	Goods	17.2	1.58	2.79
⊕ American Express Company	Financial	14.9	-13.18	2.70
⊕ International Business M	Hardware	16.2	13.20	2.62
⊕ Kimberly-Clark Corporati	Goods	17.0	5.23	2.37
⊖ PepsiCo, Inc.	Goods	20.4	23.89	2.35
⊕ The Travelers Companies,	Financial	7.8	2.37	2.26
⊕ United Parcel Service, I	Business	18.2	-3.50	2.18
⊕ Intel Corporation	Hardware	25.4	34.22	2.15
⊕ Procter & Gamble Company	Goods	23.1	16.63	1.98
⊕ Texas Instruments, Inc.	Hardware	19.2	17.01	1.96
⊖ 3M Company	Ind Mtrls	14.1	10.53	1.89
⊕ ExxonMobil Corporation	Energy	13.6	24.34	1.75
⊕ Cisco Systems, Inc.	Hardware	21.5	-0.95	1.58
⊕ Hewlett-Packard Company	Hardware	18.8	23.40	1.58
⊕ Gap, Inc.	Consumer	21.7	10.54	1.56
⊕ Bank of America Corporat	Financial	9.4	-19.25	1.56
⊕ Ecolab, Inc.	Ind Mtrls	32.3	14.21	1.38

Current Investment Style

Value Blnd Growth — Large / Mid / Small

Market Cap	%
Giant	42.8
Large	35.9
Mid	20.9
Small	0.4
Micro	0.0
Avg $mil: 40,033	

Value Measures		Rel Category
Price/Earnings	14.67	0.93
Price/Book	2.75	1.07
Price/Sales	1.65	1.33
Price/Cash Flow	10.90	1.18
Dividend Yield %	1.76	0.93

Growth Measures	%	Rel Category
Long-Term Erngs	—	—
Book Value	8.28	0.90
Sales	7.65	0.94
Cash Flow	7.48	0.86
Historical Erngs	16.00	0.96

Profitability	%	Rel Category
Return on Equity	24.17	1.09
Return on Assets	9.75	1.17
Net Margin	14.46	1.18

Sector Weightings	% of Stocks	Rel S&P 500	3 Year High	3 Year Low
Info	23.58	1.13		
Software	4.49	1.08	7	4
Hardware	15.06	1.48	16	9
Media	1.86	0.64	5	2
Telecom	2.17	0.60	3	0
Service	40.41	0.99		
Health	11.93	0.99	15	11
Consumer	6.75	1.00	7	4
Business	4.93	1.12	5	2
Financial	16.80	0.96	28	17
Mfg	36.01	0.94		
Goods	13.78	1.50	14	8
Ind Mtrls	11.81	0.91	14	10
Energy	9.35	0.74	9	5
Utilities	1.07	0.29	3	0

Composition

Cash	0.5
Stocks	99.5
Bonds	0.0
Other	0.0
Foreign (% of Stock)	0.0

Morningstar's Take by Emiko Kurotsu 12-31-07

This SRI fund offers a compelling quality proposition.

iShares KLD Select Social invests in 200-300 large companies that pass social screens that consider factors such as diversity, human rights, and corporate governance, among others. The index provider, KLD, aims to keep the portfolio's risk/reward profile roughly in line with the Russell 1000 Index's, explaining why this fund's sector weightings resemble the Russell benchmark's.

This fund's index has another trait in common with the Russell benchmark--high portfolio quality. In fact, this fund owns a slightly greater share of high-quality names than the Russell does. All told, Morningstar's equity analysts have awarded wide economic moat ratings to stocks representing nearly half of this fund's assets. Wide-moat names boast defensible competitive advantages, such as scale, barriers to entry, or brand identity, that keep rivals at bay. Examples are not hard to find: Top holding Johnson & Johnson wields a diverse portfolio of premier brand names. American Express' strong hold over high-spending card customers allows it to collect higher merchant fees than any other credit card company.

The fund's risk profile is also appealing, as most of its underlying stocks sport average or below-average business-risk ratings. Generally speaking, these firms throw off cash steadily, making their results easier to forecast and, thus, reducing the imprecision of our analysts' forecasts. For instance, Kimberly-Clark's dominance in mature product categories like diapers and tissues--which aren't as likely to see new, successful entrants--ensure steady sales year after year.

In addition to its attractive quality/risk profile, the portfolio is well-diversified across holdings and sectors. That, in turn, has tamped down volatility. As such, we wouldn't require a large margin of safety to invest here. A 9% discount to our fair value estimate--which takes the fund's expense ratio into account--should suffice.

Address:	45 Fremont Street United States 800-474-2737
Web Address:	www.ishares.com
Inception:	01-24-05*
Advisor:	Barclays Global Fund Advisers

Management Fee:	0.50%		
Expense Projections:	3Yr:$160	5Yr:$280	10Yr:$628
Income Distrib:	Annually		
Exchange:	NYSE		

iShares NYSE 100 Index NY

Market Price	Mstar Category
$75.97	Large Value

Morningstar Fair Value

Price/Fair Value Ratio	Coverage Rate %
0.87	100

Morningstar Rating	Return	Risk	Yield	NAV	Avg Daily Vol. (k)	52 wk High/Low
★★★	Average	Low	2.6%	$75.84	11	$81.81 - $72.21

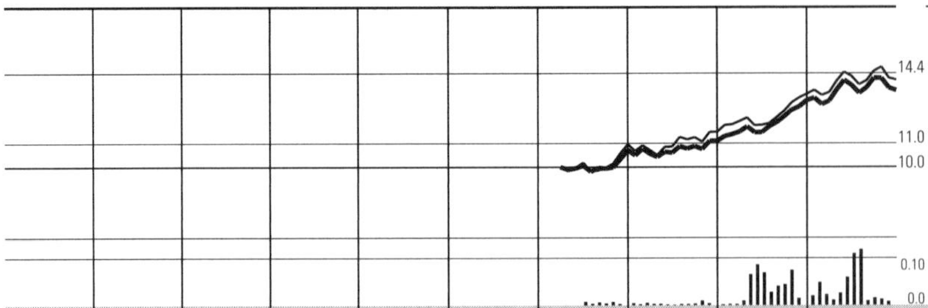

Growth of $10,000
- Investment Value of ETF
- Investment Value of Index S&P 500

Trading Volume Millions

Valuation

This ETF focuses on industry behemoths that boast intractable competitive advantages. It is also well diversified across holdings and industries. As such, we'd gladly scoop the fund up when it trades at least 8% below our fair value estimate. It's been trading at a 14% discount to fair value recently, making it a bargain.

Methodology

This ETF's benchmark is the NYSE 100, a collection of the 100 largest stocks (as measured by market capitalization) listed on the New York Stock Exchange. Because the NYSE excludes ADRs, this ETF has no foreign exposure.

History

1998	1999	2000	2001	2002	2003	2004	2005	2006	2007	History
—	—	—	—	—	—	64.27	65.14	74.91	75.84	NAV $
—	—	—	—	—	—	64.40	65.23	74.94	75.97	Market Price $
—	—	—	—	—	—	8.25*	3.52	16.96	3.81	NAV Return%
—	—	—	—	—	—	8.29*	3.45	16.85	3.94	Market Price Return%
—	—	—	—	—	—	-0.02	0.05	0.09	-0.03	Avg Premium/Discount%
—	—	—	—	—	—	—	-1.39	1.17	-1.68	NAV Rtrn% +/-S&P 500
—	—	—	—	—	—	—	2.12	2.44	2.31	NAV Rtrn% +/-NYSE 100
—	—	—	—	—	—	—	90	92	32	NAV Return% Rank in Cat
—	—	—	—	—	—	—	2.14	1.86	2.63	Income Return %
—	—	—	—	—	—	—	1.38	15.10	1.18	Capital Return %
—	—	—	—	—	—	0.84	1.36	1.20	1.95	Income $
—	—	—	—	—	—	0.00	0.00	0.00	0.00	Capital Gains $
—	—	—	—	—	—	0.20	0.20	0.20	0.20	Expense Ratio %
—	—	—	—	—	—	1.89	2.03	1.83	2.09	Income Ratio %
—	—	—	—	—	—	3	7	6	10	Turnover Rate %
—	—	—	—	—	—	26	29	345	106	Net Assets $mil

Performance 12-31-07

Historic Quarterly NAV Returns

	1st Qtr	2nd Qtr	3rd Qtr	4th Qtr	Total
2003	—	—	—	—	—
2004	—	0.58	-1.13	7.32	—*
2005	-1.43	0.37	2.50	2.08	3.52
2006	3.60	-0.25	6.27	6.51	16.96
2007	-0.20	6.13	2.80	-4.66	3.81

Trailing	NAV Return%	Market Return%	NAV Rtrn% +/-S&P 500	%Rank Cat.(NAV)
3 Mo	-4.66	-4.47	-1.33	28
6 Mo	-1.99	-1.75	-0.62	23
1 Yr	3.81	3.94	-1.68	32
3 Yr Avg	7.92	7.91	-0.70	78
5 Yr Avg	—	—	—	—
10 Yr Avg	—	—	—	—

Tax Analysis	Tax-Adj Return%	Tax-Cost Ratio
3 Yr (estimated)	7.13	0.73
5 Yr (estimated)	—	—
10 Yr (estimated)	—	—

Rating and Risk

Time Period	Morningstar Rtn vs Cat	Morningstar Risk vs Cat	Morningstar Risk-Adj Rating
3 Yr	Avg	Low	★★★
5 Yr	—	—	—
10 Yr	—	—	—

Other Measures	Standard Index S&P 500	Best Fit Index Mstar Large Cap TR
Alpha	-0.2	-0.7
Beta	0.88	0.91
R-Squared	91	92
Standard Deviation	7.17	
Mean	7.92	
Sharpe Ratio	0.50	

Portfolio Analysis 12-31-07

Share change since 11-07 Total Stocks:100	Sector	PE	Tot Ret%	% Assets
⊖ ExxonMobil Corporation	Energy	13.6	24.34	6.99
⊖ General Electric Company	Ind Mtrls	16.6	2.69	5.12
⊖ AT&T, Inc.	Telecom	21.6	20.58	3.46
⊖ Procter & Gamble Company	Goods	23.1	16.63	3.13
⊖ Chevron Corporation	Energy	11.4	30.59	2.72
⊖ Johnson & Johnson	Health	18.8	3.61	2.61
⊖ Bank of America Corporat	Financial	9.4	-19.25	2.53
⊖ Altria Group Inc.	Goods	13.2	22.10	2.17
⊖ Pfizer Inc.	Health	22.5	-8.15	2.12
⊖ J.P. Morgan Chase & Co.	Financial	9.5	-7.24	2.02
⊖ International Business M	Hardware	16.2	13.20	2.02
⊖ Citigroup, Inc.	Financial	7.9	-44.93	2.00
⊖ ConocoPhillips	Energy	13.8	25.42	1.79
⊖ Coca-Cola Company	Goods	26.3	30.44	1.78
⊖ Hewlett-Packard Company	Hardware	18.8	23.40	1.78
⊖ American International G	Financial	10.2	-17.96	1.77
⊖ Verizon Communications I	Telecom	21.7	22.19	1.73
⊖ Merck & Co., Inc.	Health	23.6	37.36	1.73
⊖ PepsiCo, Inc.	Goods	20.4	23.89	1.68
⊖ Wal-Mart Stores, Inc.	Consumer	15.4	4.91	1.63

Current Investment Style

Value Blnd Growth — Large Mid Small

Market Cap	%
Giant	74.5
Large	25.5
Mid	0.0
Small	0.0
Micro	0.0
Avg $mil: 106,827	

Value Measures		Rel Category
Price/Earnings	13.24	0.98
Price/Book	2.40	1.22
Price/Sales	1.52	1.27
Price/Cash Flow	9.77	1.17
Dividend Yield %	2.11	0.78

Growth Measures	%	Rel Category
Long-Term Erngs	—	—
Book Value	8.88	1.03
Sales	8.65	1.35
Cash Flow	9.46	1.80
Historical Erngs	18.08	1.20

Profitability	%	Rel Category
Return on Equity	23.24	1.18
Return on Assets	8.46	1.32
Net Margin	14.57	1.05

Sector Weightings	% of Stocks	Rel S&P 500	3 Year High	3 Year Low
Info	14.00	0.67		
Software	0.00	0.00	0	0
Hardware	6.08	0.60	6	5
Media	2.15	0.74	5	2
Telecom	5.77	1.59	6	4
Service	42.24	1.04		
Health	14.22	1.18	17	14
Consumer	6.00	0.88	7	6
Business	1.83	0.41	3	2
Financial	20.19	1.16	26	20
Mfg	43.77	1.14		
Goods	11.08	1.21	11	9
Ind Mtrls	14.39	1.11	14	12
Energy	16.77	1.33	17	9
Utilities	1.53	0.42	2	1

Composition

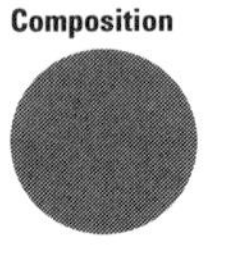

Cash	0.8
Stocks	99.2
Bonds	0.0
Other	0.0
Foreign (% of Stock)	0.0

Morningstar's Take by Sonya Morris 12-31-07

iShares NYSE 100 Index is chock-full of blue chips, so we require only a modest margin of safety to invest here.

This ETF's benchmark includes the 100 largest U.S.-based stocks (by market capitalization) that trade on the New York Stock Exchange. Limiting an index to securities that trade on a particular exchange is arbitrary, but it's hard to argue with this fund's attractive attributes. Its portfolio is a veritable who's who of U.S. corporations, featuring firms that boast prized qualities like wide brand recognition (Coca-Cola), massive scale (General Electric), global reach (ExxonMobil), and entrenched market positions (Procter & Gamble).

It's not surprising that 50 of its 100 holdings--comprising over 60% of assets--have earned wide economic moat ratings from Morningstar's equity analysts. Wide-moat firms enjoy sustainable competitive advantages that help them generate tons of free cash flow that in turn creates value for shareholders. To bestow a wide-moat rating on a firm, the analyst must believe that the company is likely to maintain its competitive edge over time. Because those advantage are likely to last, it is less likely that the forecasts that underpin our fair value estimates will prove wildly off the mark.

This ETF's high-quality portfolio has also helped damp volatility. Its standard deviation of returns (a statistical measure of volatility) is well below that of a typical large-cap fund. The stocks of larger, competitively well positioned firms tend to be relatively stable thanks in part to their solid financial performance. For instance, the average holding here generates above-average cash-flow growth of 11% per year and returns on equity of 24%. Finally, this ETF's relatively smooth ride can also be attributed to a broadly diversified portfolio that is devoid of major sector biases.

Given this ETFs' high-quality profile and steady nature, we're comfortable recommending it at an 8% or greater discount to our fair value estimate.

Address:	45 Fremont Street United States 800-474-2737
Web Address:	www.ishares.com
Inception:	03-29-04*
Advisor:	Barclays Global Fund Advisers

Management Fee:	0.20%		
Expense Projections:	3Yr:$64	5Yr:$113	10Yr:$255
Income Distrib:	Quarterly		
Exchange:	NYSE		

iShares R1000 Growth IWF

Market Price	Mstar Category
$60.78	Large Growth

Morningstar Rating	Return	Risk	Yield	NAV	Avg Daily Vol. (k)	52 wk High/Low
★★★	Average	Below Avg	0.9%	$60.93	3,714	$63.51 - $54.08

Morningstar Fair Value

Price/Fair Value Ratio	Coverage Rate %
0.95	98

Valuation

This fund is worth a look at an 8% or greater discount to our fair value estimate. It tends to be most attractive when technology and health-care stocks, which figure prominently here, fall out of favor. In late 2002, for instance, this ETF was trading at a hefty discount, although it has been hovering near fair value lately.

Methodology

This ETF tracks the Russell 1000 Growth Index--a style subset of the Russell 1000 Index--which spans 600-700 stocks that exhibit certain growth characteristics, such as loftier valuations (as measured by price/book) and higher forecasted earnings growth (based on Institutional Brokers' Estimate System data). The index ranks and weights constituents based on composite growth scores (as compiled from the above) and market cap. The index's growth bias puts sectors like technology, health care, and business- and consumer-services at the fore, while the index is light in financial services relative to other large-cap indexes.

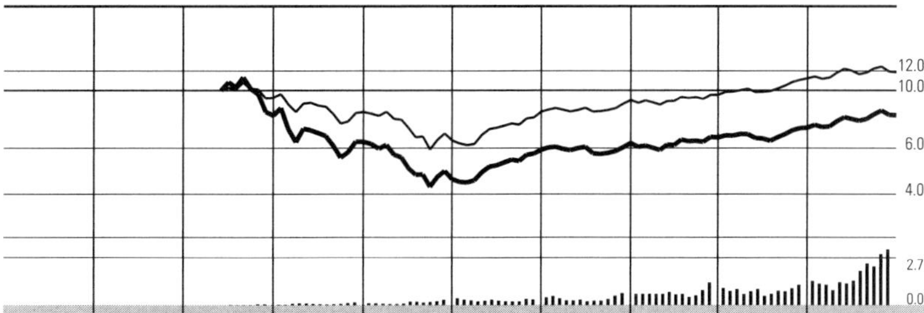

History

1998	1999	2000	2001	2002	2003	2004	2005	2006	2007	History
—	—	64.52	50.99	36.45	46.77	49.09	51.11	55.10	60.93	NAV $
—	—	64.62	50.94	36.55	46.80	49.15	51.01	55.03	60.78	Market Price $
—	—	-2.61*	-20.64	-27.99	29.46	6.10	5.08	8.86	11.63	NAV Return%
—	—	-2.64*	-20.84	-27.72	29.19	6.16	4.75	8.94	11.49	Market Price Return%
—	—	0.08	0.01	0.02	0.01	0.12	0.02	0.01	-0.01	Avg Premium/Discount%
—	—	—	-8.75	-5.89	0.78	-4.78	0.17	-6.93	6.14	NAV Rtrn% +/-S&P 500
—	—	—	-0.22	-0.11	-0.29	-0.20	-0.18	-0.21	-0.18	NAV Rtrn% +/-Russ 1000Gr
—	—	—	67	50	34	67	13	67	46	NAV Return% Rank in Cat
—	—	—	0.32	0.58	1.02	1.10	0.93	1.00	1.01	Income Return %
—	—	—	-20.96	-28.57	28.44	5.00	4.15	7.86	10.62	Capital Return %
—	—	0.09	0.21	0.29	0.37	0.51	0.45	0.51	0.56	Income $
—	—	0.11	0.00	0.00	0.00	0.00	0.00	0.00	0.00	Capital Gains $
—	—	—	0.20	0.20	0.20	0.20	0.20	0.20	0.20	Expense Ratio %
—	—	—	0.26	0.52	0.92	0.87	1.27	0.96	1.10	Income Ratio %
—	—	—	11	22	13	9	14	18	15	Turnover Rate %
—	—	106	523	744	1,492	3,144	5,399	7,675	15,553	Net Assets $mil

Performance 12-31-07

Historic Quarterly NAV Returns

	1st Qtr	2nd Qtr	3rd Qtr	4th Qtr	Total
2003	-1.11	14.22	3.86	10.35	29.46
2004	0.74	1.90	-5.26	9.10	6.10
2005	-4.12	2.41	3.96	2.94	5.08
2006	3.04	-3.95	3.89	5.87	8.86
2007	1.14	6.81	4.16	-0.79	11.63

Trailing	NAV Return%	Market Return%	NAV Rtrn% +/-S&P 500	%Rank Cat.(NAV)
3 Mo	-0.79	-1.31	2.54	30
6 Mo	3.33	3.11	4.70	35
1 Yr	11.63	11.49	6.14	46
3 Yr Avg	8.49	8.35	-0.13	23
5 Yr Avg	11.89	11.78	-0.94	40
10 Yr Avg	—	—	—	—

Tax Analysis	Tax-Adj Return%	Tax-Cost Ratio
3 Yr (estimated)	8.13	0.33
5 Yr (estimated)	11.52	0.33
10 Yr (estimated)	—	—

Rating and Risk

Time Period	Morningstar Rtn vs Cat	Morningstar Risk vs Cat	Morningstar Risk-Adj Rating
3 Yr	Avg	-Avg	★★★
5 Yr	Avg	-Avg	★★★
10 Yr	—	—	—

Other Measures	Standard Index S&P 500	Best Fit Index Russ 1000Gr
Alpha	-0.2	-0.2
Beta	1.04	1.00
R-Squared	88	100
Standard Deviation	8.65	
Mean	8.49	
Sharpe Ratio	0.49	

Portfolio Analysis 12-31-07

Share change since 11-07 Total Stocks:689	Sector	PE	Tot Ret%	% Assets
⊕ Microsoft Corporation	Software	23.4	20.83	3.76
⊕ Apple, Inc.	Hardware	50.5	133.47	2.21
⊕ Cisco Systems, Inc.	Hardware	21.5	-0.95	2.12
⊕ Google, Inc.	Business	54.0	50.17	2.04
⊕ Intel Corporation	Hardware	25.4	34.22	2.00
⊕ Hewlett-Packard Company	Hardware	18.8	23.40	1.74
⊕ PepsiCo, Inc.	Goods	20.4	23.89	1.59
⊕ International Business M	Hardware	16.2	13.20	1.51
⊕ Schlumberger, Ltd.	Energy	24.6	57.10	1.49
⊕ ExxonMobil Corporation	Energy	13.6	24.34	1.39
⊕ Merck & Co., Inc.	Health	23.6	37.36	1.34
⊕ Coca-Cola Company	Goods	26.3	30.44	1.21
⊕ Procter & Gamble Company	Goods	23.1	16.63	1.18
⊕ Altria Group Inc.	Goods	13.2	22.10	1.17
⊕ Oracle Corporation	Software	24.8	31.74	1.12
⊕ Abbott Laboratories	Health	45.7	18.04	1.11
⊕ Wal-Mart Stores, Inc.	Consumer	15.4	4.91	1.08
⊕ UnitedHealth Group, Inc.	Health	17.4	8.38	1.00
⊕ Johnson & Johnson	Health	18.8	3.61	0.93
⊕ Boeing Company	Ind Mtrls	16.9	-0.11	0.89

Current Investment Style

Value Blnd Growth; Large Mid Small

Market Cap	%
Giant	41.6
Large	36.1
Mid	21.4
Small	1.0
Micro	0.0
Avg $mil: 37,281	

Value Measures		Rel Category
Price/Earnings	16.77	0.86
Price/Book	3.55	1.05
Price/Sales	1.62	0.92
Price/Cash Flow	11.24	0.97
Dividend Yield %	1.06	1.25

Growth Measures	%	Rel Category
Long-Term Erngs	12.87	0.89
Book Value	9.25	0.91
Sales	10.51	1.08
Cash Flow	13.72	1.27
Historical Erngs	19.95	1.11

Profitability	%	Rel Category
Return on Equity	25.63	1.12
Return on Assets	10.69	1.11
Net Margin	14.10	1.09

Sector Weightings	% of Stocks	Rel S&P 500	3 Year High	3 Year Low
Info	28.10	1.35		
Software	7.49	1.81	7	6
Hardware	16.73	1.64	17	15
Media	3.16	1.09	4	3
Telecom	0.72	0.20	1	1
Service	40.78	1.00		
Health	16.11	1.34	26	16
Consumer	9.56	1.41	15	10
Business	8.24	1.87	8	5
Financial	6.87	0.39	9	6
Mfg	31.11	0.81		
Goods	9.17	1.00	11	8
Ind Mtrls	12.17	0.94	14	7
Energy	8.43	0.67	9	2
Utilities	1.34	0.36	2	0

Composition

Cash	0.3
Stocks	99.7
Bonds	0.0
Other	0.0
Foreign (% of Stock)	0.3

Morningstar's Take by Emiko Kurotsu 12-31-07

This large-growth ETF would look good at a modest discount to fair value.

iShares Russell 1000 Growth invests in the 700 or so stocks from the large-cap Russell 1000 Index that have significant growth biases, as defined by their price/book ratios and long-term growth rates.

Growth doesn't necessarily translate into quality, though, as we normally associate quality with firms that have defensible competitive advantages, or "economic moats." After all, fast-growing firms typically attract competitors eager to chip away at their profits. For instance, Yahoo surrendered its early edge in Internet advertising to rival Google. The tech bust of 2000-02 is rife with examples of investors overbidding for growth firms with no sustainable moat.

At first glance, this fund seems to follow that trend, as our analysts have awarded wide-moat ratings to just a fraction of the 619 portfolio holdings they cover. But, this fund's bias toward more-established firms that have a stranglehold on their markets lends greater permanence to their advantages. PepsiCo, for example, boasts a nearly impossible-to-replicate direct-store delivery system that spurs innovation and sales. Because the fund is market-cap-weighted, wide-moat firms like PepsiCo soak up a disproportionate percentage of assets. Thus, while wide-moat stocks don't abound here, they soak up nearly 46% of assets.

This ETF's risk profile is fairly mild, with more than 80% of assets staked in below-average and average-risk stocks. That's not too surprising given the portfolio's quality, as better-quality firms are less likely to be dislodged without warning by rivals, thereby reducing some of the uncertainty associated with our analysts' forecasts. This portfolio is also well-diversified. Taken together, that's kept a lid on volatility. As such, we wouldn't require a large margin of safety to invest here, with an 8% or greater discount to our fair value estimate sufficing.

Address:	45 Fremont Street United States 800-474-2737
Web Address:	www.ishares.com
Inception:	05-22-00 *
Advisor:	Barclays Global Fund Advisers

Management Fee:	0.20%		
Expense Projections:	3Yr:$64	5Yr:$113	10Yr:$255
Income Distrib:	Quarterly		
Exchange:	NYSE		

iShares R1000 Index IWB

Market Price	Mstar Category
$79.60	Large Blend

Morningstar Rating	Return	Risk	Yield	NAV	Avg Daily Vol. (k)	52 wk High/Low
★★★★	Above Avg	Average	1.7%	$79.88	1,045	$85.05 - $74.93

Morningstar Fair Value

Price/Fair Value Ratio	Coverage Rate %
0.89	98

Valuation

With its high-quality, moderate-risk profile, we'd invest here at an 8% margin of safety. Given this fund's large-cap bias, it tends to look cheap when money rotates to small-cap stocks or when large-caps fall out of vogue, as was the case in July and August 2007. It was recently trading at an 11% discount to our fair value estimate.

Methodology

This ETF tracks the Russell 1000 Index, a large-cap benchmark that represents about 92% of the U.S. equity market. The index, which is market-cap weighted, is a subset of the 1,000 biggest companies in the Russell 3000 Index. While the fund's top 200 names account for more than 70% of assets, the portfolio also offers a smattering of mid-cap exposure. The portfolio's sector breakdown mirrors the broad U.S. market's, with financials (nearly 20% of assets), industrials (13%), health care (11%), and energy (11%) all well-represented.

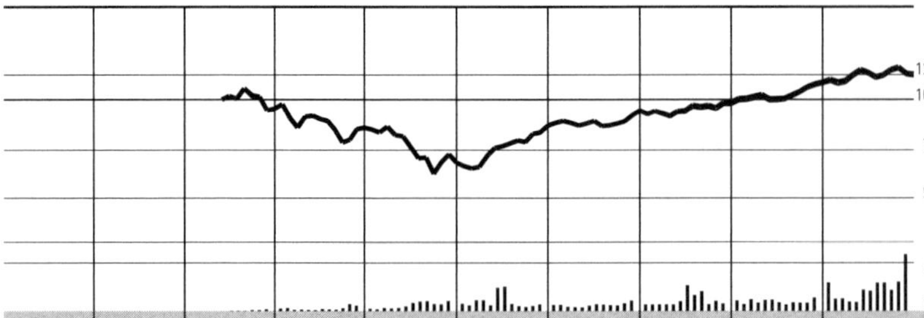

History

1998	1999	2000	2001	2002	2003	2004	2005	2006	2007	History
—	—	70.05	60.53	46.72	59.61	65.13	67.78	76.85	79.88	NAV $
—	—	70.20	60.98	46.72	59.59	64.94	67.70	76.84	79.60	Market Price $
—	—	2.10*	-12.59	-21.72	29.65	11.27	6.15	15.29	5.68	NAV Return%
—	—	2.05*	-12.13	-22.30	29.60	10.98	6.34	15.41	5.32	Market Price Return%
—	—	-0.05	0.10	-0.02	0.08	0.01	0.02	-0.03	-0.06	Avg Premium/Discount%
—	—	—	-0.70	0.38	0.97	0.39	1.24	-0.50	0.19	NAV Rtrn% +/-S&P 500
—	—	—	-0.14	-0.07	-0.24	-0.13	-0.12	-0.17	-0.09	NAV Rtrn% +/-Russ 1000
—	—	—	92	60	56	62	26	60	51	NAV Return% Rank in Cat
—	—	—	0.99	1.20	1.82	1.90	2.01	1.79	1.75	Income Return %
—	—	—	-13.58	-22.92	27.83	9.37	4.14	13.50	3.93	Capital Return %
—	—	0.45	0.69	0.72	0.85	1.12	1.30	1.21	1.33	Income $
—	—	0.00	0.00	0.00	0.00	0.00	0.00	0.00	0.00	Capital Gains $
—	—	—	0.15	0.15	0.15	0.15	0.15	0.15	0.15	Expense Ratio %
—	—	—	1.01	1.23	1.66	1.62	1.87	1.72	1.76	Income Ratio %
—	—	—	9	8	5	5	5	7	7	Turnover Rate %
—	—	238	436	726	1,860	1,869	2,413	3,051	3,762	Net Assets $mil

Performance 12-31-07

Historic Quarterly NAV Returns

	1st Qtr	2nd Qtr	3rd Qtr	4th Qtr	Total
2003	-2.97	15.66	2.96	12.20	29.65
2004	1.87	1.37	-1.82	9.75	11.27
2005	-1.92	2.02	3.93	2.08	6.15
2006	4.46	-1.69	5.02	6.90	15.29
2007	1.18	5.87	1.95	-3.24	5.68

Trailing	NAV Return%	Market Return%	NAV Rtrn% +/-S&P 500	%Rank Cat.(NAV)
3 Mo	-3.24	-3.60	0.09	46
6 Mo	-1.35	-1.67	0.02	46
1 Yr	5.68	5.32	0.19	51
3 Yr Avg	8.95	8.93	0.33	62
5 Yr Avg	13.28	13.20	0.45	46
10 Yr Avg	—	—	—	—

Tax Analysis	Tax-Adj Return%	Tax-Cost Ratio
3 Yr (estimated)	8.28	0.61
5 Yr (estimated)	12.60	0.60
10 Yr (estimated)	—	—

Rating and Risk

Time Period	Morningstar Rtn vs Cat	Morningstar Risk vs Cat	Morningstar Risk-Adj Rating
3 Yr	Avg	Avg	★★★
5 Yr	+Avg	Avg	★★★★
10 Yr	—	—	—

Other Measures	Standard Index S&P 500	Best Fit Index Russ 1000
Alpha	0.3	-0.1
Beta	1.01	1.00
R-Squared	99	100
Standard Deviation	7.90	
Mean	8.95	
Sharpe Ratio	0.59	

Portfolio Analysis 12-31-07

Share change since 11-07 Total Stocks:999	Sector	PE	Tot Ret%	% Assets
⊖ ExxonMobil Corporation	Energy	13.6	24.34	3.56
⊖ General Electric Company	Ind Mtrls	16.6	2.69	2.57
⊖ Microsoft Corporation	Software	23.4	20.83	1.97
⊖ AT&T, Inc.	Telecom	21.6	20.58	1.73
⊖ Procter & Gamble Company	Goods	23.1	16.63	1.56
⊖ Chevron Corporation	Energy	11.4	30.59	1.35
⊖ Johnson & Johnson	Health	18.8	3.61	1.30
⊖ Bank of America Corporat	Financial	9.4	-19.25	1.23
⊖ Apple, Inc.	Hardware	50.5	133.47	1.16
⊖ Cisco Systems, Inc.	Hardware	21.5	-0.95	1.11
⊖ Pfizer Inc.	Health	22.5	-8.15	1.08
⊖ Altria Group Inc.	Goods	13.2	22.10	1.07
⊖ Google, Inc.	Business	54.0	50.17	1.07
⊖ Intel Corporation	Hardware	25.4	34.22	1.04
⊖ J.P. Morgan Chase & Co.	Financial	9.5	-7.24	1.01
⊖ International Business M	Hardware	16.2	13.20	1.00
⊖ Citigroup, Inc.	Financial	7.9	-44.93	0.98
⊖ ConocoPhillips	Energy	13.8	25.42	0.97
⊖ Coca-Cola Company	Goods	26.3	30.44	0.96
⊖ Hewlett-Packard Company	Hardware	18.8	23.40	0.91

Current Investment Style

Value Blnd Growth; Large Mid Small (style box: Large Blend)

Market Cap	%
Giant	45.4
Large	33.7
Mid	19.8
Small	1.1
Micro	0.0
Avg $mil: 42,192	

Value Measures		Rel Category
Price/Earnings	14.32	0.91
Price/Book	2.38	0.93
Price/Sales	1.36	1.10
Price/Cash Flow	9.49	1.02
Dividend Yield %	1.74	0.92

Growth Measures	%	Rel Category
Long-Term Erngs	12.87	1.09
Book Value	8.02	0.87
Sales	7.48	0.91
Cash Flow	8.46	0.97
Historical Erngs	17.60	1.05

Profitability	%	Rel Category
Return on Equity	21.77	0.98
Return on Assets	8.38	1.00
Net Margin	14.02	1.14

Sector Weightings	% of Stocks	Rel S&P 500	3 Year High	3 Year Low
Info	20.73	0.99		
Software	4.19	1.01	4	3
Hardware	9.89	0.97	10	8
Media	3.16	1.09	4	3
Telecom	3.49	0.96	4	3
Service	41.37	1.02		
Health	11.94	0.99	14	11
Consumer	6.98	1.03	9	7
Business	5.24	1.19	5	4
Financial	17.21	0.99	22	17
Mfg	37.89	0.99		
Goods	8.82	0.96	9	8
Ind Mtrls	13.05	1.00	13	11
Energy	12.10	0.96	12	7
Utilities	3.92	1.07	4	3

Composition

Cash	0.6
Stocks	99.5
Bonds	0.0
Other	0.0
Foreign (% of Stock)	0.2

Morningstar's Take by Emiko Kurotsu 12-31-07

IShares Russell 1000 is worth a look at a modest discount to our fair value estimate.

This ETF tracks the Russell 1000 Index, a benchmark that's composed of the 1,000 largest U.S. companies by market cap, of the broader Russell 3000 Index.

The benchmark's catch-all nature means that it scoops up its fair share of capital-intensive or commoditylike firms. For instance, agri-science firm Dupont is vulnerable to rising oil and gas prices, yet struggles to pass those costs along given stifling price competition in many of its markets. Similarly, railroad operator Union Pacific must spend a huge chunk of its capital on track maintenance, hurting returns in the process. Firms like these detract from the portfolio's quality.

Yet, the index's large-cap tilt--the top 200 names account for more than 70% of assets--confers benefits as well. The fund's upper ranks count a number of firms boasting intractable competitive advantages, or wide "economic moats." Take Wells Fargo, which has trenched out a wide moat by amassing a geographically diverse deposit base and fortified it by grabbing a large share of each customer's wallet. While wide-moat names comprise only a fraction of the fund's holdings, they account for 42% of assets. Thus, while the portfolio's quality isn't sterling, it's hardly dismal.

The portfolio is also a mixed bag from a risk standpoint. This isn't a huge surprise given the relationship between stock quality and business risk. Put simply, dominant firms like Microsoft or Procter & Gamble are less likely to suffer jarring blows that throw their future prospects into question. Thus, while the fund's top holdings abound with below-average risk stocks, the majority of holdings fall into the average or above-average risk camps.

But the fund hasn't been too volatile owing to its wide diversification. Given this, we wouldn't demand a large discount to our fair value estimate before investing here. An 8% discount should do.

Address:	45 Fremont Street United States 800-474-2737
Web Address:	www.ishares.com
Inception:	05-15-00 *
Advisor:	Barclays Global Fund Advisers

Management Fee:	0.15%		
Expense Projections:	3Yr:$48	5Yr:$85	10Yr:$192
Income Distrib:	Quarterly		
Exchange:	NYSE		

iShares R1000 Value IWD

Market Price	Mstar Category
$80.25	Large Value

Morningstar Fair Value

Price/Fair Value Ratio	Coverage Rate %
0.84	98

Valuation

This fund looks like a bargain. It was recently trading at a 16% discount to our fair value estimate, reflecting a sharp pullback in financial stocks, which figure prominently here. We'd consider this fund attractive at an 8% or larger discount to our fair value estimate.

Methodology

This ETF tracks the Russell 1000 Value Index, a style subset of the large-cap Russell 1000 Index. The Value Index spans roughly 600 large caps that exhibit strong value traits, such as relatively low valuations (based on their price/book ratios) and less-than-torrid forecasted earning growth (based on Institutional Brokers' Estimate System data). The index ranks and weights its underlying holdings based on their combined value scores (determined by the above factors), as well as market cap. The fund is heavy in traditional value areas like financials, utilities, telecom, and, to a lesser degree, energy stocks.

Morningstar Rating	Return	Risk	Yield	NAV	Avg Daily Vol. (k)	52 wk High/Low
★★★★	Above Avg	Average	2.4%	$80.50	2,625	$89.75 - $76.19

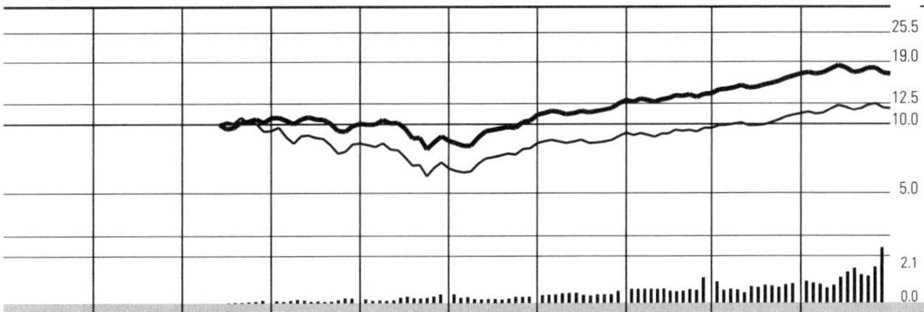

1998	1999	2000	2001	2002	2003	2004	2005	2006	2007	History
—	—	59.88	55.57	45.94	58.30	66.38	69.22	82.60	80.50	NAV $
—	—	60.03	55.40	46.05	58.37	66.37	69.03	82.70	80.25	Market Price $
—	—	7.03*	-5.73	-15.68	29.70	16.28	6.92	22.00	-0.29	NAV Return%
—	—	6.99*	-6.26	-15.22	29.55	16.12	6.64	22.48	-0.72	Market Price Return%
—	—	0.36	-0.02	-0.01	0.00	0.05	-0.05	0.03	0.00	Avg Premium/Discount%
—	—	—	6.16	6.42	1.02	5.40	2.01	6.21	-5.78	NAV Rtrn% +/-S&P 500
—	—	—	-0.14	-0.16	-0.33	-0.21	-0.13	-0.25	-0.12	NAV Rtrn% +/-Russ 1000 VI
—	—	—	40	40	80	43	10	29	63	NAV Return% Rank in Cat
—	—	—	1.45	1.78	2.44	2.25	2.58	2.47	2.36	Income Return %
—	—	—	-7.18	-17.46	27.26	14.03	4.34	19.53	-2.65	Capital Return %
—	—	0.44	0.87	0.98	1.11	1.30	1.70	1.69	1.93	Income $
—	—	0.00	0.00	0.00	0.00	0.00	0.00	0.00	0.00	Capital Gains $
—	—	—	0.20	0.20	0.20	0.20	0.20	0.20	0.20	Expense Ratio %
—	—	—	1.64	1.82	2.29	2.29	2.42	2.38	2.34	Income Ratio %
—	—	—	9	16	20	12	15	7	14	Turnover Rate %
—	—	153	639	1,123	2,326	4,710	6,185	9,177	10,489	Net Assets $mil

Performance 12-31-07

Historic Quarterly NAV Returns

	1st Qtr	2nd Qtr	3rd Qtr	4th Qtr	Total
2003	-4.92	17.20	2.01	14.10	29.70
2004	2.98	0.84	1.51	10.31	16.28
2005	0.09	1.63	3.85	1.20	6.92
2006	5.88	0.56	6.15	7.94	22.00
2007	1.21	4.88	-0.28	-5.81	-0.29

Trailing	NAV Return%	Market Return%	NAV Rtrn% +/-S&P 500	%Rank Cat.(NAV)
3 Mo	-5.81	-6.07	-2.48	55
6 Mo	-6.07	-6.35	-4.70	59
1 Yr	-0.29	-0.72	-5.78	63
3 Yr Avg	9.16	9.05	0.54	45
5 Yr Avg	14.42	14.30	1.59	25
10 Yr Avg	—	—	—	—

Tax Analysis	Tax-Adj Return%	Tax-Cost Ratio
3 Yr (estimated)	8.27	0.82
5 Yr (estimated)	13.53	0.78
10 Yr (estimated)	—	—

Rating and Risk

Time Period	Morningstar Rtn vs Cat	Morningstar Risk vs Cat	Morningstar Risk-Adj Rating
3 Yr	Avg	Avg	★★★
5 Yr	+Avg	Avg	★★★★
10 Yr	—	—	—

Other Measures	Standard Index S&P 500	Best Fit Index Russ 1000 VI
Alpha	0.6	-0.1
Beta	0.99	1.00
R-Squared	89	100
Standard Deviation	8.15	
Mean	9.16	
Sharpe Ratio	0.59	

Portfolio Analysis 12-31-07

Share change since 11-07 Total Stocks:618

Holding	Sector	PE	Tot Ret%	% Assets
⊕ ExxonMobil Corporation	Energy	13.6	24.34	5.95
⊕ General Electric Company	Ind Mtrls	16.6	2.69	4.80
⊕ AT&T, Inc.	Telecom	21.6	20.58	3.63
⊕ Chevron Corporation	Energy	11.4	30.59	2.84
⊕ Bank of America Corporat	Financial	9.4	-19.25	2.59
⊕ Pfizer Inc.	Health	22.5	-8.15	2.26
⊕ J.P. Morgan Chase & Co.	Financial	9.5	-7.24	2.11
⊕ Citigroup, Inc.	Financial	7.9	-44.93	2.06
⊕ ConocoPhillips	Energy	13.8	25.42	2.04
⊕ Procter & Gamble Company	Goods	23.1	16.63	1.98
⊕ Verizon Communications I	Telecom	21.7	22.19	1.80
⊕ American International G	Financial	10.2	-17.96	1.72
⊕ Johnson & Johnson	Health	18.8	3.61	1.71
⊕ Wells Fargo Company	Financial	11.4	-12.13	1.45
⊕ Wachovia Corporation	Financial	8.6	-29.91	1.07
⊕ Altria Group Inc.	Goods	13.2	22.10	0.97
⊕ Occidental Petroleum Cor	Energy	13.8	60.25	0.91
⊕ McDonald's Corporation	Consumer	39.5	36.38	0.79
⊕ US Bancorp	Financial	12.2	-7.89	0.78
⊕ Time Warner, Inc.	Media	13.4	-23.27	0.75

Current Investment Style

Value Blnd Growth — Large Mid Small

Market Cap	%
Giant	49.5
Large	31.1
Mid	18.1
Small	1.3
Micro	0.0
Avg $mil: 48,329	

Value Measures		Rel Category
Price/Earnings	12.31	0.91
Price/Book	1.74	0.89
Price/Sales	1.15	0.96
Price/Cash Flow	7.74	0.93
Dividend Yield %	2.49	0.92

Growth Measures	%	Rel Category
Long-Term Erngs	—	—
Book Value	7.42	0.86
Sales	5.31	0.83
Cash Flow	4.11	0.78
Historical Erngs	16.55	1.10

Profitability	%	Rel Category
Return on Equity	17.53	0.89
Return on Assets	5.84	0.91
Net Margin	13.94	1.00

Sector Weightings	% of Stocks	Rel S&P 500	3 Year High	3 Year Low
Info	12.65	0.61		
Software	0.57	0.14	2	1
Hardware	2.37	0.23	4	2
Media	3.17	1.09	5	3
Telecom	6.54	1.80	7	5
Service	42.01	1.03		
Health	7.33	0.61	8	4
Consumer	4.15	0.61	5	3
Business	1.93	0.44	3	1
Financial	28.60	1.64	37	29
Mfg	45.34	1.18		
Goods	8.44	0.92	9	6
Ind Mtrls	14.02	1.08	16	9
Energy	16.14	1.28	16	13
Utilities	6.74	1.83	7	6

Composition

Cash	0.7
Stocks	99.3
Bonds	0.0
Other	0.0
Foreign (% of Stock)	0.1

Morningstar's Take by Emiko Kurotsu 12-31-07

Given this portfolio's above-average quality and moderate risk, we'd be buyers at a modest discount to our fair value estimate.

iShares Russell 1000 Value invests in the roughly 600 stocks in the large-cap Russell 1000 Index that have strong value traits, as defined by their price/book ratios and long-term growth rates.

Of course, value doesn't always denote high quality, a trait we normally associate with firms boasting intractable competitive advantages, or wide economic moats. That said, this portfolio lays claim to a fair number of high-quality names, such as Citigroup, whose scale and unparalleled global network fortifies it against rivals. All told, our analysts award wide moats to 62 of the 562 portfolio stocks that they cover.

Modest as that tally might seem, because the fund is market-cap-weighted and most of these wide-moat firms are large caps, they account for nearly a third of the fund's assets. Thus, holdings like defense contractor General Dynamics, whose wide moat stems from its position as incumbent contractor on numerous defense department projects, loom large.

On balance, the vast majority of stocks in the portfolio court average- and below-average risk. This largely stems from the predominance of narrow- and wide-moat stocks, as such names are less likely to be dislodged by competitors in the future. That, in turn, reduces the uncertainty associated with our analysts' cash-flow forecasts (which culminate in the fair value estimates they place on every stock they cover). For instance, media giant Time Warner's voluminous film library and overall product diversity not only form part of the basis for its wide moat, but also cushion the firm's results.

The portfolio's diversification across holdings and sectors also tamps down volatility. Thus, we wouldn't demand a large margin of safety before recommending the fund, with an 8% or greater discount to our fair value estimate sufficing.

Address:	45 Fremont Street United States 800-474-2737
Web Address:	www.ishares.com
Inception:	05-22-00*
Advisor:	Barclays Global Fund Advisers

Management Fee:	0.20%		
Expense Projections:	3Yr:$64	5Yr:$113	10Yr:$255
Income Distrib:	Quarterly		
Exchange:	NYSE		

iShares R2000 Growth IWO

Market Price	Mstar Category
$83.48	Small Growth

Morningstar Fair Value

Price/Fair Value Ratio	Coverage Rate %
1.01	49

Valuation

Because our equity analysts cover less than one third of this fund's holdings, the price/fair value ratio above may not be a faithful representation of the portfolio's valuation attributes. Investors trying to gauge this ETF's attractiveness should consider the price/fair value ratio only in conjunction with other fundamental measures.

Methodology

This fund tracks the Russell 2000 Growth Index, a style subset of the small-cap Russell 2000 Index. The Growth Index encompasses between 1,200 and 1,300 stocks that have higher price/book ratios and forecasted growth than the rest of the Russell 2000. The fund's micro-cap weighting is heavier than the typical small-cap offering's, which adds to the fund's volatility relative to purer small-cap plays. Further, because the index is reconstituted just once a year, speculators have a history of running up the price of index additions and selling off deletions before indexers can, thus negatively affecting the ETF's returns.

Morningstar Rating	Return	Risk	Yield	NAV	Avg Daily Vol. (k)	52 wk High/Low
★★★	Average	Above Avg	0.6%	$83.73	4,085	$90.58 - $76.40

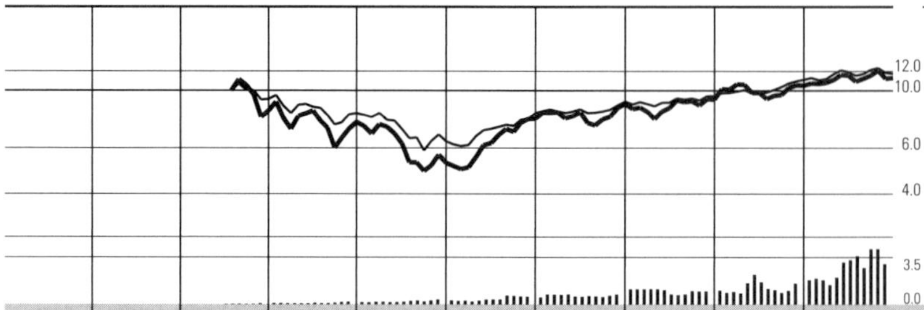

Growth of $10,000
— Investment Value of ETF
— Investment Value of Index S&P 500

Trading Volume Millions

History

1998	1999	2000	2001	2002	2003	2004	2005	2006	2007	History
—	—	64.27	57.84	40.16	59.28	67.48	69.86	78.77	83.73	NAV $
—	—	64.19	57.60	39.85	59.26	67.30	69.66	78.58	83.48	Market Price $
—	—	0.76*	-9.82	-30.29	48.19	14.13	4.04	13.13	6.93	NAV Return%
—	—	0.72*	-10.08	-30.54	49.30	13.86	4.02	13.18	6.86	Market Price Return%
—	—	-0.09	-0.14	-0.20	-0.09	-0.13	-0.11	-0.19	-0.10	Avg Premium/Discount%
—	—	—	2.07	-8.19	19.51	3.25	-0.87	-2.66	1.44	NAV Rtrn% +/-S&P 500
—	—	—	-0.59	-0.03	-0.35	-0.18	-0.11	-0.22	-0.12	NAV Rtrn% +/-Russ 2000 Gr
—	—	—	100	50	1	100	100	20	57	NAV Return% Rank in Cat
—	—	—	0.17	0.30	0.50	0.27	0.49	0.36	0.63	Income Return %
—	—	—	-9.99	-30.59	47.69	13.86	3.55	12.77	6.30	Capital Return %
—	—	0.02	0.11	0.17	0.20	0.16	0.33	0.25	0.50	Income $
—	—	0.04	0.00	0.00	0.00	0.00	0.00	0.00	0.00	Capital Gains $
—	—	—	0.25	0.25	0.25	0.25	0.25	0.25	0.25	Expense Ratio %
—	—	—	0.14	0.22	0.58	0.38	0.37	0.45	0.34	Income Ratio %
—	—	—	9	28	41	37	22	38	43	Turnover Rate %
—	—	106	414	608	1,515	2,203	2,620	2,993	3,500	Net Assets $mil

Performance 12-31-07

Historic Quarterly NAV Returns

	1st Qtr	2nd Qtr	3rd Qtr	4th Qtr	Total
2003	-3.91	24.06	10.39	12.61	48.19
2004	5.54	0.09	-6.04	14.98	14.13
2005	-6.84	3.47	6.28	1.55	4.04
2006	14.32	-7.31	-1.79	8.71	13.13
2007	2.45	6.64	-0.00	-2.13	6.93

Trailing	NAV Return%	Market Return%	NAV Rtrn% +/-S&P 500	%Rank Cat.(NAV)
3 Mo	-2.13	-1.83	1.20	13
6 Mo	-2.13	-2.40	-0.76	25
1 Yr	6.93	6.86	1.44	57
3 Yr Avg	7.97	7.95	-0.65	100
5 Yr Avg	16.31	16.42	3.48	50
10 Yr Avg	—	—	—	—

Tax Analysis	Tax-Adj Return%	Tax-Cost Ratio
3 Yr (estimated)	7.79	0.17
5 Yr (estimated)	16.14	0.15
10 Yr (estimated)	—	—

Rating and Risk

Time Period	Morningstar Rtn vs Cat	Morningstar Risk vs Cat	Morningstar Risk-Adj Rating
3 Yr	Avg	Avg	★★★
5 Yr	Avg	+Avg	★★★
10 Yr	—	—	—

Other Measures	Standard Index S&P 500	Best Fit Index Russ 2000 Gr
Alpha	-2.3	-0.1
Beta	1.55	1.00
R-Squared	69	100
Standard Deviation	14.42	
Mean	7.97	
Sharpe Ratio	0.30	

Portfolio Analysis 12-31-07

Share change since 11-07 Total Stocks:1268	Sector	PE	Tot Ret%	% Assets
⊕ Hologic, Inc.	Health	39.8	45.18	1.22
⊕ Terra Industries, Inc.	Ind Mtrls	35.3	298.66	0.64
⊕ Priceline.com, Inc.	Consumer	36.6	163.38	0.63
⊕ FLIR Systems, Inc.	Ind Mtrls	36.8	96.67	0.60
⊕ Chipotle Mexican Grill,	Consumer	63.7	136.63	0.59
⊕ Bucyrus International, I	Ind Mtrls	36.8	92.63	0.54
⊕ Equinix, Inc.	Business	—	33.55	0.53
⊕ Biomarin Pharmaceutical,	Health	—	115.99	0.49
⊕ MGI Pharma, Inc.	Health	—	120.15	0.47
⊕ Ansys, Inc.	Software	50.8	90.66	0.47
⊕ Illumina, Inc.	Health	—	50.75	0.46
⊕ DeVry, Inc.	Consumer	45.3	86.03	0.45
⊕ Onyx Pharmaceuticals, In	Health	—	425.71	0.44
⊕ FTI Consulting, Inc.	Business	33.9	121.01	0.42
⊕ Itron Inc.	Telecom	—	85.13	0.42
⊕ Micros Systems, Inc.	Software	33.8	33.13	0.41
⊕ OSI Pharmaceuticals, Inc	Health	—	38.68	0.41
⊕ Atwood Oceanics, Inc.	Energy	22.9	104.70	0.40
⊕ Alexion Pharmaceuticals,	Health	—	86.03	0.40
⊕ Time Warner Telecom, Inc	Telecom	—	1.81	0.39

Current Investment Style

Value Blnd Growth / Large Mid Small

Market Cap	%
Giant	0.0
Large	0.0
Mid	21.2
Small	62.8
Micro	16.0
Avg $mil: 1,236	

Value Measures		Rel Category
Price/Earnings	18.83	0.96
Price/Book	2.83	1.06
Price/Sales	1.40	0.98
Price/Cash Flow	9.63	0.88
Dividend Yield %	0.57	1.63

Growth Measures	%	Rel Category
Long-Term Erngs	42.33	2.03
Book Value	7.85	0.92
Sales	-2.58	NMF
Cash Flow	-7.48	NMF
Historical Erngs	6.28	0.41

Profitability	%	Rel Category
Return on Equity	11.79	0.84
Return on Assets	4.27	0.69
Net Margin	7.00	0.85

Sector Weightings	% of Stocks	Rel S&P 500	3 Year High	3 Year Low
Info	19.46	0.93		
Software	6.88	1.66	9	6
Hardware	9.15	0.90	12	9
Media	0.91	0.31	2	1
Telecom	2.52	0.69	3	2
Service	51.74	1.27		
Health	20.24	1.68	20	17
Consumer	10.58	1.56	12	10
Business	13.12	2.98	15	12
Financial	7.80	0.45	10	8
Mfg	28.80	0.75		
Goods	6.05	0.66	6	5
Ind Mtrls	16.14	1.24	16	12
Energy	6.05	0.48	8	5
Utilities	0.56	0.15	1	0

Composition

Cash	0.2
Stocks	99.8
Bonds	0.0
Other	0.0
Foreign (% of Stock)	0.6

Morningstar's Take by Emiko Kurotsu 12-31-07

Hold on to your hat here.

The fund tracks the Russell 2000 Growth Index, which sifts the Russell 2000 Index for stocks sporting above-average valuations and forecasted growth rates. While the resulting 1,300 stock portfolio is widely diversified by sector, it dips deeper into micro-cap territory than other small-growth offerings do, making it riskier. Yet, if you're looking for a low-cost, tax-efficient, widely diversified option for the small-growth slot of your portfolio, this is a decent choice, albeit not our first one. (That distinction goes to Vanguard Small Cap Growth ETF, which costs a paltry 0.12% and is less volatile than this offering.)

For others who are considering an investment here based on the portfolio's fundamental attributes, several factors give us pause, though we'd caution that our research is based on less-than-exhaustive coverage of the underlying stocks. For one, stock quality is low, as our analysts have awarded wide-moat ratings to only a handful of the 424 portfolio holdings that they cover, reflecting a dearth of competitive advantages among these companies, most of which aren't well-entrenched in their industries. Consider no-moat firm Illumina, whose genome research, while pathbreaking, is vulnerable to encroachment by rivals and resulting pricing pressure.

The portfolio's risk profile is also unappealing. Many of these firms operate in sectors marked by frequent, jarring change and low barriers to entry, such as health care or technology. Coupled with the firms' often-shaky financial state, their future prospects are more uncertain. For instance, biotech firm Human Genome Sciences has yet to bring a drug to market and continues to burn through cash, calling its future into question. All told, our analysts rate nearly two thirds of the holdings they cover at least above-average risks.

Given the portfolio's low quality and high risk, we'd need a sizable discount to our fair value estimate to invest here.

Address:	45 Fremont Street United States 800-474-2737
Web Address:	www.ishares.com
Inception:	07-24-00 *
Advisor:	Barclays Global Fund Advisers

Management Fee:	0.25%		
Expense Projections:	3Yr:$80	5Yr:$141	10Yr:$318
Income Distrib:	Quarterly		
Exchange:	NYSE		

iShares R2000 Index IWM

Market Price	Mstar Category
$75.92	Small Blend

Morningstar Fair Value

Price/Fair Value Ratio	Coverage Rate %
0.98	48

Valuation

Because our equity analysts cover less than half of this fund's holdings, the price/fair value ratio above may not be a faithful representation of the portfolio's valuation attributes. Investors trying to gauge this ETF's attractiveness should consider the price/fair value ratio only in conjunction with other fundamental measures.

Methodology

This fund tracks the Russell 2000 Index, which represents about 7% of the U.S. equity universe and consists of the roughly smallest 2,000 companies in the broader Russell 3000 Index. Although the fund is market-cap-weighted, the portfolio is widely diffused across stocks, with top holdings accounting for less than 1% of assets. Business- and consumer-services firms, as well as energy and software stocks, are well-represented here.

Morningstar Rating	Return	Risk	Yield	NAV	Avg Daily Vol. (k)	52 wk High/Low
★★★	Average	Above Avg	1.0%	$76.24	84,908	$84.94 - $70.02

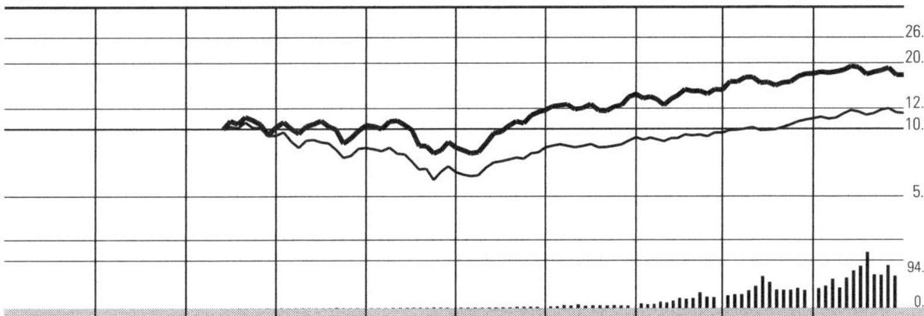

1998	1999	2000	2001	2002	2003	2004	2005	2006	2007	History
—	—	48.14	48.53	38.12	55.47	64.89	66.86	78.13	76.24	NAV $
—	—	47.88	48.17	37.91	55.40	64.75	66.72	78.03	75.92	Market Price $
—	—	7.73*	1.97	-20.51	46.94	18.16	4.46	18.17	-1.47	NAV Return%
—	—	7.67*	1.78	-20.37	47.58	18.05	4.46	18.27	-1.75	Market Price Return%
—	—	-0.16	-0.30	-0.40	-0.08	-0.13	-0.06	-0.08	-0.12	Avg Premium/Discount%
—	—	—	13.86	1.59	18.26	7.28	-0.45	2.38	-6.96	NAV Rtrn% +/-S&P 500
—	—	—	-0.52	-0.03	-0.31	-0.17	-0.09	-0.20	0.10	NAV Rtrn% +/-Russ 2000
—	—	—	100	100	1	100	100	15	34	NAV Return% Rank in Cat
—	—	—	1.09	1.03	1.16	1.08	1.36	1.25	1.00	Income Return %
—	—	—	0.88	-21.54	45.78	17.08	3.10	16.92	-2.47	Capital Return %
—	—	0.34	0.52	0.50	0.44	0.59	0.88	0.83	0.77	Income $
—	—	0.08	0.00	0.00	0.02	0.00	0.00	0.00	0.00	Capital Gains $
—	—	—	0.20	0.20	0.20	0.20	0.20	0.20	0.20	Expense Ratio %
—	—	—	1.39	1.25	1.28	1.08	1.20	1.19	1.07	Income Ratio %
—	—	—	39	20	30	26	17	20	25	Turnover Rate %
—	—	395	2,116	2,127	4,515	6,988	7,221	12,649	11,222	Net Assets $mil

Performance 12-31-07

Historic Quarterly NAV Returns

	1st Qtr	2nd Qtr	3rd Qtr	4th Qtr	Total
2003	-4.52	23.34	9.01	14.46	46.94
2004	6.21	0.47	-2.89	14.02	18.16
2005	-5.36	4.30	4.66	1.11	4.46
2006	13.90	-5.07	0.40	8.85	18.17
2007	1.91	4.55	-3.09	-4.58	-1.47

Trailing	NAV Return%	Market Return%	NAV Rtrn% +/-S&P 500	%Rank Cat.(NAV)
3 Mo	-4.58	-4.82	-1.25	18
6 Mo	-7.53	-7.94	-6.16	12
1 Yr	-1.47	-1.75	-6.96	34
3 Yr Avg	6.74	6.67	-1.88	67
5 Yr Avg	16.12	16.16	3.29	1
10 Yr Avg	—	—	—	—

Tax Analysis	Tax-Adj Return%	Tax-Cost Ratio
3 Yr (estimated)	6.31	0.40
5 Yr (estimated)	15.69	0.37
10 Yr (estimated)	—	—

Rating and Risk

Time Period	Morningstar Rtn vs Cat	Morningstar Risk vs Cat	Morningstar Risk-Adj Rating
3 Yr	Avg	+Avg	★★★
5 Yr	Avg	+Avg	★★★
10 Yr	—	—	—

Other Measures	Standard Index S&P 500	Best Fit Index Russ 2000
Alpha	-3.1	-0.1
Beta	1.45	1.00
R-Squared	72	100
Standard Deviation	13.33	
Mean	6.74	
Sharpe Ratio	0.23	

Portfolio Analysis 12-31-07

Share change since 11-07 Total Stocks:1927	Sector	PE	Tot Ret%	% Assets
⊕ Hologic, Inc.	Health	39.8	45.18	0.65
⊖ CF Industries Holdings,	Ind Mtrls	25.4	329.97	0.47
⊖ Exterran Holdings, Inc.	—	—	—	0.38
⊖ Terra Industries, Inc.	Ind Mtrls	35.3	298.66	0.34
⊖ Priceline.com, Inc.	Consumer	36.6	163.38	0.34
⊕ FLIR Systems, Inc.	Ind Mtrls	36.8	96.67	0.32
⊖ Chipotle Mexican Grill,	Consumer	63.7	136.63	0.31
⊕ Inverness Medical Innova	Health	—	45.17	0.29
⊖ Bucyrus International, I	Ind Mtrls	36.8	92.63	0.29
⊖ Equinix, Inc.	Business	—	33.55	0.28
⊖ Biomarin Pharmaceutical,	Health	—	115.99	0.26
⊕ Alexandria Real Estate E	Financial	44.0	4.43	0.25
⊖ MGI Pharma, Inc.	Health	—	120.15	0.25
⊖ Ansys, Inc.	Software	50.8	90.66	0.25
⊖ Illumina, Inc.	Health	—	50.75	0.25
⊖ DeVry, Inc.	Consumer	45.3	86.03	0.24
⊖ Onyx Pharmaceuticals, In	Health	—	425.71	0.24
⊖ Waddell & Reed Financial	Financial	24.7	35.27	0.23
⊖ Time Warner Telecom, Inc	Telecom	—	1.81	0.23
⊖ Petrohawk Energy Corpora	Energy	42.2	50.52	0.23

Current Investment Style

Value Blnd Growth; Large Mid Small

Market Cap	%
Giant	0.0
Large	0.0
Mid	15.1
Small	65.1
Micro	19.8
Avg $mil: 1,100	

Value Measures		Rel Category
Price/Earnings	15.90	1.05
Price/Book	1.84	1.08
Price/Sales	1.00	1.11
Price/Cash Flow	7.56	1.15
Dividend Yield %	1.37	0.98

Growth Measures	%	Rel Category
Long-Term Erngs	41.20	2.53
Book Value	5.31	0.70
Sales	-5.52	NMF
Cash Flow	-7.37	NMF
Historical Erngs	5.62	0.45

Profitability	%	Rel Category
Return on Equity	10.53	0.80
Return on Assets	3.92	0.67
Net Margin	8.73	0.86

Sector Weightings	% of Stocks	Rel S&P 500	3 Year High	3 Year Low
Info	16.89	0.81		
Software	5.15	1.24	6	4
Hardware	7.98	0.78	10	7
Media	1.39	0.48	2	1
Telecom	2.37	0.65	3	2
Service	52.18	1.28		
Health	13.61	1.13	14	11
Consumer	8.65	1.28	10	9
Business	10.89	2.47	12	10
Financial	19.03	1.09	23	19
Mfg	30.94	0.80		
Goods	5.92	0.65	6	5
Ind Mtrls	16.56	1.27	17	14
Energy	5.47	0.43	7	4
Utilities	2.99	0.81	3	2

Composition

Cash	0.7
Stocks	99.2
Bonds	0.0
Other	0.1
Foreign (% of Stock)	0.9

Morningstar's Take by Emiko Kurotsu 12-31-07

This fund warrants caution.

iShares Russell 2000 offers one-shot exposure to small-cap stocks, encompassing the 2,000 smallest companies in the broad-market Russell 3000 Index. Although the index is market-cap-weighted, the fund is spread widely, with the largest holdings soaking up less than 1% of assets. While the Vanguard Small Cap ETF is our favorite small-cap choice due to its dirt-cheap expense ratio, this fund is also a viable option given its low cost, wide diversificiation, and tax efficiency.

With respect to the fund's quality, risk, and valuation attributes, our analysts don't cover a significant enough portion of the portfolio holdings to allow for definitive judgments. However, some traits are evident based on our analysts' research on more than 600 of this fund's holdings. For instance, stock quality is not especially high. Just seven of the stocks covered boasted wide-moat ratings, meaning that virtually all lacked durable competitive advantages. This isn't too surprising given that many of these firms are still relatively immature in their industries, making them vulnerable to better-established rivals. Fertilizer producer CF Industries, for example, has fared well as crop demand has boomed. But our analysts are dubious that it can withstand slowing demand and encroaching competitors in its low-barrier-to-entry market.

Lesser-quality firms like these also tend to court higher levels of business risk, as their vulnerability to rivals and sometimes-fragile financial state can make future cash flows erratic. Not surprisingly, our analysts think that more than half of the 632 portfolio holdings they cover pose above-average risk. For example, database firm Sybase is waging a losing battle for market share against IBM and Oracle.

Given these traits and our less-than-comprehensive coverage of this fund's holdings, we'd invest here only at a healthy margin of safety to our fair value estimate.

Address:	45 Fremont Street United States 800-474-2737
Web Address:	www.ishares.com
Inception:	05-22-00 *
Advisor:	Barclays Global Fund Advisers

Management Fee:	0.20%		
Expense Projections:	3Yr:$64	5Yr:$113	10Yr:$255
Income Distrib:	Quarterly		
Exchange:	NYSE		

iShares R2000 Value IWN

Market Price	Mstar Category
$70.48	Small Value

Morningstar Fair Value

Price/Fair Value Ratio	Coverage Rate %
0.95	48

Valuation

Because our equity analysts cover roughly one third of this fund's holdings, the price/fair value ratio above may not be a faithful representation of the portfolio's valuation attributes. Investors trying to gauge this ETF's attractiveness should consider the price/fair value ratio only in conjunction with other fundamental measures.

Methodology

This fund tracks the Russell 2000 Value Index, which is a market-cap-weighted style subset of the small-cap Russell 2000 Index. As such, it encompasses 1,200-1,300 stocks that have lower valuations and forecasted growth rates than the norm in its parent index. This fund's micro- and mid-cap weightings are slightly smaller than the small-value category average, giving it a purer small-cap focus than many peers. The fund is widely diversified across sectors, with financials and industrials firms particularly well-represented.

Morningstar Rating	Return	Risk	Yield	NAV	Avg Daily Vol. (k)	52 wk High/Low
★★★	Above Avg	Above Avg	2.0%	$70.79	2,983	$85.45 - $65.18

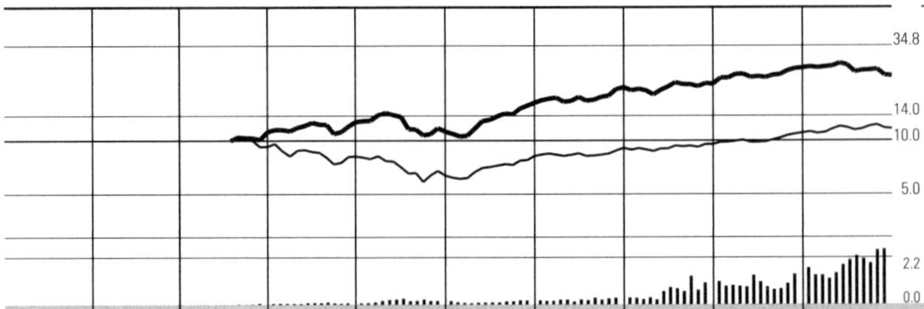

Growth of $10,000
- Investment Value of ETF
- Investment Value of Index S&P 500

Trading Volume Millions

History

1998	1999	2000	2001	2002	2003	2004	2005	2006	2007	History
—	—	38.61	42.93	37.34	53.58	64.40	66.10	80.05	70.79	NAV $
—	—	38.54	42.93	37.17	53.47	64.32	65.93	80.04	70.48	Market Price $
—	—	12.08*	13.42	-11.52	45.60	22.02	4.49	23.18	-9.92	NAV Return%
—	—	12.02*	13.62	-11.92	45.96	22.12	4.36	23.48	-10.30	Market Price Return%
—	—	-0.05	0.02	-0.30	-0.14	0.00	-0.13	-0.07	-0.16	Avg Premium/Discount%
—	—	—	25.31	10.58	16.92	11.14	-0.42	7.39	-15.41	NAV Rtrn% +/-S&P 500
—	—	—	-0.60	-0.09	-0.43	-0.23	-0.22	-0.30	-0.14	NAV Rtrn% +/-Russ 2000 VI
—	—	—	1	50	1	50	100	1	83	NAV Return% Rank in Cat
—	—	—	2.05	1.65	1.16	1.66	1.81	1.94	1.80	Income Return %
—	—	—	11.37	-13.17	44.44	20.36	2.68	21.24	-11.72	Capital Return %
—	—	0.29	0.79	0.70	0.43	0.88	1.16	1.27	1.43	Income $
—	—	0.01	0.00	0.00	0.23	0.00	0.00	0.00	0.00	Capital Gains $
—	—	—	0.25	0.25	0.25	0.25	0.25	0.25	0.25	Expense Ratio %
—	—	—	2.40	2.07	1.85	1.64	1.84	1.80	1.63	Income Ratio %
—	—	—	9	26	45	16	23	14	36	Turnover Rate %
—	—	162	560	790	1,607	2,908	3,014	4,375	3,982	Net Assets $mil

Performance 12-31-07

Historic Quarterly NAV Returns

	1st Qtr	2nd Qtr	3rd Qtr	4th Qtr	Total
2003	-5.13	22.62	7.64	16.28	45.60
2004	6.85	0.85	0.11	13.11	22.02
2005	-4.03	5.01	3.05	0.62	4.49
2006	13.42	-2.75	2.50	8.96	23.18
2007	1.39	2.26	-6.29	-7.29	-9.92

Trailing	NAV Return%	Market Return%	NAV Rtrn% +/-S&P 500	%Rank Cat.(NAV)
3 Mo	-7.29	-7.81	-3.96	75
6 Mo	-13.12	-13.54	-11.75	62
1 Yr	-9.92	-10.30	-15.41	83
3 Yr Avg	5.05	4.95	-3.57	75
5 Yr Avg	15.55	15.55	2.72	1
10 Yr Avg	—	—	—	—

Tax Analysis	Tax-Adj Return%	Tax-Cost Ratio
3 Yr (estimated)	4.40	0.62
5 Yr (estimated)	14.93	0.54
10 Yr (estimated)	—	—

Rating and Risk

Time Period	Morningstar Rtn vs Cat	Morningstar Risk vs Cat	Morningstar Risk-Adj Rating
3 Yr	Avg	+Avg	★★★
5 Yr	+Avg	+Avg	★★★
10 Yr	—	—	—

Other Measures	Standard Index S&P 500	Best Fit Index Russ 2000 VI
Alpha	-4.4	-0.2
Beta	1.37	1.00
R-Squared	69	100
Standard Deviation	12.75	
Mean	5.05	
Sharpe Ratio	0.11	

Portfolio Analysis 12-31-07

Share change since 11-07 Total Stocks:1299	Sector	PE	Tot Ret%	% Assets
⊕ CF Industries Holdings,	Ind Mtrls	25.4	329.97	0.91
⊕ Exterran Holdings, Inc.	—	—	—	0.82
⊕ Realty Income Corporatio	Financial	25.0	3.29	0.45
⊕ AptarGroup, Inc.	Goods	21.9	40.51	0.43
⊕ Westar Energy, Inc.	Utilities	14.0	4.20	0.43
⊕ SAIC, Inc.	Ind Mtrls	22.9	13.10	0.43
⊕ Aspen Insurance Holdings	Financial	5.9	11.96	0.42
⊕ Whiting Petroleum Corpor	Energy	19.5	23.73	0.40
⊕ Inverness Medical Innova	Health	—	45.17	0.38
⊕ Sybase Inc.	Software	24.0	5.63	0.36
⊕ Platinum Underwriters Ho	Financial	7.0	16.01	0.35
⊕ Apollo Investment Corpor	Financial	5.3	-15.65	0.34
⊕ Piedmont Natural Gas Com	Utilities	18.7	1.58	0.32
⊕ Bio-Rad Laboratories Inc	Health	29.0	25.57	0.32
⊕ Quanex Corporation	Ind Mtrls	15.2	51.92	0.32
⊕ Amerigroup Corporation	Health	16.9	1.56	0.32
⊕ Nicor Inc.	Utilities	13.8	-5.66	0.32
⊕ Senior Housing Prop Trus	Financial	21.0	-1.69	0.32
⊕ GrafTech International,	Ind Mtrls	13.4	156.50	0.31
⊕ Proassurance Corporation	Financial	12.7	10.02	0.30

Current Investment Style

Value Blnd Growth; Large Mid Small

Market Cap	%
Giant	0.0
Large	0.0
Mid	8.0
Small	67.8
Micro	24.2
Avg $mil: 961	

Value Measures		Rel Category
Price/Earnings	13.58	0.97
Price/Book	1.30	0.96
Price/Sales	0.75	0.96
Price/Cash Flow	5.78	0.98
Dividend Yield %	2.32	1.03

Growth Measures	%	Rel Category
Long-Term Erngs	17.00	1.44
Book Value	4.15	0.80
Sales	-7.05	NMF
Cash Flow	-6.70	NMF
Historical Erngs	8.98	1.11

Profitability	%	Rel Category
Return on Equity	9.06	0.94
Return on Assets	3.50	0.93
Net Margin	10.70	1.07

Sector Weightings	% of Stocks	Rel S&P 500	3 Year High	3 Year Low
Info	13.89	0.66		
Software	3.13	0.76	4	2
Hardware	6.63	0.65	9	4
Media	1.94	0.67	2	1
Telecom	2.19	0.60	3	1
Service	52.72	1.30		
Health	5.91	0.49	6	4
Consumer	6.40	0.94	9	6
Business	8.30	1.88	9	7
Financial	32.11	1.84	35	31
Mfg	33.40	0.87		
Goods	5.77	0.63	7	5
Ind Mtrls	17.04	1.31	19	13
Energy	4.79	0.38	7	4
Utilities	5.80	1.58	6	4

Composition

Cash	1.1
Stocks	98.7
Bonds	0.0
Other	0.2
Foreign (% of Stock)	1.1

Morningstar's Take by Emiko Kurotsu 12-31-07

This portfolio's unappealing quality and risk profile warrant caution.

iShares Russell 2000 Value sifts the small-cap Russell 2000 Index for stocks with below-average valuations and forecasted-growth rates. The resulting 1,250-plus stock portfolio doesn't look markedly different from other small-cap funds'. Thus, for those considering the fund for the small-cap slot of a portfolio, the question comes down to cost. In that respect, the fund fares well; its 0.25% expense ratio is among the lowest in its peer group, although it's not the cheapest around. (That distinction goes to Vanguard Small Cap Value ETF, which costs just 0.12%.)

That said, if it's the attractiveness of this fund's underlying stocks you're trying to gauge, there are a few factors to consider. For one, stock quality is not high; our analysts award wide-moat ratings to just three of the 424 portfolio holdings that they cover. (A wide-moat rating is what our analysts use to denote firms that possess intractable competitive advantages, like hard-to-replicate scale or brand equity.) More typical in this portfolio are lesser-quality names like no-moat jeweler Zale, which lacks qualities that distinguish it from rivals, leaving it vulnerable to competitors.

Many of these stocks are volatile as well, with a number considered above-average risks by our analysts. That's primarily a function of quality, as many of these firms have only a tenuous foothold in their markets. Moreover, some are founded on shaky finances, further heightening the uncertainty surrounding their future prospects. For instance, telecom services provider AsiaInfo Holdings' business, which isn't fortified by barriers to entry, is largely dependent on a single customer, explaining its above-average risk rating.

While the portfolio's diversification across stocks and industries has kept a lid on volatility, we'd caution investors that our analysts cover less than half this fund's assets. Thus, we'd only invest here with a healthy margin of safety.

Address:	45 Fremont Street United States 800-474-2737
Web Address:	www.ishares.com
Inception:	07-24-00*
Advisor:	Barclays Global Fund Advisers

Management Fee:	0.25%		
Expense Projections:	3Yr:$80	5Yr:$141	10Yr:$318
Income Distrib:	Quarterly		
Exchange:	NYSE		

iShares R3000 Growth IWZ

Market Price	Mstar Category
$49.54	Large Growth

Morningstar Fair Value

Price/Fair Value Ratio	Coverage Rate %
0.95	94

Valuation

Although this portfolio doesn't sport the best quality/risk profile, its wide diversification has tamped down volatility. Thus, we'd consider it at an 8% or greater discount to our fair value estimate. The fund was recently trading at a 5% discount, which isn't cheap enough to make us enthusiastic buyers of the shares.

Methodology

This fund tracks the Russell 3000 Growth Index, which consists of the roughly 2,000 stocks from the broader Russell 3000 benchmark that sport higher valuations (measured by price/book ratios) and forecasted growth rates than the norm. As its parent index is a total-market benchmark, this style subset is also well-diversified, with stocks spanning the full panoply of market sectors and market-cap strata. That said, the portfolio exhibits certain biases. For instance, it skews toward technology and health care and treads lightly in areas such as financial services, telecom, and utilities.

Performance 12-31-07

Historic Quarterly NAV Returns

	1st Qtr	2nd Qtr	3rd Qtr	4th Qtr	Total
2003	-1.33	14.86	4.33	10.50	30.66
2004	1.07	1.74	-5.36	9.58	6.65
2005	-4.37	2.47	4.16	2.79	4.92
2006	4.02	-4.28	3.37	6.09	9.19
2007	1.24	6.77	3.79	-0.91	11.18

Trailing	NAV Return%	Market Return%	NAV Rtrn% +/-S&P 500	%Rank Cat.(NAV)
3 Mo	-0.91	-0.77	2.42	35
6 Mo	2.85	2.98	4.22	41
1 Yr	11.18	11.02	5.69	54
3 Yr Avg	8.40	8.51	-0.22	34
5 Yr Avg	12.16	12.12	-0.67	20
10 Yr Avg	—	—	—	—

Tax Analysis	Tax-Adj Return%	Tax-Cost Ratio
3 Yr (estimated)	8.07	0.30
5 Yr (estimated)	11.81	0.31
10 Yr (estimated)	—	—

Morningstar Rating	Return	Risk	Yield	NAV	Avg Daily Vol. (k)	52 wk High/Low
★★★	Average	Below Avg	0.8%	$49.49	156	$51.74 - $43.96

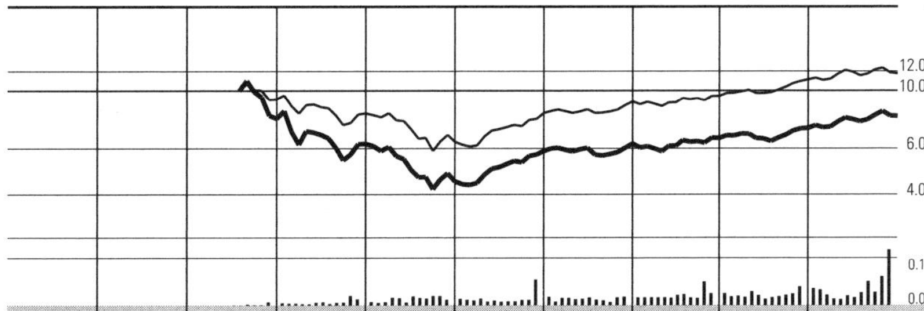

Growth of $10,000
- Investment Value of ETF
- Investment Value of Index S&P 500

Trading Volume Millions

History

1998	1999	2000	2001	2002	2003	2004	2005	2006	2007	
—	—	51.23	40.85	29.14	37.79	39.88	41.48	44.90	49.49	NAV $
—	—	51.78	40.89	29.22	37.80	39.80	41.45	45.01	49.54	Market Price $
—	—	-3.58*	-19.96	-28.15	30.66	6.65	4.92	9.19	11.18	NAV Return%
—	—	-3.57*	-20.73	-28.02	30.34	6.41	5.06	9.54	11.02	Market Price Return%
—	—	0.10	0.14	0.24	0.21	0.01	0.00	0.01	-0.01	Avg Premium/Discount%
—	—	—	-8.07	-6.05	1.98	-4.23	0.01	-6.60	5.69	NAV Rtrn% +/-S&P 500
—	—	—	-0.33	-0.12	-0.31	-0.28	-0.25	-0.27	-0.22	NAV Rtrn% +/-R3000 Growth
—	—	—	50	67	17	34	25	42	54	NAV Return% Rank in Cat
—	—	—	0.29	0.58	0.86	1.08	0.87	0.90	0.94	Income Return %
—	—	—	-20.25	-28.73	29.80	5.57	4.05	8.29	10.24	Capital Return %
—	—	0.03	0.15	0.24	0.25	0.41	0.35	0.37	0.42	Income $
—	—	0.00	0.00	0.00	0.00	0.00	0.00	0.00	0.00	Capital Gains $
—	—	—	0.25	0.25	0.25	0.25	0.25	0.25	0.25	Expense Ratio %
—	—	—	0.20	0.47	0.83	0.78	1.12	0.86	0.97	Income Ratio %
—	—	—	3	18	15	11	16	20	17	Turnover Rate %
—	—	26	49	58	128	132	214	294	436	Net Assets $mil

Rating and Risk

Time Period	Morningstar Rtn vs Cat	Morningstar Risk vs Cat	Morningstar Risk-Adj Rating
3 Yr	Avg	-Avg	★★★
5 Yr	Avg	-Avg	★★★
10 Yr	—	—	—

Other Measures	Standard Index S&P 500	Best Fit Index Russ 1000Gr
Alpha	-0.5	-0.4
Beta	1.08	1.04
R-Squared	88	99
Standard Deviation	8.99	
Mean	8.40	
Sharpe Ratio	0.47	

Portfolio Analysis 12-31-07

Share change since 11-07 Total Stocks:1957	Sector	PE	Tot Ret%	% Assets
⊕ Microsoft Corporation	Software	23.4	20.83	3.46
⊕ Apple, Inc.	Hardware	50.5	133.47	2.03
⊕ Cisco Systems, Inc.	Hardware	21.5	-0.95	1.95
⊕ Google, Inc.	Business	54.0	50.17	1.88
⊕ Intel Corporation	Hardware	25.4	34.22	1.84
⊕ Hewlett-Packard Company	Hardware	18.8	23.40	1.60
⊕ PepsiCo, Inc.	Goods	20.4	23.89	1.47
⊕ International Business M	Hardware	16.2	13.20	1.39
⊕ Schlumberger, Ltd.	Energy	24.6	57.10	1.37
⊕ ExxonMobil Corporation	Energy	13.6	24.34	1.28
⊕ Merck & Co., Inc.	Health	23.6	37.36	1.23
⊕ Coca-Cola Company	Goods	26.3	30.44	1.11
⊕ Procter & Gamble Company	Goods	23.1	16.63	1.09
⊕ Altria Group Inc.	Goods	13.2	22.10	1.08
⊕ Oracle Corporation	Software	24.8	31.74	1.03
⊕ Abbott Laboratories	Health	45.7	18.04	1.03
⊕ Wal-Mart Stores, Inc.	Consumer	15.4	4.91	1.00
⊕ UnitedHealth Group, Inc.	Health	17.4	8.38	0.92
⊕ Johnson & Johnson	Health	18.8	3.61	0.86
⊕ Boeing Company	Ind Mtrls	16.9	-0.11	0.82

Current Investment Style

Value Blnd Growth — Large Mid Small

Market Cap	%
Giant	38.3
Large	33.2
Mid	21.4
Small	5.9
Micro	1.3

Avg $mil: 28,351

Value Measures		Rel Category
Price/Earnings	16.89	0.87
Price/Book	3.48	1.03
Price/Sales	1.60	0.91
Price/Cash Flow	11.10	0.96
Dividend Yield %	1.02	1.20

Growth Measures	%	Rel Category
Long-Term Erngs	13.37	0.92
Book Value	9.12	0.90
Sales	8.55	0.88
Cash Flow	9.68	0.90
Historical Erngs	18.05	1.01

Profitability	%	Rel Category
Return on Equity	24.57	1.07
Return on Assets	10.18	1.05
Net Margin	13.55	1.05

Sector Weightings	% of Stocks	Rel S&P 500	3 Year High	3 Year Low
Info	27.39	1.31		
Software	7.43	1.79	7	6
Hardware	16.12	1.58	17	14
Media	2.97	1.02	4	3
Telecom	0.87	0.24	1	1
Service	41.68	1.03		
Health	16.44	1.37	25	16
Consumer	9.66	1.42	14	10
Business	8.64	1.96	9	6
Financial	6.94	0.40	9	6
Mfg	30.93	0.80		
Goods	8.92	0.97	11	8
Ind Mtrls	12.50	0.96	14	7
Energy	8.23	0.65	8	2
Utilities	1.28	0.35	1	0

Composition

Cash	0.2
Stocks	99.8
Bonds	0.0
Other	0.0
Foreign (% of Stock)	0.3

Morningstar's Take by Emiko Kurotsu 12-31-07

We'd invest here at a modest discount to our fair value estimate.

IShares Russell 3000 Growth sifts the Russell 3000 Index for stocks sporting higher valuations and forecasted growth rates than the norm. The resulting 2,000-stock portfolio runs the gamut of economic sectors, although technology and health care predominate. Also, while the fund dips into smaller firms, large caps take center stage, with the top 200 names accounting for the bulk of assets.

Those large caps also influence the portfolio's quality. True, size isn't always synonymous with quality; witness firms like DuPont and Prudential Financial, neither of which have trenched out durable competitive advantages, or "moats," in our analysts' view. But larger firms more often boast at least some semblance of an advantage. For instance, Wal-Mart wields its unparalleled distribution network to remain cost leader, while United Parcel Service touts a hard-to-replicate global infrastructure system. All told, this fund boasts 126 wide-moat stocks, and most of them large caps, accounting for 42% of assets.

That said, with the balance of assets spread among less-dominant firms, the portfolio's overall quality is middling. That's not surprising--the fund tracks the broad U.S. stock market and, thus, we wouldn't expect every stock to be a market titan.

The same goes for the fund's moderate risk profile. That, too, is a function of quality, as the results of more dominant firms tend to be less uncertain. For instance, visibility is high across many of wide-moat consumer giant Procter & Gamble's businesses thanks to recurring demand for its products. Yet, for every P&G, there are three other lesser-quality holdings. For instance, HIV specialist Gilead Science's fortunes are heavily tied to just one drug, explaining its above-average risk rating.

Yet, we wouldn't need a large margin of safety to invest here given the portfolio's diversification; an 8% discount to our fair value estimate will do.

Address:	45 Fremont Street United States 800-474-2737
Web Address:	www.ishares.com
Inception:	07-24-00*
Advisor:	Barclays Global Fund Advisers

Management Fee:	0.25%		
Expense Projections:	3Yr:$80	5Yr:$141	10Yr:$318
Income Distrib:	Quarterly		
Exchange:	NYSE		

iShares R3000 Index IWV

Market Price	Mstar Category
$84.40	Large Blend

Morningstar Fair Value

Price/Fair Value Ratio	Coverage Rate %
0.90	94

Morningstar Rating	Return	Risk	Yield	NAV	Avg Daily Vol. (k)	52 wk High/Low
★★★★	Above Avg	Average	1.6%	$84.66	446	$90.43 - $79.75

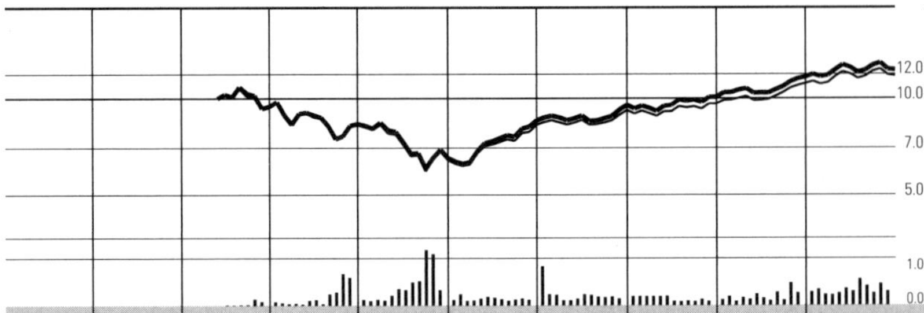

Growth of $10,000
— Investment Value of ETF
— Investment Value of Index S&P 500

Trading Volume Millions

Valuation

With many giant-cap firms falling out of vogue recently, this fund has gotten cheap: It was recently trading at a 10% discount to our fair value estimate. Given its wide diversification, we wouldn't demand a large margin of safety before investing here. An 8% discount to fair value is ample, in our view.

Methodology

This fund tracks the Russell 3000 Index, which consists of the roughly 3,000 largest companies in the U.S. by market capitalization. As such, it represents about 98% of the total U.S. equity market. Because the index is market-cap-weighted, the largest companies in the portfolio take up a significant chunk of assets, with giant and large caps accounting for nearly three quarters of the fund. Although highly similar to other total-market benchmarks like the S&P 1500 and Dow Jones U.S. indexes, the Russell 3000 dips deeper into small caps. The portfolio is well-diversified by sector and across names.

1998	1999	2000	2001	2002	2003	2004	2005	2006	2007	History
—	—	72.65	63.45	48.93	62.98	69.21	72.01	81.93	84.66	NAV $
—	—	72.44	63.50	48.96	62.96	69.15	72.02	82.04	84.40	Market Price $
—	—	2.91*	-11.78	-21.63	30.78	11.76	5.97	15.52	5.03	NAV Return%
—	—	2.86*	-11.46	-21.64	30.65	11.70	6.08	15.66	4.57	Market Price Return%
—	—	0.16	0.10	-0.19	0.02	-0.01	0.02	0.04	0.01	Avg Premium/Discount%
—	—	—	0.11	0.47	2.10	0.88	1.06	-0.27	-0.46	NAV Rtrn% +/-S&P 500
—	—	—	-0.32	-0.09	-0.28	-0.19	-0.15	-0.20	-0.11	NAV Rtrn% +/-R3000
—	—	—	61	53	44	50	39	47	64	NAV Return% Rank in Cat
—	—	—	0.88	1.36	1.81	1.77	1.86	1.64	1.72	Income Return %
—	—	—	-12.66	-22.99	28.97	9.99	4.11	13.88	3.31	Capital Return %
—	—	0.34	0.64	0.86	0.88	1.11	1.28	1.17	1.40	Income $
—	—	0.01	0.00	0.00	0.00	0.00	0.00	0.00	0.00	Capital Gains $
—	—	—	0.20	0.20	0.20	0.20	0.20	0.20	0.20	Expense Ratio %
—	—	—	1.09	1.20	1.53	1.54	1.81	1.62	1.68	Income Ratio %
—	—	—	3	6	5	4	5	5	6	Turnover Rate %
—	—	312	1,516	1,236	1,316	1,754	1,955	2,814	2,946	Net Assets $mil

Performance 12-31-07

Historic Quarterly NAV Returns

	1st Qtr	2nd Qtr	3rd Qtr	4th Qtr	Total
2003	-3.07	16.16	3.37	12.36	30.78
2004	2.17	1.30	-1.92	10.09	11.76
2005	-2.23	2.22	3.96	1.99	5.97
2006	5.27	-2.02	4.60	7.08	15.52
2007	1.24	5.73	1.53	-3.36	5.03

Trailing	NAV Return%	Market Return%	NAV Rtrn% +/-S&P 500	%Rank Cat.(NAV)
3 Mo	-3.36	-3.68	-0.03	54
6 Mo	-1.88	-2.19	-0.51	57
1 Yr	5.03	4.57	-0.46	64
3 Yr Avg	8.74	8.66	0.12	67
5 Yr Avg	13.45	13.36	0.62	39
10 Yr Avg	—	—	—	—

Tax Analysis	Tax-Adj Return%	Tax-Cost Ratio
3 Yr (estimated)	8.11	0.58
5 Yr (estimated)	12.79	0.58
10 Yr (estimated)	—	—

Rating and Risk

Time Period	Morningstar Rtn vs Cat	Morningstar Risk vs Cat	Morningstar Risk-Adj Rating
3 Yr	Avg	Avg	★★★
5 Yr	+Avg	Avg	★★★★
10 Yr	—	—	—

Other Measures	Standard Index S&P 500	Best Fit Index M* U.S. Mkt TR
Alpha	-0.1	-0.5
Beta	1.05	1.00
R-Squared	98	100
Standard Deviation	8.23	
Mean	8.74	
Sharpe Ratio	0.54	

Portfolio Analysis 12-31-07

Share change since 11-07 Total Stocks:2926	Sector	PE	Tot Ret%	% Assets
⊕ ExxonMobil Corporation	Energy	13.6	24.34	3.28
⊕ General Electric Company	Ind Mtrls	16.6	2.69	2.37
⊕ Microsoft Corporation	Software	23.4	20.83	1.81
⊕ AT&T, Inc.	Telecom	21.6	20.58	1.59
⊕ Procter & Gamble Company	Goods	23.1	16.63	1.43
⊕ Chevron Corporation	Energy	11.4	30.59	1.24
⊕ Johnson & Johnson	Health	18.8	3.61	1.20
⊕ Bank of America Corporat	Financial	9.4	-19.25	1.14
⊕ Apple, Inc.	Hardware	50.5	133.47	1.06
⊕ Cisco Systems, Inc.	Hardware	21.5	-0.95	1.02
⊕ Pfizer Inc.	Health	22.5	-8.15	0.99
⊕ Altria Group Inc.	Goods	13.2	22.10	0.99
⊕ Google, Inc.	Business	54.0	50.17	0.98
⊕ Intel Corporation	Hardware	25.4	34.22	0.96
⊕ J.P. Morgan Chase & Co.	Financial	9.5	-7.24	0.93
⊕ International Business M	Hardware	16.2	13.20	0.92
⊕ Citigroup, Inc.	Financial	7.9	-44.93	0.90
⊕ ConocoPhillips	Energy	13.8	25.42	0.90
⊕ Coca-Cola Company	Goods	26.3	30.44	0.88
⊕ Hewlett-Packard Company	Hardware	18.8	23.40	0.84

Current Investment Style

Value Blnd Growth — Large Mid Small

Market Cap	%
Giant	41.8
Large	31.0
Mid	19.5
Small	6.2
Micro	1.6
Avg $mil: 31,651	

Value Measures		Rel Category
Price/Earnings	14.42	0.91
Price/Book	2.32	0.91
Price/Sales	1.32	1.06
Price/Cash Flow	9.32	1.01
Dividend Yield %	1.71	0.90

Growth Measures	%	Rel Category
Long-Term Erngs	13.38	1.14
Book Value	7.75	0.84
Sales	5.07	0.62
Cash Flow	5.55	0.64
Historical Erngs	16.70	1.00

Profitability	%	Rel Category
Return on Equity	20.92	0.94
Return on Assets	8.04	0.96
Net Margin	13.62	1.11

Sector Weightings	% of Stocks	Rel S&P 500	3 Year High	3 Year Low
Info	20.43	0.98		
Software	4.26	1.03	4	4
Hardware	9.74	0.95	10	8
Media	3.03	1.04	4	3
Telecom	3.40	0.94	4	3
Service	42.22	1.04		
Health	12.06	1.00	14	11
Consumer	7.12	1.05	9	7
Business	5.68	1.29	6	4
Financial	17.36	1.00	22	17
Mfg	37.34	0.97		
Goods	8.60	0.94	9	8
Ind Mtrls	13.32	1.02	13	11
Energy	11.58	0.92	12	7
Utilities	3.84	1.04	4	3

Composition

Cash	0.5
Stocks	99.5
Bonds	0.0
Other	0.0
Foreign (% of Stock)	0.3

Morningstar's Take by Emiko Kurotsu 12-31-07

Mostly middling.

The iShares Russell 3000 Index spans the roughly 3,000 largest domestic companies by market cap. Like many cap-weighted indexes, large-cap stocks like ExxonMobil, General Electric, and Microsoft account for the lion's share of the fund's assets.

Because many of those well-established firms boast durable competitive advantages, the portfolio sports its fair share of high-quality names. For instance, 56 of the fund's top 100 holdings possess wide economic moats, or highly defensible advantages, in our analysts' view. Bank of America, Cisco Systems, and Pfizer are prominent representatives of that cohort. All told, wide-moat stocks soak up 40% of the fund's assets.

That tally ranks slightly behind other total-market funds like iShares S&P 1500. That's due to this fund's more-sprawling portfolio, which dips deeper into small caps where high-quality firms are less prevalent. But, on balance, stock-quality is average--not an unexpected outcome given that the fund purports to represent the entire U.S. stock market, warts and all.

The fund isn't likely to turn many heads from a risk standpoint either. The majority of its stocks court average business risk, which denotes the level of uncertainty that our analysts associate with a given business' prospects. For instance, less-established, financially shaky firms are at greater risk of being waylaid by larger rivals or felled by shifting market conditions that strain their balance sheets. Thus, while the fund is home to a number of well-fortified blue chips, some of which throw off cash flows like clockwork, many others court at least moderate business risk.

Nevertheless, we wouldn't demand a wide margin of safety here. The diversification across holdings and sectors diffuses risk widely, thus keeping the fund's overall volatility in check. We'd be buyers when the fund trades at an 8% or greater discount to our fair value estimate.

Address:	45 Fremont Street United States 800-474-2737
Web Address:	www.ishares.com
Inception:	05-22-00*
Advisor:	Barclays Global Fund Advisers

Management Fee:	0.20%		
Expense Projections:	3Yr:$64	5Yr:$113	10Yr:$255
Income Distrib:	Quarterly		
Exchange:	NYSE		

iShares R3000 Value IWW

Market Price	Mstar Category
$103.92	Large Value

Morningstar Rating	Return	Risk	Yield	NAV	Avg Daily Vol. (k)	52 wk High/Low
★★★★	Above Avg	Average	2.4%	$104.16	89	$116.94 - $98.36

Morningstar Fair Value

Price/Fair Value Ratio	Coverage Rate %
0.85	94

Valuation

This fund's price has hit bargain-basement levels, as it was recently trading at a hefty 15% discount to our fair value estimate, nearly double the discount we'd ordinarily demand. The portfolio tends to look particularly attractive when financials stocks drag, as this sector soaks up more than 30% of the fund's assets.

Methodology

This fund, which tracks the Russell 3000 Value Index, consists of roughly 2,000 stocks drawn from the all-market Russell 3000 Index, favoring those with lower valuations (measured by price/book ratios) and forecasted earnings growth rates than the norm. The fund offers exposure to the entire market-cap spectrum. However, nearly half of its assets are in giant caps, a result of its market-cap-weighting scheme. The fund is widely diversified by sector, although it's especially concentrated in financials, where it has a 31% stake, followed by industrials and energy, which account for 14% of assets apiece.

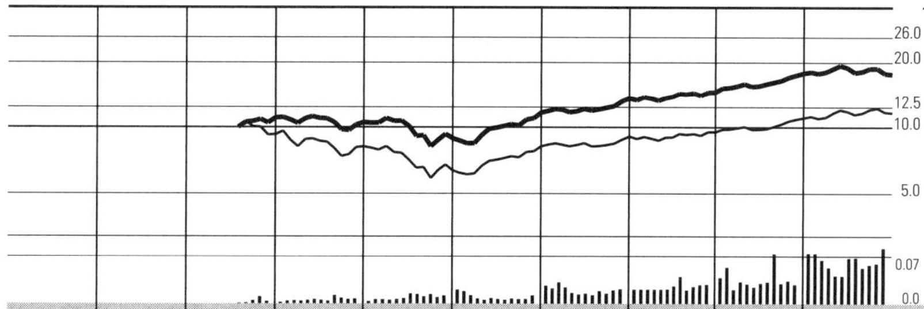

History

1998	1999	2000	2001	2002	2003	2004	2005	2006	2007	History
—	—	75.95	71.22	59.16	75.72	86.56	90.21	107.81	104.16	NAV $
—	—	76.62	71.70	59.05	75.76	86.66	90.28	107.79	103.92	Market Price $
—	—	7.69*	-4.61	-15.35	30.76	16.64	6.63	22.01	-1.17	NAV Return%
—	—	7.66*	-4.81	-16.07	31.08	16.71	6.59	21.90	-1.38	Market Price Return%
—	—	0.09	0.06	0.07	0.11	0.02	0.06	-0.02	-0.04	Avg Premium/Discount%
—	—	—	7.28	6.75	2.08	5.76	1.72	6.22	-6.66	NAV Rtrn% +/-S&P 500
—	—	—	-0.28	-0.17	-0.38	-0.30	-0.22	-0.33	-0.16	NAV Rtrn% +/-Russ 3000 VI
—	—	—	20	20	60	29	30	22	73	NAV Return% Rank in Cat
—	—	—	1.60	1.71	2.43	2.16	2.36	2.31	2.32	Income Return %
—	—	—	-6.21	-17.06	28.33	14.48	4.27	19.70	-3.49	Capital Return %
—	—	0.55	1.21	1.21	1.43	1.62	2.03	2.07	2.48	Income $
—	—	0.09	0.00	0.00	0.00	0.00	0.00	0.00	0.00	Capital Gains $
—	—	—	0.25	0.25	0.25	0.25	0.25	0.25	0.25	Expense Ratio %
—	—	—	1.67	1.79	2.20	2.19	2.33	2.26	2.23	Income Ratio %
—	—	—	4	15	16	13	16	7	14	Turnover Rate %
—	—	19	64	89	148	325	433	674	698	Net Assets $mil

Performance 12-31-07

Historic Quarterly NAV Returns

	1st Qtr	2nd Qtr	3rd Qtr	4th Qtr	Total
2003	-4.94	17.54	2.43	14.25	30.76
2004	3.26	0.83	1.37	10.51	16.64
2005	-0.31	1.89	3.78	1.15	6.63
2006	6.52	0.22	5.80	8.02	22.01
2007	1.22	4.63	-0.80	-5.94	-1.17

Trailing	NAV Return%	Market Return%	NAV Rtrn% +/-S&P 500	%Rank Cat.(NAV)
3 Mo	-5.94	-6.11	-2.61	64
6 Mo	-6.69	-6.71	-5.32	73
1 Yr	-1.17	-1.38	-6.66	73
3 Yr Avg	8.74	8.62	0.12	67
5 Yr Avg	14.42	14.41	1.59	50
10 Yr Avg	—	—	—	—

Tax Analysis	Tax-Adj Return%	Tax-Cost Ratio
3 Yr (estimated)	7.91	0.76
5 Yr (estimated)	13.56	0.75
10 Yr (estimated)	—	—

Rating and Risk

Time Period	Morningstar Rtn vs Cat	Morningstar Risk vs Cat	Morningstar Risk-Adj Rating
3 Yr	Avg	Avg	★★★
5 Yr	+Avg	Avg	★★★★
10 Yr	—	—	—

Other Measures	Standard Index S&P 500	Best Fit Index Russ 1000 VI
Alpha	0.1	-0.6
Beta	1.02	1.02
R-Squared	89	99
Standard Deviation	8.39	
Mean	8.74	
Sharpe Ratio	0.53	

Portfolio Analysis 12-31-07

Share change since 11-07 Total Stocks:1917	Sector	PE	Tot Ret%	% Assets
⊕ ExxonMobil Corporation	Energy	13.6	24.34	5.48
⊕ General Electric Company	Ind Mtrls	16.6	2.69	4.42
⊕ AT&T, Inc.	Telecom	21.6	20.58	3.34
⊕ Chevron Corporation	Energy	11.4	30.59	2.62
⊕ Bank of America Corporat	Financial	9.4	-19.25	2.39
⊕ Pfizer Inc.	Health	22.5	-8.15	2.08
⊕ J.P. Morgan Chase & Co.	Financial	9.5	-7.24	1.94
⊕ Citigroup, Inc.	Financial	7.9	-44.93	1.90
⊕ ConocoPhillips	Energy	13.8	25.42	1.88
⊕ Procter & Gamble Company	Goods	23.1	16.63	1.82
⊕ Verizon Communications I	Telecom	21.7	22.19	1.65
⊕ American International G	Financial	10.2	-17.96	1.59
⊕ Johnson & Johnson	Health	18.8	3.61	1.57
⊕ Wells Fargo Company	Financial	11.4	-12.13	1.34
⊕ Wachovia Corporation	Financial	8.6	-29.91	0.99
⊕ Altria Group Inc.	Goods	13.2	22.10	0.89
⊕ Occidental Petroleum Cor	Energy	13.8	60.25	0.84
⊕ McDonald's Corporation	Consumer	39.5	36.38	0.73
⊕ US Bancorp	Financial	12.2	-7.89	0.72
⊕ Time Warner, Inc.	Media	13.4	-23.27	0.69

Current Investment Style

Value Blnd Growth — Large Mid Small

Market Cap	%
Giant	45.6
Large	28.6
Mid	17.4
Small	6.5
Micro	1.9

Avg $mil: 35,713

Value Measures		Rel Category
Price/Earnings	12.39	0.92
Price/Book	1.70	0.87
Price/Sales	1.10	0.92
Price/Cash Flow	7.55	0.90
Dividend Yield %	2.47	0.91

Growth Measures	%	Rel Category
Long-Term Erngs	17.00	1.72
Book Value	7.10	0.82
Sales	2.66	0.42
Cash Flow	2.12	0.40
Historical Erngs	16.09	1.07

Profitability	%	Rel Category
Return on Equity	16.90	0.86
Return on Assets	5.66	0.88
Net Margin	13.69	0.99

Sector Weightings	% of Stocks	Rel S&P 500	3 Year High	3 Year Low
Info	12.75	0.61		
Software	0.76	0.18	2	1
Hardware	2.70	0.26	4	3
Media	3.08	1.06	5	3
Telecom	6.21	1.71	6	5
Service	42.83	1.05		
Health	7.22	0.60	7	4
Consumer	4.33	0.64	5	4
Business	2.41	0.55	3	2
Financial	28.87	1.66	37	29
Mfg	44.42	1.15		
Goods	8.24	0.90	8	6
Ind Mtrls	14.24	1.10	16	9
Energy	15.27	1.21	15	12
Utilities	6.67	1.81	7	6

Composition

Cash	0.8
Stocks	99.2
Bonds	0.0
Other	0.0
Foreign (% of Stock)	0.2

Morningstar's Take by Emiko Kurotsu 12-31-07

We require only a modest margin of safety for this well-diversified fund.

IShares Russell 3000 Value comprises roughly 2,000 stocks from the Russell 3000 Index that have lower valuations and forecasted growth rates than the norm. Although the portfolio spans firms of all sizes, nearly half of its assets are in familiar giant-cap names like General Electric and AT&T.

Size shouldn't be mistaken for quality, though. Indeed, many of this fund's large-cap holdings lack wide "economic moats," a term our analysts use to refer to intractable competitive advantages such as scale, brand identity, or barriers to entry. The oil patch is a case in point, as our analysts have awarded a wide moat to just one of the 15 giant-cap energy stocks in the fund, reflecting the poor returns on capital such firms typically earn.

In fact, this portfolio's quality is average on balance. About 41% of the fund's assets are tucked into firms that our analysts believe boast advantages, but fleeting ones at that. For instance, though narrow-moat holding Allstate is the third-largest property-casualty insurer, its customers can shop around for insurance policies, which reduces its pricing power.

The fund's largely middling quality carries over to its moderate risk profile. Generally speaking, dominant firms tend to throw off cash flows in a more predictable fashion, making their future results easier to forecast and, thus, lowering the uncertainty associated with our analysts fair value estimates, and vice versa. Given this portfolio's decidedly mixed quality, where wide-moat firms such as Pfizer sit alongside narrow- and no-moat stocks like Tyco and Foot Locker, it's little wonder that its typical holding courts average business risk.

Yet, given its wide diversification across stocks, industries, and market caps, the fund hasn't been very volatile. Thus, we'd only require a modest margin of safety; an 8% or greater discount to our fair value estimate would do.

Address:	45 Fremont Street United States 800-474-2737
Web Address:	www.ishares.com
Inception:	07-24-00 *
Advisor:	Barclays Global Fund Advisers

Management Fee:	0.25%		
Expense Projections:	3Yr:$80	5Yr:$141	10Yr:$318
Income Distrib:	Quarterly		
Exchange:	NYSE		

iShares Russell Microcap IWC

Market Price	Mstar Category
$52.80	Small Blend

Morningstar Fair Value

Price/Fair Value Ratio	Coverage Rate %
0.99	18

Valuation

Our equity analysts cover a small number of this ETF's stock holdings, so the price/fair value ratio above may not be a faithful representation of this portfolio's valuation attributes. Thus, investors trying to gauge this ETF's attractiveness should consider the price/fair value ratio only in conjunction with other fundamental measures.

Methodology

Management tracks the Russell Microcap Index, which includes the 1,000 smallest stocks from the Russell 2000 Index, plus the next 1,000 smallest stocks from outside the benchmark. It excludes stocks from the OTC bulletin board and Pink Sheets. The fund uses a representative sampling to track the index, which rebalances annually in June.

Morningstar Rating	Return	Risk	Yield	NAV	Avg Daily Vol. (k)	52 wk High/Low
—	—	—	0.8%	$53.04	196	$61.99 - $49.02

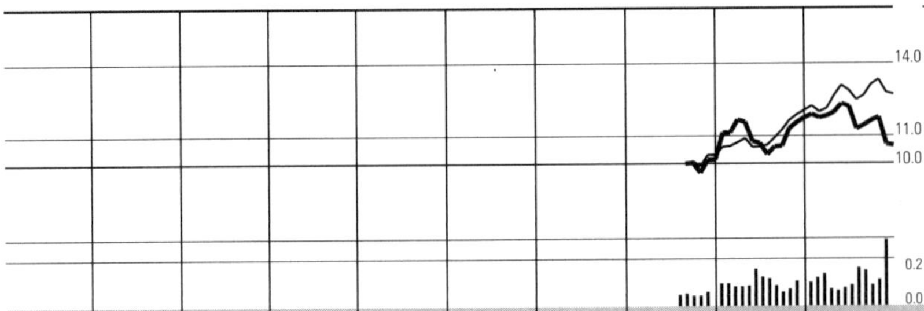

Growth of $10,000
— Investment Value of ETF
— Investment Value of Index S&P 500

Trading Volume Millions

History

1998	1999	2000	2001	2002	2003	2004	2005	2006	2007	History
—	—	—	—	—	—	—	51.31	58.56	53.04	NAV $
—	—	—	—	—	—	—	51.15	58.45	52.80	Market Price $
—	—	—	—	—	—	—	3.13*	14.75	-8.76	NAV Return%
—	—	—	—	—	—	—	2.94*	14.89	-9.00	Market Price Return%
—	—	—	—	—	—	—	-0.23	-0.14	-0.22	Avg Premium/Discount%
—	—	—	—	—	—	—	—	-1.04	-14.25	NAV Rtrn% +/-S&P 500
—	—	—	—	—	—	—	—	-1.79	-0.76	NAV Rtrn% +/-Rus Micro
—	—	—	—	—	—	—	—	100	75	NAV Return% Rank in Cat
—	—	—	—	—	—	—	—	0.59	0.72	Income Return %
—	—	—	—	—	—	—	—	14.16	-9.48	Capital Return %
—	—	—	—	—	—	—	0.10	0.30	0.42	Income $
—	—	—	—	—	—	—	0.00	0.00	0.00	Capital Gains $
—	—	—	—	—	—	—	—	0.60	0.60	Expense Ratio %
—	—	—	—	—	—	—	—	0.56	0.53	Income Ratio %
—	—	—	—	—	—	—	—	6	20	Turnover Rate %
—	—	—	—	—	—	—	103	258	310	Net Assets $mil

Performance 12-31-07

Historic Quarterly NAV Returns

	1st Qtr	2nd Qtr	3rd Qtr	4th Qtr	Total
2003	—	—	—	—	—
2004	—	—	—	—	—
2005	—	—	—	1.05	—*
2006	14.06	-7.42	-1.03	9.80	14.75
2007	0.64	3.19	-4.61	-7.90	-8.76

Trailing	NAV Return%	Market Return%	NAV Rtrn% +/-S&P 500	%Rank Cat.(NAV)
3 Mo	-7.90	-8.22	-4.57	65
6 Mo	-12.15	-12.33	-10.78	59
1 Yr	-8.76	-9.00	-14.25	75
3 Yr Avg	—	—	—	—
5 Yr Avg	—	—	—	—
10 Yr Avg	—	—	—	—

Tax Analysis	Tax-Adj Return%	Tax-Cost Ratio
3 Yr (estimated)	—	—
5 Yr (estimated)	—	—
10 Yr (estimated)	—	—

Rating and Risk

Time Period	Morningstar Rtn vs Cat	Morningstar Risk vs Cat	Morningstar Risk-Adj Rating
3 Yr	—	—	—
5 Yr	—	—	—
10 Yr	—	—	—

Other Measures	Standard Index S&P 500	Best Fit Index
Alpha	—	—
Beta	—	—
R-Squared	—	—
Standard Deviation	—	
Mean	—	
Sharpe Ratio	—	

Portfolio Analysis 12-31-07

Share change since 11-07 Total Stocks:1394	Sector	PE	Tot Ret%	% Assets
⊕ Concur Technologies, Inc	Software	—	125.75	0.38
⊕ Sigma Designs, Inc.	Hardware	38.0	116.90	0.37
⊕ Cepheid	Health	—	210.00	0.36
⊕ Arena Resources, Inc.	Energy	45.0	95.32	0.31
⊕ Savient Pharmaceuticals	Health	—	104.91	0.30
⊕ Argo Group International		—	—	0.29
⊕ CyberSource Corporation	Business	48.1	61.25	0.28
⊕ American Superconductor	Ind Mtrls	—	178.70	0.26
⊕ Synaptics, Inc.	Software	34.4	38.63	0.26
⊕ Healthcare Services Grou	Business	31.0	12.03	0.25
⊕ Kaman Corporation A	Ind Mtrls	22.0	67.23	0.24
⊕ INVESTools, Inc.	Consumer	—	28.64	0.24
⊕ Omnicell, Inc.	Hardware	26.4	44.55	0.24
⊕ RBC Bearings, Inc.	Ind Mtrls	27.3	51.64	0.24
⊕ Robbins & Myers, Inc.	Ind Mtrls	25.6	65.57	0.24
⊕ Auxilium Pharmaceuticals	Health	—	104.15	0.23
⊕ WD-40 Company	Energy	20.8	12.02	0.23
⊕ Darling International	Goods	25.1	109.80	0.23
⊕ Alnylam Pharmaceuticals,	Health	—	35.89	0.23
⊕ Standard Microsystems Co	Hardware	32.3	39.64	0.23

Current Investment Style

Value Blnd Growth; Large / Mid / Small

Market Cap	%
Giant	0.0
Large	0.0
Mid	0.0
Small	24.5
Micro	75.5
Avg $mil: 358	

Value Measures		Rel Category
Price/Earnings	15.39	1.02
Price/Book	1.66	0.98
Price/Sales	0.99	1.10
Price/Cash Flow	6.48	0.99
Dividend Yield %	1.30	0.93

Growth Measures	%	Rel Category
Long-Term Erngs	41.24	2.53
Book Value	1.92	0.25
Sales	-16.93	NMF
Cash Flow	-11.10	NMF
Historical Erngs	10.36	0.83

Profitability	%	Rel Category
Return on Equity	3.39	0.26
Return on Assets	-0.37	NMF
Net Margin	6.49	0.64

Sector Weightings	% of Stocks	Rel S&P 500	3 Year High	3 Year Low
Info	19.95	0.96		
Software	6.00	1.45	6	5
Hardware	10.44	1.02	12	9
Media	1.20	0.41	2	1
Telecom	2.31	0.64	3	2
Service	55.78	1.37		
Health	17.54	1.46	18	16
Consumer	6.66	0.98	8	6
Business	10.77	2.44	11	10
Financial	20.81	1.19	25	21
Mfg	24.28	0.63		
Goods	5.29	0.58	6	5
Ind Mtrls	12.71	0.98	14	11
Energy	5.07	0.40	5	4
Utilities	1.21	0.33	1	1

Composition

Cash	0.4
Stocks	99.4
Bonds	0.0
Other	0.1
Foreign (% of Stock)	0.5

Morningstar's Take by Annie Sorich 12-31-07

iShares Russell Microcap Index has promise, and many risks.

Investing in tiny companies has a certain cache. It's possible the next Microsoft or Genentech is lurking among the smallest of the small, those companies with market caps between $50 million and $600 million. This ETF tracks the Russell Microcap Index, which includes the bottom 1,000 stocks in the small-cap Russell 2000 Index plus an additional 1,000 firms not included in the index. It doesn't hold every stock but uses a representative sampling technique to avoid investing in those stocks with relatively little liquidity.

Although microcap investing is exciting, it's important to remember that some companies are small for a reason. These tiny firms may be in the early stages of development, with revenue dependent on few products or markets, and with limited financial backing and a lack of management experience. Even those companies destined for greatness experience bumps along the way, explaining microcaps' notoriously high volatility.

If anything, this fund's performance since inception illustrates what a wild ride shareholders must tolerate when investing here. Although it returned a respectable 14.8% in 2006, the fund was down 8% for the year through Dec. 26, 2007. It lost 8% in July, and smaller stocks have continued to lose ground as broader economic uncertainty causes investors to flee to large-cap stocks and high-quality bonds. This sort of volatility is fine for those with long time horizons (10 years or more), but can be difficult for others to stomach. One way to dampen volatility is by dollar-cost averaging into the fund. But this can be costly, given that ETF purchases and sales are subject to transaction costs, which can blunt whatever advantage the fund's low expense ratio confers.

For those very risk-tolerant investors seeking a cheap, accessible way to play microcaps, this fund is a reasonable choice. But most others should give it a wide berth.

Address:	45 Fremont Street United States 800-474-2737
Web Address:	www.ishares.com
Inception:	08-12-05*
Advisor:	Barclays Global Fund Advisers

Management Fee:	0.60%		
Expense Projections:	3Yr:$192	5Yr:$335	10Yr:$750
Income Distrib:	Quarterly		
Exchange:	NYSE		

iShares R. Midcap IWR

Market Price	Mstar Category
$103.54	Mid-Cap Blend

Morningstar Fair Value

Price/Fair Value Ratio	Coverage Rate %
0.93	93

Valuation

Due to the fund's mid-cap tilt, the fund has traded at a premium to our fair value estimate for much of the last few years. It has recently crossed into cheaper waters, though, breaching a 7% discount, which is a hair less than the 8% or more we'd demand to invest here.

Methodology

This ETF tracks the Russell Midcap Index, which consists of the 800 smallest companies in the broader Russell 1000 Index. Because it pulls in a passel of large-cap stocks, it sports a higher median market cap than other mid-cap ETFs. The fund skews toward utilities, and business- and consumer-services firms, with greater dearth in the telecom space.

Morningstar Rating	Return	Risk	Yield	NAV	Avg Daily Vol. (k)	52 wk High/Low
★★★★	Above Avg	Below Avg	1.4%	$103.94	301	$112.82 - $96.62

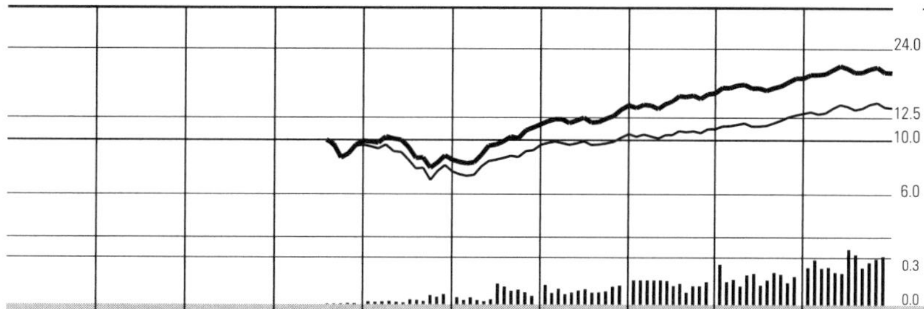

1998	1999	2000	2001	2002	2003	2004	2005	2006	2007	History
—	—	—	58.51	48.55	67.00	79.38	88.08	99.93	103.94	NAV $
—	—	—	58.92	48.63	67.12	79.33	87.93	99.84	103.54	Market Price $
—	—	—	10.43*	-16.17	39.74	19.93	12.60	15.04	5.41	NAV Return%
—	—	—	10.36*	-16.62	39.76	19.64	12.48	15.13	5.10	Market Price Return%
—	—	—	0.04	0.06	0.08	0.02	0.03	-0.04	0.00	Avg Premium/Discount%
—	—	—	—	5.93	11.06	9.05	7.69	-0.75	-0.08	NAV Rtrn% +/-S&P 500
—	—	—	—	0.02	-0.32	-0.29	-0.05	-0.22	-0.19	NAV Rtrn% +/-Rus Mid
—	—	—	—	67	34	25	17	1	47	NAV Return% Rank in Cat
—	—	—	—	0.90	1.50	1.32	1.56	1.50	1.43	Income Return %
—	—	—	—	-17.07	38.24	18.61	11.04	13.54	3.98	Capital Return %
—	—	—	0.35	0.53	0.72	0.88	1.23	1.31	1.42	Income $
—	—	—	0.00	0.00	0.00	0.00	0.00	0.00	0.00	Capital Gains $
—	—	—	—	0.20	0.20	0.20	0.20	0.20	0.20	Expense Ratio %
—	—	—	—	1.40	1.50	1.39	1.48	1.49	1.40	Income Ratio %
—	—	—	—	7	15	7	15	9	19	Turnover Rate %
—	—	—	18	165	415	1,131	1,696	2,763	3,934	Net Assets $mil

Performance 12-31-07

Historic Quarterly NAV Returns

	1st Qtr	2nd Qtr	3rd Qtr	4th Qtr	Total
2003	-2.41	18.19	6.37	13.89	39.74
2004	5.09	1.41	-0.89	13.54	19.93
2005	-0.23	4.18	5.90	2.29	12.60
2006	7.59	-2.62	2.05	7.60	15.04
2007	4.33	5.25	-0.42	-3.59	5.41

Trailing	NAV Return%	Market Return%	NAV Rtrn% +/-S&P 500	%Rank Cat.(NAV)
3 Mo	-3.59	-3.88	-0.26	54
6 Mo	-4.00	-4.25	-2.63	42
1 Yr	5.41	5.10	-0.08	47
3 Yr Avg	10.94	10.82	2.32	17
5 Yr Avg	18.01	17.88	5.18	1
10 Yr Avg	—	—	—	—

Tax Analysis	Tax-Adj Return%	Tax-Cost Ratio
3 Yr (estimated)	10.40	0.49
5 Yr (estimated)	17.46	0.47
10 Yr (estimated)	—	—

Rating and Risk

Time Period	Morningstar Rtn vs Cat	Morningstar Risk vs Cat	Morningstar Risk-Adj Rating
3 Yr	+Avg	-Avg	★★★★
5 Yr	+Avg	-Avg	★★★★
10 Yr	—	—	—

Other Measures	Standard Index S&P 500	Best Fit Index Mstar Mid Cap TR
Alpha	1.8	0.6
Beta	1.12	0.93
R-Squared	82	99
Standard Deviation	9.61	
Mean	10.94	
Sharpe Ratio	0.69	

Portfolio Analysis 12-31-07

Share change since 11-07 Total Stocks:794	Sector	PE	Tot Ret%	% Assets
⊕ Hess Corporation	Ind Mtrls	19.1	104.77	0.66
⊕ National Oilwell Varco,	Energy	21.7	132.65	0.62
⊕ Weatherford Internationa	Energy	23.4	64.15	0.55
⊕ Williams Companies, Inc.	Energy	27.7	38.70	0.51
⊕ Air Products and Chemica	Ind Mtrls	21.1	42.82	0.50
⊕ PPL Corporation	Utilities	20.0	49.31	0.47
⊕ Yum Brands, Inc.	Consumer	23.2	32.28	0.47
⊕ MEMC Electronic Material	Hardware	35.3	126.09	0.47
⊕ Allergan, Inc.	Health	40.8	7.66	0.46
⊕ CSX Corporation	Business	16.7	29.41	0.45
⊕ Precision Castparts Corp	Ind Mtrls	23.6	77.34	0.45
⊕ American Electric Power	Utilities	16.8	13.06	0.44
⊕ NVIDIA Corporation	Hardware	29.4	37.88	0.44
⊕ Constellation Energy Gro	Utilities	22.5	51.88	0.44
⊕ Principal Financial Grou	Financial	17.8	18.84	0.43
⊕ Electronic Arts, Inc.	Software	—	15.98	0.43
⊕ Chesapeake Energy Corp.	Energy	12.3	35.95	0.43
⊕ American Tower Corporati	Telecom	—	14.51	0.42
⊕ Textron, Inc.	Ind Mtrls	21.4	54.43	0.42
⊕ Edison International	Utilities	15.4	19.93	0.41

Current Investment Style

Value Blnd Growth / Large Mid Small

Market Cap	%
Giant	0.0
Large	28.7
Mid	67.3
Small	4.0
Micro	0.0
Avg $mil: 7,562	

Value Measures		Rel Category
Price/Earnings	15.00	0.94
Price/Book	2.14	0.96
Price/Sales	1.05	0.91
Price/Cash Flow	7.78	0.91
Dividend Yield %	1.39	0.84

Growth Measures	%	Rel Category
Long-Term Erngs	12.87	1.04
Book Value	7.99	0.95
Sales	6.05	1.45
Cash Flow	5.48	21.08
Historical Erngs	17.82	0.96

Profitability	%	Rel Category
Return on Equity	19.25	0.98
Return on Assets	7.20	0.93
Net Margin	12.06	1.00

Sector Weightings	% of Stocks	Rel S&P 500	3 Year High	3 Year Low
Info	16.99	0.81		
Software	4.15	1.00	4	3
Hardware	7.97	0.78	9	7
Media	2.68	0.92	3	2
Telecom	2.19	0.60	2	1
Service	41.89	1.03		
Health	8.45	0.70	12	8
Consumer	8.34	1.23	13	8
Business	8.94	2.03	9	7
Financial	16.16	0.93	22	16
Mfg	41.11	1.07		
Goods	8.99	0.98	9	7
Ind Mtrls	13.89	1.07	14	10
Energy	10.15	0.80	10	6
Utilities	8.08	2.20	8	7

Composition

Cash	0.5
Stocks	99.5
Bonds	0.0
Other	0.0
Foreign (% of Stock)	0.7

Morningstar's Take by Emiko Kurotsu 12-31-07

We'd buy iShares Russell Midcap Index at a modest discount to our fair value estimate.

Despite its moniker, this ETF isn't a pure mid-cap play. That's due to the index's construction, which lops off the top 200 stocks in the Russell 1000 Index and divvies up assets among the remaining 800 names, 84 of which are large caps. Thus, this fund invests nearly 30% of its assets in large-cap stocks.

Yet, that slug of larger firms doesn't markedly improve the quality of this fund's portfolio, which is middling on balance. Dominant firms with manifold competitive advantages, or wide economic moats, are relatively scarce here, accounting for just 57 of the 701 portfolio holdings our analysts cover; in contrast, narrow- and no-moat firms account for an overwhelming 82% of fund assets.

That's not to say that these firms are uniformly unattractive, however. For instance, some holdings, like pharmaceutical-maker Forest Laboratories which is in the process of fortifying its drug portfolio, are trenching out wider moats. Others, like El Paso, sit on the cusp of wide-moat status by dint of their profitable and highly defensible assets (natural-gas pipelines in El Paso's case). Yet, for every Forest or El Paso, there are many other holdings on less stable competitive footing. Take handbag and apparel retailer Coach which, despite efforts to carve out an "affordable luxury" niche, is still vulnerable to fickle fashion trends.

Given that many of the fund's holdings lack defensible competitive advantages, their results are more likely to be erratic in the future. That, in turn, subjects our analysts' forecasts to greater uncertainty, explaining why we consider most of the holdings to be at least average risks. That said, the fund's wide diversification has tamped down volatility. Consequently, while the portfolio does not gleam with blue-chip stocks, we wouldn't require a large margin of safety before investing here, with an 8%-plus discount to our fair value estimate sufficing.

Address:	45 Fremont Street United States 800-474-2737
Web Address:	www.ishares.com
Inception:	07-17-01 *
Advisor:	Barclays Global Fund Advisers

Management Fee:	0.20%		
Expense Projections:	3Yr:$64	5Yr:$113	10Yr:$255
Income Distrib:	Quarterly		
Exchange:	NYSE		

iShares R. Midcap Gr IWP

Market Price	Mstar Category
$113.94	Mid-Cap Growth

Morningstar Rating	Return	Risk	Yield	NAV	Avg Daily Vol. (k)	52 wk High/Low
★★★★	Average	Below Avg	0.6%	$113.93	426	$119.97 - $102.61

Morningstar Fair Value

Price/Fair Value Ratio	Coverage Rate %
0.97	93

Valuation

This fund isn't much of a bargain, trading at just a 3% discount to our fair value estimate. Given its quality and risk profile, we'd invest here when it has an 8% or greater margin of safety, a level it has never breached in its six-year history.

Methodology

This fund tracks the Russell Midcap Growth Index, a style subset of the Russell Midcap Index. As such, it's composed of roughly 550 companies with higher price/book ratios and forecasted growth rates than most other firms in its parent index. Because the Russell Midcap Index skews slightly to large caps, this fund shares that same bias, with almost 30% of assets in large caps. The fund is well-diversified across sectors, although it's heavier in health care, tech, and energy stocks than most other mid-caps, and it's much lighter in financials than its parent index.

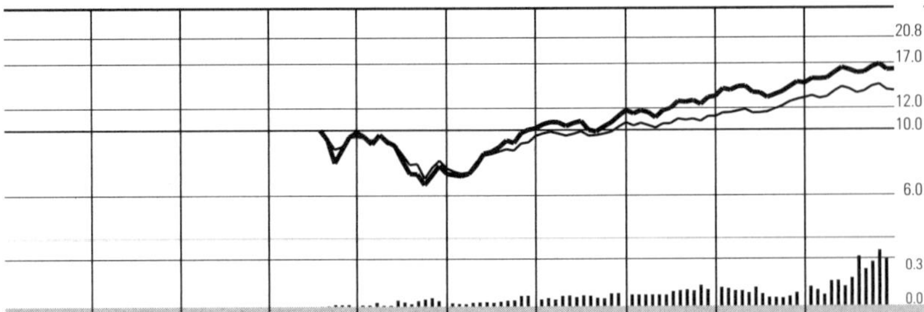

Growth of $10,000
— Investment Value of ETF
— Investment Value of Index S&P 500

Trading Volume Millions

1998	1999	2000	2001	2002	2003	2004	2005	2006	2007	History
—	—	—	71.61	51.82	73.63	84.53	94.06	103.12	113.93	NAV $
—	—	—	71.86	51.70	73.70	84.50	93.96	103.07	113.94	Market Price $
—	—	—	7.55*	-27.55	42.38	15.15	11.82	10.45	11.19	NAV Return%
—	—	—	7.55*	-27.97	42.85	15.00	11.74	10.51	11.26	Market Price Return%
—	—	—	0.43	0.16	0.07	0.09	0.01	-0.01	0.00	Avg Premium/Discount%
—	—	—	—	-5.45	13.70	4.27	6.91	-5.34	5.70	NAV Rtrn% +/-S&P 500
—	—	—	—	-0.14	-0.33	-0.33	-0.28	-0.21	-0.24	NAV Rtrn% +/-Russ MG
—	—	—	—	100	1	1	75	17	64	NAV Return% Rank in Cat
—	—	—	—	0.09	0.26	0.32	0.52	0.76	0.70	Income Return %
—	—	—	—	-27.64	42.12	14.83	11.30	9.69	10.49	Capital Return %
—	—	—	0.02	0.06	0.14	0.23	0.44	0.72	0.72	Income $
—	—	—	0.00	0.00	0.00	0.00	0.00	0.00	0.00	Capital Gains $
—	—	—	—	0.25	0.25	0.25	0.25	0.25	0.25	Expense Ratio %
—	—	—	—	0.08	0.20	0.27	0.38	0.64	0.73	Income Ratio %
—	—	—	—	5	31	10	27	14	30	Turnover Rate %
—	—	—	25	104	409	820	1,312	1,593	3,213	Net Assets $mil

Performance 12-31-07

Historic Quarterly NAV Returns

	1st Qtr	2nd Qtr	3rd Qtr	4th Qtr	Total
2003	-0.06	18.69	7.09	12.09	42.38
2004	4.76	0.99	-4.40	13.84	15.15
2005	-1.74	3.37	6.50	3.37	11.82
2006	7.59	-4.75	0.83	6.89	10.45
2007	3.90	6.68	2.08	-1.74	11.19

Trailing	NAV Return%	Market Return%	NAV Rtrn% +/-S&P 500	%Rank Cat.(NAV)
3 Mo	-1.74	-1.67	1.59	53
6 Mo	0.31	0.37	1.68	53
1 Yr	11.19	11.26	5.70	64
3 Yr Avg	11.15	11.17	2.53	50
5 Yr Avg	17.62	17.68	4.79	1
10 Yr Avg	—	—	—	—

Tax Analysis	Tax-Adj Return%	Tax-Cost Ratio
3 Yr (estimated)	10.91	0.22
5 Yr (estimated)	17.43	0.16
10 Yr (estimated)	—	—

Rating and Risk

Time Period	Morningstar Rtn vs Cat	Morningstar Risk vs Cat	Morningstar Risk-Adj Rating
3 Yr	Avg	-Avg	★★★
5 Yr	Avg	-Avg	★★★★
10 Yr	—	—	—

Other Measures	Standard Index S&P 500	Best Fit Index Russ MG
Alpha	1.7	-0.2
Beta	1.21	1.00
R-Squared	78	100
Standard Deviation	10.66	
Mean	11.15	
Sharpe Ratio	0.64	

Portfolio Analysis 12-31-07

Share change since 11-07 Total Stocks:546	Sector	PE	Tot Ret%	% Assets
⊕ National Oilwell Varco,	Energy	21.7	132.65	1.07
⊕ Weatherford Internationa	Energy	23.4	64.15	0.95
⊕ Yum Brands, Inc.	Consumer	23.2	32.28	0.82
⊕ MEMC Electronic Material	Hardware	35.3	126.09	0.81
⊕ Allergan, Inc.	Health	40.8	7.66	0.80
⊕ Precision Castparts Corp	Ind Mtrls	23.6	77.34	0.78
⊕ NVIDIA Corporation	Hardware	29.4	37.88	0.76
⊕ Electronic Arts, Inc.	Software	—	15.98	0.74
⊕ Williams Companies, Inc.	Energy	27.7	38.70	0.73
⊕ American Tower Corporati	Telecom	—	14.51	0.73
⊕ Textron, Inc.	Ind Mtrls	21.4	54.43	0.73
⊕ MasterCard Incorporated	Business	35.7	119.40	0.70
⊕ Peabody Energy Corporati	Energy	41.1	63.76	0.67
⊕ T Rowe Price Group	Financial	27.0	41.00	0.66
⊕ Express Scripts	Health	34.1	103.91	0.66
⊕ Avon Products	Goods	29.8	22.02	0.65
⊕ Cigna Corporation	Health	14.4	22.60	0.63
⊕ Noble Corporation	Energy	14.4	44.12	0.62
⊕ PPL Corporation	Utilities	20.0	49.31	0.61
⊕ Agilent Technologies, In	Hardware	23.4	5.42	0.61

Current Investment Style

Value Blnd Growth; Large Mid Small

Market Cap	%
Giant	0.0
Large	30.4
Mid	66.6
Small	3.0
Micro	0.0
Avg $mil: 7,997	

Value Measures		Rel Category
Price/Earnings	16.11	0.84
Price/Book	3.18	1.01
Price/Sales	1.46	0.95
Price/Cash Flow	9.96	0.92
Dividend Yield %	0.79	1.39

Growth Measures	%	Rel Category
Long-Term Erngs	12.87	0.80
Book Value	9.02	0.80
Sales	7.94	0.74
Cash Flow	12.28	1.28
Historical Erngs	23.38	1.08

Profitability	%	Rel Category
Return on Equity	23.21	1.08
Return on Assets	9.07	0.94
Net Margin	11.76	1.06

Sector Weightings	% of Stocks	Rel S&P 500	3 Year High	3 Year Low
Info	21.35	1.02		
Software	6.05	1.46	7	4
Hardware	10.99	1.08	15	9
Media	2.02	0.69	4	2
Telecom	2.29	0.63	3	1
Service	41.93	1.03		
Health	12.89	1.07	21	12
Consumer	9.87	1.46	17	10
Business	11.45	2.60	11	9
Financial	7.72	0.44	10	8
Mfg	36.73	0.96		
Goods	8.10	0.88	8	5
Ind Mtrls	12.71	0.98	13	7
Energy	12.70	1.01	13	5
Utilities	3.22	0.88	3	1

Composition

Cash	0.3
Stocks	99.7
Bonds	0.0
Other	0.0
Foreign (% of Stock)	0.9

Morningstar's Take by Emiko Kurotsu 12-31-07

This portfolio's quality isn't superb, but it's better than that of other mid-cap ETFs.

iShares Russell Midcap Growth doesn't look like the typical mid-cap fund. It draws its 500-plus holdings from the Russell Midcap Index, favoring those with higher valuations and forecasted growth rates. Because the parent index has a large-cap bias, this fund does too, with nearly 30% of assets devoted to such names, which is about twice the mid-cap norm.

The portfolio's quality--which is better than the typical mid-cap ETF's--also sets it apart. That's not solely due to the fund's large-cap bias, though. Indeed, 39 of the fund's 52 wide-moat holdings are mid-caps like software firm Intuit and credit checker Equifax. The index's screen for faster-growing companies means the fund pulls in roughly one third more high-quality stocks than its parent index as a percentage of assets. While growth isn't synonymous with quality, many of these names are fortified by durable advantages. For instance, wide-moat video game publisher Electronic Arts enjoys nearly unmatched clout in its market.

That said, most stocks here are of middling quality, with about 75% of assets in narrow- and no-moat names. The fund is full of firms that are poised for growth, but haven't locked in iron-clad competitive advantages. Our analysts are bullish, for instance, on the prospects of organic supermarket chain Whole Foods, but concede that the low switching costs of grocery chains leave the firm vulnerable to its finicky customer base.

The portfolio's moderate risk profile is partly a function of its middling quality. Given that many of the stocks here are vulnerable to encroaching rivals, there's at least a moderate level of uncertainty shrouding our analysts' forecasts.

Yet, the portfolio's diversification across stocks and industries has kept volatility in check. Thus, we wouldn't demand a large margin of safety. We'd invest when the fund trades at an 8% or greater discount to our fair value estimate.

Address:	45 Fremont Street United States 800-474-2737
Web Address:	www.ishares.com
Inception:	07-17-01 *
Advisor:	Barclays Global Fund Advisers

Management Fee:	0.25%		
Expense Projections:	3Yr:$80	5Yr:$141	10Yr:$318
Income Distrib:	Quarterly		
Exchange:	AMEX		

iShares R. Midcap VI IWS

Market Price	Mstar Category
$141.06	Mid-Cap Value

Morningstar Rating	Return	Risk	Yield	NAV	Avg Daily Vol. (k)	52 wk High/Low
★★★★	Above Avg	Average	2.3%	$141.19	474	$164.30 - $131.77

Morningstar Fair Value

Price/Fair Value Ratio	Coverage Rate %
0.88	94

Valuation

This portfolio hardly sports the most attractive quality/risk profile. But given its diversification across stocks and sectors, we'd consider an investment at a 9% discount to our fair value estimate. After trading at a premium for several years, the fund recently crossed into bargain territory, as it was 12% undervalued.

Methodology

This fund tracks the Russell Midcap Value Index, a style subset of the Russell Midcap Index. As such, it's composed of the roughly 500 firms from the Russell Midcap Index with lower valuations (measured by price/book ratios) and forecasted growth than the norm. Despite its moniker, the index pulls in a clutch of large-cap stocks, with over 25% of the fund's assets tucked there. The fund has a foot in every economic sector, though it's particularly well-represented in utilities, financials, and industrials and treads lightly in tech, energy, and consumer services.

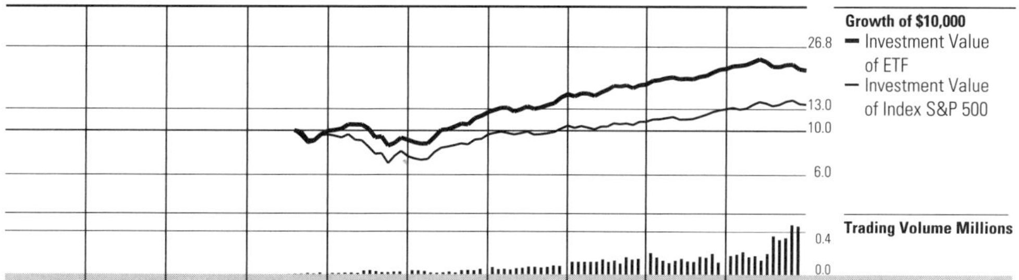

History

1998	1999	2000	2001	2002	2003	2004	2005	2006	2007	History
—	—	—	77.62	68.87	93.11	112.83	124.59	146.56	141.19	NAV $
—	—	—	77.93	68.55	93.30	112.81	124.42	146.43	141.06	Market Price $
—	—	—	11.55*	-9.69	37.70	23.26	12.68	19.95	-1.58	NAV Return%
—	—	—	11.54*	-10.46	38.62	22.99	12.54	20.00	-1.58	Market Price Return%
—	—	—	0.13	0.05	0.20	0.00	0.00	-0.02	-0.05	Avg Premium/Discount%
—	—	—	—	12.41	9.02	12.38	7.77	4.16	-7.07	NAV Rtrn% +/-S&P 500
—	—	—	—	-0.05	-0.37	-0.45	0.03	-0.27	-0.16	NAV Rtrn% +/-Russ MV
—	—	—	—	1	100	1	1	1	45	NAV Return% Rank in Cat
—	—	—	—	1.70	2.14	1.87	2.17	2.17	2.22	Income Return %
—	—	—	—	-11.39	35.56	21.39	10.51	17.78	-3.80	Capital Return %
—	—	—	0.67	1.31	1.46	1.73	2.43	2.68	3.23	Income $
—	—	—	0.00	0.00	0.00	0.00	0.00	0.00	0.00	Capital Gains $
—	—	—	—	0.25	0.25	0.25	0.25	0.25	0.25	Expense Ratio %
—	—	—	—	1.91	2.24	2.05	2.20	2.18	2.05	Income Ratio %
—	—	—	—	6	24	10	20	11	25	Turnover Rate %
—	—	—	35	96	284	1,055	2,012	3,049	3,050	Net Assets $mil

Performance 12-31-07

Historic Quarterly NAV Returns

	1st Qtr	2nd Qtr	3rd Qtr	4th Qtr	Total
2003	-4.11	17.79	5.88	15.14	37.70
2004	5.27	1.68	1.62	13.31	23.26
2005	0.83	4.70	5.34	1.31	12.68
2006	7.55	-0.60	3.47	8.43	19.95
2007	4.82	3.62	-3.58	-6.02	-1.58

Trailing	NAV Return%	Market Return%	NAV Rtrn% +/-S&P 500	%Rank Cat.(NAV)
3 Mo	-6.02	-6.09	-2.69	61
6 Mo	-9.38	-9.38	-8.01	46
1 Yr	-1.58	-1.58	-7.07	45
3 Yr Avg	9.98	9.95	1.36	1
5 Yr Avg	17.69	17.78	4.86	1
10 Yr Avg	—	—	—	—

Tax Analysis	Tax-Adj Return%	Tax-Cost Ratio
3 Yr (estimated)	9.20	0.71
5 Yr (estimated)	16.90	0.67
10 Yr (estimated)	—	—

Rating and Risk

Time Period	Morningstar Rtn vs Cat	Morningstar Risk vs Cat	Morningstar Risk-Adj Rating
3 Yr	+Avg	Avg	★★★★
5 Yr	+Avg	Avg	★★★★
10 Yr	—	—	—

Other Measures	Standard Index S&P 500	Best Fit Index Russ MV
Alpha	1.2	-0.1
Beta	1.05	1.00
R-Squared	77	100
Standard Deviation	9.24	
Mean	9.98	
Sharpe Ratio	0.61	

Portfolio Analysis 12-31-07

Share change since 11-07 Total Stocks:485	Sector	PE	Tot Ret%	% Assets
⊕ Hess Corporation	Ind Mtrls	19.1	104.77	1.56
⊕ American Electric Power	Utilities	16.8	13.06	1.03
⊕ Principal Financial Grou	Financial	17.8	18.84	0.97
⊕ Edison International	Utilities	15.4	19.93	0.97
⊕ Sempra Energy	Utilities	17.0	12.69	0.91
⊕ Spectra Energy Corporati	Utilities	—	-3.60	0.91
⊕ Murphy Oil Corporation	Energy	25.2	68.58	0.89
⊕ CSX Corporation	Business	16.7	29.41	0.89
⊕ Xerox Corporation	Ind Mtrls	15.9	-4.23	0.84
⊕ PG & E Corporation	Utilities	16.3	-6.09	0.84
⊕ Safeway Inc.	Consumer	17.0	-0.03	0.84
⊕ Liberty Capital A	Media	—	18.89	0.84
⊕ United States Steel Corp	Ind Mtrls	12.6	66.73	0.80
⊕ Bunge, Ltd.	Goods	18.6	61.80	0.78
⊕ Aon Corp.	Financial	18.6	36.99	0.78
⊕ Ford Motor Company	Goods	—	-12.65	0.76
⊕ Consolidated Edison Comp	Utilities	13.9	6.65	0.74
⊕ Parker Hannifin Corporat	Ind Mtrls	15.6	47.94	0.73
⊕ Ameriprise Financial, In	Financial	18.3	2.07	0.72
⊕ Gap, Inc.	Consumer	21.7	10.54	0.71

Current Investment Style

Value Blnd Growth / Large Mid Small

Market Cap	%
Giant	0.0
Large	26.4
Mid	68.4
Small	5.2
Micro	0.0
Avg $mil: 7,002	

Value Measures		Rel Category
Price/Earnings	13.68	1.03
Price/Book	1.48	0.97
Price/Sales	0.76	0.97
Price/Cash Flow	5.72	0.93
Dividend Yield %	2.22	0.95

Growth Measures	%	Rel Category
Long-Term Erngs	—	—
Book Value	7.44	0.90
Sales	4.71	0.73
Cash Flow	-0.31	NMF
Historical Erngs	14.63	1.11

Profitability	%	Rel Category
Return on Equity	13.88	0.93
Return on Assets	4.65	0.93
Net Margin	12.47	1.16

Sector Weightings	% of Stocks	Rel S&P 500	3 Year High	3 Year Low
Info	11.03	0.53		
Software	1.53	0.37	3	2
Hardware	3.84	0.38	5	3
Media	3.60	1.24	4	1
Telecom	2.06	0.57	2	1
Service	41.88	1.03		
Health	2.37	0.20	5	2
Consumer	6.25	0.92	11	6
Business	5.51	1.25	6	4
Financial	27.75	1.59	33	28
Mfg	47.11	1.22		
Goods	10.22	1.12	10	7
Ind Mtrls	15.50	1.19	16	11
Energy	6.64	0.53	10	5
Utilities	14.75	4.01	16	12

Composition

Cash	0.8
Stocks	99.2
Bonds	0.0
Other	0.0
Foreign (% of Stock)	0.4

Morningstar's Take by Emiko Kurotsu 12-31-07

We'd demand a moderate margin of safety before investing in this middling portfolio.

IShares Russell Midcap Value consists of roughly 500 firms with lower valuations and earnings growth rates than the mid-cap norm. The fund invests over a quarter of its assets in large-cap stocks, which is roughly double the stake of the average mid-cap offering.

That large-cap stake doesn't boost the fund's quality, though, which is mostly mediocre. Of the 426 stocks that our analysts cover here, just 18, representing about 4% of assets, garnered a wide economic moat rating, a distinction we reserve for companies boasting intractable competitive advantages. These include, for instance, Washington Post, whose profitable Kaplan educational segment and flagship paper's political clout give it a leg up over its rivals.

More common, however, are the narrow- and no-moat firms that dot the portfolio. For instance, packaged foods maker ConAgra Foods must vie for retailer shelf space with the more indelibly branded products of rivals. Similarly, asset manager Janus Capital has struggled to regain its stride amid waning demand for its bread-and-butter growth strategies, costly legal settlements, and key manager defections. While such firms don't completely lack competitive advantages, they're typically less defensible and thus less valuable. That, in turn, makes this portfolio less valuable than one teeming with higher-quality names.

It also influences the fund's risk profile. Many of these businesses are vulnerable to rivals, so their future results are more uncertain. Natural-gas distributor NiSource, for instance, is exposed to ever-changing state and federal industry regulations that affect how it does business. Yet the fund's diversification across names and sectors has tamped volatility, making the portfolio less risky on the whole. We'd be willing to invest here at a modest 9% discount to our fair value estimate.

Address:	45 Fremont Street United States 800-474-2737
Web Address:	www.ishares.com
Inception:	07-17-01 *
Advisor:	Barclays Global Fund Advisers

Management Fee:	0.25%		
Expense Projections:	3Yr:$80	5Yr:$141	10Yr:$318
Income Distrib:	Quarterly		
Exchange:	NYSE		

iShares S&P 100 Ind. OEF

Market Price	Mstar Category
$68.80	Large Blend

Morningstar Fair Value

Price/Fair Value Ratio	Coverage Rate %
0.88	100

Valuation

Given this fund's high quality and moderate risk, we wouldn't require a large discount to our fair value estimate here--8% or more is sufficient. It's not cheap enough now, but historically, it has reached these levels when blue chips have fallen out of favor.

Methodology

This ETF tracks the S&P 100, a market-cap-weighted index that's composed of 100 giant- and large-cap stocks drawn from the broader S&P 500 Index. To qualify for the S&P 500 and, in turn, this fund's index, firms must pass various capitalization and profitability screens that the index selection committee employs. The index includes many of the biggest firms in the S&P 500, representing about 45% of the total U.S. equity market capitalization. The fund is concentrated heavily in its top holdings, but it's well diversified by sector.

Morningstar Rating	Return	Risk	Yield	NAV	Avg Daily Vol. (k)	52 wk High/Low
★★	Below Avg	Below Avg	1.9%	$68.68	1,883	$73.12 - $63.46

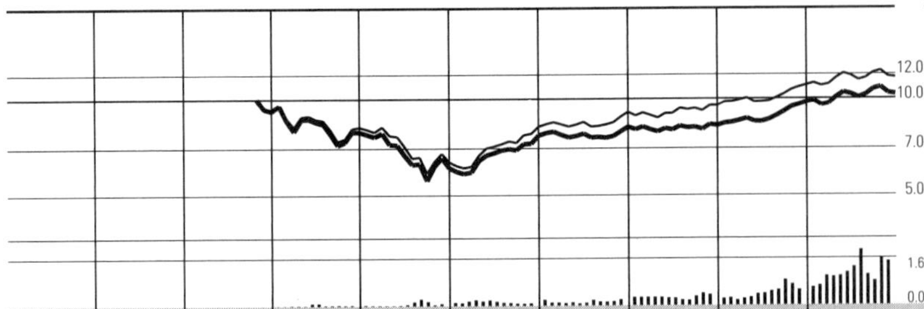

History

1998	1999	2000	2001	2002	2003	2004	2005	2006	2007	History
—	—	68.67	58.46	44.56	55.21	57.36	56.86	66.08	68.68	NAV $
—	—	68.81	58.75	44.46	55.13	57.38	56.90	66.08	68.80	Market Price $
—	—	0.74*	-13.99	-22.72	25.97	6.23	1.00	18.22	5.93	NAV Return%
—	—	0.76*	-13.74	-23.27	26.07	6.42	1.03	18.14	6.11	Market Price Return%
—	—	-0.67	0.20	0.02	0.01	0.06	0.09	0.09	0.01	Avg Premium/Discount%
—	—	—	-2.10	-0.62	-2.71	-4.65	-3.91	2.43	0.44	NAV Rtrn% +/-S&P 500
—	—	—	-0.18	-0.13	-0.28	-0.20	-0.17	-0.25	-0.19	NAV Rtrn% +/-S&P 100
—	—	—	34	17	83	50	87	20	47	NAV Return% Rank in Cat
—	—	—	0.87	1.17	1.87	2.27	1.86	1.86	2.00	Income Return %
—	—	—	-14.86	-23.89	24.10	3.96	-0.86	16.36	3.93	Capital Return %
—	—	0.15	0.59	0.68	0.83	1.25	1.06	1.05	1.31	Income $
—	—	0.00	0.00	0.00	0.00	0.00	0.00	0.00	0.00	Capital Gains $
—	—	—	0.20	0.20	0.20	0.20	0.20	0.20	0.20	Expense Ratio %
—	—	—	1.03	1.12	1.63	1.62	2.41	1.96	2.03	Income Ratio %
—	—	—	5	13	4	5	6	12	12	Turnover Rate %
—	—	185	161	196	367	608	685	3,182	4,890	Net Assets $mil

Performance 12-31-07

Historic Quarterly NAV Returns

	1st Qtr	2nd Qtr	3rd Qtr	4th Qtr	Total
2003	-3.08	14.72	2.08	10.98	25.97
2004	0.45	0.90	-2.99	8.05	6.23
2005	-1.85	-0.23	2.04	1.07	1.00
2006	3.64	-0.88	7.50	7.05	18.22
2007	-1.10	7.10	3.65	-3.52	5.93

Trailing	NAV Return%	Market Return%	NAV Rtrn% +/-S&P 500	%Rank Cat.(NAV)
3 Mo	-3.52	-3.35	-0.19	58
6 Mo	0.00	0.28	1.37	29
1 Yr	5.93	6.11	0.44	47
3 Yr Avg	8.14	8.20	-0.48	90
5 Yr Avg	11.10	11.19	-1.73	84
10 Yr Avg	—	—	—	—

Tax Analysis	Tax-Adj Return%	Tax-Cost Ratio
3 Yr (estimated)	7.46	0.63
5 Yr (estimated)	10.37	0.66
10 Yr (estimated)	—	—

Rating and Risk

Time Period	Morningstar Rtn vs Cat	Morningstar Risk vs Cat	Morningstar Risk-Adj Rating
3 Yr	Avg	-Avg	★★★
5 Yr	-Avg	-Avg	★★
10 Yr	—	—	—

Other Measures	Standard Index S&P 500	Best Fit Index Mstar Large Cap TR
Alpha	-0.3	-0.8
Beta	0.95	0.99
R-Squared	94	96
Standard Deviation	7.68	
Mean	8.14	
Sharpe Ratio	0.50	

Portfolio Analysis 12-31-07

Share change since 11-07 Total Stocks:100	Sector	PE	Tot Ret%	% Assets
⊕ ExxonMobil Corporation	Energy	13.6	24.34	6.67
⊕ General Electric Company	Ind Mtrls	16.6	2.69	4.88
⊕ Microsoft Corporation	Software	23.4	20.83	3.73
⊕ AT&T, Inc.	Telecom	21.6	20.58	3.28
⊕ Procter & Gamble Company	Goods	23.1	16.63	2.97
⊕ Chevron Corporation	Energy	11.4	30.59	2.57
⊕ Johnson & Johnson	Health	18.8	3.61	2.49
⊕ Bank of America Corporat	Financial	9.4	-19.25	2.38
⊕ Apple, Inc.	Hardware	50.5	133.47	2.26
⊕ Cisco Systems, Inc.	Hardware	21.5	-0.95	2.14
⊕ Google, Inc.	Business	54.0	50.17	2.08
⊕ Altria Group Inc.	Goods	13.2	22.10	2.07
⊕ Intel Corporation	Hardware	25.4	34.22	2.03
⊕ Pfizer Inc.	Health	22.5	-8.15	2.02
⊕ International Business M	Hardware	16.2	13.20	1.94
⊕ American International G	Financial	10.2	-17.96	1.93
⊕ Citigroup, Inc.	Financial	7.9	-44.93	1.91
⊕ J.P. Morgan Chase & Co.	Financial	9.5	-7.24	1.91
⊕ ConocoPhillips	Energy	13.8	25.42	1.84
⊕ Hewlett-Packard Company	Hardware	18.8	23.40	1.69

Current Investment Style

Value Blnd Growth (Large / Mid / Small)

Market Cap	%
Giant	81.2
Large	18.3
Mid	0.6
Small	0.0
Micro	0.0
Avg $mil: 118,326	

Value Measures		Rel Category
Price/Earnings	14.05	0.89
Price/Book	2.61	1.02
Price/Sales	1.55	1.25
Price/Cash Flow	10.47	1.13
Dividend Yield %	2.05	1.08

Growth Measures	%	Rel Category
Long-Term Erngs	—	—
Book Value	6.94	0.75
Sales	7.16	0.88
Cash Flow	6.88	0.79
Historical Erngs	16.81	1.01

Profitability	%	Rel Category
Return on Equity	24.35	1.09
Return on Assets	9.28	1.11
Net Margin	14.84	1.21

Sector Weightings	% of Stocks	Rel S&P 500	3 Year High	3 Year Low
Info	25.18	1.21		
Software	4.93	1.19	6	4
Hardware	11.99	1.17	12	9
Media	2.80	0.96	5	3
Telecom	5.46	1.50	6	4
Service	36.17	0.89		
Health	10.42	0.87	13	10
Consumer	4.52	0.67	7	4
Business	4.02	0.91	4	1
Financial	17.21	0.99	23	17
Mfg	38.66	1.01		
Goods	11.03	1.20	12	10
Ind Mtrls	11.87	0.91	15	12
Energy	13.93	1.10	14	7
Utilities	1.83	0.50	2	2

Composition

Cash	0.6
Stocks	99.4
Bonds	0.0
Other	0.0
Foreign (% of Stock)	0.0

Morningstar's Take by Emiko Kurotsu 12-31-07

This diversified large-cap ETF sports a collection of high-quality names.

This fund's underlying index tracks the 100 biggest stocks from the popular S&P 500 Index. As such, it represents the biggest of the big, with more than 82% of assets invested in giant-cap firms.

This collection of mega-caps boosts the fund's quality, which we define as firms with wide economic moats, or sustainable competitive advantages. That's not because size translates to dominance, but because many giant-cap firms are industry bellwethers that possess certain attributes, like massive scale, high barriers to entry, or a sterling brand, that keep rivals at bay. ExxonMobil, for instance, boasts formidable scale and a relentless pursuit for operational efficiency that keeps its profits protected from rivals. Microsoft's ubiquitous presence on PCs gives the software firm enormous pricing power and clout in its industry. More than half of this fund's holdings, and 64% of assets, are devoted to such heavy-hitting firms. By contrast, just 10% of the 2,000-plus equities our analysts cover garner wide-moat ratings.

This high level of quality translates to a moderate risk profile. That's because many of the fund's underlying holdings are industry leaders, meaning they're more likely to throw off predictable cash flows than an industry underdog that is still struggling to fend its turf. Fast-food giant McDonald's, for instance, earns a below-average risk rating from our analysts because its wide moat and sound financials mean it's not likely to be overrun by rivals overnight.

The portfolio's volatility also benefits from the fund's sector diversification. It has a foot in almost every economic sector, ensuring that its fortunes aren't tied to industry-specific factors, like the price of oil or the strength of the U.S. consumer.

Given these factors, we don't require a large margin of safety to invest here. We'd be enthusiastic buyers at an 8% or larger discount to our fair value estimate.

Address:	45 Fremont Street United States 800-474-2737
Web Address:	www.ishares.com
Inception:	10-23-00 *
Advisor:	Barclays Global Fund Advisers

Management Fee:	0.20%		
Expense Projections:	3Yr:$64	5Yr:$113	10Yr:$255
Income Distrib:	Quarterly		
Exchange:	CBOE		

iShares S&P 1500 Index ISI

Market Price $130.14

Mstar Category Large Blend

Morningstar Fair Value

Price/Fair Value Ratio	Coverage Rate %
0.89	96

Valuation

This fund tracks an index that aims to represent the broad U.S. stock market. As such, it tends to trade at steep discounts to fair value only amid big market corrections, like those we saw in July and August 2007. We'd recommend the fund when it's trading at an 8% or larger discount to fair value, a level it has flirted with of late.

Methodology

This ETF tracks the S&P 1500 Index, which represents approximately 90% of the U.S. equity market. The index is a composite of the widely used S&P 500, MidCap 400, and SmallCap 600 Indexes. Each index is first screened by the S&P selection committee for profitability and liquidity. As a market-cap-weighted fund, nearly 80% of the fund is tucked into giant- and large-cap stocks. Sectors diversification is in line with that of the broad domestic market: financial services dominate, with industrials, energy, and health care also strongly represented.

Morningstar Rating	Return	Risk	Yield	NAV	Avg Daily Vol. (k)	52 wk High/Low
★★★	Average	Average	1.6%	$130.33	59	$139.10 - $122.65

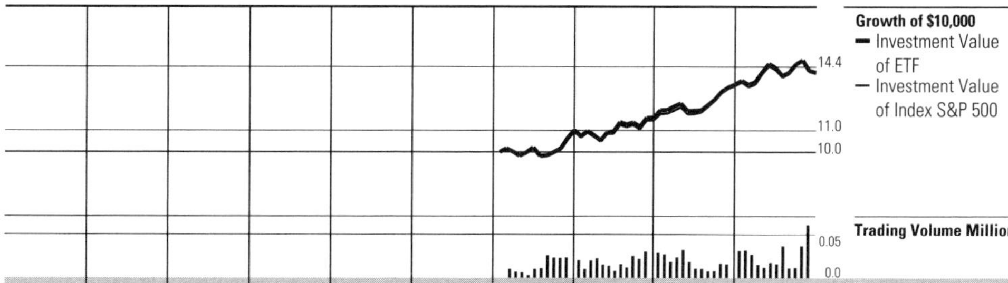

1998	1999	2000	2001	2002	2003	2004	2005	2006	2007	History
—	—	—	—	—	—	106.96	111.02	125.84	130.33	NAV $
—	—	—	—	—	—	107.07	110.98	126.57	130.14	Market Price $
—	—	—	—	—	—	8.69*	5.47	15.13	5.26	NAV Return%
—	—	—	—	—	—	8.60*	5.32	15.84	4.50	Market Price Return%
—	—	—	—	—	—	-0.09	-0.03	0.07	-0.03	Avg Premium/Discount%
—	—	—	—	—	—	—	0.56	-0.66	-0.23	NAV Rtrn% +/-S&P 500
—	—	—	—	—	—	—	-0.19	-0.21	-0.21	NAV Rtrn% +/-S&P 1500
—	—	—	—	—	—	—	44	70	62	NAV Return% Rank in Cat
—	—	—	—	—	—	—	1.62	1.68	1.71	Income Return %
—	—	—	—	—	—	—	3.85	13.45	3.55	Capital Return %
—	—	—	—	—	—	1.64	1.72	1.85	2.14	Income $
—	—	—	—	—	—	0.00	0.00	0.00	0.00	Capital Gains $
—	—	—	—	—	—	—	0.20	0.20	0.20	Expense Ratio %
—	—	—	—	—	—	—	1.73	1.61	1.68	Income Ratio %
—	—	—	—	—	—	—	5	6	4	Turnover Rate %
—	—	—	—	—	—	59	133	189	228	Net Assets $mil

Performance 12-31-07

Historic Quarterly NAV Returns

	1st Qtr	2nd Qtr	3rd Qtr	4th Qtr	Total
2003	—	—	—	—	—
2004	—	1.68	-1.89	9.56	—*
2005	-2.03	1.68	3.76	2.04	5.47
2006	4.82	-1.75	4.77	6.71	15.13
2007	1.09	6.12	1.61	-3.43	5.26

Trailing	NAV Return%	Market Return%	NAV Rtrn% +/-S&P 500	%Rank Cat.(NAV)
3 Mo	-3.43	-3.58	-0.10	57
6 Mo	-1.88	-2.00	-0.51	56
1 Yr	5.26	4.50	-0.23	62
3 Yr Avg	8.53	8.44	-0.09	76
5 Yr Avg	—	—	—	—
10 Yr Avg	—	—	—	—

Tax Analysis	Tax-Adj Return%	Tax-Cost Ratio
3 Yr (estimated)	7.92	0.56
5 Yr (estimated)	—	—
10 Yr (estimated)	—	—

Rating and Risk

Time Period	Morningstar Rtn vs Cat	Morningstar Risk vs Cat	Morningstar Risk-Adj Rating
3 Yr	Avg	Avg	★★★
5 Yr	—	—	—
10 Yr	—	—	—

Other Measures	Standard Index S&P 500	Best Fit Index M* U.S. Mkt TR
Alpha	-0.2	-0.6
Beta	1.03	0.98
R-Squared	99	100
Standard Deviation	8.03	
Mean	8.53	
Sharpe Ratio	0.53	

Portfolio Analysis 12-31-07

Share change since 11-07 Total Stocks:1500	Sector	PE	Tot Ret%	% Assets
⊕ ExxonMobil Corporation	Energy	13.6	24.34	3.50
⊕ General Electric Company	Ind Mtrls	16.6	2.69	2.56
⊕ Microsoft Corporation	Software	23.4	20.83	1.96
⊕ AT&T, Inc.	Telecom	21.6	20.58	1.72
⊕ Procter & Gamble Company	Goods	23.1	16.63	1.56
⊕ Chevron Corporation	Energy	11.4	30.59	1.35
⊕ Johnson & Johnson	Health	18.8	3.61	1.31
⊕ Bank of America Corporat	Financial	9.4	-19.25	1.25
⊕ Apple, Inc.	Hardware	50.5	133.47	1.19
⊕ Cisco Systems, Inc.	Hardware	21.5	-0.95	1.12
⊕ Google, Inc.	Business	54.0	50.17	1.10
⊕ Altria Group Inc.	Goods	13.2	22.10	1.09
⊕ Intel Corporation	Hardware	25.4	34.22	1.07
⊕ Pfizer Inc.	Health	22.5	-8.15	1.06
⊕ International Business M	Hardware	16.2	13.20	1.02
⊕ American International G	Financial	10.2	-17.96	1.01
⊕ Citigroup, Inc.	Financial	7.9	-44.93	1.01
⊕ J.P. Morgan Chase & Co.	Financial	9.5	-7.24	1.00
⊕ ConocoPhillips	Energy	13.8	25.42	0.97
⊕ Hewlett-Packard Company	Hardware	18.8	23.40	0.89

Current Investment Style

Value Blnd Growth — Large / Mid / Small

Market Cap	%
Giant	45.6
Large	32.5
Mid	17.5
Small	3.9
Micro	0.5
Avg $mil: 39,451	

Value Measures		Rel Category
Price/Earnings	14.30	0.91
Price/Book	2.36	0.92
Price/Sales	1.35	1.09
Price/Cash Flow	9.64	1.04
Dividend Yield %	1.75	0.93

Growth Measures	%	Rel Category
Long-Term Erngs	—	—
Book Value	8.05	0.87
Sales	7.57	0.93
Cash Flow	8.00	0.92
Historical Erngs	17.12	1.02

Profitability	%	Rel Category
Return on Equity	21.44	0.96
Return on Assets	8.35	1.00
Net Margin	13.85	1.13

Sector Weightings	% of Stocks	Rel S&P 500	3 Year High	3 Year Low
Info	20.20	0.97		
Software	4.14	1.00	4	3
Hardware	10.04	0.98	10	9
Media	2.66	0.91	4	3
Telecom	3.36	0.93	3	3
Service	41.62	1.02		
Health	12.15	1.01	14	12
Consumer	7.06	1.04	10	7
Business	5.19	1.18	5	4
Financial	17.22	0.99	22	17
Mfg	38.19	0.99		
Goods	8.87	0.97	9	8
Ind Mtrls	13.34	1.03	13	12
Energy	12.04	0.95	12	8
Utilities	3.94	1.07	4	3

Composition

Cash	0.6
Stocks	99.4
Bonds	0.0
Other	0.0
Foreign (% of Stock)	0.0

Morningstar's Take by Emiko Kurotsu 12-31-07

This total-market fund bears average quality.

This ETF tracks the S&P 1500 Index, which covers roughly 90% of the total U.S. stock market's capitalization and is a composite of the S&P 500, MidCap 400, and SmallCap 600 Indexes. As a market-cap-weighted index, it's extremely top-heavy, with more than 75% of assets tucked into large-cap names.

Not all large caps are quality stocks, though. That's easy to see here, where of the 264 large caps our analysts cover, just 84 boast wide economic moats, or highly defensible competitive advantages. More common are narrow-moat firms like iPod purveyor Apple and high-end jeweler Tiffany, which, despite their charms, can be dislodged by competitors over time. For instance, although Apple boasts near-legendary design prowess, it remains vulnerable to the leverage that content providers wield and must fend with rapid product cycles and pricing pressure.

The portfolio's middling quality also illustrates another principle: An index that purports to represent the entire market is bound to revert to the mean, as all companies can't outdo their rivals, and, in fact, most don't. So, for every wide-moat firm like tobacco giant Altria, there are many more like automaker Ford F and retailer J.C. Penney, which lack competitive advantages altogether.

Given the abundance of narrow- and no-moat firms here, it's not surprising that most of its underlying holdings court average business risk. After all, it's easier to estimate a business' fair value when it's dominant and, thus, throws off cash flows in more predictably. By contrast, since lesser-quality businesses are more vulnerable to rivals, their results can be significantly altered, thereby injecting uncertainty into our forecasts.

The portfolio's diversification across names and sectors does help tamp its volatility, though. Taken together with its quality and risk, then, we require only a modest margin of safety here.

Address:	45 Fremont Street United States 800-474-2737
Web Address:	www.ishares.com
Inception:	01-20-04*
Advisor:	Barclays Global Fund Advisers

Management Fee:	0.20%		
Expense Projections:	3Yr:$64	5Yr:$113	10Yr:$255
Income Distrib:	Quarterly		
Exchange:	NYSE		

iShares S&P 500 IVV

Market Price	Mstar Category
$146.74	Large Blend

Morningstar Fair Value

Price/Fair Value Ratio	Coverage Rate %
0.89	99

Valuation

Financially sturdy, dominant firms abound in this ETF. These holdings' generally temperate risk profiles and the portfolio's diversification has tamped volatility. Thus, we'd require only an 8% margin of safety to invest here. The fund recently crossed into buy territory, as it was trading at a 12% discount to our fair value estimate.

Methodology

This fund owns all the stocks in the S&P 500 Index, which includes more than 80% of the market's capitalization of U.S. stocks. The index is market-cap-weighted, which means multinational industry leaders like GE, ExxonMobil, and AT&T have a lot of influence here. To be considered for inclusion in the index by S&P's selection committee, companies most post at least four straight quarters of positive earnings. Unlike SPDRs, which is a unit investment trust, this ETF is not subject to any constraints on reinvesting dividends or lending securities, tools that indexers often use to keep pace with the benchmark.

Morningstar Rating	Return	Risk	Yield	NAV	Avg Daily Vol. (k)	52 wk High/Low
★★★	Average	Average	1.9%	$146.86	2,691	$156.79 - $137.61

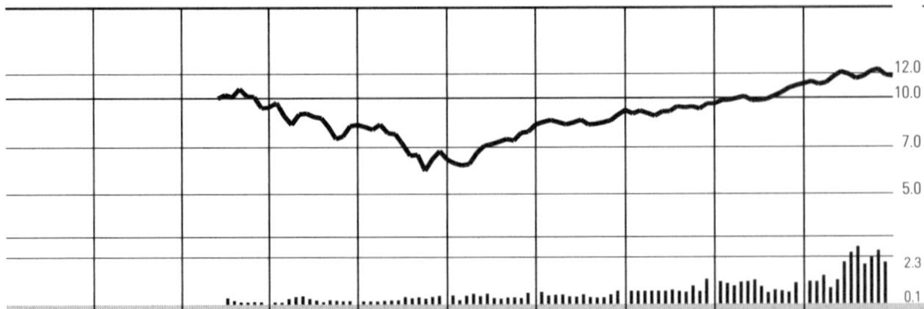

Growth of $10,000
— Investment Value of ETF
— Investment Value of Index S&P 500

Trading Volume Millions

History

1998	1999	2000	2001	2002	2003	2004	2005	2006	2007	History
—	—	132.14	115.00	88.18	111.46	121.24	124.87	141.92	146.86	NAV $
—	—	131.34	114.33	88.35	111.22	121.00	124.67	142.50	146.74	Market Price $
—	—	1.76*	-11.96	-22.15	28.53	10.77	4.83	15.69	5.44	NAV Return%
—	—	1.75*	-11.94	-21.55	28.00	10.79	4.87	16.35	4.93	Market Price Return%
—	—	-0.03	-0.07	-0.15	0.03	0.07	-0.01	0.09	0.01	Avg Premium/Discount%
—	—	—	-0.07	-0.05	-0.15	-0.11	-0.08	-0.10	-0.05	NAV Rtrn% +/-S&P 500
—	—	—	-0.07	-0.05	-0.15	-0.11	-0.08	-0.10	-0.05	NAV Rtrn% +/-S&P 500
—	—	—	77	73	62	69	52	30	56	NAV Return% Rank in Cat
—	—	—	1.01	1.30	1.87	1.90	1.78	1.91	1.98	Income Return %
—	—	—	-12.97	-23.45	26.66	8.87	3.05	13.78	3.46	Capital Return %
—	—	0.77	1.33	1.48	1.64	2.10	2.15	2.37	2.79	Income $
—	—	0.07	0.00	0.00	0.00	0.00	0.00	0.00	0.00	Capital Gains $
—	—	—	0.09	0.09	0.09	0.09	0.09	0.10	0.09	Expense Ratio %
—	—	—	1.06	1.27	1.67	1.66	2.02	1.78	1.86	Income Ratio %
—	—	—	5	3	5	3	6	7	5	Turnover Rate %
—	—	2,319	3,611	5,119	7,874	11,784	14,229	17,982	17,895	Net Assets $mil

Performance 12-31-07

Historic Quarterly NAV Returns

	1st Qtr	2nd Qtr	3rd Qtr	4th Qtr	Total
2003	-3.16	15.34	2.61	12.14	28.53
2004	1.66	1.70	-1.89	9.20	10.77
2005	-2.15	1.35	3.58	2.05	4.83
2006	4.19	-1.46	5.64	6.67	15.69
2007	0.62	6.24	2.03	-3.33	5.44

Trailing	NAV Return%	Market Return%	NAV Rtrn% +/-S&P 500	%Rank Cat.(NAV)
3 Mo	-3.33	-3.55	0.00	51
6 Mo	-1.37	-1.54	0.00	47
1 Yr	5.44	4.93	-0.05	56
3 Yr Avg	8.54	8.59	-0.08	71
5 Yr Avg	12.73	12.67	-0.10	54
10 Yr Avg	—	—	—	—

Tax Analysis	Tax-Adj Return%	Tax-Cost Ratio
3 Yr (estimated)	7.86	0.63
5 Yr (estimated)	12.03	0.62
10 Yr (estimated)	—	—

Rating and Risk

Time Period	Morningstar Rtn vs Cat	Morningstar Risk vs Cat	Morningstar Risk-Adj Rating
3 Yr	Avg	Avg	★★★
5 Yr	Avg	Avg	★★★
10 Yr	—	—	—

Other Measures	Standard Index S&P 500	Best Fit Index S&P 500
Alpha	-0.1	-0.1
Beta	1.00	1.00
R-Squared	100	100
Standard Deviation	7.77	
Mean	8.54	
Sharpe Ratio	0.55	

Portfolio Analysis 12-31-07

Share change since 11-07 Total Stocks:500	Sector	PE	Tot Ret%	% Assets
⊖ ExxonMobil Corporation	Energy	13.6	24.34	3.95
⊖ General Electric Company	Ind Mtrls	16.6	2.69	2.89
⊖ Microsoft Corporation	Software	23.4	20.83	2.21
⊖ AT&T, Inc.	Telecom	21.6	20.58	1.95
⊖ Procter & Gamble Company	Goods	23.1	16.63	1.76
⊖ Chevron Corporation	Energy	11.4	30.59	1.52
⊖ Johnson & Johnson	Health	18.8	3.61	1.47
⊖ Bank of America Corporat	Financial	9.4	-19.25	1.41
⊖ Apple, Inc.	Hardware	50.5	133.47	1.34
⊖ Cisco Systems, Inc.	Hardware	21.5	-0.95	1.27
⊖ Google, Inc.	Business	54.0	50.17	1.24
⊖ Altria Group Inc.	Goods	13.2	22.10	1.23
⊖ Intel Corporation	Hardware	25.4	34.22	1.20
⊖ Pfizer Inc.	Health	22.5	-8.15	1.20
⊖ International Business M	Hardware	16.2	13.20	1.15
⊖ American International G	Financial	10.2	-17.96	1.14
⊖ Citigroup, Inc.	Financial	7.9	-44.93	1.14
⊖ J.P. Morgan Chase & Co.	Financial	9.5	-7.24	1.13
⊖ ConocoPhillips	Energy	13.8	25.42	1.09
⊖ Hewlett-Packard Company	Hardware	18.8	23.40	1.01

Current Investment Style

Value Blnd Growth; Large Mid Small

Market Cap	%
Giant	51.5
Large	36.6
Mid	11.8
Small	0.2
Micro	0.0
Avg $mil:	56,022

Value Measures		Rel Category
Price/Earnings	14.28	0.91
Price/Book	2.43	0.95
Price/Sales	1.41	1.14
Price/Cash Flow	9.90	1.07
Dividend Yield %	1.82	0.96

Growth Measures	%	Rel Category
Long-Term Erngs	—	—
Book Value	7.92	0.86
Sales	7.73	0.94
Cash Flow	8.22	0.94
Historical Erngs	17.17	1.03

Profitability	%	Rel Category
Return on Equity	22.20	1.00
Return on Assets	8.54	1.02
Net Margin	14.20	1.16

Sector Weightings	% of Stocks	Rel S&P 500	3 Year High	3 Year Low
Info	21.00	1.01		
Software	4.16	1.00	5	3
Hardware	10.26	1.00	11	9
Media	2.93	1.01	4	3
Telecom	3.65	1.01	4	3
Service	40.86	1.01		
Health	12.08	1.00	14	12
Consumer	6.82	1.01	9	7
Business	4.44	1.01	5	3
Financial	17.52	1.01	22	18
Mfg	38.14	0.99		
Goods	9.21	1.01	9	8
Ind Mtrls	12.91	0.99	13	12
Energy	12.33	0.98	12	8
Utilities	3.69	1.00	4	3

Composition

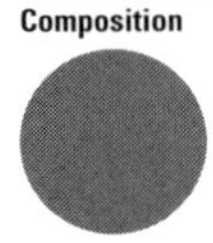

Cash	0.7
Stocks	99.3
Bonds	0.0
Other	0.0
Foreign (% of Stock)	0.0

Morningstar's Take by Sonya Morris 12-31-07

We require only a modest margin of safety to invest here.

Many investors turn to this ETF for broad exposure to U.S. stocks, but they also get a high-quality portfolio to boot. The fund's benchmark, the ubiquitous S&P 500 Index, ranks its stocks by market capitalization. Thus, the biggest U.S. corporations hold sway here.

A number of these firms have trenched out durable competitive advantages, which our analysts refer to as economic moats. For instance, ExxonMobil's massive scale and impressive operational efficiencies help insulate it from the vagaries of commodity price fluctuations. General Electric is a global titan that possesses a diversified portfolio of strong underlying businesses, many of which are leaders in their industries. Microsoft's deeply entrenched position as the world's leading software provider has turned it into a cash-generating machine. All told, almost half of the portfolio is dedicated to wide-moat firms.

The portfolio's high quality also influences its risk profile. Because wide-moat firms' competitive advantages make them harder to dislodge from their industry-leading positions, their results tend to be more predictable. Take Cisco Systems, whose business is fortified by customers' reluctance to switch network equipment vendors for fear of potentially disrupting data systems upon which they're heavily reliant. This, in turn, should ensure that Cisco's growth follows a less-jagged trajectory than is typical for tech and telecom companies. Cisco is hardly alone in this regard: 400 of the 480 portfolio holdings that we cover are rated average or below-average risk by our analysts.

Taken together with the portfolio's wide diversification across stocks and industries, these traits have made for a relatively smooth ride, as this ETF hasn't experienced a lot of turbulence. For that reason, we'd be willing to recommend it at a modest margin of safety: An 8%-plus discount to our fair value estimate is sufficient.

Address:	45 Fremont Street United States 800-474-2737
Web Address:	www.ishares.com
Inception:	05-15-00*
Advisor:	Barclays Global Fund Advisers

Management Fee:	0.09%		
Expense Projections:	3Yr:$30	5Yr:$53	10Yr:$121
Income Distrib:	Quarterly		
Exchange:	NYSE		

iShares SP 500 Growth IVW

Market Price	Mstar Category
$69.83	Large Growth

Morningstar Rating	Return	Risk	Yield	NAV	Avg Daily Vol. (k)	52 wk High/Low
★★	Below Avg	Low	1.2%	$69.89	906	$72.72 - $62.76

Morningstar Fair Value

Price/Fair Value Ratio	Coverage Rate %
0.94	100

Valuation

This ETF is loaded with blue-chip growth stocks, many of which enjoy the protection of an economic moat. It's widely diversified across stocks and sectors, putting a lid on volatility. Given this profile, we'd require only an 8% margin of safety to invest here. The fund was recently skirting that mark, at a 10% discount to our fair value

Methodology

This fund tracks the S&P 500/Citigroup Growth Index. S&P uses seven growth and valuation measures to classify the S&P 500's stocks into value, core, or growth buckets: dividend yield; price/book; price/sales; price/cash flow; and five-year earnings, sales, and internal growth rates. Stocks are allocated in equal thirds among the value, core, and growth buckets, but stocks in the middle can end up in both style indexes in proportion to their style scores. The overlap should reduce turnover caused by stocks moving from one style to another. Like other growth funds, technology and health-care stocks play prominent roles here.

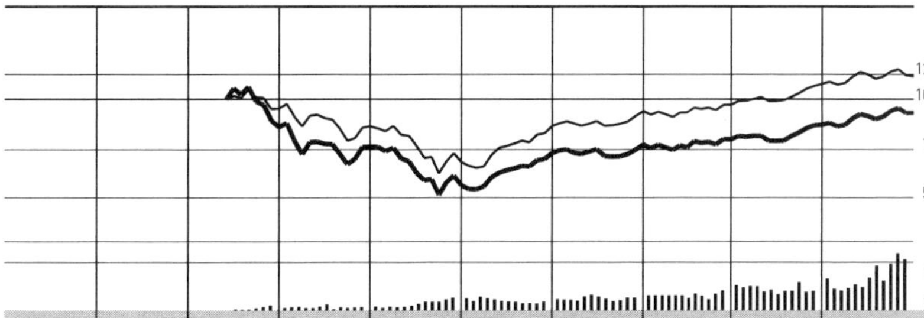

1998	1999	2000	2001	2002	2003	2004	2005	2006	2007	History
—	—	68.67	59.41	44.89	55.62	57.90	59.33	64.93	69.89	NAV $
—	—	68.25	59.31	44.91	55.60	57.75	59.28	64.92	69.83	Market Price $
—	—	-0.98*	-12.87	-23.71	25.42	5.91	3.81	10.81	8.93	NAV Return%
—	—	-0.99*	-12.48	-23.55	25.32	5.68	3.99	10.89	8.84	Market Price Return%
—	—	-0.28	-0.03	0.05	0.00	0.05	0.08	0.06	0.04	Avg Premium/Discount%
—	—	—	-0.98	-1.61	-3.26	-4.97	-1.10	-4.98	3.44	NAV Rtrn% +/-S&P 500
—	—	—	3.25	4.39	-1.66	-1.06	2.67	-0.20	-0.20	NAV Rtrn% +/-S&P 500 Gr
—	—	—	17	34	100	83	38	25	77	NAV Return% Rank in Cat
—	—	—	0.59	0.81	1.36	1.77	1.30	1.30	1.26	Income Return %
—	—	—	-13.46	-24.52	24.06	4.14	2.51	9.51	7.67	Capital Return %
—	—	0.15	0.40	0.48	0.61	0.98	0.75	0.77	0.81	Income $
—	—	0.11	0.00	0.00	0.00	0.00	0.00	0.00	0.00	Capital Gains $
—	—	—	0.18	0.18	0.18	0.18	0.18	0.18	0.18	Expense Ratio %
—	—	—	0.45	0.82	1.19	1.22	1.93	1.28	1.35	Income Ratio %
—	—	—	31	28	17	14	22	12	23	Turnover Rate %
—	—	130	398	637	1,296	2,157	3,242	4,360	6,622	Net Assets $mil

Performance 12-31-07

Historic Quarterly NAV Returns

	1st Qtr	2nd Qtr	3rd Qtr	4th Qtr	Total
2003	-0.85	12.09	2.70	9.88	25.42
2004	-0.03	2.63	-4.80	8.44	5.91
2005	-1.89	0.08	3.74	1.92	3.81
2006	2.58	-3.50	6.01	5.60	10.81
2007	-0.14	6.57	3.71	-1.31	8.93

Trailing	NAV Return%	Market Return%	NAV Rtrn% +/-S&P 500	%Rank Cat.(NAV)
3 Mo	-1.31	-1.58	2.02	47
6 Mo	2.35	2.26	3.72	65
1 Yr	8.93	8.84	3.44	77
3 Yr Avg	7.81	7.87	-0.81	45
5 Yr Avg	10.73	10.70	-2.10	80
10 Yr Avg	—	—	—	—

Tax Analysis	Tax-Adj Return%	Tax-Cost Ratio
3 Yr (estimated)	7.34	0.44
5 Yr (estimated)	10.21	0.47
10 Yr (estimated)	—	—

Rating and Risk

Time Period	Morningstar Rtn vs Cat	Morningstar Risk vs Cat	Morningstar Risk-Adj Rating
3 Yr	Avg	Low	★★★
5 Yr	-Avg	Low	★★
10 Yr	—	—	—

Other Measures	Standard Index S&P 500	Best Fit Index Mstar Large Cap TR
Alpha	-0.7	-1.2
Beta	0.99	1.02
R-Squared	94	94
Standard Deviation	7.94	
Mean	7.81	
Sharpe Ratio	0.45	

Portfolio Analysis 12-31-07

Share change since 11-07 Total Stocks:300	Sector	PE	Tot Ret%	% Assets
⊕ ExxonMobil Corporation	Energy	13.6	24.34	7.73
⊕ Microsoft Corporation	Software	23.4	20.83	4.33
⊕ Johnson & Johnson	Health	18.8	3.61	2.89
⊕ Apple, Inc.	Hardware	50.5	133.47	2.62
⊕ Cisco Systems, Inc.	Hardware	21.5	-0.95	2.48
⊕ Google, Inc.	Business	54.0	50.17	2.42
⊖ Procter & Gamble Company	Goods	23.1	16.63	2.35
☆ ConocoPhillips	Energy	13.8	25.42	2.14
⊕ PepsiCo, Inc.	Goods	20.4	23.89	1.85
⊕ Schlumberger, Ltd.	Energy	24.6	57.10	1.78
⊕ Chevron Corporation	Energy	11.4	30.59	1.70
⊖ International Business M	Hardware	16.2	13.20	1.60
⊕ Oracle Corporation	Software	24.8	31.74	1.35
⊕ Intel Corporation	Hardware	25.4	34.22	1.34
⊕ UnitedHealth Group, Inc.	Health	17.4	8.38	1.14
⊖ American International G	Financial	10.2	-17.96	1.08
⊕ Coca-Cola Company	Goods	26.3	30.44	1.07
⊕ Qualcomm, Inc.	Hardware	20.2	5.52	0.98
⊖ Wal-Mart Stores, Inc.	Consumer	15.4	4.91	0.97
⊕ American Express Company	Financial	14.9	-13.18	0.92

Current Investment Style

Value Blnd Growth — Large / Mid / Small (Large Growth)

Market Cap	%
Giant	54.0
Large	35.6
Mid	10.3
Small	0.1
Micro	0.0

Avg $mil: 63,283

Value Measures		Rel Category
Price/Earnings	15.71	0.81
Price/Book	3.34	0.99
Price/Sales	1.65	0.94
Price/Cash Flow	11.14	0.96
Dividend Yield %	1.12	1.32

Growth Measures	%	Rel Category
Long-Term Erngs	—	—
Book Value	11.71	1.15
Sales	10.96	1.13
Cash Flow	13.54	1.25
Historical Erngs	21.22	1.18

Profitability	%	Rel Category
Return on Equity	25.96	1.13
Return on Assets	11.46	1.19
Net Margin	14.37	1.11

Sector Weightings	% of Stocks	Rel S&P 500	3 Year High	3 Year Low
Info	23.74	1.14		
Software	7.59	1.83	8	5
Hardware	14.26	1.40	15	11
Media	1.81	0.62	3	1
Telecom	0.08	0.02	1	0
Service	35.13	0.86		
Health	14.39	1.20	22	14
Consumer	8.08	1.19	13	8
Business	5.44	1.23	6	3
Financial	7.22	0.41	11	2
Mfg	41.14	1.07		
Goods	9.69	1.06	16	10
Ind Mtrls	10.43	0.80	16	6
Energy	20.48	1.62	20	8
Utilities	0.54	0.15	1	1

Composition

Cash	0.4
Stocks	99.6
Bonds	0.0
Other	0.0
Foreign (% of Stock)	0.0

Morningstar's Take by Sonya Morris 12-31-07

We'd gladly scoop up shares of iShares S&P 500 Growth when they are trading at an 8% or greater discount to our fair value estimate.

This ETF, which tracks the S&P 500/Citigroup Growth Index, boasts a high-quality portfolio of industry leaders with solid growth characteristics. Consider Cisco Systems, which has generated 18% annualized revenue and earnings growth over the past decade. That profile holds across the portfolio, whose typical stock has posted nearly 20% annualized profit growth in the recent past.

Of course, growth is no guarantee of staying power. However, quality is not in short supply here. For example, Procter & Gamble's well-branded product portfolio is virtually without peer. In addition to Procter, other wide-moat holdings boast prized attributes like strong brand recognition (PepsiCo), patent protection (Medtronic), or leverage over suppliers (Wal-Mart). All told, wide-moat firms account for more than 60% of this ETF's portfolio--considerably higher than most diversified large-growth ETFs, which typically allocate less than half of their assets to such firms.

On balance, this ETF's holdings are not especially risky, either. That's not a coincidence, as competitive advantages--which abound in this portfolio--lend stability to a firm's business. Take Johnson & Johnson, whose diverse portfolio of top-tier businesses has generated healthy cash flow for decades. Similarly, hefty switching costs should keep Cisco Systems' customer base captive, thereby smoothing that firm's growth trajectory. All told, our analysts consider only a fraction of the 304 portfolio holdings that they cover to be above-average risks.

When coupled with the portfolio's wide diversification across names and industries, these traits have kept a lid on volatility. Consequently, we'd invest here at a modest margin of safety; an 8% or larger discount to our fair value estimate would suffice.

Address:	45 Fremont Street United States 800-474-2737
Web Address:	www.ishares.com
Inception:	05-22-00 *
Advisor:	Barclays Global Fund Advisers

Management Fee:	0.18%		
Expense Projections:	3Yr:$58	5Yr:$101	10Yr:$230
Income Distrib:	Quarterly		
Exchange:	NYSE		

iShares SP 500 Value IVE

Market Price	Mstar Category
$76.36	Large Value

Morningstar Fair Value

Price/Fair Value Ratio	Coverage Rate %
0.84	99

Valuation

This broadly diversified ETF is dominated by market behemoths that enjoy the protection of sizable economic moats. Furthermore, this fund hasn't experienced undue volatility. Thus, we'd be willing buyers at a modest discount (8% or more) to our fair value estimate. The fund was recently trading at a 13% discount to fair value, making it tempting.

Methodology

This fund tracks the S&P 500/Citigroup Value Index, which relies on seven growth and valuation measures (dividend yield; price/book, price/sales and price/cash flow; and five-year earnings, sales, and internal growth) to cull out the value stocks in the S&P 500 Index. As with other value benchmarks, financials play a big role here, consuming almost 30% of assets. Industrial materials, another traditional value sector, accounts for 15% of the portfolio. The index is market-cap weighted and emphasizes huge U.S. corporations. Its average market cap is approximately 15% higher than the typical large-value fund.

Morningstar Rating	Return	Risk	Yield	NAV	Avg Daily Vol. (k)	52 wk High/Low
★★★★	Above Avg	Above Avg	2.3%	$76.63	588	$84.17 - $72.52

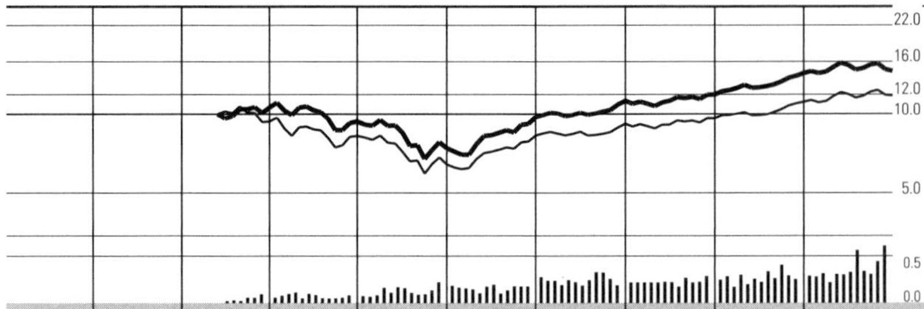

1998	1999	2000	2001	2002	2003	2004	2005	2006	2007	History
—	—	63.63	55.28	42.93	55.42	62.91	65.11	76.92	76.63	NAV $
—	—	63.38	55.28	42.90	55.33	62.88	65.05	76.89	76.36	Market Price $
—	—	5.15*	-11.85	-20.98	31.51	15.51	5.67	20.59	1.86	NAV Return%
—	—	5.10*	-11.50	-21.04	31.39	15.64	5.63	20.65	1.54	Market Price Return%
—	—	0.05	-0.01	-0.02	0.06	0.07	0.02	0.02	0.03	Avg Premium/Discount%
—	—	—	0.04	1.12	2.83	4.63	0.76	4.80	-3.63	NAV Rtrn% +/-S&P 500
—	—	—	-3.67	-4.39	1.15	0.48	-3.04	-0.21	-0.13	NAV Rtrn% +/-S&P 500 Val
—	—	—	100	80	40	57	40	43	42	NAV Return% Rank in Cat
—	—	—	1.31	1.50	2.08	1.85	2.10	2.27	2.32	Income Return %
—	—	—	-13.16	-22.48	29.43	13.66	3.57	18.32	-0.46	Capital Return %
—	—	0.45	0.83	0.83	0.89	1.02	1.31	1.47	1.77	Income $
—	—	0.15	0.00	0.00	0.00	0.00	0.00	0.00	0.00	Capital Gains $
—	—	—	0.18	0.18	0.18	0.18	0.18	0.18	0.18	Expense Ratio %
—	—	—	1.51	1.56	2.01	1.91	1.95	2.12	2.18	Income Ratio %
—	—	—	9	17	22	5	5	7	20	Turnover Rate %
—	—	229	525	702	1,477	2,931	3,015	4,530	4,456	Net Assets $mil

Performance 12-31-07

Historic Quarterly NAV Returns

	1st Qtr	2nd Qtr	3rd Qtr	4th Qtr	Total
2003	-5.54	18.76	2.49	14.38	31.51
2004	3.29	0.76	1.00	9.88	15.51
2005	-2.44	2.54	3.41	2.15	5.67
2006	5.82	0.58	5.23	7.66	20.59
2007	1.29	5.90	0.35	-5.39	1.86

Trailing	NAV Return%	Market Return%	NAV Rtrn% +/-S&P 500	%Rank Cat.(NAV)
3 Mo	-5.39	-5.70	-2.06	46
6 Mo	-5.05	-5.44	-3.68	50
1 Yr	1.86	1.54	-3.63	42
3 Yr Avg	9.08	8.97	0.46	56
5 Yr Avg	14.54	14.48	1.71	1
10 Yr Avg	—	—	—	—

Tax Analysis	Tax-Adj Return%	Tax-Cost Ratio
3 Yr (estimated)	8.28	0.73
5 Yr (estimated)	13.75	0.69
10 Yr (estimated)	—	—

Rating and Risk

Time Period	Morningstar Rtn vs Cat	Morningstar Risk vs Cat	Morningstar Risk-Adj Rating
3 Yr	Avg	Avg	★★★
5 Yr	+Avg	+Avg	★★★★
10 Yr	—	—	—

Other Measures	Standard Index S&P 500	Best Fit Index S&P 500
Alpha	0.4	0.4
Beta	1.01	1.01
R-Squared	94	94
Standard Deviation	8.09	
Mean	9.08	
Sharpe Ratio	0.59	

Portfolio Analysis 12-31-07

Share change since 11-07 Total Stocks:353	Sector	PE	Tot Ret%	% Assets
⊕ General Electric Company	Ind Mtrls	16.6	2.69	5.94
⊕ AT&T, Inc.	Telecom	21.6	20.58	4.00
⊕ Bank of America Corporat	Financial	9.4	-19.25	2.90
⊕ Altria Group Inc.	Goods	13.2	22.10	2.52
⊕ Pfizer Inc.	Health	22.5	-8.15	2.46
⊕ Citigroup, Inc.	Financial	7.9	-44.93	2.33
⊕ J.P. Morgan Chase & Co.	Financial	9.5	-7.24	2.33
⊕ Verizon Communications I	Telecom	21.7	22.19	2.00
⊕ Wells Fargo Company	Financial	11.4	-12.13	1.62
⊖ Chevron Corporation	Energy	11.4	30.59	1.35
⊖ Merck & Co., Inc.	Health	23.6	37.36	1.33
☼ American International G	Financial	10.2	-17.96	1.21
⊕ Wachovia Corporation	Financial	8.6	-29.91	1.19
☼ Procter & Gamble Company	Goods	23.1	16.63	1.15
⊖ Hewlett-Packard Company	Hardware	18.8	23.40	1.10
⊖ Intel Corporation	Hardware	25.4	34.22	1.07
⊕ Time Warner, Inc.	Media	13.4	-23.27	0.95
⊕ Morgan Stanley	Financial	6.1	-20.21	0.90
⊕ Bank of New York Mellon	Financial	21.7	26.51	0.88
⊕ Comcast Corporation A	Media	24.0	-35.29	0.88

Current Investment Style

Value Blnd Growth; Large Mid Small

Market Cap	%
Giant	48.9
Large	37.5
Mid	13.3
Small	0.3
Micro	0.0
Avg $mil: 49,507	

Value Measures		Rel Category
Price/Earnings	13.02	0.96
Price/Book	1.88	0.96
Price/Sales	1.23	1.03
Price/Cash Flow	8.67	1.04
Dividend Yield %	2.56	0.95

Growth Measures	%	Rel Category
Long-Term Erngs	—	—
Book Value	6.02	0.70
Sales	5.51	0.86
Cash Flow	3.39	0.64
Historical Erngs	14.95	0.99

Profitability	%	Rel Category
Return on Equity	18.28	0.93
Return on Assets	5.47	0.85
Net Margin	14.02	1.01

Sector Weightings	% of Stocks	Rel S&P 500	3 Year High	3 Year Low
Info	18.17	0.87		
Software	0.59	0.14	3	1
Hardware	6.05	0.59	8	5
Media	4.10	1.41	7	4
Telecom	7.43	2.05	7	5
Service	46.76	1.15		
Health	9.66	0.80	10	4
Consumer	5.47	0.81	6	4
Business	3.36	0.76	3	3
Financial	28.27	1.62	39	28
Mfg	35.06	0.91		
Goods	8.75	0.96	9	2
Ind Mtrls	15.47	1.19	18	9
Energy	3.78	0.30	10	4
Utilities	7.06	1.92	7	6

Composition

Cash	0.7
Stocks	99.3
Bonds	0.0
Other	0.0
Foreign (% of Stock)	0.0

Morningstar's Take by Sonya Morris 12-31-07

We're comfortable recommending iShares S&P 500 Value Index at a modest discount to our fair value estimate.

This ETF's benchmark applies seven different style factors to the S&P 500 Index to ferret out value stocks. Like most value indexes, it favors the financial sector, which consumes almost 30% of this ETF's portfolio. Its top-holdings list is peppered with banks that our analysts think possess wide "economic moats," such as Citigroup, Bank of America, and Wells Fargo.

To earn a wide-moat rating from our analysts, a firm must possess a durable competitive edge that allows it to wring out above-average returns over the long haul. In the banking industry, scale is a key competitive advantage. Witness Citigroup's massive global footprint. Similarly, Bank of America has a huge deposit base and the largest market share of any U.S. bank.

But this ETF's allocation to wide-moat stocks isn't confined to global financial stocks. Indeed, wide-moat stocks soak up more than one third of the portfolio and include the likes of Coca-Cola (which benefits from brand recognition across the globe), General Electric (which owns a diversified portfolio of industry leading businesses), and United Parcel Service (which has created a complex and efficient global shipping network that is difficult to duplicate).

Buoyed by stabilizing attributes like recurring demand, scale, barriers to entry, or customer switching costs, the results of competitively dominant firms typically don't run to extremes. Given the prominence of wide-moat firms in this portfolio, it's therefore not too surprising that only 11% of the fund's assets are allocated to stocks that our analysts consider above-average risks. That risk profile, coupled with the fund's wide diversification across stocks and industries, has tamped down volatility. As such, we wouldn't demand an especially large margin of safety before recommending the fund.

Address:	45 Fremont Street United States 800-474-2737
Web Address:	www.ishares.com
Inception:	05-22-00*
Advisor:	Barclays Global Fund Advisers

Management Fee:	0.18%		
Expense Projections:	3Yr:$58	5Yr:$101	10Yr:$230
Income Distrib:	Quarterly		
Exchange:	NYSE		

iShares SP MidCap400 IJH

Market Price	Mstar Category
$84.94	Mid-Cap Blend

Morningstar Fair Value

Price/Fair Value Ratio	Coverage Rate %
0.95	85

Valuation

Though this fund's portfolio includes its fair share of low-quality, above-average risk stocks, its broad diversification has helped to keep a lid on volatility. As such, we'd recommend it when it's trading at least 8% below our fair value estimate. The fund was recently trading at a 5% discount to fair value, which isn't enough to entice.

Methodology

This index-based offering mirrors the holdings and performance of the S&P MidCap 400 Index, which represents the universe of midsized U.S. companies, defined as those with market caps between $1.5 and $5.5 billion. The resulting portfolio is broadly diversified across stocks (which are market-cap weighted) and sectors. The benchmark is compiled and maintained by the S&P index committee. Constituents must have a record of at least four profitable quarters and good liquidity to be eligible.

Morningstar Rating	Return	Risk	Yield	NAV	Avg Daily Vol. (k)	52 wk High/Low
★★★	Average	Average	1.3%	$85.42	443	$92.23 - $79.28

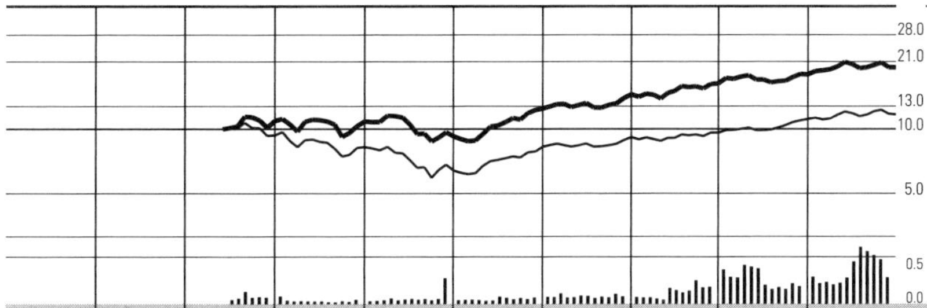

1998	1999	2000	2001	2002	2003	2004	2005	2006	2007	History
—	—	51.56	50.78	42.99	57.60	66.36	73.76	80.25	85.42	NAV $
—	—	51.64	50.58	42.93	57.53	66.16	73.80	80.17	84.94	Market Price $
—	—	9.52*	-0.68	-14.70	35.36	16.29	12.48	10.13	7.80	NAV Return%
—	—	9.44*	-1.24	-14.47	35.37	16.09	12.88	9.97	7.30	Market Price Return%
—	—	0.05	-0.07	0.00	-0.03	-0.02	-0.01	0.00	0.00	Avg Premium/Discount%
—	—	—	11.21	7.40	6.68	5.41	7.57	-5.66	2.31	NAV Rtrn% +/-S&P 500
—	—	—	-0.07	-0.17	-0.26	-0.19	-0.08	-0.19	-0.18	NAV Rtrn% +/-S&P 400 TR
—	—	—	100	1	67	75	34	71	32	NAV Return% Rank in Cat
—	—	—	0.77	0.71	1.17	1.00	1.26	1.29	1.38	Income Return %
—	—	—	-1.45	-15.41	34.19	15.29	11.22	8.84	6.42	Capital Return %
—	—	0.24	0.40	0.36	0.50	0.57	0.83	0.95	1.10	Income $
—	—	0.15	0.00	0.00	0.00	0.00	0.00	0.00	0.00	Capital Gains $
—	—	—	0.20	0.20	0.20	0.20	0.20	0.20	0.20	Expense Ratio %
—	—	—	0.86	0.87	0.98	1.02	1.21	1.19	1.44	Income Ratio %
—	—	—	32	14	12	11	10	9	12	Turnover Rate %
—	—	217	457	1,221	1,411	2,323	3,389	4,189	4,873	Net Assets $mil

Performance 12-31-07

Historic Quarterly NAV Returns

	1st Qtr	2nd Qtr	3rd Qtr	4th Qtr	Total
2003	-4.47	17.58	6.52	13.14	35.36
2004	5.01	0.93	-2.13	12.11	16.29
2005	-0.44	4.34	4.84	3.28	12.48
2006	7.67	-3.22	-1.12	6.90	10.13
2007	5.75	5.74	-0.95	-2.68	7.80

Trailing	NAV Return%	Market Return%	NAV Rtrn% +/-S&P 500	%Rank Cat.(NAV)
3 Mo	-2.68	-3.37	0.65	46
6 Mo	-3.60	-4.33	-2.23	34
1 Yr	7.80	7.30	2.31	32
3 Yr Avg	10.12	10.03	1.50	50
5 Yr Avg	16.02	15.92	3.19	67
10 Yr Avg	—	—	—	—

Tax Analysis	Tax-Adj Return%	Tax-Cost Ratio
3 Yr (estimated)	9.65	0.43
5 Yr (estimated)	15.56	0.40
10 Yr (estimated)	—	—

Rating and Risk

Time Period	Morningstar Rtn vs Cat	Morningstar Risk vs Cat	Morningstar Risk-Adj Rating
3 Yr	+Avg	Avg	★★★★
5 Yr	Avg	Avg	★★★
10 Yr	—	—	—

Other Measures	Standard Index S&P 500	Best Fit Index S&P 400 TR
Alpha	0.8	-0.1
Beta	1.18	1.00
R-Squared	76	100
Standard Deviation	10.50	
Mean	10.12	
Sharpe Ratio	0.56	

Portfolio Analysis 12-31-07

Share change since 11-07 Total Stocks:399	Sector	PE	Tot Ret%	% Assets
⊕ Intuitive Surgical, Inc.	Health	NMF	236.67	1.09
⊕ Cameron International Co	Energy	23.5	81.45	0.93
⊕ Southwestern Energy Comp	Energy	52.1	58.97	0.84
⊕ Activision	Software	57.1	72.27	0.76
⊕ Hologic, Inc.	Health	39.8	45.18	0.76
⊖ Harris Corporation	Hardware	17.6	37.98	0.76
⊕ Amphenol Corporation	Hardware	25.6	49.63	0.73
⊕ FMC Technologies, Inc.	Energy	27.5	84.00	0.65
⊕ Denbury Resources, Inc.	Energy	36.9	114.11	0.64
⊖ Joy Global, Inc.	Ind Mtrls	26.3	37.82	0.63
⊖ Grant Prideco, Inc.	Energy	13.6	39.58	0.62
⊕ Newfield Exploration Com	Energy	24.8	14.69	0.61
⊖ DENTSPLY International,	Health	27.5	51.46	0.60
⊖ Telephone and Data Syste	Telecom	26.9	15.96	0.59
⊕ Western Digital Corporat	Hardware	12.9	47.76	0.59
⊕ KBR, Inc.	Business	29.9	48.32	0.58
⊕ Equitable Resources, Inc	Energy	24.7	29.86	0.57
⊕ Energizer Holdings, Inc.	Goods	20.4	57.95	0.57
⊖ Arch Coal, Inc.	Energy	37.5	50.79	0.57
⊖ Everest Re Group, Ltd.	Financial	6.2	4.27	0.56

Current Investment Style

Value Blnd Growth; Large Mid Small

Market Cap	%
Giant	0.0
Large	0.0
Mid	81.4
Small	18.1
Micro	0.6
Avg $mil: 3,561	

Value Measures		Rel Category
Price/Earnings	14.10	0.88
Price/Book	2.02	0.90
Price/Sales	1.10	0.95
Price/Cash Flow	8.05	0.94
Dividend Yield %	1.33	0.81

Growth Measures	%	Rel Category
Long-Term Erngs	—	—
Book Value	8.46	1.01
Sales	5.99	1.43
Cash Flow	4.86	18.69
Historical Erngs	13.89	0.75

Profitability	%	Rel Category
Return on Equity	16.68	0.85
Return on Assets	7.14	0.92
Net Margin	11.61	0.96

Sector Weightings	% of Stocks	Rel S&P 500	3 Year High	3 Year Low
Info	12.97	0.62		
Software	3.32	0.80	4	3
Hardware	7.92	0.78	9	7
Media	0.74	0.25	3	1
Telecom	0.99	0.27	1	0
Service	48.22	1.19		
Health	12.80	1.06	13	10
Consumer	9.05	1.33	16	9
Business	11.68	2.65	13	10
Financial	14.69	0.84	19	14
Mfg	38.79	1.01		
Goods	5.78	0.63	7	4
Ind Mtrls	15.73	1.21	16	8
Energy	10.29	0.82	12	8
Utilities	6.99	1.90	8	6

Composition

Cash	0.4
Stocks	99.4
Bonds	0.0
Other	0.2
Foreign (% of Stock)	0.0

Morningstar's Take by Sonya Morris 12-31-07

We'd recommend iShares S&P Mid-Cap 400 at an 8% or greater discount to our fair value estimate.

This ETF focuses on stocks with market caps between $1.5 billion and $5.5 billion. Midsized firms don't often possess the economies of scale or market share of their larger counterparts. Yet, many mid-caps have managed to trench out at least a narrow economic moat. For instance, narrow-moat natural-gas explorer Southwestern Energy lacks the scale and diversified operations of a major oil company. But it has assembled a portfolio of onshore natural-gas fields with long production lives that has led to steady production gains.

Even though few of the firms represented in this ETF could be considered industry leaders, our analysts believe that a slim majority of the 313 portfolio holdings that they cover enjoy the protection of an economic moat, with 6% of those names boasting a wide moat. But, on balance, this portfolio's quality is mixed.

It's also a mixed bag from a risk standpoint. Higher-quality firms, which benefit from advantages like customer switching costs, high barriers to entry, or network effects tend to generate cash in a more predictable manner, mitigating business risk in the process. Yet, as noted, the portfolio is also home to its fair share of mediocre and below-average businesses, such as YRC Worldwide, which lacks a moat absent the scale needed to compete in the shipping business. What's more, YRC's asset- and labor-intensive business model makes its future prospects more uncertain, explaining why our analysts consider the firm an above-average risk. Though stocks like YRC don't abound, most of the fund's holdings court at least average business risk.

That said, because this ETF is so broadly diversified, volatility hasn't been extreme. Thus, we'd be buyers of the shares when they trade at an 8% or greater discount to our fair value estimate.

Address:	45 Fremont Street United States 800-474-2737
Web Address:	www.ishares.com
Inception:	05-22-00 *
Advisor:	Barclays Global Fund Advisers

Management Fee:	0.20%		
Expense Projections:	3Yr:$64	5Yr:$113	10Yr:$255
Income Distrib:	Quarterly		
Exchange:	NYSE		

iShares SP 400 Growth IJK

Market Price	Mstar Category
$89.12	Mid-Cap Growth

Morningstar Fair Value

Price/Fair Value Ratio	Coverage Rate %
1.00	88

Valuation

Although this ETF's portfolio isn't pristine from either a risk or a quality perspective, its broad diversification has mitigated volatility. As a result, we'd require only a modest margin of safety (8% or greater discount to our fair value estimate) to recommend it. The fund was recently trading at a 4% discount to our fair value estimate.

Methodology

This ETF tracks the S&P MidCap 400/Citigroup Growth Index. The bogy relies on seven growth and valuation measures to classify stocks: dividend yield; price/book, price/sales and price/cash flow; and five-year earnings, sales, and internal growth rates. A third of the index's market capitalization ends up in the value, core, or growth bucket, but stocks in the middle can end up in both style indexes in proportion to their style scores. The overlap should reduce turnover caused by stocks shifting styles.

Morningstar Rating	Return	Risk	Yield	NAV	Avg Daily Vol. (k)	52 wk High/Low
★★★	Average	Low	0.8%	$89.67	150	$94.00 - $79.59

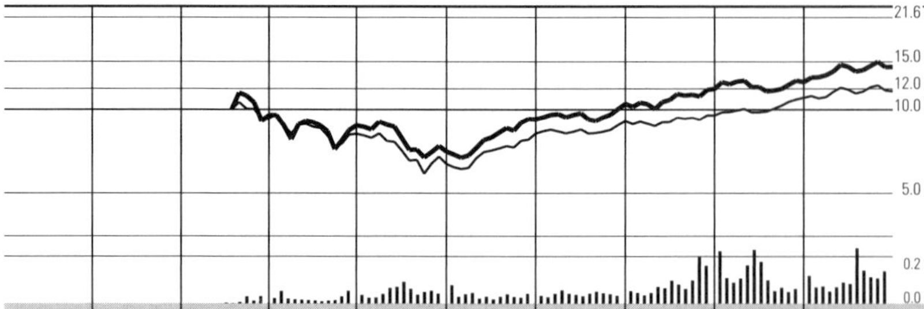

Growth of $10,000
— Investment Value of ETF
— Investment Value of Index S&P 500

Trading Volume Millions

History

1998	1999	2000	2001	2002	2003	2004	2005	2006	2007	History
—	—	61.95	56.79	45.66	59.42	67.25	75.73	79.77	89.67	NAV $
—	—	61.94	56.98	45.69	59.35	67.20	75.62	79.71	89.12	Market Price $
—	—	4.30*	-8.22	-19.40	30.66	13.71	13.31	5.75	13.35	NAV Return%
—	—	4.21*	-7.92	-19.61	30.42	13.76	13.23	5.82	12.73	Market Price Return%
—	—	-0.08	0.10	0.09	0.05	0.00	-0.03	-0.08	-0.05	Avg Premium/Discount%
—	—	—	3.67	2.70	1.98	2.83	8.40	-10.04	7.86	NAV Rtrn% +/-S&P 500
—	—	—	-5.67	0.27	-6.66	-2.07	-1.11	-0.06	-0.15	NAV Rtrn% +/-S&P Mid Gr
—	—	—	1	1	100	34	25	83	46	NAV Return% Rank in Cat
—	—	—	0.09	0.21	0.46	0.49	0.65	0.40	0.90	Income Return %
—	—	—	-8.31	-19.61	30.20	13.22	12.66	5.35	12.45	Capital Return %
—	—	0.00	0.05	0.12	0.21	0.29	0.44	0.31	0.72	Income $
—	—	0.23	0.00	0.00	0.00	0.00	0.00	0.00	0.00	Capital Gains $
—	—	—	0.25	0.25	0.25	0.25	0.25	0.25	0.25	Expense Ratio %
—	—	—	0.06	0.15	0.31	0.45	0.56	0.60	0.85	Income Ratio %
—	—	—	67	50	58	37	34	24	36	Turnover Rate %
—	—	93	250	352	612	1,083	1,787	1,751	2,314	Net Assets $mil

Performance 12-31-07

Historic Quarterly NAV Returns

	1st Qtr	2nd Qtr	3rd Qtr	4th Qtr	Total
2003	-3.07	15.95	5.92	9.76	30.66
2004	4.50	0.71	-3.48	11.94	13.71
2005	-0.13	3.60	4.32	4.98	13.31
2006	6.29	-4.43	-1.71	5.92	5.75
2007	5.87	7.17	0.70	-0.80	13.35

Trailing	NAV Return%	Market Return%	NAV Rtrn% +/-S&P 500	%Rank Cat.(NAV)
3 Mo	-0.80	-1.32	2.53	27
6 Mo	-0.10	-0.92	1.27	60
1 Yr	13.35	12.73	7.86	46
3 Yr Avg	10.74	10.54	2.12	75
5 Yr Avg	15.07	14.92	2.24	100
10 Yr Avg	—	—	—	—

Tax Analysis	Tax-Adj Return%	Tax-Cost Ratio
3 Yr (estimated)	10.51	0.21
5 Yr (estimated)	14.86	0.18
10 Yr (estimated)	—	—

Rating and Risk

Time Period	Morningstar Rtn vs Cat	Morningstar Risk vs Cat	Morningstar Risk-Adj Rating
3 Yr	Avg	-Avg	★★★
5 Yr	Avg	Low	★★★
10 Yr	—	—	—

Other Measures	Standard Index S&P 500	Best Fit Index S&P 400 TR
Alpha	1.4	0.4
Beta	1.19	1.01
R-Squared	73	97
Standard Deviation	10.74	
Mean	10.74	
Sharpe Ratio	0.61	

Portfolio Analysis 12-31-07

Share change since 11-07 Total Stocks:236	Sector	PE	Tot Ret%	% Assets
⊕ Intuitive Surgical, Inc.	Health	NMF	236.67	2.19
⊕ Cameron International Co	Energy	23.5	81.45	1.86
⊕ Southwestern Energy Comp	Energy	52.1	58.97	1.68
⊕ Hologic, Inc.	Health	39.8	45.18	1.52
⊕ Harris Corporation	Hardware	17.6	37.98	1.52
⊕ Amphenol Corporation	Hardware	25.6	49.63	1.46
⊕ FMC Technologies, Inc.	Energy	27.5	84.00	1.30
⊕ Denbury Resources, Inc.	Energy	36.9	114.11	1.28
⊕ Joy Global, Inc.	Ind Mtrls	26.3	37.82	1.25
⊕ Grant Prideco, Inc.	Energy	13.6	39.58	1.24
⊕ Newfield Exploration Com	Energy	24.8	14.69	1.22
⊕ Western Digital Corporat	Hardware	12.9	47.76	1.17
⊕ Energizer Holdings, Inc.	Goods	20.4	57.95	1.13
⊕ McAfee, Inc.	Software	32.9	32.14	1.05
⊕ Alliance Data Systems Co	Business	35.8	20.04	1.05
⊕ Pioneer Natural Resource	Energy	29.2	23.83	1.03
⊖ Steel Dynamics, Inc.	Ind Mtrls	14.7	85.99	1.02
⊕ Eaton Vance Corporation	Financial	42.9	39.33	0.99
⊕ Covance, Inc.	Health	34.4	47.04	0.97
⊕ Henry Schein, Inc.	Health	25.1	25.36	0.97

Current Investment Style

Value Blnd Growth; Large Mid Small

Market Cap	%
Giant	0.0
Large	0.0
Mid	87.2
Small	12.6
Micro	0.2

Avg $mil: 4,179

Value Measures		Rel Category
Price/Earnings	13.54	0.71
Price/Book	2.97	0.94
Price/Sales	1.50	0.97
Price/Cash Flow	10.15	0.94
Dividend Yield %	0.44	0.77

Growth Measures	%	Rel Category
Long-Term Erngs	—	—
Book Value	12.19	1.08
Sales	12.06	1.13
Cash Flow	10.87	1.13
Historical Erngs	22.72	1.05

Profitability	%	Rel Category
Return on Equity	20.87	0.97
Return on Assets	9.58	0.99
Net Margin	11.46	1.03

Sector Weightings	% of Stocks	Rel S&P 500	3 Year High	3 Year Low
Info	13.09	0.63		
Software	3.90	0.94	6	4
Hardware	8.30	0.81	10	7
Media	0.64	0.22	3	1
Telecom	0.25	0.07	0	0
Service	50.26	1.24		
Health	19.83	1.65	20	15
Consumer	12.24	1.81	22	12
Business	13.41	3.04	17	12
Financial	4.78	0.27	13	5
Mfg	36.65	0.95		
Goods	4.89	0.53	7	4
Ind Mtrls	16.36	1.26	16	4
Energy	15.20	1.20	16	9
Utilities	0.20	0.05	1	0

Composition

Cash	0.3
Stocks	99.7
Bonds	0.0
Other	0.0
Foreign (% of Stock)	0.0

Morningstar's Take by Sonya Morris 12-31-07

IShares S&P Mid-Cap 400 Growth Index's broad diversification offsets its mixed risk profile. We'd be buyers at an 8% or greater discount to our fair value estimate.

In this ETF's portfolio, high-quality stocks rub elbows with lesser fare. The fund holds a handful of wide-moat companies (which comprise 10% of assets) like Dun & Bradstreet, which has compiled a vast database of business information that would be very difficult for rivals to duplicate. But the portfolio also allocates a fourth of its assets to no-moat firms, like hard drive manufacturer Western Digital, which lacks the scale or market share to gain any pricing power in a brutally competitive industry.

Most of the holdings reside somewhere between these two extremes. Just over half of the fund's assets are dedicated to firms that have narrow economic moats. Narrow-moat firms enjoy certain competitive advantages, but they're typically less durable than those of the most-dominant firms. Take video game manufacturer Activision. Many of its titles have developed a loyal following among video gamers, but most of those games are based on licensed content that is vulnerable to competitive forces.

This portfolio is middling from a risk perspective as well. Given their vulnerability to rivals, the results of narrow and no-moat businesses tend to be less predictable than those of their wide-moat counterparts. Consequently, most such companies court at least average business-risk, meaning that our analysts believe there's a moderate chance their fair value estimate could be imprecise. Not surprisingly, average-risk stocks soak up roughly 70% of this portfolio.

Nevertheless, with assets spread over hundreds of stocks spanning disparate industries, the fund hasn't been especially volatile. Accordingly, we require only a modest margin of safety to invest here, with an 8% or greater discount to our fair value estimate sufficing.

Address:	45 Fremont Street United States 800-474-2737
Web Address:	www.ishares.com
Inception:	07-24-00 *
Advisor:	Barclays Global Fund Advisers

Management Fee:	0.25%		
Expense Projections:	3Yr:$80	5Yr:$141	10Yr:$318
Income Distrib:	Quarterly		
Exchange:	NYSE		

iShares SP 400 Value IJJ

Market Price $79.56 | **Mstar Category** Mid-Cap Value

Morningstar Fair Value

Price/Fair Value Ratio	Coverage Rate %
0.91	82

Valuation

This ETF's portfolio is of middling quality. However, it's broadly diversified across stocks and industries, which has tamped volatility. Accordingly, we'd be buyers of this fund when it dips 8% or more below our fair value estimate. It was recently trading at a 6% discount to fair value, which isn't deep enough to get us interested.

Methodology

This fund tracks the S&P MidCap 400/Citigroup Value Index. The bogy relies on seven growth and valuation measures to classify stocks. The factors are dividend yield; price/book, price/sales, and price/cash flow; and five-year earnings, sales, and internal growth rates. A third of the index's market capitalization ends up in the value, core, or growth bucket, but stocks in the middle zone can end up in both style indexes in proportion to their style scores. The overlap should reduce turnover caused by stocks moving from one style to another.

Morningstar Rating	Return	Risk	Yield	NAV	Avg Daily Vol. (k)	52 wk High/Low
★★★	Average	Above Avg	1.7%	$79.80	115	$90.23 - $73.72

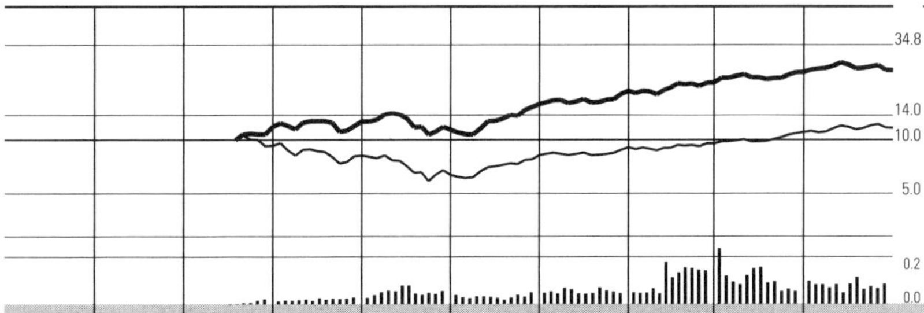

Growth of $10,000
— Investment Value of ETF
— Investment Value of Index S&P 500

Trading Volume Millions

History

1998	1999	2000	2001	2002	2003	2004	2005	2006	2007	History
—	—	42.69	45.13	39.94	55.01	64.42	70.60	79.22	79.80	NAV $
—	—	42.75	45.24	39.99	55.20	64.25	70.49	79.73	79.56	Market Price $
—	—	12.93*	7.05	-10.36	39.79	18.65	11.47	14.33	2.42	NAV Return%
—	—	12.88*	7.16	-10.46	40.05	17.94	11.59	15.25	1.46	Market Price Return%
—	—	0.28	0.01	0.15	0.10	-0.07	-0.01	0.05	-0.03	Avg Premium/Discount%
—	—	—	18.94	11.74	11.11	7.77	6.56	-1.46	-3.07	NAV Rtrn% +/-S&P 500
—	—	—	5.62	-0.93	5.99	1.47	0.70	-0.29	-0.23	NAV Rtrn% +/-S&P Mid Val
—	—	—	1	100	1	50	50	60	12	NAV Return% Rank in Cat
—	—	—	1.25	1.24	1.71	1.41	1.81	2.03	1.76	Income Return %
—	—	—	5.80	-11.60	38.08	17.24	9.66	12.30	0.66	Capital Return %
—	—	0.25	0.53	0.56	0.68	0.77	1.16	1.42	1.39	Income $
—	—	0.07	0.00	0.00	0.00	0.00	0.00	0.00	0.00	Capital Gains $
—	—	—	0.25	0.25	0.25	0.25	0.25	0.25	0.25	Expense Ratio %
—	—	—	1.58	1.43	1.50	1.47	1.78	1.68	1.82	Income Ratio %
—	—	—	17	13	11	11	10	21	20	Turnover Rate %
—	—	43	293	607	996	1,726	2,513	2,571	2,394	Net Assets $mil

Performance 12-31-07

Historic Quarterly NAV Returns

	1st Qtr	2nd Qtr	3rd Qtr	4th Qtr	Total
2003	-5.86	19.11	7.09	16.42	39.79
2004	5.46	1.14	-0.83	12.17	18.65
2005	-0.76	5.04	5.36	1.50	11.47
2006	9.00	-2.08	-0.63	7.80	14.33
2007	5.62	4.36	-2.57	-4.62	2.42

Trailing	NAV Return%	Market Return%	NAV Rtrn% +/-S&P 500	%Rank Cat.(NAV)
3 Mo	-4.62	-4.89	-1.29	31
6 Mo	-7.07	-7.34	-5.70	23
1 Yr	2.42	1.46	-3.07	12
3 Yr Avg	9.29	9.27	0.67	34
5 Yr Avg	16.71	16.60	3.88	100
10 Yr Avg	—	—	—	—

Tax Analysis	Tax-Adj Return%	Tax-Cost Ratio
3 Yr (estimated)	8.63	0.60
5 Yr (estimated)	16.05	0.57
10 Yr (estimated)	—	—

Rating and Risk

Time Period	Morningstar Rtn vs Cat	Morningstar Risk vs Cat	Morningstar Risk-Adj Rating
3 Yr	Avg	+Avg	★★★
5 Yr	Avg	+Avg	★★★
10 Yr	—	—	—

Other Measures	Standard Index S&P 500	Best Fit Index S&P 400 TR
Alpha	0.1	-0.8
Beta	1.18	0.99
R-Squared	74	97
Standard Deviation	10.59	
Mean	9.29	
Sharpe Ratio	0.49	

Portfolio Analysis 12-31-07

Share change since 11-07 Total Stocks:293	Sector	PE	Tot Ret%	% Assets
⊖ Telephone and Data Syste	Telecom	26.9	15.96	1.17
☼ Everest Re Group, Ltd.	Financial	6.2	4.27	1.11
⊖ AMB Property Corporation	Financial	21.5	1.64	1.00
⊖ Wisconsin Energy Corpora	Utilities	18.1	4.87	1.00
⊕ New York Community Banco	Financial	20.2	15.77	1.00
⊕ Pride International, Inc	Energy	13.1	12.96	0.99
⊖ Macerich Company	Financial	67.1	-15.09	0.91
⊕ MDU Resources Group, Inc	Utilities	15.9	9.94	0.88
⊖ Scana Corporation	Utilities	16.5	8.36	0.87
⊖ Northeast Utilities	Utilities	23.9	14.10	0.86
⊖ Arrow Electronics, Inc.	Business	11.6	24.50	0.85
⊖ Oneok, Inc.	Utilities	18.0	6.92	0.82
☼ Federal Realty Investmen	Financial	50.5	-0.61	0.81
⊖ Manpower, Inc.	Business	10.9	-23.33	0.81
⊖ Regency Centers Corporat	Financial	30.6	-14.56	0.79
⊖ Alliant Energy Corporati	Utilities	11.2	11.26	0.79
⊖ Forest Oil Corporation	Energy	21.2	55.57	0.78
⊖ URS Corporation	Business	21.6	26.79	0.76
⊖ Energy East Corporation	Utilities	16.3	15.05	0.76
⊖ KBR, Inc.	Business	29.9	48.32	0.74

Current Investment Style

Value Blnd Growth — Large Mid Small

Market Cap	%
Giant	0.0
Large	0.0
Mid	75.5
Small	23.6
Micro	0.9

Avg $mil: 3,038

Value Measures		Rel Category
Price/Earnings	14.73	1.11
Price/Book	1.54	1.01
Price/Sales	0.86	1.10
Price/Cash Flow	6.51	1.06
Dividend Yield %	2.23	0.95

Growth Measures	%	Rel Category
Long-Term Erngs	—	—
Book Value	6.84	0.83
Sales	3.19	0.50
Cash Flow	0.87	0.58
Historical Erngs	8.79	0.67

Profitability	%	Rel Category
Return on Equity	12.50	0.84
Return on Assets	4.69	0.94
Net Margin	11.77	1.10

Sector Weightings	% of Stocks	Rel S&P 500	3 Year High	3 Year Low
Info	12.85	0.62		
Software	2.74	0.66	3	2
Hardware	7.53	0.74	9	6
Media	0.84	0.29	3	1
Telecom	1.74	0.48	2	1
Service	46.12	1.13		
Health	5.68	0.47	7	5
Consumer	5.81	0.86	14	5
Business	9.97	2.26	11	7
Financial	24.66	1.41	25	19
Mfg	41.03	1.07		
Goods	6.68	0.73	8	4
Ind Mtrls	15.13	1.16	18	9
Energy	5.35	0.42	11	5
Utilities	13.87	3.77	15	11

Composition

Cash	0.6
Stocks	99.0
Bonds	0.0
Other	0.4
Foreign (% of Stock)	0.0

Morningstar's Take by Sonya Morris 12-31-07

We'd buy iShares S&P MidCap 400 Value at a modest discount to our fair value estimate.

This ETF spans the middle of the market-cap spectrum. It also occupies the middle ground when it comes to stock quality. Of the 215 portfolio holdings that our analysts cover, only three earn wide-moat ratings, although 105 have managed to trench out narrow moats, meaning they enjoy some competitive advantages, but ones that our analysts believe are more fleeting.

Consider semiconductor equipment maker Lam Research. The firm has developed a highly efficient structure and has a leadership position in a narrow segment of the industry. Thus, Lam has enjoyed wider profit margins and improved returns on capital over time. However, it lacks the scale and the resources of wide-moat competitor and industry leader Applied Materials, leaving it vulnerable. All told, this portfolio's abundance of middling-quality names such as Lam puts a lid on its intrinsic worth, as our analysts typically place more value on wide-moat firms.

The risk picture is also mixed. The bulk of the portfolio consists of average-risk stocks, which are firms that stand a moderate chance of being waylaid by rivals or other events in the future. True, the fund owns stakes in a clutch of riskier names such as Arch Coal, whose fate is tied to the vagaries of commodity prices, and Millennium Pharmaceuticals, which has only one product that has earned FDA approval. But on the whole, this fund lands somewhere in the middle of the business-risk spectrum, with average-risk holdings such as J.M. Smucker being the norm.

Fortunately, this risk profile hasn't translated to jarring volatility. Although not as placid as a diversified ETF teeming with wide-moat stocks, this fund isn't as racy as a concentrated sector fund either. For that reason, we wouldn't demand an especially wide margin of safety when investing here; an 8% discount to our fair value estimate would do.

Address:	45 Fremont Street United States 800-474-2737
Web Address:	www.ishares.com
Inception:	07-24-00*
Advisor:	Barclays Global Fund Advisers

Management Fee:	0.25%		
Expense Projections:	3Yr:$80	5Yr:$141	10Yr:$318
Income Distrib:	Quarterly		
Exchange:	NYSE		

iShares SP Small 600 IJR

Market Price	Mstar Category
$65.02	Small Blend

Morningstar Fair Value

Price/Fair Value Ratio	Coverage Rate %
0.98	46

Valuation

Because our equity analysts cover a relatively small number of this ETF's holdings, the price/fair value ratio above may not be a faithful representation of the portfolio's valuation attributes. Investors trying to gauge this ETF's attractiveness should consider the price/fair value ratio only in conjunction with other fundamental measures.

Methodology

This ETF is tethered to the S&P SmallCap 600 Index. That benchmark includes U.S. stocks with market caps between $300 million and $2 billion. To qualify for inclusion in the index, the stock must be sufficiently liquid and the company concerned must have posted at least four straight profitable quarters.

Morningstar Rating	Return	Risk	Yield	NAV	Avg Daily Vol. (k)	52 wk High/Low
★★★	Average	Average	1.1%	$65.06	1,752	$73.26 - $60.24

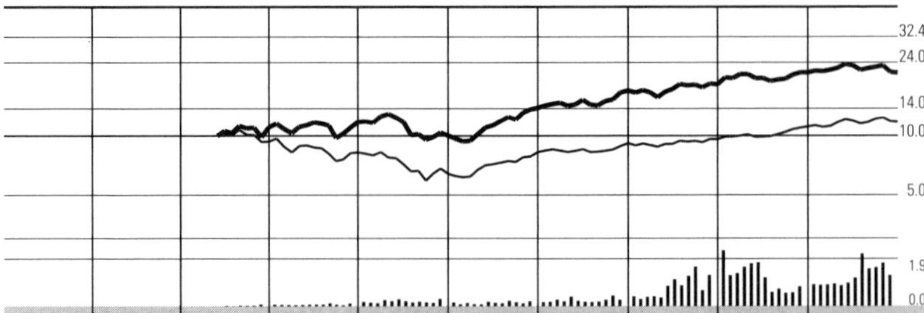

Growth of $10,000
— Investment Value of ETF
— Investment Value of Index S&P 500

Trading Volume Millions

1998	1999	2000	2001	2002	2003	2004	2005	2006	2007	History
—	—	36.27	38.35	32.51	44.73	54.34	57.89	66.01	65.06	NAV $
—	—	36.03	38.13	32.48	44.67	54.24	57.80	65.99	65.02	Market Price $
—	—	10.45*	6.34	-14.73	38.59	22.45	7.50	14.94	-0.44	NAV Return%
—	—	10.44*	6.43	-14.31	38.50	22.41	7.53	15.09	-0.48	Market Price Return%
—	—	-0.13	-0.11	-0.15	0.05	-0.05	-0.12	-0.02	-0.06	Avg Premium/Discount%
—	—	—	18.23	7.37	9.91	11.57	2.59	-0.85	-5.93	NAV Rtrn% +/-S&P 500
—	—	—	-0.20	-0.10	-0.20	-0.20	-0.18	-0.18	-0.14	NAV Rtrn% +/-S&P Small
—	—	—	1	1	100	1	34	85	25	NAV Return% Rank in Cat
—	—	—	0.53	0.55	0.84	0.89	0.93	0.88	1.05	Income Return %
—	—	—	5.81	-15.28	37.75	21.56	6.57	14.06	-1.49	Capital Return %
—	—	0.07	0.19	0.21	0.27	0.40	0.50	0.51	0.69	Income $
—	—	0.37	0.00	0.00	0.00	0.00	0.00	0.00	0.00	Capital Gains $
—	—	—	0.20	0.20	0.20	0.20	0.20	0.20	0.20	Expense Ratio %
—	—	—	0.61	0.60	0.70	0.73	0.95	0.93	0.76	Income Ratio %
—	—	—	28	16	17	11	14	16	16	Turnover Rate %
—	—	125	627	1,341	2,006	4,230	3,862	4,660	4,369	Net Assets $mil

Performance 12-31-07

Historic Quarterly NAV Returns

	1st Qtr	2nd Qtr	3rd Qtr	4th Qtr	Total
2003	-5.83	19.80	7.05	14.76	38.59
2004	6.18	3.56	-1.41	12.95	22.45
2005	-2.10	3.89	5.34	0.34	7.50
2006	12.80	-4.60	-0.93	7.82	14.94
2007	3.11	5.16	-1.87	-6.44	-0.44

Trailing	NAV Return%	Market Return%	NAV Rtrn% +/-S&P 500	%Rank Cat.(NAV)
3 Mo	-6.44	-6.51	-3.11	41
6 Mo	-8.18	-8.12	-6.81	30
1 Yr	-0.44	-0.48	-5.93	25
3 Yr Avg	7.15	7.19	-1.47	34
5 Yr Avg	15.86	15.87	3.03	100
10 Yr Avg	—	—	—	—

Tax Analysis	Tax-Adj Return%	Tax-Cost Ratio
3 Yr (estimated)	6.81	0.32
5 Yr (estimated)	15.52	0.29
10 Yr (estimated)	—	—

Rating and Risk

Time Period	Morningstar Rtn vs Cat	Morningstar Risk vs Cat	Morningstar Risk-Adj Rating
3 Yr	Avg	Avg	★★★
5 Yr	Avg	Avg	★★★
10 Yr	—	—	—

Other Measures	Standard Index S&P 500	Best Fit Index Mstar Small Cap TR
Alpha	-2.4	0.1
Beta	1.35	0.94
R-Squared	71	98
Standard Deviation	12.43	
Mean	7.15	
Sharpe Ratio	0.27	

Portfolio Analysis 12-31-07

Share change since 11-07 Total Stocks:600	Sector	PE	Tot Ret%	% Assets
⊕ Shaw Group	Ind Mtrls	—	80.42	0.93
⊕ Respironics Inc.	Health	37.9	73.46	0.92
⊕ FLIR Systems, Inc.	Ind Mtrls	36.8	96.67	0.80
⊕ Cabot Oil & Gas Corporat	Energy	25.0	33.54	0.74
⊕ Helix Energy Solutions G	Energy	10.8	32.29	0.72
⊕ Oceaneering Internationa	Energy	22.8	69.65	0.70
⊕ Trimble Navigation Ltd.	Hardware	32.1	19.22	0.69
⊖ Idexx Laboratories	Health	40.8	47.87	0.67
⊕ Southern Union Company	Energy	12.9	6.59	0.67
⊕ Pediatrix Medical Group,	Health	25.5	39.37	0.63
⊕ MGI Pharma, Inc.	Health	—	120.15	0.62
⊕ Ansys, Inc.	Software	50.8	90.66	0.61
⊕ Crocs, Inc.	Goods	20.4	70.23	0.57
⊕ Itron Inc.	Telecom	—	85.13	0.55
⊕ UGI Corporation	Utilities	14.4	2.71	0.55
⊕ Micros Systems, Inc.	Software	33.8	33.13	0.54
⊖ Massey Energy Company	Energy	29.8	54.85	0.54
⊕ Varian Semiconductor Equ	Hardware	21.4	21.92	0.53
⊕ AptarGroup, Inc.	Goods	21.9	40.51	0.53
⊕ Atwood Oceanics, Inc.	Energy	22.9	104.70	0.52

Current Investment Style

Value Blnd Growth; Large Mid Small

Market Cap	%
Giant	0.0
Large	0.0
Mid	20.7
Small	65.5
Micro	13.8
Avg $mil: 1,230	

Value Measures		Rel Category
Price/Earnings	15.14	1.00
Price/Book	1.76	1.04
Price/Sales	0.90	1.00
Price/Cash Flow	8.00	1.22
Dividend Yield %	1.00	0.71

Growth Measures	%	Rel Category
Long-Term Erngs	—	—
Book Value	10.06	1.33
Sales	7.35	1.56
Cash Flow	10.42	1.75
Historical Erngs	21.03	1.68

Profitability	%	Rel Category
Return on Equity	12.58	0.96
Return on Assets	6.35	1.09
Net Margin	10.20	1.00

Sector Weightings	% of Stocks	Rel S&P 500	3 Year High	3 Year Low
Info	15.77	0.75		
Software	5.43	1.31	5	4
Hardware	8.96	0.88	9	6
Media	0.04	0.01	0	0
Telecom	1.34	0.37	2	1
Service	46.16	1.14		
Health	12.52	1.04	13	10
Consumer	8.05	1.19	13	8
Business	9.70	2.20	12	10
Financial	15.89	0.91	17	14
Mfg	38.06	0.99		
Goods	7.19	0.78	8	6
Ind Mtrls	18.26	1.40	21	18
Energy	8.69	0.69	10	7
Utilities	3.92	1.07	4	3

Composition

Cash	0.4
Stocks	99.6
Bonds	0.0
Other	0.0
Foreign (% of Stock)	0.1

Morningstar's Take by Sonya Morris 12-31-07

There's a case to be made for iShares S&P SmallCap 600 Index.

When a market segment is firing on all cylinders--like small-cap stocks have in recent years--it's easy to lose sight of its risks. But small-cap land is home to many younger firms with few competitive advantages and limited financial resources. Consequently, small-cap stocks, and the funds that own them, experience their share of turbulence. The typical small-blend fund is almost 45% more volatile than the S&P 500, as measured by standard deviation of returns.

But this ETF's benchmark, the S&P SmallCap 600 Index, employs a methodology that helps eliminate the raciest companies in the group. Like all Standard & Poor's domestic-equity indexes, it screens out those firms that have not generated positive earnings in four straight quarters.

That financial viability screen has helped this ETF hold its own when times get tough. Witness its showing during the recent subprime meltdown this past summer. From June 1 through July 31, 2007, this fund lost 6.6% of its value. However, the Russell 2000 Index declined 8.2%. And in 2002, when the Russell 2000 Index experienced a 20.5% drop, this ETF managed to limit its losses to 14.7%. Granted, its trailing returns over the past five years are about the same as the Russell 2000's, but that's good enough to lift it above 60% of its small-blend peers.

We think this is a credible choice to fill out the small-cap slot of a long-term portfolio, particularly for cautious sorts. However those who can tolerate a bit more volatility might want to consider Vanguard Small Cap ETF, which covers virtually the same territory for half the price. Furthermore, the conventional share class of the Vanguard fund is only slightly more expensive than this ETF, and it can be had without paying a brokerage commission.

Address:	45 Fremont Street United States 800-474-2737
Web Address:	www.ishares.com
Inception:	05-22-00 *
Advisor:	Barclays Global Fund Advisers

Management Fee:	0.20%		
Expense Projections:	3Yr:$64	5Yr:$113	10Yr:$255
Income Distrib:	Quarterly		
Exchange:	NYSE		

iShares SP 600 Growth IJT

Market Price	Mstar Category
$134.86	Small Growth

Morningstar Fair Value

Price/Fair Value Ratio	Coverage Rate %
0.99	45

Valuation

Our equity analysts cover a small number of this ETF's stock holdings, so the price/fair value price ratio above may not be a faithful representation of this portfolio's valuation attributes. Thus, investors trying to gauge this ETF's attractiveness should consider the price/fair value ratio only in conjunction with other fundamental measures.

Methodology

This ETF mimics the S&P SmallCap 600/Citigroup Growth Index. That benchmark includes stocks of U.S. companies with market caps between $300 million and $2 billion. To qualify for the index, the stocks must be sufficiently liquid and the firms concerned must pass certain operating screens, including having posted at least four consecutive profitable quarters. Stocks are categorized into the growth and value camps using seven valuation measures--dividend yield; price/book, price/sales and price/cash flow; and five-year earnings, sales, and internal-growth rates.

Morningstar Rating	Return	Risk	Yield	NAV	Avg Daily Vol. (k)	52 wk High/Low
★★★	Average	Below Avg	0.3%	$134.74	181	$149.66 - $125.51

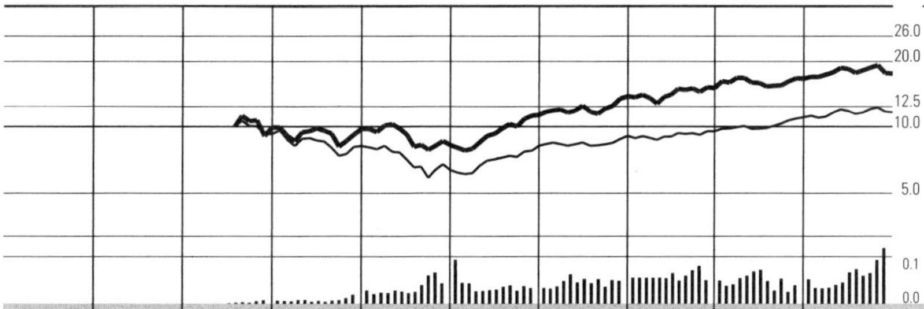

History

1998	1999	2000	2001	2002	2003	2004	2005	2006	2007	History
—	—	78.24	77.09	64.96	88.67	107.43	116.41	128.05	134.74	NAV $
—	—	78.41	76.95	65.10	88.72	107.10	116.07	127.96	134.86	Market Price $
—	—	7.10*	-1.38	-15.55	37.05	21.61	8.99	10.30	5.49	NAV Return%
—	—	7.11*	-1.77	-15.21	36.84	21.17	9.00	10.55	5.66	Market Price Return%
—	—	0.07	0.22	0.07	0.10	-0.06	-0.08	-0.13	-0.05	Avg Premium/Discount%
—	—	—	10.51	6.55	8.37	10.73	4.08	-5.49	0.00	NAV Rtrn% +/-S&P 500
—	—	—	-4.38	1.02	-1.45	-2.68	1.93	-0.24	-0.11	NAV Rtrn% +/-S&P Sm Gr
—	—	—	1	1	100	1	1	60	71	NAV Return% Rank in Cat
—	—	—	0.08	0.20	0.48	0.41	0.60	0.29	0.28	Income Return %
—	—	—	-1.46	-15.75	36.57	21.20	8.39	10.01	5.21	Capital Return %
—	—	0.00	0.06	0.16	0.31	0.36	0.65	0.34	0.35	Income $
—	—	0.62	0.00	0.00	0.00	0.00	0.00	0.00	0.00	Capital Gains $
—	—	—	0.25	0.25	0.25	0.25	0.25	0.25	0.25	Expense Ratio %
—	—	—	0.00	0.14	0.34	0.39	0.45	0.53	0.25	Income Ratio %
—	—	—	77	49	57	37	45	30	32	Turnover Rate %
—	—	35	127	513	625	1,064	1,280	1,248	1,489	Net Assets $mil

Performance 12-31-07

Historic Quarterly NAV Returns

	1st Qtr	2nd Qtr	3rd Qtr	4th Qtr	Total
2003	-3.63	16.85	7.79	12.92	37.05
2004	5.65	4.37	-3.08	13.80	21.61
2005	-1.77	3.71	6.56	0.39	8.99
2006	11.28	-5.17	-2.49	7.19	10.30
2007	4.27	6.19	1.30	-5.95	5.49

Trailing	NAV Return%	Market Return%	NAV Rtrn% +/-S&P 500	%Rank Cat.(NAV)
3 Mo	-5.95	-5.76	-2.62	75
6 Mo	-4.73	-4.52	-3.36	62
1 Yr	5.49	5.66	0.00	71
3 Yr Avg	8.24	8.38	-0.38	75
5 Yr Avg	16.15	16.12	3.32	100
10 Yr Avg	—	—	—	—

Tax Analysis	Tax-Adj Return%	Tax-Cost Ratio
3 Yr (estimated)	8.10	0.13
5 Yr (estimated)	15.99	0.14
10 Yr (estimated)	—	—

Rating and Risk

Time Period	Morningstar Rtn vs Cat	Morningstar Risk vs Cat	Morningstar Risk-Adj Rating
3 Yr	Avg	-Avg	★★★
5 Yr	Avg	-Avg	★★★
10 Yr	—	—	—

Other Measures	Standard Index S&P 500	Best Fit Index Mstar Small Cap TR
Alpha	-1.4	1.2
Beta	1.34	0.92
R-Squared	70	93
Standard Deviation	12.45	
Mean	8.24	
Sharpe Ratio	0.35	

Portfolio Analysis 12-31-07

Share change since 11-07 Total Stocks:338	Sector	PE	Tot Ret%	% Assets
⊖ Respironics Inc.	Health	37.9	73.46	1.85
⊕ FLIR Systems, Inc.	Ind Mtrls	36.8	96.67	1.62
⊖ Cabot Oil & Gas Corporat	Energy	25.0	33.54	1.49
⊖ Helix Energy Solutions G	Energy	10.8	32.29	1.44
⊕ Oceaneering Internationa	Energy	22.8	69.65	1.41
⊕ Trimble Navigation Ltd.	Hardware	32.1	19.22	1.40
⊖ Idexx Laboratories	Health	40.8	47.87	1.37
⊖ Pediatrix Medical Group,	Health	25.5	39.37	1.26
⊕ Ansys, Inc.	Software	50.8	90.66	1.24
⊕ MGI Pharma, Inc.	Health	—	120.15	1.24
⊕ Crocs, Inc.	Goods	20.4	70.23	1.16
⊕ Micros Systems, Inc.	Software	33.8	33.13	1.10
⊖ St. Mary Land & Explorat	Energy	12.4	5.07	0.93
⊖ FactSet Research Systems	Business	26.0	-0.70	0.91
⊕ Immucor, Inc.	Health	36.9	16.28	0.91
⊖ Sierra Health Services	Health	22.3	16.43	0.90
⊕ LKQ Corporation	Ind Mtrls	43.3	82.86	0.90
⊕ Philadelphia Consolidate	Financial	8.8	-11.69	0.88
⊖ Landstar System, Inc.	Business	21.6	10.74	0.87
⊖ Curtiss-Wright Corporati	Ind Mtrls	24.1	36.17	0.85

Current Investment Style

Value Blnd Growth / Large Mid Small

Market Cap	%
Giant	0.0
Large	0.0
Mid	29.9
Small	62.2
Micro	7.9
Avg $mil: 1,498	

Value Measures		Rel Category
Price/Earnings	16.45	0.84
Price/Book	2.39	0.89
Price/Sales	1.31	0.92
Price/Cash Flow	10.59	0.96
Dividend Yield %	0.35	1.00

Growth Measures	%	Rel Category
Long-Term Erngs	—	—
Book Value	13.02	1.53
Sales	12.15	11.68
Cash Flow	11.96	5.16
Historical Erngs	27.85	1.80

Profitability	%	Rel Category
Return on Equity	15.67	1.12
Return on Assets	8.29	1.34
Net Margin	10.60	1.29

Sector Weightings	% of Stocks	Rel S&P 500	3 Year High	3 Year Low
Info	16.63	0.80		
Software	8.03	1.94	8	6
Hardware	6.54	0.64	7	3
Media	0.03	0.01	0	0
Telecom	2.03	0.56	2	1
Service	47.13	1.16		
Health	18.99	1.58	20	16
Consumer	8.75	1.29	16	9
Business	11.06	2.51	13	9
Financial	8.33	0.48	13	8
Mfg	36.23	0.94		
Goods	8.10	0.88	9	6
Ind Mtrls	16.37	1.26	18	12
Energy	11.59	0.92	14	10
Utilities	0.17	0.05	1	0

Composition

Cash	0.2
Stocks	99.8
Bonds	0.0
Other	0.0
Foreign (% of Stock)	0.0

Morningstar's Take by Sonya Morris 12-31-07

IShares S&P SmallCap 600 Growth Index isn't the cheapest option, but there's a case to be made in its favor.

Some have argued that indexing doesn't work in the small-cap arena. You couldn't prove that by this ETF. Its 7.3% annualized return since its July 2000 inception surpasses nearly 90% of its small-growth rivals'. What's more, the fund has been able to deliver those returns with less volatility, as its since-inception standard deviation of returns is roughly 20% lower than the category norm.

The fund's attractive risk/reward profile is attributable to a unique aspect of the construction methodology behind its benchmark, the S&P SmallCap 600 Growth Index. Unlike many other index providers, Standards & Poor's requires that firms meet certain financial viability criteria. Specifically, a firm must string together four straight profitable quarters to qualify for inclusion in an S&P index. Because unprofitable start-ups don't make the cut, that's weighed down this fund's tech stake, which is about half that of the typical small-growth fund. That's been a boon to the fund lately, as tech stocks have largely underperformed in recent years.

Of course, investors shouldn't expect that tailwind to continue. In fact, this ETF is likely to lag its peers when tech stocks return to favor. Thankfully, however, it has a more enduring advantage: low fees. Its 0.25% expense ratio is a fraction of the cost of most small-growth funds.

Even so, this isn't the cheapest fund in the category. Vanguard Small Cap Growth ETF charges just 0.12%, and its conventional fund twin, Vanguard Small Cap Growth Index Fund costs only 0.23%, and you don't have to pay brokerage commissions to trade that fund. It worth noting, however, that the Vanguard fund has been slightly more volatile than this offering, so risk-averse investors might prefer to pay a slightly higher fee for this ETF.

Address:	45 Fremont Street United States 800-474-2737
Web Address:	www.ishares.com
Inception:	07-24-00*
Advisor:	Barclays Global Fund Advisers

Management Fee:	0.25%		
Expense Projections:	3Yr:$80	5Yr:$141	10Yr:$318
Income Distrib:	Quarterly		
Exchange:	NYSE		

iShares SP 600 Value IJS

Market Price	Mstar Category
$70.00	Small Value

Morningstar Rating	Return	Risk	Yield	NAV	Avg Daily Vol. (k)	52 wk High/Low
★★★	Average	Above Avg	1.8%	$69.97	143	$82.70 - $64.00

Morningstar Fair Value

Price/Fair Value Ratio	Coverage Rate %
0.97	47

Valuation

Because our equity analysts cover a relatively small number of this ETF's holdings, the price/fair value ratio above may not be a faithful representation of the portfolio's valuation attributes. Investors trying to gauge this ETF's attractiveness should consider the price/fair value ratio only in conjunction with other fundamental measures.

Methodology

This fund tracks the S&P SmallCap 600/Citigroup Value Index. It focuses on liquid stocks with market caps between $300 million and $2 billion. To divvy up stocks between the growth and value camps, the index methodology relies on seven growth and valuation measures--dividend yield; price/book, price/sales, and price/cash flow; and five-year earnings, sales, and internal-growth rates. Like all S&P indexes, it includes a profitability screen. Specifically, firms must have had four straight profitable quarters to be included in the index.

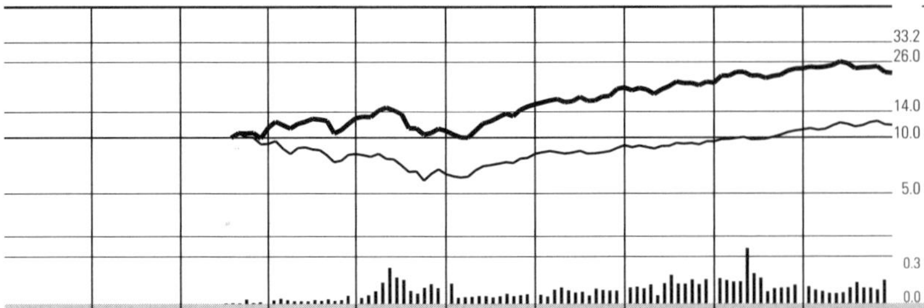

Growth of $10,000
— Investment Value of ETF
— Investment Value of Index S&P 500

Trading Volume Millions

History

1998	1999	2000	2001	2002	2003	2004	2005	2006	2007	History
—	—	38.36	42.88	36.28	50.24	61.04	63.99	75.42	69.97	NAV $
—	—	38.50	42.67	36.38	50.27	60.90	63.88	75.34	70.00	Market Price $
—	—	11.38*	12.61	-14.65	39.75	22.96	5.93	19.29	-5.70	NAV Return%
—	—	11.38*	11.68	-14.03	39.49	22.60	6.00	19.37	-5.56	Market Price Return%
—	—	-0.04	-0.01	0.03	0.11	-0.01	-0.20	-0.14	-0.15	Avg Premium/Discount%
—	—	—	24.50	7.45	11.07	12.08	1.02	3.50	-11.19	NAV Rtrn% +/-S&P 500
—	—	—	3.09	-1.72	0.55	1.87	-2.43	-0.28	-0.16	NAV Rtrn% +/-S&P Sm Val
—	—	—	50	100	100	1	25	80	34	NAV Return% Rank in Cat
—	—	—	0.77	0.81	1.05	1.35	1.07	1.35	1.66	Income Return %
—	—	—	11.84	-15.46	38.70	21.61	4.86	17.94	-7.36	Capital Return %
—	—	0.13	0.29	0.35	0.38	0.68	0.65	0.86	1.24	Income $
—	—	0.17	0.00	0.00	0.00	0.00	0.00	0.00	0.00	Capital Gains $
—	—	—	0.25	0.25	0.25	0.25	0.25	0.25	0.25	Expense Ratio %
—	—	—	0.98	0.92	0.99	0.95	1.36	1.20	1.14	Income Ratio %
—	—	—	17	14	14	12	13	16	28	Turnover Rate %
—	—	42	283	704	864	1,618	1,606	1,961	1,571	Net Assets $mil

Performance 12-31-07

Historic Quarterly NAV Returns

	1st Qtr	2nd Qtr	3rd Qtr	4th Qtr	Total
2003	-8.01	22.65	6.30	16.52	39.75
2004	6.58	2.83	0.21	11.97	22.96
2005	-2.44	4.05	4.11	0.24	5.93
2006	14.21	-4.10	0.53	8.35	19.29
2007	2.10	4.23	-4.79	-6.93	-5.70

Trailing	NAV Return%	Market Return%	NAV Rtrn% +/-S&P 500	%Rank Cat.(NAV)
3 Mo	-6.93	-6.83	-3.60	62
6 Mo	-11.39	-11.22	-10.02	25
1 Yr	-5.70	-5.56	-11.19	34
3 Yr Avg	6.02	6.11	-2.60	25
5 Yr Avg	15.41	15.36	2.58	50
10 Yr Avg	—	—	—	—

Tax Analysis	Tax-Adj Return%	Tax-Cost Ratio
3 Yr (estimated)	5.54	0.45
5 Yr (estimated)	14.93	0.42
10 Yr (estimated)	—	—

Rating and Risk

Time Period	Morningstar Rtn vs Cat	Morningstar Risk vs Cat	Morningstar Risk-Adj Rating
3 Yr	Avg	+Avg	★★★
5 Yr	Avg	+Avg	★★★
10 Yr	—	—	—

Other Measures	Standard Index S&P 500	Best Fit Index Mstar Small Core
Alpha	-3.5	-0.7
Beta	1.36	0.95
R-Squared	69	98
Standard Deviation	12.69	
Mean	6.02	
Sharpe Ratio	0.18	

Portfolio Analysis 12-31-07

Share change since 11-07 Total Stocks:449	Sector	PE	Tot Ret%	% Assets
⊕ Southern Union Company	Energy	12.9	6.59	1.33
⊕ UGI Corporation	Utilities	14.4	2.71	1.10
⊕ Massey Energy Company	Energy	29.8	54.85	1.08
⊕ Lennox International, In	Business	16.7	37.30	1.01
⊖ Shaw Group	Ind Mtrls	—	80.42	1.01
⊕ Atmos Energy Corporation	Utilities	14.6	-8.23	0.96
⊕ Essex Property Trust	Financial	60.6	-22.09	0.92
⊕ Belden CDT, Inc.	Hardware	20.0	14.29	0.77
⊕ Senior Housing Prop Trus	Financial	21.0	-1.69	0.76
⊕ Piedmont Natural Gas Com	Utilities	18.7	1.58	0.74
⊕ Acuity Brands, Inc.	Ind Mtrls	13.4	4.96	0.71
⊕ Kilroy Realty Corporatio	Financial	51.3	-27.04	0.68
⊕ Whitney Holding Corporat	Financial	11.4	-16.46	0.67
⊕ OM Group, Inc.	Ind Mtrls	36.6	27.08	0.67
⊕ Chittenden Corporation	Financial	—	—	0.66
⊕ Owens & Minor, Inc.	Health	30.3	38.24	0.66
⊕ National Retail Properti	Financial	15.7	8.15	0.64
⊕ Cleco Corporation	Utilities	11.0	14.14	0.63
⊕ Varian Semiconductor Equ	Hardware	21.4	21.92	0.62
⊕ Susquehanna Bancshares	Financial	13.4	-28.04	0.60

Current Investment Style

Value Blnd Growth — Large / Mid / Small (style box: Small Value)

Market Cap	%
Giant	0.0
Large	0.0
Mid	11.6
Small	68.8
Micro	19.6
Avg $mil: 1,014	

Value Measures		Rel Category
Price/Earnings	14.03	1.01
Price/Book	1.39	1.03
Price/Sales	0.69	0.88
Price/Cash Flow	6.28	1.07
Dividend Yield %	1.66	0.74

Growth Measures	%	Rel Category
Long-Term Erngs	—	—
Book Value	8.58	1.66
Sales	5.26	7.85
Cash Flow	9.25	2.40
Historical Erngs	15.69	1.95

Profitability	%	Rel Category
Return on Equity	9.47	0.98
Return on Assets	4.39	1.16
Net Margin	9.79	0.98

Sector Weightings	% of Stocks	Rel S&P 500	3 Year High	3 Year Low
Info	14.84	0.71		
Software	2.78	0.67	3	2
Hardware	11.39	1.12	12	8
Media	0.04	0.01	0	0
Telecom	0.63	0.17	1	0
Service	45.22	1.11		
Health	6.09	0.51	7	4
Consumer	7.31	1.08	13	7
Business	8.35	1.89	12	8
Financial	23.47	1.35	23	18
Mfg	39.94	1.04		
Goods	6.25	0.68	8	6
Ind Mtrls	20.16	1.55	27	20
Energy	5.78	0.46	7	4
Utilities	7.75	2.11	8	5

Composition

Cash	0.5
Stocks	99.5
Bonds	0.0
Other	0.0
Foreign (% of Stock)	0.2

Morningstar's Take by Sonya Morris 12-31-07

IShares S&P Small Cap 600 Value is a respectable choice for small-value exposure.

For most of the past seven years, smaller stocks have outpaced their larger brethren. But small-value stocks took a breather in 2007, which isn't particularly surprising given their long stretch of outperformance. Over time, market segments go in and out of favor, and cheap small caps couldn't continue their winning ways forever.

Index funds can often lag during inflection points in their categories. That's because unlike their active competitors, they must stay fully invested in their specified market segment. Active managers can bend the rules a bit by taking refuge in cash or by creeping up the market-cap ladder as conditions warrant.

Despite that disadvantage, this ETF held up well in 2007. That's partly because of this fund's below-average stake in the financial sector, which was hit hard in the summer amid concerns about the swooning U.S. housing market and mounting subprime loan losses. That undersized financial stake is partly due to a quirk in the methodology of this fund's benchmark. Standard & Poor's will include a stock in its indexes only if at least 50% of its outstanding shares can be traded by the general public. With heavy insider ownership not uncommon among small banks and other financial firms, many financial stocks are excluded from this fund's benchmark.

That said, this ETF's financials underweight isn't so pronounced that we would expect it to impact this fund's long-term track record. Over the long haul, it has managed to keep pace with other small-value indexes as well as the category average.

On the whole, we think this is a respectable choice for small-value exposure, but it's not our favorite ETF in the category. That distinction goes to Vanguard Small Cap Value ETF, which covers nearly identical ground for half the price.

Address:	45 Fremont Street United States 800-474-2737
Web Address:	www.ishares.com
Inception:	07-24-00 *
Advisor:	Barclays Global Fund Advisers

Management Fee:	0.25%		
Expense Projections:	3Yr:$80	5Yr:$141	10Yr:$318
Income Distrib:	Quarterly		
Exchange:	NYSE		

MidCap SPDR Trust MDY

Market Price	Mstar Category
$155.10	Mid-Cap Blend

Morningstar Fair Value

Price/Fair Value Ratio	Coverage Rate %
0.95	77

Valuation

Mid-caps have been on fire for the past few years and as a result, bargains are scarce. Not surprisingly, this ETF was recently trading at a 5% discount to our fair value estimate, which isn't cheap enough for us. This ETF is worth a look at an 8% or larger discount to fair value, a level it hasn't approached since the spring of 2003.

Methodology

This ETF tracks the S&P MidCap 400 Index. Each stock in the benchmark is screened by S&P's index selection committee on factors including profitability, liquidity, and sector representation. The portfolio's sector weightings skew toward business services, utilities, and consumer goods and services firms. This fund is organized as a unit investment trust, which means its managers can't reinvest the portfolio's dividends directly, among other constraints. This theoretically could make it more difficult for the fund to keep pace with its index, but that hasn't been the case thus far.

Morningstar Rating	Return	Risk	Yield	NAV	Avg Daily Vol. (k)	52 wk High/Low
★★★★	Above Avg	Average	1.2%	$156.63	5,194	$168.33 - $144.29

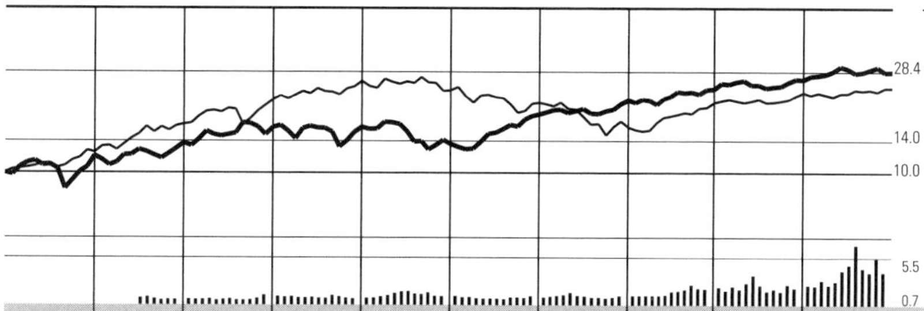

1998	1999	2000	2001	2002	2003	2004	2005	2006	2007	History
73.98	81.62	94.76	94.32	78.78	105.51	121.38	134.72	146.46	156.63	NAV $
72.75	81.12	94.38	92.80	78.65	105.40	121.00	134.69	146.35	155.10	Market Price $
18.62	14.28	17.08	0.37	-15.77	35.20	15.84	12.18	10.05	8.20	NAV Return%
17.08	15.50	17.33	-0.85	-14.53	35.29	15.60	12.50	9.99	7.22	Market Price Return%
-0.32	-0.11	-0.04	0.05	-0.17	-0.13	-0.07	-0.06	-0.04	-0.04	Avg Premium/Discount%
-9.96	-6.76	26.18	12.26	6.33	6.52	4.96	7.27	-5.74	2.71	NAV Rtrn% +/-S&P 500
-0.50	-0.44	-0.43	0.98	-1.24	-0.42	-0.64	-0.38	-0.27	0.22	NAV Rtrn% +/-S&P 400 TR
1	1	1	1	34	100	100	50	85	27	NAV Return% Rank in Cat
0.93	0.96	0.95	0.76	0.76	1.09	0.71	1.13	1.29	1.26	Income Return %
17.69	13.32	16.13	-0.39	-16.53	34.11	15.13	11.05	8.76	6.94	Capital Return %
0.60	0.71	0.78	0.71	0.72	0.86	0.75	1.37	1.72	1.84	Income $
1.50	2.00	0.00	0.00	0.00	0.00	0.00	0.00	0.00	0.00	Capital Gains $
0.30	0.26	0.28	0.26	0.25	0.25	0.25	0.25	0.25	—	Expense Ratio %
0.92	0.97	0.85	0.75	0.81	0.96	0.96	1.11	1.13	—	Income Ratio %
30	43	30	33	21	13	16	19	17	—	Turnover Rate %
—	—	—	—	5,050	6,427	7,895	8,942	8,558	10,107	Net Assets $mil

Performance 12-31-07

Historic Quarterly NAV Returns

	1st Qtr	2nd Qtr	3rd Qtr	4th Qtr	Total
2003	-4.51	17.53	6.52	13.10	35.20
2004	5.00	0.89	-2.17	11.78	15.84
2005	-0.47	4.19	4.78	3.23	12.18
2006	7.60	-3.21	-1.15	6.90	10.05
2007	5.73	5.75	-0.95	-2.31	8.20

Trailing	NAV Return%	Market Return%	NAV Rtrn% +/-S&P 500	%Rank Cat.(NAV)
3 Mo	-2.31	-3.30	1.02	29
6 Mo	-3.23	-4.34	-1.86	29
1 Yr	8.20	7.22	2.71	27
3 Yr Avg	10.13	9.88	1.51	34
5 Yr Avg	15.91	15.72	3.08	100
10 Yr Avg	10.87	10.80	4.96	1

Tax Analysis	Tax-Adj Return%	Tax-Cost Ratio
3 Yr (estimated)	9.69	0.40
5 Yr (estimated)	15.50	0.35
10 Yr (estimated)	10.32	0.50

Rating and Risk

Time Period	Morningstar Rtn vs Cat	Morningstar Risk vs Cat	Morningstar Risk-Adj Rating
3 Yr	+Avg	Avg	★★★★
5 Yr	Avg	Avg	★★★
10 Yr	+Avg	Avg	★★★★

Other Measures	Standard Index S&P 500	Best Fit Index S&P 400 TR
Alpha	0.9	-0.1
Beta	1.18	1.00
R-Squared	76	100
Standard Deviation	10.50	
Mean	10.13	
Sharpe Ratio	0.56	

Morningstar's Take by Emiko Kurotsu 12-31-07

Though not a thoroughbred, we'd invest in this fund at a modest discount to our fair value estimate.

This ETF tracks the S&P MidCap 400 Index, which targets stocks with market caps ranging from $1.5 billion to $5.5 billion. On whole, this accounts for roughly 7% of the U.S. equity market.

Dominant mid-cap firms are hard to come by. Only 8% of the mid-cap stocks that our analysts cover garner a wide economic moat, a rating that denotes the presence of durable competitive advantages. This fund doesn't buck that trend: Our analysts have awarded wide moats to only 18 of the 310 portfolio holdings that they cover.

Many firms in the portfolio boast impressive growth rates, but they haven't forged advantages that can withstand encroachment by competitors over the long haul. For instance, ValueClick claims the largest independent online advertising network in the U.S., but low customer switching costs and competitive pressures from Internet giants like Google and traditional bundled service providers make its dominance tenuous. Narrow- and no-moat firms are less valuable, on balance, than their wide-moat counterparts, so this portfolio's middling quality depresses its intrinsic worth.

The fund's quality also influences its risk profile. Given that many of its holdings aren't founded on dominant businesses with predictable cash flows, it's more difficult to forecast their results. For instance, the fortunes of narrow-moat coal producer Arch Coal are largely tied to commodity price fluctuations, which are unpredictable. In addition, smaller firms tend to be riskier given that they lack the financial wherewithal of better-established companies. This explains why our analysts consider many of this fund's holdings to be above-average risks.

That said, the portfolio's diversification across holdings and sectors tamps down volatility. Thus, we wouldn't require a wide margin of safety to invest here: An 8% or greater discount to fair value would be sufficient.

Address:	PDR Services, 86 Trinity Place United States 800-843-2639
Web Address:	www.amex.com/mdy
Inception:	05-04-95
Advisor:	PDR Services

Management Fee:	0.00%		
Expense Projections:	3Yr: —	5Yr: —	10Yr: —
Income Distrib:	Quarterly		
Exchange:	AMEX		

Portfolio Analysis 10-31-07

Share change since 09-07 Total Stocks:396	Sector	PE	Tot Ret%	% Assets
⊖ Intuitive Surgical, Inc.	Health	NMF	236.67	1.02
⊖ Lyondell Chemical Compan	Energy	—	—	1.00
⊖ Cameron International Co	Energy	23.5	81.45	0.88
⊖ Gamestop Corporation A	Goods	51.8	125.40	0.78
⊖ Southwestern Energy Comp	Energy	52.1	58.97	0.73
⊖ Harris Corporation	Hardware	17.6	37.98	0.69
⊖ Amphenol Corporation	Hardware	25.6	49.63	0.65
⊖ FMC Technologies, Inc.	Energy	27.5	84.00	0.65
✵ Hologic, Inc.	Health	39.8	45.18	0.65
⊖ Telephone and Data Syste	Telecom	26.9	15.96	0.62
⊖ KBR, Inc.	Business	29.9	48.32	0.60
⊖ Newfield Exploration Com	Energy	24.8	14.69	0.58
⊖ Denbury Resources, Inc.	Energy	36.9	114.11	0.57
⊖ Equitable Resources, Inc	Energy	24.7	29.86	0.57
⊖ Lam Research Corporation	Hardware	9.8	-14.60	0.56
⊖ Activision	Software	57.1	72.27	0.56
⊖ Everest Re Group, Ltd.	Financial	6.2	4.27	0.56
⊖ McAfee, Inc.	Software	32.9	32.14	0.55
⊖ AMB Property Corporation	Financial	21.5	1.64	0.54
⊖ Alliance Data Systems Co	Business	35.8	20.04	0.53

Current Investment Style

Value Blnd Growth — Large Mid Small

Market Cap	%
Giant	0.0
Large	0.0
Mid	82.9
Small	16.9
Micro	0.2
Avg $mil: 3,754	

Value Measures		Rel Category
Price/Earnings	15.46	0.97
Price/Book	2.36	1.05
Price/Sales	1.13	0.97
Price/Cash Flow	9.21	1.08
Dividend Yield %	1.19	0.72

Growth Measures	%	Rel Category
Long-Term Erngs	12.19	0.99
Book Value	8.00	0.95
Sales	8.28	1.98
Cash Flow	-1.99	NMF
Historical Erngs	13.72	0.74

Profitability	%	Rel Category
Return on Equity	16.00	0.81
Return on Assets	7.07	0.91
Net Margin	11.09	0.92

Sector Weightings	% of Stocks	Rel S&P 500	3 Year High	3 Year Low
Info	13.96	0.67		
Software	3.66	0.88	4	3
Hardware	8.05	0.79	9	8
Media	1.19	0.41	2	1
Telecom	1.06	0.29	1	1
Service	47.71	1.17		
Health	11.90	0.99	12	10
Consumer	9.66	1.42	13	9
Business	12.05	2.73	13	11
Financial	14.10	0.81	18	14
Mfg	38.34	1.00		
Goods	6.66	0.73	7	4
Ind Mtrls	14.74	1.13	15	9
Energy	10.43	0.83	12	8
Utilities	6.51	1.77	8	7

Composition

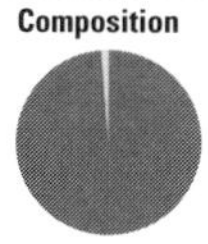

Cash	0.0
Stocks	98.6
Bonds	0.0
Other	1.4
Foreign (% of Stock)	0.0

PowerShares Dyn Lg Growth PWB

Market Price	Mstar Category
$18.75	Large Growth

Morningstar Fair Value

Price/Fair Value Ratio	Coverage Rate %
0.94	100

Valuation

Given this portfolio's diversification across stocks and industries, we'd be comfortable recommending it at a 9% or greater discount to our fair value estimate. It has never hit that level since its 2005 launch and was recently trading at a modest 6% discount to fair value, a price that's not enticing enough.

Methodology

This ETF tracks the Large Cap Growth Intellidex, a quantitatively driven benchmark that seeks large-cap stocks with a greater potential for capital appreciation than the norm. The index is based on a 25-factor model that evaluates the 2,000 biggest U.S. stocks on various technical and fundamental factors. It reconstitutes its 50-stock portfolio quarterly and thus has a much higher turnover rate and hence, greater potential tax liability than a purely passive ETF. The models favor the highest-octane large-cap stocks, explaining why the portfolio's typical name is more expensive and faster growing than the norm.

Morningstar Rating	Return	Risk	Yield	NAV	Avg Daily Vol. (k)	52 wk High/Low
—	—	—	0.2%	$18.62	269	$19.29 - $16.13

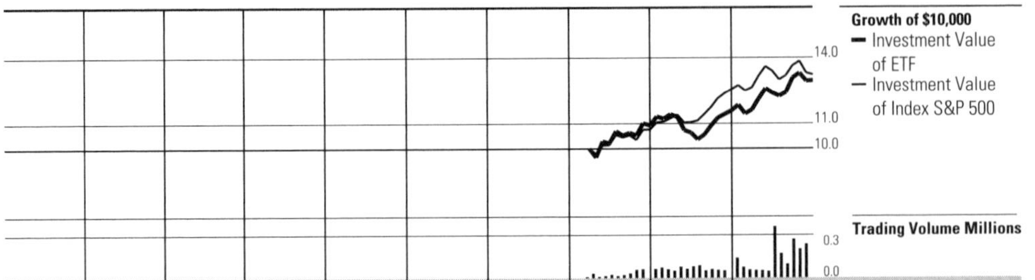

1998	1999	2000	2001	2002	2003	2004	2005	2006	2007	History
—	—	—	—	—	—	—	15.86	16.71	18.62	NAV $
—	—	—	—	—	—	—	15.86	16.72	18.75	Market Price $
—	—	—	—	—	—	—	8.51*	5.47	11.66	NAV Return%
—	—	—	—	—	—	—	8.39*	5.56	12.34	Market Price Return%
—	—	—	—	—	—	—	0.04	0.05	0.09	Avg Premium/Discount%
—	—	—	—	—	—	—	—	-10.32	6.17	NAV Rtrn% +/-S&P 500
—	—	—	—	—	—	—	—	0.09	-0.44	NAV Rtrn% +/-LG Intellidex
—	—	—	—	—	—	—	—	83	39	NAV Return% Rank in Cat
—	—	—	—	—	—	—	—	0.13	0.21	Income Return %
—	—	—	—	—	—	—	—	5.34	11.45	Capital Return %
—	—	—	—	—	—	—	0.00	0.02	0.04	Income $
—	—	—	—	—	—	—	0.00	0.00	0.00	Capital Gains $
—	—	—	—	—	—	—	0.63	0.64	0.63	Expense Ratio %
—	—	—	—	—	—	—	0.13	-0.04	0.13	Income Ratio %
—	—	—	—	—	—	—	2	73	57	Turnover Rate %
—	—	—	—	—	—	—	97	206	720	Net Assets $mil

Performance 12-31-07

Historic Quarterly NAV Returns

	1st Qtr	2nd Qtr	3rd Qtr	4th Qtr	Total
2003	—	—	—	—	—
2004	—	—	—	—	—
2005	—	1.99	3.90	2.74	—*
2006	4.10	-6.47	2.60	5.59	5.47
2007	0.31	6.39	5.71	-1.01	11.66

Trailing	NAV Return%	Market Return%	NAV Rtrn% +/-S&P 500	%Rank Cat.(NAV)
3 Mo	-1.01	-0.18	2.32	41
6 Mo	4.64	5.48	6.01	18
1 Yr	11.66	12.34	6.17	39
3 Yr Avg	—	—	—	—
5 Yr Avg	—	—	—	—
10 Yr Avg	—	—	—	—

Tax Analysis	Tax-Adj Return%	Tax-Cost Ratio
3 Yr (estimated)	—	—
5 Yr (estimated)	—	—
10 Yr (estimated)	—	—

Rating and Risk

Time Period	Morningstar Rtn vs Cat	Morningstar Risk vs Cat	Morningstar Risk-Adj Rating
3 Yr	—	—	—
5 Yr	—	—	—
10 Yr	—	—	—

Other Measures	Standard Index S&P 500	Best Fit Index
Alpha	—	—
Beta	—	—
R-Squared	—	—
Standard Deviation	—	
Mean	—	
Sharpe Ratio	—	

Portfolio Analysis 11-30-07

Share change since 10-07 Total Stocks:50	Sector	PE	Tot Ret%	% Assets
⊕ Google, Inc.	Business	54.0	50.17	4.28
⊕ Apple, Inc.	Hardware	50.5	133.47	4.18
⊕ News Corporation, Ltd. A	Media	14.9	-4.08	3.31
⊕ Hewlett-Packard Company	Hardware	18.8	23.40	3.30
⊕ Qualcomm, Inc.	Hardware	20.2	5.52	3.25
⊕ Genentech, Inc.	Health	26.2	-17.33	3.24
⊕ Bristol-Myers Squibb Com	Health	24.8	4.75	3.23
⊕ Oracle Corporation	Software	24.8	31.74	3.16
⊕ eBay, Inc.	Consumer	—	10.38	3.13
⊕ Schlumberger, Ltd.	Energy	24.6	57.10	3.08
⊕ Medtronic, Inc.	Health	20.3	-5.22	3.06
⊕ Boeing Company	Ind Mtrls	16.9	-0.11	3.04
⊕ Texas Instruments, Inc.	Hardware	19.2	17.01	2.93
⊕ Cisco Systems, Inc.	Hardware	21.5	-0.95	2.79
⊕ Walgreen Company	Consumer	18.5	-16.35	2.58
⊕ MasterCard Incorporated	Business	35.7	119.40	2.00
⊕ Monsanto Company	Ind Mtrls	67.1	114.45	1.94
⊕ Charles Schwab Corporati	Financial	30.8	40.07	1.66
⊕ Constellation Energy Gro	Utilities	22.5	51.88	1.65
⊕ Colgate-Palmolive Compan	Goods	24.7	21.94	1.65

Current Investment Style

Value Blnd Growth / Large Mid Small

Market Cap	%
Giant	40.0
Large	60.0
Mid	0.0
Small	0.0
Micro	0.0
Avg $mil: 45,440	

Value Measures		Rel Category
Price/Earnings	20.99	1.08
Price/Book	3.83	1.14
Price/Sales	1.98	1.13
Price/Cash Flow	12.70	1.10
Dividend Yield %	0.64	0.75

Growth Measures	%	Rel Category
Long-Term Erngs	16.75	1.16
Book Value	10.19	1.00
Sales	11.38	1.17
Cash Flow	17.95	1.66
Historical Erngs	22.54	1.26

Profitability	%	Rel Category
Return on Equity	24.15	1.05
Return on Assets	11.65	1.20
Net Margin	16.50	1.28

Sector Weightings	% of Stocks	Rel S&P 500	3 Year High	3 Year Low
Info	33.72	1.61		
Software	4.51	1.09	11	5
Hardware	23.11	2.26	24	8
Media	6.10	2.10	17	5
Telecom	0.00	0.00	4	0
Service	37.45	0.92		
Health	18.24	1.52	27	14
Consumer	5.71	0.84	21	6
Business	10.56	2.39	12	5
Financial	2.94	0.17	16	3
Mfg	28.82	0.75		
Goods	4.28	0.47	9	0
Ind Mtrls	13.87	1.07	14	3
Energy	6.04	0.48	10	0
Utilities	4.63	1.26	5	0

Composition

Cash	0.1
Stocks	99.9
Bonds	0.0
Other	0.0
Foreign (% of Stock)	0.0

Morningstar's Take by Emiko Kurotsu 12-31-07

We'd buy this high-octane ETF at the right price.

This ETF tracks the Large Cap Growth Intellidex, a quantitatively driven benchmark that sifts for the 50 large-cap stocks offering the greatest potential for capital appreciation based on various fundamental and technical measures. The Intellidex has a high-octane feel, as its typical stock is both more expensive (by valuation measures like price/earnings) and faster growing (by earnings or sales growth) than the norm in the Russell 1000 Growth Index. The models are most enamored with tech and health-care stocks, which soak up nearly half of the portfolio. The Intellidex also sports a higher average market cap than the Russell.

That has translated to a portfolio of respectable quality. Our analysts have awarded a wide economic moat to 19 of the fund's 51 stocks, which account for about 44% of the fund's assets. For instance, Adobe System's business software has become a necessity for many professionals, an advantage fortified by the high customer-switching costs involved. Similarly, McGraw Hill's S&P-credit rating franchise is part of a duopoly and the firm boasts scale and prestige in the lucrative educational publishing market.

Yet, this is hardly the highest-quality portfolio that we cover, as it owns a slightly smaller chunk of wide-moat stocks than the Russell index and is merely average when pitted against other large-growth ETFs. That's largely a function of the models' quest for growth. For instance, whereas preeminent semiconductor maker Intel figures prominently in the Russell index, it's absent here. Instead, faster-growing, chipmaker Nvidia--which is vulnerable to bigger rivals like Intel, explaining its narrow moat--is featured. Thus, we assign slightly less value to this portfolio's holdings than we would a higher-quality growth fund's.

Nevertheless, the portfolio's generally moderate risk profile and wide diversification doesn't argue for a wide margin of safety. We'd be buyers at a 9% discount to our fair value estimate.

Address:	301 West Roosevelt Road United States 800-983-0903
Web Address:	www.powershares.com
Inception:	03-03-05*
Advisor:	PowerShares Capital Management LLC

Management Fee:	0.50%		
Expense Projections:	3Yr:$214	5Yr:$375	10Yr:$843
Income Distrib:	Quarterly		
Exchange:	AMEX		

PowerShares Dyn Lg Value PWV

Market Price	Mstar Category
$20.35	Large Value

Morningstar Fair Value

Price/Fair Value Ratio	Coverage Rate %
0.90	100

Valuation

This ETF is a bargain. It was recently trading at a 10% discount to our fair value estimate, which exceeds the 9% discount we demand. The ETF's short history shows it tends to look cheapest when large-cap financials are out of favor, as they've been since the summer of 2007.

Methodology

This ETF tracks the Large Cap Value Intellidex, a quantitatively based benchmark that sifts the universe of larger, cheaper stocks for 50 names with the greatest potential for capital appreciation based on various technical and fundamental factors. The fund reconstitutes quarterly, but turnover here isn't as high as its large-growth sibling. Assets are spread relatively uniformly, as the top 10 holdings soak up only 35% of assets and the median position size is roughly 1.5%. The fund heavily favors financials, and to a lesser extent, energy and industrials.

Morningstar Rating	Return	Risk	Yield	NAV	Avg Daily Vol. (k)	52 wk High/Low
—	—	—	2.3%	$20.40	76	$21.56 - $19.09

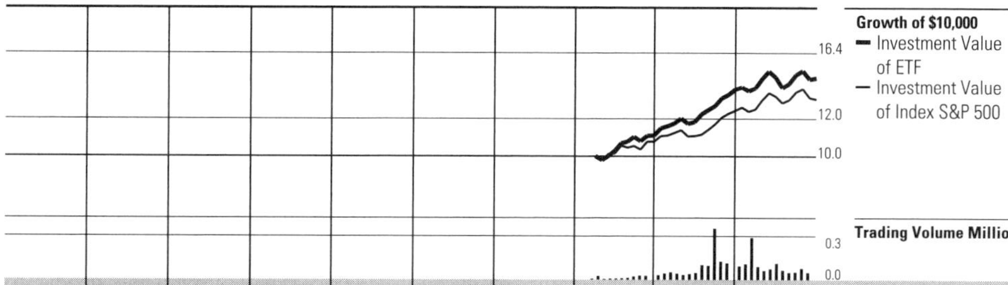

1998	1999	2000	2001	2002	2003	2004	2005	2006	2007	History
—	—	—	—	—	—	—	16.11	19.75	20.40	NAV $
—	—	—	—	—	—	—	16.12	19.77	20.35	Market Price $
—	—	—	—	—	—	—	13.50*	24.42	5.62	NAV Return%
—	—	—	—	—	—	—	12.95*	24.44	5.27	Market Price Return%
—	—	—	—	—	—	—	0.12	0.17	-0.13	Avg Premium/Discount%
—	—	—	—	—	—	—	—	8.63	0.13	NAV Rtrn% +/-S&P 500
—	—	—	—	—	—	—	—	2.32	2.04	NAV Rtrn% +/-LV Intellidex
—	—	—	—	—	—	—	—	8	21	NAV Return% Rank in Cat
—	—	—	—	—	—	—	—	1.66	2.37	Income Return %
—	—	—	—	—	—	—	—	22.76	3.25	Capital Return %
—	—	—	—	—	—	—	0.21	0.27	0.46	Income $
—	—	—	—	—	—	—	0.00	0.00	0.00	Capital Gains $
—	—	—	—	—	—	—	0.63	0.65	0.63	Expense Ratio %
—	—	—	—	—	—	—	1.99	1.75	2.00	Income Ratio %
—	—	—	—	—	—	—	—	29	16	Turnover Rate %
—	—	—	—	—	—	—	50	383	269	Net Assets $mil

Performance 12-31-07

Historic Quarterly NAV Returns

	1st Qtr	2nd Qtr	3rd Qtr	4th Qtr	Total
2003	—	—	—	—	—
2004	—	—	—	—	—
2005	—	2.72	6.71	0.66	—*
2006	5.82	0.69	7.90	8.22	24.42
2007	0.64	5.35	1.13	-1.49	5.62

Trailing	NAV Return%	Market Return%	NAV Rtrn% +/-S&P 500	%Rank Cat.(NAV)
3 Mo	-1.49	-1.59	1.84	5
6 Mo	-0.38	-0.29	0.99	5
1 Yr	5.62	5.27	0.13	21
3 Yr Avg	—	—	—	—
5 Yr Avg	—	—	—	—
10 Yr Avg	—	—	—	—

Tax Analysis	Tax-Adj Return%	Tax-Cost Ratio
3 Yr (estimated)	—	—
5 Yr (estimated)	—	—
10 Yr (estimated)	—	—

Rating and Risk

Time Period	Morningstar Rtn vs Cat	Morningstar Risk vs Cat	Morningstar Risk-Adj Rating
3 Yr	—	—	—
5 Yr	—	—	—
10 Yr	—	—	—

Other Measures	Standard Index S&P 500	Best Fit Index
Alpha	—	—
Beta	—	—
R-Squared	—	—
Standard Deviation	—	
Mean	—	
Sharpe Ratio	—	

Portfolio Analysis 11-30-07

Share change since 10-07 Total Stocks:50	Sector	PE	Tot Ret%	% Assets
⊕ Goldman Sachs Group, Inc	Financial	8.8	8.59	4.22
⊕ Altria Group Inc.	Goods	13.2	22.10	3.66
⊕ Johnson & Johnson	Health	18.8	3.61	3.59
⊕ ExxonMobil Corporation	Energy	13.6	24.34	3.41
⊕ Verizon Communications I	Telecom	21.7	22.19	3.38
⊕ J.P. Morgan Chase & Co.	Financial	9.5	-7.24	3.36
⊕ Chevron Corporation	Energy	11.4	30.59	3.28
⊕ AT&T, Inc.	Telecom	21.6	20.58	3.14
⊕ Pfizer Inc.	Health	22.5	-8.15	3.13
⊕ Bank of America Corporat	Financial	9.4	-19.25	2.98
⊕ International Business M	Hardware	16.2	13.20	2.95
⊕ Wells Fargo Company	Financial	11.4	-12.13	2.91
⊕ American International G	Financial	10.2	-17.96	2.89
⊕ Morgan Stanley	Financial	6.1	-20.21	2.77
⊕ Citigroup, Inc.	Financial	7.9	-44.93	2.33
⊕ Deere & Company	Ind Mtrls	23.3	98.60	1.77
⊕ Apache Corporation	Energy	15.9	62.91	1.76
⊕ Occidental Petroleum Cor	Energy	13.8	60.25	1.73
⊕ Principal Financial Grou	Financial	17.8	18.84	1.66
⊕ Aflac, Inc.	Financial	19.6	38.00	1.65

Current Investment Style

Value Blnd Growth — Large Mid Small

Market Cap	%
Giant	51.2
Large	48.8
Mid	0.0
Small	0.0
Micro	0.0
Avg $mil: 62,711	

Value Measures		Rel Category
Price/Earnings	11.97	0.89
Price/Book	2.03	1.04
Price/Sales	1.37	1.14
Price/Cash Flow	8.40	1.01
Dividend Yield %	2.32	0.86

Growth Measures	%	Rel Category
Long-Term Erngs	9.46	0.96
Book Value	12.53	1.45
Sales	8.44	1.32
Cash Flow	10.46	1.99
Historical Erngs	22.84	1.52

Profitability	%	Rel Category
Return on Equity	22.52	1.14
Return on Assets	6.50	1.01
Net Margin	14.72	1.06

Sector Weightings	% of Stocks	Rel S&P 500	3 Year High	Low
Info	9.47	0.45		
Software	0.00	0.00	0	0
Hardware	2.95	0.29	8	3
Media	0.00	0.00	0	0
Telecom	6.52	1.80	9	3
Service	48.63	1.20		
Health	9.67	0.80	13	5
Consumer	0.00	0.00	5	0
Business	1.28	0.29	3	0
Financial	37.68	2.16	46	33
Mfg	41.88	1.09		
Goods	9.51	1.04	12	7
Ind Mtrls	11.68	0.90	17	4
Energy	14.50	1.15	20	3
Utilities	6.19	1.68	12	4

Composition

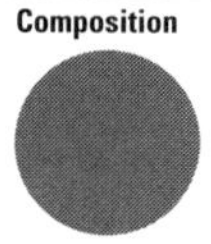

Cash	0.0
Stocks	100.0
Bonds	0.0
Other	0.0
Foreign (% of Stock)	0.0

Morningstar's Take by Emiko Kurotsu 12-31-07

Powershares Dynamic Large Cap Value's quality is neck and neck with that of the Russell 1000 Value.

This compact ETF tracks the Large Cap Value Intellidex, a quasi-actively managed index that sifts through the universe of large, cheap stocks for 50 names with the best upside potential. Powershares divvies stocks into the growth and value camps based on traits like earnings growth, price/book multiples, and dividend yield. The resulting portfolio sports purer large-cap exposure than the Russell 1000 Value Index, which stakes a sizeable 20% in mid-caps.

This fund's quality is nearly on par with iShares Russell 1000 Value's. Both ETFs are anchored in industry giants that have defensible competitive advantages, or "economic moats." These include oil major ExxonMobil, whose scale and operational efficiency are unparalleled; and Citigroup, whose global reach is hard to match. All told, nearly 40% of the Powershares fund, or 13 of the 50 stocks our analysts cover, boast wide moats, a figure that's comparable to the iShares offering's tally.

But for every top-quality stock like Pfizer, this fund is weighed down with nearly three other lesser-quality names. These narrow- and no-moat names tend to be those that have to fend with heavy capital investment demands (oil producers like Occidental Petroleum); stifling competition (telecoms like Verizon and AT&T); or regulatory constraints (utilities like Entergy and First Energy). Because such stocks generally fail to earn attractive returns on invested capital and are likely to struggle over the long haul, we view them as less valuable than wide-moat firms.

Most holdings here court at least average business risk, meaning their future results are moderately uncertain, due to their more tenuous competitive advantages. The fund's diversification tamps down volatility, though. For that reason, we'd buy this fund at a modest 9% discount to our fair value estimate.

Address:	301 West Roosevelt Road United States 800-983-0903
Web Address:	www.powershares.com
Inception:	03-03-05 *
Advisor:	PowerShares Capital Management LLC

Management Fee:	0.50%		
Expense Projections:	3Yr:$209	5Yr:$366	10Yr:$821
Income Distrib:	Quarterly		
Exchange:	AMEX		

PowerShares Dyn Market PWC

Market Price	Mstar Category
$51.86	Large Blend

Morningstar Rating	Return	Risk	Yield	NAV	Avg Daily Vol. (k)	52 wk High/Low
★★★★	Above Avg	Above Avg	1.0%	$51.55	48	$55.15 - $47.81

Morningstar Fair Value

Price/Fair Value Ratio	Coverage Rate %
0.98	92

Valuation

This ETF has traded at a premium to our fair value estimate on and off since its mid-2003 launch. That's likely due to its hefty stake in mid caps, which have been pricier. We'd be buyers when the fund is trading at a 9% or greater discount to our fair value estimate. It was recently trading at a 2% discount, which isn't cheap enough for us.

Methodology

This fund tracks the Dynamic Market Intellidex, which is based on a 25-factor quantitative model that assesses technical factors like price and volume trends alongside fundamental measures like P/E ratios and growth rates. The Intellidex, which consists of 100 stocks and is rebalanced quarterly, aims to outperform other broad-market indices. Despite its moniker, the fund isn't a perfect proxy for the broad market, as its portfolio tends to skew toward smaller, cheaper stocks. However, its sector weights mimic those of the broader market for the most part, though it has more tech, and less financials and energy.

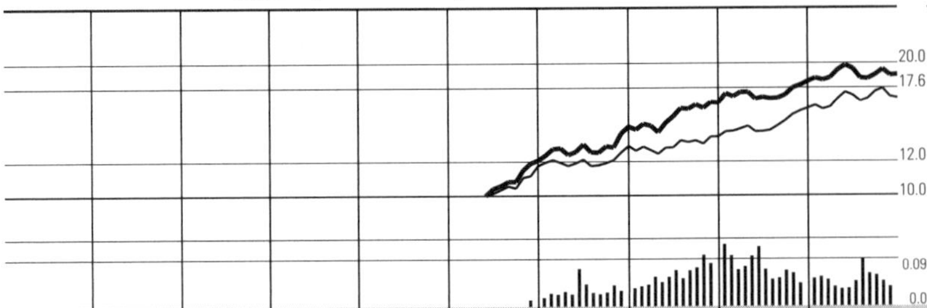

History

1998	1999	2000	2001	2002	2003	2004	2005	2006	2007	History
—	—	—	—	—	34.10	40.34	45.31	50.31	51.55	NAV $
—	—	—	—	—	34.02	40.48	45.32	50.37	51.86	Market Price $
—	—	—	—	—	15.80*	19.08	13.12	11.73	3.50	NAV Return%
—	—	—	—	—	15.97*	19.77	12.76	11.84	4.00	Market Price Return%
—	—	—	—	—	-0.01	0.22	0.12	0.03	-0.02	Avg Premium/Discount%
—	—	—	—	—	—	8.20	8.21	-4.06	-1.99	NAV Rtrn% +/-S&P 500
—	—	—	—	—	—	—	0.63	1.51	0.12	NAV Rtrn% +/-Mkt Intellidex
—	—	—	—	—	—	7	5	96	71	NAV Return% Rank in Cat
—	—	—	—	—	—	0.72	0.78	0.67	1.06	Income Return %
—	—	—	—	—	—	18.36	12.34	11.06	2.44	Capital Return %
—	—	—	—	—	0.25	0.24	0.31	0.30	0.53	Income $
—	—	—	—	—	0.00	0.00	0.00	0.00	0.00	Capital Gains $
—	—	—	—	—	—	0.60	0.60	0.60	0.60	Expense Ratio %
—	—	—	—	—	—	0.46	0.68	0.76	0.87	Income Ratio %
—	—	—	—	—	—	58	94	103	114	Turnover Rate %
—	—	—	—	—	36	230	691	958	771	Net Assets $mil

Performance 12-31-07

Historic Quarterly NAV Returns

	1st Qtr	2nd Qtr	3rd Qtr	4th Qtr	Total
2003	—	—	3.73	11.56	—*
2004	6.46	2.13	-1.08	10.70	19.08
2005	0.47	4.86	6.34	0.98	13.12
2006	5.73	-2.61	1.15	7.28	11.73
2007	1.94	4.75	-3.13	0.06	3.50

Trailing	NAV Return%	Market Return%	NAV Rtrn% +/-S&P 500	%Rank Cat.(NAV)
3 Mo	0.06	0.41	3.39	13
6 Mo	-3.07	-2.32	-1.70	67
1 Yr	3.50	4.00	-1.99	71
3 Yr Avg	9.37	9.46	0.75	34
5 Yr Avg	—	—	—	—
10 Yr Avg	—	—	—	—

Tax Analysis	Tax-Adj Return%	Tax-Cost Ratio
3 Yr (estimated)	9.07	0.27
5 Yr (estimated)	—	—
10 Yr (estimated)	—	—

Rating and Risk

Time Period	Morningstar Rtn vs Cat	Morningstar Risk vs Cat	Morningstar Risk-Adj Rating
3 Yr	+Avg	+Avg	★★★★
5 Yr	—	—	—
10 Yr	—	—	—

Other Measures	Standard Index S&P 500	Best Fit Index S&P 400 TR
Alpha	0.9	0.4
Beta	0.98	0.77
R-Squared	74	85
Standard Deviation	8.75	
Mean	9.37	
Sharpe Ratio	0.58	

Morningstar's Take by Emiko Kurotsu 12-31-07

Powershares Dynamic Market's quirks detract from the value we'd place on it.

This ETF tracks the Dynamic Market Intellidex, which uses a 25-factor quantitative model to compile 100 stocks that it expects will outperform other broad-market indices. The model uses technical metrics such as price and volume trends, as well as fundamental measures like price multiples and growth rates. With nearly 42% of assets in midcaps, this fund dips further down the market-cap ladder than its peers.

This has a noticeable impact on the portfolio's quality, which is below average. Our analysts have awarded a wide economic moat rating to only 6 of the 78 portfolio holdings that they cover, meaning the vast majority lack durable competitive advantages. True, size alone doesn't make for dominance. Three of the portfolio's half-dozen wide-moat names--fund processor SEI Investments SEIC, software provider Autodesk ADSK, and transportation concern Landstar System, Inc--are smaller firms. Yet, attributes such as scale, barriers to entry, or brand identity--all hallmarks of wide-moat businesses--are less plentiful among the firms the fund favors. Thus, shorn of bulwarks like Microsoft, it's not a huge surprise that this fund teems with lesser-quality names such as no-moat refiner Sunoco SUN or narrow-moat software provider McAfee MFE.

The portfolio's ho-hum quality doesn't indict it, but it does make it less valuable in our analysts' estimation, as we normally assign less value to firms that aren't able to defend and leverage their turf to churn out economic profits. It also increases the risk associated with the typical holding, as the future results of less-dominant firms are more uncertain, owing to the greater likelihood that such business could be waylaid by rivals.

The fund's diversification across stocks and industries has tamped down volatility. We don't need an especially wide margin of safety, but a 9% discount to our fair value estimate will do.

Address:	301 West Roosevelt Road United States 800-983-0903
Web Address:	www.powershares.com
Inception:	05-01-03*
Advisor:	PowerShares Capital Management LLC

Management Fee:	0.50%		
Expense Projections:	3Yr:$197	5Yr:$344	10Yr:$773
Income Distrib:	Quarterly		
Exchange:	AMEX		

Portfolio Analysis 11-30-07

Share change since 10-07 Total Stocks:99

Share change	Sector	PE	Tot Ret%	% Assets
⊖ Noble Energy, Inc.	Energy	17.1	63.17	4.45
⊖ Chevron Corporation	Energy	11.4	30.59	3.71
⊖ Deere & Company	Ind Mtrls	23.3	98.60	3.39
⊖ Altria Group Inc.	Goods	13.2	22.10	3.30
⊖ Constellation Energy Gro	Utilities	22.5	51.88	2.97
⊖ Owens-Illinois, Inc.	Ind Mtrls	53.2	168.29	2.96
⊖ Kellogg Company	Goods	19.0	5.70	2.90
⊖ Republic Services, Inc.	Business	22.2	17.71	2.86
⊖ Rockwell Automation	Ind Mtrls	19.5	14.90	2.59
⊖ Principal Financial Grou	Financial	17.8	18.84	2.44
⊖ Nike, Inc. B	Goods	19.4	31.48	2.42
⊖ Express Scripts	Health	34.1	103.91	2.39
⊖ McAfee, Inc.	Software	32.9	32.14	2.36
⊖ BMC Software, Inc.	Software	27.9	10.75	2.34
⊖ Hartford Financial Servi	Financial	8.9	-4.53	2.21
⊖ Autodesk, Inc.	Software	34.1	22.99	2.20
⊖ Chubb Corporation	Financial	7.9	5.20	2.20
⊖ The Travelers Companies,	Financial	7.8	2.37	2.17
⊖ Aetna, Inc.	Health	16.9	33.79	2.12
⊖ Baxter International Inc	Health	22.9	26.79	2.11

Current Investment Style

Value Blnd Growth; Large Mid Small

Market Cap	%
Giant	11.5
Large	33.4
Mid	46.3
Small	8.6
Micro	0.3
Avg $mil: 12,926	

Value Measures		Rel Category
Price/Earnings	13.78	0.87
Price/Book	2.50	0.98
Price/Sales	1.18	0.95
Price/Cash Flow	8.07	0.87
Dividend Yield %	1.19	0.63

Growth Measures	%	Rel Category
Long-Term Erngs	10.94	0.93
Book Value	11.09	1.20
Sales	10.28	1.26
Cash Flow	6.52	0.75
Historical Erngs	22.99	1.38

Profitability	%	Rel Category
Return on Equity	27.59	1.24
Return on Assets	9.23	1.11
Net Margin	12.38	1.01

Sector Weightings	% of Stocks	Rel S&P 500	3 Year High	3 Year Low
Info	18.89	0.90		
Software	8.95	2.16	9	1
Hardware	3.50	0.34	10	2
Media	2.40	0.82	3	0
Telecom	4.04	1.11	4	3
Service	39.43	0.97		
Health	12.55	1.04	14	11
Consumer	2.26	0.33	15	2
Business	6.62	1.50	11	2
Financial	18.00	1.03	22	18
Mfg	41.68	1.08		
Goods	14.59	1.59	17	6
Ind Mtrls	11.74	0.90	16	6
Energy	11.86	0.94	12	6
Utilities	3.49	0.95	4	3

Composition

Cash	0.0
Stocks	100.0
Bonds	0.0
Other	0.0
Foreign (% of Stock)	0.4

PowerShares Dyn MidGrowth PWJ

Market Price	Mstar Category
$24.26	Mid-Cap Growth

Morningstar Fair Value

Price/Fair Value Ratio	Coverage Rate %
1.04	92

Valuation

This fund's historical valuations reflect the hot streak that mid-caps have been on for the past few years. The fund has traded at a premium to our fair value estimate since mid-2003 (it was recently trading 4% above fair value, by our estimate). We'd need a 9% discount to fair value to invest here.

Methodology

This fund tracks the Mid Cap Growth Intellidex, a quantitatively based index that tracks 75 mid-cap stocks with the greatest potential for capital appreciation. The stocks are selected quarterly using a 25-factor model that focuses on a variety of technical and fundamental factors like trading volume and valuation ratios, as well as 'timeliness' and risk. The fund is well-diversified, and counts tech and business-services among its biggest sector weights. The fund has a high turnover rate due to its quarterly reconstitution; that jacks up its trading costs and potential for tax inefficiency.

Morningstar Rating	Return	Risk	Yield	NAV	Avg Daily Vol. (k)	52 wk High/Low
—	—	—	—	$23.96	231	$24.85 - $18.96

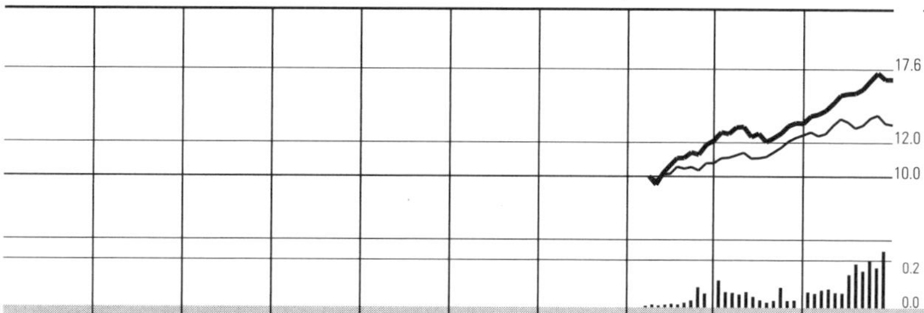

Growth of $10,000
— Investment Value of ETF
— Investment Value of Index S&P 500

Trading Volume Millions

1998	1999	2000	2001	2002	2003	2004	2005	2006	2007	History
—	—	—	—	—	—	—	17.49	19.03	23.96	NAV $
—	—	—	—	—	—	—	17.50	19.02	24.26	Market Price $
—	—	—	—	—	—	—	18.24*	9.44	25.97	NAV Return%
—	—	—	—	—	—	—	18.20*	9.34	27.56	Market Price Return%
—	—	—	—	—	—	—	0.01	0.01	0.14	Avg Premium/Discount%
—	—	—	—	—	—	—	—	-6.35	20.48	NAV Rtrn% +/-S&P 500
—	—	—	—	—	—	—	—	-0.10	-1.84	NAV Rtrn% +/-MG Intellidex
—	—	—	—	—	—	—	—	34	1	NAV Return% Rank in Cat
—	—	—	—	—	—	—	—	0.65	0.01	Income Return %
—	—	—	—	—	—	—	—	8.79	25.96	Capital Return %
—	—	—	—	—	—	—	0.00	0.11	0.00	Income $
—	—	—	—	—	—	—	0.00	0.00	0.00	Capital Gains $
—	—	—	—	—	—	—	0.63	0.65	0.63	Expense Ratio %
—	—	—	—	—	—	—	-0.20	1.56	-0.15	Income Ratio %
—	—	—	—	—	—	—	1	86	69	Turnover Rate %
—	—	—	—	—	—	—	68	126	442	Net Assets $mil

Performance 12-31-07

Historic Quarterly NAV Returns

	1st Qtr	2nd Qtr	3rd Qtr	4th Qtr	Total
2003	—	—	—	—	—
2004	—	—	—	—	—
2005	—	5.92	6.96	6.32	—*
2006	7.09	-3.05	0.09	5.31	9.44
2007	6.83	9.40	6.92	0.81	25.97

Trailing	NAV Return%	Market Return%	NAV Rtrn% +/-S&P 500	%Rank Cat.(NAV)
3 Mo	0.81	2.07	4.14	7
6 Mo	7.79	9.04	9.16	1
1 Yr	25.97	27.56	20.48	1
3 Yr Avg	—	—	—	—
5 Yr Avg	—	—	—	—
10 Yr Avg	—	—	—	—

Tax Analysis	Tax-Adj Return%	Tax-Cost Ratio
3 Yr (estimated)	—	—
5 Yr (estimated)	—	—
10 Yr (estimated)	—	—

Rating and Risk

Time Period	Morningstar Rtn vs Cat	Morningstar Risk vs Cat	Morningstar Risk-Adj Rating
3 Yr	—	—	—
5 Yr	—	—	—
10 Yr	—	—	—

Other Measures	Standard Index S&P 500	Best Fit Index
Alpha	—	—
Beta	—	—
R-Squared	—	—
Standard Deviation	—	
Mean	—	
Sharpe Ratio	—	

Morningstar's Take by Emiko Kurotsu 12-31-07

PowerShares Dynamic Mid Cap Growth offers more quality for your buck.

This ETF tracks the Mid Cap Growth Intellidex, a quantitatively driven benchmark that sifts through the universe of midsized, fast-growing stocks for 75 with the greatest potential for capital appreciation. The index's penchant for high-octane stocks is eye-catching: Its typical holding has grown faster, and trades at a higher multiple, than the norm in the Russell Mid Cap Growth Index.

High-growth stocks aren't necessarily high quality, a trait we normally associate with firms that tout defensible competitive advantages, or "economic moats." Yet, this fund owns a higher proportion of wide-moat firms than nearly all the other mid-cap ETFs we cover. These include top-holding Apollo, which has carved out a wide moat as the leader in online and for-profit education, a position fortified by the firm's scale, operating efficiency, and barriers to entry. Insurance brokerage Brown & Brown distinguishes itself through its difficult-to-replicate carrot-and-stick employee culture, which pays agents double the industry average on the condition that they churn out hefty profits at each office. All told, our analysts have awarded wide moats to 12 of the 64 holdings they cover, representing about 20% of assets.

Of course, this is far from the highest-quality portfolio we cover. In fact, for every wide-moat stock, there are several narrow-moat names like Noble Energy or Hewitt Associates, whose advantages are less clear-cut, or more fleeting. Because we normally assign greater value to firms with wide moats than to those with narrow or no moats, it means that this portfolio is less valuable, on balance, than others, particularly those that teem with larger, blue-chip stocks.

Still, these stocks carry mostly moderate risk, and are a widely diversified lot. Thus, we don't demand a large margin of safety here, with a 9% or greater discount to fair value sufficing.

Address:	301 West Roosevelt Road United States 800-983-0903
Web Address:	www.powershares.com
Inception:	03-03-05*
Advisor:	PowerShares Capital Management LLC

Management Fee:	0.50%		
Expense Projections:	3Yr:$224	5Yr:$395	10Yr:$889
Income Distrib:	Quarterly		
Exchange:	AMEX		

Portfolio Analysis 11-30-07

Share change since 10-07 Total Stocks:74	Sector	PE	Tot Ret%	% Assets
⊕ Apollo Group, Inc. A	Consumer	29.9	80.01	3.94
⊕ MEMC Electronic Material	Hardware	35.3	126.09	3.82
⊕ Express Scripts	Health	34.1	103.91	3.74
⊕ T Rowe Price Group	Financial	27.0	41.00	3.62
⊕ Allegheny Energy, Inc.	Utilities	29.6	38.90	3.56
⊕ Fluor Corporation	Business	37.3	79.23	3.50
⊕ Ecolab, Inc.	Ind Mtrls	32.3	14.21	3.48
⊕ International Game Tech.	Consumer	29.1	-4.13	3.46
⊕ Cameron International Co	Energy	23.5	81.45	3.45
⊕ McDermott International	Energy	23.0	132.13	3.30
⊕ Noble Corporation	Energy	14.4	44.12	3.21
⊕ CH Robinson Worldwide, I	Business	30.2	34.33	3.18
⊕ Rockwell Collins, Inc.	Ind Mtrls	20.9	14.77	3.17
⊕ Autodesk, Inc.	Software	34.1	22.99	3.07
⊕ CA, Inc.	Software	44.6	10.64	2.94
⊕ Telephone and Data Syste	Telecom	26.9	15.96	2.91
⊕ Laboratory Corporation o	Health	20.1	2.80	2.83
⊕ Polo Ralph Lauren Corpor	Goods	17.0	-20.23	2.76
⊕ Fidelity National Inform	Business	16.6	3.84	2.76
⊕ Electronic Data Systems	Software	14.5	-24.49	2.68

Current Investment Style

Value Blnd Growth / Large Mid Small

Market Cap	%
Giant	0.0
Large	25.3
Mid	72.6
Small	2.1
Micro	0.0
Avg $mil: 8,443	

Value Measures		Rel Category
Price/Earnings	20.93	1.09
Price/Book	3.75	1.19
Price/Sales	1.78	1.16
Price/Cash Flow	11.43	1.06
Dividend Yield %	0.49	0.86

Growth Measures	%	Rel Category
Long-Term Erngs	17.16	1.07
Book Value	10.98	0.98
Sales	10.56	0.99
Cash Flow	13.20	1.38
Historical Erngs	25.66	1.19

Profitability	%	Rel Category
Return on Equity	27.27	1.27
Return on Assets	12.31	1.28
Net Margin	13.34	1.20

Sector Weightings	% of Stocks	Rel S&P 500	3 Year High	3 Year Low
Info	23.32	1.12		
Software	9.96	2.41	13	5
Hardware	7.90	0.77	21	6
Media	0.00	0.00	3	0
Telecom	5.46	1.50	7	0
Service	46.86	1.15		
Health	13.20	1.10	24	7
Consumer	11.28	1.66	18	3
Business	16.94	3.84	18	8
Financial	5.44	0.31	17	5
Mfg	29.83	0.78		
Goods	4.42	0.48	11	2
Ind Mtrls	10.26	0.79	19	10
Energy	11.59	0.92	12	1
Utilities	3.56	0.97	6	0

Composition

Cash	0.0
Stocks	100.0
Bonds	0.0
Other	0.0
Foreign (% of Stock)	0.0

PowerShares Dyn Mid Value PWP

Market Price	Mstar Category
$18.36	Mid-Cap Value

Morningstar Fair Value

Price/Fair Value Ratio	Coverage Rate %
0.89	95

Valuation

This fund was recently trading at an 11% discount to our fair value estimate, slightly over the 9% minimum discount we'd demand. The fund has seldom been this cheap in its four-year history, reflecting the rich valuations mid-caps have garnered in the recent past.

Methodology

This ETF tracks the Mid Cap Value Intellidex, which uses a 25-factor quantitative model to sift through the universe of reasonably priced mid-cap stocks for 75 names thought to have the biggest potential upside. Powershares defines mid-value stocks as those with market caps between $1.8 and $14.4 billion and "value" characteristics deemed by a separate multifactor model. The models weight stocks based on how they score on the 25-factor model. The fund's top 20 or so holdings soak up 70% of assets. The fund reconstitutes quarterly, keeping turnover high.

Morningstar Rating	Return	Risk	Yield	NAV	Avg Daily Vol. (k)	52 wk High/Low
—	—	—	1.2%	$18.91	42	$21.36 - $17.18

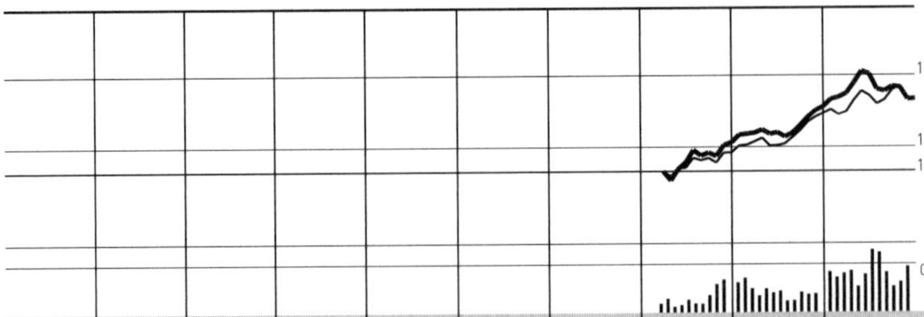

Growth of $10,000
— Investment Value of ETF
— Investment Value of Index S&P 500

Trading Volume Millions

1998	1999	2000	2001	2002	2003	2004	2005	2006	2007	History
—	—	—	—	—	—	—	16.46	18.57	18.91	NAV $
—	—	—	—	—	—	—	16.45	18.56	18.36	Market Price $
—	—	—	—	—	—	—	9.81*	14.33	3.00	NAV Return%
—	—	—	—	—	—	—	8.16*	14.33	0.05	Market Price Return%
—	—	—	—	—	—	—	-0.01	0.05	-0.29	Avg Premium/Discount%
—	—	—	—	—	—	—	—	-1.46	-2.49	NAV Rtrn% +/-S&P 500
—	—	—	—	—	—	—	—	1.35	3.67	NAV Rtrn% +/-MV Intellidex
—	—	—	—	—	—	—	—	80	1	NAV Return% Rank in Cat
—	—	—	—	—	—	—	—	1.44	1.23	Income Return %
—	—	—	—	—	—	—	—	12.89	1.77	Capital Return %
—	—	—	—	—	—	—	0.24	0.24	0.23	Income $
—	—	—	—	—	—	—	0.00	0.00	0.00	Capital Gains $
—	—	—	—	—	—	—	0.63	0.67	0.63	Expense Ratio %
—	—	—	—	—	—	—	6.34	1.33	1.64	Income Ratio %
—	—	—	—	—	—	—	1	117	43	Turnover Rate %
—	—	—	—	—	—	—	41	72	98	Net Assets $mil

Performance 12-31-07

Historic Quarterly NAV Returns

	1st Qtr	2nd Qtr	3rd Qtr	4th Qtr	Total
2003	—	—	—	—	—
2004	—	—	—	—	—
2005	—	3.39	3.68	3.89	—*
2006	3.60	0.14	2.60	7.42	14.33
2007	5.08	7.52	-4.58	-4.46	3.00

Trailing	NAV Return%	Market Return%	NAV Rtrn% +/-S&P 500	%Rank Cat.(NAV)
3 Mo	-4.46	-7.23	-1.13	23
6 Mo	-8.84	-11.45	-7.47	39
1 Yr	3.00	0.05	-2.49	1
3 Yr Avg	—	—	—	—
5 Yr Avg	—	—	—	—
10 Yr Avg	—	—	—	—

Tax Analysis	Tax-Adj Return%	Tax-Cost Ratio
3 Yr (estimated)	—	—
5 Yr (estimated)	—	—
10 Yr (estimated)	—	—

Rating and Risk

Time Period	Morningstar Rtn vs Cat	Morningstar Risk vs Cat	Morningstar Risk-Adj Rating
3 Yr	—	—	—
5 Yr	—	—	—
10 Yr	—	—	—

Other Measures	Standard Index S&P 500	Best Fit Index
Alpha	—	—
Beta	—	—
R-Squared	—	—
Standard Deviation	—	
Mean	—	
Sharpe Ratio	—	

Portfolio Analysis 11-30-07

Share change since 10-07 Total Stocks:75	Sector	PE	Tot Ret%	% Assets
⊖ Noble Energy, Inc.	Energy	17.1	63.17	3.92
⊖ Carolina Group	Goods	—	34.93	3.82
⊖ Aon Corp.	Financial	18.6	36.99	3.77
⊖ Parker Hannifin Corporat	Ind Mtrls	15.6	47.94	3.62
⊖ Clorox Company	Goods	20.0	3.86	3.54
⊖ United States Steel Corp	Ind Mtrls	12.6	66.73	3.38
⊖ Unum Group	Financial	10.5	15.99	3.32
⊖ Sara Lee Corporation	Goods	31.4	-3.41	3.31
⊖ Coventry Health Care, In	Health	15.7	18.38	3.30
⊖ ConAgra Foods, Inc.	Goods	15.9	-9.28	3.18
⊖ Genuine Parts Company	Consumer	15.8	0.58	3.16
⊖ Eaton Corporation	Ind Mtrls	15.2	31.54	3.10
⊖ Computer Sciences Corpor	Software	22.9	-6.75	3.08
⊖ VF Corporation	Goods	13.2	-14.03	3.06
⊖ AutoZone, Inc.	Consumer	13.6	3.57	3.01
⊖ Sherwin-Williams Company	Goods	12.6	-6.97	2.97
⊖ Pitney Bowes Inc.	Ind Mtrls	14.3	-15.11	2.82
⊖ CNA Financial Corporatio	Financial	8.7	-15.64	2.76
⊖ Nationwide Financial Ser	Financial	9.9	-15.31	2.73
⊖ Embarq Corporation	Telecom	—	-1.66	2.67

Current Investment Style

Value Blnd Growth — Large Mid Small

Market Cap	%
Giant	0.0
Large	10.5
Mid	87.0
Small	2.5
Micro	0.0

Avg $mil: 7,364

Value Measures		Rel Category
Price/Earnings	12.10	0.91
Price/Book	1.93	1.27
Price/Sales	0.98	1.26
Price/Cash Flow	8.62	1.40
Dividend Yield %	1.34	0.57

Growth Measures	%	Rel Category
Long-Term Erngs	10.55	1.06
Book Value	6.75	0.82
Sales	7.58	1.18
Cash Flow	4.60	3.07
Historical Erngs	23.96	1.82

Profitability	%	Rel Category
Return on Equity	24.61	1.65
Return on Assets	7.35	1.47
Net Margin	10.07	0.94

Sector Weightings	% of Stocks	Rel S&P 500	3 Year High	3 Year Low
Info	7.25	0.35		
Software	3.08	0.74	4	0
Hardware	0.42	0.04	5	0
Media	0.57	0.20	1	0
Telecom	3.18	0.88	3	0
Service	41.43	1.02		
Health	3.81	0.32	7	0
Consumer	7.81	1.15	14	3
Business	1.65	0.37	6	1
Financial	28.16	1.62	45	27
Mfg	51.32	1.33		
Goods	22.17	2.42	26	6
Ind Mtrls	21.34	1.64	28	12
Energy	7.23	0.57	8	0
Utilities	0.58	0.16	20	0

Composition

Cash	0.0
Stocks	100.0
Bonds	0.0
Other	0.0
Foreign (% of Stock)	0.0

Morningstar's Take by Emiko Kurotsu 12-31-07

Powershares Dynamic Mid Cap Value's quality is limited by its opportunity set.

This fund tracks the Mid Cap Value Intellidex, which hunts for 75 stocks with the greatest upside potential, as deemed by a 25-factor quantitative model. Its hunting ground is a pool of 300 stocks between $2 and $14 billion in market cap, which exhibit "value" traits as defined by PowerShares multifactor methodology. The resulting portfolio is among the purest mid-cap plays that we cover, as the fund keeps more than 80% of assets in midsized firms.

That allegiance does little to enhance the portfolio's quality, however. We normally associate quality with firms that boast intractable competitive advantages, or wide "economic moats." On that count, the fund ranks among the lowest of any mid-cap ETF we cover. Of the 67 portfolio stocks our analysts cover, just one--mail stream solutions provider Pitney-Bowes--garnered a wide-moat rating. In short, because the fund doesn't dabble in large caps--which are more often endowed with defensible advantages like scale or lustrous brands--it's left with fewer wide-moat holdings.

That said, many of the fund's holdings possess at least some semblance of a competitive advantage. For instance, Carolina Group's flagship Newport cigarettes earn the firm returns on capital in excess of 100%; yet its dependence on the declining U.S. cigarette market leaves it vulnerable to competition. Similarly, diversified industrial Parker Hannifin boasts attractive traits like a wide distribution system and deep customer relationships, but operates in cyclical markets. Narrow-moat stocks like these soak up 60% of assets.

Though narrow- and no-moat firms are typically riskier, as they're more vulnerable to rivals, the portfolio's diversification has tamped down volatility. Thus, we wouldn't demand a wide margin of safety to invest here, with a 9% discount to our fair value estimate sufficing.

Address:	301 West Roosevelt Road United States 800-983-0903
Web Address:	www.powershares.com
Inception:	03-03-05*
Advisor:	PowerShares Capital Management LLC

Management Fee:	0.50%		
Expense Projections:	3Yr:$242	5Yr:$428	10Yr:$968
Income Distrib:	Quarterly		
Exchange:	AMEX		

PowerShares FTSE US1000 PRF

Market Price	Mstar Category
$58.14	Large Value

Morningstar Rating	Return	Risk	Yield	NAV	Avg Daily Vol. (k)	52 wk High/Low
—	—	—	1.5%	$59.52	172	$63.75 - $55.25

Morningstar Fair Value

Price/Fair Value Ratio	Coverage Rate %
0.87	98

Valuation

This fund is cheap. It was recently trading at a 13% discount to our fair value estimate, well exceeding the 9% discount we'd ordinarily demand. Like other ETFs that track large-cap U.S. indexes, it looks most attractive when blue chips are out of favor.

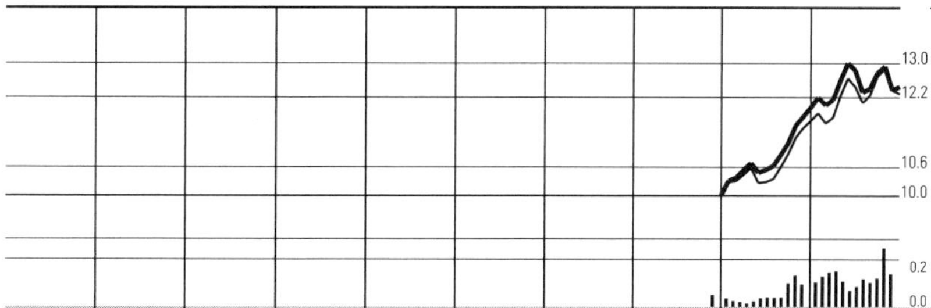

Growth of $10,000
— Investment Value of ETF
— Investment Value of Index S&P 500

Trading Volume Millions

Methodology

This fund tracks the FTSE RAFI U.S. 1000 Index, a benchmark that uses four factors (sales and cash flow over the past five years, book value, and total dividends), rather than market cap, to weight stocks. The index encompasses and ranks the 1,000 firms with the highest composite scores from the broader FTSE U.S. All Cap Index. Because it's not cap weighted, this index is less top heavy than indexes like the S&P 500, where assets are bunched up among top holdings. Relative to other large-cap indexes, the portfolio skews toward heavy-asset firms, such as industrials and utilities, and away from tech and health-care names.

1998	1999	2000	2001	2002	2003	2004	2005	2006	2007	History
—	—	—	—	—	—	—	49.29	57.93	59.52	NAV $
—	—	—	—	—	—	—	49.30	58.02	58.14	Market Price $
—	—	—	—	—	—	—	10.75*	18.86	4.25	NAV Return%
—	—	—	—	—	—	—	9.66*	19.02	1.68	Market Price Return%
—	—	—	—	—	—	—	0.02	0.05	-0.15	Avg Premium/Discount%
—	—	—	—	—	—	—	—	3.07	-1.24	NAV Rtrn% +/-S&P 500
—	—	—	—	—	—	—	—	—	—	NAV Rtrn% +/-FTSI RAFI 1000
—	—	—	—	—	—	—	—	10	27	NAV Return% Rank in Cat
—	—	—	—	—	—	—	—	1.24	1.52	Income Return %
—	—	—	—	—	—	—	—	17.62	2.73	Capital Return %
—	—	—	—	—	—	—	0.00	0.61	0.88	Income $
—	—	—	—	—	—	—	0.00	0.00	0.00	Capital Gains $
—	—	—	—	—	—	—	—	0.76	0.70	Expense Ratio %
—	—	—	—	—	—	—	—	1.38	1.40	Income Ratio %
—	—	—	—	—	—	—	—	2	8	Turnover Rate %
—	—	—	—	—	—	—	—	620	981	Net Assets $mil

Performance 12-31-07

Historic Quarterly NAV Returns

	1st Qtr	2nd Qtr	3rd Qtr	4th Qtr	Total
2003	—	—	—	—	—
2004	—	—	—	—	—
2005	—	—	—	—	—*
2006	5.11	0.06	5.47	7.16	18.86
2007	1.58	5.97	-0.50	-2.66	4.25

Trailing	NAV Return%	Market Return%	NAV Rtrn% +/-S&P 500	%Rank Cat.(NAV)
3 Mo	-2.66	-4.90	0.67	10
6 Mo	-3.15	-5.60	-1.78	32
1 Yr	4.25	1.68	-1.24	27
3 Yr Avg	—	—	—	—
5 Yr Avg	—	—	—	—
10 Yr Avg	—	—	—	—

Tax Analysis	Tax-Adj Return%	Tax-Cost Ratio
3 Yr (estimated)	—	—
5 Yr (estimated)	—	—
10 Yr (estimated)	—	—

Rating and Risk

Time Period	Morningstar Rtn vs Cat	Morningstar Risk vs Cat	Morningstar Risk-Adj Rating
3 Yr	—	—	—
5 Yr	—	—	—
10 Yr	—	—	—

Other Measures	Standard Index S&P 500	Best Fit Index
Alpha	—	—
Beta	—	—
R-Squared	—	—
Standard Deviation	—	
Mean	—	
Sharpe Ratio	—	

Portfolio Analysis 11-30-07

Share change since 10-07 Total Stocks:968	Sector	PE	Tot Ret%	% Assets
⊖ ExxonMobil Corporation	Energy	13.6	24.34	3.32
⊖ General Electric Company	Ind Mtrls	16.6	2.69	2.96
⊖ Kraft Foods, Inc.	Goods	20.0	-5.71	2.40
⊖ Microsoft Corporation	Software	23.4	20.83	1.87
⊖ Chevron Corporation	Energy	11.4	30.59	1.80
⊖ Verizon Communications I	Telecom	21.7	22.19	1.74
⊖ Bank of America Corporat	Financial	9.4	-19.25	1.51
⊖ Wal-Mart Stores, Inc.	Consumer	15.4	4.91	1.51
⊖ Altria Group Inc.	Goods	13.2	22.10	1.33
⊖ AT&T, Inc.	Telecom	21.6	20.58	1.25
⊖ Pfizer Inc.	Health	22.5	-8.15	1.22
⊖ Merrill Lynch & Company,	Financial	12.2	-41.32	1.21
⊖ Ford Motor Company	Goods	—	-12.65	1.18
⊖ General Motors Corporati	Goods	—	-16.42	1.14
⊖ J.P. Morgan Chase & Co.	Financial	9.5	-7.24	1.12
⊖ Merck & Co., Inc.	Health	23.6	37.36	1.09
⊖ ConocoPhillips	Energy	13.8	25.42	1.08
⊖ Johnson & Johnson	Health	18.8	3.61	0.99
⊖ American International G	Financial	10.2	-17.96	0.91
⊖ Reliant Energy, Inc.	Utilities	NMF	84.66	0.89

Current Investment Style

Value Blnd Growth — Large / Mid / Small

Market Cap	%
Giant	41.4
Large	34.5
Mid	20.6
Small	3.3
Micro	0.3
Avg $mil: 36,687	

Value Measures		Rel Category
Price/Earnings	15.18	1.12
Price/Book	2.09	1.07
Price/Sales	0.83	0.69
Price/Cash Flow	8.01	0.96
Dividend Yield %	2.03	0.75

Growth Measures	%	Rel Category
Long-Term Erngs	9.95	1.01
Book Value	6.91	0.80
Sales	4.63	0.72
Cash Flow	-3.41	NMF
Historical Erngs	13.60	0.90

Profitability	%	Rel Category
Return on Equity	19.96	1.01
Return on Assets	6.72	1.05
Net Margin	11.84	0.85

Sector Weightings	% of Stocks	Rel S&P 500	3 Year High	3 Year Low
Info	15.79	0.76		
Software	3.06	0.74	3	3
Hardware	5.72	0.56	6	5
Media	3.08	1.06	4	3
Telecom	3.93	1.08	5	4
Service	40.32	0.99		
Health	9.67	0.80	10	8
Consumer	8.07	1.19	10	8
Business	4.00	0.91	4	3
Financial	18.58	1.07	25	19
Mfg	43.90	1.14		
Goods	13.06	1.43	13	10
Ind Mtrls	13.40	1.03	14	12
Energy	10.56	0.84	11	7
Utilities	6.88	1.87	7	6

Composition

Cash	0.2
Stocks	99.8
Bonds	0.0
Other	0.0
Foreign (% of Stock)	0.3

Morningstar's Take by Emiko Kurotsu 12-31-07

We're not sold on PowerShares FTSE RAFI US 1000 versus its conventional rivals.

This ETF offers a different approach to indexing. Its benchmark, the FTSE RAFI U.S. 1000 Index, eschews traditional market-cap weighting and instead weights stocks based on four fundamental factors: dividends, book value, sales, and cash flow. While the resulting portfolio doesn't depart radically from its most comparable rival, iShares Russell 1000, there are some subtle differences. For instance, this fund is lighter in tech and health-care stocks, which together account for less than 20% of assets, and has a bigger mid-cap stake.

These differences drag down the fund's quality a bit. We associate quality with firms that boast intractable competitive advantages, or wide "economic moats." For instance, energy giant ExxonMobil earns a wide moat due in part to its massive scale, GE for its diversified suite of market-leading businesses, and Microsoft for its unassailable PC software franchise. While this fund invests 38% of assets in wide-moat stocks, that's slightly less than the iShares fund's stake.

That shortfall is mainly attributable to the fund's smaller weightings in large, tangible-asset-light firms, many of which--like Cisco, Intel, and Johnson & Johnson--hail from the tech and health-care sectors. While the fund's larger stakes in wide-moat stocks like Wal-Mart and Time Warner partially offsets that trend, it doesn't fully compensate. All told, this RAFI index's weighting scheme, while novel, doesn't appear to burnish the portfolio's quality.

Like the Russell 1000 offering, though, this ETF is well-diversified across stocks and industries, with its typical holding courting moderate risk. As such, we wouldn't demand a wide margin of safety. However, given the quality disparity and this fund's higher cost (0.60% expense ratio versus 0.15% for the iShares fund), it would have to be meaningfully cheaper than its iShares rival to get us interested.

Address:	301 West Roosevelt Road United States 800-843-2639
Web Address:	www.powershares.com
Inception:	12-19-05 *
Advisor:	PowerShares Capital Management LLC

Management Fee:	0.50%		
Expense Projections:	3Yr:$241	5Yr:$423	10Yr:$950
Income Distrib:	Quarterly		
Exchange:	NYSE		

PowerShares QQQ QQQQ

Market Price	Mstar Category
$51.22	Large Growth

Morningstar Rating	Return	Risk	Yield	NAV	Avg Daily Vol. (k)	52 wk High/Low
★★★★	Above Avg	High	0.3%	$51.40	153,229	$55.03 - $42.15

Morningstar Fair Value

Price/Fair Value Ratio	Coverage Rate %
0.98	99

Valuation

This ETF is tech-heavy and concentrated in its top holdings, so it has been more volatile than the typical large-cap ETF. Yet, financially sturdy firms with intractable competitive advantages dominate the portfolio. As such, we'd recommend it when it dips 8% or more below our fair value estimate. It was recently trading at a 2% discount.

Methodology

The fund, known popularly as Cubes or Qubes, tracks the Nasdaq 100 Index. The index was created in 1985 to represent the 100 largest (by market cap) nonfinancial stocks in the Nasdaq Composite Index. Because the Nasdaq is the home of many tech listings, this ETF is tech-heavy, dedicating about two thirds of its portfolio to the sector. Mega-cap tech leaders like Apple, Microsoft, Qualcomm, and Google hold sway here, as the ETF allocates more than 40% of its assets to its top 10 holdings.

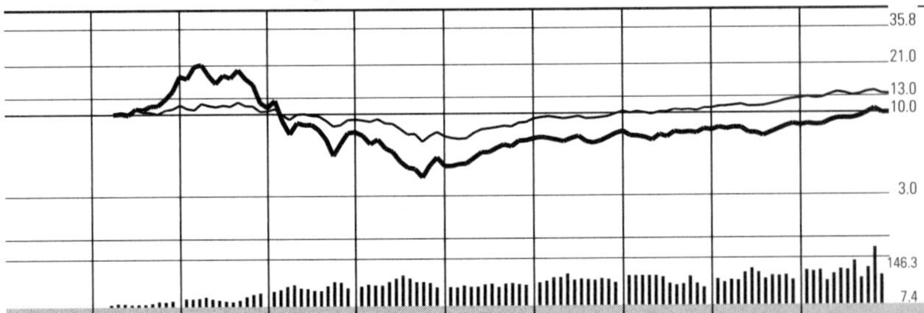

Growth of $10,000
- Investment Value of ETF
- Investment Value of Index S&P 500

Trading Volume Millions

1998	1999	2000	2001	2002	2003	2004	2005	2006	2007	History
—	92.61	58.40	40.36	24.47	36.49	39.94	40.46	43.17	51.40	NAV $
—	91.38	58.38	38.91	24.37	36.46	39.91	40.41	43.12	51.22	Market Price $
—	0.32*	-36.94	-30.89	-39.37	49.18	10.51	1.64	7.03	19.42	NAV Return%
—	0.26*	-36.11	-33.35	-37.37	49.67	10.53	1.59	7.04	19.14	Market Price Return%
—	-0.20	0.08	-0.19	-0.08	0.00	0.03	-0.02	0.00	-0.04	Avg Premium/Discount%
—	—	-27.84	-19.00	-17.27	20.50	-0.37	-3.27	-8.76	13.93	NAV Rtrn% +/-S&P 500
—	—	-0.10	1.76	-1.79	0.06	0.07	0.15	0.24	0.75	NAV Rtrn% +/-NASDAQ 100
—	—	1	100	100	1	1	87	75	8	NAV Return% Rank in Cat
—	—	0.00	0.00	0.00	0.06	1.04	0.34	0.33	0.33	Income Return %
—	—	-36.94	-30.89	-39.37	49.12	9.47	1.30	6.70	19.09	Capital Return %
—	0.00	0.00	0.00	0.00	0.01	0.38	0.14	0.13	0.14	Income $
—	0.00	0.00	0.00	0.00	0.00	0.00	0.00	0.00	0.00	Capital Gains $
—	—	0.18	0.18	0.18	0.20	0.20	0.20	0.20	—	Expense Ratio %
—	—	-0.16	-0.13	-0.13	-0.03	0.07	1.19	0.41	—	Income Ratio %
—	—	23	22	13	13	7	15	15	—	Turnover Rate %
—	—	—	—	17,034	25,632	22,196	20,311	17,957	21,767	Net Assets $mil

Performance 12-31-07

Historic Quarterly NAV Returns

	1st Qtr	2nd Qtr	3rd Qtr	4th Qtr	Total
2003	3.51	17.96	8.47	12.63	49.18
2004	-2.00	5.43	-6.82	14.79	10.51
2005	-8.51	0.78	7.28	2.76	1.64
2006	3.61	-7.53	5.08	6.32	7.03
2007	1.02	9.20	8.18	0.08	19.42

Trailing	NAV Return%	Market Return%	NAV Rtrn% +/-S&P 500	%Rank Cat.(NAV)
3 Mo	0.08	-0.27	3.41	6
6 Mo	8.26	7.77	9.63	1
1 Yr	19.42	19.14	13.93	8
3 Yr Avg	9.11	9.01	0.49	1
5 Yr Avg	16.45	16.47	3.62	1
10 Yr Avg	—	—	—	—

Tax Analysis	Tax-Adj Return%	Tax-Cost Ratio
3 Yr (estimated)	8.99	0.11
5 Yr (estimated)	16.29	0.14
10 Yr (estimated)	—	—

Rating and Risk

Time Period	Morningstar Rtn vs Cat	Morningstar Risk vs Cat	Morningstar Risk-Adj Rating
3 Yr	Avg	High	★★★
5 Yr	+Avg	High	★★★★
10 Yr	—	—	—

Other Measures	Standard Index S&P 500	Best Fit Index Mstar Large Growth
Alpha	-1.0	1.3
Beta	1.49	1.36
R-Squared	68	92
Standard Deviation	14.01	
Mean	9.11	
Sharpe Ratio	0.39	

Portfolio Analysis 10-31-07

Share change since 09-07 Total Stocks:100	Sector	PE	Tot Ret%	% Assets
⊖ Apple, Inc.	Hardware	50.5	133.47	12.31
⊖ Microsoft Corporation	Software	23.4	20.83	6.34
⊖ Google, Inc.	Business	54.0	50.17	5.35
⊖ Qualcomm, Inc.	Hardware	20.2	5.52	4.61
⊖ Cisco Systems, Inc.	Hardware	21.5	-0.95	3.83
⊖ Research in Motion, Ltd.	Hardware	NMF	166.24	3.72
⊖ Intel Corporation	Hardware	25.4	34.22	2.94
⊖ Oracle Corporation	Software	24.8	31.74	2.52
⊖ Gilead Sciences, Inc.	Health	—	41.72	2.25
⊖ eBay, Inc.	Consumer	—	10.38	1.95
⊖ Comcast Corporation A	Media	24.0	-35.29	1.63
⊖ Amgen, Inc.	Health	16.8	-32.02	1.57
⊖ Starbucks Corporation	Consumer	23.5	-42.21	1.48
⊖ Adobe Systems Inc.	Software	37.9	3.92	1.48
⊖ Teva Pharmaceutical Indu	Health	67.6	50.75	1.44
⊖ Dell, Inc.	Hardware	18.6	-2.31	1.37
⊖ Genzyme Corporation	Health	—	20.88	1.34
⊖ Celgene Corporation	Health	NMF	-19.68	1.34
⊖ Amazon.com, Inc.	Consumer	NMF	134.77	1.31
⊖ Biogen Idec, Inc.	Health	34.3	15.71	1.24

Current Investment Style

Value Blnd Growth — Large Mid Small

Market Cap	%
Giant	46.5
Large	30.9
Mid	22.6
Small	0.0
Micro	0.0

Avg $mil: 42,916

Value Measures		Rel Category
Price/Earnings	26.31	1.35
Price/Book	4.75	1.41
Price/Sales	2.93	1.66
Price/Cash Flow	16.51	1.43
Dividend Yield %	0.40	0.47

Growth Measures	%	Rel Category
Long-Term Erngs	20.76	1.43
Book Value	12.45	1.22
Sales	9.01	0.93
Cash Flow	18.36	1.70
Historical Erngs	18.98	1.06

Profitability	%	Rel Category
Return on Equity	21.19	0.92
Return on Assets	11.14	1.15
Net Margin	14.28	1.11

Sector Weightings	% of Stocks	Rel S&P 500	3 Year High	3 Year Low
Info	63.87	3.06		
Software	17.29	4.18	19	17
Hardware	39.32	3.85	39	33
Media	5.63	1.93	7	6
Telecom	1.63	0.45	2	1
Service	34.05	0.84		
Health	12.46	1.04	15	12
Consumer	11.40	1.68	15	11
Business	10.19	2.31	10	4
Financial	0.00	0.00	0	0
Mfg	2.09	0.05		
Goods	0.00	0.00	0	0
Ind Mtrls	1.92	0.15	2	2
Energy	0.17	0.01	0	0
Utilities	0.00	0.00	0	0

Composition

Cash	0.0
Stocks	100.0
Bonds	0.0
Other	0.0
Foreign (% of Stock)	7.5

Morningstar's Take by Sonya Morris 12-31-07

PowerShares QQQ can be volatile, but we'd feel comfortable recommending it at a modest discount to our fair value estimate.

This ETF attracts a lot of volume from short-term traders, but its portfolio is far from speculative. On the contrary, it tracks the Nasdaq 100 Index, a cap-weighted collection of the largest nonfinancial stocks included in the Nasdaq Composite Index. Thus, its portfolio is dominated by tech industry stalwarts like Apple, Microsoft, and Google.

More than 40% of the fund is dedicated to wide-moat firms, businesses our analysts believe have enduring competitive advantages. Cisco Systems provides a prime example. As the world's leading manufacturer of networking equipment, it has the scale to keep costs low. And because of the sensitivity of data, its customers are loath to switch to lesser-known brands.

Wide-moat companies like Cisco tend to produce more-predictable results than firms without competitive advantages, which gives us more faith in our analysts' cash flow forecasts and fair value estimates. Our confidence is further bolstered by the risk characteristics of this ETF's underlying businesses. More than 80% of its assets are dedicated to firms with average or below-average business risk ratings.

This ETF is not without risk though. It owns a handful of firms that possess no economic moat, such as NVIDIA, which, as a manufacturer of computer graphics processors, faces short product cycles, rapidly changing technologies, and intense competition from larger rivals. This fund also courts sector and stock-specific risk. Its top 10 holdings soak up more than 40% of assets, and it dedicates about two thirds of its portfolio to the tech sector. Consequently, this fund has experienced its share of ups and downs.

But this top-heavy construction is mitigated by the high quality of its portfolio. We'd willingly recommend this ETF when its market price falls 8% or more below our fair value estimate.

Address:	Nasdaq Global Fds, 9513 Key West Ave United States 800-843-2639
Web Address:	www.nasdaq.com/QQQQ
Inception:	03-10-99 *
Advisor:	PowerShares Capital Management LLC

Management Fee:	0.06%		
Expense Projections:	3Yr:$64	5Yr:$113	10Yr:$255
Income Distrib:	Annually		
Exchange:	XNMS		

PowerShares Zacks MicroCp PZI

Market Price	Mstar Category
$15.37	Small Blend

Morningstar Fair Value

Price/Fair Value Ratio	Coverage Rate %
0.98	17

Valuation

Because our equity analysts cover a relatively small number of this ETF's stock holdings, the price/fair value ratio above may not be a faithful representation of the portfolio's valuation attributes. Investors trying to gauge this ETF's attractiveness should consider the price/fair value ratio only in conjunction with other fundamental measures.

Methodology

This ETF tracks the Zacks Micro Cap Index, which is a quasi-actively managed benchmark. It includes the 300 to 500 stocks with market capitalizations between $60 million and $600 million at the time of selection. Zacks uses a computer model to select the index's constituents based on several valuation and momentum factors. The index is equal-weighted and rebalanced once per quarter, but Zacks will kick out benchmark members on a weekly basis if the stocks stop meeting the model's screens. The index omits stocks that trade over the counter or on the pink sheets. The advisor uses representative sampling.

Morningstar Rating	Return	Risk	Yield	NAV	Avg Daily Vol. (k)	52 wk High/Low
—	—	—	0.8%	$15.51	89	$19.13 - $13.92

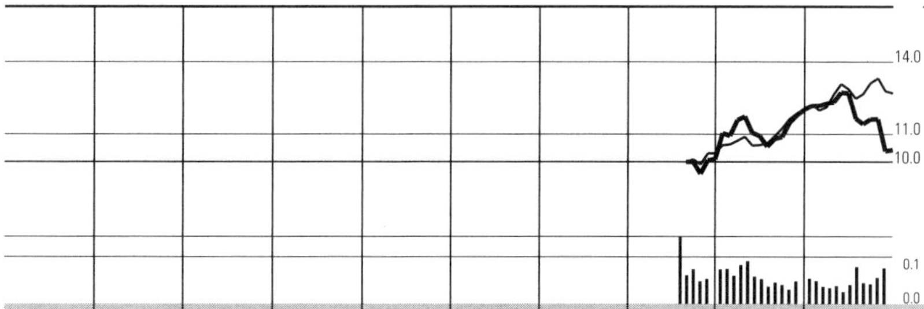

History

1998	1999	2000	2001	2002	2003	2004	2005	2006	2007	History
—	—	—	—	—	—	—	15.16	17.86	15.51	NAV $
—	—	—	—	—	—	—	15.15	17.86	15.37	Market Price $
—	—	—	—	—	—	—	2.41*	17.94	-12.55	NAV Return%
—	—	—	—	—	—	—	1.97*	18.03	-13.33	Market Price Return%
—	—	—	—	—	—	—	-0.03	-0.03	-0.16	Avg Premium/Discount%
—	—	—	—	—	—	—	—	2.15	-18.04	NAV Rtrn% +/-S&P 500
—	—	—	—	—	—	—	—	-0.43	-10.98	NAV Rtrn% +/-Russ 2000
—	—	—	—	—	—	—	—	29	91	NAV Return% Rank in Cat
—	—	—	—	—	—	—	—	0.14	0.66	Income Return %
—	—	—	—	—	—	—	—	17.80	-13.21	Capital Return %
—	—	—	—	—	—	—	0.01	0.02	0.12	Income $
—	—	—	—	—	—	—	0.00	0.00	0.00	Capital Gains $
—	—	—	—	—	—	—	—	0.72	0.71	Expense Ratio %
—	—	—	—	—	—	—	—	0.01	0.36	Income Ratio %
—	—	—	—	—	—	—	—	78	72	Turnover Rate %
—	—	—	—	—	—	—	103	175	130	Net Assets $mil

Performance 12-31-07

Historic Quarterly NAV Returns

	1st Qtr	2nd Qtr	3rd Qtr	4th Qtr	Total
2003	—	—	—	—	—
2004	—	—	—	—	—
2005	—	—	—	0.96	—*
2006	13.85	-5.20	-0.27	9.57	17.94
2007	2.05	3.46	-8.36	-9.62	-12.55

Trailing	NAV Return%	Market Return%	NAV Rtrn% +/-S&P 500	%Rank Cat.(NAV)
3 Mo	-9.62	-10.31	-6.29	88
6 Mo	-17.18	-17.79	-15.81	88
1 Yr	-12.55	-13.33	-18.04	91
3 Yr Avg	—	—	—	—
5 Yr Avg	—	—	—	—
10 Yr Avg	—	—	—	—

Tax Analysis	Tax-Adj Return%	Tax-Cost Ratio
3 Yr (estimated)	—	—
5 Yr (estimated)	—	—
10 Yr (estimated)	—	—

Rating and Risk

Time Period	Morningstar Rtn vs Cat	Morningstar Risk vs Cat	Morningstar Risk-Adj Rating
3 Yr	—	—	—
5 Yr	—	—	—
10 Yr	—	—	—

Other Measures	Standard Index S&P 500	Best Fit Index
Alpha	—	—
Beta	—	—
R-Squared	—	—
Standard Deviation	—	
Mean	—	
Sharpe Ratio	—	

Morningstar's Take by Annie Sorich 12-31-07

There are more attractive options than PowerShares Zacks Micro Cap.

The second part of 2007 has been tough for most small- and micro-cap focused ETFs, and this fund has been particularly hard-hit. Its 14.6% year-to-date loss through Nov. 19, 2007, placed it close to the bottom of small-cap blend category. The fund lost 8% in July, and smaller stocks have continued to lose ground as broader economic uncertainty causes investors to flee to large-cap stocks and high-quality bonds. In addition, the prices of micro-cap stocks tend to have dramatic ups and downs. These tiny companies may be in the early stages of development, with revenue dependent on few products or markets, and with limited financial backing and a lack of management experience. This sort of volatility is fine for those with sufficiently long time horizons (more than 10 years), but it can be difficult for others to stomach.

Volatility aside, there are other reasons we're not excited about this ETF. It tracks the Zacks Micro Cap Index, which screens companies whose market caps fall between 0.015% and 0.15% of the largest-cap U.S. companies at the time of selection (currently between $23 million and $1.1 billion) on a variety of momentum and value factors. The index is composed of the highest-ranking 300 to 500 stocks. It's rebalanced quarterly, but the constituents are reviewed weekly, and stocks that no longer measure up are dumped. As such, the fund has a higher rate of portfolio turnover than most of its peers, which can increase transaction costs and eat away at tax efficiency.

The fund's expense ratio also takes a bite out of returns. Although 0.71% of assets isn't egregious in absolute terms, it's more expensive than most other small-cap ETFs', where Vanguard Small Cap ETF comes in as the cheapest, charging 0.10%. For those intent on purchasing a micro-cap ETF, iShares Russell Microcap is more diversified (it holds 1,344 stocks as opposed to this fund's 400) and is cheaper.

Address:	301 West Roosevelt Road United States 800-843-2639
Web Address:	www.powershares.com
Inception:	08-18-05*
Advisor:	PowerShares Capital Management LLC

Management Fee:	0.50%		
Expense Projections:	3Yr:$239	5Yr:$418	10Yr:$939
Income Distrib:	Quarterly		
Exchange:	AMEX		

Portfolio Analysis 11-30-07

Share change since 10-07 Total Stocks:398	Sector	PE	Tot Ret%	% Assets
⊖ Pericom Semiconductor Co	Hardware	45.7	63.03	0.39
⊖ BioScrip, Inc.	Health	—	123.41	0.38
⊖ Axsys Technologies, Inc.	Goods	30.0	108.59	0.38
⊖ PharmaNet Development Gr	Health	62.1	77.66	0.37
⊖ RehabCare Group	Health	41.0	51.92	0.36
⊖ Carriage Services, Inc.	Consumer	23.8	73.09	0.36
⊖ AsiaInfo Holdings, Inc.	Business	32.4	43.23	0.36
⊖ Pricesmart, Inc.	Consumer	68.5	70.39	0.35
☼ Caplease, Inc.	Financial	—	-21.44	0.35
⊖ Columbus McKinnon Corpor	Ind Mtrls	16.1	55.19	0.34
⊖ Sifco Industries, Inc.	Ind Mtrls	10.1	224.32	0.34
⊖ Tecumseh Products Compan	Business	—	38.52	0.34
⊖ International Shipholdin	Business	6.2	61.38	0.34
☼ Avici Systems, Inc.	Hardware	3.3	31.56	0.34
⊖ Chiquita Brands Internat	Goods	—	15.15	0.33
⊖ Triquint Semiconductor	Hardware	60.2	47.33	0.33
⊖ Capstead Mortgage Corpor	Financial	—	63.46	0.33
⊖ EMS Technologies, Inc.	Hardware	24.4	50.88	0.33
⊖ T-3 Energy Services, Inc	Ind Mtrls	23.9	113.20	0.32
⊖ Oriental Financial Group	Financial	NMF	8.46	0.32

Current Investment Style

Value Blnd Growth — Large Mid Small

Market Cap	%
Giant	0.0
Large	0.2
Mid	0.0
Small	12.2
Micro	87.5
Avg $mil: 289	

Value Measures		Rel Category
Price/Earnings	14.49	0.96
Price/Book	1.22	0.72
Price/Sales	0.58	0.64
Price/Cash Flow	4.51	0.69
Dividend Yield %	1.26	0.90

Growth Measures	%	Rel Category
Long-Term Erngs	13.60	0.83
Book Value	1.95	0.26
Sales	-21.00	NMF
Cash Flow	-22.69	NMF
Historical Erngs	8.97	0.72

Profitability	%	Rel Category
Return on Equity	6.16	0.47
Return on Assets	2.96	0.51
Net Margin	7.38	0.72

Sector Weightings	% of Stocks	Rel S&P 500	3 Year High	3 Year Low
Info	18.47	0.88		
Software	5.02	1.21	6	4
Hardware	10.62	1.04	14	9
Media	1.33	0.46	2	0
Telecom	1.50	0.41	2	1
Service	55.23	1.36		
Health	9.71	0.81	10	5
Consumer	11.19	1.65	13	10
Business	13.90	3.15	16	12
Financial	20.43	1.17	24	18
Mfg	26.29	0.68		
Goods	5.62	0.61	6	4
Ind Mtrls	16.28	1.25	19	15
Energy	3.61	0.29	7	3
Utilities	0.78	0.21	2	0

Composition

Cash	0.1
Stocks	99.4
Bonds	0.0
Other	0.5
Foreign (% of Stock)	5.3

Rydex Russell Top 50 XLG

Market Price	Mstar Category
$110.53	Large Blend

Morningstar Fair Value

Price/Fair Value Ratio	Coverage Rate %
0.87	100

Valuation

This ETF looks like an inviting bargain: It was recently trading at a 13% discount to our fair value estimate, which exceeds the 9% discount we'd demand. Cheap stocks abound, with more than half of the portfolio holdings trading at least 15% below our fair value estimates, financials and consumer-related names being most plentiful.

Methodology

This ETF tracks the Russell Top 50 Index, which invests in the biggest 50 names from the Russell 3000, representing roughly 41% of the Russell 3000's total market capitalization. The index weights holdings by market cap and, thus, is somewhat top-heavy, with the biggest 10 holdings soaking up 40% of assets. Although the index provides exposure to most major industries, it skews toward oil majors, global banks, and drugmakers. The index reconstitutes annually.

Morningstar Rating	Return	Risk	Yield	NAV	Avg Daily Vol. (k)	52 wk High/Low
—	—	—	2.0%	$110.62	48	$117.32 - $102.40

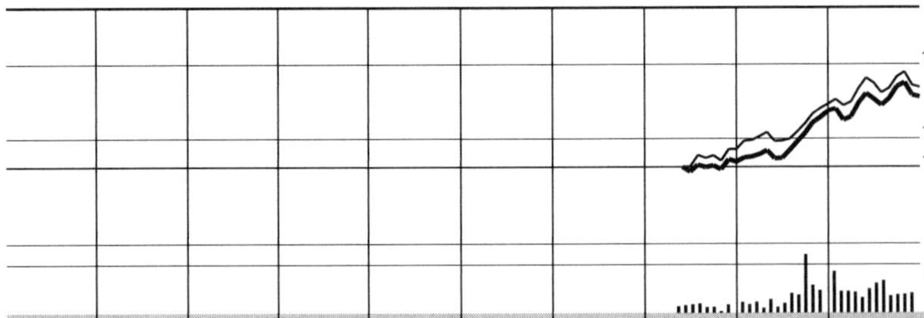

Growth of $10,000
- Investment Value of ETF
- Investment Value of Index S&P 500

Trading Volume Millions

1998	1999	2000	2001	2002	2003	2004	2005	2006	2007	History
—	—	—	—	—	—	—	93.18	107.82	110.62	NAV $
—	—	—	—	—	—	—	93.13	107.90	110.53	Market Price $
—	—	—	—	—	—	—	9.37*	17.90	4.66	NAV Return%
—	—	—	—	—	—	—	—	18.06	4.49	Market Price Return%
—	—	—	—	—	—	—	0.01	0.08	-0.03	Avg Premium/Discount%
—	—	—	—	—	—	—	—	2.11	-0.83	NAV Rtrn% +/-S&P 500
—	—	—	—	—	—	—	—	2.44	-1.11	NAV Rtrn% +/-Russ 1000
—	—	—	—	—	—	—	—	24	65	NAV Return% Rank in Cat
—	—	—	—	—	—	—	—	2.01	2.04	Income Return %
—	—	—	—	—	—	—	—	15.89	2.62	Capital Return %
—	—	—	—	—	—	—	0.93	1.86	2.18	Income $
—	—	—	—	—	—	—	0.00	0.00	0.00	Capital Gains $
—	—	—	—	—	—	—	0.20	0.20	—	Expense Ratio %
—	—	—	—	—	—	—	1.74	1.98	—	Income Ratio %
—	—	—	—	—	—	—	1	7	—	Turnover Rate %
—	—	—	—	—	—	—	140	544	647	Net Assets $mil

Performance 12-31-07

Historic Quarterly NAV Returns

	1st Qtr	2nd Qtr	3rd Qtr	4th Qtr	Total
2003	—	—	—	—	—
2004	—	—	—	—	—
2005	—	—	2.00	1.20	—*
2006	2.44	-1.20	8.29	7.58	17.90
2007	-1.94	6.00	4.02	-3.21	4.66

Trailing	NAV Return%	Market Return%	NAV Rtrn% +/-S&P 500	%Rank Cat.(NAV)
3 Mo	-3.21	-3.24	0.12	43
6 Mo	0.69	0.64	2.06	23
1 Yr	4.66	4.49	-0.83	65
3 Yr Avg	—	—	—	—
5 Yr Avg	—	—	—	—
10 Yr Avg	—	—	—	—

Tax Analysis	Tax-Adj Return%	Tax-Cost Ratio
3 Yr (estimated)	—	—
5 Yr (estimated)	—	—
10 Yr (estimated)	—	—

Rating and Risk

Time Period	Morningstar Rtn vs Cat	Morningstar Risk vs Cat	Morningstar Risk-Adj Rating
3 Yr	—	—	—
5 Yr	—	—	—
10 Yr	—	—	—

Other Measures	Standard Index S&P 500	Best Fit Index
Alpha	—	—
Beta	—	—
R-Squared	—	—
Standard Deviation	—	
Mean	—	
Sharpe Ratio	—	

Morningstar's Take by Jeffrey Ptak 12-31-07

This ETF brims with some of the highest-quality names that we cover. We'd gladly invest in the shares at a modest discount to our fair value estimate.

Investors would be hard-pressed to find a higher-quality ETF portfolio than Rydex Russell Top 50's. The fund, which is home to the 50 largest U.S. companies by market cap, teems with the stocks of blue-chip firms: Morningstar's stock analysts have bestowed wide economic moat ratings on 37 of the fund's 53 stocks, representing 72% of assets.

This reflects our analysts' collective view that these companies--which include the likes of ExxonMobil, General Electric, and Microsoft, among other market stalwarts--are founded on businesses fortified by durable competitive advantages. Generally speaking, these firms exploit their entrenched positions--which could be attributable to factors like intellectual property protection (Pfizer), near-monopolistic pricing power (Microsoft, Comcast), brand equity (Goldman Sachs, Altria), or scale (Cisco, ExxonMobil)--to consistently generate boatloads of free cash flow.

This ETF is not especially volatile. This stems from a few factors. First, the firms concerned are generally quite profitable (24% average return on equity), grow consistently via recurring revenue sources (12% three-year annualized sales growth; 17% annualized earnings growth), and boast fortresslike balance sheets. Those economics confer ballast and stability. In addition, a number of these firms are global titans. Citigroup, for instance, earned roughly 40 cents of every dollar overseas in fiscal 2006. That diversification means these firms are less levered to the U.S. economy, which, when coupled with the mix of sectors and industries represented in the list, has a cushioning effect.

As such, we'd demand only a modest margin of safety before recommending this ETF's shares. We'd be buyers when the fund trades at a 9% or greater discount to our fair value estimate.

Address:	9601 Blackwell Rd Rockville, MD 20850 800-820-0888
Web Address:	www.rydex.com
Inception:	05-04-05 *
Advisor:	Rydex Global Advisors, Inc.

Management Fee:	0.20%		
Expense Projections:	3Yr:$65	5Yr:$113	10Yr:$257
Income Distrib:	Quarterly		
Exchange:	AMEX		

Portfolio Analysis 12-31-07

Share change since 11-07 Total Stocks:53	Sector	PE	Tot Ret%	% Assets
⊕ ExxonMobil Corporation	Energy	13.6	24.34	8.30
⊕ General Electric Company	Ind Mtrls	16.6	2.69	6.00
⊕ Microsoft Corporation	Software	23.4	20.83	4.60
⊕ AT&T, Inc.	Telecom	21.6	20.58	4.03
⊕ Procter & Gamble Company	Goods	23.1	16.63	3.64
⊕ Chevron Corporation	Energy	11.4	30.59	3.16
⊕ Johnson & Johnson	Health	18.8	3.61	3.04
⊕ Bank of America Corporat	Financial	9.4	-19.25	2.88
⊕ Apple, Inc.	Hardware	50.5	133.47	2.70
⊕ Cisco Systems, Inc.	Hardware	21.5	-0.95	2.58
⊕ Pfizer Inc.	Health	22.5	-8.15	2.51
⊕ Altria Group Inc.	Goods	13.2	22.10	2.50
⊕ Google, Inc.	Business	54.0	50.17	2.50
⊕ Intel Corporation	Hardware	25.4	34.22	2.44
⊕ J.P. Morgan Chase & Co.	Financial	9.5	-7.24	2.35
⊕ International Business M	Hardware	16.2	13.20	2.32
⊕ Citigroup, Inc.	Financial	7.9	-44.93	2.29
⊕ ConocoPhillips	Energy	13.8	25.42	2.27
⊕ Coca-Cola Company	Goods	26.3	30.44	2.23
⊕ Hewlett-Packard Company	Hardware	18.8	23.40	2.13

Current Investment Style

Value Blnd Growth — Large Mid Small

Market Cap	%
Giant	96.0
Large	3.9
Mid	0.1
Small	0.0
Micro	0.0
Avg $mil: 158,005	

Value Measures		Rel Category
Price/Earnings	14.02	0.89
Price/Book	2.66	1.04
Price/Sales	1.77	1.43
Price/Cash Flow	10.50	1.13
Dividend Yield %	2.08	1.10

Growth Measures	%	Rel Category
Long-Term Erngs	—	—
Book Value	7.08	0.77
Sales	8.44	1.03
Cash Flow	8.99	1.03
Historical Erngs	16.76	1.00

Profitability	%	Rel Category
Return on Equity	24.02	1.08
Return on Assets	9.78	1.17
Net Margin	15.61	1.27

Sector Weightings	% of Stocks	Rel S&P 500	3 Year High	3 Year Low
Info	29.67	1.42		
Software	5.98	1.44	6	5
Hardware	13.50	1.32	14	10
Media	3.57	1.23	5	4
Telecom	6.62	1.82	7	3
Service	35.81	0.88		
Health	13.54	1.13	17	13
Consumer	2.64	0.39	4	3
Business	3.25	0.74	3	2
Financial	16.38	0.94	23	16
Mfg	34.51	0.90		
Goods	10.33	1.13	10	9
Ind Mtrls	8.60	0.66	10	9
Energy	15.58	1.23	16	11
Utilities	0.00	0.00	0	0

Composition

Cash	0.2
Stocks	99.8
Bonds	0.0
Other	0.0
Foreign (% of Stock)	0.0

Rydex S&P Equal Weight RSP

Market Price	Mstar Category
$47.18	Large Blend

Morningstar Fair Value

Price/Fair Value Ratio	Coverage Rate %
0.84	98

Morningstar Rating	Return	Risk	Yield	NAV	Avg Daily Vol. (k)	52 wk High/Low
★★★	Average	Above Avg	1.3%	$47.30	718	$52.67 - $43.90

Valuation

Given the portfolio's diversification and the respectable quality of its holdings, we'd be buyers at a 9% discount. This ETF was recently trading at a 13% discount to our fair value estimate. Thus, it looks like a bargain to our eyes.

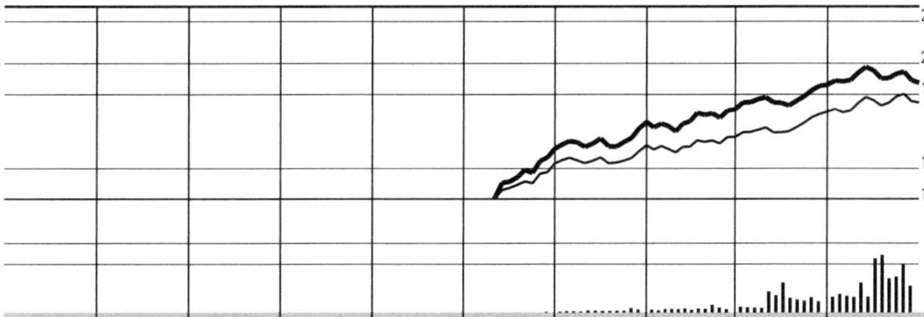

Methodology

This fund tracks the S&P Equal Weight Index, whose holdings are identical to the traditional S&P's, but equally weighted instead of market-cap-weighted. That means giant-cap holdings like ExxonMobil and General Electric don't dominate the portfolio, while mid-caps figure more prominently. Like the traditional S&P 500, this fund is very well-diversified by sector and even less-reliant on its top-holdings given the equal-weighting scheme. The index is rebalanced quarterly to ensure each stock maintains its weight, roughly 0.2% of the fund.

History

1998	1999	2000	2001	2002	2003	2004	2005	2006	2007	History
—	—	—	—	—	33.84	39.02	41.55	47.37	47.30	NAV $
—	—	—	—	—	33.86	39.04	41.48	47.34	47.18	Market Price $
—	—	—	—	—	15.62*	16.50	7.65	15.33	1.12	NAV Return%
—	—	—	—	—	15.56*	16.48	7.41	15.46	0.91	Market Price Return%
—	—	—	—	—	0.03	0.02	-0.03	0.02	-0.03	Avg Premium/Discount%
—	—	—	—	—	—	5.62	2.74	-0.46	-4.37	NAV Rtrn% +/-S&P 500
—	—	—	—	—	—	-0.45	-0.41	-0.47	-0.41	NAV Rtrn% +/-S&P 500 Eql
—	—	—	—	—	—	13	13	53	78	NAV Return% Rank in Cat
—	—	—	—	—	—	1.09	1.12	1.26	1.30	Income Return %
—	—	—	—	—	—	15.41	6.53	14.07	-0.18	Capital Return %
—	—	—	—	—	0.25	0.37	0.44	0.52	0.61	Income $
—	—	—	—	—	0.00	0.00	0.00	0.00	0.00	Capital Gains $
—	—	—	—	—	0.40	0.40	0.40	0.40	—	Expense Ratio %
—	—	—	—	—	1.13	1.09	1.11	1.21	—	Income Ratio %
—	—	—	—	—	42	55	22	17	—	Turnover Rate %
—	—	—	—	—	223	765	1,202	1,871	1,684	Net Assets $mil

Performance 12-31-07

Historic Quarterly NAV Returns

	1st Qtr	2nd Qtr	3rd Qtr	4th Qtr	Total
2003	—	—	5.14	14.91	—*
2004	3.71	2.26	-2.09	12.19	16.50
2005	-2.27	2.68	4.73	2.43	7.65
2006	6.14	-2.16	3.82	6.96	15.33
2007	2.73	5.74	-2.00	-5.02	1.12

Trailing	NAV Return%	Market Return%	NAV Rtrn% +/-S&P 500	%Rank Cat.(NAV)
3 Mo	-5.02	-5.23	-1.69	77
6 Mo	-6.92	-7.17	-5.55	78
1 Yr	1.12	0.91	-4.37	78
3 Yr Avg	7.88	7.76	-0.74	95
5 Yr Avg	—	—	—	—
10 Yr Avg	—	—	—	—

Tax Analysis	Tax-Adj Return%	Tax-Cost Ratio
3 Yr (estimated)	7.44	0.41
5 Yr (estimated)	—	—
10 Yr (estimated)	—	—

Rating and Risk

Time Period	Morningstar Rtn vs Cat	Morningstar Risk vs Cat	Morningstar Risk-Adj Rating
3 Yr	Avg	+Avg	★★★
5 Yr	—	—	—
10 Yr	—	—	—

Other Measures	Standard Index S&P 500	Best Fit Index Mstar Mid Core
Alpha	-1.1	-0.1
Beta	1.11	0.80
R-Squared	90	96
Standard Deviation	9.11	
Mean	7.88	
Sharpe Ratio	0.41	

Portfolio Analysis 12-31-07

Share change since 11-07 Total Stocks:501	Sector	PE	Tot Ret%	% Assets
☼ Range Resources Corporat	Energy	47.2	87.67	0.27
⊕ Freddie Mac	Financial	12.0	-48.20	0.22
⊕ Fannie Mae	Financial	24.1	-30.45	0.22
⊖ Hess Corporation	Ind Mtrls	19.1	104.77	0.22
⊖ United States Steel Corp	Ind Mtrls	12.6	66.73	0.22
⊕ KeyCorp	Financial	7.6	-35.39	0.21
⊕ Huntington Bancshares, I	Financial	10.0	-34.23	0.21
⊕ E*Trade Financial Corpor	Financial	3.5	-84.17	0.21
⊖ Archer Daniels Midland	Ind Mtrls	13.8	47.02	0.21
⊕ Pulte Homes, Inc.	Consumer	—	-68.29	0.21
⊕ Lennar Corporation	Consumer	—	-65.71	0.21
⊖ ProLogis Trust	Financial	14.3	7.35	0.21
⊖ Charles Schwab Corporati	Financial	30.8	40.07	0.21
⊖ Murphy Oil Corporation	Energy	25.2	68.58	0.21
⊕ Deere & Company	Ind Mtrls	23.3	98.60	0.21
⊕ Office Depot, Inc.	Consumer	7.5	-63.58	0.21
⊕ Countrywide Financial Co	Financial	—	-78.46	0.21
⊖ Schlumberger, Ltd.	Energy	24.6	57.10	0.21
⊕ Jabil Circuit, Inc.	Hardware	43.7	-37.66	0.21
⊖ Progressive Corporation	Financial	10.5	-13.42	0.21

Current Investment Style

Value Blnd Growth; Large Mid Small

Market Cap	%
Giant	10.8
Large	39.9
Mid	46.6
Small	2.7
Micro	0.0
Avg $mil: 13,602	

Value Measures		Rel Category
Price/Earnings	14.07	0.89
Price/Book	1.91	0.75
Price/Sales	0.98	0.79
Price/Cash Flow	7.14	0.77
Dividend Yield %	1.77	0.94

Growth Measures	%	Rel Category
Long-Term Erngs	—	—
Book Value	6.42	0.69
Sales	5.79	0.71
Cash Flow	4.94	0.57
Historical Erngs	13.83	0.83

Profitability	%	Rel Category
Return on Equity	18.96	0.85
Return on Assets	6.92	0.83
Net Margin	11.66	0.95

Sector Weightings	% of Stocks	Rel S&P 500	3 Year High	3 Year Low
Info	16.73	0.80		
Software	3.77	0.91	4	3
Hardware	8.14	0.80	11	8
Media	3.00	1.03	4	3
Telecom	1.82	0.50	2	2
Service	46.32	1.14		
Health	10.39	0.86	12	10
Consumer	11.21	1.65	12	11
Business	6.28	1.42	6	5
Financial	18.44	1.06	19	16
Mfg	36.94	0.96		
Goods	10.74	1.17	11	10
Ind Mtrls	12.86	0.99	14	13
Energy	7.18	0.57	7	6
Utilities	6.16	1.67	7	6

Composition

Cash	0.1
Stocks	99.9
Bonds	0.0
Other	0.0
Foreign (% of Stock)	0.0

Morningstar's Take by Emiko Kurotsu 12-31-07

Rydex S&P Equal Weight has merit, but it's not as valuable as the real thing.

This fund's holding are identical to the popular, broad-market S&P 500's with one important difference: Instead of weighting stocks by market-cap, it weights them equally. As such, giant-caps like ExxonMobil don't loom quite as large, while mid-caps figure more prominently. Whereas the cap-weighted S&P has over half its assets tucked into giant-caps and less than 12% in mid-caps; here, it's roughly the opposite.

This spin dilutes the portfolio's quality. We normally associate quality with firms wielding tell-tale advantages over rivals. While size doesn't always translate to dominance, many giant-caps boast formidable advantages, or "economic moats." Those moats, which often hinge on key attributes like scale, enviable brands, or barriers to entry, help to keep rivals at bay. Microsoft's ubiquitous presence on nearly all PCs, for instance, gives it considerable pricing power, explaining its wide moat. Certainly, smaller firms can and do possess such traits. But they're less common, reflecting not only the law of numbers (i.e, many smaller firms, only a few of which will become bulwarks) but also the less-established nature of such businesses.

In equal-weighting holdings, this fund limits the sway of these large-cap names and, in so doing, reduces the portfolio's overall quality. The numbers tell the tale: While this fund has less than 22% of assets in wide-moat stocks, the SPDR (which tracks the cap-weighted S&P) has nearly half of assets in such names. Because we ordinarily assign greater value to higher-quality stocks, it means this portfolio is less valuable than traditional S&P-trackers like the SPDR.

That said, it's hardly a dud, with nary a no-moat stock to be found. It's also well diversified, which tamps down volatility. Thus, we wouldn't demand a wider margin of safety than we do for a traditional S&P 500 ETF; we'd be buyers at a 9% discount to our fair value estimate.

Address:	9601 Blackwell Rd Rockville, MD 20850 800-820-0888
Web Address:	www.rydex.com
Inception:	04-24-03*
Advisor:	Rydex Global Advisors, Inc.

Management Fee:	0.40%		
Expense Projections:	3Yr:$129	5Yr:$225	10Yr:$508
Income Distrib:	Quarterly		
Exchange:	AMEX		

SPDR DJ Wilshire Lg Value ELV

Market Price	Mstar Category
$82.30	Large Value

Morningstar Fair Value

Price/Fair Value Ratio	Coverage Rate %
0.86	99

Valuation

This fund was recently trading at a 14% discount to our fair value estimate, largely due to the beleaguered state of the financials sector, in which it has a significant stake. Given the fund's wide diversification, above-average quality, and moderate risk, we'd be buyers when it trades at an 8% or greater discount to fair value.

Methodology

This ETF tracks the Dow Jones Wilshire Large Cap Value Index, which represents about 300 stocks drawn from the Dow Jones Wilshire 5000 Index that exhibit strong value traits (as measured by various price multiple and growth rate comparisons). This cap-weighted fund holds almost 60% in giant caps and more than a quarter in large caps. Financials make up nearly one third of the portfolio, while technology and media stocks are scarce. The Index reconstitutes twice annually, with buffer zones to prevent stocks from making abrupt changes due to small market-cap and style shifts.

Morningstar Rating	Return	Risk	Yield	NAV	Avg Daily Vol. (k)	52 wk High/Low
★★★	Average	Below Avg	2.7%	$82.53	16	$90.56 - $78.46

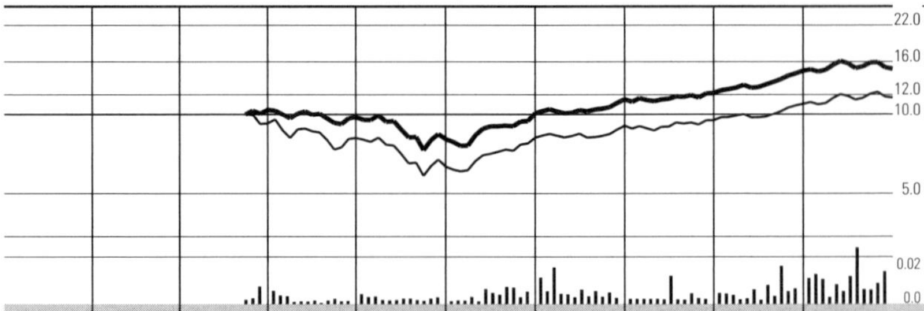

Growth of $10,000
— Investment Value of ETF
— Investment Value of Index S&P 500

Trading Volume Millions

1998	1999	2000	2001	2002	2003	2004	2005	2006	2007	History
—	—	68.28	62.84	50.38	61.81	68.26	70.13	83.31	82.53	NAV $
—	—	68.27	63.28	50.52	61.83	68.33	70.13	83.32	82.30	Market Price $
—	—	5.87*	-6.25	-17.63	25.52	13.13	5.43	21.56	1.68	NAV Return%
—	—	5.83*	-5.57	-17.98	25.21	13.21	5.33	21.58	1.38	Market Price Return%
—	—	-1.36	0.04	0.16	-0.02	0.05	-0.02	0.05	-0.15	Avg Premium/Discount%
—	—	—	5.64	4.47	-3.16	2.25	0.52	5.77	-3.81	NAV Rtrn% +/-S&P 500
—	—	—	-0.86	-2.91	-5.03	-0.42	-0.29	-0.31	-0.16	NAV Rtrn% +/-DJ Wil LV
—	—	—	60	60	100	71	60	36	53	NAV Return% Rank in Cat
—	—	—	1.66	2.30	2.58	2.54	2.67	2.55	2.70	Income Return %
—	—	—	-7.91	-19.93	22.94	10.59	2.76	19.01	-1.02	Capital Return %
—	—	0.29	1.12	1.43	1.29	1.55	1.81	1.77	2.23	Income $
—	—	0.00	0.00	0.00	0.00	0.00	0.00	0.00	0.00	Capital Gains $
—	—	—	0.21	0.24	0.23	0.21	0.21	0.21	0.20	Expense Ratio %
—	—	—	1.61	1.81	2.54	2.72	2.51	2.52	2.44	Income Ratio %
—	—	—	12	10	33	28	19	42	13	Turnover Rate %
—	—	—	—	25	87	123	98	154	120	Net Assets $mil

Performance 12-31-07

Historic Quarterly NAV Returns

	1st Qtr	2nd Qtr	3rd Qtr	4th Qtr	Total
2003	-5.51	18.25	0.16	12.15	25.52
2004	1.62	1.23	1.27	8.60	13.13
2005	-0.77	1.16	3.21	1.76	5.43
2006	4.89	0.55	7.11	7.60	21.56
2007	0.90	5.70	0.71	-5.34	1.68

Trailing	NAV Return%	Market Return%	NAV Rtrn% +/-S&P 500	%Rank Cat.(NAV)
3 Mo	-5.34	-5.55	-2.01	41
6 Mo	-4.66	-4.85	-3.29	41
1 Yr	1.68	1.38	-3.81	53
3 Yr Avg	9.23	9.09	0.61	34
5 Yr Avg	13.10	12.97	0.27	75
10 Yr Avg	—	—	—	—

Tax Analysis	Tax-Adj Return%	Tax-Cost Ratio
3 Yr (estimated)	8.28	0.87
5 Yr (estimated)	12.14	0.85
10 Yr (estimated)	—	—

Rating and Risk

Time Period	Morningstar Rtn vs Cat	Morningstar Risk vs Cat	Morningstar Risk-Adj Rating
3 Yr	Avg	-Avg	★★★
5 Yr	Avg	-Avg	★★★
10 Yr	—	—	—

Other Measures	Standard Index S&P 500	Best Fit Index Russ 1000 Vl
Alpha	0.8	0.3
Beta	0.94	0.93
R-Squared	89	96
Standard Deviation	7.73	
Mean	9.23	
Sharpe Ratio	0.63	

Portfolio Analysis 12-31-07

Share change since 11-07 Total Stocks:294	Sector	PE	Tot Ret%	% Assets
⊕ ExxonMobil Corporation	Energy	13.6	24.34	7.59
⊕ General Electric Company	Ind Mtrls	16.6	2.69	5.56
⊕ AT&T, Inc.	Telecom	21.6	20.58	3.76
⊕ Chevron Corporation	Energy	11.4	30.59	2.95
⊕ Johnson & Johnson	Health	18.8	3.61	2.83
⊕ Bank of America Corporat	Financial	9.4	-19.25	2.75
⊕ Altria Group Inc.	Goods	13.2	22.10	2.35
⊕ Pfizer Inc.	Health	22.5	-8.15	2.30
⊕ International Business M	Hardware	16.2	13.20	2.19
⊕ J.P. Morgan Chase & Co.	Financial	9.5	-7.24	2.19
⊕ Citigroup, Inc.	Financial	7.9	-44.93	2.17
⊕ ConocoPhillips	Energy	13.8	25.42	1.94
⊕ Coca-Cola Company	Goods	26.3	30.44	1.93
⊕ American International G	Financial	10.2	-17.96	1.92
⊕ Verizon Communications I	Telecom	21.7	22.19	1.88
⊕ Merck & Co., Inc.	Health	23.6	37.36	1.87
⊕ Wells Fargo Company	Financial	11.4	-12.13	1.43
⊕ Abbott Laboratories	Health	45.7	18.04	1.28
⊕ Goldman Sachs Group, Inc	Financial	8.8	8.59	1.15
⊕ Wachovia Corporation	Financial	8.6	-29.91	1.12

Current Investment Style

Value Blnd Growth; Large Mid Small

Market Cap	%
Giant	59.5
Large	26.0
Mid	14.4
Small	0.1
Micro	0.0
Avg $mil: 65,065	

Value Measures		Rel Category
Price/Earnings	12.48	0.92
Price/Book	2.04	1.04
Price/Sales	1.33	1.11
Price/Cash Flow	8.62	1.03
Dividend Yield %	2.71	1.00

Growth Measures	%	Rel Category
Long-Term Erngs	—	—
Book Value	6.64	0.77
Sales	4.73	0.74
Cash Flow	5.72	1.09
Historical Erngs	14.75	0.98

Profitability	%	Rel Category
Return on Equity	21.43	1.09
Return on Assets	6.83	1.06
Net Margin	14.71	1.06

Sector Weightings	% of Stocks	Rel S&P 500	3 Year High	Low
Info	9.74	0.47		
Software	0.36	0.09	2	0
Hardware	2.81	0.28	8	2
Media	0.46	0.16	3	0
Telecom	6.11	1.68	7	5
Service	44.07	1.08		
Health	11.35	0.94	12	7
Consumer	2.50	0.37	3	2
Business	1.77	0.40	2	1
Financial	28.45	1.63	35	28
Mfg	46.19	1.20		
Goods	9.29	1.01	9	6
Ind Mtrls	15.53	1.19	17	14
Energy	14.92	1.18	17	11
Utilities	6.45	1.75	7	4

Composition

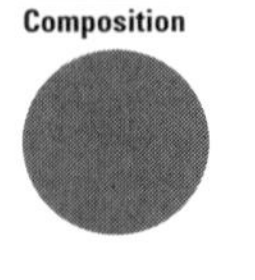

Cash	0.9
Stocks	99.1
Bonds	0.0
Other	0.0
Foreign (% of Stock)	0.0

Morningstar's Take by Emiko Kurotsu 12-31-07

We'd buy this above-average quality, moderate-risk portfolio at the right price.

SPDR Dow Jones Wilshire Large Cap Value tracks about 300 reasonably priced large caps drawn from the broader Dow Jones Wilshire 5000. The portfolio skews toward financials, which account for almost one third of assets, while largely eschewing technology and media fare. What's more, the fund's market-cap-weighting scheme means large-cap names such as ExxonMobil and Freddie Mac soak up the lion's share of assets.

The portfolio's quality is above-average, as our analysts have awarded wide economic moats, which denote durable competitive advantages, to stocks representing roughly half of this fund's assets. For instance, Goldman Sachs boasts perhaps the most prestigious nameplate on Wall Street, a pedigree that has paved the way to investment banking and other assignments. Though less glamorous, Campbell Soup is similarly dominant in the U.S. soup market, where the firm's scale helps it fend off rival private-label brands.

Most of the stocks in the portfolio aren't especially risky either, with the typical name courting average business risk. That's partly a function of quality, as more-dominant names are less likely to see their businesses torn asunder overnight by rivals. As such, we wouldn't expect Bank of America's results, which are fortified by that firm's difficult-to-replicate branch network, to be fraught with uncertainty, explaining that stock's below-average risk rating. On the flip side, narrow-moat industrial Stanley Works must fend with its dependence on a few key customers, not to mention the vagaries of input price trends; hence that firm's average risk rating.

Taken together with the portfolio's wide diversification across stocks and industries, the fund's above-average quality/moderate-risk profile has tamped down volatility. Thus, we'd demand only an 8% discount to our fair value estimate before recommending it.

Address:	One Lincoln Street United States 866-787-2257
Web Address:	www.advisors.ssga.com
Inception:	09-25-00*
Advisor:	SSgA Funds Management Inc

Management Fee:	0.20%		
Expense Projections:	3Yr:$65	5Yr:$113	10Yr:$257
Income Distrib:	Quarterly		
Exchange:	AMEX		

SPDR S&P Dividend SDY

Market Price	Mstar Category
$55.06	Large Value

Morningstar Fair Value

Price/Fair Value Ratio	Coverage Rate %
0.81	86

Valuation

Given this fund's diversification, we think it's worth a look at a 9% or greater discount to our fair value estimate. The fund has been well within our "buy" range of late, as it was trading at a 16% discount to fair value due in large part to recent weakness in the financials sector. That's the cheapest it has been in at least two years.

Methodology

This fund tracks the S&P High Yield Dividend Aristocrats Index, which represents the 50 highest dividend-yielding stocks in the S&P 1500 Index that have also increased their dividends annually for at least the past 25 years. These holdings are ranked by yield, with each capped at 4%. The fund has a larger mid-cap stake than many other dividend-focused funds have. Like other yield-focused funds, though, it owns big stakes in financials, utilities, and consumer goods stocks.

Morningstar Rating	Return	Risk	Yield	NAV	Avg Daily Vol. (k)	52 wk High/Low
—	—	—	3.5%	$55.12	55	$65.89 - $52.10

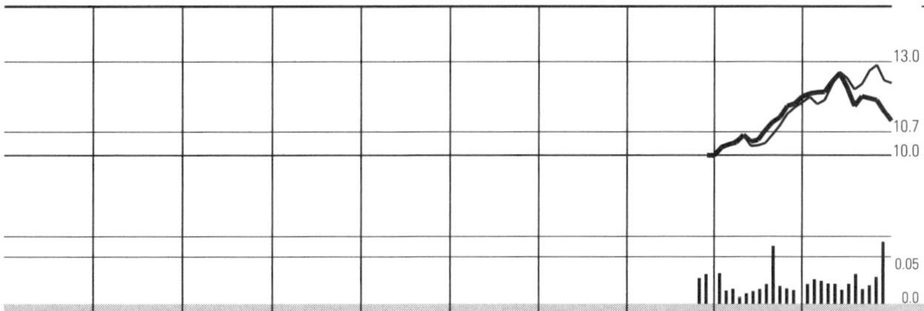

Growth of $10,000
— Investment Value of ETF
— Investment Value of Index S&P 500

Trading Volume Millions

History

1998	1999	2000	2001	2002	2003	2004	2005	2006	2007	History
—	—	—	—	—	—	—	54.09	61.79	55.12	NAV $
—	—	—	—	—	—	—	54.15	61.85	55.06	Market Price $
—	—	—	—	—	—	—	5.39*	17.74	-6.54	NAV Return%
—	—	—	—	—	—	—	5.33*	17.73	-6.74	Market Price Return%
—	—	—	—	—	—	—	0.07	0.04	-0.04	Avg Premium/Discount%
—	—	—	—	—	—	—	—	1.95	-12.03	NAV Rtrn% +/-S&P 500
—	—	—	—	—	—	—	—	3.65	3.00	NAV Rtrn% +/-S&P Arist
—	—	—	—	—	—	—	—	78	94	NAV Return% Rank in Cat
—	—	—	—	—	—	—	—	3.31	3.22	Income Return %
—	—	—	—	—	—	—	—	14.43	-9.76	Capital Return %
—	—	—	—	—	—	—	0.31	1.77	1.97	Income $
—	—	—	—	—	—	—	0.00	0.00	0.80	Capital Gains $
—	—	—	—	—	—	—	—	0.30	0.34	Expense Ratio %
—	—	—	—	—	—	—	—	3.45	3.11	Income Ratio %
—	—	—	—	—	—	—	—	25	41	Turnover Rate %
—	—	—	—	—	—	—	32	198	234	Net Assets $mil

Performance 12-31-07

Historic Quarterly NAV Returns

	1st Qtr	2nd Qtr	3rd Qtr	4th Qtr	Total
2003	—	—	—	—	—
2004	—	—	—	—	—
2005	—	—	—	—	—*
2006	3.60	0.74	6.44	5.98	17.74
2007	1.30	1.32	-3.00	-6.12	-6.54

Trailing	NAV Return%	Market Return%	NAV Rtrn% +/-S&P 500	%Rank Cat.(NAV)
3 Mo	-6.12	-6.23	-2.79	73
6 Mo	-8.94	-8.96	-7.57	82
1 Yr	-6.54	-6.74	-12.03	94
3 Yr Avg	—	—	—	—
5 Yr Avg	—	—	—	—
10 Yr Avg	—	—	—	—

Tax Analysis	Tax-Adj Return%	Tax-Cost Ratio
3 Yr (estimated)	—	—
5 Yr (estimated)	—	—
10 Yr (estimated)	—	—

Rating and Risk

Time Period	Morningstar Rtn vs Cat	Morningstar Risk vs Cat	Morningstar Risk-Adj Rating
3 Yr	—	—	—
5 Yr	—	—	—
10 Yr	—	—	—

Other Measures	Standard Index S&P 500	Best Fit Index
Alpha	—	—
Beta	—	—
R-Squared	—	—
Standard Deviation	—	
Mean	—	
Sharpe Ratio	—	

Portfolio Analysis 12-31-07

Share change since 11-07 Total Stocks:50	Sector	PE	Tot Ret%	% Assets
☼ FirstMerit Corporation	Financial	16.5	-12.29	3.12
⊕ Comerica Incorporated	Financial	9.1	-22.42	3.05
⊕ KeyCorp	Financial	7.6	-35.39	2.96
⊕ Regions Financial Corpor	Financial	10.1	-33.64	2.96
⊖ Integrys Energy Group, I	Utilities	30.0	0.35	2.95
⊕ Bank of America Corporat	Financial	9.4	-19.25	2.91
⊕ Fifth Third Bancorp	Financial	12.2	-35.42	2.75
⊕ Gannett Co., Inc.	Media	8.3	-33.49	2.72
⊖ Consolidated Edison Comp	Utilities	13.9	6.65	2.70
⊖ US Bancorp	Financial	12.2	-7.89	2.69
⊕ Pfizer Inc.	Health	22.5	-8.15	2.60
⊕ Associated Banc-Corp	Financial	11.8	-19.12	2.53
⊕ BB&T Corporation	Financial	10.7	-27.20	2.47
⊖ Vectren Corporation	Utilities	16.0	7.26	2.47
⊕ Leggett & Platt, Inc.	Ind Mtrls	11.8	-24.32	2.39
⊖ WGL Holdings, Inc.	Utilities	15.0	4.84	2.33
⊕ RPM International, Inc.	Goods	12.1	0.41	2.31
⊖ Piedmont Natural Gas Com	Utilities	18.7	1.58	2.15
⊕ Wilmington Trust Company	Financial	13.2	-13.67	2.11
☼ Pitney Bowes Inc.	Ind Mtrls	14.3	-15.11	2.06

Current Investment Style

Value Blnd Growth / Large Mid Small

Market Cap	%
Giant	18.7
Large	18.3
Mid	47.4
Small	15.6
Micro	0.0
Avg $mil: 9,591	

Value Measures		Rel Category
Price/Earnings	12.61	0.93
Price/Book	1.64	0.84
Price/Sales	1.24	1.03
Price/Cash Flow	8.47	1.01
Dividend Yield %	4.08	1.51

Growth Measures	%	Rel Category
Long-Term Erngs	—	—
Book Value	6.27	0.73
Sales	5.07	0.79
Cash Flow	6.20	1.18
Historical Erngs	7.54	0.50

Profitability	%	Rel Category
Return on Equity	17.21	0.87
Return on Assets	5.04	0.79
Net Margin	14.82	1.07

Sector Weightings	% of Stocks	Rel S&P 500	3 Year High	3 Year Low
Info	4.16	0.20		
Software	0.00	0.00	0	0
Hardware	1.37	0.13	1	0
Media	2.79	0.96	3	0
Telecom	0.00	0.00	2	0
Service	47.69	1.17		
Health	8.48	0.71	13	8
Consumer	1.46	0.22	3	1
Business	2.76	0.63	3	1
Financial	34.99	2.01	35	25
Mfg	48.15	1.25		
Goods	13.33	1.46	21	13
Ind Mtrls	15.28	1.18	15	12
Energy	1.86	0.15	3	2
Utilities	17.68	4.80	21	18

Composition

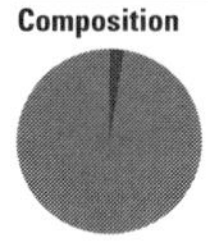

Cash	2.4
Stocks	97.6
Bonds	0.0
Other	0.0
Foreign (% of Stock)	0.0

Morningstar's Take by Emiko Kurotsu 12-31-07

This portfolio doesn't gleam with quality, but it's worth a look at the right price.

SPDR S&P Dividend tracks the S&P High Yield Dividend Aristocrats Index, which culls the S&P 1500 Index for the 50 highest-yielding stocks that have increased their dividend payouts for the past 25 years. Financials and utilities are well represented here, while the portfolio dips deeper into small- and mid-caps, which account for over half of the fund's assets.

This hunt for yield doesn't mean these stocks are all high-quality, a trait we normally associate with firms that boast intractable competitive advantages, or "economic moats," that prevent rivals from encroaching on their turf and profits. Of the 42 portfolio holdings that our analysts cover, just 15 garner a wide-moat rating, with the rest invested almost entirely in narrow-moat stocks.

While narrow-moat firms often do have some unique advantages, they tend to be more fleeting or less profitable than those of wide-moat stocks. For instance, our analysts award narrow-moat ratings to all of this fund's utilities holdings, reflecting the regulated, low-margin market that firms like Consolidated Edison operate in. Similarly, virtually every one of the fund's regional banks have narrow moats, as firms like First Horizon National lack the scale of larger financial services rivals.

Despite its average stock quality, this fund's risk profile is below average for a few reasons. First, the fund's utilities stocks don't court the risk of being dislodged by rivals given the heavily regulated nature of that industry. Second, many of the fund's financials holdings boast diversified revenue streams, making them less vulnerable to interest-rate movements than the typical spread bank. Finally, most of these firms are on sturdy financial footing.

Taken together with the fund's wide diversification, its moderate quality/risk profile has kept volatility in check. Thus, we wouldn't demand a large margin of safety before investing here.

Address:	One Lincoln Street United States 866-787-2257
Web Address:	www.advisors.ssga.com
Inception:	11-08-05*
Advisor:	SSgA Funds Management Inc

Management Fee:	0.35%		
Expense Projections:	3Yr:$113	5Yr:$197	10Yr:$446
Income Distrib:	Quarterly		
Exchange:	AMEX		

SPDR Trust Series 1 SPY

Market Price	Mstar Category
$146.21	Large Blend

Morningstar Rating	Return	Risk	Yield	NAV	Avg Daily Vol. (k)	52 wk High/Low
★★★	Average	Average	1.8%	$146.60	195,980	$156.48 - $137.35

Morningstar Fair Value

Price/Fair Value Ratio	Coverage Rate %
0.88	99

Valuation

This ETF is a diversified collection of wide-moat industry leaders. As such, it hasn't been too volatile. Accordingly, we'd require only an 8% discount to our fair value estimate to recommend it. The fund was recently trading at a 12% discount to fair value, which puts it well within our "buy" range.

Methodology

This ETF mimics the S&P 500 Index, a market-cap-weighted collection of U.S. stocks. Although it's considered a broad-market proxy, the S&P is for all intents and purposes a large-cap vehicle, with mega-caps dominating this portfolio's upper ranks. The fund is organized as a unit investment trust, so unlike most other ETFs, it cannot use futures contracts or lend securities for a fee to close the expense gap between it and its bogy. It also cannot reinvest the dividends it receives until it pays them out to investors. It has to hold the payouts in a non-interest-bearing account until they are distributed once a quarter.

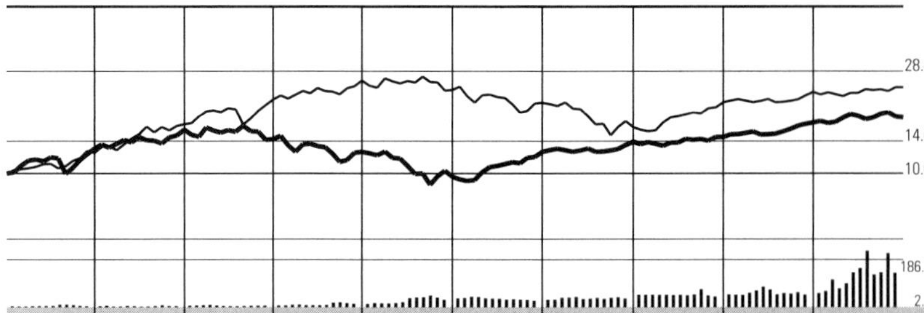

Growth of $10,000
— Investment Value of ETF
— Investment Value of Index S&P 500

Trading Volume Millions

1998	1999	2000	2001	2002	2003	2004	2005	2006	2007	History
123.00	147.08	132.21	115.05	88.21	111.45	121.10	124.70	141.64	146.60	NAV $
123.31	146.88	131.19	114.23	88.23	111.28	120.87	124.51	141.62	146.21	Market Price $
28.35	20.86	-9.15	-11.86	-22.12	28.40	10.75	4.79	15.69	5.40	NAV Return%
28.69	20.40	-9.73	-11.81	-21.54	28.18	10.70	4.83	15.85	5.14	Market Price Return%
-0.12	-0.17	-0.08	-0.09	-0.21	0.00	0.02	-0.01	0.04	0.00	Avg Premium/Discount%
-0.23	-0.18	-0.05	0.03	-0.02	-0.28	-0.13	-0.12	-0.10	-0.09	NAV Rtrn% +/-S&P 500
-0.23	-0.18	-0.05	0.03	-0.02	-0.28	-0.13	-0.12	-0.10	-0.09	NAV Rtrn% +/-S&P 500
1	40	40	69	67	69	75	56	34	60	NAV Return% Rank in Cat
1.47	1.18	1.03	1.08	1.31	1.86	1.99	1.79	1.98	1.92	Income Return %
26.88	19.68	-10.18	-12.94	-23.43	26.54	8.76	3.00	13.71	3.48	Capital Return %
1.42	1.44	1.51	1.42	1.50	1.63	2.20	2.15	2.45	2.70	Income $
0.00	0.00	0.00	0.00	0.00	0.00	0.00	0.00	0.00	0.00	Capital Gains $
0.18	0.17	0.13	0.11	0.11	0.12	0.11	0.10	0.08	—	Expense Ratio %
1.35	1.18	1.01	1.14	1.40	1.67	1.63	2.02	1.83	—	Income Ratio %
6	6	8	5	4	2	2	6	4	—	Turnover Rate %
—	—	—	—	39,273	43,815	55,944	58,539	63,997	98,152	Net Assets $mil

Performance 12-31-07

Historic Quarterly NAV Returns

	1st Qtr	2nd Qtr	3rd Qtr	4th Qtr	Total
2003	-3.20	15.31	2.60	12.11	28.40
2004	1.67	1.69	-1.89	9.18	10.75
2005	-2.16	1.33	3.58	2.05	4.79
2006	4.18	-1.45	5.63	6.67	15.69
2007	0.63	6.24	2.01	-3.36	5.40

Trailing	NAV Return%	Market Return%	NAV Rtrn% +/-S&P 500	%Rank Cat.(NAV)
3 Mo	-3.36	-3.67	-0.03	53
6 Mo	-1.41	-1.83	-0.04	49
1 Yr	5.40	5.14	-0.09	60
3 Yr Avg	8.51	8.49	-0.11	81
5 Yr Avg	12.68	12.62	-0.15	61
10 Yr Avg	5.80	5.78	-0.11	1

Tax Analysis	Tax-Adj Return%	Tax-Cost Ratio
3 Yr (estimated)	8.09	0.39
5 Yr (estimated)	12.30	0.34
10 Yr (estimated)	5.36	0.42

Rating and Risk

Time Period	Morningstar Rtn vs Cat	Morningstar Risk vs Cat	Morningstar Risk-Adj Rating
3 Yr	Avg	Avg	★★★
5 Yr	Avg	Avg	★★★
10 Yr	Avg	Avg	★★★

Other Measures	Standard Index S&P 500	Best Fit Index S&P 500
Alpha	-0.1	-0.1
Beta	1.00	1.00
R-Squared	100	100
Standard Deviation	7.77	
Mean	8.51	
Sharpe Ratio	0.54	

Portfolio Analysis 12-31-07

Share change since 11-07 Total Stocks:501	Sector	PE	Tot Ret%	% Assets
⊕ ExxonMobil Corporation	Energy	13.6	24.34	3.96
⊕ General Electric Company	Ind Mtrls	16.6	2.69	2.90
⊕ Microsoft Corporation	Software	23.4	20.83	2.22
⊕ AT&T, Inc.	Telecom	21.6	20.58	1.95
⊕ Procter & Gamble Company	Goods	23.1	16.63	1.76
⊕ Chevron Corporation	Energy	11.4	30.59	1.53
⊕ Johnson & Johnson	Health	18.8	3.61	1.48
⊕ Bank of America Corporat	Financial	9.4	-19.25	1.42
⊕ Apple, Inc.	Hardware	50.5	133.47	1.34
⊕ Cisco Systems, Inc.	Hardware	21.5	-0.95	1.27
⊕ Google, Inc.	Business	54.0	50.17	1.24
⊕ Altria Group Inc.	Goods	13.2	22.10	1.23
⊕ Intel Corporation	Hardware	25.4	34.22	1.21
⊕ Pfizer Inc.	Health	22.5	-8.15	1.20
⊕ International Business M	Hardware	16.2	13.20	1.15
⊕ American International G	Financial	10.2	-17.96	1.14
⊕ Citigroup, Inc.	Financial	7.9	-44.93	1.14
⊕ J.P. Morgan Chase & Co.	Financial	9.5	-7.24	1.13
⊕ ConocoPhillips	Energy	13.8	25.42	1.09
⊕ Hewlett-Packard Company	Hardware	18.8	23.40	1.01

Current Investment Style

Value Blnd Growth (Large Mid Small) — style box: Large Blend

Market Cap	%
Giant	51.4
Large	36.6
Mid	11.8
Small	0.2
Micro	0.0
Avg $mil: 55,998	

Value Measures		Rel Category
Price/Earnings	14.28	0.91
Price/Book	2.43	0.95
Price/Sales	1.41	1.14
Price/Cash Flow	9.91	1.07
Dividend Yield %	1.82	0.96

Growth Measures	%	Rel Category
Long-Term Erngs	—	—
Book Value	7.92	0.86
Sales	7.73	0.94
Cash Flow	8.23	0.94
Historical Erngs	17.18	1.03

Profitability	%	Rel Category
Return on Equity	22.20	1.00
Return on Assets	8.54	1.02
Net Margin	14.20	1.16

Sector Weightings	% of Stocks	Rel S&P 500	3 Year High	3 Year Low
Info	20.89	1.00		
Software	4.14	1.00	5	3
Hardware	10.21	1.00	11	9
Media	2.91	1.00	4	3
Telecom	3.63	1.00	4	3
Service	40.68	1.00		
Health	12.02	1.00	14	12
Consumer	6.79	1.00	9	7
Business	4.43	1.00	4	3
Financial	17.44	1.00	22	17
Mfg	38.43	1.00		
Goods	9.15	1.00	9	8
Ind Mtrls	13.00	1.00	13	12
Energy	12.62	1.00	13	8
Utilities	3.66	0.99	4	3

Composition

Cash	0.5
Stocks	99.5
Bonds	0.0
Other	0.0
Foreign (% of Stock)	0.0

Morningstar's Take by Sonya Morris 12-31-07

This popular ETF boasts a diversified, high-quality portfolio, so we'd be willing to hop aboard when it's trading 8% or more below our fair value estimate.

This fund, which tracks the well-known S&P 500 Index, is the oldest and among the most active ETFs on the market. Because its benchmark ranks stocks by market cap, leading multinational firms take up most of the space here (explaining, in part, why it's a favorite tool for gaining broad exposure to large caps). That gives this portfolio a high-quality look. Roughly half of its assets are dedicated to wide-moat firms, businesses that our analysts believe possess enduring competitive advantages. Some firms, such as ExxonMobil, exploit their scale to gain an edge over competitors. Others like Coca-Cola and Procter & Gamble wield powerful and diverse brands. Still others, such as Pfizer, hold patents that keep competitors at bay. These firms typically exploit these advantages to generate scads of free cash flow and enviable returns on investment.

Moreover, wide-moat firms often tend to be only moderately risky. This is due to a few factors. First, on balance, such companies are founded on entrenched businesses that generate relatively predictable results. For instance, General Electric's widely diversified suite of businesses means a downturn in one industry isn't likely to make a major dent in its overall results. In addition, wide-moat companies are typically on sturdy financial footing, with excessive leverage being the exception to the rule. To wit, software giant and top holding Microsoft recently had nearly $22 billion in cash burning a hole in its balance sheet. Taken together with the portfolio's wide diversification across names and industries, these attributes have helped to tamp down volatility.

Given the fund's high-quality, moderate-risk profile, we wouldn't demand an especially large margin of safety to invest here. An 8%-plus discount to our fair value estimate will do.

Address:	PDR Services, 86 Trinity Place United States 800-843-2639
Web Address:	www.amex.com/spy
Inception:	01-29-93
Advisor:	PDR Services

Management Fee:	0.06%		
Expense Projections:	3Yr:$31	5Yr:$54	10Yr:$124
Income Distrib:	Quarterly		
Exchange:	AMEX		

UltShort QQQ ProShares QID

Market Price	Mstar Category
$37.98	Bear Market

Morningstar Fair Value

Price/Fair Value Ratio	Coverage Rate %
—	—

Valuation

This ETF's strategy--betting with borrowed money against the Nasdaq 100 Index--is aggressive and the fund has been volatile. Given that, we'd need a wide margin of safety to invest here. We'd be buyers of the fund when it trades at a 20% or greater premium to our fair value estimate for the Nasdaq 100. It was fairly valued recently.

Methodology

This ETF seeks to deliver twice the inverse return of the Nasdaq 100 Index, a popular proxy for nonfinancial stocks listed on the Nasdaq stock exchange. To capture that return, the fund invests in derivatives, typically equity swaps, whose notional value is twice the value of assets invested in the fund. The Nasdaq 100 Index skews heavily toward tech stocks (its tech stake is roughly quadruple the S&P 500's) while treading lightly in industrials and other asset-heavy firms. It holds 100 stocks, which are weighted by market cap. The top 10 names recently soaked up 46% of assets.

Morningstar Rating	Return	Risk	Yield	NAV	Avg Daily Vol. (k)	52 wk High/Low
—	—	—	4.7%	$37.97	26,217	$57.88 - $34.04

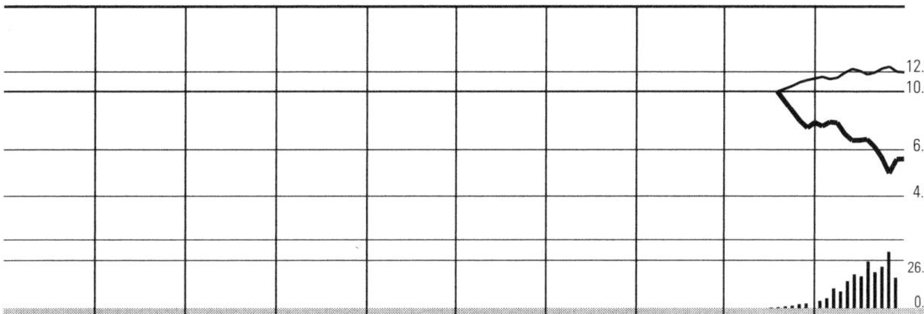

Growth of $10,000
- Investment Value of ETF
- Investment Value of Index S&P 500

Trading Volume Millions

1998	1999	2000	2001	2002	2003	2004	2005	2006	2007	History
—	—	—	—	—	—	—	—	54.34	37.97	NAV $
—	—	—	—	—	—	—	—	54.50	37.98	Market Price $
—	—	—	—	—	—	—	—	-31.60*	-27.16	NAV Return%
—	—	—	—	—	—	—	—	-31.59*	-27.36	Market Price Return%
—	—	—	—	—	—	—	—	0.10	-0.13	Avg Premium/Discount%
—	—	—	—	—	—	—	—	—	-32.65	NAV Rtrn% +/-S&P 500
—	—	—	—	—	—	—	—	—	-45.83	NAV Rtrn% +/-NASDAQ 100
—	—	—	—	—	—	—	—	—	100	NAV Return% Rank in Cat
—	—	—	—	—	—	—	—	—	3.32	Income Return %
—	—	—	—	—	—	—	—	—	-30.48	Capital Return %
—	—	—	—	—	—	—	—	0.57	1.78	Income $
—	—	—	—	—	—	—	—	0.00	0.00	Capital Gains $
—	—	—	—	—	—	—	—	—	0.95	Expense Ratio %
—	—	—	—	—	—	—	—	—	4.30	Income Ratio %
—	—	—	—	—	—	—	—	—	—	Turnover Rate %
—	—	—	—	—	—	—	—	668	1,256	Net Assets $mil

Performance 12-31-07

Historic Quarterly NAV Returns

	1st Qtr	2nd Qtr	3rd Qtr	4th Qtr	Total
2003	—	—	—	—	—
2004	—	—	—	—	—
2005	—	—	—	—	—
2006	—	—	—	-9.55	—*
2007	-0.26	-14.09	-14.09	-1.06	-27.16

Trailing	NAV Return%	Market Return%	NAV Rtrn% +/-S&P 500	%Rank Cat.(NAV)
3 Mo	-1.06	-0.78	2.27	87
6 Mo	-15.00	-14.51	-13.63	93
1 Yr	-27.16	-27.36	-32.65	100
3 Yr Avg	—	—	—	—
5 Yr Avg	—	—	—	—
10 Yr Avg	—	—	—	—

Tax Analysis	Tax-Adj Return%	Tax-Cost Ratio
3 Yr (estimated)	—	—
5 Yr (estimated)	—	—
10 Yr (estimated)	—	—

Rating and Risk

Time Period	Morningstar Rtn vs Cat	Morningstar Risk vs Cat	Morningstar Risk-Adj Rating
3 Yr	—	—	—
5 Yr	—	—	—
10 Yr	—	—	—

Other Measures	Standard Index S&P 500	Best Fit Index
Alpha	—	—
Beta	—	—
R-Squared	—	—
Standard Deviation	—	
Mean	—	
Sharpe Ratio	—	

Portfolio Analysis 11-30-07

Share change since 08-07 Total Stocks:0	Sector	PE	Tot Ret%	% Assets
☼ Nasdaq 100 Swaps	—	—	—	9.17

Morningstar's Take by Jeffrey Ptak 12-31-07

We'd invest here only with a wide margin of safety.

UltraShort QQQ ProShares seeks to deliver twice the inverse return of the Nasdaq 100 Index, which is a proxy for nonfinancial stocks listed on the Nasdaq stock exchange. That is, if the Nasdaq 100 falls 10% over a given span, the ETF should return a positive 20%, and vice versa. Suffice it to say, you'd only consider this fund if you were very bearish on the U.S. stock market.

Historically speaking, that's been a terrible bet. Although this fund launched relatively recently, the Nasdaq index has been around for a while, racking up a 13.8% return since its Jan. 1995 inception. In other words, investors in a strategy like this fund's would have suffered a nearly 28% loss by doubling down against the Nasdaq.

Of course, past isn't prologue--witness the tech-led downturn of 2000-02, which erased 78% of the Nasdaq's value. Further, it goes without saying that prices can get ahead of fundamentals, pushing the Nasdaq to unsustainably high levels and, thus, making shorting vehicles like this one more useful.

But we're still very leery. The fund makes extensive use of leverage, thereby greatly upping the stakes, not to mention volatility (it has been one of the most-volatile ETFs around during its brief existence). That's not a deal-breaker, per se. But it strongly argues for caution and explains why we would consider investing in the fund only at a wide margin of safety: We'd only dip a toe when the Nasdaq is trading at a 20% or greater premium to our fair value estimate.

Even if you can get past the fund's unpalatable risk profile, there's another trait that gives us pause: The fund is unlikely to deliver twice the inverse return over long time periods. That's due to a tick in the way returns compound over periods longer than a single day. Consequently, if you're a long-term investor, you won't get what you pay for; the fund is better suited it to those speculating on daily market gyrations.

Address:	7501 Wisconsin Avenue United States 866-776-5125
Web Address:	www.proshares.com
Inception:	07-11-06 *
Advisor:	Proshare Advisors LLC

Management Fee:	0.75%		
Expense Projections:	3Yr:$309	5Yr:$539	10Yr:$1199
Income Distrib:	Annually		
Exchange:	AMEX		

Current Investment Style

Value Blnd Growth — Large Mid Small

Market Cap	%
Giant	—
Large	—
Mid	—
Small	—
Micro	—
Avg $mil:	—

Value Measures		Rel Category
Price/Earnings	—	—
Price/Book	—	—
Price/Sales	—	—
Price/Cash Flow	—	—
Dividend Yield %	—	—

Growth Measures	%	Rel Category
Long-Term Erngs	—	—
Book Value	—	—
Sales	—	—
Cash Flow	—	—
Historical Erngs	—	—

Profitability	%	Rel Category
Return on Equity	—	—
Return on Assets	—	—
Net Margin	—	—

Sector Weightings	% of Stocks	Rel S&P 500	3 Year High	3 Year Low
Info	0.00	0.00		
Software	—	0.00	—	—
Hardware	—	0.00	—	—
Media	—	0.00	—	—
Telecom	—	0.00	—	—
Service	0.00	0.00		
Health	—	0.00	—	—
Consumer	—	0.00	—	—
Business	—	0.00	—	—
Financial	—	0.00	—	—
Mfg	0.00	0.00		
Goods	—	0.00	—	—
Ind Mtrls	—	0.00	—	—
Energy	—	0.00	—	—
Utilities	—	0.00	—	—

Composition

Cash	91.9
Stocks	8.1
Bonds	0.0
Other	0.0
Foreign (% of Stock)	100.0

Data through December 31, 2007

Vanguard Div Appr ETF VIG

Market Price	Mstar Category
$55.95	Large Blend

Morningstar Fair Value

Price/Fair Value Ratio	Coverage Rate %
0.90	96

Valuation

Financially sound companies with entrenched competitive positions anchor this ETF. Those traits, coupled with the fund's diversification, have made for a relatively tame portfolio. We'd need only an 8% discount to our fair value estimate to invest here. The fund was recently trading at a 10% discount, which puts it in "buy" territory.

Methodology

The fund tracks the Dividend Achievers Select Index, which is a subset of the broad Dividend Achievers Index. Dividend Achievers are stocks that have increased their dividends in each of the last 10 years. The index's author, Mergent, crafted this fund's benchmark specially for Vanguard, applying the firm's proprietary screens that weed out nonliquid stocks and companies that may not be able to continue growing their dividends from the broad Dividend Achievers universe. The benchmark is a modified market-cap-weighted index that includes more than 200 stocks of mostly large U.S. companies..

Morningstar Rating	Return	Risk	Yield	NAV	Avg Daily Vol. (k)	52 wk High/Low
—	—	—	1.6%	$55.92	20	$58.98 - $52.59

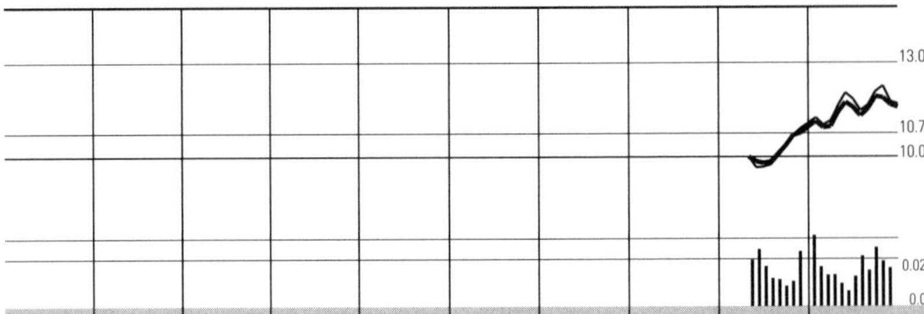

Growth of $10,000
— Investment Value of ETF
— Investment Value of Index S&P 500

Trading Volume Millions

1998	1999	2000	2001	2002	2003	2004	2005	2006	2007	History
—	—	—	—	—	—	—	—	53.77	55.92	NAV $
—	—	—	—	—	—	—	—	53.80	55.95	Market Price $
—	—	—	—	—	—	—	—	8.54*	5.63	NAV Return%
—	—	—	—	—	—	—	—	8.57*	5.63	Market Price Return%
—	—	—	—	—	—	—	—	0.05	0.02	Avg Premium/Discount%
—	—	—	—	—	—	—	—	—	0.14	NAV Rtrn% +/-S&P 500
—	—	—	—	—	—	—	—	—	-0.14	NAV Rtrn% +/-Russ 1000
—	—	—	—	—	—	—	—	—	53	NAV Return% Rank in Cat
—	—	—	—	—	—	—	—	—	1.63	Income Return %
—	—	—	—	—	—	—	—	—	4.00	Capital Return %
—	—	—	—	—	—	—	—	0.53	0.87	Income $
—	—	—	—	—	—	—	—	0.00	0.00	Capital Gains $
—	—	—	—	—	—	—	—	—	0.27	Expense Ratio %
—	—	—	—	—	—	—	—	—	1.65	Income Ratio %
—	—	—	—	—	—	—	—	—	42	Turnover Rate %
—	—	—	—	—	—	—	—	109	226	Net Assets $mil

Performance 12-31-07

Historic Quarterly NAV Returns

	1st Qtr	2nd Qtr	3rd Qtr	4th Qtr	Total
2003	—	—	—	—	—
2004	—	—	—	—	—
2005	—	—	—	—	—
2006	—	—	4.93	5.25	—*
2007	0.10	5.54	2.99	-2.92	5.63

Trailing	NAV Return%	Market Return%	NAV Rtrn% +/-S&P 500	%Rank Cat.(NAV)
3 Mo	-2.91	-2.83	0.42	35
6 Mo	-0.01	0.22	1.36	30
1 Yr	5.63	5.63	0.14	53
3 Yr Avg	—	—	—	—
5 Yr Avg	—	—	—	—
10 Yr Avg	—	—	—	—

Tax Analysis	Tax-Adj Return%	Tax-Cost Ratio
3 Yr (estimated)	—	—
5 Yr (estimated)	—	—
10 Yr (estimated)	—	—

Rating and Risk

Time Period	Morningstar Rtn vs Cat	Morningstar Risk vs Cat	Morningstar Risk-Adj Rating
3 Yr	—	—	—
5 Yr	—	—	—
10 Yr	—	—	—

Other Measures	Standard Index S&P 500	Best Fit Index
Alpha	—	—
Beta	—	—
R-Squared	—	—
Standard Deviation	—	
Mean	—	
Sharpe Ratio	—	

Portfolio Analysis 09-30-07

Share change since 06-07 Total Stocks:220

	Sector	PE	Tot Ret%	% Assets
⊕ Chevron Corporation	Energy	11.4	30.59	4.94
⊕ ExxonMobil Corporation	Energy	13.6	24.34	4.78
⊕ International Business M	Hardware	16.2	13.20	4.52
⊕ General Electric Company	Ind Mtrls	16.6	2.69	4.32
⊕ Procter & Gamble Company	Goods	23.1	16.63	4.09
⊕ Coca-Cola Company	Goods	26.3	30.44	3.99
⊕ Johnson & Johnson	Health	18.8	3.61	3.75
⊕ American International G	Financial	10.2	-17.96	3.74
⊕ Wal-Mart Stores, Inc.	Consumer	15.4	4.91	3.46
⊕ PepsiCo, Inc.	Goods	20.4	23.89	3.41
⊕ United Technologies	Ind Mtrls	18.8	24.46	2.25
⊕ Abbott Laboratories	Health	45.7	18.04	2.23
⊕ McDonald's Corporation	Consumer	39.5	36.38	2.02
⊕ 3M Company	Ind Mtrls	14.1	10.53	1.99
⊕ Medtronic, Inc.	Health	20.3	-5.22	1.93
⊕ Home Depot, Inc.	Consumer	10.7	-31.14	1.67
⊕ Target Corporation	Consumer	14.7	-11.17	1.52
⊕ Caterpillar Inc.	Ind Mtrls	14.0	20.48	1.48
⊕ Walgreen Company	Consumer	18.5	-16.35	1.40
⊕ Freddie Mac	Financial	12.0	-48.20	1.27

Current Investment Style

Value Blnd Growth / Large Mid Small

Market Cap	%
Giant	53.1
Large	31.2
Mid	13.5
Small	1.8
Micro	0.4
Avg $mil: 55,527	

Value Measures		Rel Category
Price/Earnings	15.96	1.01
Price/Book	3.11	1.21
Price/Sales	1.42	1.15
Price/Cash Flow	11.85	1.28
Dividend Yield %	1.85	0.98

Growth Measures	%	Rel Category
Long-Term Erngs	9.93	0.84
Book Value	11.04	1.19
Sales	12.36	1.51
Cash Flow	9.93	1.14
Historical Erngs	16.75	1.00

Profitability	%	Rel Category
Return on Equity	25.67	1.15
Return on Assets	9.44	1.13
Net Margin	12.92	1.05

Sector Weightings	% of Stocks	Rel S&P 500	3 Year High	3 Year Low
Info	6.12	0.29		
Software	0.00	0.00	—	—
Hardware	4.93	0.48	—	—
Media	1.04	0.36	—	—
Telecom	0.15	0.04	—	—
Service	44.72	1.10		
Health	10.64	0.89	—	—
Consumer	13.45	1.98	—	—
Business	2.35	0.53	—	—
Financial	18.28	1.05	—	—
Mfg	49.16	1.28		
Goods	16.99	1.85	—	—
Ind Mtrls	20.80	1.60	—	—
Energy	10.31	0.82	—	—
Utilities	1.06	0.29	—	—

Composition

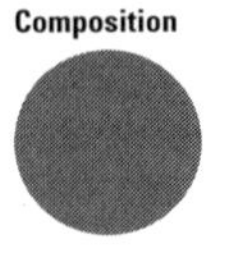

Cash	0.0
Stocks	100.0
Bonds	0.0
Other	0.0
Foreign (% of Stock)	0.0

Morningstar's Take by Dan Culloton 12-31-07

Vanguard Dividend Appreciation ETF has one of the highest-quality portfolios we cover.

The underlying holdings of this ETF, which tracks the Mergent Dividend Achievers Select Index of companies with long histories of paying and increasing their dividends, include some of the most consistently profitable companies in the U.S. That's because it's easy for corporations to fudge their earnings, but it's hard to fake a dividend which has to be paid out to stock shareholders. As a result this ETF has large positions in giant companies that have proven their ability to generate the cash needed to support rising dividends, such as General Electric, IBM, and ExxonMobil.

At Vanguard's behest, Mergent also screens its broader Dividend Achievers Universe for companies with characteristics that indicate they will be able to sustain their dividend payments over the long term. Companies that earn enough to make and increase payouts over time tend to have redoubtable competitive position, such as GE's carefully assembled portfolio of profitable businesses, IBMs nonpareil expertise at untangling and servicing large corporate software and hardware systems, and ExxonMobil's operational efficiency and economies of scale. Indeed, more than 60% of the fund's assets are invested in firms with wide moats, making it one of the highest-quality portfolios that we cover.

The ETF's focus on profitable, market-leading companies also keeps risk under control. The vast majority of assets are devoted to stocks that have weathered business cycles well, including Procter & Gamble, whose diverse stable of brands gives it something to sell in almost every environment. There are only a few of its stocks, such as oil and gas driller Helmerich & Payne, that Morningstar stock analysts think pose above-average risk. Given the superior quality of this ETF's holdings and its wide diversification across stocks and industries, we'd need only an 8% discount to our fair value estimate to invest here.

Address:	PO Box 2600 United States 800-662-6273
Web Address:	www.vanguard.com
Inception:	04-21-06*
Advisor:	The Vanguard Group, Inc.

Management Fee:	0.21%		
Expense Projections:	3Yr:$90	5Yr:$157	10Yr:$356
Income Distrib:	Quarterly		
Exchange:	AMEX		

Vanguard Growth ETF VUG

Market Price	Mstar Category
$64.48	Large Growth

Morningstar Fair Value

Price/Fair Value Ratio	Coverage Rate %
0.93	97

Valuation

This portfolio is chock-full of high-quality, low-risk growth stocks. Coupled with the fund's diversification, we'd require only a small margin of safety to invest here, with an 8% discount to our fair value estimate sufficing. Recently, the fund was flirting with "bargain" territory, as it was trading at a 7% discount to fair value.

Methodology

This exchange-traded fund tracks the MSCI U.S. Prime Market Growth Index, which sifts the 750 largest U.S. stocks--in terms of free-float market capitalization--for the fastest-growing companies. MSCI defines style (growth versus value) using an eight-factor model that includes measures ranging from dividend yield to long-term historical sales per share. MSCI employs buffer zones to limit the migration of stocks between the growth and value camps. These traits help limit turnover and make the ETF a better representation of the growth stock universe.

Morningstar Rating	Return	Risk	Yield	NAV	Avg Daily Vol. (k)	52 wk High/Low
★★★	Average	Below Avg	0.9%	$64.56	259	$66.75 - $56.95

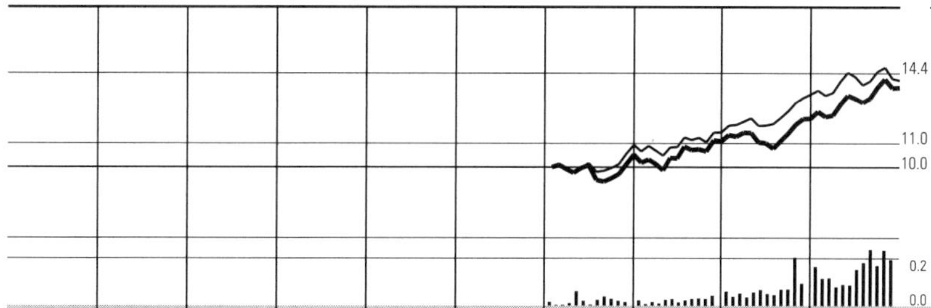

1998	1999	2000	2001	2002	2003	2004	2005	2006	2007	History
—	—	—	—	—	—	51.33	53.52	57.85	64.56	NAV $
—	—	—	—	—	—	51.40	53.50	57.86	64.48	Market Price $
—	—	—	—	—	—	7.48*	5.20	9.13	12.68	NAV Return%
—	—	—	—	—	—	7.44*	5.02	9.19	12.52	Market Price Return%
—	—	—	—	—	—	0.14	0.14	0.03	-0.01	Avg Premium/Discount%
—	—	—	—	—	—	—	0.29	-6.66	7.19	NAV Rtrn% +/-S&P 500
—	—	—	—	—	—	—	0.29	-6.66	7.19	NAV Rtrn% +/-S&P 500
—	—	—	—	—	—	—	1	50	23	NAV Return% Rank in Cat
—	—	—	—	—	—	—	0.90	0.99	1.04	Income Return %
—	—	—	—	—	—	—	4.30	8.14	11.64	Capital Return %
—	—	—	—	—	—	0.61	0.46	0.53	0.60	Income $
—	—	—	—	—	—	0.00	0.00	0.00	0.00	Capital Gains $
—	—	—	—	—	—	0.15	0.11	0.11	—	Expense Ratio %
—	—	—	—	—	—	1.22	0.86	0.97	—	Income Ratio %
—	—	—	—	—	—	24	23	28	—	Turnover Rate %
—	—	—	—	—	—	104	324	1,336	3,232	Net Assets $mil

Performance 12-31-07

Historic Quarterly NAV Returns

	1st Qtr	2nd Qtr	3rd Qtr	4th Qtr	Total
2003	—	—	—	—	—
2004	—	1.51	-4.85	9.41	—*
2005	-3.53	2.17	3.58	3.05	5.20
2006	3.34	-3.92	3.83	5.87	9.13
2007	1.23	6.66	4.38	-0.03	12.68

Trailing	NAV Return%	Market Return%	NAV Rtrn% +/-S&P 500	%Rank Cat.(NAV)
3 Mo	-0.03	-0.29	3.30	18
6 Mo	4.35	3.92	5.72	24
1 Yr	12.68	12.52	7.19	23
3 Yr Avg	8.96	8.87	0.34	12
5 Yr Avg	—	—	—	—
10 Yr Avg	—	—	—	—

Tax Analysis	Tax-Adj Return%	Tax-Cost Ratio
3 Yr (estimated)	8.75	0.19
5 Yr (estimated)	—	—
10 Yr (estimated)	—	—

Rating and Risk

Time Period	Morningstar Rtn vs Cat	Morningstar Risk vs Cat	Morningstar Risk-Adj Rating
3 Yr	Avg	-Avg	★★★
5 Yr	—	—	—
10 Yr	—	—	—

Other Measures	Standard Index S&P 500	Best Fit Index Russ 1000Gr
Alpha	0.3	0.3
Beta	1.02	0.98
R-Squared	87	99
Standard Deviation	8.55	
Mean	8.96	
Sharpe Ratio	0.55	

Portfolio Analysis 09-30-07

Share change since 06-07 Total Stocks:428	Sector	PE	Tot Ret%	% Assets
⊕ Microsoft Corporation	Software	23.4	20.83	3.37
⊕ Procter & Gamble Company	Goods	23.1	16.63	2.95
⊕ Cisco Systems, Inc.	Hardware	21.5	-0.95	2.67
⊕ Johnson & Johnson	Health	18.8	3.61	2.53
⊕ Intel Corporation	Hardware	25.4	34.22	2.00
⊕ Apple, Inc.	Hardware	50.5	133.47	1.77
⊕ Google, Inc.	Business	54.0	50.17	1.75
⊕ Schlumberger, Ltd.	Energy	24.6	57.10	1.65
⊕ PepsiCo, Inc.	Goods	20.4	23.89	1.59
⊕ International Business M	Hardware	16.2	13.20	1.51
⊕ Wal-Mart Stores, Inc.	Consumer	15.4	4.91	1.44
⊕ Oracle Corporation	Software	24.8	31.74	1.18
⊕ Hewlett-Packard Company	Hardware	18.8	23.40	1.13
⊕ Boeing Company	Ind Mtrls	16.9	-0.11	1.04
⊕ United Technologies	Ind Mtrls	18.8	24.46	1.01
⊕ Qualcomm, Inc.	Hardware	20.2	5.52	0.94
⊕ Amgen, Inc.	Health	16.8	-32.02	0.87
⊕ UnitedHealth Group, Inc.	Health	17.4	8.38	0.86
⊕ Medtronic, Inc.	Health	20.3	-5.22	0.86
⊕ Walt Disney Company	Media	14.4	-2.96	0.86

Current Investment Style

Value Blnd Growth — Large Mid Small

Market Cap	%
Giant	42.3
Large	40.7
Mid	16.8
Small	0.1
Micro	0.1
Avg $mil:	40,029

Value Measures		Rel Category
Price/Earnings	18.81	0.97
Price/Book	3.67	1.09
Price/Sales	1.67	0.95
Price/Cash Flow	12.89	1.11
Dividend Yield %	0.93	1.09

Growth Measures	%	Rel Category
Long-Term Erngs	14.14	0.98
Book Value	11.34	1.12
Sales	11.72	1.21
Cash Flow	13.05	1.21
Historical Erngs	22.84	1.27

Profitability	%	Rel Category
Return on Equity	24.19	1.06
Return on Assets	10.12	1.05
Net Margin	13.44	1.04

Sector Weightings	% of Stocks	Rel S&P 500	3 Year High	3 Year Low
Info	31.02	1.48		
Software	7.16	1.73	8	6
Hardware	17.61	1.72	18	16
Media	5.32	1.83	7	4
Telecom	0.93	0.26	2	1
Service	41.22	1.01		
Health	15.15	1.26	21	15
Consumer	11.96	1.76	15	12
Business	7.30	1.66	8	5
Financial	6.81	0.39	9	7
Mfg	27.77	0.72		
Goods	8.62	0.94	10	8
Ind Mtrls	10.79	0.83	11	7
Energy	7.09	0.56	7	4
Utilities	1.27	0.35	1	0

Composition

Cash	0.0
Stocks	100.0
Bonds	0.0
Other	0.0
Foreign (% of Stock)	0.0

Morningstar's Take by Dan Culloton 12-31-07

Vanguard Growth is full of high-quality growth stocks. We'd be buyers at a modest discount to our fair value estimate.

The ETF tracks the MSCI U.S. Prime Market Growth Index, which uses eight growth and valuation factors to sort the growth stocks out of the broader MSCI U.S. Prime Market 750. As such, this ETF's index shares the larger benchmark's penchant for established, profitable companies with strong competitive positions in their markets. Nearly half of the portfolio's assets are invested in firms with intractable competitive advantages, or wide economic moats, such as the world's largest semiconductor company Intel, which has considerable research and development resources and the scale to compete on price. The fund has big positions in some firms with slimmer advantages, such as Apple, whose success depends on its ability to set itself apart with product design and innovation in the cutthroat computer and consumer electronics businesses. But such stocks are more than offset by the firms with death grips on their markets, like the dominant PC software firm Microsoft and network-gear maker Cisco Systems.

Well-situated firms with growth winds at their back tend to be less volatile than smaller or more-cyclical companies. True, this fund's holdings include some companies that lack competitive advantages and pose more risk, such as gold miner Newmont Mining. But such names tend to be relegated to the portfolio's periphery where they can't do too much harm. Indeed, the ETF has more money in stocks with below-average risk ratings, such as consumer products giant Procter & Gamble and drug and health-care firm Johnson & Johnson, than the vast majority of equity ETFs. That risk profile, coupled with the portfolio's wide diversification, makes the ETF a compelling buy at the right price. We'd be buyers when the fund is trading at an 8% or greater discount to our fair value estimate.

Address:	PO Box 2600 United States 866-499-8473
Web Address:	www.vanguard.com
Inception:	01-26-04*
Advisor:	The Vanguard Group, Inc.

Management Fee:	0.08%		
Expense Projections:	3Yr:$35	5Yr:$62	10Yr:$141
Income Distrib:	Quarterly		
Exchange:	AMEX		

Vanguard Large Cap ETF VV

Market Price	Mstar Category
$65.70	Large Blend

Morningstar Fair Value

Price/Fair Value Ratio	Coverage Rate %
0.89	97

Valuation

This ETF has a broader reach than some large-cap ETFs, but market-leading firms dominate. Its constituents' moderate risk and the portfolio's wide diversification tempers its volatility. So, we'd need only an 8% discount to our fair value estimate to recommend it. The fund was recently trading at an 11% discount, making it a bargain.

Methodology

This ETF tracks the MSCI U.S. Prime Market 750 Index, which gives investors exposure to the 750 largest U.S.-exchange-listed stocks. Unlike the S&P 500 Index, the more well-known large-cap bogy, the MSCI U.S. Prime Market 750 Index's methodology is purely quantitative and also includes more mid-cap stocks. In contrast, the S&P 500 Index is controlled by a committee that makes some subjective decisions about the index. For instance, the panel waits six to 12 months to include IPOs, so the S&P 500 missed Google's early gains while this index didn't.

Morningstar Rating	Return	Risk	Yield	NAV	Avg Daily Vol. (k)	52 wk High/Low
★★★★	Above Avg	Average	1.7%	$65.83	171	$70.00 - $61.43

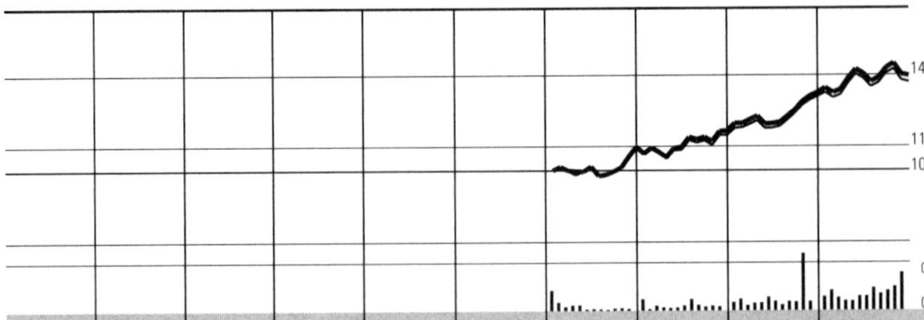

Growth of $10,000
- Investment Value of ETF
- Investment Value of Index S&P 500

Trading Volume Millions

1998	1999	2000	2001	2002	2003	2004	2005	2006	2007	History
—	—	—	—	—	—	52.99	55.40	62.92	65.83	NAV $
—	—	—	—	—	—	53.19	55.49	62.93	65.70	Market Price $
—	—	—	—	—	—	9.19*	6.26	15.61	6.44	NAV Return%
—	—	—	—	—	—	9.13*	6.03	15.44	6.21	Market Price Return%
—	—	—	—	—	—	-0.14	0.02	0.03	-0.05	Avg Premium/Discount%
—	—	—	—	—	—	—	1.35	-0.18	0.95	NAV Rtrn% +/-S&P 500
—	—	—	—	—	—	—	0.00	-0.07	0.06	NAV Rtrn% +/-MSCI Large
—	—	—	—	—	—	—	22	40	42	NAV Return% Rank in Cat
—	—	—	—	—	—	—	1.66	1.91	1.82	Income Return %
—	—	—	—	—	—	—	4.60	13.70	4.62	Capital Return %
—	—	—	—	—	—	0.96	0.87	1.05	1.14	Income $
—	—	—	—	—	—	0.00	0.00	0.00	0.00	Capital Gains $
—	—	—	—	—	—	0.12	0.07	0.07	—	Expense Ratio %
—	—	—	—	—	—	2.00	1.84	1.87	—	Income Ratio %
—	—	—	—	—	—	5	23	9	—	Turnover Rate %
—	—	—	—	—	—	48	178	587	1,162	Net Assets $mil

Performance 12-31-07

Historic Quarterly NAV Returns

	1st Qtr	2nd Qtr	3rd Qtr	4th Qtr	Total
2003	—	—	—	—	—
2004	—	1.53	-1.78	9.59	—*
2005	-1.93	1.93	3.86	2.35	6.26
2006	4.33	-1.47	5.26	6.85	15.61
2007	1.08	6.18	2.25	-3.01	6.44

Trailing	NAV Return%	Market Return%	NAV Rtrn% +/-S&P 500	%Rank Cat.(NAV)
3 Mo	-3.01	-3.19	0.32	38
6 Mo	-0.83	-0.97	0.54	40
1 Yr	6.44	6.21	0.95	42
3 Yr Avg	9.35	9.14	0.73	38
5 Yr Avg	—	—	—	—
10 Yr Avg	—	—	—	—

Tax Analysis	Tax-Adj Return%	Tax-Cost Ratio
3 Yr (estimated)	8.84	0.47
5 Yr (estimated)	—	—
10 Yr (estimated)	—	—

Rating and Risk

Time Period	Morningstar Rtn vs Cat	Morningstar Risk vs Cat	Morningstar Risk-Adj Rating
3 Yr	+Avg	Avg	★★★★
5 Yr	—	—	—
10 Yr	—	—	—

Other Measures	Standard Index S&P 500	Best Fit Index Russ 1000
Alpha	0.7	0.3
Beta	1.01	0.99
R-Squared	100	100
Standard Deviation	7.84	
Mean	9.35	
Sharpe Ratio	0.64	

Portfolio Analysis 09-30-07

Share change since 06-07 Total Stocks:750	Sector	PE	Tot Ret%	% Assets
⊕ ExxonMobil Corporation	Energy	13.6	24.34	3.52
⊕ General Electric Company	Ind Mtrls	16.6	2.69	2.87
⊕ AT&T, Inc.	Telecom	21.6	20.58	1.76
⊕ Microsoft Corporation	Software	23.4	20.83	1.71
⊕ Citigroup, Inc.	Financial	7.9	-44.93	1.56
⊕ Bank of America Corporat	Financial	9.4	-19.25	1.50
⊕ Procter & Gamble Company	Goods	23.1	16.63	1.49
⊕ Chevron Corporation	Energy	11.4	30.59	1.36
⊕ Cisco Systems, Inc.	Hardware	21.5	-0.95	1.36
⊕ Johnson & Johnson	Health	18.8	3.61	1.28
⊕ International Business M	Hardware	16.2	13.20	1.18
⊕ Pfizer Inc.	Health	22.5	-8.15	1.16
⊕ J.P. Morgan Chase & Co.	Financial	9.5	-7.24	1.06
⊕ Intel Corporation	Hardware	25.4	34.22	1.01
⊕ American International G	Financial	10.2	-17.96	1.01
⊕ Altria Group Inc.	Goods	13.2	22.10	0.99
⊕ ConocoPhillips	Energy	13.8	25.42	0.92
⊕ Apple, Inc.	Hardware	50.5	133.47	0.90
⊕ Google, Inc.	Business	54.0	50.17	0.89
⊕ Hewlett-Packard Company	Hardware	18.8	23.40	0.88

Current Investment Style

Value Blnd Growth — Large / Mid / Small

Market Cap	%
Giant	47.9
Large	34.8
Mid	17.1
Small	0.1
Micro	0.1
Avg $mil: 48,207	

Value Measures		Rel Category
Price/Earnings	15.82	1.00
Price/Book	2.67	1.04
Price/Sales	1.53	1.23
Price/Cash Flow	10.84	1.17
Dividend Yield %	1.69	0.89

Growth Measures	%	Rel Category
Long-Term Erngs	10.80	0.92
Book Value	11.38	1.23
Sales	9.31	1.14
Cash Flow	9.83	1.12
Historical Erngs	17.08	1.02

Profitability	%	Rel Category
Return on Equity	21.92	0.99
Return on Assets	8.21	0.98
Net Margin	14.57	1.19

Sector Weightings	% of Stocks	Rel S&P 500	3 Year High	3 Year Low
Info	21.32	1.02		
Software	3.83	0.93	4	4
Hardware	10.25	1.00	10	9
Media	3.38	1.16	5	3
Telecom	3.86	1.06	4	3
Service	43.00	1.06		
Health	11.73	0.98	13	12
Consumer	7.38	1.09	9	7
Business	4.45	1.01	5	3
Financial	19.44	1.12	23	19
Mfg	35.68	0.93		
Goods	8.29	0.91	9	8
Ind Mtrls	12.24	0.94	12	11
Energy	11.53	0.91	12	9
Utilities	3.62	0.98	4	3

Composition

Cash	0.3
Stocks	99.6
Bonds	0.0
Other	0.0
Foreign (% of Stock)	0.1

Morningstar's Take by Dan Culloton 12-31-07

This ETF's portfolio teems with better-than-average stocks. We'd buy it at a modest discount to our fair value estimate.

This portfolio's index, the MSCI U.S. Prime Market 750 Index, covers much of the same ground as its more renowned counterpart, the S&P 500 Index, plus a little more. Its index includes the 750 largest U.S.-exchange-listed stocks by free-float market capitalization, and, unlike the S&P 500 Index, it's constructed by quantitative methodology, meaning it will include stocks regardless of their profitability. It also dips down a bit further on the market-cap ladder to include some mid-cap stocks.

That means all the usual suspects are here, including big, well-established domestic companies with redoubtable competitive advantages, or moats, such as the dull but brutally efficient energy giant ExxonMobil and the ubiquitous PC software firm Microsoft. ExxonMobil's scale and Microsoft's vice-like grip on the PC operating system business hold competitors at bay. All told, nearly 85% of this fund's holdings boast a moat of some kind (wide or narrow), a figure that surpasses nearly all other equity ETFs.

The ETF's broader reach, however, bumps up the portfolio's risk slightly. For instance, our analysts consider Circuit City, which is struggling to turn itself around in a cutthroat consumer electronics business, to be an above-average risk. All told, more than half of the fund's above-average-risk holdings hail from the portfolio's lower reaches, where smaller, less-dominant firms coalesce.

Broad diversification mutes the impact of such holdings, though, which only represent about 11% of assets to begin with. Thus, this fund hasn't been especially volatile over time. Considering its higher-quality, moderate risk profile, we wouldn't require an especially large margin of safety. An 8% discount to our fair value estimates should do.

Address:	PO Box 2600 United States 866-499-8473
Web Address:	www.vanguard.com
Inception:	01-27-04*
Advisor:	The Vanguard Group, Inc.

Management Fee:	0.02%		
Expense Projections:	3Yr:$23	5Yr:$40	10Yr:$90
Income Distrib:	Quarterly		
Exchange:	AMEX		

Vanguard Mid Cap ETF VO

Market Price	Mstar Category
$75.61	Mid-Cap Blend

Morningstar Fair Value

Price/Fair Value Ratio	Coverage Rate %
0.94	91

Valuation

This ETF was recently trading at a 6% discount to our fair value estimate. Given its diversification across stocks and industries, we'd recommend the fund when its shares trade at an 8% or greater discount to fair value. By that standard, the fund is standing right on the cusp of bargain territory.

Methodology

This ETF tracks the MSCI U.S. Mid Cap 450 Index, which encompasses the 301st to 750th largest U.S.-listed stocks by market cap regardless of quality, profitability, or investment style. This ensures the benchmark offers an unbiased representation of the mid-cap stock universe. By contrast, the S&P MidCap 400 makes profitability an admission requirement, thereby excluding some riskier, but potentially strong-performing, stocks from the index. In addition, because the MSCI benchmark doesn't employ fundamental screens, such as sales, cash flow, or dividends, it lacks the stylistic biases that can color other mid-cap indexes.

Morningstar Rating	Return	Risk	Yield	NAV	Avg Daily Vol. (k)	52 wk High/Low
★★★★	Above Avg	Average	1.4%	$75.90	164	$83.36 - $70.19

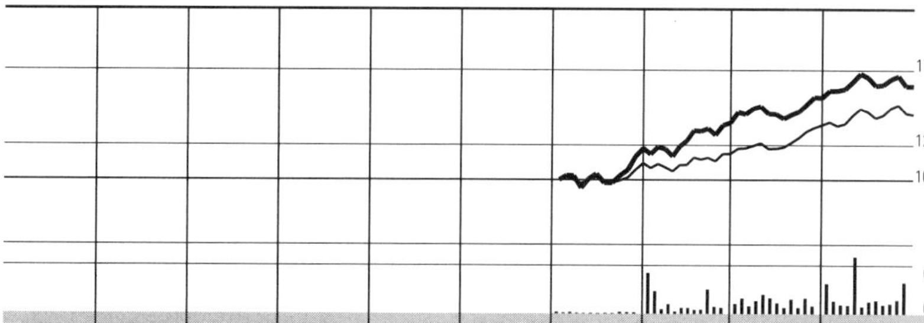

1998	1999	2000	2001	2002	2003	2004	2005	2006	2007	History
—	—	—	—	—	—	57.32	64.61	72.48	75.90	NAV $
—	—	—	—	—	—	57.35	64.61	72.63	75.61	Market Price $
—	—	—	—	—	—	12.43*	14.03	13.69	6.14	NAV Return%
—	—	—	—	—	—	12.32*	13.97	13.93	5.52	Market Price Return%
—	—	—	—	—	—	0.11	0.04	0.07	-0.03	Avg Premium/Discount%
—	—	—	—	—	—	—	9.12	-2.10	0.65	NAV Rtrn% +/-S&P 500
—	—	—	—	—	—	—	0.09	-0.06	-0.05	NAV Rtrn% +/-MSCI US Mid Cap 45
—	—	—	—	—	—	—	1	43	42	NAV Return% Rank in Cat
—	—	—	—	—	—	—	1.31	1.51	1.41	Income Return %
—	—	—	—	—	—	—	12.72	12.18	4.73	Capital Return %
—	—	—	—	—	—	0.64	0.75	0.97	1.03	Income $
—	—	—	—	—	—	0.00	0.00	0.00	0.00	Capital Gains $
—	—	—	—	—	—	0.18	0.13	0.13	—	Expense Ratio %
—	—	—	—	—	—	1.30	1.45	1.52	—	Income Ratio %
—	—	—	—	—	—	16	18	18	—	Turnover Rate %
—	—	—	—	—	—	58	1,044	1,582	1,087	Net Assets $mil

Performance 12-31-07

Historic Quarterly NAV Returns

	1st Qtr	2nd Qtr	3rd Qtr	4th Qtr	Total
2003	—	—	—	—	—
2004	—	1.05	-0.86	14.79	—*
2005	-0.38	4.41	6.41	3.03	14.03
2006	7.60	-2.88	1.30	7.40	13.69
2007	4.59	6.07	-0.93	-3.42	6.14

Trailing	NAV Return%	Market Return%	NAV Rtrn% +/-S&P 500	%Rank Cat.(NAV)
3 Mo	-3.42	-3.79	-0.09	50
6 Mo	-4.32	-4.88	-2.95	46
1 Yr	6.14	5.52	0.65	42
3 Yr Avg	11.23	11.07	2.61	1
5 Yr Avg	—	—	—	—
10 Yr Avg	—	—	—	—

Tax Analysis	Tax-Adj Return%	Tax-Cost Ratio
3 Yr (estimated)	10.73	0.45
5 Yr (estimated)	—	—
10 Yr (estimated)	—	—

Rating and Risk

Time Period	Morningstar Rtn vs Cat	Morningstar Risk vs Cat	Morningstar Risk-Adj Rating
3 Yr	+Avg	Avg	★★★★
5 Yr	—	—	—
10 Yr	—	—	—

Other Measures	Standard Index S&P 500	Best Fit Index Mstar Mid Cap TR
Alpha	1.8	0.5
Beta	1.18	1.00
R-Squared	79	99
Standard Deviation	10.28	
Mean	11.23	
Sharpe Ratio	0.67	

Portfolio Analysis 09-30-07

Share change since 06-07 Total Stocks:445	Sector	PE	Tot Ret%	% Assets
⊕ NVIDIA Corporation	Hardware	29.4	37.88	0.75
⊕ Hilton Hotels	Consumer	—	—	0.69
⊕ Ameriprise Financial, In	Financial	18.3	2.07	0.59
⊕ Smith International, Inc	Energy	23.9	81.06	0.57
⊕ T Rowe Price Group	Financial	27.0	41.00	0.56
⊕ Seagate Technology	Hardware	11.8	-2.21	0.55
⊕ NII Holdings, Inc.	Telecom	24.3	-25.02	0.54
⊕ Archstone-Smith Tr	Financial	—	—	0.53
⊕ MEMC Electronic Material	Hardware	35.3	126.09	0.53
⊕ Noble Corporation	Energy	14.4	44.12	0.52
⊕ Bunge, Ltd.	Goods	18.6	61.80	0.52
⊕ Parker Hannifin Corporat	Ind Mtrls	15.6	47.94	0.52
⊕ Express Scripts	Health	34.1	103.91	0.52
⊕ L-3 Communications Holdi	Hardware	18.5	31.08	0.51
⊕ Fluor Corporation	Business	37.3	79.23	0.51
⊕ Cummins, Inc.	Ind Mtrls	17.5	115.26	0.50
⊕ SanDisk Corporation	Hardware	NMF	-22.91	0.50
⊕ United States Steel Corp	Ind Mtrls	12.6	66.73	0.50
⊕ Murphy Oil Corporation	Energy	25.2	68.58	0.50
⊕ Boston Properties, Inc.	Financial	10.0	-10.36	0.49

Current Investment Style

Value Blnd Growth / Large Mid Small (style box: Mid Blend)

Market Cap	%
Giant	0.0
Large	11.2
Mid	88.0
Small	0.8
Micro	0.0
Avg $mil: 6,995	

Value Measures		Rel Category
Price/Earnings	15.93	1.00
Price/Book	2.39	1.07
Price/Sales	1.17	1.01
Price/Cash Flow	9.02	1.06
Dividend Yield %	1.30	0.79

Growth Measures	%	Rel Category
Long-Term Erngs	12.04	0.98
Book Value	10.10	1.20
Sales	8.23	1.97
Cash Flow	10.59	40.73
Historical Erngs	15.41	0.83

Profitability	%	Rel Category
Return on Equity	18.66	0.95
Return on Assets	7.26	0.94
Net Margin	12.84	1.06

Sector Weightings	% of Stocks	Rel S&P 500	3 Year High	3 Year Low
Info	18.08	0.87		
Software	4.22	1.02	4	4
Hardware	9.04	0.89	9	8
Media	2.05	0.70	3	2
Telecom	2.77	0.76	3	2
Service	47.86	1.18		
Health	10.08	0.84	11	9
Consumer	9.10	1.34	12	9
Business	9.37	2.12	9	6
Financial	19.31	1.11	23	19
Mfg	34.06	0.89		
Goods	7.98	0.87	8	7
Ind Mtrls	11.24	0.86	11	9
Energy	9.83	0.78	12	9
Utilities	5.01	1.36	6	5

Composition

Cash	0.0
Stocks	100.0
Bonds	0.0
Other	0.0
Foreign (% of Stock)	0.8

Morningstar's Take by Dan Culloton 12-31-07

We'd take Vanguard Mid Cap ETF at the right price.

This portfolio is quality-agnostic. That's not a coincidence, as its benchmark, the MSCI U.S. Mid Cap 450 Index, doesn't discriminate between profitable or unprofitable businesses. Rather, it takes the 301st to 750th largest U.S. stocks by market capitalization and holds them until they grow or shrink too much to be included. The index sweeps up some chaff in the process: Just 8% of its assets are devoted to companies that our stock analysts believe have wide economic moats, or easily defended competitive advantages.

The ETF's few wide-moat holdings boast enviable traits, such as T. Rowe Price's trusted brand name or Fastenal's difficult-to-duplicate store network. But no-moat and narrow-moat stocks--which together recently accounted for nearly 85% of assets--are more prevalent, reflecting the tough competition many of these firms face. For instance, computer graphics chipmaker Nvidia has no moat because it must fend with larger, better-resourced rivals in a contested market. Even narrow-moat firms can see larger rivals horn in on their turf. Big banks have chipped away at CIT Group's middle-market commercial lending business in recent years.

To be sure, there is some risk in this ETF. Nearly 30% of the fund's holdings have above-average or speculative risk ratings, including Noble, a contract oil and gas driller whose fortunes are essentially tied to the vagaries of commodity price movements. Such stocks are volatile, but here they are balanced by a large helping (constituting roughly two thirds of assets) of stocks with average or below-average risk ratings, such as logistics company Expeditors International.

That diversification helps. No one stock is going to save or sink this ETF, nor is the precision of our stock analysts' forecasts tied to a single factor, such as the price of crude oil. As such, we'd be willing buyers at an 8% or greater discount to our fair value estimate.

Address:	PO Box 2600 United States 866-499-8473
Web Address:	www.vanguard.com
Inception:	01-26-04 *
Advisor:	The Vanguard Group, Inc.

Management Fee:	0.10%		
Expense Projections:	3Yr:$42	5Yr:$73	10Yr:$166
Income Distrib:	Annually		
Exchange:	AMEX		

Vanguard Sm Cap Gr ETF VBK

Market Price	Mstar Category
$71.29	Small Growth

Morningstar Fair Value

Price/Fair Value Ratio	Coverage Rate %
1.00	59

Valuation

Because our analysts cover a relatively small number of this ETF's holdings, the price/fair value ratio above may not be a faithful representation of the portfolio's valuation attributes. As such, investors trying to gauge this ETF's attractiveness should consider the price/fair value ratio only in conjunction with other fundamental measures.

Methodology

This fund tracks the MSCI U.S. Small Cap Growth Index, which uses an eight-pronged classification system to identify small-growth stocks. The index also employs buffer zones, which limit the migration of stocks into and out of the index. The buffers should help keep portfolio turnover and trading costs low and tax efficiency high.

Morningstar Rating	Return	Risk	Yield	NAV	Avg Daily Vol. (k)	52 wk High/Low
★★★★	Above Avg	Average	0.6%	$71.18	117	$77.78 - $64.70

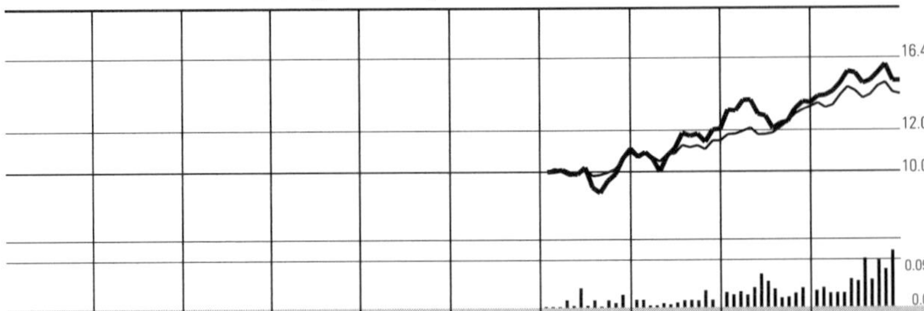

Growth of $10,000
- Investment Value of ETF
- Investment Value of Index S&P 500

Trading Volume Millions

History

1998	1999	2000	2001	2002	2003	2004	2005	2006	2007	History
—	—	—	—	—	—	53.95	58.47	65.24	71.18	NAV $
—	—	—	—	—	—	53.94	58.40	65.25	71.29	Market Price $
—	—	—	—	—	—	9.40*	8.77	12.03	9.74	NAV Return%
—	—	—	—	—	—	9.45*	8.66	12.19	9.89	Market Price Return%
—	—	—	—	—	—	-0.21	-0.06	-0.10	-0.05	Avg Premium/Discount%
—	—	—	—	—	—	—	3.86	-3.76	4.25	NAV Rtrn% +/-S&P 500
—	—	—	—	—	—	—	0.06	0.00	0.03	NAV Rtrn% +/-MSCI US Sm Cap Gr
—	—	—	—	—	—	—	25	40	29	NAV Return% Rank in Cat
—	—	—	—	—	—	—	0.40	0.45	0.64	Income Return %
—	—	—	—	—	—	—	8.37	11.58	9.10	Capital Return %
—	—	—	—	—	—	0.09	0.21	0.27	0.42	Income $
—	—	—	—	—	—	0.00	0.00	0.00	0.00	Capital Gains $
—	—	—	—	—	—	0.22	0.12	0.12	—	Expense Ratio %
—	—	—	—	—	—	0.15	0.37	0.41	—	Income Ratio %
—	—	—	—	—	—	41	39	40	—	Turnover Rate %
—	—	—	—	—	—	92	206	518	858	Net Assets $mil

Performance 12-31-07

Historic Quarterly NAV Returns

	1st Qtr	2nd Qtr	3rd Qtr	4th Qtr	Total
2003	—	—	—	—	—
2004	—	1.11	-5.73	14.85	—*
2005	-4.19	4.43	6.45	2.13	8.77
2006	13.29	-6.69	-2.35	8.53	12.03
2007	5.03	8.07	0.03	-3.34	9.74

Trailing	NAV Return%	Market Return%	NAV Rtrn% +/-S&P 500	%Rank Cat.(NAV)
3 Mo	-3.34	-3.27	-0.01	38
6 Mo	-3.31	-3.36	-1.94	38
1 Yr	9.74	9.89	4.25	29
3 Yr Avg	10.18	10.24	1.56	1
5 Yr Avg	—	—	—	—
10 Yr Avg	—	—	—	—

Tax Analysis	Tax-Adj Return%	Tax-Cost Ratio
3 Yr (estimated)	10.00	0.16
5 Yr (estimated)	—	—
10 Yr (estimated)	—	—

Rating and Risk

Time Period	Morningstar Rtn vs Cat	Morningstar Risk vs Cat	Morningstar Risk-Adj Rating
3 Yr	+Avg	Avg	★★★★
5 Yr	—	—	—
10 Yr	—	—	—

Other Measures	Standard Index S&P 500	Best Fit Index Russ 2000 Gr
Alpha	0.0	2.1
Beta	1.46	0.92
R-Squared	71	98
Standard Deviation	13.42	
Mean	10.18	
Sharpe Ratio	0.47	

Portfolio Analysis 09-30-07

Share change since 06-07 Total Stocks:918	Sector	PE	Tot Ret%	% Assets
⊕ Manitowoc Company, Inc.	Business	22.0	65.99	0.57
⊕ Cytyc	Health	—	—	0.56
⊕ Denbury Resources, Inc.	Energy	36.9	114.11	0.55
⊕ Stericycle, Inc.	Business	43.3	57.35	0.52
⊕ ITT Educational Services	Consumer	24.6	29.92	0.51
⊕ AK Steel Holding Corpora	Ind Mtrls	22.3	173.61	0.50
⊕ Trimble Navigation Ltd.	Hardware	32.1	19.22	0.48
⊕ Frontier Oil Corporation	Energy	8.7	41.82	0.47
⊕ Varian Semiconductor Equ	Hardware	21.4	21.92	0.45
⊕ Cypress Semiconductor Co	Hardware	14.8	113.57	0.45
⊕ Nalco Holding Company	Ind Mtrls	26.6	18.83	0.44
⊕ Oceaneering Internationa	Energy	22.8	69.65	0.42
⊕ Mettler-Toledo Internati	Health	26.4	44.32	0.39
⊕ BE Aerospace	Ind Mtrls	35.7	106.00	0.39
⊕ Hansen Natural Corporati	Goods	34.6	31.50	0.39
⊕ Affiliated Managers Grou	Financial	27.6	11.73	0.39
⊕ CF Industries Holdings,	Ind Mtrls	25.4	329.97	0.39
⊕ Jones Lang LaSalle, Inc.	Financial	10.3	-22.10	0.39
⊕ WellCare Health Plans, I	Health	9.7	-38.45	0.38
⊕ Helix Energy Solutions G	Energy	10.8	32.29	0.38

Current Investment Style

Value Blnd Growth — Large Mid Small

Market Cap	%
Giant	0.0
Large	0.0
Mid	43.1
Small	50.2
Micro	6.7
Avg $mil: 1,793	

Value Measures		Rel Category
Price/Earnings	19.61	1.00
Price/Book	3.05	1.14
Price/Sales	1.44	1.01
Price/Cash Flow	10.65	0.97
Dividend Yield %	0.24	0.69

Growth Measures	%	Rel Category
Long-Term Erngs	17.03	0.82
Book Value	5.28	0.62
Sales	-12.38	NMF
Cash Flow	-12.66	NMF
Historical Erngs	4.85	0.31

Profitability	%	Rel Category
Return on Equity	15.13	1.08
Return on Assets	6.56	1.06
Net Margin	8.51	1.04

Sector Weightings	% of Stocks	Rel S&P 500	3 Year High	3 Year Low
Info	21.20	1.01		
Software	6.12	1.48	8	6
Hardware	10.41	1.02	11	9
Media	1.81	0.62	2	1
Telecom	2.86	0.79	3	2
Service	48.84	1.20		
Health	17.81	1.48	21	16
Consumer	11.26	1.66	14	11
Business	14.24	3.23	15	13
Financial	5.53	0.32	7	6
Mfg	29.96	0.78		
Goods	6.22	0.68	7	5
Ind Mtrls	14.25	1.10	14	9
Energy	9.25	0.73	11	7
Utilities	0.24	0.07	1	0

Composition

Cash	0.7
Stocks	99.3
Bonds	0.1
Other	0.0
Foreign (% of Stock)	0.9

Morningstar's Take by Dan Culloton 12-31-07

Vanguard Small Cap Growth ETF has its risks, but it's still a sturdy choice.

This ETF is cheap, tax-efficient, diversified, and well-managed. The ETF's decent relative and absolute returns in recent years, however, belie some risks. Its stock universe includes some companies with weak competitive positions and immature firms whose shares trade more on the promise of profits than on actual earnings. That includes, respectively, Appalachian coal miner Massey Energy, which is threatened by cheaper Midwestern and Western coal; and biotech company Human Genome Sciences, which has yet to sell an actual drug. Such stocks tend to be volatile and could give the portfolio a few jolts.

Diversification takes a bit of that edge off. The ETF owns nearly 950 stocks across all sectors, so no one stock or area of the market will make or break the offering. Despite its preponderance of speculative, upstart businesses, the small-cap growth universe also includes its share of more mature companies with decent market positions and steadier growth trajectories, such as for-profit education firm Strayer Education and asset manager Calamos Investments. This ETF, which tracks the MSCI U.S. Small Cap Growth Index, includes those stocks too and they, along with the portfolio's broad reach, have helped prevent the fund from being more volatile than its typical peer.

The ETF currently has a larger helping of mid-cap and smaller portion of micro-cap stocks than its peers. That's because its index gradually phases stocks out of the portfolio when they grow too large instead of automatically selling them when they cross a specific size boundary. The benchmark also doesn't dip as far into the smallest of the small stocks as some other indexes. While that could make the ETF act differently from time to time, over the long run its diversified portfolio and low expense ratio gives it a good shot at posting competitive results.

Address:	PO Box 2600 United States 866-499-8473
Web Address:	www.vanguard.com
Inception:	01-26-04*
Advisor:	The Vanguard Group, Inc.

Management Fee:	0.08%		
Expense Projections:	3Yr:$39	5Yr:$68	10Yr:$154
Income Distrib:	Annually		
Exchange:	AMEX		

Vanguard TSM ETF VTI

Market Price	Mstar Category
$145.15	Large Blend

Morningstar Fair Value

Price/Fair Value Ratio	Coverage Rate %
0.90	92

Valuation

This ETF owns the entire U.S. stock market, but solid firms with real earnings and cash flow still carry more weight. That diversification gives the fund a stable risk profile. So, we'd only need an 8% discount to our fair value estimates to buy. Recently the fund was trading at a 10% discount, putting it in "bargain" territory.

Methodology

This ETF tracks the MSCI U.S. Broad Market Index, which includes almost every domestic stock. It ranks stocks by their free-float market capitalizations (or the value of all the shares that regularly trade) and covers 99.5% of the U.S. equity market. There are some differences between it and other total-market indexes. For example, unlike the Wilshire 5000 index, this benchmark includes the stocks of firms that are headquartered abroad but do most of their business in the U.S., such as Montpelier Re Holdings. In general it has and should correlate closely with other core stock indexes.

Morningstar Rating	Return	Risk	Yield	NAV	Avg Daily Vol. (k)	52 wk High/Low
★★★★	Above Avg	Average	1.8%	$145.27	389	$155.49 - $136.50

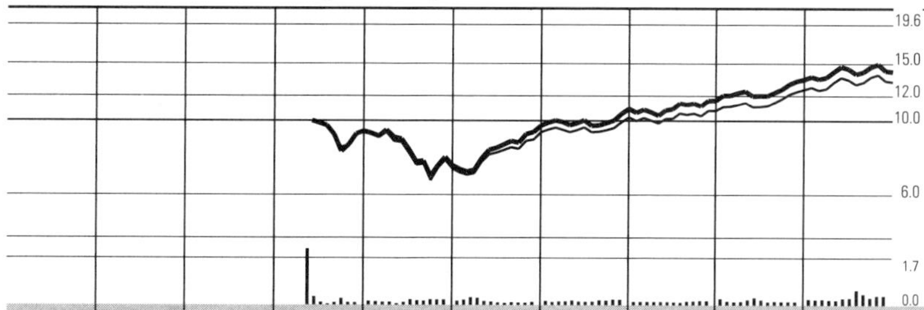

History

1998	1999	2000	2001	2002	2003	2004	2005	2006	2007	History
—	—	—	105.80	82.47	106.81	118.21	123.25	140.08	145.27	NAV $
—	—	—	105.39	82.52	106.46	118.05	123.33	140.21	145.15	Market Price $
—	—	—	4.84*	-20.93	31.44	12.55	6.10	15.66	5.56	NAV Return%
—	—	—	5.33*	-20.58	30.93	12.77	6.31	15.69	5.37	Market Price Return%
—	—	—	0.32	-0.09	-0.01	0.01	0.04	0.02	0.01	Avg Premium/Discount%
—	—	—	—	1.17	2.76	1.67	1.19	-0.13	0.07	NAV Rtrn% +/-S&P 500
—	—	—	—	—	—	0.16	-0.27	-0.06	-0.03	NAV Rtrn% +/-MSCI Tot Mkt
—	—	—	—	47	38	38	35	37	55	NAV Return% Rank in Cat
—	—	—	—	1.19	1.69	1.79	1.77	1.88	1.86	Income Return %
—	—	—	—	-22.12	29.75	10.76	4.33	13.78	3.70	Capital Return %
—	—	—	0.99	1.25	1.38	1.90	2.08	2.30	2.60	Income $
—	—	—	0.00	0.00	0.00	0.00	0.00	0.00	0.00	Capital Gains $
—	—	—	0.15	0.15	0.15	0.13	0.07	0.07	—	Expense Ratio %
—	—	—	1.26	1.38	1.54	1.79	1.74	1.78	—	Income Ratio %
—	—	—	7	4	11	4	12	4	—	Turnover Rate %
—	—	—	—	1,290	2,517	4,259	5,612	6,885	10,255	Net Assets $mil

Performance 12-31-07

Historic Quarterly NAV Returns

	1st Qtr	2nd Qtr	3rd Qtr	4th Qtr	Total
2003	-3.13	16.46	3.62	12.43	31.44
2004	2.59	1.29	-1.83	10.33	12.55
2005	-2.38	2.20	4.05	2.19	6.10
2006	5.38	-1.94	4.52	7.09	15.66
2007	1.36	6.08	1.54	-3.32	5.56

Trailing	NAV Return%	Market Return%	NAV Rtrn% +/-S&P 500	%Rank Cat.(NAV)
3 Mo	-3.32	-3.49	0.01	50
6 Mo	-1.83	-1.90	-0.46	51
1 Yr	5.56	5.37	0.07	55
3 Yr Avg	9.01	9.03	0.39	48
5 Yr Avg	13.89	13.86	1.06	23
10 Yr Avg	—	—	—	—

Tax Analysis	Tax-Adj Return%	Tax-Cost Ratio
3 Yr (estimated)	8.72	0.27
5 Yr (estimated)	13.57	0.28
10 Yr (estimated)	—	—

Rating and Risk

Time Period	Morningstar Rtn vs Cat	Morningstar Risk vs Cat	Morningstar Risk-Adj Rating
3 Yr	Avg	Avg	★★★
5 Yr	+Avg	Avg	★★★★
10 Yr	—	—	—

Other Measures	Standard Index S&P 500	Best Fit Index M* U.S. Mkt TR
Alpha	0.2	-0.3
Beta	1.05	1.01
R-Squared	98	100
Standard Deviation	8.28	
Mean	9.01	
Sharpe Ratio	0.57	

Portfolio Analysis 09-30-07

Share change since 06-07 Total Stocks:3623	Sector	PE	Tot Ret%	% Assets
⊕ ExxonMobil Corporation	Energy	13.6	24.34	3.08
⊕ General Electric Company	Ind Mtrls	16.6	2.69	2.51
⊕ AT&T, Inc.	Telecom	21.6	20.58	1.54
⊕ Microsoft Corporation	Software	23.4	20.83	1.50
⊕ Citigroup, Inc.	Financial	7.9	-44.93	1.36
⊕ Bank of America Corporat	Financial	9.4	-19.25	1.32
⊕ Procter & Gamble Company	Goods	23.1	16.63	1.31
⊕ Chevron Corporation	Energy	11.4	30.59	1.19
⊕ Cisco Systems, Inc.	Hardware	21.5	-0.95	1.19
⊕ Johnson & Johnson	Health	18.8	3.61	1.12
⊕ International Business M	Hardware	16.2	13.20	1.03
⊕ Pfizer Inc.	Health	22.5	-8.15	1.01
⊕ J.P. Morgan Chase & Co.	Financial	9.5	-7.24	0.92
⊕ Intel Corporation	Hardware	25.4	34.22	0.89
⊕ American International G	Financial	10.2	-17.96	0.88
⊕ Altria Group Inc.	Goods	13.2	22.10	0.86
⊕ ConocoPhillips	Energy	13.8	25.42	0.80
⊕ Apple, Inc.	Hardware	50.5	133.47	0.78
⊕ Google, Inc.	Business	54.0	50.17	0.78
⊕ Hewlett-Packard Company	Hardware	18.8	23.40	0.77

Current Investment Style

Value Blnd Growth / Large Mid Small

Market Cap	%
Giant	42.0
Large	30.5
Mid	19.3
Small	6.1
Micro	2.1
Avg $mil: 31,195	

Value Measures		Rel Category
Price/Earnings	15.97	1.01
Price/Book	2.58	1.01
Price/Sales	1.46	1.18
Price/Cash Flow	10.49	1.13
Dividend Yield %	1.63	0.86

Growth Measures	%	Rel Category
Long-Term Erngs	11.00	0.93
Book Value	10.20	1.10
Sales	-1.77	NMF
Cash Flow	3.02	0.35
Historical Erngs	11.78	0.70

Profitability	%	Rel Category
Return on Equity	20.72	0.93
Return on Assets	7.76	0.93
Net Margin	14.00	1.14

Sector Weightings	% of Stocks	Rel S&P 500	3 Year High	3 Year Low
Info	20.72	0.99		
Software	3.85	0.93	4	4
Hardware	10.06	0.99	10	9
Media	3.19	1.10	4	3
Telecom	3.62	1.00	4	3
Service	43.85	1.08		
Health	11.73	0.98	13	12
Consumer	7.55	1.11	10	8
Business	5.26	1.19	6	5
Financial	19.31	1.11	22	19
Mfg	35.44	0.92		
Goods	8.05	0.88	9	7
Ind Mtrls	12.83	0.99	13	11
Energy	10.95	0.87	11	8
Utilities	3.61	0.98	4	3

Composition

Cash	0.5
Stocks	99.4
Bonds	0.1
Other	0.0
Foreign (% of Stock)	0.2

Morningstar's Take by Dan Culloton 12-31-07

You'll find nearly the entire market here, warts and all. Formidable companies predominate, though, making it easy to own at a slight margin of safety.

Vanguard Total Stock Market ETF tracks the MSCI U.S. Broad Market Index, which includes nearly all publicly traded domestic stocks. Its 2,000 holdings include everything from market bellwethers such as General Electric and Bank of America, to speculative micro-caps like Human Genome Sciences and Standard Pacific.

Stocks with durable competitive advantages have the most influence, though. GE, which has a diverse portfolio of well-managed market-leading businesses, and Bank of America, which offers a hard-to-match branch system and services to retail customers, handily outweigh the profitless likes of Human Genome Sciences. In fact, the fund invests more than three quarters of assets in stocks that boast some kind of defensible advantage, or economic moat, which is higher than most equity ETFs. On balance, though, the portfolio's quality is middling, not an unexpected state of affairs considering that the fund purports to represent the entire U.S. stock market.

The portfolio's mediocre quality gives the ETF a middling risk profile, as well. Generally speaking, the more dominant the firm, the more certain its future results. In that sense, the presence of wide-moat companies like Procter & Gamble, whose unmatched and varied array of name brand consumer products help it weather economic cycles, offsets holdings like oil refiner Valero Energy, whose returns are at the mercy of the volatile spread between oil and refined products prices as well as a disappearing edge in processing high sulfur crude. All told, this fund's typical holding courts average risk in our analysts' view.

Taken together with its wide diversification across holdings and industries, the portfolio's middling-quality, moderate-risk profile has tamped down volatility. We'd be buyers at a modest 8% discount to our fair value estimate.

Address:	PO Box 2600 United States 800-662-7447
Web Address:	www.vanguard.com
Inception:	05-24-01 *
Advisor:	The Vanguard Group, Inc.

Management Fee:	0.04%		
Expense Projections:	3Yr:$23	5Yr:$40	10Yr:$90
Income Distrib:	Quarterly		
Exchange:	AMEX		

Vanguard Value ETF VTV

Market Price	Mstar Category
$66.39	Large Value

Morningstar Fair Value

Price/Fair Value Ratio	Coverage Rate %
0.85	98

Valuation

Value stocks are often associated with firms that have fallen out of favor due to industry trends or company-specific problems. But this ETF owns mostly higher-quality names that should be able to weather such troubles. We'd be buyers at an 8% or greater discount to our fair value estimate. The shares were recently trading at a hefty 15% discount.

Methodology

This exchange-traded fund tracks the MSCI U.S. Prime Market Value Index, which sifts the 750 largest U.S. companies (by free-float market capitalization) for the more attractively valued of the bunch. MSCI defines style (growth versus value) using an eight-factor model that includes measures ranging from dividend yield to long-term historical sales per share. MSCI employs buffer zones to limit the migration of stocks between the growth and value camps. These traits help limit turnover and make the ETF a better representation of the value stock universe.

Morningstar Rating	Return	Risk	Yield	NAV	Avg Daily Vol. (k)	52 wk High/Low
★★★★	Above Avg	Average	2.7%	$66.51	228	$74.26 - $63.23

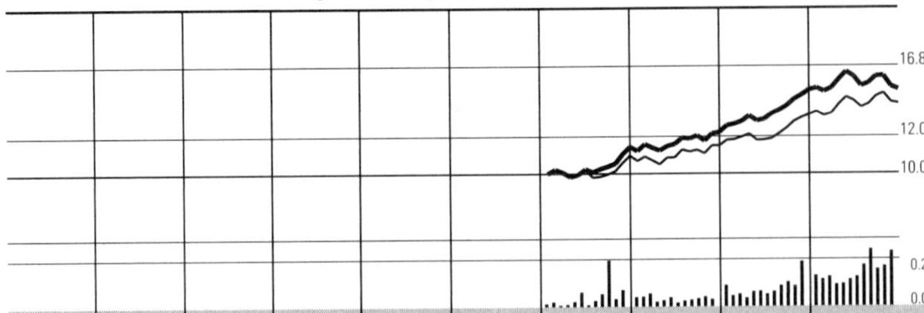

Growth of $10,000
- Investment Value of ETF
- Investment Value of Index S&P 500

Trading Volume Millions

History

1998	1999	2000	2001	2002	2003	2004	2005	2006	2007	History
—	—	—	—	—	—	54.74	57.14	68.14	66.51	NAV $
—	—	—	—	—	—	54.75	57.17	68.23	66.39	Market Price $
—	—	—	—	—	—	10.16*	7.19	22.28	0.20	NAV Return%
—	—	—	—	—	—	10.11*	7.22	22.38	-0.11	Market Price Return%
—	—	—	—	—	—	0.02	0.08	0.06	-0.03	Avg Premium/Discount%
—	—	—	—	—	—	—	2.28	6.49	-5.29	NAV Rtrn% +/-S&P 500
—	—	—	—	—	—	—	-0.07	-0.09	-0.02	NAV Rtrn% +/-MSCI US Pr Mkt Val
—	—	—	—	—	—	—	1	15	58	NAV Return% Rank in Cat
—	—	—	—	—	—	—	2.73	2.79	2.70	Income Return %
—	—	—	—	—	—	—	4.46	19.49	-2.50	Capital Return %
—	—	—	—	—	—	1.22	1.48	1.58	1.82	Income $
—	—	—	—	—	—	0.00	0.00	0.00	0.00	Capital Gains $
—	—	—	—	—	—	0.15	0.11	0.11	—	Expense Ratio %
—	—	—	—	—	—	2.46	2.72	2.58	—	Income Ratio %
—	—	—	—	—	—	18	21	20	—	Turnover Rate %
—	—	—	—	—	—	406	600	1,646	2,215	Net Assets $mil

Performance 12-31-07

Historic Quarterly NAV Returns

	1st Qtr	2nd Qtr	3rd Qtr	4th Qtr	Total
2003	—	—	—	—	—
2004	—	1.55	1.24	9.79	—*
2005	-0.37	1.73	4.08	1.60	7.19
2006	5.32	0.97	6.64	7.83	22.28
2007	0.93	5.74	0.00	-6.11	0.20

Trailing	NAV Return%	Market Return%	NAV Rtrn% +/-S&P 500	%Rank Cat.(NAV)
3 Mo	-6.11	-6.38	-2.78	68
6 Mo	-6.10	-6.27	-4.73	64
1 Yr	0.20	-0.11	-5.29	58
3 Yr Avg	9.51	9.44	0.89	23
5 Yr Avg	—	—	—	—
10 Yr Avg	—	—	—	—

Tax Analysis	Tax-Adj Return%	Tax-Cost Ratio
3 Yr (estimated)	8.74	0.70
5 Yr (estimated)	—	—
10 Yr (estimated)	—	—

Rating and Risk

Time Period	Morningstar Rtn vs Cat	Morningstar Risk vs Cat	Morningstar Risk-Adj Rating
3 Yr	+Avg	Avg	★★★★
5 Yr	—	—	—
10 Yr	—	—	—

Other Measures	Standard Index S&P 500	Best Fit Index Russ 1000 Vl
Alpha	0.9	0.2
Beta	0.99	0.99
R-Squared	89	99
Standard Deviation	8.16	
Mean	9.51	
Sharpe Ratio	0.63	

Portfolio Analysis 09-30-07

Share change since 06-07 Total Stocks:393	Sector	PE	Tot Ret%	% Assets
⊖ ExxonMobil Corporation	Energy	13.6	24.34	7.19
⊕ General Electric Company	Ind Mtrls	16.6	2.69	5.87
⊕ AT&T, Inc.	Telecom	21.6	20.58	3.60
⊕ Citigroup, Inc.	Financial	7.9	-44.93	3.18
⊕ Bank of America Corporat	Financial	9.4	-19.25	3.08
⊖ Chevron Corporation	Energy	11.4	30.59	2.77
⊖ Pfizer Inc.	Health	22.5	-8.15	2.36
⊕ J.P. Morgan Chase & Co.	Financial	9.5	-7.24	2.16
⊕ American International G	Financial	10.2	-17.96	2.06
⊕ Altria Group Inc.	Goods	13.2	22.10	2.02
⊕ ConocoPhillips	Energy	13.8	25.42	1.88
⊕ Verizon Communications I	Telecom	21.7	22.19	1.77
⊕ Wells Fargo Company	Financial	11.4	-12.13	1.56
⊕ Merck & Co., Inc.	Health	23.6	37.36	1.54
⊕ Wachovia Corporation	Financial	8.6	-29.91	1.32
⊕ Coca-Cola Company	Goods	26.3	30.44	1.07
⊖ International Business M	Hardware	16.2	13.20	0.84
⊕ Morgan Stanley	Financial	6.1	-20.21	0.82
⊕ Fannie Mae	Financial	24.1	-30.45	0.82
⊕ Merrill Lynch & Company,	Financial	12.2	-41.32	0.81

Current Investment Style

Value Blnd Growth — Large Mid Small

Market Cap	%
Giant	53.7
Large	28.6
Mid	17.4
Small	0.2
Micro	0.1
Avg $mil: 58,388	

Value Measures		Rel Category
Price/Earnings	13.58	1.01
Price/Book	2.08	1.06
Price/Sales	1.41	1.18
Price/Cash Flow	8.83	1.06
Dividend Yield %	2.48	0.92

Growth Measures	%	Rel Category
Long-Term Erngs	9.38	0.95
Book Value	11.41	1.32
Sales	7.46	1.17
Cash Flow	7.25	1.38
Historical Erngs	15.08	1.00

Profitability	%	Rel Category
Return on Equity	19.57	0.99
Return on Assets	6.22	0.97
Net Margin	15.74	1.13

Sector Weightings	% of Stocks	Rel S&P 500	3 Year High	3 Year Low
Info	11.23	0.54		
Software	0.37	0.09	2	0
Hardware	2.59	0.25	4	2
Media	1.37	0.47	4	1
Telecom	6.90	1.90	7	4
Service	44.86	1.10		
Health	8.17	0.68	9	5
Consumer	2.61	0.38	4	3
Business	1.50	0.34	2	1
Financial	32.58	1.87	37	33
Mfg	43.91	1.14		
Goods	7.96	0.87	8	7
Ind Mtrls	13.73	1.06	16	12
Energy	16.15	1.28	16	13
Utilities	6.07	1.65	7	6

Composition

Cash	0.0
Stocks	100.0
Bonds	0.0
Other	0.0
Foreign (% of Stock)	0.2

Morningstar's Take by Dan Culloton 12-31-07

Vanguard Value ETF has enough high-quality stocks in its portfolio to make it an attractive purchase at the right price.

The ETF tracks the MSCI U.S. Prime Market Value Index, which uses eight growth and valuation factors to sort the value stocks out of the broader MSCI U.S. Prime Market 750. This ETF's index shares the larger benchmark's penchant for established companies with fortified competitive positions in their respective industries.

Granted, some, such as financial conglomerate Citigroup, are under a cloud, and others, like telecom service provider Sprint Nextel, are fending off unrelenting assaults on their market redoubts. So this ETF's helping of wide-moat stocks is actually a bit smaller than those of sibling ETFs Vanguard Large Cap ETF and Vanguard Growth ETF. Still, more than 85% of the portfolio's assets are staked in stocks with either a wide or narrow economic moat, including Coca-Cola, which boasts an iconic brand and global distribution network, and AIG, which has a sprawling global footprint. Overall, this is a portfolio of solid companies.

The ETF's generally high quality keeps risks in check. True, it owns some stocks that court significant business risks, such as cigarette maker Altria and pharmaceutical company Merck, which have been locked in ceaseless litigation over the health effects of their products. However, above-average risk stocks account for only 12% of the fund's assets, leaving average- and below-average risk firms well-represented. Stocks in that latter cohort are typically more stable and thus less fraught with uncertainty. General Electric's diverse stable of businesses gives it a better shot at delivering consistent cash-flow growth through a variety of economic climates. ExxonMobil's scale, discipline, and fortress-like balance sheet give it a rare AAA credit rating, which testifies to its stability. So, we'd be buyers here when the shares traded at an 8% or greater discount to our fair value estimate.

Address:	PO Box 2600 United States 866-499-8473
Web Address:	www.vanguard.com
Inception:	01-26-04*
Advisor:	The Vanguard Group, Inc.

Management Fee:	0.08%		
Expense Projections:	3Yr:$35	5Yr:$62	10Yr:$141
Income Distrib:	Quarterly		
Exchange:	AMEX		

WisdomTree Div Top 100 DTN

Market Price	Mstar Category
$56.22	Large Blend

Morningstar Fair Value

Price/Fair Value Ratio	Coverage Rate %
0.87	99

Valuation

We'd recommend this ETF when it trades at 8% or more below our aggregate fair value estimate. At year end 2007, this ETF was well within our buy range. It allocates more than a fourth of its portfolio to financials stocks, many of which were attractively valued at the end of 2007, including holdings such as Bank of America, US Bancorp, and

Methodology

This ETF's benchmark, the WisdomTree Dividend Top 100 Index, carves out the 100 highest yielding stocks from the WisdomTree Dividend Large-Cap Index and ranks those holdings based on their dividend yields (dividends divided by stock price). That allows it to generate a higher income payout than many of its stable mates. Like most dividend-oriented funds, it winds up emphasizing sectors that are home to high-yielding stocks, like utilities and financials, and ignoring low-yielding industries, such as technology.

Morningstar Rating	Return	Risk	Yield	NAV	Avg Daily Vol. (k)	52 wk High/Low
—	—	—	3.4%	$56.28	38	$63.31 - $52.65

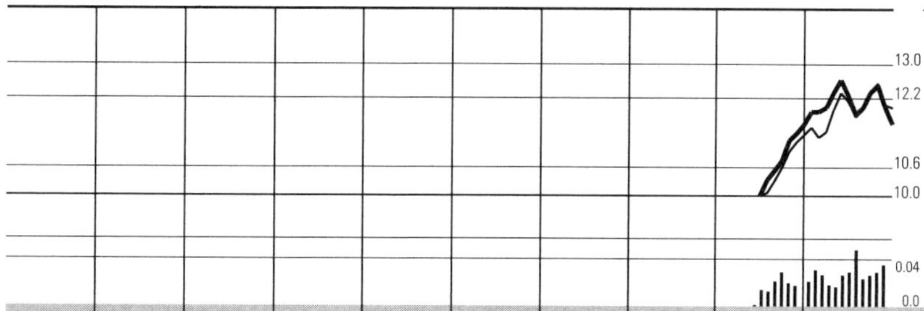

Growth of $10,000
- Investment Value of ETF
- Investment Value of Index S&P 500

Trading Volume Millions

1998	1999	2000	2001	2002	2003	2004	2005	2006	2007	History
—	—	—	—	—	—	—	—	58.04	56.28	NAV $
—	—	—	—	—	—	—	—	58.06	56.22	Market Price $
—	—	—	—	—	—	—	—	10.90*	0.11	NAV Return%
—	—	—	—	—	—	—	—	10.85*	-0.03	Market Price Return%
—	—	—	—	—	—	—	—	0.07	-0.03	Avg Premium/Discount%
—	—	—	—	—	—	—	—	—	-5.38	NAV Rtrn% +/-S&P 500
—	—	—	—	—	—	—	—	—	-5.66	NAV Rtrn% +/-Russ 1000
—	—	—	—	—	—	—	—	—	80	NAV Return% Rank in Cat
—	—	—	—	—	—	—	—	—	3.29	Income Return %
—	—	—	—	—	—	—	—	—	-3.18	Capital Return %
—	—	—	—	—	—	—	—	0.66	1.89	Income $
—	—	—	—	—	—	—	—	0.00	0.00	Capital Gains $
—	—	—	—	—	—	—	—	—	0.38	Expense Ratio %
—	—	—	—	—	—	—	—	—	3.29	Income Ratio %
—	—	—	—	—	—	—	—	—	21	Turnover Rate %
—	—	—	—	—	—	—	—	116	194	Net Assets $mil

Performance 12-31-07

Historic Quarterly NAV Returns

	1st Qtr	2nd Qtr	3rd Qtr	4th Qtr	Total
2003	—	—	—	—	—
2004	—	—	—	—	—
2005	—	—	—	—	—
2006	—	—	7.17	7.37	—*
2007	3.43	2.52	0.60	-6.15	0.11

Trailing	NAV Return%	Market Return%	NAV Rtrn% +/-S&P 500	%Rank Cat.(NAV)
3 Mo	-6.15	-6.12	-2.82	82
6 Mo	-5.59	-5.68	-4.22	75
1 Yr	0.11	-0.03	-5.38	80
3 Yr Avg	—	—	—	—
5 Yr Avg	—	—	—	—
10 Yr Avg	—	—	—	—

Tax Analysis	Tax-Adj Return%	Tax-Cost Ratio
3 Yr (estimated)	—	—
5 Yr (estimated)	—	—
10 Yr (estimated)	—	—

Rating and Risk

Time Period	Morningstar Rtn vs Cat	Morningstar Risk vs Cat	Morningstar Risk-Adj Rating
3 Yr	—	—	—
5 Yr	—	—	—
10 Yr	—	—	—

Other Measures	Standard Index S&P 500	Best Fit Index
Alpha	—	—
Beta	—	—
R-Squared	—	—
Standard Deviation	—	
Mean	—	
Sharpe Ratio	—	

Portfolio Analysis 11-30-07

Share change since 10-07 Total Stocks:94	Sector	PE	Tot Ret%	% Assets
⊖ Southern Copper Corporat	Ind Mtrls	12.1	110.56	6.33
⊖ AT&T, Inc.	Telecom	21.6	20.58	2.21
⊖ Verizon Communications I	Telecom	21.7	22.19	1.79
⊖ Bristol-Myers Squibb Com	Health	24.8	4.75	1.78
⊖ Bank of New York Mellon	Financial	21.7	26.51	1.71
⊖ Progress Energy, Inc.	Utilities	15.5	3.83	1.62
⊖ Reynolds American, Inc.	Goods	16.3	5.90	1.61
⊖ Southern Company	Utilities	17.1	9.85	1.59
⊖ Merck & Co., Inc.	Health	23.6	37.36	1.57
⊖ Public Service Enterpris	Utilities	19.1	52.10	1.51
⊖ Consolidated Edison Comp	Utilities	13.9	6.65	1.50
⊖ Ameren Corporation	Utilities	19.7	5.94	1.43
⊖ DTE Energy Holding Compa	Utilities	8.9	-5.16	1.43
⊖ American Electric Power	Utilities	16.8	13.06	1.33
⊖ PPL Corporation	Utilities	20.0	49.31	1.33
⊖ UST, Inc.	Goods	17.0	-1.53	1.31
⊖ Weyerhaeuser Company	Ind Mtrls	—	7.83	1.29
⊖ McDonald's Corporation	Consumer	39.5	36.38	1.23
⊖ Xcel Energy, Inc.	Utilities	16.1	1.95	1.22
⊖ The Dow Chemical Company	Ind Mtrls	11.3	2.55	1.22

Current Investment Style

Value Blnd Growth (Large / Mid / Small)

Market Cap	%
Giant	27.5
Large	43.8
Mid	28.7
Small	0.0
Micro	0.0
Avg $mil: 27,198	

Value Measures		Rel Category
Price/Earnings	15.64	0.99
Price/Book	1.88	0.73
Price/Sales	1.37	1.10
Price/Cash Flow	8.49	0.92
Dividend Yield %	3.30	1.75

Growth Measures	%	Rel Category
Long-Term Erngs	8.54	0.72
Book Value	7.95	0.86
Sales	3.62	0.44
Cash Flow	5.49	0.63
Historical Erngs	7.93	0.47

Profitability	%	Rel Category
Return on Equity	18.50	0.83
Return on Assets	5.46	0.65
Net Margin	14.74	1.20

Sector Weightings	% of Stocks	Rel S&P 500	3 Year High	3 Year Low
Info	5.94	0.28		
Software	0.00	0.00	—	—
Hardware	0.00	0.00	—	—
Media	0.67	0.23	—	—
Telecom	5.27	1.45	—	—
Service	38.81	0.95		
Health	6.90	0.57	—	—
Consumer	3.44	0.51	—	—
Business	1.62	0.37	—	—
Financial	26.85	1.54	—	—
Mfg	55.24	1.44		
Goods	16.07	1.75	—	—
Ind Mtrls	16.90	1.30	—	—
Energy	1.12	0.09	—	—
Utilities	21.15	5.75	—	—

Composition

Cash	0.4
Stocks	99.6
Bonds	0.0
Other	0.0
Foreign (% of Stock)	0.0

Morningstar's Take by Sonya Morris 12-31-07

Despite a few biases, WisdomTree Dividend Top 100 possesses a risk/reward profile that calls for only a modest margin of safety.

Given this ETF's focus on high-yielding stocks, it clusters the bulk of its portfolio around dividend-rich sectors like financials and utilities. Typically that's a recipe for a relatively high-quality portfolio: The utility and financials sectors are home to a disproportionately large share of firms with economic moats. Yet, only 22% of this fund's assets are dedicated to wide-moat firms. That's largely due to the outsized presence of mid-cap firms, which take up more room here because this fund ranks its portfolio by dividend yield (dividends divided by stock price). Many midsized firms boast impressive dividend payouts, yet because they don't have scale, they may not possess the competitive advantages of larger rivals. For example, this ETF holds UnionBanCal, a mid-sized regional bank that pays a healthy dividend, but it only earns a narrow moat rating because it doesn't possess the sizable geographic reach or the diversified income stream of a super-regional bank such as US Bancorp or Wells Fargo.

But even though this ETF's portfolio isn't pristine, the majority of its assets are comprised of businesses that generate positive free cash flow and respectable returns on equity. And although its benchmark doesn't explicitly screen for dividend growth as some competing dividend ETFs do, the majority of this ETF's holdings have been able to increase their dividends over time. Furthermore, only 14% of the firms of in its portfolio get an "above-average" business risk rating. Finally, because this ETF spreads its portfolio over 100 different names and because its top holdings don't consume most of the assets, we wouldn't expect this ETF to court any more volatility over time than the typical large-blend fund.

Given this ETFs modest risk profile, we'd be willing to recommend it when its market price is 8% or more below its fair value.

Address:	48 Wall Street United States 866-909-9473
Web Address:	www.wisdomtree.com
Inception:	06-16-06 *
Advisor:	WisdomTree Asset Management, Inc.

Management Fee:	0.38%		
Expense Projections:	3Yr:$122	5Yr:$213	10Yr:$480
Income Distrib:	Annually		
Exchange:	NYSE		

WisdomTree High-Yld Eqty DHS

Market Price	Mstar Category
$53.14	Large Blend

Morningstar Fair Value

Price/Fair Value Ratio	Coverage Rate %
0.84	95

Valuation

Given the fund's focus on high-quality, moderate-risk stocks and diversification across holdings and industries, we wouldn't require a large discount to our fair value estimate before recommending it. An 8% discount would suffice. By that standard, the fund has looked like a bargain of late, as it was recently trading at a hefty 16% discount.

Methodology

This ETF is tethered to the WisdomTree High-Yielding Equity Index. To construct the index, WisdomTree ranks the stocks in the WisdomTree Dividend Index by dividend yield and isolates the top 30%. It then weights those highest-yielding stocks by projected cash dividends. Thus, whereas relatively low-yielding realms like technology make the cut in the broader Dividend index, this fund is virtually devoid of such fare; instead, financial services and industrial stocks abound. In addition, this fund is more concentrated among holdings, with the top 10 stocks soaking up nearly half of assets.

Morningstar Rating	Return	Risk	Yield	NAV	Avg Daily Vol. (k)	52 wk High/Low
—	—	—	3.9%	$53.24	29	$61.50 - $50.06

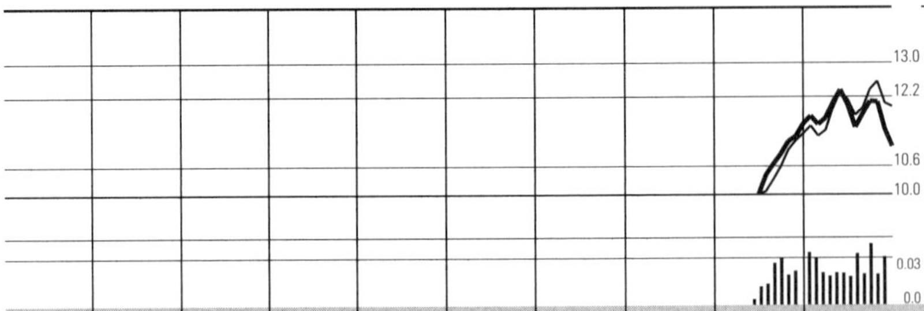

Growth of $10,000
- Investment Value of ETF
- Investment Value of Index S&P 500

Trading Volume Millions

	1998	1999	2000	2001	2002	2003	2004	2005	2006	2007	History
	—	—	—	—	—	—	—	—	57.77	53.24	NAV $
	—	—	—	—	—	—	—	—	57.73	53.14	Market Price $
	—	—	—	—	—	—	—	—	7.38*	-4.42	NAV Return%
	—	—	—	—	—	—	—	—	7.23*	-4.53	Market Price Return%
	—	—	—	—	—	—	—	—	0.04	-0.04	Avg Premium/Discount%
	—	—	—	—	—	—	—	—	—	-9.91	NAV Rtrn% +/-S&P 500
	—	—	—	—	—	—	—	—	—	-10.19	NAV Rtrn% +/-Russ 1000
	—	—	—	—	—	—	—	—	—	89	NAV Return% Rank in Cat
	—	—	—	—	—	—	—	—	—	3.65	Income Return %
	—	—	—	—	—	—	—	—	—	-8.07	Capital Return %
	—	—	—	—	—	—	—	—	0.62	2.08	Income $
	—	—	—	—	—	—	—	—	0.00	0.00	Capital Gains $
	—	—	—	—	—	—	—	—	—	0.38	Expense Ratio %
	—	—	—	—	—	—	—	—	—	3.68	Income Ratio %
	—	—	—	—	—	—	—	—	—	11	Turnover Rate %
	—	—	—	—	—	—	—	—	136	144	Net Assets $mil

Performance 12-31-07

Historic Quarterly NAV Returns

	1st Qtr	2nd Qtr	3rd Qtr	4th Qtr	Total
2003	—	—	—	—	—
2004	—	—	—	—	—
2005	—	—	—	—	—
2006	—	—	8.29	6.14	—*
2007	1.09	2.68	0.73	-8.59	-4.42

Trailing	NAV Return%	Market Return%	NAV Rtrn% +/-S&P 500	%Rank Cat.(NAV)
3 Mo	-8.59	-8.78	-5.26	87
6 Mo	-7.92	-8.01	-6.55	81
1 Yr	-4.42	-4.53	-9.91	89
3 Yr Avg	—	—	—	—
5 Yr Avg	—	—	—	—
10 Yr Avg	—	—	—	—

Tax Analysis	Tax-Adj Return%	Tax-Cost Ratio
3 Yr (estimated)	—	—
5 Yr (estimated)	—	—
10 Yr (estimated)	—	—

Rating and Risk

Time Period	Morningstar Rtn vs Cat	Morningstar Risk vs Cat	Morningstar Risk-Adj Rating
3 Yr	—	—	—
5 Yr	—	—	—
10 Yr	—	—	—

Other Measures	Standard Index S&P 500	Best Fit Index
Alpha	—	—
Beta	—	—
R-Squared	—	—
Standard Deviation	—	
Mean	—	
Sharpe Ratio	—	

Morningstar's Take by Sonya Morris 12-31-07

We're comfortable recommending WisdomTree High-Yielding Equity at a modest margin of safety.

This fund's dividend payout is well above that of the typical equity ETF and almost twice that of the S&P 500. That fat yield comes by way of its benchmark's unique methodology. Specifically, it isolates those stocks in the WisdomTree Dividend Index that rank in the top 30% in terms of dividend yield (dividends divided by stock price). Then it weights those stocks by projected cash dividends over the next 12 months.

Because it focuses on firms with the wherewithal to pay sizable cash dividends, this ETF's portfolio skews decidedly toward financially stable, established firms that frequently have enduring competitive advantages. Not surprisingly, roughly half of this fund's assets are staked in stocks that our analysts believe possess wide economic moats, many of them in the financial service sector. Consider the likes of top holdings Bank of America, Citigroup, and JP Morgan. All three are financially sturdy banks with massive geographic footprints that dwarf most of the competition.

The fund's dividend focus spurs sector biases. It sports oversized financials and utilities weightings, for example, because those sectors are home to more companies that pay dividends. By the same token it treads lightly in the technology sector as many tech companies reinvest in their businesses rather than pay dividends.

However, given the high-quality nature of this portfolio, we don't think these sector tilts significantly heighten risk. Furthermore, because this portfolio is broadly diversified across 350 dividend-paying stocks--only a small fraction of which warrant above-average risk ratings from our equity analysts--we wouldn't expect it to exhibit excessive volatility. Accordingly, we'd feel comfortable recommending this ETF with only a modest margin of safety. We'd be buyers at an 8% or greater discount to our fair value estimate.

Address:	48 Wall Street United States 866-909-9473
Web Address:	www.wisdomtree.com
Inception:	06-16-06*
Advisor:	WisdomTree Asset Management, Inc.

Management Fee:	0.38%		
Expense Projections:	3Yr:$122	5Yr:$213	10Yr:$480
Income Distrib:	Annually		
Exchange:	NYSE		

Portfolio Analysis 11-30-07

Share change since 10-07 Total Stocks:351	Sector	PE	Tot Ret%	% Assets
⊖ General Electric Company	Ind Mtrls	16.6	2.69	8.03
⊖ Bank of America Corporat	Financial	9.4	-19.25	6.15
⊖ AT&T, Inc.	Telecom	21.6	20.58	5.83
⊖ Altria Group Inc.	Goods	13.2	22.10	4.73
⊖ Citigroup, Inc.	Financial	7.9	-44.93	4.61
⊖ Pfizer Inc.	Health	22.5	-8.15	4.30
⊖ Verizon Communications I	Telecom	21.7	22.19	4.19
⊖ Chevron Corporation	Energy	11.4	30.59	3.95
⊖ J.P. Morgan Chase & Co.	Financial	9.5	-7.24	3.31
⊖ Merck & Co., Inc.	Health	23.6	37.36	3.14
⊖ Coca-Cola Company	Goods	26.3	30.44	2.80
⊖ Wachovia Corporation	Financial	8.6	-29.91	2.56
⊖ Wells Fargo Company	Financial	11.4	-12.13	2.54
⊖ Southern Copper Corporat	Ind Mtrls	12.1	110.56	2.35
⊖ Bristol-Myers Squibb Com	Health	24.8	4.75	1.86
⊖ US Bancorp	Financial	12.2	-7.89	1.62
⊖ Eli Lilly & Company	Health	26.0	5.65	1.27
⊖ The Dow Chemical Company	Ind Mtrls	11.3	2.55	1.06
⊖ E.I. du Pont de Nemours	Ind Mtrls	12.4	-6.63	0.95
⊕ Dominion Resources, Inc.	Utilities	12.3	16.98	0.86

Current Investment Style

Value Blnd Growth; Large Mid Small

Market Cap	%
Giant	62.8
Large	16.6
Mid	14.3
Small	5.0
Micro	1.3

Avg $mil: 54,075

Value Measures		Rel Category
Price/Earnings	14.67	0.93
Price/Book	1.90	0.74
Price/Sales	1.62	1.31
Price/Cash Flow	8.88	0.96
Dividend Yield %	3.98	2.11

Growth Measures	%	Rel Category
Long-Term Erngs	8.44	0.72
Book Value	9.68	1.05
Sales	2.37	0.29
Cash Flow	0.68	0.08
Historical Erngs	9.01	0.54

Profitability	%	Rel Category
Return on Equity	19.10	0.86
Return on Assets	5.66	0.68
Net Margin	17.47	1.42

Sector Weightings	% of Stocks	Rel S&P 500	3 Year High	3 Year Low
Info	11.81	0.57		
Software	0.00	0.00	—	—
Hardware	0.14	0.01	—	—
Media	0.62	0.21	—	—
Telecom	11.05	3.04	—	—
Service	47.11	1.16		
Health	10.76	0.90	—	—
Consumer	0.23	0.03	—	—
Business	0.28	0.06	—	—
Financial	35.84	2.06	—	—
Mfg	41.09	1.07		
Goods	11.91	1.30	—	—
Ind Mtrls	14.78	1.14	—	—
Energy	4.36	0.35	—	—
Utilities	10.04	2.73	—	—

Composition

Cash	0.7
Stocks	99.3
Bonds	0.0
Other	0.0
Foreign (% of Stock)	0.0

WisdomTree LargeCap Div DLN

Market Price	Mstar Category
$57.76	Large Blend

Morningstar Fair Value

Price/Fair Value Ratio	Coverage Rate %
0.86	100

Valuation

Given this ETF's high-quality, moderate-risk portfolio, we'd consider recommending it when it's trading at an 8% or greater discount to our fair value estimate. The fund was recently trading at a 13% discount to fair value, which is steep enough to make it a bona fide bargain in our view.

Methodology

This ETF tracks the WisdomTree LargeCap Dividend Index, which includes the 300 largest companies, as measured by market capitalization, in the WisdomTree Dividend Index. The LargeCap Dividend Index isn't weighted by market capitalization, though. Instead, the stocks are ranked by the dollar value of cash dividends paid to shareholders.

Morningstar Rating	Return	Risk	Yield	NAV	Avg Daily Vol. (k)	52 wk High/Low
—	—	—	2.9%	$57.95	96	$62.71 - $55.14

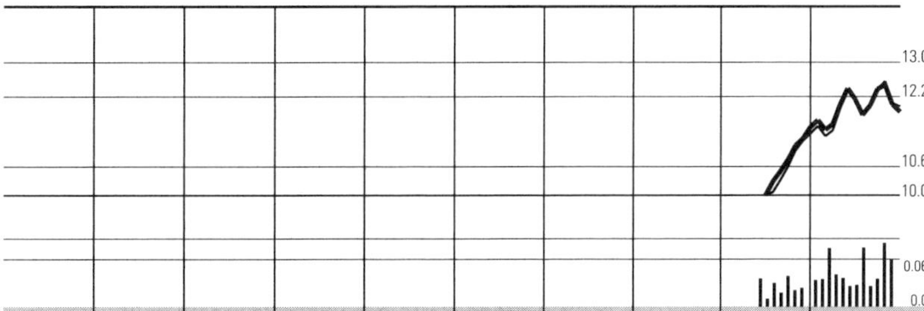

Growth of $10,000
- Investment Value of ETF
- Investment Value of Index S&P 500

Trading Volume Millions

1998	1999	2000	2001	2002	2003	2004	2005	2006	2007	History
—	—	—	—	—	—	—	—	57.88	57.95	NAV $
—	—	—	—	—	—	—	—	57.89	57.76	Market Price $
—	—	—	—	—	—	—	—	12.29*	2.99	NAV Return%
—	—	—	—	—	—	—	—	11.94*	2.64	Market Price Return%
—	—	—	—	—	—	—	—	0.07	-0.02	Avg Premium/Discount%
—	—	—	—	—	—	—	—	—	-2.50	NAV Rtrn% +/-S&P 500
—	—	—	—	—	—	—	—	—	-2.78	NAV Rtrn% +/-Russ 1000
—	—	—	—	—	—	—	—	—	74	NAV Return% Rank in Cat
—	—	—	—	—	—	—	—	—	2.93	Income Return %
—	—	—	—	—	—	—	—	—	0.06	Capital Return %
—	—	—	—	—	—	—	—	0.55	1.68	Income $
—	—	—	—	—	—	—	—	0.00	0.00	Capital Gains $
—	—	—	—	—	—	—	—	—	0.28	Expense Ratio %
—	—	—	—	—	—	—	—	—	2.65	Income Ratio %
—	—	—	—	—	—	—	—	—	13	Turnover Rate %
—	—	—	—	—	—	—	—	203	246	Net Assets $mil

Performance 12-31-07

Historic Quarterly NAV Returns

	1st Qtr	2nd Qtr	3rd Qtr	4th Qtr	Total
2003	—	—	—	—	—
2004	—	—	—	—	—
2005	—	—	—	—	—
2006	—	—	7.15	6.58	—*
2007	0.59	5.08	1.97	-4.44	2.99

Trailing	NAV Return%	Market Return%	NAV Rtrn% +/-S&P 500	%Rank Cat.(NAV)
3 Mo	-4.44	-4.69	-1.11	67
6 Mo	-2.56	-2.85	-1.19	63
1 Yr	2.99	2.64	-2.50	74
3 Yr Avg	—	—	—	—
5 Yr Avg	—	—	—	—
10 Yr Avg	—	—	—	—

Tax Analysis	Tax-Adj Return%	Tax-Cost Ratio
3 Yr (estimated)	—	—
5 Yr (estimated)	—	—
10 Yr (estimated)	—	—

Rating and Risk

Time Period	Morningstar Rtn vs Cat	Morningstar Risk vs Cat	Morningstar Risk-Adj Rating
3 Yr	—	—	—
5 Yr	—	—	—
10 Yr	—	—	—

Other Measures	Standard Index S&P 500	Best Fit Index
Alpha	—	—
Beta	—	—
R-Squared	—	—
Standard Deviation	—	
Mean	—	
Sharpe Ratio	—	

Portfolio Analysis 11-30-07

Share change since 10-07 Total Stocks:273	Sector	PE	Tot Ret%	% Assets
⊖ General Electric Company	Ind Mtrls	16.6	2.69	4.95
⊖ ExxonMobil Corporation	Energy	13.6	24.34	3.84
⊖ Bank of America Corporat	Financial	9.4	-19.25	3.81
⊖ AT&T, Inc.	Telecom	21.6	20.58	3.61
⊖ Altria Group Inc.	Goods	13.2	22.10	2.94
⊖ Citigroup, Inc.	Financial	7.9	-44.93	2.86
⊖ Pfizer Inc.	Health	22.5	-8.15	2.76
⊖ Verizon Communications I	Telecom	21.7	22.19	2.59
⊖ Chevron Corporation	Energy	11.4	30.59	2.44
⊖ J.P. Morgan Chase & Co.	Financial	9.5	-7.24	2.06
⊖ Procter & Gamble Company	Goods	23.1	16.63	2.05
⊖ Microsoft Corporation	Software	23.4	20.83	1.99
⊖ Johnson & Johnson	Health	18.8	3.61	1.98
⊖ Merck & Co., Inc.	Health	23.6	37.36	1.95
⊖ Coca-Cola Company	Goods	26.3	30.44	1.71
⊖ Southern Copper Corporat	Ind Mtrls	12.1	110.56	1.65
⊖ Wachovia Corporation	Financial	8.6	-29.91	1.64
⊖ Wells Fargo Company	Financial	11.4	-12.13	1.50
⊖ Intel Corporation	Hardware	25.4	34.22	1.45
⊖ ConocoPhillips	Energy	13.8	25.42	1.39

Current Investment Style

Value Blnd Growth / Large Mid Small

Market Cap	%
Giant	65.0
Large	28.7
Mid	6.3
Small	0.0
Micro	0.0
Avg $mil: 79,144	

Value Measures		Rel Category
Price/Earnings	14.85	0.94
Price/Book	2.30	0.90
Price/Sales	1.54	1.24
Price/Cash Flow	9.32	1.01
Dividend Yield %	2.70	1.43

Growth Measures	%	Rel Category
Long-Term Erngs	9.16	0.78
Book Value	10.86	1.18
Sales	8.28	1.01
Cash Flow	8.24	0.94
Historical Erngs	13.18	0.79

Profitability	%	Rel Category
Return on Equity	22.31	1.00
Return on Assets	7.61	0.91
Net Margin	15.21	1.24

Sector Weightings	% of Stocks	Rel S&P 500	3 Year High	3 Year Low
Info	13.86	0.66		
Software	2.09	0.50	—	—
Hardware	3.93	0.38	—	—
Media	1.35	0.46	—	—
Telecom	6.49	1.79	—	—
Service	42.24	1.04		
Health	11.40	0.95	—	—
Consumer	5.02	0.74	—	—
Business	1.85	0.42	—	—
Financial	23.97	1.38	—	—
Mfg	43.89	1.14		
Goods	12.45	1.36	—	—
Ind Mtrls	15.80	1.22	—	—
Energy	9.61	0.76	—	—
Utilities	6.03	1.64	—	—

Composition

Cash	0.4
Stocks	99.6
Bonds	0.0
Other	0.0
Foreign (% of Stock)	0.0

Morningstar's Take by Sonya Morris 12-31-07

Given WisdomTree LargeCap Dividend's diversified portfolio of financially sturdy firms, we require only a modest margin of safety to invest here.

This ETF's benchmark includes the 300 largest dividend payers in the U.S. Consequently, industry giants like General Electric, Bank of America, and AT&T dominate its portfolio, pushing its aggregate market cap almost 40% above the S&P 500's.

Because the fund focuses on industry leaders with the wherewithal to pay dividends, it's not surprising that 91% of its assets are dedicated to firms that possess competitive advantages, or "economic moats." In fact, more than half of the portfolio is dedicated to firms that earn wide economic moat ratings from our analysts. Wide-moat companies are likely to maintain their competitive edge for some time due to factors such as a huge market share (like top holdings Citigroup and Microsoft), economies of scale (Intel and ExxonMobil), or patent protection (Pfizer). Firms with sustainable competitive advantages tend to generate more predictable results than firms without economic moats, which gives us more confidence in our analysts' cash flow forecasts and fair value estimates, which in turn reduced the margin of safety we'd demand to invest here.

Furthermore, this ETF is not likely to exhibit above-average volatility. Its assets are spread over hundreds of dividend-paying stocks, and its top holdings don't consume an outsized portion of the portfolio, a common occurrence with more narrowly focused ETFs. This ETF is also broadly diversified across sectors. Granted, its emphasis on dividends means that financial stocks play a larger role here than at other large-blend funds. But its financials overweight isn't dramatic enough to significantly increase sector-specific risk.

All told, given its diversified portfolio of competitively well-positioned firms, we think this ETF is an attractive proposition when it is trading at 8% or more below our fair value estimate.

Address:	48 Wall Street United States 866-909-9473
Web Address:	www.wisdomtree.com
Inception:	06-16-06*
Advisor:	WisdomTree Asset Management, Inc.

Management Fee:	0.28%		
Expense Projections:	3Yr:$90	5Yr:$157	10Yr:$356
Income Distrib:	Quarterly		
Exchange:	NYSE		

WisdomTree MidCap Div DON

Market Price	Mstar Category
$52.02	Mid-Cap Blend

Morningstar Rating	Return	Risk	Yield	NAV	Avg Daily Vol. (k)	52 wk High/Low
—	—	—	3.0%	$52.18	32	$61.63 - $47.95

Morningstar Fair Value

Price/Fair Value Ratio	Coverage Rate %
0.91	83

Valuation

This ETF is composed largely of narrow-moat firms that court average business risk and is broadly diversified across stocks and industries. Accordingly, we'd recommend it whenever it's trading at a 9% discount to our fair value estimate. It was recently sitting right on the cusp of "buy" territory at a 9% discount to fair value.

Methodology

This ETF tracks WisdomTree MidCap Dividend Index. To create the index, WisdomTree ranks the stocks in the WisdomTree Dividend Index by market cap, removes the top 300 companies, and takes the remaining 75%. Then the index is ranked based on its constituents' planned cash dividends over the next 12 months. The index includes a large slug of REITs and utilities stocks.

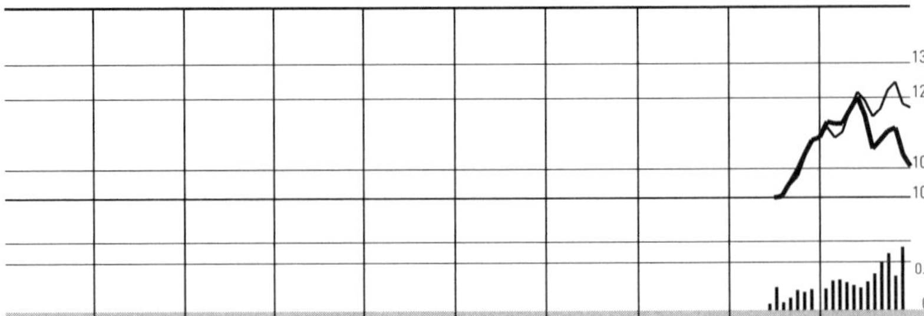

1998	1999	2000	2001	2002	2003	2004	2005	2006	2007	History
—	—	—	—	—	—	—	—	56.80	52.18	NAV $
—	—	—	—	—	—	—	—	56.84	52.02	Market Price $
—	—	—	—	—	—	—	—	5.34*	-5.49	NAV Return%
—	—	—	—	—	—	—	—	5.15*	-5.85	Market Price Return%
—	—	—	—	—	—	—	—	0.03	-0.11	Avg Premium/Discount%
—	—	—	—	—	—	—	—	—	-10.98	NAV Rtrn% +/-S&P 500
—	—	—	—	—	—	—	—	—	-13.47	NAV Rtrn% +/-S&P 400 TR
—	—	—	—	—	—	—	—	—	89	NAV Return% Rank in Cat
—	—	—	—	—	—	—	—	—	2.81	Income Return %
—	—	—	—	—	—	—	—	—	-8.30	Capital Return %
—	—	—	—	—	—	—	—	0.73	1.58	Income $
—	—	—	—	—	—	—	—	0.01	0.00	Capital Gains $
—	—	—	—	—	—	—	—	—	0.38	Expense Ratio %
—	—	—	—	—	—	—	—	—	3.47	Income Ratio %
—	—	—	—	—	—	—	—	—	12	Turnover Rate %
—	—	—	—	—	—	—	—	48	94	Net Assets $mil

Performance 12-31-07

Historic Quarterly NAV Returns

	1st Qtr	2nd Qtr	3rd Qtr	4th Qtr	Total
2003	—	—	—	—	—
2004	—	—	—	—	—
2005	—	—	—	—	—
2006	—	—	4.29	7.70	—*
2007	2.68	1.42	-2.89	-6.55	-5.49

Trailing	NAV Return%	Market Return%	NAV Rtrn% +/-S&P 500	%Rank Cat.(NAV)
3 Mo	-6.55	-6.92	-3.22	91
6 Mo	-9.25	-9.48	-7.88	75
1 Yr	-5.49	-5.85	-10.98	89
3 Yr Avg	—	—	—	—
5 Yr Avg	—	—	—	—
10 Yr Avg	—	—	—	—

Tax Analysis	Tax-Adj Return%	Tax-Cost Ratio
3 Yr (estimated)	—	—
5 Yr (estimated)	—	—
10 Yr (estimated)	—	—

Rating and Risk

Time Period	Morningstar Rtn vs Cat	Morningstar Risk vs Cat	Morningstar Risk-Adj Rating
3 Yr	—	—	—
5 Yr	—	—	—
10 Yr	—	—	—

Other Measures	Standard Index S&P 500	Best Fit Index
Alpha	—	—
Beta	—	—
R-Squared	—	—
Standard Deviation	—	
Mean	—	
Sharpe Ratio	—	

Morningstar's Take by Sonya Morris 12-31-07

WisdomTree Mid-Cap Dividend poses only moderate risks. Thus, we'd be buyers at a modest discount to our fair value estimate.

This ETF is among a new breed of index funds that weight their holdings based on fundamental factors rather than market capitalization. In this fund's case, constituents are ranked by cash dividends paid. Nevertheless, this ETF doesn't look markedly different from its market-cap-weighted rivals when it comes to portfolio quality. Although only a few of its holdings earn wide-moat ratings, it dedicates the majority of assets to companies that have managed to establish narrow economic moats. Consider Huntington Bancshares: Although it doesn't have the massive geographic footprint of wide-moat rival Bank of America, it has assembled a diversified loan portfolio and enjoys a solid position as a middle-market lender.

This fund's dividend-weighting system does influence its risk profile, however. Because it focuses on those companies with the wherewithal to pay dividends, it courts less business risk than its peers. It allocates just 10% of its portfolio to stocks with above-average business risk ratings, which is less than half that of the typical mid-blend ETF. Compared with lower-risk businesses, firms with above-average risk ratings face more uncertainty and tend to experience more erratic cash flows and are, thus, more reluctant and often less able to pay out dividends to shareholders. One of the few holdings fitting that profile is Arch Coal, which operates in a highly cyclical industry tied to fickle commodity prices, making it difficult for the firm to generate the steady cash flows necessary to support a heftier dividend payout.

Because such stocks are few and far between here and in view of the portfolio's diversification across some 400 names, we wouldn't expect this ETF to experience undue volatility. As such, we don't require a large margin of safety to invest here. We'd be buyers when the fund is trading at a 9% or greater discount to our fair value estimate.

Address:	48 Wall Street United States 866-909-9473
Web Address:	www.wisdomtree.com
Inception:	06-16-06*
Advisor:	WisdomTree Asset Management, Inc.

Management Fee:	0.38%		
Expense Projections:	3Yr:$122	5Yr:$213	10Yr:$480
Income Distrib:	Annually		
Exchange:	NYSE		

Portfolio Analysis 11-30-07

Share change since 10-07 Total Stocks:405	Sector	PE	Tot Ret%	% Assets
⊕ Windstream Corporation	Telecom	13.9	-1.74	1.59
⊕ Lyondell Chemical Compan	Energy	—	—	1.58
⊕ American Capital Strateg	Financial	4.3	-22.09	1.51
Plum Creek Timber Compan	Financial	35.1	18.26	1.26
⊕ New York Community Banco	Financial	20.2	15.77	1.22
HCP, Inc.	—	57.8	-0.33	1.16
⊕ Citizens Communications	Telecom	19.3	-4.97	1.05
⊕ Allied Capital Corporati	Financial	21.1	-27.58	1.04
⊕ Carolina Group	Goods	—	34.93	1.02
iStar Financial, Inc.	Financial	9.5	-39.78	0.90
⊕ Huntington Bancshares, I	Financial	10.0	-34.23	0.81
Pepco Holdings, Inc.	Utilities	18.1	17.09	0.78
CenterPoint Energy, Inc.	Utilities	16.5	7.35	0.74
⊕ Energy East Corporation	Utilities	16.3	15.05	0.74
Scana Corporation	Utilities	16.5	8.36	0.72
NiSource, Inc.	Utilities	15.4	-20.45	0.72
⊕ Hudson City Bancorp, Inc	Financial	27.3	10.83	0.69
Macerich Company	Financial	67.1	-15.09	0.69
⊕ MeadWestvaco Corporation	Ind Mtrls	32.3	6.73	0.68
Fidelity National Financ	Financial	13.7	-35.07	0.67

Current Investment Style

Value Blnd Growth; Large Mid Small

Market Cap	%
Giant	0.0
Large	0.2
Mid	82.7
Small	17.1
Micro	0.0
Avg $mil: 3,892	

Value Measures		Rel Category
Price/Earnings	16.66	1.04
Price/Book	1.68	0.75
Price/Sales	1.17	1.01
Price/Cash Flow	8.18	0.96
Dividend Yield %	4.07	2.47

Growth Measures	%	Rel Category
Long-Term Erngs	8.58	0.70
Book Value	6.21	0.74
Sales	8.51	2.04
Cash Flow	3.27	12.58
Historical Erngs	5.89	0.32

Profitability	%	Rel Category
Return on Equity	15.44	0.78
Return on Assets	5.39	0.70
Net Margin	16.32	1.35

Sector Weightings	% of Stocks	Rel S&P 500	3 Year High	3 Year Low
Info	6.55	0.31		
Software	0.08	0.02	—	—
Hardware	1.80	0.18	—	—
Media	1.58	0.54	—	—
Telecom	3.09	0.85	—	—
Service	51.70	1.27		
Health	2.05	0.17	—	—
Consumer	4.75	0.70	—	—
Business	4.00	0.91	—	—
Financial	40.90	2.35	—	—
Mfg	41.75	1.09		
Goods	9.76	1.07	—	—
Ind Mtrls	12.78	0.98	—	—
Energy	4.59	0.36	—	—
Utilities	14.62	3.97	—	—

Composition

Cash	0.0
Stocks	100.0
Bonds	0.0
Other	0.0
Foreign (% of Stock)	0.0

WisdomTree Total Dividend DTD

Market Price	Mstar Category
$56.75	Large Blend

Morningstar Fair Value

Price/Fair Value Ratio	Coverage Rate %
0.87	96

Valuation

This ETF looks like a bargain. It was recently trading at a 13% discount to our fair value estimate, much more than the 8% minimum we'd demand. That's the cheapest the fund has gotten in its relatively brief life. The sharp pullback in financial stocks, which loom large here, has spurred that trend.

Methodology

This fund tracks the WisdomTree Dividend Index, which compiles stocks that have paid regular cash dividends in the 12 months prior to index reconstitution. The benchmark is fundamentally weighted, which means that it ranks its roughly 750 constituents based on projected cash dividends. Thus, the stocks with the highest projected cash dividends are weighted more heavily, and vice versa. In this way, the index isn't dominated by either low-yielding, mega-cap stocks (as when strict market-cap weighting is employed) or very high-yielding, risky names (as with dividend-yield-driven approaches).

Morningstar Rating	Return	Risk	Yield	NAV	Avg Daily Vol. (k)	52 wk High/Low
—	—	—	2.7%	$56.85	19	$62.22 - $53.78

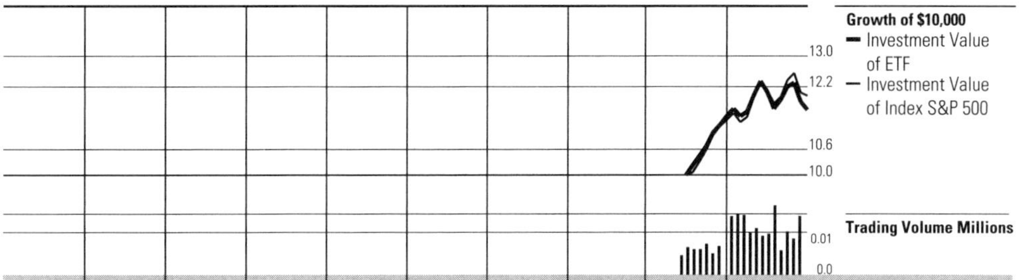

History

1998	1999	2000	2001	2002	2003	2004	2005	2006	2007	History
—	—	—	—	—	—	—	—	57.62	56.85	NAV $
—	—	—	—	—	—	—	—	57.61	56.75	Market Price $
—	—	—	—	—	—	—	—	10.89*	1.33	NAV Return%
—	—	—	—	—	—	—	—	10.64*	1.18	Market Price Return%
—	—	—	—	—	—	—	—	0.06	-0.01	Avg Premium/Discount%
—	—	—	—	—	—	—	—	—	-4.16	NAV Rtrn% +/-S&P 500
—	—	—	—	—	—	—	—	—	-4.44	NAV Rtrn% +/-Russ 1000
—	—	—	—	—	—	—	—	—	76	NAV Return% Rank in Cat
—	—	—	—	—	—	—	—	—	2.72	Income Return %
—	—	—	—	—	—	—	—	—	-1.39	Capital Return %
—	—	—	—	—	—	—	—	0.60	1.55	Income $
—	—	—	—	—	—	—	—	0.00	0.02	Capital Gains $
—	—	—	—	—	—	—	—	—	0.28	Expense Ratio %
—	—	—	—	—	—	—	—	—	2.76	Income Ratio %
—	—	—	—	—	—	—	—	—	12	Turnover Rate %
—	—	—	—	—	—	—	—	63	97	Net Assets $mil

Performance 12-31-07

Historic Quarterly NAV Returns

	1st Qtr	2nd Qtr	3rd Qtr	4th Qtr	Total
2003	—	—	—	—	—
2004	—	—	—	—	—
2005	—	—	—	—	—
2006	—	—	6.54	6.75	—*
2007	0.95	4.44	1.18	-5.00	1.33

Trailing	NAV Return%	Market Return%	NAV Rtrn% +/-S&P 500	%Rank Cat.(NAV)
3 Mo	-5.00	-5.12	-1.67	75
6 Mo	-3.88	-4.06	-2.51	70
1 Yr	1.33	1.18	-4.16	76
3 Yr Avg	—	—	—	—
5 Yr Avg	—	—	—	—
10 Yr Avg	—	—	—	—

Tax Analysis	Tax-Adj Return%	Tax-Cost Ratio
3 Yr (estimated)	—	—
5 Yr (estimated)	—	—
10 Yr (estimated)	—	—

Rating and Risk

Time Period	Morningstar Rtn vs Cat	Morningstar Risk vs Cat	Morningstar Risk-Adj Rating
3 Yr	—	—	—
5 Yr	—	—	—
10 Yr	—	—	—

Other Measures	Standard Index S&P 500	Best Fit Index
Alpha	—	—
Beta	—	—
R-Squared	—	—
Standard Deviation	—	
Mean	—	
Sharpe Ratio	—	

Portfolio Analysis 11-30-07

Share change since 10-07 Total Stocks:764	Sector	PE	Tot Ret%	% Assets
⊕ General Electric Company	Ind Mtrls	16.6	2.69	4.15
⊕ Bank of America Corporat	Financial	9.4	-19.25	3.35
⊕ ExxonMobil Corporation	Energy	13.6	24.34	3.14
⊕ AT&T, Inc.	Telecom	21.6	20.58	3.03
Altria Group Inc.	Goods	13.2	22.10	2.48
Citigroup, Inc.	Financial	7.9	-44.93	2.41
Pfizer Inc.	Health	22.5	-8.15	2.32
Verizon Communications I	Telecom	21.7	22.19	2.17
⊕ Chevron Corporation	Energy	11.4	30.59	2.10
Microsoft Corporation	Software	23.4	20.83	1.80
Merck & Co., Inc.	Health	23.6	37.36	1.78
J.P. Morgan Chase & Co.	Financial	9.5	-7.24	1.73
Procter & Gamble Company	Goods	23.1	16.63	1.71
⊕ Johnson & Johnson	Health	18.8	3.61	1.68
Southern Copper Corporat	Ind Mtrls	12.1	110.56	1.46
Coca-Cola Company	Goods	26.3	30.44	1.44
⊕ Wachovia Corporation	Financial	8.6	-29.91	1.36
Intel Corporation	Hardware	25.4	34.22	1.36
Wells Fargo Company	Financial	11.4	-12.13	1.30
Wal-Mart Stores, Inc.	Consumer	15.4	4.91	1.19

Current Investment Style

Value Blnd Growth (Large / Mid / Small) — Large Value

Market Cap	%
Giant	55.3
Large	24.2
Mid	15.6
Small	4.3
Micro	0.6
Avg $mil: 48,384	

Value Measures		Rel Category
Price/Earnings	15.08	0.96
Price/Book	2.16	0.84
Price/Sales	1.45	1.17
Price/Cash Flow	9.31	1.01
Dividend Yield %	2.92	1.54

Growth Measures	%	Rel Category
Long-Term Erngs	9.18	0.78
Book Value	9.76	1.06
Sales	8.09	0.99
Cash Flow	7.45	0.85
Historical Erngs	11.76	0.70

Profitability	%	Rel Category
Return on Equity	21.45	0.96
Return on Assets	7.38	0.88
Net Margin	15.43	1.26

Sector Weightings	% of Stocks	Rel S&P 500	3 Year High	3 Year Low
Info	12.98	0.62		
Software	1.87	0.45	—	—
Hardware	3.78	0.37	—	—
Media	1.41	0.48	—	—
Telecom	5.92	1.63	—	—
Service	44.25	1.09		
Health	10.08	0.84	—	—
Consumer	5.04	0.74	—	—
Business	2.37	0.54	—	—
Financial	26.76	1.54	—	—
Mfg	42.77	1.11		
Goods	11.91	1.30	—	—
Ind Mtrls	15.23	1.17	—	—
Energy	8.72	0.69	—	—
Utilities	6.91	1.88	—	—

Composition

Cash	0.7
Stocks	99.3
Bonds	0.0
Other	0.0
Foreign (% of Stock)	0.0

Morningstar's Take by Emiko Kurotsu 12-31-07

No matter how you cut it, this is one of the highest-quality portfolios we cover.

WisdomTree Total Dividend's secret sauce is supposedly its fundamental-weighting approach. Its underlying index looks for stocks that have paid regular dividends and ranks them by their projected cash dividends. In other words, the stocks with the biggest expected payouts are at the top of the portfolio, and vice versa.

It's a novel idea, but the fund looks pretty similar to other yield-focused funds: It's top-heavy, it favors financials, and it treads lightly in tech. What's more, this fundamental-weighting scheme doesn't seem to boost the fund's quality any more than if its holdings were cap-weighted. For instance, if we were to weight this fund's holdings by market cap instead of projected yield, we'd still end up with roughly the same-sized stake in dominant, high-quality firms, i.e., those our analysts award a wide economic moat rating. Thus, we don't view the fund's weighting scheme as a reason in and of itself to invest here.

Yet, this is still one of the highest-quality portfolios we cover. Its roughly 50% stake in wide-moat stocks is more than double that of its better-known rival, iShares Dow Jones Select Dividend. Although dividends don't necessarily translate to dominance, many of this fund's holdings are bellwethers in their industries, with top holdings General Electric, Bank of America, Pfizer, and Microsoft boasting manifold competitive advantages such as scale, barriers to entry, or lustrous brands.

Because these businesses are unlikely to be dislodged by rivals any time soon, their results tend to be more predictable, explaining why few of these names court above-average business risk. The portfolio is also well-diversified across stocks and industries, further tamping down volatility.

As such, we wouldn't demand a large margin of safety before investing here; an 8% discount to our fair value estimate would do.

Address:	48 Wall Street United States 866-909-9473
Web Address:	www.wisdomtree.com
Inception:	06-16-06*
Advisor:	WisdomTree Asset Management, Inc.

Management Fee:	0.28%		
Expense Projections:	3Yr:$90	5Yr:$157	10Yr:$356
Income Distrib:	Annually		
Exchange:	NYSE		

U.S. Stock Funds: Sector

This section offers a full-page report on each U.S. sector ETF.

Biotech HOLDRs BBH

Market Price	Mstar Category
$161.76	Specialty-Health

Morningstar Rating	Return	Risk	Yield	NAV	Avg Daily Vol. (k)	52 wk High/Low
—	—	—	—	$161.76	211	$196.90 - $159.10

Morningstar Fair Value

Price/Fair Value Ratio	Coverage Rate %
0.85	100

Valuation

Though this fund's holdings bounce around, the portfolio as a whole hasn't been too volatile and its top holdings are dominant firms, lowering their risk. As such, we wouldn't demand an especially large margin of safety to invest here; a 15% discount to our fair value estimate would do. The fund was recently trading at a 13% discount.

Methodology

This fund, like all HOLDRs, doesn't track an index. Instead, its portfolio remains static from inception, the only revisions coming as a result of mergers or bankruptcies (a not uncommon occurrence in the wild and wooly biotech world). Stock weightings fluctuate with the market. Consequently, the fund was recently packed into a mere 15 names, with its top five holdings accounting for a staggering 90% of assets. Given that, the portfolio will sink or swim with its top holdings. Investor should note that HOLDRs shares can only be purchased in round lots of 100.

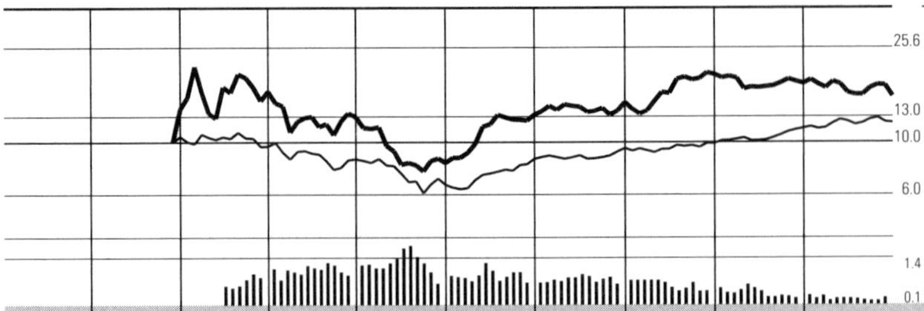

Growth of $10,000
— Investment Value of ETF
— Investment Value of Index S&P 500

Trading Volume Millions

History

1998	1999	2000	2001	2002	2003	2004	2005	2006	2007	History
161.76	143.50	170.31	132.00	84.56	135.31	152.92	200.77	183.72	161.76	NAV $
—	143.50	170.31	132.00	84.56	135.31	152.92	200.77	183.72	161.76	Market Price $
—	—	18.69	-22.50	-35.94	60.02	13.01	31.29	-8.49	-11.95	NAV Return%
—	4.97*	18.69	-22.50	-35.94	60.02	13.01	31.29	-8.49	-11.95	Market Price Return%
—	—	—	—	—	—	—	—	—	—	Avg Premium/Discount%
—	—	27.79	-10.61	-13.84	31.34	2.13	26.38	-24.28	-17.44	NAV Rtrn% +/-S&P 500
—	—	-19.15	-9.66	-15.13	40.59	8.46	22.97	-15.37	-23.18	NAV Rtrn% +/-DJ Health
—	—	1	4	5	1	1	1	9	100	NAV Return% Rank in Cat
—	—	—	—	—	—	—	—	—	—	Income Return %
—	—	—	—	—	—	—	—	—	—	Capital Return %
—	0.00	0.00	0.00	0.00	0.00	0.00	0.00	0.00	0.00	Income $
—	0.00	0.00	0.00	0.00	0.00	0.00	0.00	0.00	0.00	Capital Gains $
—	—	—	—	—	—	—	—	—	—	Expense Ratio %
—	—	—	—	—	—	—	—	—	—	Income Ratio %
—	—	—	—	—	—	—	—	—	—	Turnover Rate %
—	—	—	—	—	—	—	—	1,480	815	Net Assets $mil

Performance 12-31-07

Historic Quarterly NAV Returns

	1st Qtr	2nd Qtr	3rd Qtr	4th Qtr	Total
2003	10.28	32.17	4.70	4.86	60.02
2004	5.02	3.06	-1.33	5.83	13.01
2005	-7.93	18.83	14.00	5.27	31.29
2006	-3.55	-8.87	4.74	-0.61	-8.49
2007	-4.20	-4.49	4.57	-7.98	-11.95

Trailing	NAV Return%	Market Return%	NAV Rtrn% +/-S&P 500	%Rank Cat.(NAV)
3 Mo	-7.98	-7.98	-4.65	85
6 Mo	-3.77	-3.77	-2.40	57
1 Yr	-11.95	-11.95	-17.44	100
3 Yr Avg	1.89	1.89	-6.73	100
5 Yr Avg	13.85	13.85	1.02	1
10 Yr Avg	—	—	—	—

Tax Analysis	Tax-Adj Return%	Tax-Cost Ratio
3 Yr (estimated)	—	—
5 Yr (estimated)	—	—
10 Yr (estimated)	—	—

Rating and Risk

Time Period	Morningstar Rtn vs Cat	Morningstar Risk vs Cat	Morningstar Risk-Adj Rating
3 Yr	—	—	—
5 Yr	—	—	—
10 Yr	—	—	—

Other Measures	Standard Index S&P 500	Best Fit Index
Alpha	—	—
Beta	—	—
R-Squared	—	—
Standard Deviation	—	
Mean	1.89	
Sharpe Ratio	—	

Portfolio Analysis 12-31-07

Share change since 10-07 Total Stocks:15	Sector	PE	Tot Ret%	% Assets
Genentech, Inc.	Health	26.2	-17.33	36.62
Amgen, Inc.	Health	16.8	-32.02	18.70
Gilead Sciences, Inc.	Health	—	41.72	17.92
Biogen Idec, Inc.	Health	34.3	15.71	9.31
Genzyme Corporation	Health	—	20.88	6.46
Applera Corporation - Ap	Health	22.0	-7.04	3.78
Shire PLC ADR	Health	—	12.02	2.87
Millennium Pharmaceutica	Health	—	37.43	1.20
Sepracor, Inc.	Health	17.9	-57.37	0.96
Human Genome Sciences	Health	—	-16.08	0.55
Affymetrix, Inc.	Health	—	0.35	0.55
Applera Corporation - Ce	Health	—	13.44	0.39
Alkermes, Inc.	Health	70.9	16.60	0.37
Enzon Pharmaceuticals, I	Health	9.2	11.99	0.17
QLT, Inc.	Health	—	-47.75	0.14

Morningstar's Take by Jeffrey Ptak 12-31-07

Improbably enough, Biotech HOLDRs has one of the highest-quality portfolios we cover.

This ETF is a member of Merrill Lynch's quirky HOLDRs family. Unlike traditional ETFs, a HOLDRs portfolio doesn't track an index. Instead, it remains frozen from inception, meaning that Merrill doesn't rebalance or otherwise tinker with its holdings. Thus, a HOLDRs portfolio tends to be very concentrated. This fund is no exception, as it packs its assets into a mere 15 stocks, the top four of which--Genentech, Amgen, Gilead Sciences, and Biogen Idec--recently accounted for 85% of assets.

Biotech is not typically synonymous with "high-quality." Many of the firms that we cover are upstarts lacking FDA-approved therapies. In addition, they're vulnerable to better-resourced rivals higher up in the drugmaking food chain. All told, our analysts have awarded "wide" or "narrow" economic moat ratings to only a handful of the 64 biotechs that they cover, meaning that virtually none of these firms possess even a semblance of a competitive advantage.

This fund holds all four wide-moat biotechs--Genentech, Amgen, Biogen Idec, and Genzyme. Also, those four names soak up 73% of assets. As such, this is not only the highest-quality biotech ETF that we cover, it's one of the highest-quality portfolios that we follow, period.

Of course, with concentration comes risk. Should the wheels come off at one of these firms, it could drag the portfolio down. Yet, these wide-moat names court only average risk in our analysts' view, given their broad drug portfolios and strong balance sheets. Further, while biotechs are notoriously volatile owing to the boom-bust nature of drug development, diversification smoothes the ride to a surprising extent, reflecting the fact that one drug's odds of success are typically unrelated to another's.

That said, we'd still require a healthy margin of safety to invest here; a 15% discount to our fair value estimate would do.

Current Investment Style

Value Blnd Growth — Large Mid Small (style box: Large Growth)

Market Cap	%
Giant	36.6
Large	55.3
Mid	6.0
Small	2.0
Micro	0.2

Avg $mil: 36,348

Value Measures		Rel Category
Price/Earnings	11.30	0.53
Price/Book	4.47	1.31
Price/Sales	4.59	1.58
Price/Cash Flow	15.65	1.20
Dividend Yield %	—	—

Growth Measures	%	Rel Category
Long-Term Erngs	—	—
Book Value	2.14	0.35
Sales	20.71	2.00
Cash Flow	18.67	1.47
Historical Erngs	27.80	0.30

Profitability	%	Rel Category
Return on Equity	12.69	1.71
Return on Assets	7.51	17.07
Net Margin	13.67	2.69

Industry Weightings	% of Stocks	Rel Cat
Biotech	98.9	2.8
Drugs	1.1	0.0
Mgd Care	0.0	0.0
Hospitals	0.0	0.0
Other HC Srv	0.0	0.0
Diagnostics	0.0	0.0
Equipment	0.0	0.0
Good/Srv	0.0	0.0
Other	0.0	0.0

Composition

Cash	0.0
Stocks	100.0
Bonds	0.0
Other	0.0
Foreign (% of Stock)	3.0

Address:	4 World Financial Center United States 800-637-7455
Web Address:	www.holdrs.com
Inception:	11-22-99
Advisor:	Merrill Lynch Pierce Fenner & Smith

Management Fee:	—
Expense Projections:	3Yr: — 5Yr: — 10Yr: —
Income Distrib:	Quarterly
Exchange:	AMEX

Consumer Discr SPDR XLY

Market Price	Mstar Category
$32.70	Large Blend

Morningstar Fair Value

Price/Fair Value Ratio	Coverage Rate %
0.80	98

Morningstar Rating	Return	Risk	Yield	NAV	Avg Daily Vol. (k)	52 wk High/Low
★	Low	High	1.4%	$32.82	3,268	$40.41 - $30.35

Valuation

Given the fund's diversity of stocks, we have greater confidence in our fair-value estimate than with most sector funds. We'd feel comfortable recommending it whenever it trades at an 8% or greater discount to our fair value estimate. The fund was recently trading well below that level, at a hefty 20% discount to fair value. It looks like a bargain.

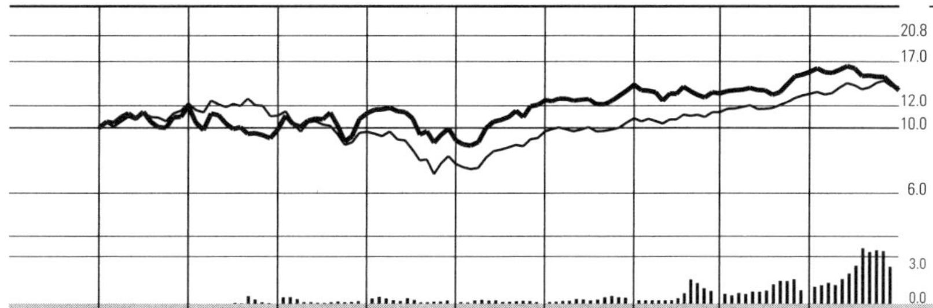

Methodology

This ETF invests passively in the consumer discretionary stocks in the S&P 500 Index. These include stocks in the media, leisure, and apparel industries, among others. The stock weightings are based on the market caps of the underlying companies, so large-cap stocks like McDonald's, Time Warner, and Walt Disney make up the top holdings. All told, the fund holds 89 stocks. Sticking to S&P 500 companies provides an initial screen for quality, as holdings must meet the standards of the S&P's selection committee.

History

1998	1999	2000	2001	2002	2003	2004	2005	2006	2007	History
26.24	30.91	25.56	28.74	23.14	31.48	35.29	32.65	38.38	32.82	NAV $
26.12	31.06	25.59	28.60	23.11	31.49	35.29	32.65	38.36	32.70	Market Price $
4.13*	18.40	-16.56	13.44	-18.96	37.00	12.90	-6.56	18.45	-13.38	NAV Return%
3.65*	19.53	-16.87	12.76	-18.67	37.20	12.88	-6.57	18.41	-13.67	Market Price Return%
-0.46	0.09	0.04	-0.05	-0.01	-0.02	0.06	-0.01	0.02	-0.02	Avg Premium/Discount%
—	-2.64	-7.46	25.33	3.14	8.32	2.02	-11.47	2.66	-18.87	NAV Rtrn% +/-S&P 500
—	-6.78	3.44	10.65	4.86	-0.42	-0.35	-0.20	-0.19	-0.17	NAV Rtrn% +/-S&P Cons Dis
—	80	100	1	34	13	31	100	14	94	NAV Return% Rank in Cat
—	0.56	0.76	0.86	0.60	0.84	0.76	0.93	0.86	1.17	Income Return %
—	17.84	-17.32	12.58	-19.56	36.16	12.14	-7.49	17.59	-14.55	Capital Return %
0.00	0.15	0.23	0.22	0.17	0.19	0.24	0.33	0.28	0.45	Income $
0.00	0.00	0.00	0.00	0.00	0.00	0.00	0.00	0.00	0.00	Capital Gains $
—	0.58	0.43	0.27	0.27	0.28	0.28	0.26	0.24	0.23	Expense Ratio %
—	0.49	0.80	0.89	0.57	0.66	0.69	0.82	0.98	0.93	Income Ratio %
—	—	16	5	42	29	3	18	12	6	Turnover Rate %
—	—	—	—	131	280	471	405	656	711	Net Assets $mil

Performance 12-31-07

Historic Quarterly NAV Returns

	1st Qtr	2nd Qtr	3rd Qtr	4th Qtr	Total
2003	-1.46	19.01	2.18	14.33	37.00
2004	1.15	-0.34	-1.24	13.40	12.90
2005	-5.73	-1.16	-0.82	1.12	-6.56
2006	3.00	-0.53	4.92	10.19	18.45
2007	-0.80	3.59	-6.32	-10.03	-13.38

Trailing	NAV Return%	Market Return%	NAV Rtrn% +/-S&P 500	%Rank Cat.(NAV)
3 Mo	-10.03	-10.58	-6.70	90
6 Mo	-15.71	-16.10	-14.34	94
1 Yr	-13.38	-13.67	-18.87	94
3 Yr Avg	-1.40	-1.52	-10.02	100
5 Yr Avg	8.20	8.14	-4.63	100
10 Yr Avg	—	—	—	—

Tax Analysis	Tax-Adj Return%	Tax-Cost Ratio
3 Yr (estimated)	-1.74	0.34
5 Yr (estimated)	7.86	0.31
10 Yr (estimated)	—	—

Rating and Risk

Time Period	Morningstar Rtn vs Cat	Morningstar Risk vs Cat	Morningstar Risk-Adj Rating
3 Yr	Low	High	★
5 Yr	Low	High	★
10 Yr	—	—	—

Other Measures	Standard Index S&P 500	Best Fit Index M* Cons Serv TR
Alpha	-10.3	-3.9
Beta	1.22	0.89
R-Squared	65	85
Standard Deviation	11.76	
Mean	-1.40	
Sharpe Ratio	-0.43	

Portfolio Analysis 12-31-07

Share change since 11-07 Total Stocks:88	Sector	PE	Tot Ret%	% Assets
⊖ McDonald's Corporation	Consumer	39.5	36.38	6.34
⊖ Walt Disney Company	Media	14.4	-2.96	5.59
⊖ Time Warner, Inc.	Media	13.4	-23.27	5.43
⊖ Comcast Corporation A	Media	24.0	-35.29	5.11
⊖ News Corporation, Ltd. A	Media	14.9	-4.08	4.32
⊖ Home Depot, Inc.	Consumer	10.7	-31.14	4.14
⊖ Target Corporation	Consumer	14.7	-11.17	3.78
⊖ Lowe's Companies Inc.	Consumer	11.4	-26.82	3.01
⊖ Viacom, Inc. B	Media	19.3	7.04	2.62
⊖ Amazon.com, Inc.	Consumer	NMF	134.77	2.59
⊖ Nike, Inc. B	Goods	19.4	31.48	2.25
⊖ Johnson Controls, Inc.	Ind Mtrls	16.7	27.49	1.95
⊖ Yum Brands, Inc.	Consumer	23.2	32.28	1.77
⊖ Carnival Corporation	Consumer	14.7	-6.83	1.77
⊖ CBS, Inc. B	Media	15.8	-10.08	1.70
⊖ Best Buy Co., Inc.	Consumer	18.9	7.38	1.68
⊖ Clear Channel Communicat	Media	21.5	-0.83	1.56
⊖ Harrah's Entertainment,	Consumer	27.2	9.32	1.51
⊖ The DIRECTV Group, Inc.	Media	19.4	-7.30	1.51
⊖ Staples, Inc.	Consumer	16.7	-12.63	1.48

Current Investment Style

Value Blnd Growth / Large Mid Small

Market Cap	%
Giant	27.0
Large	44.4
Mid	27.7
Small	0.9
Micro	0.0
Avg $mil: 21,777	

Value Measures		Rel Category
Price/Earnings	14.23	0.90
Price/Book	2.16	0.84
Price/Sales	0.74	0.60
Price/Cash Flow	6.77	0.73
Dividend Yield %	1.55	0.82

Growth Measures	%	Rel Category
Long-Term Erngs	—	—
Book Value	2.78	0.30
Sales	5.23	0.64
Cash Flow	1.98	0.23
Historical Erngs	20.40	1.22

Profitability	%	Rel Category
Return on Equity	20.54	0.92
Return on Assets	7.48	0.90
Net Margin	7.84	0.64

Sector Weightings	% of Stocks	Rel S&P 500	3 Year High	3 Year Low
Info	31.39	1.50		
Software	0.00	0.00	0	0
Hardware	0.00	0.00	0	0
Media	31.39	10.79	34	29
Telecom	0.00	0.00	0	0
Service	50.22	1.24		
Health	0.00	0.00	0	0
Consumer	48.45	7.15	55	48
Business	1.77	0.40	2	2
Financial	0.00	0.00	0	0
Mfg	18.38	0.48		
Goods	14.51	1.58	15	12
Ind Mtrls	3.87	0.30	4	3
Energy	0.00	0.00	0	0
Utilities	0.00	0.00	0	0

Composition

Cash	0.6
Stocks	99.4
Bonds	0.0
Other	0.0
Foreign (% of Stock)	0.0

Morningstar's Take by Haywood Kelly 12-31-07

Consumer Discretionary SPDR is a tame sector fund.

The theme here is discretionary consumer spending. If, for example, the U.S. housing slump or a recession sends consumer spending into a tailspin, expect poor returns from this ETF. But don't expect disaster. Although a homebuilder or bank ETF can easily crater 50%, it's extremely unlikely we'd see this portfolio suffer such a loss unless the entire U.S. stock market crashed.

Aside from a few clunkers like General Motors and Ford, the portfolio contains many high-quality names. Eight of the top 10 holdings sport wide-moat ratings, which designates firms that have excellent competitive positions. Plus, the quality is spread across several different segments of the U.S. economy. Restaurants loom large (McDonald's and Starbucks), as do retailers (Target, Amazon, and Best Buy), and media (Time Warner and Walt Disney). Overall, the companies aren't quite as profitable, when measured by ROE and ROA, as those in the S&P 500, but the earnings growth is higher and the dividend yield lower. That suggests you're getting a faster-growing portfolio than you would in an S&P 500-tracking fund.

Because the fund invests in a variety of companies and industries, it limits the exposure to any single risk factor. As such, we have more confidence in our fair value estimate for this ETF than for most sector funds. Plus, the fund isn't very concentrated among its top holdings, which means that even a disaster at a single company wouldn't set it back too far.

True, all the portfolio stocks depend to some extent on how fast dollars fly out of the U.S. consumer's wallet. But they're different enough to make this one of the more diversified--and least volatile--sector funds out there. For such a diverse portfolio of high-quality names, we'd be happy to pound the table for this ETF whenever it's cheap. We'd consider it a bargain at an 8% discount to our fair value estimate.

Address:	c/o State Street Bk&Tr, 225 Franklin St United States 800-843-2639
Web Address:	www.spdrindex.com
Inception:	12-16-98*
Advisor:	SSgA Funds Management Inc

Management Fee:	0.05%		
Expense Projections:	3Yr:$77	5Yr:$136	10Yr:$307
Income Distrib:	Quarterly		
Exchange:	AMEX		

Consumer Staple SPDR XLP

Market Price	Mstar Category
$28.80	Large Blend

Morningstar Fair Value

Price/Fair Value Ratio	Coverage Rate %
0.91	100

Morningstar Rating	Return	Risk	Yield	NAV	Avg Daily Vol. (k)	52 wk High/Low
★★★	Below Avg	Low	2.1%	$28.76	2,544	$29.49 - $25.75

Valuation

Though assets are bunched up in just a few holdings, because this portfolio focuses on mature firms across a variety of consumer-related industries, we're confident in our fair value estimate. We'd need an 8% discount to fair value before recommending this fund. It was recently trading at a 9% discount to fair value, making it a bargain.

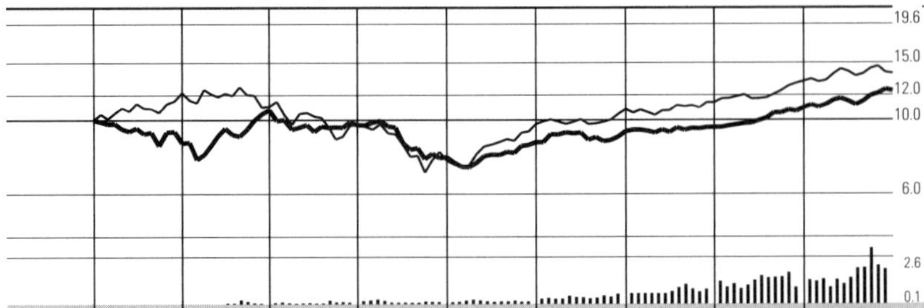

Methodology

The fund invests in the consumer staples stocks of the S&P 500, weighting the stocks by market capitalization. The top holding, Procter & Gamble, recently made up a hefty 17% of the portfolio. Sticking to S&P 500 companies provides an initial screen for quality, as holdings must meet the standards of S&P's selection committee. Constituents usually have to be leading U.S. companies that meet S&P's profitability criteria. The criteria eliminate large international companies, including Unilever and Diageo.

1998	1999	2000	2001	2002	2003	2004	2005	2006	2007	History
27.24	22.98	28.56	25.40	19.96	21.76	23.09	23.30	26.13	28.76	NAV $
27.16	23.03	28.56	25.40	19.94	21.78	23.08	23.29	26.12	28.80	Market Price $
2.77*	-14.70	25.83	-9.91	-20.02	10.95	7.79	2.84	14.49	12.47	NAV Return%
2.60*	-14.27	25.56	-9.91	-20.10	11.16	7.65	2.84	14.49	12.68	Market Price Return%
-0.29	0.04	-0.06	-0.25	-0.10	0.06	0.03	0.01	0.04	0.00	Avg Premium/Discount%
—	-35.74	34.93	1.98	2.08	-17.73	-3.09	-2.07	-1.30	6.98	NAV Rtrn% +/-S&P 500
—	0.39	9.05	-3.51	-15.76	-0.62	-0.39	-0.74	0.13	-1.71	NAV Rtrn% +/-S&P Cons Stp
—	100	1	46	40	100	93	74	76	19	NAV Return% Rank in Cat
—	1.00	1.29	1.13	1.52	1.81	1.65	1.93	2.22	2.31	Income Return %
—	-15.70	24.54	-11.04	-21.54	9.14	6.14	0.91	12.27	10.16	Capital Return %
0.00	0.27	0.30	0.32	0.38	0.36	0.36	0.44	0.51	0.60	Income $
0.00	0.00	0.00	0.00	0.00	0.00	0.00	0.00	0.00	0.00	Capital Gains $
—	0.57	0.42	0.28	0.28	0.27	0.27	0.26	0.24	0.23	Expense Ratio %
—	1.10	1.20	1.21	1.48	1.87	1.62	1.84	2.10	2.18	Income Ratio %
—	3	10	6	60	37	3	24	8	6	Turnover Rate %
—	—	—	—	230	305	761	785	1,486	2,186	Net Assets $mil

Performance 12-31-07

Historic Quarterly NAV Returns

	1st Qtr	2nd Qtr	3rd Qtr	4th Qtr	Total
2003	-6.56	8.96	1.25	7.64	10.95
2004	5.39	1.30	-5.69	7.06	7.79
2005	0.20	-0.79	2.84	0.60	2.84
2006	1.81	2.89	5.45	3.64	14.49
2007	2.26	2.44	3.80	3.44	12.47

Trailing	NAV Return%	Market Return%	NAV Rtrn% +/-S&P 500	%Rank Cat.(NAV)
3 Mo	3.44	3.45	6.77	1
6 Mo	7.37	7.60	8.74	1
1 Yr	12.47	12.68	6.98	19
3 Yr Avg	9.81	9.88	1.19	24
5 Yr Avg	9.63	9.68	-3.20	92
10 Yr Avg	—	—	—	—

Tax Analysis	Tax-Adj Return%	Tax-Cost Ratio
3 Yr (estimated)	9.03	0.71
5 Yr (estimated)	8.91	0.66
10 Yr (estimated)	—	—

Rating and Risk

Time Period	Morningstar Rtn vs Cat	Morningstar Risk vs Cat	Morningstar Risk-Adj Rating
3 Yr	+Avg	Low	★★★★
5 Yr	Low	Low	★★
10 Yr	—	—	—

Other Measures	Standard Index S&P 500	Best Fit Index M* Cons Good TR
Alpha	3.5	0.7
Beta	0.40	0.82
R-Squared	29	78
Standard Deviation	5.84	
Mean	9.81	
Sharpe Ratio	0.91	

Portfolio Analysis 12-31-07

Share change since 11-07 Total Stocks:39	Sector	PE	Tot Ret%	% Assets
⊕ Procter & Gamble Company	Goods	23.1	16.63	17.38
⊕ Altria Group Inc.	Goods	13.2	22.10	12.13
⊕ Wal-Mart Stores, Inc.	Consumer	15.4	4.91	8.56
⊕ Coca-Cola Company	Goods	26.3	30.44	5.44
⊕ CVS Caremark Corporation	Consumer	21.5	28.93	5.01
⊕ PepsiCo, Inc.	Goods	20.4	23.89	4.69
⊕ Kraft Foods, Inc.	Goods	20.0	-5.71	3.85
⊕ Colgate-Palmolive Compan	Goods	24.7	21.94	3.30
⊕ Anheuser-Busch Companies	Goods	19.1	9.06	3.15
⊕ Walgreen Company	Consumer	18.5	-16.35	3.05
⊕ Archer Daniels Midland	Ind Mtrls	13.8	47.02	2.64
⊕ Costco Wholesale Corpora	Consumer	28.5	33.21	2.56
⊕ Kimberly-Clark Corporati	Goods	17.0	5.23	2.45
⊕ General Mills, Inc.	Goods	17.2	1.58	1.68
⊕ Kroger Company	Consumer	15.3	16.82	1.65
⊕ Sysco Corporation	Consumer	18.8	-13.21	1.64
⊕ Avon Products	Goods	29.8	22.02	1.55
⊕ Safeway Inc.	Consumer	17.0	-0.03	1.44
⊕ H.J. Heinz Company	Goods	18.3	7.07	1.39
⊕ Kellogg Company	Goods	19.0	5.70	1.31

Current Investment Style

Value Blnd Growth — Large Mid Small

Market Cap	%
Giant	53.5
Large	35.1
Mid	11.4
Small	0.0
Micro	0.0
Avg $mil: 61,898	

Value Measures		Rel Category
Price/Earnings	17.26	1.09
Price/Book	3.35	1.31
Price/Sales	0.95	0.77
Price/Cash Flow	13.46	1.45
Dividend Yield %	2.25	1.19

Growth Measures	%	Rel Category
Long-Term Erngs	—	—
Book Value	7.07	0.77
Sales	9.54	1.17
Cash Flow	3.85	0.44
Historical Erngs	8.71	0.52

Profitability	%	Rel Category
Return on Equity	29.61	1.33
Return on Assets	10.36	1.24
Net Margin	9.38	0.77

Sector Weightings	% of Stocks	Rel S&P 500	3 Year High	3 Year Low
Info	0.00	0.00		
Software	0.00	0.00	0	0
Hardware	0.00	0.00	0	0
Media	0.00	0.00	0	0
Telecom	0.00	0.00	0	0
Service	25.45	0.63		
Health	0.00	0.00	0	0
Consumer	25.45	3.75	32	25
Business	0.00	0.00	0	0
Financial	0.00	0.00	0	0
Mfg	74.55	1.94		
Goods	71.90	7.85	73	66
Ind Mtrls	2.65	0.20	3	1
Energy	0.00	0.00	0	0
Utilities	0.00	0.00	0	0

Composition

Cash	0.6
Stocks	99.5
Bonds	0.0
Other	0.0
Foreign (% of Stock)	0.0

Morningstar's Take by Haywood Kelly 12-31-07

To get excited about Consumer Staples Select Sector SPDR, you need to be excited by a handful of very mature large-cap stocks.

With this ETF, you're getting a portfolio of mega-cap stocks--the average market cap is $60 billion--that are extremely mature. Consider the top two holdings. Procter & Gamble, with a 17% weighting, is a great company, but we expect its sales to grow at only a 5% to 6% clip over the next five years. The number-two holding, Altria, is milking cash flows from its hugely profitable tobacco business. We project just 3% top-line growth. There are faster-growing names in the portfolio--Walgreen and Costco, for example--but they're far outnumbered by more mature firms. As you'd expect from such a portfolio, it has a lower earnings growth and a higher dividend yield than the S&P 500.

Given the nature of the stocks in the fund, we have higher confidence in our fair value estimate for this fund than for most sector ETFs. It's relatively easy to value mature companies, especially those in noncyclical industries. Plus, 65% of the fund's assets are invested in wide-moat firms, versus 48% for the S&P 500 as a whole. The cash flows of such companies tend to be easier to forecast because of the strong competitive advantages fueling them. The standard deviation of the fund is extremely low by sector-fund standards--on a par with that of the S&P 500 as a whole. That's rather amazing considering that nearly 30% of the fund's assets are invested in just two stocks.

Keep that concentration in mind before investing. To really love this fund, you've got to be pretty confident that the top few stocks are undervalued. And if they become overvalued, this fund could be a lot more risky than its historical volatility suggests.

Address:	c/o State Street Bk&Tr, 225 Franklin St United States 800-843-2639
Web Address:	www.spdrindex.com
Inception:	12-16-98*
Advisor:	SSgA Funds Management Inc

Management Fee:	0.05%		
Expense Projections:	3Yr:$77	5Yr:$136	10Yr:$307
Income Distrib:	Quarterly		
Exchange:	AMEX		

DJ Wilshire REIT ETF RWR

Market Price	Mstar Category
$69.30	Specialty-Real Estate

Morningstar Fair Value

Price/Fair Value Ratio	Coverage Rate %
0.95	94

Morningstar Rating	Return	Risk	Yield	NAV	Avg Daily Vol. (k)	52 wk High/Low
★★★	Average	Above Avg	4.2%	$69.37	255	$99.86 - $62.37

Valuation

Though this fund spreads its assets across the various real-estate property classes, it's still captive to a single risk factor: the trajectory of the U.S. real-estate market. So, we'd demand a reasonably wide margin of safety when investing here--a 15% discount to our fair value estimate would suffice; the fund was recently trading at fair value.

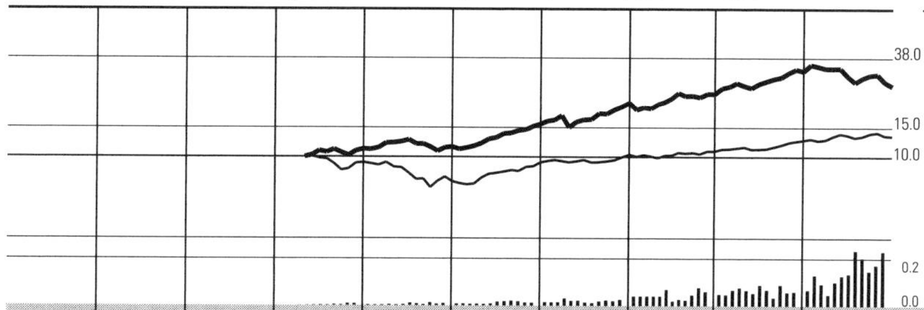

Growth of $10,000
— Investment Value of ETF
— Investment Value of Index S&P 500

Trading Volume Millions

Methodology

This exchange-traded fund tracks the Wilshire REIT Index. It's a benchmark of about 90 stocks that derive at least three quarters of their revenue from the equity ownership or operation of real estate. The bogey rebalances monthly but makes additions quarterly and deletions at year end. The index consists of straightforward exposure to retail, office, industrial, and multifamily landlords, with a smattering of self-storage and health-care REITs. It avoids more exotic stocks, such as those involved in timber. It also shuns volatile mortgage REITs that own mortgages instead of property.

History

1998	1999	2000	2001	2002	2003	2004	2005	2006	2007	History
—	—	—	39.38	38.67	49.83	62.54	67.52	87.86	69.37	NAV $
—	—	—	39.56	38.76	49.93	62.53	67.50	87.85	69.30	Market Price $
—	—	—	15.65*	2.88	35.58	32.75	13.12	35.50	-18.12	NAV Return%
—	—	—	15.63*	2.66	35.52	32.46	13.11	35.53	-18.20	Market Price Return%
—	—	—	0.07	0.23	0.06	-0.05	0.09	0.02	-0.07	Avg Premium/Discount%
—	—	—	—	24.98	6.90	21.87	8.21	19.71	-23.61	NAV Rtrn% +/-S&P 500
—	—	—	—	-0.70	-0.60	-0.41	-0.70	-0.47	-0.56	NAV Rtrn% +/-DJ Real Est
—	—	—	—	100	100	34	50	25	60	NAV Return% Rank in Cat
—	—	—	—	4.93	5.43	6.41	4.33	4.22	3.37	Income Return %
—	—	—	—	-2.05	30.15	26.34	8.79	31.28	-21.49	Capital Return %
—	—	—	1.71	1.91	2.06	3.12	2.67	2.81	2.92	Income $
—	—	—	0.23	0.00	0.16	0.00	0.45	0.54	0.00	Capital Gains $
—	—	—	0.32	0.30	0.28	0.26	0.26	0.26	0.25	Expense Ratio %
—	—	—	6.88	6.74	6.95	5.23	5.06	3.57	2.95	Income Ratio %
—	—	—	2	15	10	15	12	11	16	Turnover Rate %
—	—	—	—	87	284	535	807	1,323	1,236	Net Assets $mil

Performance 12-31-07

Historic Quarterly NAV Returns

	1st Qtr	2nd Qtr	3rd Qtr	4th Qtr	Total
2003	1.20	11.96	9.77	9.02	35.58
2004	11.99	-5.38	8.17	15.82	32.75
2005	-7.23	14.50	3.89	2.51	13.12
2006	15.65	-1.20	9.04	8.76	35.50
2007	3.66	-9.80	1.29	-13.54	-18.12

Trailing	NAV Return%	Market Return%	NAV Rtrn% +/-S&P 500	%Rank Cat.(NAV)
3 Mo	-13.54	-13.77	-10.21	55
6 Mo	-12.43	-12.76	-11.06	61
1 Yr	-18.12	-18.20	-23.61	60
3 Yr Avg	7.87	7.84	-0.75	75
5 Yr Avg	17.70	17.62	4.87	67
10 Yr Avg	—	—	—	—

Tax Analysis	Tax-Adj Return%	Tax-Cost Ratio
3 Yr (estimated)	6.39	1.37
5 Yr (estimated)	15.88	1.55
10 Yr (estimated)	—	—

Rating and Risk

Time Period	Morningstar Rtn vs Cat	Morningstar Risk vs Cat	Morningstar Risk-Adj Rating
3 Yr	Avg	+Avg	★★★
5 Yr	Avg	+Avg	★★★
10 Yr	—	—	—

Other Measures	Standard Index S&P 500	Best Fit Index DJ Real Est
Alpha	-1.6	-0.6
Beta	1.48	1.00
R-Squared	43	100
Standard Deviation	17.50	
Mean	7.87	
Sharpe Ratio	0.28	

Morningstar's Take by John Coumarianos 12-31-07

We'd like this ETF if its holdings got a little cheaper.

DJ Wilshire REIT holds a straightforward basket of retail, industrial, office, and multifamily property REITs. Many of its holdings have stumbled recently, but we'd wait for them to get a bit cheaper. Because it's difficult for REITs to build durable competitive advantages, we'd want a greater margin of safety (about 15% below our fair value estimate) before investing.

Real estate's stalwart firms occupy this ETF's top three slots. Simon Property Group, ProLogis Trust, and Vornado Realty Trust are all narrow-moat businesses because of the prime locations they've secured for their malls, distribution centers, and office buildings, respectively. Also, each firm's management team has exhibited acumen at deploying capital or developing a special niche. For example, Simon completed an opportunistic purchase of the distressed firm Mills in early 2007, while ProLogis has expanded internationally, helping its multinational clients with their supply chains overseas. Vornado has an unparalleled nose for sniffing out bargain properties that it can redevelop and re-lease at higher rental rates.

This ETF's top multifamily holdings, AvalonBay and Equity Residential, also sport narrow moat ratings for their properties in land-constrained coastal cities. However, despite recent price drops, the multifamily REITs are among the most expensive now, according to our valuation models, as investors anticipate greater profits from home buyers avoiding a still-expensive housing market. We think apartments will benefit from this factor, but only modestly.

If multifamily prices decline further, bringing this ETF's price to a 15% discount to our fair value estimate, we'd encourage investors to pick up shares. Since dividends ordinarily comprise the lion's share of REIT total returns, this ETF's 0.26% expense ratio will allow investors to keep most of that cash.

Address:	One Lincoln Street United States 866-787-2257
Web Address:	www.advisors.ssga.com
Inception:	04-23-01 *
Advisor:	SSgA Funds Management Inc

Management Fee:	0.25%		
Expense Projections:	3Yr:$81	5Yr:$141	10Yr:$320
Income Distrib:	Quarterly		
Exchange:	AMEX		

Portfolio Analysis 12-31-07

Share change since 11-07 Total Stocks:86	Sector	PE	Tot Ret%	% Assets
⊕ Simon Property Group, In	Financial	36.8	-11.34	7.70
⊕ ProLogis Trust	Financial	14.3	7.35	6.44
⊕ Vornado Realty Trust	Financial	27.3	-25.45	4.95
⊕ Boston Properties, Inc.	Financial	10.0	-10.36	4.33
⊕ Equity Residential	Financial	—	-24.90	3.92
⊕ General Growth Propertie	Financial	33.4	-18.53	3.76
⊕ Public Storage	Financial	—	-22.83	3.74
⊕ Host Hotels & Resorts, I	Financial	22.4	-27.14	3.52
⊕ Kimco Realty Corporation	Financial	26.4	-16.04	3.17
⊕ HCP, Inc.	—	57.8	-0.33	2.98
⊕ AvalonBay Communities, I	Financial	37.5	-25.42	2.96
⊕ Ventas, Inc.	Financial	33.2	12.01	2.39
⊕ AMB Property Corporation	Financial	21.5	1.64	2.26
⊕ SL Green Realty Corporat	Financial	36.8	-27.81	2.19
⊕ Macerich Company	Financial	67.1	-15.09	2.04
⊕ Developers Diversified R	Financial	20.8	-36.01	1.87
⊕ Federal Realty Investmen	Financial	50.5	-0.61	1.84
⊕ Regency Centers Corporat	Financial	30.6	-14.56	1.77
⊕ Duke Realty Corporation	Financial	35.2	-32.72	1.51
⊕ Health Care REIT, Inc.	Financial	36.9	9.65	1.50

Current Investment Style

Value Blnd Growth — Large Mid Small

Market Cap	%
Giant	0.0
Large	19.1
Mid	59.6
Small	19.2
Micro	2.0
Avg $mil: 5,129	

Value Measures		Rel Category
Price/Earnings	29.81	1.21
Price/Book	2.08	1.16
Price/Sales	3.50	0.99
Price/Cash Flow	11.53	0.75
Dividend Yield %	5.09	1.02

Growth Measures	%	Rel Category
Long-Term Erngs	—	—
Book Value	4.83	0.60
Sales	6.15	0.73
Cash Flow	2.92	0.37
Historical Erngs	13.49	0.47

Profitability	%	Rel Category
Return on Equity	14.37	0.94
Return on Assets	4.15	0.70
Net Margin	29.47	0.81

Sector Weightings	% of Stocks	Rel S&P 500	3 Year High	3 Year Low
Info	0.00	0.00		
Software	0.00	0.00	0	0
Hardware	0.00	0.00	0	0
Media	0.00	0.00	0	0
Telecom	0.00	0.00	0	0
Service	100.00	2.46		
Health	0.00	0.00	0	0
Consumer	0.00	0.00	0	0
Business	0.00	0.00	0	0
Financial	100.00	5.74	100	100
Mfg	0.00	0.00		
Goods	0.00	0.00	0	0
Ind Mtrls	0.00	0.00	0	0
Energy	0.00	0.00	0	0
Utilities	0.00	0.00	0	0

Composition

Cash	0.1
Stocks	99.9
Bonds	0.0
Other	0.0
Foreign (% of Stock)	0.0

Energy SPDR XLE

Market Price	Mstar Category
$79.35	Specialty-Natural Res

Morningstar Fair Value

Price/Fair Value Ratio	Coverage Rate %
0.99	99

Valuation

This ETF was recently trading at a 1% discount to our fair value estimate. The major driver of that fair value estimate is our energy team's oil-price forecasts. If those assumptions prove to be way off, our fair value will be wrong. Because of this exposure to a single risk factor, we'd demand a 20% margin of safety.

Methodology

This ETF owns the oil and gas and energy-services companies in the S&P 500. The weightings of each stock roughly correspond to each stock's market cap. Thus ExxonMobil, the largest oil firm in the world, makes up more than 20% of assets, and the top 10 holdings make up two thirds of the fund's assets. Constituents have to be leading U.S. companies that meet S&P's profitability criteria. These criteria eliminate non-U.S. oil companies, including Royal Dutch Petroleum, BP, and Total SA. Morningstar has fair values on all but one of the stocks in the portfolio, or about 99% of assets.

Morningstar Rating	Return	Risk	Yield	NAV	Avg Daily Vol. (k)	52 wk High/Low
★★★	Average	Below Avg	1.0%	$79.22	19,387	$80.55 - $54.06

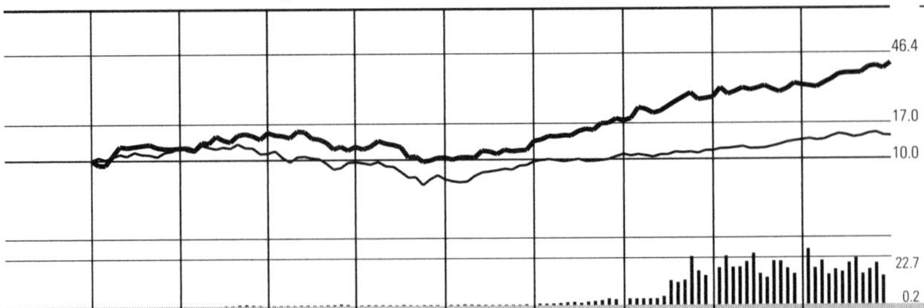

1998	1999	2000	2001	2002	2003	2004	2005	2006	2007	History
23.20	27.18	33.27	26.70	22.30	27.62	36.29	50.28	58.75	79.22	NAV $
23.34	27.09	33.19	26.70	22.33	27.55	36.32	50.31	58.63	79.35	Market Price $
16.13*	19.07	24.30	-18.33	-14.81	26.32	33.47	40.20	18.40	36.36	NAV Return%
16.33*	17.96	24.42	-18.14	-14.69	25.82	33.93	40.17	18.08	36.88	Market Price Return%
0.60	-0.04	-0.11	-0.03	0.01	0.04	-0.01	0.01	0.02	0.01	Avg Premium/Discount%
—	-1.97	33.40	-6.44	7.29	-2.36	22.59	35.29	2.61	30.87	NAV Rtrn% +/-S&P 500
—	0.34	8.62	-7.93	-3.68	0.68	1.91	8.83	-5.81	1.96	NAV Rtrn% +/-S&P Energy
—	1	1	100	75	100	25	17	45	40	NAV Return% Rank in Cat
—	1.94	1.78	1.50	1.82	2.17	1.87	1.58	1.44	1.35	Income Return %
—	17.13	22.52	-19.83	-16.63	24.15	31.60	38.62	16.96	35.02	Capital Return %
0.00	0.45	0.48	0.49	0.48	0.48	0.51	0.57	0.72	0.79	Income $
0.00	0.00	0.00	0.00	0.00	0.00	0.00	0.00	0.00	0.00	Capital Gains $
—	0.56	0.41	0.28	0.27	0.28	0.27	0.26	0.24	0.23	Expense Ratio %
—	1.73	1.71	1.56	1.82	2.06	1.70	1.36	1.18	1.19	Income Ratio %
—	20	31	17	39	7	10	10	18	7	Turnover Rate %
—	—	—	—	289	635	1,572	2,896	3,808	6,996	Net Assets $mil

Performance 12-31-07

Historic Quarterly NAV Returns

	1st Qtr	2nd Qtr	3rd Qtr	4th Qtr	Total
2003	0.67	8.18	0.30	15.65	26.32
2004	6.66	7.80	11.56	4.05	33.47
2005	18.48	4.11	20.96	-6.04	40.20
2006	8.49	4.59	-5.30	10.19	18.40
2007	2.90	15.05	8.76	5.91	36.36

Trailing	NAV Return%	Market Return%	NAV Rtrn% +/-S&P 500	%Rank Cat.(NAV)
3 Mo	5.91	6.35	9.24	35
6 Mo	15.19	15.61	16.56	30
1 Yr	36.36	36.88	30.87	40
3 Yr Avg	31.30	31.34	22.68	1
5 Yr Avg	30.72	30.73	17.89	17
10 Yr Avg	—	—	—	—

Tax Analysis	Tax-Adj Return%	Tax-Cost Ratio
3 Yr (estimated)	30.74	0.43
5 Yr (estimated)	30.06	0.50
10 Yr (estimated)	—	—

Rating and Risk

Time Period	Morningstar Rtn vs Cat	Morningstar Risk vs Cat	Morningstar Risk-Adj Rating
3 Yr	Avg	Avg	★★★
5 Yr	Avg	-Avg	★★★
10 Yr	—	—	—

Other Measures	Standard Index S&P 500	Best Fit Index M* Energy Sec TR
Alpha	20.2	0.0
Beta	1.15	1.00
R-Squared	20	99
Standard Deviation	20.05	
Mean	31.30	
Sharpe Ratio	1.25	

Portfolio Analysis 12-31-07

Share change since 11-07 Total Stocks:35	Sector	PE	Tot Ret%	% Assets
⊕ ExxonMobil Corporation	Energy	13.6	24.34	19.58
⊕ Chevron Corporation	Energy	11.4	30.59	12.12
⊕ ConocoPhillips	Energy	13.8	25.42	8.83
⊕ Schlumberger, Ltd.	Energy	24.6	57.10	5.01
⊕ Occidental Petroleum Cor	Energy	13.8	60.25	4.35
⊕ Transocean, Inc.	Energy	16.1	77.14	3.42
⊕ Marathon Oil Corporation	Energy	9.7	34.09	3.14
⊕ Devon Energy Corporation	Energy	14.7	33.51	2.87
⊕ Valero Energy Corporatio	Energy	8.1	37.91	2.73
⊕ Apache Corporation	Energy	15.9	62.91	2.73
⊕ Hess Corporation	Ind Mtrls	19.1	104.77	2.66
⊕ National Oilwell Varco,	Energy	21.7	132.65	2.48
⊕ Halliburton Company	Energy	14.4	23.33	2.39
⊕ Anadarko Petroleum Corp.	Energy	7.9	52.04	2.37
⊕ XTO Energy, Inc.	Energy	14.7	37.60	2.06
⊕ Weatherford Internationa	Energy	23.4	64.15	1.96
⊕ Baker Hughes Inc.	Energy	17.9	9.35	1.95
⊕ Williams Companies, Inc.	Energy	27.7	38.70	1.81
⊕ EOG Resources	Energy	22.9	43.55	1.80
⊕ Chesapeake Energy Corp.	Energy	12.3	35.95	1.64

Current Investment Style

Value Blnd Growth / Large Mid Small

Market Cap	%
Giant	50.0
Large	44.4
Mid	5.6
Small	0.0
Micro	0.0
Avg $mil: 74,008	

Value Measures		Rel Category
Price/Earnings	11.92	0.73
Price/Book	2.53	1.09
Price/Sales	1.26	0.91
Price/Cash Flow	8.51	1.07
Dividend Yield %	1.17	0.85

Growth Measures	%	Rel Category
Long-Term Erngs	—	—
Book Value	17.11	1.15
Sales	7.83	0.70
Cash Flow	12.30	0.76
Historical Erngs	33.80	0.93

Profitability	%	Rel Category
Return on Equity	24.91	1.22
Return on Assets	12.43	1.32
Net Margin	15.45	1.13

Industry Weightings	% of Stocks	Rel Cat
Oil & Gas	67.3	2.0
Oil/Gas Products	4.1	1.2
Oil & Gas Srv	22.1	0.9
Pipelines	4.1	3.8
Utilities	0.0	0.0
Hard Commd	0.0	0.0
Soft Commd	0.0	0.0
Misc. Indstrl	0.0	0.0
Other	2.4	0.2

Composition

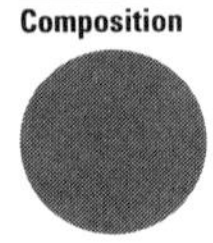

Cash	0.2
Stocks	99.8
Bonds	0.0
Other	0.0
Foreign (% of Stock)	0.0

Morningstar's Take by Haywood Kelly 12-31-07

Energy Select Sector SPDR is a high-quality portfolio, but one that deserves a large margin of safety.

The quality of the underlying companies in this ETF is high. The largest holding, at 20% of assets as of Oct. 30, is ExxonMobil, whose scale confers a wide economic moat. Each of the top 10 holdings generates positive free cash flow, and nine of those 10 pay dividends. All told, 24 of the 34 holdings have an average or below-average business risk rating.

But the shares of this ETF are volatile. Its standard deviation is among the highest among the ETFs that Morningstar covers. The stocks in the portfolio are highly levered to oil prices, and they tend to move as a group. The bulk of the assets are invested in oil producers like Exxon and Chevron, whose cash flows and share prices depend on the trajectory of oil prices. For example, if we lowered our oil-price assumptions by 10%, our fair value for Exxon would fall roughly 6% and for Chevron, 22%. And oil-services stocks--including Schlumberger and Halliburton--recently made up 22% of the portfolio. Not only are such stocks very sensitive to oil prices, but they were recently overvalued.

Volatility in itself isn't bad. What's bad is that our fair value of this ETF is so dependent on a single risk factor: our forecast of oil prices. If the oil-price forecasts built into our fair value estimates of oil stocks are imprecise, our fair value for this ETF will be wrong. With a more-diversified ETF, such forecasting errors tend to wash out. In order to recommend this ETF, we'd need to see a 20% discount to fair value.

There will undoubtedly be times when we'll pound the table for this ETF. Because our approach to forecasting commodity prices takes a long-term view--focusing on a midcycle price estimate several years out--our oil-price forecasts will be less volatile than oil prices or oil-related stocks. Given the fund's low cost (0.24%), it's an attractive way to access oil stocks when they get cheap.

Address:	c/o State Street Bk&Tr, 225 Franklin St United States 800-843-2639
Web Address:	www.spdrindex.com
Inception:	12-16-98 *
Advisor:	SSgA Funds Management Inc

Management Fee:	0.05%		
Expense Projections:	3Yr:$77	5Yr:$136	10Yr:$307
Income Distrib:	Quarterly		
Exchange:	AMEX		

Financial SPDR XLF

Market Price	Mstar Category
$28.93	Specialty-Financial

Morningstar Fair Value

Price/Fair Value Ratio	Coverage Rate %
0.76	100

Valuation

Although this ETF holds stocks from across the financial sector, many are exposed to the same risk factors: the U.S. mortgage market, the shape of the yield curve, loan-default rates, and so on. As such, we would demand at least a 15% discount to our fair value estimate before recommending it. It was recently trading at a 24% discount.

Methodology

This fund passively invests in the financial companies in the S&P 500 Index, which screens its components for profitability, industry leadership, and certain trading criteria. The stocks are weighted by market cap, so nearly half of its assets are in its largest 10 positions. The index is limited to U.S. companies, which eliminates some big international players. Banks make up roughly 43% of assets, with the remainder being in securities firms, insurance, REITs, money managers, and S&Ls.

Morningstar Rating	Return	Risk	Yield	NAV	Avg Daily Vol. (k)	52 wk High/Low
★★	Below Avg	Above Avg	3.0%	$29.10	91,694	$38.02 - $26.45

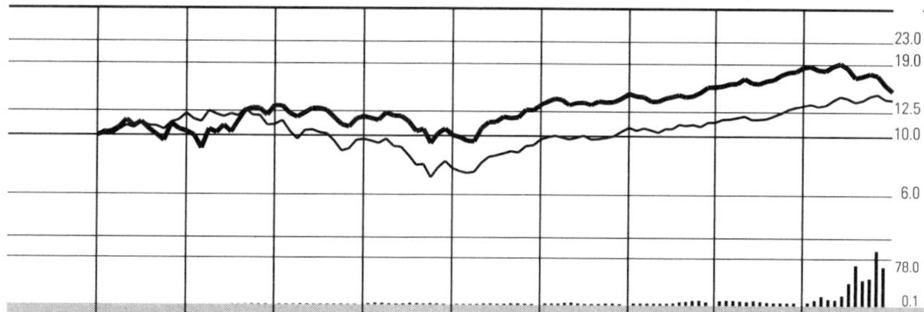

Growth of $10,000
- Investment Value of ETF
- Investment Value of Index S&P 500

Trading Volume Millions

History

1998	1999	2000	2001	2002	2003	2004	2005	2006	2007	History
23.33	23.84	29.50	26.40	22.05	28.22	30.55	31.69	36.77	29.10	NAV $
23.44	23.77	29.50	26.30	22.00	28.13	30.53	31.67	36.74	28.93	Market Price $
5.17*	3.46	25.50	-9.07	-14.88	30.60	10.58	6.20	18.90	-18.79	NAV Return%
4.44*	2.67	25.87	-9.42	-14.75	30.48	10.87	6.20	18.89	-19.19	Market Price Return%
0.47	0.02	0.42	-0.10	-0.06	-0.04	-0.06	0.00	0.01	-0.09	Avg Premium/Discount%
—	-17.58	34.60	2.82	7.22	1.92	-0.30	1.29	3.11	-24.28	NAV Rtrn% +/-S&P 500
—	-0.66	-0.20	-0.12	-0.24	-0.53	-0.33	-0.28	-0.29	-0.16	NAV Rtrn% +/-S&P Fincl
—	1	1	100	75	100	100	40	40	75	NAV Return% Rank in Cat
—	1.29	1.53	1.37	1.70	2.36	2.23	2.35	2.67	2.38	Income Return %
—	2.17	23.97	-10.44	-16.58	28.24	8.35	3.85	16.23	-21.17	Capital Return %
0.00	0.30	0.36	0.40	0.45	0.52	0.63	0.71	0.84	0.87	Income $
0.00	0.00	0.00	0.00	0.00	0.00	0.00	0.00	0.00	0.00	Capital Gains $
—	0.57	0.44	0.27	0.27	0.28	0.26	0.26	0.24	0.23	Expense Ratio %
—	1.14	1.45	1.43	1.70	2.09	2.14	2.30	2.42	2.35	Income Ratio %
—	6	7	9	11	6	9	9	11	15	Turnover Rate %
—	—	—	—	451	802	1,140	1,872	2,301	5,052	Net Assets $mil

Performance 12-31-07

Historic Quarterly NAV Returns

	1st Qtr	2nd Qtr	3rd Qtr	4th Qtr	Total
2003	-5.16	18.37	4.12	11.74	30.60
2004	4.79	-2.43	0.31	7.82	10.58
2005	-6.42	4.25	0.67	8.15	6.20
2006	3.18	-0.16	7.91	6.96	18.90
2007	-2.90	2.05	-4.31	-14.35	-18.79

Trailing	NAV Return%	Market Return%	NAV Rtrn% +/-S&P 500	%Rank Cat.(NAV)
3 Mo	-14.35	-14.95	-11.02	83
6 Mo	-18.05	-18.73	-16.68	75
1 Yr	-18.79	-19.19	-24.28	75
3 Yr Avg	0.84	0.67	-7.78	80
5 Yr Avg	8.17	8.10	-4.66	75
10 Yr Avg	—	—	—	—

Tax Analysis	Tax-Adj Return%	Tax-Cost Ratio
3 Yr (estimated)	-0.02	0.85
5 Yr (estimated)	7.30	0.80
10 Yr (estimated)	—	—

Rating and Risk

Time Period	Morningstar Rtn vs Cat	Morningstar Risk vs Cat	Morningstar Risk-Adj Rating
3 Yr	Avg	+Avg	★★★
5 Yr	-Avg	+Avg	★★
10 Yr	—	—	—

Other Measures	Standard Index S&P 500	Best Fit Index DJ Finance
Alpha	-7.5	-0.6
Beta	1.09	1.02
R-Squared	58	98
Standard Deviation	11.11	
Mean	0.84	
Sharpe Ratio	-0.26	

Portfolio Analysis 12-31-07

Share change since 11-07 Total Stocks:92	Sector	PE	Tot Ret%	% Assets
⊕ Bank of America Corporat	Financial	9.4	-19.25	8.02
⊕ American International G	Financial	10.2	-17.96	6.48
⊕ Citigroup, Inc.	Financial	7.9	-44.93	6.44
⊕ J.P. Morgan Chase & Co.	Financial	9.5	-7.24	6.42
⊕ Wells Fargo Company	Financial	11.4	-12.13	4.46
⊕ Goldman Sachs Group, Inc	Financial	8.8	8.59	3.75
⊕ Wachovia Corporation	Financial	8.6	-29.91	3.29
⊕ American Express Company	Financial	14.9	-13.18	2.66
⊕ Morgan Stanley	Financial	6.1	-20.21	2.47
⊕ Bank of New York Mellon	Financial	21.7	26.51	2.43
⊕ US Bancorp	Financial	12.2	-7.89	2.40
⊕ Merrill Lynch & Company,	Financial	12.2	-41.32	2.01
⊕ Metropolitan Life Insura	Financial	12.3	4.94	2.00
⊕ Prudential Financial, In	Financial	12.1	9.72	1.85
⊕ Fannie Mae	Financial	24.1	-30.45	1.71
⊕ Chicago Mercantile Excha	Financial	48.5	35.37	1.65
⊕ The Travelers Companies,	Financial	7.8	2.37	1.52
⊕ Lehman Brothers Holdings	Financial	8.8	-15.52	1.52
⊕ State Street Corporation	Financial	21.3	21.92	1.37
⊕ Aflac, Inc.	Financial	19.6	38.00	1.34

Current Investment Style

Value Blnd Growth; Large Mid Small

Market Cap	%
Giant	49.3
Large	37.1
Mid	13.4
Small	0.1
Micro	0.0
Avg $mil: 45,001	

Value Measures		Rel Category
Price/Earnings	10.53	0.88
Price/Book	1.37	0.93
Price/Sales	1.80	0.88
Price/Cash Flow	12.78	1.09
Dividend Yield %	3.17	1.09

Growth Measures	%	Rel Category
Long-Term Erngs	—	—
Book Value	8.15	0.76
Sales	6.54	0.84
Cash Flow	32.48	2.10
Historical Erngs	14.85	0.81

Profitability	%	Rel Category
Return on Equity	17.15	1.01
Return on Assets	2.44	0.84
Net Margin	22.30	1.00

Industry Weightings	% of Stocks	Rel Cat
Intl Banks	26.1	1.5
Banks	17.8	0.8
Real Estate	5.7	2.3
Sec Mgmt	16.0	1.2
S & Ls	1.5	0.3
Prop & Reins	13.8	0.9
Life Ins	7.7	1.2
Misc. Ins	2.4	0.8
Other	9.1	0.6

Composition

Cash	0.9
Stocks	99.1
Bonds	0.0
Other	0.0
Foreign (% of Stock)	0.0

Morningstar's Take by Haywood Kelly 12-31-07

Financial Select Sector SPDR is a bet on large-cap U.S. financials.

Going into 2007, we felt this ETF was slightly undervalued. But it's gotten cheaper ... and cheaper ... and cheaper. Financial stocks have taken a licking from the U.S. mortgage market meltdown. Three top-10 holdings--Citigroup, Merrill Lynch, and Wachovia--dropped at least 30% apiece in 2007. The fund as a whole fell 25 percentage points shy of the S&P 500 last year.

But this ETF has three things going for it. First and most obviously, its holdings are very cheap. Nine of the top 10 holdings earn 5 stars as of Dec. 31, 2007, and the overall price of the ETF is just 76% of what we think the fair value of the underlying stocks is. Even if we're wrong on the fair values, this gives us a plump margin of safety--easily exceeding the 15% threshold we demand before recommending a fund like this. Our analysts think the kind of large-cap financials that dominate this portfolio have been punished much too severely by the market.

Secondly, the portfolio is packed with high-quality financial names from across the financial sector. Wide-moat firms make up 55% of the portfolio, and you have to go down to the 14th largest holding (Prudential) before finding a company without at least a narrow moat. About 43% of the fund's assets are in banks, which tend to earn wide- or narrow-moat ratings thanks to high customer switching costs. There are several ETFs that focus exclusively on banks and therefore sport even greater exposure to wide-moat firms. The trade-off is that this ETF offers some added diversification, with hefty stakes in insurance firms, investment banks, as well as a smattering of REITs and money-management firms.

Finally, with an expense ratio of just 0.24%, the fund is a low-cost way to buy financial stocks. When financial stocks appear cheap--and they certainly do to us right now--this ETF provides a good way to gain exposure.

Address:	c/o State Street Bk&Tr, 225 Franklin St United States 800-843-2639
Web Address:	www.spdrindex.com
Inception:	12-16-98*
Advisor:	SSgA Funds Management Inc

Management Fee:	0.05%		
Expense Projections:	3Yr:$77	5Yr:$136	10Yr:$307
Income Distrib:	Quarterly		
Exchange:	AMEX		

Health Care Sel SPDR XLV

Market Price	Mstar Category
$35.31	Specialty-Health

Morningstar Fair Value

Price/Fair Value Ratio	Coverage Rate %
0.90	99

Valuation

The fund's portfolio contains high-quality firms, and many of the stock-specific risks cancel one another out. As such, it hasn't been much more volatile than the market as a whole. Thus, we'd demand only an 8% discount to our fair value estimate to recommend it. The fund was recently trading at a 10% discount, making it a bargain.

Methodology

This ETF owns the health-care companies in the S&P 500, weighted according to market cap. These include firms focused on drugs (both big pharma and biotech), health-care equipment and supplies, hospitals, medical devices, and health insurers. Because the index draws its constituents from the broader S&P 500, it has an inherent quality screen. S&P 500 holdings have to meet the standards of the S&P's selection committee, and this includes profitability and status as a leading U.S. company. The criteria eliminate foreign health-care companies.

Morningstar Rating	Return	Risk	Yield	NAV	Avg Daily Vol. (k)	52 wk High/Low
★★	Below Avg	Below Avg	1.6%	$35.25	2,086	$36.82 - $33.08

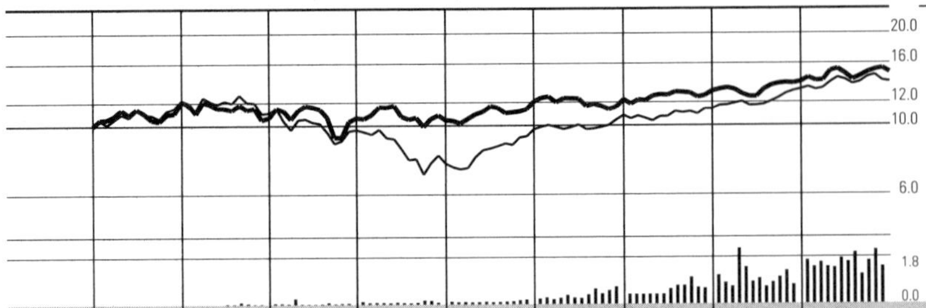

1998	1999	2000	2001	2002	2003	2004	2005	2006	2007	History
25.93	30.96	27.32	27.19	26.54	30.09	30.18	31.72	33.50	35.25	NAV $
26.00	30.89	27.25	26.95	26.55	30.15	30.19	31.72	33.49	35.31	Market Price $
5.33*	20.10	-11.57	-0.20	-1.66	14.75	1.44	6.44	7.10	6.92	NAV Return%
5.36*	19.51	-11.60	-0.82	-0.75	14.92	1.28	6.41	7.05	7.16	Market Price Return%
0.27	-0.08	-0.09	-0.24	0.10	0.01	0.10	0.01	0.02	-0.03	Avg Premium/Discount%
—	-0.94	-2.47	11.69	20.44	-13.93	-9.44	1.53	-8.69	1.43	NAV Rtrn% +/-S&P 500
—	30.76	-48.62	11.75	17.16	-0.31	-0.32	-0.02	-0.43	-0.23	NAV Rtrn% +/-S&P Health
—	60	60	31	1	93	100	75	34	59	NAV Return% Rank in Cat
—	0.00	0.17	0.27	0.73	1.31	1.14	1.32	1.42	1.71	Income Return %
—	20.10	-11.74	-0.47	-2.39	13.44	0.30	5.12	5.68	5.21	Capital Return %
0.00	0.00	0.05	0.07	0.20	0.35	0.34	0.40	0.45	0.57	Income $
0.00	0.18	0.01	0.00	0.00	0.00	0.00	0.00	0.00	0.00	Capital Gains $
—	0.57	0.42	0.28	0.28	0.28	0.27	0.26	0.24	0.23	Expense Ratio %
—	-0.11	0.10	0.26	0.49	1.21	1.20	1.20	1.40	1.64	Income Ratio %
—	15	22	28	103	6	7	3	4	10	Turnover Rate %
—	—	—	—	158	454	1,053	1,787	1,843	2,446	Net Assets $mil

Performance 12-31-07

Historic Quarterly NAV Returns

	1st Qtr	2nd Qtr	3rd Qtr	4th Qtr	Total
2003	0.94	9.86	-4.51	8.37	14.75
2004	-0.49	2.61	-5.51	5.14	1.44
2005	-0.68	4.08	1.50	1.44	6.44
2006	1.14	-5.12	10.10	1.37	7.10
2007	0.91	5.02	1.00	-0.10	6.92

Trailing	NAV Return%	Market Return%	NAV Rtrn% +/-S&P 500	%Rank Cat.(NAV)
3 Mo	-0.10	0.25	3.23	36
6 Mo	0.90	0.71	2.27	37
1 Yr	6.92	7.16	1.43	59
3 Yr Avg	6.82	6.87	-1.80	75
5 Yr Avg	7.25	7.28	-5.58	100
10 Yr Avg	—	—	—	—

Tax Analysis	Tax-Adj Return%	Tax-Cost Ratio
3 Yr (estimated)	6.29	0.50
5 Yr (estimated)	6.75	0.47
10 Yr (estimated)	—	—

Rating and Risk

Time Period	Morningstar Rtn vs Cat	Morningstar Risk vs Cat	Morningstar Risk-Adj Rating
3 Yr	Avg	Avg	★★★
5 Yr	Low	-Avg	★
10 Yr	—	—	—

Other Measures	Standard Index S&P 500	Best Fit Index DJ Health
Alpha	-0.1	-1.1
Beta	0.66	1.06
R-Squared	32	99
Standard Deviation	9.01	
Mean	6.82	
Sharpe Ratio	0.30	

Portfolio Analysis 12-31-07

Share change since 11-07 Total Stocks:51	Sector	PE	Tot Ret%	% Assets
⊖ Johnson & Johnson	Health	18.8	3.61	12.33
⊖ Pfizer Inc.	Health	22.5	-8.15	10.03
⊖ Merck & Co., Inc.	Health	23.6	37.36	8.17
⊖ UnitedHealth Group, Inc.	Health	17.4	8.38	4.90
⊖ Abbott Laboratories	Health	45.7	18.04	4.75
⊖ Wyeth	Health	13.6	-11.36	3.83
⊖ Medtronic, Inc.	Health	20.3	-5.22	3.69
⊖ Bristol-Myers Squibb Com	Health	24.8	4.75	3.41
⊖ Eli Lilly & Company	Health	26.0	5.65	3.40
⊖ WellPoint, Inc.	Health	16.4	11.49	3.32
⊖ Amgen, Inc.	Health	16.8	-32.02	3.26
⊖ Schering-Plough Corporat	Health	21.0	13.66	2.82
⊖ Gilead Sciences, Inc.	Health	—	41.72	2.77
⊖ Baxter International Inc	Health	22.9	26.79	2.41
⊖ Aetna, Inc.	Health	16.9	33.79	1.92
⊖ Medco Health Solutions,	Health	31.1	89.78	1.80
⊖ Thermo Fisher Scientific	Health	48.5	27.36	1.58
⊖ Covidien, Ltd.	Health	—	—	1.42
⊖ Cardinal Health, Inc.	Health	26.5	-9.74	1.36
⊖ Becton, Dickinson and Co	Health	24.9	20.72	1.35

Current Investment Style

Value Blnd Growth (Large Mid Small)

Market Cap	%
Giant	51.3
Large	41.0
Mid	7.7
Small	0.0
Micro	0.0

Avg $mil: 52,349

Value Measures		Rel Category
Price/Earnings	15.42	0.72
Price/Book	3.36	0.99
Price/Sales	1.60	0.55
Price/Cash Flow	12.60	0.97
Dividend Yield %	1.49	1.91

Growth Measures	%	Rel Category
Long-Term Erngs	—	—
Book Value	6.12	1.00
Sales	10.01	0.97
Cash Flow	9.16	0.72
Historical Erngs	12.97	0.14

Profitability	%	Rel Category
Return on Equity	19.27	2.59
Return on Assets	9.09	20.66
Net Margin	14.21	2.79

Industry Weightings	% of Stocks	Rel Cat
Biotech	11.2	0.3
Drugs	54.4	1.9
Mgd Care	15.2	1.8
Hospitals	0.2	0.3
Other HC Srv	0.0	0.0
Diagnostics	1.1	0.8
Equipment	14.4	0.9
Good/Srv	3.0	0.6
Other	0.5	0.2

Composition

Cash	0.5
Stocks	99.5
Bonds	0.0
Other	0.0
Foreign (% of Stock)	0.0

Morningstar's Take by Haywood Kelly 12-31-07

Health Care Select Sector SPDR is a low-cost way to buy a portfolio of drug stocks.

An ETF makes a lot of sense for health-care investors. No matter how deep your knowledge of individual stocks, you can always be shocked by a bolt from the blue. Think of Merck's Vioxx, or Wyeth's fen-phen, or Boston Scientific's drug-eluting stents. A product can be wildly successful one year, and spawn thousands of lawsuits the next.

Such company-specific risks get diversified away in the ETF format. Granted, all health-care companies face the risk of Congress changing the rules--whether it's Medicare reimbursement, nationalized health care, or stricter Food and Drug Administration guidelines--which could potentially hammer all the stocks in this portfolio to some degree. But by buying at a discount to the intrinsic value of the portfolio, an investor can mitigate even this risk.

Among health-care ETFs, the SPDR is a strong choice. Its expense ratio is just 0.24%, and its portfolio is chock-full of high-quality firms. Nine of the top 10 holdings sport wide-moat ratings; for the portfolio as a whole, 65% of assets are in wide-moat stocks. The top two holdings, Johnson & Johnson and Pfizer, generate more than $20 billion in annual free cash flow combined--an indication of just how profitable the best health-care companies are.

Given the high-quality nature of the portfolio, we'd recommend this ETF whenever it trades for more than an 8% discount to the intrinsic value of its underlying stocks. Keep in mind that although the fund invests in stocks throughout the health-care sector, you're really getting fairly concentrated exposure to drugmakers. Eight of the top 10 holdings are drugmakers, and the top 10 stocks make up a hefty 60% of the assets of the fund.

Address:	c/o State Street Bk&Tr, 225 Franklin St United States 800-843-2639
Web Address:	www.spdrindex.com
Inception:	12-16-98 *
Advisor:	SSgA Funds Management Inc

Management Fee:	0.05%		
Expense Projections:	3Yr:$77	5Yr:$136	10Yr:$307
Income Distrib:	Quarterly		
Exchange:	AMEX		

Industrial SPDR XLI

Market Price	Mstar Category
$39.16	Large Blend

Morningstar Rating	Return	Risk	Yield	NAV	Avg Daily Vol. (k)	52 wk High/Low
★★★★	Above Avg	Above Avg	1.5%	$39.11	4,085	$41.90 - $34.75

Morningstar Fair Value

Price/Fair Value Ratio	Coverage Rate %
0.92	100

Valuation

We would demand an 8% discount to our fair value estimate before recommending this ETF. Despite having 20% of assets in a single stock, the mature nature of the fund's top holdings and their exposure to many different parts of the global economy limit volatility. The fund was recently trading at a 9% discount, making it a bargain in our eyes.

Methodology

This fund owns industrial companies in the S&P 500. The holdings, which are market-cap-weighted, include manufacturers, builders, railroads, package delivery companies, and aerospace and defense contractors. The fund is top-heavy: The top 10 names soak up roughly half of assets, and one name, General Electric, recently accounted for 20% of the fund. Because the index draws its constituents from the broader S&P 500, it has an inherent quality screen. S&P 500 holdings have to meet the standards of the S&P's selection committee, which include profitability and status as a leading U.S. company.

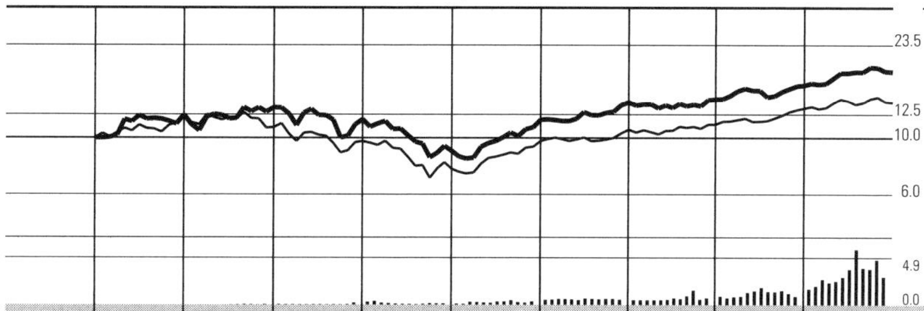

Growth of $10,000
— Investment Value of ETF
— Investment Value of Index S&P 500

Trading Volume Millions

History

1998	1999	2000	2001	2002	2003	2004	2005	2006	2007	History
24.37	29.58	31.29	27.73	20.55	26.84	31.08	31.43	35.05	39.11	NAV $
24.56	29.61	31.25	27.70	20.59	26.76	31.07	31.42	35.01	39.16	Market Price $
7.76*	23.06	6.97	-10.21	-24.81	32.50	17.44	2.75	13.61	13.20	NAV Return%
7.45*	22.23	6.73	-10.19	-24.58	31.85	17.75	2.74	13.51	13.48	Market Price Return%
0.78	0.10	0.08	0.01	0.10	0.03	0.02	0.03	-0.02	0.00	Avg Premium/Discount%
—	2.02	16.07	1.68	-2.71	3.82	6.56	-2.16	-2.18	7.71	NAV Rtrn% +/-S&P 500
—	1.56	1.09	-4.47	1.53	0.30	-0.60	0.43	0.32	1.17	NAV Rtrn% +/-S&P Industr
—	1	1	80	100	20	15	78	83	11	NAV Return% Rank in Cat
—	1.22	1.13	1.09	1.20	1.68	1.51	1.58	2.03	1.63	Income Return %
—	21.84	5.84	-11.30	-26.01	30.82	15.93	1.17	11.58	11.57	Capital Return %
0.00	0.30	0.33	0.34	0.33	0.34	0.40	0.49	0.63	0.57	Income $
0.00	0.08	0.00	0.00	0.00	0.00	0.00	0.00	0.00	0.00	Capital Gains $
—	0.57	0.44	0.28	0.28	0.27	0.28	0.25	0.24	0.23	Expense Ratio %
—	0.94	1.10	1.25	1.26	1.59	1.44	1.54	1.67	1.69	Income Ratio %
—	12	42	7	58	15	3	6	3	7	Turnover Rate %
—	—	—	—	235	586	780	886	1,070	1,663	Net Assets $mil

Performance 12-31-07

Historic Quarterly NAV Returns

	1st Qtr	2nd Qtr	3rd Qtr	4th Qtr	Total
2003	-5.88	16.18	4.48	15.97	32.50
2004	-1.00	8.41	-0.64	10.13	17.44
2005	-1.81	-3.10	2.92	4.93	2.75
2006	7.90	0.36	-0.99	5.95	13.61
2007	1.74	9.96	5.37	-3.97	13.20

Trailing	NAV Return%	Market Return%	NAV Rtrn% +/-S&P 500	%Rank Cat.(NAV)
3 Mo	-3.97	-4.22	-0.64	65
6 Mo	1.19	1.29	2.56	22
1 Yr	13.20	13.48	7.71	11
3 Yr Avg	9.73	9.79	1.11	29
5 Yr Avg	15.51	15.49	2.68	8
10 Yr Avg	—	—	—	—

Tax Analysis	Tax-Adj Return%	Tax-Cost Ratio
3 Yr (estimated)	9.11	0.57
5 Yr (estimated)	14.88	0.55
10 Yr (estimated)	—	—

Rating and Risk

Time Period	Morningstar Rtn vs Cat	Morningstar Risk vs Cat	Morningstar Risk-Adj Rating
3 Yr	+Avg	+Avg	★★★★
5 Yr	+Avg	+Avg	★★★★
10 Yr	—	—	—

Other Measures	Standard Index S&P 500	Best Fit Index M* Inds Mat TR
Alpha	1.7	-2.7
Beta	0.87	0.92
R-Squared	53	88
Standard Deviation	9.31	
Mean	9.73	
Sharpe Ratio	0.59	

Portfolio Analysis 12-31-07

Share change since 11-07 Total Stocks:56

Holding	Sector	PE	Tot Ret%	% Assets
⊖ General Electric Company	Ind Mtrls	16.6	2.69	18.23
⊖ United Technologies	Ind Mtrls	18.8	24.46	5.17
⊖ United Parcel Service, I	Business	18.2	-3.50	4.97
⊖ Boeing Company	Ind Mtrls	16.9	-0.11	4.65
⊖ 3M Company	Ind Mtrls	14.1	10.53	4.05
⊖ Caterpillar Inc.	Ind Mtrls	14.0	20.48	3.23
⊖ Honeywell International,	Ind Mtrls	20.8	38.65	3.19
⊖ Emerson Electric Company	Ind Mtrls	21.3	31.42	3.10
⊕ Deere & Company	Ind Mtrls	23.3	98.60	3.03
⊖ General Dynamics	Ind Mtrls	18.6	21.35	2.56
⊖ Lockheed Martin Corporat	Ind Mtrls	15.3	15.99	2.54
⊖ Union Pacific Corporatio	Business	18.4	38.33	2.36
⊖ FedEx Corporation	Business	13.9	-17.61	1.94
⊖ Northrop Grumman Corpora	Ind Mtrls	15.4	18.46	1.89
⊖ Raytheon Company	Ind Mtrls	21.5	17.02	1.87
⊖ Burlington Northern Sant	Business	16.5	14.30	1.84
⊖ Danaher Corporation	Ind Mtrls	23.2	21.29	1.64
⊖ Cummins, Inc.	Ind Mtrls	17.5	115.26	1.58
⊖ Illinois Tool Works, Inc	Ind Mtrls	16.4	18.00	1.55
⊖ PACCAR, Inc.	Ind Mtrls	15.2	29.91	1.53

Current Investment Style

Value Blnd Growth / Large Mid Small

Market Cap	%
Giant	37.3
Large	47.5
Mid	15.2
Small	0.0
Micro	0.0

Avg $mil: 43,661

Value Measures		Rel Category
Price/Earnings	15.49	0.98
Price/Book	3.24	1.27
Price/Sales	1.33	1.07
Price/Cash Flow	9.48	1.02
Dividend Yield %	1.88	0.99

Growth Measures	%	Rel Category
Long-Term Erngs	—	—
Book Value	4.44	0.48
Sales	8.31	1.02
Cash Flow	10.66	1.22
Historical Erngs	20.97	1.25

Profitability	%	Rel Category
Return on Equity	25.06	1.13
Return on Assets	7.71	0.92
Net Margin	9.40	0.77

Sector Weightings	% of Stocks	Rel S&P 500	3 Year High	3 Year Low
Info	0.88	0.04		
Software	0.00	0.00	0	0
Hardware	0.88	0.09	1	1
Media	0.00	0.00	0	0
Telecom	0.00	0.00	0	0
Service	23.88	0.59		
Health	0.48	0.04	1	0
Consumer	0.00	0.00	3	0
Business	23.40	5.31	26	22
Financial	0.00	0.00	0	0
Mfg	75.24	1.96		
Goods	0.00	0.00	0	0
Ind Mtrls	75.24	5.79	76	72
Energy	0.00	0.00	0	0
Utilities	0.00	0.00	0	0

Composition

Cash	0.5
Stocks	99.5
Bonds	0.0
Other	0.0
Foreign (% of Stock)	0.0

Morningstar's Take by Haywood Kelly 12-31-07

Despite its big position in one stock, Industrial Select Sector SPDR is a fairly diversified play on the global economy.

General Electric makes up 20% of this portfolio, so our opinion on that stock will weigh heavily on our opinion on this ETF as a whole. As it is, we're fairly bullish on GE's prospects. Over the next five years, we think revenues will increase at 10% annually, including acquisitions, and we also expect operating profits to increase at nearly 13% annually. Fueling GE's growth is global demand for better infrastructure. Worldwide demand for aviation, rail, energy, and water infrastructure is creating huge orders for GE products. And given the diversified nature of GE's business, parking 20% of the portfolio's assets in the stock isn't quite as risky a bet as it might seem.

What's true of GE is true to some extent of the portfolio as a whole. It's a group of firms with lots of exposure to global markets and global trade. Top five holdings Boeing, United Technologies, UPS, and 3M all have significant revenues outside the U.S., so they all benefit from strong global growth and a weak dollar. And the portfolio doesn't deviate all that far from the makeup of the S&P 500 as a whole. About 45% of the fund's assets are in wide-moat firms--not all that far from the U.S. market. The average growth rates are also right in line with those of the market.

Whether we recommend the fund, of course, comes down to valuation. Unless we thought GE was dramatically over- or undervalued, we're likely to be neutral. The other stocks in the portfolio come from a grab-bag of industries--transportation, machinery, electrical equipment, aerospace, engineering--and many of them operate in multiple geographical and product markets. With this kind of diversity, we're unlikely to think them over- or undervalued as a group. Rather, valuations will typically be all over the board and not fall to a deep discount or rise to a steep premium.

Address:	c/o State Street Bk&Tr, 225 Franklin St United States 800-843-2639
Web Address:	www.spdrindex.com
Inception:	12-16-98 *
Advisor:	SSgA Funds Management Inc

Management Fee:	0.05%		
Expense Projections:	3Yr:$77	5Yr:$136	10Yr:$307
Income Distrib:	Quarterly		
Exchange:	AMEX		

Internet HOLDRs HHH

Market Price	Mstar Category
$59.20	Large Growth

Morningstar Fair Value

Price/Fair Value Ratio	Coverage Rate %
0.90	97

Valuation

We'd demand a 15% margin of safety before recommending these shares. Although the portfolio is very concentrated, the underlying companies don't necessarily move together, which helps cancel out firm-specific risks. Our fair values on the top holdings will drive our opinion of this fund, which was recently trading at a 7% discount.

Methodology

The fund passively invests in a small group of Internet stocks. Offered by Merrill Lynch, HOLDRs differ from other ETFs in that they can be bought only in 100-share increments, investors can exchange their shares for the underlying stocks at any time (for a fee of up to $10), investors receive spin-off shares outside of their HOLDRs investment just as if they held the underlying stock directly, and rather than an annual expense ratio, the fund charges $0.08 per share in annual custody fees (which are waived if the underlying securities fail to generate enough income to cover them).

Morningstar Rating	Return	Risk	Yield	NAV	Avg Daily Vol. (k)	52 wk High/Low
—	—	—	—	$59.20	143	$67.60 - $52.43

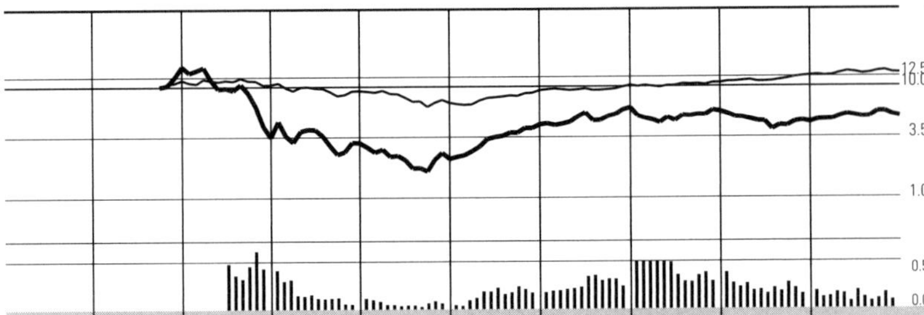

1998	1999	2000	2001	2002	2003	2004	2005	2006	2007	History
59.20	169.06	38.75	34.57	24.80	50.19	71.31	65.83	52.41	59.20	NAV $
—	169.06	38.75	34.57	24.80	50.19	71.31	65.83	52.41	59.20	Market Price $
—	—	-77.08	-10.79	-28.26	102.38	42.08	-7.68	-20.39	12.96	NAV Return%
—	-7.03*	-77.08	-10.79	-28.26	102.38	42.08	-7.68	-20.39	12.96	Market Price Return%
—	—	—	—	—	—	—	—	—	—	Avg Premium/Discount%
—	—	-67.98	1.10	-6.16	73.70	31.20	-12.59	-36.18	7.47	NAV Rtrn% +/-S&P 500
—	—	-54.66	9.63	-0.38	72.63	35.78	-12.94	-29.46	1.15	NAV Rtrn% +/-Russ 1000Gr
—	—	2	2	5	1	1	11	13	22	NAV Return% Rank in Cat
—	—	—	—	—	—	—	—	—	—	Income Return %
—	—	—	—	—	—	—	—	—	—	Capital Return %
—	0.00	0.00	0.00	0.00	0.00	0.00	0.00	0.00	0.00	Income $
—	0.00	0.00	0.00	0.00	0.00	0.00	0.00	0.00	0.00	Capital Gains $
—	—	—	—	—	—	—	—	—	—	Expense Ratio %
—	—	—	—	—	—	—	—	—	—	Income Ratio %
—	—	—	—	—	—	—	—	—	—	Turnover Rate %
—	—	—	—	—	—	—	—	343	393	Net Assets $mil

Performance 12-31-07

Historic Quarterly NAV Returns

	1st Qtr	2nd Qtr	3rd Qtr	4th Qtr	Total
2003	16.94	33.97	9.40	18.09	102.38
2004	1.41	26.48	-7.33	19.53	42.08
2005	-22.63	-1.81	13.49	7.08	-7.68
2006	-11.65	-8.36	-8.72	7.73	-20.39
2007	6.45	7.64	8.81	-9.40	12.96

Trailing	NAV Return%	Market Return%	NAV Rtrn% +/-S&P 500	%Rank Cat.(NAV)
3 Mo	-9.40	-9.40	-6.07	94
6 Mo	-1.42	-1.42	-0.05	83
1 Yr	12.96	12.96	7.47	22
3 Yr Avg	-6.02	-6.02	-14.64	100
5 Yr Avg	19.01	19.01	6.18	1
10 Yr Avg	—	—	—	—

Tax Analysis	Tax-Adj Return%	Tax-Cost Ratio
3 Yr (estimated)	—	—
5 Yr (estimated)	—	—
10 Yr (estimated)	—	—

Rating and Risk

Time Period	Morningstar Rtn vs Cat	Morningstar Risk vs Cat	Morningstar Risk-Adj Rating
3 Yr	—	—	—
5 Yr	—	—	—
10 Yr	—	—	—

Other Measures	Standard Index S&P 500	Best Fit Index
Alpha	—	—
Beta	—	—
R-Squared	—	—
Standard Deviation	—	
Mean	-6.02	
Sharpe Ratio	—	

Portfolio Analysis 12-31-07

Share change since 10-07 Total Stocks:12	Sector	PE	Tot Ret%	% Assets
Amazon.com, Inc.	Consumer	NMF	134.77	28.61
eBay, Inc.	Consumer	—	10.38	25.77
Yahoo, Inc.	Media	45.7	-8.93	20.37
Time Warner, Inc.	Media	13.4	-23.27	11.30
McAfee, Inc.	Software	32.9	32.14	4.15
Priceline.com, Inc.	Consumer	36.6	163.38	3.80
Ameritrade Holding	Financial	18.9	23.98	2.94
Earthlink, Inc.	Telecom	—	-0.42	0.81
RealNetworks, Inc.	Business	12.4	-44.33	0.79
E*Trade Financial Corpor	Financial	3.5	-84.17	0.68
CNET Networks, Inc.	Media	—	0.44	0.58
☼ Cmgi	Software	13.2	-2.02	0.21

Morningstar's Take by Haywood Kelly 12-31-07

If you like eBay, Yahoo, and Amazon, you'll like Internet HOLDRs.

Merrill Lynch's suite of Internet-related HOLDRs have been some of the worst investment vehicles ever. Launched in the heyday of the tech bubble, they're a classic case of a fund shop creating products at the worst possible time. As for this ETF, the collapse of the tech bubble devastated its returns. Since its inception in the fall of 1999, the fund has lost an annualized 23%.

The initial holdings of the fund included such illustrious names as CMGI, Exodus Communications, Inktomi, Lycos, Go2Net, and Earthlink. As such companies went bankrupt, got acquired, or simply fizzled out, the number of positions in the HOLDR has shrunk from the initial 20 to just 11 currently. (An oddity of the HOLDR structure is that the portfolio is not periodically reconstituted as with most other ETFs.) Three stocks now dominate the portfolio: eBay, Amazon, and Yahoo. Each of these bubble survivors represents about 25% of the portfolio.

Given the very different characteristics of these three firms--after all, "the Internet" is not a single industry--our opinions of them won't necessarily be congruent. As of mid-December 2007, for example, we think both eBay and Yahoo are undervalued enough to earn 5 stars. Amazon, by contrast, trades for double our fair value estimate. Adding up all the fair values and comparing them to the market price, the fund trades for about a 10% discount to what we think the underlying holdings are worth.

That's not quite enough for us to recommend the fund--we'd require a 15% discount to do that. But we certainly think the next seven years will be better for this fund than the first seven. The underlying stocks are attractively priced, and the quality of the top holdings is high. Of the top five holdings, three earn wide-moat ratings from Morningstar and two earn narrow-moat ratings.

Address:	4 World Financial Center United States 800-637-7455
Web Address:	www.holdrs.com
Inception:	09-22-99
Advisor:	Merrill Lynch Pierce Fenner & Smith

Management Fee:	—
Expense Projections:	3Yr: — 5Yr: — 10Yr: —
Income Distrib:	Quarterly
Exchange:	AMEX

Current Investment Style

Value Blnd Growth; Large Mid Small

Market Cap	%
Giant	11.3
Large	74.7
Mid	10.9
Small	3.1
Micro	0.0
Avg $mil: 29,710	

Value Measures		Rel Category
Price/Earnings	26.81	1.38
Price/Book	3.04	0.90
Price/Sales	2.73	1.55
Price/Cash Flow	17.47	1.51
Dividend Yield %	0.30	0.35

Growth Measures	%	Rel Category
Long-Term Erngs	—	—
Book Value	11.15	1.10
Sales	17.54	1.81
Cash Flow	13.55	1.25
Historical Erngs	7.85	0.44

Profitability	%	Rel Category
Return on Equity	18.85	0.82
Return on Assets	4.87	0.50
Net Margin	6.79	0.53

Sector Weightings	% of Stocks	Rel S&P 500	3 Year High	3 Year Low
Info	37.41	1.79		
Software	4.36	1.05	4	4
Hardware	0.00	0.00	0	0
Media	32.24	11.08	47	32
Telecom	0.81	0.22	1	1
Service	62.59	1.54		
Health	0.00	0.00	0	0
Consumer	58.18	8.58	58	41
Business	0.79	0.18	2	1
Financial	3.62	0.21	8	3
Mfg	0.00	0.00		
Goods	0.00	0.00	0	0
Ind Mtrls	0.00	0.00	0	0
Energy	0.00	0.00	0	0
Utilities	0.00	0.00	0	0

Composition

Cash	0.0
Stocks	100.0
Bonds	0.0
Other	0.0
Foreign (% of Stock)	0.0

iShares C&S Realty ICF

Market Price	Mstar Category
$79.14	Specialty-Real Estate

Morningstar Fair Value

Price/Fair Value Ratio	Coverage Rate %
0.98	100

Valuation

Though this portfolio is well-diversified across the main property classes, all of the holdings remain more or less subject to a common risk factor--the trajectory of the real estate market. For that reason, we'd require a 16% discount to our fair value estimate before recommending it. The fund was recently trading at a 2% discount.

Methodology

This exchange-traded fund tracks the Cohen & Steers Realty Majors Index. The benchmark includes office, industrial, apartments, and retail REITs that meet the liquidity and quality standards of real estate investment firm Cohen & Steers' investment committee--usually about 30 stocks. Index constituents can't exceed 8% of assets. The bogy is rebalanced quarterly.

Morningstar Rating	Return	Risk	Yield	NAV	Avg Daily Vol. (k)	52 wk High/Low
★★★	Above Avg	High	4.1%	$79.22	1,099	$115.76 - $70.79

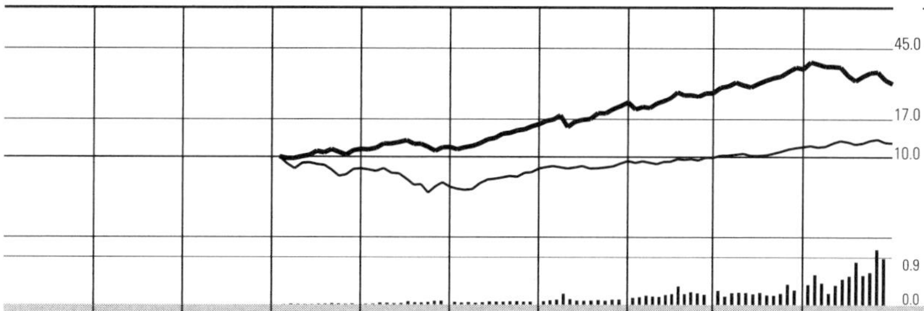

1998	1999	2000	2001	2002	2003	2004	2005	2006	2007	History
—	—	—	42.19	40.70	52.95	68.31	74.72	100.51	79.22	NAV $
—	—	—	42.15	40.77	53.04	68.16	74.84	100.30	79.14	Market Price $
—	—	—	15.74*	2.98	36.78	35.21	14.14	39.03	-18.30	NAV Return%
—	—	—	15.73*	3.26	36.75	34.68	14.57	38.52	-18.21	Market Price Return%
—	—	—	0.06	0.04	-0.02	0.00	0.10	-0.03	-0.09	Avg Premium/Discount%
—	—	—	—	25.08	8.10	24.33	9.23	23.24	-23.79	NAV Rtrn% +/-S&P 500
—	—	—	—	-0.60	0.60	2.05	0.32	3.06	-0.74	NAV Rtrn% +/-DJ Real Est
—	—	—	—	50	34	1	25	1	100	NAV Return% Rank in Cat
—	—	—	—	6.61	5.00	4.47	3.35	2.79	3.24	Income Return %
—	—	—	—	-3.63	31.78	30.74	10.79	36.24	-21.54	Capital Return %
—	—	—	2.18	2.72	2.00	2.32	2.25	2.06	3.22	Income $
—	—	—	0.00	0.10	0.36	0.52	0.72	0.90	0.00	Capital Gains $
—	—	—	0.35	0.35	0.35	0.35	0.35	0.35	0.35	Expense Ratio %
—	—	—	6.01	5.80	6.17	5.28	4.97	3.55	2.03	Income Ratio %
—	—	—	2	15	13	15	28	18	14	Turnover Rate %
—	—	—	42	208	630	1,298	1,666	2,749	2,056	Net Assets $mil

Performance 12-31-07

Historic Quarterly NAV Returns

	1st Qtr	2nd Qtr	3rd Qtr	4th Qtr	Total
2003	1.43	11.73	10.88	8.85	36.78
2004	13.03	-5.98	9.19	16.52	35.21
2005	-7.38	14.80	4.28	2.94	14.14
2006	15.69	-1.53	10.36	10.59	39.03
2007	3.46	-11.63	3.92	-14.01	-18.30

Trailing	NAV Return%	Market Return%	NAV Rtrn% +/-S&P 500	%Rank Cat.(NAV)
3 Mo	-14.01	-13.92	-10.68	64
6 Mo	-10.64	-10.62	-9.27	39
1 Yr	-18.30	-18.21	-23.79	100
3 Yr Avg	9.04	9.08	0.42	25
5 Yr Avg	19.11	19.04	6.28	34
10 Yr Avg	—	—	—	—

Tax Analysis	Tax-Adj Return%	Tax-Cost Ratio
3 Yr (estimated)	7.90	1.05
5 Yr (estimated)	17.70	1.18
10 Yr (estimated)	—	—

Rating and Risk

Time Period	Morningstar Rtn vs Cat	Morningstar Risk vs Cat	Morningstar Risk-Adj Rating
3 Yr	+Avg	High	★★★
5 Yr	+Avg	High	★★★
10 Yr	—	—	—

Other Measures	Standard Index S&P 500	Best Fit Index DJ Real Est
Alpha	-0.6	0.4
Beta	1.55	1.05
R-Squared	42	99
Standard Deviation	18.51	
Mean	9.04	
Sharpe Ratio	0.33	

Portfolio Analysis 12-31-07

Share change since 11-07 Total Stocks:30	Sector	PE	Tot Ret%	% Assets
⊕ ProLogis Trust	Financial	14.3	7.35	8.60
⊕ Simon Property Group, In	Financial	36.8	-11.34	8.16
⊕ Vornado Realty Trust	Financial	27.3	-25.45	6.69
⊕ Boston Properties, Inc.	Financial	10.0	-10.36	5.92
⊕ Equity Residential	Financial	—	-24.90	5.30
⊕ General Growth Propertie	Financial	33.4	-18.53	5.29
⊕ Host Hotels & Resorts, I	Financial	22.4	-27.14	4.61
⊖ Kimco Realty Corporation	Financial	26.4	-16.04	4.56
⊖ Public Storage	Financial	—	-22.83	4.54
⊕ AvalonBay Communities, I	Financial	37.5	-25.42	4.38
⊕ HCP, Inc.	—	57.8	-0.33	3.69
⊕ AMB Property Corporation	Financial	21.5	1.64	3.47
⊕ Ventas, Inc.	Financial	33.2	12.01	3.09
⊕ SL Green Realty Corporat	Financial	36.8	-27.81	2.79
⊕ Macerich Company	Financial	67.1	-15.09	2.75
⊕ Regency Centers Corporat	Financial	30.6	-14.56	2.60
⊕ Developers Diversified R	Financial	20.8	-36.01	2.52
⊕ Federal Realty Investmen	Financial	50.5	-0.61	2.44
⊕ Duke Realty Corporation	Financial	35.2	-32.72	2.29
⊖ Alexandria Real Estate E	Financial	44.0	4.43	2.11

Current Investment Style

Value Blnd Growth — Large Mid Small

Market Cap	%
Giant	0.0
Large	23.8
Mid	73.9
Small	2.3
Micro	0.0
Avg $mil: 7,727	

Value Measures		Rel Category
Price/Earnings	29.59	1.20
Price/Book	2.25	1.25
Price/Sales	3.96	1.13
Price/Cash Flow	12.68	0.83
Dividend Yield %	4.52	0.90

Growth Measures	%	Rel Category
Long-Term Erngs	—	—
Book Value	8.45	1.05
Sales	7.93	0.95
Cash Flow	2.92	0.37
Historical Erngs	15.01	0.52

Profitability	%	Rel Category
Return on Equity	15.70	1.03
Return on Assets	4.60	0.78
Net Margin	33.59	0.93

Sector Weightings	% of Stocks	Rel S&P 500	3 Year High	3 Year Low
Info	0.00	0.00		
Software	0.00	0.00	0	0
Hardware	0.00	0.00	0	0
Media	0.00	0.00	0	0
Telecom	0.00	0.00	0	0
Service	100.00	2.46		
Health	0.00	0.00	0	0
Consumer	0.00	0.00	0	0
Business	0.00	0.00	0	0
Financial	100.00	5.74	100	100
Mfg	0.00	0.00		
Goods	0.00	0.00	0	0
Ind Mtrls	0.00	0.00	0	0
Energy	0.00	0.00	0	0
Utilities	0.00	0.00	0	0

Composition

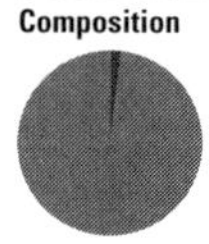

Cash	1.5
Stocks	98.5
Bonds	0.0
Other	0.0
Foreign (% of Stock)	0.0

Morningstar's Take by John Coumarianos 12-31-07

IShares Cohen & Steers Realty Majors Index makes you pay upscale prices for its meat-and-potatoes fare.

This ETF holds the largest names in the main property classes: retail, industrial, office, and multifamily. Many of its holdings have stumbled recently, but we don't think it's cheap enough to buy yet. Because it's difficult for REITs to build durable competitive advantages, we'd want a greater margin of safety (about 15% below our fair value estimate) before investing.

Real estate's stalwart firms occupy this ETF's top three slots. Simon Property Group, ProLogis Trust, and Vornado Realty Trust are all narrow-moat businesses because of the prime locations they've secured for their malls, distribution centers, and office buildings, respectively. Also, each firm's management team has exhibited acumen at deploying capital or developing a special niche. For example, Simon completed an opportunistic purchase of the distressed firm Mills in early 2007, while ProLogis has expanded internationally, helping its multinational clients with their supply chains overseas. Vornado has an unparalleled nose for sniffing out bargain properties that it can redevelop and re-lease at higher rental rates.

This ETF's top multifamily holdings, AvalonBay and Equity Residential., also sport narrow moat ratings for their properties in land-constrained coastal cities. Additionally, concentration in the standard property types means this ETF avoids more exotic and profitable segments such as timber, but it also shuns risky mortgage REITs.

Despite this ETF's strengths, low barriers to entry in real estate mean that REITs typically produce modest returns on invested capital. They can also struggle to grow because of the legal requirement to pay out 90% of their earnings as dividends. Finally, after real estate's multiyear surge, a larger percentage of this ETF's future returns may come from dividends, making its 0.35% expense ratio more onerous than before.

Address:	45 Fremont Street United States 800-474-2737
Web Address:	www.ishares.com
Inception:	01-29-01 *
Advisor:	Barclays Global Fund Advisers

Management Fee:	0.35%		
Expense Projections:	3Yr:$113	5Yr:$197	10Yr:$443
Income Distrib:	Annually		
Exchange:	NYSE		

iShares DJ BMaterial IYM

Market Price	Mstar Category
$76.96	Specialty-Natural Res

Morningstar Fair Value

Price/Fair Value Ratio	Coverage Rate %
0.98	94

Valuation

We would recommend this fund as long as it traded for at least an 8% discount to our fair value estimate. Although the underlying holdings are extremely volatile--being tied to volatile commodity markets--the portfolio's mix of different types of companies damps that volatility considerably. It was recently trading at a 2% discount to fair value.

Methodology

The fund tracks the Dow Jones U.S. Basic Materials Index. The index holds stocks in the chemicals, paper and forestry, industrial metals, and mining industries. It's market-cap-weighted--which results in very low turnover for the fund--and is adjusted for the float of the constituent companies. The index is reconstituted quarterly. The fund's biggest holdings, Monsanto and DuPont, make up 17% of the portfolio, and the top 10 names account for more than half of assets.

Morningstar Rating	Return	Risk	Yield	NAV	Avg Daily Vol. (k)	52 wk High/Low
★★	Below Avg	Low	1.4%	$76.99	209	$79.08 - $57.82

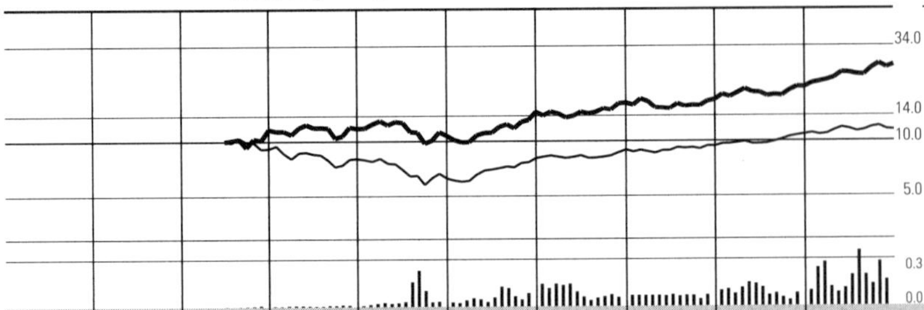

Growth of $10,000
— Investment Value of ETF
— Investment Value of Index S&P 500

Trading Volume Millions

History

1998	1999	2000	2001	2002	2003	2004	2005	2006	2007	History
—	—	38.53	38.31	34.36	45.51	50.31	51.58	59.09	76.99	NAV $
—	—	39.22	38.47	34.43	45.59	50.36	51.54	59.08	76.96	Market Price $
—	—	12.55*	1.09	-8.80	34.83	12.33	4.32	16.99	32.19	NAV Return%
—	—	12.55*	-0.28	-8.99	34.79	12.24	4.13	17.06	32.17	Market Price Return%
—	—	0.50	0.45	0.15	0.14	0.00	-0.07	0.03	-0.03	Avg Premium/Discount%
—	—	—	12.98	13.30	6.15	1.45	-0.59	1.20	26.70	NAV Rtrn% +/-S&P 500
—	—	—	-0.55	-0.48	-0.85	-0.72	-0.65	-0.64	3.78	NAV Rtrn% +/-DJ Bas Mat
—	—	—	1	1	1	85	70	85	58	NAV Return% Rank in Cat
—	—	—	1.60	1.60	1.99	1.64	1.73	2.30	1.78	Income Return %
—	—	—	-0.51	-10.40	32.84	10.69	2.59	14.69	30.41	Capital Return %
—	—	0.39	0.61	0.61	0.68	0.74	0.87	1.18	1.04	Income $
—	—	0.07	0.00	0.00	0.00	0.00	0.00	0.00	0.00	Capital Gains $
—	—	—	0.60	0.60	0.60	0.60	0.60	0.60	0.48	Expense Ratio %
—	—	—	1.77	1.42	2.10	1.70	1.53	1.83	2.00	Income Ratio %
—	—	—	16	9	6	7	6	6	13	Turnover Rate %
—	—	10	27	88	341	400	382	505	697	Net Assets $mil

Performance 12-31-07

Historic Quarterly NAV Returns

	1st Qtr	2nd Qtr	3rd Qtr	4th Qtr	Total
2003	-7.68	12.56	5.58	22.88	34.83
2004	-2.13	2.14	4.77	7.24	12.33
2005	1.89	-8.87	4.48	7.53	4.32
2006	8.67	0.55	-3.92	11.43	16.99
2007	9.21	9.62	5.93	4.24	32.19

Trailing	NAV Return%	Market Return%	NAV Rtrn% +/-S&P 500	%Rank Cat.(NAV)
3 Mo	4.24	4.25	7.57	52
6 Mo	10.42	10.45	11.79	53
1 Yr	32.19	32.17	26.70	58
3 Yr Avg	17.28	17.23	8.66	75
5 Yr Avg	19.56	19.51	6.73	83
10 Yr Avg	—	—	—	—

Tax Analysis	Tax-Adj Return%	Tax-Cost Ratio
3 Yr (estimated)	16.56	0.61
5 Yr (estimated)	18.84	0.60
10 Yr (estimated)	—	—

Rating and Risk

Time Period	Morningstar Rtn vs Cat	Morningstar Risk vs Cat	Morningstar Risk-Adj Rating
3 Yr	-Avg	Low	★★
5 Yr	Low	Low	★★
10 Yr	—	—	—

Other Measures	Standard Index S&P 500	Best Fit Index M* Inds Mat TR
Alpha	7.0	1.2
Beta	1.35	1.32
R-Squared	51	72
Standard Deviation	14.60	
Mean	17.28	
Sharpe Ratio	0.88	

Portfolio Analysis 12-31-07

Share change since 11-07 Total Stocks:74	Sector	PE	Tot Ret%	% Assets
⊖ Monsanto Company	Ind Mtrls	67.1	114.45	10.71
⊖ E.I. du Pont de Nemours	Ind Mtrls	12.4	-6.63	7.03
⊖ Freeport-McMoRan Copper	Ind Mtrls	12.1	86.51	6.92
⊖ The Dow Chemical Company	Ind Mtrls	11.3	2.55	6.60
⊖ Alcoa Inc.	Ind Mtrls	14.5	24.11	5.49
⊖ Praxair, Inc.	Ind Mtrls	25.6	52.05	4.97
⊕ Newmont Mining	Ind Mtrls	51.3	9.58	3.75
⊖ Air Products and Chemica	Ind Mtrls	21.1	42.82	3.55
⊖ Peabody Energy Corporati	Energy	41.1	63.76	2.89
⊖ Weyerhaeuser Company	Ind Mtrls	—	7.83	2.82
⊖ Nucor Corp.	Ind Mtrls	11.8	14.19	2.75
⊖ United States Steel Corp	Ind Mtrls	12.6	66.73	2.54
⊖ International Paper Co.	Ind Mtrls	5.2	-2.36	2.47
⊖ The Mosaic Company	Ind Mtrls	68.0	341.67	2.45
⊖ Consol Energy, Inc.	Energy	35.2	124.19	2.33
⊖ PPG Industries, Inc.	Ind Mtrls	14.1	12.49	2.06
⊖ Ecolab, Inc.	Ind Mtrls	32.3	14.21	1.60
⊖ Allegheny Technologies C	Ind Mtrls	11.7	-4.36	1.48
⊖ Rohm and Haas Company	Ind Mtrls	17.8	6.59	1.43
⊖ Southern Copper Corporat	Ind Mtrls	12.1	110.56	1.37

Current Investment Style

Value Blnd Growth; Large Mid Small

Market Cap	%
Giant	11.0
Large	58.0
Mid	25.8
Small	5.0
Micro	0.3
Avg $mil: 16,552	

Value Measures		Rel Category
Price/Earnings	14.14	0.87
Price/Book	2.47	1.06
Price/Sales	1.25	0.90
Price/Cash Flow	8.17	1.03
Dividend Yield %	1.33	0.96

Growth Measures	%	Rel Category
Long-Term Erngs	—	—
Book Value	8.04	0.54
Sales	8.17	0.73
Cash Flow	16.90	1.04
Historical Erngs	22.42	0.62

Profitability	%	Rel Category
Return on Equity	19.78	0.97
Return on Assets	7.38	0.78
Net Margin	8.55	0.62

Industry Weightings	% of Stocks	Rel Cat
Oil & Gas	0.0	0.0
Oil/Gas Products	0.0	0.0
Oil & Gas Srv	0.0	0.0
Pipelines	0.0	0.0
Utilities	0.0	0.0
Hard Commd	31.6	2.9
Soft Commd	8.6	3.0
Misc. Indstrl	48.8	4.6
Other	11.0	1.1

Composition

Cash	0.5
Stocks	99.5
Bonds	0.0
Other	0.0
Foreign (% of Stock)	0.6

Morningstar's Take by Haywood Kelly 12-31-07

IShares Dow Jones U.S. Basic Materials is a grab bag of commodities exposure, with a higher price tag than the competition.

The bulk of the fund's assets are in chemicals companies--firms such as DuPont, Dow Chemical, Monsanto, and Praxair. But chemicals firms are a diverse bunch, serving a variety of intermediate and end markets. Monsanto, for example, saw its stock appreciate 115% in 2007 thanks to its strong seed and herbicide business and the general strength in agricultural markets. DuPont and Dow Chemical, by contrast, are highly exposed to the construction and automotive sectors, and their stocks have been flat to down. In addition to this motley collection of chemicals holdings, this ETF has exposure to aluminum (Alcoa), gold prices (Newmont Mining), coal (Peabody Energy), steel (Nucor), forestry (Weyerhaeuser), and paper (International Paper).

Because of the diversity of the fund's holdings, the ETF does offer good diversification benefits. The fund's standard deviation is fairly tame, despite the fact that it parks half of its assets in the top 10 holdings. Plus, there's no single risk factor that would bias our ratings on the underlying stocks one way or the other. In fact, we'd expect our opinions on the underlying stocks to vary widely at any given time.

The biggest knock against this fund is that you can get a very similar portfolio--the Materials Select Sector SPDR--for half the expense ratio. Granted, the SPDR has less than half the number of holdings that this fund does, which gives this fund a slightly higher degree of diversification. But with market-cap-weighted funds like these two, that's not much of a difference. Only if this fund traded at a significantly more attractive valuation would we choose it over the competition.

Address:	45 Fremont Street United States 800-474-2737
Web Address:	www.ishares.com
Inception:	06-12-00*
Advisor:	Barclays Global Fund Advisers

Management Fee:	0.48%		
Expense Projections:	3Yr:$154	5Yr:$269	10Yr:$604
Income Distrib:	Quarterly		
Exchange:	NYSE		

iShares DJ Consumer Goods IYK

Market Price	Mstar Category
$63.92	Large Blend

Morningstar Fair Value

Price/Fair Value Ratio	Coverage Rate %
0.94	96

Valuation

Thanks to the mature nature of this portfolio's holdings, we have a high degree of confidence in our fair value estimate. As such, we'd only require a 9% discount to fair value before recommending it. The fund was recently trading at a 6% discount to fair value, which leaves it a bit shy of bargain territory.

Methodology

The fund tracks U.S. consumer goods stocks, as represented by the Dow Jones U.S. Consumer Goods Index. The index includes auto and autoparts makers, beverages, food producers, household goods, leisure goods, personal goods, and tobacco. The index is cap-weighted, which results in very low turnover, adjusted for the outstanding float of each company, and reconstituted quarterly. The portfolio contains about 150 stocks.

Morningstar Rating	Return	Risk	Yield	NAV	Avg Daily Vol. (k)	52 wk High/Low
★★	Below Avg	Below Avg	1.9%	$63.91	39	$66.24 - $58.74

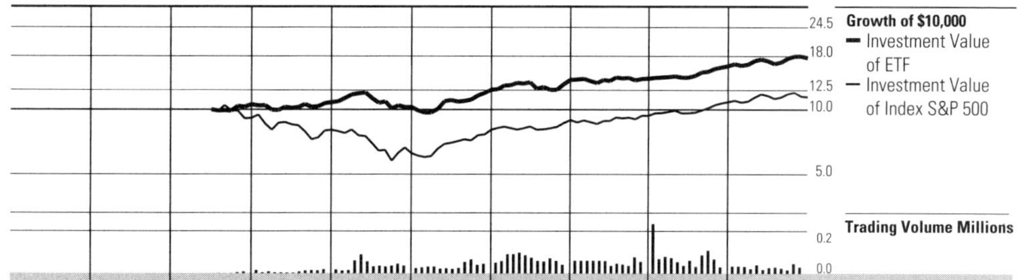

1998	1999	2000	2001	2002	2003	2004	2005	2006	2007	History
—	—	43.14	43.55	40.82	48.58	53.34	53.24	59.66	63.91	NAV $
—	—	43.44	43.60	40.65	48.30	53.32	53.26	60.00	63.92	Market Price $
—	—	7.77*	2.22	-4.95	20.83	11.39	1.44	14.32	9.17	NAV Return%
—	—	7.78*	1.63	-5.45	20.63	11.99	1.52	14.93	8.57	Market Price Return%
—	—	0.99	0.13	-0.06	0.01	-0.02	0.07	0.08	0.13	Avg Premium/Discount%
—	—	—	14.11	17.15	-7.85	0.51	-3.47	-1.47	3.68	NAV Rtrn% +/-S&P 500
—	—	—	3.32	-0.21	-3.47	-1.63	-0.60	-0.59	-2.39	NAV Rtrn% +/-DJ Con Gds
—	—	—	16	7	87	56	82	80	26	NAV Return% Rank in Cat
—	—	—	1.22	1.39	1.65	1.50	1.63	2.13	2.01	Income Return %
—	—	—	1.00	-6.34	19.18	9.89	-0.19	12.19	7.16	Capital Return %
—	—	0.25	0.52	0.60	0.67	0.73	0.86	1.12	1.19	Income $
—	—	0.00	0.00	0.00	0.00	0.00	0.00	0.00	0.00	Capital Gains $
—	—	—	0.60	0.60	0.60	0.60	0.60	0.60	0.48	Expense Ratio %
—	—	—	1.21	1.46	1.57	1.53	1.54	1.71	2.13	Income Ratio %
—	—	—	38	8	28	5	9	6	5	Turnover Rate %
—	—	15	50	100	172	344	484	343	380	Net Assets $mil

Performance 12-31-07

Historic Quarterly NAV Returns

	1st Qtr	2nd Qtr	3rd Qtr	4th Qtr	Total
2003	-5.61	14.30	0.46	11.48	20.83
2004	5.17	3.19	-7.83	11.35	11.39
2005	-1.30	0.26	3.30	-0.76	1.44
2006	1.60	-0.50	6.60	6.09	14.32
2007	1.67	3.85	2.79	0.59	9.17

Trailing	NAV Return%	Market Return%	NAV Rtrn% +/-S&P 500	%Rank Cat.(NAV)
3 Mo	0.59	0.39	3.92	9
6 Mo	3.40	3.47	4.77	9
1 Yr	9.17	8.57	3.68	26
3 Yr Avg	8.18	8.20	-0.44	85
5 Yr Avg	11.25	11.34	-1.58	77
10 Yr Avg	—	—	—	—

Tax Analysis	Tax-Adj Return%	Tax-Cost Ratio
3 Yr (estimated)	7.49	0.64
5 Yr (estimated)	10.59	0.59
10 Yr (estimated)	—	—

Rating and Risk

Time Period	Morningstar Rtn vs Cat	Morningstar Risk vs Cat	Morningstar Risk-Adj Rating
3 Yr	Avg	Low	★★★
5 Yr	-Avg	Avg	★★
10 Yr	—	—	—

Other Measures	Standard Index S&P 500	Best Fit Index M* Cons Good TR
Alpha	0.7	-2.0
Beta	0.72	1.05
R-Squared	68	96
Standard Deviation	6.78	
Mean	8.18	
Sharpe Ratio	0.57	

Morningstar's Take by Haywood Kelly 12-31-07

Our opinion of iShares Dow Jones U.S. Consumer Goods depends on our opinions of a few stocks in this highly concentrated portfolio.

With this ETF, you're getting a portfolio of mega-cap stocks--the average market cap is $37 billion--that are extremely mature. Consider the top few holdings. Procter & Gamble, with a 15% weighting, is a great company, but we expect its sales to increase at only a 5% to 6% clip over the next five years. The number-two holding, Altria, is milking cash flows from its hugely profitable tobacco business. We project just 3% top-line growth. As you'd expect from such a portfolio, its typical holding has lower earnings growth and a higher dividend yield than the S&P 500.

Given the nature of the stocks in the fund, we have higher confidence in our fair-value estimate than for most sector ETFs. It's relatively easy to value mature companies, especially those in noncyclical industries. Plus, nearly 60% of the fund's assets are invested in wide-moat firms, versus roughly 50% for the S&P 500 as a whole. The cash flows of such companies tend to be easier to forecast because of the strong competitive advantages fueling them. The standard deviation of the fund is extremely low by sector-fund standards--on a par with that of the S&P 500 as a whole. That's rather amazing, considering that 25% of the fund's assets are invested in just two stocks.

Keep that concentration in mind before investing. To really love this fund, you've got to be pretty confident that the top few stocks are undervalued. And if they become overvalued, this fund could be a lot more risky than its historical volatility suggests. But we wouldn't demand an especially large margin of safety before investing here. A 9% discount to our fair value estimate would suffice.

Address:	45 Fremont Street United States 800-474-2737
Web Address:	www.ishares.com
Inception:	06-12-00 *
Advisor:	Barclays Global Fund Advisers

Management Fee:	0.48%		
Expense Projections:	3Yr:$154	5Yr:$269	10Yr:$604
Income Distrib:	Quarterly		
Exchange:	NYSE		

Portfolio Analysis 12-31-07

Share change since 11-07 Total Stocks:147	Sector	PE	Tot Ret%	% Assets
⊕ Procter & Gamble Company	Goods	23.1	16.63	16.43
⊕ Altria Group Inc.	Goods	13.2	22.10	11.37
⊕ Coca-Cola Company	Goods	26.3	30.44	9.37
⊕ PepsiCo, Inc.	Goods	20.4	23.89	8.79
⊕ Kraft Foods, Inc.	Goods	20.0	-5.71	3.62
⊕ Colgate-Palmolive Compan	Goods	24.7	21.94	2.90
⊕ Anheuser-Busch Companies	Goods	19.1	9.06	2.75
⊕ Kimberly-Clark Corporati	Goods	17.0	5.23	2.12
⊕ Archer Daniels Midland	Ind Mtrls	13.8	47.02	1.96
⊕ Nike, Inc. B	Goods	19.4	31.48	1.68
⊕ Johnson Controls, Inc.	Ind Mtrls	16.7	27.49	1.52
⊕ General Mills, Inc.	Goods	17.2	1.58	1.37
⊕ Electronic Arts, Inc.	Software	—	15.98	1.32
⊕ Avon Products	Goods	29.8	22.02	1.23
⊕ Bunge, Ltd.	Goods	18.6	61.80	1.01
⊕ H.J. Heinz Company	Goods	18.3	7.07	1.00
⊕ Ford Motor Company	Goods	—	-12.65	0.97
⊕ Kellogg Company	Goods	19.0	5.70	0.94
⊕ Wm. Wrigley Jr. Company	Goods	26.9	15.52	0.92
⊕ Garmin, Ltd.	Hardware	29.1	75.58	0.89

Current Investment Style

Value Blnd Growth / Large Mid Small

Market Cap	%
Giant	46.2
Large	28.6
Mid	20.1
Small	4.7
Micro	0.3
Avg $mil: 40,005	

Value Measures		Rel Category
Price/Earnings	17.07	1.08
Price/Book	3.46	1.35
Price/Sales	1.00	0.81
Price/Cash Flow	10.31	1.11
Dividend Yield %	2.30	1.22

Growth Measures	%	Rel Category
Long-Term Erngs	—	—
Book Value	2.13	0.23
Sales	2.26	0.28
Cash Flow	-3.22	NMF
Historical Erngs	8.05	0.48

Profitability	%	Rel Category
Return on Equity	30.48	1.37
Return on Assets	11.09	1.33
Net Margin	10.71	0.87

Sector Weightings	% of Stocks	Rel S&P 500	3 Year High	3 Year Low
Info	3.17	0.15		
Software	2.18	0.53	2	2
Hardware	0.89	0.09	1	0
Media	0.10	0.03	0	0
Telecom	0.00	0.00	0	0
Service	3.01	0.07		
Health	0.40	0.03	0	0
Consumer	2.61	0.38	7	3
Business	0.00	0.00	1	0
Financial	0.00	0.00	1	0
Mfg	93.82	2.44		
Goods	87.03	9.50	88	82
Ind Mtrls	6.75	0.52	7	5
Energy	0.04	0.00	0	0
Utilities	0.00	0.00	0	0

Composition

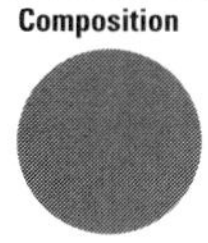

Cash	0.5
Stocks	99.5
Bonds	0.0
Other	0.0
Foreign (% of Stock)	0.2

iShares DJ Fin Sectr IYF

Market Price	Mstar Category
$94.14	Specialty-Financial

Morningstar Fair Value

Price/Fair Value Ratio	Coverage Rate %
0.77	97

Valuation

The fund holds a diverse group of financial stocks, but many of its holdings still have exposure to the same risk factors: the U.S. mortgage market and loan-default rates, to name a few. As such, we would demand at least a 16% discount to our fair value estimate before recommending it. It was recently trading at a 22% discount.

Methodology

This fund invests passively in the Dow Jones U.S. Financials Index. Holdings include stocks in the banking, securities, insurance, real estate, and money-management industries. It is market-capitalization weighted (adjusted for available float) and is reconstituted on a quarterly basis. The main difference between this fund and iShares Dow Jones U.S. Financial Services is that this one includes real estate stocks. Its portfolio holdings number about 300, as opposed to about 150 for its more narrowly focused cousin.

Morningstar Rating	Return	Risk	Yield	NAV	Avg Daily Vol. (k)	52 wk High/Low
★★★	Average	Average	2.7%	$94.36	547	$121.86 - $86.23

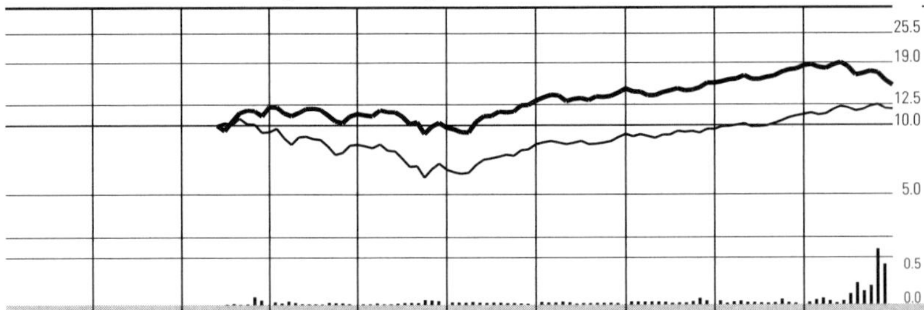

1998	1999	2000	2001	2002	2003	2004	2005	2006	2007	History
—	—	87.00	79.79	68.44	88.24	97.66	101.16	117.80	94.36	NAV $
—	—	87.00	80.49	68.21	88.04	97.68	101.09	117.67	94.14	Market Price $
—	—	5.79*	-7.07	-12.81	31.37	12.74	5.82	18.79	-17.94	NAV Return%
—	—	5.75*	-6.25	-13.86	31.51	13.02	5.72	18.74	-18.05	Market Price Return%
—	—	0.56	0.01	0.06	-0.03	-0.03	-0.01	0.00	-0.08	Avg Premium/Discount%
—	—	—	4.82	9.29	2.69	1.86	0.91	3.00	-23.43	NAV Rtrn% +/-S&P 500
—	—	—	-0.69	-0.46	-0.86	-0.65	-0.64	-0.63	-4.53	NAV Rtrn% +/-DJ Finance
—	—	—	50	50	75	50	80	50	65	NAV Return% Rank in Cat
—	—	—	1.20	1.50	2.15	1.95	2.12	2.18	2.21	Income Return %
—	—	—	-8.27	-14.31	29.22	10.79	3.70	16.61	-20.15	Capital Return %
—	—	1.44	1.04	1.19	1.46	1.71	2.05	2.19	2.58	Income $
—	—	0.39	0.00	0.00	0.00	0.00	0.00	0.00	0.00	Capital Gains $
—	—	—	0.60	0.60	0.60	0.60	0.60	0.60	0.48	Expense Ratio %
—	—	—	1.46	1.49	1.94	2.08	2.23	2.26	1.98	Income Ratio %
—	—	—	11	4	28	7	7	6	10	Turnover Rate %
—	—	22	96	140	229	303	389	548	425	Net Assets $mil

Performance 12-31-07

Historic Quarterly NAV Returns

	1st Qtr	2nd Qtr	3rd Qtr	4th Qtr	Total
2003	-4.76	17.93	4.60	11.81	31.37
2004	5.29	-2.63	1.08	8.78	12.74
2005	-6.58	4.99	0.59	7.26	5.82
2006	4.22	-0.56	7.29	6.83	18.79
2007	-2.56	1.51	-4.34	-13.28	-17.94

Trailing	NAV Return%	Market Return%	NAV Rtrn% +/-S&P 500	%Rank Cat.(NAV)
3 Mo	-13.28	-13.41	-9.95	71
6 Mo	-17.04	-17.19	-15.67	71
1 Yr	-17.94	-18.05	-23.43	65
3 Yr Avg	1.04	0.95	-7.58	60
5 Yr Avg	8.84	8.87	-3.99	50
10 Yr Avg	—	—	—	—

Tax Analysis	Tax-Adj Return%	Tax-Cost Ratio
3 Yr (estimated)	0.27	0.76
5 Yr (estimated)	8.07	0.71
10 Yr (estimated)	—	—

Rating and Risk

Time Period	Morningstar Rtn vs Cat	Morningstar Risk vs Cat	Morningstar Risk-Adj Rating
3 Yr	Avg	Avg	★★★
5 Yr	Avg	Avg	★★★
10 Yr	—	—	—

Other Measures	Standard Index S&P 500	Best Fit Index DJ Finance
Alpha	-7.4	-0.5
Beta	1.11	1.00
R-Squared	64	100
Standard Deviation	10.72	
Mean	1.04	
Sharpe Ratio	-0.25	

Portfolio Analysis 12-31-07

Share change since 11-07 Total Stocks:294	Sector	PE	Tot Ret%	% Assets
⊕ Bank of America Corporat	Financial	9.4	-19.25	7.00
⊕ J.P. Morgan Chase & Co.	Financial	9.5	-7.24	5.57
⊕ Citigroup, Inc.	Financial	7.9	-44.93	5.52
⊕ American International G	Financial	10.2	-17.96	4.90
⊕ Wells Fargo Company	Financial	11.4	-12.13	3.64
⊕ Goldman Sachs Group, Inc	Financial	8.8	8.59	2.92
⊕ Wachovia Corporation	Financial	8.6	-29.91	2.85
⊕ Bank of New York Mellon	Financial	21.7	26.51	2.09
⊕ US Bancorp	Financial	12.2	-7.89	2.07
⊕ American Express Company	Financial	14.9	-13.18	2.03
⊕ Morgan Stanley	Financial	6.1	-20.21	1.93
⊕ Merrill Lynch & Company,	Financial	12.2	-41.32	1.64
⊕ Prudential Financial, In	Financial	12.1	9.72	1.59
⊕ Fannie Mae	Financial	24.1	-30.45	1.48
⊕ Chicago Mercantile Excha	Financial	48.5	35.37	1.38
⊕ Lehman Brothers Holdings	Financial	8.8	-15.52	1.32
⊕ The Travelers Companies,	Financial	7.8	2.37	1.31
⊕ State Street Corporation	Financial	21.3	21.92	1.18
⊕ Aflac, Inc.	Financial	19.6	38.00	1.16
⊕ Allstate Corporation	Financial	6.3	-17.78	1.12

Current Investment Style

Value Blnd Growth — Large Mid Small

Market Cap	%
Giant	41.0
Large	31.8
Mid	22.0
Small	5.0
Micro	0.2
Avg $mil: 28,800	

Value Measures		Rel Category
Price/Earnings	10.88	0.91
Price/Book	1.39	0.95
Price/Sales	1.87	0.92
Price/Cash Flow	11.32	0.97
Dividend Yield %	3.30	1.13

Growth Measures	%	Rel Category
Long-Term Erngs	8.45	0.80
Book Value	7.50	0.70
Sales	5.92	0.76
Cash Flow	21.34	1.38
Historical Erngs	14.24	0.78

Profitability	%	Rel Category
Return on Equity	16.77	0.99
Return on Assets	2.80	0.96
Net Margin	22.65	1.02

Industry Weightings	% of Stocks	Rel Cat
Intl Banks	22.7	1.3
Banks	17.6	0.8
Real Estate	9.9	4.1
Sec Mgmt	15.1	1.1
S & Ls	1.9	0.3
Prop & Reins	14.9	1.0
Life Ins	6.9	1.1
Misc. Ins	2.7	0.9
Other	8.2	0.6

Composition

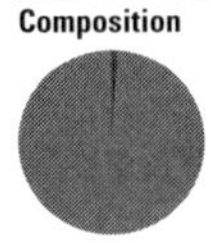

Cash	1.0
Stocks	99.0
Bonds	0.0
Other	0.0
Foreign (% of Stock)	0.4

Morningstar's Take by Haywood Kelly 12-31-07

IShares Dow Jones U.S. Financial Sector is a plain-vanilla way to track the fortunes of the U.S. financials sector.

There's not much to separate this fund's portfolio from those of other financial-focused ETFs like Vanguard Financial ETF, Financials SPDR, and iShares Dow Jones U.S. Financial Services. Each fund weights its holdings by market cap and therefore has hefty exposure to the same group of mega-caps: Bank of America, Citigroup, J.P. Morgan, and so on. Given the huge market caps of these firms, they dominate the portfolios. So when one of these funds looks cheap to us, they all will.

And at the end of 2007, they all appear cheap to us. Financial stocks have taken a licking from bad mortgage loans and the freezing of credit markets. The Morningstar financials index was down 16% year to date through late-December 2007, and many of this fund's largest holdings--Citigroup and Merrill Lynch, for example--had dropped significantly further. Our analysts feel the market is punishing many financial firms too much. As of late-December 2007, seven of the top 10 holdings of this fund were cheap enough to earn 5 stars from Morningstar.

As a way to play what could be an undervalued financials sector, an ETF like this has its merits. The portfolio is packed with high-quality financial names; wide-moat firms make up 55% of the portfolio. And by diversifying across financials, you minimize exposure to a company-specific blowup.

Our biggest knock against the fund is its 0.48% expense ratio. While not high in absolute terms, it's double that of very similar products from the Vanguard and SPDR lineups. Unless there were a significant valuation gap in favor of this fund, we'd stick to the cheaper alternatives.

Address:	45 Fremont Street United States 800-474-2737
Web Address:	www.ishares.com
Inception:	05-22-00*
Advisor:	Barclays Global Fund Advisers

Management Fee:	0.48%		
Expense Projections:	3Yr:$154	5Yr:$269	10Yr:$604
Income Distrib:	Quarterly		
Exchange:	NYSE		

iShares DJ Fin Svcs IYG

Market Price	Mstar Category
$102.14	Specialty-Financial

Morningstar Fair Value

Price/Fair Value Ratio	Coverage Rate %
0.73	98

Valuation

The fund holds a diverse group of financial stocks, but many of its holdings still have exposure to the same risk factors: the U.S. mortgage market and loan-default rates, to name a few. As such, we would demand at least a 16% discount to our fair value estimate before recommending it. It was recently trading at a 27% discount.

Methodology

This fund invests passively in the Dow Jones U.S. Financials Index. Holdings include stocks in the banking, securities, insurance, real estate, and money-management industries. It is market-capitalization weighted (adjusted for available float) and is reconstituted on a quarterly basis. The main difference between this fund and iShares Dow Jones U.S. Financial Sector is that this one excludes real estate stocks. Its portfolio holdings number about 150, as opposed to about 300 for the broader fund.

Morningstar Rating	Return	Risk	Yield	NAV	Avg Daily Vol. (k)	52 wk High/Low
★★	Below Avg	Above Avg	2.7%	$102.38	286	$137.44 - $92.24

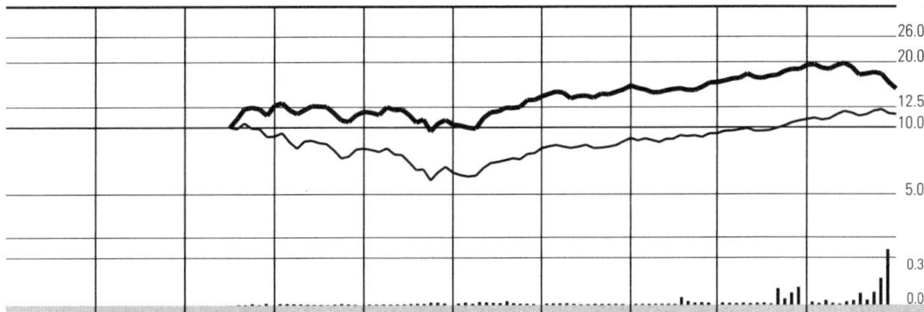

Growth of $10,000
- Investment Value of ETF
- Investment Value of Index S&P 500

Trading Volume Millions

History

1998	1999	2000	2001	2002	2003	2004	2005	2006	2007	History
—	—	98.46	91.01	78.33	103.02	112.97	114.38	133.75	102.38	NAV $
—	—	98.81	91.74	78.35	103.22	113.15	114.45	133.69	102.14	Market Price $
—	—	4.40*	-6.38	-12.41	34.04	11.92	3.46	19.32	-21.69	NAV Return%
—	—	4.37*	-5.96	-13.09	34.26	11.88	3.35	19.19	-21.84	Market Price Return%
—	—	0.06	-0.05	0.05	0.08	0.04	0.06	0.06	-0.07	Avg Premium/Discount%
—	—	—	5.51	9.69	5.36	1.04	-1.45	3.53	-27.18	NAV Rtrn% +/-S&P 500
—	—	—	-0.62	-0.49	-0.88	-0.65	-0.64	-0.61	—	NAV Rtrn% +/-DJ Fin Serv
—	—	—	1	25	50	75	100	20	80	NAV Return% Rank in Cat
—	—	—	1.16	1.62	2.22	2.12	2.09	2.22	2.09	Income Return %
—	—	—	-7.54	-14.03	31.82	9.80	1.37	17.10	-23.78	Capital Return %
—	—	0.93	1.14	1.47	1.72	2.17	2.35	2.52	2.78	Income $
—	—	0.13	0.00	0.00	0.00	0.00	0.00	0.00	0.00	Capital Gains $
—	—	—	0.60	0.60	0.60	0.60	0.60	0.60	0.48	Expense Ratio %
—	—	—	1.33	1.46	1.90	2.08	2.20	2.29	2.15	Income Ratio %
—	—	—	5	3	41	7	7	9	9	Turnover Rate %
—	—	25	59	55	124	119	177	274	261	Net Assets $mil

Performance 12-31-07

Historic Quarterly NAV Returns

	1st Qtr	2nd Qtr	3rd Qtr	4th Qtr	Total
2003	-4.10	19.41	4.74	11.75	34.04
2004	4.21	-3.22	1.37	9.47	11.92
2005	-6.79	3.37	-1.00	8.46	3.46
2006	4.53	-0.07	7.43	6.32	19.32
2007	-3.82	2.00	-5.30	-15.71	-21.69

Trailing	NAV Return%	Market Return%	NAV Rtrn% +/-S&P 500	%Rank Cat.(NAV)
3 Mo	-15.71	-15.75	-12.38	91
6 Mo	-20.17	-20.32	-18.80	91
1 Yr	-21.69	-21.84	-27.18	80
3 Yr Avg	-1.12	-1.25	-9.74	100
5 Yr Avg	7.72	7.66	-5.11	100
10 Yr Avg	—	—	—	—

Tax Analysis	Tax-Adj Return%	Tax-Cost Ratio
3 Yr (estimated)	-1.86	0.75
5 Yr (estimated)	6.94	0.72
10 Yr (estimated)	—	—

Rating and Risk

Time Period	Morningstar Rtn vs Cat	Morningstar Risk vs Cat	Morningstar Risk-Adj Rating
3 Yr	-Avg	+Avg	★★
5 Yr	-Avg	+Avg	★★
10 Yr	—	—	—

Other Measures	Standard Index S&P 500	Best Fit Index DJ Finance
Alpha	-9.3	-2.5
Beta	1.06	1.04
R-Squared	53	96
Standard Deviation	11.38	
Mean	-1.12	
Sharpe Ratio	-0.42	

Portfolio Analysis 12-31-07

Share change since 11-07 Total Stocks:144	Sector	PE	Tot Ret%	% Assets
⊕ Bank of America Corporat	Financial	9.4	-19.25	10.80
⊕ J.P. Morgan Chase & Co.	Financial	9.5	-7.24	8.60
⊕ Citigroup, Inc.	Financial	7.9	-44.93	8.52
⊕ Wells Fargo Company	Financial	11.4	-12.13	5.61
⊕ Goldman Sachs Group, Inc	Financial	8.8	8.59	4.51
⊕ Wachovia Corporation	Financial	8.6	-29.91	4.40
⊕ Bank of New York Mellon	Financial	21.7	26.51	3.23
⊕ US Bancorp	Financial	12.2	-7.89	3.19
⊕ American Express Company	Financial	14.9	-13.18	3.14
⊕ Morgan Stanley	Financial	6.1	-20.21	2.98
⊕ Merrill Lynch & Company,	Financial	12.2	-41.32	2.53
⊕ Fannie Mae	Financial	24.1	-30.45	2.28
⊕ Chicago Mercantile Excha	Financial	48.5	35.37	2.13
⊕ Lehman Brothers Holdings	Financial	8.8	-15.52	2.03
⊕ State Street Corporation	Financial	21.3	21.92	1.83
⊕ Charles Schwab Corporati	Financial	30.8	40.07	1.40
⊕ Freddie Mac	Financial	12.0	-48.20	1.31
⊕ PNC Financial Services G	Financial	12.8	-8.29	1.30
⊕ SunTrust Banks, Inc.	Financial	10.6	-23.27	1.27
⊕ Capital One Financial Co	Financial	7.0	-38.50	1.14

Current Investment Style

Value Blnd Growth; Large Mid Small

Market Cap	%
Giant	55.4
Large	26.6
Mid	13.9
Small	3.8
Micro	0.2
Avg $mil: 41,469	

Value Measures		Rel Category
Price/Earnings	11.01	0.92
Price/Book	1.35	0.92
Price/Sales	2.19	1.07
Price/Cash Flow	13.26	1.14
Dividend Yield %	3.60	1.23

Growth Measures	%	Rel Category
Long-Term Erngs	—	—
Book Value	7.97	0.74
Sales	6.39	0.82
Cash Flow	4.01	0.26
Historical Erngs	10.48	0.57

Profitability	%	Rel Category
Return on Equity	17.10	1.01
Return on Assets	2.48	0.85
Net Margin	24.51	1.10

Industry Weightings	% of Stocks	Rel Cat
Intl Banks	35.2	2.0
Banks	27.2	1.2
Real Estate	0.0	0.0
Sec Mgmt	23.4	1.7
S & Ls	3.0	0.5
Prop & Reins	0.2	0.0
Life Ins	0.0	0.0
Misc. Ins	0.1	0.0
Other	11.0	0.8

Composition

Cash	0.7
Stocks	99.3
Bonds	0.0
Other	0.0
Foreign (% of Stock)	0.0

Morningstar's Take by Haywood Kelly 12-31-07

IShares Dow Jones US Financial Services is a (slightly) purer play on banks than most financials ETFs.

The main difference between this fund and iShares U.S. Financial Sector is that this one excludes real estate stocks from the portfolio. As a result, this portfolio holds about 150 stocks, as opposed to the 300-odd stocks held by the broader iShares fund. But in practice the two portfolios are very similar. Because they're market-cap weighted, both portfolios are dominated by the same mega-cap stocks--Bank of America, Citigroup, J.P. Morgan, and so on--and those stocks drive the returns. (Most REITs sport small market caps and, thus, don't have nearly the impact you'd expect given their sheer numbers.)

Because of the tilt away from real estate, this fund had a slight valuation edge over its iShares cousin as of late-December 2007. Our analysts think that bank stocks are particularly cheap after falling so sharply in 2007 as a result of the mortgage meltdown. This fund had a price/fair value ratio of 0.74 as of December 26, compared with 0.79 for the broader iShares fund. But this, in turn, wasn't as low as the 0.70 of KBW Bank, a fund focused exclusively on bank stocks. Which fund you invest in depends on how focused a bet you want to make on banks. Right now, anyway, the greater the focus, the higher the expected return.

Like other financial-focused ETFs, this one has high exposure to the best financial companies: Wide-moat firms, which are the ones we think have the best shot at earning high returns on capital for years to come, make up 55% of the portfolio. Our biggest knock against the fund, as with many iShares offerings, is its 0.48% expense ratio. While not high in absolute terms, it's double that of very similar products from the Vanguard and SPDR lineups. Only when there's a significant valuation gap in favor of this fund would we recommend it over the alternatives.

Address:	45 Fremont Street United States 800-474-2737
Web Address:	www.ishares.com
Inception:	06-12-00 *
Advisor:	Barclays Global Fund Advisers

Management Fee:	0.48%		
Expense Projections:	3Yr:$154	5Yr:$269	10Yr:$604
Income Distrib:	Quarterly		
Exchange:	NYSE		

iShares DJ Health IYH

Market Price	Mstar Category
$70.67	Specialty-Health

Morningstar Fair Value

Price/Fair Value Ratio	Coverage Rate %
0.91	97

Valuation

The portfolio contains high-quality firms, and many stock-specific risks cancel each other out. Historically, the fund has not been much more volatile than the S&P 500. We'd demand only an 8% discount to our fair value estimate before recommending it. The fund was recently trading at a 9% discount to fair value, putting it in bargain territory.

Methodology

This exchange-traded fund tracks a subset of the Dow Jones U.S. Total Market Index that includes the health-care stocks in that broad market benchmark. Although most health-care industries are represented in the fund, drugmakers and biotech firms predominate, with such stocks recently accounting for nearly two thirds of assets. The index is market-cap-weighted, which results in heavy concentration among the fund's top holdings. The free-float-adjusted, market-capitalization-weighted index is rebalanced quarterly.

Morningstar Rating	Return	Risk	Yield	NAV	Avg Daily Vol. (k)	52 wk High/Low
★★	Below Avg	Below Avg	1.3%	$70.66	62	$73.38 - $65.55

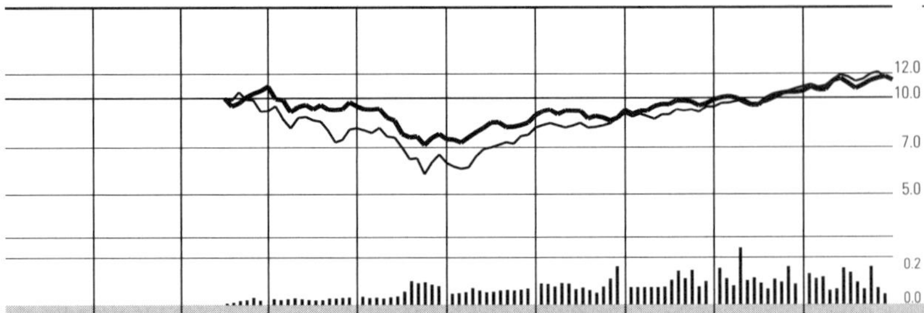

1998	1999	2000	2001	2002	2003	2004	2005	2006	2007	History
—	—	71.77	61.95	48.47	57.08	58.92	62.96	66.42	70.66	NAV $
—	—	71.91	62.10	48.53	56.98	58.99	63.04	66.32	70.67	Market Price $
—	—	3.08*	-13.34	-21.20	18.70	3.91	7.65	6.46	7.84	NAV Return%
—	—	3.09*	-13.30	-21.29	18.35	4.22	7.66	6.16	8.01	Market Price Return%
—	—	-0.13	0.14	0.15	0.05	0.05	-0.02	0.00	-0.04	Avg Premium/Discount%
—	—	—	-1.45	0.90	-9.98	-6.97	2.74	-9.33	2.35	NAV Rtrn% +/-S&P 500
—	—	—	-0.50	-0.39	-0.73	-0.64	-0.67	-0.42	-3.39	NAV Rtrn% +/-DJ Health
—	—	—	1	50	50	67	50	67	47	NAV Return% Rank in Cat
—	—	—	0.34	0.60	0.87	0.67	0.78	0.93	1.43	Income Return %
—	—	—	-13.68	-21.80	17.83	3.24	6.87	5.53	6.41	Capital Return %
—	—	0.07	0.24	0.37	0.42	0.38	0.46	0.58	0.94	Income $
—	—	0.09	0.00	0.00	0.00	0.00	0.00	0.00	0.00	Capital Gains $
—	—	—	0.60	0.60	0.60	0.60	0.60	0.60	0.48	Expense Ratio %
—	—	—	0.29	0.45	0.80	0.71	0.74	0.75	1.32	Income Ratio %
—	—	—	5	3	9	4	4	4	5	Turnover Rate %
—	—	57	223	351	491	934	1,300	1,219	975	Net Assets $mil

Performance 12-31-07

Historic Quarterly NAV Returns

	1st Qtr	2nd Qtr	3rd Qtr	4th Qtr	Total
2003	1.29	11.23	-3.05	8.67	18.70
2004	0.67	2.53	-4.78	5.73	3.91
2005	-0.62	4.85	1.84	1.44	7.65
2006	1.37	-4.91	8.71	1.59	6.46
2007	0.93	4.66	1.97	0.11	7.84

Trailing	NAV Return%	Market Return%	NAV Rtrn% +/-S&P 500	%Rank Cat.(NAV)
3 Mo	0.11	0.08	3.44	34
6 Mo	2.09	2.15	3.46	32
1 Yr	7.84	8.01	2.35	47
3 Yr Avg	7.32	7.28	-1.30	25
5 Yr Avg	8.80	8.77	-4.03	34
10 Yr Avg	—	—	—	—

Tax Analysis	Tax-Adj Return%	Tax-Cost Ratio
3 Yr (estimated)	6.94	0.35
5 Yr (estimated)	8.46	0.31
10 Yr (estimated)	—	—

Rating and Risk

Time Period	Morningstar Rtn vs Cat	Morningstar Risk vs Cat	Morningstar Risk-Adj Rating
3 Yr	Avg	-Avg	★★★
5 Yr	Low	-Avg	★★
10 Yr	—	—	—

Other Measures	Standard Index S&P 500	Best Fit Index DJ Health
Alpha	0.3	-0.5
Beta	0.65	1.00
R-Squared	36	100
Standard Deviation	8.40	
Mean	7.32	
Sharpe Ratio	0.37	

Portfolio Analysis 12-31-07

Share change since 11-07 Total Stocks:145	Sector	PE	Tot Ret%	% Assets
⊕ Johnson & Johnson	Health	18.8	3.61	10.80
⊕ Pfizer Inc.	Health	22.5	-8.15	8.79
⊕ Merck & Co., Inc.	Health	23.6	37.36	7.16
⊕ Abbott Laboratories	Health	45.7	18.04	4.89
⊕ UnitedHealth Group, Inc.	Health	17.4	8.38	4.26
⊕ Wyeth	Health	13.6	-11.36	3.34
⊕ Medtronic, Inc.	Health	20.3	-5.22	3.24
⊕ Bristol-Myers Squibb Com	Health	24.8	4.75	2.95
⊕ Eli Lilly & Company	Health	26.0	5.65	2.92
⊕ Amgen, Inc.	Health	16.8	-32.02	2.86
⊕ WellPoint, Inc.	Health	16.4	11.49	2.84
⊕ Schering-Plough Corporat	Health	21.0	13.66	2.44
⊕ Gilead Sciences, Inc.	Health	—	41.72	2.42
⊕ Baxter International Inc	Health	22.9	26.79	2.08
⊕ Genentech, Inc.	Health	26.2	-17.33	1.76
⊕ Aetna, Inc.	Health	16.9	33.79	1.64
⊕ Medco Health Solutions,	Health	31.1	89.78	1.54
⊕ Thermo Fisher Scientific	Health	48.5	27.36	1.37
⊕ Stryker Corporation	Health	32.9	36.18	1.33
⊕ Covidien, Ltd.	Health	—	—	1.24

Current Investment Style

Value Blnd Growth; Large Mid Small

Market Cap	%
Giant	47.3
Large	33.7
Mid	15.3
Small	3.5
Micro	0.2

Avg $mil: 38,322

Value Measures		Rel Category
Price/Earnings	14.81	0.70
Price/Book	3.43	1.01
Price/Sales	2.12	0.73
Price/Cash Flow	12.84	0.99
Dividend Yield %	1.35	1.73

Growth Measures	%	Rel Category
Long-Term Erngs	—	—
Book Value	6.60	1.07
Sales	9.61	0.93
Cash Flow	9.62	0.76
Historical Erngs	13.52	0.15

Profitability	%	Rel Category
Return on Equity	17.95	2.41
Return on Assets	8.51	19.34
Net Margin	13.56	2.66

Industry Weightings	% of Stocks	Rel Cat
Biotech	14.2	0.4
Drugs	48.7	1.7
Mgd Care	14.4	1.7
Hospitals	0.7	1.0
Other HC Srv	1.1	0.8
Diagnostics	1.3	0.9
Equipment	17.6	1.1
Good/Srv	2.1	0.4
Other	0.0	0.0

Composition

Cash	0.3
Stocks	99.7
Bonds	0.0
Other	0.0
Foreign (% of Stock)	0.0

Morningstar's Take by Haywood Kelly 12-31-07

Rarely would iShares Dow Jones U.S. Healthcare be our first choice for health-care investing.

An ETF makes a lot of sense for health-care investors. No matter how deep your knowledge of individual stocks, you can always be shocked by a bolt from the blue. Think of Merck's Vioxx, or Wyeth's fen-phen, or Boston Scientific's drug-eluting stents. A product can be wildly successful one year, and spawn thousands of lawsuits the next.

Such company-specific risks get diversified away in the ETF format. Granted, all health-care companies face the risk of Congress changing the rules--whether it's Medicare reimbursement, nationalized health care, or stricter Food and Drug Administration guidelines--which could potentially hammer all the stocks in this portfolio to some degree. But by buying at a discount to the intrinsic value of the portfolio, an investor can mitigate even this risk.

This portfolio is also chock-full of high-quality firms. Eight of the top 10 holdings sport wide-moat ratings; for the portfolio as a whole, 60% of assets are in wide-moat stocks. The top two holdings, Johnson & Johnson and Pfizer, generate more than $20 billion in annual free cash flow combined--an indication of just how profitable the best health-care companies are.

But among health-care ETFs, the iShares fund is not the best choice. Its expense ratio is 0.48%, double that of Health Care Select SPDR or Vanguard Health Care ETF, even though the funds' portfolios are virtually identical. Granted, the number of holdings differs across these three portfolios, but because they weight stocks by market cap, that doesn't result in meaningfully different portfolios or risk levels.

Given the high-quality nature of the portfolio, we'd recommend this ETF whenever it trades for more than an 8% discount to the intrinsic value of its underlying stocks. But considering the higher expense drag, it would rarely be our first choice.

Address:	45 Fremont Street United States 800-474-2737
Web Address:	www.ishares.com
Inception:	06-12-00 *
Advisor:	Barclays Global Fund Advisers

Management Fee:	0.48%		
Expense Projections:	3Yr:$154	5Yr:$269	10Yr:$604
Income Distrib:	Quarterly		
Exchange:	NYSE		

iShares DJ Industry IYJ

Market Price	Mstar Category
$72.80	Large Blend

Morningstar Fair Value

Price/Fair Value Ratio	Coverage Rate %
0.91	93

Morningstar Rating	Return	Risk	Yield	NAV	Avg Daily Vol. (k)	52 wk High/Low
★★★★	Above Avg	High	1.2%	$72.83	53	$77.85 - $64.80

Valuation

We would demand a 9% discount to our fair value estimate before recommending this ETF. Despite having 20% of its assets in a single stock, the mature nature of the fund's top holdings, and their exposure to many facets of the global economy, has tamped down volatility. The fund was recently trading at a 9% discount.

Methodology

This exchange-traded offering tracks the Dow Jones U.S. Industrial Sector index. The holdings include companies from a number of areas, including manufacturers, builders, railroads, package delivery companies, and aerospace and defense contractors. The constituents are cap-weighted--which results in very low turnover--and is adjusted for the free float available. However, it's very top-heavy, with 20% of assets staked in a single name, conglomerate General Electric. Thus, its fortunes are disproportionately tied to GE's. The index is reconstituted quarterly.

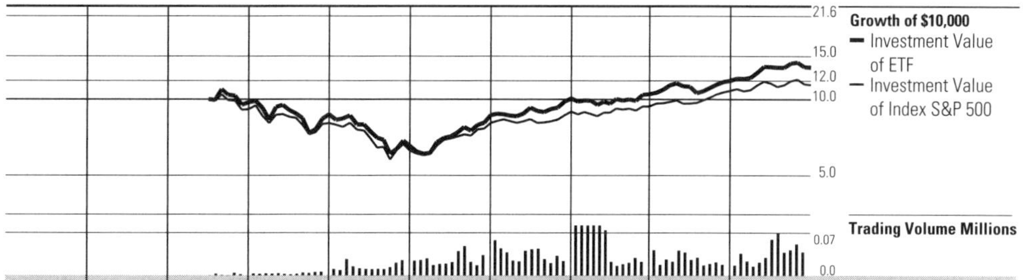

1998	1999	2000	2001	2002	2003	2004	2005	2006	2007	History
—	—	56.44	50.23	37.36	49.00	56.54	58.25	65.22	72.83	NAV $
—	—	56.50	50.51	37.43	49.08	56.60	58.24	65.60	72.80	Market Price $
—	—	4.04*	-10.43	-24.96	32.39	16.41	4.18	13.21	13.02	NAV Return%
—	—	4.03*	-10.03	-25.24	32.36	16.35	4.06	13.89	12.32	Market Price Return%
—	—	-0.92	0.25	0.24	0.04	0.02	-0.03	0.02	-0.02	Avg Premium/Discount%
—	—	—	1.46	-2.86	3.71	5.53	-0.73	-2.58	7.53	NAV Rtrn% +/-S&P 500
—	—	—	-0.27	0.58	-0.85	-0.84	-0.64	-0.66	-0.90	NAV Rtrn% +/-DJ Industr
—	—	—	54	100	31	19	61	86	13	NAV Return% Rank in Cat
—	—	—	0.53	0.72	1.05	0.95	1.13	1.20	1.35	Income Return %
—	—	—	-10.96	-25.68	31.34	15.46	3.05	12.01	11.67	Capital Return %
—	—	0.15	0.30	0.36	0.39	0.46	0.64	0.70	0.88	Income $
—	—	0.13	0.00	0.00	0.00	0.00	0.00	0.00	0.00	Capital Gains $
—	—	—	0.60	0.60	0.60	0.60	0.60	0.60	0.48	Expense Ratio %
—	—	—	0.44	0.56	1.03	0.94	0.97	1.06	1.22	Income Ratio %
—	—	—	23	27	12	3	5	7	4	Turnover Rate %
—	—	23	48	75	179	254	236	287	364	Net Assets $mil

Performance 12-31-07

Historic Quarterly NAV Returns

	1st Qtr	2nd Qtr	3rd Qtr	4th Qtr	Total
2003	-6.05	16.02	5.47	15.16	32.39
2004	-0.40	7.46	-1.20	10.08	16.41
2005	-2.03	-2.62	3.99	5.02	4.18
2006	8.53	-1.20	-1.01	6.66	13.21
2007	2.78	10.31	3.33	-3.52	13.02

Trailing	NAV Return%	Market Return%	NAV Rtrn% +/-S&P 500	%Rank Cat.(NAV)
3 Mo	-3.52	-3.45	-0.19	59
6 Mo	-0.31	-0.29	1.06	34
1 Yr	13.02	12.32	7.53	13
3 Yr Avg	10.06	10.01	1.44	19
5 Yr Avg	15.49	15.44	2.66	16
10 Yr Avg	—	—	—	—

Tax Analysis	Tax-Adj Return%	Tax-Cost Ratio
3 Yr (estimated)	9.62	0.40
5 Yr (estimated)	15.07	0.36
10 Yr (estimated)	—	—

Rating and Risk

Time Period	Morningstar Rtn vs Cat	Morningstar Risk vs Cat	Morningstar Risk-Adj Rating
3 Yr	+Avg	+Avg	★★★★
5 Yr	+Avg	High	★★★★
10 Yr	—	—	—

Other Measures	Standard Index S&P 500	Best Fit Index M* Inds Mat TR
Alpha	1.6	-2.6
Beta	0.96	0.95
R-Squared	64	91
Standard Deviation	9.39	
Mean	10.06	
Sharpe Ratio	0.62	

Portfolio Analysis 12-31-07

Share change since 11-07 Total Stocks:264	Sector	PE	Tot Ret%	% Assets
⊖ General Electric Company	Ind Mtrls	16.6	2.69	18.29
⊖ United Technologies	Ind Mtrls	18.8	24.46	3.43
⊖ Boeing Company	Ind Mtrls	16.9	-0.11	2.96
⊖ 3M Company	Ind Mtrls	14.1	10.53	2.72
⊖ United Parcel Service, I	Business	18.2	-3.50	2.36
⊖ Caterpillar Inc.	Ind Mtrls	14.0	20.48	2.29
⊖ Emerson Electric Company	Ind Mtrls	21.3	31.42	2.20
⊖ Honeywell International,	Ind Mtrls	20.8	38.65	2.06
⊕ Deere & Company	Ind Mtrls	23.3	98.60	2.00
⊖ Lockheed Martin Corporat	Ind Mtrls	15.3	15.99	1.69
⊖ Union Pacific Corporatio	Business	18.4	38.33	1.60
⊖ General Dynamics	Ind Mtrls	18.6	21.35	1.46
⊖ Burlington Northern Sant	Business	16.5	14.30	1.27
⊖ Raytheon Company	Ind Mtrls	21.5	17.02	1.27
⊖ FedEx Corporation	Business	13.9	-17.61	1.24
⊖ Illinois Tool Works, Inc	Ind Mtrls	16.4	18.00	1.22
⊖ Northrop Grumman Corpora	Ind Mtrls	15.4	18.46	1.21
⊖ Automatic Data Processin	Business	23.6	2.62	1.16
⊖ Accenture, Ltd.	Software	17.1	-1.46	1.06
⊖ Danaher Corporation	Ind Mtrls	23.2	21.29	1.06

Current Investment Style

Value Blnd Growth — Large Mid Small

Market Cap	%
Giant	29.9
Large	36.8
Mid	27.8
Small	5.2
Micro	0.3
Avg $mil: 26,261	

Value Measures		Rel Category
Price/Earnings	15.76	1.00
Price/Book	3.02	1.18
Price/Sales	1.27	1.02
Price/Cash Flow	9.18	0.99
Dividend Yield %	1.63	0.86

Growth Measures	%	Rel Category
Long-Term Erngs	—	—
Book Value	5.18	0.56
Sales	6.74	0.82
Cash Flow	10.96	1.25
Historical Erngs	23.84	1.43

Profitability	%	Rel Category
Return on Equity	23.54	1.06
Return on Assets	7.37	0.88
Net Margin	9.31	0.76

Sector Weightings	% of Stocks	Rel S&P 500	3 Year High	3 Year Low
Info	6.84	0.33		
Software	1.41	0.34	2	1
Hardware	5.17	0.51	5	4
Media	0.00	0.00	0	0
Telecom	0.26	0.07	0	0
Service	25.90	0.64		
Health	0.91	0.08	2	1
Consumer	0.27	0.04	1	0
Business	24.72	5.61	27	23
Financial	0.00	0.00	0	0
Mfg	67.26	1.75		
Goods	2.27	0.25	3	2
Ind Mtrls	64.04	4.93	66	62
Energy	0.72	0.06	1	0
Utilities	0.23	0.06	0	0

Composition

Cash	0.4
Stocks	99.6
Bonds	0.0
Other	0.0
Foreign (% of Stock)	0.7

Morningstar's Take by Haywood Kelly 12-31-07

Despite its big position in one stock, iShares Dow Jones US Industrial is a fairly diversified play on the global economy.

General Electric makes up 20% of this ETF's portfolio, so our opinion on that stock will weigh heavily on our opinion on this ETF as a whole. As it is, we're fairly bullish on GE's prospects. Over the next five years, we expect sales and operating profits to rise 10% and 13% per annum, respectively, spurred by worldwide demand for aviation, rail, energy, and water infrastructure. And given the diversified nature of GE's business, parking 20% of the portfolio's assets in the stock isn't quite as risky a bet as it might seem.

What's true of GE is true to some extent of the portfolio as a whole. It's a group of firms with lots of exposure to global markets and global trade. Top-five holdings Boeing, United Technologies, UPS, and 3M do lots of business abroad and, thus, benefit from strong global growth and a weak dollar. And the portfolio doesn't deviate all that far from the makeup of the S&P 500 as a whole. About 40% of the fund's assets are in wide-moat firms--not all that far from the U.S. market. The average growth rates are also right in line with those of the market.

Whether we recommend the fund comes down to valuation. Unless we thought GE was grossly over- or undervalued, we're likely to be neutral. The other stocks in the portfolio come from a grab-bag of industries--transportation, machinery, aerospace, engineering--and many operate in multiple geographical and product markets. With this kind of diversity, we're unlikely to think them over- or undervalued en masse. Rather, valuations will typically be all over the board.

The diversity of the portfolio does mean that we'd feel comfortable recommending the ETF at a slim 9% discount to fair value. But keep in mind that you can buy essentially the same portfolio--Industrial Select Sector SPDR--for half this fund's expense ratio.

Address:	45 Fremont Street United States 800-474-2737
Web Address:	www.ishares.com
Inception:	06-12-00 *
Advisor:	Barclays Global Fund Advisers

Management Fee:	0.48%		
Expense Projections:	3Yr:$154	5Yr:$269	10Yr:$604
Income Distrib:	Quarterly		
Exchange:	NYSE		

iShares DJ RE Index IYR

Market Price	Mstar Category
$65.70	Specialty-Real Estate

Morningstar Rating	Return	Risk	Yield	NAV	Avg Daily Vol. (k)	52 wk High/Low
★★	Below Avg	Above Avg	4.4%	$66.05	7,032	$94.57 - $59.37

Morningstar Fair Value

Price/Fair Value Ratio	Coverage Rate %
0.94	95

Valuation

Though this fund is well diversified across stocks and the various real estate industry categories, it's still more or less subject to a single risk factor: the trajectory of the real estate market. Thus, we'd seek a 16% discount to our fair value estimate. The fund was recently trading at a 6% discount, which isn't deep enough to make it a bargain.

Methodology

This fund tracks the Dow Jones U.S. Real Estate Index, which includes the REITs and the real estate operating and holding companies in the Dow Jones U.S. Financials Index. It is market-cap-weighted and adjusted for insider ownership, cross ownership, and other factors that could limit the number of stock shares that actually trade. The fund's advisor uses representative sampling to mirror the benchmark's return, which means the offering owns most but not every single stock in the index.

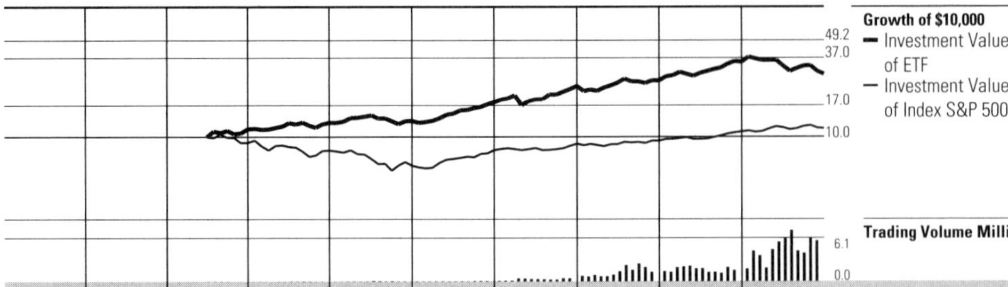

1998	1999	2000	2001	2002	2003	2004	2005	2006	2007	History
—	—	37.89	39.92	38.52	49.60	61.66	64.36	83.83	66.05	NAV $
—	—	37.98	39.90	38.65	49.63	61.60	64.15	83.35	65.70	Market Price $
—	—	14.51*	10.88	3.05	35.74	30.37	9.19	35.24	-18.15	NAV Return%
—	—	14.43*	10.56	3.46	35.37	30.15	8.94	34.91	-18.11	Market Price Return%
—	—	0.34	-0.06	0.08	-0.07	-0.14	-0.21	-0.12	-0.13	Avg Premium/Discount%
—	—	—	22.77	25.15	7.06	19.49	4.28	19.45	-23.64	NAV Rtrn% +/-S&P 500
—	—	—	-0.81	-0.58	-1.15	-0.85	-0.45	-0.26	0.00	NAV Rtrn% +/-DJ Real Est
—	—	—	1	1	67	67	100	50	80	NAV Return% Rank in Cat
—	—	—	5.37	6.44	3.93	5.35	4.64	4.55	3.50	Income Return %
—	—	—	5.51	-3.39	31.81	25.02	4.55	30.69	-21.65	Capital Return %
—	—	1.21	2.00	2.51	1.47	2.60	2.81	2.89	2.89	Income $
—	—	0.07	0.00	0.18	0.86	0.00	0.00	0.00	0.00	Capital Gains $
—	—	—	0.60	0.60	0.60	0.60	0.60	0.60	0.48	Expense Ratio %
—	—	—	6.37	5.97	6.40	5.58	5.35	3.92	2.33	Income Ratio %
—	—	—	30	10	21	20	16	19	29	Turnover Rate %
—	—	34	84	166	382	1,295	991	1,714	1,698	Net Assets $mil

Performance 12-31-07

Historic Quarterly NAV Returns

	1st Qtr	2nd Qtr	3rd Qtr	4th Qtr	Total
2003	0.15	12.66	9.20	10.17	35.74
2004	12.02	-6.56	8.25	15.06	30.37
2005	-7.71	14.28	1.93	1.57	9.19
2006	14.83	-1.51	8.68	10.03	35.24
2007	2.76	-8.71	-0.04	-12.71	-18.15

Trailing	NAV Return%	Market Return%	NAV Rtrn% +/-S&P 500	%Rank Cat.(NAV)
3 Mo	-12.71	-13.07	-9.38	37
6 Mo	-12.75	-13.36	-11.38	77
1 Yr	-18.15	-18.11	-23.64	80
3 Yr Avg	6.52	6.37	-2.10	100
5 Yr Avg	16.42	16.22	3.59	100
10 Yr Avg	—	—	—	—

Tax Analysis	Tax-Adj Return%	Tax-Cost Ratio
3 Yr (estimated)	5.04	1.39
5 Yr (estimated)	14.81	1.38
10 Yr (estimated)	—	—

Rating and Risk

Time Period	Morningstar Rtn vs Cat	Morningstar Risk vs Cat	Morningstar Risk-Adj Rating
3 Yr	-Avg	Avg	★★
5 Yr	-Avg	+Avg	★★
10 Yr	—	—	—

Other Measures	Standard Index S&P 500	Best Fit Index DJ Real Est
Alpha	-2.9	-1.7
Beta	1.47	0.94
R-Squared	47	99
Standard Deviation	16.67	
Mean	6.52	
Sharpe Ratio	0.20	

Portfolio Analysis 12-31-07

Share change since 11-07 Total Stocks:82	Sector	PE	Tot Ret%	% Assets
⊕ Simon Property Group, In	Financial	36.8	-11.34	6.61
⊕ ProLogis Trust	Financial	14.3	7.35	5.54
⊕ Vornado Realty Trust	Financial	27.3	-25.45	4.25
⊕ Boston Properties, Inc.	Financial	10.0	-10.36	3.71
⊕ Equity Residential	Financial	—	-24.90	3.39
⊕ General Growth Propertie	Financial	33.4	-18.53	3.25
⊕ Public Storage	Financial	—	-22.83	3.23
⊕ Host Hotels & Resorts, I	Financial	22.4	-27.14	3.04
⊕ Kimco Realty Corporation	Financial	26.4	-16.04	2.73
⊖ Plum Creek Timber Compan	Financial	35.1	18.26	2.72
⊕ AvalonBay Communities, I	Financial	37.5	-25.42	2.54
⊕ HCP, Inc.	—	57.8	-0.33	2.45
⊕ Annaly Capital Managemen	Financial	15.3	39.43	2.43
⊕ Ventas, Inc.	Financial	33.2	12.01	2.07
⊕ AMB Property Corporation	Financial	21.5	1.64	1.96
⊕ SL Green Realty Corporat	Financial	36.8	-27.81	1.89
⊕ Macerich Company	Financial	67.1	-15.09	1.71
⊕ Developers Diversified R	Financial	20.8	-36.01	1.62
⊕ Federal Realty Investmen	Financial	50.5	-0.61	1.60
⊕ CB Richard Ellis Group,	Financial	13.1	-34.87	1.50

Current Investment Style

Value Blnd Growth / Large Mid Small (Mid Value)

Market Cap	%
Giant	0.0
Large	18.0
Mid	65.5
Small	16.1
Micro	0.4
Avg $mil: 5,383	

Value Measures		Rel Category
Price/Earnings	23.71	0.96
Price/Book	2.11	1.17
Price/Sales	3.23	0.92
Price/Cash Flow	10.76	0.70
Dividend Yield %	4.99	1.00

Growth Measures	%	Rel Category
Long-Term Erngs	8.45	0.70
Book Value	3.06	0.38
Sales	7.49	0.89
Cash Flow	5.68	0.72
Historical Erngs	9.84	0.34

Profitability	%	Rel Category
Return on Equity	14.15	0.93
Return on Assets	4.23	0.72
Net Margin	29.61	0.82

Sector Weightings	% of Stocks	Rel S&P 500	3 Year High	3 Year Low
Info	0.00	0.00		
Software	0.00	0.00	0	0
Hardware	0.00	0.00	0	0
Media	0.00	0.00	0	0
Telecom	0.00	0.00	0	0
Service	98.69	2.43		
Health	0.00	0.00	0	0
Consumer	0.00	0.00	0	0
Business	0.00	0.00	0	0
Financial	98.69	5.66	100	98
Mfg	1.31	0.03		
Goods	0.00	0.00	0	0
Ind Mtrls	1.31	0.10	1	0
Energy	0.00	0.00	0	0
Utilities	0.00	0.00	0	0

Composition

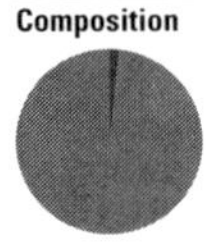

Cash	1.4
Stocks	98.6
Bonds	0.0
Other	0.0
Foreign (% of Stock)	1.4

Morningstar's Take by John Coumarianos 12-31-07

IShares Dow Jones US Real Estate provides diverse exposure to domestic real estate, but it's expensive.

This ETF has exposure to the largest names in real estate and to some unusual corners of the REIT world. Many of its holdings have also stumbled recently. However, because it's difficult for REITs to build durable competitive advantages, we'd want a greater margin of safety (about 15% below our fair value estimate) before investing.

Real estate's stalwart firms occupy this ETF's top three slots. Simon Property Group, ProLogis Trust, and Vornado Realty Trust are all narrow-moat businesses because of the prime locations they've secured for their malls, distribution centers, and office buildings, respectively. Also, each firm's management team has exhibited acumen at deploying capital or developing a special niche. For example, Simon completed an opportunistic purchase of the distressed firm Mills in early 2007, while ProLogis has expanded internationally, helping its multinational clients with their supply chains overseas. Vornado has an unparalleled nose for sniffing out bargain-basement properties that it can redevelop and re-lease at higher rental rates.

In addition to these major property types, this ETF is unusual in having exposure to timber assets via its 11th-largest holding, Plum Creek Timber. Trees are a unique commodity in that "warehousing" them when prices are soft increases a firm's assets as they continue to grow. We think this gives this ETF broader exposure to U.S real estate than its peers.

Despite this ETF's strengths, low barriers to entry in real estate mean that REITs typically produce modest returns on invested capital. They can also have difficulty growing because of the legal requirement to pay out 90% of their earnings as dividends. Finally, after real estate's multiyear surge, a larger percentage of this ETF's future total returns may come from dividends, making its 0.48% expense ratio more onerous than before.

Address:	45 Fremont Street United States 800-474-2737
Web Address:	www.ishares.com
Inception:	06-12-00*
Advisor:	Barclays Global Fund Advisers

Management Fee:	0.48%		
Expense Projections:	3Yr:$154	5Yr:$269	10Yr:$604
Income Distrib:	Quarterly		
Exchange:	NYSE		

iShares DJ Tech IYW

Market Price	Mstar Category
$62.46	Specialty-Technology

Morningstar Fair Value

Price/Fair Value Ratio	Coverage Rate %
0.95	98

Valuation

We'd require a 9% margin of safety before recommending this fund. Although it's fairly concentrated--about 60% of its assets are in the top 10 holdings--the stocks in the portfolio cater to a variety of end markets, which helps mitigate risk. It was recently trading at a 5% discount to fair value, which isn't steep enough to get excited about.

Methodology

This exchange-traded fund tracks a subset of the Dow Jones U.S. Total Market Index that includes the technology stocks in that broad market benchmark. Industries represented include software and computer services, and hardware and equipment. The fund weights holdings by market cap, resulting in very low turnover, and adjusts for the available float. Holdings are reconstituted quarterly.

Morningstar Rating	Return	Risk	Yield	NAV	Avg Daily Vol. (k)	52 wk High/Low
★★★	Average	Below Avg	0.2%	$62.48	169	$67.09 - $52.36

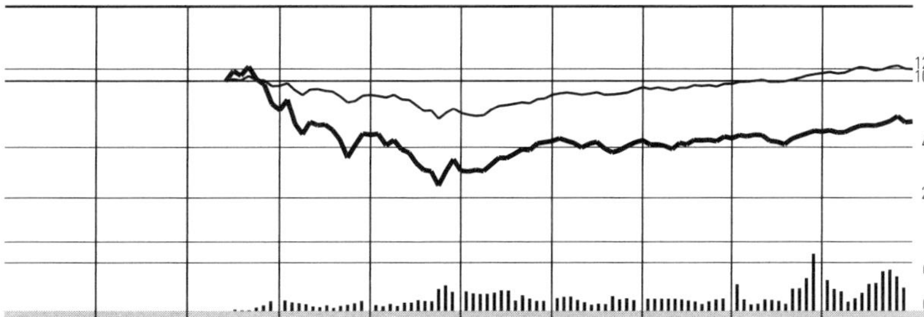

1998	1999	2000	2001	2002	2003	2004	2005	2006	2007	History
—	—	74.57	53.15	32.41	48.66	48.52	49.76	54.43	62.48	NAV $
—	—	74.56	53.20	32.50	48.51	48.46	49.72	54.45	62.46	Market Price $
—	—	-7.61*	-28.72	-39.02	50.14	1.15	2.72	9.56	15.04	NAV Return%
—	—	-7.62*	-28.65	-38.91	49.26	1.34	2.77	9.68	14.96	Market Price Return%
—	—	0.44	0.30	0.21	0.04	0.04	-0.06	0.01	0.01	Avg Premium/Discount%
—	—	—	-16.83	-16.92	21.46	-9.73	-2.19	-6.23	9.55	NAV Rtrn% +/-S&P 500
—	—	—	-0.38	-0.36	-0.90	-0.61	-0.59	-0.54	0.76	NAV Rtrn% +/-DJ Tech
—	—	—	50	20	62	87	45	43	20	NAV Return% Rank in Cat
—	—	—	0.00	0.00	0.00	1.43	0.15	0.15	0.24	Income Return %
—	—	—	-28.72	-39.02	50.14	-0.28	2.57	9.41	14.80	Capital Return %
—	—	0.00	0.00	0.00	0.00	0.70	0.07	0.08	0.13	Income $
—	—	0.00	0.00	0.00	0.00	0.00	0.00	0.00	0.00	Capital Gains $
—	—	—	0.60	0.60	0.60	0.60	0.60	0.60	0.48	Expense Ratio %
—	—	—	-0.47	-0.41	-0.22	-0.22	1.78	-0.04	0.15	Income Ratio %
—	—	—	11	8	15	5	9	7	6	Turnover Rate %
—	—	112	154	152	363	468	513	678	1,212	Net Assets $mil

Performance 12-31-07

Historic Quarterly NAV Returns

	1st Qtr	2nd Qtr	3rd Qtr	4th Qtr	Total
2003	-0.31	19.56	11.39	13.08	50.14
2004	-2.63	1.67	-10.75	14.49	1.15
2005	-7.54	2.22	6.33	2.22	2.72
2006	4.94	-9.12	8.24	6.13	9.56
2007	-0.74	9.89	5.95	-0.46	15.04

Trailing	NAV Return%	Market Return%	NAV Rtrn% +/-S&P 500	%Rank Cat.(NAV)
3 Mo	-0.46	-0.51	2.87	13
6 Mo	5.46	5.02	6.83	13
1 Yr	15.04	14.96	9.55	20
3 Yr Avg	8.99	9.02	0.37	12
5 Yr Avg	14.48	14.41	1.65	62
10 Yr Avg	—	—	—	—

Tax Analysis	Tax-Adj Return%	Tax-Cost Ratio
3 Yr (estimated)	8.92	0.06
5 Yr (estimated)	14.32	0.14
10 Yr (estimated)	—	—

Rating and Risk

Time Period	Morningstar Rtn vs Cat	Morningstar Risk vs Cat	Morningstar Risk-Adj Rating
3 Yr	Avg	-Avg	★★★
5 Yr	Avg	-Avg	★★★
10 Yr	—	—	—

Other Measures	Standard Index S&P 500	Best Fit Index
Alpha	-1.3	0.3
Beta	1.53	1.17
R-Squared	69	93
Standard Deviation	14.27	
Mean	8.99	
Sharpe Ratio	0.37	

Morningstar's Take by Haywood Kelly 12-31-07

IShares Dow Jones U.S. Technology will rarely be our top pick among tech ETFs.

The fund is a concentrated play on technology names--specifically, hardware and software. About 58% of the fund is in the hardware sector--Cisco, Intel, and the like--with the other 42% in software, including a 12% position in Microsoft, its top holding. The fund holds 200-plus names; however, because the holdings are weighted by market cap and a handful of firms dominate the software and hardware landscape, the portfolio has 60% of its assets in the top-10 names.

For investors looking for tech exposure, an ETF like this one makes sense. Technology is notoriously volatile: Products become obsolete faster than anyone thinks possible, competition is relentless, hit products can propel an also-ran to the top of the heap seemingly overnight. By buying into a group of tech names, much of that firm-specific risk cancels out. Granted, you're still exposed to the risk of tech becoming overvalued overall. When technology stocks become overvalued as a group--as they did in the late 1990s--a fund like this can be hazardous. In 2001 and 2002, as the tech bubble popped, this fund lost more than half its value. But as long as you heed the valuation of the underlying portfolio, you can sidestep that risk as well. Considering this fund's diversification across firms and end markets, we don't think it's excessively risky and thus would be willing to invest at a modest 9% discount to our fair value estimate.

We aren't crazy about this one because it's more expensive than two other tech ETFs--Technology SPDR and Vanguard Information Technology VGT. While the SPDR holds telecom stocks, which gives it a slightly different twist than this fund, the Vanguard portfolio is virtually identical. Rare will be the times when the valuation of this fund will be attractive enough relative to its peers, making it worth the heftier expense ratio.

Address:	45 Fremont Street United States 800-474-2737
Web Address:	www.ishares.com
Inception:	05-15-00*
Advisor:	Barclays Global Fund Advisers

Management Fee:	0.48%		
Expense Projections:	3Yr:$154	5Yr:$269	10Yr:$604
Income Distrib:	Quarterly		
Exchange:	NYSE		

Portfolio Analysis 12-31-07

Share change since 11-07 Total Stocks:200	Sector	PE	Tot Ret%	% Assets
⊕ Microsoft Corporation	Software	23.4	20.83	13.01
⊕ Apple, Inc.	Hardware	50.5	133.47	7.60
⊕ Cisco Systems, Inc.	Hardware	21.5	-0.95	7.23
⊕ Google, Inc.	Business	54.0	50.17	7.13
⊕ Intel Corporation	Hardware	25.4	34.22	6.81
⊕ International Business M	Hardware	16.2	13.20	6.51
⊖ Hewlett-Packard Company	Hardware	18.8	23.40	4.75
⊕ Oracle Corporation	Software	24.8	31.74	3.89
⊕ Qualcomm, Inc.	Hardware	20.2	5.52	2.85
⊖ Dell, Inc.	Hardware	18.6	-2.31	2.13
⊕ Texas Instruments, Inc.	Hardware	19.2	17.01	2.06
⊕ EMC Corporation	Hardware	26.1	40.38	1.71
⊕ Corning Inc.	Hardware	18.6	28.76	1.65
⊕ Motorola, Inc.	Hardware	NMF	-21.85	1.63
⊕ Yahoo, Inc.	Media	45.7	-8.93	1.30
⊕ Applied Materials	Hardware	14.8	-2.60	1.09
⊕ Adobe Systems Inc.	Software	37.9	3.92	1.08
⊕ MEMC Electronic Material	Hardware	35.3	126.09	0.89
⊕ NVIDIA Corporation	Hardware	29.4	37.88	0.82
⊕ American Tower Corporati	Telecom	—	14.51	0.77

Current Investment Style

Value Blnd Growth — Large Mid Small

Market Cap	%
Giant	62.1
Large	18.0
Mid	15.1
Small	4.4
Micro	0.5
Avg $mil: 58,353	

Value Measures		Rel Category
Price/Earnings	19.38	0.94
Price/Book	3.92	1.25
Price/Sales	2.39	0.98
Price/Cash Flow	13.30	0.92
Dividend Yield %	0.63	0.95

Growth Measures	%	Rel Category
Long-Term Erngs	—	—
Book Value	6.96	1.03
Sales	11.12	1.24
Cash Flow	12.67	1.30
Historical Erngs	12.07	0.85

Profitability	%	Rel Category
Return on Equity	24.50	1.43
Return on Assets	12.85	1.39
Net Margin	17.19	1.32

Industry Weightings	% of Stocks	Rel Cat
Software	26.3	1.2
Hardware	25.6	1.7
Networking Eq	10.6	1.2
Semis	16.4	0.9
Semi Equip	2.5	0.6
Comp/Data Sv	7.9	0.8
Telecom	1.8	0.7
Health Care	0.0	0.0
Other	8.9	0.5

Composition

Cash	0.3
Stocks	99.7
Bonds	0.0
Other	0.0
Foreign (% of Stock)	0.0

iShares DJ Telecom IYZ

Market Price	Mstar Category
$29.52	Specialty-Communications

Morningstar Fair Value

Price/Fair Value Ratio	Coverage Rate %
0.93	92

Morningstar Rating	Return	Risk	Yield	NAV	Avg Daily Vol. (k)	52 wk High/Low
★★	Low	Low	2.1%	$29.57	388	$35.07 - $27.58

Valuation

This fund is extremely concentrated, but we think enough of the risks cancel out so we'd be comfortable recommending it at a 9% discount to our fair value estimate. It was recently trading at a modest 3% discount to our fair value, which isn't cheap enough to get us excited.

Methodology

This fund tracks a subset of the Dow Jones U.S. Total Market Index that includes the telecom service provider stocks in that broad market benchmark. This includes both fixed-line and wireless providers. The fund weights its holdings by market cap, which results in very low turnover, and adjusts for the float outstanding. Because of the narrow slice of the market it focuses on and the fact that a handful of firms dominate telecom, the fund is extremely concentrated.

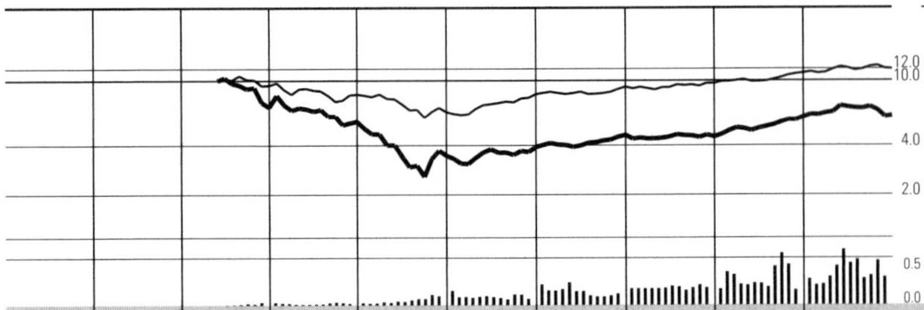

1998	1999	2000	2001	2002	2003	2004	2005	2006	2007	History
—	—	38.81	31.35	19.09	21.05	24.27	22.87	29.62	29.57	NAV $
—	—	38.81	31.53	19.06	21.05	24.30	22.86	29.59	29.52	Market Price $
—	—	-6.20*	-18.66	-38.13	12.85	18.14	-2.42	32.38	1.76	NAV Return%
—	—	-6.22*	-18.19	-38.58	13.03	18.28	-2.58	32.30	1.68	Market Price Return%
—	—	0.15	0.05	-0.02	0.14	-0.02	-0.03	0.06	-0.01	Avg Premium/Discount%
—	—	—	-6.77	-16.03	-15.83	7.26	-7.33	16.59	-3.73	NAV Rtrn% +/-S&P 500
—	—	—	-5.89	-3.58	5.52	-0.56	1.58	-4.45	-5.06	NAV Rtrn% +/-DJ Telecom
—	—	—	1	100	100	100	50	50	83	NAV Return% Rank in Cat
—	—	—	0.63	1.03	2.37	2.65	3.39	2.62	2.07	Income Return %
—	—	—	-19.29	-39.16	10.48	15.49	-5.81	29.76	-0.31	Capital Return %
—	—	0.22	0.24	0.32	0.45	0.55	0.81	0.59	0.61	Income $
—	—	0.59	0.00	0.00	0.00	0.00	0.00	0.00	0.00	Capital Gains $
—	—	—	0.60	0.60	0.60	0.60	0.60	0.60	0.48	Expense Ratio %
—	—	—	0.80	1.05	2.27	2.27	2.97	3.63	2.46	Income Ratio %
—	—	—	43	43	23	22	10	25	12	Turnover Rate %
—	—	45	58	104	144	352	497	948	856	Net Assets $mil

Performance 12-31-07

Historic Quarterly NAV Returns

	1st Qtr	2nd Qtr	3rd Qtr	4th Qtr	Total
2003	-10.86	22.40	-7.32	11.60	12.85
2004	3.35	-1.26	7.17	8.01	18.14
2005	-4.98	2.71	1.50	-1.49	-2.42
2006	13.54	-0.58	8.80	7.78	32.38
2007	5.98	8.51	0.70	-12.13	1.76

Trailing	NAV Return%	Market Return%	NAV Rtrn% +/-S&P 500	%Rank Cat.(NAV)
3 Mo	-12.13	-12.29	-8.80	100
6 Mo	-11.51	-11.54	-10.14	100
1 Yr	1.76	1.68	-3.73	83
3 Yr Avg	9.54	9.43	0.92	100
5 Yr Avg	11.87	11.87	-0.96	100
10 Yr Avg	—	—	—	—

Tax Analysis	Tax-Adj Return%	Tax-Cost Ratio
3 Yr (estimated)	8.58	0.88
5 Yr (estimated)	10.91	0.86
10 Yr (estimated)	—	—

Rating and Risk

Time Period	Morningstar Rtn vs Cat	Morningstar Risk vs Cat	Morningstar Risk-Adj Rating
3 Yr	-Avg	-Avg	★★
5 Yr	Low	Low	★★
10 Yr	—	—	—

Other Measures	Standard Index S&P 500	Best Fit Index DJ Telecom
Alpha	1.2	-2.4
Beta	1.01	0.89
R-Squared	45	93
Standard Deviation	11.76	
Mean	9.54	
Sharpe Ratio	0.47	

Portfolio Analysis 12-31-07

Share change since 11-07 Total Stocks:39	Sector	PE	Tot Ret%	% Assets
⊖ AT&T, Inc.	Telecom	21.6	20.58	16.44
⊖ Verizon Communications I	Telecom	21.7	22.19	13.42
⊖ Sprint Nextel Corporatio	Telecom	—	-30.12	6.94
⊕ MetroPCS Communications,	Telecom	70.9	—	6.07
⊖ Alltel Corp.	Telecom	—	—	5.55
⊖ NII Holdings, Inc.	Telecom	24.3	-25.02	3.96
⊖ Embarq Corporation	Telecom	—	-1.66	3.93
⊖ Leucadia National Corpor	Financial	—	67.87	3.90
⊖ Qwest Communications Int	Telecom	5.0	-16.25	3.74
⊖ Telephone and Data Syste	Telecom	26.9	15.96	3.61
⊖ Centurytel, Inc.	Telecom	12.5	-4.69	3.57
⊖ Windstream Corporation	Telecom	13.9	-1.74	3.03
⊖ Citizens Communications	Telecom	19.3	-4.97	2.87
⊖ United States Cellular C	Telecom	22.0	20.85	2.85
⊖ Virgin Media, Inc.	Media	—	-31.70	2.68
⊖ Leap Wireless Internatio	Telecom	—	-21.57	2.55
⊖ Level 3 Communications,	Telecom	—	-45.71	2.14
⊖ Dobson Communications Co	Telecom	—	—	2.02
⊖ Time Warner Telecom, Inc	Telecom	—	1.81	1.76
⊖ Cincinnati Bell, Inc.	Telecom	14.4	3.94	1.29

Current Investment Style

Value Blnd Growth — Large Mid Small

Market Cap	%
Giant	36.8
Large	8.0
Mid	42.0
Small	9.5
Micro	3.7
Avg $mil: 19,394	

Value Measures		Rel Category
Price/Earnings	17.32	0.97
Price/Book	1.72	0.77
Price/Sales	1.33	0.89
Price/Cash Flow	6.29	0.84
Dividend Yield %	1.72	0.88

Growth Measures	%	Rel Category
Long-Term Erngs	—	—
Book Value	6.99	1.32
Sales	-5.19	NMF
Cash Flow	-5.81	NMF
Historical Erngs	-2.80	NMF

Profitability	%	Rel Category
Return on Equity	15.74	0.90
Return on Assets	2.24	0.36
Net Margin	5.47	0.59

Industry Weightings	% of Stocks	Rel Cat
Telecom Srv	75.9	1.9
Wireless Srv	19.4	0.8
Network Eq	0.0	0.0
Semis	0.0	0.0
Big Media	0.0	0.0
Cable TV	0.0	0.0
Other Media	0.0	0.0
Soft/Hardwr	0.0	0.0
Other	4.7	0.7

Composition

Cash	0.8
Stocks	99.2
Bonds	0.0
Other	0.0
Foreign (% of Stock)	0.0

Morningstar's Take by Haywood Kelly 12-31-07

To like iShares Dow Jones U.S. Telecom, you need to love its top holdings.

This fund is highly concentrated even by sector-fund standards. Its top 10 holdings account for two thirds of its assets, and the top two holdings alone--AT&T and Verizon--soak up 30% of the fund. The fund only holds pure-play telecom firms focused on fixed-line and wireless. Cable companies, against which traditional telecom firms compete directly, are not in the portfolio.

So in order to fawn over the fund, you need to like the valuation of its top holdings: AT&T, Verizon, and Sprint Nextel. As of late-December 2007, we think Sprint is significantly undervalued, but that both AT&T and Verizon are slightly rich. As a result, the portfolio as a whole trades pretty close to fair value.

All three firms earn only narrow moat ratings: Competition is simply too fierce for us to have confidence that these firms can post decent returns on capital for the next 15 to 20 years. In fact, not a single holding in the portfolio warrants a wide moat rating. While that lowers the value that we'd assign to the portfolio, as dominant firms are typically more valuable than their less-established rivals, it actually makes the case for this ETF stronger. Given the risks inherent in the underlying holdings, a vehicle like this is a good way to spread the risks whenever telecom valuations are attractive. For that reason, we're comfortable recommending it when it trades at a 9% discount to our fair value estimate.

That said, like other iShares funds, this one comes with a 0.48% expense ratio. That's low in absolute terms, but when a near-identical fund comes with a 0.25% expense ratio, as Vanguard Telecom Services does, it seems quite high. Therefore, this portfolio's holdings would have to be meaningfully cheaper than Vanguard's for us to pound the table for this fund.

Address:	45 Fremont Street United States 800-474-2737
Web Address:	www.ishares.com
Inception:	05-22-00*
Advisor:	Barclays Global Fund Advisers

Management Fee:	0.48%		
Expense Projections:	3Yr:$154	5Yr:$269	10Yr:$604
Income Distrib:	Quarterly		
Exchange:	NYSE		

iShares DJ US Energy IYE

Market Price	Mstar Category
$136.97	Specialty-Natural Res

Morningstar Rating	Return	Risk	Yield	NAV	Avg Daily Vol. (k)	52 wk High/Low
★★★	Average	Below Avg	0.8%	$136.97	162	$139.07 - $93.70

Morningstar Fair Value

Price/Fair Value Ratio	Coverage Rate %
1.00	99

Valuation

This ETF was recently hovering right around our fair value estimate. The major driver of that fair value estimate is our energy team's oil price forecasts. If those assumptions prove to be way off, our fair value will be wrong. Because of this exposure to a single risk factor, we'd demand a 20% discount to fair value before recommending the fund.

Methodology

This exchange-traded fund tracks a subset of the Dow Jones U.S. Total Market Index: The Dow Jones U.S. Oil & Gas Index. The index includes the oil- and gas-company stocks from the broader-market benchmark. The fund holds more than 80 stocks, weighting the holdings by market cap (but adjusting for the outstanding float). The fund is extremely concentrated, with most of its assets in its top holdings.

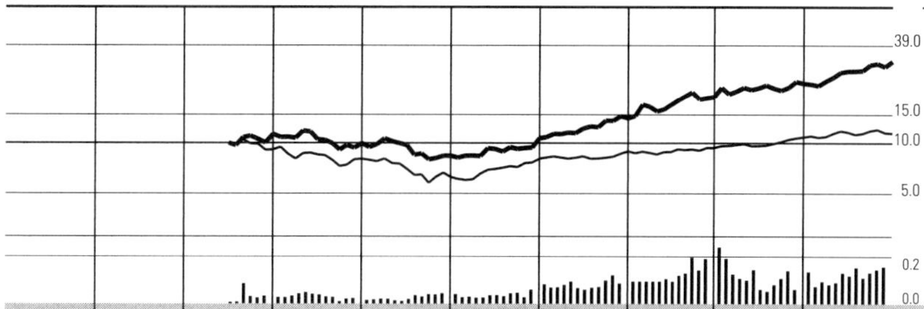

History

1998	1999	2000	2001	2002	2003	2004	2005	2006	2007	History
—	—	54.63	47.56	39.57	49.46	64.30	85.52	101.85	136.97	NAV $
—	—	54.97	47.70	39.41	49.45	64.30	85.76	101.85	136.97	Market Price $
—	—	15.47*	-11.83	-15.47	27.12	31.72	34.29	20.47	35.75	NAV Return%
—	—	15.47*	-12.12	-16.06	27.61	31.74	34.67	20.14	35.75	Market Price Return%
—	—	0.31	0.30	0.08	0.15	0.07	0.07	0.01	-0.12	Avg Premium/Discount%
—	—	—	0.06	6.63	-1.56	20.84	29.38	4.68	30.26	NAV Rtrn% +/-S&P 500
—	—	—	1.44	-0.07	4.26	1.78	2.28	-0.52	11.76	NAV Rtrn% +/-
—	—	—	1	100	75	50	67	12	42	NAV Return% Rank in Cat
—	—	—	1.14	1.46	1.86	1.54	1.24	1.26	1.11	Income Return %
—	—	—	-12.97	-16.93	25.26	30.18	33.05	19.21	34.64	Capital Return %
—	—	0.27	0.62	0.69	0.73	0.76	0.79	1.07	1.13	Income $
—	—	0.00	0.00	0.00	0.00	0.00	0.00	0.00	0.00	Capital Gains $
—	—	—	0.60	0.60	0.60	0.60	0.60	0.60	0.48	Expense Ratio %
—	—	—	0.94	1.32	1.79	1.42	1.16	1.00	1.13	Income Ratio %
—	—	—	20	18	9	2	3	2	6	Turnover Rate %
—	—	41	78	105	223	498	812	901	1,233	Net Assets $mil

Performance 12-31-07

Historic Quarterly NAV Returns

	1st Qtr	2nd Qtr	3rd Qtr	4th Qtr	Total
2003	0.12	9.41	0.23	15.79	27.12
2004	5.84	7.74	11.74	3.37	31.72
2005	17.20	2.70	18.79	-6.07	34.29
2006	8.02	4.72	-3.29	10.13	20.47
2007	3.14	14.88	9.03	5.09	35.75

Trailing	NAV Return%	Market Return%	NAV Rtrn% +/-S&P 500	%Rank Cat.(NAV)
3 Mo	5.09	5.20	8.42	45
6 Mo	14.57	14.70	15.94	33
1 Yr	35.75	35.75	30.26	42
3 Yr Avg	29.99	29.99	21.37	38
5 Yr Avg	29.75	29.85	16.92	34
10 Yr Avg	—	—	—	—

Tax Analysis	Tax-Adj Return%	Tax-Cost Ratio
3 Yr (estimated)	29.52	0.35
5 Yr (estimated)	29.20	0.42
10 Yr (estimated)	—	—

Rating and Risk

Time Period	Morningstar Rtn vs Cat	Morningstar Risk vs Cat	Morningstar Risk-Adj Rating
3 Yr	Avg	-Avg	★★★
5 Yr	Avg	-Avg	★★★
10 Yr	—	—	—

Other Measures	Standard Index S&P 500	Best Fit Index M* Energy Sec TR
Alpha	19.0	-0.5
Beta	1.17	0.97
R-Squared	21	99
Standard Deviation	19.47	
Mean	29.99	
Sharpe Ratio	1.23	

Morningstar's Take by Haywood Kelly 12-31-07

It has a good portfolio of stocks, but iShares Dow Jones U.S. Energy isn't the cheapest way to invest in them.

The quality of the underlying companies in this ETF is high. The largest holding, at 24% of assets as of Nov. 30, is Exxon-Mobil, whose scale confers a wide economic moat. Nine of the top 10 holdings generate positive free cash flow and pay dividends. Most of the fund's significant holdings have an average or below-average business risk rating.

As you'd expect, this ETF is among the most volatile that Morningstar covers. The stocks in the portfolio are highly levered to oil prices, and they tend to move as a group. The bulk of the assets are invested in oil producers like Exxon and Chevron, whose cash flows and share prices depend on the trajectory of oil prices. For example, if we lowered our oil-price assumptions by 10%, our fair value for Exxon would fall roughly 6% and for Chevron 20%. And oil-services stocks--including Schlumberger and Halliburton--recently made up about one fourth of the portfolio. Not only are such stocks uber-sensitive to oil prices, but they were recently overvalued in our opinion.

Volatility in itself isn't bad. What's bad is that our fair value of this ETF is so dependent on a single risk factor: our forecast of oil prices. If the oil-price forecasts built into our fair value estimates of oil stocks are imprecise, our fair value for this ETF will be wrong. With a more diversified ETF, such forecasting errors tend to wash out. In order to recommend this ETF, we'd need to see a 20% discount to our fair value estimate.

There will no doubt be times when this ETF gets cheap enough to recommend. But keep in mind that you can get essentially the same portfolio--Energy Select SPDR--for half the expense ratio. Unless this portfolio is more attractively valued--unlikely, given how similar the two are--you're better off in the SPDR.

Address:	45 Fremont Street United States 800-474-2737
Web Address:	www.ishares.com
Inception:	06-12-00*
Advisor:	Barclays Global Fund Advisers

Management Fee:	0.48%		
Expense Projections:	3Yr:$154	5Yr:$269	10Yr:$604
Income Distrib:	Quarterly		
Exchange:	NYSE		

Portfolio Analysis 12-31-07

Share change since 11-07 Total Stocks:86	Sector	PE	Tot Ret%	% Assets
⊕ ExxonMobil Corporation	Energy	13.6	24.34	23.73
⊕ Chevron Corporation	Energy	11.4	30.59	15.16
⊕ Schlumberger, Ltd.	Energy	24.6	57.10	6.93
⊕ Occidental Petroleum Cor	Energy	13.8	60.25	5.19
⊕ ConocoPhillips	Energy	13.8	25.42	4.77
⊕ Devon Energy Corporation	Energy	14.7	33.51	2.85
⊕ Marathon Oil Corporation	Energy	9.7	34.09	2.62
⊕ Apache Corporation	Energy	15.9	62.91	2.62
⊕ Transocean, Inc.	—	16.1	77.14	2.47
⊕ Valero Energy Corporatio	Energy	8.1	37.91	2.45
⊕ Anadarko Petroleum Corp.	Energy	7.9	52.04	2.42
⊕ Baker Hughes Inc.	Energy	17.9	9.35	2.26
⊕ Hess Corporation	Ind Mtrls	19.1	104.77	2.09
⊕ Halliburton Company	Energy	14.4	23.33	1.94
⊕ EOG Resources	Energy	22.9	43.55	1.82
⊕ Murphy Oil Corporation	Energy	25.2	68.58	1.40
⊕ XTO Energy, Inc.	Energy	14.7	37.60	1.35
⊕ National Oilwell Varco,	Energy	21.7	132.65	1.29
⊕ Weatherford Internationa	Energy	23.4	64.15	1.22
⊕ Noble Corporation	Energy	14.4	44.12	0.97

Current Investment Style

Value Blnd Growth — Large Mid Small

Market Cap	%
Giant	55.9
Large	33.1
Mid	9.5
Small	1.4
Micro	0.0
Avg $mil: 78,980	

Value Measures		Rel Category
Price/Earnings	12.05	0.74
Price/Book	2.63	1.13
Price/Sales	1.32	0.95
Price/Cash Flow	8.82	1.11
Dividend Yield %	1.17	0.85

Growth Measures	%	Rel Category
Long-Term Erngs	—	—
Book Value	17.12	1.15
Sales	7.13	0.64
Cash Flow	7.74	0.48
Historical Erngs	30.30	0.83

Profitability	%	Rel Category
Return on Equity	26.00	1.27
Return on Assets	13.34	1.42
Net Margin	15.77	1.15

Industry Weightings	% of Stocks	Rel Cat
Oil & Gas	73.0	2.1
Oil/Gas Products	3.6	1.1
Oil & Gas Srv	22.9	1.0
Pipelines	0.5	0.4
Utilities	0.0	0.0
Hard Commd	0.0	0.0
Soft Commd	0.0	0.0
Misc. Indstrl	0.0	0.0
Other	0.0	0.0

Composition

Cash	0.3
Stocks	99.7
Bonds	0.0
Other	0.0
Foreign (% of Stock)	0.0

iShares DJ Utilities IDU

Market Price	Mstar Category
$102.41	Specialty-Utilities

Morningstar Fair Value

Price/Fair Value Ratio	Coverage Rate %
0.96	94

Valuation

We'd demand an 8% discount to our fair value estimate here. Although the fund focuses on a single sector, most of the top holdings have average or below-average business risk ratings. This, coupled with the portfolio's diversification, explains why we wouldn't require a wide margin of safety. It was recently trading at a 4% discount.

Methodology

This fund tracks the Dow Jones U.S. Utilities Index, which includes power, gas, water, and other utilities stocks from the Dow Jones U.S. Total Market Index. It's market-cap-weighted--which results in very low turnover--and is adjusted for insider ownership, cross ownership, and other factors that could limit the number of stock shares that actually trade. The fund's advisor uses representative sampling to mirror the benchmark's return, which means the offering owns most, but not all, the stocks in the index.

Morningstar Rating	Return	Risk	Yield	NAV	Avg Daily Vol. (k)	52 wk High/Low
★★★	Average	Above Avg	2.3%	$102.79	69	$106.42 - $87.93

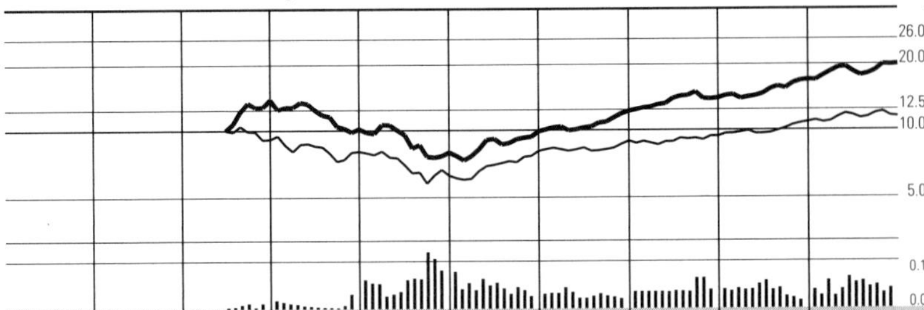

History

1998	1999	2000	2001	2002	2003	2004	2005	2006	2007	History
—	—	88.90	63.58	47.95	57.47	68.66	76.47	89.82	102.79	NAV $
—	—	88.78	63.97	48.06	57.59	68.70	76.46	89.87	102.41	Market Price $
—	—	8.49*	-26.42	-21.61	24.11	23.26	14.63	20.71	17.21	NAV Return%
—	—	8.44*	-25.87	-21.91	24.09	23.08	14.54	20.79	16.71	Market Price Return%
—	—	0.15	-0.05	0.11	0.04	-0.02	-0.04	0.02	-0.08	Avg Premium/Discount%
—	—	—	-14.53	0.49	-4.57	12.38	9.72	4.92	11.72	NAV Rtrn% +/-S&P 500
—	—	—	-0.24	-0.42	-0.80	-0.78	-0.72	-0.57	0.07	NAV Rtrn% +/-DJ Utilities
—	—	—	100	1	100	100	100	75	43	NAV Return% Rank in Cat
—	—	—	2.32	3.29	3.81	3.42	3.22	2.94	2.65	Income Return %
—	—	—	-28.74	-24.90	20.30	19.84	11.41	17.77	14.56	Capital Return %
—	—	1.12	2.05	2.07	1.80	1.94	2.19	2.23	2.36	Income $
—	—	0.14	0.00	0.00	0.00	0.00	0.00	0.00	0.00	Capital Gains $
—	—	—	0.60	0.60	0.60	0.60	0.60	0.60	0.48	Expense Ratio %
—	—	—	2.59	2.89	4.15	3.41	3.10	2.82	2.59	Income Ratio %
—	—	—	11	8	15	7	7	5	5	Turnover Rate %
—	—	37	73	276	486	560	704	786	848	Net Assets $mil

Performance 12-31-07

Historic Quarterly NAV Returns

	1st Qtr	2nd Qtr	3rd Qtr	4th Qtr	Total
2003	-3.68	19.33	-0.24	8.24	24.11
2004	5.01	-1.00	6.00	11.85	23.26
2005	4.62	9.24	6.88	-6.16	14.63
2006	-0.51	5.31	5.54	9.15	20.71
2007	8.78	-0.15	1.22	6.62	17.21

Trailing	NAV Return%	Market Return%	NAV Rtrn% +/-S&P 500	%Rank Cat.(NAV)
3 Mo	6.62	6.28	9.95	40
6 Mo	7.92	7.60	9.29	40
1 Yr	17.21	16.71	11.72	43
3 Yr Avg	17.49	17.32	8.87	100
5 Yr Avg	19.93	19.79	7.10	100
10 Yr Avg	—	—	—	—

Tax Analysis	Tax-Adj Return%	Tax-Cost Ratio
3 Yr (estimated)	16.40	0.93
5 Yr (estimated)	18.71	1.02
10 Yr (estimated)	—	—

Rating and Risk

Time Period	Morningstar Rtn vs Cat	Morningstar Risk vs Cat	Morningstar Risk-Adj Rating
3 Yr	-Avg	+Avg	★★
5 Yr	Avg	+Avg	★★★
10 Yr	—	—	—

Other Measures	Standard Index S&P 500	Best Fit Index M* Util Sect TR
Alpha	10.6	-1.1
Beta	0.43	0.98
R-Squared	11	97
Standard Deviation	10.08	
Mean	17.49	
Sharpe Ratio	1.23	

Portfolio Analysis 12-31-07

Share change since 11-07 Total Stocks:72	Sector	PE	Tot Ret%	% Assets
⊕ Exelon Corporation	Utilities	20.2	35.14	8.88
⊕ Southern Company	Utilities	17.1	9.85	4.41
⊕ Dominion Resources, Inc.	Utilities	12.3	16.98	4.27
⊕ FPL Group	Utilities	20.0	27.91	4.07
⊕ Duke Energy Corporation	Utilities	10.4	9.03	3.85
⊕ Public Service Enterpris	Utilities	19.1	52.10	3.84
⊕ Entergy Corporation	Utilities	20.0	32.55	3.75
⊕ Williams Companies, Inc.	Energy	27.7	38.70	3.48
⊕ FirstEnergy Corporation	Utilities	17.3	23.71	3.40
⊕ PPL Corporation	Utilities	20.0	49.31	3.19
⊕ American Electric Power	Utilities	16.8	13.06	3.04
⊕ Edison International	Utilities	15.4	19.93	2.78
⊕ Constellation Energy Gro	Utilities	22.5	51.88	2.76
⊕ PG & E Corporation	Utilities	16.3	-6.09	2.75
⊕ Spectra Energy Corporati	Utilities	—	-3.60	2.61
⊕ Sempra Energy	Utilities	17.0	12.69	2.29
⊕ AES Corporation	Utilities	23.3	-2.95	2.29
⊕ Consolidated Edison Comp	Utilities	13.9	6.65	2.04
⊕ Progress Energy, Inc.	Utilities	15.5	3.83	1.98
⊕ Ameren Corporation	Utilities	19.7	5.94	1.79

Current Investment Style

Value Blnd Growth; Large Mid Small

Market Cap	%
Giant	8.6
Large	55.0
Mid	32.5
Small	3.9
Micro	0.0
Avg $mil: 13,899	

Value Measures		Rel Category
Price/Earnings	15.84	0.91
Price/Book	1.44	0.87
Price/Sales	1.33	1.02
Price/Cash Flow	7.42	1.02
Dividend Yield %	2.61	0.90

Growth Measures	%	Rel Category
Long-Term Erngs	—	—
Book Value	16.21	2.16
Sales	1.97	0.59
Cash Flow	4.57	0.52
Historical Erngs	7.54	0.93

Profitability	%	Rel Category
Return on Equity	13.82	0.97
Return on Assets	4.25	1.02
Net Margin	10.72	1.06

Industry Weightings	% of Stocks	Rel Cat
Telecom Srv	0.0	0.0
Electric Utls	80.8	1.3
Nat Gas Utls	8.6	0.9
Wireless Srv	0.0	0.0
Energy	10.1	0.8
Media	0.0	0.0
Network Eq	0.0	0.0
Water	0.5	2.4
Other	0.0	0.0

Composition

Cash	0.8
Stocks	99.3
Bonds	0.0
Other	0.0
Foreign (% of Stock)	0.0

Morningstar's Take by Haywood Kelly 12-31-07

There will almost always be a better choice than iShares Dow Jones U.S. Utilities.

Despite the plodding nature of utilities, their stocks do swing in and out of favor. Over the past few years, they've definitely been in favor. This fund has returned double digits each year since 2003. Utilities have been popular as investors have hunted for yield. Plus, those utilities that came through the sector meltdown at the start of this decade have been improving their balance sheets. As a result, this fund's price multiples aren't all that far off from those of the S&P 500 as a whole.

This ETF invests passively in the utilities stocks in the Dow Jones U.S. Utilities Index. Its portfolio holds 72 stocks, but given that the index's assets are weighted by market cap, the top 10 holdings soak up 43% of assets. As you'd expect from a portfolio of utilities stocks, the growth rates of the underlying companies are low (basically GDP-like) and the dividend yield is higher than that of the market, at 2.2%.

The top holding here, at 9% of assets, is Exelon. This is an unusual utility in that it earns a wide-moat rating--the only U.S. utility to do so. The reason is Exelon's portfolio of nuclear power plants. With the concern over carbon emissions, nuclear power is back in vogue as a clean energy source. Exelon's low-cost nuclear power plants and economies of scale give it, in our view, enough of a competitive advantage to separate it from its peers. Given Exelon's hefty weighting in the portfolio, our opinion of that stock will significantly influence our view of this ETF.

One drawback with this ETF is its price tag. Its 0.48% expense ratio is double those of very similar utilities offerings from the SPDR and Vanguard families. Unless the holdings of this fund are significantly cheaper than those of its competitors--highly unlikely given the similarities of their portfolios--there's no reason to pay the premium to own these shares.

Address:	45 Fremont Street United States 800-474-2737
Web Address:	www.ishares.com
Inception:	06-12-00 *
Advisor:	Barclays Global Fund Advisers

Management Fee:	0.48%		
Expense Projections:	3Yr:$154	5Yr:$269	10Yr:$604
Income Distrib:	Quarterly		
Exchange:	NYSE		

iShares Dow Jones US Home ITB

Market Price	Mstar Category
$17.63	Large Blend

Morningstar Rating	Return	Risk	Yield	NAV	Avg Daily Vol. (k)	52 wk High/Low
—	—	—	1.7%	$17.57	371	$44.46 - $14.05

Growth of $10,000
— Investment Value of ETF
— Investment Value of Index S&P 500

Trading Volume Millions

1998	1999	2000	2001	2002	2003	2004	2005	2006	2007	History
—	—	—	—	—	—	—	—	42.35	17.57	NAV $
—	—	—	—	—	—	—	—	42.37	17.63	Market Price $
—	—	—	—	—	—	—	—	-45.74*	-58.00	NAV Return%
—	—	—	—	—	—	—	—	-45.62*	-57.87	Market Price Return%
—	—	—	—	—	—	—	—	0.07	-0.07	Avg Premium/Discount%
—	—	—	—	—	—	—	—	—	-63.49	NAV Rtrn% +/-S&P 500
—	—	—	—	—	—	—	—	—	-2.20	NAV Rtrn% +/-DJ HomeCons
—	—	—	—	—	—	—	—	—	100	NAV Return% Rank in Cat
—	—	—	—	—	—	—	—	—	0.69	Income Return %
—	—	—	—	—	—	—	—	—	-58.69	Capital Return %
—	—	—	—	—	—	—	—	0.17	0.29	Income $
—	—	—	—	—	—	—	—	0.00	0.00	Capital Gains $
—	—	—	—	—	—	—	—	—	0.48	Expense Ratio %
—	—	—	—	—	—	—	—	—	0.66	Income Ratio %
—	—	—	—	—	—	—	—	—	21	Turnover Rate %
—	—	—	—	—	—	—	—	97	215	Net Assets $mil

Morningstar Fair Value

Price/Fair Value Ratio	Coverage Rate %
0.65	78

Valuation

Most holdings in the portfolio have above-average or speculative business risk ratings. The portfolio can diversify away only so much of its biggest risk factor--the health of the U.S. housing market. As such, we'd recommend this ETF at a 20% discount to our fair value estimate. It was recently trading at a 35% discount to fair value.

Methodology

This fund tracks the Dow Jones U.S. Select Home Construction Index. The index is market-cap-weighted--which results in very low turnover for the fund--although component weights are capped for diversification. The index is adjusted for insider ownership, cross ownership, and other factors that could limit the number of stock shares that actually trade. Unlike rival homebuilder funds, which stray into home-supply and tertiary areas, this fund is focused squarely on homebuilders, making it a pure play. The portfolio is top-heavy, with the top 10 stocks accounting for nearly 60% of assets.

Performance 12-31-07

Historic Quarterly NAV Returns

	1st Qtr	2nd Qtr	3rd Qtr	4th Qtr	Total
2003	—	—	—	—	—
2004	—	—	—	—	—
2005	—	—	—	—	—
2006	—	—	-5.79	14.70	—*
2007	-19.05	-8.32	-36.41	-11.01	-58.00

Trailing	NAV Return%	Market Return%	NAV Rtrn% +/-S&P 500	%Rank Cat.(NAV)
3 Mo	-11.01	-10.78	-7.68	93
6 Mo	-43.41	-43.21	-42.04	100
1 Yr	-58.00	-57.87	-63.49	100
3 Yr Avg	—	—	—	—
5 Yr Avg	—	—	—	—
10 Yr Avg	—	—	—	—

Tax Analysis	Tax-Adj Return%	Tax-Cost Ratio
3 Yr (estimated)	—	—
5 Yr (estimated)	—	—
10 Yr (estimated)	—	—

Rating and Risk

Time Period	Morningstar Rtn vs Cat	Morningstar Risk vs Cat	Morningstar Risk-Adj Rating
3 Yr	—	—	—
5 Yr	—	—	—
10 Yr	—	—	—

Other Measures	Standard Index S&P 500	Best Fit Index
Alpha	—	—
Beta	—	—
R-Squared	—	—
Standard Deviation	—	
Mean	—	
Sharpe Ratio	—	

Morningstar's Take by Haywood Kelly 12-31-07

IShares Dow Jones U.S. Home Construction is a pure play on the beleaguered homebuilding industry.

The fund holds just 22 stocks, and each of them is narrowly focused on one thing: building homes for Americans. That's been an absolutely horrible business of late, given the mortgage debacle facing the U.S. financial industry. Through November 2007, this fund had lost 60% of its value. The portfolio as a whole trades for about 50% of book value. That's deep, deep value territory.

Of course, you get what you pay for. Some homebuilders have gone bust, and others could follow. According to Morningstar's homebuilding analyst, speculative-rated builders that aren't already in bankruptcy, such as Standard Pacific, WCI Communities, and Hovnanian, may well fall into insolvency, while a longer period of inactivity in the homebuilding market could also push above-average-risk Beazer Homes over the edge.

Most of those stocks are now small holdings in this ETF as a result of their collapsing market values. The names at the top of the portfolio--Toll Brothers, KB Home, and Ryland--should survive all but a depression-style downturn. Most of the remaining top 10 holdings should make it through as well. The advantage of the ETF format is that even if a few more homebuilders go bust, the overall portfolio could still do quite well over the long term. You don't have to precisely target the winners and losers.

With a 0.48% expense ratio, the fund is more expensive than a similar fund in the SPDR family. But the latter fund has about one quarter of its assets outside the homebuilding industry. For those gutsy investors wanting to make a contrarian investment on the U.S. home industry, this is the best vehicle we cover.

Address:	iShares Funds United States 800-474-2737			
Web Address:	www.ishares.com			
Inception:	05-01-06*			
Advisor:	Barclays Global Fund Advisers			
Management Fee:	0.48%			
Expense Projections:	3Yr:$154	5Yr:$269	10Yr:$604	
Income Distrib:	Annually			
Exchange:	NYSE			

Portfolio Analysis 12-31-07

Share change since 11-07 Total Stocks:21	Sector	PE	Tot Ret%	% Assets
⊕ Lennar Corporation	Consumer	—	-65.71	5.68
⊖ Centex Corporation	Consumer	—	-55.25	5.61
⊕ Champion Enterprises, In	Consumer	44.8	0.64	5.55
⊖ D.R. Horton Incorporated	Consumer	—	-49.13	5.50
⊖ NVR, Inc.	Consumer	8.3	-18.76	5.40
⊖ Toll Brothers, Inc.	Consumer	90.9	-37.76	5.32
⊕ Pulte Homes, Inc.	Consumer	—	-68.29	5.18
⊖ Ryland Group, Inc.	Consumer	—	-48.90	5.01
⊕ M.D.C. Holdings, Inc.	Consumer	—	-33.54	4.96
⊖ KB Home	Consumer	—	-56.69	4.72
⊕ Meritage Homes Corporati	Consumer	—	-71.99	4.56
⊕ Standard Pacific Corp.	Consumer	—	-87.41	4.55
⊕ Cavco Industries, Inc.	Consumer	29.9	-3.42	4.43
⊕ WCI Communities, Inc.	Consumer	—	-80.29	4.42
⊕ Brookfield Homes Corpora	Consumer	4.3	-57.08	4.27
⊕ Levitt Corporation A	Consumer	—	-82.26	4.13
⊕ Beazer Homes USA, Inc.	Consumer	3.9	-83.95	4.05
⊕ M/I Homes, Inc.	Consumer	—	-72.34	4.04
⊕ Palm Harbor Homes, Inc.	Consumer	—	-24.75	4.03
⊕ Hovnanian Enterprises In	Consumer	—	-78.85	3.99

Current Investment Style

Value Blnd Growth / Large Mid Small

Market Cap	%
Giant	0.0
Large	0.0
Mid	37.6
Small	15.6
Micro	46.8
Avg $mil:	810

Value Measures		Rel Category
Price/Earnings	4.20	0.27
Price/Book	0.53	0.21
Price/Sales	0.21	0.17
Price/Cash Flow	0.63	0.07
Dividend Yield %	2.25	1.19

Growth Measures	%	Rel Category
Long-Term Erngs	—	—
Book Value	-6.49	NMF
Sales	-3.96	NMF
Cash Flow	71.56	8.19
Historical Erngs	-24.88	NMF

Profitability	%	Rel Category
Return on Equity	-10.75	NMF
Return on Assets	-4.54	NMF
Net Margin	-5.88	NMF

Sector Weightings	% of Stocks	Rel S&P 500	3 Year High	3 Year Low
Info	0.00	0.00		
Software	0.00	0.00	—	—
Hardware	0.00	0.00	—	—
Media	0.00	0.00	—	—
Telecom	0.00	0.00	—	—
Service	100.00	2.46		
Health	0.00	0.00	—	—
Consumer	100.00	14.75	—	—
Business	0.00	0.00	—	—
Financial	0.00	0.00	—	—
Mfg	0.00	0.00		
Goods	0.00	0.00	—	—
Ind Mtrls	0.00	0.00	—	—
Energy	0.00	0.00	—	—
Utilities	0.00	0.00	—	—

Composition

Cash	0.6
Stocks	99.4
Bonds	0.0
Other	0.0
Foreign (% of Stock)	0.0

iShares S&P GSSI Nat Res IGE

Market Price	Mstar Category
$134.38	Specialty-Natural Res

Morningstar Fair Value

Price/Fair Value Ratio	Coverage Rate %
0.97	97

Valuation

This ETF tracks a risky sector. Plus, the accuracy of our fair value estimate depends heavily on our forecasts for volatile oil and gas prices. Consequently, we're comfortable recommending this ETF only when it's trading 20% or more below our estimate of fair value.

Methodology

This ETF mimics the Goldman Sachs Natural Resources Sector Index, a benchmark of U.S.-and Canada-based natural-resources stocks. Unlike many competing funds, this ETF includes a passel of nonenergy stocks in areas such as metals, mining, basic materials, and paper and forest products. Still, energy stocks make up about 80% of the portfolio. The index ranks stocks by market capitalization. Thus, the biggest names in the sector take up quite a bit of space here. The fund's top 10 holdings consume more than 40% of the portfolio.

Morningstar Rating	Return	Risk	Yield	NAV	Avg Daily Vol. (k)	52 wk High/Low
★★★	Average	Below Avg	0.8%	$134.41	56	$137.75 - $93.85

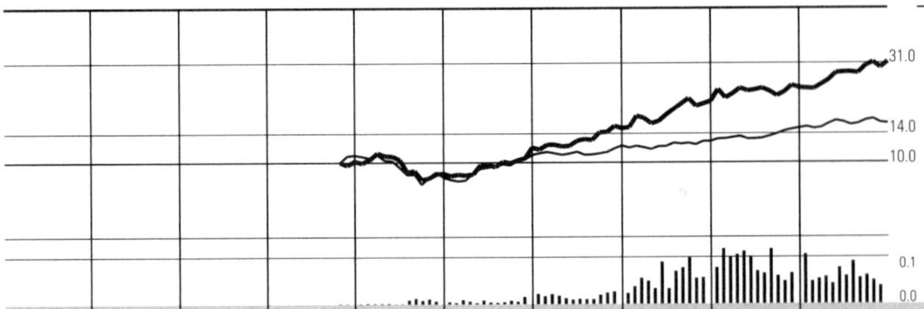

1998	1999	2000	2001	2002	2003	2004	2005	2006	2007	History
—	—	—	47.48	40.67	53.47	65.64	88.20	101.35	134.41	NAV $
—	—	—	47.80	40.70	53.41	65.64	88.33	101.60	134.38	Market Price $
—	—	—	19.84*	-13.00	33.63	24.24	35.79	16.30	33.82	NAV Return%
—	—	—	19.84*	-13.53	33.39	24.40	35.98	16.41	33.47	Market Price Return%
—	—	—	1.54	-0.36	0.05	0.09	0.08	0.05	0.07	Avg Premium/Discount%
—	—	—	—	9.10	4.95	13.36	30.88	0.51	28.33	NAV Rtrn% +/-S&P 500
—	—	—	—	-0.01	-0.77	-0.35	-0.82	-0.55	—	NAV Rtrn% +/-S&P GSSI
—	—	—	—	50	25	100	50	56	53	NAV Return% Rank in Cat
—	—	—	—	1.47	1.83	1.34	1.31	1.31	1.07	Income Return %
—	—	—	—	-14.47	31.80	22.90	34.48	14.99	32.75	Capital Return %
—	—	—	0.19	0.70	0.74	0.71	0.85	1.15	1.08	Income $
—	—	—	0.00	0.00	0.00	0.00	0.00	0.00	0.00	Capital Gains $
—	—	—	—	0.50	0.50	0.50	0.50	0.50	0.48	Expense Ratio %
—	—	—	—	1.51	1.92	1.33	1.20	1.12	1.14	Income Ratio %
—	—	—	—	12	7	7	8	7	18	Turnover Rate %
—	—	—	—	20	112	374	1,094	1,505	2,238	Net Assets $mil

Performance 12-31-07

Historic Quarterly NAV Returns

	1st Qtr	2nd Qtr	3rd Qtr	4th Qtr	Total
2003	-1.86	12.30	2.06	18.81	33.63
2004	3.35	4.53	9.86	4.68	24.24
2005	12.23	3.64	20.51	-3.13	35.79
2006	8.92	4.33	-6.48	9.43	16.30
2007	3.83	14.61	7.55	4.56	33.82

Trailing	NAV Return%	Market Return%	NAV Rtrn% +/-S&P 500	%Rank Cat.(NAV)
3 Mo	4.56	4.59	7.89	50
6 Mo	12.45	12.53	13.82	41
1 Yr	33.82	33.47	28.33	53
3 Yr Avg	28.33	28.32	19.71	50
5 Yr Avg	28.54	28.52	15.71	50
10 Yr Avg	—	—	—	—

Tax Analysis	Tax-Adj Return%	Tax-Cost Ratio
3 Yr (estimated)	27.86	0.37
5 Yr (estimated)	28.00	0.42
10 Yr (estimated)	—	—

Rating and Risk

Time Period	Morningstar Rtn vs Cat	Morningstar Risk vs Cat	Morningstar Risk-Adj Rating
3 Yr	Avg	-Avg	★★★
5 Yr	Avg	-Avg	★★★
10 Yr	—	—	—

Other Measures	Standard Index S&P 500	Best Fit Index GS NATR RES
Alpha	17.3	-0.5
Beta	1.26	1.00
R-Squared	25	100
Standard Deviation	19.43	
Mean	28.33	
Sharpe Ratio	1.17	

Morningstar's Take by Sonya Morris 12-31-07

IShares S&P GSSI Natural Resource Index is risky, so we'd need a sizable margin of safety to recommend it.

This ETF offers exposure to a broad selection of natural-resources stocks, ranging from large integrated oil firms like Chevron to small paper producers like Bowater. But its wide reach hasn't insulated it from this market segment's gyrations. Indeed, it hasn't been markedly less volatile than narrower energy ETFs. That's due partly to this fund's top-heavy profile; more than 40% of its assets are crammed into its top 10 holdings.

Moreover, this portfolio's quality isn't high. Of the 108 holdings that Morningstar equity analysts cover, only three earn a wide-moat rating and 60 possess no economic moat. Lacking a sustainable competitive advantage, these firms struggle to keep rivals at bay. For example, demand for drill-pipe manufacturer Grant Prideco's products is predicated largely on worldwide drilling activity, which depends heavily on fickle commodity prices; the firm also enjoys pricing power only near cyclical peaks. Its margins can shrivel when demand wanes and costs don't follow suit, so our analysts think it poses above-average business risk.

In fact, our analysts consider nearly half of the 108 stocks in this ETF that they cover to be above-average or speculative risks. Such firms can experience erratic results, making the task of forecasting future cash flows difficult. For instance, despite its size, Valero Energy must fend with rivals' unfettered ability to add capacity, thwarting the firm's ability to trench out an economic moat. That puts it at the mercy of the refining industry cycle, which tends to be short and unpredictable.

And because our fair value estimates for these stocks hinge significantly on one factor--our commodity price assumptions--it heightens the risk that our fair value estimate for this ETF will be wrong. For those reasons, we'd recommend this ETF only when it's trading at least 20% below our fair value estimate.

Address:	45 Fremont Street United States 800-474-2737
Web Address:	www.ishares.com
Inception:	10-22-01 *
Advisor:	Barclays Global Fund Advisers

Management Fee:	0.48%		
Expense Projections:	3Yr:$154	5Yr:$269	10Yr:$604
Income Distrib:	Quarterly		
Exchange:	NYSE		

Portfolio Analysis 12-31-07

Share change since 11-07 Total Stocks:131	Sector	PE	Tot Ret%	% Assets
⊖ Chevron Corporation	Energy	11.4	30.59	7.41
⊖ ExxonMobil Corporation	Energy	13.6	24.34	7.29
⊖ ConocoPhillips	Energy	13.8	25.42	7.22
⊖ Schlumberger, Ltd.	Energy	24.6	57.10	6.01
⊖ Occidental Petroleum Cor	Energy	13.8	60.25	3.26
⊖ EnCana Corporation	Energy	11.3	49.94	2.61
⊖ Suncor Energy, Inc.	Energy	17.0	38.36	2.57
⊕ Transocean, Inc.	—	16.1	77.14	2.32
⊖ Marathon Oil Corporation	Energy	9.7	34.09	2.21
⊖ Devon Energy Corporation	Energy	14.7	33.51	2.02
⊖ Canadian Natural Resourc	Energy	15.4	38.09	2.02
⊖ Freeport-McMoRan Copper	Ind Mtrls	12.1	86.51	2.00
⊖ Valero Energy Corporatio	Energy	8.1	37.91	1.97
⊖ Barrick Gold Corporation	Ind Mtrls	29.6	38.18	1.87
⊖ Apache Corporation	Energy	15.9	62.91	1.82
⊖ Halliburton Company	Energy	14.4	23.33	1.71
⊖ Alcoa Inc.	Ind Mtrls	14.5	24.11	1.59
⊖ Anadarko Petroleum Corp.	Energy	7.9	52.04	1.56
⊖ Hess Corporation	Ind Mtrls	19.1	104.77	1.42
⊖ Petro-Canada	Energy	17.0	32.03	1.33

Current Investment Style

Value Blnd Growth — Large Mid Small

Market Cap	%
Giant	40.7
Large	42.1
Mid	16.0
Small	1.2
Micro	0.0
Avg $mil: 37,853	

Value Measures		Rel Category
Price/Earnings	12.83	0.79
Price/Book	2.27	0.97
Price/Sales	1.42	1.02
Price/Cash Flow	7.82	0.98
Dividend Yield %	1.00	0.72

Growth Measures	%	Rel Category
Long-Term Erngs	6.98	0.54
Book Value	17.27	1.16
Sales	5.47	0.49
Cash Flow	7.29	0.45
Historical Erngs	30.89	0.85

Profitability	%	Rel Category
Return on Equity	23.01	1.12
Return on Assets	11.08	1.18
Net Margin	16.34	1.19

Industry Weightings	% of Stocks	Rel Cat
Oil & Gas	53.4	1.6
Oil/Gas Products	3.8	1.1
Oil & Gas Srv	24.4	1.0
Pipelines	3.1	2.8
Utilities	0.0	0.0
Hard Commd	7.2	0.7
Soft Commd	3.0	1.0
Misc. Indstrl	0.6	0.1
Other	4.6	0.5

Composition

Cash	0.3
Stocks	99.7
Bonds	0.0
Other	0.0
Foreign (% of Stock)	17.4

iShares S&P GSTI Semicond IGW

Market Price	Mstar Category
$59.41	Specialty-Technology

Morningstar Fair Value

Price/Fair Value Ratio	Coverage Rate %
0.96	94

Morningstar Rating	Return	Risk	Yield	NAV	Avg Daily Vol. (k)	52 wk High/Low
★	Below Avg	Above Avg	0.5%	$59.52	227	$70.88 - $51.83

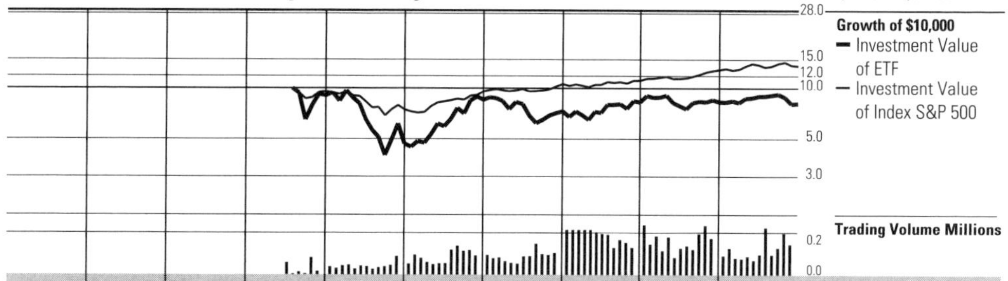

Valuation

This fund's shares are volatile, largely reflecting the cyclical ebb and flow of the semi industry. Given that many of these names are levered to similar risk factors, we'd need a sizable margin of safety before investing here, with a 15% discount to our fair value estimate doing the trick. The fund was recently hovering near fair value.

Methodology

This fund tracks the S&P GSTI Semiconductor Index. It spans roughly 50 firms, all of them either in the business of making chips (about 80% of assets) or of supplying the firms that do so (20% of assets). It omits foreign chipmakers, notably including industry behemoth Taiwan Semiconductor. But it covers all of the big U.S. semi players, including Intel, Applied Materials, and Texas Instruments. The index weights holdings by market cap and, thus, is top-heavy, with the aforementioned names accounting for 40% of assets alone. Annual portfolio turnover has typically skirted 10%.

History

1998	1999	2000	2001	2002	2003	2004	2005	2006	2007	History
—	—	—	66.55	34.56	62.94	53.85	61.01	61.03	59.52	NAV $
—	—	—	66.50	34.68	62.75	53.80	60.97	61.01	59.41	Market Price $
—	—	—	-1.39*	-48.07	82.13	-14.44	13.35	0.20	-2.00	NAV Return%
—	—	—	-1.42*	-47.85	80.95	-14.26	13.38	0.23	-2.14	Market Price Return%
—	—	—	-0.13	-0.09	-0.07	-0.02	-0.03	0.00	-0.03	Avg Premium/Discount%
—	—	—	—	-25.97	53.45	-25.32	8.44	-15.59	-7.49	NAV Rtrn% +/-S&P 500
—	—	—	—	—	-0.79	-0.47	-0.58	-0.48	—	NAV Rtrn% +/-S&P GSTI Semi
—	—	—	—	80	25	100	1	100	85	NAV Return% Rank in Cat
—	—	—	—	0.00	0.01	0.00	0.05	0.16	0.51	Income Return %
—	—	—	—	-48.07	82.12	-14.44	13.30	0.04	-2.51	Capital Return %
—	—	—	0.00	0.00	0.00	0.00	0.03	0.10	0.31	Income $
—	—	—	0.00	0.00	0.00	0.00	0.00	0.00	0.00	Capital Gains $
—	—	—	—	0.50	0.50	0.50	0.50	0.50	0.48	Expense Ratio %
—	—	—	—	-0.29	-0.20	-0.20	-0.09	0.07	0.32	Income Ratio %
—	—	—	—	8	11	6	10	6	25	Turnover Rate %
—	—	—	20	24	173	307	415	290	229	Net Assets $mil

Performance 12-31-07

Historic Quarterly NAV Returns

	1st Qtr	2nd Qtr	3rd Qtr	4th Qtr	Total
2003	1.19	25.25	19.00	20.76	82.13
2004	-1.83	-4.05	-19.11	12.28	-14.44
2005	-5.14	3.27	12.64	2.73	13.35
2006	6.69	-10.97	6.25	-0.72	0.20
2007	-1.01	9.18	2.78	-11.78	-2.00

Trailing	NAV Return%	Market Return%	NAV Rtrn% +/-S&P 500	%Rank Cat.(NAV)
3 Mo	-11.78	-12.05	-8.45	91
6 Mo	-9.32	-9.53	-7.95	83
1 Yr	-2.00	-2.14	-7.49	85
3 Yr Avg	3.64	3.60	-4.98	100
5 Yr Avg	11.64	11.52	-1.19	100
10 Yr Avg	—	—	—	—

Tax Analysis	Tax-Adj Return%	Tax-Cost Ratio
3 Yr (estimated)	3.55	0.08
5 Yr (estimated)	11.59	0.04
10 Yr (estimated)	—	—

Rating and Risk

Time Period	Morningstar Rtn vs Cat	Morningstar Risk vs Cat	Morningstar Risk-Adj Rating
3 Yr	Low	+Avg	★
5 Yr	-Avg	+Avg	★
10 Yr	—	—	—

Other Measures	Standard Index S&P 500	Best Fit Index M* Hardware TR
Alpha	-6.4	-5.4
Beta	1.74	1.09
R-Squared	50	80
Standard Deviation	19.02	
Mean	3.64	
Sharpe Ratio	0.05	

Portfolio Analysis 12-31-07

Share change since 11-07 Total Stocks:50	Sector	PE	Tot Ret%	% Assets
⊖ Texas Instruments, Inc.	Hardware	19.2	17.01	8.71
⊖ Intel Corporation	Hardware	25.4	34.22	8.61
⊕ MEMC Electronic Material	Hardware	35.3	126.09	8.45
⊖ Applied Materials	Hardware	14.8	-2.60	7.94
⊖ NVIDIA Corporation	Hardware	29.4	37.88	7.88
⊖ Broadcom Corporation	Hardware	93.5	-19.10	5.13
⊖ Analog Devices, Inc.	Hardware	21.0	-1.54	4.02
⊖ KLA-Tencor Corporation	Hardware	20.1	-2.20	3.67
⊖ Linear Technology	Hardware	22.4	7.24	2.97
⊖ Microchip Technology, In	Hardware	20.4	-0.83	2.81
⊖ Altera Corp.	Hardware	21.5	-1.30	2.71
⊖ Xilinx, Inc.	Hardware	20.2	-6.52	2.69
⊖ Lam Research Corporation	Hardware	9.8	-14.60	2.44
⊖ Cypress Semiconductor Co	Hardware	14.8	113.57	2.38
⊖ Micron Technology, Inc.	Hardware	—	-48.07	2.29
⊖ National Semiconductor	Hardware	21.1	0.44	2.23
⊖ Advanced Micro Devices	Hardware	—	-63.14	1.89
⊖ LSI Corporation	Hardware	—	-41.00	1.57
⊖ Novellus Systems, Inc.	Hardware	17.0	-19.90	1.34
⊖ Intersil Corporation	Hardware	24.2	3.77	1.33

Current Investment Style

Value Blnd Growth; Large Mid Small

Market Cap	%
Giant	8.6
Large	38.2
Mid	38.5
Small	14.6
Micro	0.1
Avg $mil: 10,752	

Value Measures		Rel Category
Price/Earnings	18.98	0.92
Price/Book	2.67	0.85
Price/Sales	2.78	1.14
Price/Cash Flow	10.96	0.76
Dividend Yield %	0.95	1.44

Growth Measures	%	Rel Category
Long-Term Erngs	—	—
Book Value	4.32	0.64
Sales	6.80	0.76
Cash Flow	13.09	1.34
Historical Erngs	16.66	1.17

Profitability	%	Rel Category
Return on Equity	17.80	1.04
Return on Assets	12.89	1.39
Net Margin	16.38	1.26

Industry Weightings	% of Stocks	Rel Cat
Software	0.0	0.0
Hardware	0.7	0.0
Networking Eq	0.0	0.0
Semis	78.4	4.4
Semi Equip	20.3	4.9
Comp/Data Sv	0.0	0.0
Telecom	0.0	0.0
Health Care	0.0	0.0
Other	0.7	0.1

Composition

Cash	0.1
Stocks	99.9
Bonds	0.0
Other	0.0
Foreign (% of Stock)	0.0

Morningstar's Take by Jeffrey Ptak 12-31-07

We'd buy iShares Goldman Sachs Semiconductor, but only with a wide margin of safety.

This ETF holds the stocks of roughly 50 semiconductor makers or the suppliers that outfit them. The index excludes foreign stocks (i.e., Taiwan Semiconductor), but the bogy covers just about all of the big domestic players, which it weights by market cap.

Semiconductor stocks are a volatile lot. Investors tend to pile into the shares on positive short-term sentiment and flee in droves when signs point to a slowdown. The cyclical nature of the semi business--which is tied to the vagaries of end-market demand and macroeconomic forces--accentuates this dynamic. Yet, this volatility can present buying opportunities, especially when the market takes an overly pessimistic view, often because the near-term outlook is hazy. Against that backdrop, this fund's attractiveness comes down to what value you'd place on it and the discount to fair value you'd demand.

This portfolio's quality--which is a key determinant of its intrinsic value--is middling. Our analysts have awarded "wide economic moat" ratings to only four of the 43 portfolio holdings they cover, and roughly one of every two names lacks a moat altogether. This reflects the rough and tumble nature of the semiconductor business, which is characterized by short product cycles and huge capital outlays. It's not surprising, therefore, that the two industry giants--Intel and Applied Materials, which account for 20% of assets--are among the few firms to trench out a wide moat.

We'd demand a 15% discount to our fair value estimate for a few reasons. First, given the semi industry's cyclical nature, our forecasts are fraught with varying degrees of uncertainty, explaining why every holding that we cover courts at least average business risk. Second, because many of these firms are levered to the same risk factors, our forecasts could prove wrong en masse.

Address:	45 Fremont Street United States 800-474-2737
Web Address:	www.ishares.com
Inception:	07-10-01 *
Advisor:	Barclays Global Fund Advisers

Management Fee:	0.48%		
Expense Projections:	3Yr:$154	5Yr:$269	10Yr:$604
Income Distrib:	Annually		
Exchange:	NYSE		

iShares S&P GSTI Technlgy IGM

Market Price	Mstar Category
$59.59	Specialty-Technology

Morningstar Fair Value

Price/Fair Value Ratio	Coverage Rate %
0.96	98

Valuation

This fund's diversification across stocks and the various tech subsectors has kept volatility from reaching extremes. As such, we wouldn't demand an especially wide margin of safety to invest here; a 9% or better discount to our fair value estimate would do.

Methodology

This fund tracks the S&P GSTI Technology Index. The benchmark spans 200-plus stocks drawn from virtually every tech subsector, though software providers and equipment makers of various stripes predominate. (The index does not include telecom service firms.) The index weights stocks by market cap. As such, assets cluster in the portfolio's biggest holdings, with the top 10 names recently soaking up more than half of assets. The index reconstitutes semiannually. Annual portfolio turnover has generally been in the single digits. The index excludes foreign-listed tech stocks as well as ADRs.

Morningstar Rating	Return	Risk	Yield	NAV	Avg Daily Vol. (k)	52 wk High/Low
★★★	Average	Average	0.2%	$59.67	137	$63.92 - $49.58

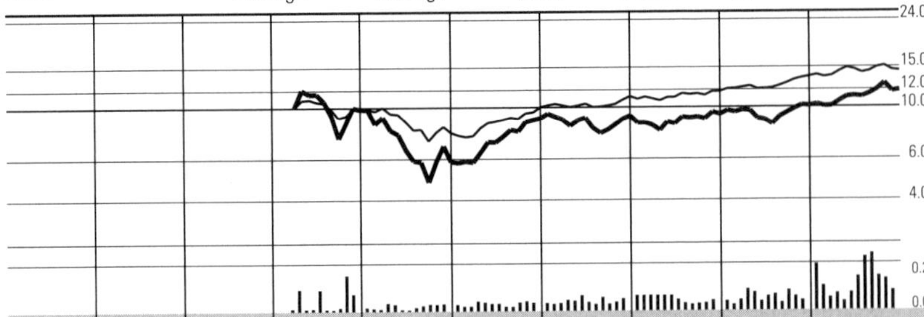

1998	1999	2000	2001	2002	2003	2004	2005	2006	2007	History
—	—	—	50.44	29.97	46.04	46.74	47.39	51.35	59.67	NAV $
—	—	—	50.69	30.04	45.85	46.71	47.35	51.42	59.59	Market Price $
—	—	—	0.92*	-40.58	53.62	2.24	1.54	8.46	16.42	NAV Return%
—	—	—	0.90*	-40.74	52.63	2.60	1.52	8.69	16.11	Market Price Return%
—	—	—	0.37	-0.11	0.06	0.04	-0.10	0.06	-0.03	Avg Premium/Discount%
—	—	—	—	-18.48	24.94	-8.64	-3.37	-7.33	10.93	NAV Rtrn% +/-S&P 500
—	—	—	—	-0.31	-0.56	-0.68	-0.48	-0.52	—	NAV Rtrn% +/-S&P GSTI Tech
—	—	—	—	40	50	75	67	71	5	NAV Return% Rank in Cat
—	—	—	—	0.00	0.00	0.71	0.14	0.09	0.22	Income Return %
—	—	—	—	-40.58	53.62	1.53	1.40	8.37	16.20	Capital Return %
—	—	—	0.00	0.00	0.00	0.33	0.07	0.04	0.11	Income $
—	—	—	0.00	0.00	0.00	0.00	0.00	0.00	0.00	Capital Gains $
—	—	—	—	0.50	0.50	0.50	0.50	0.50	0.48	Expense Ratio %
—	—	—	—	-0.30	-0.18	-0.20	0.81	0.04	0.09	Income Ratio %
—	—	—	—	8	11	5	7	5	20	Turnover Rate %
—	—	—	73	39	147	194	280	352	439	Net Assets $mil

Performance 12-31-07

Historic Quarterly NAV Returns

	1st Qtr	2nd Qtr	3rd Qtr	4th Qtr	Total
2003	-0.63	22.20	11.27	13.71	53.62
2004	-1.30	1.69	-11.15	14.64	2.24
2005	-8.83	1.42	6.85	2.78	1.54
2006	4.23	-9.32	7.29	6.96	8.46
2007	-0.10	10.24	6.34	-0.58	16.42

Trailing	NAV Return%	Market Return%	NAV Rtrn% +/-S&P 500	%Rank Cat.(NAV)
3 Mo	-0.58	-0.81	2.75	21
6 Mo	5.72	5.45	7.09	9
1 Yr	16.42	16.11	10.93	5
3 Yr Avg	8.64	8.61	0.02	56
5 Yr Avg	15.03	14.94	2.20	50
10 Yr Avg	—	—	—	—

Tax Analysis	Tax-Adj Return%	Tax-Cost Ratio
3 Yr (estimated)	8.58	0.06
5 Yr (estimated)	14.94	0.08
10 Yr (estimated)	—	—

Rating and Risk

Time Period	Morningstar Rtn vs Cat	Morningstar Risk vs Cat	Morningstar Risk-Adj Rating
3 Yr	Avg	Avg	★★★
5 Yr	Avg	Avg	★★★
10 Yr	—	—	—

Other Measures	Standard Index S&P 500	Best Fit Index M* Hardware TR
Alpha	-1.7	-0.2
Beta	1.57	0.90
R-Squared	70	93
Standard Deviation	14.57	
Mean	8.64	
Sharpe Ratio	0.35	

Portfolio Analysis 12-31-07

Share change since 11-07 Total Stocks:229	Sector	PE	Tot Ret%	% Assets
⊖ Microsoft Corporation	Software	23.4	20.83	8.89
⊖ Apple, Inc.	Hardware	50.5	133.47	6.80
⊖ Cisco Systems, Inc.	Hardware	21.5	-0.95	6.44
⊖ Google, Inc.	Business	54.0	50.17	6.27
⊖ Intel Corporation	Hardware	25.4	34.22	6.10
⊖ International Business M	Hardware	16.2	13.20	5.84
⊖ Hewlett-Packard Company	Hardware	18.8	23.40	5.11
⊖ Oracle Corporation	Software	24.8	31.74	3.50
⊖ Qualcomm, Inc.	Hardware	20.2	5.52	2.53
⊖ Dell, Inc.	Hardware	18.6	-2.31	2.16
⊖ Research in Motion, Ltd.	Hardware	NMF	166.24	2.10
⊖ Texas Instruments, Inc.	Hardware	19.2	17.01	1.84
⊖ EMC Corporation	Hardware	26.1	40.38	1.52
⊖ Corning Inc.	Hardware	18.6	28.76	1.49
⊖ eBay, Inc.	Consumer	—	10.38	1.48
⊖ Motorola, Inc.	Hardware	NMF	-21.85	1.44
⊖ Yahoo, Inc.	Media	45.7	-8.93	1.21
⊖ Amazon.com, Inc.	Consumer	NMF	134.77	1.12
⊖ Adobe Systems Inc.	Software	37.9	3.92	0.97
⊖ Applied Materials	Hardware	14.8	-2.60	0.96

Current Investment Style

Value Blnd Growth / Large Mid Small

Market Cap	%
Giant	55.9
Large	22.0
Mid	17.2
Small	4.9
Micro	0.0
Avg $mil: 47,768	

Value Measures		Rel Category
Price/Earnings	19.75	0.95
Price/Book	3.89	1.24
Price/Sales	2.28	0.93
Price/Cash Flow	13.21	0.91
Dividend Yield %	0.55	0.83

Growth Measures	%	Rel Category
Long-Term Erngs	27.89	1.76
Book Value	6.99	1.03
Sales	10.94	1.22
Cash Flow	12.70	1.30
Historical Erngs	12.52	0.88

Profitability	%	Rel Category
Return on Equity	23.21	1.35
Return on Assets	12.13	1.31
Net Margin	15.99	1.23

Industry Weightings	% of Stocks	Rel Cat
Software	23.1	1.1
Hardware	24.5	1.7
Networking Eq	10.4	1.2
Semis	14.8	0.8
Semi Equip	2.2	0.5
Comp/Data Sv	10.4	1.1
Telecom	0.1	0.1
Health Care	0.2	0.0
Other	14.3	0.9

Composition

Cash	0.2
Stocks	99.8
Bonds	0.0
Other	0.0
Foreign (% of Stock)	2.7

Morningstar's Take by Jeffrey Ptak 12-31-07

Though it boasts a high-quality portfolio, iShares S&P GSTI Technology isn't our favorite tech ETF.

This exchange-traded fund tracks an index composed of 200-plus U.S.-based tech stocks. It's a pure-play on tech, with most constituents being either software providers or gear-makers. (It doesn't hold any telecom names.) The index weights stocks by market cap. Thus, assets bunch up in its top holdings, the largest 10 of which recently soaked up more than half of assets. Accordingly, the fund's fortunes are more or less tied to this small group of tech firms.

That's not a terrible thing considering that cohort's high quality: Our analysts have awarded "wide economic moat" ratings to seven of the fund's top 10 names, meaning that these firms have trenched out formidable competitive advantages. Attractive traits like network effects (Microsoft via its ubiquitous Windows operating system), high customer switching costs (network equipment supplier Cisco System and enterprise software provider Oracle), and tall barriers to entry (Intel's massive R&D war chest, Dell's cost leadership) abound here. All told, wide-moat stocks account for 47% of this ETF's assets.

Of course, the tech sector is home to its fair share of clunky businesses, a number of which, like Priceline.com, figure into this fund's portfolio. But they're bit players for the most part, with narrow-moat firms like Apple and Google--which boast advantages, albeit less durable ones--looming larger. In addition, the fund hasn't been too volatile thanks to its diversification across names. As such, we wouldn't demand a wide margin of safety to invest here.

The problem is that there's not a lot to separate this fund's portfolio from other tech ETFs that charge less. For instance, Vanguard Information Technology's annual expense ratio is less than half this one's. As such, this portfolio would need to be meaningfully cheaper than the Vanguard fund's before we'd consider dipping a toe.

Address:	45 Fremont Street United States 800-474-2737
Web Address:	www.ishares.com
Inception:	03-13-01 *
Advisor:	Barclays Global Fund Advisers

Management Fee:	0.48%
Expense Projections:	3Yr:$154 5Yr:$269 10Yr:$604
Income Distrib:	Quarterly
Exchange:	NYSE

iShares SP Glb Fincl IXG

Market Price	Mstar Category
$79.81	Specialty-Financial

Morningstar Fair Value

Price/Fair Value Ratio	Coverage Rate %
0.90	49

Morningstar Rating	Return	Risk	Yield	NAV	Avg Daily Vol. (k)	52 wk High/Low
★★★★★	High	Above Avg	3.5%	$79.59	45	$95.64 - $74.50

Valuation

This fund is perched right on the cusp of "bargain" territory, as it was recently trading at a roughly 13% discount to our fair value estimate, which is just shy of the 16% minimum discount we'd demand. Though our analysts don't cover every last one of the stocks in the portfolio, we cover enough to feel confident in our valuation.

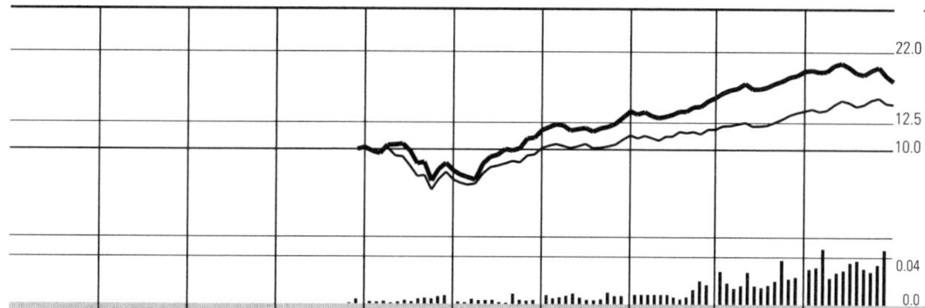

Methodology

IShares S&P Global Financial Sector tracks the financials subset of the S&P Global 1200 Index. Its holdings span the full panoply of financials subsectors, including banks, insurers, money managers, and other financial players. The fund invests roughly one third of assets in domestic financials, with the rest going to foreign names. Though the fund weights holdings by market cap, it's not especially top heavy, with the top 10 names accounting for just 14% of assets. Investments denominated in foreign currencies are not hedged back to the dollar.

1998	1999	2000	2001	2002	2003	2004	2005	2006	2007	History
—	—	—	52.35	43.03	57.96	66.56	73.13	89.32	79.59	NAV $
—	—	—	52.30	42.86	58.34	66.95	73.53	90.55	79.81	Market Price $
—	—	—	9.55*	-16.73	37.83	16.39	11.65	23.81	-7.78	NAV Return%
—	—	—	9.60*	-16.98	39.28	16.31	11.60	24.83	-8.78	Market Price Return%
—	—	—	0.73	-0.82	0.72	0.55	0.21	0.44	-0.03	Avg Premium/Discount%
—	—	—	—	5.37	9.15	5.51	6.74	8.02	-13.27	NAV Rtrn% +/-S&P 500
—	—	—	—	-0.57	-0.93	-0.85	-1.36	-0.78	-0.06	NAV Rtrn% +/-S&P Gl Fincl
—	—	—	—	100	25	25	20	10	45	NAV Return% Rank in Cat
—	—	—	—	1.09	3.05	1.54	1.80	1.66	3.11	Income Return %
—	—	—	—	-17.82	34.78	14.85	9.85	22.15	-10.89	Capital Return %
—	—	—	0.04	0.57	1.31	0.90	1.20	1.21	2.78	Income $
—	—	—	0.00	0.00	0.00	0.00	0.00	0.00	0.00	Capital Gains $
—	—	—	—	0.65	0.65	0.65	0.65	0.65	0.49	Expense Ratio %
—	—	—	—	1.44	2.04	2.14	2.11	2.17	2.13	Income Ratio %
—	—	—	—	2	8	8	5	7	5	Turnover Rate %
—	—	—	—	13	17	63	110	308	243	Net Assets $mil

Performance 12-31-07

Historic Quarterly NAV Returns

	1st Qtr	2nd Qtr	3rd Qtr	4th Qtr	Total
2003	-7.09	21.96	5.52	15.27	37.83
2004	3.97	-2.04	0.97	13.19	16.39
2005	-3.52	0.98	6.23	7.87	11.65
2006	7.79	-0.38	6.65	8.11	23.81
2007	-0.10	3.25	-2.37	-8.43	-7.78

Trailing	NAV Return%	Market Return%	NAV Rtrn% +/-S&P 500	%Rank Cat.(NAV)
3 Mo	-8.43	-8.18	-5.10	50
6 Mo	-10.59	-9.91	-9.22	46
1 Yr	-7.78	-8.78	-13.27	45
3 Yr Avg	8.43	8.31	-0.19	20
5 Yr Avg	15.38	15.54	2.55	25
10 Yr Avg	—	—	—	—

Tax Analysis	Tax-Adj Return%	Tax-Cost Ratio
3 Yr (estimated)	7.63	0.74
5 Yr (estimated)	14.58	0.69
10 Yr (estimated)	—	—

Rating and Risk

Time Period	Morningstar Rtn vs Cat	Morningstar Risk vs Cat	Morningstar Risk-Adj Rating
3 Yr	High	Avg	★★★★★
5 Yr	High	+Avg	★★★★★
10 Yr	—	—	—

Other Measures	Standard Index S&P 500	Best Fit Index MSCI World
Alpha	-0.3	-4.5
Beta	1.08	1.09
R-Squared	70	79
Standard Deviation	10.03	
Mean	8.43	
Sharpe Ratio	0.43	

Portfolio Analysis 12-31-07

Share change since 11-07 Total Stocks:234	Sector	PE	Tot Ret%	% Assets
⊖ HSBC Hldgs	Financial	—	—	2.96
⊖ Bank of America Corporat	Financial	9.4	-19.25	2.74
⊖ American International G	Financial	10.2	-17.96	2.22
⊖ Citigroup, Inc.	Financial	7.9	-44.93	2.22
⊖ J.P. Morgan Chase & Co.	Financial	9.5	-7.24	2.20
⊖ Banco Santander	Financial	—	—	2.08
⊖ UniCredito Italiano Grp	Financial	—	-5.17	1.65
⊖ Wells Fargo Company	Financial	11.4	-12.13	1.49
⊖ Allianz SE	Financial	—	—	1.47
⊖ BNP Paribas	Financial	—	—	1.47
Mitsubishi UFJ Financial	Financial	—	—	1.45
⊖ UBS	Financial	—	-21.51	1.42
⊖ Banco Bilbao Vizcaya Arg	Financial	—	—	1.36
⊖ Royal Bank of Scotland G	Financial	—	—	1.33
⊖ ING Groep	Financial	—	—	1.31
⊖ Goldman Sachs Group, Inc	Financial	8.8	8.59	1.29
⊖ Intesa Sanpaolo	Financial	—	—	1.13
⊖ Wachovia Corporation	Financial	8.6	-29.91	1.12
⊖ AXA	Financial	—	—	1.10
⊖ Deutsche Bank	Financial	7.7	-0.15	1.06

Current Investment Style

Value Blnd Growth — Large Mid Small

Market Cap	%
Giant	63.0
Large	30.3
Mid	6.6
Small	0.1
Micro	0.0
Avg $mil: 46,716	

Value Measures		Rel Category
Price/Earnings	10.77	0.90
Price/Book	1.43	0.97
Price/Sales	1.31	0.64
Price/Cash Flow	13.96	1.20
Dividend Yield %	4.00	1.37

Growth Measures	%	Rel Category
Long-Term Erngs	10.76	1.02
Book Value	10.78	1.00
Sales	11.66	1.50
Cash Flow	32.34	2.09
Historical Erngs	19.20	1.05

Profitability	%	Rel Category
Return on Equity	17.81	1.05
Return on Assets	2.03	0.70
Net Margin	23.99	1.08

Industry Weightings	% of Stocks	Rel Cat
Intl Banks	28.9	1.6
Banks	16.4	0.7
Real Estate	4.8	2.0
Sec Mgmt	16.6	1.2
S & Ls	1.3	0.2
Prop & Reins	13.8	0.9
Life Ins	7.6	1.2
Misc. Ins	2.3	0.7
Other	8.3	0.6

Composition

Cash	2.8
Stocks	97.2
Bonds	0.0
Other	0.0
Foreign (% of Stock)	64.9

Morningstar's Take by Jeffrey Ptak 12-31-07

We require a modest margin of safety to invest in iShares S&P Global Financials Sector.

This moderate risk, above-average quality portfolio tracks the financials subset of the S&P Global 1200 Index. As such, it teems with the stocks of banks, insurers, money managers, and other financial players the world over. The fund invests roughly one third of assets in domestic financials, with the rest going to foreign names.

Financial-service firms tend to enjoy inherent advantages, such as high switching costs and convenient access to cheap sources of financing. Sure enough, the fund's top holdings include a clutch of wide-moat banking powerhouses, including Bank of America, Citigroup, and J.P. Morgan Chase. These firms boast scale, global reach, and lustrous brands in spades, and they've leveraged those traits to consistently wring out value for shareholders.

But those traits aren't confined solely to the portfolio's largest holdings. In fact, many of the firms here boast at least some semblance of a competitive advantage, including a number of the fund's foreign holdings. For instance, Credit Suisse taps its reputation in the private wealth management arena to earn very attractive returns on invested capital. And while acquisitions have weighed on narrow-moat Spanish bank Banco Santander's returns, the firm still touts a hard-to-replicate branch retail network. All told, roughly 100 of the 120 or so holdings that our analysts cover boast at least a narrow economic moat.

While the portfolio's above-average quality burnishes its value, we'd still invest here only with a healthy margin of safety. Many of these names are levered to similar factors, such as the vitality of capital markets, the direction of interest rates, or the shape of the yield curve. Thus, we'd be buyers of the shares only when the fund is trading at a 16% or better discount to our fair value estimate.

Address:	45 Fremont Street United States 800-474-2737
Web Address:	www.ishares.com
Inception:	11-12-01 *
Advisor:	Barclays Global Fund Advisers

Management Fee:	0.48%		
Expense Projections:	3Yr:$154	5Yr:$269	10Yr:$604
Income Distrib:	Annually		
Exchange:	NYSE		

KBW Bank ETF KBE

Market Price	Mstar Category
$43.55	Specialty-Financial

Morningstar Fair Value

Price/Fair Value Ratio	Coverage Rate %
0.66	98

Valuation

This portfolio is loaded with wide-moat stocks that court no greater-than-average business risk. Because of its compact nature--it allocates 40% of assets to the top-five stocks--we'd require a 15% discount to our fair value to consider investing here. By that standard, this ETF is well within our buy range, recently trading at a 32%

Methodology

This fund tracks a benchmark, the KBW Bank Index, that serves as a collection of the biggest players in the U.S. banking industry. Huge institutions such as J.P. Morgan, Citigroup, and Bank of America can be found here, along with large regional banks such as PNC Financial, KeyCorp, and Fifth Third Bancorp. It uses a modified market-cap-weighting scheme (meant to ensure representative exposure to the various banking subindustries) and is reconstituted quarterly.

Morningstar Rating	Return	Risk	Yield	NAV	Avg Daily Vol. (k)	52 wk High/Low
—	—	—	5.7%	$43.56	1,704	$60.41 - $39.60

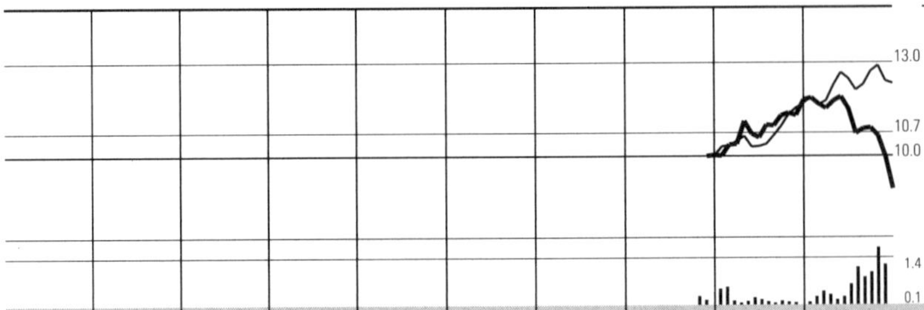

1998	1999	2000	2001	2002	2003	2004	2005	2006	2007	History
—	—	—	—	—	—	—	51.94	58.43	43.56	NAV $
—	—	—	—	—	—	—	51.96	58.25	43.55	Market Price $
—	—	—	—	—	—	—	-2.63*	16.52	-21.90	NAV Return%
—	—	—	—	—	—	—	-2.64*	16.12	-21.68	Market Price Return%
—	—	—	—	—	—	—	-0.04	0.00	0.01	Avg Premium/Discount%
—	—	—	—	—	—	—	—	0.73	-27.39	NAV Rtrn% +/-S&P 500
—	—	—	—	—	—	—	—	-2.90	-8.49	NAV Rtrn% +/-DJ Finance
—	—	—	—	—	—	—	—	70	85	NAV Return% Rank in Cat
—	—	—	—	—	—	—	—	3.85	4.32	Income Return %
—	—	—	—	—	—	—	—	12.67	-26.22	Capital Return %
—	—	—	—	—	—	—	0.13	1.97	2.48	Income $
—	—	—	—	—	—	—	0.00	0.00	0.00	Capital Gains $
—	—	—	—	—	—	—	—	0.36	0.35	Expense Ratio %
—	—	—	—	—	—	—	—	3.06	2.93	Income Ratio %
—	—	—	—	—	—	—	—	22	8	Turnover Rate %
—	—	—	—	—	—	—	49	67	364	Net Assets $mil

Performance 12-31-07

Historic Quarterly NAV Returns

	1st Qtr	2nd Qtr	3rd Qtr	4th Qtr	Total
2003	—	—	—	—	—
2004	—	—	—	—	—
2005	—	—	—	—	—*
2006	3.04	1.81	6.23	4.55	16.52
2007	-2.44	-0.08	-5.15	-15.53	-21.90

Trailing	NAV Return%	Market Return%	NAV Rtrn% +/-S&P 500	%Rank Cat.(NAV)
3 Mo	-15.53	-15.92	-12.20	87
6 Mo	-19.88	-19.96	-18.51	87
1 Yr	-21.90	-21.68	-27.39	85
3 Yr Avg	—	—	—	—
5 Yr Avg	—	—	—	—
10 Yr Avg	—	—	—	—

Tax Analysis	Tax-Adj Return%	Tax-Cost Ratio
3 Yr (estimated)	—	—
5 Yr (estimated)	—	—
10 Yr (estimated)	—	—

Rating and Risk

Time Period	Morningstar Rtn vs Cat	Morningstar Risk vs Cat	Morningstar Risk-Adj Rating
3 Yr	—	—	—
5 Yr	—	—	—
10 Yr	—	—	—

Other Measures	Standard Index S&P 500	Best Fit Index
Alpha	—	—
Beta	—	—
R-Squared	—	—
Standard Deviation	—	
Mean	—	
Sharpe Ratio	—	

Portfolio Analysis 12-31-07

Share change since 11-07 Total Stocks:24	Sector	PE	Tot Ret%	% Assets
⊖ Wells Fargo Company	Financial	11.4	-12.13	8.62
⊖ Bank of America Corporat	Financial	9.4	-19.25	8.39
⊖ J.P. Morgan Chase & Co.	Financial	9.5	-7.24	7.68
⊕ Citigroup, Inc.	Financial	7.9	-44.93	7.63
⊕ Wachovia Corporation	Financial	8.6	-29.91	7.08
⊖ State Street Corporation	Financial	21.3	21.92	4.16
⊖ Northern Trust Corporati	Financial	22.1	28.19	4.04
⊖ Bank of New York Mellon	Financial	21.7	26.51	4.03
⊖ PNC Financial Services G	Financial	12.8	-8.29	4.03
⊖ SunTrust Banks, Inc.	Financial	10.6	-23.27	3.94
⊖ US Bancorp	Financial	12.2	-7.89	3.86
⊖ BB&T Corporation	Financial	10.7	-27.20	3.72
⊖ Regions Financial Corpor	Financial	10.1	-33.64	3.67
⊖ Capital One Financial Co	Financial	7.0	-38.50	3.41
⊖ Fifth Third Bancorp	Financial	12.2	-35.42	3.17
⊖ M & T Bank Corporation	Financial	11.3	-31.53	3.07
⊖ KeyCorp	Financial	7.6	-35.39	2.91
⊖ Comerica Incorporated	Financial	9.1	-22.42	2.83
⊖ National City Corporatio	Financial	6.8	-52.59	2.68
⊖ Zions Bancorporation	Financial	8.8	-42.03	2.36

Current Investment Style

Value Blnd Growth — Large Mid Small

Market Cap	%
Giant	48.0
Large	30.5
Mid	21.5
Small	0.0
Micro	0.0
Avg $mil: 36,260	

Value Measures		Rel Category
Price/Earnings	10.17	0.85
Price/Book	1.16	0.79
Price/Sales	2.17	1.06
Price/Cash Flow	—	—
Dividend Yield %	4.86	1.66

Growth Measures	%	Rel Category
Long-Term Erngs	—	—
Book Value	6.72	0.63
Sales	3.72	0.48
Cash Flow	0.91	0.06
Historical Erngs	10.97	0.60

Profitability	%	Rel Category
Return on Equity	13.50	0.80
Return on Assets	1.24	0.43
Net Margin	23.99	1.08

Industry Weightings	% of Stocks	Rel Cat
Intl Banks	39.9	2.3
Banks	54.6	2.5
Real Estate	0.0	0.0
Sec Mgmt	0.0	0.0
S & Ls	2.3	0.4
Prop & Reins	0.0	0.0
Life Ins	0.0	0.0
Misc. Ins	0.0	0.0
Other	3.3	0.2

Composition

Cash	1.3
Stocks	98.7
Bonds	0.0
Other	0.0
Foreign (% of Stock)	0.0

Morningstar's Take by Sonya Morris 12-31-07

KBW Bank ETF is a concentrated portfolio of high-quality bank stocks that we'd gladly own at a 15% discount to our fair value estimate.

This ETF offers exposure to big U.S. banks. With the big barriers to entry in the banking industry, most of the banks in this ETF benefit from economies of scale, so it's no surprise that this ETF is full to the brim with firms that enjoy the protection of economic moats. All of the 23 stocks that we cover here possess an economic moat, and nine of those banks (comprising almost 60% of assets) earn a wide-moat rating. Consider the likes of Wells Fargo, which has built an exceedingly loyal and geographically diverse customer base. Similarly, Bank of America BAC, has a huge share of the retail banking market in the U.S. and a massive deposit base that dwarfs the competition and serves as a cheap source of financing.

These manifold competitive advantages also mitigate some of the risk these firms court. That might surprise some, considering the credit crunch that recently cast a pall over the industry, but banks tend to generate fairly predictable cash flows over time. Big U.S. banks have also used their scale to diversify their businesses beyond loan underwriting so that their fates no longer depend on the vagaries of credit or interest-rate cycles. Consequently, about 80% of this ETF's portfolio is allocated to banks with average risk ratings. The remaining 20% is dedicated to companies with below-average risk ratings.

Still, the recent turbulence among bank stocks shows that this ETF is not risk free. It's a concentrated portfolio of only 24 stocks, and it stashes about 40% of assets in its top five holdings. As a result, our fair value estimate for this ETF depends significantly on the fair value estimates of just a handful of companies. If we get those wrong, our fair value estimate for this ETF is also likely to be wrong.

Consequently, we need a respectable margin of safety to feel comfortable recommending this ETF.

Address:	One Lincoln Street United States 866-787-2257
Web Address:	www.advisors.ssga.com
Inception:	11-08-05*
Advisor:	SSgA Funds Management Inc

Management Fee:	0.35%		
Expense Projections:	3Yr:$113	5Yr:$197	10Yr:$446
Income Distrib:	Quarterly		
Exchange:	AMEX		

Materials Sel SPDR XLB

Market Price	Mstar Category
$41.70	Specialty-Natural Res

Morningstar Rating	Return	Risk	Yield	NAV	Avg Daily Vol. (k)	52 wk High/Low
★★	Below Avg	Low	2.0%	$41.67	8,718	$43.86 - $34.22

Morningstar Fair Value

Price/Fair Value Ratio	Coverage Rate %
0.90	99

Valuation

Although this fund's underlying holdings are extremely volatile--tied as they are to turbulent commodity markets--the portfolio's mix of different types of companies damps that volatility considerably. Thus, we would recommend this fund if it traded for at least an 8% discount to our fair value estimate. It was recently trading at a 10% discount.

Methodology

The fund invests passively in the materials companies within the S&P 500. The holdings are weighted by market cap, which means the top holdings can dominate the portfolio. Monsanto, for example, makes up 12% of the portfolio, and DuPont accounts for 10%. Constituents have to be leading U.S. companies that meet S&P's profitability criteria.

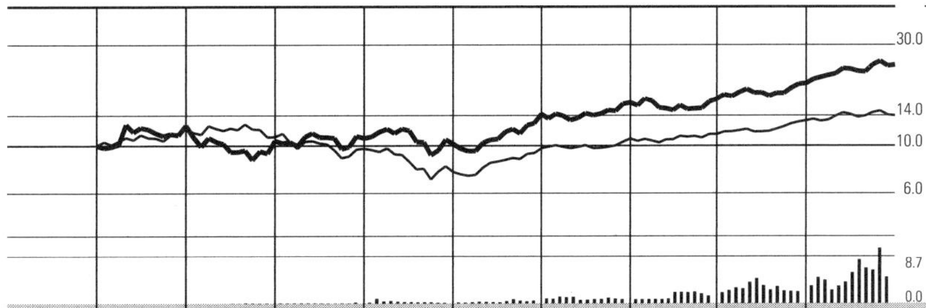

Growth of $10,000
- Investment Value of ETF
- Investment Value of Index S&P 500

Trading Volume Millions

History

	1998	1999	2000	2001	2002	2003	2004	2005	2006	2007
NAV $	21.61	26.43	21.43	21.55	19.86	26.75	29.73	30.29	34.84	41.67
Market Price $	21.92	26.58	21.41	21.42	19.84	26.69	29.73	30.28	34.81	41.70
NAV Return%	10.62*	24.28	-15.17	2.75	-5.83	37.55	13.24	4.10	18.35	21.97
Market Price Return%	10.56*	23.22	-15.73	2.22	-5.35	37.39	13.49	4.08	18.26	22.16
Avg Premium/Discount%	1.43	-0.01	0.09	-0.27	-0.03	0.00	-0.01	-0.01	-0.05	-0.02
NAV Rtrn% +/-S&P 500	—	3.24	-6.07	14.64	16.27	8.87	2.36	-0.81	2.56	16.48
NAV Rtrn% +/-S&P Mats	—	-0.98	0.55	-0.73	-0.37	-0.65	0.04	-0.32	-0.28	-0.56
NAV Return% Rank in Cat	—	20	80	8	14	7	25	80	71	84
Income Return %	—	1.58	1.51	2.05	2.12	2.42	1.90	2.15	3.11	2.35
Capital Return %	—	22.70	-16.68	0.70	-7.95	35.13	11.34	1.95	15.24	19.62
Income $	0.00	0.34	0.40	0.44	0.45	0.48	0.51	0.63	0.93	0.81
Capital Gains $	0.00	0.06	0.51	0.00	0.00	0.00	0.00	0.00	0.00	0.00
Expense Ratio %	—	0.56	0.43	0.27	0.28	0.27	0.27	0.26	0.24	0.23
Income Ratio %	—	1.44	1.73	2.12	1.96	2.39	1.96	2.01	2.57	2.26
Turnover Rate %	—	—	19	6	28	4	3	16	6	9
Net Assets $mil	—	—	—	—	254	734	708	953	1,025	1,422

Performance 12-31-07

Historic Quarterly NAV Returns

	1st Qtr	2nd Qtr	3rd Qtr	4th Qtr	Total
2003	-7.30	13.62	6.11	23.08	37.55
2004	-1.76	2.71	3.36	8.59	13.24
2005	1.78	-9.51	1.73	11.11	4.10
2006	7.47	-0.37	-0.63	11.22	18.35
2007	9.09	6.99	4.73	-0.22	21.97

Trailing	NAV Return%	Market Return%	NAV Rtrn% +/-S&P 500	%Rank Cat.(NAV)
3 Mo	-0.22	-0.05	3.11	68
6 Mo	4.50	4.40	5.87	76
1 Yr	21.97	22.16	16.48	84
3 Yr Avg	14.54	14.56	5.92	100
5 Yr Avg	18.54	18.58	5.71	100
10 Yr Avg	—	—	—	—

Tax Analysis	Tax-Adj Return%	Tax-Cost Ratio
3 Yr (estimated)	13.62	0.80
5 Yr (estimated)	17.64	0.76
10 Yr (estimated)	—	—

Rating and Risk

Time Period	Morningstar Rtn vs Cat	Morningstar Risk vs Cat	Morningstar Risk-Adj Rating
3 Yr	-Avg	Low	★★
5 Yr	Low	Low	★★
10 Yr	—	—	—

Other Measures	Standard Index S&P 500	Best Fit Index M* Inds Mat TR
Alpha	4.8	-0.5
Beta	1.26	1.22
R-Squared	54	75
Standard Deviation	13.26	
Mean	14.54	
Sharpe Ratio	0.77	

Portfolio Analysis 12-31-07

Share change since 11-07 Total Stocks:28	Sector	PE	Tot Ret%	% Assets
⊖ Monsanto Company	Ind Mtrls	67.1	114.45	14.21
⊖ E.I. du Pont de Nemours	Ind Mtrls	12.4	-6.63	9.22
⊖ Freeport-McMoRan Copper	Ind Mtrls	12.1	86.51	9.10
⊖ The Dow Chemical Company	Ind Mtrls	11.3	2.55	8.66
⊖ Alcoa Inc.	Ind Mtrls	14.5	24.11	7.21
⊖ Newmont Mining	Ind Mtrls	51.3	9.58	4.79
⊖ Praxair, Inc.	Ind Mtrls	25.6	52.05	4.65
⊖ Air Products and Chemica	Ind Mtrls	21.1	42.82	4.63
⊖ Nucor Corp.	Ind Mtrls	11.8	14.19	4.09
⊖ Weyerhaeuser Company	Ind Mtrls	—	7.83	3.72
⊖ United States Steel Corp	Ind Mtrls	12.6	66.73	3.45
⊖ International Paper Co.	Ind Mtrls	5.2	-2.36	3.35
⊖ PPG Industries, Inc.	Ind Mtrls	14.1	12.49	2.80
⊖ Allegheny Technologies C	Ind Mtrls	11.7	-4.36	2.18
⊖ Ecolab, Inc.	Ind Mtrls	32.3	14.21	2.17
⊖ Vulcan Materials Company	Ind Mtrls	15.8	-10.36	2.12
⊖ Sigma-Aldrich Corporatio	Ind Mtrls	24.5	41.94	1.78
⊖ Rohm and Haas Company	Ind Mtrls	17.8	6.59	1.63
⊖ MeadWestvaco Corporation	Ind Mtrls	32.3	6.73	1.47
⊖ Eastman Chemical Company	Ind Mtrls	17.4	5.19	1.28

Current Investment Style

Value Blnd Growth — Large Mid Small

Market Cap	%
Giant	14.3
Large	63.2
Mid	22.5
Small	0.0
Micro	0.0
Avg $mil: 22,105	

Value Measures		Rel Category
Price/Earnings	13.49	0.83
Price/Book	2.26	0.97
Price/Sales	1.25	0.90
Price/Cash Flow	8.03	1.01
Dividend Yield %	1.55	1.12

Growth Measures	%	Rel Category
Long-Term Erngs	—	—
Book Value	12.68	0.85
Sales	8.36	0.75
Cash Flow	17.45	1.07
Historical Erngs	31.08	0.86

Profitability	%	Rel Category
Return on Equity	20.13	0.98
Return on Assets	7.91	0.84
Net Margin	9.04	0.66

Industry Weightings	% of Stocks	Rel Cat
Oil & Gas	0.0	0.0
Oil/Gas Products	0.0	0.0
Oil & Gas Srv	0.0	0.0
Pipelines	0.0	0.0
Utilities	0.0	0.0
Hard Commd	33.1	3.1
Soft Commd	10.7	3.7
Misc. Indstrl	51.4	4.8
Other	4.8	0.5

Composition

Cash	0.6
Stocks	99.4
Bonds	0.0
Other	0.0
Foreign (% of Stock)	0.0

Morningstar's Take by Haywood Kelly 12-31-07

Materials Select Sector SPDR is a grab bag of commodities exposure.

The bulk of the fund's assets are in chemicals companies--firms such as DuPont, Dow Chemical, Monsanto, and Praxair. But chemicals firms are a diverse bunch, serving a variety of intermediate and end markets. Monsanto, for example, saw its stock appreciate 115% in 2007 thanks to its strong seed and herbicide business and the general strength in agricultural markets. DuPont and Dow Chemical, by contrast, are highly exposed to the construction and automotive sectors, and their stocks have been flat to down. In addition to this motley collection of chemicals holdings, this ETF has exposure to gold prices through Newmont Mining, steel through Nucor, forestry through Weyerhaeuser, and paper through International Paper.

Most of these holdings are large, mature firms. Revenues will rise if commodity prices cooperate, but not otherwise. And profitability, too, depends on the vagaries of the commodities markets and the overall global economy. Most commodities producers sport little in the way of competitive advantages, so they need a tailwind to post great profits. The portfolio contains only one wide-moat stock (Vulcan Materials), and it's just 2% of the portfolio.

Because of the diversity of the fund's holdings, the ETF does offer good diversification benefits. Its standard deviation is fairly tame, despite parking two thirds of its assets in the top 10 holdings. Plus, there's no single risk factor that would bias our ratings on the underlying stocks one way or the other. In fact, we'd expect our opinions on the underlying stocks to vary widely at any given time.

Like the other funds in the SPDR family, this one comes with a low 0.24% expense ratio. So when the portfolio holdings are cheap, this fund is an inexpensive way to gain exposure to them.

Address:	c/o State Street Bk&Tr, 225 Franklin St United States 800-843-2639
Web Address:	www.spdrindex.com
Inception:	12-16-98*
Advisor:	SSgA Funds Management Inc

Management Fee:	0.05%		
Expense Projections:	3Yr:$77	5Yr:$136	10Yr:$307
Income Distrib:	Quarterly		
Exchange:	AMEX		

Oil Services HOLDRs OIH

Market Price	Mstar Category
$189.02	Specialty-Natural Res

Morningstar Fair Value

Price/Fair Value Ratio	Coverage Rate %
1.04	71

Valuation

We'd demand a 20% discount to our fair value estimate to recommend this fund. Though we don't have every last one of this portfolio's holdings under coverage, oil-services stocks are relatively pricey in general. Not surprisingly, this portfolio was recently trading at a 4% premium to our fair value estimate. A bargain, it ain't.

Methodology

The fund passively invests in a small group of oil-services stocks. Offered by Merrill Lynch, HOLDRs differ from other ETFs in that they can be bought only in 100-share increments, investors can exchange their shares for the underlying stocks at any time (for a fee of up to $10), investors receive spin-off shares outside of their HOLDRs investment just as if they held the underlying stock directly, and rather than an annual expense ratio, the fund charges $0.08 per share in annual custody fees (which are waived if the underlying securities fail to generate enough income to cover them).

Morningstar Rating	Return	Risk	Yield	NAV	Avg Daily Vol. (k)	52 wk High/Low
—	—	—	—	$189.02	5,969	$201.11 - $126.15

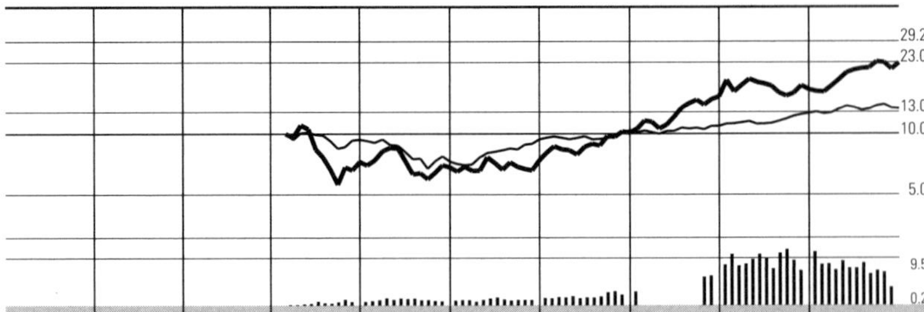

1998	1999	2000	2001	2002	2003	2004	2005	2006	2007	History
189.02	—	—	61.00	57.30	62.00	85.07	128.80	139.66	189.02	NAV $
—	—	—	61.00	57.30	62.00	85.07	128.80	139.66	189.02	Market Price $
—	—	—	—	-6.07	8.20	37.21	51.40	8.43	35.34	NAV Return%
—	—	—	11.19*	-6.07	8.20	37.21	51.40	8.43	35.34	Market Price Return%
—	—	—	—	—	—	—	—	—	—	Avg Premium/Discount%
—	—	—	—	16.03	-20.48	26.33	46.49	-7.36	29.85	NAV Rtrn% +/-S&P 500
—	—	—	—	7.19	-25.81	12.64	14.92	-8.39	0.91	NAV Rtrn% +/-GS NATR RES
—	—	—	—	3	7	1	1	12	—	NAV Return% Rank in Cat
—	—	—	—	—	—	—	—	—	—	Income Return %
—	—	—	—	—	—	—	—	—	—	Capital Return %
—	—	—	0.00	0.00	0.00	0.00	0.00	0.00	0.00	Income $
—	—	—	0.00	0.00	0.00	0.00	0.00	0.00	0.00	Capital Gains $
—	—	—	—	—	—	—	—	—	—	Expense Ratio %
—	—	—	—	—	—	—	—	—	—	Income Ratio %
—	—	—	—	—	—	—	—	—	—	Turnover Rate %
—	—	—	—	—	—	—	—	2,641	3,626	Net Assets $mil

Performance 12-31-07

Historic Quarterly NAV Returns

	1st Qtr	2nd Qtr	3rd Qtr	4th Qtr	Total
2003	-3.94	9.28	-4.24	7.64	8.20
2004	13.27	2.85	13.11	4.12	37.21
2005	13.02	5.99	21.68	3.87	51.40
2006	13.98	1.78	-13.10	7.55	8.43
2007	4.34	19.91	9.74	-1.42	35.34

Trailing	NAV Return%	Market Return%	NAV Rtrn% +/-S&P 500	%Rank Cat.(NAV)
3 Mo	-1.42	-1.42	1.91	—
6 Mo	8.18	8.18	9.55	—
1 Yr	35.34	35.34	29.85	—
3 Yr Avg	30.49	30.49	21.87	—
5 Yr Avg	26.96	26.96	14.13	—
10 Yr Avg	—	—	—	—

Tax Analysis	Tax-Adj Return%	Tax-Cost Ratio
3 Yr (estimated)	—	—
5 Yr (estimated)	—	—
10 Yr (estimated)	—	—

Rating and Risk

Time Period	Morningstar Rtn vs Cat	Morningstar Risk vs Cat	Morningstar Risk-Adj Rating
3 Yr	—	—	—
5 Yr	—	—	—
10 Yr	—	—	—

Other Measures	Standard Index S&P 500	Best Fit Index
Alpha	—	—
Beta	—	—
R-Squared	—	—
Standard Deviation	—	
Mean	30.49	
Sharpe Ratio	—	

Portfolio Analysis 12-31-07

Share change since 10-07 Total Stocks:17	Sector	PE	Tot Ret%	% Assets
⊕ Transocean Incorp.	Energy	16.1	77.14	17.30
Schlumberger, Ltd.	Energy	24.6	57.10	11.41
Baker Hughes Inc.	Energy	17.9	9.35	8.78
Halliburton Company	Energy	14.4	23.33	8.77
Diamond Offshore Drillin	Energy	21.7	89.69	7.94
Weatherford Intl	Energy	—	—	6.58
Noble Corporation	Energy	14.4	44.12	6.45
Smith International, Inc	Energy	23.9	81.06	6.16
National Oilwell Varco,	Energy	21.7	132.65	5.44
⊕ Cameron Intl	Energy	—	—	4.12
BJ Services Company	Energy	9.5	-16.80	3.51
Nabors Industries, Ltd.	Energy	8.4	-8.03	3.49
ENSCO International, Inc	Energy	9.3	19.31	3.46
Grant Prideco, Inc.	Energy	13.6	39.58	2.63
Rowan Companies, Inc.	Energy	10.9	20.14	1.65
Tidewater, Inc.	Energy	8.7	14.64	1.46
Exterran Holdings, Inc.	—	—	—	0.84

Current Investment Style

Value Blnd Growth (Large / Mid / Small)

Market Cap	%
Giant	12.8
Large	68.1
Mid	19.1
Small	0.0
Micro	0.0
Avg $mil: 24,592	

Value Measures		Rel Category
Price/Earnings	11.80	0.72
Price/Book	3.56	1.53
Price/Sales	2.63	1.89
Price/Cash Flow	9.72	1.22
Dividend Yield %	0.37	0.27

Growth Measures	%	Rel Category
Long-Term Erngs	—	—
Book Value	17.56	1.18
Sales	18.45	1.65
Cash Flow	40.03	2.46
Historical Erngs	101.46	2.79

Profitability	%	Rel Category
Return on Equity	30.96	1.51
Return on Assets	18.47	1.96
Net Margin	27.52	2.01

Industry Weightings	% of Stocks	Rel Cat
Oil & Gas	0.0	0.0
Oil/Gas Products	0.0	0.0
Oil & Gas Srv	100.0	4.3
Pipelines	0.0	0.0
Utilities	0.0	0.0
Hard Commd	0.0	0.0
Soft Commd	0.0	0.0
Misc. Indstrl	0.0	0.0
Other	0.0	0.0

Composition

Cash	0.0
Stocks	100.0
Bonds	0.0
Other	0.0
Foreign (% of Stock)	6.6

Morningstar's Take by Haywood Kelly 12-31-07

We're more bullish on Oil Services HOLDRs than we have been in some time.

In November 2007, our energy team increased its long-run oil price targets. For 2011, we're now forecasting oil prices of $68 per barrel, versus $47 previously. This change has significantly raised our fair value for this portfolio. Oil-services stocks are naturally sensitive to oil prices--the higher oil prices are, the more demand for rigs, ships, and other oil equipment. Here's a rundown of recent fair value changes to the top four holdings in this portfolio, which together account for more than 50% of the fund's assets.

Transocean: We raised our fair value estimate to $116 per share from $113 after adjusting our model for the completed merger with GlobalSantaFe. We expect the combined firm to continue to benefit from the flurry of deep-water activity and its reputation as a best-in-class operator.

Schlumberger: We raised our fair value estimate to $49 per share from $42. We're expecting 14% annual revenue growth during the next five years and for operating margins to average 29% during the same time frame.

Baker Hughes: We raised our fair value estimate to $78 from $67. We're expecting 14% annual revenue growth over the next five years and for the firm's operating margin to average 22% over the same time frame.

Halliburton: We raised our fair value estimate to $30 per share from $29. We're expecting 14% annual revenue growth over the next several years and for the firm's operating margins to average 24% over the same time frame.

We're still not recommending this ETF, however. Most oil-services stocks sport low to middling star ratings given how far their stock prices have run. Plus, given how sensitive all the stocks in the portfolio are to oil prices, we'd demand a hefty margin to fair value before recommending this fund.

Address:	4 World Financial Center United States 800-637-7455
Web Address:	www.holdrs.com
Inception:	02-06-01
Advisor:	Merrill Lynch Pierce Fenner & Smith

Management Fee:	—		
Expense Projections:	3Yr: —	5Yr: —	10Yr: —
Income Distrib:			
Exchange:	AMEX		

Pharmaceutical HOLDRs PPH

Market Price	Mstar Category
$79.19	Specialty-Health

Morningstar Fair Value

Price/Fair Value Ratio	Coverage Rate %
0.87	99

Valuation

The fund's portfolio contains high-quality firms, and many of the stock-specific risks cancel each other out. For this kind of portfolio, we have fairly high confidence in our fair value estimate, so we'd demand only an 8% discount to fair value before recommending this fund. It was recently trading at a 13% discount.

Methodology

The fund passively invests in a small group of drug stocks. Offered by Merrill Lynch, HOLDRs differ from other ETFs in that they can be bought only in 100-share increments, investors can exchange their shares for the underlying stocks at any time (for a fee of up to $10), investors receive spin-off shares outside of their HOLDRs investment just as if they held the underlying stock directly, and rather than an annual expense ratio, the fund charges $0.08 per share in annual custody fees (which are waived if the underlying securities fail to generate enough income to cover them).

Morningstar Rating	Return	Risk	Yield	NAV	Avg Daily Vol. (k)	52 wk High/Low
—	—	—	—	$79.19	699	$85.94 - $75.79

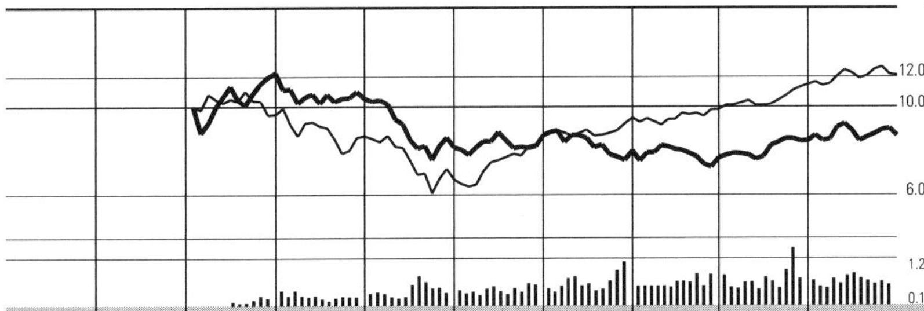

Growth of $10,000
- Investment Value of ETF
- Investment Value of Index S&P 500

Trading Volume Millions

History

1998	1999	2000	2001	2002	2003	2004	2005	2006	2007	History
79.19	—	114.25	98.50	74.10	79.50	72.69	69.65	76.90	79.19	NAV $
—	—	114.25	98.50	74.10	79.50	72.69	69.65	76.90	79.19	Market Price $
—	—	—	-13.79	-24.77	7.29	-8.57	-4.18	10.41	2.98	NAV Return%
—	—	-2.11*	-13.79	-24.77	7.29	-8.57	-4.18	10.41	2.98	Market Price Return%
—	—	—	—	—	—	—	—	—	—	Avg Premium/Discount%
—	—	—	-1.90	-2.67	-21.39	-19.45	-9.09	-5.38	-2.51	NAV Rtrn% +/-S&P 500
—	—	—	-0.95	-3.96	-12.14	-13.12	-12.50	3.53	-8.25	NAV Rtrn% +/-DJ Health
—	—	—	3	4	6	6	7	3	79	NAV Return% Rank in Cat
—	—	—	—	—	—	—	—	—	—	Income Return %
—	—	—	—	—	—	—	—	—	—	Capital Return %
—	—	0.00	0.00	0.00	0.00	0.00	0.00	0.00	0.00	Income $
—	—	0.00	0.00	0.00	0.00	0.00	0.00	0.00	0.00	Capital Gains $
—	—	—	—	—	—	—	—	—	—	Expense Ratio %
—	—	—	—	—	—	—	—	—	—	Income Ratio %
—	—	—	—	—	—	—	—	—	—	Turnover Rate %
—	—	—	—	—	—	—	—	1,915	1,990	Net Assets $mil

Performance 12-31-07

Historic Quarterly NAV Returns

	1st Qtr	2nd Qtr	3rd Qtr	4th Qtr	Total
2003	-0.04	9.22	-8.10	6.93	7.29
2004	-3.92	2.41	-9.00	2.12	-8.57
2005	-1.03	1.92	-4.17	-0.87	-4.18
2006	2.51	-1.55	10.97	-1.41	10.41
2007	1.00	5.14	-1.97	-1.07	2.98

Trailing	NAV Return%	Market Return%	NAV Rtrn% +/-S&P 500	%Rank Cat.(NAV)
3 Mo	-1.07	-1.07	2.26	49
6 Mo	-3.02	-3.02	-1.65	52
1 Yr	2.98	2.98	-2.51	79
3 Yr Avg	2.90	2.90	-5.72	67
5 Yr Avg	1.34	1.34	-11.49	100
10 Yr Avg	—	—	—	—

Tax Analysis	Tax-Adj Return%	Tax-Cost Ratio
3 Yr (estimated)	—	—
5 Yr (estimated)	—	—
10 Yr (estimated)	—	—

Rating and Risk

Time Period	Morningstar Rtn vs Cat	Morningstar Risk vs Cat	Morningstar Risk-Adj Rating
3 Yr	—	—	—
5 Yr	—	—	—
10 Yr	—	—	—

Other Measures	Standard Index S&P 500	Best Fit Index
Alpha	—	—
Beta	—	—
R-Squared	—	—
Standard Deviation	—	
Mean	2.90	
Sharpe Ratio	—	

Portfolio Analysis 12-31-07

Share change since 10-07 Total Stocks:19	Sector	PE	Tot Ret%	% Assets
Johnson & Johnson	Health	18.8	3.61	21.47
Pfizer Inc.	Health	22.5	-8.15	16.65
Merck & Co., Inc.	Health	23.6	37.36	15.81
Abbott Laboratories	Health	45.7	18.04	9.78
Wyeth	Health	13.6	-11.36	6.60
Eli Lilly & Company	Health	26.0	5.65	6.59
Bristol-Myers Squibb Com	Health	24.8	4.75	5.89
Schering-Plough Corporat	Health	21.0	13.66	4.61
Medco Health Solutions,	Health	31.1	89.78	3.88
Forest Laboratories, Inc	Health	22.9	-27.96	1.78
Zimmer Holdings, Inc.	Health	21.0	-15.60	1.67
Allergan, Inc.	Health	40.8	7.66	1.59
Hospira, Inc.	Health	62.9	26.98	1.05
Biovail	Health	—	—	0.68
King Pharmaceuticals, In	Health	14.2	-35.68	0.63
Mylan Laboratories, Inc.	Health	11.8	-29.13	0.53
Watson Pharmaceuticals I	Health	—	4.26	0.34
Advanced Medical Optics,	Health	—	-30.31	0.30
Valeant Pharmaceuticals	Health	NMF	-30.57	0.15

Current Investment Style

Value Blnd Growth — Large Mid Small

Market Cap	%
Giant	77.4
Large	17.8
Mid	4.3
Small	0.5
Micro	0.0
Avg $mil: 85,462	

Value Measures		Rel Category
Price/Earnings	14.66	0.69
Price/Book	3.50	1.03
Price/Sales	2.76	0.95
Price/Cash Flow	12.52	0.96
Dividend Yield %	2.45	3.14

Growth Measures	%	Rel Category
Long-Term Erngs	—	—
Book Value	8.03	1.31
Sales	6.09	0.59
Cash Flow	7.16	0.56
Historical Erngs	9.50	0.10

Profitability	%	Rel Category
Return on Equity	20.42	2.74
Return on Assets	10.52	23.91
Net Margin	17.97	3.53

Industry Weightings	% of Stocks	Rel Cat
Biotech	0.0	0.0
Drugs	94.1	3.3
Mgd Care	3.9	0.5
Hospitals	0.0	0.0
Other HC Srv	0.0	0.0
Diagnostics	0.0	0.0
Equipment	2.0	0.1
Good/Srv	0.0	0.0
Other	0.0	0.0

Composition

Cash	0.0
Stocks	100.0
Bonds	0.0
Other	0.0
Foreign (% of Stock)	0.7

Morningstar's Take by Haywood Kelly 12-31-07

Pharmaceutical HOLDRs offers a concentrated dose of big pharma.

The HOLDRs have characteristics that make them different from other ETFs, but in terms of the portfolio holdings, this fund has several close substitutes, including Health Care Select Sector SPDR, Vanguard Health Care ETF, and iShares Dow Jones U.S. Healthcare. Although these other funds invest in health-care stocks outside of pharmaceuticals, in practice this doesn't really differentiate them. Big pharma stocks dominate the health-care sector in terms of market cap, and thus dominate portfolios of all these ETFs.

The main difference in the portfolios is that the HOLDR is even more concentrated than its peers, with 90% of its assets in the top 10 holdings and just 19 total holdings. With positions of 15% or more in Johnson & Johnson, Merck, and Pfizer, any company-specific problems--like Merck's Vioxx disaster--will hurt this fund a bit more than its peers.

But we're comfortable concentrating on big pharma, particularly now that the group is out of favor. There's been angst over big pharma for several years: The market is worried both about former blockbusters losing patent protection and a lack of new hit products. Our equity analysts have a different take. We think drug pipelines are on the upswing thanks to a change in research strategy and solid acquisition activity. The fund's top two holdings--Johnson & Johnson and Pfizer--receive 5 stars based on their attractive valuations.

So whenever big pharma is relatively attractive, this fund will tend to be among the best choices in the crowded health-care sector-fund arena. Also keep in mind this portfolio is chock-full of high-quality, wide-moat firms. Given the high-quality nature of the portfolio, we'd recommend this ETF whenever it trades for more than an 8% discount to the intrinsic value of its underlying stocks.

Address:	4 World Financial Center United States 800-637-7455
Web Address:	www.holdrs.com
Inception:	01-31-00
Advisor:	Merrill Lynch Pierce Fenner & Smith

Management Fee:	—
Expense Projections:	3Yr: — 5Yr: — 10Yr: —
Income Distrib:	Quarterly
Exchange:	AMEX

PowerShares Water Res PHO

Market Price	Mstar Category
$21.40	Specialty-Natural Res

Morningstar Rating	Return	Risk	Yield	NAV	Avg Daily Vol. (k)	52 wk High/Low
—	—	—	0.4%	$21.26	458	$22.53 - $17.84

Morningstar Fair Value

Price/Fair Value Ratio	Coverage Rate %
0.97	60

Valuation

Because we have fair value estimates for only about half of this fund's portfolio, we don't have an investment recommendation. The fund's expense ratio shaves 0.68% off the expected returns of the underlying stocks.

Methodology

This exchange-traded fund tracks the Palisades Water Index, which represents the stock-market performance of companies in the global water industry, such as water utilities, water-treatment firms, and companies that provide related products and services. The index typically has between 30 and 40 constituents. The portfolio is equal weighted and rebalanced quarterly.

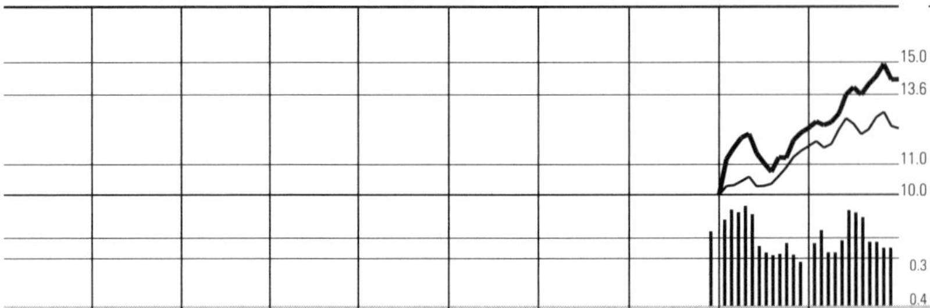

Growth of $10,000
— Investment Value of ETF
— Investment Value of Index S&P 500

Trading Volume Millions

1998	1999	2000	2001	2002	2003	2004	2005	2006	2007	History
—	—	—	—	—	—	—	15.18	18.41	21.26	NAV $
—	—	—	—	—	—	—	15.20	18.41	21.40	Market Price $
—	—	—	—	—	—	—	17.94*	22.32	15.95	NAV Return%
—	—	—	—	—	—	—	17.64*	22.17	16.73	Market Price Return%
—	—	—	—	—	—	—	0.11	0.11	0.28	Avg Premium/Discount%
—	—	—	—	—	—	—	—	6.53	10.46	NAV Rtrn% +/-S&P 500
—	—	—	—	—	—	—	—	5.50	-18.48	NAV Rtrn% +/-GS NATR RES
—	—	—	—	—	—	—	—	25	89	NAV Return% Rank in Cat
—	—	—	—	—	—	—	—	1.00	0.46	Income Return %
—	—	—	—	—	—	—	—	21.32	15.49	Capital Return %
—	—	—	—	—	—	—	0.01	0.15	0.09	Income $
—	—	—	—	—	—	—	0.00	0.00	0.00	Capital Gains $
—	—	—	—	—	—	—	—	0.67	0.66	Expense Ratio %
—	—	—	—	—	—	—	—	0.40	0.96	Income Ratio %
—	—	—	—	—	—	—	—	2	27	Turnover Rate %
—	—	—	—	—	—	—	—	1,329	2,134	Net Assets $mil

Performance 12-31-07

Historic Quarterly NAV Returns

	1st Qtr	2nd Qtr	3rd Qtr	4th Qtr	Total
2003	—	—	—	—	—
2004	—	—	—	—	—
2005	—	—	—	—	—*
2006	18.88	-7.43	1.54	9.48	22.32
2007	1.76	11.31	3.39	-0.99	15.95

Trailing	NAV Return%	Market Return%	NAV Rtrn% +/-S&P 500	%Rank Cat.(NAV)
3 Mo	-0.99	0.32	2.34	73
6 Mo	2.37	2.44	3.74	82
1 Yr	15.95	16.73	10.46	89
3 Yr Avg	—	—	—	—
5 Yr Avg	—	—	—	—
10 Yr Avg	—	—	—	—

Tax Analysis	Tax-Adj Return%	Tax-Cost Ratio
3 Yr (estimated)	—	—
5 Yr (estimated)	—	—
10 Yr (estimated)	—	—

Rating and Risk

Time Period	Morningstar Rtn vs Cat	Morningstar Risk vs Cat	Morningstar Risk-Adj Rating
3 Yr	—	—	—
5 Yr	—	—	—
10 Yr	—	—	—

Other Measures	Standard Index S&P 500	Best Fit Index
Alpha	—	—
Beta	—	—
R-Squared	—	—

Standard Deviation	—
Mean	—
Sharpe Ratio	—

Portfolio Analysis 11-30-07

Share change since 10-07 Total Stocks:35

	Sector	PE	Tot Ret%	% Assets
⊕ Veolia Environnement ADR	Business	32.6	25.01	4.17
Layne Christensen Compan	Business	23.3	49.89	3.90
⊕ Millipore Corporation	Health	36.6	9.88	3.90
⊕ Pentair, Inc.	Business	17.3	12.87	3.81
⊕ URS Corporation	Business	21.6	26.79	3.80
⊕ Pall Corporation	Health	24.0	18.14	3.65
⊕ Tetra Tech, Inc.	Business	27.3	18.85	3.64
⊕ Emerson Electric Company	Ind Mtrls	21.3	31.42	3.60
⊕ Siemens AG ADR	Hardware	26.9	62.71	3.58
⊕ Ameron International, In	Ind Mtrls	14.9	21.93	3.38
⊕ Danaher Corporation	Ind Mtrls	23.2	21.29	3.34
⊕ Agilent Technologies, In	Hardware	23.4	5.42	3.31
⊕ Aecom Technology Corpora	Business	24.8	—	3.29
⊕ Valmont Industries, Inc.	Ind Mtrls	26.5	62.51	3.27
⊕ Itron Inc.	Telecom	—	85.13	3.16
⊕ ITT Corporation	Ind Mtrls	19.5	16.61	3.11
⊕ Nalco Holding Company	Ind Mtrls	26.6	18.83	3.10
⊕ General Electric Company	Ind Mtrls	16.6	2.69	3.00
⊕ Roper Industries, Inc.	Ind Mtrls	24.7	25.05	2.89
⊕ Franklin Electric Co.	Ind Mtrls	23.9	-24.76	2.83

Current Investment Style

Value Blnd Growth — Large Mid Small

Market Cap	%
Giant	6.6
Large	14.4
Mid	36.9
Small	33.2
Micro	8.9
Avg $mil: 3,512	

Value Measures		Rel Category
Price/Earnings	22.58	1.38
Price/Book	2.27	0.97
Price/Sales	1.33	0.96
Price/Cash Flow	12.98	1.63
Dividend Yield %	0.81	0.59

Growth Measures	%	Rel Category
Long-Term Erngs	13.25	1.02
Book Value	12.43	0.83
Sales	7.69	0.69
Cash Flow	8.86	0.54
Historical Erngs	18.33	0.50

Profitability	%	Rel Category
Return on Equity	12.56	0.61
Return on Assets	5.46	0.58
Net Margin	7.17	0.52

Industry Weightings	% of Stocks	Rel Cat
Oil & Gas	0.0	0.0
Oil/Gas Products	0.0	0.0
Oil & Gas Srv	0.0	0.0
Pipelines	0.0	0.0
Utilities	13.7	4.0
Hard Commd	3.1	0.3
Soft Commd	0.0	0.0
Misc. Indstrl	44.7	4.2
Other	38.6	3.7

Composition

Cash	0.0
Stocks	100.0
Bonds	0.0
Other	0.0
Foreign (% of Stock)	9.5

Morningstar's Take by Haywood Kelly 12-31-07

We don't have fair values on enough of its holdings to have a firm opinion one way or the other about PowerShares Water Resources.

This exchange-traded fund tracks an index of industrial firms that all have something to do with water: water treatment, water utilities, pipe and pump manufacturing, and so on. The index is pure gimmickry, in our opinion. To lump companies like General Electric, Siemens, and Danaher--whose businesses are incredibly diverse--into a portfolio loaded with small-cap companies scattered across 13 industries results in one hodgepodge of a portfolio. Any commonalities based on the water theme are likely to be swamped by firm- and industry-specific factors.

What kind of portfolio do you get? For the most part, the fund equal weights its 35 or so holdings--rebalancing quarterly--so no stock ever grows to become dominant. In the fourth quarter of 2007, the weightings ranged between 4% for the top holding to 1% for the bottom holding. The average market cap of the stocks in the portfolio is $3.5 billion, putting the fund in mid-cap territory. So generally speaking, when smaller stocks do well--or when industrials and utilities stocks are hot--this fund's returns will look attractive.

So far, the fund has been blessed. It's only been around since 2005, and it has posted an 18% annualized return since inception through Dec. 1, 2007. Such flashy returns are undoubtedly a major reason why the fund has been able to amass more than $2 billion in assets.

We don't have an opinion on what future returns will be like. We have fair value estimates for only about half of the portfolio. We think that subset of the portfolio is about 7% undervalued as of mid-December, which implies healthy returns going forward, but we hesitate to assume that the rest of the portfolio is undervalued.

Unless you have a firm basis for believing the entire portfolio is underpriced, we'd avoid these shares.

Address:	301 West Roosevelt Road United States 800-843-2639
Web Address:	www.powershares.com
Inception:	12-06-05*
Advisor:	PowerShares Capital Management LLC

Management Fee:	0.50%		
Expense Projections:	3Yr:$218	5Yr:$379	10Yr:$847
Income Distrib:	Quarterly		
Exchange:	AMEX		

Regional Bank HOLDRs RKH

Market Price	Mstar Category
$131.43	Specialty-Financial

Morningstar Fair Value

Price/Fair Value Ratio	Coverage Rate %
0.72	96

Valuation

The fund holds a concentrated portfolio of banking stocks, so many of its holdings have exposure to the same risk factors, such as the U.S. mortgage market and loan-default rates. As such, we would demand at least a 15% discount to our fair value estimate before recommending the fund. It was recently trading at a 27% discount.

Methodology

The fund passively invests in a small group of bank stocks. Offered by Merrill Lynch, HOLDRs differ from other ETFs in that they can be bought only in 100-share increments, investors can exchange their shares for the underlying stocks at any time (for a fee of up to $10), investors receive spin-off shares outside of their HOLDRs investment just as if they held the underlying stock directly, and rather than an annual expense ratio, the fund charges $0.08 per share in annual custody fees (which are waived if the underlying securities fail to generate enough income to cover them).

Morningstar Rating	Return	Risk	Yield	NAV	Avg Daily Vol. (k)	52 wk High/Low
—	—	—	—	$131.43	927	$167.01 - $118.16

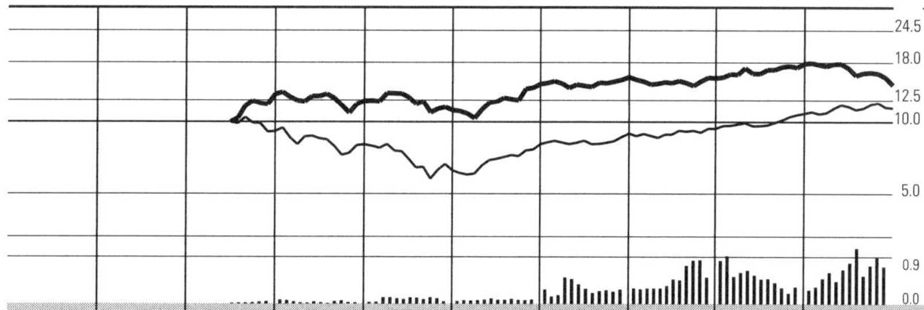

Growth of $10,000
- Investment Value of ETF
- Investment Value of Index S&P 500

Trading Volume Millions

History

1998	1999	2000	2001	2002	2003	2004	2005	2006	2007	History
131.43	—	120.00	112.25	102.75	132.61	141.95	140.48	161.52	131.43	NAV $
—	—	120.00	112.25	102.75	132.61	141.95	140.48	161.52	131.43	Market Price $
—	—	—	-6.46	-8.46	29.06	7.04	-1.04	14.98	-18.63	NAV Return%
—	—	3.96*	-6.46	-8.46	29.06	7.04	-1.04	14.98	-18.63	Market Price Return%
—	—	—	—	—	—	—	—	—	—	Avg Premium/Discount%
—	—	—	5.43	13.64	0.38	-3.84	-5.95	-0.81	-24.12	NAV Rtrn% +/-S&P 500
—	—	—	-0.08	3.89	-3.17	-6.35	-7.50	-4.44	-5.22	NAV Rtrn% +/-DJ Finance
—	—	—	3	2	5	6	7	9	—	NAV Return% Rank in Cat
—	—	—	—	—	—	—	—	—	—	Income Return %
—	—	—	—	—	—	—	—	—	—	Capital Return %
—	—	0.00	0.00	0.00	0.00	0.00	0.00	0.00	0.00	Income $
—	—	0.00	0.00	0.00	0.00	0.00	0.00	0.00	0.00	Capital Gains $
—	—	—	—	—	—	—	—	—	—	Expense Ratio %
—	—	—	—	—	—	—	—	—	—	Income Ratio %
—	—	—	—	—	—	—	—	—	—	Turnover Rate %
—	—	—	—	—	—	—	—	683	553	Net Assets $mil

Performance 12-31-07

Historic Quarterly NAV Returns

	1st Qtr	2nd Qtr	3rd Qtr	4th Qtr	Total
2003	-7.50	17.55	1.41	17.04	29.06
2004	0.56	-2.29	2.62	6.16	7.04
2005	-6.83	1.33	-2.66	7.69	-1.04
2006	3.47	0.92	6.78	3.12	14.98
2007	-2.32	-2.04	-4.02	-11.39	-18.63

Trailing	NAV Return%	Market Return%	NAV Rtrn% +/-S&P 500	%Rank Cat.(NAV)
3 Mo	-11.39	-11.39	-8.06	—
6 Mo	-14.96	-14.96	-13.59	—
1 Yr	-18.63	-18.63	-24.12	—
3 Yr Avg	-2.53	-2.53	-11.15	—
5 Yr Avg	5.05	5.05	-7.78	—
10 Yr Avg	—	—	—	—

Tax Analysis	Tax-Adj Return%	Tax-Cost Ratio
3 Yr (estimated)	—	—
5 Yr (estimated)	—	—
10 Yr (estimated)	—	—

Rating and Risk

Time Period	Morningstar Rtn vs Cat	Morningstar Risk vs Cat	Morningstar Risk-Adj Rating
3 Yr	—	—	—
5 Yr	—	—	—
10 Yr	—	—	—

Other Measures	Standard Index S&P 500	Best Fit Index
Alpha	—	—
Beta	—	—
R-Squared	—	—
Standard Deviation	—	
Mean	-2.53	
Sharpe Ratio	—	

Portfolio Analysis 12-31-07

Share change since 10-07 Total Stocks:19	Sector	PE	Tot Ret%	% Assets
J.P. Morgan Chase & Co.	Financial	9.5	-7.24	14.57
US Bancorp	Financial	12.2	-7.89	13.96
Wachovia Corporation	Financial	8.6	-29.91	11.97
Wells Fargo Company	Financial	11.4	-12.13	10.97
Bank of America Corporat	Financial	9.4	-19.25	8.92
State Street Corporation	Financial	21.3	21.92	6.20
Bank of New York Mellon	Financial	21.7	26.51	5.18
PNC Financial Services G	Financial	12.8	-8.29	4.58
SunTrust Banks, Inc.	Financial	10.6	-23.27	4.27
Northern Trust Corporati	Financial	22.1	28.19	4.07
Fifth Third Bancorp	Financial	12.2	-35.42	2.69
Keycorp	—	—	—	2.33
BB&T Corporation	Financial	10.7	-27.20	2.33
National City Corporatio	Financial	6.8	-52.59	2.21
Regions Financial Corpor	Financial	10.1	-33.64	1.83
Comerica Incorporated	Financial	9.1	-22.42	1.68
Marshall & Ilsley Corp.	Financial	7.9	-43.76	1.22
Synovus Financial Corp.	Financial	12.9	-19.65	0.68
Piper Jaffray Cos	Financial	—	—	0.35

Current Investment Style

Value Blnd Growth; Large Mid Small

Market Cap	%
Giant	67.4
Large	26.7
Mid	5.9
Small	0.0
Micro	0.0
Avg $mil: 54,303	

Value Measures		Rel Category
Price/Earnings	10.80	0.90
Price/Book	1.41	0.96
Price/Sales	2.52	1.24
Price/Cash Flow	—	—
Dividend Yield %	4.02	1.38

Growth Measures	%	Rel Category
Long-Term Erngs	—	—
Book Value	7.01	0.65
Sales	5.39	0.69
Cash Flow	0.91	0.06
Historical Erngs	14.22	0.78

Profitability	%	Rel Category
Return on Equity	15.28	0.90
Return on Assets	1.38	0.47
Net Margin	26.07	1.17

Industry Weightings	% of Stocks	Rel Cat
Intl Banks	40.0	2.3
Banks	60.0	2.7
Real Estate	0.0	0.0
Sec Mgmt	0.0	0.0
S & Ls	0.0	0.0
Prop & Reins	0.0	0.0
Life Ins	0.0	0.0
Misc. Ins	0.0	0.0
Other	0.0	0.0

Composition

Cash	0.0
Stocks	100.0
Bonds	0.0
Other	0.0
Foreign (% of Stock)	0.0

Morningstar's Take by Haywood Kelly 12-31-07

Regional Bank HOLDRs offer concentrated exposure to the U.S. banking sector.

With just 19 stocks and portfolio weightings that depend on the market cap of the underlying stocks, this fund is extremely concentrated. About 80% of its assets are in the top 10 holdings, with sizable positions in J.P. Morgan, Bank of America, and a handful of other mega-cap banking names.

Given the concentrated nature of the fund, it's a good way to bet on banking stocks when valuations are compelling. And heading into 2008, Morningstar analysts think banking stocks are trading well below fair value. As of late December 2007, four of the top five holdings in this fund were cheap enough to earn 5 stars from Morningstar, and the portfolio as a whole was 26% undervalued, in our opinion.

That's enough of a discount for us to recommend the fund. Buying a pool of banking stocks is less risky than buying one or two individual names. Plus, this portfolio is heavy on wide-moat companies, which are those we think stand an excellent chance of earning high returns on capital for years to come. Taken together, those factors lead us to demand a 15% discount to fair value to recommend this portfolio.

For those looking to bet on banking stocks, keep in mind that this portfolio is very similar to that of KBW Bank ETF. We'd expect the valuations of the two portfolios to track closely over time. The choice may come down to the structural differences between HOLDRs and more-traditional ETFs (about which, see the methodology section). In a nutshell, owning the HOLDR is more akin to owning the underlying stocks outright. For example, when Synovus Financial spins out TSYS at the end of 2007, investors in the HOLDR will receive TSYS shares in their brokerage accounts right alongside their HOLDR position.

Address:	4 World Financial Center United States 800-637-7455
Web Address:	www.holdrs.com
Inception:	06-22-00
Advisor:	Merrill Lynch Pierce Fenner & Smith

Management Fee:	—		
Expense Projections:	3Yr: —	5Yr: —	10Yr: —
Income Distrib:	None		
Exchange:	AMEX		

Retail HOLDRs RTH

Market Price	Mstar Category
$93.35	Large Blend

Morningstar Fair Value

Price/Fair Value Ratio	Coverage Rate %
0.79	100

Morningstar Rating	Return	Risk	Yield	NAV	Avg Daily Vol. (k)	52 wk High/Low
—	—	—	—	$93.35	4,712	$108.18 - $86.76

Valuation

We'd demand an 8% discount to our fair value estimate before recommending these shares. Although the portfolio is concentrated and focuses on a narrow slice of the market, the quality of the underlying holdings is very high. As of late December 2007, the fund was trading at a 21% discount to fair value, making it a bargain.

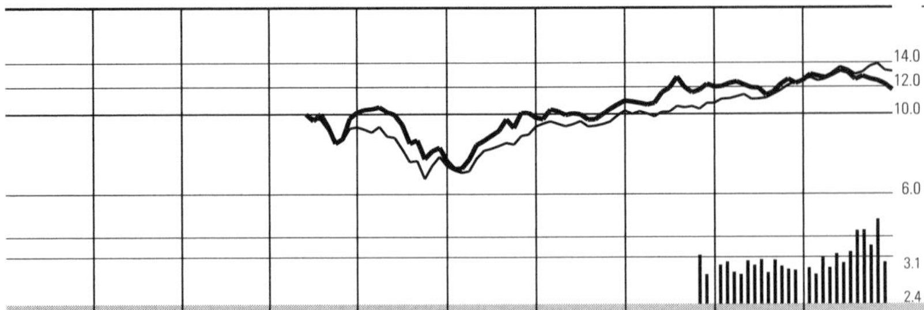

Methodology

The fund passively invests in a small group of retailers. Offered by Merrill Lynch, HOLDRs differ from other ETFs in that they can be bought only in 100-share increments, investors can exchange their shares for the underlying stocks at any time (for a fee of up to $10), investors receive spin-off shares outside of their HOLDRs investment just as if they held the underlying stock directly, and rather than an annual expense ratio, the fund charges $0.08 per share in annual custody fees (which are waived if the underlying securities fail to generate enough income to cover them).

1998	1999	2000	2001	2002	2003	2004	2005	2006	2007	History
93.35	—	—	81.06	59.38	78.25	87.30	95.38	99.35	93.35	NAV $
—	—	—	81.06	59.38	78.25	87.30	95.38	99.35	93.35	Market Price $
—	—	—	—	-26.75	31.78	11.57	9.26	4.16	-6.04	NAV Return%
—	—	—	2.17*	-26.75	31.78	11.57	9.26	4.16	-6.04	Market Price Return%
—	—	—	—	—	—	—	—	—	—	Avg Premium/Discount%
—	—	—	—	-4.65	3.10	0.69	4.35	-11.63	-11.53	NAV Rtrn% +/-S&P 500
—	—	—	—	-5.10	1.89	0.17	2.99	-11.30	-11.81	NAV Rtrn% +/-Russ 1000
—	—	—	—	15	4	10	2	30	85	NAV Return% Rank in Cat
—	—	—	—	—	—	—	—	—	—	Income Return %
—	—	—	—	—	—	—	—	—	—	Capital Return %
—	—	—	0.00	0.00	0.00	0.00	0.00	0.00	0.00	Income $
—	—	—	0.00	0.00	0.00	0.00	0.00	0.00	0.00	Capital Gains $
—	—	—	—	—	—	—	—	—	—	Expense Ratio %
—	—	—	—	—	—	—	—	—	—	Income Ratio %
—	—	—	—	—	—	—	—	—	—	Turnover Rate %
—	—	—	—	—	—	—	—	471	446	Net Assets $mil

Performance 12-31-07

Historic Quarterly NAV Returns

	1st Qtr	2nd Qtr	3rd Qtr	4th Qtr	Total
2003	0.94	16.35	5.06	6.80	31.78
2004	4.33	-2.18	0.28	9.02	11.57
2005	-2.37	11.10	-2.86	3.70	9.26
2006	3.33	-4.01	2.62	2.33	4.16
2007	1.71	3.49	-4.23	-6.80	-6.04

Trailing	NAV Return%	Market Return%	NAV Rtrn% +/-S&P 500	%Rank Cat.(NAV)
3 Mo	-6.80	-6.80	-3.47	76
6 Mo	-10.74	-10.74	-9.37	84
1 Yr	-6.04	-6.04	-11.53	85
3 Yr Avg	2.26	2.26	-6.36	95
5 Yr Avg	9.47	9.47	-3.36	85
10 Yr Avg	—	—	—	—

Tax Analysis	Tax-Adj Return%	Tax-Cost Ratio
3 Yr (estimated)	—	—
5 Yr (estimated)	—	—
10 Yr (estimated)	—	—

Rating and Risk

Time Period	Morningstar Rtn vs Cat	Morningstar Risk vs Cat	Morningstar Risk-Adj Rating
3 Yr	—	—	—
5 Yr	—	—	—
10 Yr	—	—	—

Other Measures	Standard Index S&P 500	Best Fit Index
Alpha	—	—
Beta	—	—
R-Squared	—	—
Standard Deviation	—	
Mean	2.26	
Sharpe Ratio	—	

Portfolio Analysis 12-31-07

Share change since 10-07 Total Stocks:18	Sector	PE	Tot Ret%	% Assets
Wal-Mart Stores, Inc.	Consumer	15.4	4.91	18.33
Home Depot, Inc.	Consumer	10.7	-31.14	11.34
Target	Consumer	14.7	-11.17	8.60
Walgreen Company	Consumer	18.5	-16.35	7.70
Amazon.com, Inc.	Consumer	NMF	134.77	7.32
Lowe's Companies Inc.	Consumer	11.4	-26.82	6.74
CVS Caremark Corporation	Consumer	21.5	28.93	5.98
Costco Wholesale Corpora	Consumer	28.5	33.21	5.92
Best Buy Co., Inc.	Consumer	18.9	7.38	5.01
Kroger Company	Consumer	15.3	16.82	4.18
Gap, Inc.	Consumer	21.7	10.54	3.53
Safeway Inc.	Consumer	17.0	-0.03	3.28
Macy's	Consumer	14.9	-32.65	3.26
TJX Companies	Consumer	19.0	1.97	3.04
Kohl's Corporation	Consumer	12.9	-33.10	2.92
Limited Brands, Inc.	Consumer	9.8	-32.80	1.57
SUPERVALU	Consumer	15.1	6.66	0.75
RadioShack Corporation	Consumer	10.5	1.87	0.54

Current Investment Style

Value Blnd Growth — Large Mid Small

Market Cap	%
Giant	24.3
Large	66.5
Mid	9.2
Small	0.0
Micro	0.0
Avg $mil: 40,003	

Value Measures		Rel Category
Price/Earnings	15.47	0.98
Price/Book	2.60	1.02
Price/Sales	0.53	0.43
Price/Cash Flow	9.32	1.01
Dividend Yield %	1.41	0.75

Growth Measures	%	Rel Category
Long-Term Erngs	—	—
Book Value	8.37	0.91
Sales	12.91	1.58
Cash Flow	9.19	1.05
Historical Erngs	5.90	0.35

Profitability	%	Rel Category
Return on Equity	22.38	1.01
Return on Assets	7.96	0.95
Net Margin	3.90	0.32

Sector Weightings	% of Stocks	Rel S&P 500	3 Year High	3 Year Low
Info	0.00	0.00		
Software	0.00	0.00	0	0
Hardware	0.00	0.00	0	0
Media	0.00	0.00	0	0
Telecom	0.00	0.00	0	0
Service	100.00	2.46		
Health	0.00	0.00	0	0
Consumer	100.00	14.75	100	100
Business	0.00	0.00	0	0
Financial	0.00	0.00	0	0
Mfg	0.00	0.00		
Goods	0.00	0.00	0	0
Ind Mtrls	0.00	0.00	0	0
Energy	0.00	0.00	0	0
Utilities	0.00	0.00	0	0

Composition

Cash	0.0
Stocks	100.0
Bonds	0.0
Other	0.0
Foreign (% of Stock)	0.0

Morningstar's Take by Haywood Kelly 12-31-07

Retail HOLDRs is the purest-play retail ETF we cover.

Like other members of the HOLDRs family, this fund holds a small portfolio--currently 18 stocks--and does not reconstitute or rebalance. The top five holdings make up more than 50% of the portfolio, and they're all focused on retail. This distinguishes the fund from other ETFs focused on the consumer sector, which might include food and beverage manufacturers, tobacco, auto producers, and so on.

Currently we tend to be more bullish on retailers than the market is. Take Wal-Mart, the fund's top holding at 18% of assets. Our forecasts are relatively sedate. For the next five years, we assume approximately 5% annual store expansion in the U.S. Wal-Mart business, 3% expansion for the Sam's Club chain, and about 8% annual international revenue growth. At the same time, we're assuming margins decline because of a lower ability to pass on price increases or squeeze its suppliers any further. And yet we still arrive at a fair value estimate of $60 per share, well above the stock's price as of mid-December.

What's true of Wal-Mart is true of most other stocks in the portfolio. Heading into 2008, we think this is one of the cheapest ETFs around. The top five holdings all earn 5 stars, and only one stock (Amazon.com) sports less than 2 stars. Based on the aggregate fair values of the underlying stocks, the overall portfolio is 20% undervalued, in our opinion.

We don't think an investor can go too wrong buying into this kind of portfolio, even if it isn't quite as cheap as we think. Four of the top five holdings sport wide-moat ratings, including the top position Wal-Mart. These are companies that we think will earn high returns on capital for years to come.

Address:	4 World Financial Center United States 800-637-7455
Web Address:	www.holdrs.com
Inception:	05-02-01
Advisor:	Merrill Lynch Pierce Fenner & Smith

Management Fee:	—		
Expense Projections:	3Yr: —	5Yr: —	10Yr: —
Income Distrib:	None		
Exchange:	AMEX		

Semiconductor HOLDRs SMH

Market Price	Mstar Category
$32.46	Specialty-Technology

Morningstar Fair Value

Price/Fair Value Ratio	Coverage Rate %
0.81	99

Morningstar Rating	Return	Risk	Yield	NAV	Avg Daily Vol. (k)	52 wk High/Low
—	—	—	—	$32.46	7,472	$41.00 - $28.87

Valuation

We'd require a 15% discount to fair value before recommending this fund. Although each chip firm serves a different mix of customers, they all share some common risk factors. This limits how much risk gets diversified away. The fund was recently trading at a 17% discount.

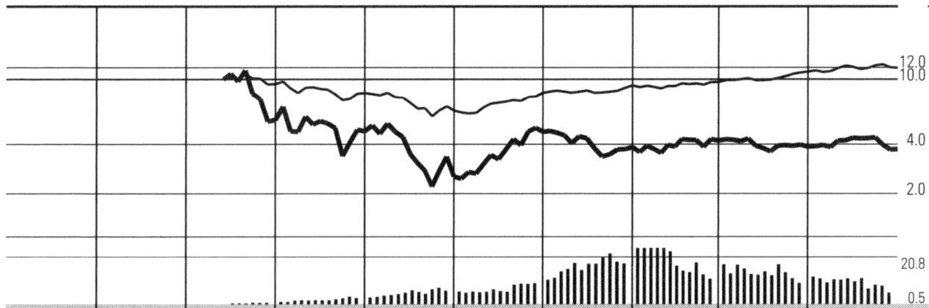

Methodology

The fund passively invests in a small group of semiconductor stocks. Offered by Merrill Lynch, HOLDRs differ from other ETFs in that they can be bought only in 100-share increments, investors can exchange their shares for the underlying stocks at any time (for a fee of up to $10), investors receive spin-off shares outside of their HOLDRs investment just as if they held the underlying stock directly, and rather than an annual expense ratio, the fund charges $0.08 per share in annual custody fees (which are waived if the underlying securities fail to generate enough income to cover them).

1998	1999	2000	2001	2002	2003	2004	2005	2006	2007	History
32.46	—	49.00	41.85	22.15	41.49	33.37	36.64	33.65	32.46	NAV $
—	—	49.00	41.85	22.15	41.49	33.37	36.64	33.65	32.46	Market Price $
—	—	—	-14.59	-47.07	87.31	-19.57	9.80	-8.16	-3.54	NAV Return%
—	—	-12.88*	-14.59	-47.07	87.31	-19.57	9.80	-8.16	-3.54	Market Price Return%
—	—	—	—	—	—	—	—	—	—	Avg Premium/Discount%
—	—	—	-2.70	-24.97	58.63	-30.45	4.89	-23.95	-9.03	NAV Rtrn% +/-S&P 500
—	—	—	1.00	-13.74	35.17	-31.30	2.44	-12.84	-10.80	NAV Rtrn% +/-PSE Tech 100
—	—	—	1	9	2	14	3	18	83	NAV Return% Rank in Cat
—	—	—	—	—	—	—	—	—	—	Income Return %
—	—	—	—	—	—	—	—	—	—	Capital Return %
—	—	0.00	0.00	0.00	0.00	0.00	0.00	0.00	0.00	Income $
—	—	0.00	0.00	0.00	0.00	0.00	0.00	0.00	0.00	Capital Gains $
—	—	—	—	—	—	—	—	—	—	Expense Ratio %
—	—	—	—	—	—	—	—	—	—	Income Ratio %
—	—	—	—	—	—	—	—	—	—	Turnover Rate %
—	—	—	—	—	—	—	—	1,434	1,390	Net Assets $mil

Performance 12-31-07

Historic Quarterly NAV Returns

	1st Qtr	2nd Qtr	3rd Qtr	4th Qtr	Total
2003	4.24	22.26	21.86	20.61	87.31
2004	-4.80	-4.23	-20.06	10.35	-19.57
2005	-2.52	3.50	9.71	-0.81	9.80
2006	-0.87	-9.39	4.19	-1.87	-8.16
2007	-0.77	13.96	0.66	-15.25	-3.54

Trailing	NAV Return%	Market Return%	NAV Rtrn% +/-S&P 500	%Rank Cat.(NAV)
3 Mo	-15.25	-15.25	-11.92	93
6 Mo	-14.69	-14.69	-13.32	96
1 Yr	-3.54	-3.54	-9.03	83
3 Yr Avg	-0.92	-0.92	-9.54	92
5 Yr Avg	7.94	7.94	-4.89	100
10 Yr Avg	—	—	—	—

Tax Analysis	Tax-Adj Return%	Tax-Cost Ratio
3 Yr (estimated)	—	—
5 Yr (estimated)	—	—
10 Yr (estimated)	—	—

Rating and Risk

Time Period	Morningstar Rtn vs Cat	Morningstar Risk vs Cat	Morningstar Risk-Adj Rating
3 Yr	—	—	—
5 Yr	—	—	—
10 Yr	—	—	—

Other Measures	Standard Index S&P 500	Best Fit Index
Alpha	—	—
Beta	—	—
R-Squared	—	—
Standard Deviation	—	
Mean	-0.92	
Sharpe Ratio	—	

Portfolio Analysis 12-31-07

Share change since 10-07 Total Stocks:18	Sector	PE	Tot Ret%	% Assets
Intel Corporation	Hardware	25.4	34.22	24.18
Texas Instruments, Inc.	Hardware	19.2	17.01	22.65
Applied Materials	Hardware	14.8	-2.60	14.41
Analog Devices, Inc.	Hardware	21.0	-1.54	5.79
Linear Technology	Hardware	22.4	7.24	4.93
KLA-Tencor Corporation	Hardware	20.1	-2.20	4.45
National Semiconductor	Hardware	21.1	0.44	4.07
Altera Corp.	Hardware	21.5	-1.30	3.53
Xilinx, Inc.	Hardware	20.2	-6.52	3.37
Broadcom Corporation	Hardware	93.5	-19.10	2.51
SanDisk Corporation	Hardware	NMF	-22.91	2.10
Micron Technology, Inc.	Hardware	—	-48.07	2.00
Novellus Systems, Inc.	Hardware	17.0	-19.90	1.69
Atmel Corporation	Hardware	—	-28.60	1.11
Teradyne, Inc.	Hardware	29.6	-30.88	0.95
Advanced Micro Devices	Hardware	—	-63.14	0.92
LSI Corporation	Hardware	—	-41.00	0.76
Amkor Technology, Inc.	Hardware	9.0	-8.67	0.54

Current Investment Style

Value Blnd Growth; Large Mid Small

Market Cap	%
Giant	24.2
Large	39.6
Mid	33.6
Small	2.6
Micro	0.0

Avg $mil: 26,596

Value Measures		Rel Category
Price/Earnings	17.12	0.83
Price/Book	3.02	0.96
Price/Sales	2.85	1.17
Price/Cash Flow	10.46	0.72
Dividend Yield %	1.47	2.23

Growth Measures	%	Rel Category
Long-Term Erngs	—	—
Book Value	1.66	0.25
Sales	8.25	0.92
Cash Flow	11.26	1.15
Historical Erngs	5.19	0.37

Profitability	%	Rel Category
Return on Equity	19.34	1.13
Return on Assets	13.85	1.50
Net Margin	16.63	1.28

Industry Weightings	% of Stocks	Rel Cat
Software	0.0	0.0
Hardware	0.0	0.0
Networking Eq	0.0	0.0
Semis	78.5	4.4
Semi Equip	21.5	5.2
Comp/Data Sv	0.0	0.0
Telecom	0.0	0.0
Health Care	0.0	0.0
Other	0.0	0.0

Composition

Cash	0.0
Stocks	100.0
Bonds	0.0
Other	0.0
Foreign (% of Stock)	0.0

Morningstar's Take by Haywood Kelly 12-31-07

Semiconductor HOLDRs are a handy way to bet on chip stocks.

Chip stocks tend to move together in cycles. These stocks often shoot past our reasonable estimate of fair value, as the market places too much emphasis on a few quarters' worth of good earnings. By waiting until chip companies report poor results and take a beating, the contrarian investor can do quite well.

This fund, given its exclusive focus on semiconductor stocks, offers a one-stop way to pursue such a strategy. The big names in chips and chip equipment are here--including the three giants Intel, Texas Instruments, and Applied Materials. The portfolio is very concentrated on these top holdings. As of late December 2007, about 60% of its assets were in that trio of stocks.

Given the portfolio's concentration, our analysts' opinions on those three stocks will drive our opinion of this ETF. As it is, we're fairly bullish on all three companies. We think Intel can boost revenues at a 10% clip over the next five years. The company appears to be on track in widening its chip-performance lead versus Advanced Micro Devices, and we have incorporated processor market-share gains in our valuation model. For Texas Instruments, we're forecasting 9% revenue growth as well as an increase in gross margins thanks to a shift toward higher-margin high-performance analog products. And we recently raised our fair value for Applied Materials by 25% thanks to our optimism about the firm's budding solar-equipment business.

Such forecasts, combined with a downturn in chip stock prices, have resulted in a cheap portfolio. As of late December, the fund appeared significantly undervalued to us, trading at a 17% discount to the aggregate fair value of its underlying holdings.

Address:	4 World Financial Center United States 800-637-7455
Web Address:	www.holdrs.com
Inception:	05-04-00
Advisor:	Merrill Lynch Pierce Fenner & Smith

Management Fee:	—		
Expense Projections:	3Yr: —	5Yr: —	10Yr: —
Income Distrib:	None		
Exchange:	AMEX		

SPDR S&P Homebuilders XHB

Market Price	Mstar Category
$19.35	Mid-Cap Value

Morningstar Fair Value

Price/Fair Value Ratio	Coverage Rate %
0.70	80

Valuation

Given the exposure to a single risk factor--the health of the U.S. housing market--the portfolio can diversify away only so much risk. As such, we'd only recommend it at a 20% discount to our fair value estimate. It was recently trading well within "buy" territory, at a hefty 31% discount to fair value.

Methodology

This fund passively tracks the S&P Homebuilders Select Index, which in turn tracks the homebuilders subindustry portion of the S&P Total Market Index. The index is equal-weighted, with assets spread across roughly 20 names, although the index does apply some liquidity screens. Although billed as a homebuilder fund, the portfolio also sweeps in a clutch of home-supply-related stocks, meaning it's not a pure play on homebuilders.

Morningstar Rating	Return	Risk	Yield	NAV	Avg Daily Vol. (k)	52 wk High/Low
—	—	—	1.5%	$19.32	3,858	$39.70 - $16.10

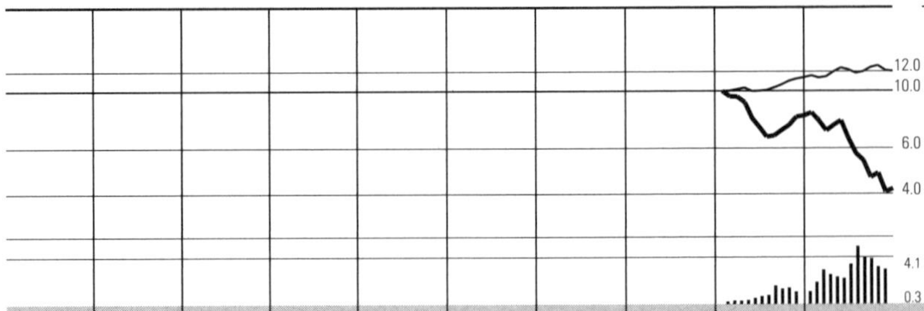

Growth of $10,000
- Investment Value of ETF
- Investment Value of Index S&P 500

Trading Volume Millions

History

1998	1999	2000	2001	2002	2003	2004	2005	2006	2007	History
—	—	—	—	—	—	—	—	37.35	19.32	NAV $
—	—	—	—	—	—	—	—	37.39	19.35	Market Price $
—	—	—	—	—	—	—	—	-36.54*	-47.69	NAV Return%
—	—	—	—	—	—	—	—	-36.48*	-47.66	Market Price Return%
—	—	—	—	—	—	—	—	0.00	-0.10	Avg Premium/Discount%
—	—	—	—	—	—	—	—	—	-53.18	NAV Rtrn% +/-S&P 500
—	—	—	—	—	—	—	—	—	0.70	NAV Rtrn% +/-S&P Home
—	—	—	—	—	—	—	—	—	100	NAV Return% Rank in Cat
—	—	—	—	—	—	—	—	—	0.79	Income Return %
—	—	—	—	—	—	—	—	—	-48.48	Capital Return %
—	—	—	—	—	—	—	—	0.21	0.30	Income $
—	—	—	—	—	—	—	—	0.00	0.00	Capital Gains $
—	—	—	—	—	—	—	—	0.36	0.35	Expense Ratio %
—	—	—	—	—	—	—	—	0.34	0.64	Income Ratio %
—	—	—	—	—	—	—	—	19	16	Turnover Rate %
—	—	—	—	—	—	—	—	295	303	Net Assets $mil

Performance 12-31-07

Historic Quarterly NAV Returns

	1st Qtr	2nd Qtr	3rd Qtr	4th Qtr	Total
2003	—	—	—	—	—
2004	—	—	—	—	—
2005	—	—	—	—	—
2006	—	-23.96	-2.69	13.81	—*
2007	-12.57	-6.56	-29.34	-9.39	-47.69

Trailing	NAV Return%	Market Return%	NAV Rtrn% +/-S&P 500	%Rank Cat.(NAV)
3 Mo	-9.39	-9.21	-6.06	92
6 Mo	-35.97	-35.55	-34.60	100
1 Yr	-47.69	-47.66	-53.18	100
3 Yr Avg	—	—	—	—
5 Yr Avg	—	—	—	—
10 Yr Avg	—	—	—	—

Tax Analysis	Tax-Adj Return%	Tax-Cost Ratio
3 Yr (estimated)	—	—
5 Yr (estimated)	—	—
10 Yr (estimated)	—	—

Rating and Risk

Time Period	Morningstar Rtn vs Cat	Morningstar Risk vs Cat	Morningstar Risk-Adj Rating
3 Yr	—	—	—
5 Yr	—	—	—
10 Yr	—	—	—

Other Measures	Standard Index S&P 500	Best Fit Index
Alpha	—	—
Beta	—	—
R-Squared	—	—
Standard Deviation	—	
Mean	—	
Sharpe Ratio	—	

Portfolio Analysis 12-31-07

Share change since 11-07 Total Stocks:22	Sector	PE	Tot Ret%	% Assets
☼ Cavco Industries, Inc.	Consumer	29.9	-3.42	5.60
⊕ Avatar Holdings Inc.	Financial	3.7	-48.27	5.06
⊕ Lennar Corporation	Consumer	—	-65.71	4.92
☼ Skyline Corporation	Consumer	—	-25.32	4.88
⊕ Pulte Homes, Inc.	Consumer	—	-68.29	4.86
⊕ Hovnanian Enterprises In	Consumer	—	-78.85	4.82
⊕ Home Depot, Inc.	Consumer	10.7	-31.14	4.79
⊖ Ryland Group, Inc.	Consumer	—	-48.90	4.76
⊖ NVR, Inc.	Consumer	8.3	-18.76	4.74
⊖ Centex Corporation	Consumer	—	-55.25	4.73
⊕ Mohawk Industries, Inc.	Goods	11.1	-0.61	4.68
⊕ Sherwin-Williams Company	Goods	12.6	-6.97	4.68
⊕ Champion Enterprises, In	Consumer	44.8	0.64	4.66
⊖ D.R. Horton Incorporated	Consumer	—	-49.13	4.65
⊕ M.D.C. Holdings, Inc.	Consumer	—	-33.54	4.61
⊕ Lowe's Companies Inc.	Consumer	11.4	-26.82	4.59
⊖ Toll Brothers, Inc.	Consumer	90.9	-37.76	4.50
⊕ KB Home	Consumer	—	-56.69	4.47
⊕ Beazer Homes USA, Inc.	Consumer	3.9	-83.95	4.09
⊕ Standard Pacific Corp.	Consumer	—	-87.41	3.99

Current Investment Style

Value Blnd Growth; Large Mid Small

Market Cap	%
Giant	0.0
Large	9.6
Mid	43.1
Small	14.3
Micro	33.0
Avg $mil: 1,665	

Value Measures		Rel Category
Price/Earnings	4.24	0.32
Price/Book	0.66	0.43
Price/Sales	0.26	0.33
Price/Cash Flow	0.87	0.14
Dividend Yield %	2.10	0.90

Growth Measures	%	Rel Category
Long-Term Erngs	—	—
Book Value	0.03	0.00
Sales	-1.85	NMF
Cash Flow	57.53	38.35
Historical Erngs	-7.55	NMF

Profitability	%	Rel Category
Return on Equity	-0.58	NMF
Return on Assets	0.27	0.05
Net Margin	-0.60	NMF

Sector Weightings	% of Stocks	Rel S&P 500	3 Year High	3 Year Low
Info	0.00	0.00		
Software	0.00	0.00	—	—
Hardware	0.00	0.00	—	—
Media	0.00	0.00	—	—
Telecom	0.00	0.00	—	—
Service	90.45	2.23		
Health	0.00	0.00	—	—
Consumer	85.28	12.58	—	—
Business	0.00	0.00	—	—
Financial	5.17	0.30	—	—
Mfg	9.55	0.25		
Goods	9.55	1.04	—	—
Ind Mtrls	0.00	0.00	—	—
Energy	0.00	0.00	—	—
Utilities	0.00	0.00	—	—

Composition

Cash	2.0
Stocks	98.0
Bonds	0.0
Other	0.0
Foreign (% of Stock)	0.0

Morningstar's Take by Haywood Kelly 12-31-07

SPDR S&P Homebuilders is an impure play on homebuilders.

With just 21 stocks in its portfolio, this fund might seem like a concentrated play on U.S. homebuilders. But that's not quite the case. Aside from homebuilders, this fund also owns positions in home-supply firms like Leggett & Platt, Mohawk Industries, Sherwin-Williams, Home Depot, and Lowe's. To be sure, each of these firms is tied to housing demand, but not nearly to the degree that pure homebuilding stocks are. Given that the fund equally weights its holdings, one fourth of the portfolio is only an indirect homebuilding play.

The diversification provided only some brake to the free-fall in housing-stock prices in 2007. This fund was down 50% through November 2007, compared with a 60% drop at rival iShares Dow Jones U.S. Home Construction. Eleven of the fund's 21 stocks had lost more than 50% of their value in the trailing 12 months. With the mortgage debacle sending new-home sales plummeting, many homebuilders will be lucky to survive the crisis. In our analysts' view, NVR, M.D.C. Holdings, KB Home, Ryland, and Toll Brothers should survive all but a depression-style downturn. Centex, D.R. Horton, and Lennar are also likely survivors, while Meritage Homes and Pulte Homes, though not as prepared, should be able to withstand a multiquarter disruption.

The portfolio trades for 60% of book value, and the old saw is that if you buy homebuilders below book value and hold on, you'll do okay. Based on Morningstar fair value estimates, the portfolio is certainly deep into bargain territory.

The advantage of the ETF format is that even if a few more homebuilders go bust, the overall portfolio could still do quite well over the long term. Thus, you don't have to select the precise winners and losers. With a 0.36% expense ratio, the fund is a cheap way to make the homebuilder bet. But for an undiluted bet, the iShares offering is a better choice.

Address:	One Lincoln Street United States 866-787-2257
Web Address:	www.advisors.ssga.com
Inception:	01-31-06*
Advisor:	SSgA Funds Management Inc

Management Fee:	0.35%		
Expense Projections:	3Yr:$113	5Yr:$197	10Yr:$446
Income Distrib:	Quarterly		
Exchange:	AMEX		

SPDR S&P Oil&Gas Expl&Pro XOP

Market Price	Mstar Category
$52.00	Specialty-Natural Res

Morningstar Rating	Return	Risk	Yield	NAV	Avg Daily Vol. (k)	52 wk High/Low
—	—	—	0.2%	$52.10	194	$53.35 - $35.42

Morningstar Fair Value

Price/Fair Value Ratio	Coverage Rate %
0.93	92

Valuation

We'd demand a 15% discount to our fair value estimate (the fund was recently trading at a 9% discount). Holdings are weighted equally, so one position won't dominate the portfolio. But all the holdings share common risk factors--importantly, the price of oil and natural gas. If our price forecasts are wrong, our fair values will be wrong.

Methodology

This fund tracks the S&P Oil & Gas Exploration & Production Select Industry Index. The index represents the oil and gas exploration and production subindustry portion of the S&P Total Market Index. The index is equal-weighted, but it does apply market-cap and liquidity screens. Because of the equal-weighting methodology, turnover is higher here than for a market-cap-weighted fund.

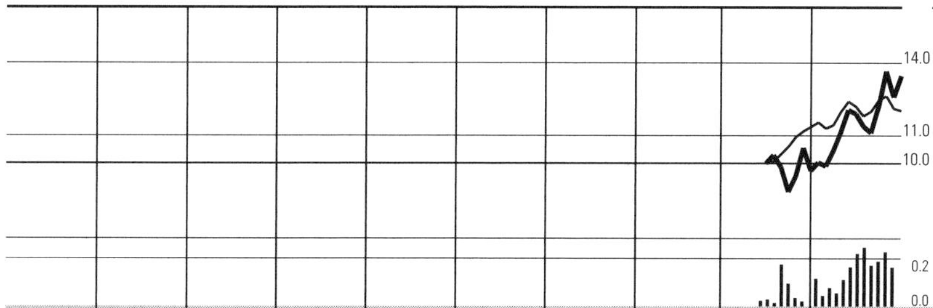

Growth of $10,000
— Investment Value of ETF
— Investment Value of Index S&P 500

Trading Volume Millions

1998	1999	2000	2001	2002	2003	2004	2005	2006	2007	History
—	—	—	—	—	—	—	—	38.15	52.10	NAV $
—	—	—	—	—	—	—	—	38.55	52.00	Market Price $
—	—	—	—	—	—	—	—	32.90*	36.90	NAV Return%
—	—	—	—	—	—	—	—	—	35.21	Market Price Return%
—	—	—	—	—	—	—	—	0.01	-0.10	Avg Premium/Discount%
—	—	—	—	—	—	—	—	—	31.41	NAV Rtrn% +/-S&P 500
—	—	—	—	—	—	—	—	—	0.29	NAV Rtrn% +/-S&P Oil/Gas
—	—	—	—	—	—	—	—	—	37	NAV Return% Rank in Cat
—	—	—	—	—	—	—	—	—	0.29	Income Return %
—	—	—	—	—	—	—	—	—	36.61	Capital Return %
—	—	—	—	—	—	—	—	0.04	0.11	Income $
—	—	—	—	—	—	—	—	0.00	0.00	Capital Gains $
—	—	—	—	—	—	—	—	0.36	0.35	Expense Ratio %
—	—	—	—	—	—	—	—	0.10	0.23	Income Ratio %
—	—	—	—	—	—	—	—	—	48	Turnover Rate %
—	—	—	—	—	—	—	—	21	81	Net Assets $mil

Performance 12-31-07

Historic Quarterly NAV Returns

	1st Qtr	2nd Qtr	3rd Qtr	4th Qtr	Total
2003	—	—	—	—	—
2004	—	—	—	—	—
2005	—	—	—	—	—
2006	—	—	-8.98	7.25	—*
2007	6.78	12.90	2.48	10.81	36.90

Trailing	NAV Return%	Market Return%	NAV Rtrn% +/-S&P 500	%Rank Cat.(NAV)
3 Mo	10.81	10.64	14.14	24
6 Mo	13.56	13.49	14.93	36
1 Yr	36.90	35.21	31.41	37
3 Yr Avg	—	—	—	—
5 Yr Avg	—	—	—	—
10 Yr Avg	—	—	—	—

Tax Analysis	Tax-Adj Return%	Tax-Cost Ratio
3 Yr (estimated)	—	—
5 Yr (estimated)	—	—
10 Yr (estimated)	—	—

Rating and Risk

Time Period	Morningstar Rtn vs Cat	Morningstar Risk vs Cat	Morningstar Risk-Adj Rating
3 Yr	—	—	—
5 Yr	—	—	—
10 Yr	—	—	—

Other Measures	Standard Index S&P 500	Best Fit Index
Alpha	—	—
Beta	—	—
R-Squared	—	—
Standard Deviation	—	
Mean	—	
Sharpe Ratio	—	

Morningstar's Take by Haywood Kelly 12-31-07

SPDR S&P Oil & Gas Exploration and Production is a pure play on oil producers.

If you're bullish on the price of oil--or if you're looking to hedge what you pay at the pump--this fund is a decent way to do it. The fund focuses on a narrow slice of the energy universe, holding only companies that explore for and produce oil and natural gas. Exposure to firm-specific risk is minimal because the index the fund tracks is equal-weighted. Each individual holding will therefore be only 2% to 3% of the portfolio. In other energy ETFs, you might see ExxonMobil account for 20%-plus of the portfolio. Here, it's on par with relative pipsqueaks such as Berry Petroleum. As a result, the top 10 holdings represent just 29% of the portfolio--low by sector-fund standards.

The big risk here is oil and natural-gas prices. Our valuation of the holdings in this ETF is highly sensitive to the trajectory we assume for these commodity prices. In November 2007, we raised our oil-price assumptions; our new assumptions make the valuation of this portfolio more attractive. In our discounted cash-flow model, we assume benchmark oil prices of $71 per barrel in 2007, $80 in 2008, $68 in 2009, $66 in 2010, and $68 in 2011. As that progression makes plain, we assume currently high oil prices will revert somewhat to the mean over the next five years. If oil prices stay high, however, this ETF will be worth much more than our current fair value estimate.

Oil prices are virtually impossible to predict, so keep that in mind before buying an ETF like this. Before recommending it, we'd demand at least a 15% discount to our fair value estimate for the portfolio. This provides some margin of safety if our oil-price forecasts are off.

Address:	One Lincoln Street United States 866-787-2257	Management Fee:	0.35%		
		Expense Projections:	3Yr:$113	5Yr:$197	10Yr:$446
Web Address:	www.advisors.ssga.com	Income Distrib:	Quarterly		
Inception:	06-19-06 *	Exchange:	AMEX		
Advisor:	SSgA Funds Management Inc				

Portfolio Analysis 12-31-07

Share change since 11-07 Total Stocks:35	Sector	PE	Tot Ret%	% Assets
⊕ Ultra Petroleum Corporat	Energy	50.8	49.77	2.97
⊕ Denbury Resources, Inc.	Energy	36.9	114.11	2.95
⊕ Cabot Oil & Gas Corporat	Energy	25.0	33.54	2.92
⊕ Newfield Exploration Com	Energy	24.8	14.69	2.91
⊕ ConocoPhillips	Energy	13.8	25.42	2.91
⊕ Range Resources Corporat	Energy	47.2	87.67	2.91
⊕ Pioneer Natural Resource	Energy	29.2	23.83	2.90
⊕ Occidental Petroleum Cor	Energy	13.8	60.25	2.90
⊕ Sunoco, Inc.	Energy	8.5	18.01	2.90
⊕ St. Mary Land & Explorat	Energy	12.4	5.07	2.89
⊕ Whiting Petroleum Corpor	Energy	19.5	23.73	2.88
⊕ Cimarex Energy Company	Energy	13.0	17.01	2.88
⊕ Quicksilver Resources, I	Energy	47.6	62.86	2.87
⊕ Chesapeake Energy Corp.	Energy	12.3	35.95	2.86
⊕ ExxonMobil Corporation	Energy	13.6	24.34	2.86
⊕ Mariner Energy, Inc.	Energy	14.2	16.73	2.86
⊕ Encore Acquisition Compa	Energy	—	36.04	2.85
⊕ Tesoro Corporation	Energy	8.7	46.04	2.85
⊕ Berry Petroleum Company	Energy	17.0	44.57	2.84
⊕ Forest Oil Corporation	Energy	21.2	55.57	2.84

Current Investment Style

Value Blnd Growth; Large Mid Small

Market Cap	%
Giant	11.5
Large	22.5
Mid	51.8
Small	14.2
Micro	0.0

Avg $mil: 9,412

Value Measures		Rel Category
Price/Earnings	14.27	0.87
Price/Book	2.08	0.89
Price/Sales	1.37	0.99
Price/Cash Flow	6.57	0.82
Dividend Yield %	0.51	0.37

Growth Measures	%	Rel Category
Long-Term Erngs	—	—
Book Value	18.98	1.27
Sales	12.03	1.08
Cash Flow	9.26	0.57
Historical Erngs	32.42	0.89

Profitability	%	Rel Category
Return on Equity	19.02	0.93
Return on Assets	8.25	0.88
Net Margin	17.85	1.30

Industry Weightings	% of Stocks	Rel Cat
Oil & Gas	84.2	2.5
Oil/Gas Products	13.0	3.9
Oil & Gas Srv	2.8	0.1
Pipelines	0.0	0.0
Utilities	0.0	0.0
Hard Commd	0.0	0.0
Soft Commd	0.0	0.0
Misc. Indstrl	0.0	0.0
Other	0.0	0.0

Composition

Cash	0.1
Stocks	99.9
Bonds	0.0
Other	0.0
Foreign (% of Stock)	0.0

streetTRACKS MS Tech MTK

Market Price	Mstar Category
$61.95	Specialty-Technology

Morningstar Rating	Return	Risk	Yield	NAV	Avg Daily Vol. (k)	52 wk High/Low
★★★	Average	Average	0.1%	$61.92	52	$68.59 - $54.40

Morningstar Fair Value

Price/Fair Value Ratio	Coverage Rate %
0.87	100

Valuation

This fund was recently trading in bargain territory, at a 12% discount to our fair value estimate, which skirts the 9% discount we'd demand. The portfolio focuses on tech stocks, but includes a wide number of industries, cutting down on firm- or industry-specific risk. The portfolio's fair value can change abruptly with each year-end

Methodology

This fund tracks the Morgan Stanley Technology Index, an equal-weighted benchmark of tech firms that is reconstituted once a year (on the third Friday of December). The index is composed of electronics-based technology companies, including firms in the following industries: computer & business services; technical software; enterprise software; Internet and PC software; telecom equipment; wireline/wireless; data networking/data security; server & enterprise hardware; PC hardware & data storage; connectors/electronics manufacturing services; semi-conductor capital equipment; and semiconductors.

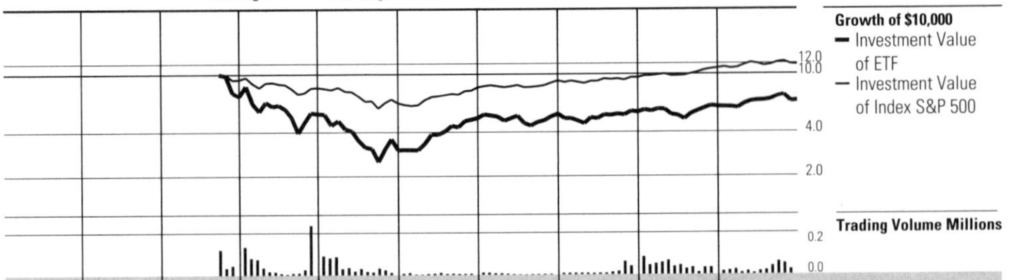

1998	1999	2000	2001	2002	2003	2004	2005	2006	2007	History
—	—	67.25	50.89	28.78	47.51	50.52	51.95	56.49	61.92	NAV $
—	—	67.25	51.10	28.65	47.49	50.52	51.90	56.60	61.95	Market Price $
—	—	-6.05*	-24.33	-43.45	65.07	6.56	2.86	8.83	9.73	NAV Return%
—	—	-6.04*	-24.01	-43.93	65.76	6.60	2.76	9.15	9.58	Market Price Return%
—	—	-0.06	0.21	0.11	0.10	0.02	-0.06	0.05	0.19	Avg Premium/Discount%
—	—	—	-12.44	-21.35	36.39	-4.32	-2.05	-6.96	4.24	NAV Rtrn% +/-S&P 500
—	—	—	—	-0.19	-0.32	-0.13	0.00	0.02	0.17	NAV Rtrn% +/-Amex MS Tech
—	—	—	25	50	38	38	34	64	45	NAV Return% Rank in Cat
—	—	—	0.00	0.00	0.00	0.21	0.02	0.08	0.12	Income Return %
—	—	—	-24.33	-43.45	65.07	6.35	2.84	8.75	9.61	Capital Return %
—	—	0.00	0.00	0.00	0.00	0.10	0.01	0.04	0.07	Income $
—	—	0.00	0.00	0.00	0.00	0.00	0.00	0.00	0.00	Capital Gains $
—	—	—	0.51	0.54	0.53	0.52	0.51	0.51	0.50	Expense Ratio %
—	—	—	-0.30	-0.30	-0.21	-0.20	0.24	0.07	0.09	Income Ratio %
—	—	—	26	37	23	17	46	23	22	Turnover Rate %
—	—	—	—	30	26	30	161	186	266	Net Assets $mil

Performance 12-31-07

Historic Quarterly NAV Returns

	1st Qtr	2nd Qtr	3rd Qtr	4th Qtr	Total
2003	-0.07	27.50	12.20	15.47	65.07
2004	2.30	1.20	-9.61	13.88	6.56
2005	-10.31	3.72	7.25	3.09	2.86
2006	4.97	-9.87	7.54	6.97	8.83
2007	-2.09	12.03	7.31	-6.78	9.73

Trailing	NAV Return%	Market Return%	NAV Rtrn% +/-S&P 500	%Rank Cat.(NAV)
3 Mo	-6.78	-6.69	-3.45	67
6 Mo	0.03	0.09	1.40	42
1 Yr	9.73	9.58	4.24	45
3 Yr Avg	7.09	7.11	-1.53	67
5 Yr Avg	16.66	16.77	3.83	25
10 Yr Avg	—	—	—	—

Tax Analysis	Tax-Adj Return%	Tax-Cost Ratio
3 Yr (estimated)	7.07	0.02
5 Yr (estimated)	16.62	0.03
10 Yr (estimated)	—	—

Rating and Risk

Time Period	Morningstar Rtn vs Cat	Morningstar Risk vs Cat	Morningstar Risk-Adj Rating
3 Yr	Avg	Avg	★★★
5 Yr	Avg	Avg	★★★
10 Yr	—	—	—

Other Measures	Standard Index S&P 500	Best Fit Index M* Hardware TR
Alpha	-3.1	-1.8
Beta	1.58	0.93
R-Squared	64	91
Standard Deviation	15.28	
Mean	7.09	
Sharpe Ratio	0.24	

Portfolio Analysis 12-31-07

Share change since 11-07 Total Stocks:35	Sector	PE	Tot Ret%	% Assets
⊖ Apple, Inc.	Hardware	50.5	133.47	2.96
⊖ Amazon.com, Inc.	Consumer	NMF	134.77	2.94
⊕ Adobe Systems Inc.	Software	37.9	3.92	2.94
⊕ Infosys Technologies, Lt	Software	30.2	-16.38	2.92
⊕ Ericsson Telephone Compa	Hardware	9.2	-41.17	2.91
⊕ Intuit	Software	24.7	3.61	2.89
⊕ Analog Devices, Inc.	Hardware	21.0	-1.54	2.89
⊖ Google, Inc.	Business	54.0	50.17	2.88
⊖ Oracle Corporation	Software	24.8	31.74	2.88
⊕ SAP Corporation ADR	Software	23.0	-2.60	2.88
⊕ Alcatel-Lucent ADR	Hardware	—	-47.71	2.88
☼ Flextronics Internationa	Hardware	15.7	5.05	2.88
⊕ Electronic Arts, Inc.	Software	—	15.98	2.88
⊖ Intel Corporation	Hardware	25.4	34.22	2.87
⊕ Automatic Data Processin	Business	23.6	2.62	2.87
⊕ Applied Materials	Hardware	14.8	-2.60	2.87
⊖ Texas Instruments, Inc.	Hardware	19.2	17.01	2.87
⊕ Broadcom Corporation	Hardware	93.5	-19.10	2.87
⊖ Microsoft Corporation	Software	23.4	20.83	2.86
⊕ Dell, Inc.	Hardware	18.6	-2.31	2.86

Current Investment Style

Value Blnd Growth — Large Mid Small

Market Cap	%
Giant	37.1
Large	45.7
Mid	17.2
Small	0.0
Micro	0.0
Avg $mil: 37,556	

Value Measures		Rel Category
Price/Earnings	21.35	1.03
Price/Book	4.24	1.35
Price/Sales	2.41	0.99
Price/Cash Flow	13.56	0.94
Dividend Yield %	0.60	0.91

Growth Measures	%	Rel Category
Long-Term Erngs	32.08	2.03
Book Value	6.38	0.94
Sales	8.29	0.92
Cash Flow	13.17	1.35
Historical Erngs	15.77	1.11

Profitability	%	Rel Category
Return on Equity	21.42	1.25
Return on Assets	11.10	1.20
Net Margin	13.27	1.02

Industry Weightings	% of Stocks	Rel Cat
Software	25.9	1.2
Hardware	23.4	1.6
Networking Eq	7.3	0.8
Semis	15.5	0.9
Semi Equip	3.0	0.7
Comp/Data Sv	7.1	0.8
Telecom	0.0	0.0
Health Care	0.0	0.0
Other	17.7	1.1

Composition

Cash	0.0
Stocks	100.0
Bonds	0.0
Other	0.0
Foreign (% of Stock)	17.2

Morningstar's Take by Haywood Kelly 12-31-07

Morgan Stanley Technology ETF is an odd duck.

The index this ETF follows is quirky. It's an equal-weighted benchmark of large-cap technology firms--spanning 35 stocks--with technology being very broadly defined. The portfolio contains retailers (Amazon.com and eBay), software firms (Microsoft and Intuit), search engines (Google and Yahoo), and tech hardware firms (Dell Computer and Intel). But the criteria for picking stocks for the index is vague.

As with any equal-weighting scheme, the fund needs to periodically rebalance, and it does this only once per year (in late December). This means the fund buys a basket of tech stocks, lets them run for a year, then reshuffles the deck--selling the winners, buying the losers--so that everything comes back to an equal weight. Most ETFs, by contrast, weight their holdings by market cap, which results in very low turnover. This fund's turnover was 22% last year--two to three times the level of most ETFs.

There's nothing inherently wrong with this approach, but it does make assessing the valuation of the fund trickier. As of late December, for example, the portfolio sported a price/fair value ratio of 0.88. On that basis, we'd typically recommend a portfolio like this. But because the portfolio will be reshuffled before the end of the year, that valuation is not necessarily indicative of what the valuation will look like in 2008.

At the very least, we'd recommend waiting until after the reconstituted portfolio is disclosed before buying this fund. That way you'll have a better idea of what you're buying. And unless this fund has a clear valuation advantage over other tech ETFs, investors can gain tech exposure through other funds with lower expense ratios without sacrificing any expected return.

Address:	One Lincoln Street United States 866-787-2257
Web Address:	www.advisors.ssga.com
Inception:	09-25-00 *
Advisor:	SSgA Funds Management Inc

Management Fee:	0.50%		
Expense Projections:	3Yr:$161	5Yr:$281	10Yr:$628
Income Distrib:	Quarterly		
Exchange:	AMEX		

Technology SPDR XLK

Market Price	Mstar Category
$26.66	Specialty-Technology

Morningstar Fair Value

Price/Fair Value Ratio	Coverage Rate %
0.94	100

Valuation

We would require an 8% discount to our fair value estimate here. Although this fund is fairly concentrated--about 60% of its assets are in the top 10 holdings--the stocks in the portfolio cater to a variety of end markets, tamping volatility. The portfolio was recently trading at a 6% discount to fair value, which is shy of bargain territory.

Methodology

This fund contains all the technology companies in the S&P 500 Index, which screens its components for profitability, industry leadership, and certain liquidity criteria. The fund weights its holdings by market cap, and is limited to U.S. companies, which eliminates some big international tech players such as Nokia. The fund holds 80 stocks, but it keeps one third of its assets in its top five stocks. Hardware makers such as Apple and IBM, and software providers such as Microsoft and Oracle, soak up more than one third of the portfolio, followed by telecom-service providers (about 17%) and semiconductor-related names (13%).

Morningstar Rating	Return	Risk	Yield	NAV	Avg Daily Vol. (k)	52 wk High/Low
★★★	Below Avg	Low	0.7%	$26.62	3,209	$28.40 - $22.64

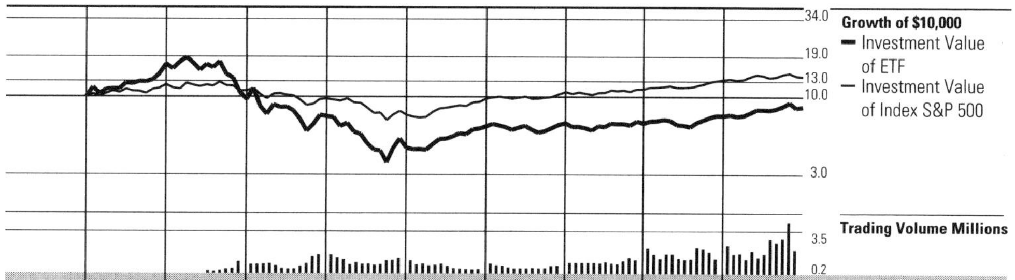

History

1998	1999	2000	2001	2002	2003	2004	2005	2006	2007	History
32.64	54.19	31.32	24.13	14.82	20.47	21.12	20.92	23.28	26.62	NAV $
32.62	53.88	31.31	24.00	14.80	20.38	21.11	20.90	23.26	26.66	Market Price $
-0.78*	66.03	-42.20	-22.96	-38.42	39.08	5.26	-0.26	12.12	15.19	NAV Return%
-1.46*	65.18	-41.89	-23.35	-38.17	38.68	5.66	-0.31	12.15	15.44	Market Price Return%
-0.06	-0.05	0.02	0.09	-0.13	-0.07	0.00	-0.05	0.00	-0.02	Avg Premium/Discount%
—	44.99	-33.10	-11.07	-16.32	10.40	-5.62	-5.17	-3.67	9.70	NAV Rtrn% +/-S&P 500
—	-12.71	-1.30	2.91	-1.01	-8.15	2.70	-1.25	3.70	-1.12	NAV Rtrn% +/-S&P Tech
—	1	1	1	10	100	50	78	22	15	NAV Return% Rank in Cat
—	0.00	0.00	0.00	0.17	0.95	2.04	0.70	0.85	0.83	Income Return %
—	66.03	-42.20	-22.96	-38.59	38.13	3.22	-0.96	11.27	14.36	Capital Return %
0.00	0.00	0.00	0.00	0.04	0.14	0.42	0.15	0.18	0.19	Income $
0.00	0.00	0.00	0.00	0.00	0.00	0.00	0.00	0.00	0.00	Capital Gains $
—	0.56	0.42	0.28	0.27	0.28	0.26	0.26	0.24	0.23	Expense Ratio %
—	-0.15	-0.16	-0.05	0.12	0.65	0.68	2.33	0.91	0.85	Income Ratio %
—	21	24	11	18	10	3	8	11	13	Turnover Rate %
—	—	—	—	972	1,101	1,236	1,541	2,018	3,009	Net Assets $mil

Performance 12-31-07

Historic Quarterly NAV Returns

	1st Qtr	2nd Qtr	3rd Qtr	4th Qtr	Total
2003	-3.24	18.76	7.18	12.92	39.08
2004	-1.22	2.12	-7.46	12.76	5.26
2005	-7.52	2.01	4.86	0.82	-0.26
2006	5.81	-8.36	8.65	6.43	12.12
2007	0.29	9.86	5.56	-0.96	15.19

Trailing	NAV Return%	Market Return%	NAV Rtrn% +/-S&P 500	%Rank Cat.(NAV)
3 Mo	-0.96	-0.70	2.37	25
6 Mo	4.55	4.82	5.92	21
1 Yr	15.19	15.44	9.70	15
3 Yr Avg	8.80	8.88	0.18	34
5 Yr Avg	13.53	13.59	0.70	87
10 Yr Avg	—	—	—	—

Tax Analysis	Tax-Adj Return%	Tax-Cost Ratio
3 Yr (estimated)	8.53	0.25
5 Yr (estimated)	13.14	0.34
10 Yr (estimated)	—	—

Rating and Risk

Time Period	Morningstar Rtn vs Cat	Morningstar Risk vs Cat	Morningstar Risk-Adj Rating
3 Yr	Avg	-Avg	★★★
5 Yr	-Avg	Low	★★★
10 Yr	—	—	—

Other Measures	Standard Index S&P 500	Best Fit Index
Alpha	-1.2	0.3
Beta	1.43	1.08
R-Squared	74	97
Standard Deviation	12.89	
Mean	8.80	
Sharpe Ratio	0.39	

Portfolio Analysis 12-31-07

Share change since 11-07 Total Stocks:80	Sector	PE	Tot Ret%	% Assets
⊕ Microsoft Corporation	Software	23.4	20.83	10.84
⊕ AT&T, Inc.	Telecom	21.6	20.58	9.54
⊕ Apple, Inc.	Hardware	50.5	133.47	6.57
⊕ Cisco Systems, Inc.	Hardware	21.5	-0.95	6.22
⊕ Google, Inc.	Business	54.0	50.17	6.06
⊕ Intel Corporation	Hardware	25.4	34.22	5.90
⊖ International Business M	Hardware	16.2	13.20	4.54
⊕ Verizon Communications I	Telecom	21.7	22.19	4.54
⊕ Hewlett-Packard Company	Hardware	18.8	23.40	4.48
⊕ Oracle Corporation	Software	24.8	31.74	3.40
⊕ Qualcomm, Inc.	Hardware	20.2	5.52	2.46
⊕ Dell, Inc.	Hardware	18.6	-2.31	2.11
⊕ Texas Instruments, Inc.	Hardware	19.2	17.01	1.79
⊕ EMC Corporation	Hardware	26.1	40.38	1.50
⊕ Corning Inc.	Hardware	18.6	28.76	1.46
⊕ eBay, Inc.	Consumer	—	10.38	1.45
⊕ Sprint Nextel Corporatio	Telecom	—	-30.12	1.44
⊕ Motorola, Inc.	Hardware	NMF	-21.85	1.41
⊕ Yahoo, Inc.	Media	45.7	-8.93	1.20
⊕ Adobe Systems Inc.	Software	37.9	3.92	0.95

Current Investment Style

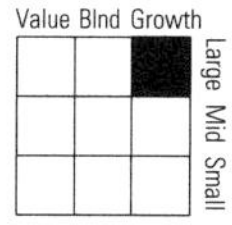

Market Cap	%
Giant	67.1
Large	21.9
Mid	10.6
Small	0.4
Micro	0.0
Avg $mil: 80,805	

Value Measures		Rel Category
Price/Earnings	18.73	0.91
Price/Book	3.43	1.09
Price/Sales	2.34	0.96
Price/Cash Flow	10.89	0.75
Dividend Yield %	0.82	1.24

Growth Measures	%	Rel Category
Long-Term Erngs	—	—
Book Value	6.98	1.03
Sales	9.98	1.11
Cash Flow	8.79	0.90
Historical Erngs	9.58	0.67

Profitability	%	Rel Category
Return on Equity	22.38	1.31
Return on Assets	11.30	1.22
Net Margin	15.79	1.22

Industry Weightings	% of Stocks	Rel Cat
Software	19.9	0.9
Hardware	21.4	1.5
Networking Eq	9.8	1.1
Semis	12.5	0.7
Semi Equip	1.6	0.4
Comp/Data Sv	8.5	0.9
Telecom	17.6	7.0
Health Care	0.0	0.0
Other	8.9	0.5

Composition

Cash	0.6
Stocks	99.4
Bonds	0.0
Other	0.0
Foreign (% of Stock)	0.0

Morningstar's Take by Haywood Kelly 12-31-07

Technology Select Sector SPDR offers easy access to the U.S. tech and telecom sectors.

Tech stocks are notoriously hard to predict. But by packaging together these stocks into a single portfolio, an ETF like this one mitigates the risk. When some of the stocks in the portfolio sputter (Dell and Sprint Nextel come to mind), others are probably going to be soaring (Google or Apple, for example). Thus the overall volatility of the portfolio is surprisingly low. And given the variety of industries (software, hardware, telecom) and end markets represented in this portfolio, it's unlikely that our fair value estimates will be systematically off.

In terms of construction, this fund is as plain-vanilla as they come. It simply invests in the technology and telecommunications stocks in the S&P 500, weighting them by market cap. This means low turnover and a bias toward more successful firms (which sport the higher market caps). Thus Google, with about $15 billion in annual revenue, gets about the same weighting as IBM, with almost $100 billion in annual revenue. The tilt toward more-successful companies puts the fund deeply in the growth column of the Morningstar Style Box. The price multiples tend to be higher than for the U.S. market as a whole, and the growth rates as well.

Keep in mind that any ETF, including this one, can be toxic if purchased at the wrong price. A case in point is when tech stocks became overvalued as a group in the late 1990s. In the 2000-02 period, as the bubble was bursting, this fund lost 70% of its value.

When the valuations are attractive, though, this fund is one of the better choices to get broad tech exposure in one package, especially when its low 0.24% expense ratio is taken into account.

Address:	c/o State Street Bk&Tr, 225 Franklin St United States 800-843-2639
Web Address:	www.spdrindex.com
Inception:	12-16-98*
Advisor:	SSgA Funds Management Inc

Management Fee:	0.05%		
Expense Projections:	3Yr:$77	5Yr:$136	10Yr:$307
Income Distrib:	Quarterly		
Exchange:	AMEX		

Utilities HOLDRs UTH

Market Price	Mstar Category
$136.23	Specialty-Utilities

Morningstar Fair Value

Price/Fair Value Ratio	Coverage Rate %
0.94	99

Valuation

We'd demand an 8% discount to fair value before recommending this fund. Although the portfolio is concentrated, the business risk of its top holdings is average or below average. This, combined with the diversification benefits of the ETF, results in the modest margin of safety. It was recently trading at a 6% discount to fair value.

Methodology

The fund passively invests in a small group of utilities stocks. Offered by Merrill Lynch, HOLDRs differ from other ETFs in that they can be bought only in 100-share increments, investors can exchange their shares for the underlying stocks at any time (for a fee of up to $10), investors receive spin-off shares outside of their HOLDRs investment just as if they held the underlying stock directly, and rather than an annual expense ratio, the fund charges $0.08 per share in annual custody fees (which are waived if the underlying securities fail to generate enough income to cover them).

Morningstar Rating	Return	Risk	Yield	NAV	Avg Daily Vol. (k)	52 wk High/Low
—	—	—	—	$136.23	75	$152.12 - $125.08

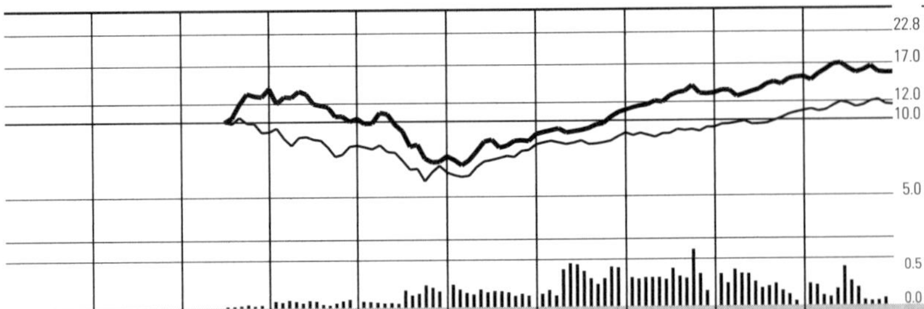

Growth of $10,000
— Investment Value of ETF
— Investment Value of Index S&P 500

Trading Volume Millions

1998	1999	2000	2001	2002	2003	2004	2005	2006	2007	History
136.23	—	120.81	91.05	64.15	78.40	97.68	114.01	131.69	136.23	NAV $
—	—	120.81	91.05	64.15	78.40	97.68	114.01	131.69	136.23	Market Price $
—	—	—	-24.64	-29.54	22.21	24.59	16.72	15.51	3.45	NAV Return%
—	—	5.03*	-24.64	-29.54	22.21	24.59	16.72	15.51	3.45	Market Price Return%
—	—	—	—	—	—	—	—	—	—	Avg Premium/Discount%
—	—	—	-12.75	-7.44	-6.47	13.71	11.81	-0.28	-2.04	NAV Rtrn% +/-S&P 500
—	—	—	1.63	-6.16	-7.18	-5.65	-8.42	-1.12	-16.66	NAV Rtrn% +/-DOWJNS UTIL
—	—	—	2	3	3	1	1	5	100	NAV Return% Rank in Cat
—	—	—	—	—	—	—	—	—	—	Income Return %
—	—	—	—	—	—	—	—	—	—	Capital Return %
—	—	0.00	0.00	0.00	0.00	0.00	0.00	0.00	0.00	Income $
—	—	0.00	0.00	0.00	0.00	0.00	0.00	0.00	0.00	Capital Gains $
—	—	—	—	—	—	—	—	—	—	Expense Ratio %
—	—	—	—	—	—	—	—	—	—	Income Ratio %
—	—	—	—	—	—	—	—	—	—	Turnover Rate %
—	—	—	—	—	—	—	—	421	440	Net Assets $mil

Performance 12-31-07

Historic Quarterly NAV Returns

	1st Qtr	2nd Qtr	3rd Qtr	4th Qtr	Total
2003	-3.66	20.71	-1.19	6.36	22.21
2004	5.13	-1.50	6.29	13.20	24.59
2005	5.21	8.09	9.88	-6.59	16.72
2006	-3.31	6.57	4.75	7.01	15.51
2007	6.93	0.59	2.18	-5.88	3.45

Trailing	NAV Return%	Market Return%	NAV Rtrn% +/-S&P 500	%Rank Cat.(NAV)
3 Mo	-5.88	-5.88	-2.55	100
6 Mo	-3.83	-3.83	-2.46	100
1 Yr	3.45	3.45	-2.04	100
3 Yr Avg	11.73	11.73	3.11	100
5 Yr Avg	16.26	16.26	3.43	100
10 Yr Avg	—	—	—	—

Tax Analysis	Tax-Adj Return%	Tax-Cost Ratio
3 Yr (estimated)	—	—
5 Yr (estimated)	—	—
10 Yr (estimated)	—	—

Rating and Risk

Time Period	Morningstar Rtn vs Cat	Morningstar Risk vs Cat	Morningstar Risk-Adj Rating
3 Yr	—	—	—
5 Yr	—	—	—
10 Yr	—	—	—

Other Measures	Standard Index S&P 500	Best Fit Index
Alpha	—	—
Beta	—	—
R-Squared	—	—
Standard Deviation	—	
Mean	11.73	
Sharpe Ratio	—	

Portfolio Analysis 12-31-07

Share change since 10-07 Total Stocks:18	Sector	PE	Tot Ret%	% Assets
Exelon Corporation	Utilities	20.2	35.14	17.86
Entergy Corporation	Utilities	20.0	32.55	8.69
Southern Company	Utilities	17.1	9.85	8.21
FPL Group	Utilities	20.0	27.91	7.89
⊕ Dominion Resources, Inc.	Utilities	12.3	16.98	7.60
Public Service Enterpris	Utilities	19.1	52.10	7.14
Edison International	Utilities	15.4	19.93	5.91
PG & E Corporation	Utilities	16.3	-6.09	5.46
FirstEnergy Corporation	Utilities	17.3	23.71	5.34
Williams Companies, Inc.	Energy	27.7	38.70	5.32
American Electric Power	Utilities	16.8	13.06	4.81
Duke Energy Corporation	Utilities	10.4	9.03	4.40
Consolidated Edison Comp	Utilities	13.9	6.65	3.22
Progress Energy, Inc.	Utilities	15.5	3.83	2.47
Reliant Energy, Inc.	Utilities	NMF	84.66	2.12
CenterPoint Energy, Inc.	Utilities	16.5	7.35	1.63
El Paso Corporation	Energy	52.4	13.97	1.28
Dynegy, Inc.	Utilities	89.3	-1.38	0.66

Current Investment Style

Value Blnd Growth — Large Mid Small

Market Cap	%
Giant	17.9
Large	74.0
Mid	8.2
Small	0.0
Micro	0.0
Avg $mil: 24,555	

Value Measures		Rel Category
Price/Earnings	16.52	0.94
Price/Book	1.75	1.05
Price/Sales	1.66	1.27
Price/Cash Flow	7.57	1.04
Dividend Yield %	2.82	0.97

Growth Measures	%	Rel Category
Long-Term Erngs	—	—
Book Value	13.76	1.83
Sales	1.62	0.48
Cash Flow	5.95	0.68
Historical Erngs	7.49	0.92

Profitability	%	Rel Category
Return on Equity	14.97	1.05
Return on Assets	3.99	0.96
Net Margin	10.41	1.02

Industry Weightings	% of Stocks	Rel Cat
Telecom Srv	0.0	0.0
Electric Utls	92.7	1.5
Nat Gas Utls	0.7	0.1
Wireless Srv	0.0	0.0
Energy	6.6	0.6
Media	0.0	0.0
Network Eq	0.0	0.0
Water	0.0	0.0
Other	0.0	0.0

Composition

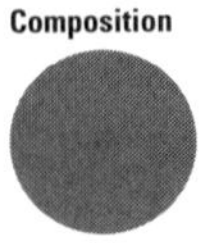

Cash	0.0
Stocks	100.0
Bonds	0.0
Other	0.0
Foreign (% of Stock)	0.0

Morningstar's Take by Haywood Kelly 12-31-07

Utilities HOLDRs offer a concentrated bet on the biggest utilities.

This ETF invests passively in a small group of utilities stocks--18 to be exact--and parks about 50% of its assets in the top five holdings alone. Exelon, the biggest holding, represents about 20% of the fund's assets. As you'd expect from a portfolio of utilities stocks, the growth rates of the underlying companies are low (basically GDP-like) and the dividend yield relatively decent, at 2.6%.

Given Exelon's hefty weighting in the portfolio, our opinion of that stock will significantly influence our view of this ETF. As of late-December 2007, our fair value estimate was $88 per share for Exelon, a tad above its share price. It's an unusual firm in that it earns a wide-moat rating from Morningstar; it's the only U.S. utility to do so. The reason is Exelon's portfolio of nuclear power plants. With the concern over carbon emissions, nuclear power is back in vogue as a clean energy source. Exelon's low-cost nuclear power plants and economies of scale give it, in our view, enough of a competitive advantage to separate it from its peers.

Overall, the portfolio trades in line with our fair value estimate, but utilities stocks do swing in and out of favor. Over the past few years, they've definitely been in favor. This fund has returned double digits each year since 2003. Utilities have been popular as investors have hunted for yield. Plus, those utilities that came through the sector meltdown at the start of this decade have been improving their balance sheets. As a result, this fund's price multiples aren't all that far off from those of the S&P 500 as a whole.

As with all HOLDRs, this ETF comes with a low price tag and some unusual structural quirks. Overall, we think it's a fine way to gain utilities exposure when the area is out of favor.

Address:	4 World Financial Center United States 800-637-7455
Web Address:	www.holdrs.com
Inception:	06-22-00
Advisor:	Merrill Lynch Pierce Fenner & Smith

Management Fee:	—		
Expense Projections:	3Yr: —	5Yr: —	10Yr: —
Income Distrib:	None		
Exchange:	AMEX		

Utilities SPDR XLU

Market Price	Mstar Category
$42.33	Specialty-Utilities

Morningstar Rating	Return	Risk	Yield	NAV	Avg Daily Vol. (k)	52 wk High/Low
★★★	Average	High	2.6%	$42.56	4,718	$44.38 - $35.98

Morningstar Fair Value

Price/Fair Value Ratio	Coverage Rate %
0.96	99

Valuation

We'd demand an 8% discount to our fair value estimate here. Although it has a large chunk of assets in its top holdings, we believe the business risk of its holdings is no greater than average. This, coupled with the fund's diversification, is why we don't demand a larger margin of safety. It was recently trading at a 4% discount to fair value.

Methodology

This exchange-traded fund owns and passively tracks the utilities stocks in the S&P 500 in proportion to their weight in the utilities sector. The fund includes companies providing water, electric, and natural-gas service. The portfolio is top-heavy, with the top 10 names soaking up nearly 60% of the fund. This is the oldest utilities ETF and also the largest by assets. It's also one of the more frequently traded ETFs focusing on stocks that fall in the large-value zone of the Morningstar Style Box.

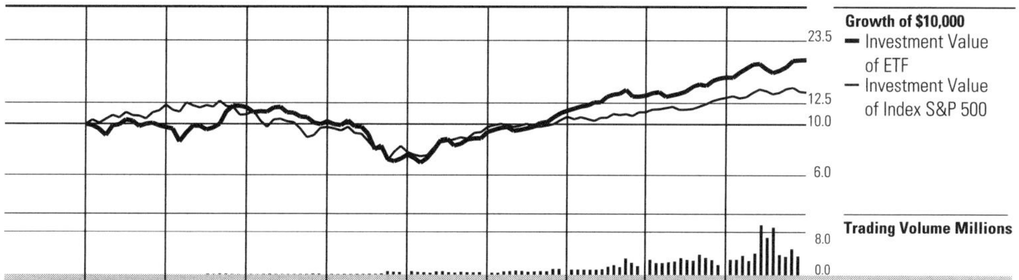

1998	1999	2000	2001	2002	2003	2004	2005	2006	2007	History
30.13	28.18	33.11	27.94	19.21	23.29	27.86	31.44	36.71	42.56	NAV $
30.23	28.14	33.19	28.03	19.15	23.33	27.85	31.39	36.73	42.33	Market Price $
7.90*	-3.33	22.03	-13.05	-28.31	25.81	23.86	16.53	20.65	19.09	NAV Return%
7.53*	-3.79	22.50	-12.98	-28.77	26.44	23.58	16.37	20.94	18.38	Market Price Return%
0.33	-0.04	0.07	-0.11	0.02	0.11	-0.01	-0.02	0.01	-0.12	Avg Premium/Discount%
—	-24.37	31.13	-1.16	-6.21	-2.87	12.98	11.62	4.86	13.60	NAV Rtrn% +/-S&P 500
—	5.85	-35.16	17.39	1.68	-0.53	-0.46	-0.34	-0.34	-0.29	NAV Rtrn% +/-S&P Utilities
—	1	1	1	100	1	1	1	100	29	NAV Return% Rank in Cat
—	2.62	3.26	2.69	3.34	4.21	3.81	3.67	3.61	3.02	Income Return %
—	-5.95	18.77	-15.74	-31.65	21.60	20.05	12.86	17.04	16.07	Capital Return %
0.00	0.78	0.91	0.88	0.92	0.80	0.87	1.01	1.12	1.10	Income $
0.00	0.18	0.25	0.00	0.00	0.00	0.00	0.00	0.00	0.00	Capital Gains $
—	0.57	0.40	0.29	0.27	0.27	0.27	0.26	0.24	0.23	Expense Ratio %
—	2.62	3.45	2.87	3.60	4.02	3.64	3.33	3.34	2.85	Income Ratio %
—	39	45	12	57	6	10	4	2	10	Turnover Rate %
—	—	—	—	534	1,284	1,686	1,752	2,982	2,504	Net Assets $mil

Performance 12-31-07

Historic Quarterly NAV Returns

	1st Qtr	2nd Qtr	3rd Qtr	4th Qtr	Total
2003	-3.26	21.21	-0.54	7.87	25.81
2004	5.07	-1.36	6.64	12.08	23.86
2005	5.36	9.22	7.17	-5.52	16.53
2006	-1.22	5.63	6.04	9.05	20.65
2007	9.20	-0.42	1.89	7.48	19.09

Trailing	NAV Return%	Market Return%	NAV Rtrn% +/-S&P 500	%Rank Cat.(NAV)
3 Mo	7.48	7.17	10.81	10
6 Mo	9.52	8.52	10.89	30
1 Yr	19.09	18.38	13.60	29
3 Yr Avg	18.75	18.55	10.13	1
5 Yr Avg	21.14	21.09	8.31	1
10 Yr Avg	—	—	—	—

Tax Analysis	Tax-Adj Return%	Tax-Cost Ratio
3 Yr (estimated)	17.48	1.07
5 Yr (estimated)	19.77	1.13
10 Yr (estimated)	—	—

Rating and Risk

Time Period	Morningstar Rtn vs Cat	Morningstar Risk vs Cat	Morningstar Risk-Adj Rating
3 Yr	Avg	+Avg	★★★
5 Yr	Avg	High	★★★
10 Yr	—	—	—

Other Measures	Standard Index S&P 500	Best Fit Index M* Util Sect TR
Alpha	12.0	-0.3
Beta	0.35	1.00
R-Squared	7	96
Standard Deviation	10.30	
Mean	18.75	
Sharpe Ratio	1.31	

Portfolio Analysis 12-31-07

Share change since 11-07 Total Stocks:31	Sector	PE	Tot Ret%	% Assets
⊖ Exelon Corporation	Utilities	20.2	35.14	11.49
⊕ Southern Company	Utilities	17.1	9.85	6.27
⊕ Dominion Resources, Inc.	Utilities	12.3	16.98	5.92
⊕ FPL Group	Utilities	20.0	27.91	5.89
⊕ Duke Energy Corporation	Utilities	10.4	9.03	5.43
⊕ Public Service Enterpris	Utilities	19.1	52.10	5.33
⊖ Entergy Corporation	Utilities	20.0	32.55	4.96
⊕ FirstEnergy Corporation	Utilities	17.3	23.71	4.71
⊖ PPL Corporation	Utilities	20.0	49.31	4.14
⊕ American Electric Power	Utilities	16.8	13.06	3.97
⊕ Constellation Energy Gro	Utilities	22.5	51.88	3.95
⊕ Edison International	Utilities	15.4	19.93	3.71
⊖ Sempra Energy	Utilities	17.0	12.69	3.45
⊕ PG & E Corporation	Utilities	16.3	-6.09	3.25
⊕ AES Corporation	Utilities	23.3	-2.95	3.05
⊕ Consolidated Edison Comp	Utilities	13.9	6.65	2.83
⊕ Progress Energy, Inc.	Utilities	15.5	3.83	2.68
⊕ Ameren Corporation	Utilities	19.7	5.94	2.40
⊕ Allegheny Energy, Inc.	Utilities	29.6	38.90	2.25
⊕ Xcel Energy, Inc.	Utilities	16.1	1.95	2.02

Current Investment Style

Value Blnd Growth / Large Mid Small

Market Cap	%
Giant	11.6
Large	67.3
Mid	20.7
Small	0.4
Micro	0.0
Avg $mil: 19,197	

Value Measures		Rel Category
Price/Earnings	16.14	0.92
Price/Book	1.55	0.93
Price/Sales	1.39	1.06
Price/Cash Flow	7.73	1.06
Dividend Yield %	2.80	0.97

Growth Measures	%	Rel Category
Long-Term Erngs	—	—
Book Value	14.56	1.94
Sales	2.80	0.84
Cash Flow	3.60	0.41
Historical Erngs	6.23	0.77

Profitability	%	Rel Category
Return on Equity	13.79	0.97
Return on Assets	3.84	0.92
Net Margin	9.64	0.95

Industry Weightings	% of Stocks	Rel Cat
Telecom Srv	0.0	0.0
Electric Utls	93.3	1.5
Nat Gas Utls	4.8	0.5
Wireless Srv	0.0	0.0
Energy	2.0	0.2
Media	0.0	0.0
Network Eq	0.0	0.0
Water	0.0	0.0
Other	0.0	0.0

Composition

Cash	0.7
Stocks	99.3
Bonds	0.0
Other	0.0
Foreign (% of Stock)	0.0

Morningstar's Take by Haywood Kelly 12-31-07

When large-cap utilities are cheap, Utilities Select Sector SPDR is a good way to play them.

Despite the plodding nature of utilities, their stocks do swing in and out of favor. Over the past few years, they've definitely been in favor. For instance, investors have favored utilities amid their clamor for higher-yielding fare. Plus, those utilities that came through the sector meltdown at the start of this decade have been improving their balance sheets. As such, this fund has returned double digits each year since 2003. Consequently, its price multiples aren't all that far off from those of the S&P 500 as a whole.

This ETF invests passively in the utilities stocks in the S&P 500. This means a concentrated portfolio--30 stocks, with about 60% of assets in the top 10 holdings--and very low turnover. As you'd expect from a portfolio of utilities stocks, the growth rates of the underlying companies are low (basically GDP-like) and the dividend yield relatively decent, at 2.6%.

The top holding here, at 12% of assets, is Exelon. This is an unusual utility in that it earns a wide-moat rating--the only U.S. utility to do so. The reason is Exelon's portfolio of nuclear power plants. With the concern over carbon emissions, nuclear power is back in vogue as a clean energy source. Exelon's low-cost nuclear power plants and economies of scale give it, in our view, enough of a competitive advantage to separate it from its peers. Given Exelon's hefty weighting in the portfolio, our opinion of that stock will significantly influence our view of this ETF.

Like other members of the SPDR family, this ETF comes with a low price tag. The expense ratio is just 0.24%. So if and when utilities stocks become attractively priced--and maybe start offering a yield closer to that of a Treasury bond--this fund will be worth a look.

Address:	c/o State Street Bk&Tr, 225 Franklin St United States 800-843-2639
Web Address:	www.spdrindex.com
Inception:	12-16-98*
Advisor:	SSgA Funds Management Inc

Management Fee:	0.05%		
Expense Projections:	3Yr:$77	5Yr:$136	10Yr:$307
Income Distrib:	Quarterly		
Exchange:	AMEX		

Vanguard Cons Stap ETF VDC

Market Price	Mstar Category
$70.79	Large Blend

Morningstar Rating	Return	Risk	Yield	NAV	Avg Daily Vol. (k)	52 wk High/Low
★★★★	Above Avg	Low	1.6%	$70.91	57	$73.77 - $63.05

Morningstar Fair Value

Price/Fair Value Ratio	Coverage Rate %
0.92	96

Valuation

High-quality firms predominate in this portfolio, which hasn't been especially volatile. As such, we'd be buyers when the fund is trading at an 8% or greater discount to our fair value estimate. It was recently trading at an 8% discount, which puts it right on the cusp of "bargain" territory.

Methodology

This ETF tracks the MSCI U.S. Investable Consumer Staples Index, a subset of the market-cap-weighted MSCI U.S. Investable Market 2500 Index. The MSCI Consumer Staples Index holds roughly 100 stocks, including manufacturers and distributors of food, beverages, and tobacco; producers of nondurable household goods and personal products; drug retailers; and consumer supercenters. It doesn't include consumer-goods stocks in the automotive or leisure industries. The index is quite top-heavy, with its top 10 holdings recently accounting for more than 60% of the fund's assets.

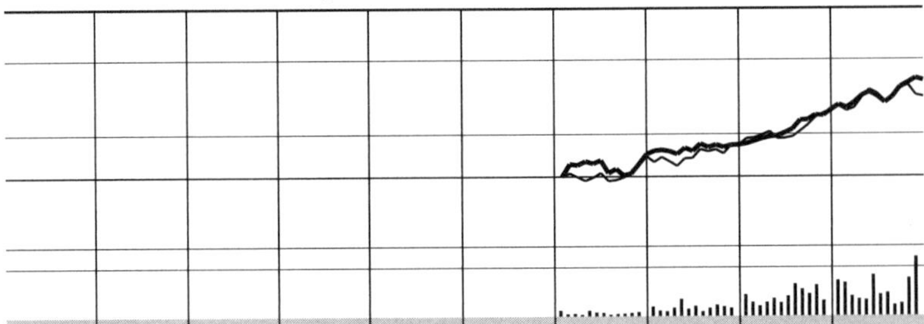

Growth of $10,000
- Investment Value of ETF
- Investment Value of Index S&P 500

Trading Volume Millions

History

	1998	1999	2000	2001	2002	2003	2004	2005	2006	2007
NAV $	—	—	—	—	—	—	54.48	55.94	63.82	70.91
Market Price $	—	—	—	—	—	—	54.57	55.93	63.84	70.79
NAV Return%	—	—	—	—	—	—	10.61*	3.95	15.81	12.92
Market Price Return%	—	—	—	—	—	—	10.56*	3.76	15.87	12.69
Avg Premium/Discount%	—	—	—	—	—	—	0.08	0.01	0.05	-0.04
NAV Rtrn% +/-S&P 500	—	—	—	—	—	—	—	-0.96	0.02	7.43
NAV Rtrn% +/-MSCI Cons St	—	—	—	—	—	—	—	-0.58	0.78	-1.00
NAV Return% Rank in Cat	—	—	—	—	—	—	—	65	27	15
Income Return %	—	—	—	—	—	—	—	1.29	1.72	1.82
Capital Return %	—	—	—	—	—	—	—	2.66	14.09	11.10
Income $	—	—	—	—	—	—	0.85	0.70	0.96	1.16
Capital Gains $	—	—	—	—	—	—	0.24	0.00	0.00	0.00
Expense Ratio %	—	—	—	—	—	—	0.28	0.26	0.25	0.22
Income Ratio %	—	—	—	—	—	—	1.51	1.71	1.93	2.20
Turnover Rate %	—	—	—	—	—	—	20	7	14	12
Net Assets $mil	—	—	—	—	—	—	22	89	255	418

Performance 12-31-07

Historic Quarterly NAV Returns

	1st Qtr	2nd Qtr	3rd Qtr	4th Qtr	Total
2003	—	—	—	—	—
2004	—	2.03	-6.05	9.17	—*
2005	1.21	0.05	2.66	-0.01	3.95
2006	2.66	2.35	5.56	4.40	15.81
2007	2.96	2.65	4.03	2.70	12.92

Trailing	NAV Return%	Market Return%	NAV Rtrn% +/-S&P 500	%Rank Cat.(NAV)
3 Mo	2.70	2.61	6.03	3
6 Mo	6.84	6.63	8.21	2
1 Yr	12.92	12.69	7.43	15
3 Yr Avg	10.77	10.65	2.15	15
5 Yr Avg	—	—	—	—
10 Yr Avg	—	—	—	—

Tax Analysis	Tax-Adj Return%	Tax-Cost Ratio
3 Yr (estimated)	10.22	0.50
5 Yr (estimated)	—	—
10 Yr (estimated)	—	—

Rating and Risk

Time Period	Morningstar Rtn vs Cat	Morningstar Risk vs Cat	Morningstar Risk-Adj Rating
3 Yr	+Avg	Low	★★★★
5 Yr	—	—	—
10 Yr	—	—	—

Other Measures	Standard Index S&P 500	Best Fit Index M* Cons Good TR
Alpha	4.2	1.5
Beta	0.45	0.83
R-Squared	38	85
Standard Deviation	5.73	
Mean	10.77	
Sharpe Ratio	1.08	

Morningstar's Take by Dan Culloton 12-31-07

Vanguard Consumer Staples Index focuses on established, profitable stocks with strong competitive positions. Because these stocks tend to be less volatile, we d be buyers at a modest discount to our fair value estimate.

This ETF tracks a benchmark that includes the shares of firms that make or distribute food, beverages, tobacco, and household and personal products. The free-float market-cap-weighted MSCI U.S. Investable Consumer Staples Index leans heavily on large companies that have built their reputations on providing consumers with things they can't or don't want to live without. Many of these companies have diverse portfolios of trusted brand names and/or hard-to-replicate distribution networks that give them defensible competitive positions. Indeed more than 45% of this ETF's assets reside in five household-name companies that have wide economic moats--Procter & Gamble, Altria, Coca-Cola, PepsiCo, and Wal-Mart.

What you get in quality you give up in growth, though. Each of the ETF's biggest holdings, and others in this portfolio for that matter, are at advanced stages of their lifecycles during which it's harder to eke out additional growth. Each stock's five-year projected earnings growth rate matches or falls below that of the S&P 500 or its respective industry.

Though concentrating assets in a few stocks can be risky, most of the fund's assets go to companies with globally recognized brand names and lots of pricing power, such as Colgate-Palmolive. Additionally, above-average risk stocks, such as debt-burdened beauty products company Revlon, take up just 15% of the portfolio. Coupled with the portfolio's diversification across various end markets, that has tamped down volatility. For that reason, we wouldn't demand a wide margin of safety when investing here. We'd be buyers of the shares when they trade at an 8% or greater discount to our fair value estimate.

Address:	PO Box 2600 United States 800-997-2798
Web Address:	www.vanguard.com
Inception:	01-26-04 *
Advisor:	Vanguard Advisers, Inc.

Management Fee:	0.17%		
Expense Projections:	3Yr:$71	5Yr:$124	10Yr:$280
Income Distrib:	Annually		
Exchange:	AMEX		

Portfolio Analysis 09-30-07

Share change since 06-07 Total Stocks:106	Sector	PE	Tot Ret%	% Assets
⊖ Procter & Gamble Company	Goods	23.1	16.63	14.66
⊖ Altria Group Inc.	Goods	13.2	22.10	9.30
⊖ Coca-Cola Company	Goods	26.3	30.44	7.35
⊖ PepsiCo, Inc.	Goods	20.4	23.89	7.33
⊖ Wal-Mart Stores, Inc.	Consumer	15.4	4.91	6.56
⊖ CVS Caremark Corporation	Consumer	21.5	28.93	4.50
⊖ Kraft Foods, Inc.	Goods	20.0	-5.71	4.03
⊖ Walgreen Company	Consumer	18.5	-16.35	3.43
⊖ Anheuser-Busch Companies	Goods	19.1	9.06	2.78
⊖ Colgate-Palmolive Compan	Goods	24.7	21.94	2.67
⊖ Kimberly-Clark Corporati	Goods	17.0	5.23	2.36
⊖ Costco Wholesale Corpora	Consumer	28.5	33.21	2.03
⊖ Sysco Corporation	Consumer	18.8	-13.21	1.64
⊖ General Mills, Inc.	Goods	17.2	1.58	1.50
⊖ Archer Daniels Midland	Ind Mtrls	13.8	47.02	1.45
⊖ Kroger Company	Consumer	15.3	16.82	1.44
⊖ Avon Products	Goods	29.8	22.02	1.24
⊕ Kellogg Company	Goods	19.0	5.70	1.18
⊖ H.J. Heinz Company	Goods	18.3	7.07	1.13
⊖ Safeway Inc.	Consumer	17.0	-0.03	1.11

Current Investment Style

Value Blnd Growth / Large Mid Small

Market Cap	%
Giant	53.7
Large	28.5
Mid	12.1
Small	4.7
Micro	1.0
Avg $mil: 43,977	

Value Measures		Rel Category
Price/Earnings	18.10	1.15
Price/Book	3.38	1.32
Price/Sales	0.93	0.75
Price/Cash Flow	13.52	1.46
Dividend Yield %	2.16	1.14

Growth Measures	%	Rel Category
Long-Term Erngs	9.64	0.82
Book Value	10.18	1.10
Sales	5.69	0.70
Cash Flow	-1.57	NMF
Historical Erngs	8.97	0.54

Profitability	%	Rel Category
Return on Equity	29.47	1.32
Return on Assets	10.58	1.27
Net Margin	9.51	0.78

Sector Weightings	% of Stocks	Rel S&P 500	3 Year High	3 Year Low
Info	0.00	0.00		
Software	0.00	0.00	0	0
Hardware	0.00	0.00	0	0
Media	0.00	0.00	0	0
Telecom	0.00	0.00	0	0
Service	24.75	0.61		
Health	0.89	0.07	1	1
Consumer	23.86	3.52	26	23
Business	0.00	0.00	0	0
Financial	0.00	0.00	1	0
Mfg	75.25	1.96		
Goods	73.41	8.01	73	71
Ind Mtrls	1.74	0.13	3	2
Energy	0.10	0.01	0	0
Utilities	0.00	0.00	0	0

Composition

Cash	0.0
Stocks	100.0
Bonds	0.0
Other	0.0
Foreign (% of Stock)	0.2

Vanguard Energy ETF VDE

Market Price	Mstar Category
$113.50	Specialty-Natural Res

Morningstar Fair Value

Price/Fair Value Ratio	Coverage Rate %
0.99	90

Morningstar Rating	Return	Risk	Yield	NAV	Avg Daily Vol. (k)	52 wk High/Low
★★★	Average	Average	0.8%	$113.58	33	$115.26 - $78.13

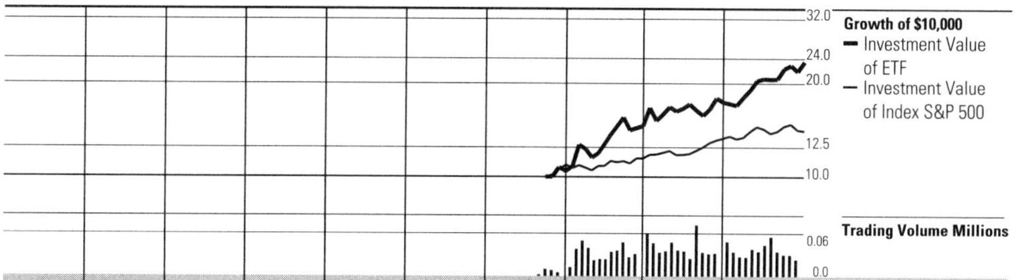

Valuation

Financially sturdy integrated oil firms sit alongside riskier fare in this ETF. Risk is also heightened here because the accuracy of our fair value estimates hinges on our commodity price forecasts. Therefore we'd only invest in this ETF when it is 20% or more below fair value. At present, it's trading at a 13% premium to our fair value estimate.

Methodology

This ETF is tethered to the MSCI U.S. Investable Market Energy Index, a market-cap-weighted benchmark that focuses on firms involved in the U.S. energy sector, including those in exploration and production, oil service, natural gas, and coal. The fund invests across the market-cap spectrum, but is dominated by major U.S. oil firms. (Its top five holdings recently accounted for nearly half of assets.) It does not have exposure to energy firms headquartered overseas.

1998	1999	2000	2001	2002	2003	2004	2005	2006	2007	History
—	—	—	—	—	—	52.39	72.16	84.94	113.58	NAV $
—	—	—	—	—	—	52.41	72.19	85.01	113.50	Market Price $
—	—	—	—	—	—	30.44*	39.05	18.98	34.87	NAV Return%
—	—	—	—	—	—	30.41*	39.05	19.03	34.66	Market Price Return%
—	—	—	—	—	—	0.02	0.01	0.04	-0.04	Avg Premium/Discount%
—	—	—	—	—	—	—	34.14	3.19	29.38	NAV Rtrn% +/-S&P 500
—	—	—	—	—	—	—	3.78	-2.05	0.45	NAV Rtrn% +/-MSCI Energy
—	—	—	—	—	—	—	34	34	47	NAV Return% Rank in Cat
—	—	—	—	—	—	—	1.34	1.29	1.11	Income Return %
—	—	—	—	—	—	—	37.71	17.69	33.76	Capital Return %
—	—	—	—	—	—	0.22	0.70	0.93	0.94	Income $
—	—	—	—	—	—	0.00	0.00	0.00	0.00	Capital Gains $
—	—	—	—	—	—	—	0.26	0.25	0.22	Expense Ratio %
—	—	—	—	—	—	—	1.97	1.23	1.20	Income Ratio %
—	—	—	—	—	—	—	16	21	15	Turnover Rate %
—	—	—	—	—	—	31	209	391	762	Net Assets $mil

Performance 12-31-07

Historic Quarterly NAV Returns

	1st Qtr	2nd Qtr	3rd Qtr	4th Qtr	Total
2003	—	—	—	—	—
2004	—	—	—	4.34	—*
2005	17.43	3.61	21.57	-5.99	39.05
2006	8.84	4.34	-4.99	10.27	18.98
2007	3.66	14.79	7.62	5.32	34.87

Trailing	NAV Return%	Market Return%	NAV Rtrn% +/-S&P 500	%Rank Cat.(NAV)
3 Mo	5.32	5.35	8.65	42
6 Mo	13.34	13.19	14.71	40
1 Yr	34.87	34.66	29.38	47
3 Yr Avg	30.67	30.62	22.05	13
5 Yr Avg	—	—	—	—
10 Yr Avg	—	—	—	—

Tax Analysis	Tax-Adj Return%	Tax-Cost Ratio
3 Yr (estimated)	30.23	0.34
5 Yr (estimated)	—	—
10 Yr (estimated)	—	—

Rating and Risk

Time Period	Morningstar Rtn vs Cat	Morningstar Risk vs Cat	Morningstar Risk-Adj Rating
3 Yr	Avg	Avg	★★★
5 Yr	—	—	—
10 Yr	—	—	—

Other Measures	Standard Index S&P 500	Best Fit Index M* Energy Sec TR
Alpha	19.5	-0.6
Beta	1.21	1.00
R-Squared	22	99
Standard Deviation	20.07	
Mean	30.67	
Sharpe Ratio	1.23	

Portfolio Analysis 09-30-07

Share change since 06-07 Total Stocks:153	Sector	PE	Tot Ret%	% Assets
⊕ ExxonMobil Corporation	Energy	13.6	24.34	19.86
⊕ Chevron Corporation	Energy	11.4	30.59	10.83
⊕ Schlumberger, Ltd.	Energy	24.6	57.10	7.32
⊕ ConocoPhillips	Energy	13.8	25.42	7.31
⊕ Occidental Petroleum Cor	Energy	13.8	60.25	2.97
⊕ Marathon Oil Corporation	Energy	9.7	34.09	2.19
⊕ Valero Energy Corporatio	Energy	8.1	37.91	2.06
⊕ Devon Energy Corporation	Energy	14.7	33.51	1.98
⊕ Halliburton Company	Energy	14.4	23.33	1.97
⊕ Transocean, Inc.	Energy	16.1	77.14	1.83
⊕ Apache Corporation	Energy	15.9	62.91	1.69
⊕ Baker Hughes Inc.	Energy	17.9	9.35	1.64
⊕ National Oilwell Varco,	Energy	21.7	132.65	1.46
⊕ Anadarko Petroleum Corp.	Energy	7.9	52.04	1.42
⊕ XTO Energy, Inc.	Energy	14.7	37.60	1.30
⊕ Weatherford Internationa	Energy	23.4	64.15	1.29
⊕ Williams Companies, Inc.	Energy	27.7	38.70	1.17
⊕ Hess Corporation	Ind Mtrls	19.1	104.77	1.09
⊕ EOG Resources	Energy	22.9	43.55	1.02
⊕ GlobalSantaFe Corporatio	Energy	—	—	1.00

Current Investment Style

Value Blnd Growth — Large Mid Small

Market Cap	%
Giant	45.5
Large	31.6
Mid	14.8
Small	7.0
Micro	1.2

Avg $mil: 46,645

Value Measures		Rel Category
Price/Earnings	12.75	0.78
Price/Book	2.56	1.10
Price/Sales	1.31	0.94
Price/Cash Flow	7.93	0.99
Dividend Yield %	1.11	0.80

Growth Measures	%	Rel Category
Long-Term Erngs	10.55	0.81
Book Value	14.49	0.97
Sales	6.35	0.57
Cash Flow	6.79	0.42
Historical Erngs	28.05	0.77

Profitability	%	Rel Category
Return on Equity	25.46	1.24
Return on Assets	12.69	1.35
Net Margin	15.36	1.12

Industry Weightings	% of Stocks	Rel Cat
Oil & Gas	65.0	1.9
Oil/Gas Products	3.6	1.1
Oil & Gas Srv	24.9	1.1
Pipelines	3.2	2.9
Utilities	0.0	0.0
Hard Commd	0.2	0.0
Soft Commd	0.0	0.0
Misc. Indstrl	0.4	0.0
Other	2.8	0.3

Composition

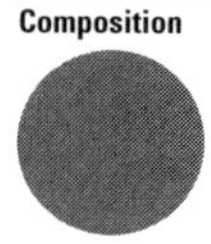

Cash	0.0
Stocks	100.0
Bonds	0.0
Other	0.0
Foreign (% of Stock)	0.0

Morningstar's Take by Sonya Morris 12-31-07

Vanguard Energy ETF has its risks, so we'd need a sizable margin of safety to invest in it.

This ETF has been more than twice as volatile as the S&P 500 Index. That turbulence stems from a couple of key factors. First, the profitability of energy firms depends heavily on commodity prices, which can gyrate wildly. Thus, these businesses' short-term profits and cash flows can be streaky, and so can their stock prices. Second, this ETF's concentrated portfolio accentuates those bumps. Its top 10 holdings consume more than 60% of assets, and two stocks alone--ExxonMobil and Chevron--account for 30% of the portfolio.

Granted, ExxonMobil and Chevron are two of the highest-quality firms in the oil patch. Thanks to economies of scale and diversified revenue streams, both have generated impressive cash flows and returns on invested capital even during cyclical downturns. But the same can't be said for other holdings in this ETF. Of the 90 stocks in this portfolio that our analysts cover, 52 lack economic moats, meaning they have no appreciable competitive advantage. Consider top-10 holding Valero Energy. Its operations are concentrated in the refining industry, and its profit margins and cash flows have fluctuated dramatically. That's why Valero is one of the 40 stocks in the portfolio with above-average business risk.

That makeup impinges on this ETF's risk profile. The future cash flows of some of the racier holdings can be difficult to predict. Plus, the precision of our fair value estimates depends heavily on one factor--our future commodity-price assumptions. Forecasting oil and gas prices is a complex and difficult task, and if we get our assumptions wrong, our fair value estimate for this ETF will also be wrong. That doesn't mean we'd never invest here. Given the fund's volatility, it will undoubtedly dip down into our buy range on occasion. But considering its risks, we wouldn't recommend it unless it was trading at least 20% below our fair value estimate.

Address:	PO Box 2600 United States 800-997-2798
Web Address:	www.vanguard.com
Inception:	09-23-04 *
Advisor:	Vanguard Advisers, Inc.

Management Fee:	0.22%		
Expense Projections:	3Yr:$71	5Yr:$124	10Yr:$280
Income Distrib:	Annually		
Exchange:	AMEX		

Vanguard Financial ETF VFH

Market Price	Mstar Category
$52.65	Specialty-Financial

Morningstar Fair Value

Price/Fair Value Ratio	Coverage Rate %
0.79	93

Valuation

Barriers to entry can be significant in the financials sector, so many of this ETF's holdings are protected by an economic moat. All the same, the firms here are exposed to many of the same risks. So we require a 15% discount to our fair value estimate to recommend this ETF. It was recently trading at a 21% discount, making it a bargain.

Methodology

This portfolio includes all of the financials stocks included in the MSCI U.S. Investable Market 2500 Index, which represents 98% of the capitalization of the U.S. equity market. That turns out to be more than 500 financial companies, ranging from global financial-services firms to small regional banks. The fund is market-cap-weighted, so the market's biggest players have larger positions in the portfolio. About one fourth of the fund's assets are in mid- and small-cap stocks.

Morningstar Rating	Return	Risk	Yield	NAV	Avg Daily Vol. (k)	52 wk High/Low
★★★	Average	Average	2.8%	$52.62	141	$67.60 - $48.00

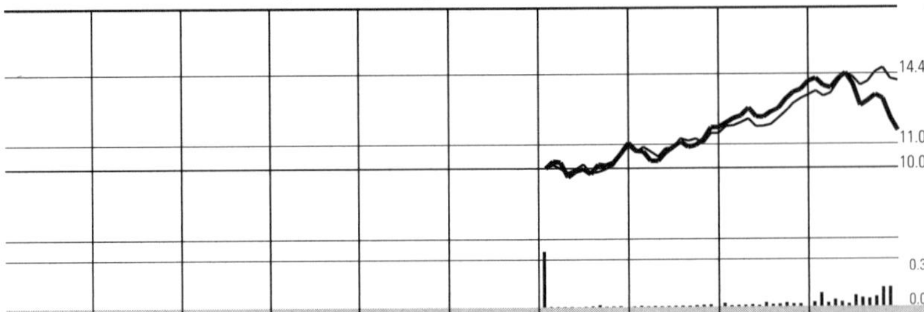

Growth of $10,000
— Investment Value of ETF
— Investment Value of Index S&P 500

Trading Volume Millions

1998	1999	2000	2001	2002	2003	2004	2005	2006	2007	History
—	—	—	—	—	—	53.75	55.95	65.33	52.62	NAV $
—	—	—	—	—	—	53.81	56.01	65.50	52.65	Market Price $
—	—	—	—	—	—	3.28*	6.07	19.25	-17.42	NAV Return%
—	—	—	—	—	—	3.30*	6.06	19.43	-17.58	Market Price Return%
—	—	—	—	—	—	0.02	-0.02	0.09	0.01	Avg Premium/Discount%
—	—	—	—	—	—	—	1.16	3.46	-22.91	NAV Rtrn% +/-S&P 500
—	—	—	—	—	—	—	-0.21	-0.25	-0.08	NAV Rtrn% +/-MSCI Fincl
—	—	—	—	—	—	—	60	30	60	NAV Return% Rank in Cat
—	—	—	—	—	—	—	1.90	2.32	2.30	Income Return %
—	—	—	—	—	—	—	4.17	16.93	-19.72	Capital Return %
—	—	—	—	—	—	1.15	1.01	1.29	1.49	Income $
—	—	—	—	—	—	0.00	0.00	0.00	0.00	Capital Gains $
—	—	—	—	—	—	0.28	0.26	0.25	0.22	Expense Ratio %
—	—	—	—	—	—	2.38	2.61	2.52	2.41	Income Ratio %
—	—	—	—	—	—	9	6	6	12	Turnover Rate %
—	—	—	—	—	—	27	62	209	406	Net Assets $mil

Performance 12-31-07

Historic Quarterly NAV Returns

	1st Qtr	2nd Qtr	3rd Qtr	4th Qtr	Total
2003	—	—	—	—	—
2004	—	-2.53	1.37	8.95	—*
2005	-6.60	5.33	0.73	7.04	6.07
2006	4.52	-0.50	7.14	7.03	19.25
2007	-2.48	1.35	-3.94	-13.02	-17.42

Trailing	NAV Return%	Market Return%	NAV Rtrn% +/-S&P 500	%Rank Cat.(NAV)
3 Mo	-13.01	-12.84	-9.68	67
6 Mo	-16.44	-16.28	-15.07	67
1 Yr	-17.42	-17.58	-22.91	60
3 Yr Avg	1.46	1.44	-7.16	40
5 Yr Avg	—	—	—	—
10 Yr Avg	—	—	—	—

Tax Analysis	Tax-Adj Return%	Tax-Cost Ratio
3 Yr (estimated)	0.80	0.65
5 Yr (estimated)	—	—
10 Yr (estimated)	—	—

Rating and Risk

Time Period	Morningstar Rtn vs Cat	Morningstar Risk vs Cat	Morningstar Risk-Adj Rating
3 Yr	Avg	Avg	★★★
5 Yr	—	—	—
10 Yr	—	—	—

Other Measures	Standard Index S&P 500	Best Fit Index DJ Finance
Alpha	-7.0	-0.1
Beta	1.11	0.99
R-Squared	66	100
Standard Deviation	10.65	
Mean	1.46	
Sharpe Ratio	-0.22	

Morningstar's Take by Sonya Morris 12-31-07

Vanguard Financials ETF is a respectable choice for broad financial exposure. We'd be buyers at a 15% discount to our fair value estimate.

This ETF is one of the most diversified financial funds on the market. It spreads its assets over more than 500 holdings. It samples from a wide variety of financial stocks, including banks (Citigroup), insurers (American International Group), investment banks (Goldman Sachs), and credit card companies (American Express). It also includes a smattering of REITs, which make up about 10% of the portfolio.

Many firms in the financial sector enjoy competitive advantages, not least of which are significant barriers to entry, which can range from large capital requirements to regulatory hurdles. As a result, the vast majority of the holdings here are protected by an economic moat. In fact, more than 45% of the portfolio is dedicated to wide-moat firms. Many of those companies gain their edge through scale. For example, many big banks, like J.P. Morgan and Bank of America, have a huge base of customers, many of whom they're able to keep in the fold by imposing high switching costs. Others, like Chicago Mercantile Exchange, benefit from network effects; specifically, the exchange's unparalleled liquidity and product diversity attracts traders, thereby creating an even deeper market, attracting other participants, and keeping rival exchanges at bay.

Although this sector's risks have been on full display lately amid the recent credit crunch, most financial firms typically don't court a lot of business risk. Many financial companies have diversified revenue streams that help them to better withstand adversity like the credit shocks we are experiencing now.

Still, many of these holdings are exposed to the same risk factors, including yield-curve shifts and credit-quality issues, so we're willing to recommend this ETF only when it's trading 15% or more below our fair value estimate.

Address:	PO Box 2600 United States 800-997-2798
Web Address:	www.vanguard.com
Inception:	01-26-04*
Advisor:	Vanguard Advisers, Inc.

Management Fee:	0.15%		
Expense Projections:	3Yr:$71	5Yr:$124	10Yr:$280
Income Distrib:	Quarterly		
Exchange:	AMEX		

Portfolio Analysis 09-30-07

Share change since 06-07 Total Stocks:514	Sector	PE	Tot Ret%	% Assets
⊕ Citigroup, Inc.	Financial	7.9	-44.93	7.12
⊕ Bank of America Corporat	Financial	9.4	-19.25	6.88
⊕ J.P. Morgan Chase & Co.	Financial	9.5	-7.24	4.83
⊕ American International G	Financial	10.2	-17.96	4.60
⊕ Wells Fargo Company	Financial	11.4	-12.13	3.50
⊕ Wachovia Corporation	Financial	8.6	-29.91	2.96
⊕ Goldman Sachs Group, Inc	Financial	8.8	8.59	2.46
⊕ American Express Company	Financial	14.9	-13.18	1.96
⊕ Morgan Stanley	Financial	6.1	-20.21	1.84
⊕ Fannie Mae	Financial	24.1	-30.45	1.83
⊕ Merrill Lynch & Company,	Financial	12.2	-41.32	1.80
⊕ US Bancorp	Financial	12.2	-7.89	1.75
⊕ Metropolitan Life Insura	Financial	12.3	4.94	1.61
☼ Bank of New York Mellon	Financial	21.7	26.51	1.54
⊕ Prudential Financial, In	Financial	12.1	9.72	1.39
⊕ Freddie Mac	Financial	12.0	-48.20	1.21
⊖ Berkshire Hathaway Inc.	Financial	15.9	29.19	1.16
☼ The Travelers Companies,	Financial	7.8	2.37	1.03
⊕ Allstate Corporation	Financial	6.3	-17.78	1.02
⊖ Washington Mutual, Inc.	Financial	5.1	-68.25	0.91

Current Investment Style

Value Blnd Growth / Large Mid Small

Market Cap	%
Giant	43.1
Large	30.5
Mid	18.9
Small	6.3
Micro	1.3
Avg $mil: 30,876	

Value Measures		Rel Category
Price/Earnings	12.19	1.02
Price/Book	1.69	1.15
Price/Sales	2.19	1.07
Price/Cash Flow	14.11	1.21
Dividend Yield %	2.83	0.97

Growth Measures	%	Rel Category
Long-Term Erngs	10.33	0.98
Book Value	11.99	1.12
Sales	7.03	0.90
Cash Flow	-11.16	NMF
Historical Erngs	14.43	0.79

Profitability	%	Rel Category
Return on Equity	17.25	1.02
Return on Assets	2.79	0.96
Net Margin	24.25	1.09

Industry Weightings	% of Stocks	Rel Cat
Intl Banks	22.4	1.3
Banks	18.1	0.8
Real Estate	10.1	4.1
Sec Mgmt	12.7	0.9
S & Ls	2.8	0.5
Prop & Reins	13.6	0.9
Life Ins	6.5	1.0
Misc. Ins	3.8	1.2
Other	10.0	0.7

Composition

Cash	0.6
Stocks	99.4
Bonds	0.0
Other	0.0
Foreign (% of Stock)	0.3

Vanguard HealthCar ETF VHT

Market Price	Mstar Category
$60.62	Specialty-Health

Morningstar Fair Value

Price/Fair Value Ratio	Coverage Rate %
0.92	94

Valuation

This ETF owns a lot of stalwart drug, medical device, managed care, and biotech stocks. Though assets are piled up in a few names, volatility hasn't been extreme. As such, we'd be buyers when the fund is trading at an 8% or greater discount to our fair value estimate, which is precisely where it was as of late-December.

Methodology

This exchange-traded fund tracks the MSCI U.S. Investable Market Health Care Index, which represents the health-care companies drawn from the largest 2,500 stocks in the U.S. equity market. Large-cap drug names dominate the benchmark, although biotechnology, medical-equipment, and health-care services stocks play supporting roles. The ETF is concentrated in its largest holdings, with about half of its assets in its top 10. Given the MSCI index's domestic focus, the fund has no exposure to foreign-domiciled health-care firms.

Morningstar Rating	Return	Risk	Yield	NAV	Avg Daily Vol. (k)	52 wk High/Low
★★★	Average	Below Avg	1.4%	$60.59	36	$63.60 - $56.37

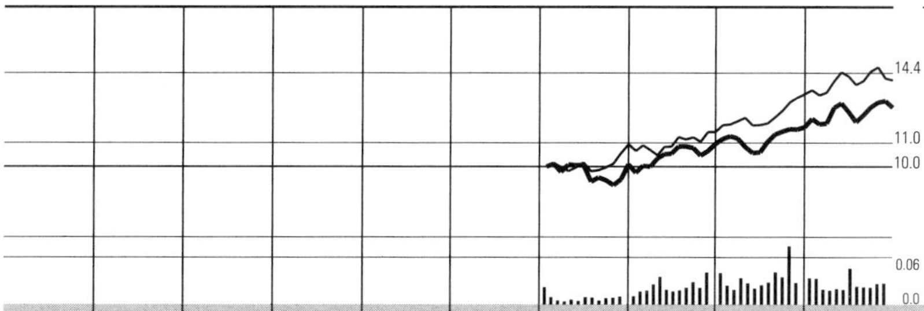

Growth of $10,000
- Investment Value of ETF
- Investment Value of Index S&P 500

Trading Volume Millions

History

1998	1999	2000	2001	2002	2003	2004	2005	2006	2007	History
—	—	—	—	—	—	50.24	54.00	56.96	60.59	NAV $
—	—	—	—	—	—	50.28	54.02	56.94	60.62	Market Price $
—	—	—	—	—	—	5.62*	8.24	6.62	7.80	NAV Return%
—	—	—	—	—	—	5.64*	8.20	6.54	7.89	Market Price Return%
—	—	—	—	—	—	0.07	0.06	0.03	-0.03	Avg Premium/Discount%
—	—	—	—	—	—	—	3.33	-9.17	2.31	NAV Rtrn% +/-S&P 500
—	—	—	—	—	—	—	-0.23	-0.23	-0.19	NAV Rtrn% +/-MSCI Health
—	—	—	—	—	—	—	1	50	53	NAV Return% Rank in Cat
—	—	—	—	—	—	—	0.77	1.14	1.44	Income Return %
—	—	—	—	—	—	—	7.47	5.48	6.36	Capital Return %
—	—	—	—	—	—	0.13	0.39	0.62	0.82	Income $
—	—	—	—	—	—	0.00	0.00	0.00	0.00	Capital Gains $
—	—	—	—	—	—	0.28	0.26	0.25	0.22	Expense Ratio %
—	—	—	—	—	—	1.09	1.13	1.15	1.46	Income Ratio %
—	—	—	—	—	—	8	9	11	10	Turnover Rate %
—	—	—	—	—	—	55	238	342	515	Net Assets $mil

Performance 12-31-07

Historic Quarterly NAV Returns

	1st Qtr	2nd Qtr	3rd Qtr	4th Qtr	Total
2003	—	—	—	—	—
2004	—	2.62	-5.60	6.30	—*
2005	-0.86	5.14	2.21	1.59	8.24
2006	2.07	-5.13	8.26	1.70	6.62
2007	1.42	4.48	1.86	-0.13	7.80

Trailing	NAV Return%	Market Return%	NAV Rtrn% +/-S&P 500	%Rank Cat.(NAV)
3 Mo	-0.13	0.00	3.20	39
6 Mo	1.73	1.83	3.10	34
1 Yr	7.80	7.89	2.31	53
3 Yr Avg	7.55	7.54	-1.07	1
5 Yr Avg	—	—	—	—
10 Yr Avg	—	—	—	—

Tax Analysis	Tax-Adj Return%	Tax-Cost Ratio
3 Yr (estimated)	7.16	0.36
5 Yr (estimated)	—	—
10 Yr (estimated)	—	—

Rating and Risk

Time Period	Morningstar Rtn vs Cat	Morningstar Risk vs Cat	Morningstar Risk-Adj Rating
3 Yr	Avg	-Avg	★★★
5 Yr	—	—	—
10 Yr	—	—	—

Other Measures	Standard Index S&P 500	Best Fit Index DJ Health
Alpha	0.4	-0.2
Beta	0.67	0.98
R-Squared	40	99
Standard Deviation	8.27	
Mean	7.55	
Sharpe Ratio	0.40	

Portfolio Analysis 09-30-07

Share change since 06-07 Total Stocks:266	Sector	PE	Tot Ret%	% Assets
⊕ Johnson & Johnson	Health	18.8	3.61	9.78
⊕ Pfizer Inc.	Health	22.5	-8.15	8.81
⊕ Merck & Co., Inc.	Health	23.6	37.36	5.76
⊕ Abbott Laboratories	Health	45.7	18.04	4.25
⊕ Amgen, Inc.	Health	16.8	-32.02	3.37
⊕ UnitedHealth Group, Inc.	Health	17.4	8.38	3.34
⊕ Medtronic, Inc.	Health	20.3	-5.22	3.33
⊕ Wyeth	Health	13.6	-11.36	3.10
⊕ Eli Lilly & Company	Health	26.0	5.65	3.01
⊕ Bristol-Myers Squibb Com	Health	24.8	4.75	2.93
⊕ WellPoint, Inc.	Health	16.4	11.49	2.51
⊕ Schering-Plough Corporat	Health	21.0	13.66	2.44
⊕ Gilead Sciences, Inc.	Health	—	41.72	1.97
⊕ Genentech, Inc.	Health	26.2	-17.33	1.91
⊕ Baxter International Inc	Health	22.9	26.79	1.89
⊕ Aetna, Inc.	Health	16.9	33.79	1.43
⊕ Celgene Corporation	Health	NMF	-19.68	1.40
⊕ Medco Health Solutions,	Health	31.1	89.78	1.31
⊕ Thermo Fisher Scientific	Health	48.5	27.36	1.26
⊕ Cardinal Health, Inc.	Health	26.5	-9.74	1.24

Current Investment Style

Value Blnd Growth; Large Mid Small

Market Cap	%
Giant	49.6
Large	26.6
Mid	16.9
Small	5.9
Micro	1.0

Avg $mil: 31,699

Value Measures		Rel Category
Price/Earnings	17.28	0.81
Price/Book	3.52	1.03
Price/Sales	1.73	0.60
Price/Cash Flow	14.06	1.08
Dividend Yield %	1.26	1.62

Growth Measures	%	Rel Category
Long-Term Erngs	11.83	0.78
Book Value	13.27	2.16
Sales	10.43	1.01
Cash Flow	10.65	0.84
Historical Erngs	11.85	0.13

Profitability	%	Rel Category
Return on Equity	17.24	2.32
Return on Assets	8.17	18.57
Net Margin	13.67	2.69

Industry Weightings	% of Stocks	Rel Cat
Biotech	15.1	0.4
Drugs	45.5	1.6
Mgd Care	12.6	1.5
Hospitals	0.6	1.0
Other HC Srv	1.3	0.9
Diagnostics	1.5	1.1
Equipment	17.0	1.1
Good/Srv	4.9	1.0
Other	1.6	0.5

Composition

Cash	0.0
Stocks	100.0
Bonds	0.0
Other	0.0
Foreign (% of Stock)	0.1

Morningstar's Take by Dan Culloton 12-31-07

Vanguard Health Care ETF leans toward the shares of mature, financially sound companies that more than hold their own in their respective markets. Because many of its holdings have defensive qualities, we'd be willing to invest at a modest margin of safety.

The ETF's benchmark, the MSCI U.S. Investable Market Health Care Index, includes the stocks of the pharmaceutical, medical device, managed care, biotech, and other health-related firms from the broad U.S. equity market. Large drugmakers, including seven of the ETF's top 10 holdings, make up the lion's share of assets. Although beset in recent years by patent expirations and competition from generic drugs, these companies still boast formidable competitive advantages. Eli Lilly invests more in research and development than most of its peers. Pfizer has enormous scale and a wide array of patented drugs in its arsenal. Johnson & Johnson gets more than half its revenue from non-pharmaceutical businesses, which gives it diversification. Indeed, this ETF stakes 57% of its assets in companies that have wide economic moats, making it one of the higher-quality funds that we cover.

With more than 30% of its assets in its five biggest holdings, a handful of stocks disproportionately influence the fund's valuation. The portfolio also includes a clutch of stocks whose future prospects are more uncertain, explaining their above-average risk ratings. For instance, Merck, faces years of litigation over the safety of its Vioxx painkiller and several patent expirations in coming years. In addition, Genentech's intrinsic worth is highly dependent on cash flow that it won't see for several years. Yet, on balance, most of these firms' risks cancel each other out, explaining the portfolio's moderate volatility.

For that reason, we'd be willing to invest in this ETF when it's trading at least 8% below our fair value estimate.

Address:	PO Box 2600 United States 800-997-2798
Web Address:	www.vanguard.com
Inception:	01-26-04*
Advisor:	Vanguard Advisers, Inc.

Management Fee:	0.20%		
Expense Projections:	3Yr:$71	5Yr:$124	10Yr:$280
Income Distrib:	Annually		
Exchange:	AMEX		

Vanguard InfoTech ETF VGT

Market Price $60.12 | **Mstar Category** Specialty-Technology

Morningstar Fair Value

Price/Fair Value Ratio	Coverage Rate %
0.94	94

Valuation

This ETF owns many tech sector bellwethers with strong competitive advantages. While the tech sector can be a wild ride at times, this fund's diversification across names has tamped volatility. Thus, we'd be willing to give the fund a look at an 8% discount to our fair value estimate. It recently was trading at a modest discount.

Methodology

This ETF tracks the MSCI U.S. Investable Information Technology Index, a subset of the market-cap-weighted MSCI U.S. Investable Market 2500 Index. The MSCI IT Index holds more than 400 stocks in the software, hardware, semiconductor, IT consulting, Internet, data processing, and outsourcing industries. The fund takes a more diversified approach than many tech portfolios, but it's still pretty concentrated.

Morningstar Rating	Return	Risk	Yield	NAV	Avg Daily Vol. (k)	52 wk High/Low
★★★	Average	Below Avg	0.3%	$60.20	68	$64.70 - $50.83

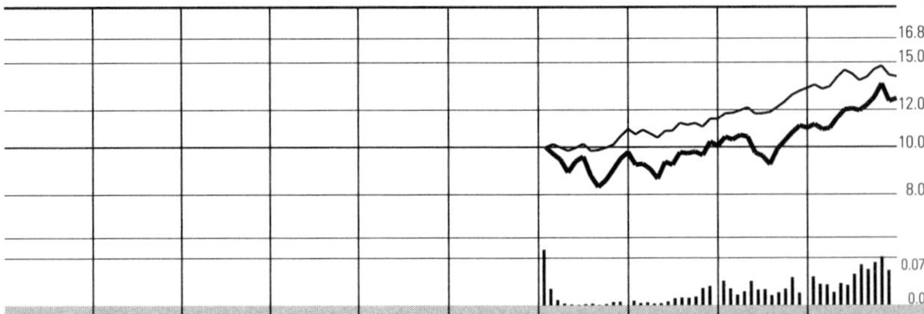

Growth of $10,000
— Investment Value of ETF
— Investment Value of Index S&P 500

Trading Volume Millions

1998	1999	2000	2001	2002	2003	2004	2005	2006	2007	History
—	—	—	—	—	—	47.04	48.31	52.50	60.20	NAV $
—	—	—	—	—	—	47.06	48.38	52.53	60.12	Market Price $
—	—	—	—	—	—	4.91*	2.89	8.95	15.00	NAV Return%
—	—	—	—	—	—	4.87*	2.99	8.86	14.78	Market Price Return%
—	—	—	—	—	—	0.11	0.00	0.03	-0.06	Avg Premium/Discount%
—	—	—	—	—	—	—	-2.02	-6.84	9.51	NAV Rtrn% +/-S&P 500
—	—	—	—	—	—	—	-0.20	-0.26	-0.13	NAV Rtrn% +/-MSCI Tech
—	—	—	—	—	—	—	23	57	25	NAV Return% Rank in Cat
—	—	—	—	—	—	—	0.19	0.28	0.33	Income Return %
—	—	—	—	—	—	—	2.70	8.67	14.67	Capital Return %
—	—	—	—	—	—	0.61	0.09	0.14	0.18	Income $
—	—	—	—	—	—	0.00	0.00	0.00	0.00	Capital Gains $
—	—	—	—	—	—	0.28	0.26	0.25	0.22	Expense Ratio %
—	—	—	—	—	—	0.12	1.28	0.36	0.42	Income Ratio %
—	—	—	—	—	—	9	7	8	8	Turnover Rate %
—	—	—	—	—	—	19	106	247	596	Net Assets $mil

Performance 12-31-07

Historic Quarterly NAV Returns

	1st Qtr	2nd Qtr	3rd Qtr	4th Qtr	Total
2003	—	—	—	—	—
2004	—	1.41	-10.56	14.08	—*
2005	-7.63	1.96	6.34	2.74	2.89
2006	5.28	-9.34	7.31	6.38	8.95
2007	-0.11	9.82	5.37	-0.50	15.00

Trailing	NAV Return%	Market Return%	NAV Rtrn% +/-S&P 500	%Rank Cat.(NAV)
3 Mo	-0.50	-0.50	2.83	17
6 Mo	4.84	4.64	6.21	17
1 Yr	15.00	14.78	9.51	25
3 Yr Avg	8.84	8.77	0.22	23
5 Yr Avg	—	—	—	—
10 Yr Avg	—	—	—	—

Tax Analysis	Tax-Adj Return%	Tax-Cost Ratio
3 Yr (estimated)	8.74	0.09
5 Yr (estimated)	—	—
10 Yr (estimated)	—	—

Rating and Risk

Time Period	Morningstar Rtn vs Cat	Morningstar Risk vs Cat	Morningstar Risk-Adj Rating
3 Yr	Avg	-Avg	★★★
5 Yr	—	—	—
10 Yr	—	—	—

Other Measures	Standard Index S&P 500	Best Fit Index
Alpha	-1.4	0.2
Beta	1.52	1.15
R-Squared	71	94
Standard Deviation	13.99	
Mean	8.84	
Sharpe Ratio	0.37	

Portfolio Analysis 09-30-07

Share change since 06-07 Total Stocks:381	Sector	PE	Tot Ret%	% Assets
⊕ Microsoft Corporation	Software	23.4	20.83	9.24
⊕ Cisco Systems, Inc.	Hardware	21.5	-0.95	7.43
⊕ International Business M	Hardware	16.2	13.20	6.47
⊕ Intel Corporation	Hardware	25.4	34.22	5.56
⊕ Apple, Inc.	Hardware	50.5	133.47	4.91
⊕ Google, Inc.	Business	54.0	50.17	4.86
⊕ Hewlett-Packard Company	Hardware	18.8	23.40	4.76
⊕ Oracle Corporation	Software	24.8	31.74	3.29
⊕ Qualcomm, Inc.	Hardware	20.2	5.52	2.61
⊕ Dell, Inc.	Hardware	18.6	-2.31	2.20
⊕ Texas Instruments, Inc.	Hardware	19.2	17.01	1.94
⊕ EMC Corporation	Hardware	26.1	40.38	1.60
⊕ eBay, Inc.	Consumer	—	10.38	1.58
⊕ Motorola, Inc.	Hardware	NMF	-21.85	1.56
⊕ Corning Inc.	Hardware	18.6	28.76	1.43
⊕ Yahoo, Inc.	Media	45.7	-8.93	1.20
⊕ Applied Materials	Hardware	14.8	-2.60	1.06
⊕ Adobe Systems Inc.	Software	37.9	3.92	0.95
⊕ Automatic Data Processin	Business	23.6	2.62	0.94
⊕ Accenture, Ltd.	Software	17.1	-1.46	0.88

Current Investment Style

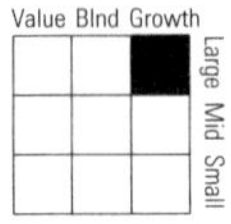

Market Cap	%
Giant	51.3
Large	22.4
Mid	18.8
Small	6.5
Micro	0.9
Avg $mil: 39,822	

Value Measures		Rel Category
Price/Earnings	21.52	1.04
Price/Book	4.02	1.28
Price/Sales	2.36	0.97
Price/Cash Flow	14.62	1.01
Dividend Yield %	0.59	0.89

Growth Measures	%	Rel Category
Long-Term Erngs	15.50	0.98
Book Value	7.77	1.15
Sales	10.70	1.19
Cash Flow	9.27	0.95
Historical Erngs	16.50	1.16

Profitability	%	Rel Category
Return on Equity	23.23	1.36
Return on Assets	11.41	1.23
Net Margin	15.38	1.18

Industry Weightings	% of Stocks	Rel Cat
Software	23.8	1.1
Hardware	23.8	1.6
Networking Eq	11.3	1.3
Semis	15.8	0.9
Semi Equip	2.8	0.7
Comp/Data Sv	9.0	0.9
Telecom	0.3	0.1
Health Care	0.2	0.0
Other	13.1	0.8

Composition

Cash	0.0
Stocks	100.0
Bonds	0.0
Other	0.0
Foreign (% of Stock)	0.3

Morningstar's Take by Dan Culloton 12-31-07

Vanguard Information Technology ETF leans on companies that have trenched out defensible competitive advantages.

This ETF's benchmark, the MSCI U.S. Investable Information Technology Index, includes software, hardware, Internet, and other tech-related stocks from the broad domestic equity market. Established tech bellwethers with enduring advantages take up much of the portfolio's assets. Microsoft generates prodigious cash flow by charging a toll on the millions of PCs running its software. Google dominates Internet search and advertising. The more people who buy and sell via eBay's auction site, the more valuable it becomes. Indeed 46% of this ETF's assets are in stocks with wide moats, which is a bigger helping than most of its rivals.

While the portfolio's decent quality mutes its risks (businesses with firm competitive advantages tend to produce more-reliable results), its holdings are subject to all of the tech sector's unique perils. Tech firms operate in a rapid-fire zone of competition and innovation. New, disruptive technologies can erode or wipe out the advantages of even wide-moat companies. Advanced Micro Devices harries Intel with new chip designs, and the dominant chipmaker pushes right back with draconian price cuts. In a few years, Sun Microsystems went from business software and hardware juggernaut to a marginal player that gives away its software to generate interest in services and hardware. All told, about three fourths of this ETF's assets are in stocks with average to above-average risk.

Yet, that's not terrible for a tech fund. Furthermore, given the portfolio's diversification across names, many of these firms-specific risks get diffused. That helps explain the portfolio's volatility, which hasn't been extreme. Consequently, we wouldn't demand a large margin of safety to invest here; an 8% discount to our fair value estimate would do.

Address:	PO Box 2600 United States 800-997-2798
Web Address:	www.vanguard.com
Inception:	01-26-04 *
Advisor:	Vanguard Advisers, Inc.

Management Fee:	0.18%		
Expense Projections:	3Yr:$71	5Yr:$124	10Yr:$280
Income Distrib:	Annually		
Exchange:	AMEX		

Vanguard Materials ETF VAW

Market Price	Mstar Category
$87.94	Specialty-Natural Res

Morningstar Fair Value

Price/Fair Value Ratio	Coverage Rate %
0.94	90

Valuation

This portfolio's quality is middling, and a slug of assets is staked in risky businesses. Yet, it's well diversified across holdings and end markets. Accordingly, we'd be willing to recommend it at an 8% or greater discount to our fair value estimate. Recently, it was trading at a 5% discount, which isn't quite steep enough.

Methodology

This ETF's benchmark, the MSCI U.S. Investible Market Materials Index, is a market-cap-weighted index of U.S.-domiciled companies in the materials sector, which spans the chemicals, paper, metals, and mining industries, among others. The portfolio holds upward of 100 stocks, making it nearly double the breadth of some competing basic-materials ETFs. The fund's top five holdings recently soaked up more than one third of assets. Many materials companies produce commodity-like products, making it very difficult to trench out an economic moat.

Morningstar Rating	Return	Risk	Yield	NAV	Avg Daily Vol. (k)	52 wk High/Low
★★	Below Avg	Low	1.5%	$87.96	32	$91.90 - $69.31

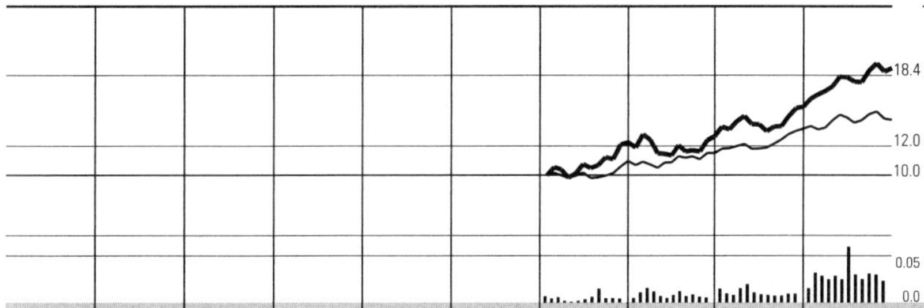

Growth of $10,000
— Investment Value of ETF
— Investment Value of Index S&P 500

Trading Volume Millions

1998	1999	2000	2001	2002	2003	2004	2005	2006	2007	History
—	—	—	—	—	—	58.81	60.03	70.60	87.96	NAV $
—	—	—	—	—	—	58.89	59.94	70.51	87.94	Market Price $
—	—	—	—	—	—	17.64*	3.71	19.50	26.42	NAV Return%
—	—	—	—	—	—	17.63*	3.42	19.52	26.55	Market Price Return%
—	—	—	—	—	—	0.05	0.03	0.01	0.00	Avg Premium/Discount%
—	—	—	—	—	—	—	-1.20	3.71	20.93	NAV Rtrn% +/-S&P 500
—	—	—	—	—	—	—	-0.23	-0.30	-0.05	NAV Rtrn% +/-MSCI Mats
—	—	—	—	—	—	—	100	23	76	NAV Return% Rank in Cat
—	—	—	—	—	—	—	1.65	1.89	1.81	Income Return %
—	—	—	—	—	—	—	2.06	17.61	24.61	Capital Return %
—	—	—	—	—	—	0.98	0.97	1.14	1.28	Income $
—	—	—	—	—	—	0.00	0.00	0.00	0.00	Capital Gains $
—	—	—	—	—	—	0.28	0.26	0.25	0.22	Expense Ratio %
—	—	—	—	—	—	1.93	1.83	2.16	1.84	Income Ratio %
—	—	—	—	—	—	8	12	13	6	Turnover Rate %
—	—	—	—	—	—	24	54	127	344	Net Assets $mil

Performance 12-31-07

Historic Quarterly NAV Returns

	1st Qtr	2nd Qtr	3rd Qtr	4th Qtr	Total
2003	—	—	—	—	—
2004	—	3.25	4.21	9.34	—*
2005	1.41	-8.80	3.13	8.74	3.71
2006	9.43	-1.86	-1.01	12.40	19.50
2007	10.21	8.62	4.18	1.36	26.42

Trailing	NAV Return%	Market Return%	NAV Rtrn% +/-S&P 500	%Rank Cat.(NAV)
3 Mo	1.36	1.47	4.69	62
6 Mo	5.60	5.71	6.97	72
1 Yr	26.42	26.55	20.93	76
3 Yr Avg	16.14	16.08	7.52	87
5 Yr Avg	—	—	—	—
10 Yr Avg	—	—	—	—

Tax Analysis	Tax-Adj Return%	Tax-Cost Ratio
3 Yr (estimated)	15.52	0.53
5 Yr (estimated)	—	—
10 Yr (estimated)	—	—

Rating and Risk

Time Period	Morningstar Rtn vs Cat	Morningstar Risk vs Cat	Morningstar Risk-Adj Rating
3 Yr	-Avg	Low	★★
5 Yr	—	—	—
10 Yr	—	—	—

Other Measures	Standard Index S&P 500	Best Fit Index M* Inds Mat TR
Alpha	5.9	0.4
Beta	1.35	1.29
R-Squared	57	76
Standard Deviation	13.88	
Mean	16.14	
Sharpe Ratio	0.84	

Portfolio Analysis 09-30-07

Share change since 06-07 Total Stocks:119	Sector	PE	Tot Ret%	% Assets
⊕ Monsanto Company	Ind Mtrls	67.1	114.45	7.56
⊕ DuPont El de Nemours & C	Ind Mtrls	12.4	-6.63	7.42
⊕ Dow Chemical Company	Ind Mtrls	11.3	2.55	6.67
⊕ Freeport-McMoRan Copper	Ind Mtrls	12.1	86.51	6.48
⊕ Alcoa Inc.	Ind Mtrls	14.5	24.11	5.51
⊕ Praxair, Inc.	Ind Mtrls	25.6	52.05	4.37
⊕ Air Products and Chemica	Ind Mtrls	21.1	42.82	3.43
⊕ Newmont Mining	Ind Mtrls	51.3	9.58	3.27
⊕ Nucor Corp.	Ind Mtrls	11.8	14.19	2.91
⊕ Weyerhaeuser Company	Ind Mtrls	—	7.83	2.52
⊕ International Paper Co.	Ind Mtrls	5.2	-2.36	2.43
⊕ United States Steel Corp	Ind Mtrls	12.6	66.73	2.03
⊕ PPG Industries, Inc.	Ind Mtrls	14.1	12.49	2.01
⊕ Lyondell Chemical Compan	Energy	—	—	1.71
⊕ Allegheny Technologies C	Ind Mtrls	11.7	-4.36	1.63
⊕ Ecolab, Inc.	Ind Mtrls	32.3	14.21	1.42
⊕ Vulcan Materials Company	Ind Mtrls	15.8	-10.36	1.37
⊕ The Mosaic Company	Ind Mtrls	68.0	341.67	1.33
⊕ Rohm and Haas Company	Ind Mtrls	17.8	6.59	1.27
⊕ Sigma-Aldrich Corporatio	Ind Mtrls	24.5	41.94	1.04

Current Investment Style

Value Blnd Growth — Large Mid Small

Market Cap	%
Giant	0.0
Large	54.5
Mid	36.7
Small	8.0
Micro	0.8
Avg $mil: 12,818	

Value Measures		Rel Category
Price/Earnings	16.44	1.01
Price/Book	2.41	1.03
Price/Sales	1.11	0.80
Price/Cash Flow	9.75	1.22
Dividend Yield %	1.34	0.97

Growth Measures	%	Rel Category
Long-Term Erngs	12.37	0.95
Book Value	9.88	0.66
Sales	7.40	0.66
Cash Flow	7.89	0.48
Historical Erngs	29.38	0.81

Profitability	%	Rel Category
Return on Equity	18.50	0.90
Return on Assets	7.25	0.77
Net Margin	8.22	0.60

Industry Weightings	% of Stocks	Rel Cat
Oil & Gas	0.0	0.0
Oil/Gas Products	0.2	0.1
Oil & Gas Srv	0.0	0.0
Pipelines	0.0	0.0
Utilities	0.0	0.0
Hard Commd	32.5	3.0
Soft Commd	10.8	3.7
Misc. Indstrl	48.4	4.5
Other	8.2	0.8

Composition

Cash	0.1
Stocks	99.9
Bonds	0.0
Other	0.0
Foreign (% of Stock)	0.7

Morningstar's Take by Sonya Morris 12-31-07

Given its moderate risk, we'd be willing to invest in Vanguard Materials ETF when it trades at least 8% below its aggregate fair value.

Wide-moat firms are few and far between in the industrial materials sector. Of the 72 stocks we cover in this portfolio, only two--Martin Marietta and Vulcan Materials--earn wide economic moat ratings from our analysts. Both companies are aggregates producers and, thus, enjoy the protection of high barriers to entry due to their strategically located quarries.

Few other firms in this ETF benefit from competitive advantages, however. The majority of this portfolio is staked in firms that have no economic moat at all, with most engaged in commodity businesses, such as steel, paper, and chemicals. Unable to differentiate their products, firms like DuPont exert little pricing power and are captive to economic cycles. As a result, few are able to consistently produce excess returns on capital over time.

Because no-moat firms such as these are more easily waylaid by rivals or by the vagaries of commodity price movements, their results are inherently less predictable. Not surprisingly, although average-risk firms soak up the bulk of this portfolio, above-average risk stocks figure prominently as well. Consider gold producer Newmont Mining, which is not only fully exposed to gold price fluctuations, but also subject to environmental and political risks, as many of its mines are located in volatile parts of the world.

Nevertheless, these riskier stocks aren't in the majority. And while this portfolio can hardly be considered high quality, it's well diversified by holdings and end markets, explaining the fund s moderate volatility. Accordingly, we'd be willing to recommend it when it's trading at least 8% below our fair value estimate.

Address:	PO Box 2600 United States 800-997-2798
Web Address:	www.vanguard.com
Inception:	01-26-04*
Advisor:	Vanguard Advisers, Inc.

Management Fee:	0.16%		
Expense Projections:	3Yr:$71	5Yr:$124	10Yr:$280
Income Distrib:	Annually		
Exchange:	AMEX		

Vanguard REIT Index ETF VNQ

Market Price	Mstar Category
$61.46	Specialty-Real Estate

Morningstar Rating	Return	Risk	Yield	NAV	Avg Daily Vol. (k)	52 wk High/Low
★★★	Average	Average	5.1%	$61.53	350	$87.27 - $55.49

Morningstar Fair Value

Price/Fair Value Ratio	Coverage Rate %
0.96	86

Valuation

This ETF was recently trading at a 4% discount to our fair value estimate, which marks a sharp turnabout from past years when many of its holdings were valued well above fair value. Nevertheless, given the fund's narrow focus, we'd demand at least a 15% discount to our fair value estimate to recommend it. By that standard, it's not a "buy."

Methodology

This ETF tracks the MSCI U.S. REIT Index, a market-cap weighted benchmark spanning virtually all equity REIT property types and geographic locales. To qualify for the index, a stock must have a total market cap of at least $100 million and be sufficiently liquid. Because those criteria sweep a passel of small caps into the index, the fund is relatively well-diversified across holdings. The index does not include mortgage or hybrid REITs (which invest in both real estate and mortgage securities) and is rebalanced quarterly.

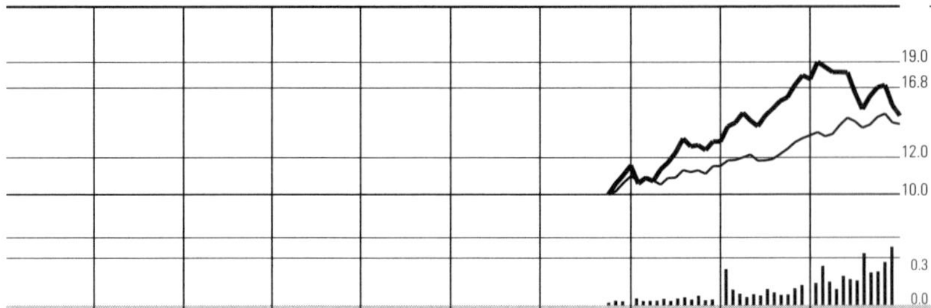

History

	1998	1999	2000	2001	2002	2003	2004	2005	2006	2007	History
	—	—	—	—	—	—	56.55	59.59	76.98	61.53	NAV $
	—	—	—	—	—	—	56.55	59.56	77.00	61.46	Market Price $
	—	—	—	—	—	—	12.78*	12.00	35.19	-16.38	NAV Return%
	—	—	—	—	—	—	12.74*	11.95	35.29	-16.50	Market Price Return%
	—	—	—	—	—	—	0.06	0.02	0.01	0.01	Avg Premium/Discount%
	—	—	—	—	—	—	—	7.09	19.40	-21.87	NAV Rtrn% +/-S&P 500
	—	—	—	—	—	—	—	-0.13	-0.73	0.44	NAV Rtrn% +/-MSCI REIT
	—	—	—	—	—	—	—	75	75	40	NAV Return% Rank in Cat
	—	—	—	—	—	—	—	5.22	3.24	4.10	Income Return %
	—	—	—	—	—	—	—	6.78	31.95	-20.48	Capital Return %
	—	—	—	—	—	—	0.68	2.89	1.90	3.11	Income $
	—	—	—	—	—	—	0.59	0.68	1.35	0.00	Capital Gains $
	—	—	—	—	—	—	—	0.18	0.12	0.12	Expense Ratio %
	—	—	—	—	—	—	—	3.60	3.00	2.36	Income Ratio %
	—	—	—	—	—	—	7	13	17	21	Turnover Rate %
	—	—	—	—	—	—	171	410	1,476	1,682	Net Assets $mil

Performance 12-31-07

Historic Quarterly NAV Returns

	1st Qtr	2nd Qtr	3rd Qtr	4th Qtr	Total
2003	—	—	—	—	—
2004	—	—	—	15.00	—*
2005	-7.31	14.65	3.59	1.73	12.00
2006	14.81	-1.37	9.41	9.10	35.19
2007	3.40	-9.35	2.39	-12.87	-16.38

Trailing	NAV Return%	Market Return%	NAV Rtrn% +/-S&P 500	%Rank Cat.(NAV)
3 Mo	-12.87	-12.57	-9.54	46
6 Mo	-10.79	-11.04	-9.42	54
1 Yr	-16.38	-16.50	-21.87	40
3 Yr Avg	8.18	8.14	-0.44	50
5 Yr Avg	—	—	—	—
10 Yr Avg	—	—	—	—

Tax Analysis	Tax-Adj Return%	Tax-Cost Ratio
3 Yr (estimated)	6.53	1.53
5 Yr (estimated)	—	—
10 Yr (estimated)	—	—

Rating and Risk

Time Period	Morningstar Rtn vs Cat	Morningstar Risk vs Cat	Morningstar Risk-Adj Rating
3 Yr	Avg	Avg	★★★
5 Yr	—	—	—
10 Yr	—	—	—

Other Measures	Standard Index S&P 500	Best Fit Index DJ Real Est
Alpha	-1.2	-0.2
Beta	1.45	0.97
R-Squared	44	100
Standard Deviation	17.02	
Mean	8.18	
Sharpe Ratio	0.30	

Portfolio Analysis 09-30-07

Share change since 06-07 Total Stocks:99

Share change	Holding	Sector	PE	Tot Ret%	% Assets
⊖	Simon Property Group, In	Financial	36.8	-11.34	6.87
⊖	ProLogis Trust	Financial	14.3	7.35	5.24
⊖	Vornado Realty Trust	Financial	27.3	-25.45	4.60
⊖	Archstone-Smith Tr	Financial	—	—	4.12
⊖	Boston Properties, Inc.	Financial	10.0	-10.36	3.80
⊖	Equity Residential	Financial	—	-24.90	3.79
⊖	General Growth Propertie	Financial	33.4	-18.53	3.64
⊖	Host Hotels & Resorts, I	Financial	22.4	-27.14	3.60
⊖	Kimco Realty Corporation	Financial	26.4	-16.04	3.15
⊖	Public Storage	Financial	—	-22.83	3.09
⊖	AvalonBay Communities, I	Financial	37.5	-25.42	2.89
⊕	Developers Diversified R	Financial	20.8	-36.01	2.15
⊖	SL Green Realty Corporat	Financial	36.8	-27.81	2.13
⊖	HCP, Inc.	—	57.8	-0.33	2.10
⊖	Macerich Company	Financial	67.1	-15.09	1.93
⊖	AMB Property Corporation	Financial	21.5	1.64	1.83
⊖	Ventas, Inc.	Financial	33.2	12.01	1.69
⊖	Regency Centers Corporat	Financial	30.6	-14.56	1.64
⊖	Federal Realty Investmen	Financial	50.5	-0.61	1.54
⊕	Duke Realty Corporation	Financial	35.2	-32.72	1.50

Current Investment Style

Value Blnd Growth; Large Mid Small

Market Cap	%
Giant	0.0
Large	28.1
Mid	50.8
Small	19.6
Micro	1.5
Avg $mil: 5,833	

Value Measures		Rel Category
Price/Earnings	29.06	1.18
Price/Book	2.42	1.34
Price/Sales	5.09	1.45
Price/Cash Flow	14.49	0.95
Dividend Yield %	4.44	0.89

Growth Measures	%	Rel Category
Long-Term Erngs	7.05	0.59
Book Value	8.34	1.03
Sales	1.48	0.18
Cash Flow	9.35	1.19
Historical Erngs	10.99	0.38

Profitability	%	Rel Category
Return on Equity	13.89	0.91
Return on Assets	4.13	0.70
Net Margin	31.74	0.88

Sector Weightings	% of Stocks	Rel S&P 500	3 Year High	3 Year Low
Info	0.00	0.00		
Software	0.00	0.00	0	0
Hardware	0.00	0.00	0	0
Media	0.00	0.00	0	0
Telecom	0.00	0.00	0	0
Service	100.00	2.46		
Health	0.00	0.00	0	0
Consumer	0.00	0.00	0	0
Business	0.00	0.00	0	0
Financial	100.00	5.74	100	100
Mfg	0.00	0.00		
Goods	0.00	0.00	0	0
Ind Mtrls	0.00	0.00	0	0
Energy	0.00	0.00	0	0
Utilities	0.00	0.00	0	0

Composition

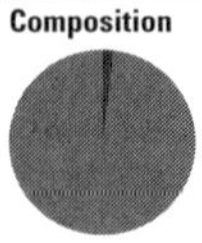

Cash	1.8
Stocks	98.2
Bonds	0.0
Other	0.0
Foreign (% of Stock)	0.0

Morningstar's Take by Andrew Gogerty 12-31-07

Vanguard REIT Index is a midquality portfolio at best, and one that we'd invest in only with a suitably large margin of safety.

The quality of this ETF's portfolio is not especially high. No holding garners a wide economic moat from Morningstar's equity analysts, meaning that none of the firms concerned boasts an enduring competitive edge in their view.

To be sure, that's hardly unique to this fund; our analysts haven't awarded a wide-moat rating to any one of the 70-plus REITs that they had under coverage recently. The inability of REITs to trench a wide moat stems from the industry's low barriers to entry; anyone can start a business and amass property. Further, brand loyalty doesn't pose the same obstacle as in other industries. Not surprisingly, then, this fund's narrow-moat holdings, like mall-operator Simon Properties, tend to boast attributes like highly sought-after properties in hard-to-replicate places.

Shorn of durable competitive advantages, these firms' results tend to be less predictable, adding an element of uncertainty to the cash flow forecasts that underpin our analysts' fair value estimates. While slow, but steady, cash flow growth from increasing rents confers some stability, REITs are cyclical by nature and few produce high returns on invested capital. Moreover, REITs are levered to similar factors, including occupancy rates, net operating income, and rent income growth. Not only does this common-factor risk heighten the potential for our forecasts to be errant en masse, it also subjects the fund to greater volatility.

True, volatility can create the opportunity to invest here at a more attractive price. Just as investors drove up REIT prices to irrational levels in recent years amid a frothy real estate market and low interest rates, they've pulled back as optimism has waned, creating some bargains. But in the end we'd take the plunge only with a healthy margin of safety--a 15% or greater discount to our fair value estimate should suffice.

Address:	PO Box 2600 United States 800-662-6273
Web Address:	www.vanguard.com
Inception:	09-23-04*
Advisor:	The Vanguard Group, Inc.

Management Fee:	0.10%		
Expense Projections:	3Yr:$39	5Yr:$68	10Yr:$154
Income Distrib:	Quarterly		
Exchange:	AMEX		

Vanguard TelcomSrv ETF VOX

Market Price	Mstar Category
$75.27	Specialty-Communications

Morningstar Fair Value

Price/Fair Value Ratio	Coverage Rate %
0.99	81

Morningstar Rating	Return	Risk	Yield	NAV	Avg Daily Vol. (k)	52 wk High/Low
★★★	Average	Below Avg	2.6%	$75.47	40	$85.06 - $70.49

Valuation

This is an ETF of middling- to poor-quality stocks. Yet, volatility hasn't been extreme, reflecting the portfolio's diversification across stocks. For that reason, we'd need only an 8% discount to our fair value estimate to invest here. Recently, it looked fairly valued.

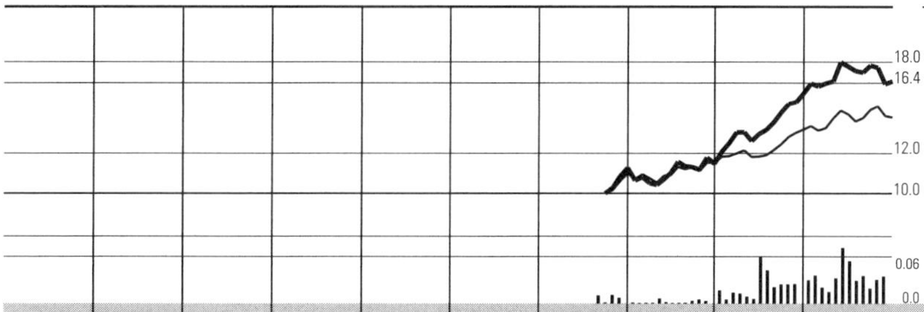

Methodology

This ETF tracks the MSCI U.S. Investable Telecommunications Services Index, a subset of the market-cap-weighted MSCI U.S. Investable Market 2500 Index. The MSCI Telecom index holds fewer than 50 stocks that offer communications services through fixed-line, cellular, wireless, high-bandwidth, or fiber-optic cable networks. The index and ETF don't include equipment makers, such as Qualcomm. The index is so concentrated that the ETF has to modify the weightings of its largest holdings to comply with IRS diversification rules. So, the fund won't exactly mimic its bogy.

History

1998	1999	2000	2001	2002	2003	2004	2005	2006	2007	History
—	—	—	—	—	—	54.93	54.45	73.47	75.47	NAV $
—	—	—	—	—	—	54.90	54.46	73.51	75.27	Market Price $
—	—	—	—	—	—	16.39*	1.92	36.65	5.49	NAV Return%
—	—	—	—	—	—	16.52*	2.00	36.70	5.15	Market Price Return%
—	—	—	—	—	—	0.02	-0.07	-0.01	-0.06	Avg Premium/Discount%
—	—	—	—	—	—	—	-2.99	20.86	0.00	NAV Rtrn% +/-S&P 500
—	—	—	—	—	—	—	3.99	-0.61	-4.99	NAV Rtrn% +/-MSCI Telecom
—	—	—	—	—	—	—	1	1	50	NAV Return% Rank in Cat
—	—	—	—	—	—	—	2.83	1.70	2.72	Income Return %
—	—	—	—	—	—	—	-0.91	34.95	2.77	Capital Return %
—	—	—	—	—	—	0.41	1.56	0.93	2.00	Income $
—	—	—	—	—	—	0.00	0.00	0.00	0.00	Capital Gains $
—	—	—	—	—	—	—	0.26	0.25	0.23	Expense Ratio %
—	—	—	—	—	—	—	2.72	3.31	2.21	Income Ratio %
—	—	—	—	—	—	—	41	32	17	Turnover Rate %
—	—	—	—	—	—	16	22	147	211	Net Assets $mil

Performance 12-31-07

Historic Quarterly NAV Returns

	1st Qtr	2nd Qtr	3rd Qtr	4th Qtr	Total
2003	—	—	—	—	—
2004	—	—	—	11.91	—*
2005	-6.55	4.75	2.57	1.52	1.92
2006	14.82	-0.74	10.15	8.85	36.65
2007	4.51	7.71	0.47	-6.73	5.49

Trailing	NAV Return%	Market Return%	NAV Rtrn% +/-S&P 500	%Rank Cat.(NAV)
3 Mo	-6.73	-6.95	-3.40	67
6 Mo	-6.29	-6.47	-4.92	67
1 Yr	5.49	5.15	0.00	50
3 Yr Avg	13.68	13.60	5.06	50
5 Yr Avg	—	—	—	—
10 Yr Avg	—	—	—	—

Tax Analysis	Tax-Adj Return%	Tax-Cost Ratio
3 Yr (estimated)	12.80	0.77
5 Yr (estimated)	—	—
10 Yr (estimated)	—	—

Rating and Risk

Time Period	Morningstar Rtn vs Cat	Morningstar Risk vs Cat	Morningstar Risk-Adj Rating
3 Yr	Avg	-Avg	★★★
5 Yr	—	—	—
10 Yr	—	—	—

Other Measures	Standard Index S&P 500	Best Fit Index M* Telecm Sec TR
Alpha	4.2	0.8
Beta	1.18	0.90
R-Squared	61	91
Standard Deviation	11.77	
Mean	13.68	
Sharpe Ratio	0.79	

Portfolio Analysis 09-30-07

Share change since 06-07 Total Stocks:45	Sector	PE	Tot Ret%	% Assets
⊖ AT&T, Inc.	Telecom	21.6	20.58	20.40
⊖ Verizon Communications I	Telecom	21.7	22.19	19.10
⊖ Sprint Nextel Corporatio	Telecom	—	-30.12	6.25
⊖ Alltel Corp.	Telecom	—	—	4.48
⊖ American Tower Corporati	Telecom	—	14.51	3.93
⊖ Qwest Communications Int	Telecom	5.0	-16.25	3.18
⊖ NII Holdings, Inc.	Telecom	24.3	-25.02	3.06
⊖ Crown Castle Internation	Telecom	—	28.79	2.67
⊖ Embarq Corporation	Telecom	—	-1.66	2.09
⊕ Level 3 Communications,	Telecom	—	-45.71	1.89
⊖ Windstream Corporation	Telecom	13.9	-1.74	1.87
⊖ Citizens Communications	Telecom	19.3	-4.97	1.53
⊖ Centurytel, Inc.	Telecom	12.5	-4.69	1.51
⊖ Leap Wireless Internatio	Telecom	—	-21.57	1.45
⊖ SBA Communications Corpo	Telecom	—	23.05	1.32
⊖ Golden Telecom, Inc.	Telecom	26.9	115.52	1.32
⊖ Dobson Communications Co	Telecom	—	—	1.26
⊖ NeuStar, Inc.	Telecom	28.1	-11.59	1.23
⊖ Time Warner Telecom, Inc	Telecom	—	1.81	1.18
⊖ United States Cellular C	Telecom	22.0	20.85	1.12

Current Investment Style

Value Blnd Growth — Large Mid Small

Market Cap	%
Giant	39.8
Large	21.1
Mid	21.3
Small	12.8
Micro	5.0
Avg $mil: 21,903	

Value Measures		Rel Category
Price/Earnings	21.36	1.20
Price/Book	2.22	1.00
Price/Sales	1.81	1.21
Price/Cash Flow	8.42	1.13
Dividend Yield %	1.53	0.78

Growth Measures	%	Rel Category
Long-Term Erngs	9.05	0.86
Book Value	7.89	1.49
Sales	-10.23	NMF
Cash Flow	-7.26	NMF
Historical Erngs	0.61	0.10

Profitability	%	Rel Category
Return on Equity	11.05	0.63
Return on Assets	2.55	0.41
Net Margin	5.56	0.60

Industry Weightings	% of Stocks	Rel Cat
Telecom Srv	77.4	2.0
Wireless Srv	21.5	0.9
Network Eq	0.0	0.0
Semis	0.0	0.0
Big Media	0.0	0.0
Cable TV	0.0	0.0
Other Media	0.0	0.0
Soft/Hardwr	0.0	0.0
Other	1.1	0.1

Composition

Cash	0.0
Stocks	100.0
Bonds	0.0
Other	0.0
Foreign (% of Stock)	1.3

Morningstar's Take by Dan Culloton 12-31-07

This is a concentrated ETF of companies with slim competitive advantages. Yet, many of the firm-specific risks cancel each other out, tamping down volatility.

Vanguard Telecom Services ETF, like many index funds focusing on this sector, might be better named the "AT&T and Verizon ETF." Those two stocks take up nearly 40% of this portfolio and, thus, go a long way in explaining this ETF's quality, risk, valuation, and performance attributes.

The quality of this ETF's holdings is below average. AT&T and Verizon are large; they've been aggressive consolidators; and they've invested heavily in wireless and broadband services to replace their dying landline phone business. They are, however, beset by competition from cable, Internet, wireless, and other players. To defend themselves they must invest heavily in projects with uncertain outcomes, such as the new broadband delivery systems they're pursuing. Given this, both firms are rated narrow-moat by our analysts. They're hardly alone in that regard: Not one of the stocks in this portfolio garners a wide-moat rating and more than one fifth of assets were staked in firms that lack competitive advantages of any kind.

The cash flows and financial health of businesses with precarious competitive positions are less reliable. Qwest Communications has lagged other phone companies in rolling out Internet and video services to answer the challenge posed by cable companies, and it still struggles under a heavy debt load. Level 3 is also saddled with heavy debt and the task of integrating various firms it acquired over a period of years. Yet, few of the firms here are significantly at risk of flaming out, explaining why our analysts believe most pose only average business risk. Furthermore, with risk diffused across a number of different firms, volatility hasn't been extreme. Given that, we'd need only an 8% discount our fair value estimate to invest here.

Address:	PO Box 2600 United States 800-997-2798
Web Address:	www.vanguard.com
Inception:	09-23-04*
Advisor:	Vanguard Advisers, Inc.

Management Fee:	0.18%		
Expense Projections:	3Yr:$74	5Yr:$130	10Yr:$293
Income Distrib:	Annually		
Exchange:	AMEX		

Vanguard Utilities ETF VPU

Market Price	Mstar Category
$87.58	Specialty-Utilities

Morningstar Fair Value

Price/Fair Value Ratio	Coverage Rate %
0.97	90

Morningstar Rating	Return	Risk	Yield	NAV	Avg Daily Vol. (k)	52 wk High/Low
★★★	Average	Above Avg	2.5%	$87.64	30	$91.18 - $75.29

Valuation

This ETF owns a mix of regulated and unregulated utilities stocks. The end result is a portfolio of average quality and risk. The fund isn't excessively volatile, so we wouldn't demand an especially wide margin of safety to invest here; an 8% discount to our fair value estimate would do. The fund was recently hovering near fair value.

Methodology

This exchange-traded fund tracks the MSCI U.S. Investable Market Utilities Index, an index of roughly 90 domestic utility stocks. This index, which is market-cap-weighted, consists almost entirely of electric and natural-gas utilities, and thus doesn't contain the telecom and energy stocks found in the portfolios of most actively managed utilities-sector funds.

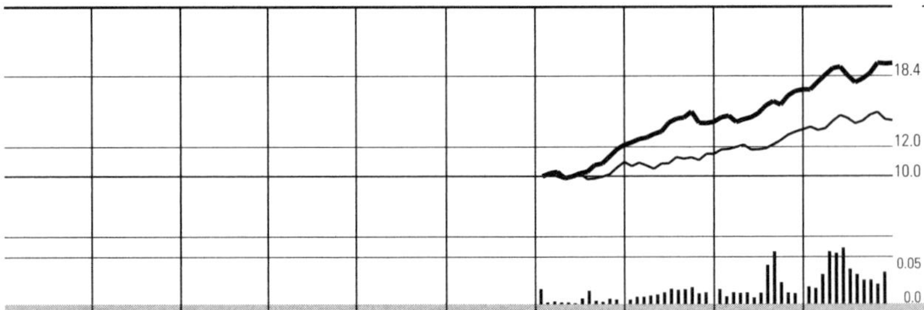

Growth of $10,000
— Investment Value of ETF
— Investment Value of Index S&P 500

Trading Volume Millions

1998	1999	2000	2001	2002	2003	2004	2005	2006	2007	History
—	—	—	—	—	—	58.46	65.15	76.77	87.64	NAV $
—	—	—	—	—	—	58.56	65.14	76.81	87.58	Market Price $
—	—	—	—	—	—	18.92*	14.75	21.58	17.15	NAV Return%
—	—	—	—	—	—	18.90*	14.54	21.66	17.01	Market Price Return%
—	—	—	—	—	—	-0.02	-0.01	0.05	0.03	Avg Premium/Discount%
—	—	—	—	—	—	—	9.84	5.79	11.66	NAV Rtrn% +/-S&P 500
—	—	—	—	—	—	—	-0.27	-0.13	-0.35	NAV Rtrn% +/-MSCI Utils
—	—	—	—	—	—	—	50	50	57	NAV Return% Rank in Cat
—	—	—	—	—	—	—	3.29	3.40	2.88	Income Return %
—	—	—	—	—	—	—	11.46	18.18	14.27	Capital Return %
—	—	—	—	—	—	1.55	1.90	2.19	2.19	Income $
—	—	—	—	—	—	0.00	0.00	0.00	0.00	Capital Gains $
—	—	—	—	—	—	0.28	0.26	0.25	0.22	Expense Ratio %
—	—	—	—	—	—	3.82	3.36	3.29	2.74	Income Ratio %
—	—	—	—	—	—	7	7	9	12	Turnover Rate %
—	—	—	—	—	—	53	105	163	335	Net Assets $mil

Performance 12-31-07

Historic Quarterly NAV Returns

	1st Qtr	2nd Qtr	3rd Qtr	4th Qtr	Total
2003	—	—	—	—	—
2004	—	-0.86	6.00	11.80	—*
2005	4.41	9.41	6.88	-6.02	14.75
2006	-0.16	5.47	5.49	9.46	21.58
2007	9.20	-0.37	1.30	6.29	17.15

Trailing	NAV Return%	Market Return%	NAV Rtrn% +/-S&P 500	%Rank Cat.(NAV)
3 Mo	6.29	6.23	9.62	50
6 Mo	7.68	7.64	9.05	50
1 Yr	17.15	17.01	11.66	57
3 Yr Avg	17.79	17.70	9.17	50
5 Yr Avg	—	—	—	—
10 Yr Avg	—	—	—	—

Tax Analysis	Tax-Adj Return%	Tax-Cost Ratio
3 Yr (estimated)	16.90	0.76
5 Yr (estimated)	—	—
10 Yr (estimated)	—	—

Rating and Risk

Time Period	Morningstar Rtn vs Cat	Morningstar Risk vs Cat	Morningstar Risk-Adj Rating
3 Yr	Avg	+Avg	★★★
5 Yr	—	—	—
10 Yr	—	—	—

Other Measures	Standard Index S&P 500	Best Fit Index M* Util Sect TR
Alpha	10.7	-1.0
Beta	0.46	0.98
R-Squared	12	97
Standard Deviation	10.17	
Mean	17.79	
Sharpe Ratio	1.25	

Portfolio Analysis 09-30-07

Share change since 06-07 Total Stocks:87	Sector	PE	Tot Ret%	% Assets
⊖ Exelon Corporation	Utilities	20.2	35.14	8.32
⊖ Txu	Utilities	—	—	5.15
⊖ Southern Company	Utilities	17.1	9.85	4.47
⊖ Dominion Resources, Inc.	Utilities	12.3	16.98	4.06
⊖ Duke Energy Corporation	Utilities	10.4	9.03	3.89
⊖ FPL Group	Utilities	20.0	27.91	3.89
⊖ Public Service Enterpris	Utilities	19.1	52.10	3.69
⊖ Entergy Corporation	Utilities	20.0	32.55	3.52
⊖ FirstEnergy Corporation	Utilities	17.3	23.71	3.19
⊖ American Electric Power	Utilities	16.8	13.06	3.04
⊖ PPL Corporation	Utilities	20.0	49.31	2.95
⊖ Edison International	Utilities	15.4	19.93	2.84
⊖ PG & E Corporation	Utilities	16.3	-6.09	2.82
⊖ Constellation Energy Gro	Utilities	22.5	51.88	2.56
⊖ Sempra Energy	Utilities	17.0	12.69	2.34
⊖ AES Corporation	Utilities	23.3	-2.95	2.12
⊖ Consolidated Edison Comp	Utilities	13.9	6.65	2.07
⊖ Progress Energy, Inc.	Utilities	15.5	3.83	1.90
⊖ Ameren Corporation	Utilities	19.7	5.94	1.80
⊖ Mirant Corporation	Utilities	7.9	23.47	1.66

Current Investment Style

Value Blnd Growth; Large Mid Small

Market Cap	%
Giant	8.4
Large	54.6
Mid	30.9
Small	6.1
Micro	0.0
Avg $mil: 13,692	

Value Measures		Rel Category
Price/Earnings	16.42	0.94
Price/Book	2.24	1.35
Price/Sales	1.30	0.99
Price/Cash Flow	6.44	0.88
Dividend Yield %	2.84	0.98

Growth Measures	%	Rel Category
Long-Term Erngs	8.06	0.87
Book Value	6.29	0.84
Sales	3.65	1.09
Cash Flow	14.44	1.65
Historical Erngs	9.04	1.11

Profitability	%	Rel Category
Return on Equity	15.91	1.12
Return on Assets	3.74	0.90
Net Margin	9.66	0.95

Industry Weightings	% of Stocks	Rel Cat
Telecom Srv	0.0	0.0
Electric Utls	84.8	1.4
Nat Gas Utls	10.2	1.0
Wireless Srv	0.0	0.0
Energy	4.1	0.3
Media	0.0	0.0
Network Eq	0.0	0.0
Water	0.9	4.3
Other	0.0	0.0

Composition

Cash	0.5
Stocks	99.5
Bonds	0.0
Other	0.0
Foreign (% of Stock)	0.0

Morningstar's Take by Dan Culloton 12-31-07

It has been a while since utility stocks were considered the favored investments of "widows and orphans," but at the right price Vanguard Utilities ETF could be a decent buy.

Deregulation has made it difficult for utilities to sustain their competitive advantages. Over the years many have gone from regulated monopolies with predictable returns to competitors in a volatile, commodity-like business saddled with high fixed costs. That's why Morningstar stock analysts give only one utility stock in their coverage universe, and in this portfolio, a wide moat. That stock is Exelon, whose large and hard-to-duplicate fleet of nuclear power generators give it a big edge as worries about carbon emissions from fossil-fuel-burning electric plants make nukes look more attractive.

Exelon is the top holding in this ETF, which tracks the MSCI U.S. Investable Utilities Index. The ETF's benchmark also is more diversified in terms of number of stocks than its biggest rival, Utilities Select Sector SPDR. Overall, however, the portfolio's quality is middling. It consists mostly of stocks with narrow moats, slow-growth profiles, and average risks. Duke Energy, for example, delivers steady earnings and a healthy yield, but it's not clear whether the company will realize the hoped-for cost savings and operational efficiencies from its 2006 acquisition of Cinergy.

The fund's risk profile is moderate as well. To be sure, there are some dicey stocks here, such as AES Corp., which runs regulated utilities and sells power generation in several fast-growing, but volatile emerging markets. Yet, the portfolio gains ballast from other, more-traditional utility companies operating in favorable regulatory environments, such as Southern Co.

Taken together with the portfolio's diversification across names, that risk profile has tamped down volatility. As such, we'd consider investing in the fund when its shares traded at an 8% or greater discount to our fair value estimate.

Address:	PO Box 2600 United States 800-997-2798
Web Address:	www.vanguard.com
Inception:	01-26-04*
Advisor:	Vanguard Advisers, Inc.

Management Fee:	0.16%		
Expense Projections:	3Yr:$71	5Yr:$124	10Yr:$280
Income Distrib:	Quarterly		
Exchange:	AMEX		

Foreign Stock Funds: Diversified

This section offers a full-page report on each diversified foreign stock ETF.

BLDRS Emerg Mkts 50 ADR ADRE

Market Price	Mstar Category
$55.04	Diversified Emerging Mk

Morningstar Fair Value

Price/Fair Value Ratio	Coverage Rate %
1.03	87

Morningstar Rating	Return	Risk	Yield	NAV	Avg Daily Vol. (k)	52 wk High/Low
★★★★	Above Avg	High	1.5%	$55.02	343	$59.97 - $35.83

Valuation

This ETF is valued too richly for our tastes. Since mid-2005, it has been trading at a premium to our fair value estimate, most recently at a 3% premium. Given this fund's volatility, we'd require a 15% or larger discount to fair value before investing here.

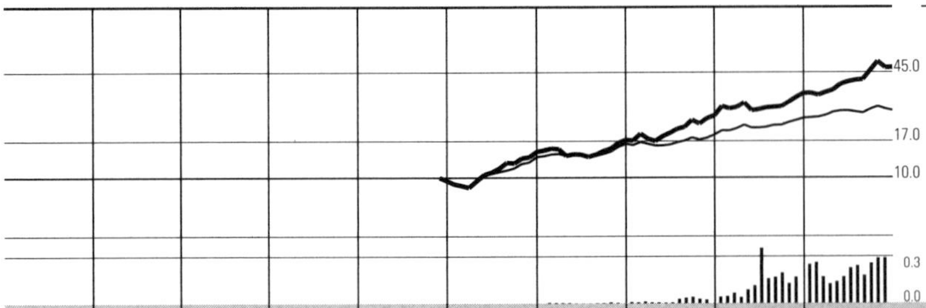

Growth of $10,000
— Investment Value of ETF
— Investment Value of Index MSCI EAFE

Trading Volume Millions

Methodology

This ETF tracks the BLDRS Emerging Markets 50 ADR Index, a cap-weighted index that tracks 50 of the most actively traded emerging-market names. Nearly 75% of the fund is in giant-caps. Firms domiciled in Brazil, South Korea, and China are most common, while telecom, industrials, financials, and energy sectors dominate. Its top 10 holdings recently accounted for nearly 50% of assets. Though assets are denominated in the dollar, the fund is still subject to currency risk given that each ADR is tied to the local-currency-denominated shares that trade on the stock's home exchange.

1998	1999	2000	2001	2002	2003	2004	2005	2006	2007	History
—	—	—	—	12.63	18.07	20.91	28.81	38.94	55.02	NAV $
—	—	—	—	12.72	18.63	20.93	28.83	38.93	55.04	Market Price $
—	—	—	—	37.65*	50.50	17.85	40.81	37.70	43.78	NAV Return%
—	—	—	—	37.48*	53.89	14.47	40.80	37.53	43.89	Market Price Return%
—	—	—	—	0.51	1.36	0.01	0.07	-0.05	0.02	Avg Premium/Discount%
—	—	—	—	—	11.91	-2.40	27.27	11.36	32.61	NAV Rtrn% +/-MSCI EAFE
—	—	—	—	—	—	-1.12	-0.84	-0.18	0.28	NAV Rtrn% +/-BONY EM
—	—	—	—	—	1	100	1	1	25	NAV Return% Rank in Cat
—	—	—	—	—	6.73	1.92	2.63	2.06	2.18	Income Return %
—	—	—	—	—	43.77	15.93	38.18	35.64	41.60	Capital Return %
—	—	—	—	0.04	0.84	0.34	0.54	0.59	0.84	Income $
—	—	—	—	0.00	0.00	0.00	0.00	0.00	0.00	Capital Gains $
—	—	—	—	—	0.30	0.30	0.30	0.30	—	Expense Ratio %
—	—	—	—	—	1.98	2.29	2.26	1.95	—	Income Ratio %
—	—	—	—	—	16	16	26	3	—	Turnover Rate %
—	—	—	—	20	4	38	282	301	911	Net Assets $mil

Performance 12-31-07

Historic Quarterly NAV Returns

	1st Qtr	2nd Qtr	3rd Qtr	4th Qtr	Total
2003	-9.30	24.14	13.56	17.70	50.50
2004	3.67	-7.33	5.04	16.77	17.85
2005	1.68	8.69	19.90	6.26	40.81
2006	12.79	-3.23	4.34	20.92	37.70
2007	1.30	16.00	17.18	4.42	43.78

Trailing	NAV Return%	Market Return%	NAV Rtrn% +/-MSCI EAFE	%Rank Cat.(NAV)
3 Mo	4.42	4.53	6.17	45
6 Mo	22.35	22.35	21.96	38
1 Yr	43.78	43.89	32.61	25
3 Yr Avg	40.74	40.72	23.91	1
5 Yr Avg	37.66	37.46	16.07	1
10 Yr Avg	—	—	—	—

Tax Analysis	Tax-Adj Return%	Tax-Cost Ratio
3 Yr (estimated)	39.80	0.67
5 Yr (estimated)	36.46	0.87
10 Yr (estimated)	—	—

Rating and Risk

Time Period	Morningstar Rtn vs Cat	Morningstar Risk vs Cat	Morningstar Risk-Adj Rating
3 Yr	High	High	★★★★★
5 Yr	Avg	High	★★★
10 Yr	—	—	—

Other Measures	Standard Index S&P 500	Best Fit Index MSCI Emg Mkt
Alpha	11.1	2.7
Beta	1.80	1.07
R-Squared	70	91
Standard Deviation	20.46	
Mean	40.74	
Sharpe Ratio	1.58	

Portfolio Analysis 10-31-07

Share change since 09-07 Total Stocks:50	Sector	Country	% Assets
⊕ China Mobile Ltd. ADR	Telecom	China	ADR
⊕ Petroleo Brasileiro S.A.	Energy	Brazil	5.48
⊕ Companhia Vale do Rio Do	Ind Mtrls	Brazil	5.07
⊕ America Mobile ADR	Telecom	Mexico	4.74
⊕ Posco ADR	Ind Mtrls	Korea	4.74
⊕ Brazilian Petroleum Corp	Energy	Brazil	4.57
⊕ PetroChina Company, Ltd.	Energy	China	4.19
⊕ China Life Insurance Com	Financial	China	4.04
⊕ Taiwan Semiconductor Man	Hardware	Taiwan	4.02
⊕ Vale Overseas Limited AD	Ind Mtrls	Brazil	3.87
⊕ Bank Bradesco ADR	Financial	Brazil	2.91
⊕ Teva Pharmaceutical Indu	Health	Israel	2.83
⊕ CNOOC, Ltd. ADR	Energy	China	2.68
⊕ Infosys Technologies, Lt	Software	India	2.47
⊕ Itau Bank Financial Hold	Financial	Brazil	2.46
⊕ ICICI Bank, Ltd. ADR	Financial	India	2.37
⊕ China Petroleum & Chemic	Business	China	2.37
⊕ Kookmin Bank ADR	Financial	Korea	2.34
⊕ Sasol, Ltd. ADR	Energy	South Africa	2.06
⊕ Cemex Corporation ADR	Ind Mtrls	Mexico	2.04

Current Investment Style

Value Blnd Growth — Large Mid Small

Market Cap	%
Giant	74.8
Large	24.6
Mid	0.5
Small	0.0
Micro	0.0
Avg $mil: 65,948	

Value Measures		Rel Category
Price/Earnings	—	—
Price/Book	—	—
Price/Sales	—	—
Price/Cash Flow	—	—
Dividend Yield %	—	—

Growth Measures	%	Rel Category
Long-Term Erngs	—	—
Book Value	22.80	1.33
Sales	23.52	1.16
Cash Flow	20.67	1.30
Historical Erngs	18.20	0.76

Composition

Cash	0.0	Bonds	0.0
Stocks	100.0	Other	0.0
Foreign (% of Stock)			100.0

Sector Weightings	% of Stocks	Rel MSCI EAFE	3 Year High	3 Year Low
Info	32.24	2.54		
Software	3.26	5.62	6	3
Hardware	6.70	1.65	9	7
Media	1.05	0.62	2	1
Telecom	21.23	3.34	25	19
Service	24.13	0.56		
Health	2.83	0.44	5	3
Consumer	0.00	0.00	0	0
Business	2.37	0.47	2	1
Financial	18.93	0.70	19	16
Mfg	43.63	0.99		
Goods	1.79	0.13	3	2
Ind Mtrls	21.40	1.23	22	17
Energy	18.97	2.44	19	12
Utilities	1.47	0.27	3	1

Regional Exposure	% Stock		
UK/W. Europe	1	N. America	0
Japan	0	Latn America	39
Asia X Japan	51	Other	9

Country Exposure	% Stock		
Brazil	30	Mexico	10
China	24	Taiwan	8
South Korea	12		

Morningstar's Take by Emiko Kurotsu 12-31-07

BLDRs Emerging Markets 50 ADR has the highest-quality emerging-markets portfolio we cover.

This ETF tracks the 50 most actively traded emerging-markets ADRs. Because these names tend to be the biggest by market cap, this fund has a distinctly large-cap feel. In fact, the fund stashes nearly 75% of assets in giant caps, with the rest mostly in large caps.

Though size doesn't automatically translate to quality, large-cap firms more often tend to boast key attributes like scale, brand equity, or high barriers to entry. In that sense, this fund's large-cap bias burnishes its quality, as virtually every one of its holdings wields at least some semblance of a competitive advantage, or "economic moat." Top-holding China Mobile, for instance, dominates the Chinese wireless industry with over 60% market share, explaining that firm's wide moat.

Of course, the portfolio hardly gleams with blue-chip, wide-moat stocks; most holdings carry a narrow-moat rating, meaning that their advantages are more modest. For instance, while energy giant Petrobras has been on a high amid a surge in crude oil prices, it still must fend with a thorny regulatory climate in its native Brazil. Likewise, Sasol is a major player in the South African fuel market and the world's leading expert in nascent gas-to-liquid and coal-to-liquid technology, yet operates in what amounts to a commodity business.

That said, the portfolio isn't a wreck. For instance, while roughly half of the emerging-markets firms that we cover lack moats, this portfolio has trace exposure to such names. Because we assign greater value to firms that possess a moat than those that don't, we think this portfolio is more valuable than one chosen at random from our emerging-markets coverage list.

Nevertheless, we'd invest here only with a healthy margin of safety--at a 15% or greater discount to our fair value estimate--as many of these firms court a good deal of risk.

Address:	Nasdaq Global Fds, 9513 Key West Ave United States 888-627-3837
Web Address:	www.bldrsfunds.com
Inception:	11-13-02 *
Advisor:	Bank of New York

Management Fee:	0.10%		
Expense Projections:	3Yr:$97	5Yr:$169	10Yr:$381
Income Distrib:	Quarterly		
Exchange:	XNMS		

iShares MSCI EAFE EFA

Market Price	Mstar Category
$78.50	Foreign Large Blend

Morningstar Fair Value

Price/Fair Value Ratio	Coverage Rate %
1.00	6

Morningstar Rating	Return	Risk	Yield	NAV	Avg Daily Vol. (k)	52 wk High/Low
★★★★	Average	Below Avg	2.5%	$78.92	12,131	$86.10 - $70.90

Valuation

Because our equity analysts cover a relatively small number of this ETF's holdings, the price/fair value ratio above may not be a faithful representation of the portfolio's valuation attributes. Investors trying to gauge this ETF's attractiveness should consider the price/fair value ratio only in conjunction with other fundamental measures.

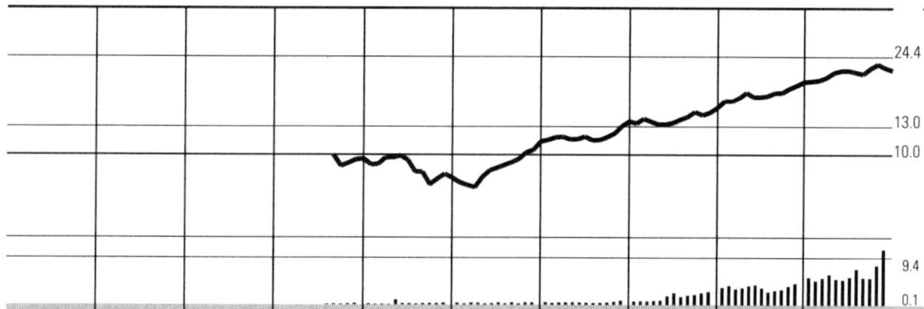

Growth of $10,000
— Investment Value of ETF
— Investment Value of Index MSCI EAFE

Trading Volume Millions

Methodology

This exchange-traded offering is a passive fund that simply attempts to match the performance of the MSCI EAFE Index. The benchmark is a free-float-adjusted market-capitalization index designed to track the developed world's stock markets outside Canada and the U.S. The index includes equities from Australia, Western Europe, Hong Kong, Japan, New Zealand, and Singapore. It uses a representative sampling method of tracking the index, so it doesn't own the thousands of securities in the benchmark. Rather, it invests in a portion of the bogy that is quantitatively constructed to match the index.

History

1998	1999	2000	2001	2002	2003	2004	2005	2006	2007	History
—	—	—	39.76	32.92	45.03	53.11	59.12	72.95	78.92	NAV $
—	—	—	39.77	33.00	45.59	53.42	59.43	73.22	78.50	Market Price $
—	—	—	12.14*	-15.61	38.45	19.75	13.39	26.00	10.97	NAV Return%
—	—	—	12.05*	-15.41	39.80	18.96	13.33	25.81	9.97	Market Price Return%
—	—	—	0.30	0.12	0.32	0.58	0.24	0.29	0.11	Avg Premium/Discount%
—	—	—	—	0.33	-0.14	-0.50	-0.15	-0.34	-0.20	NAV Rtrn% +/-MSCI EAFE
—	—	—	—	0.33	-0.14	-0.50	-0.15	-0.34	-0.20	NAV Rtrn% +/-MSCIEAFFNDT
—	—	—	—	67	75	50	75	15	94	NAV Return% Rank in Cat
—	—	—	—	1.58	1.59	1.78	2.09	2.59	2.74	Income Return %
—	—	—	—	-17.19	36.86	17.97	11.30	23.41	8.23	Capital Return %
—	—	—	0.08	0.63	0.52	0.80	1.11	1.53	2.00	Income $
—	—	—	0.00	0.00	0.00	0.00	0.00	0.00	0.00	Capital Gains $
—	—	—	—	0.35	0.35	0.35	0.36	0.35	0.34	Expense Ratio %
—	—	—	—	1.87	2.31	2.34	2.57	2.77	2.48	Income Ratio %
—	—	—	—	8	8	7	8	7	5	Turnover Rate %
—	—	—	—	2,192	5,350	13,639	22,739	37,076	51,895	Net Assets $mil

Performance 12-31-07

Historic Quarterly NAV Returns

	1st Qtr	2nd Qtr	3rd Qtr	4th Qtr	Total
2003	-8.18	19.16	8.10	17.06	38.45
2004	4.21	0.20	-0.32	15.05	19.75
2005	-0.18	-1.14	10.44	4.05	13.39
2006	9.29	0.73	3.86	10.21	26.00
2007	4.06	6.49	2.09	-1.91	10.97

Trailing	NAV Return%	Market Return%	NAV Rtrn% +/-MSCI EAFE	%Rank Cat.(NAV)
3 Mo	-1.91	-2.50	-0.16	66
6 Mo	0.14	-0.31	-0.25	85
1 Yr	10.97	9.97	-0.20	94
3 Yr Avg	16.60	16.18	-0.23	75
5 Yr Avg	21.32	21.13	-0.27	75
10 Yr Avg	—	—	—	—

Tax Analysis	Tax-Adj Return%	Tax-Cost Ratio
3 Yr (estimated)	15.73	0.75
5 Yr (estimated)	20.55	0.63
10 Yr (estimated)	—	—

Rating and Risk

Time Period	Morningstar Rtn vs Cat	Morningstar Risk vs Cat	Morningstar Risk-Adj Rating
3 Yr	Avg	-Avg	★★★
5 Yr	Avg	-Avg	★★★★
10 Yr	—	—	—

Other Measures	Standard Index S&P 500	Best Fit Index MSCI EAFE
Alpha	-0.2	-0.2
Beta	1.00	1.00
R-Squared	100	100
Standard Deviation	9.53	
Mean	16.60	
Sharpe Ratio	1.22	

Portfolio Analysis 12-31-07

Share change since 11-07 Total Stocks:812	Sector	Country	% Assets
⊕ BP	Energy	U.K.	1.65
⊕ HSBC Hldgs	Financial	U.K.	1.40
⊕ Vodafone Grp	Telecom	U.K.	1.39
⊕ TOTAL	Energy	France	1.27
⊕ Nestle	Goods	Switzerland	1.24
⊕ Royal Dutch Shell	Energy	U.K.	1.08
⊕ Toyota Motor	Goods	Japan	1.04
⊖ Nokia	Hardware	Finland	1.03
⊕ GlaxoSmithKline	Health	U.K.	1.01
⊕ Banco Santander	Financial	Spain	0.96
⊖ Telefonica	Telecom	Spain	0.96
⊕ Siemens	Hardware	Germany	0.95
⊕ E.ON	Utilities	Germany	0.93
⊕ Novartis	Health	Switzerland	0.91
⊕ Roche Holding Ltd	Health	Switzerland	0.86
⊖ BHP Billiton Ltd	Ind Mtrls	Australia	0.82
⊕ Royal Dutch Shell	Energy	U.K.	0.81
⊕ Rio Tinto	Ind Mtrls	U.K.	0.74
⊕ Allianz SE	Financial	Germany	0.69
⊕ Eni	Energy	Italy	0.69

Current Investment Style

Value Blnd Growth — Large Mid Small

Market Cap	%
Giant	56.4
Large	32.4
Mid	11.0
Small	0.2
Micro	0.0
Avg $mil: 38,073	

Value Measures		Rel Category
Price/Earnings	13.86	1.02
Price/Book	1.98	0.96
Price/Sales	1.07	1.02
Price/Cash Flow	8.18	1.06
Dividend Yield %	3.28	0.85

Growth Measures	%	Rel Category
Long-Term Erngs	11.75	0.99
Book Value	10.31	1.07
Sales	7.91	1.02
Cash Flow	10.34	1.10
Historical Erngs	19.89	1.09

Composition			
Cash	2.4	Bonds	0.0
Stocks	97.3	Other	0.3
Foreign (% of Stock)			100.0

Sector Weightings	% of Stocks	Rel MSCI EAFE	3 Year High	3 Year Low
Info	12.84	1.01		
Software	0.60	1.03	1	0
Hardware	4.00	0.99	4	4
Media	1.84	1.09	2	2
Telecom	6.40	1.01	7	5
Service	43.04	0.99		
Health	6.35	1.00	8	6
Consumer	4.95	1.00	5	5
Business	4.84	0.97	5	5
Financial	26.90	1.00	30	27
Mfg	44.12	1.00		
Goods	13.39	1.00	13	13
Ind Mtrls	17.37	1.00	18	13
Energy	8.04	1.03	9	7
Utilities	5.32	0.96	5	4

Regional Exposure	% Stock		
UK/W. Europe	70	N. America	0
Japan	20	Latn America	0
Asia X Japan	10	Other	0

Country Exposure	% Stock		
U.K.	22	Germany	9
Japan	20	Switzerland	7
France	10		

Morningstar's Take by Gregg Wolper 12-31-07

There are solid reasons for iShares MSCI EAFE Index Fund's incredible popularity--along with some reasons not to join the crowd.

This is one of the most successful exchange-traded funds ever, if gathering assets is the standard. In fact, with about $50 billion in its coffers, this fund was recently the second-largest ETF in existence--and it's nearly twice as big as number three. Only the original SPDR tops this one. Just four conventional mutual funds focusing on international stocks--three of them from American Funds--are larger.

It's understandable why this ETF has attracted attention. At the most basic level, buoyed by rising currencies as well as strong markets, international funds in general have posted mouth-watering returns, and thus have received more inflows than their domestic counterparts in the past few years. As an index-tracker following the industry's most well-established foreign-stock benchmark, this is an easy choice for institutions or others making broad asset-allocation decisions in favor of international stocks. And because it's an ETF and thus can be traded throughout the day, it's a more comfortable option than a conventional mutual fund for institutions who want the flexibility to change that allocation quickly. Finally, the fund has a low expense ratio and tracks its index quite closely.

So should you jump in? Not before considering other factors. For one thing, the EAFE Index may be well-known, but it excludes emerging markets and Canada. In addition, the EAFE-trackers from Fidelity and Vanguard cost less. It's also important to examine your reasons for being interested. If the huge gains piled up by the fund in recent years are what caught your eye, be aware those are unusually high. Don't expect the fund to necessarily produce 22.5% annualized returns for the next five years as it did over the five years ended Nov. 2, 2007.

In short, this fund can be a fine core choice, but so can many other ETF and fund options.

Address:	45 Fremont Street United States 800-474-2737
Web Address:	www.ishares.com
Inception:	08-14-01 *
Advisor:	Barclays Global Fund Advisers

Management Fee:	0.34%		
Expense Projections:	3Yr:$109	5Yr:$191	10Yr:$431
Income Distrib:	Annually		
Exchange:	NYSE		

iShares MSCI EAFE Growth EFG

Market Price	Mstar Category
$77.71	Foreign Large Growth

Morningstar Fair Value

Price/Fair Value Ratio	Coverage Rate %
1.00	3

Morningstar Rating	Return	Risk	Yield	NAV	Avg Daily Vol. (k)	52 wk High/Low
—	—	—	0.9%	$78.10	182	$83.11 - $66.20

Valuation

Because our equity analysts cover a relatively small number of this ETF's holdings, the price/fair value ratio above may not be a faithful representation of the portfolio's valuation attributes. Investors trying to gauge this ETF's attractiveness should consider the price/fair value ratio only in conjunction with other fundamental measures.

Growth of $10,000
— Investment Value of ETF
— Investment Value of Index MSCI EAFE

Trading Volume Millions

Methodology

This ETF tracks the MSCI EAFE Growth Index, a free-float-adjusted market-capitalization index designed to track developed stock markets outside Canada and the United States. The fund's portfolio is dominated by large-cap companies, and it is skewed toward growth stocks, which MSCI classifies using an eight-factor model. MSCI also employs buffer zones to limit migration between growth and value camps. The fund does not hedge its foreign-currency exposure.

1998	1999	2000	2001	2002	2003	2004	2005	2006	2007	History
—	—	—	—	—	—	—	56.31	67.94	78.10	NAV $
—	—	—	—	—	—	—	56.60	68.23	77.71	Market Price $
—	—	—	—	—	—	—	20.62*	21.88	16.11	NAV Return%
—	—	—	—	—	—	—	20.37*	21.78	15.03	Market Price Return%
—	—	—	—	—	—	—	0.36	0.40	0.26	Avg Premium/Discount%
—	—	—	—	—	—	—	—	-4.46	4.94	NAV Rtrn% +/-MSCI EAFE
—	—	—	—	—	—	—	—	-0.45	-0.34	NAV Rtrn% +/-MSCI EAFE
—	—	—	—	—	—	—	—	1	100	NAV Return% Rank in Ca
—	—	—	—	—	—	—	—	1.22	1.07	Income Return %
—	—	—	—	—	—	—	—	20.66	15.04	Capital Return %
—	—	—	—	—	—	—	0.23	0.69	0.73	Income $
—	—	—	—	—	—	—	0.00	0.00	0.02	Capital Gains $
—	—	—	—	—	—	—	—	0.40	0.40	Expense Ratio %
—	—	—	—	—	—	—	—	2.25	1.93	Income Ratio %
—	—	—	—	—	—	—	—	35	28	Turnover Rate %
—	—	—	—	—	—	—	45	408	1,156	Net Assets $mil

Performance 12-31-07

Historic Quarterly NAV Returns

	1st Qtr	2nd Qtr	3rd Qtr	4th Qtr	Total
2003	—	—	—	—	—
2004	—	—	—	—	—
2005	—	—	—	4.24	—*
2006	9.00	0.21	2.16	9.22	21.88
2007	4.78	6.70	4.29	-0.42	16.11

Trailing	NAV Return%	Market Return%	NAV Rtrn% +/-MSCI EAFE	%Rank Cat.(NAV)
3 Mo	-0.42	-1.15	1.33	50
6 Mo	3.85	3.41	3.46	100
1 Yr	16.11	15.03	4.94	100
3 Yr Avg	—	—	—	—
5 Yr Avg	—	—	—	—
10 Yr Avg	—	—	—	—

Tax Analysis	Tax-Adj Return%	Tax-Cost Ratio
3 Yr (estimated)	—	—
5 Yr (estimated)	—	—
10 Yr (estimated)	—	—

Rating and Risk

Time Period	Morningstar Rtn vs Cat	Morningstar Risk vs Cat	Morningstar Risk-Adj Rating
3 Yr	—	—	—
5 Yr	—	—	—
10 Yr	—	—	—

Other Measures	Standard Index S&P 500	Best Fit Index
Alpha	—	—
Beta	—	—
R-Squared	—	—
Standard Deviation	—	
Mean	—	
Sharpe Ratio	—	

Portfolio Analysis 12-31-07

Share change since 11-07 Total Stocks:545	Sector	Country	% Assets
☼ Nestle	Goods	Switzerland	2.56
⊕ Nokia	Hardware	Finland	2.09
⊕ GlaxoSmithKline	Health	U.K.	2.04
⊕ Telefonica	Telecom	Spain	1.97
⊕ Siemens	Hardware	Germany	1.88
☼ E.ON	Utilities	Germany	1.85
⊕ Novartis	Health	Switzerland	1.75
⊕ Roche Holding Ltd	Health	Switzerland	1.71
⊕ BHP Billiton Ltd	Ind Mtrls	Australia	1.67
⊕ Rio Tinto	Ind Mtrls	U.K.	1.49
⊕ Anglo American	Ind Mtrls	U.K.	1.18
⊕ BG Grp	Energy	U.K.	1.11
⊕ Tesco	Consumer	U.K.	1.04
⊕ BHP Billiton	Ind Mtrls	U.K.	1.03
⊕ ArcelorMittal	Ind Mtrls	Netherlands	1.01
⊕ BASF	Ind Mtrls	Germany	1.01
⊕ Bayer	Ind Mtrls	Germany	0.94
⊕ AstraZeneca	Health	U.K.	0.92
⊕ ABB Ltd	Ind Mtrls	Switzerland	0.89
⊕ British American Tobacco	Goods	U.K.	0.83

Current Investment Style

Value Blnd Growth — Large Mid Small

Market Cap	%
Giant	50.5
Large	36.2
Mid	13.0
Small	0.2
Micro	0.0
Avg $mil: 32,512	

Value Measures		Rel Category
Price/Earnings	16.89	1.29
Price/Book	2.81	1.39
Price/Sales	1.31	1.18
Price/Cash Flow	9.72	1.44
Dividend Yield %	2.37	0.71

Growth Measures	%	Rel Category
Long-Term Erngs	14.42	1.16
Book Value	9.82	0.89
Sales	7.65	0.50
Cash Flow	12.37	0.31
Historical Erngs	25.31	0.84

Composition

Cash	1.1	Bonds	0.0
Stocks	98.6	Other	0.3
Foreign (% of Stock)			100.0

Sector Weightings	% of Stocks	Rel MSCI EAFE	3 Year High	3 Year Low
Info	13.56	1.07		
Software	1.10	1.90	1	1
Hardware	7.23	1.79	7	5
Media	1.47	0.87	4	1
Telecom	3.76	0.59	11	3
Service	35.27	0.81		
Health	9.59	1.51	15	9
Consumer	7.24	1.46	8	6
Business	6.49	1.30	7	6
Financial	11.95	0.44	21	12
Mfg	51.18	1.16		
Goods	17.36	1.30	17	12
Ind Mtrls	26.23	1.51	26	15
Energy	2.49	0.32	8	2
Utilities	5.10	0.92	5	1

Regional Exposure	% Stock		
UK/W. Europe	71	N. America	0
Japan	19	Latn America	0
Asia X Japan	10	Other	0

Country Exposure	% Stock		
U.K.	21	Switzerland	10
Japan	19	France	7
Germany	11		

Morningstar's Take by Gregg Wolper 12-31-07

Investors building a diversified international portfolio could find iShares MSCI EAFE Growth Index Fund useful.

It's easy to dismiss the many exchange-traded vehicles that have come onto the market in the past few years targeting narrower and narrower segments of the stock and bond markets. The iShares family already had a fund that tracks the MSCI EAFE Index, the well-known foreign benchmark that focuses almost exclusively on big stocks in developed markets outside North America, in 2005. But it went a step further and created this and another ETF that allow investors to buy just the growth or value stocks in that index.

These two funds could come in handy, though. Of course, there's no need to rush out to buy them, especially if you already have diversified exposure to international stocks. But some of the most popular and successful international funds lean toward the value side; after the growth debacle of the early 2000s many investors had good reason to lean toward value. Investors whose international portfolios tilt heavily toward value could use this fund to ensure they won't suffer through years in the wilderness when growth takes the lead. This year provides an example of what can happen in that regard. This ETF is up 20.1% in market-price terms for the year to date through Nov. 2, 2007, while its value counterpart, iShares MSCI EAFE Value Index, has gained just 10.5%.

Another way this ETF stands out from less-worthwhile slice-and-dice funds is that it's not all that narrow. Instead of having just the most aggressive growth stocks, it is more moderate; interestingly, resource giants BHP Billiton and Rio Tinto are both among its top-10 holdings.

That said, this fund has low exposure to energy and financials compared with the broad EAFE Index. And its expense ratio is higher than many index rivals. Finally, don't expect foreign funds' huge gains of recent years to repeat automatically. All told, though, this fund has its merits.

Address:	45 Fremont Street United States 800-474-2737
Web Address:	www.ishares.com
Inception:	08-01-05*
Advisor:	Barclays Global Fund Advisers

Management Fee:	0.40%		
Expense Projections:	3Yr:$128	5Yr:$224	10Yr:$505
Income Distrib:	Annually		
Exchange:	NYSE		

iShares MSCI EAFE Value EFV

Market Price	Mstar Category
$71.95	Foreign Large Value

Morningstar Fair Value

Price/Fair Value Ratio	Coverage Rate %
0.99	8

Morningstar Rating	Return	Risk	Yield	NAV	Avg Daily Vol. (k)	52 wk High/Low
—	—	—	4.4%	$72.42	124	$81.64 - $69.64

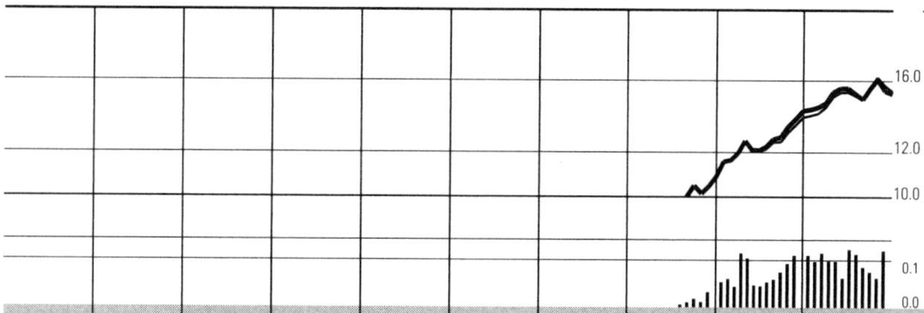

Valuation

Because our equity analysts cover a relatively small number of this ETF's holdings, the price/fair value ratio above may not be a faithful representation of the portfolio's valuation attributes. Investors trying to gauge this ETF's attractiveness should consider the price/fair value ratio only in conjunction with other fundamental measures.

Methodology

This exchange-traded fund tracks the MSCI EAFE Value Index, a free-float-adjusted market-capitalization index designed to track developed stock markets outside of Canada and the United States. The fund's portfolio is dominated by large-cap companies. This fund is skewed toward value stocks, which MSCI classifies using an eight-factor model. MSCI also employs buffer zones to limit migration between growth and value camps. The fund does not hedge its foreign-currency exposure.

History

1998	1999	2000	2001	2002	2003	2004	2005	2006	2007	History
—	—	—	—	—	—	—	56.00	71.58	72.42	NAV $
—	—	—	—	—	—	—	56.32	72.20	71.95	Market Price $
—	—	—	—	—	—	—	19.46*	29.96	7.17	NAV Return%
—	—	—	—	—	—	—	19.14*	30.34	5.56	Market Price Return%
—	—	—	—	—	—	—	0.48	0.47	0.12	Avg Premium/Discount%
—	—	—	—	—	—	—	—	3.62	-4.00	NAV Rtrn% +/-MSCI EAFE
—	—	—	—	—	—	—	—	-0.42	1.21	NAV Rtrn% +/-MSCI EAFE Free Val ND
—	—	—	—	—	—	—	—	1	100	NAV Return% Rank in Cat
—	—	—	—	—	—	—	—	2.13	4.54	Income Return %
—	—	—	—	—	—	—	—	27.83	2.63	Capital Return %
—	—	—	—	—	—	—	0.25	1.19	3.25	Income $
—	—	—	—	—	—	—	0.00	0.00	0.92	Capital Gains $
—	—	—	—	—	—	—	—	0.40	0.40	Expense Ratio %
—	—	—	—	—	—	—	—	4.34	2.95	Income Ratio %
—	—	—	—	—	—	—	—	31	21	Turnover Rate %
—	—	—	—	—	—	—	90	687	1,188	Net Assets $mil

Performance 12-31-07

Historic Quarterly NAV Returns

	1st Qtr	2nd Qtr	3rd Qtr	4th Qtr	Total
2003	—	—	—	—	—
2004	—	—	—	—	—
2005	—	—	—	3.69	—*
2006	9.70	1.14	5.42	11.11	29.96
2007	3.13	6.24	-0.10	-2.09	7.17

Trailing	NAV Return%	Market Return%	NAV Rtrn% +/-MSCI EAFE	%Rank Cat.(NAV)
3 Mo	-2.09	-2.41	-0.34	50
6 Mo	-2.19	-2.72	-2.58	100
1 Yr	7.17	5.56	-4.00	100
3 Yr Avg	—	—	—	—
5 Yr Avg	—	—	—	—
10 Yr Avg	—	—	—	—

Tax Analysis	Tax-Adj Return%	Tax-Cost Ratio
3 Yr (estimated)	—	—
5 Yr (estimated)	—	—
10 Yr (estimated)	—	—

Rating and Risk

Time Period	Morningstar Rtn vs Cat	Morningstar Risk vs Cat	Morningstar Risk-Adj Rating
3 Yr	—	—	—
5 Yr	—	—	—
10 Yr	—	—	—

Other Measures	Standard Index S&P 500	Best Fit Index
Alpha	—	—
Beta	—	—
R-Squared	—	—
Standard Deviation	—	
Mean	—	
Sharpe Ratio	—	

Portfolio Analysis 12-31-07

Share change since 11-07 Total Stocks:537	Sector	Country	% Assets
⊖ BP	Energy	U.K.	3.37
⊖ Vodafone Grp	Telecom	U.K.	2.80
⊖ HSBC Hldgs	Financial	U.K.	2.80
⊖ TOTAL	Energy	France	2.46
⊖ Royal Dutch Shell	Energy	U.K.	2.12
⊖ Toyota Motor	Goods	Japan	2.06
⊖ Banco Santander	Financial	Spain	2.00
⊖ Royal Dutch Shell	Energy	U.K.	1.58
⊖ Allianz SE	Financial	Germany	1.35
⊖ Eni	Energy	Italy	1.33
⊕ sanofi-aventis	Health	France	1.31
⊖ BNP Paribas	Financial	France	1.31
⊖ Daimler	Goods	Germany	1.28
⊕ UBS	Financial	Switzerland	1.27
⊖ Royal Bank of Scotland G	Financial	U.K.	1.20
⊕ Banco Bilbao Vizcaya Arg	Financial	Spain	1.17
⊖ Mitsubishi UFJ Financial	Financial	Japan	1.13
⊖ UniCredito Italiano Grp	Financial	Italy	1.12
⊖ ING Groep	Financial	Netherlands	1.05
⊖ Commonwealth Bank of Aus	Financial	Australia	0.95

Current Investment Style

Value Blnd Growth / Large Mid Small

Market Cap	%
Giant	63.0
Large	27.1
Mid	9.5
Small	0.3
Micro	0.1
Avg $mil: 44,242	

Value Measures		Rel Category
Price/Earnings	11.68	0.88
Price/Book	1.52	0.78
Price/Sales	0.90	0.62
Price/Cash Flow	6.72	0.82
Dividend Yield %	4.29	1.35

Growth Measures	%	Rel Category
Long-Term Erngs	9.84	0.98
Book Value	9.27	0.79
Sales	8.27	0.80
Cash Flow	4.07	0.35
Historical Erngs	16.76	0.94

Composition

Cash	4.5	Bonds	0.0
Stocks	95.2	Other	0.3
Foreign (% of Stock)			100.0

Sector Weightings	% of Stocks	Rel MSCI EAFE	3 Year High	3 Year Low
Info	11.89	0.94		
Software	0.02	0.03	0	0
Hardware	0.83	0.20	3	1
Media	2.05	1.21	2	1
Telecom	8.99	1.42	9	3
Service	51.26	1.18		
Health	3.07	0.48	4	2
Consumer	2.58	0.52	4	2
Business	3.49	0.70	4	3
Financial	42.12	1.56	43	39
Mfg	36.85	0.84		
Goods	9.25	0.69	13	9
Ind Mtrls	8.25	0.48	13	8
Energy	13.55	1.74	14	7
Utilities	5.80	1.05	9	5

Regional Exposure	% Stock		
UK/W. Europe	69	N. America	0
Japan	20	Latn America	0
Asia X Japan	10	Other	1

Country Exposure	% Stock		
U.K.	23	Germany	8
Japan	20	Australia	7
France	13		

Morningstar's Take by Gregg Wolper 12-31-07

Although it has its quirks, iShares MSCI EAFE Value Index can be useful in some situations.

It's easy to dismiss the many exchange-traded vehicles created in the past few years that target specific segments of the stock and bond markets. The iShares family already had a fund that tracks the MSCI EAFE Index, the well-known foreign benchmark that focuses almost exclusively on big stocks in developed markets outside North America, in 2005. But it went a step further and created this and another ETF that allow investors to buy just the value or growth stocks in that index.

There's no need to rush to buy these funds, especially if you already have diversified exposure to foreign stocks. But if your international holdings lean heavily toward either the growth or value realm, buying a bit of this fund or its counterpart can provide quick and easy (and cheap) balance. Sometimes that comes in handy: By having exposure to both growth and value, you won't miss out on a huge rally geared largely toward one side or the other. Conversely, you might want to buy the area that's been out of favor. This year provides an example of how the two sides of the spectrum can differ: This ETF is up 10.3% in market-price terms for the year to date through Nov. 6, 2007, but its growth counterpart, iShares MSCI EAFE Growth Index, has gained 20.6%.

Keep in mind, though, that this ETF definitely isn't as diversified as a straight EAFE fund would be. Most notably, at the end of September 2007 it had nearly 41% of its assets in financials (that's a big reason it has been lagging its growth sibling, and the EAFE Index, this year). It also has minimal weightings in health care and information technology. Another factor to note: This ETF's cost is higher than many index rivals'.

With those caveats in mind, this fund could play a role for certain investors, provided they don't expect the big gains foreign funds have amassed in recent years to keep up every year.

Address:	45 Fremont Street United States 800-474-2737
Web Address:	www.ishares.com
Inception:	08-01-05*
Advisor:	Barclays Global Fund Advisers

Management Fee:	0.40%		
Expense Projections:	3Yr:$128	5Yr:$224	10Yr:$505
Income Distrib:	Annually		
Exchange:	NYSE		

iShares MSCI Emerg Mkts EEM

Market Price	Mstar Category
$150.30	Diversified Emerging Mk

Morningstar Rating	Return	Risk	Yield	NAV	Avg Daily Vol. (k)	52 wk High/Low
★★★	Average	Average	1.3%	$151.58	17,804	$167.19 - $105.29

Morningstar Fair Value

Price/Fair Value Ratio	Coverage Rate %
1.03	34

Valuation

Because our equity analysts cover a relatively small number of this ETF's holdings, the price/fair value ratio above may not be a faithful representation of the portfolio's valuation attributes. Investors trying to gauge this ETF's attractiveness should consider the price/fair value ratio only in conjunction with other fundamental measures.

Methodology

This fund tracks the MSCI Emerging Markets Index, which spans more than 20 developing countries, including China, Korea, Brazil, Russia, South Africa, India, and Mexico (which are home to the lion's share of the fund's holdings). The index aims to capture 85% of the total market cap of stocks in those countries. Stocks in the index are weighted by free-float adjusted market capitalization. The fund doesn't own all of the 800-plus stocks in the index; rather, it uses quantitative tools to build a representative sample.

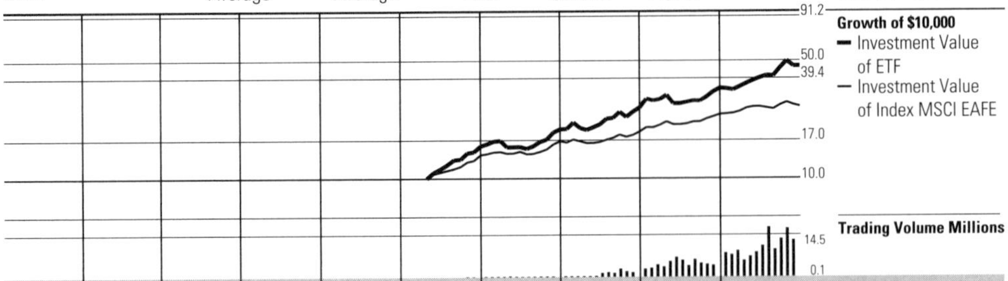

History

1998	1999	2000	2001	2002	2003	2004	2005	2006	2007	History
—	—	—	—	—	53.95	66.91	88.52	114.09	151.58	NAV $
—	—	—	—	—	54.64	67.28	88.25	114.38	150.30	Market Price $
—	—	—	—	—	38.95*	25.53	33.78	30.71	34.55	NAV Return%
—	—	—	—	—	39.16*	24.64	32.62	31.44	33.08	Market Price Return%
—	—	—	—	—	0.53	0.25	0.07	0.10	-0.14	Avg Premium/Discount%
—	—	—	—	—	—	5.28	20.24	4.37	23.38	NAV Rtrn% +/-MSCI EAFE
—	—	—	—	—	—	-0.02	-0.22	-1.46	-4.84	NAV Rtrn% +/-MSCI Emg
—	—	—	—	—	—	50	50	34	75	NAV Return% Rank in Cat
—	—	—	—	—	—	1.49	1.48	1.78	1.71	Income Return %
—	—	—	—	—	—	24.04	32.30	28.93	32.84	Capital Return %
—	—	—	—	—	0.27	0.80	0.99	1.57	1.95	Income $
—	—	—	—	—	0.00	0.00	0.00	0.00	0.00	Capital Gains $
—	—	—	—	—	0.78	0.76	0.77	0.77	0.74	Expense Ratio %
—	—	—	—	—	1.58	2.10	2.40	1.77	1.63	Income Ratio %
—	—	—	—	—	10	8	9	12	5	Turnover Rate %
—	—	—	—	—	1,076	3,894	10,264	15,694	28,854	Net Assets $mil

Performance 12-31-07

Historic Quarterly NAV Returns

	1st Qtr	2nd Qtr	3rd Qtr	4th Qtr	Total
2003	—	—	14.19	19.41	—*
2004	7.67	-7.92	6.87	18.48	25.53
2005	1.73	4.96	18.30	5.91	33.78
2006	12.19	-5.77	3.85	19.06	30.71
2007	2.02	12.62	13.96	2.77	34.55

Trailing	NAV Return%	Market Return%	NAV Rtrn% +/-MSCI EAFE	%Rank Cat.(NAV)
3 Mo	2.77	1.85	4.52	89
6 Mo	17.11	15.62	16.72	75
1 Yr	34.55	33.08	23.38	75
3 Yr Avg	33.00	32.38	16.17	50
5 Yr Avg	—	—	—	—
10 Yr Avg	—	—	—	—

Tax Analysis	Tax-Adj Return%	Tax-Cost Ratio
3 Yr (estimated)	32.42	0.44
5 Yr (estimated)	—	—
10 Yr (estimated)	—	—

Rating and Risk

Time Period	Morningstar Rtn vs Cat	Morningstar Risk vs Cat	Morningstar Risk-Adj Rating
3 Yr	Avg	Avg	★★★
5 Yr	—	—	—
10 Yr	—	—	—

Other Measures	Standard Index S&P 500	Best Fit Index MSCI Emg Mkt
Alpha	6.0	-1.7
Beta	1.72	1.00
R-Squared	77	97
Standard Deviation	18.70	
Mean	33.00	
Sharpe Ratio	1.40	

Portfolio Analysis 12-31-07

Share change since 11-07 Total Stocks:343	Sector	Country	% Assets
⊕ Gazprom OAO (EDR)	Energy	U.K.	3.70
⊕ Samsung Electnc GDR 144A	Goods	Korea	2.83
⊕ Posco ADR	Ind Mtrls	Korea	2.78
⊕ China Mobile Ltd	Telecom	China	2.66
⊕ Petroleo Brasileiro S.A.	Energy	Brazil	2.46
⊕ Taiwan Semiconductor Man	Hardware	Taiwan	2.30
⊕ Brazilian Petroleum Corp	Energy	Brazil	2.27
☼ Chunghwa Telecom	Telecom	China	1.78
⊖ Companhia Vale do Rio Do	Ind Mtrls	Brazil	1.74
⊕ Kookmin Bank ADR	Financial	Korea	1.73
⊕ Vale Overseas Limited AD	Ind Mtrls	Brazil	1.51
⊕ HDFC Bank, Ltd. ADR	Financial	India	1.44
⊕ America Movil S.A.B de C	Telecom	Mexico	1.43
⊖ Bank Bradesco ADR	Financial	Brazil	1.41
⊕ Itau Bank Financial Hold	Financial	Brazil	1.40
⊕ Reliance Inds	Ind Mtrls	India	1.38
⊕ Siliconware Precision In	Hardware	Taiwan	1.37
⊕ CEZ	Utilities	Czech Republic	1.37
⊕ Lukoil Company ADR	Energy	Russia	1.32
⊕ Korea Electric Power Cor	Utilities	Korea	1.19

Current Investment Style

Value Blnd Growth — Large / Mid / Small (style box: Large Blend)

Market Cap	%
Giant	39.8
Large	42.9
Mid	15.6
Small	1.6
Micro	0.0
Avg $mil: 23,422	

Value Measures		Rel Category
Price/Earnings	15.82	1.06
Price/Book	3.12	1.11
Price/Sales	1.78	1.07
Price/Cash Flow	10.64	1.11
Dividend Yield %	2.76	0.73

Growth Measures	%	Rel Category
Long-Term Erngs	18.01	1.00
Book Value	12.79	0.74
Sales	15.36	0.76
Cash Flow	9.82	0.62
Historical Erngs	20.47	0.86

Composition

Cash	1.4	Bonds	0.0
Stocks	98.5	Other	0.1
Foreign (% of Stock)			99.8

Sector Weightings	% of Stocks	Rel MSCI EAFE	3 Year High	3 Year Low
Info	23.67	1.87		
Software	2.21	3.81	3	2
Hardware	7.28	1.80	12	7
Media	0.95	0.56	1	1
Telecom	13.23	2.08	15	10
Service	31.05	0.72		
Health	1.82	0.29	3	2
Consumer	3.37	0.68	4	3
Business	4.91	0.98	5	2
Financial	20.95	0.78	22	19
Mfg	45.28	1.03		
Goods	5.93	0.44	14	6
Ind Mtrls	18.88	1.09	21	14
Energy	16.20	2.08	17	12
Utilities	4.27	0.77	5	3

Regional Exposure (% Stock)

UK/W. Europe	5	N. America	0
Japan	0	Latn America	21
Asia X Japan	52	Other	22

Country Exposure (% Stock)

China	18	South Africa	8
Brazil	13	Taiwan	7
South Korea	13		

Morningstar's Take by Gregg Wolper 12-31-07

The benefits of iShares MSCI Emerging Markets Index Fund are clear, and so are its shortcomings.

This has become the third-biggest exchange-traded fund by offering a quick and straightforward way to gain access to the world's hottest markets in recent years. It's likely that institutions have provided the bulk of this fund's $26 billion asset base (although the growth in asset size also owes to share appreciation). It provides an ideal option for asset allocators who simply want a specific amount of exposure to the emerging-markets rally they hope will continue and who aren't concerned about beating the index. With emerging markets seemingly unstoppable, it's understandable that an individual might be attracted to this ETF for similar reasons.

If that's you, just be careful. The most obvious reason is the length and extreme strength of the current emerging-markets rally. Despite some sharp, quick downturns, there has been no sustained decline for many years; beginning in 2003, this index has provided gains of more than 25% every calendar year. For the 12 months through Nov. 2, 2007, this ETF's market price gains are near 60%. The second reason to be cautious is that, as China's stock market has soared in the past couple of years, its percentage of this market-cap-weighted index fund has risen accordingly. That stake stood at 15.5% of assets as of Sept. 30, 2007, more than any other country. The higher that market climbs, the more shareholders will have tied up in it--an uncomfortable position should it go into reverse.

There aren't that many attractive, reasonably priced diversified emerging-markets funds, so index offerings do have their appeal. Just don't expect the rally to keep up its current pace indefinitely--and remember that other emerging-markets options, such as Vanguard Emerging Markets Stock ETF or actively managed choices, can be cheaper or more attractive in other ways.

Address:	45 Fremont Street United States 800-474-2737
Web Address:	www.ishares.com
Inception:	04-07-03 *
Advisor:	Barclays Global Fund Advisers

Management Fee:	0.75%		
Expense Projections:	3Yr:$240	5Yr:$417	10Yr:$930
Income Distrib:	Annually		
Exchange:	NYSE		

PowerShares Intl Div Ach PID

Market Price	Mstar Category
$20.58	Foreign Large Value

Morningstar Rating	Return	Risk	Yield	NAV	Avg Daily Vol. (k)	52 wk High/Low
—	—	—	2.2%	$21.22	184	$22.52 - $17.90

Morningstar Fair Value

Price/Fair Value Ratio	Coverage Rate %
0.92	97

Valuation

This fund hasn't been a screaming bargain in the past. Since its late-2005 launch, it has mostly hovered near our fair value estimate. However, it has recently been trading at an 8% discount to fair value, which puts it right on the cusp of buy territory.

Methodology

This fund tracks the International Dividend Achievers Index, which compiles 60-plus ADRs and foreign stocks trading on major U.S. exchanges that have increased their annual regular dividends for at least the past five years. The majority of the holdings are in developed markets--the United Kingdom, continental Europe, and Canada in particular--though it also owns a clutch of emerging-markets names. Like other yield-focused funds, it has a big stake in financial services stocks and treads lightly in tech. Large-cap stocks rule the roost here, accounting for more than three-quarters of assets.

Growth of $10,000
— Investment Value of ETF
— Investment Value of Index MSCI EAFE

Trading Volume Millions

History

1998	1999	2000	2001	2002	2003	2004	2005	2006	2007	History
—	—	—	—	—	—	—	15.38	18.84	21.22	NAV $
—	—	—	—	—	—	—	15.38	18.96	20.58	Market Price $
—	—	—	—	—	—	—	19.44*	26.06	15.29	NAV Return%
—	—	—	—	—	—	—	17.87*	26.90	11.09	Market Price Return%
—	—	—	—	—	—	—	0.08	0.26	0.06	Avg Premium/Discount%
—	—	—	—	—	—	—	—	-0.28	4.12	NAV Rtrn% +/-MSCI EAFE
—	—	—	—	—	—	—	—	0.35	2.85	NAV Rtrn% +/-MSCI Wd xUS
—	—	—	—	—	—	—	—	34	83	NAV Return% Rank in Cat
—	—	—	—	—	—	—	—	3.26	2.51	Income Return %
—	—	—	—	—	—	—	—	22.80	12.78	Capital Return %
—	—	—	—	—	—	—	0.09	0.50	0.47	Income $
—	—	—	—	—	—	—	0.00	0.00	0.00	Capital Gains $
—	—	—	—	—	—	—	—	0.62	0.60	Expense Ratio %
—	—	—	—	—	—	—	—	3.06	2.98	Income Ratio %
—	—	—	—	—	—	—	—	8	22	Turnover Rate %
—	—	—	—	—	—	—	27	418	745	Net Assets $mil

Performance 12-31-07

Historic Quarterly NAV Returns

	1st Qtr	2nd Qtr	3rd Qtr	4th Qtr	Total
2003	—	—	—	—	—
2004	—	—	—	—	—
2005	—	—	—	1.63	—*
2006	5.78	1.00	6.48	10.81	26.06
2007	2.80	8.37	3.18	0.30	15.29

Trailing	NAV Return%	Market Return%	NAV Rtrn% +/-MSCI EAFE	%Rank Cat.(NAV)
3 Mo	0.30	-2.82	2.05	1
6 Mo	3.48	0.21	3.09	67
1 Yr	15.29	11.09	4.12	83
3 Yr Avg	—	—	—	—
5 Yr Avg	—	—	—	—
10 Yr Avg	—	—	—	—

Tax Analysis	Tax-Adj Return%	Tax-Cost Ratio
3 Yr (estimated)	—	—
5 Yr (estimated)	—	—
10 Yr (estimated)	—	—

Rating and Risk

Time Period	Morningstar Rtn vs Cat	Morningstar Risk vs Cat	Morningstar Risk-Adj Rating
3 Yr	—	—	—
5 Yr	—	—	—
10 Yr	—	—	—

Other Measures	Standard Index S&P 500	Best Fit Index
Alpha	—	—
Beta	—	—
R-Squared	—	—
Standard Deviation	—	
Mean	—	
Sharpe Ratio	—	

Portfolio Analysis 11-30-07

Share change since 10-07 Total Stocks:66

	Sector	Country	% Assets
⊕ Nam Tai Electronics Inc.	Hardware	Hong Kong	4.78
⊖ Tomkins PLC ADR	Ind Mtrls	U.K.	3.48
⊖ Barclays PLC ADR	Financial	U.K.	3.41
⊖ HSBC Holdings PLC ADR	Financial	U.K.	2.77
⊖ Allied Irish Banks ADR	Financial	Ireland	2.68
⊖ Bank of Montreal	Financial	Canada	2.61
⊖ Volvo Corporation ADR	Ind Mtrls	Sweden	2.52
⊕ Westpac Banking Corporat	Financial	Australia	2.52
⊖ Pearson plc ADR	Media	U.K.	2.49
⊖ National Grid PLC ADR	Utilities	U.K.	2.44
⊖ Bank Bilbao Vizcaya Arge	Financial	Spain	2.42
⊕ Vodafone Group PLC ADR	Telecom	U.K.	2.40
⊖ TransCanada Corporation	Energy	Canada	2.38
⊖ British American Tobacco	Goods	U.K.	2.31
⊖ BP PLC ADR	Energy	U.K.	2.28
⊖ Unilever N.V. (ADR)	Goods	Netherlands	2.21
⊖ Unilever PLC ADR	Goods	U.K.	2.15
⊖ Banco Santander SA ADR	Financial	Spain	2.14
⊖ Bank of Nova Scotia	Financial	Canada	2.13
⊖ Diageo PLC ADR	Goods	U.K.	2.03

Current Investment Style

Value Blnd Growth / Large Mid Small

Market Cap	%
Giant	47.1
Large	38.1
Mid	8.7
Small	0.7
Micro	5.3
Avg $mil: 26,167	

Value Measures		Rel Category
Price/Earnings	11.87	0.90
Price/Book	1.90	0.98
Price/Sales	1.77	1.21
Price/Cash Flow	10.30	1.25
Dividend Yield %	2.83	0.89

Growth Measures	%	Rel Category
Long-Term Erngs	10.51	1.05
Book Value	12.35	1.05
Sales	9.64	0.93
Cash Flow	12.20	1.04
Historical Erngs	15.70	0.88

Composition

Cash	0.0	Bonds	0.0
Stocks	100.0	Other	0.0
Foreign (% of Stock)			93.8

Sector Weightings	% of Stocks	Rel MSCI EAFE	3 Year High	3 Year Low
Info	18.97	1.50		
Software	1.40	2.41	2	1
Hardware	5.50	1.36	7	2
Media	7.25	4.29	7	2
Telecom	4.82	0.76	8	0
Service	43.57	1.01		
Health	3.04	0.48	6	2
Consumer	0.00	0.00	0	0
Business	1.92	0.38	3	1
Financial	38.61	1.43	47	37
Mfg	37.47	0.85		
Goods	14.80	1.11	15	7
Ind Mtrls	8.79	0.51	12	5
Energy	9.31	1.20	14	7
Utilities	4.57	0.82	12	4

Regional Exposure % Stock

UK/W. Europe	52	N. America	28
Japan	5	Latn America	2
Asia X Japan	10	Other	3

Country Exposure % Stock

U.K.	33	Japan	5
Canada	22	Hong Kong	5
United States	6		

Morningstar's Take by Emiko Kurotsu 12-31-07

PowerShares International Dividend Achievers is one of the highest-quality foreign-stock portfolios we cover.

This fund tracks the International Dividend Achievers Index, a small group of U.S.-listed foreign stocks that have increased their dividends for the past five years. Though most firms hail from continental Europe or Canada, the fund also owns a clutch of emerging-markets names. Similarly, while large caps dominate here, the portfolio has a stake in a number of smaller firms. Thus, its holdings range from mega-bank Barclays to tiny Cayman Islands water-utility Consolidated Water Company.

That said, the fund's quality is above average, with only a few of its holdings touting some competitive advantage, or economic moat. More than half of the fund's top-quality names, denoted by a wide-moat rating, are large European and Canadian banks such as HSBC, Allied Irish, and Bank of Montreal, many of whom boast coveted attributes like hard-to-replicate scale or lustrous brands. Nearly all of the other firms here have narrow moats, indicating that they boast an edge over rivals, albeit one that's less durable or valuable than that of a more dominant business. For instance, NTT DoCoMo is Japan's largest wireless provider, yet remains under pressure from rival carriers. On balance, though, we place more value on this fund's holdings than on a portfolio skewed toward lower-quality names.

The portfolio's quality also carries over into its risk profile. Its narrow-moat holdings typically court at least moderate business risk, reflecting the uncertainty that stems from their less-entrenched competitive positions, but high-risk names are scarce. Coupled with the fund's diversification across stocks, industries, and regions and its modest stake in oft-turbulent emerging markets, that temperate risk profile has tamped volatility. Thus, we'd happily scoop up shares here when they're trading at a 9% or greater discount to our fair value estimate.

Address:	301 West Roosevelt Road United States 800-843-2639
Web Address:	www.powershares.com
Inception:	09-15-05*
Advisor:	PowerShares Capital Management LLC

Management Fee:	0.40%		
Expense Projections:	3Yr:$200	5Yr:$349	10Yr:$784
Income Distrib:	Quarterly		
Exchange:	AMEX		

SPDR DJ Global Titans DGT

Market Price	Mstar Category
$78.85	World Stock

Morningstar Fair Value

Price/Fair Value Ratio	Coverage Rate %
0.89	92

Valuation

This fund looks attractive right now. It's trading at an 11% discount to our fair value estimate, though we'd require just a 9% or more margin of safety given the portfolio's high quality and moderate risk.

Methodology

This fund tracks the Dow Jones Global Titans Index, which consists of 50 of the world's biggest companies based on market cap, assets, book value, revenue, and profits. To be included in the index, each firm must derive at least a portion of its revenue from outside of its home country. The index is composed of many U.S.-domiciled companies, with about 60% of assets tucked there, 20% in continental Europe, and 16% in the U.K. Financials dominate the portfolio, taking up nearly a fourth of the fund, while energy, health-care, and consumer-goods giants are also well represented.

Morningstar Rating	Return	Risk	Yield	NAV	Avg Daily Vol. (k)	52 wk High/Low
★	Low	Low	2.2%	$78.84	12	$82.77 - $72.46

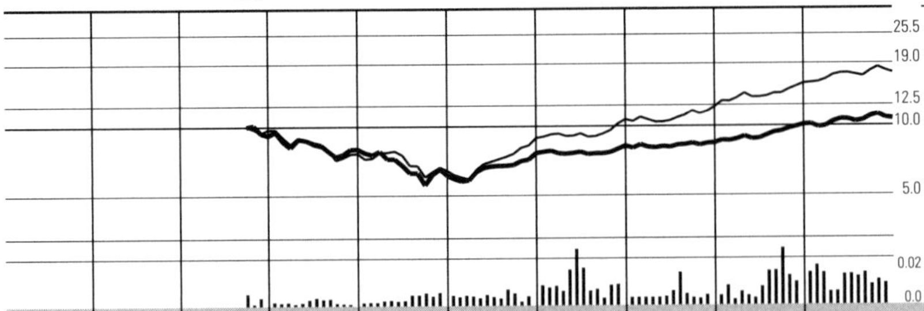

History

1998	1999	2000	2001	2002	2003	2004	2005	2006	2007	History
—	—	76.96	66.32	50.02	61.22	64.40	64.89	76.06	78.84	NAV $
—	—	76.97	66.94	50.00	61.22	64.43	65.01	76.08	78.85	Market Price $
—	—	0.92*	-12.88	-23.37	24.92	7.34	2.83	19.85	5.94	NAV Return%
—	—	0.93*	-12.08	-24.11	24.97	7.39	2.97	19.65	5.93	Market Price Return%
—	—	-0.60	0.34	0.06	0.05	0.08	0.17	0.09	0.22	Avg Premium/Discount%
—	—	—	8.56	-7.43	-13.67	-12.91	-10.71	-6.49	-5.23	NAV Rtrn% +/-MSCI EAFE
—	—	—	—	0.93	2.69	1.81	2.01	2.41	—	NAV Rtrn% +/-DJ Titans
—	—	—	100	86	81	100	100	1	75	NAV Return% Rank in Cat
—	—	—	0.93	1.25	2.28	2.06	2.06	2.39	2.26	Income Return %
—	—	—	-13.81	-24.62	22.64	5.28	0.77	17.46	3.68	Capital Return %
—	—	0.13	0.71	0.83	1.13	1.25	1.32	1.54	1.70	Income $
—	—	0.00	0.00	0.00	0.00	0.00	0.00	0.00	0.00	Capital Gains $
—	—	—	0.52	0.55	0.54	0.51	0.51	0.51	0.51	Expense Ratio %
—	—	—	0.87	1.07	1.77	1.84	2.47	2.11	2.33	Income Ratio %
—	—	—	16	12	13	15	36	9	9	Turnover Rate %
—	—	—	—	15	24	93	91	186	189	Net Assets $mil

Performance 12-31-07

Historic Quarterly NAV Returns

	1st Qtr	2nd Qtr	3rd Qtr	4th Qtr	Total
2003	-4.66	14.79	1.53	12.43	24.92
2004	-0.32	1.48	-1.64	7.88	7.34
2005	-1.28	-0.06	4.00	0.21	2.83
2006	3.86	0.59	7.30	6.91	19.85
2007	-1.48	6.84	3.27	-2.54	5.94

Trailing	NAV Return%	Market Return%	NAV Rtrn% +/-MSCI EAFE	%Rank Cat.(NAV)
3 Mo	-2.54	-2.56	-0.79	71
6 Mo	0.65	0.70	0.26	60
1 Yr	5.94	5.93	-5.23	75
3 Yr Avg	9.30	9.28	-7.53	100
5 Yr Avg	11.85	11.86	-9.74	100
10 Yr Avg	—	—	—	—

Tax Analysis	Tax-Adj Return%	Tax-Cost Ratio
3 Yr (estimated)	8.48	0.75
5 Yr (estimated)	11.03	0.73
10 Yr (estimated)	—	—

Rating and Risk

Time Period	Morningstar Rtn vs Cat	Morningstar Risk vs Cat	Morningstar Risk-Adj Rating
3 Yr	Low	Low	★★
5 Yr	Low	Low	★
10 Yr	—	—	—

Other Measures	Standard Index S&P 500	Best Fit Index MSCI World
Alpha	-2.4	-1.6
Beta	0.62	0.81
R-Squared	64	81
Standard Deviation	7.36	
Mean	9.30	
Sharpe Ratio	0.67	

Portfolio Analysis 12-31-07

Share change since 11-07 Total Stocks:50	Sector	Country	% Assets
⊖ ExxonMobil Corporation	Energy	United States	6.75
⊖ General Electric Company	Ind Mtrls	United States	4.94
⊕ Microsoft Corporation	Software	United States	3.92
AT&T, Inc.	Telecom	United States	3.34
⊖ BP PLC ADR	Energy	U.K.	3.05
Procter & Gamble Company	Goods	United States	3.02
Chevron Corporation	Energy	United States	2.62
Vodafone Group PLC ADR	Telecom	U.K.	2.61
HSBC Holdings PLC ADR	Financial	U.K.	2.60
⊖ Johnson & Johnson	Health	United States	2.52
Bank of America Corporat	Financial	United States	2.44
⊕ Nestle	Goods	Switzerland	2.39
⊖ Total SA ADR	Energy	France	2.31
Cisco Systems, Inc.	Hardware	United States	2.17
⊕ Toyota Motor Corporation	Goods	Japan	2.12
⊕ Altria Group Inc.	Goods	United States	2.09
⊖ Pfizer Inc.	Health	United States	2.05
Intel Corporation	Hardware	United States	2.04
Royal Dutch Shell PLC AD	Energy	U.K.	2.02
Nokia Corporation ADR	Hardware	Finland	1.99

Current Investment Style

Value Blnd Growth / Large Mid Small

Market Cap	%
Giant	100.0
Large	0.0
Mid	0.0
Small	0.0
Micro	0.0
Avg $mil: 178,097	

Value Measures		Rel Category
Price/Earnings	13.38	0.87
Price/Book	2.47	0.99
Price/Sales	1.66	1.44
Price/Cash Flow	10.47	1.06
Dividend Yield %	2.58	0.95

Growth Measures	%	Rel Category
Long-Term Erngs	10.37	0.90
Book Value	7.08	0.82
Sales	6.56	1.04
Cash Flow	7.56	1.48
Historical Erngs	16.29	0.90

Composition

Cash	0.6	Bonds	0.0
Stocks	99.4	Other	0.0
Foreign (% of Stock)			39.9

Sector Weightings	% of Stocks	Rel MSCI EAFE	3 Year High	3 Year Low
Info	25.92	2.05		
Software	3.94	6.79	4	3
Hardware	11.73	2.90	12	9
Media	0.79	0.47	2	1
Telecom	9.46	1.49	9	4
Service	35.36	0.82		
Health	13.49	2.12	18	13
Consumer	1.58	0.32	2	1
Business	0.00	0.00	0	0
Financial	20.29	0.75	25	20
Mfg	38.71	0.88		
Goods	13.98	1.05	14	12
Ind Mtrls	4.97	0.29	6	5
Energy	19.76	2.54	20	16
Utilities	0.00	0.00	0	0

Regional Exposure	% Stock		
UK/W. Europe	36	N. America	60
Japan	3	Latn America	0
Asia X Japan	1	Other	0

Country Exposure	% Stock		
United States	60	France	4
U.K.	16	Japan	3
Switzerland	7		

Morningstar's Take by Emiko Kurotsu 12-31-07

SPDR Dow Jones Global Titans brims with high-quality stocks.

This ETF purports to represent the world's 50 leading global companies, as selected by the Dow Jones index selection committee. In addition to market cap, the selection committee also considers fundamental factors like assets, sales, and profit.

These firms aren't tied to any one business model or industry. For instance, the portfolio includes capital-intensive stocks like U.K. oil major BP and Japan's Toyota Motors. Alongside them sit services-oriented firms like drugmaker Johnson & Johnson, consumer titan Procter & Gamble, and financials giant Bank of America.

That diversity doesn't dilute the portfolio's quality, however, as the majority of names here boast defensible competitive advantages. For example, Microsoft maintains preeminence in its market through dominant pricing power and the network effects of its widespread technology. All told, our analysts have awarded wide economic moats to 26 of the fund's 50 holdings, signifying our conviction that these companies will be able to churn out economic profits over the long haul.

In addition to increasing to our estimate of this fund's intrinsic worth, the portfolio's high-quality also tamps down risk. That's because wide-moat firms are less likely to be dislodged by competitors. For instance, while rivals can try, they're unlikely to replicate Coca-Cola's global distribution network, let alone its low-cost, low-capital manufacturing process. That should ensure that the beverage giant's cash flows remain on an even keel going forward, explaining why our analysts consider the company a below-average risk. Coke isn't alone in that regard, as our analysts consider only a handful of the fund's stocks to be above-average risks.

Given the fund's high-quality, moderate-risk profile, we'd invest in the shares at a 9% discount to our fair value estimate, a margin of safety that takes the fund's 0.50% expense ratio duly into account.

Address:	One Lincoln Street, United States, 866-787-2257
Web Address:	www.advisors.ssga.com
Inception:	09-25-00*
Advisor:	SSgA Funds Management Inc

Management Fee:	0.50%		
Expense Projections:	3Yr:$161	5Yr:$281	10Yr:$628
Income Distrib:	Quarterly		
Exchange:	AMEX		

Vanguard EmergMkts ETF VWO

Market Price	Mstar Category
$104.30	Diversified Emerging Mkts

Morningstar Fair Value

Price/Fair Value Ratio	Coverage Rate %
1.01	6

Valuation

Because our equity analysts cover a relatively small number of this ETF's holdings, the price/fair value ratio above may not be a faithful representation of the portfolio's valuation attributes. Investors trying to gauge this ETF's attractiveness should consider the price/fair value ratio only in conjunction with other fundamental measures.

Methodology

This exchange-traded fund tries to mirror the performance of the MSCI Emerging Markets Index. Prior to August 2006, it tracked a custom-made version of that index. One difference between the two had been that this fund's benchmark excluded Russia, but now Russia is included. The fund does not engage in currency hedging. Vanguard uses fair-value pricing on occasion when it deems it necessary.

Morningstar Rating	Return	Risk	Yield	NAV	Avg Daily Vol. (k)	52 wk High/Low
—	—	—	1.9%	$104.93	747	$117.28 - $71.10

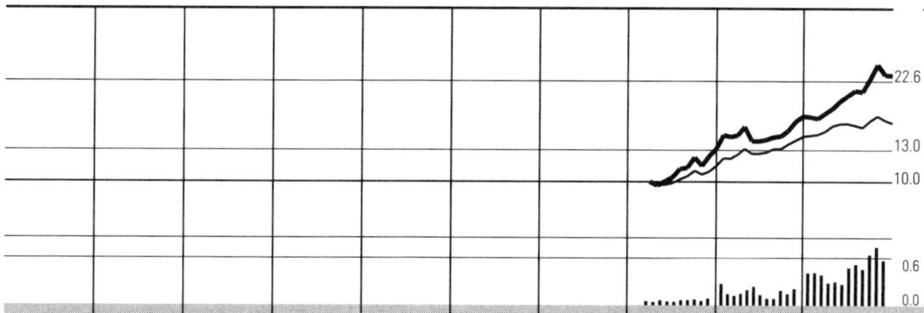

Growth of $10,000
— Investment Value of ETF
— Investment Value of Index MSCI EAFE

Trading Volume Millions

1998	1999	2000	2001	2002	2003	2004	2005	2006	2007	History
—	—	—	—	—	—	—	60.40	76.87	104.93	NAV $
—	—	—	—	—	—	—	60.88	77.39	104.30	Market Price $
—	—	—	—	—	—	—	31.99*	29.53	39.05	NAV Return%
—	—	—	—	—	—	—	32.07*	29.38	37.29	Market Price Return%
—	—	—	—	—	—	—	0.53	0.54	0.31	Avg Premium/Discount%
—	—	—	—	—	—	—	—	3.19	27.88	NAV Rtrn% +/-MSCI EAFE
—	—	—	—	—	—	—	—	-2.64	-0.34	NAV Rtrn% +/-MSCI Emg Mkt
—	—	—	—	—	—	—	—	67	50	NAV Return% Rank in Cat
—	—	—	—	—	—	—	—	2.22	2.56	Income Return %
—	—	—	—	—	—	—	—	27.31	36.49	Capital Return %
—	—	—	—	—	—	—	1.08	1.34	1.97	Income $
—	—	—	—	—	—	—	0.00	0.00	0.00	Capital Gains $
—	—	—	—	—	—	—	0.30	0.30	—	Expense Ratio %
—	—	—	—	—	—	—	2.59	2.32	—	Income Ratio %
—	—	—	—	—	—	—	15	26	—	Turnover Rate %
—	—	—	—	—	—	—	553	2,055	5,969	Net Assets $mil

Performance 12-31-07

Historic Quarterly NAV Returns

	1st Qtr	2nd Qtr	3rd Qtr	4th Qtr	Total
2003	—	—	—	—	—
2004	—	—	—	—	—
2005	—	3.73	17.22	7.15	—*
2006	11.23	-4.54	4.07	17.23	29.53
2007	2.22	15.40	14.47	2.98	39.05

Trailing	NAV Return%	Market Return%	NAV Rtrn% +/-MSCI EAFE	%Rank Cat.(NAV)
3 Mo	2.98	2.38	4.73	78
6 Mo	17.88	16.38	17.49	62
1 Yr	39.05	37.29	27.88	50
3 Yr Avg	—	—	—	—
5 Yr Avg	—	—	—	—
10 Yr Avg	—	—	—	—

Tax Analysis	Tax-Adj Return%	Tax-Cost Ratio
3 Yr (estimated)	—	—
5 Yr (estimated)	—	—
10 Yr (estimated)	—	—

Rating and Risk

Time Period	Morningstar Rtn vs Cat	Morningstar Risk vs Cat	Morningstar Risk-Adj Rating
3 Yr	—	—	—
5 Yr	—	—	—
10 Yr	—	—	—

Other Measures	Standard Index S&P 500	Best Fit Index
Alpha	—	—
Beta	—	—
R-Squared	—	—
Standard Deviation	—	
Mean	—	
Sharpe Ratio	—	

Portfolio Analysis 09-30-07

Share change since 06-07 Total Stocks:836	Sector	Country	% Assets
☼ Gazprom OAO (EDR)	Energy	—	3.20
⊕ China Mobile Ltd	Telecom	Hong Kong	2.91
⊕ America Movil S.A.B de C	Telecom	Mexico	1.77
⊕ Samsung Electronics	Goods	Korea	1.74
⊕ Companhia Vale do Rio Do	Ind Mtrls	Brazil	1.35
⊕ Petroleo Brasileiro Sa P	Energy	Brazil	1.24
⊕ Lukoil Company ADR	Energy	Russia	1.24
⊕ POSCO	Ind Mtrls	Korea	1.23
⊕ China Life Insurance	Financial	Hong Kong	1.22
⊕ Hon Hai Precision Indust	Hardware	Taiwan	1.13
⊕ Cia Vale Rio Doce	Ind Mtrls	Brazil	1.12
⊕ Reliance Industries Ltd	Ind Mtrls	India	1.11
⊕ PetroChina	Energy	Hong Kong	1.06
⊕ Taiwan Semiconductor Mfg	Hardware	Taiwan	1.05
⊕ Petroleo Brasileiro	Energy	Brazil	1.05
⊕ Teva Pharmaceutical Indu	Health	Israel	0.98
☼ MMC Norilsk Nickel ADR	Ind Mtrls	Russia	0.81
⊕ CNOOC Ltd	Energy	Hong Kong	0.78
⊕ Kookmin Bank	Financial	Korea	0.71
⊕ Sasol Limited Grp	Energy	South Africa	0.71

Current Investment Style

Value Blnd Growth — Large Mid Small

Market Cap	%
Giant	39.5
Large	41.0
Mid	17.3
Small	1.8
Micro	0.4
Avg $mil: 18,735	

Value Measures		Rel Category
Price/Earnings	15.67	1.05
Price/Book	2.56	0.91
Price/Sales	1.40	0.84
Price/Cash Flow	8.51	0.89
Dividend Yield %	2.62	0.69

Growth Measures	%	Rel Category
Long-Term Erngs	28.53	1.59
Book Value	14.60	0.85
Sales	16.34	0.80
Cash Flow	19.31	1.22
Historical Erngs	48.75	2.05

Composition

Cash	0.3	Bonds	0.0
Stocks	99.2	Other	0.5
Foreign (% of Stock)			99.4

Sector Weightings	% of Stocks	Rel MSCI EAFE	3 Year High	3 Year Low
Info	19.79	1.56		
Software	1.04	1.79	2	1
Hardware	6.43	1.59	10	6
Media	1.03	0.61	2	1
Telecom	11.29	1.78	12	10
Service	33.21	0.77		
Health	1.82	0.29	3	2
Consumer	3.36	0.68	4	3
Business	6.33	1.27	6	5
Financial	21.70	0.80	22	19
Mfg	47.01	1.07		
Goods	8.49	0.64	18	8
Ind Mtrls	20.94	1.21	21	16
Energy	14.32	1.84	14	9
Utilities	3.26	0.59	3	2

Regional Exposure	% Stock		
UK/W. Europe	4	N. America	1
Japan	0	Latn America	19
Asia X Japan	56	Other	20

Country Exposure	% Stock		
South Korea	15	Taiwan	11
Hong Kong	14	South Africa	7
Brazil	12		

Morningstar's Take by Gregg Wolper 12-31-07

After a roller-coaster third quarter, Vanguard Emerging Markets ETF strengths remain intact, but so do its risks.

In all three of the sharp global market slides during the past two years, emerging markets have been among the hardest-hit groups. As a result, in 2006's May-June drop and the declines of February-March and July-August of 2007, this fund suffered substantial losses. All three times, it bounced back quickly, recovering the losses and then some. This ETF has returned 40% on a market-price basis for the year to date through Oct. 16, 2007.

As a result, there are two ways to look at this fund now. It's a solid choice for those interested in injecting some direct emerging-markets exposure into a long-term portfolio. Few actively managed emerging-markets funds offer a compelling a mix of long-tenured, successful managers and reasonable costs. So, this low-cost index tracker has appeal.

On the other hand, this year's stunning gains represent just the latest stretch of a long-lasting, powerful rally in emerging markets. This fund's mutual-fund share class (which has a longer history than the ETF class) has posted annual gains of between 26% and 58% in each of the past four calendar years, so this marks the fifth straight year of remarkably strong performance. Anyone thinking of investing here primarily because they expect emerging markets to keep up that level of performance indefinitely should think twice before choosing this ETF--or any emerging-markets fund.

One more caution: Index tracking is more difficult with emerging markets than with, say, the S&P 500 Index. There have often been notable discrepancies between the mutual-fund version's short-term returns and the index's. Over the long term, though, the fund has matched its index well.

Address:	PO Box 2600 United States 866-499-8473
Web Address:	www.vanguard.com
Inception:	03-04-05 *
Advisor:	Vanguard Advisers, Inc.

Management Fee:	0.16%		
Expense Projections:	3Yr:$97	5Yr:$169	10Yr:$381
Income Distrib:	Annually		
Exchange:	AMEX		

Foreign Stock Funds: Country/Region

This section offers a full-page report on each country/region-focused stock ETF.

iShares Australia EWA

Market Price	Mstar Category
$28.82	Pacific/Asia ex-Japan St

Morningstar Rating	Return	Risk	Yield	NAV	Avg Daily Vol. (k)	52 wk High/Low
★★★	Average	Below Avg	4.4%	$29.13	2,343	$34.71 - $22.82

Morningstar Fair Value

Price/Fair Value Ratio	Coverage Rate %
1.00	15

Valuation

Because our analysts cover a relatively small number of this ETF's stock holdings, the price/fair value ratio may not be a faithful representation of the portfolio's valuation attributes. Accordingly, investors trying to gauge this ETF's attractiveness should consider the price/fair value ratio only in conjunction with other fundamental

Methodology

This ETF tracks the MSCI Australia Index, which covers roughly 85 stocks that trade primarily on the Australian Stock Exchange. The fund represents about 85% of the Australian market, which is dominated by banks and industrials, especially mining firms. Financials make up 40% of assets while industrials account for another 28%. As a cap-weighted index, giant and large caps take up more than 90% of assets, with more than half of the portfolio concentrated in its top 10 holdings. The fund doesn't hedge its investments back to the U.S. dollar.

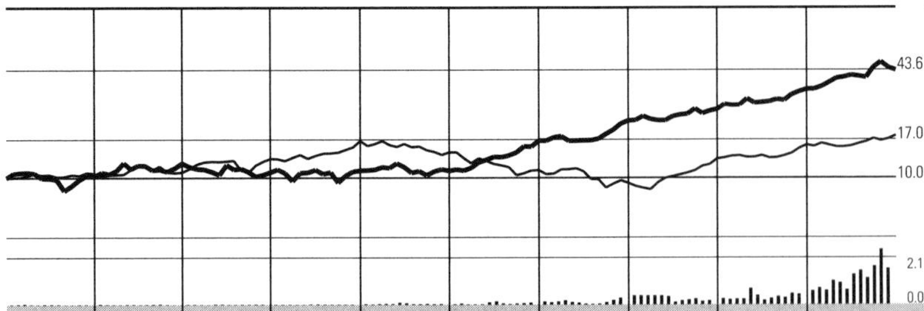

Growth of $10,000
- Investment Value of ETF
- Investment Value of Index MSCI EAFE

Trading Volume Millions

1998	1999	2000	2001	2002	2003	2004	2005	2006	2007	History
9.40	10.94	9.43	9.42	9.13	13.23	16.72	18.83	23.63	29.13	NAV $
9.50	11.06	9.50	9.45	9.08	13.36	16.70	18.81	23.50	28.82	Market Price $
2.18	19.24	-11.52	2.33	-0.28	49.82	30.86	16.66	31.42	28.96	NAV Return%
4.26	19.27	-11.83	1.90	-1.14	52.12	29.43	16.68	30.84	28.29	Market Price Return%
0.58	1.45	0.60	0.02	0.25	0.94	0.17	-0.07	0.21	0.24	Avg Premium/Discount%
-17.75	-7.79	2.65	23.77	15.66	11.23	10.61	3.12	5.08	17.79	NAV Rtrn% +/-MSCI EAFE
-3.87	1.58	-1.55	0.65	1.06	0.36	0.52	0.64	0.56	0.62	NAV Rtrn% +/-MSCI Austr
1	100	1	60	34	1	1	13	62	73	NAV Return% Rank in Cat
1.95	2.05	2.20	2.21	2.82	4.71	4.35	3.99	5.84	5.41	Income Return %
0.23	17.19	-13.72	0.12	-3.10	45.11	26.51	12.67	25.58	23.55	Capital Return %
0.18	0.19	0.24	0.21	0.27	0.43	0.58	0.67	1.10	1.28	Income $
0.00	0.06	0.03	0.02	0.00	0.00	0.00	0.00	0.00	0.00	Capital Gains $
—	—	0.95	0.84	0.84	0.84	0.79	0.57	0.54	0.51	Expense Ratio %
—	—	2.22	2.54	2.47	3.21	3.37	4.13	3.75	1.36	Income Ratio %
—	—	36	23	5	8	9	17	7	21	Turnover Rate %
43	66	58	60	75	140	244	463	770	1,893	Net Assets $mil

Performance 12-31-07

Historic Quarterly NAV Returns

	1st Qtr	2nd Qtr	3rd Qtr	4th Qtr	Total
2003	3.94	15.91	6.09	17.21	49.82
2004	6.05	-5.42	8.89	19.81	30.86
2005	2.03	3.81	10.78	-0.58	16.66
2006	5.95	3.81	2.80	16.24	31.42
2007	9.39	10.33	11.26	-3.96	28.96

Trailing	NAV Return%	Market Return%	NAV Rtrn% +/-MSCI EAFE	%Rank Cat.(NAV)
3 Mo	-3.96	-5.15	-2.21	87
6 Mo	6.84	5.90	6.45	80
1 Yr	28.96	28.29	17.79	73
3 Yr Avg	25.51	25.11	8.68	62
5 Yr Avg	31.12	30.99	9.53	1
10 Yr Avg	15.61	15.59	6.95	1

Tax Analysis	Tax-Adj Return%	Tax-Cost Ratio
3 Yr (estimated)	23.70	1.44
5 Yr (estimated)	29.37	1.33
10 Yr (estimated)	14.32	1.12

Rating and Risk

Time Period	Morningstar Rtn vs Cat	Morningstar Risk vs Cat	Morningstar Risk-Adj Rating
3 Yr	-Avg	-Avg	★★
5 Yr	Avg	-Avg	★★★
10 Yr	Avg	Low	★★★★

Other Measures	Standard Index S&P 500	Best Fit Index Pac ex-Japan
Alpha	2.5	-1.1
Beta	1.48	1.08
R-Squared	76	97
Standard Deviation	16.18	
Mean	25.51	
Sharpe Ratio	1.23	

Portfolio Analysis 11-30-07

Share change since 10-07 Total Stocks:85	Sector	Country	% Assets
⊖ BHP Billiton Ltd	Ind Mtrls	Australia	13.64
⊖ Commonwealth Bank of Aus	Financial	Australia	7.34
⊖ National Australia Bank	Financial	Australia	5.92
⊖ Westpac Banking	Financial	Australia	4.94
⊖ Australia & New Zealand	Financial	Australia	4.92
⊖ Rio Tinto Ltd	Ind Mtrls	Australia	3.94
⊖ Woolworths Ltd	Consumer	Australia	3.86
⊖ Westfield Grp	Consumer	Australia	3.38
⊖ QBE Insurance Grp Ltd	Financial	Australia	2.64
⊖ Woodside Petroleum Ltd	Energy	Australia	2.19
☼ Macquarie Grp	—	Australia	2.01
⊖ CSL Ltd	Health	Australia	1.81
⊖ AMP Ltd	Financial	Australia	1.80
⊖ Brambles Ltd	Business	Australia	1.66
⊖ Suncorp-Metway Ltd	Financial	Australia	1.63
⊖ Wesfarmers Ltd	Ind Mtrls	Australia	1.57
⊖ Newcrest Mining Ltd	Ind Mtrls	Australia	1.45
⊖ Telstra	Telecom	Australia	1.26
⊖ Stockland	Financial	Australia	1.18
⊖ Foster's Grp Ltd	Goods	Australia	1.18

Current Investment Style

Value Blnd Growth — Large Mid Small

Market Cap	%
Giant	56.8
Large	35.6
Mid	7.6
Small	0.0
Micro	0.0
Avg $mil: 24,813	

Value Measures		Rel Category
Price/Earnings	16.14	0.92
Price/Book	2.52	0.96
Price/Sales	1.97	0.90
Price/Cash Flow	8.78	1.02
Dividend Yield %	3.93	1.17

Growth Measures	%	Rel Category
Long-Term Erngs	15.36	0.92
Book Value	10.23	0.87
Sales	13.45	0.73
Cash Flow	23.34	1.29
Historical Erngs	21.23	0.73

Composition

Cash	0.5	Bonds	0.0
Stocks	99.5	Other	0.0
Foreign (% of Stock)			100.0

Sector Weightings	% of Stocks	Rel MSCI EAFE	3 Year High	Low
Info	4.12	0.33		
Software	0.51	0.88	1	0
Hardware	0.00	0.00	0	0
Media	1.84	1.09	2	1
Telecom	1.77	0.28	2	1
Service	59.65	1.38		
Health	3.23	0.51	3	2
Consumer	9.68	1.95	11	6
Business	6.87	1.38	7	6
Financial	39.87	1.48	50	40
Mfg	36.24	0.82		
Goods	3.21	0.24	5	3
Ind Mtrls	27.95	1.61	28	21
Energy	4.53	0.58	5	3
Utilities	0.55	0.10	2	0

Regional Exposure			% Stock
UK/W. Europe	0	N. America	0
Japan	0	Latn America	0
Asia X Japan	100	Other	0

Country Exposure	% Stock
Australia	100

Morningstar's Take by Emiko Kurotsu 12-31-07

IShares MSCI Australia may not be the best route to the Australian equity market.

This ETF covers the bulk of Australia's stock market through its 80 to 90 holding portfolio. The country's biggest industries--banking, mining, and real estate--dominate the fund, with financials making up nearly 40% of assets, and industrials, over a fourth.

The Australian economy has prospered in recent years, buoyed by the nation's ample natural resources and high, government-mandated savings rates. Yet, we're not very enthusiastic about this portfolio's contents. Though its two biggest mining firms, BHP Billiton and Rio Tinto (which together make up almost 20% of the fund), are industry leaders boasting diverse natural-resource portfolios, experienced management, and robust balance sheets, they're still captive to the vagaries of the economic cycle and unpredictable commodity prices.

The fund's bank holdings aren't very compelling either. Australia's so-called "Big Four" banks, which take up almost a fourth of this ETF, aren't very competitive or efficient due to regulations that limit foreign takeovers and mergers with one another. Thus, even the biggest of the lot--National Australia Bank--has tended to post lackluster results, inspiring little confidence from our stock analysts.

While we cover a relatively small number of this fund's underlying holdings, the portfolio's middling quality and volatility argue to make caution the better part of valor. Thus, if you're considering an investment here based on the fundamental attractiveness of the fund's holdings, we'd do so only with a wide margin of safety. If, on the other hand, you're weighing the fund as a potential portfolio building block, we'd think twice, as many diversified foreign funds already offer ample exposure to Australian stocks.

Address:	45 Fremont Street United States 800-474-2737
Web Address:	www.ishares.com
Inception:	03-12-96
Advisor:	Barclays Global Fund Advisers

Management Fee:	0.54%		
Expense Projections:	3Yr:$173	5Yr:$302	10Yr:$677
Income Distrib:	Annually		
Exchange:	NYSE		

iShares Brazil Index EWZ

Market Price	Mstar Category
$80.70	Latin America Stock

Morningstar Rating	Return	Risk	Yield	NAV	Avg Daily Vol. (k)	52 wk High/Low
★★★★★	High	High	1.5%	$81.55	13,985	$86.15 - $42.70

Morningstar Fair Value

Price/Fair Value Ratio	Coverage Rate %
1.00	10

Valuation

This fund is overheated. Its holdings have been trading at a premium to our fair value estimate for a while now, reflecting the market's exuberance for commodity and energy stocks. Given the portfolio's high volatility, we'd invest here only with a wide margin of safety: We'd need at least a 20% discount to our fair value estimate.

Methodology

This fund tracks the MSCI Brazil Index, which covers more than 60 firms that trade primarily on the Bolsa de Valores de Sao Paulo. The fund's holdings, which are weighted by market cap, represent about 85% of the Brazilian stock market. Large-cap stocks dominate the fund, accounting for nearly 90% of assets. The Brazilian economy is heavily tied to commodities; thus, the fund invests more than one third of assets in mining and steel producers, with another one fourth devoted to energy stocks. The fund does not hedge its investments back to the U.S. dollar.

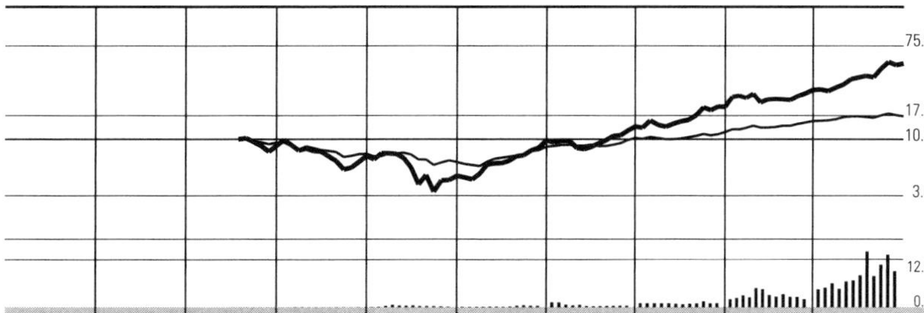

Growth of $10,000
— Investment Value of ETF
— Investment Value of Index MSCI EAFE

Trading Volume Millions

History

1998	1999	2000	2001	2002	2003	2004	2005	2006	2007	History
—	—	16.38	12.48	8.04	16.85	22.13	33.16	46.87	81.55	NAV $
—	—	16.50	12.70	7.98	17.00	22.24	33.37	46.85	80.70	Market Price $
—	—	23.41*	-19.52	-34.70	113.03	34.16	52.46	44.27	76.59	NAV Return%
—	—	23.24*	-18.69	-36.31	116.54	33.63	52.66	43.30	74.83	Market Price Return%
—	—	0.90	-0.21	0.28	0.47	0.10	-0.11	0.03	0.00	Avg Premium/Discount%
—	—	—	1.92	-18.76	74.44	13.91	38.92	17.93	65.42	NAV Rtrn% +/-MSCI EAFE
—	—	—	-2.53	-4.05	-1.98	-1.32	-3.99	-1.03	-2.97	NAV Rtrn% +/-MSCI Brazil
—	—	—	100	100	1	100	50	1	1	NAV Return% Rank in Cat
—	—	—	3.37	0.88	3.36	2.74	2.63	2.84	2.57	Income Return %
—	—	—	-22.89	-35.58	109.67	31.42	49.83	41.43	74.02	Capital Return %
—	—	0.03	0.55	0.11	0.27	0.46	0.58	0.94	1.20	Income $
—	—	0.34	0.09	0.00	0.00	0.00	0.00	0.00	0.00	Capital Gains $
—	—	—	0.99	—	0.99	0.96	0.74	0.70	0.69	Expense Ratio %
—	—	—	—	—	3.59	3.59	3.94	2.65	2.17	Income Ratio %
—	—	—	43	103	85	106	48	15	22	Turnover Rate %
—	—	—	—	53	360	389	1,224	2,958	7,580	Net Assets $mil

Performance 12-31-07

Historic Quarterly NAV Returns

	1st Qtr	2nd Qtr	3rd Qtr	4th Qtr	Total
2003	4.98	24.64	18.44	37.46	113.03
2004	-0.65	-12.07	25.82	22.06	34.16
2005	3.71	7.89	34.61	1.23	52.46
2006	21.20	-3.01	-1.03	24.01	44.27
2007	5.31	24.23	20.69	11.84	76.59

Trailing	NAV Return%	Market Return%	NAV Rtrn% +/-MSCI EAFE	%Rank Cat.(NAV)
3 Mo	11.84	11.37	13.59	1
6 Mo	34.98	33.36	34.59	1
1 Yr	76.59	74.83	65.42	1
3 Yr Avg	57.19	56.39	40.36	1
5 Yr Avg	61.83	61.74	40.24	1
10 Yr Avg	—	—	—	—

Tax Analysis	Tax-Adj Return%	Tax-Cost Ratio
3 Yr (estimated)	56.24	0.60
5 Yr (estimated)	60.82	0.62
10 Yr (estimated)	—	—

Rating and Risk

Time Period	Morningstar Rtn vs Cat	Morningstar Risk vs Cat	Morningstar Risk-Adj Rating
3 Yr	+Avg	+Avg	★★★★
5 Yr	High	High	★★★★★
10 Yr	—	—	—

Other Measures	Standard Index S&P 500	Best Fit Index MSCI Latin Am
Alpha	17.7	-1.5
Beta	2.40	1.25
R-Squared	59	95
Standard Deviation	29.72	
Mean	57.19	
Sharpe Ratio	1.54	

Portfolio Analysis 11-30-07

Share change since 10-07 Total Stocks:65	Sector	Country	% Assets
⊕ Petroleo Brasileiro Sa P	Energy	Brazil	13.61
⊕ Companhia Vale do Rio Do	Ind Mtrls	Brazil	12.23
⊕ Petroleo Brasileiro	Energy	Brazil	11.49
⊕ Vale Overseas Limited AD	Ind Mtrls	Brazil	10.37
⊖ Banco Bradesco	Financial	Brazil	6.05
⊕ Banco Itau Holding Finan	Financial	Brazil	4.99
⊕ Unibanco-Uniao De	Financial	Brazil	4.28
⊖ Companhia de Bebidas das	Goods	Brazil	3.36
⊕ Companhia Siderurgica Na	Ind Mtrls	Brazil	2.33
⊕ Gerdau	Ind Mtrls	Brazil	2.21
⊕ Usinas Siderurgicas de M	Ind Mtrls	Brazil	2.10
⊕ Cia. Energetica de Minas	Utilities	Brazil	1.46
⊕ Embraer-Empresa Brasilei	Ind Mtrls	Brazil	1.23
⊕ All Amer Latina	Business	Brazil	1.21
⊕ Tele Norte Leste Partici	Telecom	Brazil	1.15
☼ Bovespa Hldg Sa	—	Brazil	1.09
⊕ Aracruz Celulose	Ind Mtrls	Brazil	0.98
⊕ Votorantim Celulose e Pa	Ind Mtrls	Brazil	0.82
⊕ Brasil Telecom Participa	Telecom	Brazil	0.80
⊖ Centrais Eletricas Brasi	Utilities	Brazil	0.77

Current Investment Style

Value Blnd Growth — Large / Mid / Small (Large Blend)

Market Cap	%
Giant	61.9
Large	25.9
Mid	11.8
Small	0.4
Micro	0.0
Avg $mil: 43,036	

Value Measures		Rel Category
Price/Earnings	13.67	0.92
Price/Book	2.55	0.87
Price/Sales	2.05	1.22
Price/Cash Flow	8.20	0.93
Dividend Yield %	2.38	0.83

Growth Measures	%	Rel Category
Long-Term Erngs	11.11	0.80
Book Value	13.95	0.99
Sales	16.60	0.93
Cash Flow	29.00	1.48
Historical Erngs	17.40	0.74

Composition

Cash	0.0	Bonds	0.0
Stocks	99.5	Other	0.5
Foreign (% of Stock)			100.0

Sector Weightings	% of Stocks	Rel MSCI EAFE	3 Year High	3 Year Low
Info	4.95	0.39		
Software	0.00	0.00	0	0
Hardware	0.03	0.01	0	0
Media	0.64	0.38	1	0
Telecom	4.28	0.67	16	4
Service	22.09	0.51		
Health	0.20	0.03	1	0
Consumer	2.69	0.54	4	0
Business	2.36	0.47	5	0
Financial	16.84	0.62	18	5
Mfg	72.95	1.66		
Goods	5.30	0.40	9	2
Ind Mtrls	36.04	2.08	37	26
Energy	25.76	3.32	42	21
Utilities	5.85	1.06	7	5

Regional Exposure	% Stock		
UK/W. Europe	0	N. America	0
Japan	0	Latn America	100
Asia X Japan	0	Other	0

Country Exposure	% Stock
Brazil	100

Morningstar's Take by Emiko Kurotsu 12-31-07

IShares MSCI Brazil requires significant caution.

This ETF covers about 85% of the Brazilian stock market, which is heavily driven by commodity-based firms like mining behemoth Companhia Vale de Rio Doce and steel giant Gerdau. Not surprisingly, sector diversification is in short supply, with industrials taking up more than a third of assets and energy another fourth. Further, because the index is cap-weighted, the top 10 holdings make up 71% of the fund, while 25% of assets are staked in one firm alone: integrated oil major Petrobras.

Given that many of these businesses are more or less captive to commodity prices or the vagaries of the economic cycle, none has been able to trench out a durable competitive advantage over rivals. Still, some holdings have eked out at least some semblance of an advantage. For instance, narrow-moat firm Companhia Vale de Rio Doce uses its scale to dominate the world's iron-ore market and its two thirds share of Brazil's rail freight network to keep shipping costs in check.

Similarly, by owning and operating its own mine, railroad, port, and power plant, steel producer Companhia Siderugica Nacional is better able to keep its production costs in line, giving it a leg up on rivals.

Still, don't be lulled into a false sense of security. In addition to commodity-specific risks, many of the fund's holdings are saddled with uncertainties unique to their home turf. For example, energy giant Petrobras is majority-controlled by the Brazilian government, meaning other shareholder interests could take a backseat when state concerns flare. Similarly, our analysts don't think Braskem, a petrochemical firm, could keep pace with global peers if government-imposed tariffs were retracted. Uncertainties like these, coupled with the gyrations of the Brazilian real, have stoked the fund's volatility, which is among the highest of any ETF we cover. As such, we'd need a wide margin of safety before investing here.

Address:	45 Fremont Street United States 800-474-2737
Web Address:	www.ishares.com
Inception:	07-10-00*
Advisor:	Barclays Global Fund Advisers

Management Fee:	0.70%		
Expense Projections:	3Yr:$224	5Yr:$390	10Yr:$871
Income Distrib:	Annually		
Exchange:	NYSE		

iShares Canada Index EWC

Market Price	Mstar Category
$32.12	Foreign Large Value

Morningstar Fair Value

Price/Fair Value Ratio	Coverage Rate %
0.98	93

Valuation

Until recently, this fund traded at a premium to our fair value estimate for the better part of three years (it was recently trading at a modest discount). Given its heavy exposure to volatile energy and commodity-related stocks, the fund would have to trade at 16% or greater discount to fair value before we'd recommend it.

Methodology

This fund tracks the MSCI Canada Index, which represents about 100 stocks that trade primarily on the Toronto Stock Exchange and collectively account for about 85% of the total Canadian market. The fund weights holdings by market cap. As such, its blue-chip holdings dominate, with the top 10 stocks representing almost 42% of assets. The fund's sector weights reflect the Canadian economy, with banking, energy, and natural-resources-related industrials looming large. Financial firms account for almost a third of the fund. The index does not hedge investments back into the U.S. dollar.

Morningstar Rating	Return	Risk	Yield	NAV	Avg Daily Vol. (k)	52 wk High/Low
★★★★★	High	High	1.2%	$32.33	1,507	$36.42 - $24.11

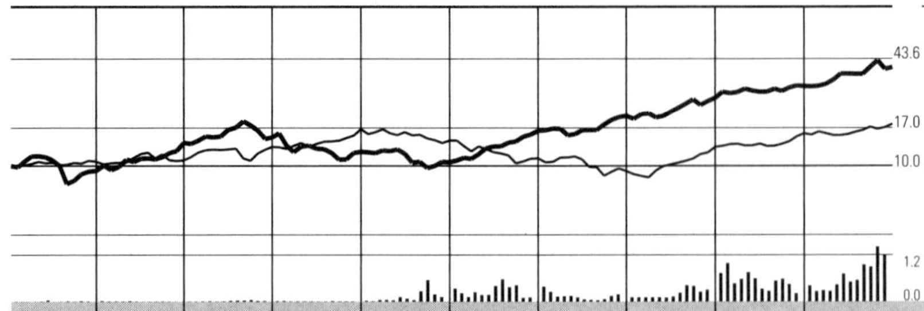

Growth of $10,000
- Investment Value of ETF
- Investment Value of Index MSCI EAFE

Trading Volume Millions

History

1998	1999	2000	2001	2002	2003	2004	2005	2006	2007	History
11.76	16.50	13.31	10.85	9.39	14.19	17.17	21.80	25.32	32.33	NAV $
11.56	16.50	13.38	10.62	9.44	14.25	17.29	21.90	25.32	32.12	Market Price $
-6.47	46.14	7.68	-17.85	-13.20	53.34	22.45	27.84	17.45	29.22	NAV Return%
-7.78	48.67	8.24	-20.01	-10.84	53.18	22.78	27.53	16.91	28.40	Market Price Return%
0.54	0.06	0.93	-0.28	0.40	0.47	0.33	0.19	0.29	0.06	Avg Premium/Discount%
-26.40	19.11	21.85	3.59	2.74	14.75	2.20	14.30	-8.89	18.05	NAV Rtrn% +/-MSCI EAFE
-0.28	-7.68	2.34	2.58	-0.01	-1.26	0.25	-0.47	-0.35	-0.35	NAV Rtrn% +/-MSCI Can
1	1	1	1	1	1	1	1	67	1	NAV Return% Rank in Cat
1.12	0.67	3.30	0.21	0.27	2.15	1.40	0.87	1.31	1.54	Income Return %
-7.59	45.47	4.38	-18.06	-13.47	51.19	21.05	26.97	16.14	27.68	Capital Return %
0.15	0.08	0.55	0.03	0.03	0.20	0.20	0.15	0.28	0.39	Income $
0.55	0.49	4.80	0.06	0.00	0.00	0.00	0.00	0.00	0.00	Capital Gains $
—	—	1.17	0.84	—	0.84	0.70	0.57	0.54	0.52	Expense Ratio %
—	—	4.07	—	—	0.98	0.81	1.00	1.09	1.32	Income Ratio %
—	—	64	63	5	10	10	9	20	8	Turnover Rate %
13	12	17	26	348	309	313	621	1,076	1,898	Net Assets $mil

Performance 12-31-07

Historic Quarterly NAV Returns

	1st Qtr	2nd Qtr	3rd Qtr	4th Qtr	Total
2003	4.79	18.19	7.05	15.65	53.34
2004	2.61	-1.92	8.05	12.61	22.45
2005	3.49	2.42	18.24	2.00	27.84
2006	8.26	0.42	1.05	6.90	17.45
2007	3.04	14.83	9.41	-0.18	29.22

Trailing	NAV Return%	Market Return%	NAV Rtrn% +/-MSCI EAFE	%Rank Cat.(NAV)
3 Mo	-0.18	-0.67	1.57	34
6 Mo	9.21	8.88	8.82	1
1 Yr	29.22	28.40	18.05	1
3 Yr Avg	24.72	24.17	7.89	1
5 Yr Avg	29.51	29.20	7.92	1
10 Yr Avg	14.35	14.31	5.69	1

Tax Analysis	Tax-Adj Return%	Tax-Cost Ratio
3 Yr (estimated)	24.29	0.34
5 Yr (estimated)	29.00	0.39
10 Yr (estimated)	13.12	1.08

Rating and Risk

Time Period	Morningstar Rtn vs Cat	Morningstar Risk vs Cat	Morningstar Risk-Adj Rating
3 Yr	High	High	★★★★★
5 Yr	High	High	★★★★★
10 Yr	High	High	★★★★

Other Measures	Standard Index S&P 500	Best Fit Index MSCI Ac Wrld ND
Alpha	3.0	4.0
Beta	1.38	1.60
R-Squared	64	72
Standard Deviation	16.46	
Mean	24.72	
Sharpe Ratio	1.17	

Portfolio Analysis 11-30-07

Share change since 10-07 Total Stocks:104	Sector	Country	% Assets
⊕ Royal Bank of Canada	Financial	Canada	6.05
⊕ Manulife Financial Corpo	Financial	Canada	5.77
⊕ Research in Motion, Ltd.	Hardware	Canada	5.10
⊕ Bank of Nova Scotia	Financial	Canada	4.67
⊕ EnCana Corporation	Energy	Canada	4.42
⊕ Suncor Energy, Inc.	Energy	Canada	3.93
⊕ Potash Corporation of Sa	Ind Mtrls	Canada	3.34
⊕ Canadian Natural Resourc	Energy	Canada	3.12
⊕ Barrick Gold Corporation	Ind Mtrls	Canada	3.11
⊕ Bank of Montreal	Financial	Canada	2.83
⊕ Sun Life Financial, Inc.	Financial	Canada	2.68
⊕ Canadian Imperial Bank o	Financial	Canada	2.67
⊕ Canadian National Railwa	Business	Canada	2.19
⊕ Petro-Canada	Energy	Canada	2.14
⊕ Goldcorp, Inc.	Ind Mtrls	Canada	2.03
⊕ TransCanada Corporation	Energy	Canada	1.90
⊕ Rogers Communications, I	Telecom	Canada	1.85
⊕ Talisman Energy, Inc.	Energy	Canada	1.65
⊕ Brookfield Asset Managem	Financial	Canada	1.59
⊕ Teck Cominco Limited Sub	Ind Mtrls	Canada	1.47

Current Investment Style

Value Blnd Growth — Large / Mid / Small

Market Cap	%
Giant	53.3
Large	37.2
Mid	9.3
Small	0.1
Micro	0.0
Avg $mil: 22,401	

Value Measures		Rel Category
Price/Earnings	16.12	1.22
Price/Book	2.40	1.24
Price/Sales	1.71	1.17
Price/Cash Flow	7.67	0.93
Dividend Yield %	2.38	0.75

Growth Measures	%	Rel Category
Long-Term Erngs	9.67	0.97
Book Value	13.66	1.16
Sales	13.26	1.28
Cash Flow	18.93	1.61
Historical Erngs	20.94	1.18

Composition

Cash	0.3	Bonds	0.0
Stocks	99.7	Other	0.0
Foreign (% of Stock)			100.0

Sector Weightings	% of Stocks	Rel MSCI EAFE	3 Year High	3 Year Low
Info	12.08	0.95		
Software	0.46	0.79	1	0
Hardware	5.89	1.45	6	2
Media	2.05	1.21	2	2
Telecom	3.68	0.58	4	3
Service	40.79	0.94		
Health	0.42	0.07	1	0
Consumer	2.78	0.56	5	3
Business	4.87	0.98	6	5
Financial	32.72	1.21	37	31
Mfg	47.13	1.07		
Goods	0.80	0.06	1	0
Ind Mtrls	17.43	1.00	20	17
Energy	27.73	3.57	32	24
Utilities	1.17	0.21	1	0

Regional Exposure			% Stock
UK/W. Europe	0	N. America	100
Japan	0	Latn America	0
Asia X Japan	0	Other	0

Country Exposure	% Stock
Canada	100

Morningstar's Take by Emiko Kurotsu 12-31-07

Canada's big banks prop up iShares MSCI Canada Index's portfolio quality, but the rest is a gamble.

This ETF tracks about 100 stocks that represent about 85% of the Canadian stock market. As such, it reflects the key drivers of the Canadian economy: banks (one third of assets), energy (one fourth), and other commodity-related industries (one fifth).

Big banks enhance the fund's quality. Of the 68 portfolio holdings that our analysts cover, five garner wide-moat ratings, which our analysts award to firms boasting defensible competitive advantages. All five of these firms are big banks like Royal Bank of Canada RY and Bank of Montreal BMO. In addition to the ready access to capital that banks typically enjoy, industry regulations that prevent foreign rivals from setting up shop fortify Canadian banks' advantages. What's more, several have succeeded in delving deeply into client pockets, spurring cross-selling opportunities and making switching costs more onerous.

Unfortunately, these firms are the exception rather than the rule in a portfolio that's loaded with commodity-sensitive, capital-intensive names. For instance, none of the energy stocks here--which range from pipeline operators to crude-oil producers--earn a wide moat. These businesses don't consistently earn high returns on capital due to their dependence on volatile oil prices, not to mention their heavy capital investment needs. Quality is in even shorter supply among the portfolio's 14 mining holdings, 12 of which lack any sort of moat. This, too, reflects the nature of the industry, as mining firms are essentially price-takers in a wildly unpredictable commodity market. Even the world's largest gold producer, Barrick Gold ABX, lacks a moat due to its high fixed costs and lack of control over prices.

The fund's heavy exposure to firms tied to commodity market gyrations has also spurred volatility. Thus, we'd need a significant margin of safety to invest here. A 16% or greater discount to our fair value would do.

Address:	45 Fremont Street United States 800-474-2737
Web Address:	www.ishares.com
Inception:	03-12-96
Advisor:	Barclays Global Fund Advisers

Management Fee:	0.54%		
Expense Projections:	3Yr:$173	5Yr:$302	10Yr:$677
Income Distrib:	Annually		
Exchange:	NYSE		

iShares EMU Index EZU

Market Price	Mstar Category
$119.32	Europe Stock

Morningstar Fair Value

Price/Fair Value Ratio	Coverage Rate %
1.00	4

Valuation

Because our equity analysts cover a relatively small number of this ETF's holdings, the price/fair value ratio above may not be a faithful representation of the portfolio's valuation attributes. Investors trying to gauge this ETF's attractiveness should consider the price/fair value ratio only in conjunction with other fundamental measures.

Methodology

This exchange-traded offering is a passive fund that simply attempts to match the performance of the MSCI EMU Index. The benchmark is a free float-adjusted market-capitalization index designed to track the stocks in member nations of the European Monetary Union. It includes companies based in Austria, Belgium, Finland, France, Germany, Greece, Ireland, Italy, the Netherlands, Portugal, and Spain, but excludes the United Kingdom, Switzerland, and others. It uses a representative sampling method of tracking the index.

Morningstar Rating	Return	Risk	Yield	NAV	Avg Daily Vol. (k)	52 wk High/Low
★★★	Average	Average	2.5%	$119.99	384	$126.89 - $99.83

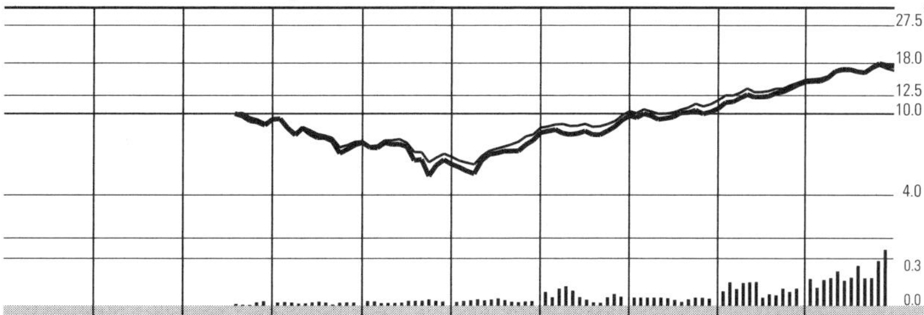

1998	1999	2000	2001	2002	2003	2004	2005	2006	2007	History
—	—	73.22	55.78	43.28	60.81	72.31	77.23	103.05	119.99	NAV $
—	—	73.25	55.99	43.50	61.25	72.60	77.65	103.35	119.32	Market Price $
—	—	7.09*	-22.96	-21.60	42.39	21.06	8.61	35.84	19.42	NAV Return%
—	—	7.01*	-22.70	-21.49	42.70	20.68	8.77	35.50	18.41	Market Price Return%
—	—	0.62	0.59	0.16	0.30	0.57	0.12	0.15	-0.08	Avg Premium/Discount%
—	—	—	-1.52	-5.66	3.80	0.81	-4.93	9.50	8.25	NAV Rtrn% +/-MSCI EAFE
—	—	—	-0.45	0.34	-0.76	-0.35	-0.19	-0.45	-0.13	NAV Rtrn% +/-MSCI EMU
—	—	—	55	82	31	36	50	20	17	NAV Return% Rank in Cat
—	—	—	0.56	0.81	1.83	2.14	1.83	2.40	2.87	Income Return %
—	—	—	-23.52	-22.41	40.56	18.92	6.78	33.44	16.55	Capital Return %
—	—	0.01	0.41	0.45	0.79	1.30	1.32	1.85	2.96	Income $
—	—	0.00	0.26	0.00	0.00	0.00	0.00	0.00	0.00	Capital Gains $
—	—	—	0.84	0.84	0.84	0.79	0.58	0.54	0.51	Expense Ratio %
—	—	—	1.13	1.44	2.08	2.29	2.50	3.23	2.60	Income Ratio %
—	—	—	24	3	7	11	8	8	5	Turnover Rate %
—	—	—	—	143	234	456	718	2,221	2,904	Net Assets $mil

Performance 12-31-07

Historic Quarterly NAV Returns

	1st Qtr	2nd Qtr	3rd Qtr	4th Qtr	Total
2003	-10.24	26.00	2.51	22.81	42.39
2004	-0.59	2.43	0.18	18.68	21.06
2005	-0.10	-1.22	7.83	2.06	8.61
2006	12.72	1.34	6.36	11.81	35.84
2007	4.55	9.84	2.13	1.82	19.42

Trailing	NAV Return%	Market Return%	NAV Rtrn% +/-MSCI EAFE	%Rank Cat.(NAV)
3 Mo	1.82	1.22	3.57	22
6 Mo	3.99	3.71	3.60	24
1 Yr	19.42	18.41	8.25	17
3 Yr Avg	20.78	20.40	3.95	22
5 Yr Avg	24.88	24.62	3.29	29
10 Yr Avg	—	—	—	—

Tax Analysis	Tax-Adj Return%	Tax-Cost Ratio
3 Yr (estimated)	19.94	0.70
5 Yr (estimated)	24.09	0.63
10 Yr (estimated)	—	—

Rating and Risk

Time Period	Morningstar Rtn vs Cat	Morningstar Risk vs Cat	Morningstar Risk-Adj Rating
3 Yr	Avg	-Avg	★★★
5 Yr	Avg	Avg	★★★
10 Yr	—	—	—

Other Measures	Standard Index S&P 500	Best Fit Index MSCI Eur
Alpha	3.1	1.4
Beta	1.03	1.04
R-Squared	87	96
Standard Deviation	10.51	
Mean	20.78	
Sharpe Ratio	1.46	

Morningstar's Take by Gregg Wolper 12-31-07

It's hard to find a rationale for owning iShares EMU Index.

This exchange-traded fund limits itself to the countries using the euro (the European Monetary Union). Those countries are developed, Western European markets boasting many excellent companies and stable governmental systems. Furthermore, this is a large-cap portfolio, so the potential volatility of smaller stocks isn't a concern.

So what's not to like? Basically, that the markets excluded from the fund's portfolio can boast all the same qualities, except for the euro. Those left out include two of Europe's biggest markets as measured by market capitalization--the United Kingdom and Switzerland. The list of notable companies headquartered thus omitted from this fund includes GlaxoSmithKline, BP, Novartis, UBS, Nestle, Credit Suisse, Vodafone, and HSBC--and that's just the biggest names. If those firms shared something in common that made them unattractive, that would make this portfolio appealing. But they don't have much in common except their bases in non-EMU European countries.

Other reasons this fund could justify itself: If firms in the euro countries only traded with each other, then an EMU-only fund would eliminate exchange-rate troubles. Or, that the fund allows investors to get pure euro exposure in one fell swoop. Yet, companies in euro countries trade with firms the world over, making the fund an imperfect hedge against currency risk. Plus, investors seeking euro exposure can get their fill from another ETF that owns the currency itself.

True, a health-care bear might like this fund. Without British and Swiss pharma firms, it has less than 3% of assets in health care, compared with more than 7% for the broader-based iShares S&P Europe 350 Index or Vanguard European Stock ETF.

This ETF has big, well-established companies and is far from the riskiest choice. It does not seem preferable, though, to broader funds, some of which are cheaper as well.

Address:	45 Fremont Street United States 800-474-2737
Web Address:	www.ishares.com
Inception:	07-25-00*
Advisor:	Barclays Global Fund Advisers

Management Fee:	0.54%		
Expense Projections:	3Yr:$173	5Yr:$302	10Yr:$677
Income Distrib:	Annually		
Exchange:	NYSE		

Portfolio Analysis 11-30-07

Share change since 10-07 Total Stocks:281	Sector	Country	% Assets
⊖ TOTAL	Energy	France	3.48
⊖ Nokia	Hardware	Finland	3.07
⊖ Telefonica	Telecom	Spain	2.89
⊖ Banco Santander	Financial	Spain	2.83
⊖ Siemens	Hardware	Germany	2.54
⊖ E.ON	Utilities	Germany	2.49
⊖ BNP Paribas	Financial	France	2.20
⊖ Banco Bilbao Vizcaya Arg	Financial	Spain	2.13
⊖ sanofi-aventis	Health	France	1.98
⊖ Daimler	Goods	Germany	1.85
⊖ Allianz SE	Financial	Germany	1.84
Eni	Energy	Italy	1.82
⊖ ING Groep	Financial	Netherlands	1.53
⊖ France Telecom	Telecom	France	1.38
⊖ Intesa Sanpaolo	Financial	Italy	1.35
⊖ BASF	Ind Mtrls	Germany	1.34
⊖ Suez	Utilities	France	1.34
⊖ ArcelorMittal	Ind Mtrls	Netherlands	1.31
⊖ AXA	Financial	France	1.27
⊖ Deutsche Telekom	Telecom	Germany	1.24

Current Investment Style

Value Blnd Growth — Large Mid Small

Market Cap	%
Giant	58.7
Large	30.8
Mid	10.1
Small	0.4
Micro	0.0
Avg $mil: 48,156	

Value Measures		Rel Category
Price/Earnings	12.96	1.01
Price/Book	1.95	0.98
Price/Sales	0.95	0.93
Price/Cash Flow	7.79	0.98
Dividend Yield %	3.58	0.92

Growth Measures	%	Rel Category
Long-Term Erngs	10.98	0.97
Book Value	11.24	1.17
Sales	8.27	0.93
Cash Flow	12.43	1.84
Historical Erngs	16.66	0.82

Composition

Cash	0.0	Bonds	0.0
Stocks	99.7	Other	0.3
Foreign (% of Stock)			100.0

Sector Weightings	% of Stocks	Rel MSCI EAFE	3 Year High	3 Year Low
Info	19.28	1.52		
Software	1.13	1.95	2	1
Hardware	6.84	1.69	7	5
Media	2.26	1.34	3	2
Telecom	9.05	1.43	10	7
Service	40.69	0.94		
Health	3.41	0.54	5	3
Consumer	3.35	0.68	4	3
Business	4.50	0.90	5	4
Financial	29.43	1.09	34	29
Mfg	40.01	0.91		
Goods	11.84	0.89	13	10
Ind Mtrls	13.70	0.79	14	10
Energy	7.06	0.91	13	7
Utilities	7.41	1.34	8	7

Regional Exposure	% Stock		
UK/W. Europe	100	N. America	0
Japan	0	Latn America	0
Asia X Japan	0	Other	0

Country Exposure	% Stock		
France	28	Italy	11
Germany	24	Netherlands	9
Spain	13		

iShares FTSE/Xinhua China FXI

Market Price $170.45

Mstar Category Pacific/Asia ex-Japan St

Morningstar Fair Value

Price/Fair Value Ratio	Coverage Rate %
1.00	1

Morningstar Rating	Return	Risk	Yield	NAV	Avg Daily Vol. (k)	52 wk High/Low
★★★★★	High	High	1.2%	$174.27	5,841	$218.51 - $91.65

Growth of $10,000
- Investment Value of ETF
- Investment Value of Index MSCI EAFE

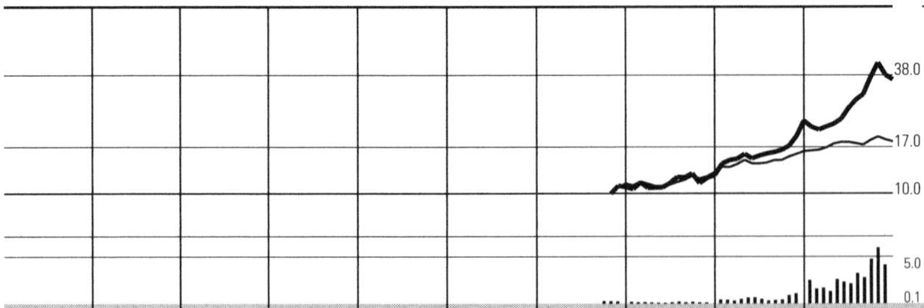

Trading Volume Millions

Valuation

As our stock analysts cover a relatively small number of holdings here, investors should consider this ETF's price/fair value ratio alongside other fundamental measures. That said, the stocks we do cover were recently trading at a 7% premium to our fair value estimate and anecdotal evidence suggests that the Chinese market is frothy.

Methodology

This fund tracks the FTSE/Xinhua China 25 Index. The benchmark encompasses 25 blue-chip Chinese companies that trade on the Hong Kong Stock Exchange and are available to international investors. Given the index's compact size and cap-weighted methodology, it's not surprising that the fund is very top heavy, with the top 10 stocks accounting for over 60% of assets. Financials and energy stakes dominate the fund, taking up 40% and 21% of the fund, respectively. Though the fund does not hedge its investments to the U.S. dollar, the Hong Kong dollar is pegged to the greenback.

1998	1999	2000	2001	2002	2003	2004	2005	2006	2007	History
—	—	—	—	—	—	54.91	61.44	111.14	174.27	NAV $
—	—	—	—	—	—	55.47	61.62	111.45	170.45	Market Price $
—	—	—	—	—	—	45.95*	14.15	83.19	58.66	NAV Return%
—	—	—	—	—	—	45.40*	13.33	83.17	54.75	Market Price Return%
—	—	—	—	—	—	0.65	0.44	0.48	-0.41	Avg Premium/Discount%
—	—	—	—	—	—	—	0.61	56.85	47.49	NAV Rtrn% +/-MSCI EAFE
—	—	—	—	—	—	—	—	—	—	NAV Rtrn% +/-FTSE Xinhu
—	—	—	—	—	—	—	38	1	19	NAV Return% Rank in Cat
—	—	—	—	—	—	—	2.28	2.12	1.88	Income Return %
—	—	—	—	—	—	—	11.87	81.07	56.78	Capital Return %
—	—	—	—	—	—	0.00	1.25	1.31	2.09	Income $
—	—	—	—	—	—	0.00	0.00	0.00	0.00	Capital Gains $
—	—	—	—	—	—	—	0.74	0.74	0.74	Expense Ratio %
—	—	—	—	—	—	—	2.97	2.62	1.74	Income Ratio %
—	—	—	—	—	—	—	13	45	36	Turnover Rate %
—	—	—	—	—	—	568	1,352	5,696	7,145	Net Assets $mil

Performance 12-31-07

Historic Quarterly NAV Returns

	1st Qtr	2nd Qtr	3rd Qtr	4th Qtr	Total
2003	—	—	—	—	—
2004	—	—	—	—	—*
2005	-0.97	5.42	11.53	-1.97	14.15
2006	19.94	3.61	6.51	38.41	83.19
2007	-6.33	22.85	41.95	-2.88	58.66

Trailing	NAV Return%	Market Return%	NAV Rtrn% +/-MSCI EAFE	%Rank Cat.(NAV)
3 Mo	-2.88	-4.19	-1.13	75
6 Mo	37.87	33.85	37.48	7
1 Yr	58.66	54.75	47.49	19
3 Yr Avg	49.15	47.55	32.32	1
5 Yr Avg	—	—	—	—
10 Yr Avg	—	—	—	—

Tax Analysis	Tax-Adj Return%	Tax-Cost Ratio
3 Yr (estimated)	48.38	0.52
5 Yr (estimated)	—	—
10 Yr (estimated)	—	—

Rating and Risk

Time Period	Morningstar Rtn vs Cat	Morningstar Risk vs Cat	Morningstar Risk-Adj Rating
3 Yr	High	High	★★★★★
5 Yr	—	—	—
10 Yr	—	—	—

Other Measures	Standard Index S&P 500	Best Fit Index MSCI Ex Jpn ND
Alpha	18.8	7.9
Beta	1.76	1.36
R-Squared	41	74
Standard Deviation	26.30	
Mean	49.15	
Sharpe Ratio	1.51	

Portfolio Analysis 12-31-07

Share change since 11-07 Total Stocks:27	Sector	Country	% Assets
⊕ China Mobile Ltd	Telecom	China	11.43
⊕ PetroChina	Energy	China	8.00
⊕ China Life Insurance	Financial	China	7.92
⊕ Industrial & Commercial	Financial	China	5.59
⊕ China Construction Bank	Financial	China	5.25
⊖ China Shenhua Energy	Energy	China	4.57
⊕ CNOOC Ltd	Energy	China	4.50
⊕ China Petroleum & Chemic	Business	China	4.28
⊕ China Communications Con	Business	China	3.97
⊕ BOC Hong Kong (Hldgs) Lt	Financial	Hong Kong	3.89
⊖ Ping An Insurance (Grp)	Financial	China	3.83
⊕ China Telecom	Telecom	China	3.79
⊕ China Merchants Bank	Financial	China	3.75
⊕ Bank of Communications	Financial	China	3.26
⊕ China Unicom Ltd	Telecom	China	3.17
⊕ China Coal Energy	Energy	China	3.11
⊕ Bank of China	Financial	China	2.86
⊕ China Merchants Hldgs (I	Ind Mtrls	China	2.54
⊖ Zijin Mining Grp Co Ltd	Ind Mtrls	China	2.15
⊕ Aluminum Corp. of China	Ind Mtrls	China	2.07

Current Investment Style

Value Blnd Growth — Large / Mid / Small (Large Blend box filled)

Market Cap	%
Giant	86.9
Large	13.1
Mid	0.0
Small	0.0
Micro	0.0
Avg $mil: 91,581	

Value Measures		Rel Category
Price/Earnings	21.70	1.23
Price/Book	3.50	1.33
Price/Sales	2.47	1.12
Price/Cash Flow	10.13	1.17
Dividend Yield %	2.52	0.75

Growth Measures	%	Rel Category
Long-Term Erngs	15.52	0.93
Book Value	15.08	1.28
Sales	25.55	1.39
Cash Flow	11.98	0.66
Historical Erngs	20.23	0.69

Composition

Cash	1.3	Bonds	0.0
Stocks	98.7	Other	0.0
Foreign (% of Stock)			100.0

Sector Weightings	% of Stocks	Rel MSCI EAFE	3 Year High	3 Year Low
Info	19.99	1.58		
Software	0.00	0.00	0	0
Hardware	0.00	0.00	0	0
Media	0.00	0.00	0	0
Telecom	19.99	3.15	24	18
Service	48.66	1.12		
Health	0.00	0.00	0	0
Consumer	0.00	0.00	0	0
Business	9.37	1.88	16	6
Financial	39.29	1.45	44	20
Mfg	31.35	0.71		
Goods	0.00	0.00	4	0
Ind Mtrls	8.84	0.51	12	9
Energy	20.45	2.63	25	17
Utilities	2.06	0.37	6	2

Regional Exposure	% Stock		
UK/W. Europe	0	N. America	0
Japan	0	Latn America	0
Asia X Japan	100	Other	0

Country Exposure	% Stock
China	96
Hong Kong	4

Morningstar's Take by Emiko Kurotsu 12-31-07

Be forewarned: IShares FTSE/Xinhua China 25 is full of risks.

This China ETF exemplifies the explosive growth of the Chinese stock market in recent years. Its 25 holdings--the biggest and most liquid publicly traded Chinese firms available to international investors--returned almost 100% in the past year alone. That growth has come with a catch, however: the fund was nearly twice as volatile as the MSCI Emerging Markets Asia Index over that span.

This volatility shouldn't be taken lightly. The fund is very concentrated by name and sector, with ten of its 25 stocks soaking up over 60% of assets, and financials and energy names dominating. When a single stock tumbles or the price of oil drops, this portfolio has nowhere to hide.

There are also fundamental risks to consider. Despite the fund's focus on some of the largest Chinese firms, only one--China Mobile--has trenched out a durable competitive advantage, or wide "economic moat." For example, though PetroChina is the biggest publicly traded energy firm, its relies heavily on the Chinese market for profits and on its state-owned parent company for exclusive exploration rights. With the Chinese energy market poised to open to foreign competitors, PetroChina's advantages are more tenuous, explaining the firm's narrow-moat rating.

Localized profits and state ties increase the intrinsic risk of many of this fund's stocks. Most rely exclusively on China for growth, which means that when that economy falters, so will profits. That raises the level of uncertainty associated with the forecasts that underpin our analysts' estimates of these firms' fair values. In view of that, we'd steer clear of this fund unless it's trading at least a 27% discount to our fair value estimate. We prefer more diversified ETFs like iShares MSCI Emerging Markets, which provides exposure to a broader range of stocks, industries, and regions, notably including China.

Address:	45 Fremont Street United States 800-474-2737
Web Address:	www.ishares.com
Inception:	10-05-04*
Advisor:	Barclays Global Fund Advisers

Management Fee:	0.74%		
Expense Projections:	3Yr:$237	5Yr:$411	10Yr:$918
Income Distrib:	Annually		
Exchange:	NYSE		

iShares Germany Indx EWG

Market Price	Mstar Category
$35.44	Europe Stock

Morningstar Fair Value

Price/Fair Value Ratio	Coverage Rate %
0.98	13

Morningstar Rating	Return	Risk	Yield	NAV	Avg Daily Vol. (k)	52 wk High/Low
★★★	Average	Above Avg	1.5%	$35.74	1,222	$36.50 - $26.33

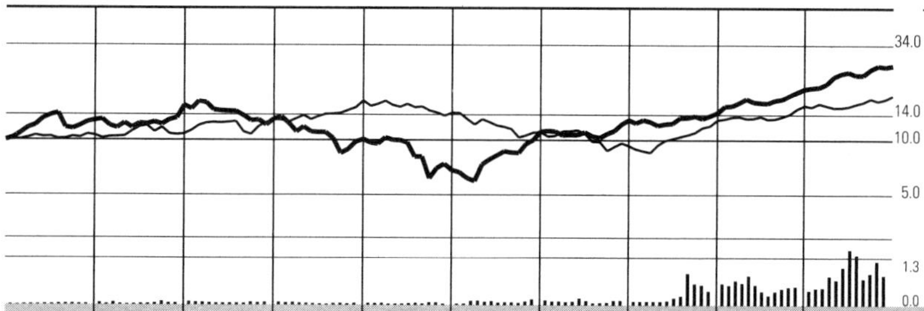

Growth of $10,000
— Investment Value of ETF
— Investment Value of Index MSCI EAFE

Trading Volume Millions

Valuation

Because our equity analysts don't cover all of this fund's holdings, our valuation assessment is not definitive. Still, judging from the valuation of the names that our analysts cover, the fund was recently trading at a 4% discount to our fair value estimate, which is hardly a bargain in our eyes.

Methodology

This fund tracks the MSCI Germany Index, which represents about 50 stocks that trade primarily on the Frankfurt Stock Exchange. Collectively, the index constituents account for about 85% of the total German stock market. The fund weights holdings by market cap. The portfolio is top-heavy, with the top 10 stocks making up a whopping 64% of assets. The fund's sector weights reflect the key drivers of the German economy, with financials, industrials, and utilities firms leading the way. The index does not hedge investments back into the U.S. dollar.

1998	1999	2000	2001	2002	2003	2004	2005	2006	2007	History
22.12	26.16	19.59	14.99	10.03	16.15	18.51	20.22	26.92	35.74	NAV $
22.25	26.69	19.50	15.10	9.85	16.19	18.63	20.31	26.90	35.44	Market Price $
28.28	20.87	-15.97	-22.57	-32.28	63.09	15.82	9.86	35.66	34.75	NAV Return%
28.08	22.59	-18.02	-21.64	-33.98	66.48	16.29	9.64	34.96	33.70	Market Price Return%
-0.03	0.29	0.29	-0.01	0.07	0.03	0.22	0.01	0.07	0.01	Avg Premium/Discount%
8.35	-6.16	-1.80	-1.13	-16.34	24.50	-4.43	-3.68	9.32	23.58	NAV Rtrn% +/-MSCI EAFE
-1.13	0.79	-0.37	-0.18	0.90	-0.71	-0.35	-0.06	-0.33	-0.46	NAV Rtrn% +/-MSCI Grmny
45	23	78	46	100	8	71	29	34	1	NAV Return% Rank in Cat
1.01	0.48	0.62	0.96	0.81	2.00	1.20	0.63	2.51	1.92	Income Return %
27.27	20.39	-16.59	-23.53	-33.09	61.09	14.62	9.23	33.15	32.83	Capital Return %
0.18	0.11	0.16	0.19	0.12	0.20	0.19	0.12	0.51	0.52	Income $
0.13	0.36	2.37	0.00	0.00	0.00	0.00	0.00	0.00	0.00	Capital Gains $
—	—	0.94	0.84	—	0.84	0.80	0.57	0.54	0.51	Expense Ratio %
—	—	0.73	—	—	1.98	1.27	1.54	2.62	2.32	Income Ratio %
—	—	56	20	9	11	9	9	12	4	Turnover Rate %
80	157	165	108	69	145	156	479	937	1,973	Net Assets $mil

Performance 12-31-07

Historic Quarterly NAV Returns

	1st Qtr	2nd Qtr	3rd Qtr	4th Qtr	Total
2003	-12.86	38.44	3.31	30.87	63.09
2004	-4.27	3.75	-1.87	18.84	15.82
2005	-2.16	-1.88	9.68	4.34	9.86
2006	13.75	-0.30	4.80	14.15	35.66
2007	6.76	16.11	3.57	4.96	34.75

Trailing	NAV Return%	Market Return%	NAV Rtrn% +/-MSCI EAFE	%Rank Cat.(NAV)
3 Mo	4.96	4.01	6.71	9
6 Mo	8.70	8.56	8.31	10
1 Yr	34.75	33.70	23.58	1
3 Yr Avg	26.17	25.54	9.34	1
5 Yr Avg	30.56	30.81	8.97	15
10 Yr Avg	9.99	9.82	1.33	56

Tax Analysis	Tax-Adj Return%	Tax-Cost Ratio
3 Yr (estimated)	25.59	0.46
5 Yr (estimated)	29.99	0.44
10 Yr (estimated)	9.20	0.72

Rating and Risk

Time Period	Morningstar Rtn vs Cat	Morningstar Risk vs Cat	Morningstar Risk-Adj Rating
3 Yr	+Avg	Avg	★★★★
5 Yr	+Avg	+Avg	★★★★
10 Yr	-Avg	+Avg	★

Other Measures	Standard Index S&P 500	Best Fit Index MSCI Eur
Alpha	6.7	4.7
Beta	1.12	1.14
R-Squared	76	84
Standard Deviation	12.28	
Mean	26.17	
Sharpe Ratio	1.63	

Portfolio Analysis 11-30-07

Share change since 10-07 Total Stocks:50	Sector	Country	% Assets
⊕ Siemens	Hardware	Germany	10.33
⊕ E.ON	Utilities	Germany	10.19
⊕ Daimler	Goods	Germany	7.57
⊕ Allianz SE	Financial	Germany	7.40
⊕ BASF	Ind Mtrls	Germany	5.58
⊕ Deutsche Bank	Financial	Germany	5.33
⊕ Deutsche Telekom	Telecom	Germany	5.01
⊕ RWE	Utilities	Germany	4.88
⊕ Bayer	Ind Mtrls	Germany	4.71
⊕ SAP	Software	Germany	3.62
⊕ Muenchener Rueckversiche	Financial	Germany	3.06
⊕ Volkswagen	Goods	Germany	3.04
⊕ Deutsche Boerse	Financial	Germany	3.03
⊕ Deutsche Post	Business	Germany	2.11
⊕ Commerzbank	Financial	Germany	1.98
⊕ ThyssenKrupp	Ind Mtrls	Germany	1.71
⊕ Continental	Ind Mtrls	Germany	1.58
⊕ Porsche Automobil Holdin	Goods	Germany	1.54
⊕ MAN	Ind Mtrls	Germany	1.46
⊕ Volkswagen AG	—	Germany	1.28

Current Investment Style

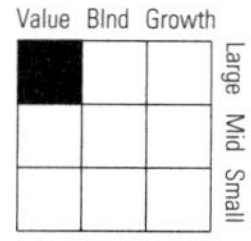

Market Cap	%
Giant	69.1
Large	24.5
Mid	6.3
Small	0.1
Micro	0.0
Avg $mil: 58,662	

Value Measures		Rel Category
Price/Earnings	13.53	1.05
Price/Book	1.90	0.95
Price/Sales	0.80	0.78
Price/Cash Flow	6.53	0.82
Dividend Yield %	3.16	0.81

Growth Measures	%	Rel Category
Long-Term Erngs	11.28	1.00
Book Value	9.45	0.98
Sales	5.64	0.64
Cash Flow	14.33	2.13
Historical Erngs	16.57	0.82

Composition

Cash	0.1	Bonds	0.0
Stocks	98.7	Other	1.3
Foreign (% of Stock)			100.0

Sector Weightings	% of Stocks	Rel MSCI EAFE	3 Year High	3 Year Low
Info	20.62	1.63		
Software	3.67	6.33	6	4
Hardware	11.42	2.82	12	10
Media	0.46	0.27	1	0
Telecom	5.07	0.80	10	4
Service	29.87	0.69		
Health	2.38	0.37	5	2
Consumer	1.34	0.27	2	1
Business	3.33	0.67	4	3
Financial	22.82	0.84	28	23
Mfg	49.51	1.13		
Goods	14.70	1.10	16	11
Ind Mtrls	19.16	1.10	20	14
Energy	0.00	0.00	0	0
Utilities	15.65	2.82	16	13

Regional Exposure	% Stock		
UK/W. Europe	100	N. America	0
Japan	0	Latn America	0
Asia X Japan	0	Other	0

Country Exposure	% Stock
Germany	100

Morningstar's Take by Emiko Kurotsu 12-31-07

IShares MSCI Germany's recent performance is impressive, but its quality less so.

This ETF is the only one we cover that offers pure exposure to German stocks. Its 50, mostly giant-cap, holdings cover roughly 85% of the German stock market. That's been a good place to invest of late, as the German market's key sectors--industrials, utilities, and financials--have posted uniformly strong earnings against a healthy economic backdrop. Indeed, this ETF breezed past every developed European market fund to return 32% in the 12 months ended mid-December 2007.

Still, quality is in short supply here. While our analysts rate relatively few stocks in the fund, they cover nine of the top 10 names, which together make up about 60% of assets. Tellingly, not a single one of these stocks boasts a wide "economic moat," our parlance for firms with unassailable competitive advantages. For instance, though automaker Daimler did well to spin off its Chrysler unit, our analysts still don't think its luxury Mercedes and trucking arms can off rivals. Similarly, Deutsche Telekom lacks a moat because of its inability to effectively protect its turf in Germany and abroad from encroaching rivals like Vodafone. Though these firms aren't necessarily representative of all of the fund's holdings, they're bellwethers of the German economy and, thus, offer more than a modicum of insight into the portfolio's overall quality, which appears to be middling at best. The upshot is that these lesser-quality firms, and thus this fund, are worth less than a basket of wide-moat stocks.

That's not to say that we wouldn't buy this fund if its holdings got cheap enough. But the portfolio's mediocre quality and lack of diversification has stoked volatility. As such, we'd require at least a 9% discount to our fair value estimate to invest here.

Address:	45 Fremont Street United States 800-474-2737
Web Address:	www.ishares.com
Inception:	03-12-96
Advisor:	Barclays Global Fund Advisers

Management Fee:	0.54%		
Expense Projections:	3Yr:$173	5Yr:$302	10Yr:$677
Income Distrib:	Annually		
Exchange:	NYSE		

iShares Hong Kong EWH

Market Price	Mstar Category
$21.93	Pacific/Asia ex-Japan S

Morningstar Rating	Return	Risk	Yield	NAV	Avg Daily Vol. (k)	52 wk High/Low
★★	Below Avg	Average	1.7%	$22.19	6,635	$24.10 - $14.82

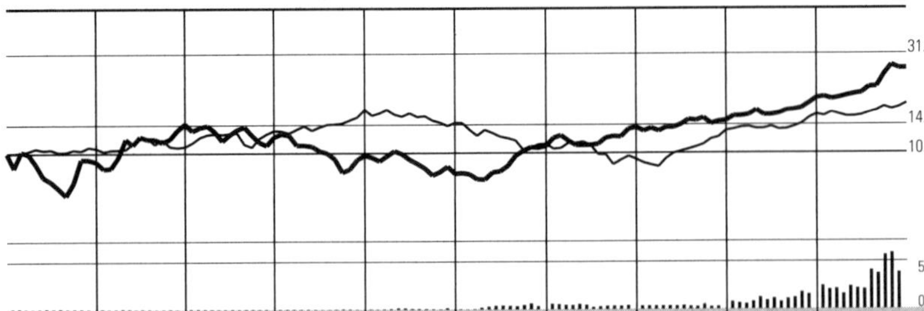

Growth of $10,000
- Investment Value of ETF
- Investment Value of Index MSCI EAFE

Trading Volume Millions

Morningstar Fair Value

Price/Fair Value Ratio	Coverage Rate %
1.00	0

Valuation

Because our equity analysts cover a relatively small number of this ETF's stock holdings, the price/fair value ratio above may not be a faithful representation of the portfolio's valuation attributes. Accordingly, investors should consider the price/fair value ratio only in conjunction with other fundamental measures.

Methodology

IShares MSCI Hong Kong tracks the MSCI Hong Kong Index, a free-float market-cap weighted benchmark that compiles stocks on the Hong Kong Stock Exchanges and Clearing Ltd. The portfolio is concentrated, with more than one half of assets typically in the top 10 names; the fund's top holding recently accounted for 10%-plus of assets. Financials figure prominently here, with real estate and investment-services firms as well as banks soaking up roughly half of the fund. Though investments are unhedged, they're denominated in Hong Kong dollars which, in turn, are pegged to the U.S. greenback.

History

1998	1999	2000	2001	2002	2003	2004	2005	2006	2007	History
9.33	13.94	11.74	9.27	7.37	9.93	12.04	12.63	16.06	22.19	NAV $
9.38	14.25	11.50	9.17	7.43	10.00	12.09	12.62	16.00	21.93	Market Price $
-9.12	54.00	-13.99	-18.98	-18.98	36.82	24.01	7.84	29.69	40.55	NAV Return%
-9.05	56.58	-17.58	-18.19	-17.43	36.67	23.65	7.31	29.30	39.42	Market Price Return%
-0.51	0.30	0.32	0.55	-0.27	0.52	0.09	0.20	-0.15	-0.12	Avg Premium/Discount%
-29.05	26.97	0.18	2.46	-3.04	-1.77	3.76	-5.70	3.35	29.38	NAV Rtrn% +/-MSCI EAFE
-5.89	-5.44	0.43	-0.37	-1.19	-1.28	-0.97	-0.56	-0.66	-0.65	NAV Rtrn% +/-MSCI HK
67	67	34	80	83	67	34	62	75	37	NAV Return% Rank in Cat
2.68	4.14	1.77	1.95	1.54	2.05	2.74	2.97	2.46	2.36	Income Return %
-11.80	49.86	-15.76	-20.93	-20.52	34.77	21.27	4.87	27.23	38.19	Capital Return %
0.29	0.38	0.25	0.23	0.14	0.15	0.27	0.36	0.31	0.38	Income $
0.12	0.00	0.02	0.01	0.00	0.00	0.00	0.00	0.00	0.00	Capital Gains $
—	—	0.94	0.84	—	0.84	0.80	0.57	0.54	0.52	Expense Ratio %
—	—	2.57	—	—	3.06	2.78	2.75	2.87	2.92	Income Ratio %
—	—	21	43	15	10	5	6	10	9	Turnover Rate %
68	89	70	60	121	413	642	639	1,359	2,590	Net Assets $mil

Performance 12-31-07

Historic Quarterly NAV Returns

	1st Qtr	2nd Qtr	3rd Qtr	4th Qtr	Total
2003	-6.24	9.55	26.16	5.59	36.82
2004	6.14	-4.65	10.45	10.94	24.01
2005	-4.24	7.98	7.71	-3.18	7.84
2006	7.05	-0.22	6.23	14.30	29.69
2007	0.44	5.64	23.71	7.08	40.55

Trailing	NAV Return%	Market Return%	NAV Rtrn% +/-MSCI EAFE	%Rank Cat.(NAV)
3 Mo	7.08	6.07	8.83	13
6 Mo	32.46	31.06	32.07	27
1 Yr	40.55	39.42	29.38	37
3 Yr Avg	25.26	24.60	8.43	87
5 Yr Avg	27.24	26.73	5.65	67
10 Yr Avg	10.17	9.99	1.51	100

Tax Analysis	Tax-Adj Return%	Tax-Cost Ratio
3 Yr (estimated)	24.33	0.74
5 Yr (estimated)	26.34	0.71
10 Yr (estimated)	9.23	0.85

Rating and Risk

Time Period	Morningstar Rtn vs Cat	Morningstar Risk vs Cat	Morningstar Risk-Adj Rating
3 Yr	-Avg	-Avg	★★
5 Yr	-Avg	-Avg	★★
10 Yr	Low	Avg	★

Other Measures	Standard Index S&P 500	Best Fit Index Pac ex-Japan
Alpha	7.5	3.0
Beta	1.01	0.84
R-Squared	42	71
Standard Deviation	14.80	
Mean	25.26	
Sharpe Ratio	1.32	

Portfolio Analysis 11-30-07

Share change since 10-07 Total Stocks:44	Sector	Country	% Assets
⊖ Hong Kong Exchanges & Cl	Financial	Hong Kong	10.11
⊖ Cheung Kong (Hldgs) Ltd	Financial	Hong Kong	8.93
⊖ Sun Hung Kai Properties	Financial	Hong Kong	8.78
⊖ Hutchison Whampoa Ltd	Telecom	Hong Kong	7.86
⊖ Esprit Hldgs Ltd	Consumer	Hong Kong	4.91
⊖ Hang Seng Bank	Financial	Hong Kong	4.64
⊖ Swire Pacific Ltd	Financial	Hong Kong	3.60
⊖ The Hong Kong & China Ga	Utilities	Hong Kong	3.36
⊖ BOC Hong Kong (Hldgs) Lt	Financial	Hong Kong	3.04
⊖ Hang Lung Properties Ltd	Financial	Hong Kong	2.96
⊖ New World Development	Financial	Hong Kong	2.94
⊖ Li & Fung Ltd	Goods	Hong Kong	2.84
⊖ CLP Hldgs Ltd	Utilities	Hong Kong	2.82
⊖ The Bank of East Asia Lt	Financial	Hong Kong	2.68
⊖ Hongkong Electric Hldgs	Utilities	Hong Kong	2.33
⊖ Henderson Land Developme	Financial	Hong Kong	2.31
⊖ Tencent Hldgs Ltd	Telecom	China	2.22
⊖ The Wharf (Hldgs) Ltd	Financial	Hong Kong	2.20
⊕ Kerry Properties Ltd	Financial	Hong Kong	1.87
⊖ Sino Land	Financial	Hong Kong	1.67

Current Investment Style (Value Blnd Growth; Large Mid Small)

Market Cap	%
Giant	51.7
Large	45.6
Mid	2.7
Small	0.0
Micro	0.0
Avg $mil: 20,803	

Value Measures		Rel Category
Price/Earnings	16.14	0.92
Price/Book	2.44	0.93
Price/Sales	4.19	1.90
Price/Cash Flow	11.43	1.32
Dividend Yield %	2.66	0.79

Growth Measures	%	Rel Category
Long-Term Erngs	15.61	0.93
Book Value	8.07	0.69
Sales	17.99	0.98
Cash Flow	24.29	1.35
Historical Erngs	21.44	0.74

Composition

Cash	0.1	Bonds	0.0
Stocks	99.9	Other	0.0
Foreign (% of Stock)			100.0

Sector Weightings	% of Stocks	Rel MSCI EAFE	3 Year High	3 Year Low
Info	12.42	0.98		
Software	0.00	0.00	0	0
Hardware	0.43	0.11	1	0
Media	0.49	0.29	1	0
Telecom	11.50	1.81	16	11
Service	71.24	1.64		
Health	0.00	0.00	0	0
Consumer	7.49	1.51	9	6
Business	3.08	0.62	4	3
Financial	60.67	2.25	61	50
Mfg	16.35	0.37		
Goods	4.49	0.34	5	3
Ind Mtrls	2.84	0.16	5	1
Energy	0.00	0.00	0	0
Utilities	9.02	1.63	17	8

Regional Exposure	% Stock		
UK/W. Europe	0	N. America	0
Japan	0	Latn America	0
Asia X Japan	100	Other	0

Country Exposure	% Stock
Hong Kong	96
China	4

Morningstar's Take by Jeffrey Ptak 12-31-07

IShares MSCI Hong Kong's dazzling recent performance isn't reason enough to take the plunge.

No question about it, this ETF has been on a tear. The fund, which tracks the MSCI Hong Kong Index, ripped off gains of 37%, 24%, 7%, and 29% from 2003 to 2006 and was up 40% for the year through Dec. 26. Consequently, the fund's 25% five-year annualized return bests nearly all ETFs.

The remarkable thing about that run is what's missing: A strong currency tailwind. The fund's investments are denominated in the Hong Kong dollar, which is pegged to the U.S. greenback. As such, the fund hasn't had the benefit of a falling dollar like other funds, meaning that stock price appreciation has fueled its rise, with heady economic growth--much of it linked to mainland China's furious expansion--propelling names like top-holding Hong Kong Exchanges and Clearing.

Yet, while the going has been good lately, there's no guarantee that it'll continue. The fund's early years provide a sobering reminder in that regard: An investment at the fund's April 1996 inception would have lost more than half its value by August 1998 and wouldn't fully recover until January 2004. That concern takes on added urgency when one considers the overheated state of the Chinese market, where bankers have gone to unusual lengths, such as curbing lending, to rein in growth.

More fundamentally, we don't see a strong reason to own the portfolio given its overlap with diversified foreign funds, such as MSCI EAFE Index trackers. And while our analysts cover only a few of this portfolio's 40-plus stock holdings, anecdotal evidence suggests that they're not exactly screaming bargains. For instance, Powershares Golden Dragon Halter USX China was recently trading at a hefty 17% premium to our analysts' estimate of its intrinsic worth while BLDRS Asia 50 ADR, which spans developed and developing Asian nations, was hovering near fair value.

Address:	45 Fremont Street United States 800-474-2737
Web Address:	www.ishares.com
Inception:	03-12-96
Advisor:	Barclays Global Fund Advisers

Management Fee:	0.54%		
Expense Projections:	3Yr:$173	5Yr:$302	10Yr:$677
Income Distrib:	Annually		
Exchange:	NYSE		

iShares Japan Index EWJ

Market Price	Mstar Category
$13.29	Japan Stock

Morningstar Fair Value

Price/Fair Value Ratio	Coverage Rate %
1.00	0

Valuation

Because our equity analysts cover a relatively small number of this ETF's holdings, the price/fair value ratio above may not be a faithful representation of the portfolio's valuation attributes. Investors trying to gauge this ETF's attractiveness should consider the price/fair value ratio only in conjunction with other fundamental measures.

Methodology

This passively run offering provides mainstream exposure to Japan. It's designed to track the MSCI Japan Index, a market-cap-weighted index that aims to replicate the top 85% of the publicly available stock universe in Japan. This ETF's biggest holdings are well-known powerhouses like Toyota, Mitsubishi UFJ Financial Group, Canon, and Sony. It has a relatively large average market cap to go along with its relatively neutral sector and style stances.

Morningstar Rating	Return	Risk	Yield	NAV	Avg Daily Vol. (k)	52 wk High/Low
★★★	Average	Below Avg	1.0%	$13.37	17,315	$15.14 - $12.83

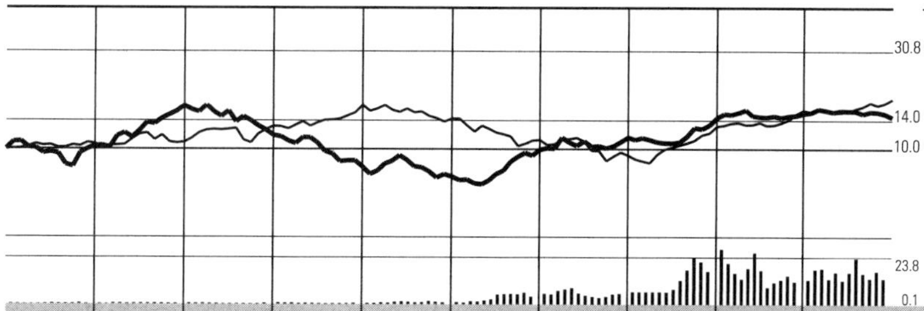

Growth of $10,000
— Investment Value of ETF
— Investment Value of Index MSCI EAFE

Trading Volume Millions

History

1998	1999	2000	2001	2002	2003	2004	2005	2006	2007	History
10.34	16.15	11.17	7.83	7.01	9.50	10.86	13.48	14.12	13.37	NAV $
10.25	16.31	11.06	7.71	6.95	9.64	10.92	13.52	14.21	13.29	Market Price $
3.53	57.89	-28.57	-29.90	-10.47	35.54	14.78	24.65	5.49	-4.33	NAV Return%
3.88	60.86	-29.97	-30.29	-9.86	38.73	13.74	24.34	5.85	-5.48	Market Price Return%
-0.07	0.31	0.53	0.37	-0.08	0.61	0.24	0.00	-0.13	-0.11	Avg Premium/Discount%
-16.40	30.86	-14.40	-8.46	5.47	-3.05	-5.47	11.11	-20.85	-15.50	NAV Rtrn% +/-MSCI EAFE
-1.52	-3.64	-0.41	-0.50	-0.19	-0.37	-1.08	-0.87	-0.75	-0.10	NAV Rtrn% +/-MSCI Japan
1	1	1	1	100	1	1	1	100	15	NAV Return% Rank in Cat
0.00	0.43	0.01	0.00	0.00	0.02	0.45	0.53	0.74	0.98	Income Return %
3.53	57.46	-28.58	-29.90	-10.47	35.52	14.33	24.12	4.75	-5.31	Capital Return %
0.00	0.04	0.00	0.00	0.00	0.00	0.04	0.06	0.10	0.14	Income $
0.01	0.11	0.45	0.00	0.00	0.00	0.00	0.00	0.00	0.00	Capital Gains $
—	0.94	0.88	0.84	0.84	0.84	0.64	0.57	0.54	0.52	Expense Ratio %
—	-0.27	-0.32	-0.11	-0.12	0.03	0.28	0.59	0.48	0.68	Income Ratio %
—	—	22	21	2	2	5	6	8	3	Turnover Rate %
310	979	650	474	542	2,890	6,624	13,042	13,787	10,313	Net Assets $mil

Performance 12-31-07

Historic Quarterly NAV Returns

	1st Qtr	2nd Qtr	3rd Qtr	4th Qtr	Total
2003	-7.56	11.42	21.47	8.34	35.54
2004	14.63	-3.95	-7.65	12.88	14.78
2005	-2.58	-3.69	18.94	11.69	24.65
2006	6.38	-4.60	-0.88	4.87	5.49
2007	3.47	-0.62	-0.90	-6.13	-4.33

Trailing	NAV Return%	Market Return%	NAV Rtrn% +/-MSCI EAFE	%Rank Cat.(NAV)
3 Mo	-6.13	-6.33	-4.38	60
6 Mo	-6.97	-7.43	-7.36	40
1 Yr	-4.33	-5.48	-15.50	15
3 Yr Avg	7.95	7.55	-8.88	100
5 Yr Avg	14.37	14.44	-7.22	1
10 Yr Avg	3.67	3.74	-4.99	1

Tax Analysis	Tax-Adj Return%	Tax-Cost Ratio
3 Yr (estimated)	7.68	0.25
5 Yr (estimated)	14.17	0.17
10 Yr (estimated)	3.48	0.18

Rating and Risk

Time Period	Morningstar Rtn vs Cat	Morningstar Risk vs Cat	Morningstar Risk-Adj Rating
3 Yr	+Avg	-Avg	★★★★
5 Yr	Avg	-Avg	★★★★
10 Yr	-Avg	-Avg	★★

Other Measures	Standard Index S&P 500	Best Fit Index MSCI Japan
Alpha	-6.2	-0.5
Beta	0.87	1.00
R-Squared	50	100
Standard Deviation	11.75	
Mean	7.95	
Sharpe Ratio	0.34	

Portfolio Analysis 11-30-07

Share change since 10-07 Total Stocks:352	Sector	Country	% Assets
⊖ Toyota Motor	Goods	Japan	5.35
⊖ Mitsubishi UFJ Financial	Financial	Japan	2.92
⊖ Nintendo	Goods	Japan	2.17
⊖ Sumitomo Mitsui Financia	Financial	Japan	1.97
⊖ SONY CORPORATION	Goods	Japan	1.93
⊖ CANON INC.	Goods	Japan	1.93
⊖ Takeda Pharmaceutical	Health	Japan	1.90
⊖ HONDA MOTOR	Goods	Japan	1.85
⊖ Mizuho Financial Grp	Financial	Japan	1.79
⊖ Matsushita Electric Indu	Ind Mtrls	Japan	1.44
⊖ Mitsui & Co.	Ind Mtrls	Japan	1.36
⊖ Mitsubishi	Ind Mtrls	Japan	1.33
⊖ Nippon Steel	Ind Mtrls	Japan	1.21
⊖ The Tokyo Electric Power	Utilities	Japan	1.14
⊖ Nomura Hldgs	Financial	Japan	1.11
⊖ JFE Hldgs	Ind Mtrls	Japan	1.04
⊖ Mitsubishi Estate	Financial	Japan	1.03
⊖ East Japan Railway	Business	Japan	0.98
⊖ Komatsu Ltd	Ind Mtrls	Japan	0.97
⊖ NTT DoCoMo	Telecom	Japan	0.92

Current Investment Style

Value Blnd Growth / Large Mid Small

Market Cap	%
Giant	51.6
Large	35.8
Mid	12.3
Small	0.2
Micro	0.0
Avg $mil: 19,335	

Value Measures		Rel Category
Price/Earnings	16.23	1.00
Price/Book	1.56	1.08
Price/Sales	0.82	1.14
Price/Cash Flow	7.12	1.02
Dividend Yield %	1.71	0.86

Growth Measures	%	Rel Category
Long-Term Erngs	9.95	0.96
Book Value	10.01	1.15
Sales	7.51	1.06
Cash Flow	7.99	1.59
Historical Erngs	16.55	1.41

Composition

Cash	0.3	Bonds	0.0
Stocks	99.5	Other	0.2
Foreign (% of Stock)			100.0

Sector Weightings	% of Stocks	Rel MSCI EAFE	3 Year High	3 Year Low
Info	9.77	0.77		
Software	0.62	1.07	1	0
Hardware	6.00	1.48	7	5
Media	0.75	0.44	1	1
Telecom	2.40	0.38	3	2
Service	35.86	0.83		
Health	5.85	0.92	6	5
Consumer	3.41	0.69	6	3
Business	7.15	1.43	8	7
Financial	19.45	0.72	25	19
Mfg	54.37	1.24		
Goods	23.83	1.79	26	21
Ind Mtrls	25.44	1.47	27	19
Energy	0.87	0.11	1	1
Utilities	4.23	0.76	5	4

Regional Exposure	% Stock		
UK/W. Europe	0	N. America	0
Japan	100	Latn America	0
Asia X Japan	0	Other	0

Country Exposure	% Stock
Japan	100
Fiji	0

Morningstar's Take by William Samuel Rocco 12-31-07

Investors seeking a straightforward Japan play will find this ETF a worthwhile option.

IShares MSCI Japan Index Fund doesn't do anything fancy or provide much exposure to smaller-cap or lesser-known names in its chosen market. It tracks its namesake index, which is a market-cap-weighted index that aims to capture the top 85% of the publicly available stock universe in Japan. Thus, its portfolio is packed with well-known and widely held blue chips such as Toyota, Honda, Canon, and Sony, and its average market cap is normally much bigger than those of most passively run Japan funds as well as those of most actively run ones.

This ETF is attractively priced. Its 0.54% expense ratio, not surprisingly, is much lower than those of all the actively managed Japan offerings. And the other passive, pure-Japan offerings have expense ratios between 0.48% and 0.54%, so the fund is competitively priced relative to its direct peers. (The two Vanguard funds in the category, Vanguard Pacific Stock Index and the ETF version of that fund, are far cheaper, but they invest roughly 25% of their assets outside Japan and thus may not satisfy those seeking pure-Japan exposure.)

This ETF also has a solid risk/reward profile. It has tracked the returns of its index reasonably well over time (after taking fees into account.) Its returns are similar to those of the one other passive, pure-Japan offering that has been around for more than a couple of years. And while it hasn't fared quite as well as the Japan category norm over the past decade, it has outperformed over the trailing three- and five-year periods and suffered less volatility.

In short, this ETF is worth a look from investors set on a pure-Japan play. But such investors should note that this ETF is likely to overlap a lot with the Japan portions of their foreign funds and that the Japanese market has been a tough place to make money, as the paltry long-term gains of Japan funds attest.

Address:	45 Fremont Street United States 800-474-2737
Web Address:	www.ishares.com
Inception:	03-12-96
Advisor:	Barclays Global Fund Advisers

Management Fee:	0.54%		
Expense Projections:	3Yr:$173	5Yr:$302	10Yr:$677
Income Distrib:	Annually		
Exchange:	NYSE		

iShares Mexico Index EWW

Market Price	Mstar Category
$56.00	Latin America Stock

Morningstar Fair Value

Price/Fair Value Ratio	Coverage Rate %
1.00	2

Valuation

Given this portfolio's lack of diversification--it has more than 20% of assets in a single name--and emerging markets' notorious volatility, we think caution is the better part of valor here. Therefore, we'd demand a 16% discount to our fair value estimate before investing in the fund. It was recently sitting right on the cusp of buy territory.

Methodology

This fund tracks the MSCI Mexico Index, which consists of 25 or so stocks that trade on the Bolsa Mexicana de Valores, the country's national stock exchange. The index, which aims to cover 85% of the publicly traded Mexican market, weights stocks by free float adjusted market cap. The portfolio is very top heavy, with roughly half of assets stuffed into the top three names and nearly one fourth of the fund staked in a single name--telecom-provider America Movil. Telecom, basic materials, and mining abound here while financial and tech are scarce. The portfolio is not hedged back to the U.S. dollar.

Morningstar Rating	Return	Risk	Yield	NAV	Avg Daily Vol. (k)	52 wk High/Low
★	Low	Low	1.9%	$56.25	3,315	$64.77 - $47.94

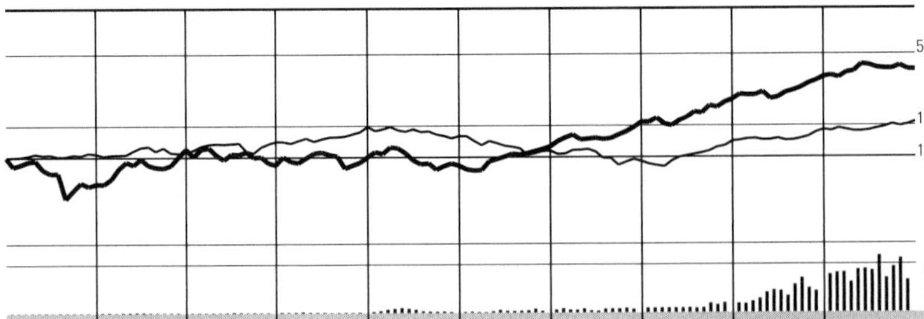

Growth of $10,000
— Investment Value of ETF
— Investment Value of Index MSCI EAFE

Trading Volume Millions

1998	1999	2000	2001	2002	2003	2004	2005	2006	2007	History
10.29	18.01	13.47	15.11	12.62	16.98	24.90	35.78	51.06	56.25	NAV $
10.25	18.06	13.31	15.18	12.45	17.08	25.16	35.71	51.25	56.00	Market Price $
-34.96	76.13	-22.77	13.49	-13.12	36.24	48.29	45.61	44.02	12.25	NAV Return%
-35.33	77.31	-23.90	15.38	-14.69	38.92	48.96	43.82	44.84	11.33	Market Price Return%
-1.14	-0.74	0.34	-0.08	0.05	-0.30	0.21	0.26	0.06	0.02	Avg Premium/Discount%
-54.89	49.10	-8.60	34.93	2.82	-2.35	28.04	32.07	17.68	1.08	NAV Rtrn% +/-MSCI EAF
—	-2.44	-2.77	-4.92	0.19	3.43	-0.03	-3.50	2.58	0.10	NAV Rtrn% +/-MSCI Mex
1	1	1	1	1	100	1	100	50	100	NAV Return% Rank in Ca
0.75	0.31	0.42	1.14	3.46	1.64	1.63	1.91	1.27	2.05	Income Return %
-35.71	75.82	-23.19	12.35	-16.58	34.60	46.66	43.70	42.75	10.20	Capital Return %
0.12	0.03	0.07	0.15	0.52	0.21	0.28	0.48	0.46	1.05	Income $
0.30	0.06	0.42	0.03	0.00	0.00	0.00	0.00	0.00	0.00	Capital Gains $
—	—	1.04	0.84	—	0.84	0.78	0.57	0.54	0.51	Expense Ratio %
—	—	0.35	—	—	1.43	1.40	1.70	2.06	1.19	Income Ratio %
—	—	24	34	8	13	12	9	12	14	Turnover Rate %
11	27	31	35	48	65	189	479	1,317	1,209	Net Assets $mil

Performance 12-31-07

Historic Quarterly NAV Returns

	1st Qtr	2nd Qtr	3rd Qtr	4th Qtr	Total
2003	-7.05	24.38	5.62	11.58	36.24
2004	20.85	-5.17	5.14	23.07	48.29
2005	-3.01	11.97	21.12	10.71	45.61
2006	7.29	-3.70	16.85	19.28	44.02
2007	6.97	13.05	-5.64	-1.64	12.25

Trailing	NAV Return%	Market Return%	NAV Rtrn% +/-MSCI EAFE	%Rank Cat.(NAV)
3 Mo	-1.64	-2.95	0.11	100
6 Mo	-7.19	-7.45	-7.58	100
1 Yr	12.25	11.33	1.08	100
3 Yr Avg	33.02	32.36	16.19	100
5 Yr Avg	36.60	36.85	15.01	100
10 Yr Avg	15.29	15.22	6.63	1

Tax Analysis	Tax-Adj Return%	Tax-Cost Ratio
3 Yr (estimated)	32.39	0.47
5 Yr (estimated)	35.98	0.45
10 Yr (estimated)	14.57	0.62

Rating and Risk

Time Period	Morningstar Rtn vs Cat	Morningstar Risk vs Cat	Morningstar Risk-Adj Rating
3 Yr	Low	Low	★
5 Yr	Low	Low	★
10 Yr	—	—	—

Other Measures	Standard Index S&P 500	Best Fit Index MSCI Latin Am
Alpha	9.8	0.4
Beta	1.41	0.68
R-Squared	47	66
Standard Deviation	19.56	
Mean	33.02	
Sharpe Ratio	1.35	

Portfolio Analysis 11-30-07

Share change since 10-07 Total Stocks:35	Sector	Country	% Assets
⊖ America Movil S.A.B de C	Telecom	Mexico	24.82
⊖ Cemex S.A. B de C.V.	Financial	Mexico	13.30
⊖ Telefonos de Mexico	Telecom	Mexico	10.88
⊖ Grupo Mexico	Ind Mtrls	Mexico	5.48
⊖ Wal-mart de Mexico S A B	Consumer	Mexico	5.12
⊖ Grupo Televisa	Media	Mexico	5.00
⊖ Fomento Economico Mexica	Goods	Mexico	4.47
⊖ Grupo Financiero Banorte	Financial	Mexico	4.27
⊖ Carso Global Telecom	Telecom	Mexico	2.94
⊖ Grupo Carso	Ind Mtrls	Mexico	2.63
⊖ Grupo Modelo	Goods	Mexico	2.06
⊖ Grupo Bimbo	Goods	Mexico	1.89
⊖ Kimberly-Clark de Mexico	Ind Mtrls	Mexico	1.87
⊖ Empresas ICA	Business	Mexico	1.71
⊖ Alfa	Ind Mtrls	Mexico	1.67
⊖ Industrias Penoles	Ind Mtrls	Mexico	1.58
⊖ Grupo Aeroportuario del	Business	Mexico	1.56
⊖ Southeast Airport Group	Business	Mexico	1.34
⊖ Controladora Comercial M	Consumer	Mexico	0.99
⊖ Urbi Desarrollos Urbanos	Consumer	Mexico	0.98

Current Investment Style

Value Blnd Growth — Large / Mid / Small

Market Cap	%
Giant	40.9
Large	44.7
Mid	13.6
Small	0.8
Micro	0.0
Avg $mil: 21,701	

Value Measures		Rel Category
Price/Earnings	13.58	0.91
Price/Book	3.22	1.10
Price/Sales	1.72	1.02
Price/Cash Flow	8.64	0.98
Dividend Yield %	3.59	1.25

Growth Measures	%	Rel Category
Long-Term Erngs	16.39	1.18
Book Value	16.20	1.15
Sales	20.38	1.14
Cash Flow	18.57	0.95
Historical Erngs	28.42	1.21

Composition

Cash	0.0	Bonds	0.0
Stocks	99.7	Other	0.2

Foreign (% of Stock) 100.0

Sector Weightings	% of Stocks	Rel MSCI EAFE	3 Year High	Low
Info	43.89	3.46		
Software	0.01	0.02	0	0
Hardware	0.00	0.00	0	0
Media	5.04	2.98	6	5
Telecom	38.84	6.12	43	37
Service	33.37	0.77		
Health	0.00	0.00	0	0
Consumer	10.54	2.13	13	10
Business	5.07	1.02	5	1
Financial	17.76	0.66	21	15
Mfg	22.74	0.52		
Goods	9.40	0.70	13	9
Ind Mtrls	13.34	0.77	15	10
Energy	0.00	0.00	0	0
Utilities	0.00	0.00	0	0

Regional Exposure	% Stock		
UK/W. Europe	0	N. America	0
Japan	0	Latn America	100
Asia X Japan	0	Other	0

Country Exposure	% Stock
Mexico	100

Morningstar's Take by Jeffrey Ptak 12-31-07

IShares MSCI Mexico is too hot to handle without a wide margin of safety.

There's nothing fancy about what this fund's benchmark, the MSCI Mexico Index, does: It holds 25 or so stocks that trade on Mexico's lone stock exchange, it weights each by market cap, and it occasionally rebalances the portfolio. That translates to lots of telecom, basic materials, and consumer-related exposure, as phone companies, cement-makers, miners, and beverage-giants dominate the economic landscape in Mexico.

What some investors might not realize, however, is the extent to which a handful of stocks determine the fund's fate. Its top holding, wireless provider America Movil, recently accounted for nearly 25% of assets. Cement-maker Cemex and phone carrier Telmex soaked up 13% and 10%, respectively. As these stocks go, so goes this portfolio.

Considering the respectable quality of these names, that's not a horrible thing. For instance, America Movil has trenched out a narrow moat by sheer virtue of its scale, which has conferred cost leadership in the Latin American wireless market. Similarly, barriers to entry allow Cemex to remain one of the world's largest cement traders while Telmex parlays its position as incumbent fixed-line provider into gobs of free cash flow. All told, our analysts have awarded at least a narrow moat to 10 of the 12 portfolio holdings that they cover, meaning that most firms have at least some semblance of a competitive advantage.

However, investors have to watch their step here. The portfolio is quite volatile owing to its concentrated nature, the often-unsteady state of these businesses, and currency gyrations. Also, Mexico is not as economically diverse as the U.S., as the portfolio's lumpy sector weightings attest. Thus, should global infrastructure demand cool, for example, the Mexican economy--and at least some of these companies--could take it on the chin.

With that in mind, we'd invest here only with a wide margin of safety.

Address:	45 Fremont Street United States 800-474-2737
Web Address:	www.ishares.com
Inception:	03-12-96
Advisor:	Barclays Global Fund Advisers

Management Fee:	0.54%		
Expense Projections:	3Yr:$173	5Yr:$302	10Yr:$677
Income Distrib:	Annually		
Exchange:	NYSE		

iShares MSCI ex-Japn EPP

Market Price	Mstar Category
$154.28	Pacific/Asia ex-Japan Stk

Morningstar Fair Value

Price/Fair Value Ratio	Coverage Rate %
1.00	13

Valuation

Because our equity analysts cover a relatively small number of this ETF's holdings, the price/fair value ratio above may not be a faithful representation of the portfolio's valuation attributes. Investors trying to gauge this ETF's attractiveness should consider the price/fair value ratio only in conjunction with other fundamental measures.

Methodology

This ETF tracks the MSCI's Pacific Free ex-Japan Index, a market-cap-weighted index composed of four developed markets. Thus, this ETF has a pronounced large-cap bias and devotes around 66% of its assets to Australia, 21% of its assets to Hong Kong, 10% of its assets to Singapore, and 2% of its assets to New Zealand. It also has atypical sectors weights, including a huge financials stake, because its underlying markets have pronounced--and similar--industry biases.

Morningstar Rating	Return	Risk	Yield	NAV	Avg Daily Vol. (k)	52 wk High/Low
★★★	Average	Low	4.7%	$155.50	332	$181.83 - $120.65

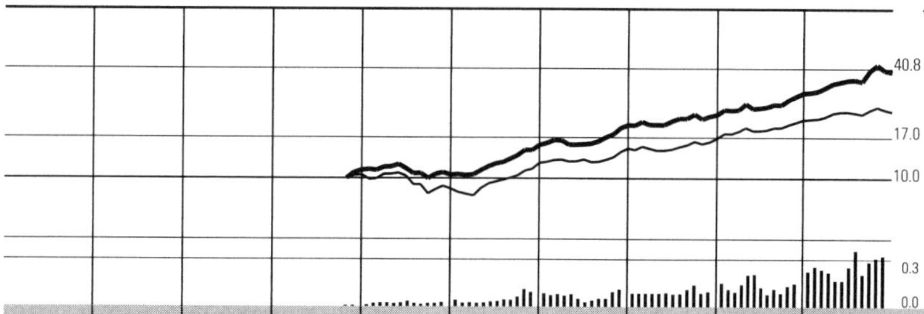

Growth of $10,000
— Investment Value of ETF
— Investment Value of Index MSCI EAFE

Trading Volume Millions

History

1998	1999	2000	2001	2002	2003	2004	2005	2006	2007	History
—	—	—	54.55	50.55	72.10	89.70	98.55	124.86	155.50	NAV $
—	—	—	54.17	50.79	72.48	90.17	98.67	125.24	154.28	Market Price $
—	—	—	24.19*	-5.73	45.73	28.68	14.03	32.07	30.82	NAV Return%
—	—	—	24.03*	-4.62	45.80	28.68	13.57	32.31	29.40	Market Price Return%
—	—	—	0.07	0.87	1.10	0.34	0.19	0.08	0.14	Avg Premium/Discount%
—	—	—	—	10.21	7.14	8.43	0.49	5.73	19.65	NAV Rtrn% +/-MSCI EAFE
—	—	—	—	0.69	-0.04	0.22	0.22	0.05	0.09	NAV Rtrn% +/-Pac ex-Japan
—	—	—	—	50	17	17	50	50	64	NAV Return% Rank in Cat
—	—	—	—	1.62	2.99	4.18	4.12	5.27	5.84	Income Return %
—	—	—	—	-7.35	42.74	24.50	9.91	26.80	24.98	Capital Return %
—	—	—	0.27	0.88	1.51	3.01	3.70	5.20	7.29	Income $
—	—	—	0.00	0.00	0.00	0.00	0.00	0.00	0.18	Capital Gains $
—	—	—	—	0.50	0.50	0.50	0.50	0.50	0.50	Expense Ratio %
—	—	—	—	2.87	3.47	3.68	4.09	3.67	3.43	Income Ratio %
—	—	—	—	5	8	8	16	8	11	Turnover Rate %
—	—	—	—	157	505	996	1,675	2,497	4,105	Net Assets $mil

Performance 12-31-07

Historic Quarterly NAV Returns

	1st Qtr	2nd Qtr	3rd Qtr	4th Qtr	Total
2003	0.65	14.86	10.76	13.80	45.73
2004	6.13	-4.78	9.47	16.33	28.68
2005	0.52	4.57	9.26	-0.72	14.03
2006	6.41	2.35	3.99	16.62	32.07
2007	7.38	9.49	12.99	-1.53	30.82

Trailing	NAV Return%	Market Return%	NAV Rtrn% +/-MSCI EAFE	%Rank Cat.(NAV)
3 Mo	-1.53	-2.55	0.22	56
6 Mo	11.26	10.62	10.87	67
1 Yr	30.82	29.40	19.65	64
3 Yr Avg	25.36	24.81	8.53	75
5 Yr Avg	29.87	29.54	8.28	34
10 Yr Avg	—	—	—	—

Tax Analysis	Tax-Adj Return%	Tax-Cost Ratio
3 Yr (estimated)	23.54	1.45
5 Yr (estimated)	28.24	1.26
10 Yr (estimated)	—	—

Rating and Risk

Time Period	Morningstar Rtn vs Cat	Morningstar Risk vs Cat	Morningstar Risk-Adj Rating
3 Yr	-Avg	-Avg	★★
5 Yr	Avg	Low	★★★
10 Yr	—	—	—

Other Measures	Standard Index S&P 500	Best Fit Index Pac ex-Japan
Alpha	3.9	0.2
Beta	1.33	0.99
R-Squared	75	100
Standard Deviation	14.69	
Mean	25.36	
Sharpe Ratio	1.33	

Morningstar's Take by William Samuel Rocco 12-31-07

This exchange-traded fund is anything but an ordinary Pacific/Asia ex-Japan offering.

IShares MSCI Pacific ex-Japan's itinerary differs considerably from most of its category peers'. It confines itself to the region's four developed exchanges--with roughly two thirds of its assets in Australia and one third divided among Hong Kong, Singapore, and New Zealand--while most of its peers invest in eight to 10 regional markets, favor the emerging ones, and shun Australia.

This ETF also has marked market-cap and sector biases. Its benchmark is market-cap weighted, so it tilts toward bigger firms and its average market cap is almost double the Pacific/Asia ex-Japan category norm. Its hardware weight is fraction of the group norm, because Taiwan and the region's other technology powers are not part of its purview. And it devotes nearly half its assets to financial stocks, while its typical peer invests approximately one quarter of its assets in such names, as the Australia, Hong Kong, and Singapore markets are packed with banks, real estate companies, and other financial firms.

This ETF has done an excellent job of replicating the performance of its benchmark, the MSCI Pacific Free ex-Japan Index since opening in late 2001, but it has posted subpar results relative to its category peers. Indeed, it did crush its typical competitor in 2004, as Australia and its developed neighbors shined, but it markedly underperformed both before and after as the region's emerging markets fared best. Thus, its three-year, five-year, and since-inception returns lag the category average by sizable margins.

In short, this ETF is not a good choice for investors seeking broad exposure to the Pacific/Asia ex-Japan region or for those who wish to benefit directly from the strong growth in China and Asia's other emerging markets. But it is a solid option for those who do want to focus on the region's developed exchanges.

Address:	45 Fremont Street United States 800-474-2737
Web Address:	www.ishares.com
Inception:	10-25-01 *
Advisor:	Barclays Global Fund Advisers

Management Fee:	0.50%		
Expense Projections:	3Yr:$160	5Yr:$280	10Yr:$628
Income Distrib:	Annually		
Exchange:	NYSE		

Portfolio Analysis 12-31-07

Share change since 11-07 Total Stocks:185	Sector	Country	% Assets
⊖ BHP Billiton Ltd	Ind Mtrls	Australia	7.93
⊖ Commonwealth Bank of Aus	Financial	Australia	4.57
⊖ National Australia Bank	Financial	Australia	3.62
⊖ Westpac Banking	Financial	Australia	3.06
⊖ Australia & New Zealand	Financial	Australia	3.02
⊖ Woolworths Ltd	Consumer	Australia	2.53
⊕ Rio Tinto Ltd	Ind Mtrls	Australia	2.38
⊖ Westfield Grp	Consumer	Australia	2.15
⊖ Sun Hung Kai Properties	Financial	Hong Kong	2.09
⊖ Hong Kong Exchanges & Cl	Financial	Hong Kong	2.00
⊖ Cheung Kong (Hldgs) Ltd	Financial	Hong Kong	1.93
⊖ Hutchison Whampoa Ltd	Telecom	Hong Kong	1.74
⊖ QBE Insurance Grp Ltd	Financial	Australia	1.67
⊖ Singapore Telecommunicat	Telecom	Singapore	1.49
⊖ Woodside Petroleum Ltd	Energy	Australia	1.40
⊖ Wesfarmers Ltd	Ind Mtrls	Australia	1.28
⊖ Macquarie Grp	—	Australia	1.22
⊖ United Overseas Bank Ltd	Financial	Singapore	1.19
⊖ CSL Ltd	Health	Australia	1.18
⊖ DBS Grp Hldgs Ltd	Financial	Singapore	1.15

Current Investment Style

Value Blnd Growth; Large Mid Small

Market Cap	%
Giant	50.6
Large	41.8
Mid	7.6
Small	0.0
Micro	0.0
Avg $mil: 21,096	

Value Measures		Rel Category
Price/Earnings	16.28	0.92
Price/Book	2.39	0.91
Price/Sales	2.26	1.03
Price/Cash Flow	7.39	0.85
Dividend Yield %	3.93	1.17

Growth Measures	%	Rel Category
Long-Term Erngs	14.88	0.89
Book Value	9.91	0.84
Sales	14.74	0.80
Cash Flow	23.05	1.28
Historical Erngs	21.83	0.75

Composition

Cash	4.8	Bonds	0.0
Stocks	94.2	Other	1.1
Foreign (% of Stock)			100.0

Sector Weightings	% of Stocks	Rel MSCI EAFE	3 Year High	3 Year Low
Info	7.05	0.56		
Software	0.32	0.55	0	0
Hardware	0.28	0.07	1	0
Media	0.98	0.58	2	1
Telecom	5.47	0.86	7	5
Service	64.61	1.49		
Health	2.38	0.37	2	1
Consumer	8.87	1.79	9	6
Business	7.01	1.40	7	6
Financial	46.35	1.72	50	46
Mfg	28.35	0.64		
Goods	3.19	0.24	4	3
Ind Mtrls	19.46	1.12	20	16
Energy	3.03	0.39	3	2
Utilities	2.67	0.48	5	2

Regional Exposure	% Stock		
UK/W. Europe	0	N. America	0
Japan	0	Latn America	0
Asia X Japan	100	Other	0

Country Exposure	% Stock		
Australia	64	New Zealand	1
Hong Kong	23	China	1
Singapore	11		

iShares S&P Euro-350 IEV

Market Price	Mstar Category
$114.34	Europe Stock

Morningstar Fair Value

Price/Fair Value Ratio	Coverage Rate %
1.00	6

Valuation

Because our equity analysts cover a relatively small number of this ETF's stock holdings, the price/fair value ratio above may not be a faithful representation of the portfolio's valuation attributes. Investors trying to gauge this ETF's attractiveness should consider the price/fair value ratio only in conjunction with other fundamental measures.

Methodology

This exchange-traded offering is a passive fund that attempts to match the performance of the S&P Europe 350 Index. The benchmark is a market-cap-weighted index designed to track leading stocks from across the developed countries of Europe. It has a very modest mid-cap stake and essentially no small caps. It uses a representative sampling method to track the index.

Morningstar Rating	Return	Risk	Yield	NAV	Avg Daily Vol. (k)	52 wk High/Low
★★★	Average	Below Avg	2.7%	$115.40	325	$124.60 - $100.00

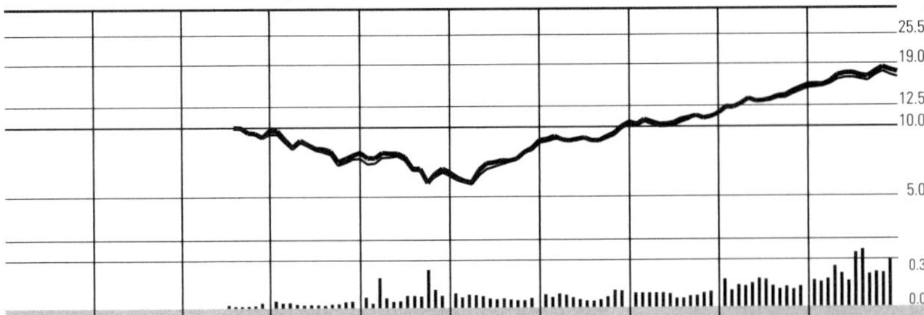

Growth of $10,000
— Investment Value of ETF
— Investment Value of Index MSCI EAFE

Trading Volume Millions

1998	1999	2000	2001	2002	2003	2004	2005	2006	2007	History
—	—	75.09	59.12	47.34	64.04	75.13	80.15	104.32	115.40	NAV $
—	—	76.69	59.09	47.48	64.15	75.25	80.77	104.87	114.34	Market Price $
—	—	7.26*	-20.05	-18.12	37.70	19.44	9.17	32.77	13.67	NAV Return%
—	—	7.13*	-21.76	-17.84	37.53	19.42	9.84	32.44	12.03	Market Price Return%
—	—	2.12	0.94	0.37	0.30	0.74	0.29	0.45	0.01	Avg Premium/Discount%
—	—	—	1.39	-2.18	-0.89	-0.81	-4.37	6.43	2.50	NAV Rtrn% +/-MSCI EAF
—	—	—	-0.47	-0.21	-1.02	-1.76	-0.71	-0.92	-1.92	NAV Rtrn% +/-S&P Europ
—	—	—	37	55	69	43	43	60	39	NAV Return% Rank in Ca
—	—	—	1.25	1.80	2.35	2.11	2.50	2.60	3.00	Income Return %
—	—	—	-21.30	-19.92	35.35	17.33	6.67	30.17	10.67	Capital Return %
—	—	0.18	0.93	1.06	1.11	1.35	1.88	2.08	3.13	Income $
—	—	0.00	0.00	0.00	0.00	0.00	0.00	0.00	0.00	Capital Gains $
—	—	—	0.60	0.60	0.60	0.60	0.60	0.60	0.60	Expense Ratio %
—	—	—	1.12	1.49	2.11	2.17	2.26	2.47	2.47	Income Ratio %
—	—	—	24	4	6	5	5	7	4	Turnover Rate %
—	—	86	195	428	647	1,082	1,270	2,384	2,891	Net Assets $mil

Performance 12-31-07

Historic Quarterly NAV Returns

	1st Qtr	2nd Qtr	3rd Qtr	4th Qtr	Total
2003	-9.42	22.08	3.51	20.29	37.70
2004	0.55	1.86	1.08	15.37	19.44
2005	0.21	-0.88	7.64	2.10	9.17
2006	10.43	2.72	5.65	10.78	32.77
2007	3.51	8.68	1.41	-0.35	13.67

Trailing	NAV Return%	Market Return%	NAV Rtrn% +/-MSCI EAFE	%Rank Cat.(NAV)
3 Mo	-0.35	-1.44	1.40	48
6 Mo	1.05	0.48	0.66	48
1 Yr	13.67	12.03	2.50	39
3 Yr Avg	18.11	17.68	1.28	50
5 Yr Avg	22.06	21.76	0.47	57
10 Yr Avg	—	—	—	—

Tax Analysis	Tax-Adj Return%	Tax-Cost Ratio
3 Yr (estimated)	17.15	0.81
5 Yr (estimated)	21.17	0.73
10 Yr (estimated)	—	—

Rating and Risk

Time Period	Morningstar Rtn vs Cat	Morningstar Risk vs Cat	Morningstar Risk-Adj Rating
3 Yr	Avg	-Avg	★★★
5 Yr	Avg	-Avg	★★★
10 Yr	—	—	—

Other Measures	Standard Index S&P 500	Best Fit Index MSCI Eur
Alpha	1.5	0.0
Beta	0.96	0.97
R-Squared	93	100
Standard Deviation	9.60	
Mean	18.11	
Sharpe Ratio	1.35	

Portfolio Analysis 12-31-07

Share change since 11-07 Total Stocks:345	Sector	Country	% Assets
⊖ BP	Energy	U.K.	2.42
⊖ HSBC Hldgs	Financial	U.K.	2.07
⊖ TOTAL	Energy	France	2.05
⊖ Vodafone Grp	Telecom	U.K.	2.04
⊖ Nestle	Goods	Switzerland	1.89
⊖ Telefonica	Telecom	Spain	1.68
⊖ Nokia	Hardware	Finland	1.58
⊖ Royal Dutch Shell	Energy	U.K.	1.58
⊖ E.ON	Utilities	Germany	1.55
⊖ Novartis	Health	Switzerland	1.55
⊖ Siemens	Hardware	Germany	1.50
⊖ GlaxoSmithKline	Health	U.K.	1.45
⊖ Banco Santander	Financial	Spain	1.40
⊖ Roche Holding Ltd	Health	Switzerland	1.26
⊖ Royal Dutch Shell	Energy	U.K.	1.19
⊕ UniCredito Italiano Grp	Financial	Italy	1.16
⊖ Rio Tinto	Ind Mtrls	U.K.	1.13
⊖ Daimler	Goods	Germany	1.05
⊖ BNP Paribas	Financial	France	1.02
⊖ Allianz SE	Financial	Germany	1.00

Current Investment Style

Market Cap	%
Giant	63.3
Large	30.2
Mid	6.5
Small	0.1
Micro	0.0
Avg $mil: 58,287	

Value Measures		Rel Category
Price/Earnings	12.88	1.00
Price/Book	2.08	1.05
Price/Sales	1.09	1.07
Price/Cash Flow	8.69	1.09
Dividend Yield %	3.70	0.95

Growth Measures	%	Rel Category
Long-Term Erngs	11.41	1.01
Book Value	10.42	1.08
Sales	7.85	0.89
Cash Flow	9.94	1.47
Historical Erngs	20.20	1.00

Composition

Cash	2.5	Bonds	0.0
Stocks	97.5	Other	0.0
Foreign (% of Stock)			100.0

Sector Weightings	% of Stocks	Rel MSCI EAFE	3 Year High	3 Year Low
Info	14.20	1.12		
Software	0.52	0.90	1	1
Hardware	4.20	1.04	4	3
Media	1.90	1.12	3	2
Telecom	7.58	1.19	9	6
Service	42.62	0.98		
Health	7.37	1.16	10	7
Consumer	4.35	0.88	5	4
Business	3.14	0.63	3	3
Financial	27.76	1.03	33	28
Mfg	43.19	0.98		
Goods	11.67	0.87	12	11
Ind Mtrls	14.12	0.81	14	10
Energy	10.56	1.36	13	9
Utilities	6.84	1.23	7	5

Regional Exposure			% Stock
UK/W. Europe	100	N. America	0
Japan	0	Latn America	0
Asia X Japan	0	Other	0

Country Exposure			% Stock
U.K.	32	Switzerland	10
France	16	Spain	7
Germany	13		

Morningstar's Take by Gregg Wolper 12-31-07

At a lower price, iShares S&P Europe 350 would be a more attractive option.

This exchange-traded fund owns about 200 fewer stocks than ETF rival Vanguard European Stock (which is the young, exchange-traded share class of the older mutual fund Vanguard European Stock Index), and it has a slightly stronger tilt toward the very biggest companies. Other than that, however, the portfolios are similar: Their sector and country weightings aren't far apart, and their top holdings also look very much alike. Both funds aim to provide shareholders with straightforward passive exposure to large Western European companies (no emerging markets here) and--not an unimportant point these days--to European currencies. Both funds' currency exposure is completely unhedged, as is the case with most index funds.

With these similarities in mind, the major difference between the two rivals stands out sharply: their cost. This ETF's 0.60% expense ratio is far higher than the Vanguard ETF's 0.12% price tag; even the mutual-fund version of the Vanguard fund is significantly cheaper than this offering.

This fund also must confront the issue faced by any regional fund: Why not pick a broader international fund that includes some holdings in Asia and elsewhere? Asset allocators may reply that they own those holdings in other funds and wish to control the percentages in each, as well as in small caps. For that purpose, this fund could work well, if it cost less. Its sector weightings are more balanced than some foreign index funds'--it has less than 30% in financials, for example, far less than some others. Its lack of emerging-markets exposure could appeal to those justifiably concerned that those markets have run up so high a sharp fall is a strong possibility.

In short, there's nothing inherently wrong with the makeup of this portfolio; but it's only for a limited audience, and it costs too much even for that group.

Address:	45 Fremont Street United States 800-474-2737
Web Address:	www.ishares.com
Inception:	07-25-00*
Advisor:	Barclays Global Fund Advisers

Management Fee:	0.60%		
Expense Projections:	3Yr:$192	5Yr:$335	10Yr:$750
Income Distrib:	Annually		
Exchange:	NYSE		

iShares SP Latin 40 ILF

Market Price	Mstar Category
$248.91	Latin America Stock

Morningstar Rating	Return	Risk	Yield	NAV	Avg Daily Vol. (k)	52 wk High/Low
★★★	Average	Low	1.4%	$249.30	478	$266.88 - $157.90

Morningstar Fair Value

Price/Fair Value Ratio	Coverage Rate %
1.07	57

Valuation

This fund's holdings aren't fraught with risk. But the portfolio is concentrated, skews to just a few sectors, and fluctuates with currency gyrations. Given that volatility, the fund would have to trade at a 20% or greater discount to our fair value estimate to get us interested. It was trading at a 7% premium recently.

Methodology

This fund tracks the S&P Latin American 40 Index, which draws together 40 of the largest firms in Mexico, Brazil, Chile, and Argentina. The index weights holdings by free-float-adjusted market cap. It's very top-heavy, with the biggest 10 names accounting for roughly two thirds of assets. In addition, the portfolio skews decidedly toward miners, telecoms, oil majors, and big banks, which loom large over the Latin American economic landscape. Technology and consumer-related issues are in short supply here. Investments are denominated in the local currency and thus subject to exchange-rate fluctuations.

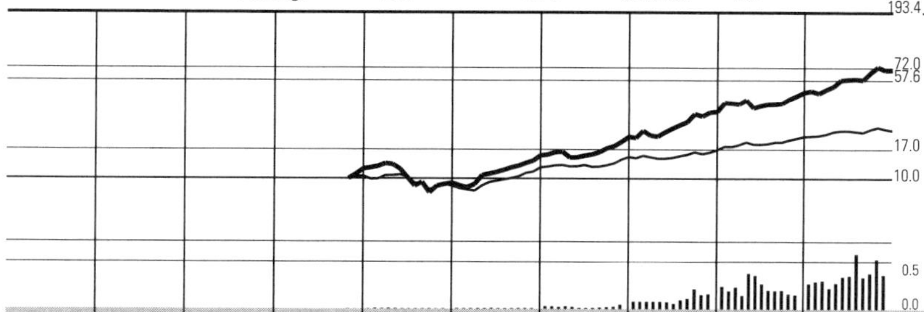

1998	1999	2000	2001	2002	2003	2004	2005	2006	2007	History
—	—	—	47.73	36.35	58.17	79.92	123.00	169.89	249.30	NAV $
—	—	—	47.69	36.59	58.84	80.55	122.85	169.93	248.91	Market Price $
—	—	—	35.85*	-21.96	62.12	39.03	56.01	40.85	48.75	NAV Return%
—	—	—	35.82*	-21.38	62.91	38.53	54.60	41.06	48.48	Market Price Return%
—	—	—	-0.05	-0.01	0.57	0.49	0.37	0.06	0.07	Avg Premium/Discount%
—	—	—	—	-6.02	23.53	18.78	42.47	14.51	37.58	NAV Rtrn% +/-MSCI EAFE
—	—	—	—	1.36	-3.69	0.31	-0.04	-1.72	-1.72	NAV Rtrn% +/-S&P Latin Am
—	—	—	—	50	50	50	1	100	50	NAV Return% Rank in Cat
—	—	—	—	1.93	2.04	1.61	2.11	2.65	2.04	Income Return %
—	—	—	—	-23.89	60.08	37.42	53.90	38.20	46.71	Capital Return %
—	—	—	0.27	0.92	0.74	0.94	1.69	3.26	3.47	Income $
—	—	—	0.00	0.00	0.00	0.00	0.00	0.00	0.00	Capital Gains $
—	—	—	—	0.50	0.50	0.50	0.50	0.50	0.50	Expense Ratio %
—	—	—	—	2.94	2.42	2.61	2.00	2.58	2.08	Income Ratio %
—	—	—	—	2	9	13	6	12	7	Turnover Rate %
—	—	—	—	9	61	224	1,224	1,580	3,091	Net Assets $mil

Performance 12-31-07

Historic Quarterly NAV Returns

	1st Qtr	2nd Qtr	3rd Qtr	4th Qtr	Total
2003	-2.12	23.78	11.72	19.78	62.12
2004	6.91	-6.54	13.99	22.07	39.03
2005	2.40	13.04	29.39	4.16	56.01
2006	14.37	-3.08	4.47	21.64	40.85
2007	5.06	19.60	12.57	5.16	48.75

Trailing	NAV Return%	Market Return%	NAV Rtrn% +/-MSCI EAFE	%Rank Cat.(NAV)
3 Mo	5.16	4.48	6.91	34
6 Mo	18.38	18.34	17.99	34
1 Yr	48.75	48.48	37.58	50
3 Yr Avg	48.41	47.94	31.58	50
5 Yr Avg	49.09	48.85	27.50	50
10 Yr Avg	—	—	—	—

Tax Analysis	Tax-Adj Return%	Tax-Cost Ratio
3 Yr (estimated)	47.60	0.55
5 Yr (estimated)	48.35	0.50
10 Yr (estimated)	—	—

Rating and Risk

Time Period	Morningstar Rtn vs Cat	Morningstar Risk vs Cat	Morningstar Risk-Adj Rating
3 Yr	+Avg	-Avg	★★★
5 Yr	Avg	Low	★★★
10 Yr	—	—	—

Other Measures	Standard Index S&P 500	Best Fit Index MSCI Latin Am
Alpha	15.4	1.1
Beta	1.95	0.98
R-Squared	65	98
Standard Deviation	22.93	
Mean	48.41	
Sharpe Ratio	1.67	

Portfolio Analysis 12-31-07

Share change since 11-07 Total Stocks:37	Sector	Country	% Assets
⊕ Brazilian Petroleum Corp	Energy	Brazil	11.66
⊕ Companhia Vale do Rio Do	Ind Mtrls	Brazil	10.94
⊕ Vale Overseas Limited AD	Ind Mtrls	Brazil	9.53
⊕ America Movil S.A.B de C	Telecom	Mexico	9.50
⊖ Bank Bradesco ADR	Financial	Brazil	4.78
⊖ Itau Bank Financial Hold	Financial	Brazil	4.68
⊕ Unibanco - Union of Braz	Financial	Brazil	3.88
⊕ Cemex S.A. B de C.V.	Financial	Mexico	3.84
⊕ Petroleo Brasileiro S.A.	Energy	Brazil	3.79
⊕ Companhia Siderurgica Na	Ind Mtrls	Brazil	3.34
⊕ American Beverage Compan	Goods	Brazil	3.24
⊕ Telefonos de Mexico	Telecom	Mexico	2.92
⊕ Wal-mart de Mexico S A B	Consumer	Mexico	2.49
⊕ Gerdau SA ADR	Ind Mtrls	Brazil	2.21
⊕ Tenaris SA ADR	Ind Mtrls	Luxembourg	2.16
⊕ Grupo Televisa	Media	Mexico	1.95
⊕ Fomento Economico Mexica	Goods	Mexico	1.86
⊖ National Electricity Com	Utilities	Chile	1.37
⊕ Tele Norte Leste Holding	Telecom	Brazil	1.19
⊕ Brazilian Aviation Compa	Ind Mtrls	Brazil	1.14

Current Investment Style

Value Blnd Growth / Large Mid Small

Market Cap	%
Giant	62.7
Large	30.9
Mid	6.4
Small	0.0
Micro	0.0
Avg $mil: 52,961	

Value Measures		Rel Category
Price/Earnings	15.19	1.02
Price/Book	3.76	1.28
Price/Sales	1.92	1.14
Price/Cash Flow	9.89	1.12
Dividend Yield %	2.52	0.88

Growth Measures	%	Rel Category
Long-Term Erngs	13.43	0.97
Book Value	16.96	1.20
Sales	16.51	0.93
Cash Flow	18.07	0.92
Historical Erngs	26.28	1.12

Composition

Cash	1.5	Bonds	0.0
Stocks	98.5	Other	0.1
Foreign (% of Stock)			100.0

Sector Weightings	% of Stocks	Rel MSCI EAFE	3 Year High	3 Year Low
Info	17.02	1.34		
Software	0.00	0.00	0	0
Hardware	0.00	0.00	0	0
Media	1.98	1.17	3	2
Telecom	15.04	2.37	23	14
Service	22.21	0.51		
Health	0.00	0.00	0	0
Consumer	3.23	0.65	5	3
Business	0.00	0.00	0	0
Financial	18.98	0.70	26	19
Mfg	60.77	1.38		
Goods	5.87	0.44	8	6
Ind Mtrls	33.90	1.95	35	21
Energy	15.97	2.06	16	9
Utilities	5.03	0.91	8	5

Regional Exposure % Stock

UK/W. Europe	2	N. America	0
Japan	0	Latn America	98
Asia X Japan	0	Other	0

Country Exposure % Stock

Brazil	66	Luxembourg	2
Mexico	26	Argentina	0
Chile	6		

Morningstar's Take by Jeffrey Ptak 12-31-07

This fund would have to be plenty cheap to get us interested.

IShares S&P Latin America 40 invests in 40 of the largest firms drawn from major sectors of the Mexican, Brazilian, Chilean, and Argentinean markets. The index, which is market-cap-weighted, reflects the regional economic biases, so it's heavy in basic materials, energy, financial services, and telecom, light in tech, media, and consumer-related fare.

To love the fund, you'll have to be enamored with its biggest holdings: The top 10 names soak up two thirds of assets. That prospect isn't too far-fetched, as virtually every one of these firms boasts at least some semblance of a competitive advantage, or "moat." Take the top holding, Brazilian miner Vale Overseas, which has the largest share of the iron-ore trade, a quintessential scale business. That has paved the way to attractive returns on capital. Similarly, Brazilian upstream oil producer Petrobras has exclusive rights to harvest oil from its existing properties, explaining its narrow moat. All told, only one of the fund's top 10 names lacks a moat altogether.

Yet, this portfolio doesn't exactly gleam with the highest-quality stocks. Vale Overseas and Petrobras, for instance, are largely tied to the vagaries of the commodity cycle, making it difficult to trench out a durable competitive edge. They're not alone in that regard. For instance, Mexican wireless giant America Movil benefits from its enormous scale, yet it still must fend with rivals like Telefonica in a difficult pricing environment. The upshot is that the holdings' middling quality makes the portfolio less valuable in our eyes.

Of course, if these stocks got cheap enough, we'd be enthusiastic buyers. But the fund has been volatile, owing to the portfolio's top-heavy construction, narrow sector focus, and exposure to currency gyrations. For that reason, we'd invest here only at a 20% or greater discount to our fair value estimate.

Address:	45 Fremont Street United States 800-474-2737
Web Address:	www.ishares.com
Inception:	10-25-01 *
Advisor:	Barclays Global Fund Advisers

Management Fee:	0.50%		
Expense Projections:	3Yr:$160	5Yr:$280	10Yr:$628
Income Distrib:	Annually		
Exchange:	NYSE		

iShares Singapore EWS

Market Price	Mstar Category
$13.79	Pacific/Asia ex-Japan St

Morningstar Rating	Return	Risk	Yield	NAV	Avg Daily Vol. (k)	52 wk High/Low
★★	Below Avg	Average	3.7%	$13.80	4,436	$15.90 - $11.01

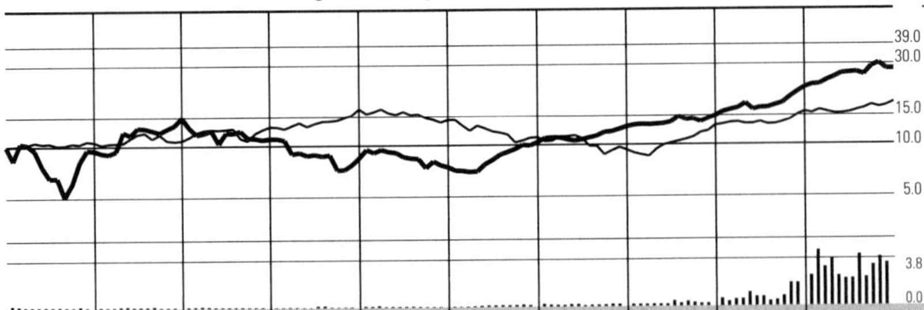

Morningstar Fair Value

Price/Fair Value Ratio	Coverage Rate %
1.00	0

Valuation

Because our equity analysts cover a relatively small number of this ETF's stock holdings, the price/fair value ratio above may not represent the portfolio's true valuation attributes. Accordingly, investors should consider the price/fair value ratio only in conjunction with other fundamental measures.

Methodology

This fund tracks the MSCI Singapore Index, a collection of 30 or so stocks that trade on that nation's major stock exchanges. The benchmark aims to cover 85% of Singapore's total market cap. It weights holdings by free-float adjusted market cap. The portfolio is top heavy, with roughly one third of assets packed into the fund's top three holdings. It also skews heavily to financial services, real estate, and telecom firms, which together recently accounted for more than 60% of assets. Investments are denominated in the Singapore dollar.

History

1998	1999	2000	2001	2002	2003	2004	2005	2006	2007	History
6.10	9.31	6.71	5.08	4.39	6.01	7.09	7.90	11.22	13.80	NAV $
6.12	9.19	6.50	5.07	4.27	6.00	7.17	7.90	11.20	13.79	Market Price $
-5.41	55.35	-25.01	-23.22	-12.02	39.70	22.62	15.57	46.06	27.78	NAV Return%
-5.10	52.84	-26.41	-20.90	-14.25	43.38	24.21	14.28	45.80	27.92	Market Price Return%
0.62	-0.14	-1.31	-1.16	-0.27	0.22	0.05	0.40	0.07	0.06	Avg Premium/Discount%
-25.34	28.32	-10.84	-1.78	3.92	1.11	2.37	2.03	19.72	16.61	NAV Rtrn% +/-MSCI EAFE
-1.38	-4.85	2.39	0.20	-0.97	2.10	0.35	1.20	-0.65	-0.57	NAV Rtrn% +/-MSCI SF N
34	34	100	100	67	50	50	25	25	82	NAV Return% Rank in Cat
1.60	2.33	0.72	0.79	1.53	2.71	4.59	4.10	3.91	4.54	Income Return %
-7.01	53.02	-25.73	-24.01	-13.55	36.99	18.03	11.47	42.15	23.24	Capital Return %
0.11	0.14	0.07	0.05	0.08	0.12	0.28	0.29	0.31	0.51	Income $
0.01	0.01	0.22	0.02	0.00	0.00	0.00	0.00	0.00	0.00	Capital Gains $
—	—	0.94	0.84	—	0.84	0.79	0.57	0.54	0.51	Expense Ratio %
—	—	1.60	—	—	2.67	3.50	5.19	4.74	3.80	Income Ratio %
—	—	52	32	9	14	9	8	6	8	Turnover Rate %
90	131	69	74	75	162	193	393	1,074	2,124	Net Assets $mil

Performance 12-31-07

Historic Quarterly NAV Returns

	1st Qtr	2nd Qtr	3rd Qtr	4th Qtr	Total
2003	-6.15	17.23	15.53	9.90	39.70
2004	5.82	-2.36	10.14	7.74	22.62
2005	2.54	3.58	4.25	4.38	15.57
2006	11.01	0.23	6.71	23.01	46.06
2007	10.16	10.36	8.72	-3.33	27.78

Trailing	NAV Return%	Market Return%	NAV Rtrn% +/-MSCI EAFE	%Rank Cat.(NAV)
3 Mo	-3.33	-3.33	-1.58	81
6 Mo	5.11	5.04	4.72	86
1 Yr	27.78	27.92	16.61	82
3 Yr Avg	29.20	28.69	12.37	38
5 Yr Avg	29.87	30.58	8.28	17
10 Yr Avg	10.65	10.64	1.99	67

Tax Analysis	Tax-Adj Return%	Tax-Cost Ratio
3 Yr (estimated)	27.68	1.18
5 Yr (estimated)	28.43	1.11
10 Yr (estimated)	9.64	0.91

Rating and Risk

Time Period	Morningstar Rtn vs Cat	Morningstar Risk vs Cat	Morningstar Risk-Adj Rating
3 Yr	-Avg	-Avg	★★★
5 Yr	Avg	Low	★★★
10 Yr	-Avg	+Avg	★

Other Measures	Standard Index S&P 500	Best Fit Index Pac ex-Japan
Alpha	9.7	6.7
Beta	1.09	0.82
R-Squared	53	71
Standard Deviation	14.40	
Mean	29.20	
Sharpe Ratio	1.58	

Portfolio Analysis 11-30-07

Share change since 10-07 Total Stocks:36	Sector	Country	% Assets
⊖ Singapore Telecommunicat	Telecom	Singapore	13.37
⊖ United Overseas Bank Ltd	Financial	Singapore	10.55
⊖ DBS Grp Hldgs Ltd	Financial	Singapore	9.85
⊖ Oversea-Chinese Banking	Financial	Singapore	8.64
⊖ Keppel	Ind Mtrls	Singapore	6.14
⊖ Singapore Exchange Ltd	Financial	Singapore	5.46
⊖ CapitaLand Ltd	Financial	Singapore	4.75
⊖ Singapore Airlines Ltd	Business	Singapore	4.28
⊖ City Developments Ltd	Financial	Singapore	3.49
⊖ Singapore Press Hldgs Lt	Media	Singapore	3.30
⊖ Cosco Corp. (Singapore)	Business	Singapore	2.42
⊖ Singapore Technologies E	Ind Mtrls	Singapore	2.38
⊖ Fraser & Neave Ltd	Ind Mtrls	Singapore	2.26
SembCorp Industries Ltd	Business	Singapore	2.24
SembCorp Marine Ltd	Business	Singapore	1.71
⊖ ComfortDelGro	Business	Singapore	1.67
⊖ CapitaMall Trust Managem	Financial	Singapore	1.56
⊖ Venture	Hardware	Singapore	1.28
⊖ Jardine Cycle & Carriage	Consumer	Singapore	1.24
⊖ Keppel Land Ltd	Financial	Singapore	1.19

Current Investment Style

Value Blnd Growth — Large Mid Small

Market Cap	%
Giant	23.8
Large	61.7
Mid	14.6
Small	0.0
Micro	0.0
Avg $mil: 9,485	

Value Measures		Rel Category
Price/Earnings	15.15	0.86
Price/Book	2.11	0.80
Price/Sales	2.07	0.94
Price/Cash Flow	2.12	0.25
Dividend Yield %	4.66	1.39

Growth Measures	%	Rel Category
Long-Term Erngs	14.67	0.88
Book Value	9.67	0.82
Sales	20.72	1.13
Cash Flow	19.97	1.11
Historical Erngs	29.99	1.03

Composition

Cash	0.1	Bonds	0.0
Stocks	99.9	Other	0.0
Foreign (% of Stock)			100.0

Sector Weightings	% of Stocks	Rel MSCI EAFE	3 Year High	3 Year Low
Info	18.40	1.45		
Software	0.00	0.00	0	0
Hardware	1.71	0.42	6	2
Media	3.30	1.95	5	3
Telecom	13.39	2.11	14	11
Service	68.59	1.58		
Health	1.11	0.17	1	1
Consumer	2.14	0.43	2	1
Business	14.42	2.89	15	10
Financial	50.92	1.89	56	47
Mfg	13.01	0.30		
Goods	0.00	0.00	1	0
Ind Mtrls	12.27	0.71	13	10
Energy	0.74	0.10	1	0
Utilities	0.00	0.00	0	0

Regional Exposure	% Stock		% Stock
UK/W. Europe	0	N. America	0
Japan	0	Latn America	0
Asia X Japan	100	Other	0

Country Exposure	% Stock
Singapore	100

Morningstar's Take by Jeffrey Ptak 12-31-07

Tread carefully with iShares MSCI Singapore.

This ETF tracks the MSCI Singapore Index, a benchmark that aims to cover 85% of that nation's stock market. Assets are spread across 35 or so names, which are weighted by market cap. The fund skews toward financial and telecom firms, which dot its upper ranks. Like many country-specific funds, it's concentrated, with its top three holdings recently soaking up about one third of assets.

If you're considering the fund as a portfolio building block, there are a few factors to weigh. First, if you already invest in a broadly diversified foreign fund, you might already own a stake in Singaporean stocks. For instance, iShares MSCI EAFE owns roughly two of every three stocks in this portfolio. Second, even if you don't have Singapore exposure elsewhere, it's not like you're cheating yourself: Singaporean stocks are a trace weighting in the EAFE index, reflecting the country's modest role on the world stage.

True, the fund is one of a kind--there are no other pure-play Singapore-country ETFs on the market. It's also inexpensive, as it levies a modest 0.54% expense ratio. But we don't think those are reasons enough to make the fund even a fringe player in a diversified portfolio.

If you're eyeing the fund as a way to wager on, or against, the Singaporean economy, we'd tread carefully. Because our analysts cover only one of the fund's holdings, we can't speak definitively as to the portfolio's overall quality or risk. Singapore is not resource-rich, making it reliant on trade with other nations, primarily its Asian neighbors. Thus, while banks, real estate, and telecom firms--which abound here--typically aren't crummy businesses, the fund's fortunes will turn to a large degree on the health of the Asian economy.

Coupled with the portfolio's focused nature and currency gyrations (assets are denominated in Singapore dollars), we think that's ample reason to invest here only with a wide margin of safety.

Address:	45 Fremont Street United States 800-474-2737
Web Address:	www.ishares.com
Inception:	03-12-96
Advisor:	Barclays Global Fund Advisers

Management Fee:	0.54%
Expense Projections:	3Yr:$173 5Yr:$302 10Yr:$677
Income Distrib:	Annually
Exchange:	NYSE

iShares S.Korea Indx EWY

Morningstar Rating	Return	Risk	Yield	NAV	Market Price	Avg Daily Vol. (k)	Mstar Category	52 wk High/Low
★★	Below Avg	High	0.6%	$64.75	$64.70	2,372	Pacific/Asia ex-Japan Stk	$74.76 - $46.45

Morningstar Fair Value

Price/Fair Value Ratio	Coverage Rate %
1.00	2

Valuation

Because our equity analysts cover a relatively small number of this ETF's stock holdings, the price/fair value ratio above may not be a faithful representation of the portfolio's valuation attributes. Accordingly, investors should consider the price/fair value ratio only in conjunction with other fundamental measures.

Methodology

IShares MSCI South Korea tracks the MSCI Korea Index, a free-float market-cap-weighted benchmark consisting of stocks on the South Korean Stock Exchange. Like most country-specific ETFs, this fund's portfolio is top heavy, with the top three holdings recently accounting for more than 25% of assets. The benchmark largely mirrors the Korean economy, which is heavy in consumer-goods, industrials, and financials. Investments, which are denominated in the South Korean won, are unhedged.

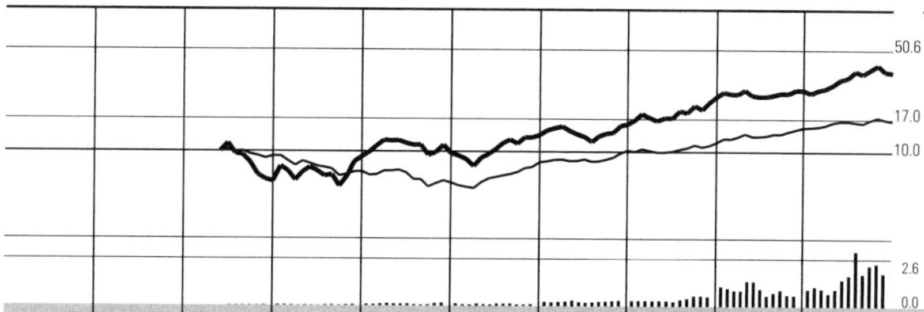

Growth of $10,000
— Investment Value of ETF
— Investment Value of Index MSCI EAFE

Trading Volume Millions

History

1998	1999	2000	2001	2002	2003	2004	2005	2006	2007	History
—	—	12.03	17.52	18.58	24.61	28.99	44.67	49.30	64.75	NAV $
—	—	12.25	17.71	18.35	25.04	29.25	44.75	49.40	64.70	Market Price $
—	—	16.94*	46.74	6.05	33.74	18.22	55.00	11.10	32.08	NAV Return%
—	—	16.92*	45.66	3.61	37.79	17.23	53.89	11.13	31.71	Market Price Return%
—	—	0.83	-0.29	-0.18	0.10	0.19	0.41	-0.33	0.03	Avg Premium/Discount%
—	—	—	68.18	21.99	-4.85	-2.03	41.46	-15.24	20.91	NAV Rtrn% +/-MSCI EAFE
—	—	—	-1.28	-2.24	-1.28	-3.84	-1.97	-1.54	0.23	NAV Rtrn% +/-MSCI Korea
—	—	—	1	1	83	67	1	100	55	NAV Return% Rank in Cat
—	—	—	0.29	0.00	1.28	0.40	0.90	0.75	0.75	Income Return %
—	—	—	46.45	6.05	32.46	17.82	54.10	10.35	31.33	Capital Return %
—	—	0.00	0.03	0.00	0.24	0.10	0.26	0.33	0.37	Income $
—	—	0.00	0.07	0.00	0.00	0.00	0.00	0.00	0.00	Capital Gains $
—	—	—	0.99	—	0.99	0.94	0.74	0.70	0.68	Expense Ratio %
—	—	—	—	—	0.98	0.87	1.49	0.71	0.96	Income Ratio %
—	—	55	39	25	39	29	30	47	20	Turnover Rate %
—	—	—	—	117	197	489	1,380	1,619	3,668	Net Assets $mil

Performance 12-31-07

Historic Quarterly NAV Returns

	1st Qtr	2nd Qtr	3rd Qtr	4th Qtr	Total
2003	-18.30	30.50	9.19	14.89	33.74
2004	14.22	-14.87	4.97	15.82	18.22
2005	10.93	-0.37	21.38	15.54	55.00
2006	4.39	-3.50	5.27	4.77	11.10
2007	2.72	18.56	13.86	-4.74	32.08

Trailing	NAV Return%	Market Return%	NAV Rtrn% +/-MSCI EAFE	%Rank Cat.(NAV)
3 Mo	-4.74	-4.40	-2.99	93
6 Mo	8.46	7.90	8.07	73
1 Yr	32.08	31.71	20.91	55
3 Yr Avg	31.51	31.09	14.68	25
5 Yr Avg	29.17	29.47	7.58	50
10 Yr Avg	—	—	—	—

Tax Analysis	Tax-Adj Return%	Tax-Cost Ratio
3 Yr (estimated)	31.24	0.21
5 Yr (estimated)	28.89	0.22
10 Yr (estimated)	—	—

Rating and Risk

Time Period	Morningstar Rtn vs Cat	Morningstar Risk vs Cat	Morningstar Risk-Adj Rating
3 Yr	Avg	+Avg	★★★
5 Yr	-Avg	High	★★
10 Yr	—	—	—

Other Measures	Standard Index S&P 500	Best Fit Index MSCI Ex Jpn ND
Alpha	8.3	-0.2
Beta	1.46	1.11
R-Squared	43	75
Standard Deviation	21.18	
Mean	31.51	
Sharpe Ratio	1.20	

Portfolio Analysis 11-30-07

Share change since 10-07 Total Stocks:96	Sector	Country	% Assets
⊕ Samsung Electronics	Goods	Korea	13.35
⊕ POSCO	Ind Mtrls	Korea	9.44
⊕ Kookmin Bank	Financial	Korea	4.84
⊕ Hyundai Heavy Industries	Business	Korea	4.32
⊕ Shinhan Financial Grp	Financial	Korea	3.42
⊕ Hyundai Motor	Goods	Korea	2.30
⊕ Shinsegae	Consumer	Korea	2.20
⊕ Korea Electric Power	Utilities	Korea	2.15
⊕ NHN	Business	Korea	2.11
⊕ Sk Engy	Energy	Korea	2.05
⊕ LG Electronics	Goods	Korea	1.98
⊕ Samsung	Consumer	Korea	1.95
⊕ KT&G	Goods	Korea	1.87
⊕ Samsung Fire & Marine In	Financial	Korea	1.80
⊕ Samsung Electnc	—	Korea	1.73
⊕ SK Hldgs Co, Ltd	Energy	Korea	1.62
⊕ Samsung Heavy Industry	Ind Mtrls	Korea	1.62
⊕ GS Engineering & Constru	Business	Korea	1.27
⊕ LG Chem Ltd	Ind Mtrls	Korea	1.16
⊕ Hyundai Development	Business	Korea	1.16

Current Investment Style

Value Blnd Growth; Large Mid Small

Market Cap	%
Giant	44.6
Large	43.9
Mid	11.5
Small	0.0
Micro	0.0
Avg $mil: 14,876	

Value Measures		Rel Category
Price/Earnings	13.57	0.77
Price/Book	1.70	0.65
Price/Sales	0.81	0.37
Price/Cash Flow	5.90	0.68
Dividend Yield %	2.65	0.79

Growth Measures	%	Rel Category
Long-Term Erngs	14.10	0.84
Book Value	13.48	1.15
Sales	8.27	0.45
Cash Flow	11.36	0.63
Historical Erngs	5.28	0.18

Composition

Cash	0.1	Bonds	0.0
Stocks	97.6	Other	2.3
Foreign (% of Stock)			100.0

Sector Weightings	% of Stocks	Rel MSCI EAFE	3 Year High	3 Year Low
Info	4.84	0.38		
Software	0.00	0.00	0	0
Hardware	0.78	0.19	3	1
Media	0.00	0.00	0	0
Telecom	4.06	0.64	6	3
Service	41.51	0.96		
Health	0.75	0.12	1	0
Consumer	6.06	1.22	6	4
Business	16.23	3.25	17	7
Financial	18.47	0.68	22	15
Mfg	53.65	1.22		
Goods	25.41	1.90	42	23
Ind Mtrls	21.38	1.23	24	12
Energy	4.65	0.60	5	3
Utilities	2.21	0.40	4	2

Regional Exposure	% Stock		
UK/W. Europe	0	N. America	0
Japan	0	Latn America	0
Asia X Japan	100	Other	0

Country Exposure	% Stock
South Korea	100

Morningstar's Take by Jeffrey Ptak 12-31-07

Passive portfolio-builders can do without iShares MSCI South Korea.

This ETF tracks the MSCI Korea Index, which aims to cover 85% of the total value of stocks listed on the South Korea Stock Exchange. The index weights holdings based on free-float-adjusted market cap. Consequently, the portfolio is top heavy, with the top three names recently soaking up 26% of assets. It also skews toward consumer goods and industrial names.

Investors considering this fund as a building block in a portfolio should think twice before purchasing. The fund substantially overlaps with better diversified offerings focusing on the broader developing markets. For instance, this fund's sibling, iShares MSCI Emerging Markets, already owns a number of the stocks in this portfolio. In addition, even if you're hellbent on using the fund to plug a hole in your portfolio, bear in mind that South Korea typically plays a supporting, not a feature, role in most broadly diversified portfolios.

Of course, investors could also be mulling an investment here based on the attractiveness of the fund's underlying stocks. Because our analysts cover a relatively small number of the fund's holdings, we can't definitively assess the stocks' credentials. That said, at first blush, top-holding Samsung Electronic's quality looks like a mixed bag, as its low-return mobile handset and consumer-electronics businesses offset its attractive semiconductor manufacturing franchise. Similarly, while metals-maker Posco and ship-builder Hyundai operate in high barrier-to-entry markets, heavy industrials rarely earn high returns on invested capital.

In addition to the portfolio's mottled quality, investors also should be mindful of its breakneck volatility, which is partially attributable to currency gyrations. We'd seek a 20% or greater discount to any estimate of the portfolio's intrinsic worth before dipping a toe here.

Address:	45 Fremont Street United States 800-474-2737
Web Address:	www.ishares.com
Inception:	05-09-00*
Advisor:	Barclays Global Fund Advisers

Management Fee:	0.70%		
Expense Projections:	3Yr:$224	5Yr:$390	10Yr:$871
Income Distrib:	Annually		
Exchange:	NYSE		

iShares Taiwan Index EWT

Market Price	Mstar Category
$15.03	Pacific/Asia ex-Japan St

Morningstar Fair Value

Price/Fair Value Ratio	Coverage Rate %
1.00	0

Valuation

Because our equity analysts cover a small number of this ETF's stock holdings, the price/fair value price ratio above may not be a faithful representation of this portfolio's valuation attributes. Investors trying to gauge this ETF's attractiveness should consider the price/fair value ratio only in conjunction with other fundamental measures.

Methodology

This fund tracks the MSCI Taiwan Index, which represents about 110 stocks that trade on the Taiwan Stock Exchange. Collectively, the index accounts for about 85% of the Taiwanese stock market. As a market-cap-weighted fund, giant and large caps make up more than three quarters of the portfolio, with many names hailing from Taiwan's biggest industries: technology and industrials. In fact, hardware firms (ranging from semiconductors to consumer electronics), make up more than half of the portfolio, while industrials account for another 15%. The fund does not hedge its investments back to the U.S. dollar.

Morningstar Rating	Return	Risk	Yield	NAV	Avg Daily Vol. (k)	52 wk High/Low
★	Low	Average	2.6%	$15.20	7,753	$18.19 - $13.08

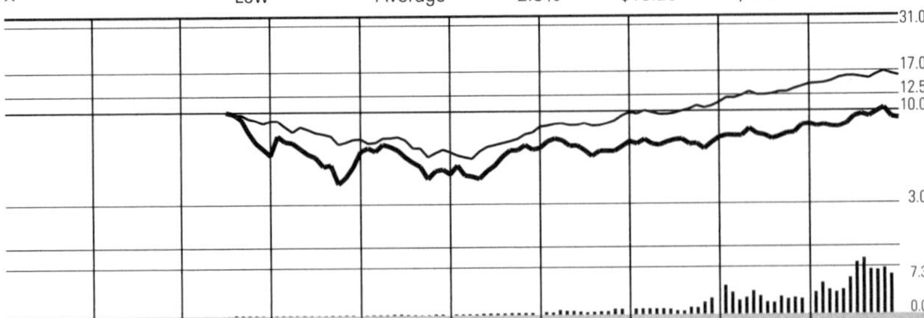

Growth of $10,000
- Investment Value of ETF
- Investment Value of Index MSCI EAFE

Trading Volume Millions

1998	1999	2000	2001	2002	2003	2004	2005	2006	2007	History
—	—	10.21	10.72	7.97	11.13	12.00	12.45	14.50	15.20	NAV $
—	—	10.56	10.78	8.15	11.24	12.06	12.48	14.40	15.03	Market Price $
—	—	-1.82*	5.00	-25.65	39.92	8.56	4.89	18.94	7.64	NAV Return%
—	—	-1.97*	2.08	-24.40	38.19	8.03	4.62	17.84	7.17	Market Price Return%
—	—	1.67	0.60	1.58	1.58	-0.29	0.43	-0.02	-0.36	Avg Premium/Discount%
—	—	—	26.44	-9.71	1.33	-11.69	-8.65	-7.40	-3.53	NAV Rtrn% +/-MSCI EAFE
—	—	—	-5.05	-0.96	-1.99	-0.43	-1.49	-1.03	-0.74	NAV Rtrn% +/-MSCI Taiw
—	—	—	20	100	34	100	75	87	100	NAV Return% Rank in Cat
—	—	—	0.00	0.00	0.27	0.71	1.13	2.42	2.69	Income Return %
—	—	—	5.00	-25.65	39.65	7.85	3.76	16.52	4.95	Capital Return %
—	—	0.32	0.00	0.00	0.02	0.08	0.14	0.30	0.39	Income $
—	—	0.54	0.00	0.00	0.00	0.00	0.00	0.00	0.00	Capital Gains $
—	—	—	0.99	—	1.31	1.19	1.03	0.85	0.77	Expense Ratio %
—	—	—	—	—	0.43	1.23	2.34	2.74	2.61	Income Ratio %
—	—	—	30	11	15	19	20	29	35	Turnover Rate %
—	—	—	—	138	342	720	1,522	2,158	2,657	Net Assets $mil

Performance 12-31-07

Historic Quarterly NAV Returns

	1st Qtr	2nd Qtr	3rd Qtr	4th Qtr	Total
2003	-3.01	15.01	21.93	2.88	39.92
2004	9.97	-11.93	-1.02	13.24	8.56
2005	-3.50	5.53	-4.66	8.04	4.89
2006	2.17	0.47	2.43	13.13	18.94
2007	-3.45	14.00	6.20	-7.92	7.64

Trailing	NAV Return%	Market Return%	NAV Rtrn% +/-MSCI EAFE	%Rank Cat.(NAV)
3 Mo	-7.92	-8.14	-6.17	100
6 Mo	-2.21	-3.55	-2.60	100
1 Yr	7.64	7.17	-3.53	100
3 Yr Avg	10.33	9.73	-6.50	100
5 Yr Avg	15.32	14.55	-6.27	100
10 Yr Avg	—	—	—	—

Tax Analysis	Tax-Adj Return%	Tax-Cost Ratio
3 Yr (estimated)	9.58	0.68
5 Yr (estimated)	14.79	0.46
10 Yr (estimated)	—	—

Rating and Risk

Time Period	Morningstar Rtn vs Cat	Morningstar Risk vs Cat	Morningstar Risk-Adj Rating
3 Yr	Low	-Avg	★
5 Yr	Low	Avg	★
10 Yr	—	—	—

Other Measures	Standard Index S&P 500	Best Fit Index MSCI Ex Jpn ND
Alpha	-6.1	-14.9
Beta	1.12	0.94
R-Squared	36	76
Standard Deviation	17.95	
Mean	10.33	
Sharpe Ratio	0.40	

Morningstar's Take by Emiko Kurotsu 12-31-07

We would steer clear of this offering.

IShares MSCI Taiwan covers most of the Taiwanese stock market through its roughly 110 holdings. Compared with other market-cap-weighted, single-country funds, this fund dips further down the market-cap range, with more than 20% in mid-caps. But assets are clustered in just a few industries, including technology and industrials.

The fund's tech stake warrants a great deal of caution. More than half of this portfolio is invested in various technology firms ranging from makers of semiconductors (Taiwan Semiconductor) to LCD panels (AU Optronics) to consumer electronics (Hon Hai Precision). Though our analysts cover just a few of these stocks, their take on these industries is telling. For instance, although AU Optronics commands about 20% of the LCD market, our analysts believe it has no defensible advantages in a fiercely competitive, highly cyclical industry fraught with high fixed costs. And although Taiwan Semi is the world's largest chip foundry and manages to differentiate itself somewhat by producing slightly higher-cost, higher-quality chips, it still must compete in a climate characterized by very short product cycles and hefty capital requirements. Given that big firms like these have managed to carve out relatively flimsy moats, we'd be even more leery of smaller, lesser-equipped firms in the same or similar industries. Many such firms dot this fund's portfolio.

The fund's narrow country and sector focus, coupled with currency gyrations, has made it one of the most volatile around. For those not willing to stomach such a ride, we'd strongly suggest looking at more diversified offerings, such as iShares MSCI Emerging Markets, which sweeps in many of this fund's holdings.

Address:	45 Fremont Street United States 800-474-2737
Web Address:	www.ishares.com
Inception:	06-20-00*
Advisor:	Barclays Global Fund Advisers

Management Fee:	0.70%		
Expense Projections:	3Yr:$224	5Yr:$390	10Yr:$871
Income Distrib:	Annually		
Exchange:	NYSE		

Portfolio Analysis 11-30-07

Share change since 10-07 Total Stocks:109	Sector	Country	% Assets
⊖ Taiwan Semiconductor Mfg	Hardware	Taiwan	10.96
⊖ Hon Hai Precision Indust	Hardware	Taiwan	8.86
⊖ Nan Ya Plastics	Ind Mtrls	Taiwan	3.60
⊖ Cathay Financial Holding	Financial	Taiwan	3.47
⊖ AU Optronics	Hardware	Taiwan	3.30
⊖ China Steel	Ind Mtrls	Taiwan	3.16
⊖ MediaTek	Hardware	Taiwan	3.02
⊖ Formosa Plastics	Ind Mtrls	Taiwan	3.00
⊖ Chunghwa Telecom	Telecom	Taiwan	2.90
⊖ ASUSTEK Computer	Business	Taiwan	2.67
⊖ High Tech Computer	Hardware	Taiwan	2.34
⊖ Innolux Display	Hardware	Taiwan	2.02
⊖ United Microelectronics	Hardware	Taiwan	2.02
⊖ Formosa Chemicals & Fibr	Goods	Taiwan	1.92
⊖ Chi Mei Optoelectronics	Hardware	Taiwan	1.52
⊖ Mega Financial Holding	—	Taiwan	1.44
⊖ Formosa Petrochemical	Energy	Taiwan	1.43
⊖ Chinatrust Financial Hol	Financial	Taiwan	1.42
⊖ Delta Electronics	Goods	Taiwan	1.41
⊖ Acer	Goods	Taiwan	1.33

Current Investment Style

Value Blnd Growth — Large Mid Small

Market Cap	%
Giant	31.8
Large	46.5
Mid	21.2
Small	0.5
Micro	0.0
Avg $mil: 9,328	

Value Measures		Rel Category
Price/Earnings	13.20	0.75
Price/Book	1.90	0.72
Price/Sales	1.05	0.48
Price/Cash Flow	6.52	0.75
Dividend Yield %	3.49	1.04

Growth Measures	%	Rel Category
Long-Term Erngs	21.42	1.28
Book Value	10.91	0.93
Sales	20.98	1.14
Cash Flow	11.55	0.64
Historical Erngs	15.20	0.52

Composition

Cash	0.2	Bonds	0.0
Stocks	99.1	Other	0.7
Foreign (% of Stock)			100.0

Sector Weightings	% of Stocks	Rel MSCI EAFE	3 Year High	3 Year Low
Info	55.23	4.36		
Software	0.23	0.40	1	0
Hardware	51.12	12.62	54	40
Media	0.00	0.00	0	0
Telecom	3.88	0.61	4	3
Service	20.00	0.46		
Health	0.00	0.00	0	0
Consumer	0.35	0.07	1	0
Business	8.01	1.61	10	7
Financial	11.64	0.43	21	11
Mfg	24.77	0.56		
Goods	8.76	0.66	9	8
Ind Mtrls	14.54	0.84	16	12
Energy	1.47	0.19	1	0
Utilities	0.00	0.00	0	0

Regional Exposure	% Stock		% Stock
UK/W. Europe	0	N. America	0
Japan	0	Latn America	0
Asia X Japan	100	Other	0

Country Exposure	% Stock
Taiwan	100

iShares U.K. Index EWU

Market Price	Mstar Category
$24.08	Europe Stock

Morningstar Rating	Return	Risk	Yield	NAV	Avg Daily Vol. (k)	52 wk High/Low
★★	Low	Low	3.5%	$24.10	829	$27.22 - $22.14

Morningstar Fair Value

Price/Fair Value Ratio	Coverage Rate %
1.00	0

Valuation

Although we don't cover enough of the fund's holdings here to make a definitive assessment of its valuation, this ETF was recently trading at a 4% discount to our fair value estimate. Given fund's quality and risk profile, we'd require at least a 9% discount before investing here.

Methodology

This ETF tracks the MSCI United Kingdom Index, which consists of roughly 150 stocks that trade primarily on the London Stock Exchange. Taken together, these stocks account for about 85% of the U.K.'s total market capitalization. As a cap-weighted fund, this portfolio is top heavy, with the fund's top 10 holdings accounting for almost half of all assets. The portfolio's sector composition represents the U.K.'s major players, including banks, energy, and pharma, as well as British-based mining companies. The fund does not hedge back into the U.S. dollar.

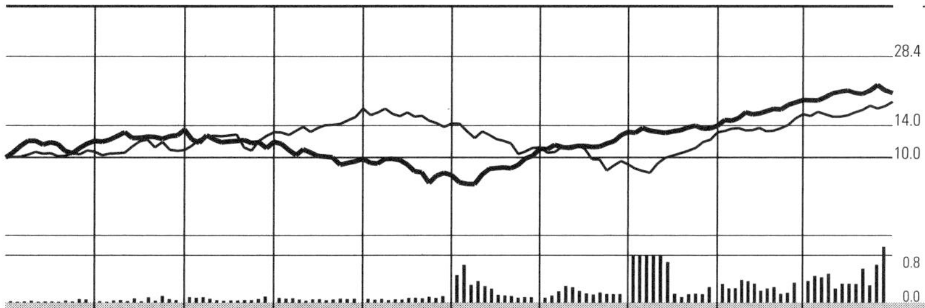

Growth of $10,000
— Investment Value of ETF
— Investment Value of Index MSCI EAFE

Trading Volume Millions

History

1998	1999	2000	2001	2002	2003	2004	2005	2006	2007	History
20.39	21.41	17.99	14.65	12.13	15.37	17.88	18.49	23.19	24.10	NAV $
20.44	21.44	17.62	14.69	12.15	15.58	18.09	18.58	23.41	24.08	Market Price $
18.42	12.14	-11.66	-15.93	-15.25	30.74	18.59	6.63	29.82	7.59	NAV Return%
19.52	12.02	-13.60	-13.93	-15.34	32.31	18.36	5.91	30.41	6.48	Market Price Return%
0.02	0.83	0.94	0.32	0.50	0.74	1.11	-0.03	0.70	0.24	Avg Premium/Discount%
-1.51	-14.89	2.51	5.51	0.69	-7.85	-1.66	-6.91	3.48	-3.58	NAV Rtrn% +/-MSCI EAFE
0.45	-0.30	-0.01	-1.88	-0.02	-1.32	-0.98	-0.72	-0.79	-0.77	NAV Rtrn% +/-MSCI UK
67	34	56	28	46	92	50	85	80	67	NAV Return% Rank in Cat
1.97	1.64	1.16	2.63	1.93	3.92	2.24	3.24	4.40	3.64	Income Return %
16.45	10.50	-12.82	-18.56	-17.18	26.82	16.35	3.39	25.42	3.95	Capital Return %
0.35	0.33	0.25	0.47	0.28	0.48	0.34	0.58	0.81	0.84	Income $
0.24	1.04	0.70	0.01	0.00	0.00	0.00	0.00	0.00	0.00	Capital Gains $
—	—	0.94	0.84	—	0.84	0.77	0.57	0.54	0.51	Expense Ratio %
—	—	—	—	—	3.23	3.11	3.39	4.81	3.51	Income Ratio %
—	—	33	30	14	6	6	11	10	8	Turnover Rate %
86	124	180	123	119	172	587	514	992	1,171	Net Assets $mil

Performance 12-31-07

Historic Quarterly NAV Returns

	1st Qtr	2nd Qtr	3rd Qtr	4th Qtr	Total
2003	-8.74	17.71	3.22	17.91	30.74
2004	1.63	1.22	2.59	12.37	18.59
2005	1.23	-0.61	5.95	0.03	6.63
2006	8.11	4.75	4.11	10.11	29.82
2007	2.85	7.34	0.00	-2.54	7.59

Trailing	NAV Return%	Market Return%	NAV Rtrn% +/-MSCI EAFE	%Rank Cat.(NAV)
3 Mo	-2.54	-3.12	-0.79	78
6 Mo	-2.54	-2.44	-2.93	76
1 Yr	7.59	6.48	-3.58	67
3 Yr Avg	14.20	13.72	-2.63	85
5 Yr Avg	18.22	18.16	-3.37	100
10 Yr Avg	6.80	6.86	-1.86	89

Tax Analysis	Tax-Adj Return%	Tax-Cost Ratio
3 Yr (estimated)	12.89	1.15
5 Yr (estimated)	17.00	1.03
10 Yr (estimated)	5.62	1.10

Rating and Risk

Time Period	Morningstar Rtn vs Cat	Morningstar Risk vs Cat	Morningstar Risk-Adj Rating
3 Yr	Low	-Avg	★★
5 Yr	Low	Low	★
10 Yr	Low	Low	★★

Other Measures	Standard Index S&P 500	Best Fit Index MSCI EASExJ
Alpha	-1.3	-2.9
Beta	0.92	0.89
R-Squared	82	87
Standard Deviation	9.68	
Mean	14.20	
Sharpe Ratio	0.99	

Portfolio Analysis 11-30-07

Share change since 10-07 Total Stocks:152	Sector	Country	% Assets
⊖ BP	Energy	U.K.	7.31
⊖ HSBC Hldgs	Financial	U.K.	6.29
⊖ Vodafone Grp	Telecom	U.K.	6.24
⊖ GlaxoSmithKline	Health	U.K.	4.77
⊖ Royal Dutch Shell	Energy	U.K.	4.67
⊖ Rio Tinto	Ind Mtrls	U.K.	3.66
⊖ Royal Dutch Shell	Energy	U.K.	3.49
⊖ Royal Bank of Scotland G	Financial	U.K.	2.98
⊖ Anglo American	Ind Mtrls	U.K.	2.86
⊖ Tesco	Consumer	U.K.	2.46
⊖ BHP Billiton	Ind Mtrls	U.K.	2.40
⊖ Barclays	Financial	U.K.	2.39
⊖ AstraZeneca	Health	U.K.	2.24
⊖ BG Grp	Energy	U.K.	2.24
⊖ HBOS	Financial	U.K.	1.93
⊖ Diageo	Goods	U.K.	1.88
⊖ British American Tobacco	Goods	U.K.	1.88
⊖ Lloyds TSB Grp	Financial	U.K.	1.81
⊖ BT Grp	Telecom	U.K.	1.52
⊖ Unilever	Goods	U.K.	1.51

Current Investment Style

Value Blnd Growth (style box: Large Value)

Market Cap	%
Giant	64.6
Large	21.2
Mid	13.9
Small	0.3
Micro	0.0
Avg $mil: 58,519	

Value Measures		Rel Category
Price/Earnings	12.71	0.99
Price/Book	2.29	1.15
Price/Sales	1.27	1.25
Price/Cash Flow	9.75	1.23
Dividend Yield %	4.10	1.06

Growth Measures	%	Rel Category
Long-Term Erngs	11.51	1.02
Book Value	6.27	0.65
Sales	5.23	0.59
Cash Flow	4.26	0.63
Historical Erngs	24.63	1.21

Composition

Cash	0.2	Bonds	0.0
Stocks	99.8	Other	0.0
Foreign (% of Stock)			100.0

Sector Weightings	% of Stocks	Rel MSCI EAFE	3 Year High	3 Year Low
Info	11.17	0.88		
Software	0.07	0.12	0	0
Hardware	0.17	0.04	0	0
Media	2.72	1.61	4	3
Telecom	8.21	1.29	9	6
Service	41.53	0.96		
Health	7.57	1.19	11	7
Consumer	7.02	1.42	9	7
Business	3.24	0.65	4	3
Financial	23.70	0.88	29	24
Mfg	47.30	1.08		
Goods	9.27	0.69	10	9
Ind Mtrls	15.03	0.87	15	9
Energy	18.05	2.32	21	14
Utilities	4.95	0.89	5	4

Regional Exposure	% Stock		
UK/W. Europe	99	N. America	0
Japan	0	Latn America	0
Asia X Japan	0	Other	1

Country Exposure	% Stock
U.K.	99
South Africa	1

Morningstar's Take by Emiko Kurotsu 12-31-07

We'd happily invest in iShares MSCI United Kingdom at a modest margin of safety.

This ETF is the one to own if you want pure exposure to large, U.K.-based firms. As a cap-weighted ETF, the biggest stocks take center stage here, with the top 10 holdings alone accounting for almost half of the portfolio.

Though the U.K. market is more diversified than many, it's still heavily driven by its biggest players: banks, oil majors, miners, and pharmaceuticals, which together account for well over half of the portfolio. Some of these giant-caps are high-quality firms that boast superior advantages, or wide "economic moats." HSBC earns a wide-moat rating, for instance, in part due to its extensive footprint in emerging markets like Hong Kong and Latin America. GlaxoSmithKline's sheer scale allows it to dig deep into its pockets to fund an extensive drug lineup at varying stages of development. Yet others, such as integrated oil concern BP and global miner Rio Tinto, operate in capital intensive industries that are closely tied to commodity markets, thereby dulling their advantages.

On balance, though, the portfolio's quality is above average. Of the 60% of fund assets that our analysts cover, roughly one fourth are invested in wide-moat stocks in a variety of industries, ranging from banking (Barclays) to consumer goods (Diageo) and media (British Sky Broadcasting). The balance of the portfolio is staked in narrow-moat firms that boast at least some competitive advantages, including scale or brand prestige. For instance though our analysts believe Unilever ought to be split into two pieces, its packaged food division is the world's largest, while its personal-care division boasts more than a few popular brands, including Dove and Ponds.

Given the portfolio's quality and generally moderate risk, we wouldn't demand a wide margin of safety to invest here. We'd be enthusiastic buyers at a 9% or greater discount to our fair value estimate.

Address:	45 Fremont Street United States 800-474-2737
Web Address:	www.ishares.com
Inception:	03-12-96
Advisor:	Barclays Global Fund Advisers

Management Fee:	0.54%		
Expense Projections:	3Yr:$173	5Yr:$302	10Yr:$677
Income Distrib:	Annually		
Exchange:	NYSE		

PowerShares Halter USX PGJ

Market Price	Mstar Category
$34.25	Pacific/Asia ex-Japan St

Morningstar Fair Value

Price/Fair Value Ratio	Coverage Rate %
1.14	93

Morningstar Rating	Return	Risk	Yield	NAV	Avg Daily Vol. (k)	52 wk High/Low
★★★	Average	Above Avg	0.6%	$34.95	1,111	$38.72 - $18.68

Valuation

Given China's hot growth, we're not surprised this fund's valuation was recently overvalued, as it was trading at a 14% premium to our fair value estimate. With the many risks inherent in the portfolio, though, we'd steer clear until it's trading at least 20% below our fair value estimate.

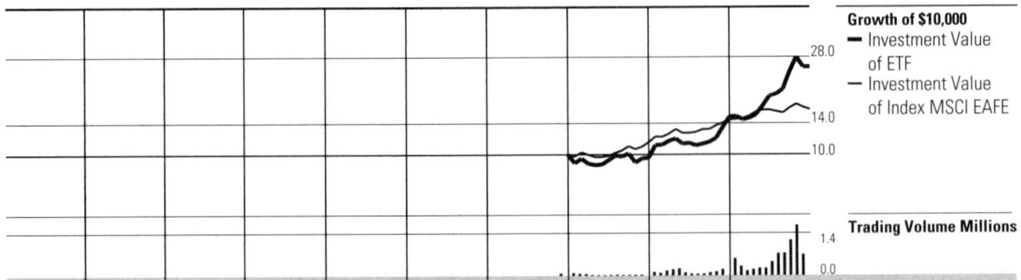

Methodology

This fund tracks the Halter USX China Index, which represents roughly 75 firms that trade on major U.S. stock exchanges but conduct most of their business within mainland China . The index weights stocks by market cap, excluding any below $50 million. Compared to some other China-focused funds, this portfolio has a bigger midcap stake and places less emphasis on financials, and more on business-services and telecom firms, though energy still looms large. While investments are denominated in dollars, they're linked to the yuan-denominated ordinary shares.

1998	1999	2000	2001	2002	2003	2004	2005	2006	2007	History
—	—	—	—	—	—	14.49	13.85	20.92	34.95	NAV $
—	—	—	—	—	—	14.51	13.87	21.15	34.25	Market Price $
—	—	—	—	—	—	34.64*	-3.29	53.10	68.42	NAV Return%
—	—	—	—	—	—	33.55*	-3.29	54.56	63.27	Market Price Return%
—	—	—	—	—	—	0.14	0.14	0.27	-0.15	Avg Premium/Discount%
—	—	—	—	—	—	—	-16.83	26.76	57.25	NAV Rtrn% +/-MSCI EAFE
—	—	—	—	—	—	—	-21.15	24.63	35.04	NAV Rtrn% +/-MSCIAC FE
—	—	—	—	—	—	—	100	13	10	NAV Return% Rank in Cat
—	—	—	—	—	—	—	1.13	1.52	1.02	Income Return %
—	—	—	—	—	—	—	-4.42	51.58	67.40	Capital Return %
—	—	—	—	—	—	0.00	0.16	0.21	0.21	Income $
—	—	—	—	—	—	0.00	0.00	0.00	0.00	Capital Gains $
—	—	—	—	—	—	—	0.70	0.71	0.70	Expense Ratio %
—	—	—	—	—	—	—	1.24	1.18	1.06	Income Ratio %
—	—	—	—	—	—	—	9	21	17	Turnover Rate %
—	—	—	—	—	—	25	79	354	748	Net Assets $mil

Performance 12-31-07

Historic Quarterly NAV Returns

	1st Qtr	2nd Qtr	3rd Qtr	4th Qtr	Total
2003	—	—	—	—	—
2004	—	—	—	—	—*
2005	-8.97	3.71	7.01	-4.28	-3.29
2006	19.21	-2.17	0.99	29.99	53.10
2007	-1.38	25.80	29.42	4.89	68.42

Trailing	NAV Return%	Market Return%	NAV Rtrn% +/-MSCI EAFE	%Rank Cat.(NAV)
3 Mo	4.89	2.76	6.64	25
6 Mo	35.74	33.17	35.35	20
1 Yr	68.42	63.27	57.25	10
3 Yr Avg	35.61	34.64	18.78	13
5 Yr Avg	—	—	—	—
10 Yr Avg	—	—	—	—

Tax Analysis	Tax-Adj Return%	Tax-Cost Ratio
3 Yr (estimated)	35.08	0.39
5 Yr (estimated)	—	—
10 Yr (estimated)	—	—

Rating and Risk

Time Period	Morningstar Rtn vs Cat	Morningstar Risk vs Cat	Morningstar Risk-Adj Rating
3 Yr	Avg	+Avg	★★★
5 Yr	—	—	—
10 Yr	—	—	—

Other Measures	Standard Index S&P 500	Best Fit Index MSCI Ex Jpn ND
Alpha	9.7	2.4
Beta	1.64	1.14
R-Squared	45	66
Standard Deviation	23.27	
Mean	35.61	
Sharpe Ratio	1.25	

Portfolio Analysis 11-30-07

Share change since 10-07 Total Stocks:74

Holding	Sector	Country	% Assets
⊖ China Mobile Ltd. ADR	Telecom	Hong Kong	6.37
⊖ Suntech Power Holdings C	Ind Mtrls	China	6.01
⊖ PetroChina Company, Ltd.	Energy	China	5.92
⊖ China Petroleum & Chemic	Business	China	5.31
⊖ Baidu.com, Inc. ADR	Media	China	5.29
⊖ China Netcom Group Corp.	Telecom	China	5.26
⊖ China United Telecommuni	Telecom	China	5.10
⊖ China Telecom Corporatio	Telecom	China	5.03
⊖ CNOOC, Ltd. ADR	Energy	Hong Kong	4.80
⊖ China Life Insurance Com	Financial	China	4.42
⊖ Yanzhou Coal Mining Comp	Energy	China	4.00
⊖ Huaneng Power Internatio	Utilities	China	3.67
⊖ Aluminum Corp of China,	Ind Mtrls	China	3.45
⊖ Focus Media Holding, Ltd	Business	China	3.18
⊖ China Southern Airlines	Business	China	2.75
⊖ Guangshen Railway Compan	Business	China	2.62
⊖ China Eastern Airlines C	Business	China	2.35
⊖ Sinopec Shanghai Petroch	Energy	China	2.29
⊖ Mindray Medical Internat	Health	China	2.12
⊖ Ctrip.com International,	Business	China	1.98

Current Investment Style

Value Blnd Growth — Large / Mid / Small

Market Cap	%
Giant	43.3
Large	12.2
Mid	32.5
Small	7.2
Micro	4.9
Avg $mil: 15,778	

Value Measures		Rel Category
Price/Earnings	—	—
Price/Book	—	—
Price/Sales	—	—
Price/Cash Flow	—	—
Dividend Yield %	—	—

Growth Measures	%	Rel Category
Long-Term Erngs	—	—
Book Value	—	—
Sales	—	—
Cash Flow	—	—
Historical Erngs	—	—

Composition

Cash	0.0	Bonds	0.0
Stocks	100.0	Other	0.0
Foreign (% of Stock)			97.2

Sector Weightings	% of Stocks	Rel MSCI EAFE	3 Year High	3 Year Low
Info	34.11	2.69		
Software	0.25	0.43	2	0
Hardware	4.52	1.12	11	4
Media	7.06	4.18	7	3
Telecom	22.28	3.51	23	20
Service	34.27	0.79		
Health	3.38	0.53	4	0
Consumer	2.16	0.44	2	0
Business	24.25	4.86	26	22
Financial	4.48	0.17	6	4
Mfg	31.63	0.72		
Goods	0.22	0.02	2	0
Ind Mtrls	10.43	0.60	11	7
Energy	17.26	2.22	22	17
Utilities	3.72	0.67	5	4

Regional Exposure	% Stock		% Stock
UK/W. Europe	0	N. America	3
Japan	0	Latn America	0
Asia X Japan	97	Other	0

Country Exposure	% Stock		% Stock
China	84	Canada	0
Hong Kong	12	—	
United States	3		

Morningstar's Take by Emiko Kurotsu 12-31-07

PowerShares Golden Dragon Halter USX China looks different than peers, but still warrants great caution.

This ETF pulls together roughly 75 Chinese stocks that trade on U.S. exchanges and weights them by market cap. That's not exactly an original formula as country-specific ETFs go. But it sets the fund apart from other China-focused funds in a few ways. It's better-diversified by market-cap, with more than 30% in midcaps. At the same time, it branches out from the typical bank and energy fare--mainstays of the Chinese economy--to encompass a number of telecom and business-services names.

This portfolio's quality is average at best. About 60% of assets are in narrow-moat firms, which wield competitive advantages, albeit ones that confer modest, or fleeting, economic benefits. These include China Life Insurance, which has first-mover advantage and a sales force that's 640,000 members strong, to fortify its position as an incumbent insurance provider. Yet even that firm must fend off challenges from fast-growing rivals spurred by evolving regulations allowing new entrants on its turf. Similarly, Baidu.com's status as China's biggest search engine faces threats from foreign rivals like Google and Microsoft, who are eager to take some of its market share.

Though the portfolio's middling quality isn't by itself a reason not to invest here, it makes the fund less valuable, as we place greater value in firms that boast durable competitive advantages. It also has a secondary effect: Most firms here carry above-average business risk, reflecting the uncertain regulatory and fluid market in which they operate. Furthermore, the fund's holdings tend to derive all of its profits from China and are thus likely to falter when the Chinese economy slows.

Given these significant risks, we wouldn't invest here without a significant margin of safety. We'd need a 20% or greater discount to our fair value estimate in order to dip a toe.

Address:	301 West Roosevelt Road United States 800-983-0903
Web Address:	www.powershares.com
Inception:	12-09-04*
Advisor:	PowerShares Capital Management LLC

Management Fee:	0.50%		
Expense Projections:	3Yr:$231	5Yr:$404	10Yr:$905
Income Distrib:	Quarterly		
Exchange:	AMEX		

Vanguard Euro Stk ETF VGK

Market Price	Mstar Category
$74.82	Europe Stock

Morningstar Rating	Return	Risk	Yield	NAV	Avg Daily Vol. (k)	52 wk High/Low
—	—	—	3.1%	$74.76	307	$81.91 - $65.60

Morningstar Fair Value

Price/Fair Value Ratio	Coverage Rate %
1.00	3

Valuation

Our equity analysts cover a small number of this ETF's stock holdings, so the price/fair value price ratio above may not be a faithful representation of this portfolio's valuation attributes. Thus, investors trying to gauge this ETF's attractiveness should consider the price/fair value ratio only in conjunction with other fundamental measures.

Methodology

This exchange-traded fund is designed to mirror the performance of the MSCI Europe Index, a capitalization-weighted benchmark of the region's largest markets and stocks. The portfolio is dominated by familiar global leaders such as BP, Nestle, and Novartis, but the large number of holdings dilutes exposure to individual names. The fund has a fair amount of mid-cap exposure but does not own stocks from Central or Eastern Europe. Vanguard does not hedge foreign-currency exposure.

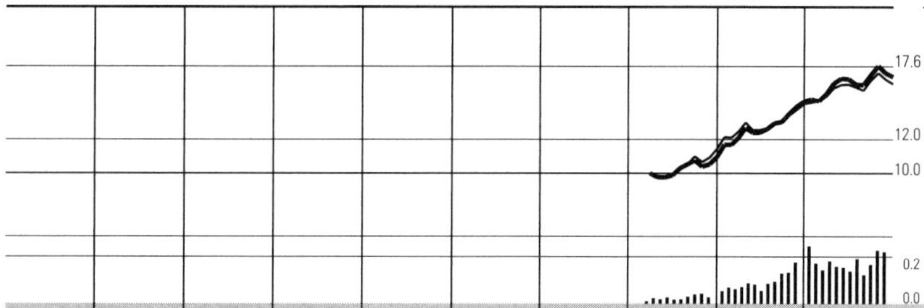

Growth of $10,000
— Investment Value of ETF
— Investment Value of Index MSCI EAFE

Trading Volume Millions

1998	1999	2000	2001	2002	2003	2004	2005	2006	2007	History
—	—	—	—	—	—	—	52.05	67.70	74.76	NAV $
—	—	—	—	—	—	—	52.60	68.16	74.82	Market Price $
—	—	—	—	—	—	—	17.98*	33.57	13.93	NAV Return%
—	—	—	—	—	—	—	—	33.07	13.25	Market Price Return%
—	—	—	—	—	—	—	0.54	0.64	0.42	Avg Premium/Discount%
—	—	—	—	—	—	—	—	7.23	2.76	NAV Rtrn% +/-MSCI EAFE
—	—	—	—	—	—	—	—	-0.15	0.07	NAV Rtrn% +/-MSCI Eur
—	—	—	—	—	—	—	—	47	34	NAV Return% Rank in Cat
—	—	—	—	—	—	—	—	3.48	3.48	Income Return %
—	—	—	—	—	—	—	—	30.09	10.45	Capital Return %
—	—	—	—	—	—	—	1.38	1.81	2.36	Income $
—	—	—	—	—	—	—	0.00	0.00	0.00	Capital Gains $
—	—	—	—	—	—	—	0.18	0.18	—	Expense Ratio %
—	—	—	—	—	—	—	2.93	3.44	—	Income Ratio %
—	—	—	—	—	—	—	5	6	—	Turnover Rate %
—	—	—	—	—	—	—	277	1,507	3,100	Net Assets $mil

Performance 12-31-07

Historic Quarterly NAV Returns

	1st Qtr	2nd Qtr	3rd Qtr	4th Qtr	Total
2003	—	—	—	—	—
2004	—	—	—	—	—
2005	—	-1.10	8.18	1.78	—*
2006	10.61	2.69	5.72	11.24	33.57
2007	4.14	8.10	2.19	-0.96	13.93

Trailing	NAV Return%	Market Return%	NAV Rtrn% +/-MSCI EAFE	%Rank Cat.(NAV)
3 Mo	-0.96	-1.29	0.79	61
6 Mo	1.21	1.13	0.82	43
1 Yr	13.93	13.25	2.76	34
3 Yr Avg	—	—	—	—
5 Yr Avg	—	—	—	—
10 Yr Avg	—	—	—	—

Tax Analysis	Tax-Adj Return%	Tax-Cost Ratio
3 Yr (estimated)	—	—
5 Yr (estimated)	—	—
10 Yr (estimated)	—	—

Rating and Risk

Time Period	Morningstar Rtn vs Cat	Morningstar Risk vs Cat	Morningstar Risk-Adj Rating
3 Yr	—	—	—
5 Yr	—	—	—
10 Yr	—	—	—

Other Measures	Standard Index S&P 500	Best Fit Index
Alpha	—	—
Beta	—	—
R-Squared	—	—
Standard Deviation	—	
Mean	—	
Sharpe Ratio	—	

Portfolio Analysis 09-30-07

Share change since 06-07 Total Stocks:560	Sector	Country	% Assets
⊕ HSBC Hldgs	Financial	U.K.	2.19
⊕ BP	Energy	U.K.	2.13
⊕ Vodafone Grp	Telecom	U.K.	1.83
⊕ Nestle	Goods	Switzerland	1.82
⊕ TOTAL	Energy	France	1.76
⊕ Nokia	Hardware	Finland	1.57
⊕ GlaxoSmithKline	Health	U.K.	1.53
⊕ Royal Dutch Shell	Energy	U.K.	1.53
⊕ Novartis	Health	Switzerland	1.29
⊕ Roche Holding Ltd	Health	Switzerland	1.29
⊕ Telefonica	Telecom	Spain	1.24
⊕ Banco Santander	Financial	Spain	1.23
⊕ Siemens	Hardware	Germany	1.18
⊕ E.On	Utilities	Germany	1.16
⊕ Royal Dutch Shell	Energy	U.K.	1.14
⊕ UBS AG	Financial	Switzerland	1.10
⊕ Allianz SE	Financial	Germany	1.06
⊕ Royal Bank of Scotland G	Financial	U.K.	1.04
⊕ ENI	Energy	Italy	0.97
⊕ ABN AMRO Holding	Financial	Netherlands	0.96

Current Investment Style

Style box: Value Blnd Growth / Large Mid Small

Market Cap	%
Giant	60.3
Large	28.0
Mid	11.3
Small	0.4
Micro	0.0
Avg $mil: 49,293	

Value Measures		Rel Category
Price/Earnings	13.22	1.03
Price/Book	2.19	1.10
Price/Sales	1.12	1.10
Price/Cash Flow	8.79	1.11
Dividend Yield %	3.62	0.93

Growth Measures	%	Rel Category
Long-Term Erngs	11.08	0.98
Book Value	8.83	0.92
Sales	8.34	0.94
Cash Flow	11.75	1.74
Historical Erngs	20.09	0.99

Composition

Cash	0.3	Bonds	0.0
Stocks	97.5	Other	2.3
Foreign (% of Stock)			100.0

Sector Weightings	% of Stocks	Rel MSCI EAFE	3 Year High	3 Year Low
Info	14.60	1.15		
Software	0.69	1.19	1	1
Hardware	4.37	1.08	4	3
Media	2.24	1.33	3	2
Telecom	7.30	1.15	9	6
Service	43.68	1.01		
Health	7.44	1.17	10	7
Consumer	4.54	0.92	5	4
Business	3.88	0.78	4	4
Financial	27.82	1.03	31	28
Mfg	41.73	0.95		
Goods	11.73	0.88	12	10
Ind Mtrls	14.49	0.84	14	10
Energy	10.14	1.31	13	9
Utilities	5.37	0.97	5	5

Regional Exposure	% Stock		
UK/W. Europe	100	N. America	0
Japan	0	Latn America	0
Asia X Japan	0	Other	0

Country Exposure	% Stock		
U.K.	32	Switzerland	10
France	14	Netherlands	6
Germany	12		

Morningstar's Take by Dan Lefkovitz 12-31-07

Vanguard European Stock ETF has the feel of an old standby.

A number of new Europe-focused ETFs have launched since this one came out in March 2005. That's a testament to the ETF market's explosive growth as well as to the strong performance of European stocks, boosted by the appreciation of European currencies against the U.S. dollar.

At first glance, those upstarts look like stiff competition, as this fund sports a subpar since-inception record versus the Europe-stock category. Perhaps other benchmarks are superior to the MSCI Europe Index that this fund tracks, or passive management doesn't work in Europe.

Yet, there are a few things to consider. First, very few actively managed funds that play in the same field as this fund--meaning Western European large-cap stocks--have proved that they can add value. Second, the Europe-stock category is home to a grab bag of funds, including offerings focused on Eastern Europe and small-cap shares. Many of these niche funds have put up spectacular numbers since 2001, as risky fare has trumped developed-market blue chips. Not surprisingly, some of the new Europe-focused ETFs target those same red-hot, but risky, niches.

This fund is actually more battle-tested than its inception date implies. Typical of Vanguard's ETFs, it's an exchange-traded share class of mutual fund Vanguard European Stock Index, around since 1990. The new ETFs are far less-proven. Also, performance has perked up here. Western European large caps recorded nice gains in 2006 and have held up relatively well during 2007's ups and downs. This fund also stacks up well versus other broad Europe-focused ETFs, such as iShares MSCI EMU and iShares S&P Europe 350, as it's cheaper and more complete.

Although investors should of course weigh this fund's role carefully, it's a solid choice for those seeking to augment a portfolio's exposure to large European firms.

Address:	PO Box 2600 United States 866-499-8473
Web Address:	www.vanguard.com
Inception:	03-04-05*
Advisor:	Vanguard Advisers, Inc.

Management Fee:	0.14%		
Expense Projections:	3Yr:$58	5Yr:$101	10Yr:$230
Income Distrib:	Annually		
Exchange:	AMEX		

Vanguard Pacif Stk ETF VPL

Market Price	Mstar Category
$67.75	Japan Stock

Morningstar Fair Value

Price/Fair Value Ratio	Coverage Rate %
1.00	3

Valuation

Because our equity analysts cover a relatively small number of this ETF's holdings, the price/fair value ratio above may not be a faithful representation of the portfolio's valuation attributes. Investors trying to gauge this ETF's attractiveness should consider the price/fair value ratio only in conjunction with other fundamental measures.

Methodology

This ETF tracks the MSCI Pacific Index, a capitalization-weighted benchmark of the region's largest stocks in developed markets, as defined by MSCI. Though its roughly 70%-80% Japan stake lands it in the Japan-stock category, it puts the remainder of its assets in Australia, Hong Kong, Singapore, and New Zealand. It does not have any exposure to other popular Asian markets such as Taiwan, Korea, India, or Thailand. Its bogy gives it hefty exposure to its markets' biggest stocks. It does not hedge its currency exposure.

Morningstar Rating	Return	Risk	Yield	NAV	Avg Daily Vol. (k)	52 wk High/Low
—	—	—	2.5%	$67.33	133	$75.22 - $65.01

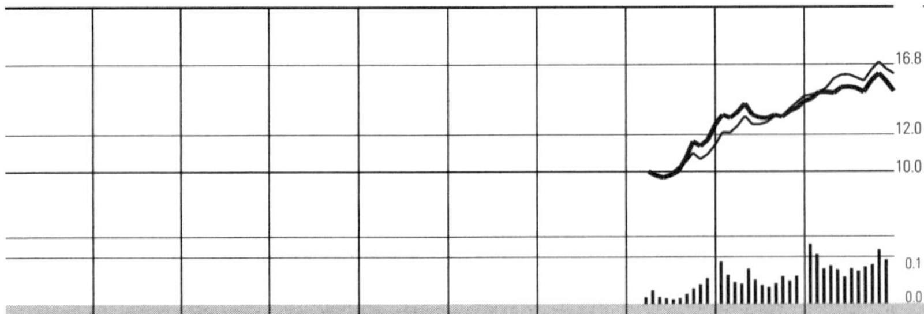

Growth of $10,000
- Investment Value of ETF
- Investment Value of Index MSCI EAFE

Trading Volume Millions

History

1998	1999	2000	2001	2002	2003	2004	2005	2006	2007	History
—	—	—	—	—	—	—	60.03	65.81	67.33	NAV $
—	—	—	—	—	—	—	60.89	66.47	67.75	Market Price $
—	—	—	—	—	—	—	13.02*	12.10	4.85	NAV Return%
—	—	—	—	—	—	—	13.00*	11.63	4.45	Market Price Return%
—	—	—	—	—	—	—	0.81	0.50	0.21	Avg Premium/Discount%
—	—	—	—	—	—	—	—	-14.24	-6.32	NAV Rtrn% +/-MSCI EAFE
—	—	—	—	—	—	—	—	-0.10	-0.45	NAV Rtrn% +/-MSCI Pac
—	—	—	—	—	—	—	—	1	1	NAV Return% Rank in Cat
—	—	—	—	—	—	—	—	2.45	2.54	Income Return %
—	—	—	—	—	—	—	—	9.65	2.31	Capital Return %
—	—	—	—	—	—	—	0.93	1.47	1.67	Income $
—	—	—	—	—	—	—	0.00	0.00	0.00	Capital Gains $
—	—	—	—	—	—	—	0.18	0.18	—	Expense Ratio %
—	—	—	—	—	—	—	1.89	1.82	—	Income Ratio %
—	—	—	—	—	—	—	7	2	—	Turnover Rate %
—	—	—	—	—	—	—	312	816	1,414	Net Assets $mil

Performance 12-31-07

Historic Quarterly NAV Returns

	1st Qtr	2nd Qtr	3rd Qtr	4th Qtr	Total
2003	—	—	—	—	—
2004	—	—	—	—	—
2005	—	-1.58	17.33	8.21	—*
2006	6.55	-2.78	0.37	7.83	12.10
2007	4.48	2.55	2.96	-4.96	4.85

Trailing	NAV Return%	Market Return%	NAV Rtrn% +/-MSCI EAFE	%Rank Cat.(NAV)
3 Mo	-4.96	-4.68	-3.21	20
6 Mo	-2.14	-1.55	-2.53	10
1 Yr	4.85	4.45	-6.32	1
3 Yr Avg	—	—	—	—
5 Yr Avg	—	—	—	—
10 Yr Avg	—	—	—	—

Tax Analysis	Tax-Adj Return%	Tax-Cost Ratio
3 Yr (estimated)	—	—
5 Yr (estimated)	—	—
10 Yr (estimated)	—	—

Rating and Risk

Time Period	Morningstar Rtn vs Cat	Morningstar Risk vs Cat	Morningstar Risk-Adj Rating
3 Yr	—	—	—
5 Yr	—	—	—
10 Yr	—	—	—

Other Measures	Standard Index S&P 500	Best Fit Index
Alpha	—	—
Beta	—	—
R-Squared	—	—
Standard Deviation	—	
Mean	—	
Sharpe Ratio	—	

Morningstar's Take by William Samuel Rocco 12-31-07

It's crucial to examine the big picture at Vanguard Pacific Stock ETF.

This young exchange-traded fund looks good relative to its category rivals. Indeed, while the typical Japan fund is down 1% for the year to date through Sept. 28, 2007, this ETF is up 10%. And its older mutual fund clone has handily outpaced the average Japan fund over the trailing three-, five-, and 10-year periods.

But that record isn't as meaningful as one might think because this ETF and its clone have a broader geographic purview than their category peers. This fund tracks the MSCI Pacific Index and thus normally has a sizable stake in Australia and small stakes in Hong Kong, Singapore, and New Zealand on top of a hefty position in Japan. This geographic breadth has been quite advantageous over time, as the non-Japanese markets have generally performed much better than the Japanese market during the past decade. The Australia market has a 14% annualized 10-year return, for example, while the Japan market has a 2% annualized 10-year return.

The fact that this ETF and its clone invest roughly 20% to 30% of assets outside Japan means that it also makes sense to compare them to diversified Pacific/Asia offerings. And the mutual fund share class of this ETF has lagged the typical offering of that type by sizable margins over the trailing three-, five-, and 10-year periods, as its zero exposure to Asia's emerging markets and its oversized Japan stake have hurt.

Finally, it's tough to fit this ETF into a portfolio. Its unusual geographic range means it doesn't work well as a pure-Japan play or a pan-Asia play. Thus, we think most investors can comfortably steer clear of this ETF, even though it's cheap and has done a good job of tracking its benchmark.

Address:	PO Box 2600 United States 866-499-8473
Web Address:	www.vanguard.com
Inception:	03-04-05*
Advisor:	Vanguard Advisers, Inc.

Management Fee:	0.14%		
Expense Projections:	3Yr:$58	5Yr:$101	10Yr:$230
Income Distrib:	Annually		
Exchange:	AMEX		

Portfolio Analysis 09-30-07

Share change since 06-07 Total Stocks:536	Sector	Country	% Assets
⊕ Toyota Motor	Goods	Japan	3.64
⊕ BHP Billiton Ltd	Ind Mtrls	Australia	3.01
⊕ Mitsubishi UFJ Financial	Financial	Japan	1.68
⊕ Commonwealth Bank of Aus	Financial	Australia	1.49
⊕ Takeda Pharmaceutical	Health	Japan	1.36
⊕ CANON INC.	Goods	Japan	1.33
⊕ National Australia Bank	Financial	Australia	1.32
⊕ Mizuho Financial Grp	Financial	Japan	1.28
⊕ HONDA MOTOR	Goods	Japan	1.19
⊕ Nintendo	Goods	Japan	1.18
⊕ Sumitomo Mitsui Financia	Financial	Japan	1.17
⊕ Australia & New Zealand	Financial	Australia	1.12
⊕ SONY CORPORATION	Goods	Japan	1.11
⊕ Westpac Banking	Financial	Australia	1.07
⊕ Mitsubishi	Ind Mtrls	Japan	0.98
⊕ Nippon Steel	Ind Mtrls	Japan	0.95
⊕ Mitsui & Co.	Ind Mtrls	Japan	0.94
⊕ JFE Hldgs	Ind Mtrls	Japan	0.94
⊕ Matsushita Electric Indu	Ind Mtrls	Japan	0.84
⊕ Westfield Grp	Consumer	Australia	0.77

Current Investment Style

Value Blnd Growth / Large Mid Small

Market Cap	%
Giant	53.0
Large	35.8
Mid	11.1
Small	0.1
Micro	0.0
Avg $mil: 20,293	

Value Measures		Rel Category
Price/Earnings	16.93	1.04
Price/Book	1.87	1.30
Price/Sales	1.07	1.49
Price/Cash Flow	7.88	1.13
Dividend Yield %	2.33	1.18

Growth Measures	%	Rel Category
Long-Term Erngs	13.67	1.31
Book Value	9.67	1.11
Sales	8.38	1.18
Cash Flow	9.68	1.93
Historical Erngs	17.67	1.50

Composition

Cash	0.3	Bonds	0.1
Stocks	97.6	Other	2.1
Foreign (% of Stock)			100.0

Sector Weightings	% of Stocks	Rel MSCI EAFE	3 Year High	3 Year Low
Info	9.32	0.74		
Software	0.43	0.74	1	0
Hardware	4.51	1.11	5	4
Media	0.99	0.59	1	1
Telecom	3.39	0.53	4	3
Service	44.02	1.02		
Health	4.56	0.72	5	4
Consumer	5.47	1.10	6	5
Business	6.99	1.40	7	6
Financial	27.00	1.00	30	27
Mfg	46.66	1.06		
Goods	16.62	1.25	19	17
Ind Mtrls	25.01	1.44	25	20
Energy	1.75	0.23	2	1
Utilities	3.28	0.59	5	3

Regional Exposure	% Stock		
UK/W. Europe	0	N. America	0
Japan	67	Latn America	0
Asia X Japan	33	Other	0

Country Exposure	% Stock		
Japan	67	Singapore	4
Australia	22	New Zealand	0
Hong Kong	7		

Fixed Income Funds

This section offers a full-page report on each fixed income ETF.

iShares iBoxx$ Corp Bd LQD

Market Price	Mstar Category
$104.84	Long-Term Bond

Morningstar Fair Value

Price/Fair Value Ratio	Coverage Rate %
NA	NA

Valuation

This ETF primarily holds bonds, not stocks. That explains why the fund's price/fair value ratio does not appear above.

Methodology

The fund's benchmark, the iBoxx $ Liquid Investment Grade Index, uses sampling techniques to mimic the corporate-bond market. The index includes bonds from companies that meet Goldman Sachs' definition of liquid, long-term corporate debt. The issuers must have headquarters in the U.S., Canada, Western Europe, or Japan; have investment-grade ratings; have at least $500 million in outstanding debt; be less than five years old; and have at least three years until maturity. The managers can also differ from the index by up to 10% to add value on the margins.

Morningstar Rating	Return	Risk	Yield	NAV	Avg Daily Vol. (k)	52 wk High/Low
★	Below Avg	Below Avg	5.5%	$104.35	153	$108.65 - $102.66

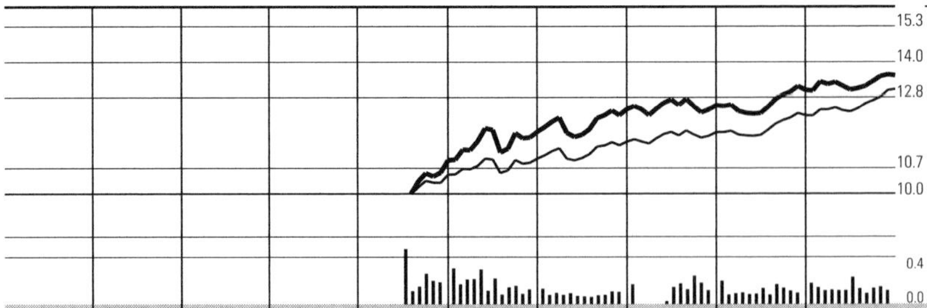

1998	1999	2000	2001	2002	2003	2004	2005	2006	2007	History
—	—	—	—	107.99	110.38	111.53	107.50	106.21	104.35	NAV $
—	—	—	—	109.69	110.57	111.53	107.69	106.68	104.84	Market Price $
—	—	—	—	5.37*	7.43	5.91	1.00	3.96	3.73	NAV Return%
—	—	—	—	5.47*	5.94	5.73	1.18	4.24	3.76	Market Price Return%
—	—	—	—	0.92	0.24	0.25	0.09	0.09	0.41	Avg Premium/Discount%
—	—	—	—	—	3.33	1.57	-1.43	-0.37	-3.24	NAV Rtrn% +/-LB Aggreg
—	—	—	—	—	1.56	-2.65	-4.33	1.25	1.73	NAV Rtrn% +/-LB LongTerm
—	—	—	—	—	1	1	1	1	1	NAV Return% Rank in Cat
—	—	—	—	—	5.20	4.81	4.70	5.12	5.51	Income Return %
—	—	—	—	—	2.23	1.10	-3.70	-1.16	-1.78	Capital Return %
—	—	—	—	2.48	5.48	5.19	5.13	5.37	5.71	Income $
—	—	—	—	0.00	0.00	0.00	0.00	0.00	0.00	Capital Gains $
—	—	—	—	—	0.15	0.15	0.15	0.15	0.15	Expense Ratio %
—	—	—	—	—	5.38	5.38	4.71	4.75	5.26	Income Ratio %
—	—	—	—	—	20	20	32	71	89	Turnover Rate %
—	—	—	—	1,857	2,307	2,520	2,419	2,719	3,235	Net Assets $mil

Performance 12-31-07

Historic Quarterly NAV Returns

	1st Qtr	2nd Qtr	3rd Qtr	4th Qtr	Total
2003	2.60	5.26	-0.81	0.29	7.43
2004	3.71	-4.26	5.04	1.55	5.91
2005	-1.52	4.04	-1.66	0.25	1.00
2006	-1.46	-0.55	4.79	1.24	3.96
2007	1.47	-1.38	2.12	1.50	3.73

Trailing	NAV Return%	Market Return%	NAV Rtrn% +/-LB Aggreg	%Rank Cat.(NAV)
3 Mo	1.50	1.18	-1.50	100
6 Mo	3.65	3.50	-2.28	100
1 Yr	3.73	3.76	-3.24	1
3 Yr Avg	2.89	3.05	-1.67	1
5 Yr Avg	4.38	4.16	-0.04	1
10 Yr Avg	—	—	—	—

Tax Analysis	Tax-Adj Return%	Tax-Cost Ratio
3 Yr (estimated)	1.08	1.76
5 Yr (estimated)	2.58	1.72
10 Yr (estimated)	—	—

Rating and Risk

Time Period	Morningstar Rtn vs Cat	Morningstar Risk vs Cat	Morningstar Risk-Adj Rating
3 Yr	-Avg	Avg	★★
5 Yr	-Avg	-Avg	★
10 Yr	—	—	—

Other Measures	Standard Index S&P 500	Best Fit Index LB Credit
Alpha	-1.6	-0.8
Beta	1.31	1.15
R-Squared	87	98
Standard Deviation	3.96	
Mean	2.89	
Sharpe Ratio	-0.35	

Morningstar's Take by Lawrence Jones 12-31-07

IShares iBoxx $ Investment Grade Corporate Bond can get the job done, but there are better options.

There are relatively few fixed-income mutual fund offerings, either indexed or actively managed, that focus solely on the investment-grade corporate bond sector, but with more than $3 billion in assets, this exchange-traded fund has become prominent among them. Fund management attempts to track the iBoxx $ Liquid Investment Grade Index, a subset of the 1,000 issue iBoxx $ Corporates Index, using a sampling technique involving a 100-bond portfolio of the most liquid, and long-term, bonds in the corporate universe. Moreover, one of the fund's most compelling advantages is its rock-bottom 0.15% expense ratio, which allows for more total return to flow to investors.

While the fund offers good exposure to investment-grade corporate bonds, we have some concerns. For instance, the fund is fairly concentrated in certain industry areas of the corporate bond market, which can hurt returns should those regions stumble. In mid- to late 2007, for example, when the subprime mortgage meltdown and liquidity crisis hurt the bonds of many financials and banking firms (which represent more than 40% of the portfolio here), fund returns suffered. Also, while the fund's long-term market return is reasonably close to its NAV return, meaningful deviations have occurred over shorter periods, introducing tracking error risk and raising the possibility the team may have trouble matching the benchmark. And some variations can be introduced from the team's ability to invest 10% in non-index issues (to reflect changes to the index), adding an uncertain active element. Finally, the fund hasn't kept pace with some actively managed corporate-bond-focused mutual funds.

So while we like the fund's cost and think it could serve as a good diversifier for a government-heavy bond portfolio, we think investors should consider other options before climbing aboard.

Address:	45 Fremont Street United States 800-474-2737
Web Address:	www.ishares.com
Inception:	07-22-02*
Advisor:	Barclays Global Fund Advisers

Management Fee:	0.15%		
Expense Projections:	3Yr:$48	5Yr:$85	10Yr:$192
Income Distrib:	Annually		
Exchange:	AMEX		

Portfolio Analysis 12-31-07

Total Fixed-Income:102	Date of Maturity	Amount $000	Value $000	% Net Assets
Amer Express Bk Fsb Mtn	10-17-12	35,650	36,192	1.13
Telecom Italia Cap 7.2%	07-18-36	32,550	35,229	1.10
Comcast 6.95%	08-15-37	32,550	34,448	1.08
JOHNSON & JOHNSON	08-15-17	32,550	34,273	1.07
GENERAL ELEC CAP	08-07-37	32,550	34,216	1.07
Johnson & Johnson 5.15%	08-15-12	32,550	34,130	1.07
Shell Intl Fin Bv 5.625%	06-27-11	32,550	34,019	1.06
Embarq 7.995%	06-01-36	32,550	34,014	1.06
Toyota Mtr Cr 5.45%	05-18-11	32,550	33,853	1.06
At&T 6.8%	05-15-36	31,000	33,500	1.05
Astrazeneca 5.4%	09-15-12	32,550	33,481	1.05
Deutsche Bk Ag London 6%	09-01-17	32,550	33,453	1.04
Astrazeneca 6.45%	09-15-37	31,000	33,452	1.04
Cisco Sys 5.25%	02-22-11	32,550	33,443	1.04
Cisco Sys 5.5%	02-22-16	32,550	33,386	1.04
General Elec Cap 5.625%	09-15-17	32,550	33,343	1.04
Bhp Billiton Fin Usa 5.1	03-29-12	32,550	33,306	1.04
Amer Express 6.15%	08-28-17	32,550	33,264	1.04
Abbott Labs 5.6%	11-30-17	32,550	33,150	1.04
CITIGROUP	08-15-17	32,550	33,056	1.03

Current Investment Style

Duration: Short Int Long; Quality: High Med Low

[1] figure provided by fund

Avg Eff Duration[1]	6.8 Yrs
Avg Eff Maturity	11.4 Yrs
Avg Credit Quality	A
Avg Wtd Coupon	5.86%
Avg Wtd Price	100.27% of par

Coupon Range	% of Bonds	Rel Cat
0% PIK	0.0	0.0
0% to 6%	66.1	1.5
6% to 8%	33.9	0.7
8% to 10%	0.0	0.0
More than 10%	0.0	0.0

1.00=Category Average

Credit Analysis	% bonds 12-31-07		
US Govt	0	BB	0
AAA	6	B	0
AA	28	Below B	0
A	29	NR/NA	7
BBB	30		

Sector Breakdown	% of assets
US Treasuries	0
TIPS	0
US Agency	0
Mortgage Pass-Throughs	0
Mortgage CMO	0
Mortgage ARM	0
US Corporate	97
Asset-Backed	0
Convertible	0
Municipal	0
Corporate Inflation-Protected	0
Foreign Corporate	2
Foreign Govt	0

Composition

Cash	0.6	Bonds	99.0
Stocks	0.0	Other	0.5

Special Securities	
Restricted/Illiquid Secs	Trace
Exotic Mortgage-Backed	0
Emerging-Markets Secs	0
Options/Futures/Warrants	No

iShares Lehman 1-3 T SHY

Market Price $82.19

Mstar Category Short Government

Morningstar Fair Value

Price/Fair Value Ratio	Coverage Rate %
NA	NA

Valuation

This ETF holds bonds, not stocks. That explains why the fund's price/fair value ratio does not appear above.

Methodology

The fund tries to match the returns and yield of its index, the Lehman Brothers U.S. Treasury: 1-3 Year Index. The index includes U.S. Treasury bonds that have between one and three years until maturity; at least $250 million in par outstanding. On the margins, the managers can also differ from the index by up to 10% if these investments better help track the index.

Morningstar Rating	Return	Risk	Yield	NAV	Avg Daily Vol. (k)	52 wk High/Low
★★★★	Above Avg	Average	4.3%	$82.05	822	$82.66 - $79.68

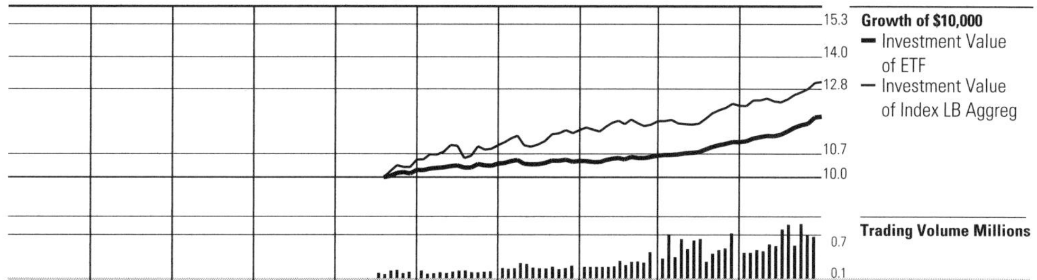

1998	1999	2000	2001	2002	2003	2004	2005	2006	2007	History
—	—	—	—	82.21	82.35	81.42	80.16	79.86	82.05	NAV $
—	—	—	—	82.27	82.47	81.43	80.21	79.96	82.19	Market Price $
—	—	—	—	3.19*	1.78	0.80	1.48	3.83	7.30	NAV Return%
—	—	—	—	3.22*	1.86	0.66	1.53	3.89	7.36	Market Price Return%
—	—	—	—	0.06	0.07	0.04	-0.09	-0.05	-0.03	Avg Premium/Discount%
—	—	—	—	—	-2.32	-3.54	-0.95	-0.50	0.33	NAV Rtrn% +/-LB Aggreg
—	—	—	—	—	—	—	—	—	4.30	NAV Rtrn% +/-LB 1-3 US Treas
—	—	—	—	—	1	1	1	1	1	NAV Return% Rank in Cat
—	—	—	—	—	1.61	1.94	3.05	4.20	4.48	Income Return %
—	—	—	—	—	0.17	-1.14	-1.57	-0.37	2.82	Capital Return %
—	—	—	—	0.64	1.31	1.58	2.45	3.30	3.51	Income $
—	—	—	—	0.00	0.00	0.00	0.00	0.00	0.00	Capital Gains $
—	—	—	—	—	0.15	0.15	0.15	0.15	0.15	Expense Ratio %
—	—	—	—	—	1.80	1.63	2.11	3.36	4.28	Income Ratio %
—	—	—	—	—	44	21	106	83	64	Turnover Rate %
—	—	—	—	904	1,326	2,247	4,401	5,662	9,517	Net Assets $mil

Performance 12-31-07

Historic Quarterly NAV Returns

	1st Qtr	2nd Qtr	3rd Qtr	4th Qtr	Total
2003	0.57	0.68	0.40	0.12	1.78
2004	1.00	-1.16	0.98	-0.01	0.80
2005	-0.33	1.12	0.03	0.66	1.48
2006	0.35	0.61	1.96	0.87	3.83
2007	1.40	0.68	2.64	2.41	7.30

Trailing	NAV Return%	Market Return%	NAV Rtrn% +/-LB Aggreg	%Rank Cat.(NAV)
3 Mo	2.41	2.59	-0.59	50
6 Mo	5.11	5.18	-0.82	50
1 Yr	7.30	7.36	0.33	1
3 Yr Avg	4.18	4.23	-0.38	1
5 Yr Avg	3.01	3.03	-1.41	1
10 Yr Avg	—	—	—	—

Tax Analysis	Tax-Adj Return%	Tax-Cost Ratio
3 Yr (estimated)	2.79	1.33
5 Yr (estimated)	1.93	1.05
10 Yr (estimated)	—	—

Rating and Risk

Time Period	Morningstar Rtn vs Cat	Morningstar Risk vs Cat	Morningstar Risk-Adj Rating
3 Yr	+Avg	Avg	★★★★
5 Yr	+Avg	Avg	★★★★
10 Yr	—	—	—

Other Measures	Standard Index S&P 500	Best Fit Index LB 1-5 YR GOVT
Alpha	-0.3	-0.2
Beta	0.40	0.77
R-Squared	67	98
Standard Deviation	1.41	
Mean	4.18	
Sharpe Ratio	-0.14	

Portfolio Analysis 12-31-07

Total Fixed-Income:32	Date of Maturity	Amount $000	Value $000	% Net Assets
US Treasury Note	08-15-09	649,600	667,516	7.07
US Treasury Note	05-15-10	625,240	646,148	6.85
US Treasury Note 4.75%	02-15-10	464,000	479,976	5.09
US Treasury Note 4.75%	12-31-08	464,000	470,380	4.98
US Treasury Note 3.875%	07-15-10	448,920	458,096	4.85
US Treasury Note 4.5%	03-31-09	426,880	433,932	4.60
US Treasury Note 4.875%	05-15-09	406,000	415,659	4.40
US Treasury Note 3.25%	01-15-09	412,960	413,604	4.38
US Treasury Note 2.625%	03-15-09	408,320	405,850	4.30
US Treasury Note 4.5%	04-30-09	371,200	377,826	4.00
US Treasury Note 4.5%	02-15-09	364,240	369,605	3.92
US Treasury Note 4.625%	11-15-09	348,000	358,022	3.79
US Treasury Note 4%	06-15-09	320,160	324,351	3.44
US Treasury Note 3.5%	08-15-09	293,480	295,429	3.13
US Treasury Note 6.5%	02-15-10	230,840	246,872	2.62
US Treasury Note 4.875%	01-31-09	232,000	236,079	2.50
US Treasury Note 3.875%	05-15-09	220,400	222,622	2.36
US Treasury Note 3.625%	01-15-10	214,600	217,098	2.30
US Treasury Note 4%	03-15-10	208,800	213,064	2.26
US Treasury Note 3.625%	07-15-09	211,120	212,777	2.25

Current Investment Style

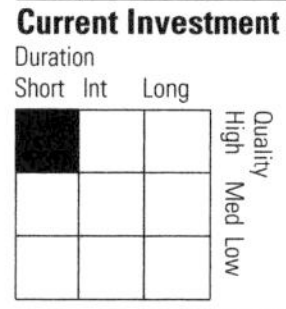

[1] figure provided by fund

Avg Eff Duration[1]	1.7 Yrs
Avg Eff Maturity	1.8 Yrs
Avg Credit Quality	AAA
Avg Wtd Coupon	4.19%
Avg Wtd Price	101.99% of par

Coupon Range	% of Bonds	Rel Cat
0% PIK	0.0	0.0
0% to 6%	97.1	1.0
6% to 8%	2.9	2.0
8% to 10%	0.0	0.0
More than 10%	0.0	0.0

1.00=Category Average

Credit Analysis		% bonds 12-31-07	
US Govt	0	BB	0
AAA	100	B	0
AA	0	Below B	0
A	0	NR/NA	0
BBB	0		

Sector Breakdown	% of assets
US Treasuries	97
TIPS	0
US Agency	0
Mortgage Pass-Throughs	0
Mortgage CMO	0
Mortgage ARM	0
US Corporate	0
Asset-Backed	0
Convertible	0
Municipal	0
Corporate Inflation-Protected	0
Foreign Corporate	0
Foreign Govt	0

Composition			
Cash	2.9	Bonds	97.1
Stocks	0.0	Other	0.0

Special Securities	
Restricted/Illiquid Secs	0
Exotic Mortgage-Backed	—
Emerging-Markets Secs	0
Options/Futures/Warrants	No

Morningstar's Take by Paul Herbert 12-31-07

IShares Lehman 1-3 Year Treasury Bond is at the top of its game--but it won't always be.

This ETF might appeal to investors who want to steer clear of credit risk. It tracks the Lehman Brothers 1-3 Year Treasury Bond Index, a collection of 40-some U.S. Treasury bonds maturing in 12 to 36 months. Because these bonds are backed by the full faith and credit of the government, they are perceived as among the safest around.

The advantages of hanging around in this neighborhood have been apparent in 2007. Bloodied by subprime-related losses, fixed-income investors have fled many types of assets perceived as risky. The primary beneficiaries of this shakeout have been Treasury-bond holders. Treasuries' prices have benefited from the flight to quality, and they've also received a shot in the arm as the U.S. Federal Reserve has hacked away at short-term yields. The fund has gained 7.3% for the year to date through Dec. 3, 2007, which tops the rises of the typical short-term bond and short-government funds.

These results aren't indicative of what the fund will deliver in a given year, though. While it has played some good defense in 2007, it's more likely that it will return an amount closer to its yield--4.09% according to its advisor. The fund could fare worse if interest rates rise, too, as Treasuries are more sensitive to rate changes than other bonds. As rates rose from 2004 to 2006, for instance, the fund's returns were paltry. In sunnier economic times, bond funds that take more risk should again outperform it.

That's not to say that this fund isn't doing its job: Barclay's has kept its expenses low and its managers have tracked its index well. ETF investors should keep in mind that cheaper option Vanguard Short-Term Bond ETF BSV is among the legions of fixed-income ETFs to come out in 2007, though. And traditional mutual fund fans have plenty of other worthwhile short-term Treasury-focused and diversified offerings to choose from as well.

Address:	45 Fremont Street United States 800-474-2737
Web Address:	www.ishares.com
Inception:	07-22-02*
Advisor:	Barclays Global Fund Advisers

Management Fee:	0.15%		
Expense Projections:	3Yr:$48	5Yr:$85	10Yr:$192
Income Distrib:	Annually		
Exchange:	AMEX		

iShares Lehman 7-10 IEF

Market Price	Mstar Category
$87.01	Long Government

Morningstar Rating	Return	Risk	Yield	NAV	Avg Daily Vol. (k)	52 wk High/Low
★★	Below Avg	Low	4.3%	$86.78	285	$88.39 - $79.59

Morningstar Fair Value

Price/Fair Value Ratio	Coverage Rate %
NA	NA

Valuation

This ETF holds bonds, not stocks. That explains why the fund's price/fair value ratio does not appear above.

Methodology

The fund tries to match the returns and yield of its index, the Lehman Brothers U.S. Treasury 7-10 Year Index. The index includes U.S. Treasury bonds that have between seven and 10 years until maturity and at least $250 million in par outstanding. On the margins, the managers can also differ from the index by up to 10% if these investments better help track the index.

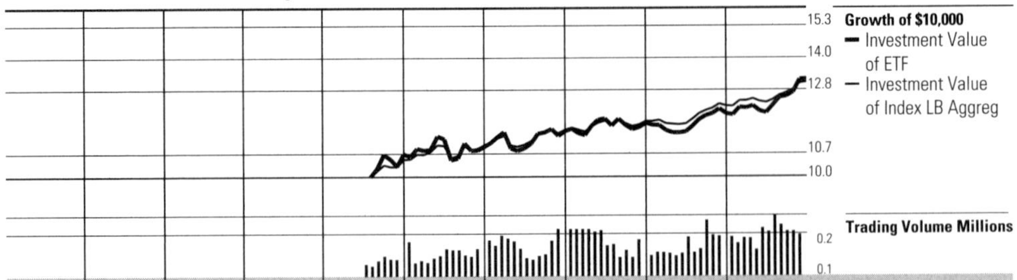

History

1998	1999	2000	2001	2002	2003	2004	2005	2006	2007	History
—	—	—	—	86.05	84.56	85.06	83.71	82.35	86.78	NAV $
—	—	—	—	86.15	84.70	84.95	83.91	82.44	87.01	Market Price $
—	—	—	—	5.22*	2.05	4.44	2.27	2.65	10.21	NAV Return%
—	—	—	—	5.27*	2.10	4.13	2.64	2.52	10.38	Market Price Return%
—	—	—	—	0.12	0.09	0.03	-0.13	-0.02	-0.01	Avg Premium/Discount%
—	—	—	—	—	-2.05	0.10	-0.16	-1.68	3.24	NAV Rtrn% +/-LB Aggreg
—	—	—	—	—	0.17	0.03	-0.16	-5.46	0.07	NAV Rtrn% +/-LB 7-10 US Treas
—	—	—	—	—	1	1	1	1	1	NAV Return% Rank in Cat
—	—	—	—	—	3.81	3.82	3.89	4.25	4.63	Income Return %
—	—	—	—	—	-1.76	0.62	-1.62	-1.60	5.58	Capital Return %
—	—	—	—	1.78	3.22	3.18	3.25	3.49	3.74	Income $
—	—	—	—	0.00	0.00	0.00	0.00	0.00	0.00	Capital Gains $
—	—	—	—	—	0.15	0.15	0.15	0.15	0.15	Expense Ratio %
—	—	—	—	—	3.79	3.59	3.75	4.02	4.50	Income Ratio %
—	—	—	—	—	54	74	121	94	45	Turnover Rate %
—	—	—	—	602	397	638	1,164	1,787	2,525	Net Assets $mil

Performance 12-31-07

Historic Quarterly NAV Returns

	1st Qtr	2nd Qtr	3rd Qtr	4th Qtr	Total
2003	1.04	3.21	-1.12	-1.03	2.05
2004	4.17	-4.39	4.51	0.33	4.44
2005	-1.13	4.77	-1.82	0.56	2.27
2006	-2.03	-0.38	4.61	0.54	2.65
2007	1.61	-1.35	4.71	5.01	10.21

Trailing	NAV Return%	Market Return%	NAV Rtrn% +/-LB Aggreg	%Rank Cat.(NAV)
3 Mo	5.01	5.22	2.01	80
6 Mo	9.96	10.12	4.03	100
1 Yr	10.21	10.38	3.24	1
3 Yr Avg	4.98	5.12	0.42	100
5 Yr Avg	4.28	4.31	-0.14	100
10 Yr Avg	—	—	—	—

Tax Analysis	Tax-Adj Return%	Tax-Cost Ratio
3 Yr (estimated)	3.45	1.46
5 Yr (estimated)	2.82	1.40
10 Yr (estimated)	—	—

Rating and Risk

Time Period	Morningstar Rtn vs Cat	Morningstar Risk vs Cat	Morningstar Risk-Adj Rating
3 Yr	-Avg	Low	★★
5 Yr	-Avg	Low	★★
10 Yr	—	—	—

Other Measures	Standard Index S&P 500	Best Fit Index LB Govt
Alpha	0.3	-0.1
Beta	1.64	1.50
R-Squared	92	99
Standard Deviation	4.77	
Mean	4.98	
Sharpe Ratio	0.14	

Portfolio Analysis 12-31-07

Total Fixed-Income:14	Date of Maturity	Amount $000	Value $000	% Net Assets
US Treasury Note 4.125%	05-15-15	413,802	421,830	16.92
US Treasury Note 4.75%	08-15-17	262,773	277,512	11.13
US Treasury Note 4.875%	08-15-16	256,953	273,606	10.97
US Treasury Note	05-15-17	263,646	273,182	10.96
US Treasury Bond 11.25%	02-15-15	154,521	225,802	9.06
US Treasury Note 4.625%	11-15-16	189,732	198,676	7.97
US Treasury Bond 9.25%	02-15-16	116,400	158,920	6.37
US Treasury Note 5.125%	05-15-16	127,458	137,939	5.53
US Treasury Note 4.5%	02-15-16	119,310	124,172	4.98
US Treasury Note 4.625%	02-15-17	115,818	121,047	4.86
US Treasury Note 4.25%	11-15-17	116,400	118,437	4.75
US Treasury Bond 7.25%	05-15-16	71,877	88,371	3.54
US Treasury Note 4.5%	11-15-15	38,412	40,007	1.60
US Treasury Bond 9.875%	11-15-15	23,280	32,612	1.31

Morningstar's Take by Paul Herbert 12-31-07

Rivals have moved in on iShares Lehman 7-10 Year Treasury Bond's turf.

ETF providers have been particularly busy in 2007, bringing an astonishing 268 new funds to market through Dec. 3. And, unlike in years past, many of these new offerings track fixed-income indexes. Though there were just half a dozen bond ETFs out there when the ball dropped to ring in this year, now there are 45. Six of these newbies track indexes of long-term bonds, as this fund does.

For all of these funds, this year has been a strong one. With subprime concerns roiling the bond market's more credit-sensitive areas, Treasuries have stolen the show. And longer-term bonds have been shining since it became apparent that the U.S. Federal Reserve would move to cut interest rates--as it did in September and again in October. This fund mimics the Lehman Brothers 7-10 Year Treasury Bond Index, which includes 21 bonds that are public obligations of the U.S. Treasury maturing in that range. It has gained 10.8% on an NAV basis so far in 2007, nearly 4 percentage points more than the broad Lehman Brothers Aggregate Bond Index. The other funds have fared better during their short lives, as each tracks an index that includes longer-term bonds than this fund's, and thus each courts added interest-rate sensitivity.

It's unlikely that this advantage will be so pronounced over time. Plus, because they are much more sensitive to changes in interest rates, bonds with longer durations--duration is a measure of rate sensitivity--tend to be more volatile than those with shorter-dated ones. As a result, this fund shouldn't treat investors to the severe ups and downs that some rivals will.

Investors who stick with funds for the long term should keep an eye on expenses, too. This fund comes in pretty cheap, as its expense ratio is 0.15%. But new entrants from State Street and Vanguard charge even less, which makes them attractive alternatives to this offering.

Address:	45 Fremont Street United States 800-474-2737
Web Address:	www.ishares.com
Inception:	07-22-02*
Advisor:	Barclays Global Fund Advisers

Management Fee:	0.15%		
Expense Projections:	3Yr:$48	5Yr:$85	10Yr:$192
Income Distrib:	Annually		
Exchange:	AMEX		

Current Investment Style

Duration: Short Int Long; Quality: High Med Low

1 figure provided by fund

Avg Eff Duration1	6.6 Yrs
Avg Eff Maturity	8.4 Yrs
Avg Credit Quality	AAA
Avg Wtd Coupon	5.72%
Avg Wtd Price	111.31% of par

Coupon Range	% of Bonds	Rel Cat
0% PIK	0.0	0.0
0% to 6%	77.2	1.6
6% to 8%	4.0	0.1
8% to 10%	8.6	0.4
More than 10%	10.2	7.0

1.00=Category Average

Credit Analysis		% bonds 12-31-07	
US Govt	0	BB	0
AAA	100	B	0
AA	0	Below B	0
A	0	NR/NA	0
BBB	0		

Sector Breakdown	% of assets
US Treasuries	100
TIPS	0
US Agency	0
Mortgage Pass-Throughs	0
Mortgage CMO	0
Mortgage ARM	0
US Corporate	0
Asset-Backed	0
Convertible	0
Municipal	0
Corporate Inflation-Protected	0
Foreign Corporate	0
Foreign Govt	0

Composition			
Cash	0.0	Bonds	100.0
Stocks	0.0	Other	0.0

Special Securities	
Restricted/Illiquid Secs	0
Exotic Mortgage-Backed	—
Emerging-Markets Secs	0
Options/Futures/Warrants	No

iShares Lehman 20+ TLT

Market Price	Mstar Category
$93.05	Long Government

Morningstar Fair Value

Price/Fair Value Ratio	Coverage Rate %
NA	NA

Valuation

This ETF holds bonds, not stocks. That explains why the fund's price/fair value ratio does not appear above.

Methodology

This exchange-traded fund attempts to mimic the behavior of the Lehman Brothers 20+ Year Treasury Bond Index. The index, and the fund, own about a dozen long-term Treasury issues. The fund's return has trailed the index's by less than the amount of its expense ratio over time. As Treasury bonds are issued by the U.S. government, investors need not worry about credit risk, but the tradeoff is that interest-rate risk is a major concern.

Morningstar Rating	Return	Risk	Yield	NAV	Avg Daily Vol. (k)	52 wk High/Low
★★★	Average	Average	4.5%	$92.91	1,651	$95.58 - $82.35

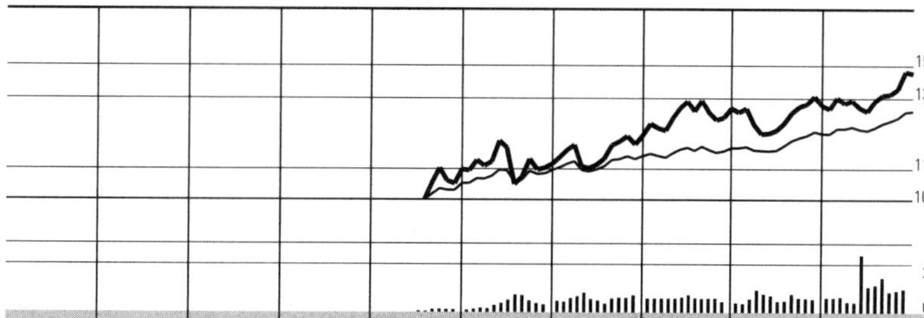

1998	1999	2000	2001	2002	2003	2004	2005	2006	2007	History
—	—	—	—	88.35	85.34	88.57	91.78	88.42	92.91	NAV $
—	—	—	—	88.57	85.45	88.55	91.90	88.43	93.05	Market Price $
—	—	—	—	7.17*	1.75	8.88	8.44	0.83	10.15	NAV Return%
—	—	—	—	7.20*	1.63	8.71	8.61	0.71	10.30	Market Price Return%
—	—	—	—	0.13	0.11	0.02	-0.18	-0.20	-0.11	Avg Premium/Discount%
—	—	—	—	—	-2.35	4.54	6.01	-3.50	3.18	NAV Rtrn% +/-LB Aggreg
—	—	—	—	—	-0.05	-0.11	-0.13	-0.10	-0.61	NAV Rtrn% +/-LB 20+ US Treas
—	—	—	—	—	1	1	1	100	100	NAV Return% Rank in Cat
—	—	—	—	—	5.26	4.96	4.82	4.44	4.84	Income Return %
—	—	—	—	—	-3.51	3.92	3.62	-3.61	5.31	Capital Return %
—	—	—	—	1.94	4.53	4.14	4.18	3.99	4.19	Income $
—	—	—	—	0.00	0.00	0.00	0.00	0.00	0.00	Capital Gains $
—	—	—	—	—	0.15	0.15	0.15	0.15	0.15	Expense Ratio %
—	—	—	—	—	4.92	4.84	4.71	4.42	4.70	Income Ratio %
—	—	—	—	—	7	31	18	25	25	Turnover Rate %
—	—	—	—	504	282	585	817	1,432	1,487	Net Assets $mil

Performance 12-31-07

Historic Quarterly NAV Returns

	1st Qtr	2nd Qtr	3rd Qtr	4th Qtr	Total
2003	1.09	5.53	-3.29	-1.39	1.75
2004	5.79	-5.75	7.16	1.90	8.88
2005	1.43	9.22	-3.37	1.30	8.44
2006	-4.71	-1.78	7.34	0.37	0.83
2007	0.64	-2.39	5.37	6.41	10.15

Trailing	NAV Return%	Market Return%	NAV Rtrn% +/-LB Aggreg	%Rank Cat.(NAV)
3 Mo	6.41	6.58	3.41	1
6 Mo	12.13	12.34	6.20	1
1 Yr	10.15	10.30	3.18	100
3 Yr Avg	6.40	6.46	1.84	1
5 Yr Avg	5.94	5.92	1.52	1
10 Yr Avg	—	—	—	—

Tax Analysis	Tax-Adj Return%	Tax-Cost Ratio
3 Yr (estimated)	4.70	1.60
5 Yr (estimated)	4.19	1.65
10 Yr (estimated)	—	—

Rating and Risk

Time Period	Morningstar Rtn vs Cat	Morningstar Risk vs Cat	Morningstar Risk-Adj Rating
3 Yr	+Avg	Avg	★★★★
5 Yr	Avg	Avg	★★★
10 Yr	—	—	—

Other Measures	Standard Index S&P 500	Best Fit Index LB Long Tr
Alpha	1.7	0.1
Beta	2.88	1.22
R-Squared	88	99
Standard Deviation	8.55	
Mean	6.40	
Sharpe Ratio	0.26	

Portfolio Analysis 12-31-07

Total Fixed-Income:9	Date of Maturity	Amount $000	Value $000	% Net Assets
US Treasury Bond 4.5%	02-15-36	241,440	242,746	16.56
US Treasury Bond 5.375%	02-15-31	184,320	207,638	14.17
US Treasury Bond 6.25%	05-15-30	156,320	195,080	13.31
US Treasury Bond 4.75%	02-15-37	182,720	191,235	13.05
US Treasury Bond 5%	05-15-37	150,560	163,829	11.18
US Treasury Bond 5.5%	08-15-28	131,040	148,415	10.13
US Treasury Bond 5.25%	02-15-29	114,720	126,206	8.61
US Treasury Bond 6.125%	08-15-29	93,920	114,907	7.84
US Treasury Bond 5.25%	11-15-28	68,000	74,807	5.10

Morningstar's Take by Paul Herbert 12-31-07

IShares Lehman 20+ Year Treasury's bright recent results shouldn't be considered typical.

It doesn't get much better than this for fixed-income fund investors. This ETF, which tracks the Lehman Brothers 20+ Year Treasury Bond Index, a 10-bond collection of very long-term U.S. Treasury obligations, has gained 11.65% for the year to date through Dec. 4, 2007. (Nearly all of the funds that have done better this year use leverage or invest in foreign bonds on an unhedged basis.) The fund has benefited from other bond groups' misfortunes: In the wake of the subprime mess, investors sold risky fare such as junk bonds in favor of the safest options. And, when it became likely that the U.S. Federal Reserve would reduce rates to stabilize fractured credit markets, securities with the most interest-rate sensitivity--namely long-dated Treasuries--fared the best.

This performance is great, but conditions won't always be so good for the fund. Long Treasury bonds' rate responsiveness can cut both ways. At times when market yields are rising, portfolios of these securities can sock investors with losses. For instance, this fund struggled to break even in 2006, as the Fed was wrapping up its previous rate-hiking campaign. Plus, investors shouldn't bank on a flight to quality such as the one that gripped the bond market in 2007. At a point, investors will view the selling in other areas as overdone and swap Treasuries for other types of bonds.

For those who can handle some extra volatility--i.e. investors who intend to stick around for more than a few years--holding a portfolio of long-term bonds can pay off, given their yield advantage over shorter-term paper. Those looking to pick one up should make sure to consider mutual fund alternatives, such as our long-bond and long-government Analyst Picks. The roster of long-term ETFs has grown lately, too. New options from State Street and Vanguard are cheaper than this one.

Current Investment Style

Duration: Short Int Long — Quality: High Med Low

[1] figure provided by fund

Avg Eff Duration[1]	13.4 Yrs
Avg Eff Maturity	23.9 Yrs
Avg Credit Quality	AAA
Avg Wtd Coupon	5.41%
Avg Wtd Price	111.25% of par

Coupon Range	% of Bonds	Rel Cat
0% PIK	0.0	0.0
0% to 6%	72.1	1.5
6% to 8%	27.9	0.9
8% to 10%	0.0	0.0
More than 10%	0.0	0.0

1.00=Category Average

Credit Analysis		% bonds 12-31-07	
US Govt	0	BB	0
AAA	100	B	0
AA	0	Below B	0
A	0	NR/NA	0
BBB	0		

Sector Breakdown	% of assets
US Treasuries	100
TIPS	0
US Agency	0
Mortgage Pass-Throughs	0
Mortgage CMO	0
Mortgage ARM	0
US Corporate	0
Asset-Backed	0
Convertible	0
Municipal	0
Corporate Inflation-Protected	0
Foreign Corporate	0
Foreign Govt	0

Composition			
Cash	0.1	Bonds	100.0
Stocks	0.0	Other	0.0

Special Securities	
Restricted/Illiquid Secs	0
Exotic Mortgage-Backed	—
Emerging-Markets Secs	0
Options/Futures/Warrants	No

Address:	45 Fremont Street United States 800-474-2737
Web Address:	www.ishares.com
Inception:	07-22-02 *
Advisor:	Barclays Global Fund Advisers

Management Fee:	0.15%		
Expense Projections:	3Yr:$48	5Yr:$85	10Yr:$192
Income Distrib:	Annually		
Exchange:	AMEX		

iShares Lehman Aggregate AGG

Market Price	Mstar Category
$101.17	Intermediate-Term Bond

Morningstar Fair Value

Price/Fair Value Ratio	Coverage Rate %
NA	NA

Valuation

This ETF primarily holds fixed-income securities, not stocks. That explains why the fund's price/fair value ratio does not appear above.

Methodology

The fund strives to approximate the performance of the Lehman Brothers Aggregate Bond Index, which is a commonly used proxy for the broad, investment-grade U.S. bond market. It uses representative sampling to do this because owning every fixed-income security in the domestic market would be unwieldy and costly because some of the issues are illiquid.

Morningstar Rating	Return	Risk	Yield	NAV	Avg Daily Vol. (k)	52 wk High/Low
★★★★	Above Avg	Above Avg	4.9%	$100.88	598	$102.52 - $97.20

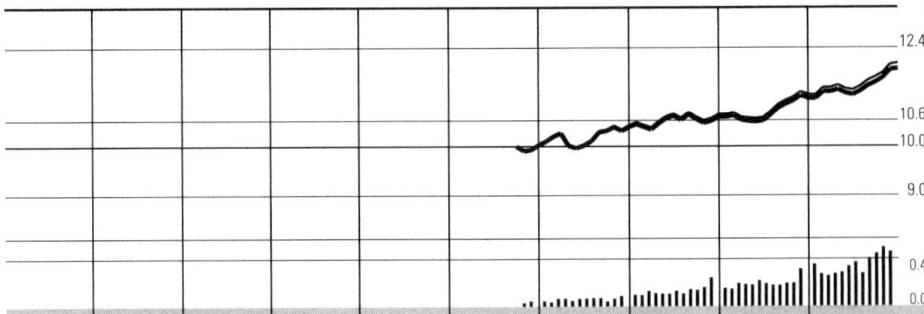

Growth of $10,000
- Investment Value of ETF
- Investment Value of Index LB Aggreg

Trading Volume Millions

1998	1999	2000	2001	2002	2003	2004	2005	2006	2007	History
—	—	—	—	—	101.61	102.05	100.13	99.45	100.88	NAV $
—	—	—	—	—	102.15	102.40	100.59	99.70	101.17	Market Price $
—	—	—	—	—	4.31*	3.99	2.16	4.13	6.57	NAV Return%
—	—	—	—	—	4.38*	3.79	2.28	3.91	6.61	Market Price Return%
—	—	—	—	—	0.50	0.25	0.12	0.16	0.24	Avg Premium/Discount%
—	—	—	—	—	—	-0.35	-0.27	-0.20	-0.40	NAV Rtrn% +/-LB Aggreg
—	—	—	—	—	—	-0.35	-0.27	-0.20	-0.40	NAV Rtrn% +/-LB Aggreg
—	—	—	—	—	—	1	1	1	1	NAV Return% Rank in Cat
—	—	—	—	—	—	3.54	4.08	4.77	5.06	Income Return %
—	—	—	—	—	—	0.45	-1.92	-0.64	1.51	Capital Return %
—	—	—	—	—	0.92	3.54	4.09	4.68	4.91	Income $
—	—	—	—	—	0.00	0.00	0.00	0.00	0.00	Capital Gains $
—	—	—	—	—	—	0.20	0.20	0.20	0.20	Expense Ratio %
—	—	—	—	—	—	2.47	2.90	3.89	4.76	Income Ratio %
—	—	—	—	—	—	165	457	456	483	Turnover Rate %
—	—	—	—	—	213	990	2,894	4,913	7,738	Net Assets $mil

Performance 12-31-07

Historic Quarterly NAV Returns

	1st Qtr	2nd Qtr	3rd Qtr	4th Qtr	Total
2003	—	—	—	0.28	—*
2004	2.59	-2.66	3.22	0.88	3.99
2005	-0.60	3.01	-0.74	0.51	2.16
2006	-0.69	-0.16	3.73	1.24	4.13
2007	1.38	-0.63	2.71	2.99	6.57

Trailing	NAV Return%	Market Return%	NAV Rtrn% +/-LB Aggreg	%Rank Cat.(NAV)
3 Mo	2.99	2.82	-0.01	25
6 Mo	5.79	5.93	-0.14	38
1 Yr	6.57	6.61	-0.40	1
3 Yr Avg	4.27	4.25	-0.29	1
5 Yr Avg	—	—	—	—
10 Yr Avg	—	—	—	—

Tax Analysis	Tax-Adj Return%	Tax-Cost Ratio
3 Yr (estimated)	2.62	1.58
5 Yr (estimated)	—	—
10 Yr (estimated)	—	—

Rating and Risk

Time Period	Morningstar Rtn vs Cat	Morningstar Risk vs Cat	Morningstar Risk-Adj Rating
3 Yr	+Avg	+Avg	★★★★
5 Yr	—	—	—
10 Yr	—	—	—

Other Measures	Standard Index S&P 500	Best Fit Index LB Aggreg
Alpha	-0.3	-0.3
Beta	1.00	1.00
R-Squared	100	100
Standard Deviation	2.81	
Mean	4.27	
Sharpe Ratio	-0.03	

Portfolio Analysis 12-31-07

Total Fixed-Income:168	Date of Maturity	Amount $000	Value $000	% Net Assets
FNMA 5.5%	01-01-38	449,462	448,619	4.29
US Treasury Note 6%	08-15-09	385,801	403,359	3.86
FHLMC 4.75%	03-05-09	368,160	373,239	3.57
FHLMC 5%	01-01-38	323,674	315,734	3.02
FNMA 6%	01-01-38	297,596	302,153	2.89
US Treasury Bond 7.625%	02-15-25	216,294	296,522	2.84
FHLMC 5.5%	01-01-38	292,227	291,496	2.79
FNMA 6.5%	01-01-38	260,780	268,033	2.56
US Treasury Note 3.5%	02-15-10	238,537	240,674	2.30
US Treasury Note 4.5%	02-15-09	233,935	237,381	2.27
FHLMC 6%	01-01-38	201,721	204,652	1.96
US Treasury Bond 8.125%	08-15-19	122,720	165,429	1.58
FHLMC 4.5%	01-15-13	157,235	160,894	1.54
US Treasury Note 4.75%	05-15-14	148,798	158,195	1.51
FHLMC 5.5%	01-01-23	136,526	138,126	1.32
FNMA 7.25%	01-15-10	124,254	133,074	1.27
FNMA 5%	01-01-23	128,856	128,916	1.23
FNMA 4.5%	01-01-23	123,487	121,500	1.16
FHLMC 4.5%	01-01-23	123,487	121,422	1.16
FHLMC 5%	02-01-23	117,351	117,351	1.12

Current Investment Style

Duration: Short Int Long

Quality: High Med Low

[1] figure provided by fund

Avg Eff Duration[1]	4.6 Yrs
Avg Eff Maturity	7.1 Yrs
Avg Credit Quality	AA
Avg Wtd Coupon	5.59%
Avg Wtd Price	104.16% of par

Coupon Range	% of Bonds	Rel Cat
0% PIK	0.0	0.0
0% to 6%	77.2	1.1
6% to 8%	19.7	0.9
8% to 10%	3.1	0.7
More than 10%	0.0	0.0

1.00=Category Average

Credit Analysis		% bonds 12-31-07	
US Govt	0	BB	0
AAA	74	B	0
AA	8	Below B	0
A	10	NR/NA	1
BBB	8		

Sector Breakdown	% of assets
US Treasuries	18
TIPS	0
US Agency	9
Mortgage Pass-Throughs	27
Mortgage CMO	0
Mortgage ARM	0
US Corporate	18
Asset-Backed	0
Convertible	0
Municipal	0
Corporate Inflation-Protected	0
Foreign Corporate	1
Foreign Govt	1

Composition			
Cash	26.8	Bonds	73.2
Stocks	0.0	Other	0.0

Special Securities	
Restricted/Illiquid Secs	Trace
Exotic Mortgage-Backed	0
Emerging-Markets Secs	Trace
Options/Futures/Warrants	No

Morningstar's Take by Annie Sorich 12-31-07

IShares Lehman Aggregate Bond doesn't stand up to the competition.

Although this ETF was the first to offer diversified fixed-income exposure, it's no longer the only choice. In April, Vanguard introduced an ETF share class of its Vanguard Total Bond Market Index mutual fund called Vanguard Total Bond Market ETF, and State Street followed by launching SPDR Lehman Aggregate Bond in May. Each fund tracks the Lehman Aggregate Bond Index.

Unlike stock index funds, bond index funds are not typically mirror images of their benchmark indexes, many of which would be prohibitively expensive to duplicate bond for bond. The Lehman Aggregate Index contains more than 6,000 securities, making it virtually impossible to mimic. Although bond index funds do replicate the major characteristics of the index, there is room for managers to add value with issue selection and sector allocation.

Overall, the Vanguard fund looks better from a replication standpoint. It owned 2,300 issues through September 2007, while this fund's portfolio contained fewer than 170 securities on the same date, perhaps making it easier for the Vanguard fund to replicate the index's returns. When we compare this ETF's returns with those of the mutual fund version of the Vanguard ETF, which carries the same 0.20% expense ratio, the difference is obvious. This fund trailed the Lehman Aggregate by 0.31% since its September 2003 inception through the end of September 2007. In contrast, the mutual fund version of the Vanguard ETF trailed the index by only 0.12%.

On the expense front, the Vanguard ETF is also a clear winner. This fund's 0.20% expense ratio is not unreasonable, but the Vanguard ETF charges only 0.11% of assets, leaving more return for investors than even its mutual fund counterpart.

Given the strengths of the Vanguard ETF on replication and expenses, few reasons remain to invest in this ETF.

Address:	45 Fremont Street United States 800-474-2737
Web Address:	www.ishares.com
Inception:	09-22-03*
Advisor:	Barclays Global Fund Advisers

Management Fee:	0.20%		
Expense Projections:	3Yr:$77	5Yr:$135	10Yr:$306
Income Distrib:	Annually		
Exchange:	AMEX		

iShares Lehman TIPS Bond TIP

Market Price	Mstar Category
$105.80	Inflation-Protected Bond

Morningstar Fair Value

Price/Fair Value Ratio	Coverage Rate %
NA	NA

Valuation

This ETF holds inflation-indexed Treasury bonds, not stocks. That explains why the fund's price/fair value ratio does not appear above.

Methodology

The fund's index, the Lehman Brothers U.S. Treasury Inflation Notes Index, holds all TIPS that have at least one year until maturity and at least $250 million par outstanding. The managers can also deviate from the index by up to 5% in order to add value on the margins.

Morningstar Rating	Return	Risk	Yield	NAV	Avg Daily Vol. (k)	52 wk High/Low
★★★★	Above Avg	Above Avg	4.3%	$105.35	281	$107.90 - $97.33

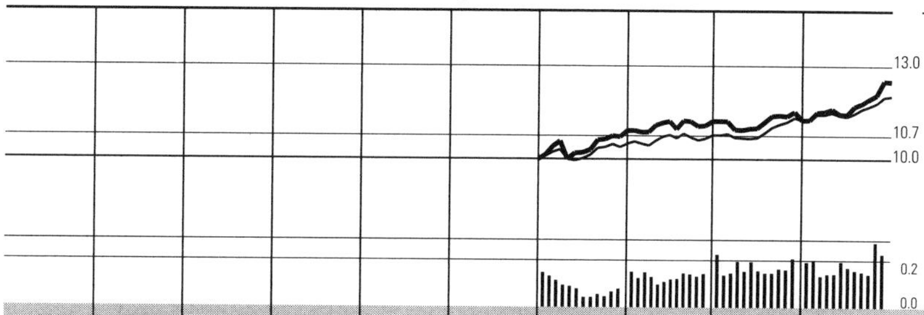

Growth of $10,000
- Investment Value of ETF
- Investment Value of Index LB Aggreg

Trading Volume Millions

History

1998	1999	2000	2001	2002	2003	2004	2005	2006	2007	History
—	—	—	—	—	101.61	105.64	102.80	98.79	105.35	NAV $
—	—	—	—	—	101.71	105.81	102.82	98.80	105.80	Market Price $
—	—	—	—	—	5.66*	8.21	2.65	0.29	11.46	NAV Return%
—	—	—	—	—	5.77*	8.28	2.50	0.28	11.93	Market Price Return%
—	—	—	—	—	0.10	0.18	0.06	0.04	0.06	Avg Premium/Discount%
—	—	—	—	—	—	3.87	0.22	-4.04	4.49	NAV Rtrn% +/-LB Aggreg
—	—	—	—	—	—	-0.25	-0.19	-0.12	-0.35	NAV Rtrn% +/-LB TIPS
—	—	—	—	—	—	1	1	1	1	NAV Return% Rank in Cat
—	—	—	—	—	—	4.15	5.41	4.23	4.64	Income Return %
—	—	—	—	—	—	4.06	-2.76	-3.94	6.82	Capital Return %
—	—	—	—	—	0.12	4.14	5.58	4.27	4.49	Income $
—	—	—	—	—	0.00	0.00	0.00	0.00	0.00	Capital Gains $
—	—	—	—	—	—	0.20	0.20	0.20	0.20	Expense Ratio %
—	—	—	—	—	—	-0.25	3.60	4.12	4.09	Income Ratio %
—	—	—	—	—	—	2	32	13	17	Turnover Rate %
—	—	—	—	—	142	1,511	3,310	4,001	5,299	Net Assets $mil

Performance 12-31-07

Historic Quarterly NAV Returns

	1st Qtr	2nd Qtr	3rd Qtr	4th Qtr	Total
2003	—	—	—	—	—*
2004	5.07	-3.14	3.79	2.44	8.21
2005	-0.37	2.98	-0.01	0.06	2.65
2006	-2.30	0.44	3.60	-1.35	0.29
2007	2.40	-0.82	4.56	4.96	11.46

Trailing	NAV Return%	Market Return%	NAV Rtrn% +/-LB Aggreg	%Rank Cat.(NAV)
3 Mo	4.96	5.39	1.96	1
6 Mo	9.75	10.09	3.82	1
1 Yr	11.46	11.93	4.49	1
3 Yr Avg	4.69	4.78	0.13	1
5 Yr Avg	—	—	—	—
10 Yr Avg	—	—	—	—

Tax Analysis	Tax-Adj Return%	Tax-Cost Ratio
3 Yr (estimated)	2.99	1.62
5 Yr (estimated)	—	—
10 Yr (estimated)	—	—

Rating and Risk

Time Period	Morningstar Rtn vs Cat	Morningstar Risk vs Cat	Morningstar Risk-Adj Rating
3 Yr	+Avg	+Avg	★★★★
5 Yr	—	—	—
10 Yr	—	—	—

Other Measures	Standard Index S&P 500	Best Fit Index LB Govt
Alpha	0.1	-0.3
Beta	1.42	1.31
R-Squared	75	81
Standard Deviation	4.57	
Mean	4.69	
Sharpe Ratio	0.09	

Portfolio Analysis 12-31-07

Total Fixed-Income:23	Date of Maturity	Amount $000	Value $000	% Net Assets
US Treasury Bond 2.375%	01-15-25	362,378	381,008	7.22
US Treasury Bond 3.875%	04-15-29	279,349	370,123	7.01
US Treasury Note 0.875%	04-15-10	348,360	347,301	6.58
US Treasury Note 3%	07-15-12	301,587	326,800	6.19
US Treasury Note 2%	01-15-14	305,981	316,249	5.99
US Treasury Bond 3.625%	04-15-28	242,349	307,704	5.83
US Treasury Note 1.875%	07-15-13	288,375	297,375	5.63
US Treasury Note 1.625%	01-15-15	274,076	275,224	5.21
US Treasury Note 2%	07-15-14	262,585	271,303	5.14
US Treasury Note 2.375%	04-15-11	248,838	259,441	4.92
US TREASURY NOTE	07-15-15	217,728	221,986	4.21
US Treasury Note 3.875%	01-15-09	213,379	219,786	4.16
US Treasury Note	01-15-16	213,905	219,648	4.16
US Treasury Bond 2%	01-15-26	219,729	219,138	4.15
US Treasury Note 2.5%	07-15-16	202,940	216,571	4.10
US Treasury Note 2.375%	01-15-17	195,414	206,419	3.91
US Treasury Note 3.5%	01-15-11	160,610	172,758	3.27
US Treasury Note 4.25%	01-15-10	127,421	136,006	2.58
US Treasury Bond 2.375%	01-15-27	113,600	120,301	2.28
US Treasury Note 3.375%	01-15-12	102,387	111,739	2.12

Current Investment Style

Duration: Short Int Long — Quality: High Med Low

[1] figure provided by fund

Avg Eff Duration[1]	6.6 Yrs
Avg Eff Maturity	9.5 Yrs
Avg Credit Quality	AAA
Avg Wtd Coupon	2.53%
Avg Wtd Price	107.75% of par

Coupon Range	% of Bonds	Rel Cat
0% PIK	0.0	0.0
0% to 6%	100.0	1.0
6% to 8%	0.0	0.0
8% to 10%	0.0	0.0
More than 10%	0.0	0.0

1.00=Category Average

Credit Analysis		% bonds 12-31-07	
US Govt	0	BB	0
AAA	100	B	0
AA	0	Below B	0
A	0	NR/NA	0
BBB	0		

Sector Breakdown	% of assets
US Treasuries	21
TIPS	78
US Agency	0
Mortgage Pass-Throughs	0
Mortgage CMO	0
Mortgage ARM	0
US Corporate	0
Asset-Backed	0
Convertible	0
Municipal	0
Corporate Inflation-Protected	0
Foreign Corporate	0
Foreign Govt	0

Composition			
Cash	0.6	Bonds	99.4
Stocks	0.0	Other	0.0

Special Securities	
Restricted/Illiquid Secs	0
Exotic Mortgage-Backed	—
Emerging-Markets Secs	0
Options/Futures/Warrants	No

Morningstar's Take by Karen Dolan 12-31-07

IShares Lehman TIPS Bond serves a useful purpose and it's been the one to beat.

This exchange-traded fund's goal hasn't been top of mind for most investors. Who needs protection from inflation when it has remained benign and other corners of the market have had such handsome gains over the past several years? Yet, that's exactly what this fund offers and now is a good time to take note of its benefits. The low inflation of the past decade says nothing about the next 10 years. Whether inflation ends up being 2%, 10%, or somewhere in the middle will have a big impact on investors' future purchasing power.

The benefits of TIPS are clear and the competition to provide exposure to them has been heating up. When the U.S. Treasury started offering TIPS bonds in 1997, only a handful of mutual funds focused on them. Times have changed. At last count, there were 41 distinct mutual funds and two ETFs (this one included) investing mostly in bonds whose principal value, and thus coupons, adjust for inflation.

This ETF's value proposition holds strong amidst the growing competition: Its 0.20% expense ratio makes it dirt cheap and its exposure is clear-cut. The fund tracks the Lehman Brothers U.S. Treasury Inflation Notes Index, which at the end of Nov. 2007 included 23 U.S. TIPS bonds. As simple as that sounds, most of the alternatives have indeed had a hard time beating this fund. Returns here have been near the top of the pack for the trailing one and three years and since its 2003 inception.

This fund is an all-around good way to access TIPS. While investors could just as easily buy Treasury Inflation-Protected Securities directly from the government, we think owning a low-cost, diversified bundle of TIPS makes sense and can help mitigate the added interest-rate risk that would come with owning a single longer-dated TIPS bond directly. All said, this ETF is an attractively priced, well-constructed option for TIPS exposure.

Address:	45 Fremont Street United States 800-474-2737
Web Address:	www.ishares.com
Inception:	12-04-03*
Advisor:	Barclays Global Fund Advisers

Management Fee:	0.20%		
Expense Projections:	3Yr:$64	5Yr:$113	10Yr:$255
Income Distrib:	Annually		
Exchange:	NYSE		

iShares S&P Nat Muni Bd MUB

Market Price	Mstar Category
$101.96	Muni National Interm

Morningstar Fair Value

Price/Fair Value Ratio	Coverage Rate %
NA	NA

Valuation

This ETF primarily holds municipal bonds not stocks. That explains why the fund's price/fair value ratio does not appear above.

Methodology

The ETF tracks the S&P National Muni Bond Index. The index is a collection of more than 3,000 individual securities issued by states, counties, and local governments. This ETF holds a representative sample of about 50 bonds. The interest payouts on all its holdings are exempt from federal income taxes. It also steers clear of bonds that might trigger the alternative minimum tax. The index focuses solely on bonds with ratings of BBB or higher. About 70% of its portfolio is dedicated to AAA-rated muni bonds. The index rebalances monthly.

Morningstar Rating	Return	Risk	Yield	NAV	Avg Daily Vol. (k)	52 wk High/Low
—	—	—	—	$100.71	62	$102.28 - $99.53

History

1998	1999	2000	2001	2002	2003	2004	2005	2006	2007	History
—	—	—	—	—	—	—	—	—	100.71	NAV $
—	—	—	—	—	—	—	—	—	101.96	Market Price $
—	—	—	—	—	—	—	—	—	1.58*	NAV Return%
—	—	—	—	—	—	—	—	—	3.64*	Market Price Return%
—	—	—	—	—	—	—	—	—	0.73	Avg Premium/Discount%
—	—	—	—	—	—	—	—	—	—	NAV Rtrn% +/-LB Muni
—	—	—	—	—	—	—	—	—	—	NAV Rtrn% +/-LB Muni 10YR
—	—	—	—	—	—	—	—	—	—	NAV Return% Rank in Cat
—	—	—	—	—	—	—	—	—	—	Income Return %
—	—	—	—	—	—	—	—	—	—	Capital Return %
—	—	—	—	—	—	—	—	—	1.17	Income $
—	—	—	—	—	—	—	—	—	0.00	Capital Gains $
—	—	—	—	—	—	—	—	—	—	Expense Ratio %
—	—	—	—	—	—	—	—	—	—	Income Ratio %
—	—	—	—	—	—	—	—	—	—	Turnover Rate %
—	—	—	—	—	—	—	—	—	332	Net Assets $mil

Performance 12-31-07

Historic Quarterly NAV Returns

	1st Qtr	2nd Qtr	3rd Qtr	4th Qtr	Total
2003	—	—	—	—	—
2004	—	—	—	—	—
2005	—	—	—	—	—
2006	—	—	—	—	—
2007	—	—	—	1.56	—*

Trailing	NAV Return%	Market Return%	NAV Rtrn% +/-LB Muni	%Rank Cat.(NAV)
3 Mo	1.56	2.42	0.19	1
6 Mo	—	—	—	—
1 Yr	—	—	—	—
3 Yr Avg	—	—	—	—
5 Yr Avg	—	—	—	—
10 Yr Avg	—	—	—	—

Tax Analysis	Tax-Adj Return%	Tax-Cost Ratio
3 Yr (estimated)	—	—
5 Yr (estimated)	—	—
10 Yr (estimated)	—	—

Rating and Risk

Time Period	Morningstar Rtn vs Cat	Morningstar Risk vs Cat	Morningstar Risk-Adj Rating
3 Yr	—	—	—
5 Yr	—	—	—
10 Yr	—	—	—

Other Measures	Standard Index S&P 500	Best Fit Index
Alpha	—	—
Beta	—	—
R-Squared	—	—
Standard Deviation	—	
Mean	—	
Sharpe Ratio	—	

Portfolio Analysis 12-31-07

Total Fixed-Income:54	Date of Maturity	Amount $000	Value $000	% Net Assets
Oregon St Dept Administr	09-01-11	18,365	19,521	5.94
North Carolina St Go Ref	03-01-12	15,545	16,642	5.07
Oregon St Go Bds 4.5%	08-01-32	15,815	15,675	4.77
Regl Transn Dist 4.5%	11-01-34	15,175	14,880	4.53
Massachusetts St Sch Bld	08-15-35	13,400	13,109	3.99
California St Go Bds 5%	06-01-17	11,135	11,941	3.64
Citizens Ppty Ins 5%	03-01-17	10,000	10,719	3.26
Los Angeles Calif Uni Sc	07-01-18	9,000	9,795	2.98
Chicago Ill 5.5%	01-01-38	8,255	8,886	2.71
California St Dept Wtr R	05-01-17	7,975	8,864	2.70
Illinois St Go Bonds 5%	03-01-34	8,595	8,838	2.69
North Carolina St Ref Go	04-01-13	8,000	8,668	2.64
Maryland St Cap Impt 5.2	02-15-12	8,000	8,633	2.63
California St Go Ref Bd	03-01-19	7,725	8,094	2.46
Puerto Rico Comwlth Infr	07-01-25	7,275	8,019	2.44
New York N Y City Mun Wt	06-15-38	7,200	7,430	2.26
Florida Hurricane Catast	07-01-12	5,900	6,288	1.91
New Jersey St Transn Tr	12-15-22	6,000	5,961	1.81
Utah St 5.375%	07-01-10	5,635	5,943	1.81
Chicago Ill Skyway Toll	01-01-31	5,500	5,917	1.80

Current Investment Style

Duration: Short Int Long; Quality: High Med Low

¹ figure provided by fund

Avg Eff Duration¹	7.0 Yrs
Avg Eff Maturity	10.8 Yrs
Avg Credit Quality	AA
Avg Wtd Coupon	5.01%
Avg Wtd Price	104.92% of par

Coupon Range	% of Bonds	Rel Cat
0% PIK	0.0	0.0
0% to 6%	100.0	1.0
6% to 8%	0.0	0.0
8% to 10%	0.0	0.0
More than 10%	0.0	0.0

1.00=Category Average

Credit Analysis	% bonds 12-31-07		
US Govt	0	BB	0
AAA	68	B	0
AA	16	Below B	0
A	14	NR/NA	2
BBB	0		

Sector Breakdown	% of assets
US Treasuries	—
TIPS	—
US Agency	—
Mortgage Pass-Throughs	—
Mortgage CMO	—
Mortgage ARM	—
US Corporate	—
Asset-Backed	—
Convertible	—
Municipal	—
Corporate Inflation-Protected	—
Foreign Corporate	—
Foreign Govt	—

Composition			
Cash	1.2	Bonds	98.8
Stocks	0.0	Other	0.0

Special Securities	
Restricted/Illiquid Secs	0
Exotic Mortgage-Backed	—
Emerging-Markets Secs	0
Options/Futures/Warrants	No

Morningstar's Take by Sonya Morris 12-31-07

The case for iShares National Municipal Bond isn't open-and-shut.

When this fund, which tracks the S&P National Municipal Bond Index, was introduced in Sept. 2007, it became the first ETF to provide exposure to municipal securities (though competing ETFs were launched just days later).

There are some notable differences between this ETF and most conventional muni-bond mutual funds. First, it's more concentrated: It holds roughly 50 bonds and stashes half of its assets in its top 10 holdings. In comparison, the typical muni mutual fund spans more than 180 issues and allocates about 20% of assets to its top securities. So this ETF courts more issue-specific risk than most of the competition.

Second, this is an index fund, whereas all open-end mutual funds are actively managed. Index funds face more challenges in the complex, less-transparent muni bond arena. For example, it remains to be seen how closely muni ETFs will track their benchmarks. Muni investors also tend to buy and hold, thereby reducing secondary market volume. If liquidity problems emerge, muni ETFs' prices could stray from their net asset values.

Despite these uncertainties, muni ETFs have one major advantage--they're cheap. This ETF costs just 0.25%, which is far lower than the 0.64% levy charged by the typical conventional no-load muni fund. Expenses loom large in the muni fund world where returns are modest at best. So this ETF's low-cost advantage is a big plus.

That said, this ETF isn't the cheapest way to gain muni exposure. A couple of mutual funds charge even less, most notably Vanguard Intermediate-Term Tax Exempt, which has an expense ratio of 0.17%. Thus, with muni ETFs still in their infancy, we'd like to see how they fare in this less liquid and less transparent marketplace before giving them a thumbs up. In the meantime, the Vanguard fund is a viable alternative, given its proven track record and lower expense ratio.

Address:	45 Fremont Street United States 800-474-2737
Web Address:	www.ishares.com
Inception:	09-07-07*
Advisor:	Barclays Global Fund Advisers

Management Fee:	0.30%		
Expense Projections:	3Yr:$80	5Yr: —	10Yr: —
Income Distrib:	Annually		
Exchange:	AMEX		

SPDR Lehman Agg Bond LAG

Market Price	Mstar Category
$53.72	Intermediate-Term Bond

Morningstar Rating	Return	Risk	Yield	NAV	Avg Daily Vol. (k)	52 wk High/Low
—	—	—	—	$53.56	30	$54.44 - $51.54

Morningstar Fair Value

Price/Fair Value Ratio	Coverage Rate %
NA	NA

Valuation

This ETF holds bonds, not stocks. That explains why the fund's price/fair value ratio does not appear above.

Methodology

This fund tracks the Lehman U.S. Aggregate Bond Index, the most commonly cited proxy for the broad domestic investment-grade bond market. The index spans investment grade securities only and excludes inflation-indexed Treasuries and non-dollar bonds as well. But pretty much everything else--including plain-vanilla Treasuries, agencies, mortgage-backed securities, and corporate bonds--can be found here. Treasuries, agencies, and mortgages recently accounted for nearly three quarters of the index. Credit quality skews toward the highest rung, with AAA bonds soaking up 80% of the benchmark.

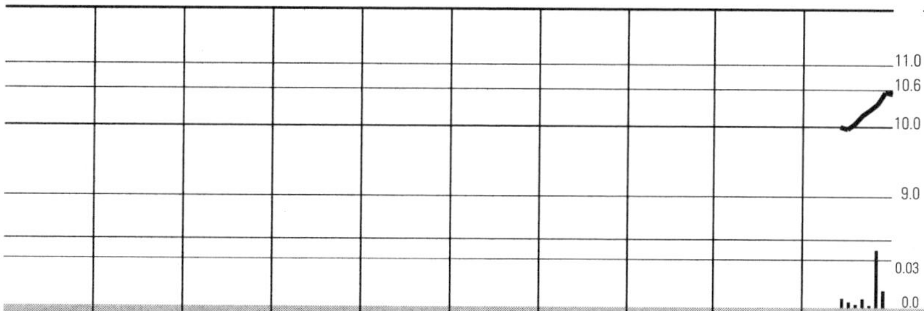

History

1998	1999	2000	2001	2002	2003	2004	2005	2006	2007	History
—	—	—	—	—	—	—	—	—	53.56	NAV $
—	—	—	—	—	—	—	—	—	53.72	Market Price $
—	—	—	—	—	—	—	—	—	4.99*	NAV Return%
—	—	—	—	—	—	—	—	—	5.31*	Market Price Return%
—	—	—	—	—	—	—	—	—	0.30	Avg Premium/Discount%
—	—	—	—	—	—	—	—	—	—	NAV Rtrn% +/-LB Aggreg
—	—	—	—	—	—	—	—	—	—	NAV Rtrn% +/-LB Aggreg
—	—	—	—	—	—	—	—	—	—	NAV Return% Rank in Cat
—	—	—	—	—	—	—	—	—	—	Income Return %
—	—	—	—	—	—	—	—	—	—	Capital Return %
—	—	—	—	—	—	—	—	—	1.37	Income $
—	—	—	—	—	—	—	—	—	0.00	Capital Gains $
—	—	—	—	—	—	—	—	—	0.13	Expense Ratio %
—	—	—	—	—	—	—	—	—	4.42	Income Ratio %
—	—	—	—	—	—	—	—	—	17	Turnover Rate %
—	—	—	—	—	—	—	—	—	64	Net Assets $mil

Performance 12-31-07

Historic Quarterly NAV Returns

	1st Qtr	2nd Qtr	3rd Qtr	4th Qtr	Total
2003	—	—	—	—	—
2004	—	—	—	—	—
2005	—	—	—	—	—
2006	—	—	—	—	—
2007	—	—	2.92	2.53	—*

Trailing	NAV Return%	Market Return%	NAV Rtrn% +/-LB Aggreg	%Rank Cat.(NAV)
3 Mo	2.53	2.68	-0.47	75
6 Mo	5.52	5.77	-0.41	75
1 Yr	—	—	—	—
3 Yr Avg	—	—	—	—
5 Yr Avg	—	—	—	—
10 Yr Avg	—	—	—	—

Tax Analysis	Tax-Adj Return%	Tax-Cost Ratio
3 Yr (estimated)	—	—
5 Yr (estimated)	—	—
10 Yr (estimated)	—	—

Rating and Risk

Time Period	Morningstar Rtn vs Cat	Morningstar Risk vs Cat	Morningstar Risk-Adj Rating
3 Yr	—	—	—
5 Yr	—	—	—
10 Yr	—	—	—

Other Measures	Standard Index S&P 500	Best Fit Index
Alpha	—	—
Beta	—	—
R-Squared	—	—
Standard Deviation	—	
Mean	—	
Sharpe Ratio	—	

Portfolio Analysis 11-30-07

Total Fixed-Income:109	Date of Maturity	Amount $000	Value $000	% Net Assets
FNMA 5.5%		5,100	5,108	7.74
FHLMC 6%		3,800	3,858	5.85
FHLMC 5%		3,500	3,434	5.20
US Treasury Note 4.5%	04-30-12	2,993	3,129	4.74
US Treasury Note 4%	04-15-10	2,368	2,420	3.67
FNMA 6.5%		1,425	1,465	2.22
US Treasury Bond 6%	02-15-26	1,164	1,389	2.10
US Treasury Bond 8.875%	08-15-17	998	1,382	2.09
FHLMC 5%	01-16-09	1,320	1,337	2.03
US Treasury Note 4.875%	08-15-16	1,248	1,333	2.02
FHLMC 4.5%		1,350	1,328	2.01
FNMA 6%		1,250	1,278	1.94
KREDITANSTALT FUR WIEDER	03-30-09	1,250	1,242	1.88
Jpmorgan & Chase 6.625%	03-15-12	1,050	1,115	1.69
FHLBA 5.375%	08-19-11	925	973	1.47
US Treasury Note 4.5%	03-31-09	914	930	1.41
FNMA 5%		900	900	1.36
GNMA 6%		800	820	1.24
GNMA 5.5%		800	810	1.23
European Invt Bk 5%	02-08-10	750	772	1.17

Current Investment Style

Duration: Short Int Long; Quality: High Med Low

[1] figure provided by fund

Avg Eff Duration[1]	4.3 Yrs
Avg Eff Maturity	—
Avg Credit Quality	AAA
Avg Wtd Coupon	5.50%
Avg Wtd Price	103.18% of par

Coupon Range	% of Bonds	Rel Cat
0% PIK	0.0	0.0
0% to 6%	80.3	1.1
6% to 8%	16.8	0.7
8% to 10%	2.9	0.7
More than 10%	0.0	0.0

1.00=Category Average

Credit Analysis		% bonds 11-30-07	
US Govt	0	BB	0
AAA	73	B	0
AA	11	Below B	0
A	11	NR/NA	0
BBB	6		

Sector Breakdown	% of assets
US Treasuries	15
TIPS	0
US Agency	7
Mortgage Pass-Throughs	28
Mortgage CMO	0
Mortgage ARM	0
US Corporate	21
Asset-Backed	0
Convertible	0
Municipal	0
Corporate Inflation-Protected	0
Foreign Corporate	1
Foreign Govt	1

Composition			
Cash	19.5	Bonds	80.5
Stocks	0.0	Other	0.0

Special Securities	
Restricted/Illiquid Secs	Trace
Exotic Mortgage-Backed	0
Emerging-Markets Secs	0
Options/Futures/Warrants	No

Morningstar's Take by Jeffrey Ptak 12-31-07

Good, but not the best.

SPDR Lehman Aggregate Bond tracks the Lehman U.S. Aggregate Bond Index, the most popular proxy for the domestic investment-grade bond market. The Lehman spans virtually every investment-grade sector, including Treasuries, bonds issued by government-sponsored entities such as Fannie Mae, and corporate bonds. It does not include inflation-indexed Treasuries, non-dollar securities, or high-yield bonds.

We're typically fond of bond index funds like this one for a few reasons. For one, they're very cheap. That holds especially true for bond ETFs, which aren't saddled with certain types of costs common to mutual funds. This fund is no exception, as it levies a paltry 0.13% expense ratio. That gives it a big leg up in the return-constrained fixed-income world, where every basis point counts. In addition, the fund's simplicity and pleasing diversification can't be beat, as its holdings cover just about every nook and cranny in the bond market.

Of course, there are managers, like PIMCO's Bill Gross or Loomis Sayles' Dan Fuss, who have consistently shown the ability to beat the bond market even after fees. They, along with the other fine managers on our Fund Analyst Picks list are certainly viable alternatives to a bond index fund, which simply aims to deliver the market return. But you have to do your homework to monitor even the best managers.

If that doesn't appeal to you, this fund is certainly a strong option to consider. However, it's not our top choice. That distinction goes to Vanguard Total Bond Market ETF, which also tracks the Lehman index. It's a bit cheaper than this offering, as it costs only 0.11% per annum. In addition, whereas this fund holds a mere 121 of the 9,100-plus bonds in the Lehman index, the Vanguard offering's portfolio spans over 3,000 issues. That more-comprehensive coverage gives us greater comfort that the Vanguard fund's returns will hew closely to the index's over time.

Address:	One Lincoln Street United States 866-787-2257
Web Address:	www.advisors.ssga.com
Inception:	05-23-07*
Advisor:	SSgA Funds Management Inc

Management Fee:	0.18%		
Expense Projections:	3Yr:$54	5Yr: —	10Yr: —
Income Distrib:	Monthly		
Exchange:	AMEX		

SPDR Lehman Muni Bd TFI

Market Price	Mstar Category
$22.26	Muni National Long

Morningstar Fair Value

Price/Fair Value Ratio	Coverage Rate %
NA	NA

Valuation

This ETF primarily holds municipal bonds, not stocks. That explains why the fund's price/fair value ratio does not appear above.

Methodology

This ETF mimics the Lehman Brothers Municipal Managed Money Index, which aims to reflect the long-term tax-exempt bond market. It is composed of bonds issued by cities, counties, and states that are exempt from federal income taxes. To be included in the index, a bond must be rated AA- or higher. It excludes bonds exposed to the alternative minimum tax. It also omits airline bonds, tobacco bonds, hospital bonds, housing bonds, and all floaters and derivatives. This fund uses representative sampling to track the benchmark. Thus, while the index spans thousands of bonds, this portfolio holds less than 50 securities.

Morningstar Rating	Return	Risk	Yield	NAV	Avg Daily Vol. (k)	52 wk High/Low
—	—	—	—	$22.16	44	$22.61 - $21.85

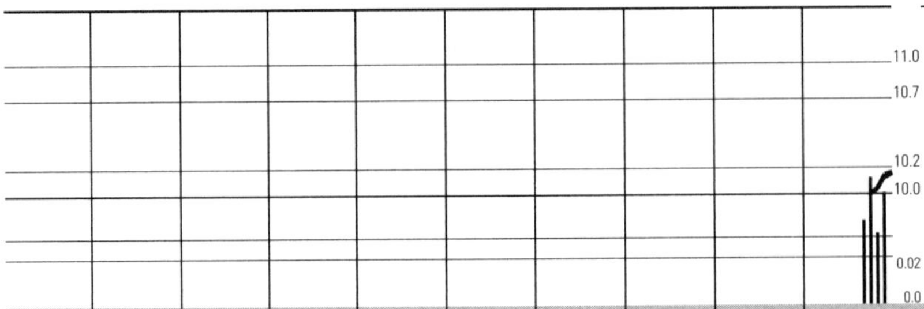

Growth of $10,000
- Investment Value of ETF
- Investment Value of Index LB Muni

Trading Volume Millions

1998	1999	2000	2001	2002	2003	2004	2005	2006	2007	History
—	—	—	—	—	—	—	—	—	22.16	NAV $
—	—	—	—	—	—	—	—	—	22.26	Market Price $
—	—	—	—	—	—	—	—	—	0.88*	NAV Return%
—	—	—	—	—	—	—	—	—	—	Market Price Return%
—	—	—	—	—	—	—	—	—	0.20	Avg Premium/Discount%
—	—	—	—	—	—	—	—	—	—	NAV Rtrn% +/-LB Muni
—	—	—	—	—	—	—	—	—	—	NAV Rtrn% +/-LB Muni 20YR
—	—	—	—	—	—	—	—	—	—	NAV Return% Rank in Cat
—	—	—	—	—	—	—	—	—	—	Income Return %
—	—	—	—	—	—	—	—	—	—	Capital Return %
—	—	—	—	—	—	—	—	—	0.18	Income $
—	—	—	—	—	—	—	—	—	0.00	Capital Gains $
—	—	—	—	—	—	—	—	—	—	Expense Ratio %
—	—	—	—	—	—	—	—	—	—	Income Ratio %
—	—	—	—	—	—	—	—	—	—	Turnover Rate %
—	—	—	—	—	—	—	—	—	71	Net Assets $mil

Performance 12-31-07

Historic Quarterly NAV Returns

	1st Qtr	2nd Qtr	3rd Qtr	4th Qtr	Total
2003	—	—	—	—	—
2004	—	—	—	—	—
2005	—	—	—	—	—
2006	—	—	—	—	—
2007	—	—	—	1.53	—*

Trailing	NAV Return%	Market Return%	NAV Rtrn% +/-LB Muni	%Rank Cat.(NAV)
3 Mo	1.53	1.83	0.16	1
6 Mo	—	—	—	—
1 Yr	—	—	—	—
3 Yr Avg	—	—	—	—
5 Yr Avg	—	—	—	—
10 Yr Avg	—	—	—	—

Tax Analysis	Tax-Adj Return%	Tax-Cost Ratio
3 Yr (estimated)	—	—
5 Yr (estimated)	—	—
10 Yr (estimated)	—	—

Rating and Risk

Time Period	Morningstar Rtn vs Cat	Morningstar Risk vs Cat	Morningstar Risk-Adj Rating
3 Yr	—	—	—
5 Yr	—	—	—
10 Yr	—	—	—

Other Measures	Standard Index S&P 500	Best Fit Index
Alpha	—	—
Beta	—	—
R-Squared	—	—
Standard Deviation	—	
Mean	—	
Sharpe Ratio	—	

Portfolio Analysis 12-31-07

Total Fixed-Income:56	Date of Maturity	Amount $000	Value $000	% Net Assets
Massachusetts St Wtr Pol	08-01-33	2,000	2,290	3.26
Williamson Cnty Tex G O	02-15-18	2,000	2,209	3.14
Charleston Cnty S C Go T	11-01-18	2,000	2,199	3.13
Georgia St Go Bds 5%	04-01-12	2,000	2,141	3.05
Central Puget Sound Wash	11-01-36	2,000	2,082	2.96
Commonwealth Fing Auth 5	06-01-25	1,925	2,028	2.89
Minnesota St Go State 5%	06-01-15	1,820	2,000	2.85
Missouri St Regl Convent	08-15-16	1,800	1,952	2.78
Michigan Mun Bd Auth 5%	10-01-22	1,700	1,818	2.59
San Francisco Calif Bay	08-01-22	1,500	1,632	2.32
Long Island Pwr Auth 5%	05-01-18	1,500	1,622	2.31
Kentucky St Tpk Auth 5%	07-01-25	1,500	1,573	2.24
Bay Area Toll Auth 5%	04-01-31	1,500	1,569	2.23
Port Auth 5%	12-01-29	1,500	1,557	2.22
New York N Y Go Bds 5%	10-01-12	1,400	1,489	2.12
San Jose Evergreen Calif	09-01-20	2,500	1,437	2.05
New Jersey St Transn Tr	06-15-12	1,305	1,413	2.01
Maryland St 5%	08-01-12	1,250	1,344	1.91
Engy Northwest Wash Elec	07-01-12	1,200	1,305	1.86
Phoenix Ariz Var Purp 5%	07-01-17	1,000	1,103	1.57

Current Investment Style

Duration: Short Int Long — Quality: High Med Low

[1] figure provided by fund

Avg Eff Duration[1]	7.8 Yrs
Avg Eff Maturity	—
Avg Credit Quality	AAA
Avg Wtd Coupon	4.98%
Avg Wtd Price	105.46% of par

Coupon Range	% of Bonds	Rel Cat
0% PIK	0.0	0.0
0% to 6%	100.0	1.0
6% to 8%	0.0	0.0
8% to 10%	0.0	0.0
More than 10%	0.0	0.0

1.00=Category Average

Credit Analysis	% bonds 12-31-07		
US Govt	0	BB	0
AAA	71	B	0
AA	29	Below B	0
A	0	NR/NA	0
BBB	0		

Sector Breakdown	% of assets
US Treasuries	—
TIPS	—
US Agency	—
Mortgage Pass-Throughs	—
Mortgage CMO	—
Mortgage ARM	—
US Corporate	—
Asset-Backed	—
Convertible	—
Municipal	—
Corporate Inflation-Protected	—
Foreign Corporate	—
Foreign Govt	—

Composition			
Cash	1.2	Bonds	98.8
Stocks	0.0	Other	0.0

Special Securities	
Restricted/Illiquid Secs	0
Exotic Mortgage-Backed	—
Emerging-Markets Secs	0
Options/Futures/Warrants	No

Morningstar's Take by Sonya Morris 12-31-07

We think there's reason to take a wait-and-see approach with SPDR Lehman Municipal Bond ETF.

Muni bond ETFs face more challenges than equity ETFs do. The muni bond market is vast, and unlike stocks, which are bought and sold over an organized exchange, muni bonds trade over the counter, making pricing less transparent. Also, investors tend to hold muni bonds until they mature, so secondary-market trading activity is modest. If muni ETFs face liquidity constraints, there's a chance their market prices and NAVs could differ materially. Plus, with a less liquid and less transparent market, muni bond ETFs may have a tougher time tracking their benchmarks than equity ETFs. This fund and its rival muni ETFs launched just a few months ago, so their short track records don't give us much to go on. No conventional muni mutual fund employs an indexing approach, so we can't turn to an existing index fund for guidance.

Furthermore, muni bond ETFs court more concentration risk than the typical muni bond mutual fund. The ETF uses representative sampling to track its benchmark, so while the index includes more than 20,000 individual securities, the ETF's portfolio consists of just 39 bonds. That's a much smaller portfolio than the typical muni bond mutual fund, which includes more than 180 issues.

That's not to say that this ETF doesn't have its strong points--most notably a low expense ratio. With annual fees of just 0.20%, it's the cheapest muni ETF on the market, and it's far cheaper than the typical muni mutual fund, which charges 0.64%. That's powerful in muni land because expenses eat up a large portion of the modest total returns generated by the typical muni fund.

That said, you can get similar exposure for even less from Vanguard Long-Term Tax-Exempt, which charges just 0.16% in expenses, and you don't have to pay brokerage commissions to buy it.

Given the existence of a solid alternative, there's no reason to hop aboard here until we've seen more from muni ETFs.

Address:	One Lincoln Street United States 866-787-2257
Web Address:	www.advisors.ssga.com
Inception:	09-11-07*
Advisor:	SSgA Funds Management Inc

Management Fee:	0.30%		
Expense Projections:	3Yr:$86	5Yr: —	10Yr: —
Income Distrib:	Monthly		
Exchange:	AMEX		

Vanguard Ttl Bnd Mkt ETF BND

Market Price $77.38

Mstar Category Intermediate-Term Bond

Morningstar Rating	Return	Risk	Yield	NAV	Avg Daily Vol. (k)	52 wk High/Low
—	—	—	—	$76.61	199	$77.65 - $73.40

Morningstar Fair Value

Price/Fair Value Ratio	Coverage Rate %
NA	NA

Valuation

This ETF holds bonds, not stocks. That explains why the fund's price/fair value ratio does not appear above.

Methodology

The exchange-traded fund strives to approximate the performance of the Lehman Brothers Aggregate Bond Index, which is a commonly used proxy for the broad, investment-grade U.S. bond market. The duration (a measure of interest-rate sensitivity) and other key characteristics of the index are carefully replicated, but the fund does not hold every security in the index. Instead, in an effort to pick up additional yield and return, it tends to hold a higher percentage of short-term corporate bonds or asset-backed securities and fewer short Treasuries than does its index.

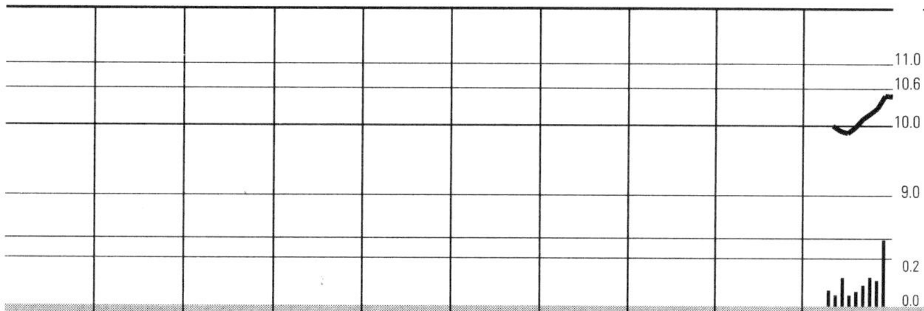

1998	1999	2000	2001	2002	2003	2004	2005	2006	2007	History
—	—	—	—	—	—	—	—	—	76.61	NAV $
—	—	—	—	—	—	—	—	—	77.38	Market Price $
—	—	—	—	—	—	—	—	—	5.09*	NAV Return%
—	—	—	—	—	—	—	—	—	6.08*	Market Price Return%
—	—	—	—	—	—	—	—	—	0.27	Avg Premium/Discount%
—	—	—	—	—	—	—	—	—	—	NAV Rtrn% +/-LB Aggreg
—	—	—	—	—	—	—	—	—	—	NAV Rtrn% +/-LB Aggreg
—	—	—	—	—	—	—	—	—	—	NAV Return% Rank in Cat
—	—	—	—	—	—	—	—	—	—	Income Return %
—	—	—	—	—	—	—	—	—	—	Capital Return %
—	—	—	—	—	—	—	—	—	2.09	Income $
—	—	—	—	—	—	—	—	—	0.00	Capital Gains $
—	—	—	—	—	—	—	—	—	—	Expense Ratio %
—	—	—	—	—	—	—	—	—	—	Income Ratio %
—	—	—	—	—	—	—	—	—	—	Turnover Rate %
—	—	—	—	—	—	—	—	—	1,095	Net Assets $mil

Performance 12-31-07

Historic Quarterly NAV Returns

	1st Qtr	2nd Qtr	3rd Qtr	4th Qtr	Total
2003	—	—	—	—	—
2004	—	—	—	—	—
2005	—	—	—	—	—
2006	—	—	—	—	—
2007	—	—	2.95	2.68	—*

Trailing	NAV Return%	Market Return%	NAV Rtrn% +/-LB Aggreg	%Rank Cat.(NAV)
3 Mo	2.68	3.41	-0.32	62
6 Mo	5.71	6.56	-0.22	50
1 Yr	—	—	—	—
3 Yr Avg	—	—	—	—
5 Yr Avg	—	—	—	—
10 Yr Avg	—	—	—	—

Tax Analysis	Tax-Adj Return%	Tax-Cost Ratio
3 Yr (estimated)	—	—
5 Yr (estimated)	—	—
10 Yr (estimated)	—	—

Rating and Risk

Time Period	Morningstar Rtn vs Cat	Morningstar Risk vs Cat	Morningstar Risk-Adj Rating
3 Yr	—	—	—
5 Yr	—	—	—
10 Yr	—	—	—

Other Measures	Standard Index S&P 500	Best Fit Index
Alpha	—	—
Beta	—	—
R-Squared	—	—
Standard Deviation	—	
Mean	—	
Sharpe Ratio	—	

Portfolio Analysis 09-30-07

Total Fixed-Income:11067	Date of Maturity	Amount $000	Value $000	% Net Assets
US Treasury Note 6.5%	02-15-10	697,025	736,017	1.43
US Treasury Note 4.5%	09-30-11	572,395	579,819	1.12
US TREASURY NOTE	10-31-11	428,145	435,569	0.84
US Treasury Bond 6.75%	08-15-26	349,355	428,288	0.83
US Treasury Note 4.5%	04-30-09	403,575	406,856	0.79
US Treasury Bond 8.75%	08-15-20	294,125	404,331	0.78
US Treasury Bond 8.75%	05-15-17	305,390	402,495	0.78
US Treasury Note 4%	02-15-15	381,975	371,650	0.72
US TREASURY NOTE	10-31-08	336,550	339,390	0.66
US Treasury Note 4.25%	08-15-14	341,450	338,889	0.66
US Treasury Note 4.875%	07-31-11	307,675	315,751	0.61
US Treasury Bond 8.875%	08-15-17	236,010	314,594	0.61
US Treasury Bond 7.5%	11-15-16	257,469	312,825	0.61
US Treasury Note 4.75%	05-31-12	298,005	304,662	0.59
US Treasury Note 4.5%	11-30-11	263,175	266,465	0.52
US Treasury Note 4.875%	05-31-09	257,475	261,177	0.51
US Treasury Note 3.125%	10-15-08	259,075	256,686	0.50
FNMA 6%	10-01-37	251,600	251,915	0.49
Chase Issuance Tr 2005-1	12-15-10	244,486	244,283	0.47
US Treasury Bond 8.125%	08-15-21	164,625	218,617	0.42

Current Investment Style

Duration: Short Int Long; Quality: High Med Low

[1] figure provided by fund

Avg Eff Duration[1]	4.6 Yrs
Avg Eff Maturity	7.3 Yrs
Avg Credit Quality	AAA
Avg Wtd Coupon	5.52%
Avg Wtd Price	102.33% of par

Coupon Range	% of Bonds	Rel Cat
0% PIK	0.0	0.0
0% to 6%	74.8	1.0
6% to 8%	19.8	0.9
8% to 10%	4.5	1.1
More than 10%	0.9	1.0

1.00=Category Average

Credit Analysis		% bonds 09-30-07	
US Govt	0	BB	0
AAA	80	B	0
AA	6	Below B	0
A	7	NR/NA	0
BBB	7		

Sector Breakdown	% of assets
US Treasuries	24
TIPS	0
US Agency	9
Mortgage Pass-Throughs	37
Mortgage CMO	1
Mortgage ARM	0
US Corporate	18
Asset-Backed	6
Convertible	0
Municipal	0
Corporate Inflation-Protected	0
Foreign Corporate	1
Foreign Govt	1

Composition			
Cash	2.4	Bonds	97.5
Stocks	0.0	Other	0.0

Special Securities	
Restricted/Illiquid Secs	Trace
Exotic Mortgage-Backed	0
Emerging-Markets Secs	Trace
Options/Futures/Warrants	No

Morningstar's Take by Michael Herbst 12-31-07

Vanguard Total Bond Index has few legs up on the competition.

This fund has been nearly perfect lately. Its 5.38% gain for six months leading up to November 29 falls within 0.1% of its Lehman Brothers Aggregate Bond Index bogy. That's not too surprising: Although it only launched April 3, 2007, it's the ETF share class of intermediate-bond category Analyst Pick Vanguard Total Bond Market Index. That fund's performance over the trailing three- and five-year periods has been more than 99% correlated to that of its benchmark.

Fractions of a percentage point may not seem like much, yet the fund's showing is impressive because bond index funds are built to mimic a benchmark rather than match it bond-for-bond. The fund's portfolio contains more than 3,000 bonds--versus the roughly 160 holdings of its rival iShares Lehman Aggregate Bond--so we think management here stands a better chance of minimizing tracking error. We also don't take for granted the skill necessary to track a benchmark and overcome expenses. Earlier in the year, for example, one of the fund's competitors, Fidelity U.S. Bond Index, had a slice of assets parked in an internal ultrashort bond fund that got stung due to its exposure to subprime loans. As a result, that fund's year-to-date gain trails the funds' shared benchmark by more than a full percentage point. Here, manager Ken Volpert's team has added value recently by buying new corporate bonds at a slight discount before they enter the index. It has also slightly underweighted and overweighted a number of corporate bonds relative to the benchmark.

Beyond management's skill, the fund's rock-bottom 0.11% expense ratio is the lowest levy we've seen for ETF and mutual-fund intermediate-bond offerings. That means Volpert can take on even less risk in transcending the fund's lower fee hurdle. That advantage, in addition to our confidence in Vanguard's crack indexing team, have us recommending this fund.

Address:	PO Box 2600, United States, 866-499-8473
Web Address:	www.vanguard.com
Inception:	04-03-07 *
Advisor:	The Vanguard Group, Inc.

Management Fee:	0.09%		
Expense Projections:	3Yr:$35	5Yr:$62	10Yr:$141
Income Distrib:	Monthly		
Exchange:	AMEX		

Specialty/Other Funds

This section offers a full-page report on each currency, commodity, and precious metals ETF.

CurrencyShares Euro Trust FXE

Market Price	Mstar Category
$146.40	World Bond

Morningstar Fair Value

Price/Fair Value Ratio	Coverage Rate %
NA	NA

Valuation

Trading currencies as a tactical play is risky. For that reason, most investors should consider this fund only as a part of a long-term currency hedging strategy. (The price/fair value ratio does not appear above because the fund doesn't own stocks.)

Methodology

This ETF is designed to track the price of the euro, the currency for 13 European Union countries. The fund invests its assets in two euro-denominated U.K.-based deposit accounts. The primary account earns interest, accrued daily, at the initial annual rate of EONIA (Euro OverNight Index Average) minus 27 basis points. The secondary account receives the primary account's interest, pays trust expenses and fees (0.4% expense ratio), and distributes excess income to shareholders monthly, which is taxable as ordinary income. The fund does not utilize derivative instruments to gain currency exposure.

Morningstar Rating	Return	Risk	Yield	NAV	Avg Daily Vol. (k)	52 wk High/Low
—	—	—	3.0%	$146.45	200	$149.23 - $129.10

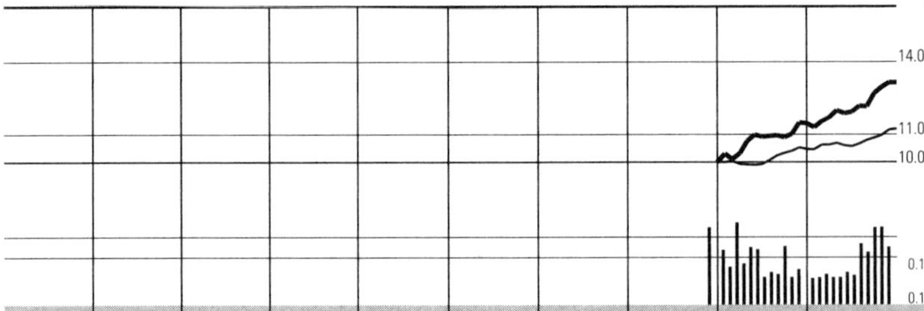

1998	1999	2000	2001	2002	2003	2004	2005	2006	2007	History
—	—	—	—	—	—	—	118.56	131.99	146.45	NAV $
—	—	—	—	—	—	—	118.15	131.99	146.40	Market Price $
—	—	—	—	—	—	—	13.82*	13.65	14.57	NAV Return%
—	—	—	—	—	—	—	13.20*	14.04	14.54	Market Price Return%
—	—	—	—	—	—	—	-0.34	0.00	0.05	Avg Premium/Discount%
—	—	—	—	—	—	—	—	9.32	7.60	NAV Rtrn% +/-LB Aggreg
—	—	—	—	—	—	—	—	6.71	12.22	NAV Rtrn% +/-SB Wld Govt
—	—	—	—	—	—	—	—	1	61	NAV Return% Rank in Cat
—	—	—	—	—	—	—	—	2.22	3.39	Income Return %
—	—	—	—	—	—	—	—	11.43	11.18	Capital Return %
—	—	—	—	—	—	—	0.00	2.61	4.40	Income $
—	—	—	—	—	—	—	0.00	0.00	0.00	Capital Gains $
—	—	—	—	—	—	—	—	—	—	Expense Ratio %
—	—	—	—	—	—	—	—	—	—	Income Ratio %
—	—	—	—	—	—	—	—	—	—	Turnover Rate %
—	—	—	—	—	—	—	89	939	981	Net Assets $mil

Performance 12-31-07

Historic Quarterly NAV Returns

	1st Qtr	2nd Qtr	3rd Qtr	4th Qtr	Total
2003	—	—	—	—	—
2004	—	—	—	—	—
2005	—	—	—	—	—*
2006	2.96	5.62	-0.18	4.70	13.65
2007	2.07	1.90	6.36	3.58	14.57

Trailing	NAV Return%	Market Return%	NAV Rtrn% +/-LB Aggreg	%Rank Cat.(NAV)
3 Mo	3.58	3.22	0.58	16
6 Mo	10.16	9.72	4.23	37
1 Yr	14.57	14.54	7.60	61
3 Yr Avg	—	—	—	—
5 Yr Avg	—	—	—	—
10 Yr Avg	—	—	—	—

Tax Analysis	Tax-Adj Return%	Tax-Cost Ratio
3 Yr (estimated)	—	—
5 Yr (estimated)	—	—
10 Yr (estimated)	—	—

Rating and Risk

Time Period	Morningstar Rtn vs Cat	Morningstar Risk vs Cat	Morningstar Risk-Adj Rating
3 Yr	—	—	—
5 Yr	—	—	—
10 Yr	—	—	—

Other Measures	Standard Index S&P 500	Best Fit Index
Alpha	—	—
Beta	—	—
R-Squared	—	—
Standard Deviation	—	
Mean	—	
Sharpe Ratio	—	

Portfolio Analysis 10-31-07

	Date of Maturity	Amount $000	Value $000	% Net Assets
Total Fixed-Income:0				

Morningstar's Take by Emiko Kurotsu 12-31-07

CurrencyShares Euro Trust provides a viable way to hedge your currency exposure, though it's hardly a necessary route for all.

This ETF offers unadulterated exposure to the euro, the common currency for 13 European Union countries, by investing cash in euro-denominated accounts. These accounts bear interest at the EU inter-bank rate (EONIA), and investors reap that interest, less fund fees, monthly. When those monies are translated back into the dollar, investors reap any currency appreciation as well. That formula has worked wonders lately: The euro has appreciated more than 30% against the dollar in the past year alone.

Yet, that isn't a sufficient reason to invest here. Indeed, currency investing is an inexact science at best. Exchange-rate gyrations are notoriously unpredictable, tied as they are to a multitude of macro- and microeconomic variables, such as trade deficits, inflation rates, or other sociopolitical factors. While that shouldn't preclude opportunistic currency investments, any wager on the good times continuing is a bet on the interplay of these complex variables, long odds and all.

A sounder reason to invest in a currency fund like this one is to protect a portfolio's value, or at least reduce its volatility, by hedging its currency exposure. In that respect, this fund is a viable option for a few reasons. First, because it doesn't use derivatives, you know exactly what you're investing in. Second, unlike non-dollar-denominated bond funds, this ETF is largely shorn of credit and interest-rate risk. Finally, with a 0.4% expense ratio (plus brokerage costs), it's cheaper than many competing options. For instance, spot market transactions and currency accounts are typically subject to high fees and commissions.

For those compelled to hedge their portfolio's euro exposure, this fund is well worth a look. For others, especially those who lack meaningful exposure to European securities, it's not necessary.

Address:	9601 Blackwell Rd United States 800-820-0888
Web Address:	www.rydex.com
Inception:	12-09-05*
Advisor:	Rydex Investments

Management Fee:	0.40%
Expense Projections:	3Yr: — 5Yr: — 10Yr: —
Income Distrib:	Monthly
Exchange:	NYSE

Current Investment Style

Duration: Short Int Long; Quality: High Med Low

[1] figure provided by fund

Avg Eff Duration[1]	—
Avg Eff Maturity	—
Avg Credit Quality	—
Avg Wtd Coupon	—
Avg Wtd Price	107.75% of par

Coupon Range	% of Bonds	Rel Cat
0% PIK	—	0.0
0% to 6%	0.0	0.0
6% to 8%	0.0	0.0
8% to 10%	0.0	0.0
More than 10%	0.0	0.0

1.00=Category Average

Credit Analysis		% bonds 10-31-07	
US Govt	—	BB	—
AAA	—	B	—
AA	—	Below B	—
A	—	NR/NA	—
BBB	—		

Sector Breakdown	% of assets
US Treasuries	—
TIPS	—
US Agency	—
Mortgage Pass-Throughs	—
Mortgage CMO	—
Mortgage ARM	—
US Corporate	—
Asset-Backed	—
Convertible	—
Municipal	—
Corporate Inflation-Protected	—
Foreign Corporate	—
Foreign Govt	—

Composition			
Cash	100.0	Bonds	0.0
Stocks	0.0	Other	0.0

Special Securities	
Restricted/Illiquid Secs	0
Exotic Mortgage-Backed	—
Emerging-Markets Secs	0
Options/Futures/Warrants	No

iPath DJ-AIGCom Id TR ETN DJP

Market Price	Mstar Category
$56.23	Specialty-Natural Res

Morningstar Fair Value

Price/Fair Value Ratio	Coverage Rate %
—	—

Valuation

This is an exchange-traded note that tracks the performance of a commodity index. It does not hold stocks. That explains why the fund's price/fair value ratio does not appear above.

Methodology

IPath ETNs offer a transparent way to invest in commodities. Whereas traditional mutual funds have to employ complicated derivative strategies, iPath ETNs are 30-year notes backed by Barclays Bank PLC. The bank promises to pay the return of the Dow Jones-AIG Commodity Total Return Index, less an annual fee of 0.75%. The index is well-diversified between 18 different commodities and limits its exposure to energy-related raw goods to a third of its value. The notes trade on the NYSE and a daily arbitrage mechanism should ensure they track close to their underlying value.

Morningstar Rating	Return	Risk	Yield	NAV	Avg Daily Vol. (k)	52 wk High/Low
—	—	—	—	$56.19	173	$58.08 - $45.81

Growth of $10,000
- Investment Value of ETF
- Investment Value of Index S&P 500

Trading Volume Millions

History

1998	1999	2000	2001	2002	2003	2004	2005	2006	2007	History
—	—	—	—	—	—	—	—	48.65	56.19	NAV $
—	—	—	—	—	—	—	—	48.94	56.23	Market Price $
—	—	—	—	—	—	—	—	7.72*	15.50	NAV Return%
—	—	—	—	—	—	—	—	7.78*	14.90	Market Price Return%
—	—	—	—	—	—	—	—	0.31	0.14	Avg Premium/Discount%
—	—	—	—	—	—	—	—	—	10.01	NAV Rtrn% +/-S&P 500
—	—	—	—	—	—	—	—	—	-0.73	NAV Rtrn% +/-DJ/AIG Comm
—	—	—	—	—	—	—	—	—	92	NAV Return% Rank in Cat
—	—	—	—	—	—	—	—	—	0.00	Income Return %
—	—	—	—	—	—	—	—	—	15.50	Capital Return %
—	—	—	—	—	—	—	—	0.00	0.00	Income $
—	—	—	—	—	—	—	—	0.00	0.00	Capital Gains $
—	—	—	—	—	—	—	—	—	—	Expense Ratio %
—	—	—	—	—	—	—	—	—	—	Income Ratio %
—	—	—	—	—	—	—	—	—	—	Turnover Rate %
—	—	—	—	—	—	—	—	835	2,634	Net Assets $mil

Performance 12-31-07

Historic Quarterly NAV Returns

	1st Qtr	2nd Qtr	3rd Qtr	4th Qtr	Total
2003	—	—	—	—	—
2004	—	—	—	—	—
2005	—	—	—	—	—
2006	—	—	-6.66	5.21	—*
2007	4.44	-0.33	6.10	4.58	15.50

Trailing	NAV Return%	Market Return%	NAV Rtrn% +/-S&P 500	%Rank Cat.(NAV)
3 Mo	4.58	4.56	7.91	48
6 Mo	10.96	10.78	12.33	52
1 Yr	15.50	14.90	10.01	92
3 Yr Avg	—	—	—	—
5 Yr Avg	—	—	—	—
10 Yr Avg	—	—	—	—

Tax Analysis	Tax-Adj Return%	Tax-Cost Ratio
3 Yr (estimated)	—	—
5 Yr (estimated)	—	—
10 Yr (estimated)	—	—

Rating and Risk

Time Period	Morningstar Rtn vs Cat	Morningstar Risk vs Cat	Morningstar Risk-Adj Rating
3 Yr	—	—	—
5 Yr	—	—	—
10 Yr	—	—	—

Other Measures	Standard Index S&P 500	Best Fit Index
Alpha	—	—
Beta	—	—
R-Squared	—	—
Standard Deviation	—	
Mean	—	
Sharpe Ratio	—	

Portfolio Analysis 00-00-00

Share change since 00-00	Total Stocks:0	Sector	PF	Tot Ret%	% Assets

Current Investment Style

Value Blnd Growth; Large Mid Small

Market Cap	%
Giant	—
Large	—
Mid	—
Small	—
Micro	—
Avg $mil:	—

Value Measures		Rel Category
Price/Earnings	—	—
Price/Book	—	—
Price/Sales	—	—
Price/Cash Flow	—	—
Dividend Yield %	—	—

Growth Measures	%	Rel Category
Long-Term Erngs	—	—
Book Value	—	—
Sales	—	—
Cash Flow	—	—
Historical Erngs	—	—

Profitability	%	Rel Category
Return on Equity	—	—
Return on Assets	—	—
Net Margin	—	—

Industry Weightings	% of Stocks	Rel Cat
Oil & Gas	—	—
Oil/Gas Products	—	—
Oil & Gas Srv	—	—
Pipelines	—	—
Utilities	—	—
Hard Commd	—	—
Soft Commd	—	—
Misc. Indstrl	—	—
Other	—	—

Composition

Graph is not avaliable.

Cash	—
Stocks	0.0
Bonds	0.0
Other	0.0
Foreign (% of Stock)	0.0

Morningstar's Take by Karen Dolan 12-31-07

IPath Dow Jones-AIG Commodity Index finds itself in the middle of some tax-related controversy.

This exchange-traded note has a notably unique structure. Unlike commodity mutual funds or exchange-traded funds, ETN owners don't actually have a claim on a portfolio of commodity-related securities. Rather, they hold a 30-year note backed by Barclays Bank PLC where Barclays promises to pay the return of the Dow Jones-AIG Commodity Index, less an annual fee of 0.75%.

The ETN's tax-friendly status has been a big selling point, but it's unclear whether that benefit will hold in the IRS' eyes. Barclay's interpretation is that investors of this ETN are subject to capital gains tax based on when they buy and sell the notes. So an investor could buy today, hold for 10 years and face the favorable long-term capital gains tax rate when they actually sell the note. That's in marked contrast to competing commodity funds that use futures or structured notes to track their index and are thus forced to make annual distributions, portions of which are taxed at higher rates.

ETNs' favorable tax status became uncertain when the IRS issued a ruling on ETN's linked to single currencies in December 2007. The ruling concluded that interest accrued must be taxed as ordinary income annually and that gains or losses realized when the notes are sold also be taxed at ordinary income rates. That ruling doesn't apply here, but the IRS is reviewing this structure, so it's possible this ETN could wind up being taxed more like its fund rivals.

Tax issues aside, this ETN does offer useful exposure to commodities. It tracks a diversified index and its transparent structure means investors don't have to assume the risk that the note will trail the benchmark by more than its fees. An unfavorable tax ruling would put this ETN more on par with competing ETFs and active managers who have a chance at making up the fee differential, but it doesn't break the case for it entirely.

Address:	1 Churchill Place United Kingdom 877-764-7284
Web Address:	
Inception:	06-06-06*
Advisor:	Barclays Bank

Management Fee:	0.75%		
Expense Projections:	3Yr: —	5Yr: —	10Yr: —
Income Distrib:	None		
Exchange:	NYSE		

iPath S&P GSCI TotRet ETN GSP

Market Price	Mstar Category
$53.17	Specialty-Natural Res

Morningstar Rating	Return	Risk	Yield	NAV	Avg Daily Vol. (k)	52 wk High/Low
—	—	—	—	$53.18	21	$55.05 - $36.11

Morningstar Fair Value

Price/Fair Value Ratio	Coverage Rate %
—	—

Valuation

This is an exchange-traded note that tracks the performance of a commodity index. It does not hold stocks. That explains why the fund's price/fair value ratio does not appear above.

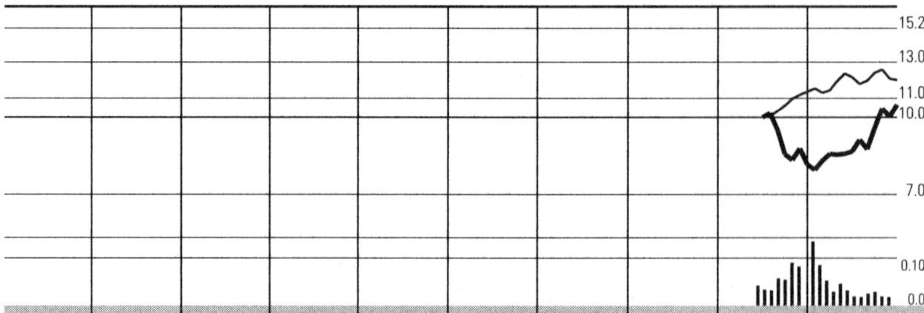

Growth of $10,000
- Investment Value of ETF
- Investment Value of Index S&P 500

Trading Volume Millions

Methodology

IPath ETNs offer a transparent way to invest in commodities. Whereas traditional mutual funds have to employ complicated derivative strategies, iPath ETNs are 30-year notes backed by Barclays Bank PLC. The bank promises to pay the return of the S&P Goldman Sachs Commodity Total Return Index , less an annual fee of 0.75%. Energy commodities usually take up more than 70% of the index's value and drive its returns and volatility. The notes trade on the NYSE and a daily arbitrage mechanism should ensure they track close to their underlying value.

History

1998	1999	2000	2001	2002	2003	2004	2005	2006	2007	History
—	—	—	—	—	—	—	—	40.29	53.18	NAV $
—	—	—	—	—	—	—	—	40.40	53.17	Market Price $
—	—	—	—	—	—	—	—	4.01*	31.99	NAV Return%
—	—	—	—	—	—	—	—	4.00*	31.61	Market Price Return%
—	—	—	—	—	—	—	—	0.25	-0.17	Avg Premium/Discount%
—	—	—	—	—	—	—	—	—	26.50	NAV Rtrn% +/-S&P 500
—	—	—	—	—	—	—	—	—	-0.68	NAV Rtrn% +/-S&P GSCI
—	—	—	—	—	—	—	—	—	60	NAV Return% Rank in Cat
—	—	—	—	—	—	—	—	—	0.00	Income Return %
—	—	—	—	—	—	—	—	—	31.99	Capital Return %
—	—	—	—	—	—	—	—	0.00	0.00	Income $
—	—	—	—	—	—	—	—	0.00	0.00	Capital Gains $
—	—	—	—	—	—	—	—	—	—	Expense Ratio %
—	—	—	—	—	—	—	—	—	—	Income Ratio %
—	—	—	—	—	—	—	—	—	—	Turnover Rate %
—	—	—	—	—	—	—	—	208	260	Net Assets $mil

Performance 12-31-07

Historic Quarterly NAV Returns

	1st Qtr	2nd Qtr	3rd Qtr	4th Qtr	Total
2003	—	—	—	—	—
2004	—	—	—	—	—
2005	—	—	—	—	—
2006	—	—	-15.68	-4.68	—*
2007	5.04	1.16	11.38	11.54	31.99

Trailing	NAV Return%	Market Return%	NAV Rtrn% +/-S&P 500	%Rank Cat.(NAV)
3 Mo	11.54	11.42	14.87	19
6 Mo	24.22	24.14	25.59	19
1 Yr	31.99	31.61	26.50	60
3 Yr Avg	—	—	—	—
5 Yr Avg	—	—	—	—
10 Yr Avg	—	—	—	—

Tax Analysis	Tax-Adj Return%	Tax-Cost Ratio
3 Yr (estimated)	—	—
5 Yr (estimated)	—	—
10 Yr (estimated)	—	—

Rating and Risk

Time Period	Morningstar Rtn vs Cat	Morningstar Risk vs Cat	Morningstar Risk-Adj Rating
3 Yr	—	—	—
5 Yr	—	—	—
10 Yr	—	—	—

Other Measures	Standard Index S&P 500	Best Fit Index
Alpha	—	—
Beta	—	—
R-Squared	—	—
Standard Deviation	—	
Mean	—	
Sharpe Ratio	—	

Portfolio Analysis 00-00-00

Share change since 00-00 Total Stocks:0	Sector	PE	Tot Ret%	% Assets

Morningstar's Take by Karen Dolan 12-31-07

IPath S&P GSCI Total Return could lose one of its advantages.

This exchange-traded note has a notably unique structure. Unlike commodity mutual funds or exchange-traded funds, ETN owners don't actually have a claim on a portfolio of commodity-related securities. Rather, they hold a 30-year note backed by Barclays Bank PLC where Barclays promises to pay the return of the S&P GSCI Total Return Index, less an annual fee of 0.75%.

The ETN's tax-friendly status has been a big selling point, but it's unclear whether that benefit will hold in the IRS' eyes. Barclay's interpretation is that investors here are subject to capital gains tax based on when they buy and sell the notes. So an investor could buy today, hold for 10 years, and face the favorable long-term capital gains tax rate when they actually sell the note. That's in marked contrast to competing commodity funds that use futures or structured notes to track their index and are thus forced to make annual distributions, portions of which are taxed at higher rates.

ETNs' favorable tax status became uncertain when the IRS issued a ruling on ETN's linked to single currencies in Dec. 2007. The ruling held that interest accrued must be taxed as ordinary income annually and that gains or losses realized when the notes are sold also be taxed at ordinary rates. That ruling doesn't apply here, but the IRS is reviewing this structure, so it's possible this ETN could wind up being taxed more like its fund rivals.

Tax issues aside, this ETN can be a useful portfolio diversifier for investors comfortable with the index's heavy energy weight and accompanying volatility. The note's transparent structure means investors don't have to assume the risk that the note will trail the index by more than its fees. An unfavorable tax ruling would put this ETN more on par with competing ETFs and active managers who have a chance at making up the fee differential, but it doesn't break the case for it entirely.

Address:	1 Churchill Place United Kingdom 877-764-7284
Web Address:	
Inception:	06-06-06 *
Advisor:	Barclays Bank

Management Fee:	0.75%		
Expense Projections:	3Yr: —	5Yr: —	10Yr: —
Income Distrib:	None		
Exchange:	NYSE		

Current Investment Style

Value Blnd Growth — Large Mid Small

Market Cap	%
Giant	—
Large	—
Mid	—
Small	—
Micro	—
Avg $mil:	—

Value Measures		Rel Category
Price/Earnings	—	—
Price/Book	—	—
Price/Sales	—	—
Price/Cash Flow	—	—
Dividend Yield %	—	—

Growth Measures	%	Rel Category
Long-Term Erngs	—	—
Book Value	—	—
Sales	—	—
Cash Flow	—	—
Historical Erngs	—	—

Profitability	%	Rel Category
Return on Equity	—	—
Return on Assets	—	—
Net Margin	—	—

Industry Weightings	% of Stocks	Rel Cat
Oil & Gas	—	—
Oil/Gas Products	—	—
Oil & Gas Srv	—	—
Pipelines	—	—
Utilities	—	—
Hard Commd	—	—
Soft Commd	—	—
Misc. Indstrl	—	—
Other	—	—

Composition

Graph is not avaliable.

Cash	—
Stocks	0.0
Bonds	0.0
Other	0.0
Foreign (% of Stock)	0.0

iShares COMEX Gold Trust IAU

Market Price	Mstar Category
$82.45	Specialty-Precious Metals

Morningstar Fair Value

Price/Fair Value Ratio	Coverage Rate %
—	—

Valuation

This fund invests directly in gold bullion. There's no way to assign an intrinsic value to gold, so we have no opinion as to the timeliness of this investment. We would simply caution that the stellar performance of the past few years is in no way indicative of future results.

Methodology

This fund invests in gold bullion stored in various locations throughout the world. Barclays Global Investors is the trust sponsor. The amount of gold backing each share will decrease gradually over time to cover fund expenses. The annual expense ratio is 0.40%. Consult your tax advisor before making an investment here. Under current tax laws, gains on this investment are taxed as ordinary income, at a maximum of 28%, regardless of an investors' holding period.

Morningstar Rating	Return	Risk	Yield	NAV	Avg Daily Vol. (k)	52 wk High/Low
—	—	—	—	$82.52	194	$86.88 - $60.54

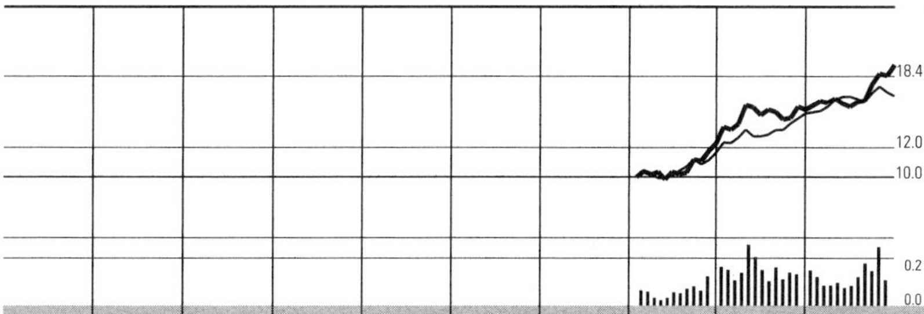

History

1998	1999	2000	2001	2002	2003	2004	2005	2006	2007	History
—	—	—	—	—	—	—	51.52	63.03	82.52	NAV $
—	—	—	—	—	—	—	51.73	63.25	82.45	Market Price $
—	—	—	—	—	—	—	25.14*	22.35	30.91	NAV Return%
—	—	—	—	—	—	—	25.11*	22.27	30.36	Market Price Return%
—	—	—	—	—	—	—	0.09	0.30	0.11	Avg Premium/Discount%
—	—	—	—	—	—	—	—	-3.99	19.74	NAV Rtrn% +/-MSCI EAFE
—	—	—	—	—	—	—	—	-0.85	6.94	NAV Rtrn% +/-Gold Price
—	—	—	—	—	—	—	—	100	1	NAV Return% Rank in Cat
—	—	—	—	—	—	—	—	0.00	0.00	Income Return %
—	—	—	—	—	—	—	—	22.35	30.91	Capital Return %
—	—	—	—	—	—	—	0.00	0.00	0.00	Income $
—	—	—	—	—	—	—	0.00	0.00	0.00	Capital Gains $
—	—	—	—	—	—	—	—	—	—	Expense Ratio %
—	—	—	—	—	—	—	—	—	—	Income Ratio %
—	—	—	—	—	—	—	—	—	—	Turnover Rate %
—	—	—	—	—	—	—	368	908	1,481	Net Assets $mil

Performance 12-31-07

Historic Quarterly NAV Returns

	1st Qtr	2nd Qtr	3rd Qtr	4th Qtr	Total
2003	—	—	—	—	—
2004	—	—	—	—	—
2005	—	1.56	7.49	10.16	—*
2006	12.40	5.34	-2.52	6.01	22.35
2007	4.27	-2.35	14.49	12.29	30.91

Trailing	NAV Return%	Market Return%	NAV Rtrn% +/-MSCI EAFE	%Rank Cat.(NAV)
3 Mo	12.29	11.98	14.04	13
6 Mo	28.56	28.01	28.17	25
1 Yr	30.91	30.36	19.74	1
3 Yr Avg	—	—	—	—
5 Yr Avg	—	—	—	—
10 Yr Avg	—	—	—	—

Tax Analysis	Tax-Adj Return%	Tax-Cost Ratio
3 Yr (estimated)	—	—
5 Yr (estimated)	—	—
10 Yr (estimated)	—	—

Rating and Risk

Time Period	Morningstar Rtn vs Cat	Morningstar Risk vs Cat	Morningstar Risk-Adj Rating
3 Yr	—	—	—
5 Yr	—	—	—
10 Yr	—	—	—

Other Measures	Standard Index S&P 500	Best Fit Index
Alpha	—	—
Beta	—	—
R-Squared	—	—
Standard Deviation	—	
Mean	—	
Sharpe Ratio	—	

Portfolio Analysis 08-31-07

Share change since 06-07 Total Stocks:0	Sector	Country	% Assets
⊕ Gold Bullion	—	—	100.00

Morningstar's Take by Haywood Kelly 12-31-07

IShares COMEX Gold Trust is a decent way to gain gold exposure.

There are good reasons and bad reasons to invest in gold. As a hedge against the loss in purchasing power of paper currencies, gold makes sense. Governments have historically been lousy stewards of the value of their currencies, and a gold position can help hedge a portfolio against such losses. Unfortunately, many investors are terrible at deciding when to invest in gold. When bullion prices are soaring, it's all too easy to jump on the gilded bandwagon. Many investors lost their shirts buying krugerrands back in the late 1970s, the last time gold prices soared.

As a way to invest in gold the right way, this fund does the job. Each share of the trust represents about one tenth of an ounce of gold bullion at current market prices. And thanks to the ETF format, the fund offers direct exposure to the value of gold in a more liquid and convenient format than burying gold bullion in your basement. Instead of buying guard dogs and a security system, you pay 0.40% in annual expenses.

Unlike most precious-metals funds, this one does not invest in the stocks of gold producers. That's an important distinction. Shares in a company--which are backed by the cash flows generated by a business--have an intrinsic value. Gold does not. It's worth what people will pay for it, and that's inherently unpredictable. The next 10 years could be great for gold prices or they could be horrible. No one knows. The historical returns of this fund are therefore completely irrelevant to making an investment decision.

Are investors using this fund intelligently? As gold has soared to $800 an ounce--the highest it's been since 1980--the fund's assets have ballooned to $1.4 billion from $400 million in 2005. This suggests performance chasing. The fund's trailing one-year return is a hefty 26%. Keep in mind that should gold prices falter, this fund's performance will tail off considerably.

Address:	45 Fremont Street United States 800-474-2737
Web Address:	www.ishares.com
Inception:	01-21-05*
Advisor:	Barclays Global Investors

Management Fee:	0.40%		
Expense Projections:	3Yr: —	5Yr: —	10Yr: —
Income Distrib:	Annually		
Exchange:	AMEX		

Current Investment Style

Value Blnd Growth — Large Mid Small

Market Cap	%
Giant	—
Large	—
Mid	—
Small	—
Micro	—
Avg $mil:	—

Value Measures		Rel Category
Price/Earnings	—	—
Price/Book	—	—
Price/Sales	—	—
Price/Cash Flow	—	—
Dividend Yield %	—	—

Growth Measures	%	Rel Category
Long-Term Erngs	—	—
Book Value	—	—
Sales	—	—
Cash Flow	—	—
Historical Erngs	—	—

Composition

Cash	0.0	Bonds	0.0
Stocks	0.0	Other	100.0
Foreign (% of Stock)			0.0

Sector Weightings	% of Stocks	Rel MSCI EAFE	3 Year High	3 Year Low
Info	0.00	0.00		
Software	—	0.00	—	—
Hardware	—	0.00	—	—
Media	—	0.00	—	—
Telecom	—	0.00	—	—
Service	0.00	0.00		
Health	—	0.00	—	—
Consumer	—	0.00	—	—
Business	—	0.00	—	—
Financial	—	0.00	—	—
Mfg	0.00	0.00		
Goods	—	0.00	—	—
Ind Mtrls	—	0.00	—	—
Energy	—	0.00	—	—
Utilities	—	0.00	—	—

Regional Exposure	% Stock		
UK/W. Europe	0	N. America	0
Japan	0	Latn America	0
Asia X Japan	0	Other	100

Country Exposure % Stock

iShares Silver Trust SLV

Market Price	Mstar Category
$146.97	Specialty-Precious Metals

Morningstar Fair Value

Price/Fair Value Ratio	Coverage Rate %
—	—

Valuation

This ETF primarily invests directly in silver--the physical commodity--rather than stocks. That explains why the fund's price/fair value ratio does not appear above.

Methodology

Unlike most ETFs, this fund does not track an index. Instead, the fund directly owns silver bullion, held at the London branch of J.P. Morgan Chase. Its price will reflect the market price of silver, less the expenses of the fund.

Morningstar Rating	Return	Risk	Yield	NAV	Avg Daily Vol. (k)	52 wk High/Low
—	—	—	—	$146.38	418	$155.90 - $115.10

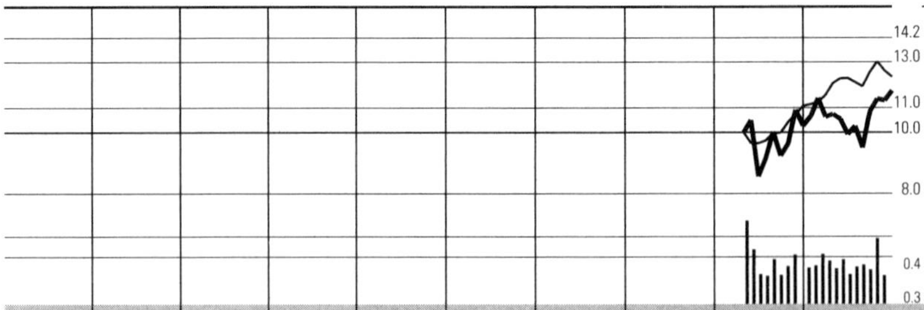

Growth of $10,000
— Investment Value of ETF
— Investment Value of Index MSCI EAFE

Trading Volume Millions

1998	1999	2000	2001	2002	2003	2004	2005	2006	2007	History
—	—	—	—	—	—	—	—	128.57	146.38	NAV $
—	—	—	—	—	—	—	—	128.64	146.97	Market Price $
—	—	—	—	—	—	—	—	11.43*	13.85	NAV Return%
—	—	—	—	—	—	—	—	11.69*	14.25	Market Price Return%
—	—	—	—	—	—	—	—	1.84	0.20	Avg Premium/Discount%
—	—	—	—	—	—	—	—	—	2.68	NAV Rtrn% +/-MSCI EAFE
—	—	—	—	—	—	—	—	—	-26.21	NAV Rtrn% +/-MSCI W Me&M
—	—	—	—	—	—	—	—	—	100	NAV Return% Rank in Cat
—	—	—	—	—	—	—	—	—	0.00	Income Return %
—	—	—	—	—	—	—	—	—	13.85	Capital Return %
—	—	—	—	—	—	—	—	0.00	0.00	Income $
—	—	—	—	—	—	—	—	0.00	0.00	Capital Gains $
—	—	—	—	—	—	—	—	—	—	Expense Ratio %
—	—	—	—	—	—	—	—	—	—	Income Ratio %
—	—	—	—	—	—	—	—	—	—	Turnover Rate %
—	—	—	—	—	—	—	—	1,562	2,488	Net Assets $mil

Performance 12-31-07

Historic Quarterly NAV Returns

	1st Qtr	2nd Qtr	3rd Qtr	4th Qtr	Total
2003	—	—	—	—	—
2004	—	—	—	—	—
2005	—	—	—	—	—
2006	—	—	7.82	11.55	—*
2007	3.36	-6.19	8.72	8.00	13.85

Trailing	NAV Return%	Market Return%	NAV Rtrn% +/-MSCI EAFE	%Rank Cat.(NAV)
3 Mo	8.00	7.63	9.75	50
6 Mo	17.41	19.00	17.02	100
1 Yr	13.85	14.25	2.68	100
3 Yr Avg	—	—	—	—
5 Yr Avg	—	—	—	—
10 Yr Avg	—	—	—	—

Tax Analysis	Tax-Adj Return%	Tax-Cost Ratio
3 Yr (estimated)	—	—
5 Yr (estimated)	—	—
10 Yr (estimated)	—	—

Rating and Risk

Time Period	Morningstar Rtn vs Cat	Morningstar Risk vs Cat	Morningstar Risk-Adj Rating
3 Yr	—	—	—
5 Yr	—	—	—
10 Yr	—	—	—

Other Measures	Standard Index S&P 500	Best Fit Index
Alpha	—	—
Beta	—	—
R-Squared	—	—
Standard Deviation	—	
Mean	—	
Sharpe Ratio	—	

Portfolio Analysis 08-31-07

Share change since 06-07 Total Stocks:0	Sector	Country	% Assets
⊕ Silver Bullion	—	—	100.00

Morningstar's Take by Sonya Morris 12-31-07

This ETF isn't a must-own.

With inflation fears mounting, investors are increasingly turning to precious metals like gold and silver. IShares Silver Trust provides a convenient way to gain exposure to silver: It invests directly in the actual metal, held in the London branch of J.P. Morgan Chase.

However, it should be noted that silver isn't a foolproof inflation hedge. Unlike gold, silver has industrial applications, which means it's more likely to fluctuate with economic ups and downs. If companies that use silver in their manufacturing process produce fewer products, silver prices--and this ETF--are likely to suffer. More importantly, over the long haul, precious metals haven't returned much more than inflation. Historically, stocks have offered better protection against inflation.

A better argument for investing in this ETF is for diversification purposes, since silver prices aren't correlated with stocks. But to benefit from those properties, you need a long-term view and a stomach for some volatility. Indeed, this is one turbulent ETF. Double-digit monthly swings are not unusual. To illustrate, in its second full month of trading, this ETF plunged 18.5% in June 2006. Two months later, it jumped 10%. All told, this ETF has been twice as volatile as the S&P 500 Index and more turbulent than diversified commodity funds.

This ETF's streaky nature should be enough to warn off anyone tempted to use it as a vehicle to speculate on unpredictable silver prices. For those undeterred, the trend in silver prices is at least worth considering, as the metal was recently flirting with 25-year highs. In other words, the downside risk is likely more pronounced than any upside potential.

Finally, this ETF is less tax efficient than many other investments. If you hold a stock longer than a year, capital gains are taxed at a maximum rate of 15%. However, silver is taxed as a collectible, subjecting gains to a 28% maximum tax rate.

We'd take a pass.

Address:	iShares Funds United States 800-474-2737
Web Address:	www.ishares.com
Inception:	04-21-06*
Advisor:	Barclays Global Investors

Management Fee:	0.50%		
Expense Projections:	3Yr: —	5Yr: —	10Yr: —
Income Distrib:	Annually		
Exchange:	AMEX		

Current Investment Style

Value Blnd Growth — Large / Mid / Small

Market Cap	%
Giant	—
Large	—
Mid	—
Small	—
Micro	—
Avg $mil:	—

Value Measures		Rel Category
Price/Earnings	—	—
Price/Book	—	—
Price/Sales	—	—
Price/Cash Flow	—	—
Dividend Yield %	—	—

Growth Measures	%	Rel Category
Long-Term Erngs	—	—
Book Value	—	—
Sales	—	—
Cash Flow	—	—
Historical Erngs	—	—

Composition

Cash	0.0	Bonds	0.0
Stocks	0.0	Other	100.0
Foreign (% of Stock)			0.0

Sector Weightings	% of Stocks	Rel MSCI EAFE	3 Year High	3 Year Low
Info	0.00	0.00		
Software	—	0.00	—	—
Hardware	—	0.00	—	—
Media	—	0.00	—	—
Telecom	—	0.00	—	—
Service	0.00	0.00		
Health	—	0.00	—	—
Consumer	—	0.00	—	—
Business	—	0.00	—	—
Financial	—	0.00	—	—
Mfg	0.00	0.00		
Goods	—	0.00	—	—
Ind Mtrls	—	0.00	—	—
Energy	—	0.00	—	—
Utilities	—	0.00	—	—

Regional Exposure			% Stock
UK/W. Europe	0	N. America	0
Japan	0	Latn America	0
Asia X Japan	0	Other	100

Country Exposure % Stock

Market Vectors Gld Miners GDX

Market Price	Mstar Category
$45.83	Specialty-Precious Metals

Morningstar Rating	Return	Risk	Yield	NAV	Avg Daily Vol. (k)	52 wk High/Low
—	—	—	1.6%	$46.24	2,019	$52.25 - $34.49

Morningstar Fair Value

Price/Fair Value Ratio	Coverage Rate %
1.01	84

Valuation

All of this fund's holdings are levered to essentially one factor: the price of gold. Thus, our forecasts hinge on our gold price projection, which could be off. As such, we'd need a large margin of discount to invest here, with a 27% discount to our fair value estimate doing the trick. The fund was recently trading at a 1% premium.

Methodology

This fund tracks the Amex Gold Miners Index, a market-cap-weighted benchmark of U.S.-listed gold miners with market caps of at least $100 million. Though the index purports to invest solely in firms that are involved "primarily in the mining of gold," the index includes a clutch of diversified miners, such as Pan American Silver. The index weights holdings by market cap. Though the index recently spanned more than 30 names, it's very top heavy, with roughly half of assets in the five biggest holdings. The vast majority of these firms are domiciled and mine abroad.

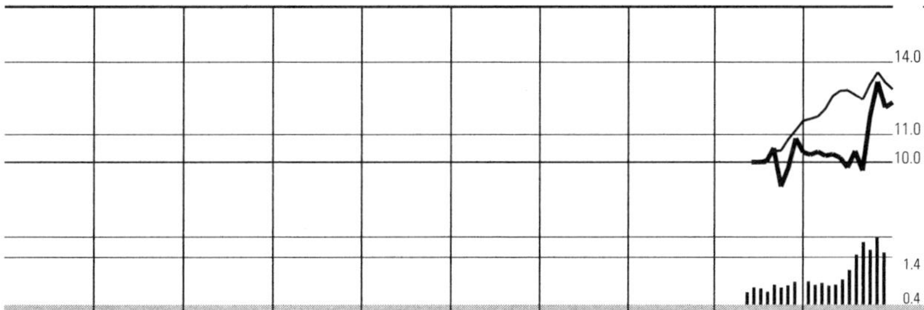

Growth of $10,000
— Investment Value of ETF
— Investment Value of Index MSCI EAFE

Trading Volume Millions

1998	1999	2000	2001	2002	2003	2004	2005	2006	2007	History
—	—	—	—	—	—	—	—	39.87	46.24	NAV $
—	—	—	—	—	—	—	—	39.91	45.83	Market Price $
—	—	—	—	—	—	—	—	11.13*	17.92	NAV Return%
—	—	—	—	—	—	—	—	—	16.76	Market Price Return%
—	—	—	—	—	—	—	—	0.13	0.07	Avg Premium/Discount%
—	—	—	—	—	—	—	—	—	6.75	NAV Rtrn% +/-MSCI EAFE
—	—	—	—	—	—	—	—	—	1.06	NAV Rtrn% +/-Amex Gold
—	—	—	—	—	—	—	—	—	75	NAV Return% Rank in Cat
—	—	—	—	—	—	—	—	—	1.87	Income Return %
—	—	—	—	—	—	—	—	—	16.05	Capital Return %
—	—	—	—	—	—	—	—	0.12	0.75	Income $
—	—	—	—	—	—	—	—	0.00	0.00	Capital Gains $
—	—	—	—	—	—	—	—	0.55	—	Expense Ratio %
—	—	—	—	—	—	—	—	0.69	—	Income Ratio %
—	—	—	—	—	—	—	—	4	—	Turnover Rate %
—	—	—	—	—	—	—	—	422	1,436	Net Assets $mil

Performance 12-31-07

Historic Quarterly NAV Returns

	1st Qtr	2nd Qtr	3rd Qtr	4th Qtr	Total
2003	—	—	—	—	—
2004	—	—	—	—	—
2005	—	—	—	—	—
2006	—	—	-7.81	12.11	—*
2007	-1.19	-3.87	19.02	4.30	17.92

Trailing	NAV Return%	Market Return%	NAV Rtrn% +/-MSCI EAFE	%Rank Cat.(NAV)
3 Mo	4.30	2.76	6.05	87
6 Mo	24.14	22.99	23.75	62
1 Yr	17.92	16.76	6.75	75
3 Yr Avg	—	—	—	—
5 Yr Avg	—	—	—	—
10 Yr Avg	—	—	—	—

Tax Analysis	Tax-Adj Return%	Tax-Cost Ratio
3 Yr (estimated)	—	—
5 Yr (estimated)	—	—
10 Yr (estimated)	—	—

Rating and Risk

Time Period	Morningstar Rtn vs Cat	Morningstar Risk vs Cat	Morningstar Risk-Adj Rating
3 Yr	—	—	—
5 Yr	—	—	—
10 Yr	—	—	—

Other Measures	Standard Index S&P 500	Best Fit Index
Alpha	—	—
Beta	—	—
R-Squared	—	—
Standard Deviation	—	
Mean	—	
Sharpe Ratio	—	

Portfolio Analysis 10-31-07

Share change since 08-07 Total Stocks:34	Sector	Country	% Assets
⊕ Barrick Gold Corporation	Ind Mtrls	Canada	14.59
⊕ Goldcorp, Inc.	Ind Mtrls	Canada	10.17
⊕ Newmont Mining	Ind Mtrls	United States	9.43
⊕ Yamana Gold, Inc.	Ind Mtrls	Canada	9.42
⊕ Kinross Gold Corporation	Ind Mtrls	Canada	5.99
⊕ Anglogold Ashanti, Ltd.	Ind Mtrls	South Africa	5.36
⊕ Gold Fields, Ltd. ADR	Ind Mtrls	South Africa	4.84
⊖ Buenaventura Mining Comp	Ind Mtrls	Peru	4.72
⊖ Agnico-Eagle Mines	Ind Mtrls	Canada	4.57
⊕ Harmony Gold Mining Comp	Ind Mtrls	South Africa	3.79
⊕ Silver Standard Resource	Ind Mtrls	Canada	2.63
⊕ Iamgold Corporation	Ind Mtrls	Canada	2.56
⊕ Pan American Silver Corp	Ind Mtrls	Canada	2.52
⊕ Randgold Resources, Ltd.	Ind Mtrls	U.K.	2.46
⊕ Eldorado Gold Corporatio	Ind Mtrls	Canada	2.37
⊕ Miramar Mining Corporati	Ind Mtrls	Canada	1.47
⊕ Seabridge Gold, Inc.	Ind Mtrls	Canada	1.32
⊕ Gammon Gold, Inc.	Ind Mtrls	Canada	1.21
⊕ Apex Silver Mines, Ltd.	Ind Mtrls	United States	1.20
⊕ Hecla Mining Company	Ind Mtrls	United States	1.15

Current Investment Style

Value Blnd Growth — Large / Mid / Small

Market Cap	%
Giant	15.6
Large	51.7
Mid	21.7
Small	10.8
Micro	0.2
Avg $mil: 7,687	

Value Measures		Rel Category
Price/Earnings	33.12	1.00
Price/Book	1.78	1.00
Price/Sales	3.26	1.00
Price/Cash Flow	15.79	1.00
Dividend Yield %	0.36	1.00

Growth Measures	%	Rel Category
Long-Term Erngs	10.82	1.00
Book Value	35.57	1.00
Sales	27.37	1.00
Cash Flow	32.80	1.00
Historical Erngs	56.49	1.00

Composition

Cash	0.0	Bonds	0.0
Stocks	100.0	Other	0.0

Foreign (% of Stock) 85.9

Sector Weightings	% of Stocks	Rel MSCI EAFE	3 Year High	3 Year Low
Info	0.00	0.00		
Software	0.00	0.00	—	—
Hardware	0.00	0.00	—	—
Media	0.00	0.00	—	—
Telecom	0.00	0.00	—	—
Service	0.00	0.00		
Health	0.00	0.00	—	—
Consumer	0.00	0.00	—	—
Business	0.00	0.00	—	—
Financial	0.00	0.00	—	—
Mfg	100.00	2.27		
Goods	0.00	0.00	—	—
Ind Mtrls	100.00	5.76	—	—
Energy	0.00	0.00	—	—
Utilities	0.00	0.00	—	—

Regional Exposure			% Stock
UK/W. Europe	2	N. America	79
Japan	0	Latn America	5
Asia X Japan	0	Other	14

Country Exposure			% Stock
Canada	65	Peru	5
United States	14	U.K.	2
South Africa	14		

Morningstar's Take by Jeffrey Ptak 12-31-07

Though Market Vectors Gold Miners isn't a good inflation hedge, we'd be buyers if its underlying holdings looked attractive. But considering the risks, we'd need a large margin of safety to do so.

This ETF differs from other gold ETFs in an important respect: Rather than own bullion directly, as funds like StreetTracks Gold and iShares Comex Gold do, it invests in the shares of firms that mine the precious metal. Of course, the fortunes of gold miners are inextricably linked to the trajectory of gold prices. In that sense, the fund offers a not-so-indirect play on gold.

Yet, this would hardly be our first choice for investors seeking a precious metals fund as an inflation hedge. An investment here doesn't afford perfect exposure to the metal. In fact, some firms, like Barrick Gold, hedge a portion of their precious metals reserves, meaning that the company's performance will not necessarily be in lockstep with gold itself. Also, because these firms have enormous fixed operating costs, their cash flows--which is what you're ultimately investing in when you buy this fund--can swing much more dramatically than metal prices. Coupled with currency gyrations (virtually all of the world's gold reserves can only be found abroad), that's made this fund's index roughly twice as volatile as the spot price of gold.

Of course, the shares of these miners can get cheap from time to time. In that respect, the fund can be quite useful. But we'd take the plunge only with a large margin of safety for a few reasons. First, not one of the 18 portfolio holdings that our analysts cover possesses even a semblance of a competitive advantage, reflecting the fact that these firms are captive to commodity prices. Second, because our forecasts depend, to a large extent, on our gold price projection, there's a chance that our fair value estimates could be wrong en masse. Thus, we'd need a 27% discount to our fair value estimate to invest here.

Address:	99 Park Avenue - 8th Floor United States 888-658-8287
Web Address:	vaneck.com/etf
Inception:	05-16-06*
Advisor:	Van Eck Associates Corp.

Management Fee:	0.50%		
Expense Projections:	3Yr:$204	5Yr: —	10Yr: —
Income Distrib:	Annually		
Exchange:	AMEX		

PowerShares DB Com Idx Fd DBC

Market Price	Mstar Category
$31.56	Specialty-Natural Res

Morningstar Fair Value

Price/Fair Value Ratio	Coverage Rate %
—	—

Morningstar Rating	Return	Risk	Yield	NAV	Avg Daily Vol. (k)	52 wk High/Low
—	—	—	—	$31.46	409	$32.68 - $22.61

Valuation

This ETF holds financial derivatives that track commodities, not stocks. That explains why the fund's price/fair value ratio does not appear above.

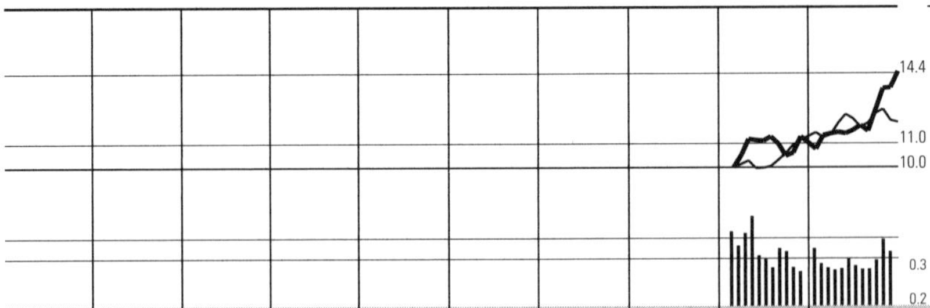

Growth of $10,000
- Investment Value of ETF
- Investment Value of Index S&P 500

Trading Volume Millions

Methodology

This ETF tracks the Deutsche Bank Commodity Index, which is composed of crude oil, heating oil, aluminum, gold, corn, and wheat. The index leaves out certain commodities, such as natural gas, livestock, copper, and nickel. Competing indexes have a broader basket of 20 or more commodities. Deutsche Bank argues that the six raw goods represented here are the most liquid, are correlated with other commodities in their respective sectors, and are thus the best representation. It primarily relies on futures contracts to gain exposure to commodities.

1998	1999	2000	2001	2002	2003	2004	2005	2006	2007	History
—	—	—	—	—	—	—	—	24.55	31.46	NAV $
—	—	—	—	—	—	—	—	24.58	31.56	Market Price $
—	—	—	—	—	—	—	—	18.05*	31.35	NAV Return%
—	—	—	—	—	—	—	—	18.25*	31.60	Market Price Return%
—	—	—	—	—	—	—	—	0.24	0.21	Avg Premium/Discount%
—	—	—	—	—	—	—	—	—	25.86	NAV Rtrn% +/-S&P 500
—	—	—	—	—	—	—	—	—	4.52	NAV Rtrn% +/-DB Commod
—	—	—	—	—	—	—	—	—	66	NAV Return% Rank in Cat
—	—	—	—	—	—	—	—	—	0.00	Income Return %
—	—	—	—	—	—	—	—	—	31.35	Capital Return %
—	—	—	—	—	—	—	—	0.61	0.00	Income $
—	—	—	—	—	—	—	—	0.00	0.76	Capital Gains $
—	—	—	—	—	—	—	—	—	—	Expense Ratio %
—	—	—	—	—	—	—	—	—	—	Income Ratio %
—	—	—	—	—	—	—	—	—	—	Turnover Rate %
—	—	—	—	—	—	—	—	712	1,535	Net Assets $mil

Performance 12-31-07

Historic Quarterly NAV Returns

	1st Qtr	2nd Qtr	3rd Qtr	4th Qtr	Total
2003	—	—	—	—	—
2004	—	—	—	—	—
2005	—	—	—	—	—
2006	—	5.76	-5.60	5.19	—*
2007	3.52	1.24	8.25	15.78	31.35

Trailing	NAV Return%	Market Return%	NAV Rtrn% +/-S&P 500	%Rank Cat.(NAV)
3 Mo	15.78	15.07	19.11	14
6 Mo	25.34	25.87	26.71	16
1 Yr	31.35	31.60	25.86	66
3 Yr Avg	—	—	—	—
5 Yr Avg	—	—	—	—
10 Yr Avg	—	—	—	—

Tax Analysis	Tax-Adj Return%	Tax-Cost Ratio
3 Yr (estimated)	—	—
5 Yr (estimated)	—	—
10 Yr (estimated)	—	—

Rating and Risk

Time Period	Morningstar Rtn vs Cat	Morningstar Risk vs Cat	Morningstar Risk-Adj Rating
3 Yr	—	—	—
5 Yr	—	—	—
10 Yr	—	—	—

Other Measures	Standard Index S&P 500	Best Fit Index
Alpha	—	—
Beta	—	—
R-Squared	—	—
Standard Deviation	—	
Mean	—	
Sharpe Ratio	—	

Portfolio Analysis 11-30-07

Share change since 10-07 Total Stocks:0	Sector	PE	Tot Ret%	% Assets
⊖ Crude Oil (Fut)	—	—	—	33.24
⊖ Heating Oil (Fut)	—	—	—	19.26
⊖ Wheat (Fut)	—	—	—	12.60
☼ Lme Alum (Fut)	—	—	—	12.32
☼ Corn (Fut)	—	—	—	11.15
⊖ Gold 100 (Fut)	—	—	—	9.35

Current Investment Style

Value Blnd Growth — Large Mid Small

Market Cap	%
Giant	—
Large	—
Mid	—
Small	—
Micro	—
Avg $mil:	—

Value Measures		Rel Category
Price/Earnings	—	—
Price/Book	—	—
Price/Sales	—	—
Price/Cash Flow	—	—
Dividend Yield %	—	—

Growth Measures	%	Rel Category
Long-Term Erngs	—	—
Book Value	—	—
Sales	—	—
Cash Flow	—	—
Historical Erngs	—	—

Profitability	%	Rel Category
Return on Equity	—	—
Return on Assets	—	—
Net Margin	—	—

Industry Weightings	% of Stocks	Rel Cat
Oil & Gas	—	—
Oil/Gas Products	—	—
Oil & Gas Srv	—	—
Pipelines	—	—
Utilities	—	—
Hard Commd	—	—
Soft Commd	—	—
Misc. Indstrl	—	—
Other	—	—

Composition

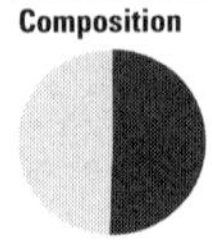

Cash	50.5
Stocks	0.0
Bonds	0.0
Other	49.5
Foreign (% of Stock)	0.0

Morningstar's Take by Karen Dolan 12-31-07

PowerShares DB Commodity Index Fund is different, and it leaves a few things to be desired.

Most commodity funds track either the S&P Goldman Sachs Commodity Index or the Dow Jones AIG Commodity Index. This exchange-traded fund follows a less mainstream bogy, the Deutsche Bank Liquid Commodity Index, which is composed of crude oil, heating oil, aluminum, corn, gold, and wheat. We think it leaves some important ones out. Natural gas, livestock, and copper are excluded, for example. The fund's narrow selection chips away at its appeal for investors seeking a broad basket of raw goods.

None of the commodity funds (this one included) hold the actual physical commodities. They instead use derivatives such as structured notes and futures to track their price movements. One key difference between this fund and its competitors is that it tries to take advantage of the price differences between futures with varying maturities. All else held constant, when the price of a longer-dated futures contract is above the current price of the commodity, the higher futures price will converge to the lower current price as its maturity nears. That phenomenon is known as a negative roll yield or contango. The opposite holds true if the longer-dated futures price is lower than the current price, which results in a positive roll yield or backwardation. This fund tracks an enhanced version of its index that tries to minimize negative roll yields and maximize positive roll yields. It's unclear whether it will add additional value doing so. The enhanced index has been around only since May 2006, so we don't have much of a track record to rely on.

Unfortunately, this fund doesn't set itself apart in one important way. Like most of its commodity ETF rivals, it levies a 0.75% management fee, which seems high for simply tracking an index. In short, this ETF, and its newfangled benchmark, still have much to prove.

Address:	301 West Roosevelt Road Wheaton, IL 60187 877-369-4617
Web Address:	www.dbfunds.db.com
Inception:	02-03-06 *
Advisor:	DB Commodity Services, LLC

Management Fee:	0.75%
Expense Projections:	3Yr: — 5Yr: — 10Yr: —
Income Distrib:	None
Exchange:	AMEX

streetTRACKS Gold Shares GLD

Market Price	Mstar Category
$82.46	Specialty-Precious Metals

Morningstar Fair Value

Price/Fair Value Ratio	Coverage Rate %
—	—

Valuation

This fund invests directly in gold bullion. There's no way to assign an intrinsic value to gold, so we have no opinion as to the timeliness of this investment. We would simply caution that the stellar performance of the past few years is in no way indicative of future results.

Methodology

This fund issues shares equal in value to roughly one tenth of an ounce of gold. The fund's expenses are 0.40% per year, and the fund sells gold held by the trust on an as-needed basis to pay the trust's expenses. As a result, the amount of gold represented by each share will be reduced over time. The fund is sponsored by the World Gold Council and marketed by State Street Global Advisors. Consult your tax advisor before making an investment here. Under current tax laws, gains on this investment are taxed as ordinary income, at a maximum of 28%, regardless of an investors' holding period.

Morningstar Rating	Return	Risk	Yield	NAV	Avg Daily Vol. (k)	52 wk High/Low
★★★	Low	Low	—	$79.07	7,561	$86.78 - $60.48

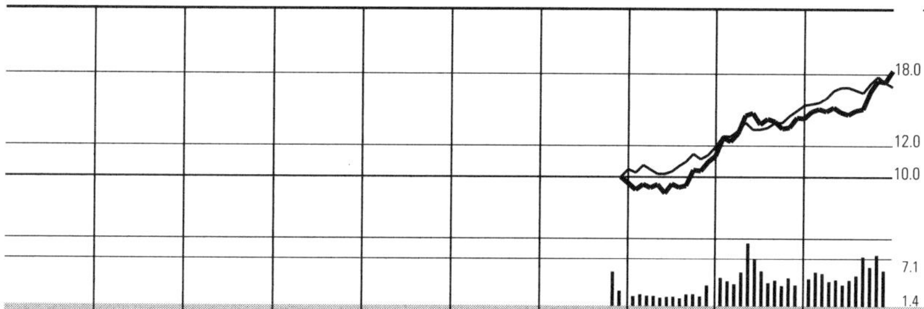

Growth of $10,000
- Investment Value of ETF
- Investment Value of Index MSCI EAFE

Trading Volume Millions

History

1998	1999	2000	2001	2002	2003	2004	2005	2006	2007	History
—	—	—	—	—	—	43.78	51.07	63.04	79.07	NAV $
—	—	—	—	—	—	43.80	51.58	62.90	82.46	Market Price $
—	—	—	—	—	—	20.52*	16.65	23.44	25.43	NAV Return%
—	—	—	—	—	—	22.00*	17.76	21.95	31.10	Market Price Return%
—	—	—	—	—	—	-0.21	-0.04	0.52	0.01	Avg Premium/Discount%
—	—	—	—	—	—	—	3.11	-2.90	14.26	NAV Rtrn% +/-MSCI EAFE
—	—	—	—	—	—	—	-1.12	0.24	1.46	NAV Rtrn% +/-Gold Price
—	—	—	—	—	—	—	100	50	25	NAV Return% Rank in Cat
—	—	—	—	—	—	—	0.00	0.00	0.00	Income Return %
—	—	—	—	—	—	—	16.65	23.44	25.43	Capital Return %
—	—	—	—	—	—	0.00	0.00	0.00	0.00	Income $
—	—	—	—	—	—	0.00	0.00	0.00	0.00	Capital Gains $
—	—	—	—	—	—	—	—	—	—	Expense Ratio %
—	—	—	—	—	—	—	—	—	—	Income Ratio %
—	—	—	—	—	—	—	—	—	—	Turnover Rate %
—	—	—	—	—	—	1,335	4,341	9,261	16,826	Net Assets $mil

Performance 12-31-07

Historic Quarterly NAV Returns

	1st Qtr	2nd Qtr	3rd Qtr	4th Qtr	Total
2003	—	—	—	—	—
2004	—	—	—	—	—*
2005	-2.49	2.13	8.17	8.29	16.65
2006	13.35	5.30	-2.42	5.98	23.44
2007	3.99	-1.80	14.10	12.48	25.43

Trailing	NAV Return%	Market Return%	NAV Rtrn% +/-MSCI EAFE	%Rank Cat.(NAV)
3 Mo	7.64	12.18	9.39	62
6 Mo	22.82	28.30	22.43	75
1 Yr	25.43	31.10	14.26	25
3 Yr Avg	21.78	23.48	4.95	100
5 Yr Avg	—	—	—	—
10 Yr Avg	—	—	—	—

Tax Analysis	Tax-Adj Return%	Tax-Cost Ratio
3 Yr (estimated)	21.78	0.00
5 Yr (estimated)	—	—
10 Yr (estimated)	—	—

Rating and Risk

Time Period	Morningstar Rtn vs Cat	Morningstar Risk vs Cat	Morningstar Risk-Adj Rating
3 Yr	Low	Low	★★★
5 Yr	—	—	—
10 Yr	—	—	—

Other Measures	Standard Index S&P 500	Best Fit Index Amex Gold
Alpha	8.4	10.5
Beta	0.82	0.37
R-Squared	27	56
Standard Deviation	15.19	
Mean	21.78	
Sharpe Ratio	1.20	

Portfolio Analysis 09-30-07

Share change since 06-07 Total Stocks:0	Sector	Country	% Assets
☼ Gold Bullion	Ind Mtrls	Australia	100.00

Morningstar's Take by Haywood Kelly 12-31-07

StreetTRACKS Gold Trust is a decent way to gain gold exposure.

There are good reasons and bad reasons to invest in gold. As a hedge against the loss in purchasing power of paper currencies, gold makes sense. Governments have historically been lousy stewards of the value of their currencies, and a gold position can help hedge a portfolio against such losses. Unfortunately, many investors are horrible at deciding when to invest in gold. When bullion prices are soaring, it's all too easy to jump on the gilded bandwagon. Many investors lost their shirts buying Krugerrands back in the late 1970s, the last time gold prices soared.

As a way to invest in gold the right way, this fund does the job. Each share represents about one tenth of an ounce of bullion at current market prices. And thanks to the ETF format, the fund offers direct exposure to the value of gold in a more liquid and convenient package than burying gold in your basement. Instead of buying guard dogs and a security system, you pay 0.40% per year.

Unlike most precious-metals funds, this one does not invest in the stocks of gold producers. That's an important distinction. Shares in a company--which are backed by the cash flows generated by a business--have an intrinsic value. Gold does not. It's worth what people will pay for it, and that's inherently unpredictable. The next 10 years could be great for gold prices or they could be horrible. No one knows. The historical returns of this fund are therefore completely irrelevant to making an investment decision.

Are investors using this fund intelligently? As gold has gone from $400 to $800 an ounce--the highest it's been since 1980--over the past four years, the fund's assets have ballooned to $15 billion from $1.3 billion. This suggest performance-chasing. The fund's trailing three-year return is a hefty 22% annualized. Keep in mind that should gold prices falter, this fund's performance will tail off.

Address:	444 Madison Ave, 3rd Fl United States 866-320-4053
Web Address:	www.streettracksgoldshares.com
Inception:	11-18-04*
Advisor:	Bank of New York

Management Fee:	0.40%
Expense Projections:	3Yr: — 5Yr: — 10Yr: —
Income Distrib:	None
Exchange:	NYSE

Current Investment Style

Value Blnd Growth — Large Mid Small

Market Cap	%
Giant	—
Large	—
Mid	—
Small	—
Micro	—
Avg $mil: —	

Value Measures		Rel Category
Price/Earnings	—	—
Price/Book	—	—
Price/Sales	—	—
Price/Cash Flow	—	—
Dividend Yield %	—	—

Growth Measures	%	Rel Category
Long-Term Erngs	—	—
Book Value	—	—
Sales	—	—
Cash Flow	—	—
Historical Erngs	—	—

Composition

Cash	0.0	Bonds	0.0
Stocks	0.0	Other	100.0
Foreign (% of Stock)			0.0

Sector Weightings	% of Stocks	Rel MSCI EAFE	3 Year High	3 Year Low
Info	0.00	0.00		
Software	—	0.00	—	—
Hardware	—	0.00	—	—
Media	—	0.00	—	—
Telecom	—	0.00	—	—
Service	0.00	0.00		
Health	—	0.00	—	—
Consumer	—	0.00	—	—
Business	—	0.00	—	—
Financial	—	0.00	—	—
Mfg	0.00	0.00		
Goods	—	0.00	—	—
Ind Mtrls	—	0.00	—	—
Energy	—	0.00	—	—
Utilities	—	0.00	—	—

Regional Exposure % Stock

UK/W. Europe	0	N. America	0
Japan	0	Latn America	0
Asia X Japan	0	Other	100

Country Exposure % Stock

Tables and Charts

This section compiles performance portfolio, cost, and other data on all U.S.-listed exchange-traded funds.

Performance Summary
190 U.S.-Listed ETFs
214 Indexes
217 Best & Worst Performing ETFs

Morningstar Research
218 Cheapest & Dearest Stock ETFs
219 Highest & Lowest Quality Stock ETFs
220 Least & Most Risky Stock ETFs

Size & Popularity Stats
221 Largest & Most Heavily-Traded ETFs
222 Most & Least Popular ETFs

Yield & Cost Data
223 Highest-Yielding ETFs
224 ETFs with Lowest Annual Expenses

Portfolio & Volatility Data
225 Valuation Measures
226 Growth Measures
227 Profitability Measures
228 Least & Most Volatile

Performance Summary

U.S.-Listed ETFs

Page	Name	Cat	Style Box	NAV ($)	Market Price ($)	2007 Avg. Prem. Discount%	NAV Return% through 12-31-07 1Yr	NAV Return% Annualized 3Yr	NAV Return% Annualized 5Yr	Mkt Price Rtn% through 12-31-07 1Yr	Mkt Price Rtn% Annualized 3Yr	Mkt Price Rtn% Annualized 5Yr	Morningstar Rating	Risk Statistics Standard Deviation	Risk Statistics Sharpe Ratio
—	✶ Adelante Shares RE Classc ACK	SR		21.20	21.25	3.47	—	—	—	—	—	—	—	—	—
—	✶ Adelante Shares RE Compst ACB	SR		20.48	20.40	0.26	—	—	—	—	—	—	—	—	—
—	✶ Adelante Shares RE Growth AGV	SR		21.10	21.63	4.58	—	—	—	—	—	—	—	—	—
—	✶ Adelante Shares RE Kings AKB	SR		21.64	21.34	–0.51	—	—	—	—	—	—	—	—	—
—	✶ Adelante Shares RE Shelt AQS	SR		19.93	20.31	0.31	—	—	—	—	—	—	—	—	—
—	✶ Adelante Shares RE Value AVU	SR		20.32	20.28	3.18	—	—	—	—	—	—	—	—	—
—	✶ Adelante Shares RE Yld Pl ATY	SR		21.42	21.81	0.71	—	—	—	—	—	—	—	—	—
—	✶ Ameristock/Ryan 1 Yr Trs GKA	GS		25.13	25.59	0.62	—	—	—	—	—	—	—	—	—
—	✶ Ameristock/Ryan 10 Yr Trs GKD	GL		25.83	25.78	–0.18	—	—	—	—	—	—	—	—	—
—	✶ Ameristock/Ryan 2 Yr Trs GKB	GS		25.30	25.27	0.09	—	—	—	—	—	—	—	—	—
—	✶ Ameristock/Ryan 20 Yr Trs GKE	GL		26.20	25.88	–0.24	—	—	—	—	—	—	—	—	—
—	✶ Ameristock/Ryan 5 Yr Trs GKC	GI		25.41	25.39	–0.78	—	—	—	—	—	—	—	—	—
—	B2B Internet HOLDRs BHH	ST		—	2.36	—	—	—	—	3.96	–6.42	–1.77	—	—	—
88	Biotech HOLDRs BBH	SH		161.76	161.76	—	–11.95	1.89	13.85	–11.95	1.89	13.85	—	—	—
—	BLDRS Asia 50 ADR Index ADRA	DP		36.01	34.22	–0.36	10.93	17.07	19.84	5.24	15.05	18.59	★	13.48	0.92
—	BLDRS Dev Mkts 100 ADR ADRD	FB		33.15	31.53	–0.35	15.59	16.59	20.15	9.73	14.65	19.09	★★★	9.81	1.19
138	BLDRS Emerg Mkts 50 ADR ADRE	EM		55.02	55.04	0.02	43.78	40.74	37.66	43.89	40.72	37.46	★★★★	20.46	1.58
—	BLDRS Europe 100 ADR ADRU	ES		34.47	32.23	–0.42	18.91	17.86	21.35	11.07	15.20	19.89	★★★	9.89	1.29
—	Broadband HOLDRs BDH	ST		—	13.96	—	—	—	—	–11.20	–5.80	13.08	—	—	—
—	✶ Claymore S&P Global Water CGW	SN		25.41	25.88	0.84	—	—	—	—	—	—	—	—	—
—	✶ Claymore/BDD High Inc LVL	LB		20.82	19.92	–0.81	—	—	—	—	—	—	—	—	—
—	✶ Claymore/BIR Ldrs Mid Val BMV	MV		23.97	23.50	–0.44	—	—	—	—	—	—	—	—	—
—	✶ Claymore/BIR Ldrs Sm Core BES	SB		23.28	22.95	–0.15	—	—	—	—	—	—	—	—	—
—	✶ Claymore/BIR Leaders 50 BST	LB		25.07	24.60	–0.08	—	—	—	—	—	—	—	—	—
—	Claymore/BNY BRIC EEB	EM		52.90	53.39	0.12	67.75	—	—	67.30	—	—	—	—	—
—	✶ Claymore/Clear Glb Exch EXB	SF		26.83	26.90	0.26	—	—	—	—	—	—	—	—	—
—	✶ Claymore/Clear Glb Timber CUT	SN		24.53	24.25	–0.01	—	—	—	—	—	—	—	—	—
—	✶ Claymore/Clear Glb Vacc JNR	SH		24.81	23.26	–0.55	—	—	—	—	—	—	—	—	—
—	✶ Claymore/Clear Mid-Cap Gr MCG	MG		24.95	25.26	0.39	—	—	—	—	—	—	—	—	—
—	Claymore/Clear Spin-Off CSD	MB		27.25	26.84	–0.14	9.48	—	—	7.79	—	—	—	—	—
—	✶ Claymore/Great Comp Lg Gr XGC	LG		24.47	24.05	–0.19	—	—	—	—	—	—	—	—	—
—	✶ Claymore/IndexIQ Sm Value SCV	SV		21.33	20.55	0.18	—	—	—	—	—	—	—	—	—
—	✶ Claymore/KLD Lg Core KSF	LB		24.51	24.15	–0.95	—	—	—	—	—	—	—	—	—
—	Claymore/LGA Green GRN	LB		26.03	25.21	–0.26	6.65	—	—	2.68	—	—	—	—	—
—	✶ Claymore/Morningstar Info MZN	LB		25.58	26.04	–1.07	—	—	—	—	—	—	—	—	—
—	✶ Claymore/Morningstar Mfg MZG	LB		26.83	27.38	0.06	—	—	—	—	—	—	—	—	—
—	✶ Claymore/Morningstar Svc MZO	LB		24.79	23.17	–1.71	—	—	—	—	—	—	—	—	—
—	✶ Claymore/Ocean Tomo Grwth OTR	LG		28.44	28.37	–0.19	—	—	—	—	—	—	—	—	—
—	Claymore/Ocean Tomo Paten OTP	LB		29.01	28.45	–0.22	17.42	—	—	14.79	—	—	—	—	—
—	✶ Claymore/Robb Report Glbl ROB	WS		24.72	24.02	–0.08	—	—	—	—	—	—	—	—	—
—	✶ Claymore/Robeco BP LgVal CLV	LV		23.75	23.41	0.33	—	—	—	—	—	—	—	—	—
—	✶ Claymore/Robeco Dev Intl EEN	FB		26.23	24.40	–0.74	—	—	—	—	—	—	—	—	—
—	✶ Claymore/Robeco Dev World EEW	WS		26.69	25.30	0.01	—	—	—	—	—	—	—	—	—
—	Claymore/Sabrient Defend DEF	LB		26.58	25.90	–0.24	7.62	—	—	4.84	—	—	—	—	—
—	Claymore/Sabrient Insider NFO	MB		29.76	29.27	–0.24	10.85	—	—	8.94	—	—	—	—	—
—	Claymore/Sabrient Stealth STH	SB		23.50	22.93	–0.35	–13.98	—	—	–16.19	—	—	—	—	—
—	✶ Claymore/SWM Cdn Enrg ENY	SN		24.79	25.72	0.72	—	—	—	—	—	—	—	—	—
—	✶ Claymore/Zacks Country Ro CRO	FB		26.07	24.95	–0.55	—	—	—	—	—	—	—	—	—
—	✶ Claymore/Zacks Div Rotat IRO	LB		23.67	22.65	–1.52	—	—	—	—	—	—	—	—	—
—	✶ Claymore/Zacks Gr & Inc CZG	LB		25.27	24.50	–0.92	—	—	—	—	—	—	—	—	—
—	✶ Claymore/Zacks Intl Yld HGI	FB		23.88	22.22	–1.50	—	—	—	—	—	—	—	—	—
—	✶ Claymore/Zacks Mid Core CZA	MB		25.93	25.84	0.03	—	—	—	—	—	—	—	—	—
—	Claymore/Zacks Sector Rot XRO	LB		31.80	32.28	0.20	15.40	—	—	17.09	—	—	—	—	—
—	Claymore/Zacks Yield Hog CVY	LB		24.47	23.27	–0.46	–2.61	—	—	–7.35	—	—	—	—	—
89	Consumer Discr SPDR XLY	LB		32.82	32.70	–0.02	–13.38	–1.40	8.20	–13.67	–1.52	8.14	★	11.76	–0.4

✶ New in 2007

Performance Summary

U.S.-Listed ETFs

Portfolio				Morningstar Valuation		Costs		Trading Information	
Top 3 Sectors	Avg. Mkt. Cap. ($mil)	P/E Ratio	P/B Ratio	Price/ Fair Value	Coverage Rate %	Expense Ratio %	Tax-Cost Ratio	52-week High/Low	Avg. Daily Vol.
	4,243	30.51	2.11	0.89	91.72	0.58	—	26.55–19.64	7,715
	3,456	28.53	2.15	0.92	84.27	0.58	—	26.41–19.00	300
	2,527	27.24	1.67	0.88	75.25	0.58	—	26.31–19.78	442
	4,104	30.60	2.36	0.94	91.49	0.58	—	26.66–20.05	1,219
	2,390	29.32	2.02	0.89	91.42	0.58	—	26.13–18.46	9,180
	1,425	24.87	1.87	0.89	65.23	0.58	—	26.25–18.95	1,562
	3,112	26.42	2.07	0.93	75.21	0.58	—	26.39–19.90	1,712
—	—	—	—	—	—	0.15	—	25.63–25.00	595
—	—	—	—	—	—	0.15	—	27.68–24.91	914
—	—	—	—	—	—	0.15	—	26.19–25.00	1,166
—	—	—	—	—	—	0.15	—	28.34–24.90	1,795
—	—	—	—	—	—	0.15	—	27.20–24.96	1,100
	592	—	2.30	1.00	—	—	—	—	22,663
	36,348	11.30	4.47	0.85	100.00	—	—	—	211,279
	66,790	—	—	0.98	88.11	0.30	0.53	38.60–31.01	25,025
	92,532	12.76	1.87	0.92	95.74	0.30	0.87	34.24–28.10	32,298
	65,947	—	—	1.03	86.59	0.30	0.67	60.00–35.87	342,899
	91,545	12.90	1.90	0.92	97.62	0.30	0.94	35.64–28.35	14,186
	30,939	16.17	2.83	0.80	92.25	—	—	—	61,814
	6,768	18.75	2.55	0.97	24.16	0.65	—	26.30–23.02	101,332
	1,598	12.32	1.46	0.87	64.23	0.60	—	25.50–19.04	6,113
	5,832	12.88	1.63	0.92	90.29	0.60	—	26.58–22.07	2,730
	1,295	12.39	1.67	0.97	46.31	0.60	—	27.21–21.66	2,772
	31,262	10.91	2.20	0.88	98.53	0.60	—	27.10–23.32	1,745
	58,514	—	—	1.12	81.56	0.60	—	57.82–28.24	674,553
	19,909	16.66	2.05	1.01	62.87	0.65	—	28.29–21.89	47,649
	3,643	18.67	1.33	1.03	43.29	0.75	—	24.98–22.59	24,495
	14,903	15.57	2.67	0.95	68.50	0.65	—	25.70–23.20	586
	4,475	18.51	3.13	1.02	79.64	0.60	—	26.49–22.66	2,060
	4,952	14.34	1.12	0.84	85.48	0.60	—	31.52–24.90	12,710
	33,984	12.57	2.21	0.87	100.00	0.60	—	27.03–22.67	3,192
	639	14.52	1.33	0.96	40.78	0.60	—	25.54–19.06	2,243
	33,853	15.03	2.43	0.89	97.68	0.50	—	25.86–22.87	730
	35,041	15.41	2.59	0.90	98.84	0.60	—	27.52–24.24	1,596
	49,585	17.68	2.81	0.93	97.30	0.49	—	27.74–23.42	4,713
	38,772	14.37	2.64	0.96	94.23	0.49	—	27.69–24.79	10,166
	25,663	13.34	2.02	0.84	95.73	0.49	—	26.70–22.39	257
	65,381	18.61	6.61	1.01	98.67	0.60	—	29.95–25.00	1,416
	69,809	15.22	2.89	0.91	99.20	0.60	—	30.10–24.54	1,676
	22,185	15.62	2.39	0.98	34.28	0.70	—	26.63–22.26	4,634
	54,641	11.25	1.81	0.87	99.26	0.89	—	25.94–22.42	3,152
	31,621	13.09	1.80	1.00	3.03	0.65	—	27.60–23.40	2,466
	35,954	13.83	2.04	0.96	52.36	0.65	—	27.69–23.56	1,854
	13,541	14.35	2.26	0.96	97.55	0.60	—	28.12–24.89	8,531
	4,019	13.78	1.90	0.94	72.45	0.60	—	31.89–26.66	9,512
	447	10.14	1.39	0.93	10.88	0.60	—	29.76–21.80	12,249
	7,395	17.45	1.88	0.96	75.80	0.65	—	29.35–22.04	14,574
	39,294	13.89	1.94	1.00	0.64	0.65	—	27.31–21.84	5,240
	3,633	11.19	1.49	0.81	69.14	0.50	—	25.53–21.15	2,125
	6,208	15.82	2.03	0.96	86.80	0.60	—	27.31–23.22	537
	16,810	12.43	1.79	0.97	28.24	0.65	—	25.53–21.44	2,356
	5,028	14.02	1.90	0.94	86.00	0.60	—	27.83–24.36	1,524
	17,058	16.59	3.26	1.06	96.29	0.60	—	33.02–27.23	63,553
	6,680	11.75	1.33	0.81	76.63	0.60	—	28.54–22.42	25,155
	21,777	14.23	2.16	0.80	98.34	0.24	0.34	40.39–30.36	3,267,554

Performance Summary

U.S.-Listed ETFs

Page	Name	Cat	Style Box	NAV ($)	Market Price ($)	2007 Avg. Prem. Discount %	NAV Return% through 12-31-07 1Yr	NAV Return% Annualized 3Yr	NAV Return% Annualized 5Yr	Mkt Price Rtn% through 12-31-07 1Yr	Mkt Price Rtn% Annualized 3Yr	Mkt Price Rtn% Annualized 5Yr	Morningstar Rating	Risk Statistics Standard Deviation	Risk Statistics Sharpe Ratio
90	Consumer Staple SPDR XLP	LB		28.76	28.80	0.00	12.47	9.81	9.63	12.68	9.88	9.68	★★★	5.84	0.91
—	CurrencyShares Aus Dollar FXA	IB	—	88.14	88.03	0.18	18.00	—	—	17.58	—	—	—	—	—
—	CurrencyShares BP Strlng FXB	IB	—	199.27	199.62	0.23	6.68	—	—	6.94	—	—	—	—	—
—	CurrencyShares Can Dollar FXC	IB	—	101.50	100.95	0.18	22.53	—	—	22.05	—	—	—	—	—
180	CurrencyShares Euro Trust FXE	IB	—	146.45	146.40	0.05	14.57	—	—	14.54	—	—	—	—	—
—	★ CurrencyShares Japan Yen FXY	IB	—	89.39	89.60	0.09	—	—	—	—	—	—	—	—	—
—	CurrencyShares Mex Peso FXM	IB	—	92.01	91.98	0.16	5.55	—	—	5.57	—	—	—	—	—
—	CurrencyShares Swe Krona FXS	IB	—	155.32	155.04	0.14	8.89	—	—	8.93	—	—	—	—	—
—	CurrencyShares Swi Franc FXF	IB	—	88.36	88.38	0.09	9.19	—	—	9.14	—	—	—	—	—
30	DIAMONDS Trust DIA	LV		132.50	132.55	0.07	8.71	9.77	12.22	8.79	9.85	12.23	★★★	8.12	0.67
—	DJ Euro STOXX 50 ETF FEZ	ES		63.22	62.66	–0.13	21.78	20.08	23.70	20.37	19.85	23.61	★★★	10.22	1.44
—	DJ STOXX 50 ETF FEU	ES		52.85	52.91	0.10	13.63	15.66	19.30	13.45	15.78	19.98	★★	9.38	1.15
91	DJ Wilshire REIT ETF RWR	SR		69.37	69.30	–0.07	–18.12	7.87	17.70	–18.20	7.84	17.62	★★★	17.50	0.28
—	★ ELEMENTS DOD HiYld ETN DOD	LV	—	9.78	10.19	2.05	—	—	—	—	—	—	—	—	—
—	★ ELEMENTS Mstar Wide Moat WMW	LB		9.19	9.16	–0.51	—	—	—	—	—	—	—	—	—
—	★ ELEMENTS Rogers Agric ETN RJA	SN	—	10.86	10.93	0.58	—	—	—	—	—	—	—	—	—
—	★ ELEMENTS Rogers Enrgy ETN RJN	SN	—	11.22	11.21	–0.11	—	—	—	—	—	—	—	—	—
—	★ ELEMENTS Rogers Metal ETN RJZ	SN	—	9.33	9.36	0.26	—	—	—	—	—	—	—	—	—
—	★ ELEMENTS Rogers TR ETN RJI	SN	—	10.70	10.77	0.48	—	—	—	—	—	—	—	—	—
—	★ ELEMENTS SPECTRUM Lg ETN EEH	LB	—	10.55	10.55	–0.20	—	—	—	—	—	—	—	—	—
92	Energy SPDR XLE	SN		79.22	79.35	0.01	36.36	31.30	30.72	36.88	31.34	30.73	★★★	20.05	1.25
—	Europe 2001 HOLDRs EKH	ES		—	88.68	—	—	—	—	6.33	11.69	16.23	—	—	—
—	Fidelity Nasdaq Comp Trac ONEQ	LG		103.95	103.91	–0.06	10.08	7.32	—	9.94	7.30	—	★★	12.51	0.28
93	Financial SPDR XLF	SF		29.10	28.93	–0.09	–18.79	0.84	8.17	–19.19	0.67	8.10	★★	11.11	–0.3
—	First Tr NASDAQ-100 Eq Id QQEW	LB		22.08	22.09	–0.02	9.73	—	—	9.63	—	—	—	—	—
—	First Tr NASDAQ100 Tech QTEC	ST		21.50	21.51	0.03	7.66	—	—	7.55	—	—	—	—	—
—	First Trust AMEX Bio Indx FBT	SH		24.41	24.37	0.05	3.65	—	—	3.53	—	—	—	—	—
—	★ First Trust ConDsc AlpDEX FXD	MG		16.99	16.95	–0.90	—	—	—	—	—	—	—	—	—
—	★ First Trust ConStp AlpDEX FXG	MV		19.08	19.24	0.12	—	—	—	—	—	—	—	—	—
—	First Trust DB Strat Val FDV	LV		24.12	24.17	0.01	10.25	—	—	10.33	—	—	—	—	—
—	First Trust DJ Intrnt Idx FDN	ST		25.09	25.13	0.02	11.18	—	—	11.30	—	—	—	—	—
—	First Trust DJ S MicroCap FDM	SB		22.35	22.06	–0.06	–6.04	—	—	–7.36	—	—	—	—	—
—	★ First Trust DJ STOXX 30 FDD	ES		29.69	30.25	1.03	—	—	—	—	—	—	—	—	—
—	★ First Trust Energy AlpDEX FXN	SN		23.02	22.99	0.02	—	—	—	—	—	—	—	—	—
—	★ First Trust Fincls AlpDEX FXO	SF		15.76	15.79	–0.09	—	—	—	—	—	—	—	—	—
—	★ First Trust FTSE EPRA/NAR FFR	SR		46.80	46.90	0.00	—	—	—	—	—	—	—	—	—
—	★ First Trust HlthCr AlpDEX FXH	SH		20.19	20.27	0.15	—	—	—	—	—	—	—	—	—
—	★ First Trust Indust AlpDEX FXR	MB		19.44	19.51	–0.47	—	—	—	—	—	—	—	—	—
—	First Trust IPOX-100 Indx FPX	LG		25.36	25.41	–0.12	14.48	—	—	14.76	—	—	—	—	—
—	★ First Trust ISE Chindia FNI	PJ		27.73	27.71	–0.03	—	—	—	—	—	—	—	—	—
—	★ First Trust ISE NatGas FCG	SN		22.31	22.24	0.03	—	—	—	—	—	—	—	—	—
—	★ First Trust ISE Water FIW	SN		22.38	22.43	0.21	—	—	—	—	—	—	—	—	—
—	★ First Trust LgCore AlpDEX FEX	LB		28.15	28.23	0.03	—	—	—	—	—	—	—	—	—
—	★ First Trust LgGrOp AlpDEX FTC	LG		30.66	30.58	–0.05	—	—	—	—	—	—	—	—	—
—	★ First Trust LgVaOp AlpDEX FTA	LV		26.15	26.20	–0.01	—	—	—	—	—	—	—	—	—
—	★ First Trust Matrl AlpDEX FXZ	SN		22.11	21.91	–0.09	—	—	—	—	—	—	—	—	—
—	★ First Trust MidCr AlpDEX FNX	MB		28.08	28.14	–0.01	—	—	—	—	—	—	—	—	—
—	First Trust MStar Div Ld FDL	LV		20.20	20.14	–0.02	–10.68	—	—	–10.98	—	—	—	—	—
—	★ First Trust MultGr AlpDEX FAD	MG		30.40	30.39	–0.34	—	—	—	—	—	—	—	—	—
—	★ First Trust MultVa AlpDEX FAB	MV		25.77	25.98	0.20	—	—	—	—	—	—	—	—	—
—	★ First Trust NASDAQ Clean QCLN	SN		30.86	33.00	0.63	—	—	—	—	—	—	—	—	—
—	★ First Trust NASDAQ ExTech QQXT	LB		21.18	21.30	–1.00	—	—	—	—	—	—	—	—	—
—	★ First Trust S&P REIT FRI	SR		15.69	15.85	–0.65	—	—	—	—	—	—	—	—	—
—	★ First Trust SmCore AlpDEX FYX	SB		26.55	26.75	–0.10	—	—	—	—	—	—	—	—	—
—	★ First Trust Tech AlpDEX FXL	ST		20.68	20.83	–0.56	—	—	—	—	—	—	—	—	—

★ New in 2007

Performance Summary

U.S.-Listed ETFs

Portfolio				Morningstar Valuation		Costs		Trading Information	
Top 3 Sectors	Avg. Mkt. Cap. ($mil)	P/E Ratio	P/B Ratio	Price/ Fair Value	Coverage Rate %	Expense Ratio %	Tax-Cost Ratio	52-week High/Low	Avg. Daily Vol.
	61,897	17.26	3.35	0.91	100.00	0.24	0.71	29.52–25.77	2,543,628
—	—	—	—	—	—	0.40	—	93.79–77.34	92,266
—	—	—	—	—	—	0.40	—	211.27–192.47	44,619
—	—	—	—	—	—	0.40	—	109.16–84.44	109,474
—	—	—	—	—	—	0.40	—	148.98–129.16	199,569
—	—	—	—	—	—	0.40	—	92.33–80.54	316,003
—	—	—	—	—	—	0.40	—	93.84–88.98	7,200
—	—	—	—	—	—	0.40	—	160.74–140.77	15,297
—	—	—	—	—	—	0.40	—	90.95–79.83	81,039
	113,594	14.32	3.38	0.88	100.00	0.17	0.84	141.61–120.51	13,890,707
	87,487	12.31	1.94	0.99	15.02	0.32	1.04	65.66–51.58	261,158
	114,082	12.03	2.11	0.99	13.07	0.31	1.14	55.60–46.13	29,154
	5,128	29.81	2.08	0.95	94.15	0.25	1.37	99.84–62.28	255,125
—	—	—	—	—	—	0.75	—	10.26–9.46	11,079
	16,001	16.21	2.04	0.66	100.00	0.75	—	10.08–8.76	1,216
—	—	—	—	—	—	0.75	—	11.16–9.94	184,555
—	—	—	—	—	—	0.75	—	11.66–9.87	16,215
—	—	—	—	—	—	0.75	—	10.29–9.01	17,412
—	—	—	—	—	—	0.75	—	11.06–9.29	100,175
—	—	—	—	—	—	0.75	—	10.75–9.40	8,310
	74,008	11.92	2.53	0.99	99.03	0.24	0.43	80.36–54.02	19,386,650
	30,534	17.45	2.26	1.02	77.35	—	—	—	1,017
	14,056	20.81	3.07	0.97	79.20	0.30	0.20	112.24–92.02	27,744
	45,001	10.53	1.37	0.76	99.72	0.24	0.85	37.99–26.53	91,693,652
	13,235	21.46	3.34	0.93	98.96	0.60	—	24.32–19.72	40,230
	19,757	22.87	3.60	0.95	100.00	0.60	—	24.08–19.35	16,428
	5,469	29.37	3.91	0.99	100.00	0.60	—	26.42–22.14	37,805
	7,437	17.66	1.98	0.86	91.52	0.70	—	20.64–15.86	1,111
	12,340	19.33	2.46	0.86	97.22	0.70	—	20.36–18.28	1,045
	41,814	14.48	2.34	0.86	100.00	0.65	—	25.80–21.67	27,034
	12,803	28.24	3.15	1.01	92.86	0.60	—	28.04–22.45	54,451
	496	16.56	1.64	1.00	22.48	0.60	—	26.02–20.87	6,973
	23,736	11.27	1.81	0.99	3.17	0.60	—	32.17–29.09	3,300
	10,579	10.95	1.95	0.94	87.12	0.70	—	23.67–19.06	2,373
	7,248	11.31	1.21	0.80	92.99	0.70	—	20.45–14.89	1,276
	6,823	22.19	1.43	0.98	30.42	0.60	—	55.16–44.49	1,544
	9,142	20.38	2.87	1.02	93.92	0.70	—	20.90–19.08	2,139
	7,307	17.19	2.55	0.98	82.54	0.70	—	20.79–17.31	1,860
	11,777	20.83	2.38	0.99	89.43	0.60	—	25.88–21.87	6,909
	22,549	26.99	3.01	1.09	95.50	0.60	—	31.70–19.23	86,545
	4,133	17.76	2.11	0.89	73.76	0.60	—	22.94–18.00	11,051
	2,334	21.07	2.15	0.97	52.23	0.60	—	23.58–19.99	8,206
	15,982	15.15	1.93	0.90	97.91	0.70	—	30.99–26.90	4,355
	21,893	19.34	3.37	0.99	99.63	0.70	—	31.82–27.63	5,063
	12,016	12.57	1.37	0.82	96.21	0.70	—	30.91–24.79	2,441
	6,952	15.68	2.28	1.02	85.25	0.70	—	22.62–18.12	1,618
	2,740	15.82	1.68	0.94	80.31	0.70	—	31.21–26.57	3,041
	51,682	13.20	1.63	0.77	97.64	0.45	—	24.99–19.39	15,592
	7,457	19.49	3.15	1.01	82.50	0.70	—	32.03–27.99	7,106
	4,033	12.70	1.23	0.85	79.97	0.70	—	30.87–24.29	3,595
	3,682	28.83	2.97	1.32	75.10	0.60	—	32.01–18.91	27,876
	10,567	20.48	3.23	0.92	98.28	0.60	—	23.14–18.77	4,163
	5,223	26.21	2.24	0.97	91.52	0.50	—	20.30–14.60	3,875
	893	14.66	1.45	0.97	39.00	0.70	—	31.04–24.99	5,002
	8,934	19.17	2.34	1.00	93.23	0.70	—	22.74–18.90	2,149

Disclosure: Morningstar licenses its indexes to certain ETF providers, including Barclays Global Investors (BGI) and First Trust, for use in exchange-traded funds. These ETFs are not sponsored, issued, or sold by Morningstar. Morningstar does not make any representation regarding the advisability of investing in ETFs that are based on Morningstar indexes.

Performance Summary

U.S.-Listed ETFs

Page	Name	Cat	Style Box	NAV ($)	Market Price ($)	2007 Avg. Prem. Discount%	NAV Return% through 12-31-07 1Yr	NAV Return% Annualized 3Yr	NAV Return% Annualized 5Yr	Mkt Price Rtn% through 12-31-07 1Yr	Mkt Price Rtn% Annualized 3Yr	Mkt Price Rtn% Annualized 5Yr	Morningstar Rating	Risk Statistics Standard Deviation	Risk Statistics Sharpe Ratio
—	★ First Trust Util AlpDEX FXU	SU		18.23	18.35	–0.31	—	—	—	—	—	—	—	—	—
—	First Trust Value Line Dv FVD	LV		15.75	15.56	–0.25	–3.43	7.03	—	–4.37	10.36	—	★★★	7.32	0.38
—	First Trust Value Line Eq FVI	MB		20.45	20.44	0.01	4.64	—	—	4.43	—	—	—	—	—
—	First Trust Value Line100 FVL	MG		17.91	17.91	–1.06	19.90	12.20	—	29.75	14.23	—	★★★	13.98	0.59
94	Health Care Sel SPDR XLV	SH		35.25	35.31	–0.03	6.92	6.82	7.25	7.16	6.87	7.28	★★	9.01	0.30
—	★ HealthShares Auto-Inflam HHA	SH		23.93	24.08	–0.07	—	—	—	—	—	—	—	—	—
—	★ HealthShares Cancer HHK	SH		32.91	33.34	0.64	—	—	—	—	—	—	—	—	—
—	★ HealthShares Cardio Dvcs HHE	SH		24.95	24.90	0.07	—	—	—	—	—	—	—	—	—
—	★ HealthShares Cardiology HRD	SH		22.45	22.50	0.68	—	—	—	—	—	—	—	—	—
—	★ HealthShares Composite HHQ	SH		26.56	26.74	0.82	—	—	—	—	—	—	—	—	—
—	★ HealthShares Derm & Wound HRW	SH		22.57	22.45	–0.12	—	—	—	—	—	—	—	—	—
—	★ HealthShares Diagnostics HHD	SH		32.86	32.99	0.45	—	—	—	—	—	—	—	—	—
—	★ HealthShares Emerg Cancer HHJ	SH		18.23	18.17	–0.01	—	—	—	—	—	—	—	—	—
—	★ HealthShares Enablng Tech HHV	SH		31.85	31.87	0.16	—	—	—	—	—	—	—	—	—
—	★ HealthShares Euro Drugs HRJ	SH		22.97	23.18	0.10	—	—	—	—	—	—	—	—	—
—	★ HealthShares EuroMed&Dvcs HHT	SH		23.12	23.03	–0.57	—	—	—	—	—	—	—	—	—
—	★ HealthShares Gl/Gender HHU	SH		22.12	22.74	0.78	—	—	—	—	—	—	—	—	—
—	★ HealthShares Inf Disease HHG	SH		18.97	19.51	0.65	—	—	—	—	—	—	—	—	—
—	★ HealthShares Meta-Endo HHM	SH		21.00	21.00	0.77	—	—	—	—	—	—	—	—	—
—	★ HealthShares Neuroscience HHN	SH		22.47	22.37	0.01	—	—	—	—	—	—	—	—	—
—	★ HealthShares Ophthal HHZ	SH		21.23	21.28	1.53	—	—	—	—	—	—	—	—	—
—	★ HealthShares Ortho Repair HHP	SH		25.54	25.92	0.57	—	—	—	—	—	—	—	—	—
—	★ HealthShares Patient Care HHB	SH		25.25	25.25	–0.04	—	—	—	—	—	—	—	—	—
—	★ HealthShares Resp/Pulmon HHR	SH		21.70	21.80	0.09	—	—	—	—	—	—	—	—	—
95	Industrial SPDR XLI	LB		39.11	39.16	0.00	13.20	9.73	15.51	13.48	9.79	15.49	★★★★	9.31	0.59
—	Internet Arch HOLDRs IAH	ST		—	50.90	—	—	—	—	19.20	10.33	14.68	—	—	—
96	Internet HOLDRs HHH	LG		59.20	59.20	—	12.96	–6.02	19.01	12.96	–6.02	19.01	—	—	—
—	Internet Infr HOLDRs IIH	ST		—	5.55	—	—	—	—	1.65	6.46	18.45	—	—	—
—	★ iPath CBOE S&P500 B/W ETN BWV	LB	—	51.33	51.39	0.12	—	—	—	—	—	—	—	—	—
—	★ iPath DJ AIG Agric ETN JJA	SN	—	56.19	56.32	0.20	—	—	—	—	—	—	—	—	—
—	★ iPath DJ AIG Copper ETN JJC	SN	—	42.99	43.08	–0.58	—	—	—	—	—	—	—	—	—
—	★ iPath DJ AIG Energy ETN JJE	SN	—	53.95	53.59	3.88	—	—	—	—	—	—	—	—	—
—	★ iPath DJ AIG Grains ETN JJG	SN	—	57.31	57.50	0.17	—	—	—	—	—	—	—	—	—
—	★ iPath DJ AIG Livstock ETN COW	SN	—	47.37	47.49	–3.53	—	—	—	—	—	—	—	—	—
—	★ iPath DJ AIG Metals ETN JJM	SN	—	43.88	43.89	–0.24	—	—	—	—	—	—	—	—	—
—	★ iPath DJ AIG Nat Gas ETN GAZ	SN	—	47.40	47.50	0.96	—	—	—	—	—	—	—	—	—
—	★ iPath DJ AIG Nickel ETN JJN	SN	—	41.28	41.15	–0.07	—	—	—	—	—	—	—	—	—
181	iPath DJ-AIGCom Id TR ETN DJP	SN	—	56.19	56.23	0.14	15.50	—	—	14.90	—	—	—	—	—
—	★ iPath EUR/USD ETN ERO	IB	—	55.34	55.04	–0.02	—	—	—	—	—	—	—	—	—
—	★ iPath GBP/USD ETN GBB	IB	—	51.93	51.24	–0.32	—	—	—	—	—	—	—	—	—
—	★ iPath JPY/USD ETN JYN	IB	—	53.59	53.54	0.16	—	—	—	—	—	—	—	—	—
—	iPath MSCI India Idx ETN INP	PJ		90.08	97.79	2.49	72.01	—	—	86.44	—	—	—	—	—
—	iPath S&P GSCI CrOil ETN OIL	SN	—	55.94	56.15	–0.36	46.75	—	—	47.53	—	—	—	—	—
182	iPath S&P GSCI TotRet ETN GSP	SN	—	53.18	53.17	–0.17	31.99	—	—	31.61	—	—	—	—	—
148	iShares Australia EWA	PJ		29.13	28.82	0.24	28.96	25.51	31.12	28.29	25.11	30.99	★★★	16.18	1.23
—	iShares Austria Index EWO	ES		37.20	36.88	–0.25	3.96	19.72	35.97	1.69	18.99	35.58	★★★★	15.64	0.96
—	iShares Belgium Indx EWK	ES		24.55	24.40	–0.02	–1.20	13.22	24.13	–1.83	12.84	24.25	★★	11.03	0.80
149	iShares Brazil Index EWZ	LS		81.55	80.70	0.00	76.59	57.19	61.83	74.83	56.39	61.74	★★★★★	29.72	1.54
97	iShares C&S Realty ICF	SR		79.22	79.14	–0.09	–18.30	9.04	19.11	–18.21	9.08	19.04	★★★	18.51	0.33
150	iShares Canada Index EWC	FV		32.33	32.12	0.06	29.22	24.72	29.51	28.40	24.17	29.20	★★★★★	16.46	1.17
183	iShares COMEX Gold Trust IAU	SP	—	82.52	82.45	0.11	30.91	—	—	30.36	—	—	—	—	—
98	iShares DJ BMaterial IYM	SN		76.99	76.96	–0.03	32.19	17.28	19.56	32.17	17.23	19.51	★★	14.60	0.88
—	iShares DJ Cons Services IYC	LG		62.00	61.83	–0.01	–7.42	0.97	8.62	–7.70	0.86	8.61	★	10.31	–0.3
99	iShares DJ Consumer Goods IYK	LB		63.91	63.92	0.13	9.17	8.18	11.25	8.57	8.20	11.34	★★	6.78	0.57
—	★ iShares DJ EPAC Sel Div IDV	FB		46.42	46.26	0.68	—	—	—	—	—	—	—	—	—

★ New in 2007

Performance Summary

U.S.-Listed ETFs

Portfolio				Morningstar Valuation		Costs		Trading Information	
Top 3 Sectors	Avg. Mkt. Cap. ($mil)	P/E Ratio	P/B Ratio	Price/Fair Value	Coverage Rate %	Expense Ratio %	Tax-Cost Ratio	52-week High/Low	Avg. Daily Vol.
	7,258	16.74	1.08	0.94	93.62	0.70	—	20.27–17.78	638
	11,206	15.16	1.77	0.86	92.57	0.70	2.17	17.81–15.10	20,209
	12,225	15.06	2.24	0.98	87.49	0.70	—	21.83–18.91	7,282
	8,459	24.92	4.14	1.12	84.20	0.70	2.95	18.61–15.34	74,700
	52,349	15.42	3.36	0.90	99.33	0.24	0.50	36.79–33.08	2,085,732
	1,044	7.77	5.06	0.98	41.89	0.75	—	27.98–21.42	1,576
	2,583	34.15	5.35	1.04	72.52	0.75	—	34.64–24.90	11,544
	653	35.96	3.00	1.03	40.43	0.75	—	27.48–23.99	370
	1,891	17.95	2.61	0.84	83.62	0.75	—	26.43–21.67	1,220
	3,614	22.07	3.38	0.99	73.67	0.75	—	28.45–25.03	3,392
	940	15.91	2.48	0.86	59.79	0.75	—	26.01–21.06	750
	1,975	35.10	3.82	1.06	49.04	0.75	—	34.44–23.19	25,425
	306	73.81	4.27	0.94	43.97	0.75	—	28.85–17.48	7,110
	2,017	30.18	3.57	1.10	65.70	0.75	—	34.38–24.64	3,154
	2,550	24.49	4.05	1.04	9.69	0.95	—	28.07–22.83	3,276
	1,361	26.43	3.94	1.00	—	0.95	—	25.22–22.20	5,680
	1,247	10.17	2.54	0.99	61.14	0.75	—	27.26–21.55	1,894
	1,676	13.22	2.49	0.83	74.41	0.75	—	27.34–18.75	1,342
	765	8.88	4.23	0.86	45.61	0.75	—	27.00–19.72	2,504
	3,268	16.38	2.34	0.92	74.99	0.75	—	27.04–21.06	1,988
	628	22.40	2.85	0.94	42.12	0.75	—	27.44–20.39	2,758
	671	31.62	2.86	1.01	19.69	0.75	—	27.25–24.67	755
	3,113	17.42	2.58	1.06	60.47	0.75	—	28.17–24.29	4,423
	924	17.74	1.90	0.91	48.40	0.75	—	29.32–21.53	3,348
	43,661	15.49	3.24	0.92	99.58	0.24	0.57	41.83–34.69	4,084,786
	103,491	17.52	4.65	0.94	87.85	—	—	—	31,682
	29,709	26.81	3.04	0.90	96.83	—	—	—	142,967
	5,308	47.93	3.05	1.16	94.70	—	—	—	51,306
—	—	—	—	—	—	0.75	—	51.72–47.51	2,938
—	—	—	—	—	—	0.75	—	58.24–49.32	39,873
—	—	—	—	—	—	0.75	—	50.35–40.74	2,444
—	—	—	—	—	—	0.75	—	56.04–47.92	8,268
—	—	—	—	—	—	0.75	—	59.97–49.15	30,603
—	—	—	—	—	—	0.75	—	55.37–46.18	5,909
—	—	—	—	—	—	0.75	—	50.24–42.72	4,500
—	—	—	—	—	—	0.75	—	55.19–44.98	3,157
—	—	—	—	—	—	0.75	—	53.32–40.26	3,531
—	—	—	—	—	—	0.75	—	58.04–45.54	172,798
—	—	—	—	—	—	0.40	—	55.89–49.17	9,200
—	—	—	—	—	—	0.40	—	54.23–49.52	5,983
—	—	—	—	—	—	0.40	—	55.38–48.23	11,767
	20,021	25.47	4.59	1.00	—	0.89	—	93.49–46.32	638,188
—	—	—	—	—	—	0.75	—	58.09–31.80	83,904
—	—	—	—	—	—	0.75	—	55.00–36.09	20,826
	24,812	16.14	2.52	1.00	14.58	0.54	1.44	34.16–22.68	2,342,765
	8,927	12.36	1.49	1.00	0.33	0.54	0.58	41.60–34.35	190,128
	20,513	10.83	1.37	1.00	0.09	0.54	1.02	28.48–23.63	119,690
	43,035	13.67	2.55	1.00	9.88	0.70	0.60	85.37–42.93	13,985,347
	7,727	29.59	2.25	0.98	100.00	0.35	1.05	115.52–70.80	1,099,294
	22,401	16.12	2.40	0.98	92.66	0.54	0.34	36.25–24.13	1,506,791
—	—	—	—	—	—	0.40	—	85.63–60.76	194,312
	16,551	14.14	2.47	0.98	94.29	0.48	0.61	79.16–57.82	208,575
	20,896	15.78	2.17	0.81	98.18	0.48	0.18	72.39–57.46	91,930
	40,005	17.07	3.46	0.94	95.87	0.48	0.64	66.26–58.80	39,016
	9,108	11.58	1.96	1.00	7.01	0.50	—	52.62–43.97	9,158

Performance Summary

U.S.-Listed ETFs

Page	Name	Cat	Style Box	NAV ($)	Market Price ($)	2007 Avg. Prem. Discount%	NAV Return% through 12-31-07 1Yr	NAV Return% Annualized 3Yr	NAV Return% Annualized 5Yr	Mkt Price Rtn% through 12-31-07 1Yr	Mkt Price Rtn% Annualized 3Yr	Mkt Price Rtn% Annualized 5Yr	Morningstar Rating	Risk Statistics Standard Deviation	Risk Statistics Sharpe Ratio
100	iShares DJ Fin Sectr IYF	SF		94.36	94.14	–0.08	–17.94	1.04	8.84	–18.05	0.95	8.87	★★★	10.72	–0.3
101	iShares DJ Fin Svcs IYG	SF		102.38	102.14	–0.07	–21.69	–1.12	7.72	–21.84	–1.25	7.66	★★	11.38	–0.4
102	iShares DJ Health IYH	SH		70.66	70.67	–0.04	7.84	7.32	8.80	8.01	7.28	8.77	★★	8.40	0.37
103	iShares DJ Industry IYJ	LB		72.83	72.80	–0.02	13.02	10.06	15.49	12.32	10.01	15.44	★★★★	9.39	0.62
104	iShares DJ RE Index IYR	SR		66.05	65.70	–0.13	–18.15	6.52	16.42	–18.11	6.37	16.22	★★	16.67	0.20
31	iShares DJ Sel Dividend DVY	LV		64.72	64.49	–0.05	–5.37	5.18	—	–5.67	5.02	—	★★	7.62	0.14
105	iShares DJ Tech IYW	ST		62.48	62.46	0.01	15.04	8.99	14.48	14.96	9.02	14.41	★★★	14.27	0.37
106	iShares DJ Telecom IYZ	SC		29.57	29.52	–0.01	1.76	9.54	11.87	1.68	9.43	11.87	★★	11.76	0.47
107	iShares DJ US Energy IYE	SN		136.97	136.97	–0.12	35.75	29.99	29.75	35.75	29.99	29.85	★★★	19.47	1.23
—	iShares DJ US Health Prov IHF	SH		63.26	63.23	–0.02	18.25	—	—	18.15	—	—	—	—	—
—	iShares DJ US Medical Dev IHI	SH		60.68	60.62	–0.03	18.84	—	—	18.75	—	—	—	—	—
—	iShares DJ US Oil & Gas IEO	SN		66.57	66.50	–0.15	39.72	—	—	39.62	—	—	—	—	—
—	iShares DJ US Oil Equip IEZ	SN		64.37	64.36	0.00	42.67	—	—	42.64	—	—	—	—	—
—	iShares DJ US Pharma IHE	SH		53.72	53.79	0.02	2.19	—	—	2.37	—	—	—	—	—
108	iShares DJ Utilities IDU	SU		102.79	102.41	–0.08	17.21	17.49	19.93	16.71	17.32	19.79	★★★	10.08	1.23
—	iShares Dow Jones TransAv IYT	MB		81.85	81.25	–0.10	1.15	6.95	—	0.39	6.65	—	★★	15.50	0.23
—	iShares Dow Jones US Aero ITA	MB		67.91	67.93	–0.01	27.56	—	—	27.62	—	—	—	—	—
—	iShares Dow Jones US BrDl IAI	SF		51.22	51.16	–0.05	–4.11	—	—	–4.29	—	—	—	—	—
109	iShares Dow Jones US Home ITB	LB		17.57	17.63	–0.07	–58.00	—	—	–57.87	—	—	—	—	—
32	iShares Dow Jones US Idx IYY	LB		71.60	71.54	–0.04	5.81	9.00	13.55	5.78	8.94	13.53	★★★★	8.11	0.58
—	iShares Dow Jones US Insr IAK	SF		49.64	49.65	–0.02	–7.46	—	—	–7.42	—	—	—	—	—
—	iShares Dow Jones US RegB IAT	SF		37.57	37.60	0.07	–25.54	—	—	–25.48	—	—	—	—	—
151	iShares EMU Index EZU	ES		119.99	119.32	–0.08	19.42	20.78	24.88	18.41	20.40	24.62	★★★	10.51	1.46
—	iShares France Index EWQ	ES		38.29	38.03	–0.10	13.00	18.37	22.36	12.14	18.16	22.28	★★★	10.97	1.21
—	★ iShares FTSE DevSmCp exNA IFSM	FR		46.52	46.67	0.18	—	—	—	—	—	—	—	—	—
—	★ iShares FTSE EPRA Asia IFAS	SR		46.34	46.19	0.03	—	—	—	—	—	—	—	—	—
—	★ iShares FTSE EPRA Europe IFEU	SR		47.87	47.55	–1.12	—	—	—	—	—	—	—	—	—
—	★ iShares FTSE EPRA Glbl RE IFGL	SR		46.82	47.30	0.60	—	—	—	—	—	—	—	—	—
—	★ iShares FTSE EPRA Nrth Am IFNA	SR		46.72	46.65	–1.05	—	—	—	—	—	—	—	—	—
—	★ iShares FTSE NAREIT Ind/O FIO	SR		39.48	39.39	0.16	—	—	—	—	—	—	—	—	—
—	★ iShares FTSE NAREIT Mortg REM	SR		29.66	29.60	–0.09	—	—	—	—	—	—	—	—	—
—	★ iShares FTSE NAREIT RE 50 FTY	SR		39.07	39.14	–0.09	—	—	—	—	—	—	—	—	—
—	★ iShares FTSE NAREIT Resdn REZ	SR		38.36	38.34	–0.17	—	—	—	—	—	—	—	—	—
—	★ iShares FTSE NAREIT Retl RTL	SR		36.78	36.67	–0.02	—	—	—	—	—	—	—	—	—
152	iShares FTSE/Xinhua China FXI	PJ		174.27	170.45	–0.41	58.66	49.15	—	54.75	47.55	—	★★★★★	26.30	1.51
153	iShares Germany Indx EWG	ES		35.74	35.44	0.01	34.75	26.17	30.56	33.70	25.54	30.81	★★★	12.28	1.63
154	iShares Hong Kong EWH	PJ		22.19	21.93	–0.12	40.55	25.26	27.24	39.42	24.60	26.73	★★	14.80	1.32
—	★ iShares iBoxx $ HiYld Cor HYG	HY		98.53	100.72	1.57	—	—	—	—	—	—	—	—	—
168	iShares iBoxx$ Corp Bd LQD	CL		104.35	104.84	0.41	3.73	2.89	4.38	3.76	3.05	4.16	★	3.96	–0.4
—	iShares Italy Index EWI	ES		33.43	32.94	–0.20	5.41	12.44	21.14	3.77	11.89	21.03	★★	10.23	0.78
155	iShares Japan Index EWJ	JS		13.37	13.29	–0.11	–4.33	7.95	14.37	–5.48	7.55	14.44	★★★	11.75	0.34
—	iShares KLD 400 Social DSI	LB		51.97	52.15	0.13	3.19	—	—	3.17	—	—	—	—	—
33	iShares KLD Sel Soc Idx KLD	LB		60.62	60.82	0.12	4.03	—	—	4.31	—	—	—	—	—
—	★ iShares Lehman 1-3 Credit CSJ	CS		100.71	101.04	0.21	—	—	—	—	—	—	—	—	—
169	iShares Lehman 1-3 T SHY	GS		82.05	82.19	–0.03	7.30	4.18	3.01	7.36	4.23	3.03	★★★★	1.41	–0.1
—	★ iShares Lehman 10-20 Trea TLH	GL		104.77	105.01	–0.07	—	—	—	—	—	—	—	—	—
171	iShares Lehman 20+ TLT	GL		92.91	93.05	–0.11	10.15	6.40	5.94	10.30	6.46	5.92	★★★	8.55	0.26
—	★ iShares Lehman 3-7 Treas IEI	GI		105.26	105.52	0.11	—	—	—	—	—	—	—	—	—
170	iShares Lehman 7-10 IEF	GL		86.78	87.01	–0.01	10.21	4.98	4.28	10.38	5.12	4.31	★★	4.77	0.14
172	iShares Lehman Aggregate AGG	CI		100.88	101.17	0.24	6.57	4.27	—	6.61	4.25	—	★★★★	2.81	–0.0
—	★ iShares Lehman Credit CFT	CI		99.53	99.99	0.38	—	—	—	—	—	—	—	—	—
—	★ iShares Lehman Govt/Cred GBF	CI		101.90	102.00	0.14	—	—	—	—	—	—	—	—	—
—	★ iShares Lehman Int Credit CIU	CI		100.00	100.97	0.34	—	—	—	—	—	—	—	—	—
—	★ iShares Lehman Int Gov/Cr GVI	CI		102.23	102.86	0.18	—	—	—	—	—	—	—	—	—
—	★ iShares Lehman MBS Bond MBB	CI		101.57	101.80	0.04	—	—	—	—	—	—	—	—	—

★ New in 2007

Performance Summary

U.S.-Listed ETFs

Portfolio				Morningstar Valuation		Costs		Trading Information	
Top 3 Sectors	Avg. Mkt. Cap. ($mil)	P/E Ratio	P/B Ratio	Price/ Fair Value	Coverage Rate %	Expense Ratio %	Tax-Cost Ratio	52-week High/Low	Avg. Daily Vol.
	28,799	10.88	1.39	0.77	97.39	0.48	0.76	121.99–86.12	547,165
	41,469	11.01	1.35	0.73	97.92	0.48	0.75	137.60–92.13	286,017
	38,321	14.81	3.43	0.91	97.10	0.48	0.35	73.41–65.59	62,440
	26,260	15.76	3.02	0.91	92.93	0.48	0.40	77.83–64.85	52,677
	5,382	23.71	2.11	0.94	94.88	0.48	1.39	94.79–59.43	7,032,156
	10,256	12.52	1.36	0.82	85.73	0.40	1.13	75.58–60.95	836,041
	58,352	19.38	3.92	0.95	97.55	0.48	0.06	67.18–52.49	169,211
	19,393	17.32	1.72	0.93	91.55	0.48	0.88	35.05–27.67	387,805
	78,979	12.05	2.63	1.00	98.80	0.48	0.35	139.11–93.77	161,596
	13,261	15.96	2.86	1.06	90.26	0.48	—	64.48–53.07	66,237
	7,990	22.63	2.99	0.95	84.73	0.48	—	62.11–50.62	55,621
	13,388	12.46	2.08	0.92	90.67	0.48	—	67.95–44.64	87,356
	13,234	11.50	2.77	1.09	84.21	0.48	—	66.72–40.80	62,328
	15,549	7.45	2.94	0.88	94.54	0.48	—	58.81–52.16	29,356
	13,898	15.84	1.44	0.96	93.84	0.48	0.93	106.32–87.97	69,070
	9,442	13.88	1.96	0.90	88.40	0.48	0.25	97.45–74.25	756,538
	10,776	17.09	2.92	1.00	78.11	0.48	—	71.62–53.63	77,766
	14,011	13.37	1.52	0.97	93.98	0.48	—	57.85–45.02	1,127,663
	810	4.20	0.53	0.65	77.76	0.48	—	44.49–14.27	371,046
	36,729	14.44	2.37	0.90	96.67	0.20	0.54	76.36–67.13	54,708
	24,093	8.71	1.30	0.85	95.43	0.48	—	57.57–46.96	20,202
	9,509	11.59	1.25	0.70	90.82	0.48	—	53.46–33.92	74,701
	48,156	12.96	1.95	1.00	3.73	0.54	0.70	126.69–100.11	383,919
	53,234	12.93	1.75	1.00	0.13	0.54	0.41	39.85–32.79	362,087
	1,934	13.25	1.68	1.00	1.98	0.50	—	49.53–44.37	13,262
	11,579	22.32	1.50	1.00	0.76	0.48	—	50.69–43.67	4,943
	3,643	13.12	0.71	1.00	0.32	0.48	—	51.60–45.02	1,482
	7,544	18.67	1.15	1.00	2.71	0.48	—	50.53–44.35	7,067
	4,527	28.68	2.07	0.96	84.54	0.48	—	51.82–42.15	3,723
	4,436	27.04	1.70	0.97	91.34	0.48	—	50.59–35.52	4,670
	1,124	7.13	1.43	0.93	53.35	0.48	—	51.08–26.17	14,376
	6,620	25.89	2.20	0.97	98.34	0.48	—	50.06–35.07	8,103
	2,963	54.39	2.14	1.05	93.42	0.48	—	54.01–34.70	4,996
	5,007	29.74	3.09	0.98	88.48	0.48	—	50.00–32.71	7,545
	91,581	21.70	3.50	1.00	1.29	0.74	0.52	216.00–92.99	5,841,341
	58,662	13.53	1.90	0.98	12.76	0.54	0.46	36.54–26.31	1,221,756
	20,803	16.14	2.44	1.00	0.07	0.54	0.74	23.90–15.08	6,634,597
—	—	—	—	—	—	0.50	—	104.95–96.42	41,107
—	—	—	—	—	—	0.15	1.76	108.03–103.05	152,757
	48,522	12.77	1.75	1.00	0.44	0.54	0.98	36.30–31.31	133,905
	19,334	16.23	1.56	1.00	0.33	0.54	0.25	15.28–12.95	17,314,793
	46,067	15.50	2.49	0.88	98.24	0.50	—	55.33–48.80	18,796
	40,032	14.67	2.75	0.88	98.55	0.50	—	65.38–57.06	9,566
—	—	—	—	—	—	0.20	—	101.61–99.52	29,065
—	—	—	—	—	—	0.15	1.33	82.54–79.64	822,077
—	—	—	—	—	—	0.15	—	107.14–95.54	18,877
—	—	—	—	—	—	0.15	1.60	95.78–82.46	1,650,579
—	—	—	—	—	—	0.15	—	106.59–98.35	37,784
—	—	—	—	—	—	0.15	1.46	88.16–79.63	285,302
—	—	—	—	—	—	0.24	1.58	101.90–97.06	597,657
—	—	—	—	—	—	0.20	—	102.05–97.16	3,957
—	—	—	—	—	—	0.20	—	103.20–97.49	6,550
—	—	—	—	—	—	0.20	—	101.44–97.89	32,123
—	—	—	—	—	—	0.20	—	103.20–98.23	10,569
—	—	—	—	—	—	0.35	—	102.53–97.86	18,976

Performance Summary

U.S.-Listed ETFs

Page	Name	Cat	Style Box	NAV ($)	Market Price ($)	2007 Avg. Prem. Discount%	NAV Return% through 12-31-07 1Yr	NAV Return% Annualized 3Yr	NAV Return% Annualized 5Yr	Mkt Price Rtn% through 12-31-07 1Yr	Mkt Price Rtn% Annualized 3Yr	Mkt Price Rtn% Annualized 5Yr	Morningstar Rating	Risk Statistics Standard Deviation	Risk Statistics Sharpe Ratio
—	★ iShares Lehman Short Trea SHV	CS	—	109.55	109.60	0.00	—	—	—	—	—	—	—	—	—
173	iShares Lehman TIPS Bond TIP	IP	—	105.35	105.80	0.06	11.46	4.69	—	11.93	4.78	—	★★★★	4.57	0.09
—	iShares Malaysia EWM	PJ		12.91	12.73	–0.23	45.46	26.26	23.55	44.59	25.16	23.75	★	14.95	1.36
156	iShares Mexico Index EWW	LS		56.25	56.00	0.02	12.25	33.02	36.60	11.33	32.36	36.85	★	19.56	1.35
—	★ iShares MSCI BRIC BKF	EM		59.01	59.50	0.96	—	—	—	—	—	—	—	—	—
—	★ iShares MSCI Chile ECH	LS		48.16	48.57	0.77	—	—	—	—	—	—	—	—	—
139	iShares MSCI EAFE EFA	FB		78.92	78.50	0.11	10.97	16.60	21.32	9.97	16.18	21.13	★★★★	9.53	1.22
140	iShares MSCI EAFE Growth EFG	FG		78.10	77.71	0.26	16.11	—	—	15.03	—	—	—	—	—
141	iShares MSCI EAFE Value EFV	FV		72.42	71.95	0.12	7.17	—	—	5.56	—	—	—	—	—
142	iShares MSCI Emerg Mkts EEM	EM		151.58	150.30	–0.14	34.55	33.00	—	33.08	32.38	—	★★★	18.70	1.40
157	iShares MSCI ex-Japn EPP	PJ		155.50	154.28	0.14	30.82	25.36	29.87	29.40	24.81	29.54	★★★	14.69	1.33
—	★ iShares MSCI Kokusai Indx TOK	FB		48.79	48.90	0.23	—	—	—	—	—	—	—	—	—
—	iShares MSCI South Africa EZA	EM		131.58	130.11	–0.12	17.29	21.04	—	14.96	20.28	—	★	25.56	0.71
—	iShares MstarLargeCore JKD	LB		80.57	80.46	–0.01	8.46	9.01	—	8.23	8.92	—	★★★	7.13	0.65
—	iShares MstarLargeGrowth JKE	LG		71.49	71.48	0.00	12.05	6.81	—	12.05	6.77	—	★★	9.87	0.28
—	iShares MstarLargeValue JKF	LV		80.77	80.71	–0.05	–0.55	9.96	—	–0.65	9.92	—	★★★★	8.68	0.65
—	iShares MstarMidCore JKG	MB		82.77	82.63	–0.04	1.73	8.53	—	1.51	8.30	—	★★★	11.18	0.40
—	iShares MstarMidGrowth JKH	MG		100.23	100.09	–0.02	19.42	14.82	—	19.40	14.76	—	★★★★	11.51	0.89
—	iShares MstarMidValue JKI	MV		79.05	78.68	0.03	–5.79	7.57	—	–6.21	7.31	—	★★★	9.38	0.37
—	iShares MstarSmallCore JKJ	SB		80.66	80.70	–0.08	–5.60	6.52	—	–5.68	6.60	—	★★★	13.20	0.22
—	iShares MstarSmallGrowth JKK	SG		81.83	81.82	–0.07	10.85	8.65	—	10.92	8.63	—	★★★	14.34	0.35
—	iShares MstarSmallValue JKL	SV		74.00	74.00	–0.06	–8.36	4.72	—	–8.28	4.66	—	★★★	12.45	0.09
—	iShares NASD Biotech IBB	SH		81.21	81.18	–0.10	4.37	2.54	10.38	4.52	2.53	10.49	★	15.04	–0.1
—	iShares Netherlands EWN	ES		30.08	29.96	–0.11	18.58	20.88	20.30	18.12	20.62	20.48	★★	11.98	1.30
34	iShares NYSE 100 Index NY	LV		75.84	75.97	–0.03	3.81	7.92	—	3.94	7.91	—	★★★	7.17	0.50
—	iShares NYSE Composite NYC	LB		89.12	89.14	0.24	8.81	12.55	—	8.62	12.44	—	★★★★★	8.33	0.96
45	iShares R. Midcap IWR	MB		103.94	103.54	0.00	5.41	10.94	18.01	5.10	10.82	17.88	★★★★	9.61	0.69
46	iShares R. Midcap Gr IWP	MG		113.93	113.94	0.00	11.19	11.15	17.62	11.26	11.17	17.68	★★★★	10.66	0.64
47	iShares R. Midcap Vl IWS	MV		141.19	141.06	–0.05	–1.58	9.98	17.69	–1.58	9.95	17.78	★★★★	9.24	0.61
35	iShares R1000 Growth IWF	LG		60.93	60.78	–0.01	11.63	8.49	11.89	11.49	8.35	11.78	★★★	8.65	0.49
36	iShares R1000 Index IWB	LB		79.88	79.60	–0.06	5.68	8.95	13.28	5.32	8.93	13.20	★★★★	7.90	0.59
37	iShares R1000 Value IWD	LV		80.50	80.25	0.00	–0.29	9.16	14.42	–0.72	9.05	14.30	★★★★	8.15	0.59
38	iShares R2000 Growth IWO	SG		83.73	83.48	–0.10	6.93	7.97	16.31	6.86	7.95	16.42	★★★	14.42	0.30
39	iShares R2000 Index IWM	SB		76.24	75.92	–0.12	–1.47	6.74	16.12	–1.75	6.67	16.16	★★★	13.33	0.23
40	iShares R2000 Value IWN	SV		70.79	70.48	–0.16	–9.92	5.05	15.55	–10.30	4.95	15.55	★★★	12.75	0.11
41	iShares R3000 Growth IWZ	LG		49.49	49.54	–0.01	11.18	8.40	12.16	11.02	8.51	12.12	★★★	8.99	0.47
42	iShares R3000 Index IWV	LB		84.66	84.40	0.01	5.03	8.74	13.45	4.57	8.66	13.36	★★★★	8.23	0.54
43	iShares R3000 Value IWW	LV		104.16	103.92	–0.04	–1.17	8.74	14.42	–1.38	8.62	14.41	★★★★	8.39	0.53
44	iShares Russell Microcap IWC	SB		53.04	52.80	–0.22	–8.76	—	—	–9.00	—	—	—	—	—
48	iShares S&P 100 Ind. OEF	LB		68.68	68.80	0.01	5.93	8.14	11.10	6.11	8.20	11.19	★★	7.68	0.50
49	iShares S&P 1500 Index ISI	LB		130.33	130.14	–0.03	5.26	8.53	—	4.50	8.44	—	★★★	8.03	0.53
50	iShares S&P 500 IVV	LB		146.86	146.74	0.01	5.44	8.54	12.73	4.93	8.59	12.67	★★★	7.77	0.55
—	★ iShares S&P Asia 50 AIA	DP		47.99	48.09	0.46	—	—	—	—	—	—	—	—	—
—	★ iShares S&P CA Muni Bond CMF	MF		103.92	104.34	0.51	—	—	—	—	—	—	—	—	—
158	iShares S&P Euro-350 IEV	ES		115.40	114.34	0.01	13.67	18.11	22.06	12.03	17.68	21.76	★★★	9.60	1.35
—	iShares S&P Glb 100 IOO	WS		80.67	80.97	0.15	10.82	11.60	14.73	11.11	11.58	14.69	★★	8.21	0.86
—	iShares S&P GSCI Commdty GSG	SN	—	52.37	52.74	–0.24	31.44	—	—	31.62	—	—	—	—	—
110	iShares S&P GSSI Nat Res IGE	SN		134.41	134.38	0.07	33.82	28.33	28.54	33.47	28.32	28.52	★★★	19.43	1.17
—	iShares S&P GSTI Network IGN	ST		34.00	34.03	–0.05	5.78	3.87	20.34	5.42	3.96	20.15	★★	21.10	0.08
111	iShares S&P GSTI Semicond IGW	ST		59.52	59.41	–0.03	–2.00	3.64	11.64	–2.14	3.60	11.52	★	19.02	0.05
—	iShares S&P GSTI Software IGV	ST		51.59	51.60	0.07	15.69	6.58	15.40	14.92	6.59	15.46	★★★	15.32	0.21
112	iShares S&P GSTI Technlgy IGM	ST		59.67	59.59	–0.03	16.42	8.64	15.03	16.11	8.61	14.94	★★★	14.57	0.35
174	★ iShares S&P Nat Muni Bd MUB	MI		100.71	101.96	0.73	—	—	—	—	—	—	—	—	—
—	★ iShares S&P NY Muni Bond NYF	MN		101.92	101.90	0.08	—	—	—	—	—	—	—	—	—
—	★ iShares S&P U.S. Prfd Stk PFF	LB	—	40.98	41.50	0.10	—	—	—	—	—	—	—	—	—

★ New in 2007

Performance Summary

U.S.-Listed ETFs

Portfolio				Morningstar Valuation		Costs		Trading Information	
Top 3 Sectors	Avg. Mkt. Cap. ($mil)	P/E Ratio	P/B Ratio	Price/ Fair Value	Coverage Rate %	Expense Ratio %	Tax-Cost Ratio	52-week High/Low	Avg. Daily Vol.
—	—	—	—	—	—	0.15	—	110.04–108.60	74,540
—	—	—	—	—	—	0.20	1.62	107.70–97.28	280,817
	4,994	15.08	2.25	1.00	2.52	0.54	1.11	13.54–9.27	2,646,387
	21,700	13.58	3.22	1.00	2.42	0.54	0.47	64.34–48.44	3,314,637
	41,282	17.07	3.41	1.02	19.78	0.75	—	61.05–55.05	22,305
	5,846	18.03	2.35	1.00	0.18	0.74	—	51.17–45.33	35,985
	38,072	13.86	1.98	1.00	5.57	0.34	0.75	85.64–71.40	12,131,294
	32,512	16.89	2.81	1.00	3.25	0.40	—	82.35–66.51	181,920
	44,241	11.68	1.52	0.99	8.12	0.40	—	81.29–69.99	124,253
	23,422	15.82	3.12	1.03	33.72	0.75	0.44	165.39–105.77	17,804,252
	21,096	16.28	2.39	1.00	13.48	0.50	1.45	179.66–121.21	331,932
	46,851	14.11	2.30	0.94	58.85	0.25	—	50.29–46.87	1,922
	11,292	12.69	2.44	1.00	2.11	0.70	0.73	152.65–107.18	276,638
	68,820	15.11	2.86	0.90	99.61	0.20	0.54	83.71–73.11	14,121
	56,547	19.04	3.39	0.96	100.00	0.25	0.15	75.65–62.78	74,280
	99,267	11.07	1.82	0.83	100.00	0.25	0.93	90.64–76.66	44,848
	5,979	14.88	2.26	0.91	95.49	0.25	0.41	93.79–76.44	8,774
	6,219	17.35	3.48	1.03	86.29	0.30	0.10	103.88–84.25	30,812
	5,312	11.38	1.31	0.80	93.74	0.30	0.80	95.52–73.04	10,420
	1,283	14.65	1.83	0.91	56.30	0.25	0.29	95.53–73.50	18,078
	1,367	21.80	2.88	1.01	56.98	0.30	0.03	87.83–72.24	23,266
	1,252	12.63	1.19	0.88	58.01	0.30	0.76	89.25–67.91	13,699
	4,143	10.99	4.26	0.99	82.39	0.48	0.01	87.26–73.10	1,159,192
	24,981	12.23	1.81	1.00	0.11	0.54	0.87	32.94–25.52	109,890
	106,826	13.24	2.40	0.87	100.00	0.20	0.73	81.89–72.28	10,786
	45,943	13.94	2.19	0.91	96.02	0.25	0.63	94.52–81.08	13,393
	7,561	15.00	2.14	0.93	93.44	0.20	0.49	112.99–96.61	300,531
	7,996	16.11	3.18	0.97	93.37	0.25	0.22	120.07–102.95	425,796
	7,001	13.68	1.48	0.88	93.53	0.25	0.71	164.22–131.60	474,307
	37,281	16.77	3.55	0.95	97.91	0.20	0.33	63.64–54.08	3,714,388
	42,191	14.32	2.38	0.89	98.12	0.15	0.61	85.12–75.07	1,044,595
	48,329	12.31	1.74	0.84	98.35	0.20	0.82	89.77–76.27	2,625,202
	1,236	18.83	2.83	1.01	48.72	0.25	0.17	90.50–76.49	4,084,946
	1,100	15.90	1.84	0.98	48.23	0.20	0.40	85.15–70.18	84,907,686
	961	13.58	1.30	0.95	47.64	0.25	0.62	85.60–65.16	2,982,597
	28,351	16.89	3.48	0.95	93.95	0.25	0.30	51.77–44.03	156,292
	31,650	14.42	2.32	0.90	94.16	0.20	0.58	90.47–79.85	446,312
	35,713	12.39	1.70	0.85	94.37	0.25	0.76	116.94–98.47	89,468
	357	15.39	1.66	0.99	18.37	0.60	—	61.88–49.07	195,793
	118,326	14.05	2.61	0.88	100.00	0.20	0.63	73.10–63.35	1,882,750
	39,450	14.30	2.36	0.89	96.46	0.20	0.56	139.22–122.68	59,261
	56,021	14.28	2.43	0.89	99.46	0.09	0.63	156.65–137.97	2,690,598
	47,066	15.54	2.34	1.00	1.13	0.50	—	50.28–45.78	15,807
—	—	—	—	—	—	0.25	—	105.09–102.73	6,316
	58,287	12.88	2.08	1.00	5.53	0.60	0.81	124.29–101.04	324,815
	131,526	13.11	2.38	0.94	55.13	0.40	0.62	85.38–70.88	168,478
—	—	—	—	—	—	0.75	—	54.14–36.08	106,314
	37,853	12.83	2.27	0.97	96.98	0.48	0.37	137.64–93.91	55,578
	9,135	19.45	2.58	0.94	95.03	0.48	0.00	38.30–29.71	173,450
	10,752	18.98	2.67	0.96	94.33	0.48	0.08	70.84–51.70	226,733
	13,115	23.59	3.58	1.02	93.68	0.48	0.01	53.86–43.14	211,195
	47,767	19.75	3.89	0.96	97.52	0.48	0.06	64.03–49.73	136,616
—	—	—	—	—	—	0.25	—	101.84–99.49	62,204
—	—	—	—	—	—	0.25	—	103.12–100.66	2,190
	—	—	—	1.00	0.52	0.48	—	50.45–40.94	27,166

Performance Summary

U.S.-Listed ETFs

Page	Name	Cat	Style Box	NAV ($)	Market Price ($)	2007 Avg. Prem. Discount %	NAV Return% through 12-31-07 1Yr	NAV Annualized 3Yr	NAV Annualized 5Yr	Mkt Price Rtn% through 12-31-07 1Yr	Mkt Annualized 3Yr	Mkt Annualized 5Yr	Morningstar Rating	Risk Statistics Standard Deviation	Sharpe Ratio
—	★ iShares S&P World exUS Pr WPS	SR		48.92	49.36	0.73	—	—	—	—	—	—	—	—	—
161	iShares S.Korea Indx EWY	PJ		64.75	64.70	0.03	32.08	31.51	29.17	31.71	31.09	29.47	★★	21.18	1.20
184	iShares Silver Trust SLV	SP	—	146.38	146.97	0.20	13.85	—	—	14.25	—	—	—	—	—
160	iShares Singapore EWS	PJ		13.80	13.79	0.06	27.78	29.20	29.87	27.92	28.69	30.58	★★	14.40	1.58
54	iShares SP 400 Growth IJK	MG		89.67	89.12	–0.05	13.35	10.74	15.07	12.73	10.54	14.92	★★★	10.74	0.61
55	iShares SP 400 Value IJJ	MV		79.80	79.56	–0.03	2.42	9.29	16.71	1.46	9.27	16.60	★★★	10.59	0.49
51	iShares SP 500 Growth IVW	LG		69.89	69.83	0.04	8.93	7.81	10.73	8.84	7.87	10.70	★★	7.94	0.45
52	iShares SP 500 Value IVE	LV		76.63	76.36	0.03	1.86	9.08	14.54	1.54	8.97	14.48	★★★★	8.09	0.59
57	iShares SP 600 Growth IJT	SG		134.74	134.86	–0.05	5.49	8.24	16.15	5.66	8.38	16.12	★★★	12.45	0.35
58	iShares SP 600 Value IJS	SV		69.97	70.00	–0.15	–5.70	6.02	15.41	–5.56	6.11	15.36	★★★	12.69	0.18
—	iShares SP Glb Cons Discr RXI	WS		54.71	54.76	0.22	–3.75	—	—	–3.83	—	—	—	—	—
—	iShares SP Glb Cons Stpls KXI	WS		62.53	62.94	0.46	18.44	—	—	18.86	—	—	—	—	—
—	iShares SP Glb Enrgy IXC	SN		141.82	141.88	0.07	30.40	26.63	27.23	29.80	26.69	27.33	★★	18.73	1.13
113	iShares SP Glb Fincl IXG	SF		79.59	79.81	–0.03	–7.78	8.43	15.38	–8.78	8.31	15.54	★★★★★	10.03	0.43
—	iShares SP Glb Hlth IXJ	SH		58.33	58.31	0.03	3.89	7.31	8.70	3.34	6.97	8.63	★★	7.84	0.39
—	iShares SP Glb Industrial EXI	WS		63.57	63.32	0.37	14.86	—	—	14.08	—	—	—	—	—
—	iShares SP Glb Materials MXI	SN		77.31	77.55	0.25	37.21	—	—	37.66	—	—	—	—	—
—	iShares SP Glb Tech IXN	ST		65.38	65.40	0.09	13.18	8.77	14.23	12.53	8.52	14.10	★★★	12.77	0.39
—	iShares SP Glb Tele IXP	SC		77.61	77.43	0.22	25.86	16.27	18.54	24.70	15.73	18.32	★★★	10.15	1.13
—	iShares SP Glb Utilities JXI	SU		69.24	69.38	0.26	22.48	—	—	22.46	—	—	—	—	—
159	iShares SP Latin 40 ILF	LS		249.30	248.91	0.07	48.75	48.41	49.09	48.48	47.94	48.85	★★★	22.93	1.67
53	iShares SP MidCap400 IJH	MB		85.42	84.94	0.00	7.80	10.12	16.02	7.30	10.03	15.92	★★★	10.50	0.56
56	iShares SP Small 600 IJR	SB		65.06	65.02	–0.06	–0.44	7.15	15.86	–0.48	7.19	15.87	★★★	12.43	0.27
—	iShares SP TOPIX 150 ITF	JS		117.73	116.64	–0.22	–4.48	8.70	14.13	–5.77	8.21	14.07	★★★★	12.08	0.39
—	iShares Spain Index EWP	ES		64.22	63.65	–0.18	22.31	24.08	31.13	20.94	23.58	31.06	★★★★	11.88	1.54
—	iShares Sweden Index EWD	ES		31.07	30.72	–0.13	0.50	16.65	28.75	–1.30	16.10	28.60	★★	16.69	0.75
—	iShares Switzerland EWL	ES		26.17	25.99	–0.03	6.99	16.55	19.52	5.51	15.71	19.33	★★	9.79	1.19
162	iShares Taiwan Index EWT	PJ		15.20	15.03	–0.36	7.64	10.33	15.32	7.17	9.73	14.55	★	17.95	0.40
163	iShares U.K. Index EWU	ES		24.10	24.08	0.24	7.59	14.20	18.22	6.48	13.72	18.16	★★	9.68	0.99
114	KBW Bank ETF KBE	SF		43.56	43.55	0.01	–21.90	—	—	–21.68	—	—	—	—	—
—	KBW Capital Markets ETF KCE	SF		67.08	66.93	–0.10	0.94	—	—	0.61	—	—	—	—	—
—	KBW Insurance ETF KIE	SF		52.78	52.76	0.01	–5.82	—	—	–5.73	—	—	—	—	—
—	KBW Regional Banking ETF KRE	SF		37.07	37.08	0.03	–22.25	—	—	–23.15	—	—	—	—	—
—	MACROshares Oil Down DCR	SN	—	8.01	10.04	9.67	–57.87	—	—	–45.29	—	—	—	—	—
—	MACROshares Oil Up UCR	SN	—	32.00	30.05	–0.23	61.37	—	—	44.88	—	—	—	—	—
—	Market 2000 HOLDRs MKH	LB		—	63.74	—	—	—	—	3.29	4.48	7.27	—	—	—
—	★ Market Vectors GlbAlt Ene GEX	SN		59.50	59.96	0.78	—	—	—	—	—	—	—	—	—
—	★ Market Vectors Glbl Agri MOO	WS		56.73	57.45	0.56	—	—	—	—	—	—	—	—	—
—	★ Market Vectors Glbl Nclr NLR	SN		35.62	35.60	0.63	—	—	—	—	—	—	—	—	—
185	Market Vectors Gld Miners GDX	SP		46.24	45.83	0.07	17.92	—	—	16.76	—	—	—	—	—
—	★ Market Vectors Russia ETF RSX	EM	—	49.59	50.94	1.10	—	—	—	—	—	—	—	—	—
—	Market Vectors Steel ETF SLX	SN		84.55	85.04	0.00	83.34	—	—	84.35	—	—	—	—	—
115	Materials Sel SPDR XLB	SN		41.67	41.70	–0.02	21.97	14.54	18.54	22.16	14.56	18.58	★★	13.26	0.77
59	MidCap SPDR Trust MDY	MB		156.63	155.10	–0.04	8.20	10.13	15.91	7.22	9.88	15.72	★★★★	10.50	0.56
—	Mkt Vectors Environmental Serv EVX	MB		53.38	51.93	–0.23	21.05	—	—	17.84	—	—	—	—	—
—	★ NYSE Arca Tech 100 ETF NXT	ST		26.25	26.28	0.06	—	—	—	—	—	—	—	—	—
116	Oil Services HOLDRs OIH	SN		189.02	189.02	—	35.34	30.49	26.96	35.34	30.49	26.96	—	—	—
117	Pharmaceutical HOLDRs PPH	SH		79.19	79.19	—	2.98	2.90	1.34	2.98	2.90	1.34	—	—	—
—	★ PowerShares 1-30 Ladder PLW	GL	—	26.61	26.50	0.06	—	—	—	—	—	—	—	—	—
—	PowerShares Aero&Defense PPA	LG		23.11	22.65	–0.11	24.86	—	—	22.28	—	—	—	—	—
—	PowerShares Buyback Achv PKW	LB		24.79	24.34	–0.15	–0.07	—	—	–2.27	—	—	—	—	—
—	PowerShares Cleantech PZD	SG		33.99	35.70	0.44	35.33	—	—	41.95	—	—	—	—	—
—	★ PowerShares DB Agricultur DBA	SN	—	32.90	32.99	0.14	—	—	—	—	—	—	—	—	—
—	★ PowerShares DB Base Metal DBB	SN	—	22.37	21.90	–0.08	—	—	—	—	—	—	—	—	—
186	PowerShares DB Com Idx Fd DBC	SN	—	31.46	31.56	0.21	31.35	—	—	31.60	—	—	—	—	—

★ New in 2007

Performance Summary

U.S.-Listed ETFs

Portfolio				Morningstar Valuation		Costs		Trading Information	
Top 3 Sectors	Avg. Mkt. Cap. ($mil)	P/E Ratio	P/B Ratio	Price/ Fair Value	Coverage Rate %	Expense Ratio %	Tax-Cost Ratio	52-week High/Low	Avg. Daily Vol.
	7,021	18.25	1.14	1.00	1.34	0.48	—	55.78–46.47	42,120
	14,875	13.57	1.70	1.00	1.50	0.70	0.21	73.25–46.25	2,372,044
—	—	—	—	—	—	0.50	—	157.01–115.94	418,125
	9,485	15.15	2.11	1.00	0.10	0.54	1.18	15.79–11.01	4,436,258
	4,179	13.54	2.97	1.00	87.72	0.25	0.21	94.01–79.73	150,161
	3,037	14.73	1.54	0.91	82.06	0.25	0.60	90.31–73.78	114,881
	63,283	15.71	3.34	0.94	99.65	0.18	0.44	72.69–62.91	906,365
	49,506	13.02	1.88	0.84	99.28	0.18	0.73	84.24–72.52	588,437
	1,498	16.45	2.39	0.99	45.35	0.25	0.13	149.56–125.70	181,276
	1,013	14.03	1.39	0.97	47.07	0.25	0.45	82.73–64.06	142,861
	25,918	14.29	1.98	0.90	51.12	0.48	—	63.00–50.93	5,673
	58,326	18.77	3.42	0.95	54.30	0.48	—	64.10–52.77	52,927
	107,233	12.22	2.70	0.98	69.18	0.48	0.55	145.03–102.18	53,974
	46,716	10.77	1.43	0.90	49.31	0.48	0.74	95.63–75.11	45,078
	59,201	15.47	3.21	0.93	65.82	0.48	0.37	62.02–56.13	66,119
	35,149	15.00	2.62	0.95	52.35	0.48	—	68.20–55.28	32,842
	34,232	13.92	2.29	0.99	45.16	0.48	—	82.57–54.43	68,364
	63,836	19.42	3.63	0.96	77.12	0.48	0.07	70.14–55.35	41,287
	91,950	16.42	2.21	0.99	45.07	0.48	0.78	82.64–61.74	45,811
	35,222	17.27	1.98	0.98	37.62	0.48	—	71.92–55.14	42,749
	52,961	15.19	3.76	1.07	57.35	0.50	0.55	266.27–158.82	478,184
	3,561	14.10	2.02	0.95	84.88	0.20	0.43	92.27–79.31	443,235
	1,230	15.14	1.76	0.98	46.16	0.20	0.32	73.38–60.15	1,751,518
	27,503	15.48	1.51	1.00	1.09	0.50	0.23	134.34–114.15	17,792
	54,250	14.22	3.01	1.00	0.16	0.54	0.52	68.61–51.74	283,243
	17,738	13.43	2.33	1.00	0.08	0.54	0.75	39.00–29.34	296,496
	55,157	15.07	2.55	0.99	8.35	0.54	0.29	27.68–24.20	205,331
	9,327	13.20	1.90	1.00	0.17	0.70	0.68	18.03–13.25	7,753,488
	58,518	12.71	2.29	1.00	0.17	0.54	1.15	27.13–22.29	828,778
	36,259	10.17	1.16	0.66	97.76	0.35	—	60.39–39.66	1,703,553
	18,294	14.24	1.82	1.01	100.00	0.35	—	72.24–59.01	863,110
	21,298	8.74	1.27	0.83	100.00	0.35	—	61.53–49.98	203,095
	1,615	13.45	1.34	0.87	69.72	0.35	—	51.01–33.15	1,983,855
—	—	—	—	—	—	1.60	—	22.97–6.79	42,213
—	—	—	—	—	—	1.60	—	33.22–17.11	10,867
	113,685	14.86	2.73	0.92	70.10	—	—	—	8,451
	6,883	43.91	3.57	1.15	37.92	0.65	—	60.61–38.69	81,907
	14,925	19.16	3.44	1.13	73.56	0.65	—	57.94–40.48	268,957
	4,593	25.53	1.71	1.00	23.32	0.65	—	44.43–35.26	61,676
	7,686	33.12	1.78	1.01	84.41	0.55	—	52.47–34.32	2,018,797
	26,394	—	—	1.03	17.01	0.69	—	53.22–36.26	452,408
	28,179	12.50	2.53	1.02	84.72	0.55	—	89.26–44.21	120,213
	22,104	13.49	2.26	0.90	98.75	0.24	0.80	43.83–34.23	8,718,063
	3,754	15.46	2.36	0.95	77.40	0.25	0.40	168.54–145.87	5,193,688
	2,485	25.26	2.69	0.89	77.75	0.55	—	56.26–42.38	7,308
	15,384	19.46	3.25	0.93	93.48	0.50	—	28.40–24.67	11,762
	24,591	11.80	3.56	1.04	70.90	—	—	—	5,969,352
	85,461	14.66	3.50	0.87	99.33	—	—	—	698,935
—	—	—	—	—	—	0.25	—	26.90–25.15	18,003
	11,736	18.96	2.92	0.98	85.95	0.60	—	24.19–18.64	149,344
	19,725	15.74	2.63	0.88	94.67	0.60	—	27.00–23.17	20,893
	3,334	27.09	2.84	1.13	62.93	0.60	—	36.84–24.37	66,805
—	—	—	—	—	—	0.75	—	34.13–24.58	499,999
—	—	—	—	—	—	0.75	—	29.03–21.44	67,371
—	—	—	—	—	—	0.83	—	32.54–22.43	408,826

Performance Summary

U.S.-Listed ETFs

Page	Name	Cat	Style Box	NAV ($)	Market Price ($)	2007 Avg. Prem. Discount%	NAV Return% through 12-31-07 1Yr	Annualized 3Yr	5Yr	Mkt Price Rtn% through 12-31-07 1Yr	Annualized 3Yr	5Yr	Morningstar Rating	Risk Statistics Standard Deviation	Sharpe Ratio
—	★ PowerShares DB Energy DBE	SN	—	35.17	35.30	–0.01	—	—	—	—	—	—	—	—	—
—	PowerShares DB G10 Currcy DBV	IB	—	27.47	27.48	0.41	9.40	—	—	8.98	—	—	—	—	—
—	★ PowerShares DB Gold DGL	SP	—	31.74	31.58	0.00	—	—	—	—	—	—	—	—	—
—	★ PowerShares DB Oil DBO	SN	—	34.62	34.71	0.33	—	—	—	—	—	—	—	—	—
—	★ PowerShares DB Prec Metal DBP	SP	—	31.06	30.97	–0.02	—	—	—	—	—	—	—	—	—
—	★ PowerShares DB Silver DBS	SP	—	27.83	27.79	0.08	—	—	—	—	—	—	—	—	—
—	★ PowerShares DB USD Bear UDN	IB	—	27.54	27.58	0.09	—	—	—	—	—	—	—	—	—
—	★ PowerShares DB USD Bull UUP	IB	—	23.86	23.70	–0.02	—	—	—	—	—	—	—	—	—
—	PowerShares Div Achievers PFM	LV		17.09	16.74	–0.23	2.00	—	—	–0.41	—	—	—	—	—
—	★ PowerShares DWA Technical PDP	MB		26.80	27.29	0.28	—	—	—	—	—	—	—	—	—
—	PowerShares Dyn Agg Grwth PGZ	MG		28.55	28.60	0.04	15.10	—	—	14.95	—	—	—	—	—
—	★ PowerShares Dyn Asia Pac PUA	DP		29.28	27.80	0.19	—	—	—	—	—	—	—	—	—
—	PowerShares Dyn Banking PJB	SF		19.12	19.19	0.27	–22.25	—	—	–21.87	—	—	—	—	—
—	PowerShares Dyn Basic Mat PYZ	SN		34.40	35.00	0.13	25.37	—	—	27.43	—	—	—	—	—
—	PowerShares Dyn Bio&Genom PBE	SH		19.63	18.73	–0.51	11.00	—	—	5.82	—	—	—	—	—
—	PowerShares Dyn Building PKB	LB		18.32	18.26	–0.16	11.14	—	—	10.84	—	—	—	—	—
—	PowerShares Dyn Cons Disc PEZ	MB		24.83	23.65	–0.56	–6.56	—	—	–11.17	—	—	—	—	—
—	PowerShares Dyn Cons Stpl PSL	LB		27.82	27.29	–0.12	7.54	—	—	5.03	—	—	—	—	—
—	PowerShares Dyn Deep Val PVM	MV		24.84	24.62	–0.12	1.36	—	—	0.32	—	—	—	—	—
—	★ PowerShares Dyn DevIntOpp PFA	FB		24.70	23.75	0.50	—	—	—	—	—	—	—	—	—
—	PowerShares Dyn Energy PXI	SN		36.03	36.16	–0.01	29.58	—	—	30.13	—	—	—	—	—
—	PowerShares Dyn Engy Exp PXE	SN		25.37	25.37	–0.08	35.12	—	—	34.90	—	—	—	—	—
—	★ PowerShares Dyn Europe PEH	ES		24.21	23.57	0.26	—	—	—	—	—	—	—	—	—
—	PowerShares Dyn Financial PFI	SF		25.44	25.03	–0.23	–1.01	—	—	–2.63	—	—	—	—	—
—	PowerShares Dyn Food&Bev PBJ	LB		17.10	16.92	–0.19	7.09	—	—	6.23	—	—	—	—	—
—	PowerShares Dyn Hard&Elec PHW	ST		18.80	17.81	–0.41	10.78	—	—	4.86	—	—	—	—	—
—	PowerShares Dyn Health PTH	SH		29.67	30.07	0.05	14.58	—	—	16.01	—	—	—	—	—
—	PowerShares Dyn Hlth Svcs PTJ	SH		29.14	29.61	0.15	14.48	—	—	16.25	—	—	—	—	—
—	PowerShares Dyn Indust PRN	MB		30.86	30.86	–0.12	15.66	—	—	15.44	—	—	—	—	—
—	PowerShares Dyn Insurance PIC	SF		17.68	17.10	–0.25	–2.22	—	—	–5.55	—	—	—	—	—
—	PowerShares Dyn Leisr&Ent PEJ	LB		16.71	15.82	–0.44	–3.37	—	—	–8.66	—	—	—	—	—
—	PowerShares Dyn Lg Cp PJF	LB		27.68	27.82	0.17	9.08	—	—	9.23	—	—	—	—	—
60	PowerShares Dyn Lg Growth PWB	LG		18.62	18.75	0.09	11.66	—	—	12.34	—	—	—	—	—
61	PowerShares Dyn Lg Value PWV	LV		20.40	20.35	–0.13	5.62	—	—	5.27	—	—	—	—	—
—	PowerShares Dyn MagniQuan PIQ	MB		26.94	26.75	–0.12	2.37	—	—	1.48	—	—	—	—	—
62	PowerShares Dyn Market PWC	LB		51.55	51.86	–0.02	3.50	9.37	—	4.00	9.46	—	★★★★	8.75	0.58
—	PowerShares Dyn Media PBS	SC		14.95	14.25	–0.44	–5.65	—	—	–10.21	—	—	—	—	—
—	PowerShares Dyn Mid Cap PJG	MB		27.24	27.02	–0.01	7.02	—	—	5.61	—	—	—	—	—
64	PowerShares Dyn Mid Value PWP	MV		18.91	18.36	–0.29	3.00	—	—	0.05	—	—	—	—	—
63	PowerShares Dyn MidGrowth PWJ	MG		23.96	24.26	0.14	25.97	—	—	27.56	—	—	—	—	—
—	PowerShares Dyn Network PXQ	ST		18.08	18.04	–0.10	3.23	—	—	2.15	—	—	—	—	—
—	PowerShares Dyn Oil & Gas PXJ	SN		27.72	27.70	0.03	39.54	—	—	39.34	—	—	—	—	—
—	PowerShares Dyn OTC PWO	MG		52.76	52.82	–0.02	1.16	5.62	—	1.35	5.60	—	★	12.39	0.16
—	PowerShares Dyn Pharma PJP	SH		18.87	18.22	–0.31	4.22	—	—	0.65	—	—	—	—	—
—	PowerShares Dyn Retail PMR	LB		16.00	15.67	–0.27	–17.40	—	—	–19.14	—	—	—	—	—
—	PowerShares Dyn Semicond PSI	ST		17.05	17.26	0.04	–0.86	—	—	0.41	—	—	—	—	—
—	PowerShares Dyn Sm Growth PWT	SG		17.51	17.47	–0.15	–0.94	—	—	–0.96	—	—	—	—	—
—	PowerShares Dyn Sm Value PWY	SV		17.05	15.95	–0.65	–2.37	—	—	–8.82	—	—	—	—	—
—	PowerShares Dyn Small Cap PJM	SB		24.65	24.25	0.10	–2.08	—	—	–4.58	—	—	—	—	—
—	PowerShares Dyn Software PSJ	ST		20.03	20.06	–0.07	4.11	—	—	4.37	—	—	—	—	—
—	PowerShares Dyn Tech PTF	ST		27.46	27.23	–0.04	6.08	—	—	5.26	—	—	—	—	—
—	PowerShares Dyn Tele&Wire PTE	SC		19.31	18.61	–0.34	3.07	—	—	–0.76	—	—	—	—	—
—	PowerShares Dyn Utilities PUI	SU		19.89	19.79	–0.18	7.97	—	—	7.30	—	—	—	—	—
—	★ PowerShares EmgMkts Debt PCY	EB	—	25.42	26.44	2.26	—	—	—	—	—	—	—	—	—
—	PowerShares Finc Prefer PGF	SF	—	20.70	19.78	–0.30	–11.84	—	—	–15.93	—	—	—	—	—

★ New in 2007

Performance Summary

U.S.-Listed ETFs

Portfolio				Morningstar Valuation		Costs		Trading Information	
Top 3 Sectors	Avg. Mkt. Cap. ($mil)	P/E Ratio	P/B Ratio	Price/ Fair Value	Coverage Rate %	Expense Ratio %	Tax-Cost Ratio	52-week High/Low	Avg. Daily Vol.
—	—	—	—	—	—	0.75	—	36.48–22.52	35,841
—	—	—	—	—	—	0.75	—	29.72–25.78	168,411
—	—	—	—	—	—	0.50	—	32.71–24.15	18,709
—	—	—	—	—	—	0.50	—	35.88–21.87	57,435
—	—	—	—	—	—	0.75	—	32.06–24.19	25,349
—	—	—	—	—	—	0.50	—	30.23–22.66	20,135
—	—	—	—	—	—	0.50	—	28.50–23.47	67,280
—	—	—	—	—	—	0.50	—	25.22–23.32	202,711
	69,403	14.80	2.49	0.86	97.52	0.50	—	18.19–16.17	32,807
	9,481	20.80	3.68	1.06	85.65	0.60	—	27.88–23.08	237,960
	4,188	23.46	3.43	1.06	73.50	0.60	—	30.45–24.33	7,603
	6,404	13.23	1.91	1.00	0.91	0.80	—	32.41–22.85	24,376
	4,477	12.61	1.59	0.87	66.55	0.60	—	25.48–17.96	34,558
	5,652	14.81	2.21	1.02	77.88	0.60	—	36.59–27.11	15,967
	3,945	31.64	5.44	0.95	88.14	0.60	—	20.29–17.10	39,226
	3,788	16.79	2.59	0.96	60.81	0.60	—	21.45–16.04	40,023
	4,777	14.56	2.79	0.87	83.00	0.60	—	29.62–22.07	43,333
	9,704	17.49	3.02	0.93	90.27	0.60	—	28.89–26.11	5,539
	7,881	11.30	1.66	0.94	83.90	0.60	—	27.46–23.30	2,618
	8,262	10.67	1.57	1.00	1.92	0.75	—	26.89–22.43	31,763
	7,210	11.67	1.92	1.00	75.49	0.60	—	36.73–25.86	8,111
	10,847	12.87	1.89	0.97	82.26	0.60	—	25.87–17.46	42,793
	9,251	10.31	1.67	1.00	1.49	0.75	—	26.48–22.12	7,468
	6,767	10.66	1.47	0.97	81.26	0.60	—	27.69–23.51	16,172
	8,687	17.86	2.96	0.93	91.30	0.60	—	18.03–16.11	21,390
	7,047	19.10	2.62	0.93	80.63	0.60	—	21.43–16.01	15,613
	6,797	20.18	2.57	1.04	84.84	0.60	—	30.73–25.95	13,245
	6,803	18.68	3.13	1.10	84.58	0.60	—	30.27–25.02	15,660
	5,080	16.28	2.83	0.97	80.35	0.60	—	33.38–26.64	17,685
	7,271	9.56	1.32	0.92	88.77	0.60	—	19.54–16.50	17,377
	6,292	18.08	2.60	0.87	83.16	0.60	—	19.36–14.67	36,869
	58,025	15.10	2.60	0.93	100.00	0.60	—	28.57–25.03	13,089
	45,440	20.99	3.83	0.94	100.00	0.60	—	19.28–16.20	268,919
	62,710	11.97	2.03	0.90	100.00	0.60	—	21.55–19.17	76,217
	7,125	13.59	2.21	0.99	84.69	0.60	—	29.28–25.53	26,460
	12,926	13.78	2.50	0.98	91.78	0.60	0.27	55.18–47.99	47,973
	5,821	19.47	1.70	0.91	89.80	0.60	—	17.62–13.34	32,460
	7,935	14.61	2.52	0.99	92.44	0.60	—	29.55–25.55	11,214
	7,364	12.10	1.93	0.89	95.33	0.60	—	21.35–17.55	42,329
	8,443	20.93	3.75	1.04	91.84	0.60	—	24.79–18.93	231,352
	3,267	20.73	2.67	0.92	80.70	0.60	—	21.12–16.23	9,887
	7,974	11.33	2.39	1.05	72.66	0.60	—	28.76–17.92	160,882
	5,940	18.74	2.94	0.95	77.35	0.60	0.03	58.38–49.88	11,545
	17,042	18.99	3.24	0.87	94.58	0.60	—	19.91–17.59	20,188
	5,082	14.47	2.26	0.80	78.17	0.60	—	21.17–14.45	46,557
	4,415	8.25	2.25	1.03	90.13	0.60	—	20.59–15.46	68,281
	1,426	16.88	2.53	1.03	56.93	0.60	—	19.31–16.57	24,608
	1,466	12.80	1.51	0.94	38.32	0.60	—	19.87–15.04	72,846
	1,427	14.53	1.78	0.98	48.89	0.60	—	28.13–22.94	7,671
	3,696	18.71	3.28	1.00	79.95	0.60	—	21.55–18.39	13,045
	5,188	18.01	2.85	1.00	82.93	0.60	—	29.59–24.99	9,349
	7,409	16.28	2.24	0.96	82.62	0.60	—	21.94–17.66	12,591
	7,248	17.35	1.19	0.97	89.51	0.60	—	21.26–18.03	11,728
—	—	—	—	—	—	0.50	—	25.92–25.21	36,793
	—	—	—	1.00	0.17	0.60	—	25.10–19.53	127,100

Performance Summary

U.S.-Listed ETFs

Page	Name	Cat	Style Box	NAV ($)	Market Price ($)	2007 Avg. Prem. Discount%	NAV Return% through 12-31-07 1Yr	NAV Annualized 3Yr	NAV Annualized 5Yr	Mkt Price Rtn% through 12-31-07 1Yr	Mkt Annualized 3Yr	Mkt Annualized 5Yr	Morningstar Rating	Risk Statistics Standard Deviation	Risk Statistics Sharpe Ratio
—	★ PowerShares FTSE AsPc exJ PAF	PJ		58.99	57.84	0.79	—	—	—	—	—	—	—	—	—
—	★ PowerShares FTSE AsPc S/M PDQ	PJ		25.07	25.30	0.72	—	—	—	—	—	—	—	—	—
—	PowerShares FTSE BasMtrls PRFM	SN		66.11	66.76	0.04	21.03	—	—	21.86	—	—	—	—	—
—	PowerShares FTSE ConsGds PRFG	LB		52.00	48.77	–0.63	5.94	—	—	0.39	—	—	—	—	—
—	PowerShares FTSE ConsSrvs PRFS	LB		50.89	49.25	–0.42	–6.41	—	—	–9.98	—	—	—	—	—
—	★ PowerShares FTSE Dvp exUS PXF	FB		50.99	50.63	0.69	—	—	—	—	—	—	—	—	—
—	★ PowerShares FTSE Dvp S/M PDN	FR		24.94	24.37	–0.17	—	—	—	—	—	—	—	—	—
—	★ PowerShares FTSE Em Mrkts PXH	FB		26.24	26.04	0.86	—	—	—	—	—	—	—	—	—
—	PowerShares FTSE Energy PRFE	SN		76.74	77.24	0.08	34.64	—	—	35.46	—	—	—	—	—
—	★ PowerShares FTSE Eur S/M PWD	ES		24.66	24.32	0.32	—	—	—	—	—	—	—	—	—
—	★ PowerShares FTSE Europe PEF	ES		52.19	51.61	–0.72	—	—	—	—	—	—	—	—	—
—	PowerShares FTSE Fin PRFF	SF		46.05	43.42	–0.58	–12.84	—	—	–18.17	—	—	—	—	—
—	PowerShares FTSE Hth Care PRFH	SH		55.57	54.08	–0.29	12.15	—	—	8.99	—	—	—	—	—
—	PowerShares FTSE Ind PRFN	LB		60.26	59.87	–0.15	12.44	—	—	11.74	—	—	—	—	—
—	★ PowerShares FTSE Japan PJO	JS		48.96	50.15	1.61	—	—	—	—	—	—	—	—	—
—	PowerShares FTSE Tel&Tech PRFQ	SC		58.62	59.55	0.04	9.17	—	—	10.77	—	—	—	—	—
65	PowerShares FTSE US1000 PRF	LV		59.52	58.14	–0.15	4.25	—	—	1.68	—	—	—	—	—
—	PowerShares FTSE US1500 PRFZ	SB		53.92	53.45	0.02	–0.11	—	—	–1.06	—	—	—	—	—
—	PowerShares FTSE Utility PRFU	SU		59.91	59.80	–0.05	12.46	—	—	11.53	—	—	—	—	—
—	★ PowerShares GlbCleanEnrgy PBD	SN		29.99	31.70	1.81	—	—	—	—	—	—	—	—	—
—	★ PowerShares Global Water PIO	SN		24.38	24.72	0.96	—	—	—	—	—	—	—	—	—
164	PowerShares Halter USX PGJ	PJ	—	34.95	34.25	–0.15	68.42	35.61	—	63.27	34.64	—	★★★	23.27	1.25
—	PowerShares High Gr Div PHJ	LB		15.63	14.98	–0.30	–5.25	—	—	–9.35	—	—	—	—	—
—	★ PowerShares HY Corp Bd PHB	HY	—	24.56	25.24	3.43	—	—	—	—	—	—	—	—	—
—	PowerShares HY Div Achiev PEY	MV		13.85	13.31	–0.49	–11.87	0.48	—	–15.32	–0.84	—	★	9.06	–0.4
—	★ PowerShares Ins CA Muni PWZ	MC	—	24.99	25.09	0.18	—	—	—	—	—	—	—	—	—
—	★ PowerShares Ins Nat Muni PZA	ML	—	25.11	25.15	–0.01	—	—	—	—	—	—	—	—	—
—	★ PowerShares Ins NY Muni PZT	MY	—	24.93	25.09	0.41	—	—	—	—	—	—	—	—	—
143	PowerShares Intl Div Ach PID	FV		21.22	20.58	0.06	15.29	—	—	11.09	—	—	—	—	—
—	★ PowerShares Intl LstPvtEq PFP	FG		23.62	23.96	1.45	—	—	—	—	—	—	—	—	—
—	PowerShares List Pvt Eqty PSP	MB		23.13	22.03	–0.44	–9.47	—	—	–13.75	—	—	—	—	—
—	PowerShares Lux Nanotech PXN	ST		16.12	15.67	–0.16	–8.15	—	—	–9.05	—	—	—	—	—
66	PowerShares QQQ QQQQ	LG		51.40	51.22	–0.04	19.42	9.11	16.45	19.14	9.01	16.47	★★★★	14.01	0.39
—	PowerShares Val Line Indu PYH	LB		29.18	29.62	0.24	12.69	—	—	14.16	—	—	—	—	—
—	PowerShares Val Line Time PIV	MG		18.03	18.66	0.27	12.81	—	—	16.77	—	—	—	—	—
—	★ PowerShares VRDO Tax-Free PVI	MS	—	25.02	25.06	0.17	—	—	—	—	—	—	—	—	—
118	PowerShares Water Res PHO	SN		21.26	21.40	0.28	15.95	—	—	16.73	—	—	—	—	—
—	PowerShares WilderHill PBW	SN		27.66	27.69	0.34	59.46	—	—	58.50	—	—	—	—	—
—	PowerShares WilderHill Pr PUW	SN		29.63	29.81	0.06	15.03	—	—	15.79	—	—	—	—	—
67	PowerShares Zacks MicroCp PZI	SB		15.51	15.37	–0.16	–12.55	—	—	–13.33	—	—	—	—	—
—	PowerShares Zacks Sm Cap PZJ	SB		26.04	25.93	–0.19	–2.40	—	—	–3.90	—	—	—	—	—
119	Regional Bank HOLDRs RKH	SF		131.43	131.43	—	–18.63	–2.53	5.05	–18.63	–2.53	5.05	—	—	—
120	Retail HOLDRs RTH	LB		93.35	93.35	—	–6.04	2.26	9.47	–6.04	2.26	9.47	—	—	—
—	★ Rydex 2x Russell 2000 RRY	SB	—	69.36	69.51	0.09	—	—	—	—	—	—	—	—	—
—	★ Rydex 2x S&P 500 RSU	LB	—	70.89	70.75	–0.19	—	—	—	—	—	—	—	—	—
—	★ Rydex 2x S&P MidCap 400 RMM	MB	—	70.50	70.81	0.60	—	—	—	—	—	—	—	—	—
—	★ Rydex Inv 2x Russell 2000 RRZ	BM	—	77.72	77.00	–0.56	—	—	—	—	—	—	—	—	—
—	★ Rydex Inv 2x S&P 500 RSW	BM	—	77.72	77.79	0.61	—	—	—	—	—	—	—	—	—
—	★ Rydex Inv2x S&P Mid 400 RMS	BM	—	78.08	77.31	–0.33	—	—	—	—	—	—	—	—	—
68	Rydex Russell Top 50 XLG	LB		110.62	110.53	–0.03	4.66	—	—	4.49	—	—	—	—	—
—	Rydex S&P 500 Pure Growth RPG	LG		37.90	37.95	0.07	6.34	—	—	6.45	—	—	—	—	—
—	Rydex S&P 500 Pure Value RPV	LV		31.59	31.54	–0.02	–4.10	—	—	–4.27	—	—	—	—	—
69	Rydex S&P Equal Weight RSP	LB		47.30	47.18	–0.03	1.12	7.88	—	0.91	7.76	—	★★★	9.11	0.41
—	Rydex S&P EqWght Cons Dis RCD	LB		38.88	39.01	–0.08	–16.13	—	—	–16.04	—	—	—	—	—
—	Rydex S&P EqWght Cons Stp RHS	LB		52.22	52.74	–0.01	8.46	—	—	8.93	—	—	—	—	—

★ New in 2007

Performance Summary

U.S.-Listed ETFs

Portfolio				Morningstar Valuation		Costs		Trading Information	
Top 3 Sectors	Avg. Mkt. Cap. ($mil)	P/E Ratio	P/B Ratio	Price/ Fair Value	Coverage Rate %	Expense Ratio %	Tax-Cost Ratio	52-week High/Low	Avg. Daily Vol.
	28,041	15.91	2.33	1.00	8.47	0.80	—	63.52–44.52	3,715
	2,704	15.25	1.72	1.00	0.26	0.80	—	27.36–23.55	7,089
	15,515	15.36	2.33	0.93	93.40	0.60	—	70.69–54.77	4,117
	23,901	17.25	2.69	0.89	97.10	0.60	—	55.62–46.89	1,293
	21,768	16.40	2.01	0.80	97.91	0.60	—	59.24–45.86	3,317
	36,794	13.63	1.81	1.00	6.93	0.75	—	53.05–46.65	15,436
	1,833	15.12	1.41	1.00	1.80	0.75	—	26.47–23.25	8,216
	26,509	14.51	2.91	1.03	49.94	0.85	—	28.21–24.54	32,172
	66,427	11.77	2.16	0.97	99.12	0.60	—	77.86–52.92	6,228
	2,150	13.33	1.83	1.00	0.60	0.75	—	26.61–22.71	3,853
	54,651	12.80	2.02	1.00	2.91	0.75	—	54.24–45.53	2,307
	36,898	12.04	1.40	0.76	97.60	0.60	—	55.68–41.05	11,368
	56,310	18.63	3.47	0.91	99.15	0.60	—	56.32–50.16	3,324
	30,130	16.84	2.81	0.91	95.52	0.60	—	64.40–54.02	6,938
	15,846	15.84	1.38	1.00	0.07	0.75	—	50.89–45.88	3,130
	69,878	17.60	2.68	0.94	99.23	0.60	—	63.87–52.55	5,785
	36,687	15.18	2.09	0.87	97.57	0.60	—	63.84–56.06	172,194
	1,358	16.52	1.80	0.98	51.56	0.60	—	60.25–50.47	20,202
	12,211	19.75	1.33	0.96	95.02	0.60	—	62.80–53.85	1,831
	3,782	29.89	2.46	1.10	24.77	0.75	—	31.93–23.71	92,239
	3,861	18.78	2.70	0.98	15.99	0.75	—	26.79–22.71	115,787
	15,778	—	—	1.14	92.51	0.60	0.39	38.72–18.69	1,110,773
	41,809	14.65	2.39	0.81	97.46	0.50	—	17.45–14.35	16,754
	—	—	—	—	—	0.50	—	24.88–24.05	2,559
	3,348	12.54	1.29	0.84	62.39	0.50	1.29	16.48–12.70	140,542
—	—	—	—	—	—	0.28	—	25.31–24.49	3,971
—	—	—	—	—	—	0.28	—	25.36–24.56	12,306
—	—	—	—	—	—	0.28	—	25.22–24.51	3,096
	26,166	11.87	1.90	0.92	96.81	0.50	—	22.41–17.88	183,536
	3,181	9.31	1.22	1.00	—	0.75	—	27.32–22.76	9,817
	2,294	13.78	1.23	0.95	57.26	0.60	—	29.33–20.97	76,796
	2,201	20.40	2.21	0.97	59.03	0.60	—	18.25–14.80	40,305
	42,916	26.31	4.75	0.98	99.29	0.20	0.11	55.04–42.14	153,228,746
	7,958	22.08	3.76	1.11	80.81	0.60	—	30.94–25.77	35,790
	7,973	24.18	4.28	1.16	77.39	0.60	—	19.33–15.87	120,581
—	—	—	—	—	—	0.25	—	25.09–24.99	13,060
	3,512	22.58	2.27	0.97	60.15	0.60	—	22.51–17.84	458,472
	2,060	27.82	2.14	1.19	64.84	0.60	—	28.66–16.75	945,689
	3,799	15.82	1.75	0.91	64.64	0.60	—	31.47–25.24	15,974
	288	14.49	1.22	0.98	16.72	0.60	—	19.15–14.29	89,475
	663	16.99	1.67	0.98	32.02	0.60	—	29.44–24.35	34,434
	54,302	10.80	1.41	0.72	96.24	—	—	—	927,182
	40,003	15.47	2.60	0.79	100.00	—	—	—	4,711,594
—	—	—	—	0.99	21.37	0.70	—	77.09–58.51	4,642
—	—	—	—	0.91	−6.15	0.70	—	76.78–63.46	5,564
—	—	—	—	0.97	−20.78	0.70	—	76.84–60.56	870
—	—	—	—	—	—	0.70	—	91.50–72.00	11,716
—	—	—	—	—	—	0.70	—	86.48–73.08	10,605
—	—	—	—	—	—	0.70	—	90.27–72.44	2,484
	158,005	14.02	2.66	0.87	100.00	0.20	—	117.34–102.48	48,273
	16,327	15.61	3.21	0.89	97.97	0.35	—	39.74–35.46	31,000
	7,523	10.18	0.90	0.67	95.04	0.35	—	37.44–28.41	17,058
	13,601	14.07	1.91	0.84	97.61	0.40	0.41	52.68–44.01	717,876
	8,261	12.69	1.75	0.77	95.60	0.50	—	51.18–35.23	34,393
	19,456	16.71	3.14	0.88	100.00	0.50	—	53.80–48.78	1,834

Performance Summary

U.S.-Listed ETFs

Page	Name	Cat	Style Box	NAV ($)	Market Price ($)	2007 Avg. Prem. Discount%	NAV Return% through 12-31-07 1Yr	NAV Annualized 3Yr	NAV Annualized 5Yr	Mkt Price Rtn% through 12-31-07 1Yr	Mkt Annualized 3Yr	Mkt Annualized 5Yr	Morningstar Rating	Risk Statistics Standard Deviation	Risk Statistics Sharpe Ratio
—	Rydex S&P EqWght Energy RYE	SN		68.52	68.37	0.01	41.22	—	—	40.18	—	—	—	—	—
—	Rydex S&P EqWght Financls RYF	SF		40.78	41.20	0.31	–18.24	—	—	–17.38	—	—	—	—	—
—	Rydex S&P EqWght HlthCare RYH	SH		56.36	56.29	–0.19	10.81	—	—	10.37	—	—	—	—	—
—	Rydex S&P EqWght Industr RGI	LB		56.14	56.29	0.32	15.50	—	—	15.81	—	—	—	—	—
—	Rydex S&P EqWght Material RTM	SN		55.77	56.00	–0.10	10.18	—	—	10.52	—	—	—	—	—
—	Rydex S&P EqWght Tech RYT	ST		50.19	50.14	0.05	1.81	—	—	0.98	—	—	—	—	—
—	Rydex S&P EqWght Util RYU	SU		61.12	61.05	0.20	10.32	—	—	10.00	—	—	—	—	—
—	Rydex S&P Midcap 400 Gr RFG	MG		56.58	56.91	0.02	9.97	—	—	10.56	—	—	—	—	—
—	Rydex S&P Midcap 400 Val RFV	MV		32.81	32.68	–0.07	–3.19	—	—	–3.77	—	—	—	—	—
—	Rydex S&P Smallcap 600 Gr RZG	SG		40.94	40.97	0.29	1.28	—	—	–0.05	—	—	—	—	—
—	Rydex S&P Smallcap 600 Va RZV	SV		33.38	33.43	–0.06	–18.85	—	—	–19.06	—	—	—	—	—
121	Semiconductor HOLDRs SMH	ST		32.46	32.46	—	–3.54	–0.92	7.94	–3.54	–0.92	7.94	—	—	—
—	Short Dow30 ProShares DOG	BM	—	59.30	59.35	0.02	–1.49	—	—	–1.36	—	—	—	—	—
—	Short MidCap400 ProShares MYY	BM	—	59.73	59.70	0.06	–1.23	—	—	–0.71	—	—	—	—	—
—	★ Short MSCI EAFE ProShares EFZ	BM	—	72.37	72.20	0.05	—	—	—	—	—	—	—	—	—
—	★ Short MSCI EmMkts ProShar EUM	BM	—	72.67	72.50	–0.01	—	—	—	—	—	—	—	—	—
—	Short QQQ ProShares PSQ	BM	—	53.24	53.21	0.05	–11.34	—	—	–11.39	—	—	—	—	—
—	★ Short Russell2000 ProShrs RWM	BM	—	72.01	72.10	0.05	—	—	—	—	—	—	—	—	—
—	★ Short S&P SmCap600 ProShr SBB	BM	—	70.91	70.71	–0.05	—	—	—	—	—	—	—	—	—
—	Short S&P500 ProShares SH	BM	—	60.72	60.77	0.07	1.31	—	—	1.99	—	—	—	—	—
—	Software HOLDRs SWH	ST		—	43.85	—	—	—	—	8.16	2.91	10.19	—	—	—
—	★ SPA MarketGrader 100 SIH	LB		23.11	23.10	0.00	—	—	—	—	—	—	—	—	—
—	★ SPA MarketGrader 200 SNB	LB		22.89	23.08	0.30	—	—	—	—	—	—	—	—	—
—	★ SPA MarketGrader 40 SFV	LB		22.37	22.32	–0.19	—	—	—	—	—	—	—	—	—
—	★ SPA MarketGrader Lrg 100 SZG	LB		22.36	24.12	3.59	—	—	—	—	—	—	—	—	—
—	★ SPA MarketGrader Mid 100 SVD	MB		22.79	23.11	0.46	—	—	—	—	—	—	—	—	—
—	★ SPA MarketGrader Smll 100 SSK	SB		23.63	22.60	–2.28	—	—	—	—	—	—	—	—	—
—	★ SPDR Barclays Cap TIPS IPE	IP	—	50.70	50.92	0.31	—	—	—	—	—	—	—	—	—
144	SPDR DJ Global Titans DGT	WS		78.84	78.85	0.22	5.94	9.30	11.85	5.93	9.28	11.86	★	7.36	0.67
—	SPDR DJ Wilshire Intl RE RWX	SR		56.70	56.95	0.59	–6.88	—	—	–7.30	—	—	—	—	—
—	SPDR DJ Wilshire Large Cp ELR	LB		67.60	67.43	0.00	6.19	—	—	5.89	—	—	—	—	—
—	SPDR DJ Wilshire Lg Grwth ELG	LG		58.69	58.71	–0.03	10.50	7.43	10.94	10.49	7.34	10.82	★★	8.68	0.38
70	SPDR DJ Wilshire Lg Value ELV	LV		82.53	82.30	–0.15	1.68	9.23	13.10	1.38	9.09	12.97	★★★	7.73	0.63
—	SPDR DJ Wilshire Mid Cap EMM	MB		56.10	55.94	–0.05	5.29	—	—	5.13	—	—	—	—	—
—	SPDR DJ Wilshire Mid Gr EMG	MG		66.07	65.91	–0.13	10.94	—	—	10.66	—	—	—	—	—
—	SPDR DJ Wilshire Mid Val EMV	MV		56.35	56.44	–0.04	–1.54	—	—	–1.96	—	—	—	—	—
—	SPDR DJ Wilshire Sm Grwth DSG	SG		98.28	98.29	–0.15	7.78	9.94	17.76	7.69	9.93	17.64	★★★★	12.73	0.47
—	SPDR DJ Wilshire Sm Value DSV	SV		66.01	66.07	–0.11	–4.29	6.55	15.35	–4.19	6.50	15.35	★★★	11.95	0.23
—	SPDR DJ Wilshire Small Cp DSC	SB		61.40	61.51	0.19	1.67	—	—	1.84	—	—	—	—	—
—	SPDR DJ Wilshire Tot Mkt TMW	LB		105.65	105.45	–0.06	5.42	8.96	12.50	5.20	8.76	12.55	★★★	7.94	0.58
—	★ SPDR FTSE/Macq Glb Inf100 GII	SU		60.58	60.53	0.25	—	—	—	—	—	—	—	—	—
—	★ SPDR Lehman 1-3 Mo BIL	UB		45.78	45.79	0.03	—	—	—	—	—	—	—	—	—
175	★ SPDR Lehman Agg Bond LAG	CI		53.56	53.72	0.30	—	—	—	—	—	—	—	—	—
—	★ SPDR Lehman Cali Muni Bd CXA	MC	—	22.27	22.45	0.53	—	—	—	—	—	—	—	—	—
—	★ SPDR Lehman Int Term ITE	GI		54.76	54.93	0.20	—	—	—	—	—	—	—	—	—
—	★ SPDR Lehman Intl Tr Bd BWX	IB	—	53.13	53.80	0.75	—	—	—	—	—	—	—	—	—
—	★ SPDR Lehman Long-Term TLO	GL		53.49	53.65	0.21	—	—	—	—	—	—	—	—	—
176	★ SPDR Lehman Muni Bd TFI	ML		22.16	22.26	0.20	—	—	—	—	—	—	—	—	—
—	★ SPDR Lehman NY Muni Bd INY	MY	—	22.00	22.28	1.15	—	—	—	—	—	—	—	—	—
—	★ SPDR Lehman Sh Term Muni SHM	MS	—	22.73	22.79	0.30	—	—	—	—	—	—	—	—	—
—	★ SPDR MSCI ACWI (ex-US) CWI	FB		41.38	41.26	0.38	—	—	—	—	—	—	—	—	—
—	SPDR Russell/Nomura PRIME JPP	JS		50.71	50.17	–0.21	–4.97	—	—	–6.54	—	—	—	—	—
—	SPDR Russell/Nomura Sm Jp JSC	JS		44.27	44.15	0.13	–11.56	—	—	–13.00	—	—	—	—	—
—	SPDR S&P Biotech XBI	SH		59.40	59.36	–0.08	29.09	—	—	29.02	—	—	—	—	—
—	★ SPDR S&P BRIC 40 BIK	EM		32.29	32.05	0.49	—	—	—	—	—	—	—	—	—

★ New in 2007

Performance Summary

U.S.-Listed ETFs

Portfolio				Morningstar Valuation		Costs		Trading Information	
Top 3 Sectors	Avg. Mkt. Cap. ($mil)	P/E Ratio	P/B Ratio	Price/ Fair Value	Coverage Rate %	Expense Ratio %	Tax-Cost Ratio	52-week High/Low	Avg. Daily Vol.
	24,060	12.20	2.47	0.98	97.15	0.50	—	69.46–46.31	7,213
	14,361	11.08	1.20	0.74	98.95	0.50	—	53.50–36.62	6,737
	17,044	16.54	3.03	0.91	98.00	0.50	—	58.29–51.17	18,221
	15,621	15.35	2.91	0.94	98.17	0.50	—	61.51–50.53	4,064
	10,355	13.74	2.30	0.88	92.95	0.50	—	61.54–50.80	3,632
	12,727	18.53	2.56	0.86	98.55	0.50	—	56.30–44.88	12,211
	12,836	16.05	1.29	0.94	97.52	0.50	—	65.60–55.89	8,188
	3,090	8.86	2.82	0.94	89.76	0.35	—	59.75–51.66	12,387
	1,531	13.15	0.94	0.77	77.50	0.35	—	38.94–29.40	10,110
	911	14.33	2.11	0.96	41.76	0.35	—	45.68–37.74	6,557
	423	12.28	0.78	0.86	45.86	0.35	—	45.38–29.81	16,062
	26,596	17.12	3.02	0.81	98.93	—	—	—	7,471,961
—	—	—	—	—	—	0.95	—	65.45–55.84	219,373
—	—	—	—	—	—	0.95	—	63.91–56.01	31,317
—	—	—	—	—	—	0.95	—	74.73–67.81	11,665
—	—	—	—	—	—	0.95	—	79.38–69.02	21,756
—	—	—	—	—	—	0.95	—	65.21–50.07	99,221
—	—	—	—	—	—	0.95	—	76.39–65.30	52,185
—	—	—	—	—	—	0.95	—	74.93–63.64	7,537
—	—	—	—	—	—	0.95	—	65.02–57.22	212,561
	48,463	21.21	4.85	1.00	81.23	—	—	—	214,114
	4,003	12.33	2.51	1.02	65.40	1.12	—	24.92–21.90	8,200
	3,699	13.90	2.55	1.01	62.13	1.12	—	24.69–21.53	2,914
	3,131	12.09	2.74	1.04	57.21	1.12	—	25.07–21.39	1,047
	20,109	14.65	3.00	1.00	96.64	1.12	—	24.90–20.95	3,290
	3,195	13.15	2.42	1.02	66.76	1.12	—	24.77–21.76	1,383
	741	13.71	2.10	0.97	29.21	1.12	—	24.61–21.77	975
—	—	—	—	—	—	0.18	—	52.02–47.06	9,520
	178,096	13.38	2.47	0.89	91.96	0.50	0.75	82.85–72.29	12,195
	5,919	16.00	0.94	1.00	1.64	0.60	—	70.41–53.70	274,878
	48,636	14.47	2.42	0.89	99.01	0.20	—	71.88–63.25	5,523
	36,698	16.87	2.92	0.93	98.96	0.20	0.24	61.22–52.45	42,782
	65,064	12.48	2.04	0.86	98.95	0.20	0.87	90.57–78.60	15,590
	3,849	13.80	1.91	0.95	85.38	0.25	—	64.64–51.98	5,507
	4,087	13.87	2.52	0.96	84.52	0.25	—	72.38–60.76	8,824
	3,534	13.76	1.42	0.92	85.31	0.25	—	65.99–52.49	2,355
	1,667	16.61	2.44	0.98	62.83	0.25	0.17	108.73–90.86	16,107
	1,609	13.78	1.37	0.93	61.88	0.25	1.04	77.99–61.02	20,331
	1,643	15.09	1.78	0.96	62.07	0.25	—	68.54–56.76	6,587
	34,330	14.38	2.37	0.90	95.21	0.20	0.55	112.61–99.32	17,720
	27,651	17.50	2.00	0.99	44.55	0.60	—	63.33–50.35	11,757
—	—	—	—	—	—	0.13	—	45.96–45.74	139,276
—	—	—	—	—	—	0.13	—	54.11–51.48	29,697
—	—	—	—	—	—	0.20	—	22.58–21.97	3,500
—	—	—	—	—	—	0.13	—	55.33–52.05	4,961
—	—	—	—	—	—	0.50	—	54.58–51.23	79,668
—	—	—	—	—	—	0.13	—	54.85–48.39	9,645
—	—	—	—	—	—	0.20	—	22.45–21.84	43,561
—	—	—	—	—	—	0.20	—	22.30–21.80	2,163
—	—	—	—	—	—	0.20	—	22.88–22.50	16,913
	35,952	14.38	2.10	1.00	18.57	0.35	—	44.88–35.60	117,833
	14,535	15.93	1.46	1.00	4.35	0.51	—	59.72–49.10	8,698
	990	16.15	1.16	1.00	1.41	0.56	—	55.03–42.54	23,549
	3,786	25.01	5.26	0.96	86.08	0.35	—	62.08–45.76	192,199
	105,132	18.45	4.11	1.06	33.97	0.40	—	35.39–21.96	222,788

Performance Summary

U.S.-Listed ETFs

Page	Name	Cat	Style Box	NAV ($)	Market Price ($)	2007 Avg. Prem. Discount%	NAV Return% through 12-31-07 1Yr	NAV Annualized 3Yr	NAV Annualized 5Yr	Mkt Price Rtn% through 12-31-07 1Yr	Mkt Annualized 3Yr	Mkt Annualized 5Yr	Morningstar Rating	Risk Statistics Standard Deviation	Risk Statistics Sharpe Ratio
—	★ SPDR S&P China GXC	PJ		91.63	89.85	–0.10	—	—	—	—	—	—	—	—	—
71	SPDR S&P Dividend SDY	LV		55.12	55.06	–0.04	–6.54	—	—	–6.74	—	—	—	—	—
—	★ SPDR S&P Emerging Europe GUR	ES	—	70.54	70.88	0.13	—	—	—	—	—	—	—	—	—
—	★ SPDR S&P Emerging Markets GMM	EM		77.20	76.69	0.10	—	—	—	—	—	—	—	—	—
—	★ SPDR S&P Emrg Asia Pacif GMF	PJ		88.16	87.28	0.36	—	—	—	—	—	—	—	—	—
—	★ SPDR S&P Emrg Latin Am GML	LS		81.39	80.90	–0.10	—	—	—	—	—	—	—	—	—
—	★ SPDR S&P Emrg MidE & Afr GAF	EM		70.24	70.63	0.13	—	—	—	—	—	—	—	—	—
122	SPDR S&P Homebuilders XHB	MV		19.32	19.35	–0.10	–47.69	—	—	–47.66	—	—	—	—	—
—	★ SPDR S&P Intl Small Cap GWX	FR		33.96	34.44	0.81	—	—	—	—	—	—	—	—	—
—	SPDR S&P Metals & Mining XME	SN		69.54	69.12	–0.09	42.57	—	—	41.74	—	—	—	—	—
—	SPDR S&P Oil&Gas Equ&Svcs XES	SN		40.60	40.58	–0.08	38.81	—	—	38.61	—	—	—	—	—
123	SPDR S&P Oil&Gas Expl&Pro XOP	SN		52.10	52.00	–0.10	36.90	—	—	35.21	—	—	—	—	—
—	SPDR S&P Pharmaceuticals XPH	SH		33.65	33.70	–0.04	–1.38	—	—	–1.02	—	—	—	—	—
—	SPDR S&P Retail XRT	MG		33.99	33.56	–0.40	–16.15	—	—	–17.03	—	—	—	—	—
—	SPDR S&P Semiconductor XSD	ST		46.53	46.51	–0.08	–5.05	—	—	–5.12	—	—	—	—	—
—	★ SPDR S&P World ex-US GWL	FB		32.67	32.84	–0.13	—	—	—	—	—	—	—	—	—
72	SPDR Trust Series 1 SPY	LB		146.60	146.21	0.00	5.40	8.51	12.68	5.14	8.49	12.62	★★★	7.77	0.54
187	streetTRACKS Gold Shares GLD	SP	—	79.07	82.46	0.01	25.43	21.78	—	31.10	23.48	—	★★★	15.19	1.20
124	streetTRACKS MS Tech MTK	ST		61.92	61.95	0.19	9.73	7.09	16.66	9.58	7.11	16.77	★★★	15.28	0.24
—	★ TDAX Independence 2010 TDD	TA	—	25.07	25.22	0.64	—	—	—	—	—	—	—	—	—
—	★ TDAX Independence 2020 TDH	TB	—	24.82	24.91	0.59	—	—	—	—	—	—	—	—	—
—	★ TDAX Independence 2030 TDN	TC	—	24.56	24.65	0.98	—	—	—	—	—	—	—	—	—
—	★ TDAX Independence 2040 TDV	TC	—	24.47	24.66	0.64	—	—	—	—	—	—	—	—	—
—	★ TDAX Independence In-Tgt TDX	CA		25.20	25.35	0.62	—	—	—	—	—	—	—	—	—
125	Technology SPDR XLK	ST		26.62	26.66	–0.02	15.19	8.80	13.53	15.44	8.88	13.59	★★★	12.89	0.39
—	Telecom HOLDRs TTH	SC		—	37.97	—	—	—	—	7.32	9.17	7.16	—	—	—
—	★ Ultra Basic Mat ProShares UYM	SN		95.72	95.00	–0.04	—	—	—	—	—	—	—	—	—
—	★ Ultra Cons Goods ProShar UGE	LB		73.96	74.49	–0.14	—	—	—	—	—	—	—	—	—
—	★ Ultra Cons Services ProSh UCC	LB		52.34	52.72	0.13	—	—	—	—	—	—	—	—	—
—	Ultra Dow30 ProShares DDM	LB		84.95	85.17	0.13	4.36	—	—	4.25	—	—	—	—	—
—	★ Ultra Financials ProShar UYG	SF		41.36	41.55	0.14	—	—	—	—	—	—	—	—	—
—	★ Ultra Health Care ProShr RXL	SH		70.53	70.50	0.10	—	—	—	—	—	—	—	—	—
—	★ Ultra Industrials ProShr UXI	LB		77.03	76.05	0.11	—	—	—	—	—	—	—	—	—
—	Ultra MidCap400 ProShares MVV	MB		78.97	77.78	–0.16	1.58	—	—	0.14	—	—	—	—	—
—	★ Ultra Oil & Gas ProShares DIG	SN		109.67	109.60	0.21	—	—	—	—	—	—	—	—	—
—	Ultra QQQ ProShares QLD	LB		99.16	99.22	0.09	22.42	—	—	22.45	—	—	—	—	—
—	★ Ultra Real Estate ProShar URE	SR		34.46	34.50	0.44	—	—	—	—	—	—	—	—	—
—	★ Ultra Russell Mid Gr ProS UKW	MG		67.72	68.10	0.32	—	—	—	—	—	—	—	—	—
—	★ Ultra Russell Mid Val Pro UVU	MV		54.08	54.85	0.34	—	—	—	—	—	—	—	—	—
—	★ Ultra Russell1000 Gr ProS UKF	LG		71.86	71.78	0.09	—	—	—	—	—	—	—	—	—
—	★ Ultra Russell1000 Val Pro UVG	LV		59.37	59.35	–0.23	—	—	—	—	—	—	—	—	—
—	★ Ultra Russell2000 Gr Pro UKK	SG		65.11	65.36	–0.03	—	—	—	—	—	—	—	—	—
—	★ Ultra Russell2000 ProShrs UWM	SB		60.62	60.54	–0.25	—	—	—	—	—	—	—	—	—
—	★ Ultra Russell2000 Val Pro UVT	SV		47.05	47.25	–0.48	—	—	—	—	—	—	—	—	—
—	★ Ultra S&P SmCap600 ProShr SAA	SB		60.14	60.08	–0.04	—	—	—	—	—	—	—	—	—
—	Ultra S&P500 ProShares SSO	LB		83.16	82.80	–0.01	–2.22	—	—	–2.81	—	—	—	—	—
—	★ Ultra Semiconductor ProSh USD	ST		71.12	71.00	0.21	—	—	—	—	—	—	—	—	—
—	★ Ultra Technology ProShar ROM	ST		80.81	80.87	0.07	—	—	—	—	—	—	—	—	—
—	★ Ultra Utilities ProShares UPW	SU		83.81	83.34	–0.09	—	—	—	—	—	—	—	—	—
—	★ UltraShort FTSE/Xinhua 25 FXP	BM	—	76.73	76.87	0.79	—	—	—	—	—	—	—	—	—
—	★ UltraShort MSCI Jpn Pro EWV	BM	—	75.50	76.25	0.55	—	—	—	—	—	—	—	—	—
—	★ UltShort Basic Mat ProSh SMN	SN	—	40.51	40.65	–0.25	—	—	—	—	—	—	—	—	—
—	★ UltShort Cons Goods ProSh SZK	BM	—	63.26	63.24	–0.07	—	—	—	—	—	—	—	—	—
—	★ UltShort Cons Svcs ProSh SCC	BM	—	85.44	85.60	–0.13	—	—	—	—	—	—	—	—	—
—	UltShort Dow30 ProShares DXD	BM	—	50.12	50.18	0.10	–8.94	—	—	–8.73	—	—	—	—	—

★ New in 2007

Performance Summary

U.S.-Listed ETFs

Portfolio				Morningstar Valuation		Costs		Trading Information	
Top 3 Sectors	Avg. Mkt. Cap. ($mil)	P/E Ratio	P/B Ratio	Price/ Fair Value	Coverage Rate %	Expense Ratio %	Tax-Cost Ratio	52-week High/Low	Avg. Daily Vol.
	46,376	20.54	3.36	1.01	6.30	0.60	—	111.41–52.68	186,455
	9,591	12.61	1.64	0.81	86.04	0.35	—	65.83–52.13	55,015
	—	—	—	1.01	3.08	0.60	—	73.40–54.44	24,104
	16,881	15.72	3.02	1.02	16.48	0.60	—	84.38–56.30	17,439
	15,384	17.98	2.99	1.00	13.93	0.60	—	99.89–60.92	28,561
	34,875	13.91	2.69	1.06	40.73	0.60	—	87.33–57.77	22,933
	9,038	13.08	2.38	1.00	1.94	0.60	—	76.06–58.78	26,542
	1,664	4.24	0.66	0.70	79.80	0.35	—	39.72–15.90	3,857,560
	1,061	15.77	1.64	1.00	3.37	0.60	—	38.74–32.78	137,438
	5,181	13.62	2.56	1.03	83.37	0.35	—	71.20–47.12	526,031
	10,420	11.11	2.65	0.99	87.13	0.35	—	41.89–26.83	59,246
	9,412	14.27	2.08	0.93	91.61	0.35	—	53.35–35.48	194,067
	10,490	4.51	2.89	0.82	95.36	0.35	—	37.55–32.04	6,397
	3,259	14.25	1.88	0.78	83.07	0.35	—	45.38–30.41	3,378,877
	5,537	17.84	1.90	0.89	86.26	0.35	—	57.10–40.64	31,900
	25,301	14.13	1.93	1.00	15.34	0.35	—	35.50–30.14	2,628
	55,998	14.28	2.43	0.88	99.46	0.09	0.39	156.39–137.71	195,979,587
—	—	—	—	—	—	0.40	0.00	84.83–60.32	7,561,079
	37,556	21.35	4.24	0.87	100.00	0.50	0.02	68.57–54.41	51,934
	41,588	15.60	2.54	0.98	27.55	0.65	—	25.52–24.92	7,177
	41,089	15.61	2.56	0.96	44.52	0.65	—	25.75–24.34	14,970
	38,992	15.61	2.55	0.94	59.62	0.65	—	25.95–23.81	11,806
	39,030	15.53	2.52	0.94	64.01	0.65	—	26.00–23.65	12,547
	47,090	15.03	2.46	0.99	54.02	0.65	—	25.39–25.06	6,909
	80,804	18.73	3.43	0.94	99.79	0.24	0.25	28.51–22.56	3,209,052
	128,228	15.27	1.89	1.05	100.00	—	—	—	110,991
	16,002	15.87	2.40	0.98	94.45	0.95	—	108.19–67.99	18,362
	40,538	18.40	3.53	0.94	94.58	0.95	—	80.02–65.50	8,285
	21,416	17.57	2.26	0.84	98.09	0.95	—	75.02–46.21	8,186
	113,158	15.73	3.41	0.90	90.24	0.95	—	102.41–76.89	653,773
	30,619	12.30	1.47	0.81	97.65	0.95	—	73.97–36.58	477,031
	40,302	19.43	3.53	0.93	95.35	0.95	—	78.59–64.54	6,567
	26,967	17.43	3.04	0.92	93.98	0.95	—	94.53–67.56	7,124
	3,602	16.76	2.05	0.96	77.73	0.95	—	101.06–71.14	95,265
	79,946	12.37	2.46	0.99	98.29	0.95	—	120.26–64.01	59,825
	40,415	23.64	4.27	0.99	91.52	0.95	—	122.60–75.96	4,310,454
	5,734	23.91	2.23	0.96	95.51	0.95	—	76.97–29.33	47,262
	7,862	18.98	3.17	0.97	94.19	0.95	—	79.36–60.50	9,706
	7,050	14.50	1.50	0.89	93.76	0.95	—	76.02–48.81	5,863
	37,062	19.02	3.58	0.95	98.14	0.95	—	81.84–61.76	10,869
	48,179	13.56	1.77	0.87	98.47	0.95	—	76.71–54.93	8,893
	1,220	19.46	2.85	1.01	56.42	0.95	—	78.65–57.73	11,083
	1,090	16.60	1.85	0.99	49.47	0.95	—	81.22–53.70	457,157
	959	14.29	1.32	0.96	53.35	0.95	—	72.22–41.47	10,473
	1,238	16.27	1.77	0.98	53.33	0.95	—	84.21–53.68	17,696
	55,972	15.75	2.45	0.91	89.63	0.95	—	100.34–76.78	2,037,876
	24,873	21.16	2.89	0.95	96.49	0.95	—	97.99–55.18	34,956
	56,468	20.25	3.93	0.96	97.93	0.95	—	97.76–62.90	44,351
	14,802	18.37	1.44	0.97	95.18	0.95	—	94.69–70.00	14,104
—	—	—	—	—	—	0.95	—	93.69–61.83	1,168,272
—	—	—	—	—	—	0.95	—	80.64–66.50	12,854
—	—	—	—	—	—	0.95	—	71.61–38.63	146,605
—	—	—	—	—	—	0.95	—	74.95–59.68	22,695
—	—	—	—	—	—	0.95	—	96.33–66.02	35,101
—	—	—	—	—	—	0.95	—	61.96–44.80	2,699,438

Performance Summary

U.S.-Listed ETFs

Page	Name	Cat	Style Box	NAV ($)	Market Price ($)	2007 Avg. Prem. Discount %	NAV Return% through 12-31-07 1Yr	NAV Return% Annualized 3Yr	NAV Return% Annualized 5Yr	Mkt Price Rtn% through 12-31-07 1Yr	Mkt Price Rtn% Annualized 3Yr	Mkt Price Rtn% Annualized 5Yr	Morningstar Rating	Risk Statistics Standard Deviation	Risk Statistics Sharpe Ratio
—	★ UltShort Financials ProSh SKF	BM	—	99.90	99.88	–0.02	—	—	—	—	—	—	—	—	—
—	★ UltShort Hlth Care ProSh RXD	BM	—	66.00	65.60	–0.27	—	—	—	—	—	—	—	—	—
—	★ UltShort Industrial ProSh SIJ	BM	—	56.14	56.29	0.22	—	—	—	—	—	—	—	—	—
—	UltShort Mid400 ProShares MZZ	BM	—	54.59	54.84	0.05	–8.97	—	—	–7.07	—	—	—	—	—
—	★ UltShort MSCI EmMkts ProS EEV	BM	—	73.03	73.07	0.35	—	—	—	—	—	—	—	—	—
—	★ UltShort Oil & Gas ProSh DUG	BM	—	36.05	35.98	–0.05	—	—	—	—	—	—	—	—	—
73	UltShort QQQ ProShares QID	BM	—	37.97	37.98	–0.13	–27.16	—	—	–27.36	—	—	—	—	—
—	★ UltShort Real Estat ProSh SRS	BM	—	110.47	110.78	0.50	—	—	—	—	—	—	—	—	—
—	★ UltShort Russell Mid Gr SDK	BM	—	64.38	63.85	–0.32	—	—	—	—	—	—	—	—	—
—	★ UltShort Russell Mid Val SJL	BM	—	82.30	82.05	–0.24	—	—	—	—	—	—	—	—	—
—	★ UltShort Russell1000 Gr SFK	BM	—	62.67	62.60	0.02	—	—	—	—	—	—	—	—	—
—	★ UltShort Russell1000 Val SJF	BM	—	76.04	76.27	–0.27	—	—	—	—	—	—	—	—	—
—	★ UltShort Russell2000 Gr SKK	BM	—	66.58	66.44	0.17	—	—	—	—	—	—	—	—	—
—	★ UltShort Russell2000 ProS TWM	BM	—	70.08	70.33	0.12	—	—	—	—	—	—	—	—	—
—	★ UltShort Russell2000 Val SJH	BM	—	89.22	89.67	–0.02	—	—	—	—	—	—	—	—	—
—	UltShort S&P500 ProShares SDS	BM	—	53.86	54.18	0.10	–3.94	—	—	–3.70	—	—	—	—	—
—	★ UltShort Semicon ProShar SSG	BM	—	56.68	56.25	–0.21	—	—	—	—	—	—	—	—	—
—	★ UltShort SmCap600 ProShrs SDD	BM	—	70.18	70.09	0.09	—	—	—	—	—	—	—	—	—
—	★ UltShort Tech ProShares REW	BM	—	53.09	53.79	0.21	—	—	—	—	—	—	—	—	—
—	★ UltShort Utilities ProSh SDP	BM	—	50.71	50.69	0.00	—	—	—	—	—	—	—	—	—
—	★ UltShrt MSCI EAFE Proshar EFU	BM	—	74.01	73.90	0.04	—	—	—	—	—	—	—	—	—
—	★ United States Natural Gas UNG	SN	—	36.18	36.25	0.30	—	—	—	—	—	—	—	—	—
—	United States Oil USO	SN	—	75.81	75.76	–0.14	46.15	—	—	46.82	—	—	—	—	—
126	Utilities HOLDRs UTH	SU		136.23	136.23	—	3.45	11.73	16.26	3.45	11.73	16.26	—	—	—
127	Utilities SPDR XLU	SU		42.56	42.33	–0.12	19.09	18.75	21.14	18.38	18.55	21.09	★★★	10.30	1.31
—	Vanguard Cons Disc ETF VCR	LG		53.24	53.18	–0.07	–11.53	–0.42	—	–11.79	–0.48	—	★	11.97	–0.3
128	Vanguard Cons Stap ETF VDC	LB		70.91	70.79	–0.04	12.92	10.77	—	12.69	10.65	—	★★★★	5.73	1.08
74	Vanguard Div Appr ETF VIG	LB		55.92	55.95	0.02	5.63	—	—	5.63	—	—	—	—	—
145	Vanguard EmergMkts ETF VWO	EM		104.93	104.30	0.31	39.05	—	—	37.29	—	—	—	—	—
129	Vanguard Energy ETF VDE	SN		113.58	113.50	–0.04	34.87	30.67	—	34.66	30.62	—	★★★	20.07	1.23
165	Vanguard Euro Stk ETF VGK	ES		74.76	74.82	0.42	13.93	—	—	13.25	—	—	—	—	—
—	★ Vanguard Europe Pacific VEA	FB		47.92	47.92	0.23	—	—	—	—	—	—	—	—	—
—	Vanguard ExMkt ETF VXF	MB		105.24	105.15	–0.03	4.49	9.73	17.63	4.46	9.67	17.54	★★★★	11.17	0.50
130	Vanguard Financial ETF VFH	SF		52.62	52.65	0.01	–17.42	1.46	—	–17.58	1.44	—	★★★	10.65	–0.2
—	★ Vanguard FTSE All-W ex-US VEU	FB		58.53	58.61	0.37	—	—	—	—	—	—	—	—	—
75	Vanguard Growth ETF VUG	LG		64.56	64.48	–0.01	12.68	8.96	—	12.52	8.87	—	★★★	8.55	0.55
131	Vanguard HealthCar ETF VHT	SH		60.59	60.62	–0.03	7.80	7.55	—	7.89	7.54	—	★★★	8.27	0.40
—	Vanguard High Dividend Yi VYM	LV		51.24	51.10	0.02	1.68	—	—	1.39	—	—	—	—	—
—	Vanguard Indstrls ETF VIS	LB		73.19	73.09	0.05	13.52	11.24	—	13.20	11.20	—	★★★★	9.55	0.72
132	Vanguard InfoTech ETF VGT	ST		60.20	60.12	–0.06	15.00	8.84	—	14.78	8.77	—	★★★	13.99	0.37
—	★ Vanguard Int-Term Bnd ETF BIV	CI		76.96	77.32	0.24	—	—	—	—	—	—	—	—	—
76	Vanguard Large Cap ETF VV	LB		65.83	65.70	–0.05	6.44	9.35	—	6.21	9.14	—	★★★★	7.84	0.64
—	★ Vanguard Lng-Term Bnd ETF BLV	CL		76.38	76.80	0.08	—	—	—	—	—	—	—	—	—
133	Vanguard Materials ETF VAW	SN		87.96	87.94	0.00	26.42	16.14	—	26.55	16.08	—	★★	13.88	0.84
77	Vanguard Mid Cap ETF VO	MB		75.90	75.61	–0.03	6.14	11.23	—	5.52	11.07	—	★★★★	10.28	0.67
—	Vanguard Mid Growth ETF VOT	MG		64.85	64.80	–0.02	17.44	—	—	17.16	—	—	—	—	—
—	Vanguard Mid Value ETF VOE	MV		53.16	53.14	–0.01	–4.27	—	—	–4.33	—	—	—	—	—
166	Vanguard Pacif Stk ETF VPL	JS		67.33	67.75	0.21	4.85	—	—	4.45	—	—	—	—	—
134	Vanguard REIT Index ETF VNQ	SR		61.53	61.46	0.01	–16.38	8.18	—	–16.50	8.14	—	★★★	17.02	0.30
—	★ Vanguard Sht-Term Bnd ETF BSV	CS		76.88	77.05	0.12	—	—	—	—	—	—	—	—	—
78	Vanguard Sm Cap Gr ETF VBK	SG		71.18	71.29	–0.05	9.74	10.18	—	9.89	10.24	—	★★★★	13.42	0.47
—	Vanguard Sm Cp Val ETF VBR	SV		64.65	64.64	–0.08	–6.96	5.67	—	–6.93	5.67	—	★★★	11.48	0.16
—	Vanguard Small Cap ETF VB	SB		68.07	68.07	–0.02	1.27	8.04	—	1.36	7.97	—	★★★★	12.25	0.34
135	Vanguard TelcomSrv ETF VOX	SC		75.47	75.27	–0.06	5.49	13.68	—	5.15	13.60	—	★★★	11.77	0.79
79	Vanguard TSM ETF VTI	LB		145.27	145.15	0.01	5.56	9.01	13.89	5.37	9.03	13.86	★★★★	8.28	0.57

★ New in 2007

Performance Summary

U.S.-Listed ETFs

Portfolio				Morningstar Valuation		Costs		Trading Information	
Top 3 Sectors	Avg. Mkt. Cap. ($mil)	P/E Ratio	P/B Ratio	Price/ Fair Value	Coverage Rate %	Expense Ratio %	Tax-Cost Ratio	52-week High/Low	Avg. Daily Vol.
—	—	—	—	—	—	0.95	—	112.32–66.46	2,679,753
—	—	—	—	—	—	0.95	—	76.19–61.88	1,707
—	—	—	—	—	—	0.95	—	72.56–49.98	14,142
—	—	—	—	—	—	0.95	—	63.13–48.19	797,462
—	—	—	—	—	—	0.95	—	88.19–66.16	216,215
—	—	—	—	—	—	0.95	—	76.30–35.05	984,681
—	—	—	—	—	—	0.95	—	57.77–33.93	26,216,812
—	—	—	—	—	—	0.95	—	128.44–63.64	893,270
—	—	—	—	—	—	0.95	—	80.35–58.43	6,275
—	—	—	—	—	—	0.95	—	90.87–64.90	8,775
—	—	—	—	—	—	0.95	—	79.15–57.74	8,821
—	—	—	—	—	—	0.95	—	83.42–63.62	6,561
—	—	—	—	—	—	0.95	—	82.63–58.04	31,041
—	—	—	—	—	—	0.95	—	78.74–59.53	4,956,170
—	—	—	—	—	—	0.95	—	100.70–67.34	52,041
—	—	—	—	—	—	0.95	—	62.56–48.27	16,882,961
—	—	—	—	—	—	0.95	—	74.22–47.28	13,828
—	—	—	—	—	—	0.95	—	78.25–57.19	59,390
—	—	—	—	—	—	0.95	—	77.72–47.10	30,273
—	—	—	—	—	—	0.95	—	70.00–47.81	8,889
—	—	—	—	—	—	0.95	—	78.52–65.57	40,122
—	—	—	—	—	—	0.60	—	53.67–34.03	1,051,263
—	—	—	—	—	—	0.50	—	78.70–43.13	3,244,978
	24,555	16.52	1.75	0.94	99.35	—	—	—	75,370
	19,197	16.14	1.55	0.96	99.16	0.24	1.07	44.38–35.84	4,718,119
	13,293	17.78	2.29	0.82	90.25	0.22	0.26	65.13–49.73	39,679
	43,976	18.10	3.38	0.92	96.35	0.22	0.50	73.73–63.14	56,661
	55,527	15.96	3.11	0.90	96.32	0.28	—	58.98–52.52	20,382
	18,735	15.67	2.56	1.01	5.76	0.30	—	116.62–71.11	746,525
	46,645	12.75	2.56	0.99	89.70	0.22	0.34	115.20–78.04	33,308
	49,292	13.22	2.19	1.00	3.21	0.18	—	81.66–65.31	306,879
	37,147	14.17	2.09	1.00	2.94	0.15	—	52.28–44.57	342,312
	2,532	17.22	2.27	0.97	65.59	0.08	0.25	115.56–99.77	40,272
	30,875	12.19	1.69	0.79	92.95	0.22	0.65	67.58–49.56	140,661
	33,722	14.49	2.16	1.00	15.60	0.25	—	63.32–48.95	278,324
	40,029	18.81	3.67	0.93	97.05	0.11	0.19	66.84–56.82	259,397
	31,698	17.28	3.52	0.92	94.16	0.22	0.36	63.57–56.40	36,497
	68,350	14.43	2.41	0.86	95.56	0.25	—	55.75–49.56	27,175
	30,012	17.70	3.25	0.93	90.39	0.22	0.38	79.23–64.85	21,366
	39,822	21.52	4.02	0.94	93.78	0.22	0.09	64.74–50.79	68,235
—	—	—	—	—	—	0.11	—	77.97–72.67	28,529
	48,206	15.82	2.67	0.89	97.42	0.07	0.47	70.00–61.37	170,841
	—	—	—	1.00	0.75	0.11	—	78.35–71.15	19,509
	12,818	16.44	2.41	0.94	90.38	0.22	0.53	91.93–69.38	32,247
	6,995	15.93	2.39	0.94	91.35	0.13	0.45	83.40–72.00	163,935
	7,615	16.86	3.38	1.01	91.13	0.13	—	66.98–55.34	42,128
	6,370	15.03	1.81	0.87	92.12	0.13	—	63.56–50.31	54,397
	20,293	16.93	1.87	1.00	3.29	0.18	—	75.17–64.72	132,538
	5,833	29.06	2.42	0.96	86.16	0.12	1.53	87.06–56.87	350,450
—	—	—	—	—	—	0.11	—	77.45–74.37	53,321
	1,793	19.61	3.05	1.00	58.51	0.12	0.16	77.75–64.65	116,805
	1,602	15.48	1.61	0.94	57.28	0.12	0.72	77.34–60.83	166,656
	1,698	17.29	2.12	0.97	58.00	0.10	0.44	76.59–64.26	142,090
	21,903	21.36	2.22	0.99	81.46	0.23	0.77	85.03–72.14	40,310
	31,195	15.97	2.58	0.90	91.91	0.07	0.27	155.31–136.72	389,382

Performance Summary

U.S.-Listed ETFs

Page	Name	Cat	Style Box	NAV ($)	Market Price ($)	2007 Avg. Prem. Discount%	NAV Return% through 12-31-07 1Yr	NAV Return% Annualized 3Yr	NAV Return% Annualized 5Yr	Mkt Price Rtn% through 12-31-07 1Yr	Mkt Price Rtn% Annualized 3Yr	Mkt Price Rtn% Annualized 5Yr	Morningstar Rating	Risk Statistics Standard Deviation	Risk Statistics Sharpe Ratio
177	★ Vanguard Ttl Bnd Mkt ETF BND	CI		76.61	77.38	0.27	—	—	—	—	—	—	—	—	—
136	Vanguard Utilities ETF VPU	SU		87.64	87.58	0.03	17.15	17.79	—	17.01	17.70	—	★★★	10.17	1.25
80	Vanguard Value ETF VTV	LV		66.51	66.39	–0.03	0.20	9.51	—	–0.11	9.44	—	★★★★	8.16	0.63
—	Wireless HOLDRs WMH	SC		—	72.33	—	—	—	—	20.15	6.94	15.59	—	—	—
—	WisdomTree DEFA DWM	FB		69.86	69.40	0.20	15.06	—	—	13.90	—	—	—	—	—
—	WisdomTree DEFA HiYld Eq DTH	FB		66.55	66.25	0.15	11.37	—	—	10.53	—	—	—	—	—
81	WisdomTree Div Top 100 DTN	LB		56.28	56.22	–0.03	0.11	—	—	–0.03	—	—	—	—	—
—	★ WisdomTree Earnings 100 EEZ	LB		50.34	50.45	0.10	—	—	—	—	—	—	—	—	—
—	★ WisdomTree Earnings 500 EPS	LB		50.72	50.55	0.18	—	—	—	—	—	—	—	—	—
—	★ WisdomTree Emrg Hi-Yld Eq DEM	EM		53.49	52.76	0.60	—	—	—	—	—	—	—	—	—
—	★ WisdomTree Emrg SmCap Div DGS	EM		47.41	47.17	0.63	—	—	—	—	—	—	—	—	—
—	WisdomTree Eur SmCap Div DFE	ES		60.70	59.14	–0.60	–0.13	—	—	–2.92	—	—	—	—	—
—	WisdomTree Eur Total Div DEB	ES		68.08	67.95	0.14	12.89	—	—	12.54	—	—	—	—	—
—	WisdomTree Euro Hi-Yld Eq DEW	ES		65.02	64.73	0.21	8.93	—	—	8.34	—	—	—	—	—
82	WisdomTree High-Yld Eqty DHS	LB		53.24	53.14	–0.04	–4.42	—	—	–4.53	—	—	—	—	—
—	WisdomTree IntDiv Top 100 DOO	FB		70.56	69.76	0.24	14.05	—	—	12.41	—	—	—	—	—
—	WisdomTree Intl Basic Mat DBN	SN		37.55	37.50	0.42	32.28	—	—	32.14	—	—	—	—	—
—	WisdomTree Intl Comm DGG	SC		35.58	35.06	0.49	27.37	—	—	25.78	—	—	—	—	—
—	WisdomTree Intl Con Cycl DPC	FB		29.12	28.96	0.03	5.26	—	—	4.71	—	—	—	—	—
—	WisdomTree Intl Con NonCy DPN	FB		30.07	30.16	0.58	14.76	—	—	14.52	—	—	—	—	—
—	WisdomTree Intl Energy DKA	SN		34.36	34.03	0.22	25.46	—	—	23.39	—	—	—	—	—
—	WisdomTree Intl Financial DRF	SF		26.85	26.76	0.28	1.52	—	—	0.61	—	—	—	—	—
—	WisdomTree Intl Hlth Care DBR	SH		26.64	26.75	0.38	3.50	—	—	3.13	—	—	—	—	—
—	WisdomTree Intl Indust DDI	FB		32.57	32.28	0.40	16.57	—	—	14.80	—	—	—	—	—
—	WisdomTree Intl LgCap Div DOL	FB		68.72	68.16	0.19	15.46	—	—	14.08	—	—	—	—	—
—	WisdomTree Intl MdCap Div DIM	FA		67.33	66.68	0.13	9.05	—	—	7.68	—	—	—	—	—
—	★ WisdomTree Intl RealEst DRW	SR		48.27	49.35	1.04	—	—	—	—	—	—	—	—	—
—	WisdomTree Intl SmCap Div DLS	FA		65.47	64.25	0.20	6.82	—	—	4.00	—	—	—	—	—
—	WisdomTree Intl Tech DBT	ST		24.76	24.70	0.53	–6.11	—	—	–6.74	—	—	—	—	—
—	WisdomTree Intl Utilities DBU	SU		35.02	35.05	0.63	24.21	—	—	23.28	—	—	—	—	—
—	WisdomTree Japan HiYld Eq DNL	JS		53.15	52.18	–0.28	–5.48	—	—	–7.75	—	—	—	—	—
—	WisdomTree Japan SmCp Div DFJ	JS		45.94	44.80	–0.42	–7.63	—	—	–10.60	—	—	—	—	—
—	WisdomTree Japan Tot Div DXJ	JS		51.71	50.80	–0.31	–4.89	—	—	–7.32	—	—	—	—	—
83	WisdomTree LargeCap Div DLN	LB		57.95	57.76	–0.02	2.99	—	—	2.64	—	—	—	—	—
—	★ WisdomTree Low P/E EZY	LB		48.73	48.66	–0.01	—	—	—	—	—	—	—	—	—
84	WisdomTree MidCap Div DON	MB		52.18	52.02	–0.11	–5.49	—	—	–5.85	—	—	—	—	—
—	★ WisdomTree MidCap Earning EZM	MB		46.32	46.18	0.00	—	—	—	—	—	—	—	—	—
—	WisdomTree Pac ex-Jp HYEq DNH	PJ		71.24	70.49	–0.09	21.67	—	—	19.59	—	—	—	—	—
—	WisdomTree Pac ex-Jp TDiv DND	PJ		82.66	82.00	0.12	34.80	—	—	33.10	—	—	—	—	—
—	WisdomTree SmallCap Div DES	SB		48.54	48.53	–0.12	–12.50	—	—	–12.43	—	—	—	—	—
—	★ WisdomTree SmCap Earning EES	SB		42.03	42.22	–0.08	—	—	—	—	—	—	—	—	—
85	WisdomTree Total Dividend DTD	LB		56.85	56.75	–0.01	1.33	—	—	1.18	—	—	—	—	—
—	★ WisdomTree Total Earnings EXT	LB		50.15	50.00	–0.06	—	—	—	—	—	—	—	—	—

Fund Categories

BM	Bear Market	GI	Intermediate-Term Government Bond	MF	Muni California Interm/Short	SP	Specialty–Precious Metals
CA	Conservative Allocation	GL	Long-Term Government Bond	MG	Mid-Cap Growth	SN	Specialty–Natural Resources
CI	Intermediate-Term Bond	GS	Short-Term Government Bond	MI	Muni National Interm	SR	Specialty–Real Estate
CL	Long-Term Bond	HY	High-Yield Bond	ML	Muni National Long	ST	Specialty–Technology
CS	Short-Term Bond	IB	World Bond	MS	Muni National Short	SU	Specialty–Utilities
DP	Diversified Pacific Stock	IP	Inflation-Protected Bond	MY	Muni New York Long	SV	Small-Cap Value
EB	Emerging Markets Bond	JS	Japan Stock	MN	Muni New York Interm/Short	TC	Target-Date 2030+
EM	Diversified Emerging Markets	LB	Large-Cap Blend	MV	Mid-Cap Value	TA	Target-Date 2000–2014
ES	Europe Stock	LG	Large-Cap Growth	PJ	Pacific ex-Japan Stock	TB	Target-Date 2015–2029
FB	Foreign Large Growth	LS	Latin America Stock	SB	Small-Cap Blend	UB	Ultrashort Bond
FG	Foreign Large Growth	LV	Large-Cap Value	SC	Specialty–Communications	WS	World Stock
FR	Foreign Small Mid Growth	MA	Moderate Allocation	SF	Specialty–Financials		
FA	Foreign Small Mid Value	MB	Mid-Cap Blend	SG	Small-Cap Growth		
FV	Foreign Large Value	MC	Muni California Long	SH	Specialty–Health		

Performance Summary

U.S.-Listed ETFs

Portfolio				Morningstar Valuation		Costs		Trading Information	
Top 3 Sectors	Avg. Mkt. Cap. ($mil)	P/E Ratio	P/B Ratio	Price/ Fair Value	Coverage Rate %	Expense Ratio %	Tax-Cost Ratio	52-week High/Low	Avg. Daily Vol.
Financial	—	—	—	1.00	2.42	0.11	—	77.41–73.27	198,536
Utilities, Energy	13,692	16.42	2.24	0.97	89.73	0.22	0.76	91.00–75.31	29,542
Financial, Energy, Industrial Materials	58,387	13.58	2.08	0.85	97.87	0.11	0.70	74.25–64.13	228,227
Hardware, Telecom	65,501	20.24	2.92	1.03	87.86	—	—	—	10,742
Financial, Industrial Materials, Telecom	40,151	13.20	2.00	1.00	2.55	0.48	—	74.72–60.03	79,819
Financial, Telecom, Energy	47,038	11.82	1.92	1.00	2.65	0.58	—	72.85–59.36	22,046
Financial, Utilities, Industrial Materials	27,197	15.64	1.88	0.87	98.95	0.38	—	63.28–53.40	37,945
Financial, Industrial Materials, Energy	30,161	11.78	1.77	0.87	99.87	0.38	—	54.75–47.25	4,412
Financial, Energy, Industrial Materials	61,044	14.20	2.26	0.88	99.29	0.28	—	53.60–47.13	18,459
Industrial Materials, Energy, Telecom	11,630	12.00	2.24	0.99	2.13	0.63	—	56.85–43.07	47,270
Industrial Materials, Business Svs, Financial	1,537	11.06	1.85	1.00	0.11	0.63	—	51.80–44.61	19,695
Industrial Materials, Business Svs, Financial	1,069	13.09	1.91	1.00	0.01	0.58	—	76.41–58.22	15,452
Financial, Energy, Consumer Goods	48,101	12.43	2.03	1.00	1.83	0.48	—	72.92–59.51	15,562
Financial, Telecom, Energy	62,280	11.22	1.86	1.00	0.04	0.58	—	70.96–59.02	11,027
Financial, Industrial Materials, Consumer Goods	54,075	14.67	1.90	0.84	94.95	0.38	—	61.51–50.83	29,465
Financial, Telecom, Utilities	45,161	11.88	2.01	1.00	2.53	0.58	—	77.03–61.74	53,023
Industrial Materials, Healthcare, Consumer Goods	24,642	13.43	2.24	1.00	9.02	0.58	—	40.78–27.33	40,136
Telecom, Media, Hardware	62,081	16.86	2.47	1.00	5.38	0.58	—	37.94–27.42	27,826
Consumer Goods, Consumer Svs, Industrial Materials	15,985	13.10	1.67	1.00	6.39	0.58	—	33.64–27.20	3,828
Consumer Goods, Healthcare, Consumer Svs	39,657	17.72	3.06	1.00	—	0.58	—	31.32–26.42	10,321
Energy, Business Svs, Consumer Svs	49,424	12.65	2.33	1.00	—	0.58	—	36.97–26.17	16,438
Financial, Business Svs, Industrial Materials	43,769	10.32	1.53	0.99	3.11	0.58	—	30.28–25.82	15,933
Healthcare, Industrial Materials, Consumer Svs	23,587	17.89	2.77	1.00	—	0.58	—	28.42–25.35	11,002
Industrial Materials, Business Svs, Hardware	10,613	15.44	2.19	1.00	—	0.58	—	36.06–27.96	13,130
Financial, Telecom, Energy	73,473	12.97	2.12	1.00	3.64	0.48	—	73.60–58.76	24,230
Industrial Materials, Financial, Business Svs	7,537	14.96	2.03	1.00	0.01	0.58	—	75.07–62.28	34,606
Financial, Consumer Svs, Business Svs	7,449	19.09	1.18	1.00	—	0.58	—	55.66–43.42	55,647
Industrial Materials, Business Svs, Financial	1,256	14.53	1.64	1.00	0.11	0.58	—	74.23–61.77	73,067
Software, Consumer Goods, Business Svs	10,337	16.93	2.29	1.00	—	0.58	—	28.97–23.57	5,693
Utilities, Energy, Business Svs	36,547	18.13	2.58	1.00	—	0.58	—	36.25–27.60	82,264
Consumer Goods, Industrial Materials, Utilities	12,184	15.77	1.35	1.00	0.01	0.58	—	62.37–51.44	10,690
Industrial Materials, Consumer Goods, Financial	1,005	17.12	1.06	1.00	0.04	0.58	—	54.35–44.68	15,909
Industrial Materials, Consumer Goods, Financial	15,001	15.83	1.44	1.00	0.02	0.48	—	59.57–50.19	8,414
Financial, Industrial Materials, Consumer Goods	79,143	14.85	2.30	0.86	99.87	0.28	—	62.70–55.87	96,293
Financial, Energy, Industrial Materials	44,311	11.82	1.83	0.85	95.76	0.38	—	54.11–46.27	6,181
Financial, Utilities, Industrial Materials	3,891	16.66	1.68	0.91	83.06	0.38	—	61.60–49.11	31,558
Industrial Materials, Financial, Consumer Svs	2,651	14.39	1.74	0.91	74.48	0.38	—	53.52–43.73	19,091
Financial, Industrial Materials, Telecom	13,286	14.45	2.45	1.00	8.57	0.58	—	83.15–59.93	14,066
Financial, Telecom, Industrial Materials	22,137	16.53	2.61	1.00	8.20	0.48	—	92.85–61.46	82,079
Financial, Industrial Materials, Consumer Goods	789	15.78	1.50	0.94	32.41	0.38	—	59.67–45.45	64,698
Financial, Industrial Materials, Business Svs	584	13.20	1.45	0.96	29.71	0.38	—	51.13–39.13	7,693
Financial, Industrial Materials, Consumer Goods	48,384	15.08	2.16	0.87	96.03	0.28	—	62.20–54.59	18,569
Financial, Energy, Industrial Materials	39,297	14.26	2.16	0.88	95.61	0.28	—	53.56–47.24	5,063

Equity Style Box

Val Blnd Grth

Lg Mid Sm

Sectors

- Information
- Software
- Hardware
- Media
- Telecom
- Service
- Healthcare
- Consumer Svs
- Business Svs
- Financial
- Manufacturing
- Consumer Goods
- Industrial Materials
- Energy
- Utilities

Performance Summary

Indexes

Page(s)	Index	Annualized Total Return% 3 Yr	5 Yr	10 Yr	Annual Total Return % 2007	2006	2005	2004	2003	2002	2001	2000	1999	1998
	U.S. Diversified													
30	DJ Industrial Average TR USD	9.66	12.24	7.43	8.88	19.05	1.72	5.31	28.28	–15.01	–5.44	–4.85	27.21	18.13
31	DJ US Select Dividend TR USD	5.57	12.59	9.40	–5.16	19.56	3.77	18.14	30.16	–3.94	13.09	24.86	–4.08	4.33
32	DJ US TR USD	9.21	13.79	6.18	6.01	15.57	6.32	12.01	30.75	–22.08	–11.95	–9.23	22.72	24.90
—	DJ Wilshire 4500 Full Cap TR USD	10.63	18.20	7.86	5.78	16.07	10.27	18.57	43.72	–17.81	–9.30	–15.77	35.49	8.63
—	DJ Wilshire 5000 Full Cap TR USD	9.21	14.07	6.34	5.73	15.88	6.32	12.62	31.64	–20.86	–10.97	–10.89	23.56	23.43
70	DJ Wilshire US Large Cap Value TR USD	9.48	14.23	7.56	1.84	21.87	5.72	13.55	30.55	–14.72	–5.39	6.88	4.80	17.92
60	Dynamic Large Cap Grth Intellidex PR USD	7.37	—	—	12.10	5.38	4.78	—	—	—	—	—	—	—
61	Dynamic Large Cap Valu Intellidex PR USD	11.57	—	—	3.58	22.10	9.83	—	—	—	—	—	—	—
62	Dynamic Market Intellidex PR USD	8.63	—	—	3.38	10.22	12.49	—	—	—	—	—	—	—
63	Dynamic Mid Cap Growth Intellidex PR USD	17.47	—	—	27.81	9.54	15.80	—	—	—	—	—	—	—
64	Dynamic Mid Cap Value Intellidex PR USD	7.64	—	—	–0.67	12.98	11.13	—	—	—	—	—	—	—
33	KLD Select Social PR USD	5.32	—	—	2.68	11.52	2.04	—	—	—	—	—	—	—
79	MSCI US Broad Market GR USD	9.13	—	—	5.59	15.72	6.37	12.39	—	—	—	—	—	—
77	MSCI US Mid Cap 450 GR USD	11.23	18.19	10.02	6.19	13.75	13.94	20.52	39.05	–16.46	–6.38	–1.85	34.32	9.26
76	MSCI US Prime Market 750 GR USD	9.35	13.53	6.15	6.38	15.68	6.26	11.41	29.45	–21.93	–12.84	–11.89	24.56	28.90
—	MSCI US Prime Market Growth	9.02	12.44	4.27	12.73	9.20	5.25	7.38	29.20	–27.30	–22.14	–27.79	43.96	43.62
80	MSCI US Prime Market Value GR USD	9.57	14.52	7.70	0.22	22.37	7.26	15.44	29.72	–16.95	–3.33	9.02	6.25	14.63
134	MSCI US REIT	8.23	17.91	10.37	–16.82	35.92	12.13	31.49	36.74	3.64	12.83	26.81	–4.55	–16.90
78	MSCI US Small Cap Growth GR USD	10.14	18.46	8.50	9.71	12.03	8.71	16.13	50.37	–29.31	–6.29	–8.25	49.55	6.63
—	Morningstar Dividend Leaders TR USD	5.14	11.02	10.47	–10.34	25.64	3.16	13.80	27.53	–7.28	5.03	48.75	–13.77	28.53
—	Morningstar Large Cap TR USD	9.05	12.53	5.10	6.69	15.91	4.87	9.54	27.04	–23.47	–15.10	–11.38	21.05	30.74
—	Morningstar Large Core TR USD	9.23	13.13	6.22	8.64	15.54	3.82	13.99	24.71	–23.82	–14.35	4.24	17.81	23.18
—	Morningstar Large Growth TR USD	7.08	9.96	0.89	12.34	5.68	3.43	0.19	30.65	–33.15	–29.07	–33.51	42.59	51.23
—	Morningstar Large Value TR USD	10.27	14.06	7.09	–0.43	25.78	7.05	14.05	26.26	–15.05	–3.38	5.66	0.57	17.85
—	Morningstar Mid Cap TR USD	10.68	17.55	8.68	5.23	14.32	12.70	19.66	38.38	–18.06	–4.63	6.94	15.55	6.01
—	Morningstar Mid Core TR USD	8.78	16.27	9.03	1.95	14.72	10.05	19.05	38.68	–12.42	6.05	14.77	1.89	2.87
—	Morningstar Mid Growth TR USD	15.13	19.79	6.83	19.70	9.63	16.27	15.45	40.02	–32.54	–21.59	–11.10	52.46	9.49
—	Morningstar Mid Value TR USD	7.78	16.17	9.41	–5.52	18.81	11.54	24.30	35.94	–10.00	5.06	24.59	–6.83	5.85
—	Morningstar Small Cap TR USD	7.14	16.95	8.13	–0.66	17.05	5.76	20.44	47.70	–20.36	5.26	7.66	17.78	–6.01
—	Morningstar Small Core TR USD	6.80	16.51	10.88	–5.43	21.16	6.30	23.61	42.59	–14.16	14.60	23.21	16.74	–7.55
—	Morningstar Small Growth TR USD	8.94	17.50	4.03	11.08	10.04	5.77	13.48	52.65	–36.87	–12.92	–12.10	46.80	–6.55
—	Morningstar Small Value TR USD	5.04	16.43	9.70	–8.15	20.03	5.12	24.03	48.87	–8.24	18.58	18.65	–5.19	–3.67
—	Morningstar US Core TR USD	9.03	14.03	7.14	6.44	15.76	5.19	15.62	28.63	–21.18	–9.31	7.10	14.67	17.75
—	Morningstar US Growth TR USD	8.97	12.62	2.57	13.82	6.83	6.41	4.37	34.12	–33.20	–26.32	–28.45	44.51	39.76
—	Morningstar US Market TR USD	9.29	13.90	6.14	5.92	15.70	6.52	12.35	30.73	–22.17	–11.88	–7.02	19.79	23.86
—	Morningstar US Value TR USD	9.49	14.75	7.78	–1.91	24.10	7.82	16.85	29.75	–13.68	–0.68	10.06	–1.27	14.13
—	Morningstar Wide Moat Focus TR USD	—	—	—	–1.31	17.72	4.67	27.82	36.20	—	—	—	—	—
66,73	NASDAQ 100 PR USD	8.75	16.20	7.72	18.67	6.79	1.49	10.44	49.12	–37.58	–32.65	–36.84	101.95	85.31
—	NYSE Composite PR	10.34	14.27	6.07	6.58	17.86	6.95	12.16	29.28	–19.83	–10.21	1.01	9.15	16.55
34	NYSE US 100 PR	5.63	8.69	—	1.50	14.52	1.40	6.68	20.61	—	—	—	—	—
35	Russell 1000 Growth TR USD	8.68	12.11	3.83	11.81	9.07	5.26	6.30	29.75	–27.88	–20.42	–22.42	33.16	38.71
36	Russell 1000 TR USD	9.08	13.43	6.20	5.77	15.46	6.27	11.40	29.89	–21.65	–12.45	–7.79	20.91	27.02
37	Russell 1000 Value TR USD	9.32	14.63	7.68	–0.17	22.25	7.05	16.49	30.03	–15.52	–5.59	7.01	7.35	15.63
38	Russell 2000 Growth TR USD	8.11	16.50	4.32	7.05	13.35	4.15	14.31	48.54	–30.26	–9.23	–22.43	43.09	1.23
39	Russell 2000 TR USD	6.80	16.25	7.08	–1.57	18.37	4.55	18.33	47.25	–20.48	2.49	–3.02	21.26	–2.55
40	Russell 2000 Value TR USD	5.27	15.80	9.06	–9.78	23.48	4.71	22.25	46.03	–11.43	14.02	22.83	–1.49	–6.45
41	Russell 3000 Growth TR USD	8.64	12.42	3.83	11.40	9.46	5.17	6.93	30.97	–28.03	–19.63	–22.42	33.83	35.02
42	Russell 3000 TR USD	8.89	13.63	6.22	5.14	15.72	6.12	11.95	31.06	–21.54	–11.46	–7.46	20.90	24.14
43	Russell 3000 Value TR USD	8.97	14.69	7.73	–1.01	22.34	6.85	16.94	31.14	–15.18	–4.33	8.04	6.65	13.50
44	Russell Micro Cap TR USD	3.22	15.87	—	–8.00	16.54	2.57	14.14	66.36	–16.10	17.58	—	—	—
46	Russell Mid Cap Growth TR USD	11.39	17.90	7.59	11.43	10.66	12.10	15.48	42.71	–27.41	–20.15	–11.75	51.29	17.86
45	Russell Mid Cap TR USD	11.09	18.21	9.91	5.60	15.26	12.65	20.22	40.06	–16.19	–5.62	8.25	18.23	10.09
47	Russell Mid Cap Value TR USD	10.11	17.92	10.18	–1.42	20.22	12.65	23.71	38.07	–9.64	2.33	19.18	–0.11	5.08
48	S&P 100 TR	8.35	11.31	5.84	6.12	18.47	1.17	6.43	26.25	–22.59	–13.81	–12.55	32.79	33.21
49	S&P 1500 TR	8.72	13.23	6.35	5.47	15.34	5.66	11.78	29.59	–21.31	–10.64	–6.98	20.26	26.35

Performance Summary

Indexes

		Annualized Total Return%			Annual Total Return %									
Page(s)	Index	3 Yr	5 Yr	10 Yr	2007	2006	2005	2004	2003	2002	2001	2000	1999	1998
69	S&P 500 Equal Weighted TR	8.31	15.94	8.93	1.53	15.80	8.06	16.95	40.97	−18.18	−0.39	9.64	12.03	12.19
50,72	S&P 500 TR	8.62	12.83	5.91	5.49	15.79	4.91	10.88	28.68	−22.10	−11.89	−9.10	21.04	28.58
51	S&P 500/Citi Growth TR	7.01	10.74	4.42	9.13	11.01	1.14	6.97	27.08	−28.10	−16.12	−19.14	37.38	38.16
52	S&P 500/Citi Value TR	10.23	14.97	6.68	1.99	20.80	8.71	15.03	30.36	−16.59	−8.18	−0.51	4.88	18.91
71	S&P High Yield Divdend Aristocrats	—	—	—	−9.54	14.09	—	—	—	—	—	—	—	—
53,59	S&P MidCap 400 TR	10.27	16.20	11.19	7.98	10.32	12.56	16.48	35.62	−14.53	−0.61	17.51	14.72	19.12
54	S&P MidCap 400/Citi Growth TR	11.17	16.92	13.97	13.50	5.81	14.42	15.78	37.32	−19.67	−2.55	15.77	36.10	37.19
55	S&P MidCap 400/Citi Value TR	9.23	15.36	8.52	2.65	14.62	10.77	17.18	33.80	−9.43	1.43	19.51	−2.63	3.71
56	S&P SmallCap 600 TR	7.32	16.04	9.03	−0.30	15.12	7.68	22.65	38.79	−14.63	6.54	11.80	12.40	−1.31
57	S&P SmallCap 600/Citi Growth TR	7.71	16.56	9.05	5.60	10.54	7.06	24.29	38.50	−16.57	3.00	7.59	19.72	−0.08
58	S&P SmallCap 600/Citi Value TR	6.97	15.58	8.81	−5.54	19.57	8.36	21.09	39.20	−12.93	9.52	15.77	4.91	−2.63
	U.S. Sector													
185	AMEX Gold Miners PR USD	22.49	19.58	—	16.86	21.86	29.08	−9.56	47.07	—	—	—	—	—
124	AMEX Morgan Stanley Technology PR USD	7.03	16.69	—	9.56	8.81	2.86	6.69	65.39	−43.26	—	—	—	—
98	DJ US Basic Materials TR USD	16.91	18.34	8.24	32.86	17.63	4.97	13.05	35.68	−8.32	1.64	−15.67	27.10	−8.27
99	DJ US Consumer Goods TR USD	11.41	12.63	6.45	9.69	14.91	2.04	13.02	24.30	−4.74	−1.10	4.49	−10.21	10.80
101	DJ US Financial Services TR USD	—	—	—	−21.41	19.93	4.10	12.57	34.92	−11.92	−5.76	23.86	2.40	8.98
100	DJ US Financial TR USD	4.69	9.49	7.09	−17.66	19.42	6.46	13.39	32.23	−12.35	−6.38	26.94	1.52	7.51
102	DJ US Health Care TR USD	10.94	9.18	7.73	8.36	6.88	8.32	4.55	19.43	−20.81	−12.84	37.84	−4.03	39.09
109	DJ US Home Const PR USD	−26.14	—	—	−55.80	−20.61	14.81	—	—	—	—	—	—	—
103	DJ US Industrials TR USD	11.84	15.12	6.20	13.57	13.87	4.82	17.25	33.24	−25.54	−10.16	−9.14	26.72	10.98
—	DJ US Oil&Gas TR USD	30.45	29.88	15.07	34.84	22.77	34.09	32.43	25.74	−13.52	−11.66	26.56	20.18	−5.20
104	DJ US Real Estate TR USD	6.73	16.91	9.20	−18.15	35.50	9.64	31.22	36.89	3.63	11.69	27.64	−5.31	−21.12
105	DJ US Technology TR USD	10.22	11.28	4.97	15.70	10.10	3.31	1.76	51.04	−38.66	−28.34	−36.99	83.68	70.30
106	DJ US Telecom TR USD	12.92	10.62	1.21	10.04	36.83	−4.00	18.70	7.33	−34.55	−12.77	−40.27	18.41	51.82
108	DJ US Utilities TR USD	18.98	21.41	9.39	17.76	21.28	15.35	24.04	24.91	−21.19	−26.18	56.07	−13.19	13.32
91	DJ Wilshire REIT TR USD	8.46	18.27	11.05	−17.56	35.97	13.82	33.16	36.18	3.58	12.35	31.04	−2.58	−17.01
128	MSCI US IMI/Cons Staple GR USD	11.06	11.32	5.90	13.92	15.03	4.53	9.29	14.18	−3.99	−4.64	17.17	−15.04	13.89
129	MSCI US IMI/Energy GR USD	30.07	29.70	15.08	34.42	21.03	35.27	33.20	25.21	−9.70	−10.77	25.99	19.17	−8.23
130	MSCI US IMI/Financials GR USD	1.64	—	—	−17.34	19.50	6.28	—	—	—	—	—	—	—
131	MSCI US IMI/Health Care GR USD	7.77	—	—	7.99	6.85	8.47	—	—	—	—	—	—	—
132	MSCI US IMI/Info Tech GR USD	9.03	—	—	15.13	9.21	3.09	—	—	—	—	—	—	—
133	MSCI US IMI/Materials GR USD	16.34	—	—	26.47	19.80	3.94	—	—	—	—	—	—	—
135	MSCI US IMI/Tele Svcs GR USD	14.09	—	—	10.48	37.26	−2.07	—	—	—	—	—	—	—
136	MSCI US IMI/Utilities GR USD	18.04	—	—	17.50	21.71	15.02	—	—	—	—	—	—	—
89	S&P 500 Sec/Cons Disc TR	−1.21	8.46	5.20	−13.21	18.64	−6.36	13.25	37.42	−23.82	2.79	−20.00	25.18	41.14
90	S&P 500 Sec/Cons Staples TR	10.59	10.30	5.32	14.18	14.36	3.58	8.18	11.57	−4.26	−6.40	16.78	−15.09	15.76
92	S&P 500 Sec/Energy TR	29.92	29.38	14.84	34.40	24.21	31.37	31.56	25.64	−11.13	−10.40	15.68	18.73	0.63
93	S&P 500 Sec/Financials TR	1.08	8.48	5.46	−18.63	19.19	6.48	10.91	31.13	−14.64	−8.95	25.70	4.12	11.42
94	S&P 500 Sec/Health Care TR	7.05	7.51	6.10	7.15	7.53	6.46	1.76	15.06	−18.82	−11.95	37.05	−10.66	43.88
95	S&P 500 Sec/Industrials TR	9.10	15.17	7.21	12.03	13.29	2.32	18.04	32.20	−26.34	−5.74	5.88	21.50	10.87
125	S&P 500 Sec/Information Technology TR	8.39	13.97	5.32	16.31	8.42	0.99	2.56	47.23	−37.41	−25.87	−40.90	78.74	78.14
115	S&P 500 Sec/Materials TR	14.92	18.88	8.69	22.53	18.63	4.42	13.20	38.20	−5.46	3.48	−15.72	25.26	−6.18
127	S&P 500 Sec/Utilities TR	19.07	21.53	7.79	19.38	20.99	16.87	24.32	26.34	−29.99	−30.44	57.19	−9.18	14.84
110	S&P GSSI Natural Resources TR	—	—	—	34.44	16.85	36.61	24.59	34.40	−12.99	−15.59	15.79	27.23	−14.19
111	S&P GSTI Semiconductor TR	—	—	—	−1.51	0.68	13.93	−13.97	82.92	—	—	—	—	—
112	S&P GSTI Technology TR	—	—	—	16.94	8.98	2.02	2.92	54.18	−40.27	−28.58	−37.84	88.87	69.16
122	S&P Homebuilders Select Industry	—	—	—	−48.39	—	—	—	—	—	—	—	—	—
123	S&P Oil&Gas Explor&Prodn Select Industry	—	—	—	36.61	—	—	—	—	—	—	—	—	—

NDTR_D = the index is listed in US dollars, with net dividends reinvested. ID = the index is listed in dollars, without net dividends reinvested. TR = Total Return

Performance Summary

Indexes

Page(s)	Index	Annualized Total Return% 3 Yr	5 Yr	10 Yr	Annual Total Return % 2007	2006	2005	2004	2003	2002	2001	2000	1999	1998
	Foreign Diversified													
138	BONY Emerging Markets 50 ADR TR USD	40.99	—	—	43.50	37.88	41.65	18.97	—	—	—	—	—	—
144	DJ Titans Global 50 PR USD	—	—	—	3.99	17.44	0.82	5.53	22.23	−24.30	—	—	—	—
140	MSCI EAFE Free Growth NR USD	17.29	19.85	—	16.45	22.33	13.28	16.12	31.99	−16.02	−24.58	−24.43	29.89	—
139	MSCI EAFE Free NR USD	16.83	21.59	8.65	11.17	26.34	13.54	20.25	38.59	−15.94	−21.44	−14.16	26.94	19.87
141	MSCI EAFE Free Value NR USD	16.27	23.21	—	5.96	30.38	13.80	24.33	45.30	−15.91	−18.52	−3.03	23.55	—
142,145	MSCI EM NR USD	35.15	37.02	—	39.39	32.17	34.00	25.55	55.82	−6.17	−2.62	−30.56	67.44	—
	Foreign Country/Region													
148	MSCI Australia NR USD	24.90	30.57	15.64	28.34	30.86	16.02	30.34	49.46	−1.34	1.68	−9.97	17.66	6.05
149	MSCI Brazil NR USD	59.81	64.07	—	79.56	45.30	56.45	35.48	115.01	−30.65	−16.99	−11.50	71.21	—
150	MSCI Canada NR USD	25.11	29.91	14.53	29.57	17.80	28.31	22.20	54.60	−13.19	−20.43	5.34	53.82	−6.19
151	MSCI EMU NR USD	21.03	25.24	—	19.55	36.29	8.80	21.41	43.15	−21.94	−22.51	−8.38	19.05	—
165	MSCI Europe NR USD	18.55	22.78	9.55	13.86	33.72	9.42	20.88	38.54	−18.38	−19.90	−8.40	15.93	28.50
153	MSCI Germany NR USD	26.43	30.92	10.09	35.21	35.99	9.92	16.17	63.80	−33.18	−22.39	−15.60	20.08	29.41
154	MSCI Hong Kong NR USD	25.89	28.06	11.77	41.20	30.35	8.40	24.98	38.10	−17.79	−18.61	−14.42	59.44	−3.23
155	MSCI Japan NR USD	8.50	15.00	4.50	−4.23	6.24	25.52	15.86	35.91	−10.28	−29.40	−28.16	61.53	5.05
161	MSCI Korea NR USD	32.60	30.89	—	31.85	12.64	56.97	22.06	35.02	8.29	48.02	−49.75	93.20	—
156	MSCI Mexico NR USD	33.24	36.04	—	12.15	41.44	49.11	48.32	32.81	−13.31	18.41	−20.00	78.57	—
157	MSCI Pacific Ex Japan NR USD	25.24	29.76	13.30	30.73	32.02	13.81	28.46	45.77	−6.42	−9.88	−15.42	42.64	−6.85
166	MSCI Pacific NR USD	13.16	19.01	6.83	5.30	12.20	22.64	18.98	38.48	−9.29	−25.40	−25.76	57.63	2.41
160	MSCI Singapore Free NR USD	29.14	29.37	10.67	28.35	46.71	14.37	22.27	37.60	−11.05	−23.42	−27.40	60.20	−4.03
162	MSCI Taiwan NR USD	11.42	16.43	—	8.38	19.97	6.38	8.99	41.91	−24.69	10.05	−44.75	52.10	—
163	MSCI UK NR USD	14.96	19.13	7.43	8.36	30.61	7.35	19.57	32.06	−15.23	−14.05	−11.65	12.44	17.97
158	S&P Europe 350 TR USD	19.30	23.34	9.97	15.59	33.69	9.88	21.20	38.72	−17.91	−19.58	−7.12	16.94	26.32
113	S&P Global 1200 Sec/Financials TR	9.12	16.15	—	−7.72	24.59	13.01	17.24	38.76	−16.16	−14.06	14.59	8.57	—
159	S&P Latin America 40 TR	49.59	50.42	20.79	50.47	42.57	56.05	38.72	65.81	−23.32	3.42	−8.62	78.31	−33.53
	Fixed Income													
169	LB 1-3 Yr US Treasury PR USD	—	—	—	2.89	—	—	—	—	—	—	—	—	—
172,175,177	LB US Agg Bond TR USD	4.56	4.42	5.97	6.97	4.33	2.43	4.34	4.10	10.25	8.44	11.63	−0.82	8.69
171	LB US Treasury 20+ Yr TR USD	7.64	7.04	7.57	10.15	0.93	8.57	8.99	1.80	17.00	3.63	21.50	−10.06	14.22
170	LB US Treasury 7-10 Yr TR USD	7.30	6.03	6.94	10.20	8.11	2.43	4.41	1.88	14.49	6.82	14.74	−5.33	12.36
173	LB US Treasury US TIPS TR USD	5.52	7.01	7.43	11.64	0.41	2.84	8.46	8.40	16.57	7.90	13.18	2.39	3.95
	Specialty/Other													
181	DJ AIG Commodity TR USD	12.92	14.26	8.97	16.23	2.07	21.36	9.15	23.93	25.91	−19.51	31.84	24.35	−27.03
186	Deutsche Bank Liquid Commodity	—	—	—	26.83	—	—	—	—	—	—	—	—	—
183,187	IA Gold Price PR USD	20.00	19.68	10.19	—	23.20	17.77	4.40	20.18	25.57	0.75	−5.44	0.85	−0.82
182	S&P GSCI Commodity TR	12.25	14.90	9.33	32.67	−15.09	25.55	17.28	20.72	32.07	−31.93	49.74	40.92	−35.75

Performance Summary

Best & Worst Performing ETFs

Best Performing

Page	Name	Total Return %*	Investor Return%
One Year (12-31-07)			
—	Market Vectors Steel ETF SLX	83.34	59.21
149	iShares Brazil Index EWZ	76.59	70.79
—	iPath MSCI India Idx ETN INP	72.01	80.01
164	PowerShares Halter USX PGJ	68.42	61.27
—	Claymore/BNY BRIC EEB	67.75	53.66
—	MACROshares Oil Up UCR	61.37	58.97
—	PowerShares WilderHill PBW	59.46	61.19
152	iShares FTSE/Xinhua China FXI	58.66	53.87
159	iShares SP Latin 40 ILF	48.75	47.07
—	iPath S&P GSCI CrOil ETN OIL	46.75	48.58
—	United States Oil USO	46.15	35.20
—	iShares Malaysia EWM	45.46	41.47
138	BLDRS Emerg Mkts 50 ADR ADRE	43.78	43.82
—	iShares DJ US Oil Equip IEZ	42.67	36.84
—	SPDR S&P Metals & Mining XME	42.57	32.57
Three Year (12-31-07)			
149	iShares Brazil Index EWZ	57.19	55.63
152	iShares FTSE/Xinhua China FXI	49.15	55.75
159	iShares SP Latin 40 ILF	48.41	44.48
138	BLDRS Emerg Mkts 50 ADR ADRE	40.74	38.84
164	PowerShares Halter USX PGJ	35.61	47.85
156	iShares Mexico Index EWW	33.02	27.27
142	iShares MSCI Emerg Mkts EEM	33.00	31.61
161	iShares S.Korea Indx EWY	31.51	23.36
92	Energy SPDR XLE	31.30	30.80
129	Vanguard Energy ETF VDE	30.67	26.48
116	Oil Services HOLDRs OIH	30.49	—
107	iShares DJ US Energy IYE	29.99	27.53
160	iShares Singapore EWS	29.20	28.85
110	iShares S&P GSSI Nat Res IGE	28.33	25.91
—	iShares SP Glb Enrgy IXC	26.63	22.70
Five Year (12-31-07)			
149	iShares Brazil Index EWZ	61.83	57.05
159	iShares SP Latin 40 ILF	49.09	44.94
138	BLDRS Emerg Mkts 50 ADR ADRE	37.66	38.15
156	iShares Mexico Index EWW	36.60	29.61
—	iShares Austria Index EWO	35.97	21.01
—	iShares Spain Index EWP	31.13	28.98
148	iShares Australia EWA	31.12	25.98
92	Energy SPDR XLE	30.72	31.28
153	iShares Germany Indx EWG	30.56	31.43
160	iShares Singapore EWS	29.87	28.99
157	iShares MSCI ex-Japn EPP	29.87	27.27
107	iShares DJ US Energy IYE	29.75	28.54
150	iShares Canada Index EWC	29.51	28.21
161	iShares S.Korea Indx EWY	29.17	23.07
—	iShares Sweden Index EWD	28.75	12.00

Worst Performing

Page	Name	Total Return %*	Investor Return%
One Year (12-31-07)			
109	iShares Dow Jones US Home ITB	–58.00	–59.93
—	MACROshares Oil Down DCR	–57.87	–58.35
122	SPDR S&P Homebuilders XHB	–47.69	–51.22
73	UltShort QQQ ProShares QID	–27.16	–25.24
—	iShares Dow Jones US RegB IAT	–25.54	–34.68
—	KBW Regional Banking ETF KRE	–22.25	–31.67
—	PowerShares Dyn Banking PJB	–22.25	–31.76
114	KBW Bank ETF KBE	–21.90	–33.96
101	iShares DJ Fin Svcs IYG	–21.69	–20.77
—	Rydex S&P Smallcap 600 Va RZV	–18.85	–25.27
93	Financial SPDR XLF	–18.79	–21.81
119	Regional Bank HOLDRs RKH	–18.63	—
97	iShares C&S Realty ICF	–18.30	–18.78
—	Rydex S&P EqWght Financls RYF	–18.24	–20.74
104	iShares DJ RE Index IYR	–18.15	–19.90
Three Year (12-31-07)			
96	Internet HOLDRs HHH	–6.02	—
119	Regional Bank HOLDRs RKH	–2.53	—
89	Consumer Discr SPDR XLY	–1.40	–3.40
101	iShares DJ Fin Svcs IYG	–1.12	0.91
121	Semiconductor HOLDRs SMH	–0.92	—
—	Vanguard Cons Disc ETF VCR	–0.42	–5.34
—	PowerShares HY Div Achiev PEY	0.48	1.96
93	Financial SPDR XLF	0.84	–3.62
—	iShares DJ Cons Services IYC	0.97	1.45
100	iShares DJ Fin Sectr IYF	1.04	0.46
130	Vanguard Financial ETF VFH	1.46	–8.23
88	Biotech HOLDRs BBH	1.89	—
120	Retail HOLDRs RTH	2.26	—
—	iShares NASD Biotech IBB	2.54	1.84
168	iShares iBoxx$ Corp Bd LQD	2.89	2.93
Five Year (12-31-07)			
117	Pharmaceutical HOLDRs PPH	1.34	—
169	iShares Lehman 1-3 T SHY	3.01	4.35
170	iShares Lehman 7-10 IEF	4.28	5.74
168	iShares iBoxx$ Corp Bd LQD	4.38	4.18
119	Regional Bank HOLDRs RKH	5.05	—
171	iShares Lehman 20+ TLT	5.94	8.28
94	Health Care Sel SPDR XLV	7.25	6.63
101	iShares DJ Fin Svcs IYG	7.72	6.60
121	Semiconductor HOLDRs SMH	7.94	—
93	Financial SPDR XLF	8.17	1.86
89	Consumer Discr SPDR XLY	8.20	3.33
—	iShares DJ Cons Services IYC	8.62	7.06
—	iShares SP Glb Hlth IXJ	8.70	7.12
102	iShares DJ Health IYH	8.80	7.77
100	iShares DJ Fin Sectr IYF	8.84	6.16

* Three- and five-year returns are annualized.

Morningstar Research

Cheapest & Dearest Stock ETFs

Cheapest Stock ETFs

Page	Name	Morningstar Coverage Rate*	Price per Share	Morningstar Fair Value per Share	Morningstar Price/Fair Value
U.S. Stock-Diversified					
—	ELEMENTS Mstar Wide Moat WMW	100.00	9.16	13.92	0.66
—	First Trust MStar Div Ld FDL	97.64	20.14	26.24	0.77
—	PowerShares High Gr Div PHJ	97.46	14.98	18.53	0.81
71	SPDR S&P Dividend SDY	86.04	55.06	68.00	0.81
31	iShares DJ Sel Dividend DVY	85.73	64.49	78.44	0.82
U.S. Stock-Sector					
114	KBW Bank ETF KBE	97.76	43.55	66.00	0.66
—	iShares Dow Jones US RegB IAT	90.82	37.60	53.65	0.70
119	Regional Bank HOLDRs RKH	96.24	131.43	183.74	0.72
101	iShares DJ Fin Svcs IYG	97.92	102.14	140.24	0.73
93	Financial SPDR XLF	99.72	28.93	38.04	0.76
Foreign Stock-Diversified					
144	SPDR DJ Global Titans DGT	91.96	78.85	88.78	0.89
—	BLDRS Dev Mkts 100 ADR ADRD	95.74	31.53	34.22	0.92
143	PowerShares Intl Div Ach PID	96.81	20.58	22.41	0.92
Foreign Stock-Country/Region					
—	BLDRS Europe 100 ADR ADRU	97.62	32.23	35.15	0.92
—	BLDRS Asia 50 ADR Index ADRA	88.11	34.22	34.99	0.98

Dearest Stock ETFs

Page	Name	Morningstar Coverage Rate*	Price per Share	Morningstar Fair Value per Share	Morningstar Price/Fair Value
U.S. Stock-Diversified					
—	First Trust Value Line100 FVL	84.20	17.91	16.02	1.12
—	PowerShares Val Line Indu PYH	80.81	29.62	26.78	1.11
—	PowerShares DWA Technical PDP	85.65	27.29	25.83	1.06
—	Claymore/Zacks Sector Rot XRO	96.29	32.28	30.53	1.06
63	PowerShares Dyn MidGrowth PWJ	91.84	24.26	23.34	1.04
U.S. Stock-Sector					
—	Internet Infr HOLDRs IIH	94.70	5.55	4.77	1.16
—	PowerShares Dyn Hlth Svcs PTJ	84.58	29.61	26.86	1.10
—	iShares DJ US Oil Equip IEZ	84.21	64.36	58.81	1.09
—	iShares DJ US Health Prov IHF	90.26	63.23	59.64	1.06
—	iShares FTSE NAREIT Resdn REZ	93.42	38.34	36.49	1.05
Foreign Stock-Diversified					
—	Market Vectors Glbl Agri MOO	73.56	57.45	50.84	1.13
138	BLDRS Emerg Mkts 50 ADR ADRE	86.59	55.04	53.44	1.03
—	Claymore/Robeco Dev World EEW	52.36	25.30	26.25	0.96
Foreign Stock-Country/Region					
164	PowerShares Halter USX PGJ	92.51	34.25	30.05	1.14
—	Claymore/BNY BRIC EEB	81.56	53.39	47.87	1.12

Limited to U.S.-focused ETFs with at least 80% coverage rates and foreign-focused funds with at least 50% coverage rates.

Morningstar Research

Highest & Lowest Quality Stock ETFs

Highest Quality Stock ETFs

Page	Name	Morningstar Coverage Rate %	% Wide Moat	% Narrow Moat	% No Moat	% Unrated
U.S. Stock-Diversified						
—	ELEMENTS Mstar Wide Moat WMW	100.00	99.99	0.00	0.00	0.00
30	DIAMONDS Trust DIA	100.00	72.37	22.85	4.61	0.00
68	Rydex Russell Top 50 XLG	100.00	72.17	25.68	0.00	1.04
—	PowerShares High Gr Div PHJ	97.46	70.58	26.07	1.16	1.97
—	iShares MstarLargeCore JKD	99.61	66.94	23.57	7.86	1.53
U.S. Stock-Sector						
117	Pharmaceutical HOLDRs PPH	99.33	90.52	4.81	3.70	0.97
—	B2B Internet HOLDRs BHH	0.00	74.80	0.00	0.00	25.19
88	Biotech HOLDRs BBH	100.00	73.49	23.83	2.69	0.00
—	PowerShares FTSE Hth Care PRFH	99.15	69.49	14.66	12.85	2.49
90	Consumer Staple SPDR XLP	100.00	65.53	24.34	9.98	0.00
Foreign Stock						
144	SPDR DJ Global Titans DGT	91.96	56.95	30.97	3.59	8.43
—	iShares SP Glb Hlth IXJ	65.82	42.53	16.79	4.62	35.95
—	Claymore/Clear Glb Vacc JNR	68.50	42.45	9.34	16.98	31.21
—	iShares S&P Glb 100 IOO	55.13	38.31	11.89	3.28	46.33
—	iShares SP Glb Cons Stpls KXI	54.30	38.22	11.17	4.19	45.48
—	iShares SP Glb Tech IXN	77.12	37.47	32.51	3.04	26.82
—	Claymore/Clear Glb Exch EXB	62.87	29.93	14.17	5.89	48.56
143	PowerShares Intl Div Ach PID	96.81	29.26	49.79	17.23	3.73
—	iShares SP Glb Industrial EXI	52.35	25.06	18.70	6.61	49.32
—	Claymore/Robeco Dev World EEW	52.36	17.48	20.31	10.71	49.49

Lowest Quality Stock ETFs

Page	Name	Morningstar Coverage Rate %	% Wide Moat	% Narrow Moat	% No Moat	% Unrated
U.S. Stock-Diversified						
—	Rydex S&P Midcap 400 Val RFV	77.50	0.00	33.60	43.27	23.29
55	iShares SP 400 Value IJJ	82.06	1.32	39.68	40.61	18.36
—	PowerShares Dyn Mid Cap PJG	92.44	10.98	40.39	40.51	7.78
—	PowerShares Val Line Time PIV	77.39	13.00	21.33	39.10	26.60
—	iShares MstarMidValue JKI	93.74	3.20	51.49	38.53	6.64
U.S. Stock-Sector						
185	Market Vectors Gld Miners GDX	84.41	0.00	0.00	86.66	13.35
—	SPDR S&P Oil&Gas Equ&Svcs XES	87.13	0.00	13.47	71.69	14.75
109	iShares Dow Jones US Home ITB	77.76	0.00	7.25	68.30	24.33
—	PowerShares FTSE BasMtrls PRFM	93.40	0.00	31.07	64.30	4.41
116	Oil Services HOLDRs OIH	70.90	0.00	26.47	62.54	10.98
Foreign Stock						
—	Market Vectors Glbl Agri MOO	73.56	0.00	26.69	41.32	31.99
164	PowerShares Halter USX PGJ	92.51	0.00	66.74	20.46	12.81
—	Europe 2001 HOLDRs EKH	77.35	13.66	45.27	19.16	18.69
—	First Trust ISE Chindia FNI	95.50	0.00	78.37	17.02	4.62
150	iShares Canada Index EWC	92.66	16.22	49.01	15.00	15.53
—	PowerShares FTSE Em Mrkts PXH	49.94	0.58	32.04	14.68	43.99
—	iShares SP Glb Enrgy IXC	69.18	17.03	36.27	9.39	35.76
—	Claymore/BNY BRIC EEB	81.56	1.54	69.26	8.53	20.60
138	BLDRS Emerg Mkts 50 ADR ADRE	86.59	1.13	75.79	7.47	13.66
159	iShares SP Latin 40 ILF	57.35	3.44	42.85	7.29	46.24

Limited to U.S.-focused ETFs with at least 80% coverage rates and foreign-focused funds with at least 50% coverage rates.

Morningstar Research

Least & Most Risky Stock ETFs

Least Risky Stock ETFs

Page	Name	Morningstar Coverage Rate %	% Below Avg Business Risk	% Average Business Risk	% Above Avg Business Risk	% Speculative Business Risk	% Unrated
U.S. Stock-Diversified							
74	Vanguard Div Appr ETF VIG	96.32	55.04	39.77	2.27	0.01	2.91
30	DIAMONDS Trust DIA	100.00	49.57	40.14	8.31	1.81	0.00
—	PowerShares High Gr Div PHJ	97.46	46.60	48.61	2.60	0.00	1.97
71	SPDR S&P Dividend SDY	86.04	46.51	34.40	3.09	0.00	15.87
—	PowerShares Div Achievers PFM	97.52	43.57	49.74	3.88	0.00	2.58
U.S. Stock-Sector							
90	Consumer Staple SPDR XLP	100.00	58.93	26.97	13.95	0.00	0.00
128	Vanguard Cons Stap ETF VDC	96.35	55.72	26.26	14.37	0.25	3.39
99	iShares DJ Consumer Goods IYK	95.87	52.19	25.01	17.17	2.28	3.29
—	Ultra Cons Goods ProShar UGE	94.58	46.56	22.32	15.34	2.03	2.90
120	Retail HOLDRs RTH	100.00	46.48	45.98	3.62	0.00	3.92
Foreign Stock							
—	iShares SP Glb Cons Stpls KXI	54.30	33.96	11.93	7.69	0.00	45.48
144	SPDR DJ Global Titans DGT	91.96	28.24	58.19	5.08	0.00	8.43
—	iShares S&P Glb 100 IOO	55.13	23.29	26.34	3.50	0.35	46.33
—	iShares SP Glb Enrgy IXC	69.18	18.18	37.57	6.94	0.00	35.76
—	iShares SP Glb Tech IXN	77.12	16.53	48.67	7.82	0.00	26.82
—	iShares SP Glb Hlth IXJ	65.82	16.41	34.45	13.08	0.00	35.95
—	iShares SP Glb Cons Discr RXI	51.12	16.19	30.43	1.42	1.28	50.25
—	BLDRS Europe 100 ADR ADRU	97.62	12.84	78.91	4.77	0.75	0.01
—	iShares MSCI Kokusai Indx TOK	58.85	12.70	38.57	5.95	0.16	0.23
143	PowerShares Intl Div Ach PID	96.81	11.80	64.85	19.35	0.28	3.73

Most Risky Stock ETFs

Page	Name	Morningstar Coverage Rate %	% Below Avg Business Risk	% Average Business Risk	% Above Avg Business Risk	% Speculative Business Risk	% Unrated
U.S. Stock-Diversified							
—	PowerShares Dyn Sm Growth PWT	56.93	0.00	17.94	32.49	0.39	48.73
—	Vanguard Mid Growth ETF VOT	91.13	5.12	54.60	32.35	1.81	5.04
—	iShares MstarSmallGrowth JKK	56.98	0.45	24.02	31.54	1.83	42.05
78	Vanguard Sm Cap Gr ETF VBK	58.51	1.12	27.92	28.71	1.69	39.96
—	First Trust NASDAQ ExTech QQXT	98.28	8.15	58.69	24.93	5.84	2.37
U.S. Stock-Sector							
185	Market Vectors Gld Miners GDX	84.41	0.00	0.00	78.51	8.15	13.35
—	First Trust AMEX Bio Indx FBT	100.00	0.00	24.91	65.16	5.01	4.93
—	HealthShares Cancer HHK	72.52	0.00	8.38	63.41	3.33	24.88
—	SPDR S&P Biotech XBI	86.08	0.00	12.97	59.63	5.28	22.01
—	HealthShares Cardiology HRD	83.62	0.00	21.85	45.14	16.29	16.72
Foreign Stock							
—	First Trust ISE Chindia FNI	95.50	0.00	16.14	77.56	1.69	4.62
164	PowerShares Halter USX PGJ	92.51	0.00	10.08	75.02	2.10	12.81
—	Claymore/BNY BRIC EEB	81.56	0.00	9.00	65.77	4.56	20.60
138	BLDRS Emerg Mkts 50 ADR ADRE	86.59	0.00	19.07	63.08	2.24	13.66
159	iShares SP Latin 40 ILF	57.35	0.00	0.78	52.68	0.12	46.24
—	Market Vectors Glbl Agri MOO	73.56	0.00	33.33	34.68	0.00	31.99
—	PowerShares FTSE Em Mrkts PXH	49.94	0.00	13.75	27.76	5.79	43.99
150	iShares Canada Index EWC	92.66	3.06	58.37	18.62	0.18	15.53
—	Claymore/Clear Glb Exch EXB	62.87	0.00	35.02	14.97	0.00	48.56
—	Claymore/Robeco Dev World EEW	52.36	7.80	33.77	6.93	0.00	49.49

Limited to U.S.-focused ETFs with at least 80% coverage rates and foreign-focused funds with at least 50% coverage rates.

Size & Popularity Stats

Largest & Most Heavily Traded ETFs

Largest ETFs

Page	Name	Assets ($mil)
U.S. Stock-Diversified		
72	SPDR Trust Series 1 SPY	98,152
66	PowerShares QQQ QQQQ	21,766
50	iShares S&P 500 IVV	17,894
35	iShares R1000 Growth IWF	15,553
39	iShares R2000 Index IWM	11,221
37	iShares R1000 Value IWD	10,488
79	Vanguard TSM ETF VTI	10,254
59	MidCap SPDR Trust MDY	10,106
30	DIAMONDS Trust DIA	8,574
31	iShares DJ Sel Dividend DVY	6,912
U.S. Stock-Sector		
92	Energy SPDR XLE	6,995
93	Financial SPDR XLF	5,051
116	Oil Services HOLDRs OIH	3,626
125	Technology SPDR XLK	3,009
127	Utilities SPDR XLU	2,504
94	Health Care Sel SPDR XLV	2,446
110	iShares S&P GSSI Nat Res IGE	2,237
90	Consumer Staple SPDR XLP	2,186
118	PowerShares Water Res PHO	2,134
97	iShares C&S Realty ICF	2,055
Foreign Stock-Diversified		
139	iShares MSCI EAFE EFA	51,895
142	iShares MSCI Emerg Mkts EEM	28,853
145	Vanguard EmergMkts ETF VWO	5,968
—	Vanguard FTSE All-W ex-US VEU	1,322
141	iShares MSCI EAFE Value EFV	1,187
140	iShares MSCI EAFE Growth EFG	1,155
—	iShares S&P Glb 100 IOO	976
138	BLDRS Emerg Mkts 50 ADR ADRE	911
143	PowerShares Intl Div Ach PID	745
—	WisdomTree Intl SmCap Div DLS	576
Foreign Stock-Country/Region		
155	iShares Japan Index EWJ	10,312
149	iShares Brazil Index EWZ	7,579
152	iShares FTSE/Xinhua China FXI	7,145
157	iShares MSCI ex-Japn EPP	4,105
161	iShares S.Korea Indx EWY	3,668
165	Vanguard Euro Stk ETF VGK	3,100
159	iShares SP Latin 40 ILF	3,091
151	iShares EMU Index EZU	2,903
158	iShares S&P Euro-350 IEV	2,890
162	iShares Taiwan Index EWT	2,657

Most Heavily Traded ETFs

Page	Name	Avg Daily Volume
U.S. Stock-Diversified		
72	SPDR Trust Series 1 SPY	195,979,587
66	PowerShares QQQ QQQQ	153,228,746
39	iShares R2000 Index IWM	84,907,686
73	UltShort QQQ ProShares QID	26,216,812
30	DIAMONDS Trust DIA	13,890,707
59	MidCap SPDR Trust MDY	5,193,688
38	iShares R2000 Growth IWO	4,084,946
35	iShares R1000 Growth IWF	3,714,388
40	iShares R2000 Value IWN	2,982,597
50	iShares S&P 500 IVV	2,690,598
U.S. Stock-Sector		
93	Financial SPDR XLF	91,693,652
92	Energy SPDR XLE	19,386,650
115	Materials Sel SPDR XLB	8,718,063
121	Semiconductor HOLDRs SMH	7,471,961
104	iShares DJ RE Index IYR	7,032,156
116	Oil Services HOLDRs OIH	5,969,352
127	Utilities SPDR XLU	4,718,119
120	Retail HOLDRs RTH	4,711,594
95	Industrial SPDR XLI	4,084,786
122	SPDR S&P Homebuilders XHB	3,857,560
Foreign Stock-Diversified		
142	iShares MSCI Emerg Mkts EEM	17,804,252
139	iShares MSCI EAFE EFA	12,131,294
145	Vanguard EmergMkts ETF VWO	746,525
138	BLDRS Emerg Mkts 50 ADR ADRE	342,899
—	Vanguard FTSE All-W ex-US VEU	278,324
—	Market Vectors Glbl Agri MOO	268,957
143	PowerShares Intl Div Ach PID	183,536
140	iShares MSCI EAFE Growth EFG	181,920
141	iShares MSCI EAFE Value EFV	124,253
—	BLDRS Dev Mkts 100 ADR ADRD	32,298
Foreign Stock-Country/Region		
155	iShares Japan Index EWJ	17,314,793
149	iShares Brazil Index EWZ	13,985,347
162	iShares Taiwan Index EWT	7,753,488
154	iShares Hong Kong EWH	6,634,597
152	iShares FTSE/Xinhua China FXI	5,841,341
160	iShares Singapore EWS	4,436,258
156	iShares Mexico Index EWW	3,314,637
161	iShares S.Korea Indx EWY	2,372,044
148	iShares Australia EWA	2,342,765
150	iShares Canada Index EWC	1,506,791

Size & Popularity Stats

Most & Least Popular ETFs

Most Popular ETFs

Page	Name	Assets ($mil)	Est. 2007 Net Inflows	Price/Fair Value	Coverage Rate %
U.S. Stock-Diversified					
72	SPDR Trust Series 1 SPY	98,152	30,584,399,925	0.88	99.46
35	iShares R1000 Growth IWF	15,553	6,954,432,839	0.95	97.91
79	Vanguard TSM ETF VTI	10,254	6,913,748,497	0.90	91.91
75	Vanguard Growth ETF VUG	3,231	2,054,697,748	0.93	97.05
51	iShares SP 500 Growth IVW	6,622	1,882,539,682	0.94	99.65
80	Vanguard Value ETF VTV	2,214	1,502,810,595	0.85	97.87
48	iShares S&P 100 Ind. OEF	4,889	1,454,558,374	0.88	100.00
46	iShares R. Midcap Gr IWP	3,212	1,422,569,640	0.97	93.37
37	iShares R1000 Value IWD	10,488	1,413,484,548	0.84	98.35
—	UltShort S&P500 ProShares SDS	1,652	1,349,542,497	—	—
U.S. Stock-Sector					
93	Financial SPDR XLF	5,051	4,003,349,097	0.76	99.72
92	Energy SPDR XLE	6,995	2,316,926,530	0.99	99.03
—	UltShort Financials ProSh SKF	966	777,832,260	—	—
125	Technology SPDR XLK	3,009	668,963,150	0.94	99.79
95	Industrial SPDR XLI	1,662	588,589,373	0.92	99.58
118	PowerShares Water Res PHO	2,134	560,749,515	0.97	60.15
—	PowerShares WilderHill PBW	1,731	513,203,347	1.19	64.84
94	Health Care Sel SPDR XLV	2,446	508,197,047	0.90	99.33
90	Consumer Staple SPDR XLP	2,186	470,942,850	0.91	100.00
—	UltShort Real Estat ProSh SRS	579	469,074,819	—	—
Foreign Stock-Diversified					
139	iShares MSCI EAFE EFA	51,895	10,563,736,370	1.00	5.57
142	iShares MSCI Emerg Mkts EEM	28,853	7,862,225,886	1.03	33.72
145	Vanguard EmergMkts ETF VWO	5,968	4,382,778,349	1.01	5.76
—	Vanguard FTSE All-W ex-US VEU	1,322	1,310,653,985	1.00	15.60
140	iShares MSCI EAFE Growth EFG	1,155	686,302,872	1.00	3.25
Foreign Stock-Country/Region					
165	Vanguard Euro Stk ETF VGK	3,100	4,087,720,587	1.00	3.21
166	Vanguard Pacif Stk ETF VPL	1,414	2,402,312,241	1.00	3.29
149	iShares Brazil Index EWZ	7,579	2,201,113,805	1.00	9.88
161	iShares S.Korea Indx EWY	3,668	1,594,652,959	1.00	1.50
148	iShares Australia EWA	1,893	829,083,988	1.00	14.58
—	Vanguard Europe Pacific VEA	653	805,923,839	1.00	2.94
—	Market Vectors Russia ETF RSX	800	764,583,923	1.03	17.01

Least Popular ETFs

Page	Name	Assets ($mil)	Est. 2007 Net Inflows	Price/Fair Value	Coverage Rate %
U.S. Stock-Diversified					
39	iShares R2000 Index IWM	11,221	–3,460,738,405	0.98	48.23
50	iShares S&P 500 IVV	17,894	–918,451,612	0.89	99.46
31	iShares DJ Sel Dividend DVY	6,912	–364,201,950	0.82	85.73
—	First Trust Value Line100 FVL	2	–320,625,256	1.12	84.20
56	iShares SP Small 600 IJR	4,368	–317,769,975	0.98	46.16
58	iShares SP 600 Value IJS	1,570	–293,569,873	0.97	47.07
—	First Trust Value Line Dv FVD	180	–266,982,508	0.86	92.57
34	iShares NYSE 100 Index NY	106	–258,615,462	0.87	100.00
62	PowerShares Dyn Market PWC	771	–217,946,561	0.98	91.78
55	iShares SP 400 Value IJJ	2,394	–207,415,711	0.91	82.06
U.S. Stock-Sector					
127	Utilities SPDR XLU	2,504	–1,165,608,449	0.96	99.16
—	United States Oil USO	485	–553,486,095	—	—
—	iShares NASD Biotech IBB	1,538	–440,083,101	0.99	82.39
102	iShares DJ Health IYH	975	–343,352,260	0.91	97.10
—	KBW Regional Banking ETF KRE	57	–154,004,299	0.87	69.72
97	iShares C&S Realty ICF	2,055	–134,981,071	0.98	100.00
106	iShares DJ Telecom IYZ	856	–98,874,619	0.93	91.55
—	iShares S&P GSTI Network IGN	166	–69,021,021	0.94	95.03
108	iShares DJ Utilities IDU	848	–61,880,805	0.96	93.84
—	iShares SP Glb Hlth IXJ	708	–57,488,323	0.93	65.82
Foreign Stock-Diversified					
—	Claymore/Robeco Dev World EEW	5	–11,330,017	0.96	52.36
—	Claymore/Robeco Dev Intl EEN	5	–5,409,569	1.00	3.03
144	SPDR DJ Global Titans DGT	189	–4,268,250	0.89	91.96
—	Claymore/Zacks Intl Yld HGI	9	–403,895	0.97	28.24
—	Claymore/Zacks Country Ro CRO	5	–212,104	1.00	0.64
Foreign Stock-Country/Region					
155	iShares Japan Index EWJ	10,312	–3,165,982,004	1.00	0.33
152	iShares FTSE/Xinhua China FXI	7,145	–1,400,429,754	1.00	1.29
156	iShares Mexico Index EWW	1,209	–144,580,754	1.00	2.42
—	SPDR Russell/Nomura PRIME JPP	60	–99,837,493	1.00	4.35
—	iShares SP TOPIX 150 ITF	247	–96,462,044	1.00	1.09
—	iShares Austria Index EWO	383	–66,848,739	1.00	0.33
—	iShares Italy Index EWI	185	–35,322,480	1.00	0.44

Yield & Cost Data

Highest Yielding ETFs

Highest Yielding

Page	Name	Category	12 Month Yield	Moringstar Price/Fair Value	Moringstar Coverage Rate (%)
U.S. Stock-Diversified					
82	WisdomTree High-Yld Eqty DHS	Large Blend	3.91	0.84	94.95
31	iShares DJ Sel Dividend DVY	Large Value	3.66	0.82	85.73
71	SPDR S&P Dividend SDY	Large Value	3.52	0.81	86.04
81	WisdomTree Div Top 100 DTN	Large Blend	3.35	0.87	98.95
84	WisdomTree MidCap Div DON	Mid-Cap Blend	3.02	0.91	83.06
83	WisdomTree LargeCap Div DLN	Large Blend	2.90	0.86	99.87
80	Vanguard Value ETF VTV	Large Value	2.74	0.85	97.87
85	WisdomTree Total Dividend DTD	Large Blend	2.73	0.87	96.03
70	SPDR DJ Wilshire Lg Value ELV	Large Value	2.70	0.86	98.95
34	iShares NYSE 100 Index NY	Large Value	2.57	0.87	100.00
U.S. Stock-Sector					
114	KBW Bank ETF KBE	Specialty-Financial	5.70	0.66	97.76
134	Vanguard REIT Index ETF VNQ	Specialty-Real Estate	5.06	0.96	86.16
104	iShares DJ RE Index IYR	Specialty-Real Estate	4.38	0.94	94.88
91	DJ Wilshire REIT ETF RWR	Specialty-Real Estate	4.21	0.95	94.15
97	iShares C&S Realty ICF	Specialty-Real Estate	4.06	0.98	100.00
93	Financial SPDR XLF	Specialty-Financial	2.99	0.76	99.72
130	Vanguard Financial ETF VFH	Specialty-Financial	2.83	0.79	92.95
100	iShares DJ Fin Sectr IYF	Specialty-Financial	2.74	0.77	97.39
101	iShares DJ Fin Svcs IYG	Specialty-Financial	2.71	0.73	97.92
135	Vanguard TelcomSrv ETF VOX	Specialty-Communications	2.65	0.99	81.46
Foreign Stock-Diversified					
143	PowerShares Intl Div Ach PID	Foreign Large Value	2.21	0.92	96.81
144	SPDR DJ Global Titans DGT	World Stock	2.16	0.89	91.96
138	BLDRS Emerg Mkts 50 ADR ADRE	Diversified Emerging Mkts	1.53	1.03	86.59
Foreign Stock-Country/Region					
159	iShares SP Latin 40 ILF	Latin America Stock	1.39	1.07	57.35
150	iShares Canada Index EWC	Foreign Large Value	1.20	0.98	92.66
164	PowerShares Halter USX PGJ	Pacific/Asia ex-Japan Stk	0.61	1.14	92.51
Fixed Income					
168	iShares iBoxx$ Corp Bd LQD	Long-Term Bond	5.47	—	—
172	iShares Lehman Aggregate AGG	Intermediate-Term Bond	4.87	—	—
171	iShares Lehman 20+ TLT	Long Government	4.51	—	—
170	iShares Lehman 7-10 IEF	Long Government	4.30	—	—
169	iShares Lehman 1-3 T SHY	Short Government	4.27	—	—

Yield & Cost Data

ETFs with Lowest Annual Expenses

U.S. Stock Diversified

Page	Name	Expense Ratio %
Large Blend		
79	Vanguard TSM ETF VTI	0.07
76	Vanguard Large Cap ETF VV	0.07
72	SPDR Trust Series 1 SPY	0.09
50	iShares S&P 500 IVV	0.09
36	iShares R1000 Index IWB	0.15
Large Growth		
75	Vanguard Growth ETF VUG	0.11
51	iShares SP 500 Growth IVW	0.18
66	PowerShares QQQ QQQQ	0.20
35	iShares R1000 Growth IWF	0.20
—	SPDR DJ Wilshire Lg Grwth ELG	0.20
Large Value		
80	Vanguard Value ETF VTV	0.11
30	DIAMONDS Trust DIA	0.17
52	iShares SP 500 Value IVE	0.18
37	iShares R1000 Value IWD	0.20
70	SPDR DJ Wilshire Lg Value ELV	0.20
Mid-Cap Blend		
—	Vanguard ExMkt ETF VXF	0.08
77	Vanguard Mid Cap ETF VO	0.13
53	iShares SP MidCap400 IJH	0.20
45	iShares R. Midcap IWR	0.20
59	MidCap SPDR Trust MDY	0.25
Mid-Cap Growth		
—	Vanguard Mid Growth ETF VOT	0.13
54	iShares SP 400 Growth IJK	0.25
46	iShares R. Midcap Gr IWP	0.25
—	SPDR DJ Wilshire Mid Gr EMG	0.25
—	iShares MstarMidGrowth JKH	0.30

Page	Name	Expense Ratio %
Mid-Cap Value		
—	Vanguard Mid Value ETF VOE	0.13
55	iShares SP 400 Value IJJ	0.25
47	iShares R. Midcap VI IWS	0.25
—	SPDR DJ Wilshire Mid Val EMV	0.25
—	iShares MstarMidValue JKI	0.30
Small Blend		
—	Vanguard Small Cap ETF VB	0.10
56	iShares SP Small 600 IJR	0.20
39	iShares R2000 Index IWM	0.20
—	iShares MstarSmallCore JKJ	0.25
—	SPDR DJ Wilshire Small Cp DSC	0.25
Small Growth		
78	Vanguard Sm Cap Gr ETF VBK	0.12
57	iShares SP 600 Growth IJT	0.25
38	iShares R2000 Growth IWO	0.25
—	SPDR DJ Wilshire Sm Grwth DSG	0.25
—	iShares MstarSmallGrowth JKK	0.30
Small Value		
—	Vanguard Sm Cp Val ETF VBR	0.12
58	iShares SP 600 Value IJS	0.25
40	iShares R2000 Value IWN	0.25
—	SPDR DJ Wilshire Sm Value DSV	0.25
—	iShares MstarSmallValue JKL	0.30

U.S. Stock Sector

Page	Name	Expense Ratio %
Specialty-Communication		
135	Vanguard TelcomSrv ETF VOX	0.23
106	iShares DJ Telecom IYZ	0.48
Specialty-Financial		
130	Vanguard Financial ETF VFH	0.22
93	Financial SPDR XLF	0.24
Specialty-Health		
131	Vanguard HealthCar ETF VHT	0.22
94	Health Care Sel SPDR XLV	0.24

Page	Name	Expense Ratio %
Specialty-Natural Res		
129	Vanguard Energy ETF VDE	0.22
133	Vanguard Materials ETF VAW	0.22
Specialty-Technology		
132	Vanguard InfoTech ETF VGT	0.22
125	Technology SPDR XLK	0.24
Specialty-Utilities		
136	Vanguard Utilities ETF VPU	0.22
127	Utilities SPDR XLU	0.24

Portfolio & Volatility Data

Valuation Measures

Lowest Valuation

Page	Name	Category	Measure	Rel to Category	3-Year Average
Price/Cash					
109	iShares Dow Jones US Home ITB	Large Blend	0.63	0.07	—
122	SPDR S&P Homebuilders XHB	Mid-Cap Value	0.87	0.14	—
—	Claymore/Clear Glb Timber CUT	Specialty-Natural Res	1.69	0.21	—
160	iShares Singapore EWS	Pacific/Asia ex-Japan Stk	2.12	0.25	6.54
—	Rydex S&P 500 Pure Value RPV	Large Value	2.87	0.34	—
Price/Prospective Earnings					
109	iShares Dow Jones US Home ITB	Large Blend	4.20	0.27	—
122	SPDR S&P Homebuilders XHB	Mid-Cap Value	4.24	0.32	—
—	SPDR S&P Pharmaceuticals XPH	Specialty-Health	4.51	0.21	—
—	iShares FTSE NAREIT Mortg REM	Specialty-Real Estate	7.13	0.29	—
—	iShares DJ US Pharma IHE	Specialty-Health	7.45	0.35	—
Price/Book					
109	iShares Dow Jones US Home ITB	Large Blend	0.53	0.21	—
122	SPDR S&P Homebuilders XHB	Mid-Cap Value	0.66	0.43	—
—	iShares FTSE EPRA Europe IFEU	Specialty-Real Estate	0.71	0.39	—
—	Rydex S&P Smallcap 600 Va RZV	Small Value	0.78	0.58	—
—	Rydex S&P 500 Pure Value RPV	Large Value	0.90	0.46	—
Price/Sales					
109	iShares Dow Jones US Home ITB	Large Blend	0.21	0.17	—
—	Rydex S&P Smallcap 600 Va RZV	Small Value	0.25	0.32	—
122	SPDR S&P Homebuilders XHB	Mid-Cap Value	0.26	0.33	—
—	PowerShares FTSE ConsGds PRFG	Large Blend	0.33	0.27	—
—	Rydex S&P Midcap 400 Val RFV	Mid-Cap Value	0.40	0.51	—

Highest Valuation

Page	Name	Category	Measure	Rel to Category	3-Year Average
Price/Cash					
—	B2B Internet HOLDRs BHH	Specialty-Technology	55.25	3.82	21.38
—	iShares FTSE EPRA Asia IFAS	Specialty-Real Estate	41.38	2.71	—
—	WisdomTree Intl RealEst DRW	Specialty-Real Estate	38.55	2.52	—
—	iShares FTSE EPRA Glbl RE IFGL	Specialty-Real Estate	28.35	1.86	—
—	Internet Infr HOLDRs IIH	Specialty-Technology	26.47	1.83	13.89
Price/Prospective Earnings					
—	HealthShares Emerg Cancer HHJ	Specialty-Health	73.81	3.47	—
—	iShares FTSE NAREIT Resdn REZ	Specialty-Real Estate	54.39	2.20	—
—	Internet Infr HOLDRs IIH	Specialty-Technology	47.93	2.32	32.79
—	Market Vectors GlbAlt Ene GEX	Specialty-Natural Res	43.91	2.69	—
—	HealthShares Cardio Dvcs HHE	Specialty-Health	35.96	1.69	—
Price/Book					
—	Claymore/Ocean Tomo Grwth OTR	Large Growth	6.61	1.96	—
—	PowerShares Dyn Bio&Genom PBE	Specialty-Health	5.44	1.60	4.07
—	HealthShares Cancer HHK	Specialty-Health	5.35	1.57	—
—	SPDR S&P Biotech XBI	Specialty-Health	5.26	1.54	—
—	HealthShares Auto-Inflam HHA	Specialty-Health	5.06	1.48	—
Price/Sales					
—	PowerShares Dyn Bio&Genom PBE	Specialty-Health	7.50	2.59	5.58
—	SPDR S&P Biotech XBI	Specialty-Health	6.44	2.22	—
—	First Trust ISE Chindia FNI	Pacific/Asia ex-Japan Stk	6.20	2.82	—
—	HealthShares Cancer HHK	Specialty-Health	6.07	2.09	—
—	HealthShares Auto-Inflam HHA	Specialty-Health	5.63	1.94	—

Portfolio & Volatility Data

Growth Measures

Fastest Growth

Page	Name	Category	Measure (%)	Rel to Category	3-Year Average
Earnings Growth					
38	iShares R2000 Growth IWO	Small Growth	42.33	2.03	18.09
44	iShares Russell Microcap IWC	Small Blend	41.24	2.53	15.46
39	iShares R2000 Index IWM	Small Blend	41.20	2.53	14.10
—	HealthShares EuroMed&Dvcs HHT	Specialty-Health	34.01	2.25	—
124	streetTRACKS MS Tech MTK	Specialty-Technology	32.08	2.03	15.82
Sales Growth					
—	First Trust ISE Chindia FNI	Pacific/Asia ex-Japan Stk	32.02	1.74	—
—	iPath MSCI India Idx ETN INP	Pacific/Asia ex-Japan Stk	29.62	1.61	—
—	SPDR S&P China GXC	Pacific/Asia ex-Japan Stk	27.95	1.52	—
—	Claymore/SWM Cdn Enrg ENY	Specialty-Natural Res	27.57	2.47	—
185	Market Vectors Gld Miners GDX	Specialty-Precious Metals	27.37	1.00	—
Cash Flow Growth					
—	iShares Dow Jones US BrDI IAI	Specialty-Financial	265.69	17.15	—
109	iShares Dow Jones US Home ITB	Large Blend	71.56	8.19	—
—	PowerShares Intl LstPvtEq PFP	Foreign Large Growth	67.98	1.69	—
—	iShares Dow Jones US Insr IAK	Specialty-Financial	51.25	3.31	—
—	PowerShares Dyn Oil & Gas PXJ	Specialty-Natural Res	50.69	3.11	—
Book Value Growth					
—	Market Vectors Steel ETF SLX	Specialty-Natural Res	53.92	3.61	—
185	Market Vectors Gld Miners GDX	Specialty-Precious Metals	35.57	1.00	—
—	First Trust Energy AlpDEX FXN	Specialty-Natural Res	24.38	1.63	—
—	PowerShares Dyn Engy Exp PXE	Specialty-Natural Res	23.78	1.59	21.28
—	Claymore/SWM Cdn Enrg ENY	Specialty-Natural Res	23.22	1.56	—

Slowest Growth

Page	Name	Category	Measure (%)	Rel to Category	3-Year Average
Earnings Growth					
—	Telecom HOLDRs TTH	Specialty-Communications	3.00	0.28	6.96
—	Adelante Shares RE Value AVU	Specialty-Real Estate	5.48	0.46	—
—	Claymore/SWM Cdn Enrg ENY	Specialty-Natural Res	6.02	0.46	—
—	Claymore/Clear Mid-Cap Gr MCG	Mid-Cap Growth	6.09	0.38	—
—	Adelante Shares RE Classc ACK	Specialty-Real Estate	6.56	0.54	—
Sales Growth					
—	B2B Internet HOLDRs BHH	Specialty-Technology	–22.75	–2.53	–2.92
67	PowerShares Zacks MicroCp PZI	Small Blend	–21.00	4.47	–3.96
—	First Trust IPOX-100 Indx FPX	Large Growth	–19.40	–2.00	—
—	WisdomTree SmCap Earning EES	Small Blend	–19.38	4.12	—
—	Claymore/Sabrient Stealth STH	Small Blend	–17.79	3.79	—
Cash Flow Growth					
—	iShares FTSE NAREIT Resdn REZ	Specialty-Real Estate	–54.35	–6.89	—
—	PowerShares List Pvt Eqty PSP	Mid-Cap Blend	–52.94	–203.62	—
—	First Trust IPOX-100 Indx FPX	Large Growth	–29.90	–2.77	—
—	PowerShares FTSE ConsGds PRFG	Large Blend	–23.25	–2.66	—
67	PowerShares Zacks MicroCp PZI	Small Blend	–22.69	3.81	–5.44
Book Value Growth					
—	B2B Internet HOLDRs BHH	Specialty-Technology	–21.24	–3.14	–5.80
—	HealthShares Emerg Cancer HHJ	Specialty-Health	–20.86	–3.40	—
—	iShares FTSE NAREIT Mortg REM	Specialty-Real Estate	–17.47	–2.16	—
—	Claymore/Clear Spin-Off CSD	Mid-Cap Blend	–15.03	–1.79	—
—	HealthShares Auto-Inflam HHA	Specialty-Health	–11.00	–1.79	—

Portfolio & Volatility Data

Profitability Measures

Most Profitable

Page	Name	Category	Measure (%)	Rel to Category	3-Year Average
Return on Equity					
159	iShares SP Latin 40 ILF	Latin America Stock	35.16	1.26	29.41
—	Market Vectors Steel ETF SLX	Specialty-Natural Res	34.68	1.69	—
—	Claymore/Ocean Tomo Grwth OTR	Large Growth	34.39	1.50	—
—	SPA MarketGrader 40 SFV	Large Blend	33.48	1.50	—
—	SPDR S&P Emrg Latin Am GML	Latin America Stock	31.50	1.13	—
Return on Assets					
116	Oil Services HOLDRs OIH	Specialty-Natural Res	18.47	1.96	14.80
—	SPA MarketGrader 40 SFV	Large Blend	18.46	2.21	—
—	SPA MarketGrader 100 SIH	Large Blend	16.81	2.01	—
—	PowerShares Dyn Oil & Gas PXJ	Specialty-Natural Res	15.53	1.65	12.17
—	iShares DJ US Oil Equip IEZ	Specialty-Natural Res	15.42	1.64	—
Net Margin					
—	iShares FTSE EPRA Europe IFEU	Specialty-Real Estate	65.70	1.82	—
—	WisdomTree Intl RealEst DRW	Specialty-Real Estate	58.79	1.63	—
—	SPDR DJ Wilshire Intl RE RWX	Specialty-Real Estate	57.99	1.60	—
—	iShares S&P World exUS Pr WPS	Specialty-Real Estate	50.86	1.41	—
—	iShares FTSE EPRA Glbl RE IFGL	Specialty-Real Estate	50.49	1.40	—

Least Profitable

Page	Name	Category	Measure (%)	Rel to Category	3-Year
Return on Equity					
—	HealthShares Emerg Cancer HHJ	Specialty-Health	–44.03	–5.92	—
—	HealthShares Ophthal HHZ	Specialty-Health	–13.56	–1.82	—
109	iShares Dow Jones US Home ITB	Large Blend	–10.75	–0.48	—
—	HealthShares Cancer HHK	Specialty-Health	–9.75	–1.31	—
—	HealthShares Meta-Endo HHM	Specialty-Health	–8.24	–1.11	—
Return on Assets					
—	HealthShares Emerg Cancer HHJ	Specialty-Health	–33.27	75.61	—
—	HealthShares Auto-Inflam HHA	Specialty-Health	–23.36	53.09	—
—	HealthShares Meta-Endo HHM	Specialty-Health	–22.01	50.02	—
—	HealthShares Inf Disease HHG	Specialty-Health	–13.54	30.77	—
—	PowerShares Dyn Bio&Genom PBE	Specialty-Health	–11.82	26.86	–4.61
Net Margin					
—	HealthShares Cancer HHK	Specialty-Health	–15.67	–3.08	—
—	B2B Internet HOLDRs BHH	Specialty-Technology	–11.65	–0.90	4.11
—	HealthShares Ophthal HHZ	Specialty-Health	–10.10	–1.98	—
—	SPDR S&P Biotech XBI	Specialty-Health	–8.99	–1.77	—
—	HealthShares Inf Disease HHG	Specialty-Health	–8.37	–1.64	—

Portfolio & Volatility Data

Least & Most Volatile ETFs

Least Volatile

Page	Name	Category	Standard Deviation	Rel to Category
One Year (12-31-07)				
169	iShares Lehman 1-3 T SHY	Short Government	1.67	1.00
172	iShares Lehman Aggregate AGG	Intermediate-Term Bond	2.66	1.00
168	iShares iBoxx$ Corp Bd LQD	Long-Term Bond	3.42	1.00
173	iShares Lehman TIPS Bond TIP	Inflation-Protected Bond	4.83	1.00
—	CurrencyShares Mex Peso FXM	World Bond	4.94	0.54
—	CurrencyShares BP Strlng FXB	World Bond	5.12	0.56
170	iShares Lehman 7-10 IEF	Long Government	5.15	0.78
180	CurrencyShares Euro Trust FXE	World Bond	5.65	0.62
—	CurrencyShares Swi Franc FXF	World Bond	5.88	0.64
—	WisdomTree Japan HiYld Eq DNL	Japan Stock	6.91	0.85
Three Year (12-31-07)				
169	iShares Lehman 1-3 T SHY	Short Government	1.41	1.00
172	iShares Lehman Aggregate AGG	Intermediate-Term Bond	2.81	1.00
168	iShares iBoxx$ Corp Bd LQD	Long-Term Bond	3.96	1.00
173	iShares Lehman TIPS Bond TIP	Inflation-Protected Bond	4.57	1.00
170	iShares Lehman 7-10 IEF	Long Government	4.77	0.72
128	Vanguard Cons Stap ETF VDC	Large Blend	5.73	0.68
90	Consumer Staple SPDR XLP	Large Blend	5.84	0.70
99	iShares DJ Consumer Goods IYK	Large Blend	6.78	0.81
—	iShares MstarLargeCore JKD	Large Blend	7.13	0.85
34	iShares NYSE 100 Index NY	Large Value	7.17	0.90
Five Year (12-31-07)				
169	iShares Lehman 1-3 T SHY	Short Government	1.48	1.00
168	iShares iBoxx$ Corp Bd LQD	Long-Term Bond	5.52	1.00
170	iShares Lehman 7-10 IEF	Long Government	6.14	0.75
90	Consumer Staple SPDR XLP	Large Blend	7.28	0.77
51	iShares SP 500 Growth IVW	Large Growth	8.16	0.80
144	SPDR DJ Global Titans DGT	World Stock	8.27	0.95
48	iShares S&P 100 Ind. OEF	Large Blend	8.43	0.89
—	SPDR DJ Wilshire Tot Mkt TMW	Large Blend	8.55	0.90
—	iShares SP Glb Hlth IXJ	Specialty-Health	8.56	0.77
72	SPDR Trust Series 1 SPY	Large Blend	8.59	0.90

Most Volatile

Page	Name	Category	Standard Deviation	Rel to Category
One Year (12-31-07)				
—	MACROshares Oil Down DCR	Specialty-Natural Res	53.44	2.97
152	iShares FTSE/Xinhua China FXI	Pacific/Asia ex-Japan Stk	35.16	1.59
109	iShares Dow Jones US Home ITB	Large Blend	32.46	2.89
—	Claymore/BNY BRIC EEB	Diversified Emerging Mkts	28.84	1.33
164	PowerShares Halter USX PGJ	Pacific/Asia ex-Japan Stk	28.73	1.30
—	iPath MSCI India Idx ETN INP	Pacific/Asia ex-Japan Stk	28.69	1.30
122	SPDR S&P Homebuilders XHB	Mid-Cap Value	28.67	2.22
—	United States Oil USO	Specialty-Natural Res	28.44	1.58
149	iShares Brazil Index EWZ	Latin America Stock	27.32	1.22
—	iPath S&P GSCI CrOil ETN OIL	Specialty-Natural Res	27.24	1.52
Three Year (12-31-07)				
149	iShares Brazil Index EWZ	Latin America Stock	29.72	1.23
152	iShares FTSE/Xinhua China FXI	Pacific/Asia ex-Japan Stk	26.30	1.45
—	iShares MSCI South Africa EZA	Diversified Emerging Mkts	25.56	1.18
164	PowerShares Halter USX PGJ	Pacific/Asia ex-Japan Stk	23.27	1.28
159	iShares SP Latin 40 ILF	Latin America Stock	22.93	0.95
161	iShares S.Korea Indx EWY	Pacific/Asia ex-Japan Stk	21.18	1.16
—	iShares S&P GSTI Network IGN	Specialty-Technology	21.10	1.33
138	BLDRS Emerg Mkts 50 ADR ADRE	Diversified Emerging Mkts	20.46	0.95
129	Vanguard Energy ETF VDE	Specialty-Natural Res	20.07	1.09
92	Energy SPDR XLE	Specialty-Natural Res	20.05	1.08
Five Year (12-31-07)				
149	iShares Brazil Index EWZ	Latin America Stock	28.29	1.26
—	iShares S&P GSTI Network IGN	Specialty-Technology	27.06	1.42
111	iShares S&P GSTI Semicond IGW	Specialty-Technology	24.51	1.28
161	iShares S.Korea Indx EWY	Pacific/Asia ex-Japan Stk	22.11	1.36
159	iShares SP Latin 40 ILF	Latin America Stock	20.85	0.93
162	iShares Taiwan Index EWT	Pacific/Asia ex-Japan Stk	20.15	1.24
138	BLDRS Emerg Mkts 50 ADR ADRE	Diversified Emerging Mkts	18.95	1.00
156	iShares Mexico Index EWW	Latin America Stock	18.37	0.82
92	Energy SPDR XLE	Specialty-Natural Res	18.35	1.03
107	iShares DJ US Energy IYE	Specialty-Natural Res	17.91	1.01

Glossary

This section explains how to use the data found in this publication to make better investment decisions.

Glossary

A

Average Credit Quality

see also Credit Analysis

Average credit quality gives a snapshot of the portfolio's overall credit quality. It is an average of each bond's credit rating, adjusted for its relative weighting in the portfolio. For the purposes of Morningstar's calculations, U.S. government securities are considered AAA bonds, nonrated municipal bonds generally are classified as BB, and other nonrated bonds generally are considered B.

Average Daily Volume

The average number of shares of an ETF traded per day, usually measured over the previous 12 months. This number, in addition to total net assets, can be a rough gauge of an ETF's popularity in the market.

Average Effective Duration

Average effective duration provides a measure of a fund's interest-rate sensitivity. The longer a fund's duration, the more sensitive the fund is to shifts in interest rates. The relationship among funds with different durations is straightforward: A fund with a duration of 10 years is expected to be twice as volatile as a fund with a five-year duration. Duration also gives an indication of how a fund's net asset value (NAV) will change as interest rates change. A fund with a five-year duration would be expected to lose 5% of its NAV if interest rates rose by 1 percentage point, or gain 5% if interest rates fell by 1 percentage point. Morningstar surveys fund companies for this information.

Average Effective Maturity

Average effective maturity is a weighted average of all the maturities of the bonds in a portfolio, computed by weighting each bond's effective maturity by the market value of the security. Average effective maturity takes into consideration all mortgage prepayments, puts, and adjustable coupons. (Because Morningstar uses fund company calculations for this figure and because different companies use varying interest-rate assumptions in determining call likelihood and timing, we ask that companies not adjust for call provisions.) Funds with longer maturity are generally considered more interest-rate sensitive than their shorter counterparts.

Average Return

see also Total Return and Market Return

The annualized return of the ETF over a multiyear period, such as three or five years. This represents the annual return that an investor would have received if the fund's returns were evenly spread across the time period.

Average Stock Percentage

see also Composition

For stock-oriented funds, we provide a yearly average stock position calculated by averaging all reported composition numbers for the year. These averages provide a valuable complement to the current composition numbers; investors can compare a fund's current level of market participation with its historical averages.

Average Weighted Coupon

see also Coupon Range

Average weighted coupon is computed by averaging each bond's coupon rate adjusted for its relative weighting in the portfolio. This figure indicates whether the fund is opting for a high- or low-coupon strategy, and it may serve as an indicator of interest-rate sensitivity, particularly for mortgage-backed funds or other funds with callable bonds. A high coupon frequently indicates less sensitivity to interest rates; a low coupon, the opposite.

Average Weighted Price

Average weighted price is computed for most bond funds by weighting the price of each bond by its relative size in the portfolio. This number reveals whether the fund favors bonds selling at prices above or below face value (premium or discount securities, respectively) and can also serve as an indicator of interest-rate sensitivity. This statistic is expressed as a percentage of par (face) value. This statistic is not calculated for international-bond funds, because their holdings are often expressed in terms of foreign currencies.

B

Best Fit Index

see also Modern Portfolio Theory Statistics

The Best Fit Index is the market index whose monthly returns have correlated the most closely with a given fund's in the most recent 36 consecutive months. Morningstar regresses the fund's monthly excess returns against monthly excess returns of several well-known market indexes. Best Fit signifies the index that provides the highest R-squared, or correlation with a given fund.

Beta

see Modern Portfolio Theory Statistics

Bid/Ask Spread

The difference in the price at which an investor can buy and sell ETF shares. A wide bid/ask spread allows market makers to buy at a lower price and sell at a higher price.

Business Risk

Morningstar Business Risk is a measure of the uncertainty associated with the forecasts that underpin our fair value estimate on a given stock. In evaluating business risk, analysts consider the existence and durability of a firm's competitive advantages (which we refer to as "economic moats") along with event risk, or the chance that a non-financial issue could materially affect the company's fortunes. Based on these two factors, we classify the company's level of business risk as above average, average, below average, or speculative. The riskier a firm, the wider the margin of safety

we demand when investing in the shares. ("Margin of safety" refers to our recommended practice of buying stocks at a discount to fair value; in that way, we duly allow for uncertainty and a range of potential outcomes.)

C

Capital Gains

Capital gains are the profits received and distributed from the sale of securities within a portfolio. This line shows a summary of the ETF's annual capital gains distributions expressed in per-share dollar amounts. Both short- and long-term gains are included, as are options premiums and distributions from paid-in capital. Most ETFs realize and distribute fewer capital gains than conventional mutual funds because ETFs do not have to sell securities to satisfy redemptions. As a result, ETFs are often considered to be more tax-efficient than mutual funds.

Capital Return %

see also Income Return % and Total Return

Morningstar provides the portion of a fund's total returns that was generated by realized and unrealized increases in the value of securities in the portfolio. Frequently, a stock fund's returns will be derived entirely from capital return. By looking at capital return and income return, an investor can see whether the fund's returns come from capital, from income, or from a combination of both. Adding capital and income return will produce the fund's total return.

Category

see Morningstar Category

Composition

see also Average Stock Percentage

The composition percentages provide a simple breakdown of the fund's portfolio holdings, as of the date listed, into general investment classes at the bottom of the Portfolio Analysis section. Cash encompasses both the actual cash and the cash equivalents (fixed-income securities with maturities of one year or less) held by the portfolio. A negative percentage of cash indicates that the portfolio is leveraged, meaning it has borrowed against its own assets to buy more securities or that it has used other techniques to gain additional exposure to the market. The percentage listed as Stocks incorporates only the portfolio's straight common stocks. Bonds include every fixed-income security with a maturity of more than one year, from government notes to high-yield corporate bonds. Other includes preferred stocks (equity securities that pay dividends at a specified rate), as well as convertible bonds and convertible preferreds, which are corporate securities that are exchangeable for a set amount of another form of security (usually shares of common stock) at a prestated price. Other also includes all those not-so-neatly categorized securities, such as warrants and options.

Cost of Equity

In deciding the rate to discount future cash flows, Morningstar analysts ignore stock-price volatility (which drives most estimates of beta). We welcome volatility, as it offers opportunities to buy a stock at a discount to our estimate of its fair value. Instead, Morningstar analysts focus on the fundamental risks facing a company's business. Ideally, we'd like our discount rates to reflect the risk of permanent capital loss to the investor. When assigning a cost of equity to a stock, our analysts consider a firm's financial leverage, the cyclicality of its business, its size, and the sustainability of cash flows that it generates. Based on that assessment, our analysts assign a cost of equity to each stock, thus establishing the minimum return that we would require to invest in it. A stock ETF's cost of equity is derived by calculating the weighted-average cost of equity for the portfolio using the percentage weightings and cost of equity of each stock in the portfolio that our analysts cover.

Country Exposure

For each international portfolio the country exposure information displays the top five countries in which the ETF is invested. This information is gathered directly from the portfolios given by the fund companies.

Coupon Range

see also Average Weighted Coupon

Taxable-bond funds feature a table listing the breakdown of each portfolio's bond coupons, or rates of interest payments. The coupon range is designed to help an investor complete the picture suggested by the average weighted coupon statistic. These ranges differ according to Morningstar category and, due to changing interest rates, are subject to alteration over time. Whatever the breakdown may be, the first number is always exclusive and the second number is always inclusive. A range of 8% to 10% for example, would exclude bonds that have a weighted coupon rate of exactly 8% but would include bonds with a weighted coupon rate of 10%. High-yield bond funds include PIKs in their coupon breakdown, which are payment-in-kind issues that make interest payments in the form of additional securities rather than cash.

The overall percentage of bond assets that fall within each coupon range is noted in the % of Bonds column. The Rel Cat column compares a fund with others in its Morningstar Category. The category average is set at 1.0.

Coverage Rate

The percentage of stocks in an ETF's portfolio under coverage by Morningstar stock analysts. These stocks for which Morningstar equity analysts have researched and estimated fair values. The coverage rate helps investors determine the relevance of an ETF's Price/Fair Value Measure. Coverage rates of less than 60% are not relevant. Coverage rates of 50% to 60% are somewhat relevant. Coverage rates of more than 66% to 80% are considered fair and moderately relevant. Coverage rates of 80% or better are considered fully relevant.

Credit Analysis

see also Average Credit Quality

This section depicts the quality of bonds in a bond fund's portfolio. The credit analysis shows the percentage of fixed-income securities that fall within each credit-quality rating as assigned by Standard & Poor's or Moody's.

At the top of the ratings are U.S. government bonds. Bonds issued and backed by the government, as well as those backed by government-linked organizations such as Fannie Mae and Freddie Mac, are of extremely high quality and thus are considered equivalent to bonds rated AAA, which is the highest possible rating a corporate issue can receive. Morningstar gives U.S. government bonds a credit rating separate from AAA securities to allow for a more accurate credit analysis of a portfolio's holdings. Bonds with a BBB rating are the lowest grade that are still considered to be investment grade. Bonds that are rated BB or lower (often called junk bonds or high-yield bonds) are considered to be speculative. Any bonds that appear in the NR/NA category are either not rated by Standard & Poor's or Moody's, or did not have a rating available at the time of publication.

Current Investment Style

see also Investment Style Box

For equity funds, this section lists a fund portfolio's current averages for various portfolio statistics, including price/earnings, price/cash flow, and historical earnings growth. To provide perspective, we compare these measures with the funds' category average.

For bond funds, this section lists a portfolio's current duration, as well as averages for effective maturity, credit quality, weighted coupon, and price. These numbers are helpful in determining how much interest-rate and credit risk the portfolio currently has. For example, funds with high durations typically are very sensitive to changes in interest rates, whereas those with durations of just a year or two tend to be relatively insensitive to interest-rate changes. Funds with AAA or AA average credit-quality rankings take on less credit risk than those with, for example, B ratings, which indicate the portfolio holds a lot of high-yield (or junk) debt.

Morningstar currently uses price/cash flow, price/book, and median market capitalization to categorize foreign funds. This section also compares international-stock funds' current valuations with those of the MSCI EAFE Index, which is the most widely used benchmark for international offerings. Funds with low valuations typically hold stocks that aren't expected to grow rapidly, and therefore land in one of the value style boxes. By contrast, portfolios with high valuations typically hold fast-growing issues.

D

Discount to NAV

Unlike regular open-end mutual funds, which are bought and sold directly from the fund company at the net asset value (NAV) of their portfolio securities, ETFs and closed-end funds trade at prices determined by the market forces of supply and demand. A fund that trades at a price less than its NAV is said to trade at a discount to its NAV. Any discount or premium should be small and short-lived due to the arbitrage mechanisms inherent in ETF structures.

Dividend

The portion of a company's profit paid directly to shareholders, generally expressed in a per-share amount. Most ETFs pay dividends at least semiannually or annually. Some ETFs such as the iShares Dow Jones Select Dividend Index, actively mimic indexes that identify high dividend-paying stocks. The way in which an ETF pays out its dividends depends on the legal structure of the ETF. The open-end index ETFs automatically reinvest dividends and pay shareholders through a quarterly cash distribution; unit investment trust ETFs do not reinvest dividends, instead putting them in a non-interest-bearing account until quarterly payout; and grantor trust ETFs allow investors to receive dividends directly from the companies of the underlying securities, instead of from the authorized participant. For an ETF's specific distribution policy, you must read the ETF's prospectus or consult with your financial advisor.

Duration

see Average Effective Duration

E

Economic Moat

The idea of an economic moat refers to how likely companies are to keep competitors at bay for an extended period. One of the keys to finding superior long-term investments is buying companies that will be able to stay one step ahead of their competitors, and it's this characteristic—think of it as the strength and sustainability of a firm's competitive advantage—that we're trying to capture with the economic moat rating.

One of the first things we do when we're thinking about the size of a firm's economic moat is look at the company's historical financial performance. Companies that have generated returns on capital higher than their cost of capital for many years running usually have a moat, especially if their returns on capital have been rising or are fairly stable.

Of course, the past is a highly imperfect predictor of the future, so we look carefully at the source of a company's excess economic profits before assigning a moat rating. For example, a competitive advantage created by a hot new technology usually isn't very sustainable, because it won't be too long until someone comes along and invents a better widget.

Here are some of the attributes that can give companies economic moats:

Huge Market Share: When a firm enjoys economies of scale in areas like manufacturing, sales, and marketing, it can be pretty tough for a competitor to catch up.

Low-Cost Producer: The ability to produce products or services at a lower cost than competitors is an advantage that's especially potent in commodity industries.

Patents, Copyrights, or Governmental Approvals and Licenses: Some companies generate enormous profits when the government artificially protects their products or markets.

Unique Corporate Culture: Although you should be careful of placing too much emphasis on this attribute, since it's such a "soft" method of determining competitive advantage, there's no question it can make a difference.

High Customer-Switching Costs: If you can make it tough for your customers to use a competitor, it's usually easy to keep ratcheting prices up just a bit year after year—which can lead to big profits.

The Network Effect: This is a relatively rare, but potentially quite potent, source of competitive advantage, and often accrues by the first mover in an emerging technology. Because a network's value increases as more people use it, the company that creates the network can create a massive economic moat.

Exchange Traded Fund (ETF)
see also Open-Index
An abbreviation for exchange-traded funds. ETFs are baskets of securities that are traded on an exchange and, unlike open-end mutual funds, can be bought and sold throughout the trading day. They can also be sold short and bought on margin. In brief, anything you might do with a stock, you can do with an ETF. Currently most ETFs are index funds and are composed of holdings that mimic a given index or specialize in certain commodities. They offer diversification, low costs, and trading flexibility to investors. Unlike mutual funds, there are options available on many ETFs. There are three different legal structures for ETFs: open-end funds, unit investment trusts, and grantor trusts. The first two structures are registered with the SEC under the Investment Company Act of 1940, while the third is not. The primary differences among these three structures regard their dividend distribution schedules and purchase/redemption policies.

ETF Star Rating
see Historical Profile, Star Rating, and Risk

Equity Style
see Investment Style Box

Exchange Traded Note (ETNs)
Exchange Traded Notes are 30-year senior, unsecured debt securities that track indexes and can be bought and sold on the New York Stock Exchange through a broker at market prices that are set throughout the day by supply and demand. ETNs don't necessarily invest in the indexes they track, but their issuers promise to pay investors what they would have gained or lost if they had invested directly in the index (minus commission costs and the ETNs' fees). As such, there is little risk that the ETN will not track its index, but there is credit risk, or the possibility that the issuer will go bankrupt before it has to meet its obligations to ETN holders.

ETNs are not ETFs, but like ETFs they have an arbitrage mechanism that theoretically should keep their market prices close to the intrinsic value of their benchmarks. Large institutional investors who can amass 50,000 notes can redeem them directly back to the issuer once per day or week, which gives them a chance to take advantage of premiums or discounts.

ETNs, like their ETF cousins, could offer tax advantages because they don't make income or capital gains distributions. Investors have to pay capital gains taxes only when they sell their notes in the secondary market or accept payment when the securities mature (Note that the Internal Revenue Service has never actually opined on how this kind of structured product should be taxed and could rule ETNs need to be taxed differently in the future.)

Expense Projections (Three-, Five-, and 10-Year)
The SEC mandates that each fund administered by a registered investment company list its expense projections. Found in the fund's prospectus, these figures show how much an investor would expect to pay in expenses, sales charges (loads), and fees over the next three, five, and 10 years, assuming a $10,000 investment that grows by 5% per year with redemption at the end of each time period. Expense projections are commonly based on the past year's incurred fees or an

estimate of the current fiscal year's fees, should a portion of the overall fee structure change as of the printing of the fund's most current prospectus. Newer funds are required to print expense projections for only one- and three-year time periods, as longer-term projections may not be possible to estimate.

Expense Ratio

The annual fee that all ETFs charge their shareholders. It is taken from the ETF's annual report and expressed as a percentage of the ETF's average daily net assets deducted each fiscal year for fund expenses. It may include such items as the management fee, trustee's fee, and license fee, among others. The expense ratio is deducted from the ETF's average net assets and accrued on a daily basis. It does not include the commissions paid to trade ETF shares, or the costs incurred by the fund in trading its underlying securities. If the ETF's assets are small, its expense ratio can be quite high because the ETF must meet its expenses from a restricted asset base. Conversely, as the net assets of the fund grow, the expense percentage should ideally diminish because expenses are spread across the wider base. To note, HOLDRs do not express their fees as expense ratios, but instead charge a flat quarterly fee per 100 shares.

F

Fixed-Income Style

see Investment Style Box

Fair Value

see also Morningstar Price/Fair Value Measure

Morningstar stock analysts estimate a stock's fair value using a discounted cash flow model that takes into account their estimates of the company's growth, profitability, risk, and many other factors over the next five years. This fair value is then compared with the stock's market price to gauge its attractiveness.

Morningstar uses the fair values its analysts set for stocks to help determine if an ETF's portfolio holdings are over- or undervalued.

Free Cash Flow

A company's cash flows from operations less capital expenditures. Operating cash flows are the cash flows a company generates from its ongoing business activities. Capital expenditures are, broadly speaking, the money that a firm has to spend to maintain and expand its business. Sometimes referred to as "owner earnings", free cash flows represent the money that the owner of a company could withdraw from the treasury without harming the company's ongoing business. In valuing stocks, Morningstar analysts forecast free cash flows into the future and then discount those cash flows back to the present at a certain discount rate. Therefore, the more free cash a business throws off, all things being equal, the more money that's left for shareholders and, thus, the more valuable the company as a whole.

G

Growth of $10,000

The Growth of $10,000 graph shows an ETF's performance based on how $10,000 invested in the fund would have grown over time. The returns used in the graph are not load-adjusted. The growth of $10,000 begins at the date of the fund's inception, or the first year listed on the graph, whichever is appropriate. Located alongside the ETF's graph line is a line that represents the growth of $10,000 in either the S&P 500 Index (for stock funds and hybrid funds) or the LB Aggregate Index (for bond funds). The third line represents the fund's Morningstar category average (see definition below). These lines allow investors to compare the performance of the fund with the performance of a benchmark index and the ETF's Morningstar category. Both lines are plotted on a logarithmic scale, so that identical percentage changes in the value of an investment have the same vertical distance on the graph. For example, the vertical distance between $10,000 and $20,000 is the same as the distance between $20,000 and $40,000 because both represent a 100% increase in investment value. This provides a more accurate representation of performance than would a simple arithmetic graph. The graphs are scaled so that the full length of the vertical axis represents a tenfold increase in investment value. For securities with returns that have exhibited greater than a tenfold increase over the period shown in the graph, the vertical axis has been compressed accordingly.

Growth Measures

Long-Term Earnings Growth

Earnings are what are left of a firm's revenues after it pays all of its expenses, costs, and taxes. Companies whose earnings grow faster than those of their industry peers usually see better price performance for their stocks. Projected earnings growth is an estimate of a company's expected long-term growth in earnings, derived from all polled analysts' estimates. When reported for an ETF, it shows the weighted average of the projected growth in earnings for each stock in the ETF's portfolio. This measure helps determine Morningstar's growth score for each stock and the overall growth orientation of the ETF.

Historical Earnings Growth

Historical earnings growth shows the rate of increase in a company's earnings per share, based on up to four time periods. When reported for an ETF, it shows the weighted average of the growth in earnings for each stock in the ETF's portfolio. This measure helps determine Morningstar's growth score for each stock and the overall growth orientation of the ETF.

Sales Growth

Sales growth shows the rate of increase in a company's sales per share, based on up to four time periods, and it is considered the best gauge of how rapidly a company's core business is growing. When reported for an ETF, it shows the weighted average of the sales-growth rates for each stock in the ETF's portfolio. This measure helps determine Morningstar's growth score for each stock and the overall growth orientation of the ETF.

Cash Flow Growth

Cash flow tells you how much cash a business is actually generating—in other words, its earnings before depreciation, amortization, and noncash charges. Sometimes called cash earnings, it's considered a gauge of liquidity and solvency. Cash flow growth shows the rate of increase in a company's cash flow per share, based on up to four time periods. When reported for an ETF, it shows the weighted average of the growth in cash flow for each stock in the ETF's portfolio. This measure helps determine Morningstar's growth score for each stock and the overall growth orientation of the ETF.

Book Value Growth

Book value is, in theory, what would be left over for shareholders if a company shut down its operations, paid off all its creditors, collected from all its debtors, and liquidated itself. In practice, however, the value of assets and liabilities can change substantially from when they are first recorded. Book value growth shows the rate of increase in a company's book value per share, based on up to four time periods. When reported for an ETF it shows the weighted average of the growth rates in book value for each stock in the ETF's portfolio. This measure helps determine Morningstar's growth score for each stock and the overall growth orientation of the ETF.

H

Historical Profile, Star Rating, and Risk

see also Morningstar Category

The star rating displayed in the Historical Profile section is an ETF's overall risk-adjusted star rating. The star ratings for the three time periods in the Rating and Risk section are combined here. In ascending order, these categories are Lowest (★), Below Average (★★), Neutral (★★★), Above Average (★★★★), and Highest (★★★★★). ETFs less than three years old are listed as Not Rated.

Hurdle Rate

A stock ETF's hurdle rate refers to the minimum return that we would accept to invest in it. We calculate the hurdle rate as the sum of the ETF's cost of equity, annual expenses, and a diversification factor. We derive an ETF's cost of equity as the weighted-average cost of equity of the portfolio stocks that we cover.
An ETF's annual expenses are equivalent to the annual expense ratio that's disclosed in the fund's annual report (it does not include brokerage commissions or other transaction costs). The diversification factor is intended to reflect an ETF's diversification potential. If the Morningstar analyst believes that an ETF portfolio's diversification warrants a lower hurdle rate, then the analyst will reduce the hurdle rate by the amount of the diversification factor.

I

Inception

The date on which the ETF commenced operations by offering its shares for sale to investors.

Income $

Income reflects the dividends and interest generated by an ETF's holdings. This area shows a fund's yearly income distribution expressed in per-share dollar amounts.

Income Distribution

The number of times per year that an ETF intends to make income payments (from either dividends or interest). This will differ according to the legal structure of the ETF and is specified in the ETF's prospectus or marketing documents.

Income Ratio %

The fund's income ratio reveals the percentage of current income earned per share. It is calculated by dividing the ETF's net investment income by its average net assets. (Net investment income is the total income of the ETF, less expenses.) An income ratio can be negative if an ETF's expenses exceed its income, which can occur with funds that have high costs or that tend to emphasize capital gains rather than income. Because the income ratio is based on an ETF's fiscal year and is taken directly from the fund's annual shareholder report, it may not exactly correspond with other calendar-year information on the page.

Income Return %

see also Capital Return % and Total Return

Income return is that portion of an ETF's total returns that was derived from income distributions. Income return will often be higher than capital return for bond-tracking ETFs, and typically lower for equity-tracking ETFs. Adding the income return and the capital return together will produce the fund's total return.

Industry Weightings

see also Relative Comparisons and Sector Weightings

For specialty ETFs (also called sector ETFs), we replace the standard sector weightings, which include broad industry classifications such as hardware, with a breakdown of the ETF's weightings in the sector's subindustries, or subsectors. Each sector has its own breakdown of subsectors, which can help investors decide which specific areas of an industry the ETF invests in, and how pure its focus is. The industry weightings show at a glance whether an ETF is conservatively diversified across a sector, betting on just a couple of risky subsectors to charge up returns, or crouching defensively in the mildest corner of the specialty. The ETF's weightings relative to its category average are also shown.

Each specialty ETF's breakdown also includes an Other classification, but a large weighting there shouldn't be interpreted as meaning the ETF is investing outside of its specialty. This is merely a catchall designation to classify the stocks that don't meet the exact criteria for any specific subsector. It's impossible to capture every nook and cranny of the sprawling technology category, for example, in the eight subsectors included on the page. Thus, a fair number of tech stocks fall into Other.

Investment Style Box

see also Current Investment Style, Growth, Market Capitalization, Morningstar Category, and Value

To help investors cut through the confusion and profusion of mutual funds and ETFs, Morningstar designed the style box, a visual tool for better understanding a fund's true investment strategy. Based on an analysis of a fund's portfolio, the Morningstar style box is a snapshot of the types of securities held by the fund. The style box is calculated with methodology similar to that used to assign the Morningstar Categories. By providing an easy-to-understand visual representation of stock and fund characteristics, the Morningstar style box allows for informed comparisons and portfolio construction based on actual holdings, as opposed to assumptions based on a fund's name or how it is marketed. The style box also forms the basis for Morningstar's style-based fund categories and market indexes.

Domestic-Stock Style Box

The Morningstar domestic-stock style box is a nine-square grid that provides a graphical representation of the "investment style" of stocks, mutual funds, and ETFs. It classifies securities according to market capitalization (the vertical axis) and growth and value factors (the horizontal axis). Note: Fixed-income funds are classified according to credit quality (the vertical axis) and sensitivity to changes in interest rates (the horizontal axis).

How It Works

Style box assignments begin at the individual stock level. Morningstar determines the investment style of each individual stock in its database. The style attributes of individual stocks are then used to determine the style classification of stock ETFs.

The Horizontal Axis

The scores for a stock's value and growth characteristics determine its placement on the horizontal axis of the stock style box:

Value Score Components and Weights	
Forward-looking measures	
Price/projected earnings	50.0%
Historical-based measures	
Price/book	12.5%
Price/sales	12.5%
Price/cash flow	12.5%
Dividend yield	12.5%

Growth Score Components and Weights	
Forward-looking measures	
Long-term projected earnings growth	50.0%
Historical-based measures	
Historical earnings growth	12.5%
Sales growth	12.5%
Cash flow growth	12.5%
Book value growth	12.5%

Growth and value characteristics for each individual stock are compared with those of other stocks within the same capitalization band and are scored from zero to 100 for both value and growth. To determine the overall style score, the value score is subtracted from the growth score.

The resulting number can range from 100 (for low-yield, extremely growth-oriented stocks) to -100 (for high-yield, low-growth stocks). A stock is classified as growth if the net score equals or exceeds the "growth threshold" (normally about 25 large-cap stocks). It is deemed value if its score equals or falls below the "value threshold" (normally about -15 for large-cap stocks). And if the score lies between the two thresholds, the stock is classified as "core."

Stock Style Box

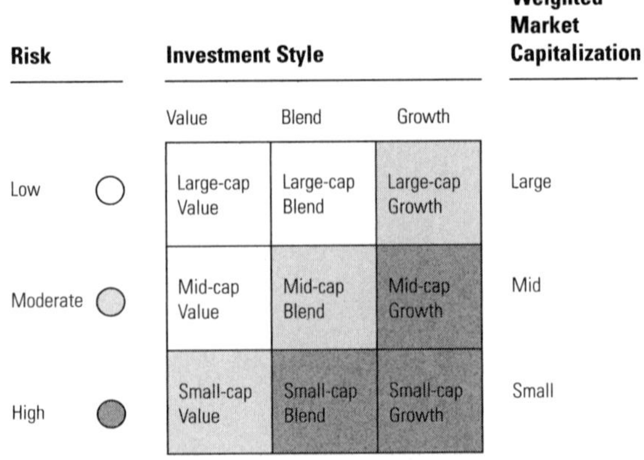

Within the stock style box grid, nine possible combinations exist, ranging from large-cap value for the safest funds to small-cap growth for the riskiest.

The thresholds between value, core, and growth stocks vary to some degree over time, as the distribution of stock styles changes in the market. However, on average, the three stock styles each account for approximately one third of the total free float in each size category.

The Vertical Axis

Rather than a fixed number of large-cap or small-cap stocks, Morningstar uses a flexible system that isn't adversely affected by overall movements in the market to classify stocks as small, medium, or large. Large-cap stocks are defined as the group that accounts for the top 70% capitalization of the Morningstar domestic-stock universe; mid-cap stocks represent the next 20%; and small-cap stocks represent the balance. The Morningstar stock universe represents approximately 99% of the U.S. market for actively traded stocks.

Moving from Individual Stocks to Funds

A stock-tracking ETF is an aggregation of individual stocks and its style is determined by the style assignments of the stocks it owns. By plotting all of an ETF's stocks on the stock style grid, the range of stock styles included in the fund immediately becomes apparent. An asset-weighted average of the stocks' net value/growth scores determines a fund's horizontal placement-value, growth, or blend.

A fund's vertical placement is determined by its "market cap," which is defined as the geometric mean of the market capitalization (or average weighted market cap) for the stocks it owns.

Cap1 = the capitalization of stock 1 and W1 = the % weight in the portfolio and the geometric mean of market capitalization $= (Cap1^{W1})(Cap2^{W2})(Cap3^{W3})(Cap4^{W4})\ldots(CapN^{WN})$

For a simple example, consider a fund that owns just three stocks:

25% stake in Stock A, market cap = $1.85 Billion
35% stake in Stock B, market cap = $3.56 Billion
40% stake in Stock C, market cap = $8.58 Billion

Its geometric mean of market capitalization would equal:

$(\$1.85\text{ bil}^{.25})(\$3.56\text{ bil}^{.35})(\$8.58\text{ bil}^{.40}) = \$4.30$ Billion

Note that this number is larger than the fund's median market cap-the capitalization of the median stock in its portfolio. That's because stock C, with a relatively higher market cap, occupies the biggest slice of the portfolio. The geometric mean better identifies the portfolio's "center of gravity." In other words, it provides more accurate insight into how market trends (as defined by capitalization) might affect the portfolio.

Style box assignments for stocks are updated each month. Assignments for ETFs are recalculated whenever Morningstar receives updated portfolio holdings for the ETF.

Using the Style Box

In general, a growth-oriented ETF will hold the stocks of companies that the portfolio manager believes will increase earnings faster than the rest of the market. A value-oriented ETF contains mostly stocks the manager thinks are currently undervalued in price and will eventually see their worth recognized by the market. A blend fund might be a mix of growth stocks and value stocks, or it may contain stocks that exhibit both characteristics.

Understanding how different types of stocks behave is crucial for building a diversified, style-controlled portfolio of stocks, mutual funds, or ETFs. The Morningstar style box helps investors construct portfolios based on the characteristics, or style factors, of all the stocks and funds that portfolio includes.

International-Stock Style Box

These style boxes are similar to the domestic-stock style boxes described above, although the methodology is different.

On the vertical axis, international-stock ETFs are grouped as small, medium, or large. ETFs with median market capitalizations of less than $1 billion are grouped in the small-cap box. ETFs with median market caps equal to or greater than $1 billion but less than or equal to $5 billion are labeled as mid-cap offerings. ETFs with median market caps exceeding $5 billion are large cap. On the horizontal axis, international-stock ETFs, like their domestic counterparts, are separated into value, blend, or growth ETFs. We take the stock portfolio's average price/cash-flow ratio relative to the MSCI EAFE Index and add it to the portfolio's average price/book figure relative to the MSCI EAFE Index. (The MSCI EAFE average in each case is set equal to 1.00.) If the sum of the relative price/cash flow and the relative price/book is less than 1.75, the ETF is defined as a value offering if the sum lands from 1.75 to 2.25 the ETF is classified as a blend vehicle; if the sum is greater than 2.25 the ETF falls into the growth column.

Bond Style Box

Domestic- and international-bond ETFs feature their own Morningstar style box, which focuses on two pillars of bond performance: interest-rate sensitivity and credit quality. Morningstar splits bond ETFs into three groups of rate sensitivity as determined by duration (short, intermediate, and long) and three credit-quality groups (high, medium, and low). These groupings graphically display a portfolio's average effective duration and credit quality. As with stock funds, nine possible combinations exist, ranging from short duration/high quality for the safest funds to long duration/low quality for the most volatile.

Along the horizontal axis of the style box lies the interest-rate sensitivity of an ETF's bond portfolio based on average effective duration. This figure, which is calculated by the ETF sponsors, weights each bond's duration by its relative size within the portfolio. Duration provides a more accurate description of a bond's true interest-rate sensitivity than does maturity because it takes into consideration all mortgage prepayments, puts and call options, and adjustable coupons. ETFs with an average effective duration of less than 3.5 years qualify as short term. ETFs with an average effective duration of greater than or equal to 3.5 years and less than or equal to six years are classified as intermediate. ETFs with an average effective duration of greater than six years are considered long term.

Along the vertical axis of a bond style box lies the average credit-quality rating of a bond portfolio. ETFs that have an average credit rating of AAA or AA are categorized as high quality. Bond portfolios with average ratings of A or BBB are medium quality, and those rated BB and below are categorized as low quality. For the purposes of Morningstar's calculations, U.S. government securities are considered AAA bonds, nonrated municipal bonds generally are classified as BB, and all other nonrated bonds generally are considered B.

Investor Return %

Morningstar investor returns (also known as dollar-weighted returns) measure how the typical investor in that fund fared over time, incorporating the impact of cash inflows and outflows from purchases and sales. In contrast to total returns, investor returns account for all cash flows into and out of the fund to measure how the average investor performed over time. Investor return is calculated in a similar manner as internal rate of return. Investor return measures the compound growth rate in the value of all dollars invested in the fund over the evaluation period. Investor return is the growth rate that will link the beginning total net assets plus all intermediate cash flows to the ending total net assets.

M

Management Fee

The management fee is the maximum percentage deducted from a ETF's average net assets to pay an advisor or subadvisor. Often, as the ETF's net assets grow, the percentage deducted for management fees decreases. Alternatively, the ETF may compute the fee as a flat percentage of average net assets. Management fees for ETFs should be relatively low compared with mutual funds, with most being well under 1.00%.

Bond Style Box

Risk	Duration			Quality
	Value	Blend	Growth	
Low	Short-term High Quality	Interm-term High Quality	Long-term High Quality	High
Moderate	Short-term Medium Quality	Interm-term Medium Quality	Long-term Medium Quality	Medium
High	Short-term Low Quality	Interm-term Low Quality	Long-Term Low Quality	Low

Within the bond style box grid, nine possible combinations exist, ranging from short duration or maturity/high quality for the safest funds to long duration or maturity/low quality for the riskiest.

Margin of Safety

Though we aim to buy stocks for less than their intrinsic worth, or fair value, it's easy to estimate a stock's value too optimistically. To compensate for this all-too-human tendency, we try to buy stocks only when they're trading at a substantial discount to our fair value estimate. The difference between the market's price for a stock and our fair value estimate is the margin of safety. Our analysts' assessment of business risk dictates the margin of safety that we demand, with riskier stocks warranting wider margins of safety and vice versa for less risky stocks. This same principle applies to stock ETFs—we're not content to invest in ETFs that are trading at slight discounts to our fair value estimate. Instead, we aim to buy at a certain discount to fair value. Basic portfolio theory holds that the diversification of an ETF portfolio should diffuse some of the uncertainty associated with our forecasts. Stated differently, whereas there's significant uncertainty that a stock's price will converge to our fair value estimate over a certain time horizon, there's less uncertainty that the prices of a basket of stocks will converge, in aggregate, to our weighted-average fair value estimate. Therefore, the margins of safety that we apply to our ETF fair value estimates tend to be narrower than those we place around our single-stock fair value estimates.

Market Cap

Shown for domestic-stock ETFs, this section gives investors a view of the different sizes of companies in a fund's portfolio. Every month, we break down a stock portfolio into five different sizes of companies by their market capitalization and show what percentage of a fund's stock assets is devoted to each. Instead of using stationary market-cap cut-offs, we base our boundaries on percentiles: We call the largest 1% of U.S. companies Giant, the next 4% Large, the next 15% Medium, the next 30% Small, and the bottom 50% Micro. The Market Cap section is designed to help investors complete the picture suggested by the median market cap statistic. While average weighted market cap pinpoints the size of the average holding, this section allows investors to see the whole range of companies held by the fund.

Market Price

An ETF's share price as determined by market supply and demand. The market price can be expressed as the bid or offer price, the midpoint between the bid/offer spread, or the last sale price. Its expression depends on the policy of the quoting entity.

Market Return

see also Total Return and NAV Return

The total return of an ETF based on its market price at the beginning and end of the holding period. This may differ from the ETF's NAV return. The market return is the return earned by ETF investors, except for those who hold creation units (authorized participants).

Maturity

see Average Effective Maturity

Mean

see Standard Deviation

Methodology

While the Morningstar Category gives investors an idea of what sorts of investments an ETF makes, it does not fully capture the nuances of the construction methodology of the ETF's underlying index. In this section, Morningstar analysts explain the criteria ETF bogies use in selecting securities and how risky a given methodology may be. On the equity side, the strategy description often focuses on what size and type of company an index keys on, or a discussion regarding how a style-based benchmark, for instance, defines growth and value stocks. With bond ETFs, the strategy section explains how the ETF manager goes about tracking the often wide-ranging fixed-income indexes. Strategy section also often notes whether an ETF manager uses representative sampling to track the underlying index and the benchmarks rebalancing schedule.

Modern Portfolio Theory Statistics (MPT Statistics)

Developed in the 1950s by Harry Markowitz, Modern Portfolio Theory statistics (or MPT statistics) are standard financial and academic statistical tools for assessing the risk and return of a portfolio relative to its benchmark. The main theory behind MPT is that a certain risk level will produce a certain corresponding return. Its statistical tools are best-fit beta, alpha, and R-squared. Morningstar bases alpha, beta, and R-squared on a least-squares regression of the portfolio's excess return over Treasury bills compared with the excess returns of the fund's benchmark index. These calculations are computed for the trailing 36-month period. For ETFs, the benchmark index should have a high R-squared, because index-tracking ETF's underlying portfolio should replicate the composition of its target index.

Alpha

Alpha represents the amount by which a portfolio has outperformed or underperformed what was expected based on its risk (beta). If alpha is positive, it means the portfolio's returns were higher than its regression line predicted. With mutual funds, investors often view alpha as a measurement of the value added or subtracted by active fund managers. With index-tracking ETFs, the alpha should correlate with the accepted beta of the benchmark. There are limitations to alpha's ability to accurately depict a fund's added or subtracted value. In some cases, a negative alpha can result from the expenses that are present in the fund figures but are not present in the figures of the comparison index. Alpha is completely dependent on the accuracy of beta: If the investor accepts beta as a conclusive definition of risk, a positive alpha would be a conclusive indicator of good fund performance.

Beta

Beta is a measure of a fund's sensitivity to market movements. It measures the relationship between a fund's excess return over T-bills and the excess return of the benchmark index. Morningstar calculates beta using the same regression equation as the one used for alpha, which regresses excess return for the fund against excess return for the index. This approach differs slightly from other methodologies that rely on a regression of raw returns. By definition, the beta of the benchmark (in this case, an index) is 1.00. Accordingly, a fund with beta 1.10 has performed 10% better than its benchmark index after deducting the T-bill rate in up markets and 10% worse in down markets, assuming all other factors remain constant. Conversely, a beta of 0.85 indicates that the fund has performed 15% worse than the index in up markets and 15% better in down markets. A low beta does not imply that the fund has a low level of volatility, though; rather, a low beta means only that the fund's market-related risk is low. A specialty fund that invests primarily in gold, for example, will usually have a low beta (and a low R-squared), as its performance is tied more closely to the price of gold and gold-mining stocks than to the overall stock market. Thus, although the specialty fund might fluctuate wildly because of rapid changes in gold prices, its beta will remain low. With index-tracking ETFs, the beta coefficient should not deviate greatly from 1.00 because the portfolio aims to replicate the composition of the underlying benchmark. Hence, its volatility should also approximate that of the benchmark.

R-Squared

R-squared ranges from zero to 100 and reflects the percentage of an ETF's movements that are explained by movements in its benchmark index. An R-squared of 100 means that all movements of an ETF are completely correlated with movements in the index. Thus, index ETFs that invest only in S&P 500 stocks will have an R-squared very close to 100. Conversely, a low R-squared indicates that very few of the ETF's movements are explained by movements in its benchmark index. An R-squared measure of 25, for example, means that only 25% of the ETF's movements can be explained by movements in its benchmark index. Therefore, R-squared can be used to ascertain the significance of a particular beta or alpha. Generally, a high R-squared will indicate a more reliable beta figure. If the R-squared is low, then the beta explains less of the ETF's performance.

Morningstar Category

see also Investment Style Box

While the investment objective stated in a fund's prospectus may or may not reflect how the ETF actually invests, the Morningstar Category is assigned based on the underlying securities in each portfolio. Morningstar assigns categories based on three years of composition and style boxes. For ETFs that are not yet three years old an average of the portfolios since the ETF's inception is used.

The Morningstar Category helps investors make meaningful comparisons between mutual funds and ETFs. The categories make it easier to build well-diversified portfolios, assess potential risk, and identify the top-performing mutual funds and ETFs.

The following is a list and explanation of the categories. We place funds in a given category based on their portfolio statistics and compositions over the past three years. If the fund is new and has no portfolio history, we estimate where it will fall before giving it a more permanent category assignment. When necessary, we may change a category assignment based on recent changes to the portfolio.

Stock ETFs

Domestic-Stock ETFs

ETFs with at least 70% of assets in domestic stocks are categorized based on the style and size of the stocks they typically own. The style and size divisions reflect those used in the investment style box: value, blend, or growth style and small, medium, or large. Based on their investment style over the past three years, diversified domestic-stock funds are placed in one of the nine categories shown below:

Large Growth	Mid-cap Growth	Small Growth
Large Blend	Mid-cap Blend	Small Blend
Large Value	Mid-cap Value	Small Value

Morningstar also includes several other domestic-stock categories: Communications, Financial, Health Care, Natural Resources, Precious Metals, Real Estate, Technology, Utilities, Convertible Bond (convertible-bond funds have at least 50% of their assets invested in convertible securities), Conservative Allocation (conservative-allocation funds invest in both stocks and bonds, with just 20% to 50% of assets in stocks), and Moderate Allocation (moderate-allocation funds invest in both stocks and bonds, with more than 50% in stocks).

International-Stock ETFs

Stock funds and ETFs that have invested 40% or more of their equity holdings in foreign stocks (on average over the past three years) are placed in an international-stock category, based on the following parameters:

Europe: at least 75% of stocks invested in Europe.

Latin America: at least 75% of stocks invested in Latin America.

Diversified Emerging Markets: at least 50% of stocks invested in emerging markets.

Diversified Asia/Pacific: at least 65% of stocks invested in Pacific countries, with at least an additional 10% of stocks invested in Japan.

Asia/Pacific ex-Japan: at least 75% of stocks in Pacific countries, with less than 10% of stocks invested in Japan.

Japan: at least 75% of stocks invested in Japan.

Foreign Large Value: a majority of assets invested in large-cap foreign stocks that are value-oriented (based on low price/book and price/cash flow ratios, relative to the MSCI EAFE Index).

Foreign Large Blend: a majority of assets invested in large-cap foreign stocks, where neither growth nor value characteristics predominate.

Foreign Large Growth: a majority of assets invested in large-cap foreign stocks that are growth-oriented (based on high price/book and price/cash flow ratios, relative to the MSCI EAFE Index).

Foreign Small/Mid-Cap Value: a majority of assets invested in small- and mid-cap foreign stocks that are value-oriented (based on low price/book and price/cash flow ratios, relative to the MSCI EAFE Index).

Foreign Small/Mid-Cap Growth: a majority of assets invested in small- and mid-cap foreign stocks that are growth-oriented (based on high price/book and price/cash flow ratios, relative to the MSCI EAFE Index).

World : at least 40% of stock holdings invested in foreign stocks, with at least 10% of stocks invested in the United States.

World Allocation: a fund with stock holdings of greater than 20% but less than 70% of the portfolio where 40% of the stocks and bonds are foreign. Also, must have at least 10% of assets invested in bonds.

Bond ETFs

ETFs with 80% or more of their assets invested in bonds are classified as bond ETFs. Note: For all bond funds, maturity figures are used only when duration figures are unavailable.

Taxable-Bond ETFs

Long-Term Government: at least 90% of bond portfolio invested in government issues with a duration of greater than six years, or an average effective maturity of greater than 10 years.

Intermediate-Term Government: at least 90% of bond portfolio invested in government issues with a duration of greater than or equal to 3.5 years and less than or equal to six years, or an average effective maturity of greater than or equal to four years and less than or equal to 10 years.

Short-Term Government: at least 90% of bond portfolio invested in government issues with a duration of greater than or equal to one year and less than 3.5 years, or an average effective maturity of greater than or equal to one year and less than four years.

Long-Term Bond: focuses on corporate and other investment-grade issues with an average duration of more than six years, or an average effective maturity of more than 10 years.

Intermediate-Term Bond: focuses on corporate and other investment-grade issues with an average duration of greater than or equal to 3.5 years but less than or equal to six years, or an average effective maturity of greater than or equal to four but less than or equal to 10 years.

Short-Term Bond: focuses on corporate and other investment-grade issues with an average duration of greater than or equal to one but less than 3.5 years, or an average effective maturity of greater than or equal to one but less than four years.

Ultrashort Bond: used for ETFs with an average duration or an average effective maturity of less than one year. This category includes general corporate and government bond funds, and excludes any international, convertible, multisector, and high-yield bond funds.

High-Yield Bond: at least 65% of assets in bonds rated below BBB.

Multisector Bond: seeks income by diversifying assets among several fixed-income sectors, usually U.S. government obligations, foreign bonds, and high-yield domestic debt securities.

Morningstar Return vs. Category
An assessment of a fund's excess return over a risk-free rate (the return of the 90-day Treasury bill) in comparison to similar ETFs and conventional open-end funds after adjusting for an assumed 0.20% commission. (ETF commissions are treated like front- and back-end loads. The 0.20% commission represents Morningstar's $20 estimate of the average retail commission paid and the $10,000 average investment amount, per SEC guidelines for expense projections.) Morningstar uses NAVs to calculate returns rather than market prices. ETF market prices are set throughout the day by supply and demand, and tend to stick close to their NAVs, which are set at the end of the trading day. NAVs are a better measure of performance because if ETFs don't trade often, their market prices grow stale.

In each Morningstar Category, the top 10% of funds earn a High Morningstar Return, the next 22.5% Above Average, the middle 35% Average, the next 22.5% Below Average, and the bottom 10% Low. Morningstar Return is measured for up to three time periods (three, five, and 10 years). These separate measures are then weighted and averaged to produce an overall measure for the fund. Funds with less than three years of performance history are not rated.

Morningstar Risk vs. Category
As assessment of the variations in a fund's monthly returns in comparison to similar ETFs and conventional open-end funds, with an emphasis on downward variation. The greater the variation, the higher the risk score. If two funds have precisely the same return, the one with the greater variations in its return is given the larger risk score.

In each Morningstar Category, the 10% of funds with the lowest measure of risk are described as Low Risk, the next 22.5% Below Average, the middle 35% Average, the next 22.5% Above Average, and the top 10% High. Morningstar Risk is measured for up to three time periods (three, five, and 10 years). These separate measures are then weighted and averaged to produce an overall measure for the fund. Funds with less than three years of performance history are not rated.

Morningstar Price/Fair Value Measure
A ratio that offers a bottom-up assessment of whether an ETF portfolio is cheap or expensive by gauging if its holdings, on average, are trading above or below their Morningstar fair value estimates. The process draws on the research of Morningstar's stable of 100-plus in-house equity analysts who research and estimate fair values for more than 2,000 stocks. Morningstar calculates the market value of all the holdings in a given ETF for which it has fair value estimates. Then it uses the fair value estimates of those stocks to calculate a fair value of the same portfolio. Lastly, Morningstar compares the two numbers and calculates the percentage premium or discount of the market value compared to the fair value. The result is expressed as a ratio. A measure higher than 1.0 means the ETF is overvalued, according to Morningstar estimates. A reading lower than 1.0 means the offering is undervalued. Because Morningstar does not estimate a fair value for every stock an ETF might own, the relevance of the results of the price/fair value depends on how many stocks in a given portfolio have received a fair value estimate and the percentage of that portfolio's assets these stocks represent.

Morningstar Fair Value Per Share
The aggregate fair value of the stocks in an ETF portfolio that are under coverage by Morningstar equity analysts, divided by the ETF's shares outstanding. Depending on the coverage rate, the fair value may not include all of the stocks in the ETF portfolio.

Price/Fair Value Premium/Discount
The percent by which the aggregate fair value of an ETF's portfolio exceeds or trails the aggregate market price of the stocks in the portfolio for which Morningstar has estimated fair values.

Price Per Share
An ETF's quoted market price.

Morningstar Style Box
see Investment Style Box

Morningstar's Take
Morningstar's analysis of a fund that interprets and enhances the numerical data in an effort to provide an assessment of an ETF's worth. To accomplish this, a Morningstar analyst scrutinizes past shareholder reports, puts historical performance into the perspective of market trends, and whenever possible, interviews an ETF manager or other fund official. Although many people are involved in producing this Morningstar page, the analyst is ultimately responsible for its content.

N

NAV
see Net Asset Value

NAV Return
see also Market Return and Total Return
The total return of an ETF, based on its NAV at the beginning and end of the holding period and assuming reinvested dividends. This may be different from the ETF's market return. The market return, not the NAV return, is the return actually earned by ETF investors, except for those who hold creation units (authorized participants).

Net Assets
see Total Net Assets

Net Asset Flows
The difference between asset inflows—monies that investors invest in a fund—and asset outflows. Though ETFs trade in the secondary market, they are not closed to net new investment in the same way closed-end mutual funds are. Rather, a market-market, such as a brokerage house or investment bank, is able to issue and redeem new fund shares to whet investor appetite, or lack thereof. Thus, when investors are pumping more money into an ETF than they're pulling away, the net asset inflows swell the ETF's overall size. The higher the level of inflows, the more popular an ETF is thought to be with investors.

Net Asset Value
An ETF's net asset value (NAV) represents its per-share price. An ETF's NAV is derived by dividing the total net assets of the ETF by the number of shares outstanding. Note that the Net Asset Value of ETFs may differ from the market price, which is the price at which the ETF shares are traded on an intraday market.

P

Percentile Rank (% Rank)
see also Performance
Located in the Performance and History sections these rankings allow investors to compare a fund's total returns with those of other funds.

In the Performance section we compare the fund's total return for various time periods against the same Morningstar Category (% Rank Cat). In the History section, we compare a fund's calendar-year total returns with its category's (Total Rtn % Rank Cat). In both sections, a fund's total returns are ranked on a scale from 1 to 100 where 1 represents the highest-returning 1% of funds and 100 represents the lowest-returning 1% of funds. Thus, in the performance section, a Percentile rank of 15 under the % Rank Cat column for the trailing three-month period indicates that the fund's three-month return placed in the top 15% of all funds in its category for that time period.

Performance
see also Percentile Rank, Tax Analysis, and Total Return
A fund's total return figures for various time periods.

Investment Value Graph
The Investment Value graph line shows a fund's performance trend, derived from the fund's historical growth of $10,000. It provides a visual depiction of how a fund has amassed its returns, including the performance swings its shareholders have endured along the way. The growth of $10,000 begins at the date of the fund's inception; if the fund has been in existence for more than 12 years, the growth of $10,000 begins at the first year listed on the graph. Also, featured in the graph is the performance of an index (S&P 500 or MSCI EAFE) that allows investors to compare the performance of the fund with the performance of the benchmark index.

Quarterly Returns
The first section provides the fund's quarterly and year-end total returns for the past five years. The quarterly returns are compounded to obtain the year-end total return shown on the right. (Calculating the sum of the

four quarterly returns will not produce the year-end total return because simple addition does not take into account the effects of compounding.)

Total Return %
This figure is calculated by taking the change in net asset value, reinvesting all income and capital-gains distributions during the period, and dividing by the starting net asset value.

+/- S&P 500
This statistic measures the difference between a stock ETF's total return and the total return of the S&P 500 Index. A negative number indicates that the ETF underperformed the index by the given amount, while a positive number indicates that the ETF outperformed the index by the given amount. For example, a listing of -2.0 indicates that the fund underperformed the index by 2 percentage points. The difference between each stock ETF's performance and the S&P 500 Index is listed. Bond ETFs are compared with the Lehman Brothers Aggregate Bond Index. The next column shows the same performance figure relative to another more specialized benchmark index.

% Rank Cat:
see also Percentile Rank
Morningstar lists each ETF's total return for various time periods against the funds in the same Morningstar Category (% Rank Cat). One is the highest or best percentile ranking and 100 is the lowest, or worst.

Portfolio Analysis
Occupying much of the right side of the Morningstar page is the Portfolio Analysis section. Prominent in this section are an ETF's most recently reported top securities (excluding cash and cash equivalents for all but short-term bond funds), ranked in descending order by the percentage of the portfolio's net assets they occupy. With this information, investors can more clearly identify what drives the fund's performance.

Morningstar makes every effort to gather the most up-to-date portfolio information from a fund. By law, however, funds need only report this information four times during a calendar year, and they have two months after the report date to actually release the shareholder report and portfolio. Therefore, it is possible that a fund's portfolio could be up to five months old or more at the time of publication. We print the date the portfolio was reported. Older portfolios should not be disregarded, however; although the list may not represent the exact current holdings of the fund, it may still provide a good picture of the overall nature of the fund's management style.

Total Stocks/Total Fixed-Income
Total Stock indicates the total number of stock securities in a fund's portfolio, and Total Fixed-Income denotes the number of bond securities a fund holds. Theses do not simply refer to the stocks or bonds listed on the page; rather, they represent all stocks and bonds in the portfolio. These listings can be quite useful for gaining greater insight into the portfolio's diversification.

Share Change
Applied only to common stocks, the share change entry indicates the change in the number of shares of each stock from the previously reported portfolio. If the change column shows a minus sign for one of the portfolio's stocks, that means the ETF's manager sold shares of that stock since the previous portfolio was reported. Similarly, a plus sign next to the holding means that management added shares of that stock to the portfolio. The sunshine symbol indicates that the stock is a new addition to the portfolio. We list the date of the previously reported portfolio in the column heading, so that you know how much time has passed between the current portfolio and the previously reported portfolio.

Security
This column lists the names of the stock or bond securities held as of the portfolio date. For stock holdings, this line typically displays just the name of the issuing company. Other stock labels are included where appropriate, such as ADR, which distinguishes an American Depository Receipt. Bond holdings, however, will usually include more information to differentiate among the many types of bonds available. For most bonds, the coupon rate is listed as a percentage figure after the name of the bond. Adjustable-rate mortgages and floating-rate notes will have ARM or FRN (or IFRN for inverse-floating rate notes) listed after the name of the bond to indicate that the coupon rate is variable. Some adjustable-rate bond listings will include the formula by which the coupon rate is calculated, which is usually a fixed percentage plus some benchmark value.

Securities followed by the abbreviation IO are interest-only securities, or those that consist only of the interest portion of a security, not the principal portion. PO indicates a principal-only security that sells at a discount to par and carries a coupon rate of zero.

Sector: see also Sector Weighting and Industry Weightings
The industry sector of each stock holding is reported in this column this gives investors greater insight into where an ETF's top holdings are concentrated and where its vulnerabilities lie.

P/E: see also Price/Earnings Ratio and Value Measures
To add depth to the average P/E number for the entire portfolio (listed under Current Investment Style), the P/E ratio for each stock is reported here. NMF means the stock's p/e is 100 or more. A minus sign means the company has no earnings or the figure is not available.

YTD Return %
The year-to-date stock returns show whether one or two big winners (or losers) are driving fund performance, or a lot of little successes. In some cases, losses in top holdings can suggest a bargain-hunting strategy if a position in a losing stock is new or expanded.

% Assets
The % Assets column indicates what percentage of the portfolio's net assets a given security constitutes. Morningstar calculates the percentage of net assets figure by dividing the market value of the security by the ETF's total net assets. If a given security makes up a large percentage of the fund's net assets, the fund uses a concentrated portfolio strategy, at least with respect to the security in question. If, however, the percentage figures are low, then the manager is simply not willing to bet heavily on a particular security.

Date of Maturity
Maturity, located in the portfolio section for bond ETFs only, indicates the date on which a bond or note comes due. This information can be used in determining the portfolio's basic fixed-income strategy. For example, if most of these dates are a year or two away, the fund is taking a conservative, short-term approach. The maturity dates listed here, however, are not adjusted for calls (rights an issuer may have to redeem outstanding bonds before their scheduled maturity) or for the likelihood of mortgage prepayments. Thus, they might not accurately state the actual time to repayment of a bond, and might overstate a portfolio's sensitivity to interest-rate changes.

Amount
Found on bond ETF pages, the amount column refers to the size of the fund's investment in a given security as to the portfolio dates listed above. This figure reflects the principal value of the security in thousands of dollars.

Value
Value simply gives the market value of a particular security in thousands of dollars as of the portfolio date. The value column allows investors to gauge whether a fixed-income security is selling at a premium or a discount to its face value, as reflected in the amount column.

Premium
see also NAV and Discount to NAV
The amount by which an ETF's market price is greater than its net asset value (NAV). Any discount or premium is usually small and short-lived because ETFs' in-kind redemption process allows market makers to arbitrage away the difference.

Profitability Measures
Return on Assets (ROA)
This measures how effectively companies use their assets to generate profits. The formula for an individual firm is net income divided by assets. Companies with high returns on assets include software firms and beverage companies. Both types of companies frequently generate high profits but have relatively small investments in plant, equipment, and other assets. Firms with low returns on assets are typically in manufacturing or other capital-intensive industries. Companies with low returns on assets tend to have low valuations and are mostly held by value ETFs; by contrast, growth managers favor firms with high returns on assets. An ETF's ROA is equal to the weighted average ROA of its individual holdings.

Return on Equity (ROE)
This calculation reveals how effectively management has invested shareholders' equity, which is the amount of money initially invested in the business plus

retained earnings. ROE is simply net income divided by average shareholder equity. A high ROE is often a sign that a company's management uses its resources wisely, and the company is often located in a growing industry with high barriers to entry. For example, thanks to its dominance of the software operating-systems market, Microsoft usually has high ROEs. By contrast, companies with low ROEs frequently operate in stagnant industries in which there is overcapacity. For example, automakers frequently earn low returns on equity. Companies with high ROEs generally have better business models, but as a reflection of that, their share prices are often expensive. Growth managers typically prefer companies with high and rising ROEs, while valuation concerns may lead value managers to buy firms with low ROEs. A fund's ROE is the weighted average of its individual holdings' ROEs.

Net Margin
We arrive at net margin by dividing a firm's net income (after all expenses, including taxes) by its sales. This measures how effective a company is at wringing profits out of each dollar of revenues. Companies with high net margins tend to have strong competitive positions, while those with low net margins often operate in highly price-competitive industries such as retailing. Companies that consistently earn high net margins include pharmaceuticals and successful software companies.

Low-margin businesses include supermarkets and other retailers. High-margin firms earn superior returns but also garner premium valuations, so the stocks are often too expensive for value managers. At the ETF level, net margin represents the weighted average of the individual stocks' net margins.

R

Rank
see Percentile Rank

Rating and Risk
see also Historical Profile
In this section, Morningstar includes commission-adjusted returns and several risk measures and proprietary statistics.

Regional Exposure
All international stock funds feature a regional exposure listing. This table displays the percentage of the fund's total net assets invested in the U.K./Western Europe, Japan, Asia ex-Japan, North America, and Latin America. Below the regional information on each page we list the five largest country exposures. The information in this section is gathered from portfolios and is the most recent available.

Relative Comparisons
see also Industry Weightings and Market Capitalization
At various places in the Portfolio Analysis section, Morningstar shows how an individual ETF compares with the average of all ETFs within its category (Rel Cat) or a benchmark index (Rel S&P 500). The category average (or index) is always set equal to 1.00. For example, a domestic-stock ETF with a utilities weighting of 1.50 relative to its category has 50% more in utilities issues than its average peer. Stock statistics are displayed in comparison with the S&P Index. In this case, 1.00 represents the index. A relative price/book ratio of 0.43, for example, indicates that the fund's price/book is 57% lower than that of the index.

Restricted/Illiquid Securities
see Special Securities

Return
see Total Return

Risk
see Business Risk Modern Portfolio Theory Statistics and Standard Deviation

S

Sector Breakdown for Fixed-Income Funds
The fixed-income sector illustrates the type of bonds a fund owns. These sectors help investors compare and understand the sector exposure of each mutual fund. These data are especially useful for comparing two funds that may be in the same Morningstar Category. The fixed-income sectors are calculated for all domestic taxable-bond portfolios. It is based on the securities in the most recent portfolio. This information shows the percentage of bond and cash assets invested in each of the 14 fixed-income sectors.

Morningstar groups all fixed-income assets into the following sectors:

U.S. Government

U.S. Treasuries

This sector includes all conventional fixed-rate debt issued by the Treasury department of the United States government (i.e. this sector excludes tips). Some examples of this type of debt are Treasury bonds and Treasury notes. Treasury bills are included under % Cash, because they mature in less than 12 months.

TIPS

TIPS are inflation-indexed debt issued by the U.S. Treasury. (The term TIPS derives from their former name, Treasury Inflation-Protected Securities.) These bonds have principal and coupon payments that are linked to movements in the Consumer Price Index. They are a defensive measure against expectations of inflation, which typically erodes the real yield of conventional bonds. Even if inflation fears are in check, these bonds can benefit when the yields fall on traditional Treasuries. These unique securities act very differently than any other fixed-rate bond, and their volatility can change over time, depending on the level of interest rates.

U.S. Agency

This sector includes debt securities issued by government agencies-such as the Federal National Mortgage Association (FNMA), also known as Fannie Mae, or the Federal Home Loan Mortgage Corporation (FHLMC), also known as Freddie Mac-to raise capital and finance their operations. These "debentures" are not secured by physical assets, so they differ from most of the mortgage bonds that are issued by these agencies.

Mortgage

Mortgage Pass-Throughs

These are fixed-income securities that represent a claim to the cash flows associated with a pool of mortgages. The bondholders are entitled to a share of the principal and interest payments paid by the homeowners.
The majority of these bonds are issued by a government agency such as FNMA, GNMA, or FHLMC. A few private corporations and banks also securitize and package mortgages in this way, and those are also included in this sector.

Mortgage CMO

Collateralized mortgage obligations (CMO) are similar to pass-through mortgage securities, but investors have more control over whether they will be paid sooner or later. CMOs are structured by time, so that some investors can line up for the first series of cash flow payments, while others may choose to put themselves at the end of the line. A fund manager would buy a late-paying CMO if he or she believed that there would be a lot of mortgage refinancing in the near term. This would protect the fund from getting its money back too early, which would require it to be reinvested at a lower interest rate. Most CMOs are based on mortgages from government agencies, such as FNMA or GNMA.

Mortgage ARM

Adjustable-rate mortgage (ARM) securities are backed by residential home mortgages where the interest rate is reset periodically in relation to a benchmark. Most ARMs are from government agencies, such as FNMA and GNMA.

Credit

U.S. Corporate

This sector includes all fixed-income securities that are issued by corporations domiciled in the United States. Corporate bonds are issued with a wide range of coupon rates and maturity dates.

Asset-Backed

Asset-backed securities are based on the expected cash flow from such things as auto loans, credit-card receivables, and computer leases. The cash flows for asset-backed securities can be fixed (e.g. auto loans have a defined payment schedule and a fixed maturity) or variable (credit-card debt is paid at random intervals). These securities typically range in maturity from two to seven years.

Convertible

Convertible bonds give the owner an opportunity to convert the bond to a certain number of shares of common stock at a certain price. As the stock approaches that price, the option to convert becomes more valuable and the price of the convertible bond also rises. These securities usually provide lower interest payments, because the option to convert to stock could potentially be quite valuable at some point in the future.

Municipal
Local and state governments issue municipal bonds in order to raise money for operations and development. This financing is sometimes used to build or upgrade hospitals, sewer systems, schools, housing, stadiums, or industrial complexes. Some municipal bonds are backed by the issuing entity while others are linked to a revenue stream, such as from a tollway or a utility. Municipal bonds are exempt from federal tax and often from state and local taxes, too. The tax break allows municipal governments to sell the bonds at a lower interest rate, because the investor gets an additional tax benefit. Currently there are no municipal-bond ETFs.

Corporate Inflation-Protected
Inflation-protected securities are similar to TIPS, but they are issued by a private entity rather than by the U.S. government. These bonds are linked to an index of inflation, and the principal and coupon payments increase when inflation increases. As with TIPS, these securities behave quite differently from conventional bonds.

Foreign
Foreign Corporate
These fixed-income securities are issued by corporations that are based outside of the United States.

Foreign Government
These fixed-income securities are issued by governments outside the United States.

Cash
Cash can be cash in the bank, certificates of deposit, currency, or money market holdings. Cash can also be any fixed-income securities that mature in less than 12 months. Cash also includes commercial paper and any repurchase agreements held by the ETF. Because this data point is based on only the cash and bond assets in the ETF, it can be different than the % Cash in the composition breakdown, which is expressed as a percent of total assets.

Sector Weightings/Super Sectors
Morningstar divides the stock market into three broad "super sectors," each of which contains four specific industry sectors. Sectors are based on what companies actually do. That is, unlike some other sector classification systems, sectors aren't based on expected behavior of the stocks of these companies.

The super sectors with their major inclusive sectors are as follows:

Information Sphere
Made up of the Software, Hardware, Media, and Telecommunications sectors.

Service Sphere
Made up of the Health Care, Consumer Services, Business Services, and Financial Services sectors.

Manufacturing Sphere
Made up of the Consumer Goods, Industrial Materials, Energy, and Utilities sectors.

The sectors with their major inclusive industries are as follows:

Software
Companies engaged in the design and marketing of computer operating systems and applications. Examples include Microsoft, and Oracle.

Hardware
Manufacturers of computer equipment, communication equipment, semiconductors, and components. Examples include IBM, Cisco Systems, and Intel.

Media
Companies that own and operate broadcast networks and those that create content or provide it for other media companies. Examples include Time Warner, Walt Disney, and Washington Post.

Telecommunications
Companies that provide communication services using fixed-line networks or those that provide wireless access and services. Examples include AT&T and Verizon.

Health Care
Includes biotechnology, pharmaceuticals, research services, HMOs, home health, hospitals, assisted living, and medical equipment and supplies. Examples include Abbott Laboratories, Merck, and Cardinal Health.

Consumer Services
Includes retail stores, personal services, home builders, home supply, travel and entertainment companies,

and educational providers. Examples include Wal-Mart, Home Depot, and Expedia.

Business Services
Includes advertising, printing, publishing, business support, consultants, employment, engineering and construction, security services, waste management, distributors, and transportation. Examples include Manpower, R.R. Donnelley, and Southwest Airlines.

Financial Services
Includes banks, finance companies, money-management firms, savings and loans, securities brokers, and insurance companies. Examples include Citigroup, Washington Mutual, and Fannie Mae.

Consumer Goods
Companies that manufacture or provide food, beverages, household and personal products, apparel, shoes, textiles, autos and auto parts, consumer electronics, luxury goods, packaging, and tobacco. Examples include PepsiCo, Ford Motor, and Kraft Foods.

Industrial Materials
Includes aerospace and defense firms, companies that provide or manufacture chemicals, machinery, building materials, and commodities. Examples include Boeing, DuPont, and Alcoa.

Energy
Companies that produce or refine oil and gas, oilfield services and equipment companies, and pipeline operators. Examples include ExxonMobil, Schlumberger, and BP.

Utilities
Electric, gas, and water utilities. Examples include Duke Energy, Exelon, and El Paso.

Share Change
see Portfolio Analysis

Sharpe Ratio
The Sharpe ratio is a risk-adjusted measure developed by Nobel Laureate William Sharpe. It is calculated using standard deviation and excess return to determine reward per unit of risk. First, the average monthly return of the 90-day Treasury bill (over a 36-month period) is subtracted from the fund's average monthly return. The difference in total return represents the fund's excess return beyond that of the 90-day Treasury bill, a risk-free investment. An arithmetic annualized excess return is then calculated by multiplying this monthly return by 12. To show a relationship between excess return and risk, this number is then divided by the standard deviation of the ETF's annualized excess returns. The higher the Sharpe ratio, the better the ETF's historical risk-adjusted performance.

Special Securities
This section shows an ETF's exposure to a variety of complex or illiquid securities, including derivatives. The percentage of total net assets represented by each type of security is listed to the right of each group. Some securities may fall under more than one type.

Restricted/Illiquid Securities
Restricted and illiquid securities are issues that may be hard to accurately price and difficult to sell because an investor may be unable to find a buyer quickly. Private placement issues and 144(a) securities are both included here. Both types have varying degrees of liquidity and are exempt from some of the cumbersome registration and disclosure requirements that public offerings usually face.

Exotic Mortgage-Backed Securities
This section indicates how much of an ETF's net assets are held in unusual mortgage-backed derivatives. Specifically, we delineate those securities that see their price changes magnified when interest rates or mortgage-prepayment speeds change. Because not all mortgage-backed derivatives have these traits, we include the following: interest-only (IOs) and principal-only paper (POs), inverse floating-rate securities (IFRNs), and Z-tranche collateralized mortgage obligation issues, all of which are fairly clearly labeled in a fund's shareholder reports. Kitchen-sink bonds, a complex mix of interest-only, principal-only bonds, and cast-off CMO tranches, are also tallied here. For stock funds, which rarely hold mortgage-backed issues of any kind, we combine exotic mortgage-backed securities with structured notes.

Emerging-Markets Securities
Debt or equity securities from emerging markets are listed here. These figures are calculated from the most recently available portfolio. Morningstar classifies as an emerging market anything aside from the following developed markets: Australia, Austria, Belgium, Canada, Denmark, Finland, France, Germany, Greece, Hong Kong, Ireland, Italy, Japan, the Netherlands, New Zealand, Norway, Portugal, Singapore, South Korea, Spain, Sweden, Switzerland, Taiwan, the United Kingdom, and the United States. This list is subject to change as markets become more developed or vice versa.

Options/Futures/Warrants
Options and futures may be used speculatively, to leverage a portfolio, or cautiously, as a hedge against risk. We don't show the percentage of assets devoted to options or futures because it is difficult to determine from shareholder reports how much of a portfolio is affected by an options or futures contract. We also include forward contracts and warrants in this area.

Standard Deviation
A statistical measure of the range of an ETF's performance. When an ETF has a high standard deviation, its range of performance has been very wide, indicating greater volatility. Investors use the standard deviation of historical performance to try to predict the range of returns that are most likely for a given portfolio. Standard deviation is based on a bell-curve distribution, so approximately 68% of the time, returns will fall within one standard deviation of the mean return for the portfolio, and 95% within two standard deviations. The most important thing to note is that the greater the standard deviation, the greater the fund's volatility has been.

For example, an investor can compare two ETFs with the same average monthly return of 5%, but with different standard deviations. The first ETF has a standard deviation of 2, which means that its range of returns for the past 36 months has typically remained between 1% and 9%. On the other hand, assume that the second ETF has a standard deviation of 4 for the same period. This higher deviation indicates that this ETF has experienced returns fluctuating between -3% and 13%. With the second ETF, an investor can expect greater volatility.

Mean
The mean represents the annualized average monthly return from which the standard deviation is calculated. The mean will be the same as the annualized trailing, three-year return figure for the same time period.

Style Box
see Investment Style Box

T

Tax-Adjusted Return %
see Tax Analysis

Tax Analysis
The information provided in the Tax Analysis section can be used to evaluate an ETF's aftertax returns and its efficiency in achieving them. Additionally, the potential capital gains exposure figure can provide a glimpse at a shareholder's vulnerability to taxation. All these figures can help an investor judge which ETFs have been tax-friendly.

Tax-Adjusted Return
The Tax-Adj Rtn % column shows an estimate of an ETF's annualized aftertax total return for the three-, five-, and 10-year periods, excluding any capital gains effects that would result from selling the ETF at the end of the period. Consistent with SEC guidance regarding tax-adjusted returns, these figures reflect the maximum load paid by fund shareholders. To determine this figure, all income and short-term (less than one year) capital-gain distributions are taxed at the maximum federal rate at the time of distribution. Long-term (more than one year) capital gains are taxed at a 20% rate. The aftertax portion is then reinvested in the fund. The category percentile rank (% Rank Cat) for each fund's tax-adjusted return is also listed. This ranking helps investors compare a fund's estimated aftertax performance with that of other funds in the category.

Tax-Cost Ratio
This represents the estimated percentage-point reduction in an annualized return that has resulted from income taxes over the past three-, five-, and 10-year periods. The calculation assumes investors pay the maximum federal rate on capital gains and ordinary income.

Ticker
A ticker is the symbol assigned to the ETF based on the exchange on which it's sold. ETF tickers range from three to four characters and are commonly used to locate a fund on electronic price-quoting systems.

Total Net Assets (TNA)
see also Average Daily Volume
This figure gives the ETF's asset base, net of fees and any expenses, at year end of past calendar years and at month end for the current year. Both total net assets and average daily volume can indicate the popularity of an ETF with investors.

Total Return
see also Capital Return %, Income Return %, and Market Return
All references to total return represent an ETF's gains over a specified period of time. Total return includes both income (in the form of dividends or interest payments) and capital gains or losses (the increase or decrease in the value of a security). Morningstar calculates total return by taking the change in an ETF's NAV, assuming the reinvestment of all income and capital-gains distributions (on the actual reinvestment date used by the ETF) during the time period, and then dividing the initial NAV. The quarterly returns, listed in the Performance section, express the ETF's return for each individual quarter; the total shown on the right is the compounded return for the four quarters of that year. An asterisk next to the total return number indicates that the return is calculated for a partial quarter or partial year because the ETF began operations during that time period.

Note that market return calculates total return by using market prices in place of the ETF's net asset value (NAV). Thus, the market total return and NAV total return may differ slightly.

Total Stocks/Total Fixed-Income
see Portfolio Analysis

Tracking Error
As applied to index exchange-traded funds, this refers to the amount by which the ETF portfolio's returns differ from that of the benchmark it tries to follow. In general, an index ETF's tracking error should be no greater than its expense ratio. That shows the fund is doing a good job tracking its underlying index before expenses are deducted. Tracking error greater than an ETF's expense ratio could indicate the fund's manager isn't doing a good job running the fund, or that the fund has selected an inefficient index to follow.

Turnover Rate
The rate that represents, roughly, the percentage of the portfolio's holdings that have changed over the past year, this number provides a rough measure of the ETF's level of trading activity. This publicly reported figure is calculated by funds in accordance with SEC regulations, and Morningstar gathers the information from fund shareholder reports. An ETF divides the lesser of purchases or sales (expressed in dollars and excluding all securities with maturities of less than one year) by the ETF's average monthly assets. The resulting percentage can be loosely interpreted to represent the percentage of the portfolio's holdings that have changed over the past year. The turnover ratio is most accurate, however, when an ETF's asset base remains stable. A low turnover figure (typically less than 30%) might indicate that the manager is following a buy-and-hold strategy. High turnover (more than 100%) could be an indication of an investment strategy involving considerable buying and selling of securities. For index-tracking ETFs, the turnover ratio should be low (ie. generally in single digits) because they are not actively managed; however, the turnover rate can be greater based on the methodology of the particular index tracked.

V

Value Measures
Price/Projected Earnings
Projected earnings are the consensus analyst opinion of how much a company will earn during its next fiscal year. Price/projected earnings represents the amount investors are paying for each dollar of expected earnings per share. When reported for an ETF, it shows the weighted average of the price/projected earnings ratio for each stock in the ETF's portfolio. This measure helps determine Morningstar's value score for each stock and the overall value orientation of the ETF.

Price/Book Value
Book value is, in theory, what would be left over for shareholders if a company shut down its operations, paid off all of its creditors, collected from all of its debtors, and liquidated itself. In practice, however, the value of assets and liabilities can change substantially from when they are first recorded. Many investors use the price/book ratio-the ratio of a company share price to its total book value per share-as a way to value a stock. If the share price is less than total equity per share, the company is selling for less than its break-up value. When reported for an ETF, it shows the weighted average of the price/book ratio for each stock in the ETF's portfolio. This measure helps determine Morningstar's value score for each stock and the overall value orientation of the ETF.

Price/Sales
Price/sales represents the amount investors are paying for each dollar of sales generated by the company. Price/sales is usually a less volatile measure than either price/earnings or price/book and can be especially useful when evaluating companies with volatile earnings. When reported for an ETF, it shows the weighted average of the price/sales ratio for each stock in the ETF's portfolio. This measure helps determine Morningstar's value score for each stock and the overall value orientation of the ETF.

Price/Cash Flow
Cash flow tells you how much cash a business is actually generating-its earnings before depreciation, amortization, and noncash charges. Sometimes called cash earnings, it's considered a gauge of liquidity and solvency. Price/cash flow represents the amount investors are paying for each dollar generated from a company's operations. When reported for an ETF, it shows the weighted average of the price/cash flow ratio for each stock in the ETF's portfolio. This measure helps determine Morningstar's value score for each stock and the overall value orientation of the ETF.

Dividend Yield
Dividends are the per-share amount taken from a company's profits and paid to shareholders. Dividend yield is equal to a company's annual dividend divided by its share price. It works as a kind of valuation measure-the lower the yield, the more investors have to pay for each dollar of dividends. Investors often consider stocks with high dividend yields potentially undervalued investments. When reported for an ETF, it shows the weighted average of the dividend yield for each stock in the ETF's portfolio.

This measure helps determine Morningstar's value score for each stock and the overall value orientation of the ETF.

Y

YTD
An abbreviation for year to date, or since the beginning of the current calendar or fiscal year. When evaluating YTD total returns, for example, the beginning price is the first day of the current calendar or last day of the current calendar (usually December 31 or January 1) to the present date.

Yield
Yield, expressed as a percentage, represents a fund's income return on capital investment for the past 12 months. This figure refers only to interest distributions from fixed-income securities and dividends from stocks. Money generated from the sale of securities, from options and futures transactions, and from currency transactions are considered capital gains, not income. Return of capital is also not considered income. NMF (No Meaningful Figure) appears in this space for ETFs that do not properly label distributions. N/A appears if an ETF is less than one year old, in which case we cannot calculate yield. Morningstar computes yield by dividing the sum of the fund's income distributions for the past 12 months by the previous month's NAV (adjusted upward for any capital gains distributed over the same period).